Routledge International Handbook of Rural Studies

Rural societies around the world are changing in fundamental ways, both at their own initiative and in response to external forces. The *Routledge International Handbook of Rural Studies* examines the organisation and transformation of rural society in more developed regions of the world, taking an interdisciplinary and problem-focused approach. Written by leading social scientists from many countries, it addresses emerging issues and challenges in innovative and provocative ways to inform future policy. This volume is organised around eight emerging social, economic and environmental challenges:

- Demographic change
- Economic transformations
- Food systems and land
- Environment and resources
- Changing configurations of gender and rural society
- Social and economic equality
- Social dynamics and institutional capacity
- Power and governance

Cross-cutting these challenges are the growing interdependence of rural and urban; the rise in inequality within and between places; the impact of fiscal crisis on rural societies; neoliberalism, power and agency; and rural areas as potential sites of resistance. The *Routledge International Handbook of Rural Studies* is required reading for anyone concerned with the future of rural areas.

Mark Shucksmith is Director of the Newcastle University Institute for Social Renewal, UK, where he is also Professor of Planning. His main areas of research include rural development, social exclusion in rural areas, rural housing, agricultural change and rural policy. His books include *Rural Transformations and Rural Policies in the US and UK* (Routledge, 2012), *Future Directions in Rural Development* (Carnegie UK Trust, 2012), *Comparing Rural Development: Continuity and Change in the Countryside of Western Europe* (Ashgate, 2009), *CAP and the Regions: The Territorial Impact of the CAP* (CABI, 2005), *Young People and Rural Policy in Europe* (Ashgate,

2004), *Housing in the European Countryside* (Routledge, 2003) and *Exclusive Countryside? Social Inclusion and Regeneration in Rural Britain* (JRF, 2000). In 2007–2008 he chaired the Scottish Government's Committee of Inquiry into Crofting, which led to the Crofting Reform Act 2010. He has also served on the UK Government's Commission for Rural Communities, Affordable Rural Housing Commission, and Countryside Agency. He directed the Joseph Rowntree Foundation's programme on *Action in Rural Areas* 1996–2000. Mark was vice president of the International Rural Sociological Association from 2004 to 2008, and was programme chair for the XI World Rural Sociology Congress in Norway in 2004. He has provided advice to governments and agencies in several countries, and to the OECD. He was awarded the OBE by the Queen in 2009 for services to rural development and to crofting.

David L. Brown is International Professor of Development Sociology, and co-director of the Community & Regional Development Institute at Cornell University in Ithaca, New York. Professor Brown is a social demographer whose research focuses on migration and development, and the production and reproduction of spatial inequalities. He has published over 50 scholarly articles and written or edited 11 books on rural population and society. His most recent books include *Rural Transformations and Rural Policies in the UK and US* (Routledge, 2012) (co-edited), *Rural Communities in the 21st Century: Resilience and Transformation* (Polity, 2011) (with Kai Schafft), *Rural Retirement Migration* (Springer, 2008) (with Nina Glasgow), *Population Change and Rural Society* (Springer, 2006) (co-edited) and *Challenges for Rural America in the 21st Century* (Penn State, 2003) (co-edited). He is past president of the Rural Sociological Society, was elected to the Executive Committee of the European Society for Rural Sociology, and was chair of the American Sociological Association's section on the Sociology of Development in 2015. He received the Distinguished Rural Sociologist Award from the Rural Sociological Society, the Chancellor's Award for Sustained Professional Service from the State University of New York, and was awarded an honorary doctorate from Rousse University in Bulgaria in 2007 recognising his contributions to that university's rural and regional development educational programmes.

Routledge International Handbook of Rural Studies

Edited by Mark Shucksmith and David L. Brown

SECTION EDITORS

NEIL ARGENT
BETTINA B. BOCK
LYNDA CHESHIRE
DAVID FRESHWATER
GEOFFREY LAWRENCE
KATRINA RØNNINGEN
KAI A. SCHAFFT
SALLY SHORTALL

Routledge
Taylor & Francis Group

LONDON AND NEW YORK

First published 2016 by Routledge

2 Park Square, Milton Park, Abingdon, Oxfordshire OX14 4RN
52 Vanderbilt Avenue, New York, NY 10017

Routledge is an imprint of the Taylor & Francis Group, an informa business

First issued in paperback 2019

British Library Cataloguing-in-Publication Data
A catalogue record for this book is available from the British Library

Library of Congress Cataloging in Publication Data
Names: Shucksmith, Mark, editor. | Brown, David L. (David Louis), 1945-
editor.
Title: Routledge international handbook of rural studies / edited by Mark
Shucksmith and David Brown.
Description: Abingdon, Oxon ; New York, NY : Routledge, [2016]
Identifiers: LCCN 2015048216| ISBN 9781138804371 (hardback) |
ISBN 9781315753041 (ebook)
Subjects: LCSH: Sociology, Rural. | Rural development.
Classification: LCC HT421 .R68 2016 | DDC 307.1/412--dc23
LC record available at http://lccn.loc.gov/2015048216

ISBN: 978-1-138-80437-1 (hbk)
ISBN: 978-0-367-33584-7 (pbk)

Typeset in Bembo
by Saxon Graphics Ltd, Derby

To rural scholars, past, present and future

Contents

Contents

Contents

Conclusion   661

Figures

Tables

Acknowledgements

The preparation of this Handbook over the last two years has been a massive undertaking, and as Editors we are indebted to many colleagues for helping bring this volume to fruition. Our section editors have made a very substantial contribution and we would like to formally acknowledge our gratitude to Neil Argent, Bettina Bock, Lynda Cheshire, David Freshwater, Geoff Lawrence, Katrina Rønningen, Kai Schafft and Sally Shortall. They have done a fantastic job. Of course, we also want to thank the over 70 scholars who contributed chapters to the Handbook.

We are indebted to Fiona Simmons and Kate O'Neill, of Newcastle University's Institute for Social Renewal, for clerical support above and beyond the call of duty – liaising with authors, keeping track of successive drafts and finally preparing the manuscript for delivery to the publishers. Jenny Hasenfuss, also of NISR, gave strong support to this endeavour, as did Gerhard Boomgaarden and Alyson Claffey of Routledge. Finally, we would like to thank Mike Woods, Ann Tickamyer and Sally Shortall for helpful comments on our introductory chapter, and all of our colleagues in Newcastle and Cornell universities for their support.

Contributors

Neil Argent is Professor of Human Geography in the Division of Geography and Planning at the University of New England, Armidale, Australia. His research interests focus on the social, economic and demographic factors driving change in rural societies, and their interrelationships with each other and rural environments.

Loka Ashwood is an Assistant Professor in the Department of Agricultural Economics and Rural Sociology at Auburn University. She is currently co-editing a Special Issue in the *Journal of Rural Studies* on the rural as a dimension of environmental injustice. She is writing a book on the alternative politics of rural protest that affront conjoined corporate and state environmental injustices.

Jane Atterton is manager and policy researcher in the Rural Policy Centre, SRUC (Scotland's Rural College). She has over 15 years' research experience in both academic and policy environments. Her research interests focus broadly on rural and regional development issues, with a particular focus on rural businesses, rural communities and the rural policy-making process.

Unn-Doris K. Bæck holds a PhD in Sociology from the University of Tromsø, Norway. Her research includes studies in sociocultural perspectives on learning and education, sociology of education and sociology of youth, with special emphasis on aspects related to social class, cultural diversity and urban/rural dimensions. Bæck currently works as a Professor in Education at the Department of Education at UiT The Arctic University of Norway and as an Adjunct Professor in Sociology at the Department of Sociology, University of Oulu, Finland.

Cathy Banwell has a Master's degree in anthropology and a PhD in health sciences through the University of Melbourne. Her most significant contribution to public health research has been to bring social science theories and research methods to the development of explanations for new patterns of health risks and outcomes.

Fabio Bartolini is Assistant Professor in Agricultural Economics. His main research topic focuses on assessment of agricultural policy impacts on multiple dimensions: environmental, productive factor demands and innovation and new technology adoption. Other research interests are in agricultural structural changes, factors markets, bio-economy and agro-energy.

Michael M. Bell is Vilas Distinguished Achievement Professor of Community and Environmental Sociology and Director of the Center for Integrated Agricultural Systems at the University of

Wisconsin-Madison. Mike is also an agroecologist, ethnographer and social theorist, as well as a composer and performer of classical and grassroots music.

Bettina B. Bock currently works as Associate Professor of Rural Sociology at the Department of Social Science of Wageningen University and as Professor for Population Decline and Quality of Rural Life at Groningen University, both in the Netherlands. Her research projects include rural development and rural marginalisation, looking in particular at the opportunities for social innovation, rural gender relations, sustainable food production and consumption and animal welfare. Since 2014 she has been chief editor of *Sociologia Ruralis*.

Berit Brandth is a Professor of Sociology at the Norwegian University of Science and Technology. One of her main research subjects is rural studies, an area where she has published widely on various aspects of gender and agriculture through inroads such as technology, organisation, media, embodiment, family and tourism. Her other area of interest is gender, work and care politics with a special focus on fathers and parental leave.

David L. Brown is Professor of Development Sociology at Cornell University, USA. He is a social demographer whose scholarship is motivated by an interest in explaining the determinants of spatial inequality in more developed nations. In particular, he is interested in how processes of uneven national development shape opportunity structures and life chances of people living in various types of areas. Recent research also focuses on how various mobilities structure and restructure the rural–urban interface. His work is conducted in the USA, UK, and Central and Eastern Europe.

Gianluca Brunori is Professor of Food Policy at Pisa University in the Department of Agriculture, Food and Environment. He has served as president of RC40 and vice president of the European Society of Rural Sociology. His research activities focus on rural development strategies, on rural innovation and on the performance of food systems.

Joseph T. Campbell focuses his research and professional interest on the balance between community economic development and natural resource management in rural areas of the USA and abroad. He oversees Ohio State University's Social Responsibility Initiative and conducts applied research on the social impacts of energy development and climate change adaptation. Joe has managed dozens of community development research projects in mining and agricultural communities in the USA and in Ghana.

Majda Černič Istenič is an Associate Professor of Sociology at the University of Ljubljana, Biotechnical Faculty, Agronomy Department, and Senior Research Fellow at the Scientific Research Centre of the Slovenian Academy of Sciences and Arts. Her research encompasses topics from the sociological domain which relate to various cross-cutting subjects. In her research she focuses on gender and intergenerational relations, social aspects of reproductive behaviour, comparisons of different aspects of the lives of rural and urban populations and positions of different actors in the food chain (farmers, extension services, consumers and agricultural policy makers).

Chrysanthi Charatsari earned her PhD degree in Agricultural Education from Aristotle University of Thessaloniki and worked as a postdoctoral research fellow at the National Agricultural Organization DEMETRA and at Aristotle University of Thessaloniki, where she is currently a research associate. She has participated in several research projects funded by the European Union targeted at adult education, vocational education and rural development. Her primary research interests include agricultural education and extension, rural women, rural and community development, gender stereotypes in rural communities, rural cultures and identities, and research methods.

Lynda Cheshire is an Associate Professor in Sociology in the School of Social Science at the University of Queensland. Her research interests lie in the areas of rural studies, housing and neighbourhoods, with a particular focus on the changing relations between the state and civil society as understood through the lens of government. She has applied her work to various domains including the dominance of self-help in contemporary rural development policies, the rising role of the corporate (mining) sector in the governance of rural areas and the changing role of rural local government. She is author of *Governing Rural Development* (2006) and co-editor of *Rural Governance: International Perspectives* (2007).

Michael Corbett is Professor of Rural and Remote Education at the University of Tasmania. Corbett's research investigates the way we think about rural space, and how this thinking influences education policy, teacher education and literacies. His work is principally interested in the implicit connection between education and mobility, and particularly the geographic and social mobility of rural youth and how it influences school-to-work transitions.

Jane Dixon is Associate Professor and Senior Fellow at the National Centre for Epidemiology and Population Health, Australian National University. Her research takes place at the intersection of sociology and public health, and focuses on transformations within national food systems with a special interest in food retailing and food producer livelihoods.

Kim Donehower is Associate Professor of English at the University of North Dakota, where she researches the relationship between literacy and the sustainability of rural communities. She is the co-author or co-editor of *Rural Literacies*, *Reclaiming the Rural: Essays on Literacy, Rhetoric, and Pedagogy* and *Re-Reading Appalachia: Literacy, Place, and Cultural Resistance*. Her essays have appeared in *Women and Literacy: Local and Global Inquiries for a New Century*, *Rethinking Rural Literacies: Transnational Perspectives* and *Doing Educational Research in Rural Settings: Methodological Issues, International Perspectives, and Practical Solutions*.

David J. A. Douglas has worked in public service, management consulting and the academy. Formally a partner in what is now Cap Gemini, management consulting, he was Director of the former graduate University School of Rural Planning and Development, University of Guelph, Canada (1985–1992), and Professor in the School of Environmental Design and Rural Development (Guelph), 1992–2009. He continues as an active university instructor, facilitator, researcher and writer. He specialises in rural development policy and planning, community development, local government and governance, economic development and strategic planning and management. He has worked throughout Canada, the EU, Iran, China, Japan, Pakistan, Ukraine, Indonesia and other international contexts.

Jo-Anne Everingham is a Sociologist and Senior Research Fellow at the University of Queensland. She is particularly interested in assessing the cumulative impacts of extractive industries and the social impacts of mining, oil and gas projects in predominantly agricultural regions. Her work also examines collaborative governance of 'wicked problems' as disparate as regional development, inclusion of women and Indigenous people and population ageing.

Susan C. Faircloth (an enrolled member of the Coharie Tribe of North Carolina) is a Professor and Chair of the Educational Leadership Department at the University of North Carolina Wilmington. She is also a former Fulbright Senior Scholar to New Zealand. Her research interests include Indigenous education, the education of culturally and linguistically diverse students with special educational needs, and the moral and ethical dimensions of school leadership.

Frode Flemsæter has a PhD in Geography from the Norwegian University of Science and Technology (NTNU). Flemsæter has particular interests within the fields of legal geography and moral landscapes, which includes work on land ownership and property relations, commodification of natural resources, access to and recreation in the outdoors, second home ownership, and the power geometries related to use and protection of valuable landscapes.

David Freshwater is a Professor at the University of Kentucky with a joint appointment in Agricultural Economics and the Martin School of Public Policy. He is also an adjunct professor in the Geography Department at the Memorial University of Newfoundland. His main research interests are agricultural and rural policy in the OECD countries. In addition to his academic research he has been a consultant to the OECD and a number of government agencies, and was Head of the OECD Rural Programme in 2009. In the 1990s he led TVA Rural Studies, a rural research programme that was jointly funded by the Tennessee Valley Authority and the University of Kentucky.

Charles Geisler focuses on the sociology of property, its abiding controversies, and emergent forms. His work extends to land concentration and land use planning in times of crisis; new enclosures; land reform; property rights and human rights; ownership in stateless places; occupation theory; the public trust doctrine; and post-property theory. He has studied land displacement and dispossession in Bangladesh, the United States, Ethiopia, the Dominican Republic, Scotland, Vietnam and Japan. His most recent co-edited books are, with Shelley Feldman and Gayatri Menon, *Accumulating Insecurity, Securing Accumulation: Violence and Dispossession in the Making of Everyday Life* (2011) and, with Stefano Ruzza and Anja Jakobi, *Non-State Challenges in a Re-Ordered World: The Jackals of Westphalia* (2015).

Jörg Gertel is Professor of Economic Geography and Global Studies at the University of Leipzig. His recent books include *Seasonal Workers in Mediterranean Agriculture: The Social Costs of Eating Fresh*, co-edited with Sarah Ruth Sippel (2014); *Disrupting Territories: Land, Commodification and Conflict in Sudan*, co-edited with Richard Rottenburg and Sandra Calkins (2014); and *Economic Spaces of Pastoral Production and Commodity Systems: Markets and Livelihoods*, co-edited with Richard Le Heron (2011).

Menelaos Gkartzios is a Lecturer in Rural Planning and Development at the Centre for Rural Economy, Newcastle University. He has a PhD in Regional and Urban Planning from University College Dublin. His research interests include rural housing policy, mobilities and urban–rural transformations, and international comparative analysis.

Contributors

Leland Glenna is Associate Professor of Rural Sociology and Science, Technology, and Society at the Pennsylvania State University. His teaching and research interests are in the areas of social and environmental impacts of agricultural science and technologies, the role of science and technology in agricultural and natural resource policy making, and the social and ethical implications of democratising science and technology research.

Krzysztof Gorlach is Professor of Sociology at Jagiellonian University. His areas of interest include family farming, social stratification and social movements theories.

Anne Green is a Professor at the Institute for Employment Research, University of Warwick. She has substantial experience of researching employment, non-employment, skills, local and regional labour market issues, migration and commuting, and associated policy issues in rural and urban contexts. She regularly undertakes research for the UK government and agencies, the European Commission, the OECD and research councils and foundations.

Bill Green is Emeritus Professor of Education at Charles Sturt University, Bathurst, New South Wales, Australia. His research interests are in literacy studies and curriculum enquiry, rural education, doctoral research education and professional practice education. Recent publications include *Rethinking Rural Literacies: Transnational Perspectives* (2013), co-edited with Michael Corbett, and *The Body in Professional Practice, Learning and Education: Body/Matters* (2015), co-edited with Nick Hopwood.

Greg Halseth is a Professor in the Geography Program at the University of Northern British Columbia, where he is also the Canada Research Chair in Rural and Small Town Studies and Director of UNBC's Community Development Institute. His research examines rural and small town community development, and community strategies for coping with social and economic change, all with a focus upon northern BC's resource-based towns. His recent books include *Building Community in an Instant Town* and *Building for Success*, which talk about rural and small town community development and community economic development, as well as an edited volume, *Next Rural Economies*, which includes contributions from 12 OECD countries. His latest book is *Investing in Place: Economic Renewal in Northern British Columbia*.

Neil Hanlon is a Professor of Geography at the University of Northern British Columbia (Canada). His research interests include rural and remote health service provision, regional health governance, community-level adaptations to population ageing, and the changing role of the voluntary sector in health and social care. His work has been published in leading journals such as *Health and Place*, *Social Science and Medicine* and *Health and Social Care in the Community*.

Marit S. Haugen is a Senior Researcher at the Centre for Rural Research and is Adjunct Professor of sociology at the Norwegian University of Science and Technology. Her research focuses on rural gender studies, gender and agriculture, rural tourism, and the relation between rural and urban communities and rural ageing.

Allison Hayes-Conroy examines the relationship between the human body and other aspects of social and environmental life (e.g., food, land, territory, community). She has published widely on the politics of food and bodies. She has regional interests in Latin America, especially Colombia, where she maintains a long-term research commitment with community organisations in the city of Medellín.

Jessica Hayes-Conroy explores the intersection of health, bodies and socio-environmental change. Her work often centres on food and nourishment, exploring critical and feminist approaches to questions of nutrition and healthy eating. She recently conducted research on radiation contamination in post-disaster Fukushima, Japan, where she investigated the impacts of the nuclear accident of 11 March 2011 on residents' daily life choices.

Gregory Hooks is Professor and Chair of Sociology at McMaster University, Canada. His research examines spatial inequality across a range of phenomena, including environmental inequality, military and criminal justice facilities, and local governmental services.

Anne S. Hynds is a Pākehā researcher and teacher. Her work is grounded in the context of contemporary schooling in Aotearoa New Zealand and the contribution that quality teaching can make to a socially just society. Her interests include teacher understandings of culturally responsive and inclusive pedagogies, collaborative enquiry and evidence-based practice in the work of change. She is currently the Director of Research for the University of Auckland's Starpath Project for Tertiary Participation and Success, which aims to find evidence-based ways of transforming current patterns of student underachievement for Māori, Pacific Island and other students from high poverty communities.

David Kay provides leadership for CaRDI programming in areas including energy, land use, community economics and local governance. He contributes through applied research, outreach and training efforts that attempt to build community-based decision-making capacity and to help weave local policy into a regionally coherent fabric. David holds an MS in Agricultural Economics from Cornell University.

Robin Kearns has, for almost three decades, analysed dimensions of New Zealand's changing cities and rural regions. His interests span social, cultural and health geography. His latest book is *The Afterlives of the Psychiatric Asylum* (2015, with Graham Moon and Alun Joseph).

Geoffrey Lawrence is Emeritus Professor of Sociology at the University of Queensland, Australia, and President of the International Rural Sociology Association (2012–2016). His current research investigates the impacts of globalisation, neoliberalism and financialisation upon food and farming both in Australia and internationally. He is a Fellow of the Academy of Social Sciences in Australia.

Jo Little is Professor of Gender and Geography at the University of Exeter. Her main areas of research include gender identities in rural communities, rural women's employment and rural domestic violence. She is author of several academic books on rural society and gender including *Contested Countryside Cultures* (with Paul Cloke) and *Gender and Rural Geography*. Her most recent book is a co-edited collection (with Barbara Pini and Berit Brandth) entitled *Feminism and Ruralities*.

Linda M. Lobao is a Professor of Rural Sociology, sociology and Geography at the Ohio State University. With Gregory Hooks and Ann Tickamyer, she edited *The Sociology of Spatial Inequality* (2007) and is a current co-editor of *The Cambridge Journal of Regions, Economy, and Society*. Lobao is a past president of the Rural Sociological Society and a Fellow of the American Association for the Advancement of Science.

Áine Macken-Walsh is a Sociologist at Teagasc, Ireland's Agriculture and Food Authority. Her research interests are socio-cultural dimensions of agriculture and fishing; qualitative and action research methodologies; and governance approaches to rural development.

Ruth McAreavey is a Lecturer in Spatial Planning and has worked previously for a housing agency, a charity and in local government. Her research interests include migration, ethnicity, rural development, community regeneration and research methods and ethics.

Lori McVay has a Master's degree in Organizational Leadership from Azusa Pacific University in California. She received her PhD in Sociology from Queen's University, Belfast, Northern Ireland, where she focused on the development of leadership skills among rural women. Lori lives and works in Michigan, and is currently serving as Coordinator of Early Career Connections for the Trans-Atlantic Rural Research Network.

Michelle A. Meyer researches and teaches in areas including environmental sociology, sociology of disaster, community, sustainability and social stratification. Her research has been funded by the US National Science Foundation, Rural Sociological Society and Midwest Sociological Society. She also works with local governments and non-profit organisations to support disaster preparedness, mitigation and recovery planning, especially for marginalised populations.

Paul Milbourne is professor of human geography in the School of Geography and Planning at Cardiff University. He has research interests that lie mainly in the field of social geography and, more specifically, the geographies of welfare and poverty. He is also interested in the interplay between social and environmental forms of (in)justice within contemporary society. Paul has published widely on these themes, including several books on poverty, homelessness and welfare reform in rural places.

Caitríona Ní Laoire is a Lecturer in Applied Social Studies and deputy director of the Institute for Social Sciences in the 21st Century at University College Cork. Her research interests coalesce around the areas of migration, young people, gender and rurality. Her research has explored issues such as rural youth out-migration, rural return migration and rural social change, and she has published widely in these areas.

Joan Noguera is Professor of Regional Geography and leads the research group LocSus on local sustainability at the University of Valencia. His doctoral dissertation presented the results of research on the evaluation of rural development policies in Spain. From 1994 he has been involved in competitive research projects on territorial development (development policies, public–private partnerships, periferality and new factors for territorial development, knowledge and local development, etc.). He has participated in official evaluations of rural development policies by the EU and has been invited to OECD projects such as RURBAN (2013) on building partnerships between rural and urban areas, among others. He has several R&D projects in Latin American countries.

Eamon O'Shea is a personal professor in the School of Business and Economics at NUI Galway, Ireland. He is author/co-author of numerous books and monographs, mainly in the field of ageing and social policy, and has been influential in setting the agenda for the ongoing reform of the long-stay sector in Ireland. His current research addresses the economics of dementia, health care evaluation, and rural ageing.

Giorgio Osti is a rural sociologist and Associate Professor in the Department of Political and Social Sciences, University of Trieste, Italy. He is interested in sociospatial relationships, especially in how reciprocity works in different places. He has been involved in research concerning local development in fragile areas and environmental issues like waste management and energy transition.

Jeremy Phillipson is a Reader in rural enterprise and knowledge exchange and Director of research in the School of Agriculture, Food and Rural Development at Newcastle University. His research considers expertise exchange within rural land management and the development needs of rural and marine economies. Jeremy is a member of the DECC/Defra Social Science Expert Panel, board member of the Scottish Government RESAS Strategic Research Board and a member of the European Commission's FARNET advisory group that advises on the future development of fishing communities.

Elizabeth P. Ransom has taught at the University of Richmond since 2003, with a year away in 2005–2006 for the position of the Science & Technology Policy Fellow at the American Association for the Advancement of Science and the US Department of Agriculture. Ransom's research interests are in the areas of international development and globalization, the sociology of agriculture and food, and social studies of science and technology. Her latest co-edited book is *Rural America in a Globalizing World: Problems and Prospects for the 2010s*. The book covers agriculture and food; natural resources; demographic change; the multifaceted dimensions of diversity; and issues of rural economics, community and quality of life.

Katrina Rønningen is a geographer, research manager and senior researcher at the Center for Rural Research in Trondheim, Norway. Her research interests are within rural land use and natural resources including cultural landscape management, international agricultural policies, multifunctionality in agriculture, conservation and land use discourses and controversies linked to, for example, food security and climate change, great carnivores, land use rights, indigenous land use, coastal planning for fish farming and conservation, and rural development, commodification and transformation processes more widely.

Stuart A. Rosenfeld, Founder of Regional Technology Strategies, Inc., has over 40 years' experience in public policy research, analysis, and implementation concerning education and training, rural and industrial development, and technology strategies in the United States and Europe. Previous positions have included deputy director of the Southern Growth Policies Board, director of the Southern Technology Council, Senior Associate at the National Institute of Education, and manager of operations research for divisions of General Electric. Rosenfeld has an EdD in Planning and Social Policy from Harvard and a BS in Chemical Engineering from the University of Wisconsin-Madison.

Kai A. Schafft is an Associate Professor of Education at Penn State. Trained as a rural sociologist, his work examines the relationship between social and spatial inequality. He edits the *Journal of Research in Rural Education* and has authored or edited three books, and over 70 journal articles, reports and reviews related to rural scholarship.

Thomas Scharf is Professor of Social Gerontology, Institute for Ageing, Newcastle University. He was previously director of the Irish Centre for Social Gerontology, NUI Galway, where he led a programme of work on rural ageing. He is currently engaged in a variety of projects on issues around poverty in later life, loneliness and social isolation, aspects of intergenerational solidarity, and the experiences of people ageing in different types of community, both rural and urban.

Jeff Sharp is a rural sociologist at Ohio State University who conducts research related to community and development. His work has been particularly attentive to the community and agricultural change at the rural–urban interface.

Sally Shortall is a Sociologist based at Queen's University Belfast. She is recognised internationally for her scholarship on agriculture, rural development theory and practice, gender and farming, and rural communities. She is currently President of the European Society for Rural Sociology.

Mark Shucksmith is Director of the Newcastle University Institute for Social Renewal and Professor of Planning at Newcastle University. Mark was Programme Chair for the World Rural Sociology Congress in Trondheim in 2004 and for the European Society of Rural Sociology Congress in 2015, as well as being the author of many books and articles. He is a Trustee of Action with Communities in Rural England (ACRE) and was a Commissioner at the Commission for Rural Communities from 2005 to 2013. Mark chaired the Scottish Government's Committee of Inquiry into Crofting, which led to the Crofting Reform Act 2010. He was awarded the OBE in 2009 by the Queen for services to rural development and to crofting.

Ajay S. Singh teaches at Ohio State University. His research pertains to human adaptation to climate change in the contexts of water resources, food systems and the protection of endangered species.

Sarah Ruth Sippel holds a PhD in Geography and is a Senior Researcher at the University of Leipzig, Germany. She has done extensive research on intensive agriculture and rural livelihood security in the Mediterranean and North Africa and, together with Jörg Gertel, co-edited the volume *Seasonal Workers in Mediterranean Agriculture: The Social Costs of Eating Fresh* (2014). Currently, her research interests lie in the nexus between global food security, financialisation of agriculture and food, and new solidarities within global agri-food systems.

Kiah Smith is a Research Associate in the School of Social Science, University of Queensland, specialising in environment and development sociology. Her research explores connections between food security, climate change, resilience and governance, with specific focus on food justice, the right to food, fair/ethical trade, gender, resilience and green economy. She is also a Future Earth Fellow and has previously worked with the United Nations Research Institute for Social Development in Geneva.

Paweł Starosta is Associate Professor of Sociology at the University of Łódź. His areas of interest include local communities, social capital and rural sociology issues.

Aileen Stockdale is Professor of Environmental Planning at Queen's University Belfast. Her research examines population change with a specific focus on rural migration processes: the decision making of migrants, the relationship with life course events, migrant experiences, and the consequences for rural areas. Most recently her work has investigated migration at mid-life and retirement.

David Symes is Reader Emeritus at the University of Hull (UK) where he taught in the geography department. He has published extensively on the changing social structures of farming in Europe and on fisheries development in the northeast Atlantic and has advised the European Commission, UK and Scottish governments on matters relating to fisheries governance.

Annette Aagaard Thuesen conducts research in relation to the EU Rural Development Programme and Fisheries Programme, local community councils, village action plans, partnerships, governance, democracy, gender, institutional capacity, participatory processes and evaluation methods. She has recently worked on an evaluation of the Danish LAG and FLAG development strategies 2007–2013, conducted for the Ministry of Housing, Urban and Rural Affairs, as well as an investigation for the Ministry of Food, Agriculture and Fisheries on the added value of the LEADER approach for rural and coastal development.

Ann R. Tickamyer is Professor of Rural Sociology, Sociology, and Women's and Gender Studies and Head of the Department of Agricultural Economics, Sociology, and Education at Penn State University. Her research interests are in the areas of spatial inequalities, rural poverty, livelihood practices, and gender and development in the USA and Southeast Asia.

Flaminia Ventura is Associate Professor at Perugia University. She has a PhD in rural sociology from Wageningen University. Her research interests include agricultural and rural sociology, development intervention and rural transformation, contemporary rural politics and governance. She was head of the technical cabinet of the Italian agricultural minister in the period 2002–2006 and from 2008 she has been one of the national rural networks coordinators.

Jo Vergunst is a lecturer in Social Anthropology at the University of Aberdeen, Scotland. He has research interests in human–environment relations, landscape and mobilities and has carried out ethnographic fieldwork amongst communities in Orkney and elsewhere in Scotland.

Kieran Walsh is deputy director of the Irish Centre for Social Gerontology at NUI Galway, Ireland, where he currently leads an applied interdisciplinary project in urban communities drawing on life course approaches. Much of his research explores the relationship between older people and their surrounding environment within institutional and community settings and the social, health and well-being outcomes of this relationship.

Bruce A. Weber is Professor of Applied Economics and director of the Rural Studies Program at Oregon State University. He has taught courses, conducted research and developed educational programmes in rural studies, rural development economics and rural poverty at Oregon State University for over 40 years.

Tony Weis is the author of *The Ecological Hoofprint: The Global Burden of Industrial Livestock* (2013) and *The Global Food Economy: The Battle for the Future of Farming* (2007). His research is broadly located in the field of political ecology, with a focus on agriculture and food systems.

Timothy R. Wojan earned a PhD in Agricultural and Applied Economics from the University of Wisconsin-Madison. He has spent most of his professional life doing research on rural economic development at the Economic Research Service in Washington, DC and spent two years at the OECD coordinating reviews of regional development policy in member countries.

His research is currently focused on rural innovation in non-farm tradable sectors using data from the first establishment survey of self-reported innovation in the USA.

Michael Woods is Professor of Human Geography at Aberystwyth University and co-director of the Wales Institute of Social and Economic Research, Data and Methods (WISERD). He has researched extensively on topics of rural restructuring, politics and governance, particularly in the context of globalisation, and he is editor of the *Journal of Rural Studies*.

Nathan Young is a sociologist by training with a correspondingly wide range of research interests, including rural sociology, environmental sociology, science and technology studies, media sociology, and natural resource management. His current work focuses on oceans policy and governance, marine resource management, climate change and rural coastal communities.

Ann C. Ziebarth is a Professor in the Housing Studies Program at the University of Minnesota College of Design. As a rural sociologist she studies the impact of economic, social and political change on people living in small towns and rural areas. Her work focuses on housing issues as an indicator of these changes. Ann has been a member of the Rural Sociological Society since 1983 as well as actively participating in other professional organisations.

Abbreviations

ABA	American Bar Association
ACLU	American Civil Liberties Union
ACS	American Community Survey
BC	British Columbia
CA	census agglomeration
CAFOs	concentrated animal feeding operations
CAP	Common Agricultural Policy of the European Union
CBD	central business district
CCS	Census Consolidated Subdivisions
CEDAW	Convention to Eliminate all forms of Discrimination Against Women
CERCLA	Comprehensive Environmental Response, Compensation and Liability Act
CETA	Canada–EU Trade Agreement
CFP	Common Fisheries Policy of the European Union
CFS	Committee on World Food Security
CFTC	Commodity Futures Trading Commission
CGIAR	Consultative Group on International Agricultural Research
CIKR	Critical Infrastructure and Key Reserves
CIMMYT	International Centre for the Improvement of Maize and Wheat
CIP	Critical Infrastructure Protection
CIS	Community Innovation Survey
CMA	Census Metropolitan Area
CMLUCA	California Military Land Use Compatibility Analyst
CSA	community-supported agriculture
CSM	civil society mechanism
DAC	Development Assistance Committee (USA)
DHS	Department of Homeland Security (USA)
DOD	Department of Defense (USA)
DOE	Department of Education (USA)
DOE	Department of Energy (USA)
EEZs	exclusive economic zones
EIP	European Innovation Partnership
EQLS	European Quality of Life Survey
ERO	Education Review Office
EU	European Union
FAO	Food and Agriculture Organization of the UN
FERC	Federal Energy Regulatory Commission

Abbreviations

FIFO	first in, first out
FLAGs	fisheries local action groups of the European Union
FNS	food and nutrition security
FP	Fisheries Programme
GAO	Government Accountability Office
GATT	General Agreement on Tariffs and Trade
GDP	gross domestic product
GE crops	genetically engineered crops
GHGs	greenhouse gases
GMO	genetically modified organisms
GNI	gross national income
GRAIN	Genetic Resources Action International
HACCP	Hazard Analysis Critical Control Point
HDI	Human Development Index
ICT	information and communication technology
IFAD	International Fund for Agricultural Development
ILO	International Labor Organization
ILRI	International Livestock Research Institute
IMF	International Monetary Fund
IPCC	International Panel on Climate Change
IRRI	International Rice Research Institute
ITQs	individual transferable quotas
LAGs	local action groups (under the EU LEADER programme)
LEADER	Liaisons Entre Actions de Developpement de l'Économie Rurale – the EU's rural development programme based on community-led action
LESO	Law Enforcement Support Office
LGB	lesbian, gay and bisexual
MA	metropolitan area
MSA	Metropolitan Statistical Area
NAFTA	North American Free Trade Agreement
NARI	National Agricultural Research Institute
NAV Eures	Norwegian Labour and Welfare Administration, European Employment Services
NEPA	National Environmental Policy Act (USA)
NERC	North American Electric Reliability Corporation
NGOs	non-governmental organisations
NIETC	National Interest Electric Transmission Corridor
NIMBY	not in my back yard
NIPP	National Infrastructure Protection Plan (USA)
NLS	New Literacy Studies
NORTHCOM	US Northern Command
NPM	new public management
OECD	Organisation for Economic Co-operation and Development
OGs	Operational Groups
OPEC	Organisation of the Petroleum Exporting Countries
PES	Payments for Ecosystem Services
POs	producer organisations
PPP	public–private partnerships

PRWORA	Personal Responsibility and Work Opportunity Reconciliation Act (US)
R&D	research and development
RDP	Rural Development Programme of each EU member state under the CAP
RIG	research interest group
ROWs	rights of way
RSS	Rural Sociological Society (North America)
RST CCS	Rural and Small Town Census Consolidated Subdivision
SBI	Secure Borders Initiative (USA)
SMEs	small and medium-sized enterprises
STEM	science, technology, engineering and mathematics
TFCs	transnational food corporations
TNCs	transnational corporations
TSA	Transportation Security Administration (USA)
TVA	Tennessee Valley Authority
UDD	urban distance discount
UMIC	upper middle income country
UNCLOS	UN Convention on the Law of the Sea
UNHCR	UN High Commissioner for Refugees
USDA	US Department of Agriculture
VET	vocational education and training
WTO	World Trade Organization
YTS	Youbou Timberless Society

Framing Rural Studies in the Global North

Mark Shucksmith and David L. Brown

Introduction

In 2011, the United Nations (UN) announced that one half of the world's population lived in urban areas. More developed regions attained this level in the late 1940s, and typically exceeded 75% by the turn of the 21st century.[1] However, the fact that population is concentrated in urban areas does not diminish the continuing importance of rural people, communities and environments. The vast majority of the world's land and water is rural; most food and fibre is produced on rural land; energy and other natural resources are extracted in rural environments; major infrastructure such as transportation and communication is largely located in rural space; and, while a minority, rural population is still numerically significant even in highly developed and urbanised nations. Accordingly, rural population, economy and space still play a major role in producing national development and well-being. This book examines the organisation and transformation of rural society in more developed regions of the world. Moreover, while the book's various chapters contribute to disciplinary knowledge of rural structure and change, they also provide a synthesis of current knowledge on various aspects of rural society, economy and environment that might inform public and private decisions and policies. Our focus is on the global north even though we agree with Woods (2012) that there is an 'unbridged divide' between rural studies in Europe, America and Australasia (the 'global north') and the rest of the world.

Over the past 80 years, rural studies has developed into an international and interdisciplinary endeavour that examines a wide range of social, economic and environmental issues as well as policy responses to such processes and changes.[2] This book is timely. In the decade since scholars last took stock of rural challenges and opportunities (Cloke, Marsden & Mooney, 2006), a global economic crisis has erupted and persisted; globalisation has penetrated ever more deeply into rural regions, economies and communities; new technologies for extracting natural resources have been deployed; and evidence that human activities, including those occurring in rural environments, are contributing to climate change has increased. All of these developments prompt much new thinking about the role of rural people, communities and environments in relation to economic prosperity, food security, global warming, environmental degradation, energy exploration, social justice and human rights.

What is 'rural'?

But first, what do we mean by 'rural'? This seemingly simple question is notoriously difficult to answer. Despite many critiques, rural and urban continue to be portrayed, if not as polar opposites, then at least as distinctly different entities. Many see the rural as epitomising the good life and being the antithesis of modernity. Others see rural in a less positive light, setting rural communities in opposition to the supposedly creative, dynamic, innovative and fluid nature of urban relations. As Murdoch, Lowe, Ward and Marsden (2003) have observed, two main conflicting narratives, pastoralism and pre-modernity, shape our perceptions of rurality. Pastoralists often see rural areas as repositories of cultural values or even national identities and seek to protect their romantic notion of rural life from outside influences. In contrast, modernists see rural areas as essentially backward and requiring transformation and development so that their residents can enjoy the tangible benefits of the modern world. A further view is that our separation of urban and rural is merely a construct of capitalism: rather than describing surface appearances we should focus on the underlying social and economic processes of global capitalist exploitation, 'enclosure' and land ownership (Levitas, 2015).

Not all social scientists conceptualise and define rural and urban in a similar manner. Often a distinction is drawn between social constructivism and a more structural/demographic approach. The demographic approach came first and is still influential in research and analysis conducted by national and international statistical agencies throughout the world, and among a large share of rural scholars in North America, Australia and elsewhere. In contrast, the social constructivist framework is associated with the cultural turn in rural studies in the UK in the 1980s and 1990s, and to some extent can be understood as a critique of the structural/demographic practice. However, neither approach is hegemonic, even in the USA and UK, let alone across Europe and internationally. Moreover, the view of rural as a social representation has itself been critiqued, as we shall see. The authors and editors of this Handbook acknowledge both these approaches and their critiques.

Social scientists in North America and elsewhere examine rural society and rural social change as part of the urbanisation process. Late 19th- and early 20th-century scholars were concerned with the impact of urbanisation and industrialisation on social life, social relationships and social control (Durkheim, 1938; Wirth, 1938). While this scholarly tradition's legacy lingers, contemporary scholars and researchers are less interested in examining the nature of rural social life, and more concerned with the implications of living and working in rural environments on life chances and opportunities, as well as the role played by rural communities, economies and natural environments in a nation's overall development trajectory and prospects. Accordingly, social scientific analysis of rural issues in present-day North America tends to focus on the determinants and consequences of structural transformations of rural economy and society, and on the interpenetration of urban and rural society that results from increased mobility of people, workers, capital, information and goods.

The structural/demographic approach typically uses quantitative or mixed methods research approaches. Most studies begin with a descriptive-comparative analysis that demonstrates how an outcome such as poverty, life expectancy, school dropout, underemployment, etc. varies across rural–urban spatial units. It should be noted that the vast majority of scholars in this tradition reject the notion of a rural–urban dichotomy, and rather operationalise rurality as a variable that spans from the most highly urbanised metropolises to hamlets and isolated dwellings (Champion & Hugo, 2003). Accordingly, the impact of rurality on socially, economically and environmentally important outcomes is not taken for granted, but is rather an hypothesis to be examined in theoretically shaped and motivated analysis. The main question is whether observed urban–rural variation is simply a reflection of differences in population composition (age, race, etc.) and economic organisation (the kinds of occupations and industries that make up local economies), as argued by Hoggart (1990), or whether more rural areas are different from their more urban counterparts net of these differences in composition. In other words, the social scientific question focuses on the role that rural place may play in determining life chances, health, other aspects of social well-being and economic security. More recently, attention has focused on the blurring of rural–urban boundaries that results from a wide variety of mobilities that occur in the rural–urban interface, a social and economic space that both unites and separates rural from urban (Lichter & Brown, 2014).

The structural/demographic approach to rural social science depends on being able to differentiate rural from urban as well as distinguishing important differences within the urban and rural categories themselves. Even the most hard-core analyst deploying this form of research would admit that quantitative distinctions among spatial units are somewhat arbitrary. However, this is true of virtually any classification of the natural, physical or social world. Most adherents to this approach would argue: (a) that classification schemes must be theoretically driven, for example, shaped by criteria such as population density, population size, and demonstrated interactions with external settlements, that are known to affect economy, society and environment; and (b) that the goal is to produce a classification system where within-category differentiation is less important than variability across the categories.[3] More fundamentally, examinations of rural–urban variability, and change therein, must be shaped and motivated by theoretical conceptualisations of the roles played by space and place in producing and reproducing locality-based social structure and social change.

Meanwhile, some European social scientists, especially rural geographers and sociologists in the UK, have been involved in a discursive journey to unravel the concept of rural. The main dimensions of this process are captured in Halfacree's (1993) identification of four approaches to examining rural society and rural social change, and more recently in Halfacree (2006) and Woods (2009).

Descriptive studies rely on the premise that a clear distinction can be drawn between rural and urban areas that can be statistically measured, but these are tautological insofar as they rely on an intuitive sense of what is rural. The *spatial determinism* approach goes further, imbuing the environment with the power to determine social behaviour and relations, widely understood as an urban or a rural 'way of life' (Tonnies, 1887; Wirth, 1938). Whilst such approaches have been criticised as empirically deficient (Pahl, 1965, 1968), the tendency to appeal to a rural identity remains important not least because of its common-sense appeal and political saliency. *Rural locality studies* drew on structuralist political economy approaches in the 1980s. These argued that forces of global restructuring had clear local manifestations and that these were different in rural areas, but Hoggart (1990) argued that causal processes transgress rural–urban divides and so the restructuring thesis undermined the notion of rural–urban distinction. A growing consensus then emerged within rural studies in the UK, associated with the cultural turn, that rural cannot be understood as a specific type of space, but had to be seen instead in terms of social representation (Halfacree, 1993; see also Mormont, 1990; Murdoch & Pratt, 1993; Pratt, 1996). Of course, this argument applies equally to urban space and to cities as social imaginaries (Amin & Thrift, 2002). Attention shifted, accordingly, to what people think of as rural, and the symbols, signs and images which people conceive of as rural. Such *social constructivist* approaches reinvigorated rural studies by examining what rurality means, and to whom. A focus emerged upon the social relations which overlie physical space, including their power-infused character; and upon the interconnections between different meanings of rurality and the institutional structures and processes of rural change. Building upon this are the deconstructivist approaches which stress the detachment of symbols of rurality from the practices of everyday life.

The view of rural as social representation has itself been critiqued since the 1990s, for example by Cloke (2006), with calls for the 're-materialising of the rural'. One response has been the emergence of a 'relational' approach to rural studies (Murdoch, 2003; Heley & Jones, 2012; Copus & De Lima, 2014), drawing on actor-network theory, hybridity and planning theory. Another attempt to rematerialise the rural is Halfacree's (2006) threefold model of rural space as practised, represented and material, following Lefebvre (1991). This focuses on the interplay between distinctive spatial practices linked to production or consumption, everyday experiences of (rural) life, informal and formal representations of rurality, and the images and symbols which surround this. As the symbolic begins to take precedence over the material, the construction of rurality is contested between different groups – it becomes a site of social struggle with very real consequences. For example, rurality in England may be constructed in such a way as to increase demand for rural residence while preventing supply, hence inflating property values and excluding middle- and lower income groups from the countryside (Sturzaker & Shucksmith, 2011). Halfacree himself illustrates his model with the example of the centrality of productivist agriculture in postwar rural Britain and its demise.

In summary, academic scholarship on rural studies in more developed nations is shaped and motivated by numerous contrasting conceptual/analytical approaches. Each approach offers different insights, and has its own strengths and weaknesses that readers must keep in mind when considering the results of empirical investigations. Regardless of their perspective, however, virtually all contemporary rural scholars reject the idea of essential differences between rural and urban areas, largely because economic, social and technological processes transcend such boundaries and empirical studies have exploded simplistic rural/urban dualities. The social constructivist arguments accordingly view rurality as an imaginary which has different meanings to different people, and whose meanings and symbols may be manipulated and contested as part of social struggles. Against this, 'rurality' has a powerful and continuing resonance in lay discourses, such that rurality may be invisible only to the clever: the idea of rural only becomes problematic under close scrutiny by academics. More structural/materialist scholars focus attention on 'mobilities' and how the increased velocity, volume and variety of movement in society and economy produces and reproduces places; restructures interactions within and among places; and transforms power relationships both within and between places, be they urban, rural or some combination of both.

Narratives of rural change

Change not stability is the normal situation for rural communities and regions. But change is not necessarily part of a 'natural process'. The fact that rural communities experience a wide variety of development trajectories is evidence that rural growth or decline is not simply part of a grand development narrative where natural endowments, geographic situation and other ascribed attributes determine a place's future. Rather, rural places can be extremely active in shaping their own destinies. Hence, since rural places have highly variable assets, including social assets like institutional capacities, social relationships that contribute or inhibit mobilisation, and/or leadership, rural social and economic change typically results in spatial differentiation. However, while all places, rural and urban, have their own histories, it is possible to identify a number of meta-narratives that can serve as a heuristic framework for understanding rural change in the world's more developed regions, and the competing, power-infused ways in which these are represented. The six narratives we identify are not exhaustive of the varieties of rural change, but they capture many of the accounts of rural change that has been experienced during recent decades in Europe, North America, Oceania and other parts of the 'global north'. The first three narratives are borrowed from Shucksmith, Talbot and Lee (2011); the last three are original to this chapter.

An agri-centric narrative: Many accounts of rural change view this from an agri-centric perspective, viewing rural areas essentially as agricultural, and therefore privileging the agricultural sector in their account. For example, the EU (DG Agriculture) consultation on CAP (Common Agricultural Policy) reform (CEC, 2010) asserts that 'agriculture remains an essential driver of the rural economy in much of the EU. The vitality and potential of many rural areas remain closely linked to the presence of a competitive and dynamic farming sector, which is attractive to young farmers' (p. 5). Consequently, the objective of 'balanced territorial development' can best be pursued through maintaining farm subsidies and promoting farm diversification. Marsden's (2003) three models of agricultural and rural development in Europe – an agro-industrial model, an alternative post-productivist model, and a nascent rural development model based on local food production – may each be seen as variations on this narrative.

An urban–rural access narrative: An alternative perspective prioritises urban–rural interactions in explaining change, according to spheres of urban influence, generally measured in terms of distance or travel-to-work areas. One detailed investigation of this approach (Copus et al., 2006) drew attention to two large-scale processes of change: a long-established 'urbanisation' trend drawing population and economic activity out of more remote rural areas into urban and accessible rural areas, and a more recent 'counter-urbanisation' flow out of urban regions into accessible rural areas. As a result of these two flows, the report argued, accessible rural regions represent a zone of growth, while the more remote parts of the EU are still being depleted of population and economic activity through cumulative self-perpetuating cycles of decline – a reference back to Myrdal's cumulative causation thesis. Another branch of the EU (DG Regional) tends towards this narrative, and so prioritises investment in transport infrastructure and physical accessibility to bring more remote rural areas within urban zones of influence and prosperity. In a later paper, Copus (2010) called into question much of our established thinking about urban–rural relations, showing how little evidence basis there is for the 'stylised fallacy' that growth originates in urban centres and trickles out to rural hinterlands.

A competitive economy narrative: A third narrative emphasises the role of global competition and capital. Thus, the fortunes of any given locality (rural or urban) may be profoundly affected by the manner in which global capital seeks to exploit local resources such as land and labour, unless local capital itself is able to underpin development. Rural areas characterised by low wages, a compliant, non-unionised workforce and lower levels of regulation may be particularly prone to exploitation by international capital, leading to increased dependency and peripherality. On the other hand, rural areas with highly educated and skilled populations, strong institutions and social capital may be sites of innovation, prosperity and security. The post-Soviet transition of the EU's new member states (NMS) has capitalist penetration very clearly at its heart, such that rural regions in the NMS have been fundamentally affected by the ways in which global capital have sought to exploit their resources and their developing markets. These dimensions of capital are, in principle, independent of distance to urban centres and of reliance on agriculture, although in practice there may be historically contingent associations with these factors. This emphasis on global competitiveness in a world where localities are increasingly interconnected and interdependent is also the main thrust of the EU's Lisbon Strategy and of many member states' economic policies. 'The whole of the Union faces challenges arising from a likely acceleration in economic restructuring as a result of globalisation, trade opening, the technological revolution, the development of the knowledge economy and society, an ageing population and a growth in immigration' (CEC, 2004, p. 2). The Lisbon Strategy accordingly sets out the EU's aspiration to become the most competitive and dynamic knowledge-based economy, capable of sustainable economic growth with more and better jobs and greater social cohesion, and rural areas of Europe are expected to contribute to, and benefit from, this strategy. From this perspective, the CAP is largely irrelevant to the future of rural regions (Court of Auditors, 2006).

A places left behind narrative: It is important to distinguish between poor people and poor places (Lobao, Hooks & Tickamayer, 2007; Bertolini & Peragine, 2009). Place-based inequality may arise because, in some cases, places have been reliant on large-scale extractive industries which once in decline leave a degraded landscape and communities 'blighted by widespread unemployment, long-term sickness and poverty a decade after the collapse' (Bennett, Hudson & Benyon, 2000). In other places, the decline of agriculture may lead to 'land abandonment' and an out-migration of young people. Here, the problem is that some (vulnerable) people remain trapped by their lack of opportunity and their lack of human capital (Carr & Kefalis, 2009; Shucksmith & Rønningen, 2011; Duncan, 2014). The latter process is especially prominent in particular depressed regions such as Appalachia or the Mississippi Delta in the United States, or in Eastern Europe, where post-socialist restructuring of agriculture, privatisation of industries and cuts in public spending led to rapid losses in rural employment while offering few alternatives. By contrast, in some other regions, notably in the UK, the land and property market and development regulation have served to perpetuate rural areas as elite spaces with hidden poverty and social exclusion (Philip & Shucksmith, 2003), so that the issue is not one of poor places but of 'poverty amongst affluence'. Processes underlying spatial inequalities thus operate at a number of scales (Copus et al., 2006; Copus & Hörnström, 2011), from macro-scale processes of centralisation within the Eurozone, for example, to micro-scale processes of territorial stigmatisation (Wacquant, 2007) and settlement restructuring. How people in rural areas respond to these processes and negotiate and mediate change is an important theme for later chapters in this Handbook.

An amenity-based economy narrative: The high discretionary income of many households in the global north,[4] notwithstanding the recent recession and increasing inequality, has enabled the development of markets for luxury, travel and entertainment. This has an impact in selected rural economies, especially those with attractive natural amenities. Research has shown that communities that commodify their natural environment in the form of recreation and tourism have experienced superior economic and demographic performance in recent decades. In fact, in the United States, such places are the only category of rural place to experience consistent growth during the past 20 years (McGranahan, 1999; Hunter, Boardman & Saint Onge, 2005). Ironically, however, while economic dependence on recreation and tourism produces economic advantages for local economies, it also depends on a large supply of low-wage, low-skill workers, many of whom have insecure part-time and/or seasonal jobs. Hence, while amenity-based economies perform relatively well, they tend to generate inequality and displacement since workers are often unable to afford housing locally given the overheated housing market that often accompanies such growth. Hence, while policies promoting amenity development in rural areas induce population and economic growth, they may inadvertently produce economic winners and losers, increased inequality and political contention that weakens community cohesion. This narrative promoting recreation and tourism as an economic panacea for rural development is also common amongst policy makers. Such proposals should critically consider the pros and cons of amenity-based development, and how its benefits might be distributed throughout the community, and potential environmental externalities associated with tourism and recreation industries (USDA, 2001). Similarly, attracting well-off retirees has also been promoted as an amenity-based development strategy in many parts of the United States and elsewhere (Brown & Glasgow, 2008). Yet in-migration of older persons without concurrent in-migration at younger ages yields non-sustainable ageing-in place and eventual demographic decline. A number of studies have explored such aspects of rural social change through the concept of mobilities (Halfacree, 2012; Shucksmith, Brown & Vergunst, 2012; Milbourne & Kitchen, 2014), as proposed by Urry (2007).

A narrative of society–nature interrelationships: Rural society and economy affect and are affected by the natural environment. While these interdependencies have been recognised since at least the 1970s (for example, see Firey, 1978; Shoard, 1980), the nature of society–environment interactions has intensified and new vulnerabilities, to society and nature, have recently emerged. This is because many society–nature interactions take place via 'trans-boundary mediums' such as water, the atmosphere, labour markets and global circuits of capital. As Fortman (2014, p. 159) has observed, human activities in one locality 'can come back and bite you via natural processes'. We would add that changes in natural processes such as sea level rise, increasingly erratic weather systems and more widespread and persistent drought can 'come back and bite us' via natural systems.

Natural resource extraction has affected rural communities in both positive and negative ways since large-scale mining developed during the Industrial Revolution in the United Kingdom and across Europe. Yet, with each technological *advance*, energy and mineral extraction brings new vulnerabilities to both society and nature. Three examples – offshore oil drilling, high-volume horizontal gas drilling ('fracking') and wind power generation – are particularly salient at the present time. Each brings benefits, but each challenges both the socioeconomic and natural environments. Each of these technologies produces local jobs and a wide variety of other economic benefits, but each is also problematic. Offshore drilling – for example, in the USA Gulf of Mexico or off the California coast – poses the danger of spills which foul beaches, kill marine life and negatively affect tourism and other aspects of local economy. Spills also occur during fracking, and this technique is thought to degrade water quality and increase seismic instability. Moreover, since fracking often occurs in isolated areas lacking a large local workforce or supply infrastructure, boom and bust cycles of growth often occur which bring a multitude of social disruptions (Krannich, Gentry, Luloff & Robertson, 2104). Wind turbines are a major aspect of green energy generation, yet they also pose potential problems including landscape degradation and high mortality among migratory bird populations. The long and the short of it is that all new technologies, whether it's the computer chip, the mouldboard plough or fracking, affect society, the economy and the environment in many ways, some anticipated, some not.

Globalisation has enhanced and deepened society–nature interrelationships. First and foremost, mining and natural resource exploration are deeply embedded in the global economy, which has implications for control over production, labour policies, adherence to safety regulations and – perhaps most critically – the retention and local investment of the social surplus in local economies (Duncan, 2014). Just as local economies are embedded in international systems that are shaped and controlled by multinational corporations and transnational institutions, communities are embedded in global environmental systems. While this is nothing new, the impact of global climatic variation on local areas is more dramatic than in previous years. In 2011, for example, the United States experienced 14 extreme weather events, each costing $1 billion or more (Morello, 2011). There is a scientific consensus that the increased prevalence of extreme weather events is a result of human activities, often directed by global corporations that are penetrating deeper and deeper into low-income, less developed regions. The impacts on rural communities and populations are undeniable (Walthall et al., 2012).

Lower snowpack in high mountain areas reduces run-off thereby affecting agriculture and rural community viability. Melting glaciers increase sea level thereby submerging low-lying areas of coastal communities, destroying coastal fisheries and disrupting recreational economies. Higher risk of storm surges associated with hurricanes and other extreme weather also adversely affect coastal communities. Forest ecosystems, and the communities that depend on them, are at increased risk from longer fire seasons, and new weeds, diseases and insect pests.[5]

Growing concern about the impact of human activity on climate change may, in turn, be deployed to the detriment of groups in rural societies. For example, a letter to *The Economist* argued that no one should be allowed to live in settlements of fewer than 32,000 people, on the grounds that large nucleated settlements allegedly have a smaller carbon footprint. Similar ideas underpin the 'new urbanism' (US) or 'sustainable urbanism' (UK) movement, which 'expropriates the *gemeinschaft* characteristics once ascribed to the rural, while also being in essence a political movement against suburbs and rural settlements, which are presented as inherently unsustainable because of their reliance on private cars and a lack of services' (Shucksmith, 2009, p. 4). In the UK an elite pressure group 'ecologised' their campaign against development in rural areas (Murdoch & Lowe, 2003) so as to embed a vested discourse into national and local planning policies that rural communities are inherently unsustainable (Sturzaker & Shucksmith, 2011).

These narratives raise issues of power, agency and governance. As Morton and Rudel (2014, p. 182) have observed, 'The unprecedented numbers of extreme weather events in recent years have raised questions about the resilience of rural communities in the face of these disturbances.' Why can some rural communities respond in ways that ensure their survival while others fail? This is a key question for rural social science in the future. The perspective of coupled human and natural systems is a powerful conceptual lens for such research (Collins et al., 2011).

A thematic approach

Interdependence of places (and of nature/society)

Many scholars have commented on the world's increasing connectivity. Since rural places were once thought to have been 'protected by distance', increased connectivity is thought to make them more vulnerable to external forces. However, 'protection of distance' is a counter-intuitive idea since lack of physical access has generally been thought to contribute to rural underdevelopment and lack of opportunities. Hence, greater connectivity would seem to increase rural accessibility, even as it may expose rural places to national, global and regional forces, some of which can be deleterious. Recognition of the double-edged impacts of increasing connectivity echoes sociological debates of the 1970s between the modernisation thesis and the dependency thesis (Frank, 1971). Applying dependency theory to rural Scotland, then, Carter (1974) argued that the Highlands and Islands of Scotland were impoverished not by a lack of development but rather by neocolonial development in the form of capitalist penetration and exploitation. Similar arguments have been made to explain the historical underdevelopment of Appalachia in the United States (Caudil, 1962).

The increased interdependence of rural places can be explored at a number of levels and across a number of dimensions. In this section we will discuss rural–urban interdependence, global–local interdependence, and interdependencies between rural society and nature.

Rural–urban interdependence: The conventional view of urban regions involves a dominant city and its dependent rural hinterland. Urban dominance is assumed, with rural-to-urban workforce commuting a typical indicator of the magnitude and direction of urban–rural interdependence.

In contrast, the perspective we suggest here is more inductive. In our view, the rural–urban interface, while a geographic space, is given meaning by the interactions that take place within it, and these interactions are continually changing. Rather than starting with a preconceived notion of urban dominance and rural dependency, we let the social and economic life that occurs in the interface define the nature of urban–rural relationships. We contend that these relationships are constructed through 'mobilities', for example, through various transactions occurring between rural and urban populations, communities, economies and environments (Urry, 2007). This idea is not new. In fact, as early as 1989, Potter and Unwin discussed how the urban–rural interface is constructed through interactions, linkages and flows of people, money, ideas, information and material. Following a similar logic, Lichter and Brown (2011) identified ten different types of boundary-crossing behaviour that define and redefine urban–rural relationships in the United States.

In our conceptualisation, the urban–rural interface is a zone or a field of interdependence, not a clear border of separation. In addition, the interface is a 'space', not a 'place'; that is, a space of intense social and economic interaction where urban and rural come together, as well as where they are divided from each other. As Logan (2012) observes, space is a relational concept. The distribution of power embedded in these relationships is dynamic and variable, hence rural communities have potential agency in interactions with their urban counterparts, agency that can increase or decrease over time, and thus urban dominance cannot be assumed. As we observed previously, 'This new landscape of rural–urban relationships sets the conditions for communities to act and/or be acted upon' (Shucksmith, Brown & Vergunst, 2012, p. 292).

Global–local interdependence: As indicated above, exogenous forces that affect rural communities originate in other, typically urban, regions within the same nation state, but they also come from beyond national borders. In other words, rural communities are embedded in global circuits of capital, information and labour, in environmental and climatic conditions originating across the globe, in an increasingly interconnected global climatic, and in an international epidemiological system comprised of disease vectors that affect people, animals and plants. Given the extent of global–local interdependencies in the contemporary world, the notion of separate rural societies seems somewhat quaint and perhaps even mythologised. Rural communities are not now – nor were they ever – truly independent of social, economic, technological and natural forces from without.

Global–local relationships play out in a wide variety of ways. Neoliberalism, and in particular the relatively unregulated activities of transnational corporations, is of particular concern for rural economies. Foreign direct investment has become the principal source of capital supporting rural employment in many countries. While international capital can flow to rural economies bringing jobs (including well-paying jobs in auto assembly and other durable manufactures), it can just as easily flow in the opposite direction. Moreover, international capital tends to flow to places with initial advantage, thereby contributing to the further underdevelopment of historically poorer areas (Brown, Greskovits & Kulcsar, 2007).

The reverse flow of capital out of rural economies often involves the offshoring of establishments as employers seek cheaper and less organised labour, and laxer regulations in the global south. Rural manufacturing is especially vulnerable to offshoring because it tends to utilise low-skill labour to produce non-durable goods. Since these kinds of jobs can be easily replicated for a lower price abroad, many employers are quick to pull up stakes and move to the global south. The logic of international capital is that investors seek the highest returns regardless of where products are produced and under what conditions. Hence, global capital has no sentiment for locality. To keep capital in an underperforming location would be to risk capital flight as investors switch their money to higher performing firms.

Acknowledging the strength of global forces, however, does not mean that rural community autonomy is mechanistically or automatically undermined by global capital or by trade and other rules promulgated by transnational institutions. New sociological conceptualisations of global–local relationships promote a more complex and nuanced picture. In particular, the notion of neo-endogenous development focuses attention on the mobilisation of local resources and capabilities which, when combined with effective external relationships, can empower rural localities in their interactions with external institutions and agents. Neo-endogenous development involves bottom-up deliberative governance, territorial place shaping and institutional capacity building (Shucksmith, Brown & Vergunst, 2012). Some critics observe that the endogenous approach may exacerbate inequalities both within and between places because the initially uneven playing field disadvantages weaker and poorer places' ability to mobilise resources and form effective external relationships (Arnason, Shucksmith & Vergunst, 2009). In addition, the potential for local agency varies across and within nations. In the UK, for example, the national state is a strong actor in local affairs, while in the USA the national government lacks the authority, and often the will, to intervene at the local level (Shucksmith, Brown & Vergunst, 2012). Accordingly, local communities are left to go it alone in the USA and in Australia (Cheshire, 2006) while they have received some support in the UK. Moreover, resources, institutional capacity, leadership and other attributes vary widely across localities in the USA, hence leading to differential agency when dealing with predatory forces from the outside. Neo-endogenous development is predicated on the ability to produce an effective interaction between internal and external resources. Communities are more vulnerable where one or both are weak. The result of this interaction can be uneven development and a perpetuation of spatial inequality between rural and urban as well as within the rural itself.

Nature–society interdependence: Until recently, social science often treated nature and society as separate spheres. This dualistic perspective fundamentally affects the way in which we examine important rural questions such as natural resource management, the impacts of population growth, the growth of leisure activities in rural regions, energy exploration and extraction, agriculture and food systems, the value of protecting endangered species. As Ramutsindela (2005, p. 3) has observed, 'It is fruitless to encourage the development of practices that foster the society–nature nexus while our thought systems emphasize the society–nature dichotomy.'

In 1995, Raymond Murphy called attention to this dualism in his classic article, 'Sociology As If Nature Did Not Matter.' His main point, in his own words, is that 'Reality is both a social construction and a construction of nature.' He observed that 'Human activities take place in a dynamic ecosystem in which human activity is but one element … Humans exert an effect on nature by manipulating it according to their goals and in the process unleash forces of nature and new forms of social–nature interaction, which affect social action' (Murphy, 1995, p. 704). Goldman and Schurman (2000, p. 565) make a similar point, arguing that 'Studies of nature–society relations need to consider ecological processes, political-economic structures, meanings, values and agency as necessary and complimentary components of analysis.' Hence, the dualistic, nature–society binary masks the reality of coupled human–natural systems.

Recognition of the dynamic, fluid and mutually constitutive aspects of society and nature is particularly relevant to rural social science. Human activities such as excess application of chemical fertilisers, mountain top removal mining practices, second home development in fragile environments, and careless waste management practices can adversely affect the natural environment's capacity to support human settlement. Accordingly, populations are displaced, streams are polluted requiring expensive reclamation efforts, and prime farmland is permanently removed from production. While human activities often initiate the causal process by altering the natural ecosystem, they can also induce natural forces such as air and water pollution, acid rain, landslides and so on which make continued human activity in affected areas expensive or impossible. Hence, complex infrastructure is required to mediate the impacts of human-induced environmental change. In extreme instances, population displacement can occur. While social science is only recently acknowledging the mutually constitutive nature of society and environment, public policy is even later to the game. Few environmental impact statements require meaningful social impact analyses, and virtually none recognise that the impacts of human activities on ecological processes, and vice versa, are cumulative in nature.

Rising inequality

Inequality, poverty and social exclusion are increasing worldwide following the recent economic crisis, but also for long-standing reasons. These widening disparities affect many aspects of society. Regardless of urban, suburban or rural location, inequalities in life chances, living conditions and healthy life expectancy are increasing. Many studies (Kerbo, 2003; Eurostat, 2012) have documented widening income inequalities in the USA and Europe since the 1980s, but Piketty (2014) has offered a much longer historical perspective on income and wealth inequalities in the USA, France, Italy, UK, Germany, Switzerland, Japan and many other countries. His argument is based on the tendency of returns on capital to exceed returns to labour and rates of economic growth. His empirical analysis shows that high and widening inequality, based mainly on inherited wealth, has been a persistent feature of developed countries for at least 200 years, apart from an aberrant period of greater equality between 1914 and the 1970s due to the effects on wealth and inheritance of the two world wars and the Great Depression and of the high taxes and social reforms that accompanied reconstruction. But since the 1970s there has been a resurgence of the dynamic of inherited wealth (or 'patrimonial capitalism') around the world, while in some countries the neoliberal hegemony and associated cuts in top marginal rates of tax have also permitted 'supermanagers' to enjoy highly inflated salaries. Thus, in the USA the share of pre-tax income enjoyed by the top 1% has increased from less than 10% in 1970 to 22.5% in 2012. There have been even bigger gains for the top 0.1% and 0.001% (Saez & Piketty, 2013). Wealth inequality, on the other hand, is now wider in Europe than in the USA, notably in France, Italy and the UK (Piketty, 2014).

Moreover, there is a spatial aspect to inequality. Modernisation theory contends that geographic differences in economic well-being will diminish over time as societies grow and develop. This view is rooted in the belief that improved internal factor mobility should tend to eliminate geographic dualism or spatial polarisation. Williamson's (1965) '24 nation study' is generally cited as evidence that national development diminishes spatial inequality as interregional linkages emerge, facilitating the spread of development from initially wealthier to poorer regions. However, most research fails to demonstrate this convergence, as areas of initial advantage tend to retain their privilege. Mandel (1976, p. 43) and other critics contend that 'the unequal development between regions and nations is the very essence of capitalism'. Or as Neil Smith (1990, p. 148) has observed, 'The mobility of capital brings about the development of areas with a high rate of profit, and underdevelopment of those with a low rate of profit.'

In the USA and in Eastern Europe, for example, the 'places left behind' are disproportionally rural (Rural Sociological Society, 1993; Brown & Lee, 1999; Sherman, 2014). In the UK and elsewhere in Western Europe, this is not necessarily true, at least with respect to income inequality, although many rural places experience high levels of social exclusion. US rural poverty tends to be higher because of deindustrialisation and offshoring of jobs in the context of thin economies with few alternatives to jobs lost to economic restructuring. In addition, rural economies tend to contain a disproportionate share of low-wage, low-skill jobs which may be less than full time and generally insecure. The legacy of past practices such as slavery, sharecropping and tenant farming, exploitative mining and mineral extraction also hold many rural regions back (Sherman, 2014). In post-socialist Eastern Europe, rural poverty tends to be high because communist-era industrialisation practices drained rural regions of human and other forms of capital. In the post-socialist era, job growth is highly dependent on the availability of foreign direct investment, and risk-averse international capitalists tend to invest in safe locations, such as economies that are already performing relatively well (Brown, Greskovits & Kulcsar, 2007).

Sociological analysis provides a complementary micro-level examination of the dynamics of poverty and inequality at the household and individual levels. Rank, Hirschl and Foster (2014) exemplify such analysis. Using 40 years of income data in combination with focus groups and interviews, the authors show that the risk of economic vulnerability has increased substantially over the past four decades in the USA, and the 'American dream' (economic security, enhanced life chances for one's children, etc.) is becoming harder to reach and harder to keep. Their analysis reveals the astonishing rate at which individuals move in and out of poverty and affluence and how initial advantages and disadvantages translate into patterns of cumulative inequality which define their lives.

Sociologists tend to explain inequalities in terms of social class, ethnicity, gender and age. Class derives from the social relations of production (the ownership of capital in particular, but also occupation), but this has received less attention than other social divisions in recent years as many developed countries were thought to have evolved from 'work-based societies' toward more affluent 'consumption-based societies' (Ransome, 2005). Race and ethnicity are fundamental to understandings of inequality in many countries, such as the USA and Australia, along with legacies of colonialism, slavery and exploitation. Similarly, inequalities based on gender, age and other aspects of cultural identity are widely recognised. These comprise the principal dimensions through which to pursue a relational understanding of the dynamics of rising inequality, poverty and social exclusion around the world.

Some scholars have contended that race has declined as a basis of inequality in society, yet research shows that race persists as a principal determinant of unequal opportunity and rewards across the life course. While the extent of race-based inequality may have diminished somewhat during recent decades, racial subordination persists because it is historically entrenched in narratives of social relations in the USA, Canada, Australia, New Zealand and other postcolonial regions of the global north. William Julius Wilson's (1980) influential book, *The Declining Significance of Race*, initiated a contentious examination of the structural and cultural mechanisms through which race divides societies. Wilson's later works, such as *When Work Disappears* (1996) and studies such as Massey and Denton's *American Apartheid* (1993) show how the hyper-segregation of blacks in 'jobless ghettos' produced both structural and cultural isolation from opportunity structures and cultural resources necessary for societal advancement. Cynthia Duncan (1999, 2014) extended this analysis to rural areas, and convincingly demonstrated that while the 'ghetto' metaphor may not exactly pertain in rural areas, structural and social isolation produces and reproduces racial inequality there as well as in urban central cities. Lichter and his colleagues (2012) have examined the intersection of race, segregation and concentrated poverty, characterising it as the 'geography of exclusion'.

Gender is also a persisting basis for social inequality in rural areas of the global north. In the USA, for example, the poverty rate in 2007 (prior to the recent recession) was over 14% for women compared with 11.5% for men. In rural areas the respective figures were 18.6% and 14.5%, and single women with children are particularly disadvantaged. As Carolyn Sachs (2014) observes, women's persisting disadvantage in rural economies is a product of the global drivers of changes in rural employment, and the resulting displacement from productive work to reproductive work, or, as Sachs characterises it, 'from bad jobs to worse' (2014, p. 422). Aside from the material disadvantage, women continue to be isolated from many social and economic roles and opportunities simply because of deeply entrenched gender stereotypes, and resulting discrimination across institutional realms.

In addition to gender per se, gender identity is a new basis of inequality in many societies. While public attitudes toward homosexuals have improved in many nations (see, for example, Smith, 2011) and notable advances in social relations surrounding gender identity have recently occurred such as Ireland's legalisation of same-sex marriage and the USA Supreme Court's decision making same-sex marriage legal in all 50 states, prejudice and discrimination based on sexual orientation are still deeply entrenched in many urban and rural communities across the global north. Moreover, homosexual relations are still broadly condemned in some world regions such as Eastern and Central Europe and Russia (Takac & Szalma, 2014). Even within nations with relatively progressive attitudes toward homosexuality, rural areas tend to be more conservative than their urban counterparts, a difference often attributed to stronger adherence to fundamentalist religion (Dillon & Savage, 2006). Guaranteeing equality to gays, lesbians and transgender persons is an evolving challenge for social and economic institutions throughout urban and rural regions in the global north.

Because the social bases of inequality are so diverse, contemporary scholarship has begun to explore the *intersectionality* of these factors. Crenshaw (1991) coined this term to describe how race and gender interact to affect women's experiences. Similarly, we observe that the experiences of rural persons are affected by class, race, gender, sexual orientation and citizenship, and that these factors cannot be examined separately. Moreover, it is important to examine whether living in a rural area per se has an impact on life chances or whether rural areas are simply containers for social relationships based on gender, race, sexual orientation, citizenship and so on. In other words, does rurality have an independent effect on life chances, or is the 'rural effect' simply selectivity, that is, the concentration of persons with various social and demographic characteristics associated with poverty and exclusion in such places.

Accounts of the growth of inequality along these social divisions since the 1970s tend to emphasise the crisis of Keynesian economic management after 1973, the ascendancy of the 'new right' in offering radical explanations and remedies for this, and the rapid globalisation and pervasive doctrine of neoliberalism which subsequently gained hegemonic status. To varying degrees, and in different forms, Western governments embraced aspects of neoliberal policy, reducing marginal tax rates, 'rolling back' their welfare state provisions, marketising what remained of the public sector, and cutting social security budgets. In Eastern Europe too, governments were forced to abandon universal welfare provisions and full employment guaranteed by the state. And since 2007, the economic crisis and accompanying cuts in public spending and the turn towards 'austerity' have reduced public assistance and welfare entitlements even further, as well as public spending on health, education, infrastructure and many other aspects of state provision. The effects are variable and uncertain so far, but it is clear that certain social groups (e.g., young people) and certain places (e.g., southern and eastern Europe) are most adversely affected. Rural areas have been unevenly affected by these forces, in ways which research is only now revealing.

Fiscal crisis of the state

The period since the global banking crisis began in 2007 is commonly termed an age of austerity, as governments in many parts of the global north bailed out the banks, suffered economic shocks and then sought to balance their budgets through cutting public expenditure and investment. In some countries, notably in the weaker economies of the Eurozone, austerity was imposed from outside by their creditors and by fears of downgrading by powerful risk-rating agencies. This has had major consequences for people who live in rural areas in several respects.

A first wave of consequences derived from the banking crisis itself, as credit became hard to access and markets responded to the increased uncertainty and falls in property prices. The construction industry was hard hit with declines in both prices and building activity. In turn, consumer confidence suffered and falling aggregate demand reduced profitability in many sectors of developed economies, though these effects varied from country to country.

The banking crisis, and the associated impacts on rural and urban economies, soon became translated into a fiscal crisis as governments moved to save banks from failure by taking on their bad debts. In the UK, for example, bailing out the banks increased the national debt as a proportion of GDP (gross domestic product) from 37% in 2007 to 80% in 2014 (ONS, 2015). The interest payments on these debts worsened fiscal deficits and led in many countries (but not all) to the adoption of austerity policies whereby public expenditure was cut in accordance with neoliberal orthodoxies. How this has affected rural populations and economies is still emerging, and countries across the world have implemented widely different policies: those ideologically committed to reducing the size of the state (such as the UK Coalition government) have used the fiscal crisis as justification for 'shock doctrine' reductions in welfare and public services and for privatisation (Klein, 2007; Toynbee & Walker, 2015); some, such as Greece and Ireland, have had shock doctrine thrust upon them by international creditors, such as the IMF, World Bank and European Central Bank; while others, such as the USA, have been less doctrinaire, perhaps even recalling Keynesian lessons from the interwar years on the virtues of public spending during a recession.

Hadjimichalis and Hudson (2014, p. 209) have shown how the crisis spread around the world, taking on 'various forms depending on local conditions and on the form of geo-economic and geo-political integration in each particular country and region into the international division of labour'. Thus, for East–Central European countries and regions, 'offensive privatisations and dispossession of public assets, internationalisation of the financial sector, cheap credit, and increasing reliance on exports and foreign investments paved the way for rapid crisis' (p. 209). In southern Europe, deregulation and delocalisation in the 1990s exacerbated structural weaknesses and increased economic vulnerability and weakened tax bases; while the subsequent formation of the Eurozone removed the possibility of currency devaluation, leaving these economies highly exposed to the global crisis. After several years of rescue plans based on ultra-austerity, these 'countries and their regions continue to face negative growth, increasing public debt, high unemployment and deep impoverishment of their population' (p. 211).

So far there is only a little evidence of the various ways in which the economic crisis has affected people in rural areas. One consequence has been loss of employment, notably in the public sector (with gendered impacts), and often hitting young people especially hard. Youth unemployment rates are especially high in rural areas of eastern and southern Europe (Shucksmith, this volume). Services of general interest are also likely to have been reduced, or centralised, and in many countries these impacts are also related to privatisation. Rising household poverty levels, especially in the rural regions of the poorer countries, are frequently accompanied by cuts in welfare support, with a widespread shift towards ever greater conditionality of such support. Voluntary and community organisations are also likely to have lost public funding, and private donations, at a time when their support is most needed. Finally, there are consequences for slowing or even reversing migration to rural areas – sometimes transnational, sometimes from rural to urban, but also in some cases from urban back to rural, as shown in a number of recent studies in Greece, for example (Gkartzios, 2013; Kasimis & Papadopoulos, 2013). No doubt more reliable and detailed evidence will emerge from rural studies about the spatial and social effects of the economic crisis and the resulting fiscal crisis in the next few years, and some emerging findings are presented in the chapters which follow.

Rural as a site of resistance to neoliberalism

One reason for these restrictions on public spending in many countries is that the period since the 1973 oil shock has been characterised by policies of neoliberalism ('a contradictory regime of market-centric rule' [Peck, 2014, p. 133]), privatisation and deregulation. That oil crisis led in many countries to a rejection of the Keynesian economic management and social contract that underpinned the postwar consensus, in favour of the monetarist theories of the New Right which sought to 'roll back the state' and give greater freedoms to market capitalism. Competitive economic growth was prioritised, and individualism, self-help and frugality were emphasised in place of social solidarity, regulation and a welfare state. Nowhere is this more prominent than in the USA, which in the 1990s replaced its needs-based income transfer system with a highly individualistic 'welfare to work' policy featuring strict time limits on income benefits. At the same time the USA devolved the management and conduct of many of its social welfare programs from the federal to the state and local levels even though localities generally lacked the fiscal, technical and other resources to manage these programs on their own. It also heralded 'market-oriented and voluntarist modes of governance, based on the principles of devolved and outsourced responsibility' (Peck, 2014, p. 147). These reforms are now seen to have increased 'deep poverty' in the USA to 'staggering' levels, with 1.5 million families surviving on under $2 a day (Edin & Shaefer, 2015).

Peck, Theodore and Brenner (2010, p. 112) argued that as a result of the 2007 banking crisis and the ensuing sovereign debt crisis, neoliberalism lost all intellectual and moral authority, but that, notwithstanding this, neoliberalism is so politically and institutionally entrenched that it will survive in a 'zombie phase', 'in which residual neoliberal impulses are sustained not by intellectual or moral leadership, or even by hegemonic forces, but by underlying macroeconomic and macro-institutional conditions'.

Indeed, Peck (2014, p. 133) subsequently acknowledged that neoliberalism remains undiminished, both as a political-economic-cultural phenomenon, and as an explanatory concept: 'The sobering failure, to date anyway, of post-neoliberal "alternatives" to gain much meaningful traction, either extra-locally or in mainstream discourse, has meant that neoliberalism appears to have scored a most audacious (yet at the same time hollow) victory.' And he quotes Centeno and Cohen's (2012, p. 312) conclusion that 'the crisis and ensuing Great Recession may have shaken neoliberalism's supremacy, but it remains unchallenged by serious alternatives and continues to shape post-2008 policy'. While Peck and others have pointed to contradictions inherent within neoliberalism, notably its failure to recognise the socially embedded nature of the capitalist economy (Cahill, 2012, p. 115), Peck no longer expects these contradictions to bring about neoliberalism's eventual collapse, given its apparent facility for shape-shifting survival and its incapacitation of ideological opposition.

This 'zombie phase' of neoliberalism is highly relevant to rural society and economy in the global north because while such a climate will constrain the transformative potential of progressive post-neoliberal alternatives, it offers opportunities for 'the (re)mobilisation, recognition and valuation of multiple, *local* forms of development, rooted in local cultures, values and movements' – what Peck and colleagues have called the 'progressively variegated economy' (2010, p. 111), and Wright (2010) has termed 'real utopias'. This more positive view is supported by a number of recent studies of rural practice: for example, Mackenzie (2006, 2013), and Shucksmith and Rønningen (2011) find evidence for post-neoliberal possibilities in their studies of community-based land reform and the role of small farms in upland areas, in Scotland and Norway. Other examples of resistance to neoliberalism in rural studies include work on alternative food networks (Jarsoz, 2008; Fairbairn, 2012) and on 'transition cultures' (Neal, 2013). Such instances may suggest alternatives to neoliberalism on an intellectual and moral level, and may perhaps open up new possibilities for place-based rural communities around the world to 'spur the post-neoliberal imagination' (Peck, Theodore & Brenner 2010, p. 111). Meanwhile, however, the rural is also a site for the reproduction of neoliberalism both through the electoral support of rural voters for neoliberal parties and through the role of some academics, for example, in promoting neoliberalism in countries such as Australia. Major rural-oriented institutions, including Land-Grant universities, have also been criticised as being overly influenced by transnational agribusiness in ways that produce new technologies, production processes, and marketing systems which systematically undermine rural agency and the viability of smaller scale, locality-based agriculture (Lacy et al., 2014).

One central question is how far such endogenous or neo-endogenous actions, offering spaces of resistance to overwhelming neoliberal exogenous forces, have broader transformative traction. How can we tell if these are 'oases in the desert' or potentially transformative sources of alternative post-neoliberal futures? Another important question concerns how such agency or resistance might be fostered and supported, by whom, and in whose interest?

In contrast to individualising neoliberal doctrines of self-help, widely advocated and applied in rural development (Cheshire, 2006), it has been argued that new forms of governance and community empowerment can build agency while simultaneously placing limits on it (Swindal & McAreavey, 2012). New forms of environmental governance are also spheres in which these themes are playing out (Potter & Wolf, 2012; Vergunst, Geisler & Steadman, 2012). Other alternatives may perhaps be built on new mobilities and networked rural development (Lowe, Murdoch & Ward, 1995; Shucksmith, 2012), such as those engendered by entrepreneurial in-migrants and return migrants (Bosworth & Glasgow, 2012), or through partnership with extra-local actors such as universities and NGOs (non-governmental organisations). There is potential for government to play an enabling role, however imperfectly, building the capacity of local communities to engage with, resist and subvert broader forces of neoliberalism. A corollary is that removing state support, often under the cloak of neoliberal-induced austerity, is unlikely to foster empowerment (Shucksmith, 2012).

In thinking about neoliberalism and rural places as sites of resistance, Peck (2014, p. 153) articulates a further challenge for researchers, explaining that neoliberalism 'should never be a fig leaf for preemptive explanation, neither should invocations of neoliberalism be a prelude to unbounded analytical (or indeed political) fatalism, of the "we're all doomed to endless market rule" variety'. His argument is that we should study non-neoliberal alternatives or post-neoliberal trajectories not in isolation but relationally, understanding these emergent developments 'in relation to hegemonically neoliberalised fields of power and their associated domains of transformative practice'. How exactly do they challenge the governing imperatives of financialised and corporative market rule?

Conclusion: a problem-oriented approach to rural studies

It is common now to talk of global challenges or societal challenges. Around the world, globalisation, technological change, population growth or decline, ageing, migration, escalating demand for energy, foodstuffs and other raw materials, and the unevenness and volatility of capitalist economic growth together have presented governments and citizens with challenges of great magnitude to which there are no simple or obvious answers. The old certainties and big assumptions about the world order that have tended to govern our thinking since the end of the Second World War no longer seem valid, and there is a dearth of fresh thinking about how best to respond to the unresolved insecurities resulting from the war, let alone the new challenges of the current age such as government debt, faltering economic growth, rising unemployment (especially amongst young people), communities in decline, and rising inequalities in income, health, education and wealth. For many people, the failure to provide convincing responses to these challenges has exacerbated their sense of powerlessness, in turn threatening to undermine politics and the legitimate authority of government at all levels.

A key role for universities and scholars: How might rural social science, and researchers more generally, respond to these challenges? A crucial role for universities and scholars is, of course, to gather research-based evidence with which to inform action to address these societal challenges. Equally important is to foster deliberation and debate in public about what we understand to be 'a good life' and 'a good society'. Unless we do this, as Sandel (2013) has argued, we risk 'outsourcing our morality to the market', leaving neoliberal values unchallenged. The public value of universities has recently been addressed by several social scientists, notably by Burawoy (2005, 2011), by Brewer (2013, 2014) and in a collection edited by Holmwood (2011). Brewer, in particular, has argued the case for a value-infused, problem-oriented, post-disciplinary approach to 'the fundamental problems of culture, the market and the state in the 21st century' (Brewer, 2014). In accordance with the approach advocated by Brewer (2013, pp. 170–175) for the 'new public social science', this volume will therefore encourage relevance and post-disciplinarity by adopting a problem-oriented, rather than a strictly discipline-oriented approach. This will include challenging how problems are framed and the assumptions underlying policy.

Brewer argues that the 'wicked' nature of these societal challenges, or in other words their complexity and intractability (Head, 2008; Head & Alford, 2013), often requires the insights of more than a single discipline. Indeed he argues for post-disciplinary approaches – problem-oriented as opposed to discipline-oriented – superseding inter-disciplinarity and multi-disciplinarity. 'Problems are no longer defined in terms of the received wisdom of individual disciplines, but by the technical features required to understand, analyse, explain and ameliorate them', drawing on disciplinary ideas of all kinds used in combination as the problem determines (Brewer, 2014, p. 9). He suggests that this may not necessarily mean collaboration with others across disciplinary boundaries, if individual researchers are able themselves to transcend such boundaries and approach the topic from perspectives outside their own discipline. This is a major challenge for rural studies in the future.

The status of social science in universities is precarious for many reasons, not the least of which is that demonstrating the impacts of social science research is difficult. Some claim that social science research lacks 'concrete results', and that impacts are difficult to measure in a causal way. However, social scientists can demonstrate that its studies contribute to changes in social process – enhanced decision making, greater civic engagement, empowered civil society actors, more rigorous and informed discussion of contentious issues such as poverty and inequality, discrimination, community decline or failing institutions. In other words, social scientific research contributes to deeper democracy. Changes in social process are important 'impacts', and should be evaluated for their intrinsic worth, not whether they are comparable to a drought-resistant strain of rice or a faster microprocessor. Comparison with the biological and physical sciences misses the point.

Co-production of knowledge: Brewer also argues that in addressing these wicked problems 'public social science' must collaborate with other social actors and publics, including government, NGOs and civil society, through co-production of knowledge to lessen the gap between researchers and the 'real world' of wicked problems. Necessarily this requires social scientists 'to write to make themselves understood rather than for professional acclaim' (Brewer, 2014, p. 11) and for their research activity to be engaged and accessible. This is an issue for rural studies, where findings too often tend to be 'written for and consumed by academics' (Milbourne, 2000), often in 'a language that made sense only to the cognoscenti' with 'little if any talk of the political purchase of critical ideas beyond the walls of the classroom or the pages of academic journals' (Blomley, 1994, p. 383), although Milbourne (2000) has called for 'critical' geographers to seek out new audiences beyond the walls of the academy. But connecting with other social actors and publics goes beyond effective dissemination, communication and open access, Brewer argues, requiring genuine involvement of different publics in the formulation of the research problem and subsequent conversations with relevant publics at all stages of the research process (Brewer, 2013, p. 187). Examples of such co-production of knowledge from rural studies include Marika, Yunupingu, Marika-Mununggiritj and Muller (2009) and Ramzan, Pini and Bryant (2009). Lichter and Brown (2014) contend that research at the urban–rural interface provides a platform for interdisciplinary research by natural, physical and social scientists and deeper engagement between land grant universities and society. Ironically, they observe that 'the land grant system was a populist project that arose from the need to produce research-based information and education in support of the nation's development' (p. 5). Rural studies can reclaim this role by transcending boundaries between disciplines, perspectives and problem areas.

Transcending boundaries: Transcending boundaries is a major theme, therefore, whether these are boundaries between disciplines, boundaries between universities and society, or boundaries between research, teaching and engagement. It also means transcending the boundaries between nations if we are to engage with global society and address global challenges, but this raises the question of how far knowledge can travel – in other words, how do we distinguish between the universal and the particular?

Lowe (2012) has observed that, while research is necessarily produced in and of its time and place, globalisation is intensifying pressures to internationalise knowledge systems:

> The second half of the 20th century was a phase of strongly formalistic universalism, encapsulated in notions of modernisation, but which through association with the global projection of the dominant values of the Western world evoked counter charges of parochialism (including Eurocentrism and gender bias) ... Comparative analysis offers an alternative. It explores the different socio-cultural contexts in which knowledge is produced – where knowledge comes from, what is its currency and how it is used. Instead of denying the parochialism of knowledge, it seeks to appreciate its very groundedness and boundedness. While this is an acknowledgement of the limitation of the social sciences, it may also be the key to what distinctively they have to offer to the globalisation of scientific knowledge generally.
>
> *(Lowe, 2012, pp. 19–20)*

Dialogue between researchers in different countries is therefore one of the principal means by which we might distinguish between the *universal and the particular,* understanding the partiality and boundedness of our findings. Qualifying our findings in this way may also reveal new avenues for research by highlighting the significance of particular contingencies. Another major benefit of international comparisons is that, quite apart from gaining insights into other countries, it often enables the researcher to see their own country or region in new ways, making visible that which was hitherto taken for granted and thus invisible.

How do rural studies transcend boundaries between disciplines and between nations? While disciplines of rural sociology, rural geography and agricultural economics retain their distinctive identities, there has been a growing tendency towards interdisciplinarity and indeed post-disciplinarity. Today, rural studies draws from an array of parent disciplines, including sociology, anthropology, economics, geography, planning, demography, history, law, politics, education, gender studies, public health, ecology and the natural sciences. Nevertheless, the scope of rural studies is contested, with debates about the meaning and salience of rurality as an analytical concept noted above, and different intellectual traditions and institutional expressions dominating in different countries and disciplines (again, see Lowe, 2012).

In the USA, for example, scholarship on rural issues has continued to be defined along disciplinary lines, each of which has its own association and journal (for example, rural sociology, rural health, agricultural economics, community development). Moreover, US rural research tends to remain more structuralist and quantitative than elsewhere. In contrast, in the UK and elsewhere in Europe, rural research has often taken a 'cultural turn', influenced by postmodern and post-structuralist conceptual perspectives, but this is far from universal. In 1985 the *Journal of Rural Studies* (*JRS*) was launched with an editorial that highlighted not only debates over definitions, concepts and methods but also fragmentation between disciplines and between national research cultures and concerns. A new editor of *JRS* in 2012 reflected that rural studies had indeed become more international and interdisciplinary since 1985, but that the 'unbridged divide' between rural studies in Europe, America and Australasia (the 'global north') and the rest of the world has widened (Woods, 2012). These continuing differences are acknowledged in this Handbook, even though our focus will often be on the global north. It is important also to recognise the contribution to internationalisation of scholarship provided by bodies such as the International Rural Sociology Association (IRSA), founded in 1976 to promote international cooperation in rural sociology, and which holds a World Congress every four years.

Transcending the gap between academic research and the worlds of policy and practice represents another challenge, of great importance if rural social science aspires to help address the societal challenges of the 21st century. It is widely recognised that most potential users of research evidence will be unaware of our research findings – 'thirsty for knowledge while drowning in a sea of information', according to one recent study (McCormick, 2014). That study found that while university research is the most trusted by policy and practice users, paradoxically it was a relatively unused source of evidence. Shortall (2013a, p. 267) notes the findings of research by Reimer and Brett (2013) and by Shortall (2013b) that community leaders, civil servants and politicians involved in rural development and rural policy rarely use social science evidence to justify their claims, and more often use personal anecdotal experience to validate arguments.

In her work on sociology, knowledge and evidence in rural policy making, Shortall (2013a) has drawn on the wider literature on the sociology of scientific knowledge to question the ability of science (including social science) to make 'truth claims' on the basis of objective facts. She calls for reflexivity from rural researchers in considering how policy priorities are socially constructed, how research questions are framed politically, how evidence is used, the inherent knowledge power struggles, and the tensions in relating empirical knowledge to normative knowledge (Shortall, 2013a, p. 270).

Stevens's (2011, p. 237) ethnographic study of British civil servants' use of research evidence focuses more on the research users. Despite their commitment to the use of evidence in formulating 'evidence-based policy', civil servants were 'hampered by the huge volume of various kinds of evidence and by the unsuitability of much academic research in answering policy questions. Faced with this deluge of inconclusive information, they used evidence to create persuasive policy stories', often involving the use of 'killer charts', excising uncertainty and simplifying complexity in support of maintenance and enhancement of the prevailing order and of their own status and advancement. Social inequality was 'silently silenced'. Stevens concludes that this selective, narrative use of policy-infused evidence (rather than evidence-based policy) 'is ideological in that it supports systematically asymmetrical relations of power' and then plays a part in the reproduction of inequality (2011, p. 251). More positive accounts are offered in Bastow, Dunleavy and Tinkler's (2014) reports of academics' work with third-sector organisations in advocacy coalitions, and in several authors' recognition of the role which academics can play as 'boundary spanners', translating knowledge by linking academia with worlds of policy and practice (Sebba, 2013; Talbot & Talbot, 2014; Bastow, Dunleavy & Tinkler, 2014).

The challenge for social scientists engaged in rural studies to make a difference to policy and practice through their research is therefore not straightforward, and it may be easier to retreat to the ivory tower than to seek to 'speak truth to power' or to challenge powerful interests. Despite this, we maintain that researchers have a responsibility to society to do precisely this if we are to realise the public value of our universities and justify our public funding and academic freedoms.

The Handbook's organisation

This Handbook is organised around eight problem-oriented focal areas. Moreover, each discussion of each theme is shaped by four principal cross-cutting themes of enquiry, namely:

- the growing interdependence of places, and specifically of rural and urban societies and environments;
- the rise in social and economic inequality within and between places;
- the fiscal crisis of the state, and how this affects rural societies and their governance;
- neoliberalism, power and agency: rural areas as potential sites of resistance.

Weaving these cross-cutting themes through the individual contributions not only makes the book more coherent, but also ensures each essay's relevance to emerging issues and challenges and policy discourse.

The Handbook's sections represent critical substantive, problem-oriented domains of rural studies. Each section has been prepared under the guidance of a distinguished section editor who elaborates the issue at the beginning of their respective section. To the extent possible, our choice of section editors reflects the disciplinary and geographic range of rural studies. The book's first half comprises four sections, namely: Demographic Change, Economic Transformations, Food Systems and Land, and Environment and Resources. These chapters engage with major transformations in the material aspects of rural society, economy and environment. The second half begins with two sections focusing on particular aspects of rural inequality and exclusion, namely Changing Configurations of Gender and Rural Society, and Social and Economic Equality. The final two sections concern institutions and institutional change: Social Dynamics and Institutional Capacity, and Power and Governance. We believe that this Handbook addresses the most crucial issues for rural studies and rural societies in innovative and provocative ways, through an approach which is both problem oriented and theoretically informed. Each chapter synthesises recent research in the area, identifies emerging issues for research and articulates policy concerns associated with the particular issues.

Notes

1   There is no universal statistical standard for delineating rural and urban. Each nation reports data to the UN using its own definition. We will discuss this in some detail later in this introduction.
2   Three main scholarly associations examine rural social and economic transformations in the 'global north'. These are the European Society for Rural Sociology, the Rural Sociological Society and the International Rural Sociology Association. In addition, there are more specialised associations in agricultural economics, rural health, and environmental studies and so on, and many national governments have internal research organisations that conduct research on rural issues.
3   Recently, the USDA-ERS (United States Department of Agriculture Economic Research Service) commissioned the US National Academy of Sciences to host an interdisciplinary workshop to examine the reliability, and continued utility, of its four rural classification systems.
4   Discretionary income is defined as spendable income that exceeds subsistence needs of households with similar demographic features.
5   Of course, while global warming will negatively affect the prospects for agriculture in some areas, the result may be just the opposite in others: growing seasons may increase, water supply may increase, pollinators and beneficial insects may take up residence, etc.

References

Amin, A & Thrift, N (2002). *Cities: Reimagining the urban*. Cambridge: Polity.
Arnason, A, Shucksmith, M & Vergunst, J (2009). *Comparing rural development: Continuity and change in the countryside of Western Europe*. Aldershot: Ashgate.
Bastow, S, Dunleavy, P & Tinkler, J (2014). *The impact of the social sciences: How academics and their research make a difference*. London: Sage.
Bennett, K, Hudson, R & Benyon, H (2000). *Rural areas learning from the coalfields*. York: York Publishing Services.
Bertolini, P and Peragine, V (2009). *Poverty and social exclusion in rural areas*. Report to CEC Directorate General for Employment, Social Affairs and Equal Opportunities.
Blomley, N (1994). Activism and the academy. *Environment and Planning D: Society and Space* 12, 383–385.
Bosworth, G & Glasgow, N (2012). Entrepreneurial behavior among rural in-migrants. In M Shucksmith, DL Brown, S Shortall, J Vergunst & M Warner (Eds), *Rural transformations and rural policies in the US and UK* (pp. 138–155). New York: Routledge.
Brewer, J (2013). *The public value of the social sciences*. London: Bloomsbury.
Brewer, J (2014). *Society as a vocation: Renewing social science for social renewal*. Annual Lord Patten Lecture, Newcastle University Institute for Social Renewal, Newcastle University.
Brown, DL and Glasgow, N (2008). *Rural retirement migration*. Dordrecht: Springer.
Brown, DL, Greskovits, B & Kulcsar, L (2007). Leading sectors and leading regions: Economic restructuring and regional inequality in Hungary since 1990. *International Journal of Urban and Regional Research* 31(3), 1245–1260.
Brown, DL & Lee, M (1999). Persisting inequality between metropolitan and nonmetropolitan America: Implications for theory and policy. In P Moen, D Demster-McClain & H Walker (Eds), *A nation divided: Poverty, inequality and community in American society* (pp. 151–170). Ithaca, NY: Cornell University Press.
Burawoy, M (2005). For public sociology. *American Sociological Review* 70, 4–28.
Burawoy, M (2011). Redefining the public university: Global and national connections. In J Holmwood (Ed.), *A manifesto for the public university* (pp. 27–41). London: Bloomsbury.
Cahill, D (2012). The embedded neoliberal economy. In D Cahill, L Edwards & F Stilwell (Eds), *Neoliberalism: Beyond the free market* (pp. 110–127). Cheltenham: Edward Elgar.
Carr, P & Kefalis, M (2009). *Hollowing out the middle*. New York: Beacon Press.
Carter, I (1974). The Highlands of Scotland as an underdeveloped region. In E De Kalt & G Williams (Eds), *Sociology and development* (pp. 279–314). London: Tavistock Publications.
Caudil, H (1962). *Night comes to the Cumberlands*. Lexington: University of Kentucky Press.

CEC (2004). *Third report on economic and social cohesion*. COM (2004) 107 Final. Luxembourg: Commission of the European Communities.

CEC (2010). *Europe 2020: A strategy for smart, sustainable and inclusive growth*. COM (2010) 2020 final. Brussels: Commission of the European Communities.

Centeno, M & Cohen, J (2012). The arc of neoliberalism. *Annual Review of Sociology* 38(1), 317–340.

Champion, A & Hugo, G (Eds). (2003). *New forms of urbanization: Beyond the urban–rural dichotomy*. London: Ashgate.

Cheshire, L (2006). *Governing local development*. Aldershot: Ashgate.

Cloke, P (2006). Conceptualising rurality. In P Cloke, T Marsden & P Mooney (Eds), *The handbook of rural studies* (pp. 18–28). London: Sage.

Cloke, P, Marsden, T & Mooney, P (Eds). (2006). *The handbook of rural studies*. London: Sage.

Collins, S, Carpenter, S, Swinton, S, Orenstein, D, Childers, D, Gragson, T, Grimm, N, Grove, J, Harlan, S & Kaye, J (2011). An integrated conceptual framework for long-term social-ecological research. *Frontiers in Ecology and Environment* 9(6), 351–357.

Copus, A (2010). New relationships between rural and urban areas in EU countries. Invited paper presented at the conference 'The territorial approach in agricultural and rural policies: An international review', Rome, 4–5 November.

Copus, A & De Lima, P (Eds). (2014). *Territorial cohesion in rural Europe: The relational turn in rural development*. Abingdon: Routledge.

Copus, A, Hall, C, Barnes, A, Dalton, H, Cook, P, Weingarten, P, Baum, S, Stange, H, Lidnder, C, Hill, A, Eiden, G, McQaid, R, Grief, M & Johansson, M (2006). *Study on employment in rural Areas (SERA)*. Final deliverable. Brussels: DG Agriculture.

Copus, A & Hörnström, L (Eds) (2011). *The new rural Europe: Towards a rural cohesion policy*. Stockholm: Nordregio.

Court of Auditors. (2006). *Rural development investments: Do they effectively address the problems of rural areas?* Available at www.eca.europa.eu/audit_reports/special_reports/docs/2006/rs07_06en.pdf.

Crenshaw, K (1991). Mapping the margins: Intersectionality, identity, politics and violence against women of color. *Stanford Law Review* 43(6), 1241–1299.

Dillon, M & Savage, S (2006). Values and religion in rural America: Attitudes toward abortion and same sex marriage. *Issue Brief* no. 1. University of New Hampshire: Carsey Institute.

Duncan, C (1999). *Worlds apart: Why poverty persists in rural America*. New Haven, CT: Yale University Press.

Duncan, M (2014). *Worlds apart* (2nd edn). New Haven, CT: Yale University Press.

Durkheim, E (1938). *The rules of sociological method*. Free Press.

Edin, K & Shaefer, L (2015). *$2 a day: Living on almost nothing in America*. New York: Houghton Mifflin Harcourt.

Eurostat. (2012). *Labour force survey: Youth unemployment 2009 and 2012 by degree of urbanisation*. Labour Force Survey. Brussels: Eurostat.

Fairbairn, M (2012). Framing transformation: The counter-hegemonic potential of food sovereignty in the US context. *Agriculture and Human Values* 29(2), 217–230.

Firey, W (1978). Some contributions of sociology to the study of natural resources. In M Barnabas, S Hulbe & P Jacob (Eds), *Challenges of societies in transition* (pp. 162–174). Delhi: Maxmillan Co.

Fortman, L (2014). Connections: The next decade of rural sociological research on natural resources and the environment. In C Bailey, L Jensen & E Ransom (Eds), *Rural America in a globalizing world* (pp. 159–171). Morgantown: University of West Virginia Press.

Frank, AG (1971). *Sociology of development and underdevelopment*. New York: Monthly Review Press.

Gkartzios, M (2013). 'Leaving Athens': Narratives of counterurbanisation in times of crisis. *Journal of Rural Studies* 32, 158–167.

Goldman, M & Schurman, R (2000). Closing the great divide: New social theory on society and nature. *Annual Review of Sociology* 26, 563–584.

Hadjimichalis, C & Hudson, R (2014). Contemporary crisis across Europe and the crisis of regional development theories. *Regional Studies* 48(1), 208–218.

Halfacree, K (1993). Locality and social representation: Space, discourse and alternative definitions of the rural. *Journal of Rural Studies* 9, 1–15.

Halfacree, K (2006). Rural space: Constructing a threefold architecture. In P Cloke, T Marsden & P Mooney (Eds), *The handbook of rural studies* (pp. 44–62). London: Sage.

Halfacree, K (2012). Heterolocal identities? Counter-urbanisation, second homes, and rural consumption in the era of mobilities. *Population, Space and Place* 18, 209–224.

Head, B (2008). Wicked problems in public policy. *Public Policy* 3(2), 101–118.

Head, B & Alford, J (2013). Wicked problems: Implications for public policy and management. *Administration and Society* 45(3), 1–29.

Heley, J & Jones, L (2012). Relational rurals. *Journal of Rural Studies* 28, 208–217.

Hoggart, K (1990). Let's do away with rural. *Journal of Rural Studies* 6(3), 245–257.

Holmwood, J (Ed.). (2011). *A manifesto for the public university*. London: Bloomsbury.

Hunter, L, Boardman, J & Saint Onge, J (2005). The association between natural amenities, rural population growth and long-term residents' economic well-being. *Rural Sociology* 70(4), 452–469.

Jarsoz, L (2008). The city in the country: Growing alternative food networks in metropolitan areas. *Journal of Rural Studies* 24(3), 231–244.

Kasimis, C & Papadopoulos, A (2013). Rural transformations and family farming in contemporary Greece. In D Ortiz-Miranda, A Moragues-Faus & E Arnalte-Alegre (Eds), *Agriculture in Mediterranean Europe: Between old and new paradigms* (pp. 263–193). Research in Rural Sociology and Development 19. Bingley: Emerald Group.

Kerbo, H (2003). *Social stratification and inequality*. McGraw-Hill.

Klein, N (2007). *Shock doctrine: The rise of disaster capitalism*. Canada: Knopf.

Krannich, R, Gentry, B, Luloff, A & Robertson, P (2014). Resource dependency in rural America. In C Bailey, L Jensen & E Ransom (Eds), *Rural America in a globalizing world* (pp. 208–225). Morgantown: University of West Virginia Press.

Lacy, WB., Glenna, LL, Biscotti, D, Welsh, R & Clancy, K (2014). The two cultures of science: Implications for university–industry relationships in US agriculture biotechnology. *Journal of Integrative Agriculture* 12(1), 60345–60347.

Lefebvre, H (1991). *The production of space*. Oxford: Blackwell. (Originally published in 1974 in French)

Levitas, R (2015). The rural, the urban and the utopian. Address to European Utopian Studies Society conference, Newcastle University.

Lichter, D & Brown, DL (2011). Rural America in urban society: Changing spatial and social boundaries. *Annual Review of Sociology* 37, 565–592.

Lichter, D & Brown, DL (2014). The new rural–urban interface: Lessons for higher education. *Choices* 29(1), 1–6.

Lichter, D, Parisi, D & Taquino, M (2012). The geography of exclusion: Race, segregation, and concentrated poverty. *Social Problem* 59, 364–388.

Lobao, L, Hooks, G & Tickamayer, A (Eds). (2007). *The sociology of spatial inequality*. New York: SUNY Press.

Logan, J (2012). Making a place for space: Spatial thinking in social science. *Annual Review of Sociology* 38, 507–524.

Lowe, P (2012). The agency of rural research in comparative context. In M Shucksmith, DL Brown, S Shortall, J Vergunst & M Warner (Eds), *Rural transformations and rural policies in the US and UK* (pp. 18–38). New York: Routledge.

Lowe, P, Murdoch, J & Ward, N (1995). Networks in rural development: Beyond exogenous and endogenous models. In JD van der Ploeg & C van Dijk (Eds), *Beyond modernisation* (pp. 87–105). Assen: Van Gorcum.

Mackenzie, F (2006). A working land: Crofting communities, place and the politics of the possible in post-Land Reform Scotland. *Transactions of the Institute of British Geographers* NS 31, 383–398.

Mackenzie, AFD (2013). *Places of possibility: Property, nature and community land ownership*. Chichester: Wiley-Blackwell.

Mandel, E (1976). Capitalism and regional disparities. *Southwest Economy and Society* 1, 41–46.

Marika, R, Yunupingu, Y, Marika-Mununggiritj, R & Muller, S (2009). Leaching the poison – the importance of process and partnership in working with Yolngu. *Journal of Rural Studies* 24, 404–413.

Marsden, T (2003). *The condition of rural sustainability*. Assen, Netherlands: Van Gorcum.

Massey, D & Denton, N (1993). *American apartheid*. Cambridge, MA: Harvard University Press.

McCormick, J (2014). *Evidence exchange: Learning from social policy across the UK*. Dunfermline: Carnegie UK Trust.

McGranahan, D (1999). Natural amenities drive rural population change. AER-781. Washington, DC: USDA-ERS.

Milbourne, P (2000). Exporting 'other' rurals: New audiences for qualitative research. In A Hughes, C Morris & S Seymour (Eds), *Ethnography and rural research* (pp. 179–197). Cheltenham: Countryside and Community Press.

Milbourne, P & Kitchen, L (2014). Rural mobilities: Connecting movement and fixidity in rural places. *Journal of Rural Studies* 34, 326–336.

Morello, L (2011). NOAA makes it official: 2011 among most extreme weather years in history. *Scientific American*, June 17. Retrieved 30 June 2015 from http://www.scientificamerican.com/article/noaa-makes-2011-most-extreme-weather-year/.

Mormont, M (1990). Who is rural? or How to be rural: Towards a sociology of the rural. In T Marsden, P Lowe & S Whatmore (Eds), *Rural restructuring* (pp. 21–44). London: David Fulton.

Morton, L & Rudel, T (2014). Impacts of climate change on people and communities of rural America. In C Bailey, L Jensen & E Ransom (Eds), *Rural America in a globalizing world* (pp. 172–189). Morgantown: University of West Virginia Press.

Murdoch, J (2003). Co-constructing the countryside: Hybrid networks and the extensive self. In P Cloke (Ed.), *Country visions* (pp. 263–282). Harlow: Pearson.

Murdoch, J & Lowe, P (2003). The preservationist paradox: Modernism, environmentalism and the politics of spatial division. *Transactions of the Institute of British Geographers* NS28, 318–332.

Murdoch, J, Lowe, P, Ward, N & Marsden, T (2003). *The differentiated countryside*. London: Routledge.

Murdoch, J & Pratt, A (1993). Rural studies: Modernism, postmodernism and the 'post-rural'. *Journal of Rural Studies* 9, 411–427.

Murphy, R (1995). Sociology as if nature did not matter: An ecological critique. *British Journal of Sociology* 46(4), 688–707.

Neal, S (2013). Transition culture: Politics, localities and ruralities. *Journal of Rural Studies* 32, 60–69.

ONS (Office for National Statistics). (2015). *Public expenditure statistical analysis* (PESA). London: HMSO.

Pahl, RE (1965). *Urbs in rure: The Metropolitan fringe in Hertfordshire*. Geographical Papers No. 2, London: LSE.

Pahl, RE (1968). The rural–urban continuum. In RE Pahl (Ed.), *Readings in urban sociology* (pp. 263–297). Oxford: Pergamon.

Peck, J (2014). Explaining (with) neoliberalism. *Territory, Politics, Governance* 1(2), 132–157.

Peck, J, Theodore, N & Brenner, N (2010). Postneoliberalism and its malcontents. *Antipode* 41(1), 94–116.

Philip, L & Shucksmith, M (2003). Conceptualising social exclusion. *European Planning Studies* 11(4), 461–480.

Piketty, T. (2014). *Capital in the 21st century*. Cambridge, MA: Belknap Press.

Potter, C & Wolf, S (2012). Agri-environmental policy, rural environment and forks in the road. In M Shucksmith, DL Brown, S Shortall, J Vergunst & M Warner (Eds), *Rural transformations and rural policies in the US and UK* (pp. 216–232). New York: Routledge.

Potter, R. & Unwin, T. (1989) (Eds) (1989). *The geography of urban–rural interaction in developing countries*. London: Routledge.

Pratt, A (1996). Discourses of rurality: Loose talk or social struggle. *Journal of Rural Studies* 12, 69–78.

Ramutsindela, M (2005). Society–nature dualism and human gradation. In M Ramutsindela (Ed.), *Parks and people in post-colonial society* (pp. 1–17). Dordrecht: Springer.

Ramzan, B, Pini, B & Bryant, L (2009). Experiencing and writing indigeneity, rurality and gender. *Journal of Rural Studies* 24, 435–443.

Rank, M, Hirschl, T & Foster, K (2014). *Chasing the American dream: Understanding what shapes our fortunes*. Oxford: Oxford University Press.

Ransome, P (2005). *Work, consumption and culture: Affluence and social change in the 21st century*. London: Sage.

Reimer, W & Brett, M (2013). Scientific knowledge and rural policy: A long distant relationship. *Sociologia Ruralis* 53(3), 272–290.

Rural Sociological Society. (1993). *Persistent rural poverty*. Boulder, CO: Westview Press.

Sachs, C (2014). Gender, race, ethnicity, class and sexuality in Rural America. In C Bailey, L Jensen & E Ransom (Eds), *Rural America in a globalizing world* (pp. 412–434). Morgantown: West Virginia University Press.

Saez, E & Piketty, T (2013). Top incomes and the great recession: Recent evolutions and policy implications. *International Monetary Fund Economic Review* 61(3), 456–478.

Sandel, M (2013). *What money can't buy? The moral limits of markets*. London: Penguin.

Sebba, J (2013). An exploratory review of the role of research mediators in social science. *Evidence & Policy* 9(3), 391–408.

Sherman, J (2014). Rural poverty: The great recession, rising unemployment, and the under-utilized safety net. In C Bailey, L Jensen & E Ransom (Eds), *Rural America in a globalizing world* (pp. 523–542). Morgantown: West Virginia University Press.

Shoard, M (1980). *The theft of the countryside*. London: Temple Smith.

Shortall, S (2013a). The role of subjectivity and knowledge power struggles in the formation of public policy. *Sociology* 47(6), 1088–1103.

Shortall, S (2013b). Using scientific knowledge in policy making: The importance of organisational culture. *Sociologia Ruralis* 53(3), 349–368.

Shucksmith, M (2009). Sustainable rural communities: Constructing sustainable places beyond cities. Plenary paper to ESRS Congress, Vaasa, 1999. Available at http://www.researchgate.net/publication/264489776_Sustainable_Rural_Communities_constructing_sustainable_places_beyond_cities.

Shucksmith, M (2012). Class, power and inequality in rural areas: Beyond social exclusion? *Sociologia Ruralis* 52(4), 377–397.

Shucksmith, M, Brown, DL & Vergunst, J (2012). Constructing the rural–urban interface. Place still matters in a highly mobile society. In M Shucksmith, DL Brown, S Shortall, J Vergunst & M Warner (Eds), *Rural transformations and rural policies in the US and UK* (pp. 287–303). New York: Routledge.

Shucksmith, M & Rønningen, K (2011). The uplands after neoliberalism? The role of the small farm in rural sustainability. *Journal of Rural Studies*. Published online, April 2011.

Shucksmith, M, Talbot, H & Lee, R (2011). Meta-narratives as heuristic generalisations of rural change. In A Copus & L Hörnström (Eds), *The new rural Europe: Towards rural cohesion policy* (pp.19–36). Stockholm: Nordregio.

Smith, N (1990). *Uneven development*. Cambridge, MA: Blackwell.

Smith, T (2011). Public attitudes toward homosexuality. Chicago: NORC. Retrieved 7 July 2015 from http://www.norc.org/NewsEventsPublications/PressReleases/Pages/american-acceptance-of-homosexuality-gss-report.aspx.

Stevens, A (2011). Telling policy stories: An ethnographic study of the use of evidence in policy-making in the UK. *Journal of Social Policy* 40, 237–255.

Sturzaker, J & Shucksmith, M (2011). Planning for housing in rural England: Discursive power and spatial exclusion. *Town Planning Review* 82(2), 169–193.

Swindal, M & McAreavey, R (2012). Rural governance: Participation, power and possibilities for action. In M Shucksmith, D Brown, S Shortall, M Vergunst & M Warner (Eds), *Rural policies and rural transformations in the US and UK*. New York: Routledge.

Takac, J & Szalma, I (2014). Gays in the neighborhood? European attitudes about homosexuality a quarter century after the fall of the Soviet Union. *CritCom*, 8 May. Retrieved 7 July 2015 from http://councilforeuropeanstudies.org/critcom/gays-in-the-neighborhood-european-attitudes-about-homosexuality-a-quarter-century-after-the-fall-of-the-soviet-union/.

Talbot, C & Talbot, C (2014). *Sir Humphrey and the professors: What does Whitehall want from academics?* Manchester University: Policy@Manchester.

Tonnies, F. (1887). *Gemeinschaft und Gessellschaft*. Translated as *Community and associations*, Routledge & Kegan Paul, 1955.

Toynbee, P & Walker, D (2015). *Cameron's coup: How the Tories took Britain to the brink*. London: The Guardian.

Urry, J (2007). *Mobilities*. Cambridge: Polity.

USDA (2001). Stories across America: Opportunities for rural tourism. National Trust for Historic Reservation. http://www.nal.usda.gov/ric/ricpubs/stories.htm.

Vergunst, J, Geisler, C & Steadman, R (2012). Nature conservation and environmental management: Working landscapes in Adirondack Park and Cairngorms National Park. In M Shucksmith, D Brown, S Shortall, M Vergunst & M Warner (Eds), *Rural policies and rural transformations in the US and UK* (pp. 233–252). New York: Routledge.

Wacquant, L (2007). Territorial stigmatization in the age of advanced marginality. *Thesis Eleven* 91, 66–77.

Walthall, C, Hatfield, J, Backlund, P, Lengnick, L, Marshall, E, Walsh, M, Adkins, S, Aillery, M, Ainsworth, E & Ammann, C (2012). Climate change and agriculture in the United States: Effects and adaptation. *USDA Technical Bulletin* 1935. Washington, DC: USDA.

Williamson, J (1965). Regional inequality and the process of national development: A description of patterns. *Economic Development and Cultural Change* 13, 3–45.

Wilson, WJ (1980). *The declining significance of race*. Chicago: University of Chicago Press.

Wilson, WJ (1996). *When work disappears*. New York: Knopf.

Wirth, L (1938). Urbanism as a way of life. *American Journal of Sociology* 44, 1–24.

Woods, M (2009). Rural geography: Blurring boundaries and making connections. *Progress in Human Geography* 33, 849–858.

Woods, M (2012). *Rural*. Abingdon: Routledge.

Wright, E (2010). *Envisioning real utopias*. London: Verso.

Part I
Demographic Change

Section editor: Neil Argent

2

Demographic Change

Beyond the Urban–Rural Divide

Neil Argent

Introduction

At the most basic level of analysis, rural societies are constituted by the people that live within their spaces and places. Of course, it is the many and various social, cultural and economic relationships among these people as well as their demographic characteristics that can be said to shape the distinctiveness of rural places (Panelli, 2006). Increasingly, these places are being moulded by relationships that are 'stretched out' across space, from the local through to global scales. Rapidly increasing levels of personal migration and mobility into and out of rural regions across the globe, emanating from seemingly ineluctable processes of modernisation, industrialisation and urbanisation, are drawing rural and urban together, unsettling long-established dichotomous notions of the two entities' apparently separate natures. Simultaneously, and given that voluntary human *physical* mobility is always inextricably intertwined with *social* mobility, these population shifts are centrally implicated in the creation, or persistence, of sociospatial inequality. This intertwining of demographic, socioeconomic and political change can be seen in such diverse instances as the 'gentrification of the countryside' in Western, high-amenity rural regions and localities, and the plight of the 'left behind' populations in rural China and in other, Western nations, as the young migrate to take up more remunerative employment in burgeoning industrial cities. Rural populations within these different societies are also changing across time and space in *structural* terms. For example, long-term, secular trends towards declining fertility and smaller household sizes are combining with variegated patterns of international and internal migration to produce altered national and regional population growth trajectories and age–sex structures. One of the key outcomes of these dynamics is accelerated and structural ageing of rural communities, a demographic trend that is raising a number of challenges for service provision and community development, particularly in more remote areas.

In these contexts, this chapter introduces this section of the Handbook by, first, briefly considering the long-standing but increasingly blurred spatial and social taxonomies regarding rural and urban, second, offering a broad account of the diverse 'shapes' of global north rural populations and contemporary demographic issues and, finally, providing a brief synopsis of each of the section chapters.

'Rural populations' or 'populations in rural areas' or just 'populations'?

As Shucksmith and Brown (this volume) have already outlined, the precise nature of 'rural' and 'rurality' has been subject to much social scientific and philosophical debate since the mid-1980s for two key reasons. First, the set of intellectual approaches applied to 'rural studies' (broadly construed) from that time expanded, greatly influenced by postmodernist and post-structuralist standpoints. Second, the material reality of rural areas underwent significant changes in the wake of counter-urbanisation flows of people, capital and commodities, and a concomitant shift to a more pluralistic use and governance of rural space (see Wilson, 2001; Argent, 2002, 2011; Woods, 2003; Holmes, 2006). There seems little doubt that the growing multifunctionality of rural space has helped precipitate an oftentimes radical reconsideration of long-standing conventions regarding the definition and ontological status of 'the rural'. According to this notion, rural areas are valorised by a wide range of local and non-local, agricultural and non-agricultural interests, for their consumption- and protection-oriented values as well as their productive capacities (see Holmes, 2006).

Naturally, the ensuing debates over the legacies and likely future benefits of competing stances caused controversy and polarisation, such that adherents of the various old and new approaches effectively formed oppositional 'camps' or 'tribes', defending the supremacy of their own *Weltanschauung* against the attacks of the others. A helpful intervention in this respect, then, was Halfacree's rural spatial triad (Halfacree, 2006) which, rather than seek to denigrate or elevate any one perspective at the expense of the others, incorporated positivist, post-positivist, phenomenological, structuralist and post-structuralist knowledges within a single conceptual framework in an attempt to better explain the totality of rural lived experience. Taking inspiration from Lefebvre's tripartite framework (Lefebvre, 1991), Halfacree's rural triad (2006) explicitly recognises three domains: the lived, conceived and perceived. These domains are termed, respectively, 'everyday lives of the rural', 'formal representations of the rural' and 'rural localities' (Halfacree, 2006). Halfacree has previously argued that demographers and population geographers have until relatively recently approached their work from within the comfortable certainties of positivistic spatial and social science: the realm of the conceived and 'formal representations of the rural'. However, along with rural geography and sociology, population studies has since undergone substantial change with the introduction of more post-positivist and post-structuralist stances and qualitative approaches (see Smith, 2007). Halfacree's (2006) triadic framework, therefore, offers a means for not just advancing new or hitherto marginal or marginalised perspectives on rural society but also acknowledging that what we know of rural society is a product of a range of different modes of representation – official, lay, formal, informal, positivistic and non-positivistic. It provides a crucial recognition that a comprehensive understanding of the complex influences and outcomes of demographic, sociocultural and economic change requires a carefully calibrated combination of this range of perspectives.

Thus, understandings and representations of demographic change do not occur in a social, economic nor political vacuum (Brown, 2013). Each of the chapters included in this section provide unique insights into a particular demographic issue. So as to provide a broader context for the varying foci of this section, this chapter next sets out the major post-Second World War global north 'rural' demographic trends, and the growing dilemmas surrounding their measurement.

Broad demographic trends and processes in the global north

The 2008 World Bank announcement that the globe's population had recently become predominantly urban provoked a range of responses. For most, the passing of this milestone was a mere inevitability, for others it re-emphasised the relative (and in some cases, the absolute) demographic decline facing rural areas. As Figure 2.1 shows, although each nation – or regional bloc, as in the case of Europe – varied in terms of its degree of urbanisation at the mid-point of the last century, all began the period with predominantly urbanised populations. Highly concentrated populations have long been a feature of both Australian and New Zealand settlement systems, a situation that has only been reinforced since the 1950s. Interestingly, the biggest proportional increases in urbanisation for these nations occurred during the 'long boom' between the conclusion of the Second World War and the crisis that beset the early 1970s. For most of these countries this is an era of sustained prosperity and very rapid development (and creative destruction) with the application of revolutionary new mechanical and chemical engineering and genetic technologies to agriculture, facilitating the search for greatly expanded economies of scale amongst farmers and in other predominantly rural, resource-based industries – including corporate operations – and the consequent flight of the rural population to the opportunities afforded by city and, to a lesser degree, town life. For the non-European nations shown in Figure 2.1, this was also a period of very substantial and sustained immigration – emanating largely from Europe – which overwhelmingly became concentrated in the major cities (Castles & Miller, 2009), providing a major fillip to the urbanisation process. The pace of urbanisation tapered off appreciably after the 1970s for all nations, consistent with the OPEC oil price crisis-inspired recession and the advent of counter-urbanisation across most Western nations (Champion, 2011; Ní Laoire & Stockdale, this volume).

Of course, such milestones pose (or perhaps beg) as many questions as they provide answers for, not least because of national differences in defining 'urban' and 'rural' as discrete settlement categories. The uncertainty is further compounded by counter-urbanisation processes and commuting behaviour which have both served to practically enlarge the thresholds of many cities, creating swathes of peri-urban space, 'edge cities' and the like, further smudging the boundaries of urban and rural (Champion & Hugo, 2004).

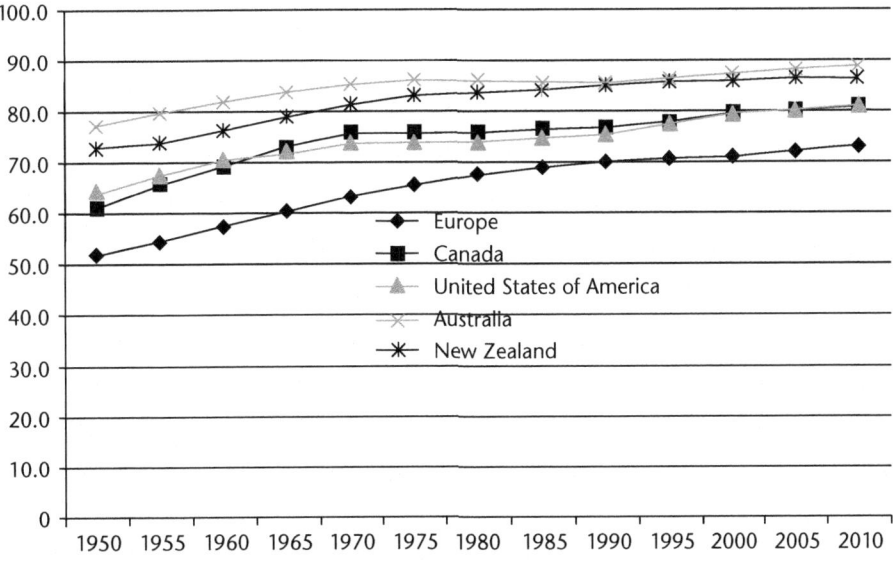

Figure 2.1　Urbanisation levels within Europe, United States of America, Canada, Australia and New Zealand, 1950–2010

Source: United Nations, Department of Economic and Social Affairs, Population Division, 2014.

The overall trend of increased urbanisation does not necessarily equate to rural depopulation, as Table 2.1 shows. Although European nations (except the UK) have experienced continued if fluctuating rural population decline over the 60 years from 1951, the fortunes of the rural societies of the remaining nations (UK, USA and the former 'settler states' of Canada, New Zealand and Australia) have been far more positive. Interestingly, the 1950s was generally a decade of growth or relative stability in rural populations, perhaps as agricultural frontiers continued to expand to meet growing international concerns regarding food and fibre shortages and, in nations like Australia and New Zealand at least, so as to meet strategic national goals concerning population distribution and economic development. The 1970s and 1980s encompassed a period of generally strong rural population growth for the non-European nations, with the exception of New Zealand, which again is consonant with the first wave of counter-urbanisation. The 1990s saw a reversal of this trend – except for New Zealand, which experienced relatively rapid growth – while the first decade of the new millennium witnessed a return to growth across most, though not all, countries.

The complex trends outlined in Table 2.1, particularly those following the turn of the current century, may seem odd at first. For many Western developed nations, the general post-1970s discourse surrounding rural demography is one of decline, crisis and negativity. Yet, as discussed above, there is no singular, homogenous 'rural'. While long-term population loss has been felt in particular categories of rural region and locality – commonly those with economic bases centred on broad-acre, capital-intensive farming or basic manufacturing – some rural regions have also seen relatively rapid and sustained population increase. In this last-mentioned case, typical candidates can be found in the counter-urbanisation 'hot spots' of the peri-metropolitan fringe, the high-amenity zones along favoured coastlines, mountainous resort areas, inland lake and riverine zones and mining towns/settlements. And as noted previously, there is little in the way of international consistency in the definition of 'urban' and 'rural' (Champion & Hugo, 2004).

Until relatively recently, the demographic features of many global north populations seemed to lag behind those of the broader societies of which they were a part by a generation or so, perhaps confirming their status as 'residual societies'. For instance, rural societies were often associated with larger than average family sizes, higher than average fertility and lower than average[1] ethnic and racial diversity than the host society, and official data sources often bore these generalisations out. More recently, though, as rural regions across the developed world confront rapidly ageing populations, and at least a share of international migration is destined for rural locales, historic rural conventions are being supplanted by a new set of defining characteristics.

Table 2.1 Rural population change (%) in Europe, United Kingdom, United States of America, Canada, Australia and New Zealand, 1951–2010

	1951–1960	1961–1970	1971–1980	1981–1990	1991–2000	2001–2010
Europe	−2.42	−5.80	−6.37	−3.32	−2.13	−4.34
United Kingdom	6.16	11.32	−5.50	3.72	0.23	−7.72
Canada	2.56	−5.96	14.52	7.69	−3.80	3.98
United States of America	−0.77	−1.18	8.17	3.58	−4.59	0.55
Australia	0.32	0.33	10.60	17.17	−2.25	2.63
New Zealand	7.24	−6.37	−1.88	−0.67	6.43	8.66

Source: United Nations, Department of Economic and Social Affairs, Population Division, 2014.

With the waning of the post-Second World War 'baby boom' during the late 1960s and early 1970s, Western developed nations entered a period of sustained fertility decline, with many seemingly destined to remain at below replacement levels for the foreseeable future. As contemporary socioeconomic and gender equity preference structures have diffused throughout Western societies – spatially and socially – so aggregate fertility rates between urban and rural have slowly converged toward a lower secular level (Hakim, 2000). In aggregate, this is a highly portentous trend, given the chronic net migration loss of young (19–24-year-old) men and women from almost all categories of rural region, and the associated impending drop in the overall number of rural births which further exacerbates regional ageing. Rural ageing is so extreme in some nations that places are experiencing natural population decrease – more deaths than births. This is a result of the chronic net out-migration of young adults, regardless of the fertility rates of the population left behind. There simply are not enough potential parents remaining in affected rural communities compared with the proportion of older persons. However, it is important to recognise that substantial fertility differentials persist within global north rural societies. For example, as Johnson and Lichter (2011) show in the United States, Hispanic migrant populations tend to have higher fertility than resident white populations, a situation that, together with the former's younger age structure, has bolstered local rural populations that would otherwise be undergoing natural decrease. In Australia a strong positive correlation persists between, on the one hand, the degree of remoteness – and the level of indigeneity of the population – and fertility, on the other. Very substantial age-specific fertility rate differentials between remote and metropolitan populations persist with, for instance, 2009 fertility levels among remote area under-20-year-old women over five times higher than for women of the same age living in Australia's cities. Regional areas – situated geographically and on the accessibility gradient somewhere midway between these two extremes – exhibited fertility rates that also fell between the relatively high levels of the remote zone and the below replacement levels of the major cities (Australian Bureau of Statistics, 2010).

The section chapters

As a set, the chapters in this section present highly informed and contemporary perspectives on the changing demographic face of rural areas, inclusive of the critical dynamics driving rural demographic change, and the multifarious policy, practice and social issues emerging from these changes.

Caitríona Ní Laoire and Aileen Stockdale's chapter on rural migration and the life course perspective begins with an acknowledgement that preferences and propensities for living in, or moving from, rural settings vary over the span of a lifetime. Their chapter demonstrates how a life course framework permits a holistic conceptualisation of rural migration (in-, out-, return) influences and outcomes; one that moves beyond conventional taxonomies of 'migrant' and 'movement' associated with counter-urbanisation and other specific migration currents.

Bettina Bock, Giorgio Osti and Flaminia Ventura's chapter centres on the interrelationships between heightened rural mobility and processes and patterns of social exclusion and integration in Europe. Their discussion focuses on the experiences of migrants from central-eastern member states to rural northwest and southern Europe in search of employment and a better quality of life. In the context of the post-global financial crisis austerity drive gripping most EU countries, Bock and colleagues note these migrants' conflicting reception in their new destinations: welcomed as agricultural and domestic workers and as a service population, but also subjected to xenophobia and discrimination.

As noted above, one significant element common to all global north rural populations is accelerated ageing (structural and numerical). The chapter by Thomas Scharf, Kieran Walsh and Eamon O'Shea notes the recent but growing research and public policy interest in rural ageing. Adopting a rural gerontology approach, Scharf, Walsh and O'Shea identify two important challenges to the development of a rural ageing research agenda. The first relates to how 'the rural' is defined conceptually and as an empirical category, a point discussed above. Relatedly, the second challenge concerns the need to move beyond the 'urban–rural divide' as an explanatory framework for differences in experiences of ageing and social and physical infrastructure provision for the elderly. In summary, they argue that rural ageing research needs to recognise that the rural aged's experiences of social inclusion or exclusion is multiply determined by individual-scale capacities together with broader scale political, economic and technological forces.

The complex interrelationships between health, health care provision and rural places are addressed by Neil Hanlon and Robin Kearns. Drawing on examples from New Zealand and Canada, their chapter argues the need for more nuanced conceptualisations of, and policy responses to, the diversity of rural health fortunes. Stressing the importance of regional and local context in health influences and outcomes, Hanlon and Kearns discuss rural health service environments from the perspective of providers and examine factors that influence the attractiveness of rural places for health professional practice.

Rural populations both influence and reflect long- and short-term political, economic, sociocultural and technological changes. It is this reflexive character of population–society relationships that David Brown and Neil Argent explore in their chapter. Central to the chapter's concerns are the complex ways in which the three vital dynamics of demographic change both shape, and are shaped by, changes in household and family structures, labour markets, service demand and economic vitality across heterogeneous rural landscapes. In addition, Brown and Argent focus on how institutional structures mediate the impacts of population change on society and economy and vice versa, contending that population change matters, but 'demography is not destiny'.

In summary, then, and consistent with the key points made earlier in this chapter regarding the heterogeneous and socially constructed nature of rural society, space and place, this section's chapters provide 'state of the art' explorations of the interrelationships between demographic processes and structures, on the one hand, and shifting political, institutional and cultural settings of global north nations, on the other, all within the opportunities and constraints afforded by the particular locational and physical environments of rural regions.

Note

1 In industrial and post-industrial societies the mean of any demographic indicator will naturally be dominated by the sheer population size of the major cities in the national settlement system.

References

Argent, N (2002). From pillar to post? In search of the post-productivist countryside in Australia. *Australian Geographer* 33, 97–114.

Argent, N (2011). Trouble in paradise: Governing Australia's multifunctional landscapes. *Australian Geographer* 42, 183–205.

Australian Bureau of Statistics. (2010). One for the country: Recent trends in fertility. *Australian social trends* (Cat. No. 4102.0). Belconnen: Australian Bureau of Statistics.

Brown, D (2013). European rural population change matters, but demography is not destiny. *Przeglad Socjologiczny* 30, 135–150.

Castles, S & Miller, M (2009). *The age of migration: International population movements in the modern world* (4th edn). Basingstoke: Palgrave Macmillan.

Champion, A (2011). Europe's rural demography. In L Kulcsár & K Curtis (Eds), *International handbook of rural demography* (pp. 81–93). Dordrecht: Springer.

Champion, T & Hugo, G (2004). *New forms of urbanization: Beyond the urban–rural dichotomy.* Farnham: Ashgate.

Hakim, C (2000). *Work–lifestyle choices in the 21st century.* Oxford: Oxford University Press.

Halfacree, K (2006). Rural space: Constructing a three-fold architecture. In P Cloke, T Marsden & P Mooney (Eds), *Handbook of rural studies* (pp. 44–62). London: Sage.

Holmes, J (2006). Impulses towards a multifunctional transition in rural Australia: Gaps in the research agenda. *Journal of Rural Studies* 22, 142–160.

Johnson, K & Lichter, D (2011). Rural natural increase in the new century: America's third demographic transition. In L Kulcsár & K Curtis (Eds), *International handbook of rural demography* (pp. 17–34). Dordrecht: Springer.

Lefebvre, H (1991). *The production of space.* Oxford: Blackwell.

Panelli, R (2006). Rural society. In P Cloke, T Marsden & P Mooney (Eds), *Handbook of rural studies* (pp. 63–90). London: Sage.

Smith, D (2007). The changing faces of rural populations: '(re)Fixing the gaze' or 'eyes wide shut'? *Journal of Rural Studies* 23, 275–282.

United Nations, Department of Economic and Social Affairs, Population Division (2014). World Urbanization Prospects: The 2014 Revision, CD-ROM edition.

Wilson, G (2001). From productivism to post-productivism … and back again? Exploring the (un)changed natural and mental landscapes of European agriculture. *Transactions of the Institute of British Geographers* 26, 77–102.

Woods, M (2003). Deconstructing rural protest: The emergence of a new social movement. *Journal of Rural Studies* 19, 309–325.

3

Migration and the Life Course in Rural Settings

Caitríona Ní Laoire and Aileen Stockdale

Introduction

It is increasingly acknowledged that the preferences and propensities for living in, or moving from, rural settings vary across the life course. These reflect the complex interplay between economic, cultural, social and lifestyle factors evident in several life domains (work, family, health, leisure), which in turn give rise to complex sets of competing influences, considerations and motivations that cut across life course stages and transitions. There is, therefore, an emerging interest in how life events (such as education, employment, family formation, empty nest, retirement, widowhood, increasing frailty or ill health) intersect with different rural migration flows and processes. In this chapter we adopt such an approach. We begin by conceptualising migration and the life course, before progressing to use a life course lens to review contemporary rural migration processes. Finally, the chapter concludes by highlighting the value of a life course approach to better understand the dynamics of contemporary rural migration processes and change.

Conceptualising migration and the life course

In the simplest of terms, '[m]igration involves the movement of a person (a *migrant*) between two places for a certain period of time. The problem is defining how far someone needs to move and for how long' (Boyle, Halfacree & Robinson, 1998, p. 34). The distance moved distinguishes migration from residential and daily/weekly mobility. The latter includes short-term movement around a fixed address, while residential mobility commonly involves short intra-area changes of address; migration, by contrast, is associated with longer inter-area moves. The geographical unit of investigation may include movement within and/or between neighbourhoods, settlements, regions and nations. Here, we define migration as a residential move which has crossed a geographical boundary. By doing so, we include the internal and international migration of individual persons and households whose associated origin or destination is rural.

According to Feijten, Hooimeijer and Mulder (2008), whether or not a desire to move is realised is determined by financial resources, restrictions (such as the distance to work or family ties), and the opportunities and constraints at the preferred destination (such as the availability of housing and employment). The determinants of migration, however, will not remain constant over the course of an individual's life and their variability affects the likelihood, direction (to or from rural settings) and distance of a move. For example, employment-motivated moves are more likely over long distances while housing considerations frequently result in short relocations. Moreover, 'the power of labour market stimuli is found to decline with migrant age whilst the relative importance of amenity and housing effects shows a corresponding increase' (Millington, 2000, p. 521). This knowledge helps to explain rural youth out-migration (for employment) and the in-migration of amenity-seeking older age cohorts. Accordingly 'migration decision-making is mainly driven by life-course events and by perceived opportunities in several life domains' (Kley & Mulder, 2010, p. 90).

Traditionally the likelihood of moving was related to age, with the age-specific migration schedule (Rossi, 1955) well known: migration peaks among younger age groups with smaller spikes evident later in life. Nevertheless, there have been calls for migration research to replace this age focus with life course stages and a continuum of life course stages specifically (Geist & McManus, 2008; Plane & Jurjevich, 2009). Among previous generations specific life events occurred within particular age parameters: today there is a greater fluidity within and between life course stages. The average age at which a woman conceives her first child has risen, and early/flexible retirement options mean that retirement is no longer the abrupt life course stage only undertaken at the state pension age. Life events, therefore, rather than age affect the likelihood of moving. Sandefur and Scott (1981) observed that the rates of migration decrease significantly as family size increases. This is because the cost of a move rises with the number of persons in the family, and the presence of additional members means that more ties must be broken at the place of origin and established at the destination. Bures (2009) alleges that there is a greater likelihood of making a long-distance move as the age of the youngest child at home increases, and Wulff, Champion and Lobo (2010) calculate that 'empty nest' status confers a mobility premium.

Different rural migration flows (into the rural, within the rural, and from the rural), therefore, emerge depending on the perceived ability of the rural to provide opportunities for individuals and households in different life domains and at different life course stages. Research adopting a life course approach has utilised mixed (Hardill & Monk, 2015) and biographical (Ní Laoire, 2008) methods. Biographical studies, in particular, help in nuancing understandings of the ways in which life and migration events intersect. They reveal how factors (beyond age) shape, and are shaped by, migration decision making and experiences.

Migration and the life course in rural settings

In this section we offer a critical 'state of knowledge' review of how life course events intersect with different rural migration flows. This draws on an extensive literature pertaining to the global north.

In-migration

Since the 1970s, rural in-migration has largely been conceptualised within a counter-urbanisation framework. It has been defined as 'a process of population deconcentration; it implies a movement from a state of more concentration to a state of less concentration' (Berry, 1976, p. 17), and 'is deemed to be the prevailing tendency when the distribution of population is shifting from larger to smaller places' (Champion, 1989, p. 32). Despite the myriad of definitions that have since appeared in the literature (Mitchell, 2004), counter-urbanisation and its associated rural in-migration was observed throughout the global north: in the UK (Perry,

Dean & Brown, 1986), Europe (Vining & Kontuly, 1978; Fielding, 1982), North America (Beale, 1975; Berry, 1976; Vining & Strauss, 1977) and Australia (Hugo & Smailes, 1985).

Rural in-migration is frequently stereotyped as involving the long-distance movement of wealthy, middle-aged and retired persons from metropolitan and city regions to scenically attractive rural and coastal locations in search of an improved quality of life or rural idyll. Such migration is linked with images and representations of the rural, where the rural idyll 'presents happy, healthy and problem-free images of rural life safely nestling with both a close social community and a contiguous natural environment' (Cloke & Milbourne, 1992: 359). It is often couched in anti-urban (crime, congestion, house prices, lacking a sense of community) and pro-rural (better environment, tranquil lifestyle) terms (Halliday & Coombes, 1995). Bolton and Chalkley (1990) and Bijker, Haartsen and Strijker (2012), nevertheless, make an important distinction between the reasons for moving (which commonly relate to lifestyle, personal or environmental factors) and the choice of destination (which is more often about jobs and house prices). The household is the level at which family/couple decision making occurs with net household (rather than individual) gain assumed to drive migration behaviour (Mincer, 1978). Inevitably there may be a lack of consensus between partners on both the desirability of a move and the preferred destination: negotiation and compromise will be necessary (Cooke, 2008). Children (if present in the household) may, or may not, also be consulted (Bushin, 2009). Specific aspects of the rural deemed attractive are identified by McGranahan (1999) and van Dam, Heins and Elbersen (2002). These vary at different stages of the life course. Nevertheless, 'the stereotypical rural in-migrant is routinely portrayed as someone who escapes the harried city for a more "down-to-earth" way of life' (Grimsrud, 2011, p. 642). Some have moved 'back to the land' (Halfacree, 2001), 'back to the water' (Smith, 2007) or 'to the sunbelt' (Brown & Glasgow, 2008) with rural in-migration commonly thought of as amenity (Abrams, Gosnell, Gill & Klepeis, 2012) and lifestyle migration (Benson & O'Reilly, 2009).

Notwithstanding this dominant counter-urbanisation narrative, a key point is that contemporary rural in-migration now involves a more diverse set of processes and consequently multiple migration flows, groups, motivations and destinations. It is no longer solely thought of as an urban to rural migration flow (leading largely to scenically attractive destinations) or an exclusively internal migration phenomenon. Instead, other in-migration flows have been observed: to less popular rural (Bijker, Haartsen & Strijker, 2013) and fringe areas (Andersen, 2011), from one rural area to another (Bijker & Haartsen, 2012; Stockdale, 2015), stepped moves (Champion, 2005), return migration to rural areas (Ní Laoire, 2007) and including international mobility (Hedberg & Haandrikman, 2014). Examples of the latter include Dutch (Eimermann, Lundmark & Muller, 2012; Eimermann, 2013) migration to rural Sweden, retirement migration from the UK to Europe (King, Warnes & Williams, 2000; Benson, 2010) and from the United States to Mexico (Sunil, Rojas & Bradley, 2007), and international labour migration (Jentsch & Simard, 2009). A wider range of migrant groups are also participating, in contrast to the perceived middle-class and retired in-migrant dominance of the past. Australian high amenity rural areas are especially attractive to the creative classes (Argent, Tonts, Jones & Holmes, 2013) and artists have been observed moving into the Canadian countryside (Mitchell, Bunting & Piccioni, 2004). Those of working age (Bijker & Haartsen, 2012), on relatively low incomes (Hugo & Bell, 1998; Bijker, Haartsen & Strijker, 2012) and ethnic groups (Johnson & Lichter, 2012) have also been observed.

In addition, rural in-migration involves multiple drivers. Erickson (1976) and Keeble and Tyler (1995) allege that people have followed jobs into rural areas. Similarly, Dahms and McComb (1999, p. 144) report that '[n]ew mobility and economic opportunity have encouraged moves to areas providing both amenities and employment', while others show that rural in-migrants create jobs which in turn attract further migrants (Beyers & Nelson, 2000). Moreover, whereas quality of life values have long been recognised as an important motivation to explain a residential move to rural areas, Johnson and Rasker (1995) and Bosworth and Willett (2011) point to their importance in the business location decision making of rural business owners too. And, in contrast to the pro-rural motivations that have dominated many rural in-migration studies, Gkartzios (2013) observes a crisis driven counter-urbanisation triggered by unemployment at origin. Similarly, Grimsrud (2011) finds that in-migration is strongly motivated by family relations and economic factors rather than pro-rural considerations.

Taking a life course approach helps to explain this contemporary diversity of rural in-flows, groups and motivations. Until recently scant attention has been paid to life course dimensions. This is now changing with the emergence of a literature which confirms rural settings as popular destinations for migrants experiencing different life events who accordingly are drawn into the rural at multiple life course stages.

Union and family formation life course stages have been observed to increase the likelihood of moving to a rural setting (Courgeau, 1989; Lindgren, 2003). Kulu's (2008) Austrian study, for example, shows that the birth of a first child triggers housing and environment-related residential moves and includes migration from cities to rural areas, with the likelihood of such a move increasing significantly with the birth of a second and third child. Such migration is linked to the availability and affordability (relative to cities) of family housing, a perception of rural areas being safe places to bring up children, and that rural areas possess a sense of community which is conducive to family life. It may also include a move to exclusive rural school catchment areas (Smith & Higley, 2012). Working-class families too at the union and family formation life course stage move to what Bijker, Haartsen and Strijker (2013) call 'less-popular' rural locations. These young families emphasise the social qualities of the rural setting (friendliness, lots of things going on) so that 'it is useful to distinguish between the physical and social aspects of the rural to explain moving to different types of rural areas' (Bijker, Haartsen & Strijker, 2013, p. 589) by different migrant groups and at different life course stages.

A move may also be undertaken in preparation for a forthcoming life event (Michielin & Mulder, 2008) such as starting a family (Kulu, 2008) or retirement. Bures (1997), Stockdale (2006) and Stockdale and MacLeod (2013) identify a retirement transition life course stage whereby the migration behaviours of pre-retirement age migrants are similar to those of retirees. An impending retirement may correspond with an empty-nest life course stage. Freed from dependent responsibilities and possessing a degree of affluence (for example, an existing mortgage may have been paid) it may signal a realisation for 'a place in the country' (Hardill, 2006) or 'dreaming of a smallholding' (Blekesaune, Haugen & Villa, 2010). For others at this stage a move permits the release of property equity through downsizing (Stockdale, 2014). Indeed, Haas and Serow (2002) allege that the baby-boom generation is more likely to move on retirement than previous cohorts. Skelley (2004) expects them to be amenity-seeking migrants and, therefore, favour rural destinations (Brown & Glasgow, 2008; Cromartie & Nelson, 2009). Conflicting evidence is provided by Cribier (2005) who observes declining retirement migration among Parisians. While she offers a growth in second home ownership as a possible explanation, others have associated a component of rural retirement in-migration with a permanent move to a previous holiday or second home (Muller & Marjavaara, 2012). Migration is also influenced by earlier residential experiences. Han and Moen (1999, p. 197) explain that 'to understand behaviour at any one life stage requires knowledge of prior transitions and trajectories', and Stockdale, MacLeod and Philip (2013) amply demonstrate the connections between life course stages when it comes to rural migration decision making. This helps to explain return migration – either to a specific place

(Lundholm, 2012) or 'to the rural' (Bijker, Haartsen & Strijker, 2012) – as a component of rural in-migration. Finally, there is evidence of a further move by rural in-migrants at the time of increasing illness, personal frailty and widowhood (that is, at later life course stages). According to Wenger (2001) migrants who have moved into rural areas, especially if they have left potential later life family and friend support systems behind, move from the countryside to larger villages and small towns. In other words, later-life migration is to destinations possessing the necessary housing types, services, facilities and support networks for a comfortable old age. Elsewhere, older rural in-migrants are found to combine amenity and proximity to family motivations in selecting destination communities (Brown & Glasgow, 2008), thereby negating a future move.

Out-migration

The association of rural out-migration with youth and the young-adulthood phase of the life course is well-established (Easthope & Gabriel, 2006; Gibson & Argent, 2008; Thissen, Droogleever Fortuijn, Strijker & Haartsen, 2010; Nugin, 2014). Research across a range of diverse contexts has identified that young adults are those most likely to migrate from rural areas and those who comprise the largest proportion of rural outflows (Stockdale, 2002b; Domina, 2006; Argent & Walmsley, 2008). While this is clearly related to age, it is more specifically related to life transitions typically from youth to adulthood, and from childhood/youth to work, education and independence. The necessity of moving from rural to urban areas for work and educational opportunities reflects the ongoing marginalisation of many rural regions in the context of global capitalist processes of urbanisation and capital accumulation, which have resulted in disinvestment and declining employment opportunities in many rural regions. Lack of employment continues to be a major explanatory factor for rural out-migration, as traditional rural sectors such as agriculture experience declining labour demands, and young people migrate to urban centres for employment reasons (Domina, 2006; Bell et al., 2009).

Rural areas also tend to lack higher education opportunities, with research in different contexts finding that higher education is a key motivation for rural out-migration among young adults (Domina, 2006; Corbett, 2007b). Stockdale (2002a) has highlighted that education may provide an initial impetus for youth out-migration, and that, subsequently, a lack of suitable employment opportunities in the rural place of origin is a factor mitigating against return, thus reinforcing the out-migration trend. In particular, the lack of graduate or professional employment opportunities in rural areas has been highlighted as a key factor. As remote or economically marginal rural regions continue to be dominated by agricultural, manual and low-skill service sectors of employment, the out-migration (and staying away) of young people is reinforced by the lack of opportunities for graduate employment. Corbett (2007b, p. 20) refers to this as the 'migration imperative of rural schooling', arguing that rural education prepares rural youth for social and spatial mobility that is inevitably about leaving rural areas. 'Social mobility increasingly presupposes geographical mobility, especially in rural areas' (Thissen, Droogleever Fortuijn, Strijker & Haartsen, p. 428).

Social and cultural factors play an important role in out-migration decisions. Limited services and facilities in rural areas are considered to contribute to the impetus for youth out-migration (Argent & Walmsley, 2008; Bell et al., 2009). Research also shows that particular social and cultural characteristics of rural places can be both exacerbated by, and contribute to, youth out-migration. Rural areas are characterised as highly gendered and heteronormative spaces from which many, including sexual minorities, seek to escape (Little, 2003; Annes & Redlin, 2012). Ní Laoire (1999) has demonstrated how gendered social and cultural norms in rural places can contribute to high female out-migration, while Jones's research (1999) highlights some experiences of oppressive or exclusionary dimensions of growing up in rural areas that contribute to young people's aspirations for out-migration.

Some research associates this with powerful discursive constructions of rural (versus urban) life which construct rural life as typically backward or marginal in comparison to the urban (Nugin, 2014). It could be argued that there is in fact a normative association between stages of the life course and urban/rural residence. Rural places tend to be discursively associated with the family formation, mid-life and later-life stages of the life course, while urban areas are associated with the young-adult stage (Ní Laoire, 2008). Giddings and Yarwood (2005) have pointed to an association between the 'growing up' and the 'growing out' of the countryside among children in rural England, linking transitions from youth to adulthood with rural–urban migration. Thus, some suggest that migration decision making is an inevitable part of transitions to adulthood and independence for rural youth (Argent & Walmsley, 2008; Thissen, Droogleever Fortuijn, Strijker & Haartsen, 2010). This notion of inevitability contributes to the construction of rural youth out-migration as a normative rite of passage in certain cultures and regions. However, as Ní Laoire (2000) argues, it is important to acknowledge the structures of power and inequality that underlie rural youth out-migration processes and to challenge its normalisation in popular discourses. Rural out-migration is bound up with geographical processes of dis/investment and economic marginalisation, which intersect with structures of gender, age, family and social class in geographically contingent ways. It is necessary therefore to understand the complexity underlying oversimplified associations between rural out-migration and the young-adult stage of the life course.

While rural youth out-migration is associated with a particular life course transition phase, it is also intersected by gender, social class and educational attainment. Gender is a significant factor in rural out-migration processes, with females generally being more likely to out-migrate from rural areas than males (Ní Laoire, 1999; Bjarnason & Thorlindsson, 2006; Corbett, 2007a; Argent & Walmsley, 2008). This is associated with a relative lack of employment opportunities for women compared to men in rural areas dominated by traditionally male employment sectors such as agriculture and other primary industries. It has also been associated with the patriarchal nature of rural societies and with the gendered nature of rural familial and kin structures which often tend to encourage the social (and hence spatial) mobility of young women (Ní Laoire, 1999). However, the role of gender in rural out-migration is also quite complex, with some research suggesting that women are much more likely than men to move short distances to nearby towns and villages, and that men and women are at least equally likely to move long distances (Stockdale, 2002a; Corbett, 2007a). This suggests that gender is implicated in rural out-migration differently at local and regional scales.

A deeper understanding of the ways in which gender shapes rural out-migration is provided by a life course perspective that focuses on transitions through family structures. Stockdale (2002b) investigates the role of social and family networks and ties in migrant decision-making processes in rural Scotland, concluding that family ties are particularly important to migrants in their initial moves away from home, and again at later stages in the life course when they have children and as their own parents age. Given the close connections between gender and family in rural social structures, there is a need for more research which explicitly explores how gender, family and the life course intersect in rural migration decision making.

Many studies show that rural out-migration is closely linked to education levels, with the more highly educated being more likely to out-migrate. For example, Domina (2006) shows that non-metropolitan out-migration in the United States is strongly associated with educational attainment, with bachelor's degree graduates being more likely to migrate than those with high-school qualifications only. Other studies have found that educational opportunities feature very prominently as stated motivations for migration among rural out-migrants (Stockdale, 2002a) or as stated motivations among rural youth intending to migrate (Drozdzewski, 2008). Parental education may also be associated with increased migration intentions (Bjarnason & Thorlindsson, 2006).

The latter suggests that there may be a social class dimension to rural out-migration processes, given the close associations between education levels and social class (see Bourdieu & Passeron, 1990; Whelan & Hannan, 1999; Ball, 2003). Few studies of rural out-migration explicitly engage with questions of social class. However, Corbett (2007b) provides a convincing analysis of the way in which social class both shapes, and is shaped by, the educational, labour market and discursive structures which propel middle-class rural youth along a trajectory of education and out-migration, while simultaneously restricting the opportunities of working-class youth to the low-skill sectors of rural labour markets. In a different context, Jones's (1999) research based in Scotland links social class to family migration history, showing that rural youth out-migration is more common among those who have grown up in in-migrant families, which tend to be more middle class, than in native families, which tend to be more working class. These social class dynamics are clearly geographically contingent on local class structures. Others have highlighted the ways in which out-migration may be associated with social class mobility; for example, Gabriel (2006) explores the experiences of social advancement among young rural migrants from economically depressed rural regions in Tasmania, suggesting that rural out-migration is associated with social class mobility.

In seeking to understand contemporary rural out-migration dynamics, it is increasingly recognised that migrants' own experiences, understandings and narratives of rural out-migration need to be understood. Thus, many studies are concerned with identifying young people's own motivations, or with the perceptions/attitudes of young people and rural residents towards their rural areas. This literature has identified a range of factors that influence young people's attitudes towards their rural places of origin/residence – from economic to cultural and environmental. In particular, attention is drawn to the strong attachments formed by people to rural areas – emphasising attachments to community, lifestyle and environment, for example – and thus to the desire to stay (Wiborg, 2004; Thissen, Droogleever Fortuijn, Strijker & Haartsen, 2010; Trell, van Hoven & Huigen, 2012; Ulrich-Schad, Henly & Safford, 2013; McLaughlin, Shoff & Demi, 2014). This points to the competing forces at play in out-migration decision-making processes, shifting attention away from emphasis on motivations for out-migration and towards complex decision making about staying or migrating (Ní Laoire, 2000; Stockdale, 2002a; Drozdzewski, 2008). In other words, young migrants and non-migrants are recognised as social agents actively making (often difficult) decisions in different rural contexts, and actively involved in reproducing or resisting migration processes. Thus is it argued that young people growing up in rural areas negotiate competing pressures and influences in their decision-making processes in relation to staying or leaving. A biographical approach to these complex decision-making processes reveals how rural and urban places, and rural–urban dynamics, are interpreted, experienced and produced by actors/agents making sense of different geographical contexts (Ní Laoire, 2000; Stockdale, 2002a).

While there is a clear association between life course transitions typically associated with young adulthood, and rural out-migration, research also highlights the diversity among rural out-migrants (Stockdale, 2002a; Drozdzewski, 2008). Stockdale's (2002a) research on out-migration from rural Scotland has found that age at migration can vary from the late teens to the early thirties. In particular, her research highlights the role of social and family networks in migration decision making. Having family or friendship connections in the destination area can be a motivating factor for out-migration; similarly Drozdzewski (2008) and Jones (1999) have both found that the previous migration of older siblings, or a family history of migration, are associated with greater propensity for out-migration. This body of research highlights the complexity of rural out-migration as well as the fluidity of the life course, and argues for a life course approach which acknowledges the fluid, unorthodox and diverse ways in which life course stages intersect with decisions to migrate.

Return migration

Return migration is increasingly acknowledged as a key component of counter-urbanisation and rural in-migration processes in the global north, although it has until recently been relatively under-recognised. The acknowledgement of the circularity and complexity of rural migration patterns, often involving return and remigration flows, challenges dominant narratives of in- and out-migration. Rural return is usually associated with particular life course stages or events, namely family formation, caring for ageing parents, relationship breakdown or a more general 'settling down' (Stockdale, 2002b; Ní Laoire, 2008; Rérat, 2014; von Reichert, Cromartie & Arthun, 2014b). Much research with rural returnees has highlighted the close association between family formation and rural return, as many migrants choose to return to the rural in order to raise their children, often citing the perceived benefits of the rural environment for children (Ní Laoire, 2008). This phenomenon is closely associated with wider family ties, as family connections to parents, siblings and others reinforce the attraction of the rural environment for return migrants. Returning to spend time with, or to care for, ageing parents, either temporarily or permanently, is also a significant dimension to rural return processes, reflecting the strength of family networks in migration decision making at particular stages of the life course (Stockdale, 2002b). Some research also suggests that a relationship breakdown can trigger a return move by rural out-migrants (Ní Laoire, 2008; Wall & von Reichert, 2013). Therefore, while economic and educational considerations are particularly important in out-migration decisions, family and lifestyle considerations seem to gain more weight in return decisions. However, some research also points out that economic reasons (combined with family factors) can be a motivating factor in rural return migration decisions, such as in Greece during the economic crisis in reaction to unemployment and urban decline (Gkartzios, 2013). Indeed, considering rural return as an element of counter-urbanisation contributes to efforts to challenge the dominant narratives of counter-urbanisation as a middle-class idyll-driven phenomenon (Ní Laoire, 2007; Gkartzios, 2013).

The impact of return migration on rural areas has been a focus of interest for some time in studies of international and regional migration, with studies in the 1970s and 1980s examining the link between return migration and 'modernisation' in rural areas, and concerns being raised about conflict between non-movers and returnees in rural communities (see, for example, Lewis & Williams, 1985; King, 1986). While some have argued that return migration does not in fact bring a demographic or economic dividend to rural areas, recent research by von Reichert, Cromartie and Arthun (2014a) in the USA suggests that return migrants contribute to demographic, social and economic vitality in rural communities. Attracting young migrants back to rural areas is often viewed as a potential solution to the negative effects of out-migration. Recent research has also explored identity processes and experiences of rural returnees from their own perspectives, frequently finding that return to the rural can involve a difficult process of adjustment and feelings of outsiderness in the place thought of as 'home' (Easthope & Gabriel, 2006), thus questioning assumptions about inherent benefits of rural return migration.

Conclusion

Contemporary rural settings are characterised by diverse migration flows, processes, groups and motivations. Adopting a life course perspective – or relating migration to and from rural settings to principal life events and transitions – permits greater understandings of the complex and multiple considerations and influences evident across the life course and how they intersect with different rural migration flows. In particular, a life course approach helps us to challenge normative associations between age/life stage and rural migration, and in this chapter has allowed us to highlight the fluid, unorthodox and diverse ways in which life course stages intersect with decisions to migrate.

In-migration is no longer viewed as the preserve of middle-class, middle-aged or older 'urban escapees'. Instead, rural areas have something to offer more diverse economic and social groups at different stages of the life course. There is also in-migration from other rural as well as urban locations (including overseas) to more varied rural area types (accessible, scenically attractive, less popular and remote locations). Similarly, there is greater acknowledgement of diversity among out-migrants in terms of their characteristics, influences and decisions.

A number of different migration processes are evident. While in-migration is commonly conceptualised in terms of counter-urbanisation, might the movement of people at different life course stages (family formation, retirement) and involving different migration flows (for example, retirement, return, inter-rural, international) represent particular components of counter-urbanisation or separate and distinctive migratory processes? A life course perspective offers an opportunity to unravel processes which are frequently fused together into one 'catch all' counter-urbanisation category.

These diverse migration flows to and from rural areas give rise to highly variable demographic, economic, social and cultural consequences depending upon the life course stage at which the move has occurred (alongside the relative importance of economic, social and lifestyle factors at work). It has long been acknowledged that tensions exist between in-migrants and long-term local rural residents (Cloke & Goodwin, 1992; Woods, 2005; Brown & Glasgow, 2008). Issues of 'geriatrification' (Philip, 1999), housing affordability (Taylor, 2008), gentrification (Phillips, 2005; Stockdale, 2010), local service provision (Divoudi & Wishardt, 2004) and community cohesion (Murdoch, Lowe, Ward & Marsden, 2003) have been reported. Against these, however, there are positive aspects to in-migration. Migrants bring rural economic development potential; they create businesses (Bosworth, 2010) and stimulate demand for housing, goods and services. In addition, they are active volunteers in community activities. Indeed, such are the perceived benefits (associated with middle-aged and retiree life course stage migrants in particular) that some have called for specific policies designed to attract such migrants (Reeder, 1998; Atterton, 2006; Brown & Glasgow, 2008; Jauhiainen, 2009; Murakami, Gilroy & Atterton, 2009). Youth out-migration too is commonly viewed in problematic terms for the places left behind: ageing populations, social conservatism, gender imbalance, population decline, contraction in rural services/facilities and declining social capital (Stockdale, 2004; Argent & Walmsley, 2008). There have been calls for employment creation and cultural initiatives (Gibson, 2008) and policies to make these communities more attractive in an attempt to encourage young people to stay, or to attract return migrants to rural areas (for example, Stockdale, 2004; Jauhiainen, 2009; McLaughlin, Shoff & Demi, 2014). This emphasis, however, tends to overlook the positive impact of out-migration on these young people's own lives (Argent & Walmsley, 2008), although for some migration can be problematic (Stockdale, 2004). Returning too may give rise to difficulties, although encouragement of return migration is often considered a potential solution to the problems of youth out-migration in declining rural areas.

This chapter acknowledges that there are multiple life course triggers for migration. The factors contributing to rural in- or out-migration involve complex intersections between life course events and wider social, economic and structural processes shaping, and shaped by, rural and urban areas. Migration processes are key to understanding the complex interconnections between the rural and the urban in the contemporary global north, as powerful constructions of rurality (and its other, the urban) are produced, reproduced and resisted, through diverse migration flows to and from rural places. Spatial inequalities are reinforced and also reshaped in part through the movements of people at different life course stages to and from rural places, as migration processes contribute to processes such as marginalisation, gentrification, geriatrification, as well as development of rural places. A life course perspective facilitates an understanding of these processes which recognises the interconnection of urban–rural dynamics with family, gender, age, caring and other socio-biographical imperatives, providing a complex and rich perspective on migration and rurality.

References

Abrams, J, Gosnell, H, Gill, N & Klepeis, P (2012). Re-creating the rural reconstructing nature: An international literature review of the environmental implications of amenity migration. *Conservation and Society* 10(3), 270–284.

Andersen, H (2011). Explanations for long-distance counter-urban migration into fringe areas in Denmark. *Population, Space and Place* 17(5), 627–641.

Annes, A & Redlin, M (2012). Coming out and coming back: Rural gay migration and the city. *Journal of Rural Studies* 28, 56–68.

Argent, N, Tonts, M, Jones, R & Holmes, J (2013). A creativity-led rural renaissance? Amenity-led migration, the creative turn and the uneven development of rural Australia. *Applied Geography* 44, 88–98.

Argent, N & Walmsley, J (2008). Rural youth migration trends in Australia: An overview of recent trends and two inland case studies. *Geographical Research* 46(2), 139–152.

Atterton, J (2006). *Ageing and coastal communities*. Centre for Rural Economy, University of Newcastle upon Tyne.

Ball, S (2003). *Class strategies and the educational market: The middle-classes and social advantage*. London: Routledge.

Beale, C (1975). *The revival of population growth in non-metropolitan America*. Report ERS 605, Economic Research Service, United States Department of Agriculture, Washington, DC.

Bell, S, Montarzino, A, Aspinall, P, Peneze, Z & Nikodemus, O (2009). Rural society, social inclusion and landscape change in Central and Eastern Europe: A case study of Latvia. *Sociologia Ruralis* 49(3), 295–326.

Benson, M (2010). The context and trajectory of lifestyle migration. *European Societies* 12(1), 45–64.

Benson, M & O'Reilly, K (Eds). (2009). *Lifestyle migration: Expectations, aspirations and experiences*. Farnham: Ashgate.

Berry, B (1976). *Urbanisation and counterurbanisation*. Beverly Hills, CA: Sage.

Beyers, W & Nelson, P (2000). Contemporary development forces in the nonmetropolitan West. *Journal of Rural Studies* 16(4), 459–474.

Bijker, R A & Haartsen, T (2012). More than counterurbanisation: Migration to popular and less-popular rural areas in the Netherlands. *Population, Space and Place* 18(5), 643–657.

Bijker, R, Haartsen, T & Strijker, D (2012). Migration to less-popular rural areas in the Netherlands: Exploring the motivations. *Journal of Rural Studies* 28(4), 490–498.

Bijker, R, Haartsen, T & Strijker, D (2013). Different areas, different people? Migration to popular and less-popular rural areas in the Netherlands. *Population, Space and Place* 19(5), 580–593.

Bjarnason, T & Thorlindsson, T (2006). Should I stay or should I go? Migration expectations among youth in Icelandic fishing and farming communities. *Journal of Rural Studies* 22, 290–300.

Blekesaune, A, Haugen, M & Villa, M (2010). Dreaming of a smallholding. *Sociologia Ruralis* 50(3), 225–241.

Bolton, N & Chalkley, B (1990). The rural population turnround: A case-study of North Devon. *Journal of Rural Studies* 6(1), 29–43.

Bosworth, G (2010). Commercial counterurbanisation: An emerging force in rural economic development. *Environment and Planning A* 42, 966–981.

Bosworth, G & Willett, J (2011). Embeddedness or escapism? Rural perceptions and economic development in Cornwall and Northumberland. *Sociologia Ruralis* 51(2), 195–214.

Bourdieu, P & Passeron, J-C (1990). *Reproduction in education, society and culture*. London: Sage.

Boyle, P, Halfacree, K & Robinson, V (1998). *Exploring contemporary migration*. London: Addison Wesley Longman.

Brown, D & Glasgow, N (2008). *Rural retirement migration*. Dordrecht: Springer.

Bures, R (1997). Migration and the life course: Is there a retirement transition? *International Journal of Population Geography* 3(2), 109–120.

Bures, R (2009). Moving the nest: The impact of coresidential children on mobility in later midlife. *Journal of Family Issues* 30(6), 837–851.

Bushin, N (2009). Researching family migration decision-making: A children-in-families approach. *Population, Space and Place* 15, 429–443.

Champion, A (1989). *Counterurbanization: The changing pace and nature of population deconcentration*. London: Edward Arnold.

Champion, A (2005). The counterurbanisation cascade in England and Wales since 1991: The evidence of a new migration dataset. *Revue Belge de Geographie* 1–2, 85–101.

Cloke, P & Goodwin, M (1992). Conceptualising countryside change: From post-Fordism to rural structured coherence. *Transactions of the Institute of British Geographers* 17, 321–336.

Cloke, P & Milbourne, P (1992). Deprivation and lifestyles in rural Wales. II: Rurality and the cultural dimension. *Journal of Rural Studies* 8, 359–371.

Cooke, T (2008). Migration in a family way. *Population, Space and Place* 14, 255–265.

Corbett, M (2007a). All kinds of potential: Women and out-migration in an Atlantic Canadian coastal community. *Journal of Rural Studies* 23, 430–442.

Corbett, M (2007b). *Learning to leave: The irony of schooling in a coastal community*. Halifax, NS: Fernwood.

Courgeau, D (1989). Family formation and urbanization. *Population: An English Selection*, 44, 123–146.

Cribier, F (2005). Changes in the experiences of life between two cohorts of Parisian pensioners, born circa 1907 and 1921. *Ageing and Society* 25(5), 637–654.

Cromartie, J & Nelson, P (2009). Baby boom migration tilts towards rural America. *Amber Waves* 7(3), 16–22.

Dahms, F & McComb, J (1999). 'Counterurbanization', interaction and functional change in a rural amenity area – a Canadian example. *Journal of Rural Studies* 15(2), 129–146.

Divoudi, S & Wishardt, M (2004). Counterurbanisation and its implications for Ryedale. *Yorkshire and Humber Regional Review*.

Domina, T (2006). What clean break?: Education and nonmetropolitan migration patterns, 1989–2004. *Rural Sociology* 71(3), 373–398.

Drozdzewski, D (2008). 'We're moving out': Youth out-migration intentions in coastal non-metropolitan New South Wales. *Geographical Research* 46(2), 153–161.

Easthope, H & Gabriel, M (2006). Turbulent lives: Exploring the cultural meaning of regional youth migration. *Geographical Research* 46(2), 172–182.

Eimermann, M (2013). Lifestyle migration to the North: Dutch families and the decision to move to rural Sweden. *Population, Space and Place*. doi: 10.002/psp.1807.

Eimermann, M, Lundmark, M & Muller, D (2012). Exploring Dutch migration to rural Sweden: International counterurbanisation in the EU. *Tijdschrift voor Economische en Sociale Geografie* 103(3), 330–346.

Erickson, R (1976). The filtering-down process: Industrial location in a nonmetropolitan area. *The Professional Geographer* 28, 245–260.

Feijten, P, Hooimeijer, P & Mulder, C (2008). Residential experience and residential environment choice over the life-course. *Urban Studies* 45(1), 141–162.

Fielding, A (1982). Counterurbanisation in Western Europe. *Progress in Planning* 17, 1–52.

Gabriel, M (2006). Youth migration and social advancement: How young people manage emerging differences between themselves and their hometown. *Journal of Youth Studies* 9, 33–46.

Geist, C & McManus, P (2008). Geographical mobility over the life course: Motivations and implications. *Population, Space and Place* 14, 283–303.

Gibson, C (2008). Youthful creativity in regional Australia: Panacea for unemployment and out-migration? *Geographical Research* 46(2), 183–195.

Gibson, C & Argent, N (2008). Getting on, getting up and getting out? Broadening perspectives on rural youth migration. *Geographical Research* 46, 135–138.

Giddings, R & Yarwood, R (2005). Growing up, going out and growing out of the countryside: Childhood experiences in rural England. *Children's Geographies* 3, 101–114.

Gkartzios, M (2013). 'Leaving Athens': Narratives of counterurbanisation in times of crisis. *Journal of Rural Studies* 32, 158–167.

Grimsrud, GM (2011). How well does the 'counterurbanisation story' travel to other countries? The case of Norway. *Population, Space and Place* 17(5), 642–655.

Haas, WH & Serow, WJ (2002). The baby boom, amenity retirement migration, and retirement communities: Will the golden age of retirement continue? *Research on Aging* 24, 150–164.

Halfacree, K (2001). Going 'back-to-the-land' again; extending the scope of counterurbanisation. *Espace, Populations, Societies* 19(1/2), 161–170.

Halliday, J & Coombes, M (1995). In search of counterurbanisation: Some evidence from Devon on the relationship between patterns of migration and motivation. *Journal of Rural Studies* 11, 433–446.

Han, SK & Moen, P (1999). Clocking out: Temporal patterning of retirement. *American Journal of Sociology* 105(1), 191–236.

Hardill, I (2006). 'A place in the country' – migration and the construction of rural living. In P Lowe & L Speakman (Eds), *The ageing countryside* (pp. 51–68). London: Age Concern.

Hardill, I & Monk, J (2015). Life course approach. In D Richardson (Ed.), *International encyclopedia of geography: People, the Earth, environment, and technology*. Washington, DC: Wiley-Association of American Geographers.

Hedberg, C & Haandrikman, K (2014). Repopulation of the Swedish countryside: Globalisation by international migration. *Journal of Rural Studies* 34, 128–138.

Hugo, G & Bell, M (1998). The hypothesis of welfare-led migration to rural areas: The Australian Case. In P Boyle & K Halfacree (Eds), *Migration into rural areas: Theories and issues* (pp. 107–133). Chichester: John Wiley & Sons.

Hugo, G & Smailes, P (1985). Urban–rural migration in Australia: A process view of the turnaround. *Journal of Rural Studies* 1(1), 11–30.

Jauhiainen, J (2009). Will the retiring baby boomers return to rural periphery? *Journal of Rural Studies* 25, 25–34.

Jentsch, B & Simard, M (2009). *International migration and rural areas*. Farnham: Ashgate.

Johnson, J & Rasker, R (1995). The role of economic and quality of life values in rural business location. *Journal of Rural Studies* 11(4), 405–416.

Johnson, K & Lichter, D (2012). Rural retirement destinations: Natural decrease and the shared demographic destinies of elderly and Hispanics. In N Glasgow & E Berry (Eds), *Rural aging in 21st century America* (pp. 275–294). Dordrecht: Springer.

Jones, G (1999). 'The same people in the same places?' Socio-spatial identities and migration in youth. *Sociology* 33, 1–22.

Keeble, D & Tyler, P (1995). Enterprising behaviour and the urban–rural shift. *Urban Studies* 32(6), 975–997.

King, R (Ed.). (1986). *Return migration and regional economic problems*. London: Croom Helm.

King, R, Warnes, T & Williams, A (2000). *Sunset lives: British retirement migration to the Mediterranean*. Oxford: Berg.

Kley, S & Mulder, C (2010). Considering, planning, and realizing migration in early adulthood. The influence of life-course events and perceived opportunities on leaving the city in Germany. *Journal of Housing and the Built Environment* 25, 73–94.

Kulu, H (2008). Fertility and spatial mobility in the life course: Evidence from Austria. *Environment and Planning A* 40(3), 632–652.

Lewis, J & Williams, A (1985). Portugal: The decade of return. *Geography* 70, 175–178.

Lindgren, U. (2003). Who is the counter–urban mover? Evidence from the Swedish urban system. *International Journal of Population Geography* 9, 399–418.

Little, J (2003). 'Riding the rural love train': Heterosexuality and the rural community. *Sociologia Ruralis* 43, 401–417.

Lundholm, E (2012). Returning home? Migration to birthplace among migrants after age 55. *Population, Space and Place* 18(1), 74–84.

McGranahan, D (1999). *Natural amenities drive rural population change*. Agricultural Economic Report No. 781. Washington, DC: US Department of Agriculture.

McLaughlin, D, Shoff, C & Demi, MA (2014). Influence of perceptions of current and future community on residential aspirations of rural youth. *Rural Sociology* 79(4), 453–477.

Michielin, F & Mulder, C (2008). Family events and the residential mobility of couples. *Environment and Planning A* 40(11), 2770–2790.

Millington, J (2000). Migration and age: The effect of age on sensitivity to migration stimuli. *Regional Studies* 34(6), 521–533.

Mincer, J (1978). Family migration decisions. *Journal of Political Economy* 86, 749–773.

Mitchell, C (2004). Making sense of counterurbanisation. *Journal of Rural Studies* 20, 15–34.

Mitchell, C, Bunting, T & Piccioni, M (2004). Visual artists: Counterurbanites in the Canadian countryside? *The Canadian Geographer* 48(2), 152–167.

Muller, D & Marjavaara, R (2012). From second home to primary residence: Migration towards recreational properties in Sweden 1991–2005. *Tijdschrift voor Economische en Sociale Geografic* 103(1), 53–68.

Murakami, K, Gilroy, R & Atterton, J (2009). Planning for the ageing countryside in Japan: The potential impact of multi-habitation. *Planning, Practice and Research* 24(3), 285–299.

Murdoch, J, Lowe, P, Ward, N & Marsden, T (2003). *The differentiated countryside*. London: Routledge.

Ní Laoire C (1999). Gender issues in Irish rural out-migration. In P Boyle & K Halfacree (Eds), *Migration and gender in the developed world* (pp. 223–237). London: Routledge.

Ní Laoire, C (2000). Conceptualising rural youth migration: A biographical approach. *International Journal of Population Geography* 6, 229–243.

Ní Laoire, C (2007). The green green grass of home? Return migration to rural Ireland. *Journal of Rural Studies* 23, 332–344.

Ní Laoire, C (2008). 'Settling back'? A biographical and life-course perspective on Ireland's recent return migration. *Irish Geography* 41(2), 195–210.

Nugin, R (2014). 'I think that they should go. Let them see something'. The context of rural youth's out-migration in post-socialist Estonia. *Journal of Rural Studies* 34, 51–64.

Perry, R, Dean, K & Brown, B (1986). *Counterurbanisation: Case studies of urban–rural movement*. Norwich: Geobooks.

Philip, M (1999). Migration and social change. In M Shucksmith & C Murphy (Eds), *Rural audit: A health check on rural Britain* (pp. 27–29). Aberdeen University: Arkleton Centre for Rural Development Research.

Phillips, M (2005). Differential productions of rural gentrification: Illustrations from North and South Norfolk. *Geoforum* 36(4), 477–494.

Plane, D & Jurjevich, J (2009). Ties that no longer bind? The patterns and repercussions of age-articulated migration. *The Professional Geographer* 61(1), 4–20.

Reeder, RJ (1998). *Retiree-attraction policies for rural development*. Agriculture Information Bulletin No. 741. Washington, DC: US Department of Agriculture, Economic Research Service.

Rérat, P (2014). The selective migration of young graduates: Which of them return to their rural home region and which do not? *Journal of Rural Studies* 35, 123–132.

Rossi, P (1955). *Why families move: A study in the social psychology of urban residential mobility*. Glencoe, IL: Free Press.

Sandefur, G & Scott, W (1981). A dynamic analysis of migration: An assessment of the effects of age, family and career variables. *Demography* 18, 355–367.

Skelley, D (2004). Retiree-attraction policies: Challenges for local governance in rural regions. *Public Administration and Management* 9(3), 212–223.

Smith, D (2007). The 'buoyancy' of 'other' geographies of gentrification: Going 'back-to-the-water' and the commodification of marginality. *Tijdschrift voor Economische en Sociale Geografie* 98(1), 53–67.

Smith, D & Higley, R (2012). Circuits of education, rural gentrification, and family migration from the global city. *Journal of Rural Studies* 28(1), 49–55.

Stockdale, A (2002a). Towards a typology of out-migration from peripheral areas: A Scottish Case Study. *International Journal of Population Geography* 8, 345–364.

Stockdale, A (2002b). Out-migration from rural Scotland: The importance of family and social networks. *Sociologia Ruralis* 42(1), 41–64.

Stockdale, A (2004). Rural out-migration: Community consequences and individual migrant experiences. *Sociologia Ruralis* 44(2), 167–194.

Stockdale, A (2006). The role of a *retirement transition* in the repopulation of rural areas. *Population, Space and Place* 12, 1–13.

Stockdale, A (2010). The diverse geographies of rural gentrification in Scotland. *Journal of Rural Studies* 26(1), 31–40.

Stockdale, A (2014). Unravelling the migration decision-making process: English early retirees moving to rural mid–Wales. *Journal of Rural Studies* 34, 161–171.

Stockdale, A (2015). Contemporary and 'messy' rural in-migration processes: Comparing counterurban and lateral rural migration. *Population, Space and Place*. doi: 10.1002/psp. 1947.

Stockdale, A & MacLeod, M (2013). Pre-retirement age migration to remote rural areas. *Journal of Rural Studies* 32, 80–92.

Stockdale, A, MacLeod, M & Philip, L (2013). Connected life courses: Influences on and experiences of 'mid life' in-migration to rural areas. *Population, Space and Place* 19(3), 239–257.

Sunil, T, Rojas, V & Bradley, D (2007). United States' international retirement migration: The reasons for retiring to the environs of Lake Chapala, Mexico. *Ageing and Society* 27, 489–510.

Taylor, M (2008). *Living working countryside: The Taylor Review of rural economy and affordable housing.* London: Department for Communities and Local Government.

Thissen, F, Droogleever Fortuijn, J, Strijker, D & Haartsen, T (2010). Migration intentions of rural youth in the Westhoek, Flanders, Belgium and the Veenkoloniën, The Netherlands. *Journal of Rural Studies* 26, 428–436.

Trell, E-M, van Hoven, B & Huigen, P (2012). 'It's good to live in Järva-Jaani but we can't stay here': Youth and belonging in rural Estonia. *Journal of Rural Studies* 28, 139–148.

Ulrich-Schad, JD, Henly, M & Safford, TG (2013). The role of community assessments, place, and the Great Recession in the migration intentions of rural Americans. *Rural Sociology* 78(3), 371–398.

van Dam, F, Heins, S & Elbersen, B (2002). Lay discourses of the rural and stated and revealed preferences for rural living. Some evidence of the existence of a rural idyll in the Netherlands. *Journal of Rural Studies* 18(4), 461–476.

Vining, D & Kontuly, T (1978). Population dispersal from major metropolitan regions: An international comparison. *International Regional Science Review* 3(1), 49–73.

Vining, D & Strauss, A (1977). A demonstration that the current deconcentration of population in the United States is a clean break with the past. *Environment and Planning A* 9, 751–758.

von Reichert, C, Cromartie, JB & Arthun, RO (2014a). Impacts of return migration on rural U.S. communities. *Rural Sociology* 79, 200–226.

von Reichert, C, Cromartie, JB & Arthun, RO (2014b). Reasons for returning and not returning to rural U.S. communities. *The Professional Geographer* 66(1), 58–70.

Wall, T & von Reichert, C (2013). Divorce as an influence in return migration to rural areas. *Population, Space and Place* 19, 350–363.

Wenger, C (2001). Myths and realities of ageing in rural Britain. *Ageing and Society* 21, 117–130.

Whelan, C & Hannan, D (1999). Class inequalities in educational attainment among the adult population in the Republic of Ireland. *The Economic and Social Review* 30(3), 285–307.

Wiborg, A (2004) Place, nature and migration: Students' attachment to their rural home places. *Sociologia Ruralis* 44(4), 416–432.

Woods, M (2005). *Rural geography.* London: Sage.

Wulff, M, Champion, A & Lobo, M (2010). Household diversity and migration in mid-life: Understanding residential mobility among 45–64 year olds in Melbourne, Australia. *Population, Space and Place* 16, 307–321.

4

Ageing in Rural Places

Thomas Scharf, Kieran Walsh and Eamon O'Shea

Introduction: the emerging field of rural gerontology

Ageing in rural places and the variety of issues facing older people who live in rural communities are long-standing topics of interest in social gerontology. Indeed, a number of pioneering studies have become key reference points of European and North American research on ageing. This is reflected, for example, in early work by Blume (1969) and Rosenmayr (1960, 1982) on family relations of older people in rural areas respectively of Germany and Austria, in Cribier's (1973) influential research on urban dwellers with second homes in the French countryside, in Arensberg and Kimball's (1940/2001) study of intergenerational farming relationships in the rural west of Ireland, and in the extensive body of work developed by Wenger (1984) in rural communities in North Wales (United Kingdom). A similarly strong North American tradition of rural gerontology is illustrated in a range of edited collections (e.g., Youmans, 1967; Coward & Lee, 1985; Rowles, Beaulieu & Myers, 1996; Coward & Krout, 1998). These studies emerged at a time when social gerontology, still in its relative infancy as a multidisciplinary field of study, sought to draw attention to the sociospatial implications of population ageing and to distinguish characteristics of rural older people from those of urban or, in the predominantly urbanised societies of the global north, general populations of ageing adults.

By 2000, research on rural ageing had matured to the point where, underpinned by an influential preparatory report undertaken by experts associated with the International Rural Aging Project (1999), it was possible to convene a first international conference dedicated to the theme of rural ageing. Around 2,100 participants from more than 40 nations and drawn from policy, practice and a range of scientific disciplines explored a wide array of issues concerning ageing in rural places (Hermanova, Brown, Goins & Briggs, 2001). Seven key topics in rural ageing were considered priority areas for the international research community: demography, health, intergenerational relationships, life course perspectives, participation of rural elders, impact of technology, and evidence of successful rural policies. Although one of the goals of the International Rural Aging Project was to establish a promising agenda for rural ageing research, 13 years later, in a review paper that followed up the Project's work, Burholt and Dobbs (2012) argued that there was still a substantial way to go in these and other topic areas. While there might have been an increase in the number of studies on these topics in rural areas, generally research lacked a critical and analytical focus. In many cases, 'rural' continued to be viewed more as a research setting rather than being seen as an ever-changing context that can potentially shape experiences and outcomes for older people.

Notwithstanding such a critique, and Wahl's (2015, p. 21) observation that social gerontology is largely blind in its 'rural eye', there is recent evidence of an upsurge of research on ageing in rural places. This is reflected, for example, in a number of journal special issues (see Milbourne, 2012) as well as in edited collections and monographs that draw primarily on research conducted in Western nations (e.g., Lowe & Speakman, 2006; Brown & Glasgow, 2008; Keating, 2008; Glasgow & Berry, 2013; Hagan Hennessy, Means & Burholt, 2014; Hash, Jurkowski & Krout, 2014; Fachinger & Künemund, 2015).

The recent proliferation of research on ageing in rural places can be attributed to at least three factors. First, and perhaps decisively, the environmental context of ageing, and issues relating to place and space, has itself become mainstreamed as a core theme in social gerontology (e.g., Kendig, 2003; Wahl, Scheidt & Windley, 2003; Davies & James, 2011; Wahl, Iwarsson & Oswald, 2012; Rowles & Bernard, 2013; Scheidt & Schwarz, 2013). Inspired by classic studies conducted by Rosow (1967), Rowles (1978), Lawton (1980) and others, the mission of environmental gerontology has been to 'understand the continually changing interrelations between aging people and their sociophysical environment and how these relationships shape the human aging progression' (Scheidt & Schwarz, 2013, p. 1). In this respect, the burgeoning field of environmental gerontology has provided the necessary incubation space for research which casts light on key issues faced by adults who are ageing in diverse rural settings across a range of countries. As noted by Wahl and Lang (2004, p. 7), relevant environmental challenges include 'preserving as-independent-as-possible everyday life in the face of physical and mental impairments by using environmental resources outside the home environment ("aging in place"), initiating processes of relocation if desired or necessary, and adapting to new living environment settings (such as nursing homes or other planned housing) after relocation'.

A second factor underpinning the growing interest in rural ageing concerns the ways in which environmental experiences are themselves being reshaped by processes associated with globalisation (Urry, 2000). This is characterised most notably by accelerated rates of migration and mobility across the globe, growing sociospatial inequalities, the impacts of new information and communications technologies, and welfare state retrenchment. The impacts of such processes on rural communities have provided fertile ground for rural gerontologists and others to explore an expanding range of topics (Woods, 2007), including how rural older adults are affected by changes in population composition (e.g., Hedberg & Haandrikman, 2014), features of poverty and social exclusion amongst rural older people (e.g., Scharf & Bartlam, 2008; Milbourne & Doheny, 2012; Walsh, O'Shea, Scharf & Shucksmith, 2014), the potential for new technologies to support social relations of rural elders (e.g., Warburton, Cowan & Bathgate, 2013; Kilpeläinen & Seppänen, 2014), and the changing nature of voluntarism in rural ageing communities (e.g., Joseph & Skinner, 2012; Skinner, Joseph & Herron, 2013; Winterton & Warburton, 2014). In countries such as Ireland, the global financial crisis of 2007–2008 has encouraged research which assesses the varied impacts of the recession and austerity policies on older people ageing in both rural and urban communities (Walsh, 2015; Walsh, Carney & Ni Leime, 2015).

Third, the burgeoning field of rural gerontology can also be attributed to research and policy discussions which increasingly acknowledge the ways in which demographic ageing intersects with other long-standing challenges facing declining and under-served rural communities. Resolving the different problems facing rural areas, whilst also building on the multifarious contributions that older people make in rural places, is increasingly viewed as central to research and policy development. In this context, for example, the World Health Organization's (2007) *Global Age-friendly Cities* project, established in 2006, has rapidly been transformed into a project that also has a powerful rural dimension (Keating, Eales & Phillips, 2013; Walsh, O'Shea, Scharf

& Shucksmith, 2014; Menec et al., 2015; Spina & Menec, 2015). This is best reflected in work undertaken in Canada to produce an *Age-friendly Rural and Remote Communities* guide (Federal/ Provincial/Territorial Ministers Responsible for Seniors, 2009). But it is also a feature of strategic planning for age-friendly communities in predominantly rural places in Ireland (e.g., Galway Age-Friendly Programme, 2014; Walsh, 2015).

Against this background, this chapter examines key themes in research on rural ageing. It reviews the challenges faced by researchers working in this field, and highlights recent developments in terms of an emerging critical perspective on ageing in rural places. The chapter concludes with a discussion of potential future directions for research on ageing in rural places.

Key themes in rural gerontology

Over time, research on ageing in rural places in Western nations has evolved to encompass a broad range of themes, disciplines and perspectives. In part, this draws on growing awareness of, and interest in, the ways in which rural places are themselves experiencing profound change. This arises not only from the impact of processes of globalisation, which have had a highly differentiated impact on rural communities (Terluin, 2003), but also from continuing demographic shifts. Demographic ageing has become a major feature of population change in the global north, where populations are ageing in both numerical and structural terms. While the absolute numbers of people aged 65 and over are continuing to increase as a result of rising life expectancies, the growing proportions of older people within national populations can be attributed primarily to reduced fertility rates. The demographic outcome is profound. In 2012, 18% of the population of the European Union, around 93 million people, were aged 65 and over. By 2060, this proportion is projected to reach 28% and the number of people to grow to 148 million people (European Commission, 2015). These changes have spatial dimensions, affecting both urban and rural areas. Despite a general increase in social, economic and cultural urbanisation, just under half (48%) of the world's older population lives in rural areas. Moreover, in most countries, the proportions of older people are greater in rural than urban areas (United Nations, 2009). This population distribution is primarily the outcome of migration patterns rather than of differences in fertility and mortality patterns. A lack of employment and education opportunities in many declining rural regions encourages younger people to move away to seek work or to pursue their studies. Such areas contrast with amenity-rich regions that are attractive sources of retirement in-migration (Brown, 2010). In purely demographic terms, and with evidence of complex patterns of counter-urbanisation, retirement migration and return migration, rural elders, therefore, continue to represent a significant group in the ageing population. Within rural regions, there is further diversity in population structures. In Europe, rural, relatively remote and sparsely populated regions typically have the highest proportions of older people (Eurostat, 2014).

Although developing world regions are responsible for the largest segment of the older rural population, rural ageing is far from being an exclusive feature of the global south. In Ireland, for example, despite a gradual decline over time, 42% of the country's population aged 65 and over were living in rural places in 2011 (Connolly, Finn & O'Shea, 2012). Relatively high proportions of people aged 65 and over live in rural and remote regions of Greece, Spain, France, Portugal, and in parts of eastern Germany. In 2013, 32% of people in the Portuguese region of Pinhal Interior Sul were aged 65 and over, representing the highest share in the European Union nations. Four Greek rural regions had over 28% of their populations in this age range (Eurostat, 2014). Past migration processes also mean that the population profile of particular types of rural area within such regions is likely to change quite significantly in the years ahead. For example, processes of suburbanisation since the 1960s are predicted to lead to a substantial ageing of rural areas close to the edge of major towns and cities in Western nations. In the German context, this phenomenon has been referred to as a process of 'ageing into the countryside' (Bucher, Kocks & Siedhoff, 1998).

Such demographic trends have encouraged social gerontologists to explore features of diverse ageing populations in different types of rural community, as proposed by Schulz-Nieswandt (2000) and by Phillipson and Scharf (2005). In Ireland, for example, Burholt, Scharf and Walsh (2013) have examined a range of issues facing older people who are ageing in small island communities. Elsewhere, a major focus for research has been on the impacts of retirement migration from northern Europe on predominantly rural regions of the Mediterranean (Casado-Díaz, Kaiser & Warnes, 2004). In the Arctic region of Europe, recent research has addressed the sociodemographic characteristics of ageing populations that live in the often harsh environmental conditions of northern Russia (Emelyanova & Rautio, 2013). While European research often frames retirement migration as a challenge for receiving rural communities, in North America there has been a stronger focus on the economic and social opportunities that emerge from such demographic processes (Brown & Glasgow, 2008). Glasgow and Brown (2012, p. 427) make the point that in-migrants to retirement destinations for older people tend to be younger, wealthier and healthier than residents who are ageing in place, and that they often migrate as married couples. As a result, 'older in-migrants stimulate the demand for housing; commercial goods and services; are active as leaders and volunteers in the community; and they often provide professional and technical assistance to the community free of charge'.

Another enduring feature of research on ageing in rural places, and partly related to the demographic processes described above, has been the investigation of ways in which a changing social and economic infrastructure has affected ageing populations. By contrast, the impact of ageing populations on such infrastructures has largely been under-researched. Infrastructural aspects are highly differentiated both between and within nations, pointing to the specificities of rural ageing environments. In some countries, the presence of local facilities such as a shop, a post office or public transport are regarded as central features of a vibrant local community and as elements of the physical environment that render communities 'age friendly'. However, while thriving rural communities might be able to sustain such facilities, in many countries the lack of economic resources in places marked by population decline and the loss of employment opportunities make these services rather more difficult to maintain (e.g., Heenan, 2010; Dwyer & Hardill, 2011; Walsh, O'Shea, Scharf & Murray, 2012; Krout, 2014). As a result, in England, for example, a survey conducted in 1997 identified that 42% of rural parishes had no shop, 43% had no post office and 75% lacked a daily bus service (Countryside Agency, 1999, p. 26). Indeed, in countries such as Canada, Ireland, New Zealand and the United Kingdom, transport features heavily in many older people's accounts of the principal challenges associated with living in rural settings (McDonagh, 2006; Davey, 2007; Ryser & Halseth, 2012; Shergold, Parkhurst & Musselwhite, 2012).

In similar vein, almost constant budgetary pressures faced by many Western nations from the middle of the 1970s to the present day have led to a restructuring of social policy and an increasingly explicit emphasis in health and social care policies on support provided by individuals, their families and a range of community and voluntary services. In rural areas, where health and social care provision has traditionally been weakest, older people may become even more vulnerable to the absence or gradual loss of what might be regarded as essential services. Again, England serves to provide an illustration of this issue. In 1997, 91% of rural parishes had no day care for older people, and 80% had no form of residential care (Countryside Agency, 1999, p. 27). Indeed, while the cost of providing social care in rural communities is typically higher than in urban areas – not least due to the higher transport costs incurred in rural places – funding arrangements may be imbalanced towards meeting the needs of older people in urban places. In England, the per capita social care expenditure on people aged 65 and over in 2009–2010 was more than twice as much in parts of inner London as in predominantly rural counties (Commission for Rural Communities, 2012). Where gaps in service provision exist, the community and voluntary sector is often expected to intervene to meet older people's care and support needs. However, in their empirical study of six contrasting community-based services in England, Hardill and Dwyer (2011) showed that the community and voluntary sector was seriously challenged by the precarious nature of funding regimes and an over-reliance on volunteer labour. Simply put, without volunteers, many rural services would be unsustainable. Parallel arguments have been made regarding the focus on voluntarism in rural places in Canada, Australia and New Zealand (Skinner & Joseph, 2011; Skinner, Joseph & Herron, 2013; Winterton & Warburton, 2014).

Underlying shortcomings in rural service provision is a widely held assumption that older people in the countryside are securely embedded within supportive social networks and that demand for formal services is lower in rural than in urban places (Wenger, 2001). While research generally points to the multiple benefits of positive social relations in later life (e.g., Bowling, 2005), Wenger's (1984) work in rural North Wales points not only to different types of social network, with some being much more supportive than others at times of crisis, but also to a substantial level of unmet care needs in rural places. While out-migration from rural communities and losses arising from bereavement or relationship breakdown may make older people vulnerable to social isolation and/or loneliness, evidence about urban–rural distinctions in the nature and quality of older adults' social relationships is inconsistent. While some studies report generally lower rates of loneliness in rural than urban places, Burholt's (2011) analysis of comparable survey data from six European nations showed that this pattern applied only in Austria, Sweden and the UK. In the Netherlands, Luxembourg and Italy, no differences in rates of loneliness were reported between urban and rural communities. Where studies address the social relations of particular groups of rural older people, they identify heightened risks of loneliness for some. In rural Appalachia, for example, one study showed chronic ill health to be associated with high rates of loneliness amongst ageing adults, and that this was in turn correlated with depression, reduced quality of life, and low levels of social support (Theeke, Goins, Moore & Campbell, 2012).

Challenges for rural gerontology

Given the need to understand how the general changes outlined above impact upon older people in rural places, researchers seeking to develop an agenda on rural ageing have often struggled to respond to two key challenges. The first challenge, likely to be shared in other rural research, concerns a fundamental difficulty in rural gerontology associated with the theorisation of rural change. While social geographers have consistently warned against overgeneralised interpretations of rurality (e.g., Pratt, 1996), and highlighted cultural variation in the meanings and significance of such terms as 'rural' and 'rurality' (Hoggart, Buller & Black, 1995; Scharf, Wenger, Thissen & Burholt, 2005; Edmondson & Scharf, 2015), there remains a need for social gerontologists to take a more critical look at what they mean when they describe their work as being rural. Lack of clarity concerning definitions of rurality (Schulz-Nieswandt, 2000; Scharf, Wenger, Thissen & Burholt, 2005) often means that researchers seeking to report on data collected in rural places are typically obliged to take for granted that the research group responsible for collecting the primary data had a robust means of distinguishing the 'urban' from the 'rural'. Many studies that purport to focus on ageing in rural places have paid surprisingly little attention to issues of definition or meaning. It is further argued that the somewhat disparate nature of research into aspects of rural ageing might itself be responsible for generating contradictory research findings. Such research may also serve to foster a number of myths and sustain stereotypical views in relation to the experience of ageing in rural areas (see Wenger, 2001).

In the field of gerontology, a second challenge to be addressed in rural gerontology concerns the (sometimes implicit) comparisons that are drawn between the contrasting experiences of older age in rural and urban areas. Underlying such research is the basic assumption that in some way ageing in rural places can be differentiated from ageing in urban contexts (see Edmondson & Scharf, 2015). This idea has been the focus of a long-standing debate in German research on ageing in different types of community settings (e.g., Arbeitsgruppe Gesundheitsanalysen, 1991; Garms-Homolová & Korte, 1993, Schulz-Nieswandt, 2000). In an early contribution to the debate, Tews (1987) hypothesised that there were two types of explanation of differences in terms of the situation of older people in urban and rural areas. The first explanation suggested that rural areas were engaged in an ongoing process of catch-up with urban areas. Drawing on modernisation theory, Tews (1987) made the point that rural areas might be regarded as being somewhat 'delayed' in their socioeconomic development. In time, rural places would acquire modern, urban characteristics. Thus the larger, multigenerational family structures that were reported by scholars such as Blume (1969) and Rosenmayr (1982) as being more common in rural areas (of Germany and Austria) would gradually give way to the more urban nuclear family form. In time, intergenerational relations in urban and rural places would come to resemble one another. This 'delay hypothesis' contrasted with an alternative view which suggested that despite the ongoing process of modernisation, differences between urban and rural areas would persist in relation to the nature and experience of ageing. According to the so-called 'level hypothesis', certain features of the situation in rural and urban areas cannot be equalised. This type of explanation is particularly closely associated with differences between urban and rural areas in terms of aspects of rural infrastructures that are important to older people, including housing arrangements, health and social care provision, and transport services (Tews, 1987).

While these dual explanations may have been useful as a means of providing a conceptual framework for comparing the experiences of ageing adults in rural and urban places, they are marked by the fundamental weakness that they identify urban areas as the destination point in terms of sociodemographic change and as the model to which rural areas should aspire (Garms-Homolová & Korte, 1993; Schulz-Nieswandt, 2000; Schweppe, 2000). One outcome of this type of approach, often reflected implicitly in comparable research in other Western nations, is that similarities between central features of the ageing process in urban and rural areas – for example, in relation to normative aspects of intergenerational relationships – tend to be underplayed. In an important contribution to this field, when Garms-Homolová and Korte (1993) reviewed relevant research on aspects of urban and rural infrastructures and intergenerational relationships in Germany, they noted a marked absence of urban–rural differences. This point was subsequently backed up by analysis of the German Ageing Survey (Brauer, 2002). In similar vein, Gallagher (2008) found fewer cultural differences than she had expected between older people living in Dublin and those in the relatively remote rural area of Donegal she studied. In this respect, it can be argued that such differences may often be assumed and subsequently overplayed in social gerontology (Golant, 2004). Reflecting the cultural 'turn' in the social sciences, the burgeoning field of cultural gerontology (Twigg & Martin, 2015) can justifiably pose questions about how fundamentally separate these two types of environmental setting actually are (Edmondson & Scharf, 2015). Indeed, Graham Rowles was probably ahead of his time when he asked explicitly in 1988, with reference to Appalachian communities in the United States, 'What's rural about rural ageing?'

While there continues to be potential for research to compare the experiences of people who are ageing in urban and rural places, especially where this draws attention to differential distribution of and access to goods and services, at another level, urban–rural comparisons may be less meaningful. This is especially likely to apply when the argument is developed that draws upon modernisation theory to suggest that 'the urban' represents the destination of 'the rural'.

Towards a critical perspective in rural gerontology

One of the major achievements of what has become known as 'critical gerontology' has been to raise awareness of the increasing heterogeneity of later life in Western societies (Bernard & Scharf, 2007; Phillipson, 2013; Baars, Dohmen, Grenier & Phillipson, 2014). Changing demographic and family structures, and variations in lifestyles and access to life chances, have served to differentiate the older population much more along the lines of the key social locations associated with such variables as age, socioeconomic status, gender, race and ethnicity, and health and disability. Such factors substantially shape the experiences of and meanings attached to later life. In general, where the influence of environmental context has featured at all in critical gerontology approaches, it has tended to focus disproportionately on urban settings (e.g., Phillipson, Berhard, Phillips & Ogg, 1998; Scharf, Phillipson, Smith & Kingston, 2002; Phillipson, 2007; Buffel, Phillipson & Scharf, 2012). More recently, however, critical gerontology perspectives have also been applied to the field of rural gerontology. For example, a growing body of work has emerged that is exploring themes around the ways in which later life in rural places can be marked by forms of social inclusion and exclusion (Philip & Shucksmith, 2003; Shucksmith, 2012; Spoor, 2013). Relevant research draws on conceptual understandings of exclusion as a multidimensional phenomenon to highlight processes and power relations that are associated with disadvantage experienced by rural older people (e.g., Moffatt & Glasgow, 2009; Milbourne & Doheny, 2012). Such work can challenge public perceptions regarding the seeming invisibility of disadvantage in rural communities. This work is important in extending earlier research in Europe and North America that examines experiences of poverty in rural places. For example, Glasgow's (1993) study of poverty among rural elders in the USA not only highlighted the disproportionately high rates of poverty experienced by older people in non-metropolitan communities, but also drew attention to the need to adopt a life course perspective in terms of explaining the accumulated risks of poverty that arise from residence in rural places.

Building on an initial pilot project in England (Scharf & Bartlam, 2008), a much deeper understanding of rural social exclusion has emerged in the context of studies undertaken in diverse rural communities in Ireland and Northern Ireland (Walsh et al., 2010; Walsh, O'Shea & Scharf, 2012; Walsh, O'Shea, Scharf & Shucksmith, 2014). Drawing on an empirical study conducted in ten rural communities on the island of Ireland, five in the Republic of Ireland and five in Northern Ireland, Walsh, O'Shea and Scharf (2012) used in-depth interviews and focus groups with community stakeholders and older people to develop and refine a model of social exclusion that specifically applies to ageing in rural places. They identified five domains of social exclusion that could characterise the lives of rural-dwelling older people, encompassing the themes of: social connections and social resources; services; transport and mobility; safety, security and crime; and income and financial resources. The work not only demonstrated the potential for these domains of exclusion to intersect to bring about multiple disadvantage for individual rural elders, but it also showed how exclusion could be mediated by individual capacities (e.g., sense of personal agency and independence), life course trajectories, characteristics of rural places and communities, and macroeconomic forces (e.g., emigration or economic recession) (Walsh, O'Shea & Scharf, 2012).

In subsequent work, the potential for rural communities themselves to act as a source of social exclusion has also been identified (Walsh, O'Shea, Scharf & Shucksmith, 2014).

The development of a more critical approach, as reflected in the emerging body of work on social exclusion and inclusion, can assist in challenging distorted views and myths in relation to rural ageing (Wenger, 2001). The approach might also address the often contradictory nature of research findings relating to ageing in rural places that has been noted by some scholars (e.g., Schweppe, 2000; Wahl, Schilling & Oswald, 2000; Phillipson & Scharf, 2005). For example, depending upon the topic under analysis, and the subjective interpretation of the researcher, older people living in rural areas have often been portrayed in starkly binary terms, as being either 'favoured' or 'disadvantaged', as being either 'well integrated' or 'socially isolated', as being either 'included' or 'excluded'. A good example of this comes from a German text on ageing policy which drew attention to the apparent 'problem' of rural ageing. Without reference to empirical evidence, Ritter and Hohmeier (1999, p. 39) suggested that, 'The situation of the elderly in rural areas is also made more difficult by the weakening of family networks, because the stability of families is declining and the number of small families and single people is increasing'. The proliferation of new research on ageing in rural places, underpinned by empirical evidence arising from major (often longitudinal) studies and a range of well-crafted qualitative investigations, has at the very least opened the door to the application of more meaningful, critical perspectives.

Conclusion: future directions for research on ageing in rural places

In concluding, and recognising the value of examining ageing in rural settings within the framework of broader debates around ageing, it is helpful to identify potentially fruitful directions for research on ageing in rural places. These suggestions are also underpinned by recognition of an ongoing need for an enrichment of theoretical perspectives, with rural gerontology, as part of the growing field of environmental gerontology, drawing closer links with developments in human geography, critical gerontology and cultural studies of ageing (Phillipson & Scharf, 2005; Edmondson & Scharf, 2015).

At a basic level, and reflecting the ambition of experts associated with the International Rural Aging Project (1999), there continues to be scope to develop research on particular topic areas associated with rural ageing. The review undertaken by Burholt and Dobbs (2012) identified a number of areas worthy of closer scrutiny, including topics addressing a range of social, economic and political, and technological themes, as well as issues relating to climate change and to agriculture and food security. Given the pace of change in rural communities, and the growing focus on diversity of ageing populations within diverse types of community, there is an equally important ongoing need for research to engage with some of the traditional themes of rural ageing. This would include attention to demographic characteristics, to the ways in which services and supports can be designed to meet the needs of ageing populations, and to the nature of intergenerational family relations in rural settings. The need for such research is important in terms of challenging preconceived ideas about ageing in rural places. The absence of recent research on major themes means that gerontology inevitably reaches back to findings arising from disparate, and often non-comparable, historical studies of rural ageing. Where studies rely on data generated 20 or even 30 years ago, they might inadvertently contribute to reinforcing the impression that rural areas are not prone to change, thus perpetuating one of the key stereotypes about rural ageing.

In some ways, the capacity to respond to these and other questions has never been better than at the present time. Major longitudinal studies of ageing across Western nations provide opportunities for researchers to focus specifically on rural ageing questions, examining change over time between cohorts of rural elders and across individual life courses. However, the lack of attention in some longitudinal studies to the diversity of rural environments means that there remains a need for other types of research approach, including qualitative and mixed-methods studies, to examine central features of the lives of older people in rural areas. This points to the potential for innovation not only in terms of theory development and the substantive focus of research, but also in relation to the application of methods with which to explore ageing in rural places.

References

Arbeitsgruppe Gesundheitsanalysen. (1991). *Alte Menschen in der Stadt und auf dem Land*. AG Gesundheitsanalysen und soziale Konzepte an der FU Berlin and Interdisziplinäre AG für Angewandte Soziale Gerontologie an der GHS Kassel. Berlin: Deutsches Zentrum für Altersfragen.

Arensberg, C & Kimball, S (1940/2001). *Family and community in Ireland*. Eds A Byrne, R Edmondson & T Varley. Ennis: CLASP Press.

Baars, J, Dohmen, J, Grenier, A & Phillipson, C (Eds). (2014). *Ageing, meaning and social structure: Connecting critical and humanistic gerontology*. Bristol: Policy Press.

Bernard, M & Scharf, T (Eds). (2007). *Critical perspectives on ageing societies*. Bristol: Policy Press.

Blume, O (1969). Zur Situation der älteren Menschen auf dem Lande. *Neues Beginnen* 3, 15–21.

Bowling, A (2005). *Ageing well: quality of life in old age*. Maidenhead: Open University Press.

Brauer, K (2002). Ein Blick zurück nach vorn. Generationenbeziehungen im Stadt-Land-Vergleich. In G Burkart & J Wolf (Eds), *Lebenszeiten. Erkundungen zur Soziologie der Generationen* (pp. 175–194). Opladen: Leske & Budrich.

Brown, DL (2010). *Rethinking the OECD's new rural demography*. Centre for Rural Economy Discussion Paper Series 26. Newcastle: Centre for Rural Economy.

Brown, DL & Glasgow, N (2008). *Rural retirement migration*. Dordrecht: Springer.

Bucher, H, Kocks, M & Siedhoff, M (1998). Regionale Alterung, Haushalts- und Wohnungsmarktentwicklung. In Deutsches Zentrum für Altersfragen (Ed.), *Regionales Altern und Mobilitätsprozesse Älterer. Expertisenband 2 zum Zweiten Altenbericht der Bundesregierung* (pp. 14–69). Frankfurt: Campus.

Buffel, T, Phillipson, C & Scharf, T (2012). Ageing in urban environments: Developing 'age-friendly' cities. *Critical Social Policy* 32(4), 597–617.

Burholt, V (2011). Loneliness of older men and women in rural areas of the UK. In Age Concern Oxfordshire (Ed.), *Safeguarding the convoy: A call to action from the Campaign to End Loneliness* (pp. 35–39). Oxford: Age Concern Oxfordshire.

Burholt, V & Dobbs, C (2012). Research on rural ageing: Where have we got to and where are we going? *Journal of Rural Studies* 28(4), 432–446.

Burholt, V, Scharf, T & Walsh, K (2013). Imagery and imaginary of islander identity: Older people and migration in Irish small-island communities. *Journal of Rural Studies* 3, 1–12.

Casado-Díaz, MA, Kaiser, C & Warnes, AM (2004). Northern European retired residents in nine southern European areas: Characteristics, motivations and adjustment. *Ageing and Society* 24(3), 353–381.

Connolly, S, Finn, C & O'Shea, E (2012). *Rural ageing in Ireland: Key trends and issues*. Rural Ageing Observatory Working Paper 1. Galway: Irish Centre for Social Gerontology, NUI Galway.

Commission for Rural Communities. (2012). *Social isolation experienced by older people in rural communities*. Gloucester: Commission for Rural Communities.

Countryside Agency. (1999). *The state of the countryside*. Cheltenham: Countryside Agency.

Coward, RT & Krout, JA (Eds). (1998). *Aging in rural settings*. New York: Springer.

Coward, RT & Lee, G (1985). *The elderly in rural society*. New York: Springer.

Cribier, F (1973). The second homes of urbanites in the French countryside. In *Étude rurales: revue trimestrielle d'histoire, géographie, sociologie et économie des campagnes* (pp. 181–204). Paris: Mouton.

Davey, J (2007). Older people and transport: Coping without a car. *Ageing and Society* 27(1), 49–65.

Davies, A & James, A (2011). *Geographies of ageing: Social processes and the spatial unevenness of population ageing*. Aldershot: Ashgate.

Dwyer, P & Hardill, I (2011). Promoting social inclusion? The impact of village services on the lives of older people living in rural England. *Ageing and Society* 31(2), 243–264.

Edmondson, R & Scharf, T (2015). Rural and urban ageing: Contributions of cultural gerontology. In J Twigg & W Martin (Eds), *Routledge handbook of cultural gerontology* (pp. 412–419). London: Routledge.

Emelyanova, A & Rautio, A (2013). Perspectives for population ageing in the Russian North. *Journal of Population Ageing* 6(3), 161–187.

European Commission. (2015). *The 2015 ageing report: Underlying assumptions and projection methodologies.* Brussels: European Commission.

Eurostat (2014). *Eurostat regional yearbook 2014.* Luxembourg: Publications Office of the European Union.

Fachinger, U & Künemund, H (Eds). (2015). *Altern im ländlichen Raum. Lebensbedingungen, Veränderungsprozesse und Gestaltungsmöglichkeiten.* Wiesbaden: Springer.

Federal, Provincial and Territorial Ministers Responsible for Seniors. (2009). *Age-friendly rural and remote communities: A guide.* Ottawa: Public Health Agency of Canada.

Gallagher, C (2008). *The community life of older people in Ireland.* Bern: Peter Lang.

Galway Age-Friendly Programme. (2014). *Galway age-friendly programme: Strategy 2014–2019.* Galway: Galway City and County Age Friendly Alliance.

Garms-Homolová, V & Korte, W (1993). Altern in der Stadt und auf dem Lande – Unterschiede oder Angleichung? In G Naegele & HP Tews (Eds), *Lebenslagen im Strukturwandel des Alters. Alternde Gesellschaft - Folgen für die Politik* (pp. 215–233). Opladen: Westdeutscher Verlag.

Glasgow, N (1993). Poverty among rural elders: Trends, context, and directions for policy. *Journal of Applied Gerontology* 12(3), 302–319.

Glasgow, N & Berry, EH (Eds). (2013). *Rural aging in 21st century America.* Dordrecht: Springer.

Glasgow, N & Brown, DL (2012). Rural ageing in the United States: Trends and contexts. *Journal of Rural Studies* 28(4), 422–431.

Golant, SM (2004). The urban–rural distinction in gerontology: An update of research. In H-W Wahl, R Scheidt & P Windley (Eds), *Aging in context: Socio-physical environments. Annual Review of Gerontology and Geriatrics* 3 (pp. 280–312). New York: Springer.

Hagan Hennessy, C, Means, R & Burholt, V (Eds). (2014). *Countryside connections: Older people, community and place in rural Britain.* Bristol: Policy Press.

Hardill, I & Dwyer, P (2011). Delivering public services in the mixed economy of welfare: Perspectives from the voluntary and community sector in rural England. *Journal of Social Policy* 40(1), 157–172.

Hash, KM, Jurkowski, ET & Krout, JA (Eds). (2014). *Aging in rural places: Programs, policies, and professional practice.* New York: Springer.

Hedberg, C & Haandrikman, K (2014). Repopulation of the Swedish countryside: Globalisation by international migration. *Journal of Rural Studies* 34, 128–138.

Heenan, D (2010). *Rural ageing in Northern Ireland: Quality of life amongst older people.* Belfast: Office of the First Minister and Deputy First Minister.

Hermanova, H, Brown, DK, Goins, RT & Briggs, R (2001). The first international conference on rural aging: A global challenge. *The Journal of Rural Health* 17, 303–304.

Hoggart, K, Buller, H & Black, R (1995). *Rural Europe: Identity and change.* London: Edward Arnold.

International Rural Aging Project. (1999). *Shepherdstown report on rural aging: The result of the expert group meeting,* May 22–25, 1999. Shepherdstown, WV: University of West Virginia.

Joseph, AE & Skinner, MW (2012). Voluntarism as a mediator of the experience of growing old in evolving rural spaces and changing rural places. *Journal of Rural Studies* 28(4), 380–388.

Keating, N (Ed.). (2008). *Rural ageing: A good place to grow old?* Bristol: Policy Press.

Keating, N, Eales, J & Phillips, JE (2013). Age-friendly rural communities: Conceptualizing 'best-fit'. *Canadian Journal on Aging* 32(4), 319–332.

Kendig, H (2003). Directions in environmental gerontology: A multidisciplinary field. *The Gerontologist* 43, 611–615.

Kilpeläinen, A & Seppänen, M (2014). Information technology and everyday life in ageing rural villages. *Journal of Rural Studies* 33, 1–8.

Krout, JA (2014). Providing services to rural older adults. In KM Hash, ET Jurkowski & JA Krout (Eds), *Aging in rural places: Programs, policies, and professional practice* (pp. 119–134). New York: Springer.

Lawton, MP (1980). *Environment and aging.* California: Brooks-Cole.

Lowe, P & Speakman, L (Eds). (2006). *The ageing countryside: The growing older population of rural England.* London: Age Concern England.

McDonagh, J (2006). Transport policy instruments and transport-related social exclusion in rural Republic of Ireland. *Journal of Transport Geography* 14(5), 355–366.

Menec, VH, Hutton, L, Newall, N, Nowicki, S, Spina, J & Veselyuk, D (2015). How 'age-friendly' are rural communities and what community characteristics are related to age-friendliness? The case of rural Manitoba, Canada. *Ageing and Society* 35(1), 203–223.

Milbourne, P (2012). Editorial. Growing old in rural places. *Journal of Rural Studies* 28(4), 315–317.

Milbourne, P & Doheny, S (2012). Older people and poverty in rural Britain: Material hardships, cultural denials and social inclusions. *Journal of Rural Studies* 28(4), 389–397.

Moffatt, S & Glasgow, N (2009). How useful is the concept of social exclusion when applied to rural older people in the United Kingdom and the United States? *Regional Studies* 43(10), 1291–1303.

Philip, LJ & Shucksmith, M (2003). Conceptualizing social exclusion in rural Britain. *European Planning Studies* 11(4), 461–480.

Phillipson, C (2007). The 'elected' and the 'excluded': Sociological perspectives on the experience of place and community in old age. *Ageing and Society* 27(3), 321–342.

Phillipson, C (2013). *Ageing*. Cambridge: Polity.

Phillipson, C, Bernard, M, Phillips, J & Ogg, J (1998). The family and community life of older people: Household composition and social networks in three urban areas. *Ageing and Society* 18(30), 259–289.

Phillipson, C & Scharf, T (2005). Rural and urban perspectives on growing old: Developing a new research agenda. *European Journal of Ageing* 2(2), 67–75.

Pratt, AC (1996). Discourses of rurality: Loose talk or social struggle? *Journal of Rural Studies* 12, 69–78.

Ritter, UP & Hohmeier, J (1999). *Alterspolitik: eine sozio-ökonomische Perspektive*. Munich: Oldenbourg.

Rosenmayr, L (1960). Selected problems of the family in urban and rural Austria. *International Journal of Comparative Sociology* 1(1), 89–102.

Rosenmayr, L (1982). Ältere Menschen in kleinen Gemeinden. *Soziale Sicherheit* 9, 364–368.

Rosow, I (1967). *The social integration of the aged*. New York: Free Press.

Rowles, GD (1978). *Prisoners of space? Exploring the geographical experience of older people*. Boulder, CO: Westview.

Rowles, GD (1988). What's rural about rural ageing? An Appalachian perspective. *Journal of Rural Studies* 4(2), 115–124.

Rowles, GD, Beaulieu, JE & Myers, WW (Eds). (1996). *Long-term care for the rural elderly*. New York: Springer Publishing Company.

Rowles, GD & Bernard, M (Eds). (2013). *Environmental gerontology: Making meaningful places in old age*. New York: Springer.

Ryser, L & Halseth, G (2012). Resolving mobility constraints impeding rural seniors' access to regionalized services. *Journal of Aging & Social Policy* 24(3), 328–344.

Scharf, T & Bartlam, B (2008). Ageing and social exclusion in rural communities. In N Keating (Ed.), *Rural ageing: A good place to grow old?* (pp. 97–108). Bristol: Policy Press.

Scharf, T, Phillipson, C, Smith, AE & Kingston, P (2002). *Growing older in socially deprived areas: Social exclusion in later life*. London: Help the Aged.

Scharf, T, Wenger, GC, Thissen, G & Burholt, V (2005). Older people in rural Europe: A comparative analysis. In D Schmied (Ed.), *Winning and losing: The changing geography of Europe's rural areas* (pp. 187–202). Aldershot: Ashgate.

Scheidt, RJ & Schwarz, B (2013). *Environmental gerontology: What now?* London: Routledge.

Schulz-Nieswandt, F (2000). Altern im ländlichen Raum - eine Situationsanalyse. In U Walter & T Altgeld (Eds), *Altern im ländlichen Raum: Ansätze für eine vorausschauende Alten- und Gesundheitspolitik* (pp. 21–39). Frankfurt: Campus.

Schweppe, C (2000). *Biographie und Alter(n) auf dem Land: Lebenssituation und Lebensentwürfe*. Opladen: Leske & Budrich.

Shergold, I, Parkhurst, G & Musselwhite, C (2012). Rural car dependence: An emerging barrier to community activity for older people. *Transportation Planning and Technology* 35(1), 69–85.

Shucksmith, M (2012). Class, power and inequality in rural areas: Beyond social exclusion? *Sociologia Ruralis* 52(4), 377–397.

Skinner, MW & Joseph, AE (2011). Placing voluntarism within evolving spaces of care in ageing rural communities. *GeoJournal* 76(2), 151–162.

Skinner, MW, Joseph, AE & Herron, RV (2013). Spaces of resistance or acquiescence? Learning from media discourses on the role of voluntarism in ageing communities. *Environment and Planning A* 45(2) 438–450.

Spina, J, & Menec, VH (2015). What community characteristics help or hinder rural communities in becoming age-friendly? Perspectives from a Canadian prairie province. *Journal of Applied Gerontology* 34(4), 444–464.

Spoor, M (2013). Multidimensional social exclusion and the 'rural–urban divide' in Eastern Europe and Central Asia. *Sociologia Ruralis* 53(2), 139–157.

Terluin, IJ (2003). Differences in economic development in rural regions of advanced countries: An overview and critical analysis of theories. *Journal of Rural Studies* 19(3), 327–344.

Tews, HP (1987). Altern auf dem Lande. *Der Landkreis* 8–9, 446–452.

Theeke, LA, Goins, RT, Moore, J & Campbell, H (2012). Loneliness, depression, social support, and quality of life in older chronically ill Appalachians. *The Journal of Psychology* 146(1–2), 155–171.

Twigg, J & Martin, W (Eds). (2015). *Routledge handbook of cultural gerontology*. London: Routledge.

United Nations (2009). *World population ageing 2009*. New York: United Nations.

Urry, J (2000). *Sociology beyond societies*. London: Routledge.

Wahl, H–W (2015). Einführung. Bedeutung und Überlegungen zur sozialgerontologischer Forschung in ländlichen Räumen. In U Fachinger & H Künemund (Eds), *Altern im ländlichen Raum. Lebensbedingungen, Veränderungsprozesse und Gestaltungsmöglichkeiten* (pp. 17–24). Wiesbaden: Springer.

Wahl, H–W, Iwarsson, S & Oswald, F (2012). Aging well and the environment: Toward an integrative model and research agenda for the future. *The Gerontologist* 52(3), 306–316.

Wahl, H–W & Lang, F (2004). Ageing in context across the adult life course: Integrating physical and social environmental research perspectives. In *Aging in context: Socio-physical environments. Annual Review of Gerontology and Geriatrics* 23 (pp. 1–34). New York: Springer.

Wahl, H–W, Scheidt, R & Windley, P (2003). *Aging in context: Socio-physical environments. Annual Review of Gerontology and Geriatrics* 23. New York: Springer.

Wahl, H–W, Schilling, O & Oswald, F (2000). Wohnen im Alter – spezielle Aspekte im ländlichen Raum. In U Walter & T Altgeld (Eds), *Altern im ländlichen Raum: Ansätze für eine vorausschauende Alten- und Gesundheitspolitik* (pp. 245–262). Frankfurt: Campus.

Walsh, K (2015). Interrogating the 'age-friendly community' in austerity: Myths, realities and the influence of place context. In K Walsh, G Carney & A Ni Leime (Eds), *Ageing through austerity: Critical perspectives from Ireland* (pp. 79–96). Bristol: Policy Press.

Walsh, K, Carney, G & Ni Leime, A (Eds). (2015). *Ageing through austerity: Critical perspectives from Ireland*. Bristol: Policy Press.

Walsh, K, Connolly, S, Gavin, M, Maguire, C, McDonagh, J, Murray, M, O'Shea, E & Scharf, T (2010). *Older people in rural communities: Exploring attachment, contribution and diversity in rural Ireland and Northern Ireland*. Galway: Healthy Ageing in Rural Communities (HARC) Research Network.

Walsh, K, O'Shea, E & Scharf, T (2012). *Social exclusion and ageing in diverse rural communities in Ireland, Northern Ireland and Scotland*. Galway: Healthy Ageing in Rural Communities (HARC) Research Network.

Walsh, K, O'Shea, E, Scharf, T & Murray, M (2012). Ageing in changing community contexts: Cross-border perspectives from rural Ireland and Northern Ireland. *Journal of Rural Studies* 28(4), 347–357.

Walsh, K, O'Shea, E, Scharf, T & Shucksmith, M (2014). Exploring the impact of informal practices on social exclusion and age-friendliness for older people in rural communities. *Journal of Community & Applied Social Psychology* 24(1), 37–49.

Warburton, J, Cowan, S and Bathgate, T (2013). Building social capital among rural, older Australians through information and communication technologies: A review article. *Australasian Journal on Ageing* 32(1), 8–14.

Wenger, GC (1984). *The supportive network*. London: Allen & Unwin.

Wenger, GC (2001). Myths and realities of ageing in rural Britain. *Ageing and Society* 21(1), 117–130.

Winterton, R & Warburton, J (2014). Healthy ageing in Australia's rural places: The contribution of older volunteers. *Voluntary Sector Review* 5(2), 181–201.

Woods, M (2007). Engaging the global countryside: Globalization, hybridity and the reconstitution of rural place. *Progress in Human Geography* 31(4), 485–507.

World Health Organization (2007). *Global age-friendly cities: A guide*. Geneva: WHO Press.

Youmans, EG (Ed.). (1967). *Older rural Americans*. Kentucky: University of Kentucky Press.

5

Health and Rural Places

Neil Hanlon and Robin Kearns

Introduction

More than four decades have passed since the publication of *The Country and the City*, Raymond Williams's (1993 [1973]) brilliant study of literary and cultural constructions of the English countryside as a bucolic and virtuous landscape. According to Williams, the 'country' idyll served as a constant counterpoint to literary representations of modern city life as worldly and ever changing. His concern was to illuminate the contradictions of these cultural constructions, and to undermine the idea of the 'rural' as a refuge from wider forces of change in English society. In the spirit of this critical analysis, we seek to challenge the notion that 'rural' is a homogeneous category, that rural populations are static, that rural ways of life operate independently of wider social and economic processes, and that there are uniquely 'rural' determinants of health. This is not to suggest that we regard 'rural' as a meaningless category, but rather that it must be understood in relational terms.

This chapter begins from the position that rural health must take account of the forces of globalisation. Rural hinterland regions are a central and necessary focus of the workings of global capitalism. They supply global commodity chains with abundant (and invariably cheap) inputs of energy, raw materials, 'surplus' labour and food staples. Extractive industries have been at the forefront of restructuring for decades, helping to shape neoliberal policy, lean production techniques and the practices of flexible accumulation (Hayter, Barnes & Bradshaw, 2003). Social relations of dependence, underpinned by neocolonialism and uneven development, are present and visibly expressed in hinterland regions of the global north and south. For these reasons, what is happening in, and to, rural landscapes – and more importantly, the people occupying these landscapes – has a major influence on patterns of health and well-being.

While there is a great deal of diversity of rural experiences, populations residing outside of larger urban places across the globe tend to exhibit various forms of health disadvantage relative to their urban counterparts (Strasser, 2003; Canadian Institute for Health Information, 2006). Clear rural disadvantages based on broad measures of population health such as life expectancy at birth and age-standardised rates of all causes of mortality have been reported in countries such as Australia, Canada and the USA while, in other countries (e.g., New Zealand), rural–urban comparisons reveal no consistent differentials, but rather a 'mixed picture' warranting more nuanced interpretations and policy responses (Smith, Humphries & Wilson, 2008). The variety of rural conditions notwithstanding, the tendency towards rural health disadvantage flies in the face of another persistent idyll: that the countryside is an inherently healthy and health-supporting environment. While specific sites of retreat in rural settings have been deemed radically therapeutic (e.g., Kearns & Collins, 2000; Conradson, 2005), the ordinary spaces of rural life do not necessarily share such codings.

Any account of rural health, however, must take account of the following features of the present global age. First, 'rural' is, and always was, a very heterogeneous category of places and populations. Second, the diversity of rural experience is now deeply influenced by forces of globalisation. Third, inequality and disadvantage are structural features of rural experience for all but a select few rural locales and residents. Fourth, and finally, in spite of these macro-level forces of power and inequality, there is still scope for rural resistance and amelioration of the worst excesses and by-products of global capitalist relations.

The chapter is organised in three sections. The first provides an account of the complexity of rural health determinants and the diversity of rural health experiences. The second section offers a discussion of rural health service environments, and explores the particular challenges and opportunities presented by this distinct context for the provision of health and social care. The third section focuses on the idea that collective mobilisation for health and wellness is possible, through community development processes that span local and non-local actors, but that such mobilisations require particular kinds of policy and support that are not typically evident in rural hinterland areas.

The diversity and complexity of rural health experiences

Comparative epidemiological analyses of urban–rural health differentials in life expectancy suggest there is no consistent pattern of rural disparity across countries of the global north, and provide evidence of only a limited number of particular causes of death (e.g., cardiovascular disease, suicide, motor vehicle accidents, obesity, and certain forms of cervical, prostate and skin cancers) (Smith, Humphries & Wilson, 2008). What these studies suggest is that the health issues facing rural populations vary considerably over time and space, creating the need for more nuanced conceptualisations of, and policy responses to, the diversity of rural health experiences. The factors that determine rural population health are closely tied to material and social conditions of rural places themselves, such as housing quality, income levels and distributions, environmental and occupational hazards, levels of social cohesion, and the availability of health services. The particular mix of factors influencing health outcomes will vary from one place to the next, thus complicating, if not undermining, the ability to generalise about rural health disparities. In light of this variability, it is useful to employ a conceptualisation of rural health, adapted from Macintyre, Ellaway and Cummins (2002), that distinguishes between sociodemographic *composition* of rural places (i.e., the concentration of individual circumstances known to influence health outcomes) and the sociocultural *context* of rural places (i.e., the aspects of the social and physical environment of place that are known to influence health outcomes).

In contrast to the 'mixed picture' emerging in the wealthier nations of the world, it is commonly held that rural places in the global south are amongst the least healthy on the planet, as reflected in major indicators of population health (e.g., life expectancy, infant and maternal mortality, risk of communicable disease). Such are the characterisations on which considerable international aid and policy effort has been mobilised to address the rural health gap in 'developing' countries. Mobilisation has been enacted through means including investments in primary health care, education, housing and sanitation, and as reflected in the United Nations Millennium Development Goals (Desai & Potter, 2008). Yet, a similar case can be made for 'at risk' populations in rapidly burgeoning 'shanty' settlements throughout the global south (Hardoy & Satterthwaite, 2014). Health disparities within societies of the global south are thus best explained by compositional factors (e.g., concentrations of extremely impoverished individuals) that may be exacerbated by, but do not depend upon, a rural context.

The category 'rural' is in many ways an inadequate one that masks the contingency of non-urban conditions and experiences. While there are certain rural commonalities (e.g., smaller populations, lower densities) and tendencies (e.g., natural resource and primary production dependence, boom/bust economic cycles), not all rural places experience the same risks and disadvantages. Differences in political economic development (e.g., welfare and infrastructure investment), amenities and geographical proximity to larger centres, for example, are factors that offer some rural communities an advantage in promoting population health.

Rural hinterlands are sites of major restructuring and economic change in the global era, and the outcomes of economic and service sector restructuring have significant implications for population health and wellness. One way to take account of the heterogeneity of rural restructuring is to employ Marsden's (1999) distinction between rural spaces of (e.g., staples resource) production and rural places of amenity (e.g., touristic) consumption. The globalisation of finance, trade and investment has favoured certain hinterland regions over others. For instance, spaces of energy production with access to large and relatively easily exploitable reserves of crude oil, gas and coal have received vast infusions of investment capital in the decades since the OPEC oil crisis of the early 1970s. Likewise, places that have positioned themselves as global tourism destinations have likewise had a comparatively favourable experience in attracting investment capital. Other rural areas have capitalised on geographic advantages (e.g., climate, scenery, access to major metropolitan centres) to 'rebrand' themselves as retirement migration destinations. Most rural areas, however, are not inherently blessed in these ways. For less privileged areas, the more limited opportunities to attract investment capital come down to factors such as community cohesion and the coordination of local interests to achieve competitive advantage in relatively less lucrative areas of production or consumption.

Rural areas are also often sites of ongoing co-presence and, at times, outright conflict between indigenous populations and settler groups. The history, status and beliefs of indigenous populations vary greatly across globally diverse rural spaces, ranging from their near-absence in places like Tasmania (due to attempts at eradication during colonisation) to political and economic ascendancy in some regions of New Zealand (aided by the settlement of land claims). Common features of indigenous rural geographies across nations, however, are twofold: their robust expressions of place attachment that are linked to health beliefs (Wilson, 2003), and their poorer health statistics vis-à-vis settler populations (Rhoades & Cravatt, 2004).

A common expression of poorer health outcomes is inadequate housing. Due to remote and often sparsely settled regions (and arguably influenced by a measure of institutional racism), the phenomenon of rural housing need and homelessness is more frequently accounted for by estimate and anecdote than enumeration. Inadequate housing is deeply implicated in a host of diseases and determinants of ill health, however, and has been linked to what Scott and Conn (1987) evocatively called 'socio-political morbidity', in reference to the Innu in Labrador. To these authors, tuberculosis, alcoholism and suicide are more than individualised pathologies. Rather, these health issues should be seen as a fundamental expression of social, political, economic and cultural alienation.

Recent scholarship provides fresh insights into the multidimensional ways in which rural places are affected by wider social processes. Invoking the 'relational turn' in the social sciences, Milbourne and Kitchen (2014) employ the notion of 'mobilities' to challenge static notions of rural society and account for the impacts of migration, global circulations and broader forces of social change. Migration has long been recognised as a self-selective process, with younger and better educated individuals on the move in search of employment and older retirees moving in search of amenities, services and support. From a health perspective, those on the move are typically in better health than those who stay behind, with implications for the health status of communities sending and receiving migrants. Rural places are also affected by the increasing circulation of ideas and influences made possible by travel and global communications that connect people in distant places. The many dimensions of mobility in the global age thus remind us that rural places are complex, dynamic and connected.

For our purposes, it is necessary to recognise the complexity of conditions of 'rural' living and what this means for the health conditions, expectations and behaviours of those living in rural environments. One important aspect of the rural condition is the organisation and delivery of health and social care. In the next section, we examine the interrelationship of rural place and health and social care delivery from the vantage point of those providing these social goods.

Rural health service environments

Rural places and regions are unique contexts for supporting the health and well-being of populations. Smaller and more dispersed client bases, lack of specialists and advanced equipment, funding shortcomings, and centrally driven policy are just some of the challenges of rural health service environments (Weinhold & Gurtner, 2014). On the other hand, greater visibility and connectivity in the community, opportunities for coordination across sectors, and commitment to place are features that offer real advantages for service delivery in rural environments.

Questions of access to care and support are critical in rural settings. Access is a multidimensional concept, but at its core it refers to the degree to which populations are able to obtain the health and social care they need to maintain or improve their health and quality of life. Access has many aspects, including quality, spatiotemporal availability, affordability, acceptability, continuity, stability and connectivity (Hanlon, 2009). It is not realistic to expect that all needed services can be placed at one's disposal in any location, let alone a rural community, and thus there is the need for regional coordination and mechanisms for connectivity.

In especially rural settings, access is too easily regarded as fundamentally an issue of overcoming physical distance and barriers (e.g., mountains, waterways). However, the notion of acceptability proposed by Penchansky and Thomas (1981) illuminates another potent dimension of health care accessibility experience. Indigenous people, for instance, may well defer or avoid contact with formal health care provision if the significance of traditional beliefs is overlooked and services are deemed 'culturally unsafe' (Wepa, 2005).

New technologies, collectively termed 'telehealth', are also acting to dilute the barriers hitherto posed by topography and distance and, in turn, contributing to the amelioration of health disparities (Whitacre, Hartman, Boggs & Schott, 2009). Telehealth involves making clinical, educational, administrative and research-related services available 'to populations with limited access' (Grigsby & Goetz, 2004, p. 237). It involves moving information rather than participants, hence generating 'virtual regions' (Cutchin, 2002), and has been gaining prominence since the early 1990s (Whitacre, Hartman, Boggs & Schott, 2009).

Telehealth raises complex issues since it involves the direct participation of patients and hence implies privacy, as well as cost and quality of care aspects (Grigsby & Goetz, 2004). Yet, if implemented, telemedicine can expand access to clinical specialists for rural residents in a timely and coordinated manner (Goetz & Debertin, 1996). Indeed telemedicine has been hailed as a saving grace for health services in rural communities, with benefits ranging from improving the perception of health care quality to offering a larger variety of services (Whitacre, Hartman, Boggs & Schott, 2009; Morthland & Scogin, 2011). Yet despite its potential, telehealth has had only limited impact on rural health care (Grigsby & Goetz, 2004). Insufficient demand to justify rural investment in telehealth (e.g., by hospitals and telecommunication service providers), policies and research agendas that marginalise the rural dimensions of telehealth, and lack of integration into established health and educational systems are key reasons for its limited impact.

The shortcomings of telehealth implementation may be seen as one instance of broader policy shortcomings. Health policy in general is often centrally directed and developed with little consideration of rural realities. As a result, reform initiatives tend to impact rural places differently, often owing to a lack of attention to rural conditions rather than intended policy directions. Many states in the global north have pursued policies of health care cost containment and austerity over the past three decades. These often involve the imposition of efficiency targets (e.g., length of stay reductions) and supply management benchmarks (e.g., bed closures) that systemically disadvantage health facilities serving more rural and remote populations (e.g., Hanlon & Rosenberg, 1998; Hanlon & Halseth, 2005).

Centrally driven and decontextualised policy undermines the potential to develop meaningfully local systems of care and support. Such decontextualisation is particularly noticeable in rural places, where boundaries between sectors of care and support are less rigid and barriers to coordinated effort are fewer, partly out of necessity (i.e., resource limitations). Nevertheless, these and other aspects of rural environments of health care and social support present unique possibilities for primary health care development.

Key nodes for generating and maintaining locally generated care and support are not only health clinics but also schools. At such sites, formal delivery of services is invariably complemented by informal relationships, local knowledge and outreach. To this extent, rural schools and clinics are more than elements of the institutional fabric; they are also relational places (i.e., informally constituted by the social relations they produce and support) (Kearns & Neuwelt, 2009). The sparseness of settlement and fragile elements of rural infrastructure, particularly in areas that have borne the brunt of service sector restructuring and economic downturn, means that closures can be highly traumatic. In the case of school closure, the loss of a community resource, site of information exchange and place of collective history all contribute to the need to see such an event as deeply connected to the health of rural places (Kearns, Lewis, McCreanor & Witten, 2009). Thus, the closure of rural schools can not only shut down a crucial focal point and meeting place for the community, but it can also block the paths to recruiting other resources (e.g., attracting medical professionals).

The interrelationships between service providers and place are critical in any context, but arguably more so in rural environments (Bourke, Humphreys, Waterman & Taylor, 2012). Recruitment and retention literature strongly suggest that it is necessary to consider the ways in which rural health service providers (health care professionals, volunteers, informal support providers) shape and are shaped by the environments in which they do their work (Humphreys et al., 2012). The fit between provider and place is especially important to the long-term stability of rural health systems (Cutchin, 1997). For this reason, recognising the co-evolution of care and place is critical for comprehending and responding to considerations of health and social care recruitment and retention, and for the planning and delivery of integrated care and support in rural settings. Another key aspect of the provider–place relationship is the provision of contextually sensitive training and socialisation, such as various models of rural and distributed medical education that self-select for practitioners wishing to practice rural general practice (Snadden & Casiro, 2008). Practitioner and place interrelationships also extend to conditions that affect the personal and family life of rural health providers. For instance, employment opportunities for spouses and adequate availability of 'cover' to allow breaks away from the often unrelenting demands of rural health care practice have been shown to influence provider–place attachments (Kearns et al., 2006). Cutchin (1997) identified 'place integration' as the processes of becoming 'at home' and reconciling place and personal aspirations. Its many dimensions interact to reinforce the stability, suitability and adaptability of rural health practice.

Towards healthy rural communities

In this final section, we develop the idea that community development processes can be mobilised to address rural health disparities. In doing so, we consider the interrelationships of community development and place integration in local potential to reorganise for health and well-being. More than this, health and wellness are issues that span populations and are mutually beneficial to civic, political and economic spheres.

Community development and mobilisation for health and wellness resonates well with the population health approach. Place is a central and organising force in population health, as it is the nexus of environmental and personal determinants of well-being. Community development is the result of social processes and the vision and leadership of those in local government, health care, business and the civic and voluntary sectors (Skinner et al., 2014). New areas of enquiry are enhancing our understanding of the interconnections of place attachments and community development initiative, once again through the concept of place integration (Hanlon et al., 2014).

Community-wide efforts to mobilise for wellness have the potential to help address persistent economic vulnerabilities of rural places. Stabilising health service environments and making rural places attractive for health professionals have benefits beyond rural health service environments, such as helping to attract capital investment and skilled workers. Even in the absence of helping solve economic development concerns, the very act of mobilising across sectors and interests in the community has direct benefits. In times of rural restructuring and economic uncertainty, collective mobilising for health can be a community anchor or stabiliser, galvanising local identity and place attachment.

The networks and partnerships that emerge from such collective efforts produce social capital that can act as a springboard for rural renewal with, in some instances, activity and expertise crossing between sectors (Kearns, 1998). If issues of isolation and under-resourcing can be toxic to the well-being of rural populations, the counter trend can be the trust and sense of collective enterprise that can develop in small communities when expertise is shared and a sense of 'we're all in it together' develops.

By way of example, in the Hokianga district of northern New Zealand, approximately 300 km north of Auckland, the community struggled successfully in the early 1990s to retain their free health service and remain outside the newly rationalised and commercialised regional health service surrounding them (Kearns, 1998). This mixed Maori and pakeha (white) community had a long history of cooperative health care with community clinics acting not only as medical centres, but also as important social institutions. This was confirmed with field research that identified residents who came to the clinic waiting rooms to interact with others, rather than necessarily seek medical attention (Kearns, 1991). This multifunctional importance of the local health system meant that, through the 1990s, competing discourses prevailed: a regionally based medical efficiency narrative coexisted alongside the locally held health significance of the service itself. When confronted with the threat of amalgamation into the regional health care system and a lack of local autonomy, protest was swift with a planned march to the national capital. A solution to this political embarrassment was the formation of the community-based Hokianga Health Enterprise Trust, comprising representatives from each of the ten rural clinic areas. The trust is owner of *Hauora Hokianga* (or Hokianga Health) which a quarter-century later continues to offer a wide range of integrated health services at no charge to those enrolled within the approximately 6,500 people who reside within the catchment area of the Hokianga Harbour. This trust is now regarded as a leader in community-owned health care in New Zealand and is evidence that not all governable spaces and subjects will acquiesce to attempts to decentre place and participation in primary health care (Prince, Kearns & Craig, 2006).

Conclusion

Much as Raymond Williams saw the need to question idyllic literary constructions of the English countryside, so too we feel it is important to resist sweeping generalisations about the health and wellness of rural populations. Where efforts have been made to pinpoint evidence of distinctly rural health conditions, the picture that emerges is rather one of variability. This suggests a need for more attention to the heterogeneity of rural populations and the specificities of place and region. This concern for acknowledging rural diversity extends to considerations of emerging technologies that hold promise to transform rural health service environments (e.g., ongoing advances in telecommunications, genomics, pharmaceuticals, prosthetics). The somewhat muted experience of telehealth as a means to enhance accessibility, however, gives us pause to temper such expectations in the absence of a more nuanced appreciation of rural conditions and capacities.

Likewise, we think it is important for future rural health research to pay more attention to processes of community development, agency and collective mobilisations around themes of community health and wellness. Mobilising for health is one of the few public issues with the potential to bridge local social divides (especially given increasing social divisiveness and conflict *within* rural populations over future rural land use and economic development), and offers a potential springboard for local initiative to achieve rural renewal and revitalisation. We also see an opportunity for research and policy to pay more attention to innovations already occurring in rural health service environments, especially in the area of primary health care development. Rural and small town settings offer unique opportunities for inter-professional collaboration and the engagement of different elements of local society, including indigenous communities, economic interests and broader elements of civil society. While networking and partnering are possible in any health service environment, we contend that rural environments offer a much less cluttered setting in which to observe the processes and outcomes of primary health care development.

This overview of rural health and place, therefore, stresses the need to recognise the diverse conditions of rural living, the distinctiveness of rural health service environments, and the possibilities and potentials for rural healthy community development. We also stress the extent to which rural populations and the activities they pursue are influenced by wider social, political and economic forces. We hope that this overview also plays a role in inspiring new directions and approaches in rural health research. We have offered examples from our own work in New Zealand and Canada, primarily as these are locations most familiar to us. Obviously, attention is warranted in other rural settings, especially those in non-Anglo societies and all throughout the global south. We also look forward to insights offered by scholarship that explores other place–health interconnections, such as those involving relational cleavages like gender, ethnicity, (dis)ability and sexuality.

References

Bourke, L, Humphreys, J, Wakerman, J & Taylor, J (2012). Understanding rural and remote health: A framework for analysis in Australia. *Health & Place* 18, 496–503.

Canadian Institute for Health Information. (2006). *How healthy are rural Canadians? An assessment of their health status and health determinants*. Ottawa: The Author.

Conradson, D (2005). Landscape, care and the relational self: Therapeutic encounters in rural England. *Health & Place* 11(4), 337–348.

Cutchin, M (1997). Physician retention in rural communities: The perspective of experiential place integration. *Health & Place* 3(1), 25–41.

Cutchin, M (2002). Virtual medical geographies: Conceptualizing telemedicine and regionalization. *Progress in Human Geography* 26, 19–39.

Desai, V & Potter, R (2008). *The companion to development studies* (2nd edn). London: Hodder.

Goetz, S & Debertin, D (1996). Rural–urban locational choices of medical doctors: A county-level analysis. *Review of Agricultural Economics* 18, 547–563.

Grigsby, W & Goetz, S (2004). Telehealth: What promise does it hold for rural areas? In N Glasgow, L Morton & N Johnson (Eds), *Critical issues in rural health* (pp. 237–250). Ames, IA: Blackwell.

Hanlon, N (2009). Access and utilization reconsidered: Towards a broader understanding of the spatial ordering of primary health care. In G Andrews & V Crooks (Eds), *Primary health care: People, practice, place* (pp. 43–56). Aldershot: Ashgate.

Hanlon, N & Halseth, G (2005). The greying of resource communities in northern British Columbia: Implications for health delivery in already under-serviced communities. *The Canadian Geographer* 49(1), 1–24.

Hanlon, NT & Rosenberg, MW (1998). Not so new public management and the denial of geography: Ontario health care reform in the 1990s. *Environment and Planning C: Government & Policy* 16(5), 559–572.

Hanlon, N, Skinner, M, Joseph, A, Ryser, L & Halseth, G (2014). Place integration through efforts to support healthy aging in British Columbia's interior: The role of voluntary sector leadership. *Health & Place* 29, 132–139.

Hardoy, JE & Satterthwaite, D (2014). *Squatter citizen: Life in the urban third world*. New York: Routledge.

Hayter, R, Barnes, T & Bradshaw, M (2003). Relocating resource peripheries to the core of economic geography's theorizing: Rationale and agenda. *Area* 35, 15–23.

Humphreys, JS, McGrail, MR, Joyce, CM, Scott, A & Kalb, G (2012). Who should receive recruitment and retention incentives? Improved targeting of rural doctors using medical workforce data. *Australian Journal of Rural Health* 20, 3–10.

Kearns, RA (1991). The place of health in the health of place: The case of the Hokianga special medical area. *Social Science and Medicine* 33, 519–530.

Kearns, RA (1998). Going it alone: Community resistance to health reforms in Hokianga, New Zealand In RA Kearns & WM Gesler (Eds), *Putting health into place: Landscape, identity and well-being* (pp. 226–247). Syracuse, NY: Syracuse University Press.

Kearns, RA & Collins, DCA (2000). New Zealand Children's Health Camps: Therapeutic landscapes meet the contract state. *Social Science and Medicine* 51, 1047–1059.

Kearns, RA, Lewis, N, McCreanor, T & Witten, K (2009). 'The status quo is not an option': Community impacts of school closure in South Taranaki, New Zealand. *Journal of Rural Studies* 25, 131–140.

Kearns, RA, Myers, J, Coster, H, Coster, G and Adair, V (2006). What makes 'place' attractive to overseas-trained doctors in rural New Zealand? *Health & Social Care in the Community* 14, 532–540.

Kearns, RA & Neuwelt, P (2009). Within and beyond clinics: Primary health care and community participation. In G Andrews & V Crooks (Eds), *Primary health care: People, practice, place* (pp. 203–220). Aldershot: Ashgate.

Macintyre, S, Ellaway, A & Cummins, S (2002). Place effects on health: How can we conceptualise, operationalise and measure them? *Social Science and Medicine* 55(1), 125–139.

Marsden, T (1999). Rural futures: The consumption countryside and its regulation. *Sociologica Ruralis*, 39(4), 501–520.

Milbourne, P & Kitchen, L (2014). Rural mobilities: Connecting movement and fixity in rural places. *Journal of Rural Studies* 34, 326–336.

Morthland, M & Scogin, F (2011). Mental health concerns for caregivers in rural communities. In R Talley, K Chwalisz & K Buckwalter (Eds), *Rural caregiving in the United States: Research, practice, policy* (pp. 85–102). New York: Springer.

Penchansky, R & Thomas, J (1981). The concept of access: Definition and relationship to consumer satisfaction. *Medical Care* 19(2), 127–140.

Prince, R, Kearns, RA & Craig, D (2006). Governmentality, discourse and space in the New Zealand health care system, 1991–2003. *Health & Place* 12, 253–266.

Rhoades, ER & Cravatt, K (2004). American Indians and Alaskan natives. In N Glasgow, L Wright Morton & NE Johnson (Eds), *Critical issues in rural health* (pp. 127–140). Ames, IA: Blackwell.

Scott, RT & Conn, S (1987). The failure of scientific medicine: Davis Inlet as an example of sociopolitical morbidity. *Canadian Family Physician* 33, 1649–1653.

Skinner, MW, Joseph, A, Hanlon, N, Ryser, L & Halseth, G (2014). Growing old in aging resource communities: Linking voluntarism, aging in place and community development. *The Canadian Geographer* 58(4), 418–428.

Smith, KB, Humphries, JS & Wilson, MGA (2008). Addressing the health disadvantage of rural populations: How does epidemiological evidence inform rural health policies and research? *Australian Journal of Rural Health* 16, 56–66.

Snadden, D & Casiro, O (2008). Maldistribution of physicians in BC: What are we trying to do about it? *British Columbia Medical Journal* 50(7), 371–372.

Strasser, R (2003). Rural health around the world: Challenges and solutions. *Family Practice* 20(4), 457–463.

Weinhold, I & Gurtner, S (2014). Understanding shortages of sufficient health care in rural areas. *Health Policy* 118, 201–214.

Wepa, D (Ed.). (2005). *Cultural safety in Aotearoa New Zealand*. Auckland: Pearson Education.

Whitacre, B, Hartman, P, Boggs, S & Schott, V (2009). A community perspective on quantifying the economic impact of teleradiology and telepsychiatry. *The Journal of Rural Health* 25(2), 194–197.

Williams, R (1993) [1973]. *The country and the city*. London: Hogarth Press.

Wilson, K (2003). Therapeutic landscapes and First Nations peoples: An exploration of culture. *Health & Place* 9, 83–93.

6

Rural Migration and New Patterns of Exclusion and Integration in Europe

Bettina B. Bock, Giorgio Osti and Flaminia Ventura

Introduction: the problem at hand

Migration into rural areas is an increasingly important phenomenon in the global north. It is significant in terms of rising numbers of rural immigrants and the demographic and socioeconomic shifts it causes in host and home regions. Yet its importance results also from the processes of social change that it reflects as well as produces, and the new chances and risks it generates in terms of social equality and social integration. Moreover, current trends of rural immigration grant new insights into modern migration as well as rural development. It is insightful as it portrays a modern, mobile image of the rural that contradicts the traditional notion of the rural as stagnant and immobile, points at the importance of extra-local relations and mobile residents, and underlines the interrelationships between urban and rural regions.

This chapter discusses the new patterns of international rural-to-rural and urban-to-rural migration that are being witnessed in the global north. It focuses in particular on Europe and the steady increase of migration into rural areas in the European Union following EU enlargement (Eurostat, 2011) as well as effects of rural mobility on patterns and processes of social exclusion and integration at various scales. Intra-European rural mobility concerns mostly urban and rural citizens of the central-eastern member states who move to rural areas in the northwest and south of Europe in search of employment and a better quality of life (Favell, 2008). Their mobility is viewed with ambivalent feelings. On the one hand, European immigrants are welcomed where there is a shortage of labour for agricultural and domestic work and where depopulating areas need new residents (Osti & Ventura, 2012). On the other hand, the increasing presence of immigrants causes social unrest as citizens perceive their communities as being intruded upon by 'strangers'. With the current global financial crisis, concerns about job competition have increased too. The idea that immigrants from the east may 'take away' jobs is used by populist politicians to fuel both anti-European and anti-migrant feelings. However, such ideas are based on an outdated idea of migration as permanent relocation of residence that ignores recent trends towards circular mobility and transnational styles of living (Vertovec, 2009; Cresswell, 2010).

Migration rates tend to change with the economic cycle even though there are differences across countries. In the UK, recent internal migration figures increased and fell with the peaks and depths of the economic cycle (Champion, 2005). In the United States, however, internal migration rates declined even prior to the 2008 debt crisis (Molloy, Smith & Wozniak, 2011). With the global financial crisis net migration rates have fallen across many countries, though OECD countries remain popular destinations for migrants (OECD, 2014). Levels of migration into Europe remain high although movement from 'new' to 'old' member states following EU enlargement accounts for a substantial proportion of intra-EU mobility (Zaiceva & Zimmermann, 2008). Generally speaking, however, and notwithstanding fluctuating migration statistics, modern society is undeniably a mobile society, characterised by high levels of mobility and, through modern technology, the maintenance of social relations across the globe. This mobility fundamentally changes social and economic life (Urry, 2007) and facilitates social practices 'without geographical contiguity' (Castells, 2000, p. 14). Social scientists describe normal, modern life as being in constant motion and modern residents as travellers and nomads who are constantly 'on the move' (Cresswell, 2010). Contemporary rural migration is part of that development and necessitates the development of a novel approach, one that conceives of mobility as a newly emergent mobile style of life and citizenship; one that allows for pluri-local senses of belonging and engagement, and which looks into mobility as spinning new networks of relations.

The chapter is structured as follows: the next section briefly discusses recent developments in migration theory and introduces a relational perspective on rural mobility. It then presents results from recent research that briefly sketches the development of increasing rural mobility, its diversity in groups and direction. The chapter then turns to the main social changes associated with this heightened and increasingly complex mobility, such as integration and exclusion at the level of the migrant households and the level of regions of origin and destination, as well as the relations between the sending and receiving EU member states. The chapter closes with conclusions regarding the exclusionary effects of increasing rural mobility and the need for more comparative, transnational and translocal research.

The framework of change: novel conceptual approaches

Migration and mobility as lifestyle

Traditional (international) migration research is underpinned by a definition of migration as changing residence from one place to another, with residence assumed to be fixed in one place (Brown, 2012). With the concept of transnationality (Portes, 2003; Glick-Schiller & Caglar, 2009), the understanding of migration substantially changes. With new, cheaper means of transportation and communication migrants may continue to maintain social relations in the sending countries and feel at home 'here and there'. Transnationality conceptualises how modern life may take place in multiple places and across borders and develops a relational approach to migration. Following Faist and colleagues (2013, p. 1), 'A transnational perspective means that migration is not an irrevocable process but may entail repeated movements and, above all, continued transactions – bounded communication between actors – between migrants and non-migrants across the borders of states.' These transnational social ties and practices constitute a 'transnational social space': a spatial framework that is relationally (and not nationally) organised. It is built through material and immaterial exchanges, the sharing of objects and relations as well as shared identities and feelings of belonging and solidarity (Levitt & Schiller, 2004). The dynamic of the relationships may vary in time and across groups, with transnationality expressed in different degrees. This chapter takes up the idea of transnationality but focuses on the network of relations that migration spins between places rather than countries. Hence, it departs from the idea of a translocal social space that connects both mobile and relatively immobile residents through recursive cross-border practices, ties and shared senses of belonging (Smith, 2011).

In addition, the chapter considers migration as one of many forms of mobility that characterise modern life. In doing so it links up with novel sociological thinking about hypermobility and the network society (Castells, 2000). Following Urry (2007), mobility includes ongoing corporeal travelling of people and objects between places, the pluri-local senses of belonging to and engagements in places that create social networks, and the imaginative, virtual and communicative 'travelling' that vivifies and invigorates those networks. Looked upon from this perspective, 'migration' is not a singular livelihood strategy but a new mobile mode of living and citizenship that alters the functioning of communities. With this conceptualisation of mobility the meaning of place alters too. *Place* no longer refers to a fixed spot in a geographically defined territory; it becomes defined through the social relations of people, their perceptions and ideas, and the meaning and significance given to places by people (Massey, 2004). The translocal spaces referred to above are relationally defined but are more than representational and encompass material practices and material flows (Anghel, 2008).

Migration and rural development

Translocality offers a useful lens for understanding how migration relates to development. Ongoing translocal ties and practices and plural modes of belonging constitute pluri-local, mobile forms of citizenship and engagement, and support the emergence of translocal civil societies (Faist, Fauser & Reisenauer, 2013). The so-called migration–development nexus and issue of co-development has been passionately discussed among migration scientists for many years (De Haas, 2010). Research provides conflicting evidence, most of it focusing on the global south (Portes, 2003). Scholars describe how migrants contribute to local development by transferring financial remittances that support relatives left behind, and sometimes allow for local economic development (Fox, 2005; Ho, Hickey & Yeoh, 2015); often, though, remittances are spent on consumption and not invested in production, which keeps households dependent on remittances (Faist, Fauser & Reisenauer, 2013). Migrants and their associations may successfully collaborate with policy makers in the improvement of local infrastructure; however, 'the degree to which the development potential of migration is exploited fundamentally depends on the more general investment environment' (De Haas, 2010, p. 251). Social remittances (ideas, behaviours, identities, contacts) may promote social change but in many cases migration encourages others to migrate as well (De Haas, 2010).

Critics of the migration–development 'buzz' describe the discussion as a façade that hides the destructive impact of out-migration on the productive capacity and social cohesion in sending places (De Haas, 2010). It may also divert the eye from the hard reality of social exclusion that many migrants face in the place of destination. This chapter examines processes of social exclusion in host places as well as at home at the level of migrant households, but also considers how the presence (and absence) of migrants as 'mobile residents' may enhance or hinder processes of local development 'here and there'. In doing so it aims to contribute not only to migration research but also to the body of knowledge on rural development.

So far, European rural development research shows little interest in mobility (Bell & Osti, 2010). This may in part be explained through the discourse of endogenous rural development that characterises rural development policy and research since the late 1980s (Saraceno, 2013), and which sees sustainable rural development as best assured when built on local resources and discourses, independent of external resources and markets (Van der Ploeg & Marsden, 2008).

Recently there is more recognition of the importance of external networks and 'connectivity', such as expressed in discussions of a neo-endogenous development paradigm and network-based relational place-shaping (Shucksmith, 2013). This resonates also in Woods's (2013) discussion of the globalising countryside, where rural enterprises and communities profit from their participation in global networks that give access to new markets and new knowledge. Still, rural development studies tend to focus on the 'sedentary' residents who are supposed to offer the resources, networks and collective action needed for local development (Van der Ploeg & Marsden, 2008). Explicit recognition of migrants as development agents is there for the highly educated urban population moving into rural areas, from within the country or from countries in the northwest of Europe. These generally highly educated newcomers are acknowledged for their contribution to local development as new rural entrepreneurs (Bosworth & Atterton, 2012), 'social entrepreneurs' and brokers of new ideas and networks (Bock, 2012), as well as prosperous residents and consumers ('grey gold') in the case of rural retirement migrants (Brown et al., 2011, p. 44). Other immigrants may figure as 'demographic refill' (Hedberg, Forsberg & Najib, 2012, p. 127), but are not considered as development actors. Those who have left the area are not taken into account either, unless they return (Stockdale, 2006). Rural out-migration is generally considered as a risk factor and indicator of marginality and decline (Barca, 2009). The loss of residents is seen as undermining the socioeconomic and demographic structure. It is also interpreted as a loss of social capital and developmental potential (Bock, 2010). There is little recognition yet that many out-migrants keep an interest in and a vivid sense of belonging to their original home, maintain social relations, return regularly and may better be described as mobile citizens (Marcu, 2014). Mobility and its development potential is, hence, not taken into account for both sending and receiving places, whereas in both cases there is evidence that mobile residents contribute to local development (White, 2010; Osti & Ventura, 2012).

Rural migration and social exclusion

In order to understand how rural migration influences processes and patterns of social exclusion and integration in Europe, the following three domains of societal integration, based on the triadic model of Powell (1990), are important to distinguish:

1   Legal integration as reflected in the presence of institutional or legal barriers of integration.
2   Market integration as reflected in income and employment.
3   Civil society integration as reflected in social embeddedness and the development of horizontal social relationships.

The first entry point focuses on formal legal frameworks and examines, for instance, the (national or regional) regulation of access to social services, such as housing and education. Here it often concerns matters of micro-discrimination, hidden in the detail of rules, because the 'embedded liberalism' of European constitutions usually protects migrants from explicit, macro forms of discrimination (Hollifield, 1992). The main problem is the protection of displaced people and migrants without permit of residence who are increasingly placed in detention camps without sufficient protection of human rights (Carr, 2012).

The second entry point looks into the ease of integration in business and employment, depending again on legislation but varying also across local agro-system regimes (Landsteiner & Langthaler, 2012). Rural areas present a particular case due to the large presence of seasonal jobs and the dominance of small firms. Migrants often end up in labour relationships that are characterised by very low wages, absence of formal contracts, illegal job brokerage, but also diffuse borders between family and work life with lodging offered as part of employment that may support integration into family and community life. In many cases, rural migrant workers have little bargaining power, resulting in their relatively weak position in market structures. This is the result of weak legal protection of flexible seasonal labour, lack of enforcement because of remoteness and/or because of the strong presence of criminal organisations such as the Mafia in southern Italy (Corrado, 2012).

The third line of research is more difficult to detect. Integration in civil society, such as reflected in the participation in community activities or associations or the establishment of social relations offering mutual help and support are generally effectively stratified by origin and ethnic descent (Hyden, 1997) as well as class and culture (Cloke & Thrift, 1987). The activities offering the best chances of integration are linked to sport, especially football, in which foreigners may even be particularly welcomed. Still, this seems an exception that confirms the rule of civil society segmentation.

Empirics: overview of existing research in Europe

Research into European rural migration varies in scope. It is a mixed body of work which includes studies on national rural-to-urban (Ní Laoire, 2001) and urban-to-rural migration (Halfacree, 2012) as well as international rural-to-urban migration (Stenning & Dawley, 2009). So far, there is little research on international and in particular European urban-to-rural and rural-to-rural migration (McAreavey, 2012), whereas it has a longer tradition in the United States (e.g., Duran, Massey & Zenteno, 2001; Riosmena & Massey, 2012). Most studies on rural-to-rural migration within Europe as well as rural immigration from other countries and continents (De Lima, 2012) unravel the experiences of individual migrants and their families, generally at either the place of origin or destination: migrants' encounters of discrimination (Hedberg, Forsberg & Najib, 2012), the loneliness of family members left behind (Andrezejewska & Ryc, 2012) and the dependence of rural families on remittances (King & Vullnetari, 2009). Others look into demographic dynamics and labour market impact (Stockdale, 2006; Green, de Hoyos, Jones & Owen, 2009), generally, however, without interpreting their findings in terms of local development. Moreover, extant studies on rural migration tend to focus on the situation in one place – or, as Milbourne (2007, p. 384, original emphasis) concludes: 'the dominant focus is on *uni-directional flows* of people *to* rural areas'. Little attention has been given to continuous and circular migratory movements (Stenning & Dawley, 2009) and their trans-territorial dimensions and development effects, probably because this requires expensive longitudinal research.[1] There is also little recognition of the particularities of rural mobility within the European Union, that crosses national borders within a common 'homeland' with shared European citizenship (King, 2002).

The studies referred to above and also European statistics (Eurostat, 2011) indicate that migration into rural areas has increased, and remains substantial across OECD countries also during the financial crisis (Kurek, 2011) even though overall net migration rates have fallen (OECD, 2014). Following Osti and Ventura (2012), this may be explained by the fact that national labourers are unwilling to work in agriculture or rural domestic services even now, as a result of which labour demand in agriculture and domestic services remains high. The dominant migratory movement is from (especially peripheral) rural and urban areas in the Central and Eastern European countries towards rural areas in the northwest and south of Europe. Quantitatively, most migrants come from Poland, Romania and Bulgaria. Romanians and Bulgarians tend to move south – to Italy, Spain and Greece, where they work in agriculture, construction, industry, tourism, domestic services and elderly care (Sandu, 2005; Osti & Ventura, 2012; Marcu, 2014). The Polish often move towards the northwest and countries such as Germany, Sweden, the Netherlands and the UK (Engbersen et al., 2013), and in particular Northern Ireland (Russel, 2012). In the Netherlands most migrants find work in agriculture, construction and transport (Dagevos, 2011), whereas in Northern Ireland agriculture and the food processing industry are the main employers (McAreavey, 2012). Many do not change places permanently but engage in circular ('shuttle') migration (Anghel, 2008). Among the migrants are men and women, with some difference in migration directions also related to the jobs applied for. Cieślinńska (2012), for instance, reports that Polish women were among the first to migrate to Belgium and Italy in search of caring and cleaning jobs, whereas migration rates among men and women were more balanced for Germany and the United States. Globally, there is a trend towards the feminisation of migration (Bock, 2006). In 2010 female migrants outnumbered male in a number of European countries (Ireland, Greece, France, Italy and Denmark): this reflects the increasing demand for paid care/domestic work during the crisis (Farris, 2015).

For many (young) men and women in Central and Eastern Europe, and especially in Poland and Romania, moving is the obvious gateway to employment and modern life (Horváth, 2008), and functions as an initiation to adulthood (White, 2010). Marcu (2014) discovered that the way the experience of migration affected the sense of self of those young Romanian migrants differed from the experience of previous cohorts. The young Romanians who are currently migrating refer to themselves as cosmopolitans who move back and forth between Romania and other countries. However, those migrants who left Romania between 1990 and 2002 remain firmly attached to their places of origin and still consider themselves as Romanians. Romanians who emigrated between 2002 and 2007 developed a 'transnational identity' with feelings of belonging to both the country of origin and the country of destination.

Integration in receiving places

In the receiving places the interpretation of migratory effects varies, with national migration history and policy playing a role as well as local shortages of labour and residents. In the Netherlands the national public debate is generally pejorative, with populist parties accusing immigrants of 'social benefit tourism' and unfair job competition (Dagevos, 2011). In Northern Ireland reactions vary. There is empathy, rooted in Northern Ireland's own history of emigration and its current political sensitivity to issues of inequality. There is, however, also social unrest due to the economic crisis, which at times results in outbursts of racism (McAreavey, 2012). In Spain and Italy immigration is seen as an instrument that helps to counter the continuous depopulation of remote rural areas (Osti & Ventura, 2012; Collantes, Pinilla, Sáez & Silvestre, 2013). The relationship between the local communities and immigrants is also dynamic. While immigrants' experiences in and with a place will shape their employment (and other) opportunities, their presence will impact on the socioeconomic development of the communities (Danson & Jentsch, 2009). This dynamic may lead towards both integration and exclusion of immigrants.

In this process the above-defined second entry point of market integration through work and employment plays a key role. The most important reason for hiring migrants – instead of local/native workers – is their readiness to accept jobs for which vacancies have been difficult to fill; often this means jobs that are physically demanding, with unpredictable working schedules, long hours of work, offering poor pay and low social status (Danson & Jentsch, 2009). The median income gap between natives and migrants is very large but smaller in rural compared to urban areas: 'In very large urban areas, the median income gap is very large, at 67%. In small urban areas, the gap falls to 32%, while in small towns and rural areas the gap is only 20%' (Bernard, 2008, p. 8).

A general feature of rural migration in Europe is surely job specialisation: while in urban contexts migrants may be involved in many different jobs and sectors, rural migrants are generally much more concentrated in one single sector, which makes them highly visible. In some mining or quarry rural zones they have completely replaced the local workforce, forming a sort of ethnic colony (Barberis, 2011); they resemble the miners' community, a well-known sociological *topos* (Bulmer, 1975) deeply entrenched with historical migration waves (Lucassen, 2005; Bade, 2008). The same has happened among farm workers employed in dairy production, with the difference that they are more spatially dispersed, working and living on farms (Sahai & Lum, 2013). In northern and central Italy it is often Romanian and Bulgarian migrants who are employed in forest management, because they introduce new knowledge and new practices. Female migrants are appreciated for their indispensable role in domestic services and especially elderly care (Viruela, 2008; Osti & Ventura, 2012). The spatial dispersion is even more marked for shepherds and forestry workers. In any case, migrants tend to monopolise the manual labour of a rural economy, leaving the control of capital and means of production in the hands of local entrepreneurs (Brown, 2010). The marked job specialisation of migrants in European rural areas is 'pleasure and pain' for them (Ambrosini, 2013). On the one hand, concentration is coupled with increased competence or professionalism; on the other, it provides a sort of obliged destiny. Migrants are called and appreciated only for specific kinds of job. The situation can change dramatically when foreigners are able to create a 'rural enclave', in which an internal articulation of work positions and economic sector differentiation starts (Portes & Manning, 1986; Alba et al., 2014). That provides a more flourishing economy but at the same time increases competition with local people. Migrants are no longer confined to marginal jobs and demonstrate success by ascending the social ladder. This, however, may cause resentment among locals.

For the moment in Europe, the tendency to create economic enclaves among migrants appears to be weak and limited to urban areas (Werbner, 2001). Successful (labour) market integration depends on migrants' knowledge and skills, possibly guaranteed by education certificates, as well as their flexibility and capability to adapt. Yet market integration is also closely linked to legal integration and recognition, primarily reflected in the duration of migrants' permit of residence. Time plays an important role, as clearly expressed in the greater likelihood and chance of social inclusion among second- and third-generation migrants (Silberman, Alba & Fournier, 2007; Alba & Foner, 2014). Children's acculturation through life at school plays an important role, as discussed in more detail below. In addition, their generally higher professional qualification paves the way to better work compared with their parents.

Kasimis and Papadopoulos (2005) identified two main paths for upward social mobility of migrants in southern Europe, both of which involve improved market integration. The first is intra-sectoral (within agriculture), and includes moving from unskilled tasks with little responsibility to more skilled and responsible tasks. The second path is inter-sectoral, that is, moving from agricultural labour to employment in construction and/or services. In most cases migrant labourers find their first job in agriculture and then move on to other jobs usually with the ambition to eventually enter non-agricultural employment that promises improvement in pay and working conditions. Again, this is closely linked to legal integration. Once a migrant's stay is legalised they do their best to move to other sectors and/or seek higher wages in more developed labour markets. This often includes searching for work in urban areas without, however, necessarily moving there. Housing conditions are an important reason for migrants to stay in rural areas, even when seeking urban employment. Research indicates that migrants are often not welcomed as new residents in urban areas, with areas with a concentration of migrants abandoned by locals, leading to increasing degradation of the area and social isolation of migrants (Vargas-Silva, 2014). In rural areas, long-established and ongoing trends of rural depopulation have led to many abandoned houses both in village centres and in the countryside, creating a more favourable housing market, especially for migrant families (Osti & Ventura, 2012). Civic integration may, hence, be more easily realised in rural areas compared to urban areas, with housing being more easily obtained in rural areas even in the absence of legal recognition and integration.

Migrant families with children generally integrate more successfully than single migrants, both economically and socially. In this process the presence of school-aged children and engagement in self-employment are two recurring elements promoting social inclusion in terms of market and civil integration. Married migrants tend to adopt a more highly developed employment and integration strategy, resulting in greater success in securing a full-time job and professional and social mobility (Baker & Benjamin, 1997). In EU Mediterranean regions such progress is often reflected in working for a respectable employer in the local community (with men generally in agriculture or construction and women in services) (Papadopoulos, 2009).

Children often become socially integrated through sports and recreational activities, which promotes a sense of belonging to the local community that is shared by both local and immigrant children, and may then include their wider families (D'Alessandro, Rampelli & Spagnolo, 2011; Osti & Ventura, 2012). Regional and local authorities play an important role here through their facilitation and financing of recreational and cultural activities (Eurydice, 2004). Schools and parishes are very important too as they often host community centres managed by social services and/or NGOs. Canadian research reveals how the development of personal ties in the communities leads to local neighbours defending the rights of migrant workers in confrontations with their employers, their home country government officials, and the Canadian state (Preibisch, 2014). This may serve as an example for the achievement of civil integration in the absence of legal and market integration. For example, in southern Italy local citizens and local farmers organised activities to demonstrate their solidarity with migrant agricultural workers and to protest against their exploitation by the Mafia and neglect by the regional authorities (Corrado, 2012). Such examples of civic initiative and social innovation have also been found in Northern Ireland (McAreavey, 2012). The reaction of local residents varies also according to the group of migrants. In Spain, for instance, local residents may protest against the arrival of single male migrants whereas they may welcome immigrant families (Viruela, 2008), because their children ensure the continuity of village schools in peripheral rural areas.

Another strong promoter of migrant social integration regards the start-up of a business and the transition from employee to entrepreneur. Setting up a successful business requires the maintenance of relationships with the local population, resulting in the development of trust and a sense of belonging on both sides when becoming aware of their mutual economic dependence (Bosworth & Atterton, 2012). Once again, migrants often fill spaces abandoned by native entrepreneurs. In Italy migrants from North Africa have entered the fresh food distribution chains based on whole markets and low-price shops both as workers and entrepreneurs. Food in itself is becoming an important space of interactions. Migrants are substituting farmers in internal and mountainous areas where difficult natural conditions and isolation have resulted in the abandonment of land and farms. These migrants start to produce both local traditional food (such as sheep's milk cheese in the Apennine Mountains) and ingredients for ethnic food for the migrant markets and ethnic food chains (Benvenuti & Cordini, 2013; Milone & Ventura, 2013).

More generally, it is important to keep in mind that the integration of migrants is a gradual and intergenerational process. It is not singular factors that promote integration by themselves; it is in interrelation and mutual influence that these factors constitute the path towards integration. This may most effectively be demonstrated through the experiences of the second and third generation of migrants. Children of migrants who are born in the host community commonly integrate more firmly and more easily; they benefit from acculturation through education and the many opportunities school offers for social interaction with native children. The degree of integration differs across migrant groups and boys and girls, which again demonstrates the importance of education. In addition, research points to the importance of spatial assimilation and the opportunity of migrant families to move into mixed neighbourhoods (Levitt & Waters, 2006; Alba et al., 2014).

Migrants' social exclusion should not only be understood as an ongoing conflict with the local population. In many cases it emerges as the coexistence of parallel lives: the presence of strong ethnic and religious networks produces forms of social segmentation often impenetrable to institutions and local services (Patacchini & Zenou, 2012). These networks operate as both legal and illegal intermediaries within the labour market through the creation of ethnic labour organisations/cooperatives specialised in specific services (seasonal work in agriculture as picking, pruning, porterage, slaughter, etc.). There are documented case studies in which immigrants do not wish to integrate but rather develop their own isolated areas of residence and work where they can maintain their cultural practices regardless of their acceptability in the local civil society (Osti & Ventura, 2012). The most frequent risk is the reproduction of social segmentation that separates natives and migrants, which nurtures intolerance and migrants' marginalisation and exclusion. In times of financial crisis, such phenomena become increasingly common, fuelled by fear about rising unemployment rates. The first to lose their jobs are immigrants, given the accepted right of priority of locals, the seasonality of jobs where immigrants are overly represented and the obvious precariousness of illegal forms of migrant recruitment (Beets & Willekens, 2009). As a result, migrants leave the crisis-ridden rural areas in search of employment in the cities.

Integration in sending places

There is great fear that rural emigration undermines the vitality of sending places due to the loss of population, and especially the younger, more entrepreneurial people. Emigration is thought to weaken social cohesion and social capital, moving places into a cycle of continuous decline (Barca, 2009). Newspapers regularly publish articles that fit this line of argument when reporting on elderly people and children being left behind. The Dutch 'adopt a grandmother' fund, which raises money to support impoverished grandmothers in rural Moldavia, is a clear example.[2] Research into migration between Mexico and the USA demonstrates that there are rural places and areas which suffer from decline as a result of emigration and where migration increases their marginality (see Brown & Argent, this volume). Rural decline does not follow automatically or instantaneously from emigration, though.

Researchers demonstrate how migration constrains production 'at home' due to the lack of labour power (Horváth, 2008) and encourages people to rely on remittances instead of investing in the creation of business and new jobs. The latter then may motivate others to emigrate as well, which, in turn, contributes to continuous depopulation and ageing since it is predominantly young men and women of reproductive age who will leave (Kurek, 2011). This, once again, demonstrates the strong interrelation between market and civil integration.

Others underline how remittances support household consumption budgets, increase savings, and are invested in commerce and the construction of houses (White, 2010) or are spent on 'conspicuous consumption' (Anghel, 2008). In time, this may contribute to the development of sending communities also through the social remittances migrants bring home – that is, new knowledge and experiences, and new contacts which improve the connectivity of places (Fox, 2005; de Lange, 2013). Such research gives clear evidence of translocal citizenship, where migrants remain integrated in their original home communities in terms of feelings of belonging and actual long-distance contributions to the community's development and governance. The emigration and market integration of some groups may also offer new opportunities to hitherto excluded groups. In Poland, for instance, there is evidence that the absence of men leads to women taking over community positions, such as village representatives (Matysiak, 2014). Overall, however, we still have little insight into the impact of mobility on social integration at the level of the local sending communities. The discourse at the national level of the 'sending' countries varies: there is evidence of criticism of mothers leaving their children behind for 'career motives' (Tyldum, 2015) and worry about how this affects the well-being of children (Timmerman, Martiniello, Rea & Wets, 2015). But migration for employment is also understood as a necessity since the financial crisis, with national governments defending the right of free mobility against the opposition of some of the receiving countries and standing up against the discrimination of their mobile citizens in the political rhetoric of populist and increasingly mainstream politicians in the older member states.[3] Integration is, therefore, a matter of interaction at the (macro) level of states and their legal, economic and political recognition, as well as at the micro level of migrants and their families and the meso level of rural places. More research is needed to better understand to what extent and how migrants become included in rural civic and economic networks and which factors influence the impact of rural migration on development processes in sending places.

Conclusion

This chapter reported on the increasing level of migration into rural areas in Europe following fundamental political changes such as the enlargement of the European Union as well as the economic shock of the worldwide financial crisis. It discussed the modern features of rural migration and highlighted the fact that migrants tend to maintain relationships with home and often live at multiple places at the same time, 'here and there'. There is a need for multi-sited research into social integration following migration that explores the migratory effects in sending and receiving places at the same time and takes account of these transnational and translocal bonds. Social integration and its opposite, social exclusion, are moreover not only taking place at the micro level of migrants and their families, although it is the focus of most of the current research. There are also effects at the meso level of the sending and receiving places, reflected, among others, in how migration and the social and economic remittances it produces facilitates or hinders local development. Research produces evidence of both but more insight is needed to better understand how the process unfolds and how it may be affected by policy. Last but not least, migration importantly matters for relations at the macro level of states, and leads to arguments about the right of free mobility and its limitation for residents of certain countries (Favell & Hansen, 2002). This also points to processes of territorial exclusion and stigmatisation. Distinguishing between legal, market and civil integration helps us to understand the multidimensionality of social integration. It also demonstrates how the three levels interrelate. To give just one example: the troubled relationship between EU member states with regard to the right of free mobility – the competition for jobs, social benefits and housing between migrants and local residents, and the concern about the identity of communities in ethnic and religious terms.

In conclusion, the multidimensionality and differentiation of migration may be summarised in the following ways.

The level, direction and process of migration into European rural areas varies across countries of origin but also migrants' social class and education: in receiving areas the result varies between gentrification, on the one hand, and ghettoisation of destitute migrants, on the other.

Processes of inclusion and exclusion vary across domains of integration, with, for example, civil integration potentially being combined with market exclusion. They differ also across migrant groups, with some groups having better chances of integration than others. They also diverge between countries, regions and places. Hence, there is no generalised pattern of migrant inclusion or exclusion across national contexts even if in specific situations (i.e., seasonal work in southern Europe) quasi slavery relationships occur.

Generally speaking, rural migrants are not excluded at the level of the sending places as they tend to maintain social relations, and return home regularly. The place itself may suffer or benefit from the effects of migration depending, among other factors, on the use of social and economic remittances. More research is needed to better understand this process.

Migration has a great impact on rural areas because of their low population density and relative homogeneity compared to urban areas which affect identity formation and demographic stratification. Both become more easily disrupted in smaller compared to bigger places through the loss of citizen groups as well as the influx of new groups, which are often – at least initially – perceived as 'strangers'.

Nevertheless, the concentration of international migrants in rural areas does not immediately cause social exclusion and segregation. Even though migrants may not always be fully integrated, this may also result in the recognition of difference and in toleration of parallel lives. Integration and exclusion, then, is a matter of degree and dimension, and depends on the extent to which exclusion accumulates or eliminates in the intersection of legal, market and civil integration at different levels. Most important at this point is to better understand this process and how the potential benefits of rural migration 'here and there' may be supported, as it is an illusion to think that rural migration may be curtailed or reduced in this era of high mobility.

Notes

1 Again, much more of this kind of research has been done in the USA, especially for what is regarded as circular migration of Mexican migrants (e.g., Sana & Massey, 2005; Stephen, 2007).
2 http://dorcas.net/favicon.ico (accessed 29 January 2015).
3 For a scientific analysis of discrimination against migrants in contexts that guarantee free movement, such as the EU, the United States and Canada, see Maas (2013).

References

Alba, R, Deane, G, Denton, N, Disha, I, McKenzie, B & Napierala, J (2014). The role of immigrant enclaves for Latino residential inequalities. *Journal of Ethnic and Migration Studies* 40(1), 1–20.

Alba, R & Foner, N (2014). Comparing immigrant integration in North America and Western Europe: How much do the grand narratives tell us? *International Migration Review* 48(1), 263–291.

Ambrosini, M (2013). *Irregular migration and invisible welfare*. New York: Palgrave Macmillan.

Andrezejewska, J & Rye, JF (2012). Lost in transnational space: Migrant farm workers in rural districts. *Mobilities* 7(2), 247–268.

Anghel, G (2008). Changing statuses. *Journal of Ethnic and Migration Studies* 34(5), 787–802.

Bade, KJ (2008). *Migration in European history*. Malden: John Wiley & Sons.

Baker, M & Benjamin, D (1997). The role of the family in immigrants' labor-market activity: An evaluation of alternative explanations. *American Economic Review* 87, 705–727.

Barberis, E (2011). Imprenditori cinesi in Italia. Fra kinship networks e legami territoriali. *Mondi Migranti* 2, 101–124.

Barca, F (2009). *Towards a territorial social agenda for the European Union*. Rome: Ministry of Economy.

Beets, G & Willekens, F (2009). The global economic crisis and international migration: An uncertain outlook. In D Coleman & D Ediev (Eds), *Vienna yearbook of population research* (pp. 19–38). Vienna: Vienna Institute of Demography/Austrian Academy of Science.

Bell, MM & Osti, G (2010). Mobilities and ruralities: An introduction. *Sociologia Ruralis* 50, 199–204.

Benvenuti, V & Cordini, M (2013). *Le imprese straniere nel settore agricolo in italia INEA*. Rome: INEA.

Bernard, A (2008). *Immigrants in the hinterlands*. Statistics Canada – Catalogue no. 75-001-X. Retrieved 15 October 2010 from http://www.statcan.gc.ca/pub/75-001-x/2008101/article/10505-eng.htm#a5.

Bock, BB (2006). Gender and rural migration: An overview. In BB Bock & S Shortall (Eds), *Rural gender relations: Issues and case studies* (pp. 155–164). Cambridge: CABI.

Bock, BB (2010). *Personal and social development of women in rural areas of Europe*. Brussels: European Parliament, COMAGRI (IP/B/AGRI/IC/2010_089; PE 438/608).

Bock, BB (2012). Social innovation and sustainability. *Studies in Agricultural Economics* 114(2), 57–63.

Bosworth, G & Atterton, J (2012). Entrepreneurial in-migration and neo-endogenous rural development. *Rural Sociology* 77(2), 254–279.

Brown, DL (2010). *Rethinking the OECD's new rural demography*. Centre for Rural Economy Discussion Paper Series No. 26, Newcastle University, UK.

Brown, DL (2012). How 'mobilities' are restructuring the rural–urban periphery. Keynote at the Agriculture in an Urbanizing Society Conference 1–4 April 2012, Wageningen University, the Netherlands.

Brown DL, Bolender, BC, Kulcsar, LJ, Glasgow, S & Sanders, S (2011). Intercounty variability of net migration at older ages as a path-dependent process. *Rural Sociology* 76(1), 44–73.

Bulmer, MIA (1975). Sociological models of the mining community. *The Sociological Review* 23, 61–92.

Carr, M (2012). *Fortress Europe: Dispatches from a gated continent*. New York: New Press.

Castells, M (2000). Materials for an exploratory theory of the network society. *British Journal of Sociology* 51(1), 5–25.

Champion, T (2005). Population movement within the UK. *Focus on People and Migration*, 91–113.

Cieślinńska B (2012). The experience of labour emigration in the life of married women: The case of Polasie, Poland. *International Migration* 52(1), 56–73.

Cloke, P & Thrift, N (1987). Intra-class conflict in rural areas. *Journal of Rural Studies* 3(4), 321–333.

Collantes, F, Pinilla, V, Sáez, LA & Silvestre, J (2013). Reducing depopulation in rural Spain: the impact of immigration. *Population, Space, and Place* 20(7), 606–621. doi: 10/1002/psp.1797.

Corrado, A (2012). Ruralità differenziate e migrazioni del sud Italia. *Agriregionieuropa* 8(28), 72–74.

Cresswell, T (2010). Towards a politics of mobility. *Environment and Planning D* 28 (1), 17–31.

Dagevos, J (Ed.). (2011). *Poolse migranten*. The Hague: Sociaal Cultureel Planbureau.

D'Alessandro, S, Rampelli, E & Spagnolo, A (Eds). (2011). *Identità, immigrazione e cittadinanza*. Rome: ISFOL.

Danson, M & Jentsch, B (2009). The new Scottish rural labour market: Processes of inclusion and exclusion. In B Jentsch & M Simard (Eds), *International migration and rural areas. Cross-national comparative perspectives* (pp. 127–150). Farnham: Ashgate.

De Haas, H (2010). The internal dynamics of migration processes. *Journal of Ethnic and Migration Studies* 36, 1587–1617.

De Lange, DE (2013). Embedded diasporas: Shaping the geopolitical landscape. *Journal of International Management* 19(1), 14–25.

De Lima, P (2012). Boundary crossing. In C Hedberg & E De Carmo (Eds), *Translocal ruralism* (pp. 203–217). Dordrecht: Springer.

Duran, J, Massey, DS & Zenteno, RM (2001). Mexican immigration to the United States: Continuities and changes. *Latin American Research Review* 26(1), 107–127.

Engbersen, G, Leerkes, A, Grabowska-Lusinka, I, Snel, E & Burgers, J (2013). On the differential attachments of migrants from Central and Eastern Europe. *Journal of Ethnic and Migration Studies* 39(6), 959–981.

Eurostat. (2011). *Migrants in Europe*. Luxembourg: European Union.

Eurydice (2004). *Integrating immigrant children in school in Europe*. Brussels: European Commission, Directorate-General for Education and Culture.

Faist, T, Fauser, M & Reisenauer, E (2013). *Transnational migration*. Cambridge: Polity.

Farris, SR (2015). Migrants' regular army of labour: Gender dimensions of the impact of the global economic crisis on migrant labour in Western Europe. *The Sociological Review* 63, 121–143.

Favell, A (2008). The new face of East–West migration in Europe. *Journal of Ethnic and Migration Studies* 34(5), 701–716.

Favell, A & Hansen, R (2002). Markets against politics: Migration, EU enlargement and the idea of Europe. *Journal of Ethnic and Migration Studies* 28, 581–601.

Fox, J (2005). Unpacking 'transnational citizenship'. *Annual Review of Political Sciences* 8, 171–201.

Glick Schiller, N & Caglar, A (2009). Towards a comparative theory of locality in migration studies. *Journal of Ethnic and Migration Studies* 35(2), 177–202.

Green, A, de Hoyos, M, Jones, P & Owen, D (2009). Rural development and labour supply challenges in the UK: The role of non-UK migrants. *Regional Studies* 43(10), 1261–1273.

Halfacree, K (2012). Heterolocal identities? *Population, Space and Place* 18, 209–224.

Hedberg, G, Forsberg, G & Najib, A (2012). When the world goes rural. In C Hedberg & RM do Carmo (Eds), *Translocal ruralism* (pp. 125–142). Dordrecht: Springer.

Ho, ELE, Hockey, M & Yeoh, BSA (2015). Special issue introduction: New research directions and critical perspectives on diaspora strategies. *Geoforum* 59, 153–158.

Hollifield, J (1992). *Immigrants, markets, and states: The political economy of postwar Europe*. Cambridge, MA: Harvard University Press.

Horváth, I (2008). The culture of migration among Romanian youth. *Journal of Ethnic and Migration Studies* 34(5), 771–786.

Hyden, G (1997). Civil society, social capital, and development: Dissection of a complex discourse. *Studies in Comparative International Development* 32(1), 3–30.

Kasimis, C & Papadopoulos, AG (2005). The multifunctional role of migrants in Greek countryside: Implications for the rural economy and society. *Journal of Ethnic and Migration Studies* 31(1), 99–127.

King, R 2002. Towards a new map of European migration. *International Journal of Population Geography* 8, 89–106.

King, R & Vullnetari, J (2009). The intersections of gender and generation in Albanian migration. *Geografiska Annaler: Series B* 91, 19–38.

Kurek, S. (2011). Double transitions? Regional patterns of population ageing in Poland. *Geografiska Annaler: Series B*, 163–184.

Landsteiner, E & Langthaler, E (Eds). (2012). *Agrosystems and labour relations in European rural societies (middle ages–twentieth century)*. Turnhout: Brepols.

Levitt, P & Schiller, NG (2004). Conceptualizing simultaneity. *International Migration Review* 38(3), 1002–1039.

Levitt, P & Waters, MC (2006). Introduction. In P Levitt & MC Waters (Eds), *The changing face of home: The transnational lives of the second generation* (pp. 1–30). New York: Russell Sage Foundation.

Lucassen, L (2005). *The immigrant threat: The integration of old and new migrants in Western Europe since 1850*. Champaign: University of Illinois Press.

Maas, W (2013). Free movement and discrimination: Evidence from Europe, the United States, and Canada. *European Journal of Migration and Law* 15, 91–110.

Marcu, S. (2014). From the marginal immigrant to the mobile citizen. *Population, Space and Place* 21(6), 506–517. doi: 10.1002/psp.1845.

Massey, D (2004). Geographies of responsibilities. *Geografiska Annaler: Series B* 86, 5–18.

Matysiak, I (2014). The feminization of governance in rural communities in Poland. *Gender, Place, and Culture* 22(5), 700–716. doi: 10.1080/0966369X.2013.879104.

McAreavey, R (2012). Resistance or resilience? *Sociologia Ruralis* 52(4), 488–506.

Milbourne, P (2007). Repopulating rural studies. *Journal of Rural Studies* 23(3), 381–386.

Milone, P & Ventura, F (2013). *Immigrazione, imprenditorialità e nuovi mercati*. Working paper. Perugia: Università di Perugia.

MIPEX. (2011). *Migrant integration policy index, MIPEX III*. Available at http://www.mipex.eu/.

Molloy, R, Smith, CL & Wozniak, AK (2011). *Internal migration in the United States*. Working paper 17307. Cambridge: National Bureau of Economic Research.

Ní Laoire, CN (2001). A matter of life and death? Men, masculinities and staying 'behind' in rural Ireland. *Sociologia Ruralis* 41, 220–236.

OECD (2014). *International migration outlook 2014*. Paris: OECD Publishing.

Osti, G & Ventura, F (2012). *Vivere da stranieri in aree fragili*. Naples: Liguori Editore.

Papadopoulos, A (2009). 'Begin from the bottom and move up': Social mobility of immigrant labour in rural Greece. *Méditerranée: Revue géographique des pays méditerranées* 113, 25–39.

Patacchini, E & Zenou, Y (2012). Ethnic networks and employment outcomes. *Regional Science and Urban Economics* 42, 938–949.

Portes, A (2003). Conclusion. *International Migration Review* 37(3), 874–892.

Portes, A & Manning, RD (1986). The immigrant enclave: Theory and empirical examples. In O Olzak & J Nagel (Eds), *Competitive ethnic relations* (pp. 47–68). Orlando, FL: Academic Press.

Powell, WW (1990). Neither market nor hierarchy: Network forms of organization. *Research in Organizational Behavior* 12, 295–336.

Preibisch, KL (2014). Migrant agricultural workers and processes of social inclusion in rural Canada: Encuentros and desencuentros. *Canadian Journal of Latin American and Caribbean Studies*. Routledge.

Riosmena, F & Massey, DS (2012). Pathways to El Norte: Origins, destinations, and characteristics of Mexican migrations to the United States. *International Migration Review* 46(1), 3–36.

Russel, R (2012). *Migration in Northern Ireland: An update*. Belfast: Northern Ireland Assembly.

Sahai, P & Lum, KD (2013). *Migration from Punjab to Italy in the dairy sector: The quiet Indian revolution*. CARIM-India Research Report 2013/10. Florence: European University Institute.

Sana, M & Massey, DS (2005). Household composition, family migration, and community context: Migrant remittances in four countries. *Social Science Quarterly* 86, 509–528.

Sandu, D (2005). Emerging transnational migration from Romanian villages. *Current Sociology* 53, 555–582.

Saraceno, E (2013). Disparity and diversity: Their use in EU rural policies. *Sociologia Ruralis* 53(3), 331–348.

Shucksmith, M (2013). *Future directions in rural development?* Dunfermline: Carnegie Trust.

Silberman, R, Alba, R & Fournier, I (2007). Segmented assimilation in France? Discrimination in the labour market against the second generation. *Ethnic and Racial Studies* 30(1), 1–27.

Smith, MP (2011). Translocality: A critical reflection. In K Brickell & A Datta (Eds.), *Translocal geographies: Spaces, places, connections* (pp. 181–198). Farnham: Ashgate.

Stenning, A & Dawley, S (2009). Poles to Newcastle. *European Urban and Regional Studies* 16, 273–294.

Stephen, L (2007). *Transborder lives: Indigenous Oaxacans in Mexico, California, and Oregon*. Durham, NC: Duke University Press.

Stockdale, A (2006). Migration. *Journal of Rural Studies* 22, 354–366.

Timmerman, C, Martiniello, M, Rea, A & Wets, J (Eds). (2015). *A new dynamics in female migration and integration*. New York: Routledge.

Tyldum, G (2015). Motherhood, Agency and sacrifice in narratives on female migration for care work. *Sociology* 49(1), 56–71.

Urry, J (2007). *Mobilities*. Cambridge: Polity.

Van der Ploeg, JD & Marsden, T (Eds). (2008). *Unfolding webs, the dynamics of regional rural development*. Assen: van Gorcum.

Vargas-Silva, C (2014). *Migrants and housing in the UK: Experiences and impacts*. The Migrants Observatory, Oxford University.

Vertovec, S (2009). *Transnationalism*. London: Routledge.

Viruela, R (2008). De Este a Oueste: la inmigración desde los nuevos países comunitarios (Rumania y Bulgaria). *Cuadernos de Geografía* 84, 127–134.

Werbner, P (2001). Metaphors of spatiality and networks in the plural city: A critique of the ethnic enclave economy debate. *Sociology* 35(3), 671–693.

White, A (2010). Young people and migration from contemporary Poland. *Journal of Youth Studies* 13(5), 565–580.

Woods, M (2013). Rural development, globalization and European regional policy: Perspectives from the DERREG project. *Geographica Polonica* 86(2), 99–109.

Zaiceva, A & Zimmermann, KF (2008). Scale, diversity, and determinants of labour migration in Europe. *Oxford Review of Economic Policy* 24(3), 427–451.

7

The Impacts of Population Change on Rural Society and Economy

David L. Brown and Neil Argent

Introduction

It seems intuitively obvious that changes in population size and composition affect local society and economy. More people means more consumers and service users; fewer school-age children and more elders translates into fewer teachers and school rooms on the one hand but more physicians on the other. However, in reality, the association between changes in population and changes in economy and society is neither simple nor mechanistic. Similar demographic changes in different places do not necessarily translate into the same social and economic outcomes. In this chapter, we develop a conceptual framework for examining the association between population dynamics and social and economic changes in rural areas.

Further complicating this complex set of relationships is the fact that the association between population change and societal outcomes may move in both directions. Economic development, for example, may produce conditions conducive to population growth, while the opposite is also true – for example, places experiencing population growth may experience a growth in jobs, establishments and so on. While acknowledging this mutually causative process, we focus primarily on population change as the independent variable in this chapter, and examine the pathways through which changes in the size and composition of population may induce changes in social and economic organisation.

Rural population trends

While no universal pattern of rural population dynamics characterises the global north during recent decades (Kulcsar & Curtis, 2012), some overall trends can be identified.[1] Perhaps most obvious is that economic development has been accompanied by urbanisation (Chen, Zhang, Liu & Zhang, 2014). According to the UN Population Division (United Nations, 2012), 77.7% of persons living in more developed nations resided in urban areas in 2011, and this level is projected to increase to 85.9% in 2050. There is very little variation among continents in the percentage of urban dwellers in 2011, ranging from 69.0% in Europe to 70.7% in Oceania and 82.2% in North America. Interestingly, less developed regions of the world have also been urbanising more rapidly than more developed although they still lag in percent urban (46.7% vs 77.7%). As a result, the percentage of persons living in urban areas now exceeds 50% worldwide (52.1%).[2]

However, after acknowledging the overall association between economic development and the level of urbanisation, more developed nations tend to differ with respect to the direction of population redistribution at the present time. For example, counter-urbanisation, an inverse association between population size and the rate of population growth (Fielding, 1982), was identified in several highly developed nations. While initially thought to be at odds with conventional theories of internal economic development and urban agglomeration, theoretical explanations were developed for the underlying social and economic processes giving rise to the demographic phenomenon. In particular, Zelinsky's (1971) mobility transition hypothesis proposed that as development proceeds, people become more geographically mobile, but fewer move from rural to urban areas. While not precisely predicting the advent of counter-urbanisation, Zelinsky's hypothesis made conceptual sense of declining urbanisation rates in more developed nations, and provided a bridge to understanding the urban-to-rural mobility that would soon be observed in a number of nations (Vining & Kontuly, 1978). Rather than simply reflecting the conventional notion that people move to maximise their income, counter-urbanisation opened the possibility of migration that was motivated by preferences for amenities and lifestyle attributes among economically secure populations in more developed nations (Gottman, 1961; Smailes & Hugo, 1985; Walmsley, Epps & Duncan, 1998).

Counter-urbanisation was initially recognised in the 1970s by Calvin Beale (1975) in the USA. Since then, however, the net balance of urban and rural population growth in that nation has fluctuated dramatically. At the present time, urban population growth rates in the United States significantly exceed those in rural regions (Johnson, 2014). Similarly, the direction of net internal migration favours urban areas. The UK, in contrast, experienced continuous counter-urbanisation from the 1950s through 2011. Even now, while the relative rates of urban and rural population growth are about equal, net internal migration favours rural areas at the expense of their urban counterparts (Champion, 2013). In the more 'metrocentric' new settler states of Canada, Australia and New Zealand, counter-urbanisation's dividends for rural areas have become more muted and spatially selective over time, with higher amenity areas characterised by scenic natural environments and good accessibility to major cities increasingly seen as exurban migration 'hot spots' (Hugo, 1994; Burnley & Murphy, 2004; Argent, Tonts, Jones & Holmes, 2011). At the same time, the growth rates of non-metropolitan regions across these nations has generally lagged those of the major – including the capital – cities (McGuirk & Argent, 2011).

Developing precise measures of the relative growth (and decline) trajectories of rural and urban components of settlement systems is complicated by the often rapid spatial expansion of suburban and exurban nodes (e.g., 'edge cities') into sprawling conurbations such that, in definitional terms, separating out urban and rural is no easy task (Champion & Hugo, 2004). For example, currently some of the fastest growing places in Australia are major regional centres within commuting range of the capital cities (McGuirk & Argent, 2011); their growth is driven primarily by natural increase and net internal migration.

In addition to counter-urbanisation, rural populations in more developed nations are likely to experience several other demographic trends although the prevalence, extent and timing of these situations varies across countries. Population ageing in excess of that experienced in urban areas, natural population decrease, amenity- and lifestyle-motivated migration, the attraction of retirement-age migrants and, in some cases, growing racial/ethnic diversity mainly resulting from international migration that increasingly ranges beyond traditional gateway cities – all characterise rural populations in the world's more developed regions (Brown, 2014). All of these demographic trends are hypothetically associated with changes in various aspects of local society and economy.

Population impact on what?

Population change affects virtually every aspect of society, but the impacts of greatest interest tend to be those that are associated with major institutional complexes such as the labour market, education, the social welfare system, consumer product markets, housing and community services, and roads, bridges, sidewalks/footpaths and other mobility-related infrastructure.[3] As early as Malthus, scholars have commented on the relationship between population change and human welfare, yet this analysis has often been short-sighted in that it has tended to privilege the impact of changes in population size while neglecting the possible impacts of changes in population structure and composition (Brown & Eloundou-Enyegue, forthcoming). Yet, it is through changes in population composition that demand shifts in consumer markets are most directly felt; that changes in the need for particular kinds of services are experienced; and where changes in preferences and lifestyles that affect every institutional sphere are articulated.

These population-related impacts seem intuitive. More people (and households) surely translates into more housing units; an increasing share of non-native speakers in classrooms should, *ceteris paribus*, result in more bilingual education programmes; chronic out-migration of well-prepared workers results in the loss of high-wage, high-skill jobs; and an increasing share of elders undoubtedly induces changes in the mix of medical services offered in a community. But it is not that simple. These same demographic trends can result in different outcomes in different places, or in the same place at different times. In other words, the impacts of changes in population size and composition are mediated by institutional settings and social and economic structures – structures that vary between communities and are transformed over time (Brown, 2013). Hence, we contend that the impacts of population change are seldom direct or mechanistic. Rather, they tend to be indirect and contingent. If this is the case, how might one examine population impacts at the local level so that public and private activities can respond in meaningful ways? In the next section, we develop a framework for examining the impact of population change at the community level.

A framework for examining the impact of population change on society and economy

Our general perspective is that the impacts of population change on rural society and economy are usually indirect and mediated by local institutions and social structure. The framework we propose is illustrated in Figure 7.1. Although our focus is on demographic characteristics and dynamics, along with their interrelationships with local social and economic change, our starting point is to acknowledge that local demographic change is itself produced or at least influenced to a greater or lesser degree by a host of economic, technological, social and cultural 'drivers', often emanating from and operating through geographical scales (Lyson, 2006; Woods, 2007; Halseth, Markey & Bruce, 2010). In some cases, the effects of these may be felt directly as in the closure and offshore relocation of a manufacturing plant with the associated job loss and out-migration. In other instances, these broader scale processes have more subtle impacts on rural population, as when a state or regional government introduces relocation grants and allowances. These are generally only mildly stimulatory in their effects, and operate through regional housing markets, private and public transport networks, regional labour market conditions, and the like. Moreover, as indicated in Figure 7.1, the social and economic outcomes of population change – for example, a school closure or the introduction of geriatric health services at local or regional hospitals – can influence population attraction and/or retention

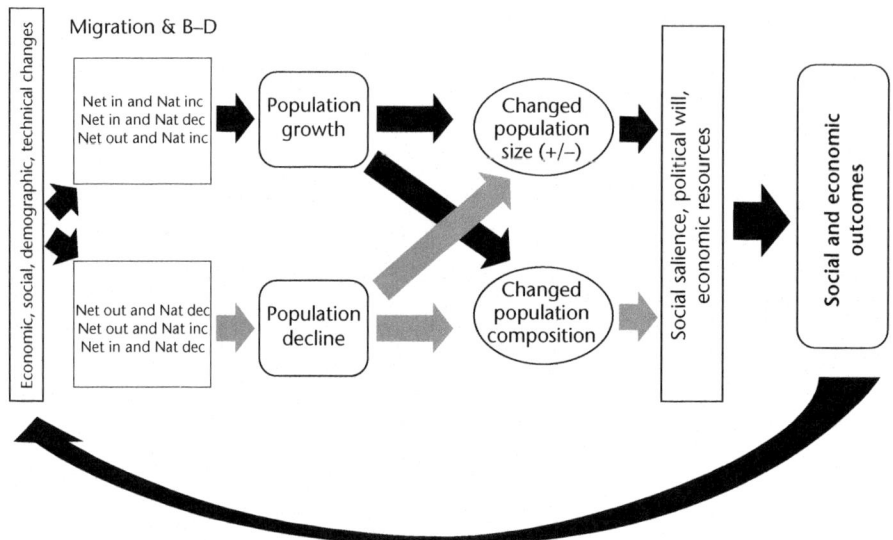

Figure 7.1 A framework for examining the impact of population change on society and economy

and/or fertility rates thereby setting the population change/social change process in motion once again. As indicated earlier, however, our primary interest in this chapter is to examine how population change affects society and economy, not vice versa.

Components of population change

Regardless of the force or direction of the stimulus when examining the impacts of population growth or decline, it is necessary to disaggregate the demographic change into its two components, net migration and natural increase/decrease, and examine the influences of these processes separately. Net migration can be either positive or negative depending on whether the balance of people moving to a place exceeds the number moving out. Natural population change is positive when births exceed deaths or negative when deaths exceed births. As shown in Figure 7.2, population growth can result from three different combinations of net migration and natural change. Similarly, there are three combinations of migration and natural change that can produce population decline.

The implication is that growing places with both net in-migration and natural increase are categorically different from places experiencing population growth where one or the other component of growth is negative. The reason for this is because the determinants of migration and of natural change differ in ways that have implications for the impacts of population growth or decline. Net in-migration, for example, typically results from economic opportunities and/ or amenities that are relatively more attractive than those possessed by other places.[4] Hence growing places with net in-migration, regardless of natural increase, typically have sufficient economic resources to provide services, initiate community improvement schemes and so on. In contrast, natural population decrease reflects a distorted age structure where women of childbearing age are relatively scarce and sometimes, but not necessarily, have low fertility rates.[5] Hence, while net out-migration generally reflects a lack of economic opportunities and resources, natural decrease sometimes occurs in relatively well-off contexts, for example in

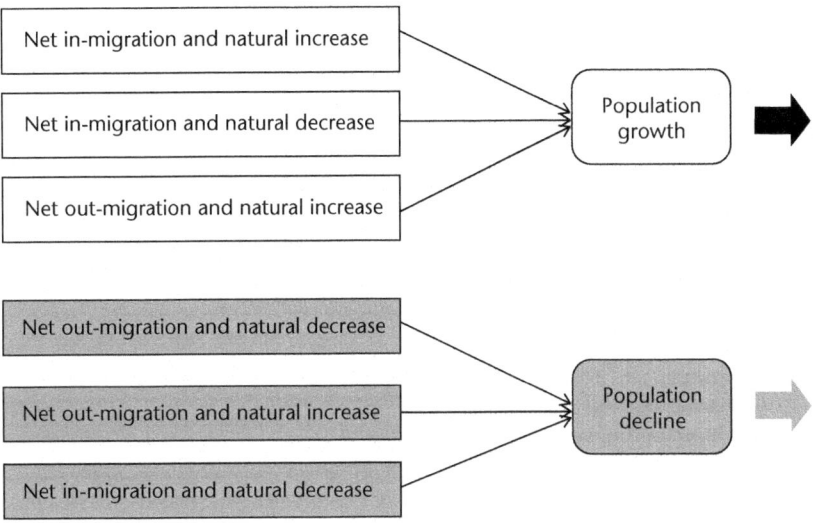

Figure 7.2 Decomposing population change

high-amenity regions which have a history of late middle-aged and retiree in-migration but also net migration loss of the young. Accordingly, population decline in places with net out-migration is generally more challenging than decline driven by natural decrease alone. Of course, population decline is most problematic where both migration and natural change are negative. This is because, consistent with our conceptual model, these twin and reinforcing dynamics of decline reflect a downward spiral in, *inter alia*, local economic and/or social opportunity and/or environmental amenity, but also greatly influence the capacity of affected regions to attract sufficient human capital to regain demographic vitality. Conversely, growing places with both net in-migration and more births than deaths tend to be advantaged in comparison with growing places with either natural decrease or net out-migration.[6] The main point we are making here is that the community-level impacts of population change are contingent on the combination of population dynamics producing the overall growth or decline.

Population size and population composition

Returning to Figure 7.1, the next step in the framework is that population growth and decline affects *both* population size and population structure/composition. Once again, these impacts are contingent on the combination of migration and natural change that produce population growth or decline. Obviously, the impacts on changes in population size are immediate and direct. Growing places have more consumers, voters, drivers, etc., while declining places experience shrinkage in these domains. However, the *rate* of growth or decline can condition the impact of changing population size. Slowly growing places are generally able to adapt incrementally (Johnson, 1985), while places experiencing growth booms must expand infrastructure or add entirely new services and facilities (Wetzel, 2012). Similarly, rapid and sustained local depopulation is generally more acutely felt than the 'slow burn' of gradual population decline and can lead to local disinvestment, disenchantment and declining morale, triggering further out-migration (Argent, 2008). Moreover, these are not 'closed systems', so that even a decline in population need not mean economic decline, as discussed further below.

Age- and race-specific net out-migration, an excess of deaths over births, net in-migration of college-educated professionals and so on affect not only population size, but also a population's age structure, racial/ethnic composition, income distribution and educational attainment. For example, chronic out-migration of young, well-prepared adults contributes to population ageing and reduces a community's human capital. If net out-migration of young adults continues over time, the relative share of young adults and elders will become so distorted that the population will produce more deaths than births (i.e., structural ageing). This is a phenomenon commonly felt across the productivist broadacre farming regions of the developed world (Halseth & Hanlon, 2005; Davies & James, 2011; Smailes, Griffin & Argent, 2014). In fact, chronic out-migration of young adults and resulting distortions of age structure will result in natural decrease even if remaining young adults have higher than average fertility rates (Johnson, 2011).

Similarly, dramatic changes in the spatial location of the US meat-packing industry has attracted young adult Hispanic immigrants from Mexico as well as from other parts of the USA. As a result of this migration, and of the higher fertility among Hispanics of childbearing age, the racial/ethnic composition of many US rural communities has become increasingly diverse (Johnson & Lichter, 2012). One final example involves education-specific out-migration. As Carr and Kefalas have described in their trenchant book, *Hollowing Out the Middle* (2009), many rural communities in the USA are suffering from a dramatic brain drain that leaves behind an under-educated workforce that is mismatched with present-day employment in high-tech, high-skill industry (also see Corbett, 2007).

Local society mediates the impacts of population change

Referring back to Figure 7.1, we now arrive at the interface between changes in population size and composition and particular aspects of community such as schools, health care, the labour market or social welfare. However, rather than proposing a mechanistic response to these demographic changes, our framework indicates that different outcomes are possible depending on the capacity of local institutions, the nature of civic engagement and social mobilisation, and other aspects of local social organisation (Brown, 2002). Accordingly, fewer school-age children does not automatically result in fewer teachers and closed schools; more Spanish-speaking children does not necessarily result in more bilingual education programmes; nor does the in-movement of retirees automatically presage high public costs for pensions and care. At one level, these outcomes depend on decisions made in local communities that are experiencing demographic change. In such instances, communities must consider the potential costs and benefits of various responses. How socially salient are potential changes such as keeping schools open in the face of declining enrolments and rising per pupil costs? Regardless of perceived salience, is there sufficient political will, resources and unity of purpose to respond affirmatively? And, of course, even when salience is perceived to be high, and local leaders are willing to expend political capital, the community must possess sufficient economic resources to respond. Consider the situation of older in-migration to rural communities. Research conducted across Europe (King, Warnes & Williams, 2000; Champion & Sheppard, 2006), in Australia (Garlick, Waterman & Soar, 2006) and in the United States (Brown & Glasgow, 2008) indicates that while older persons are less likely to migrate than younger persons, those who do move are likely to move to a rural destination. Moreover, in all of these instances older in-migrants tend to be positively selected and motivated by amenities and quality of life attributes associated with rural community living. Interestingly, older in-migration tends to be considered as a 'pensions and care issue' in England but a social and economic opportunity in the USA. Experience in the USA indicates that older in-migrants are relatively healthy and well off compared with the longer term residents they join in destinations. Accordingly, while older in-migrants increase the need for health, transportation and other ageing-related services, they generally have the resources to pay for them.

Equally as important, older in-migrants tend to be extremely active in volunteer service. In fact, Brown and Glasgow (2008) reported that older in-migrant respondents to their survey of 14 rural retirement destinations distributed across the United States were equally likely to volunteer compared with longer term older residents of the same places who had lived there for an average of over 20 years. However, as we have emphasised throughout this chapter, in-migration of highly educated and experienced older persons does not automatically translate into a deep pool of highly engaged volunteers who reduce the costs of procuring professional and technical services needed by local government. In order to benefit in this way from older in-migration, destination communities must develop facilitative structures that enhance access to volunteer opportunities. In other words, the positive impact of older in-migration is contingent on decisions and investments made by the local community.[7]

Local institutional capacity is a difficult concept to conceptualise and measure (Cocklin & Alston, 2003; Flora & Flora, 2003). Speaking generically, capable institutions are able to manage and resource their own affairs, mobilise their residents towards the common good, and plan for the future. For example, consider local government. Effective governments are able to conduct general governance and policymaking, raise revenue and prepare budgets, provide essential services and plan for the future. To do this they need effective leadership, sufficient fiscal resources, an effective organisational structure, access to and ability to analyse information, technical expertise (hard and soft), and a future orientation and planning process. Communities with high capacity are able to take advantage of opportunities, such as the in-migration of older persons, while places lacking capacity are more likely to be overwhelmed by the challenges posed by change, including demographic change. Moreover, as Warner (2003) has indicated, effective local communities are able to balance government, the private sector and civil society. She contends that communities that are able to balance the cooperative and competitive pressures among these three domains are more likely to experience a virtuous cycle of local development, while communities that fail to do so tend to fall further behind.

Local community is embedded in multilevel systems

Thus far, we have treated local communities as if they were predominantly closed systems. Their populations become larger or smaller, older or younger, more or less diverse through some combination of migration and/or natural change; and these demographic transformations pose social, political and economic challenges for local people and institutions. But, in reality, local communities are embedded in multilevel domestic and global systems (Brown, 2013). As our model suggests, though, the ability to respond to population change is both facilitated and constrained by regulations and resources available from higher levels of government. Hence, high local social capital and community activism are necessary but insufficient conditions for the establishment of new, or maintenance of existing, services (see Joseph & Chalmers, 1995; Chalmers & Joseph, 2006; Woods, 2006). In fact, for many, if not most, societies, constitutional and, hence, political and financial responsibility for the provision and administration of key services lies with government agencies and departments beyond the scale of the local – and even the region in some nations – meaning that localities are not independent of higher levels. This insight is consistent with the notion of 'neo-endogenous development' whereby local and non-local actors interact to produce rural change (Shucksmith, 2010). Consider public education. In the USA, for example, education is mostly financed by local property taxes while in most other highly developed nations education is generally financed by national budgets. Hence, the decision to keep schools open in areas with declining enrolment is a national- or state/provincial-level decision in many nations, but a largely local decision in the United States. Moreover, since the USA is a federal system, each of the 50 states has its own rules regulating public school curriculum and performance standards and – perhaps more importantly – its own local taxing authority. In New York State, for example, local property tax increases are strictly restricted thereby limiting local school districts' abilities to launch new educational initiatives or shore up schools with declining enrolment. Accordingly, the same demographic situation, for example, net out-migration of young families with school-age children, can result in dramatically different outcomes in different nations – and in some nations like the USA – across communities. This issue is particularly salient for many rural communities because they often experience declines in school-age population.

Local communities, both urban and rural, are also embedded in global as well as national systems. Global–local relationships affect most aspects of local society, and in particular the competitiveness of the local economy. It is well known that many rural jobs throughout the more developed world have been lost to international competition as transnational corporations offshore manufacturing employment to low-wage nations (Slack, 2014). Globalisation has changed the calculus of economic location for national and international firms, and in relatively high-wage regions such as much of Europe, Oceania and North America has placed increased importance on labour quality as indicated by educational levels and occupational experience. To maintain strong economies in the global world, local communities must stem out-migration of well-prepared young workers, maintain investments in public education so that new cohorts entering the labour force can compete for high-skill jobs, and provide skills training and updating across the life course. As indicated above, deciding to make these kinds of investments requires a recognition that economic security depends on maintaining a competitive workforce, the political will to establish costly educational and job training programmes, and sufficient economic resources to establish and maintain programmes that support local workers and their families. Failure to make these investments results in a vicious cycle as localities become less and less competitive and more and more youth seek employment and residence elsewhere (Warner, 2003; Carr & Kefalas, 2009). Moreover, regardless of capacity, mobilisation and resources, localities must operate in an intergovernmental system that facilitates adaptation to change, and permits innovative solutions to complex problems. Contrary to the prevailing neoliberal approach to regional and local development, local rural communities are rarely in a position to summon all of the resources to make these political, social and economic investments on their own. However, with the aid of sympathetic communities, organisations and governments, often at broader scales, they can form collaborative arrangements to share resources and/or attract the kind of financial and political capital to maintain or gain new services and attempt to hold onto their populations.

Concluding observations

To understand how population growth or decline may affect society or economy, we recommend that population change be disaggregated in two important ways. First, population growth or decline should be disaggregated into different combinations of migration and natural increase. Second, we observe that changes in population size and population composition both have implications for social and economic change. With respect to disaggregating migration and natural change, the social and economic impacts of population growth resulting from a combination of net in-migration and natural increase may be different than growth that results from natural increase in combination with net out-migration. In the first example, 'all systems are go', while population may be increasing in the second example because of momentum of previous growth even if the economy is collapsing. The distinction between changes in size and composition is important because more or fewer older persons presents categorically different challenges and opportunities than more or fewer college graduates, non-native speakers or racial/ethnic minorities.

Ever since Malthus (1989 [1803]), population change has been identified as causing a wide variety of social and economic problems. While we do not dispute that population change may contribute to such problems, we observe that population change can also have positive results. In fact, more or fewer persons and/or different kinds of persons can stimulate beneficial transformations of society and economy. Moreover, challenges sometimes become opportunities. What we argue in this chapter is that the impact of population change on society and economy is complex and contingent. Localities, both urban and rural, that have similar population dynamics often experience different results depending on their institutional capacity, other resources and civic engagement, as well as their situation with respect to higher level governments and other institutions and the global economy. As Brown (2013, p. 135) has noted elsewhere, 'population matters, but demography is not destiny'.

The framework developed in this chapter has at least two critical shortcomings that we have acknowledged, but that should be reiterated: (a) our framework's direction of causation flows from population to social and economic change when, of course, we know that the relationships between population and society are bidirectional; and (b) our framework treats local communities as relatively closed systems, while we recognise that they are embedded in multilevel domestic and global processes. We purposely removed this causal process from the more complex reality of bidirectional relationships and feedbacks for heuristic reasons. We hope that this framework will contribute to more thoughtful, rigorous and conceptually informed examinations of the impacts of population change on rural society and economy. Throughout this chapter we have emphasised the importance of local capacity for effective adaptation to rural change, and fundamental to this is accurate information about current and projected future changes in a community's population, economy and social structure. We contend that understanding the nature of population–community relationships contributes to such understanding, thereby enhancing the quality of decision making at the local rural level.

Notes

1   See section introduction for a detailed account of rural population dynamics.
2   The population threshold, and other factors, delineating urban and rural varies significantly between the world's nations. UN statistics on urbanisation reflect individual country reports based on the urban definitions used in the respective countries.
3   Note: Population change also has potential impacts on the environment and natural resources, but we will not focus on them in this chapter.
4   It should be noted that social networks and pre-existing social ties to destination areas are also important motivations for moving, and for destination choice. Similarly, social ties often moor persons who might otherwise move from underdeveloped places regardless of the relative absence of economic opportunities in such places.
5   Of course, since migration is selective of young adults, chronic out-migration typically distorts age structure, thereby contributing to natural decrease in the future.
6   Note: It is not possible for a growing place to have both net out-migration and natural decrease, nor is it possible for a declining place to have net in-migration and natural increase.
7   It should be noted that if older in-migration continues over time and is not accompanied by in-migration at younger ages, natural population decrease is likely to occur as older in-migrants age in place (Glasgow & Brown, 2012). This can be a more problematic situation.

References

Argent, N (2008). Perceived density, social interaction and morale in New South Wales rural communities. *Journal of Rural Studies* 24, 245–261.

Argent, N, Tonts, M, Jones, R & Holmes, J (2011). Amenity-led migration in rural Australia: A new driver of local demographic and environmental change? In G Luck, R Black & D Race (Eds), *Demographic change in rural landscapes: What does it mean for society and the environment?* (pp. 23–44). Dordrecht: Springer.

Beale, C (1975). The revival of rural population growth in non-metropolitan America. ERS Report 605. Washington, DC: USDA-Economic Research Service.

Brown, DL (2002). Migration and community: Social networks in a multilevel world. *Rural Sociology* 67(1), 1–23.

Brown, DL (2013). European rural population change matters, but demography is not destiny. *Przeglad Socjologiczny* 30, 135–150.

Brown, DL (2014). Rural population change in social context. In C Bailey, L Jensen & E Ransom (Eds), *Rural America in a globalizing world* (pp. 299–310). Morgantown: West Virginia University Press.

Brown, DL & Eloundou-Enyegue, P (forthcoming). Age structure and development: Beyond Malthus. In G Hooks (Ed.), *The handbook of development sociology*. Berkeley, CA: University of California Press.

Brown, DL & Glasgow, N (2008). *Rural retirement migration*. Dordrecht: Springer.

Burnley, I & Murphy, P (2004). *Sea change: Movement from metropolitan to Arcadian Australia*. Oxford: Oxford University Press.

Carr, P & Kefalas, M (2009). *Hollowing out the middle: The rural brain drain and what it means for America*. Boston, MA: Beacon Press.

Chalmers, A & Joseph, A (2006). Rural change and the production of otherness: The elderly in New Zealand. In P Cloke, T Marsden & P Mooney (Eds), *Handbook of rural studies* (pp. 388–400). London: Sage.

Champion, A (2013). Changing patterns of migration: Looking back and looking forward. Presentation to the TWRI Policy & Research Conference, St William's College, York, 18 October.

Champion, A & Sheppard, J (2006). Demographic change in rural England. In P Lowe & L Speakman (Eds), *The ageing countryside: The growing older population of rural England* (pp. 29–50). London: Age Concern.

Champion, T & Hugo, G (2004). *New forms of urbanization: Beyond the urban–rural dichotomy*. Farnham: Ashgate.

Chen, M, Zhang, H, Liu, W & Zhang, W (2014). The global pattern of urbanization and economic growth: Evidence from the last three decades. PLOS One. Retrieved 19 February 2015 from http://journals.plos.org/plosone/article?id=10.1371/journal.pone.0103799.

Cocklin, C & Alston, M (2003). *Community sustainability in rural Australia: A question of capital?* Wagga Wagga: Centre for Rural Social Research.

Corbett, M (2007). *Learning to leave: The irony of schooling in a coastal community*. Halifax: Fernwood Publishing.

Davies, A & James, A (2011). *Geographies of ageing: Social processes and the spatial unevenness of population ageing*. Farnham: Ashgate.

Fielding, AJ (1982). Counter-urbanization in Western Europe. *Progress in Planning* 17(1), 3–52.

Flora, CB & Flora, JL (2003). Social capital. In DL Brown & LE Swanson (Eds), *Challenges for rural America in the twenty-first century* (pp. 214–227). University Park, PA: Pennsylvania State University Press.

Garlick, S, Waterman, P & Soar, J (2006). Human capital, regional growth and productive ageing: New perspectives for policy and practice. In Australian Local Government Association (Ed.), *Ageing in place: Implications for local government* (pp. 59–68). Deakin ACT.

Glasgow, N & Brown, DL (2012). Rural ageing in the United States: Trends and contexts. *Journal of Rural Studies* 28, 422–431.

Gottman, J (1961). *Megalopolis: The urbanized northeastern seaboard of the United States*. Cambridge, MA: MIT Press.

Halseth, G & Hanlon, N (2005). The greying of resource communities in northern British Columbia: Implications for healthcare delivery in already-underserviced communities. *The Canadian Geographer* 49(1), 1–24.

Halseth, G, Markey, S & Bruce, D (Eds). (2010). *The next rural economies: Constructing rural place in global economies*. Wallingford: CABI Publishing.

Hugo, G (1994). The turnaround in Australia: Some first observations from the 1991 Census. *Australian Geographer* 25, 1–17.

Johnson, KJ (1985). *The impact of population change on business activity in rural America*. Boulder, CO: Westview.

Johnson, KJ (2011). The continuing incidence of natural decrease in American counties. *Rural Sociology* 76(1), 74–100.

Johnson, KJ (2014). Demographic trends in nonmetropolitan America: 2000 to 2010. In C Bailey, L Jensen & E Ransom (Eds), *Rural America in a globalizing world* (pp. 311–329). Morgantown: West Virginia University Press.

Johnson, KJ & Lichter, D (2012). Rural natural increase in the new century: America's third demographic transition. In LJ Kulcsar & K Curtis (Eds), *International handbook of rural demography* (pp. 17–35). Dordrecht: Springer.

Joseph, A & Chalmers, A (1995). Growing old in place: A view from New Zealand. *Health and Place* 1(2): 79–90.

King, R, Warnes, A & Williams, A (2000). *Sunset lives: British retirement migration to the Mediterranean*. New York: Berg.

Kulcsar, LJ & Curtis, K (Eds). (2012). *International handbook of rural demography*. Dordrecht: Springer.

Lyson, T (2006). Global capital and the transformation of rural communities. In P Cloke, T Marsden & P Mooney (Eds), *Handbook of rural studies* (pp. 292–303). London: Sage.

Malthus, T (1989 [1803]). *An essay on the principle of population* (with the Variora of 1806, 1807, 1817, 1826). 2 vols. Ed. P. James. Cambridge: Cambridge University Press.

McGuirk, P & Argent, N (2011). Population growth and change: Implications for Australia's cities and regions. *Geographical Research* 49, 317–335.

Shucksmith, M (2010). Disintegrated rural development? Neo-endogenous rural development, planning and place-shaping in diffused power contexts. *Sociologia Ruralis* 50(1), 1–14.

Slack, T (2014). Work in rural America in the era of globalization. In C Bailey, L Jensen & E Ransom (Eds), *Rural America in a globalizing world* (pp. 573–590). Morgantown: West Virginia University Press.

Smailes, P, Griffin, T & Argent, N (2014). Demographic change, differential ageing, and public policy in rural and regional Australia: A three-state case study. *Geographical Research* 52, 229–249.

Smailes, P & Hugo, G (1985). A process view of the population turnaround: An Australian rural case study. *Journal of Rural Studies* 1, 31–43.

United Nations (2012). *Urban and rural areas, 2011*. New York: UN Population Division.

Vining, D & Kontuly, T (1978). Population dispersal from major metropolitan regions: An international comparison. *International Regional Science Review* 3(1), 49–73.

Walmsley, D, Epps, R & Duncan, C (1998). Migration to the New South Wales north coast 1986–1991: Lifestyle motivated counterurbanisation. *Geoforum* 29, 105–118.

Warner, M (2003). Competition, cooperation and local governance. In DL Brown & L Swanson (Eds), *Challenges for rural America in the twenty-first century* (pp. 262–271). University Park, PA: Penn State University Press.

Wetzel, D (2012). North Dakota's oil boomtowns struggle with massive population growth. AP Wire Service. Retrieved 20 February 2015 from http://www.huffingtonpost.com/2012/01/27/oil-boom-towns-western-north-dakota-struggle-deal-population-influx_n_1236472.html.

Woods, M (2006). Political articulation: The modalities of new critical politics of rural citizenship. In P Cloke, T Marsden & P Mooney (Eds), *Handbook of rural studies* (pp. 457–471). London: Sage.

Woods, M (2007). Engaging the global countryside: Globalization, hybridity and the reconstitution of rural place. *Progress in Human Geography* 31, 485–507.

Zelinsky, W (1971). The hypothesis of the mobility transition. *Geographical Review* 61(2), 219–249.

Part II
Economic Transformations

Section editor: David Freshwater

8

Economic Transformations

Understanding the Determinants of Rural Growth

David Freshwater

An ongoing global process of urbanisation has led to an increased focus on cities as the drivers of economic growth and on a reshaping of how modern economies are organised. This belief is reinforced in a number of ways. For example, in 2009 the World Bank in its flagship annual report on global development embraced the ideas of the New Economic Geography and showed that large global cities were the dominant location for economic activity when measured by GDP per square kilometre (World Bank, 2008). Similarly, the OECD has produced a number of studies showing that large urban regions account for the majority of economic growth in its member countries (OECD, 2012, 2015). And urban-focused think-tanks, such as the Brookings Institute and McKinsey in the USA, and METREX in Europe, as well as numerous academic studies, all reinforce this sense that the modern economy is an urban economy.

However, how does this modern economy actually affect rural areas, and do measures based on the spatial density of GDP (gross domestic product), such as those promoted by the World Bank, provide adequate evidence that metropolitan regions are the only drivers of economic growth? For rural regions these are important questions, because without evidence that rural regions can make effective contributions to national economic development efforts, there is a good chance that economic development investments will not be made in rural places. And, without investment in rural areas, the urban-focused story will almost certainly become true and rural regions will be marginalised, becoming producers of low-value natural resources and providers of low-skill labour to thriving metropolitan centres.

Ward (2006) describes the challenge by recognising that only if rural regions are able to demonstrate that they can contribute to national growth in a way that is complementary to metropolitan growth will the negative perspective on the role of rural be dispelled (p. 4). This positive story has two elements. The first is anecdotal and consists of examples of rural economic success. The second is a more general narrative, or model of rural economic growth, that provides a conceptual approach to rural economic development. Interestingly, Ward's comment occurred in 2006, the same year that the OECD published *The New Rural Paradigm*, which makes a similar argument for an investment-based approach to rural policy that allows rural regions to contribute to national economies.

The modern economy

Three key attributes characterise discussions of the modern economy.[1] They are: (a) the importance of *networks*; (b) the critical role of *agglomeration* effects in improving productivity; and (c) the importance of *innovation* as a driver of growth. While all three attributes are connected, they are distinct. Networks consist of electronic media, such as the Internet, high-speed data links, social media and telephones; physical connections, such as good road and rail networks, the presence of an airport with multiple direct connections, and perhaps a port; supply or value chains that link firms through various relationships that supplement pure market exchanges; and social networks, including business or professional networks that facilitate spontaneous encounters as well as formal meetings.

Agglomeration effects can be loosely thought of as the benefits of proximity and density to a particular industry, and were first identified by Alfred Marshall in the 19th century (Marshall, 1920). He described three types of agglomeration effects that benefit firms and workers: (a) the presence of a large and specialised workforce and multiple employers that provide a 'thick' labour market; (b) the presence of a diverse set of support firms that provide necessary goods and services to all the firms in an industry; and finally, (c) opportunities for managers and other decision makers to interact with each other on both a formal and informal basis. While Marshall developed his ideas on the basis of a single industry, the idea of agglomeration has more recently been extended to refer to the benefits all firms can enjoy from close proximity, recognising that linkages across industries may be as important as linkages within a single industry.

Innovation is roughly the generation of new products and processes that either creates something new, or introduces a better way of providing something that already exists. Innovation, particularly technological innovation, is a major source of productivity because it allows more or better outputs to be produced with the same set of inputs. This increases productivity – each worker produces more output. And, higher productivity increases both national wealth and worker incomes. Where induced technological change is possible, the systematic investment of resources in research and development efforts leads to new products or processes that increase social welfare. While innovation can come from the ideas of individuals, it is increasingly seen as being based on formal innovation systems – large teams of scientists and engineers who focus on a systematic search for a solution to a specific problem.

Beyond these three key drivers, another important aspect of the modern economy is that it is open. Transport costs continue to fall both for goods and people, facilitating trade; and, in recent decades, trade barriers have been reduced with an integral part of trade liberalisation being regulatory harmonisation, for example EU single market regulations. Similarly, better information provided by the Internet and e-commerce allows buyers to seek products and services from around the world. The result is not quite a 'global economy', but it is an economy where few firms and regions are able to protect their markets from competition.

The modern economy is also characterised as being 'post-industrial' in that the service sector accounts for the largest share of output and employment. Finally, the modern economy is characterised by a core workforce of highly skilled, well-paid individuals who have both high levels of formal education and/or specific occupational skills. Outside the core workforce are a large number of individuals with weaker formal education, and, perhaps, occupational skills that are not highly valued. These fringe workers compete for a declining share of employment, and experience low wages and bouts of economic insecurity.

When these characteristics of a modern economy are put together, the end result is a picture that associates the modern economy with large urban regions. Not surprisingly, leaders of large cities have seized this notion and argue that major urban centres now drive national economies, and indeed major urban centres may be more important than national economies. This lies at the core of popular narratives, such as those of Jane Jacobs (1961 1969), Richard Florida (2003), Edward Glaeser (2011) and Bruce Katz (2013). These ideas also underpin the New Economic Geography, which is based largely on assumptions about differences in productivity due to agglomeration effects and economies of scale (Krugman, 1998; Fujita & Krugman, 2004).

If the modern economy is largely seen as being urban, driven by science-based innovation, increasingly dependent upon highly skilled workers, and mainly focused on the production of services, then rural areas seem remarkably unsuited to exert much agency in this perspective. Certainly, the three historically dominant challenges of rural areas – long distance, sparse populations and lack of critical mass – remain, and are possibly even more relevant today than in the past. Yet, the premise of this section of the book is that there is a modern rural economy that can provide a decent quality of life for rural residents, and that rural firms can be competitive in larger regional, national and international contexts.

Identifying the modern rural economy

In this part of the chapter various attributes of the modern economy, described above, will be assessed in terms of their relevance for rural regions. Some attributes will be shown to be difficult, if not impossible, for rural regions to attain. Others can be shown to be relatively independent of size of place and can be achieved in rural as well as urban regions. Still others may be possible, but may need to be achieved through a different mechanism than is used in urban regions. Most importantly, while the usual narrative for the modern economy ignores most of the strengths of rural regions, it is possible to see that in many rural regions the traditional economic base is in fact part of the modern economy and is well integrated into national and international trade.

Networks and rural economies

One aspect of rurality is weak physical connectivity. Rural places have limited transport connections and distances to external markets for exports and imports are expensive both in terms of travel cost and travel time. In particular, scheduled air service is essentially non-existent in most rural places. As the degree of remoteness increases, the magnitude of the barrier caused by weak transport connections grows. Transport is important because rural economies are small and unable to produce the majority of the goods and services that residents want, so these all have to be imported at significant additional cost. On the other side of the equation, the products that rural regions export also incur high transport costs, which reduces the profit margin for rural firms.

However, electronic networks impose a relatively small penalty on rural places (see Weber & Freshwater, this volume). Indeed, at one time electronic networks were thought to lead to the 'death of distance' because places everywhere would be linked timelessly. However, while cable and satellite television and the Internet are largely available in most rural regions, the connections are often of lower quality than are found in urban places. Nevertheless, electronic networks provide greatly improved connectivity. For example, a bed and breakfast business in a remote village can have the same Internet presence as an urban hotel. Similarly, the manufacture of specialised custom fly fishing rods can market the product globally through a website.

David Freshwater

Agglomeration and rural economies

Almost by definition it is impossible for rural places to provide Marshallian agglomeration effects. The very demographic characteristics that define rurality are the opposite of the characteristics that support agglomeration. Similarly, the associated benefit of a large home market does not exist in rural regions. Irrespective of the type of industry, rural firms face a limited local market. This means that they may be forced to be inefficient producers if they cannot reach minimum efficient scale. Where transport costs are high enough to block the import of cheaper goods or services these inefficient firms may survive, but at a significant cost to their local customers. In other cases, rural firms may be able to export goods or services into a larger market to improve scale economies. Rural places near to metropolitan regions are less penalised in this respect than more remote places (see Weber & Freshwater, and Noguera & Freshwater, this volume).

Innovation and rural economies

Innovation is now seen as one of the main drivers of economic growth (HM Treasury, 2000; Aghion & Howitt, 2009). The link between increased productivity and innovation is widely recognised at both the regional and national level (Cooke & Morgan, 1993; OECD, 2011). Productivity is crucially important to regions that are not experiencing population increases, such as is true of many rural areas, because without an increase in the number of workers the only path for economic growth is through increases in worker productivity.

While there is nothing about innovation that strictly makes it an urban phenomenon, the common belief is that innovation now takes place almost exclusively in large metropolitan regions. This is largely an artefact of how innovation is commonly measured – patent counts and expenditure on research and development. Both of these are highly biased to metropolitan areas where large university, government and corporate research facilities are located. Consequently, the research efforts of small and medium-sized enterprises (SMEs) and individuals are not captured in most national or regional studies of innovation, nor are any unpatented innovations, which leaves rural innovation unmeasured because the vast majority of rural firms are SMEs.

In contrast, Baumol (2010) identifies two complementary types of innovation. The first is the formal science-based research program that invests large amounts of money and effort in a structured search for a solution to a specific problem. The other type of innovation is less structured and is based on the ideas or inspiration of an individual or small group. It is unlikely to be based on a formal research program and in many cases the innovation is not patented.

While it is true that Baumol's first type of innovation is not typically to be found in most rural regions, there is ample evidence that a significant number of disruptive innovations come from individuals and small firms located in rural regions (Freshwater & Wojan, 2014). North and Smallbone (2006) suggest that in rural regions it is difficult to separate entrepreneurship from innovation since for many rural entrepreneurs the impetus to start a business comes from having innovated as a result of being unable to find an existing product or process that resolved a problem they were experiencing (see Atterton, this volume for more on rural innovation).

Services and rural economies

In almost all developed countries the share of services in rural regions is roughly the same as the share of services in urban regions when measured at a high level of aggregation. For example, if we choose health care or education, in most OECD countries we would find that these two industries have roughly the same share of employment across urban and rural territories. From this there has been a tendency to conclude that there are only small differences in economic structure between urban and rural in developed nations and that both rural and urban have entered the post-industrial economy.

This is, however, an incorrect conclusion. A high level of aggregation – for example, the term 'manufacturing' – encompasses many different and distinct sub-categories, and masks important differences between urban and rural regions. Returning to the same two examples given above, we find that in rural regions there are only primary care hospitals, and general practitioners, while the school system is restricted to basic primary and secondary education. In urban regions all the forms of health care and education that are available in rural regions are also available. But, in addition, there are secondary and tertiary care hospitals, a full range of medical specialists and medical research facilities. Similarly, for education, there are specialised primary and secondary schools, colleges and universities, trade schools and a host of other educational services. These more advanced entities serve both the urban population where they are located, and they also serve rural people who must travel to take advantage of the services.

Openness and rural economies

The vast majority of rural regions have always been exposed to trade effects. Because they are small economies they cannot produce all the goods and services they need. Because they have to import large amounts they must also export in order to raise the funds required to buy the goods and services that cannot be produced locally. This 'export base' model has existed for centuries, but in the last 50 years the degree of exposure to trade has increased significantly, as a result of trade agreements and improved productivity in developing countries that are the main competitors for rural regions in the OECD nations. A key strength of rural economies – the natural resource-related sectors – has always been export oriented and while its relative contribution to overall GDP has declined, it remains a source of traditional and new commodities and services that cannot be produced in urban areas (see Halseth, this volume).

Insiders and outsiders in the rural workforce

The rural workforce in almost all OECD countries is older, has less formal education and earns lower incomes than its urban counterpart. More detailed analysis by Green (this volume) points to significant problems in matching workers and employer needs and the presence of significant levels of unemployment for lower-skilled workers in many rural regions. In aggregate, this suggests that in rural regions, just as in the modern urban economy, a major problem is declining employment opportunities for the majority of rural workers who lack strong skills. In rural regions this problem can be exacerbated by low geographic mobility, particularly among older workers who sensibly believe that they have limited prospects of finding work even if they move to urban areas. Staying is a preferred option where they have housing, family support and there is the possibility of occasional work found through local contacts.

Typically all rural areas, except those within a metropolitan region, have only a small group of core workers with high skills and high incomes. Many of these workers are found in regions where traditional resource industries have modernised and adopted advanced technology, replacing large numbers of unskilled workers with a few skilled operators of machines. Examples include mining-dependent regions such as the copper mining region of Antofagasta in Chile or the Alberta oil sands in Canada; forestry-dependent regions such as Karelia in Finland or the

Pacific Northwest in the USA; highly advanced farming regions, such as the dairy industry in New Zealand or large grain farms in the Ile de France region near Paris; and specialised fishing communities, such as the crab fishery in Newfoundland Canada, and ground fish in Iceland.

Summing up

It is relatively easy to find rural places that have prospered in the modern economy through a variety of strategies and in multiple countries. This provides the anecdotal evidence that 'rural' is not synonymous with economic decline. The second task of providing a narrative of modern rural economic growth is also possible. Many of the elements that are seen as defining the modern urban economy can be found in rural regions including innovation, skilled workers and the extensive use of modern ICT.

Clearly, agglomeration effects are absent in rural regions and this is what makes the rural economic development process different. The three defining characteristics of rural – distance, density and lack of critical mass – are the antithesis of agglomeration. While rural areas in close proximity to urban centres are often able to borrow capacities from their urban neighbour, and some may even become integrated into a metropolitan economy, this is not possible for more remote rural regions.

This suggests that the idea of the modern economy has some relevance for rural regions, but the modern rural economy is qualitatively different from the modern urban economy. The differences are actually an advantage for rural regions, for if the impact of the modern economy was the same in both types of regions then rural places would only be smaller versions of urban places. Instead, the differences can convey the possibility that rural regions can be complementary to urban regions. Both have different economic strengths and functions.

Positioning new rural economies for success

This final section of the introductory chapter considers how rural regions might better position themselves for economic success. Three broad principles are offered as a way to think about constructing a place-specific rural economic development approach. This lack of specificity in the advice reflects the reality that while the modern economy, irrespective of how it is described, is fundamentally changing the larger socioeconomic environment in which all regions exist, the ways in which these changes manifest themselves varies from rural region to rural region. Diversity of conditions may be increasing among rural regions in OECD countries as a result of rapid economic change: at the global level, within nations, and in specific industries and firms.

Connected

The first of the principles is the importance of improving connectivity. For rural regions, better connectivity exposes firms and residents to new ideas and new opportunities that they might otherwise not have encountered. To be sure, it also exposes them to more competition, as will be discussed later in the section. Ultimately, better connectivity is an important way to alter the impacts of long distance, low density and lack of critical mass by: bridging distance, bringing people and market participants into contact, and expanding the number of people and firms that are accessible in any rural place.

Economists, sociologists and geographers all stress the importance of networks, whether it is as market integration, social capital, or transport and communication links. One of the old defining concepts of 'rural' was a lack of connectivity due to distance, but many rural regions have overcome this barrier. Farmers in the far outback of Australia are now as aware of global commodity price movements as traders at the Chicago Mercantile Exchange. Flowers are sent by air from greenhouses in Chile, Israel and many other countries to the flower auctions in Amsterdam, and then forwarded around the world. With a combination of the Internet, websites and rapid parcel delivery by UPS, FedEx, DHL and other carriers, small, niche, rural businesses can serve global markets and grow to be significant factors in their local economy even though they sell nothing to local firms or residents.

Conserving

Conserving is the second key principle. Rural regions are hosts and guardians of the vast majority of the natural resources in every country. The role of natural resources has evolved from only extraction and transformation to include in situ non-consumptive uses. This is most evident in the forestry sector where multiple-use management practices have been the dominant strategy for public forests in most OECD countries for decades (see Halseth, this volume). But increasingly, agriculture and fisheries are under pressure to adopt management practices that go well beyond increasing production of food and fibre.

Outdoor tourism is now a far larger source of employment in many rural regions than traditional resource extraction. And urban residents, who are by far the majority of the population in developed countries, are increasingly interested in accessing rural environments for recreation and for environmental services. With this rise in urban interest there is also increased pressure for management practices that may require reductions in extraction and greater efforts at preservation.

Resolving conflicts over natural resource management is increasingly important for rural development. Important consequences include the ability to continue to extract natural resources both to meet urban demands and provide income and employment in rural regions, expanding the income and employment opportunities in rural regions from tourism, renewable energy and the provision of environmental services as new sources of income and employment, and ensuring that rural regions contribute to larger global and national commitments to green growth and mitigating climate change.

Competitive

By definition, thriving rural economies must be competitive. Rural regions have small, specialised economies that require them to be able to export a few goods and services in order to be able to import the vast majority of the goods and services they require. But success in exports is not assured. It requires that local firms be able to produce high enough quality outputs at low enough costs that they can be priced competitively in distant markets after the producing firm absorbs the transportation costs. Over the long run the standard measure of competiveness is productivity.

The OECD has demonstrated for over 25 years that some rural regions have higher productivity, GDP per worker or growth in GDP per worker than many urban regions (OECD 1994, 2012). Yet most rural regions have lower productivity than the average for urban regions. Improving productivity is central to increasing competitiveness and meeting the challenge identified by Ward and the OECD. And, competitiveness is crucial to rural regions being able to increase employment and improve incomes.

A secondary benefit of increased productivity, particularly labour productivity, is that it leads to higher local wages. Without higher productivity rural regions will face downward pressure on wages in order to maintain jobs as local firms respond to competition by controlling costs. Rural workers with few other local employment options and high relocation costs to places where jobs might be available often have no alternative to accepting low wages to maintain employment.

The necessity to be competitive is the main factor in making the economic development strategy of each rural region unique. Each region has its own specific set of resources and its own opportunities. But it also faces a specific set of competing regions and firms both urban and rural that it must contend with and specific transport costs to each market it wants to sell in. A successful economic development strategy has to consider all of these aspects and identify appropriate investments.

The rural challenge

We must expect that only some rural regions will be successful in adapting to the modern economy, and those that do not will shrink or disappear as their economic function ends. But this is equally true for some cities, which have also failed to redefine their role in the modern economy. The big challenge for rural regions is that each usually only has one chance to identify a niche that it can occupy in the larger national and global economy. For, if rural development is an investment process, most rural places only have the resources to make one investment to transform their role. If something goes wrong in the transformation, because of a bad choice or simply bad luck, there will not be a second chance. This is nothing new. History shows that many rural places have boomed and collapsed in the past. History also shows that a large number of rural places have prospered through time, many by reinventing themselves on a periodic basis.

Note

1   This chapter provides a perspective on the modern rural economy that provides a context for the other chapters in the section. However, it largely ignores the role of macroeconomic policy. While it is true that monetary, fiscal and trade policy can have a huge impact on rural economies, these policies come as exogenous shocks that are difficult to anticipate. While specific macro regimes alter opportunities and constraints for specific rural regions, the reality of rural development is that they are something that has to be adapted to.

References

Aghion, P & Howitt, P (2009). *The economics of growth*. Cambridge, MA: MIT Press.
Baumol, W (2010). *The microtheory of innovative entrepreneurship*. Princeton, NJ: Princeton University Press.
Cooke, P & Morgan, K (1993). The network paradigm: New departures in corporate and regional development. *Environment and Planning* (D) 11(5), 543–564.
Florida, R (2003). *The rise of the creative class*. New York: Basic Books.
Freshwater, D & Wojan, T (2014). User entrepreneurship: Defining and identifying an explicit type of innovation. Paper presented at the North American Regional Science Council Meetings, Bethesda, MD, December 2014.
Fujita, M & Krugman, P (2004). The new economic geography: Past, present and future. *Papers in Regional Science* 83(1), 139–164.
Glaeser, E (2011). *The triumph of the city: How urban spaces make us human*. New York: Macmillan.
HM Treasury (2000). *Productivity in the UK: The evidence and the government's approach*. London: HM Treasury.
Jacobs, J (1961). *The death and life of great American cities*. New York: Vintage.
Jacobs, J (1969). *The economy of cities*. New York: Random House.

Katz, B (2013). *The metropolitan revolution*. Washington, DC: Brookings Institution.

Krugman, P (1998). What's new about the new economic geography? *Oxford Review of Economic Policy* 14(2), 7–17.

Marshall, A (1920). *Principles of economics*. London: Macmillan.

North, D & Smallbone, D (2006). Developing entrepreneurship and enterprise in European peripheral rural areas: Some issues facing policy makers. *European Planning Studies* 14(1), 41–60.

OECD (1994). *Creating rural indicators for shaping territorial policies*. Paris: OECD.

OECD (2006). *The new rural paradigm*. Paris: OECD.

OECD (2011). *Regions and innovation policy*. Paris: OECD.

OECD (2012). *Promoting growth in all regions*. Paris: OECD.

OECD (2015). *The metropolitan century*. Paris: OECD.

Ward, N (2006). Rural development and the economies of rural areas. In J Midgely (Ed.), *A new rural agenda* (pp. 46–67). London: Institute for Public Policy Research.

World Bank (2008). *World development report 2009*. New York: World Bank.

9

The Changing Nature of Resource Economies

A Focus on the Example of Forestry

Greg Halseth

Introduction

Industrial resource commodity production provides an important lens through which to look at rural community change because the export of natural resources as inputs into advanced manufacturing processes has long been a key economic function of rural places. Such exports include fuels, minerals and ores, food and agricultural products, forest products, and others. In this chapter, the focus is on forest products as the illustrative example of broader and more general trends. Like other types of rural and small town places, those places focused on natural resource production are challenged to engage with community and regional change as a result of their narrow economic foundations – defined as single industry (and sometimes even single company) dependent.

Before moving into the chapter, it is useful to consider the topic of 'change'. While rural places and regions are enmeshed in a suite of social, economic, cultural and environmental changes, a longer term perspective reminds us that change is nothing new. In developed economies, one can trace significant ebbs and flows to dramatic social, economic, political, demographic, cultural, technological, organisational, product, market, corporate and environmental change for most of the past 100 years. Fitchen (1991, p. 259) once wrote that it is only by being immersed in change that 'the past appears stable and unchanging by contrast'. Perhaps it is better to approach the matter of contemporary (and even accelerating) change by reminding ourselves that perhaps the only 'constant' is 'change'.

Understanding the rise of the postwar commodity economy

To start, it is important to understand the rise of the industrial resource commodity economy in the immediate post-Second World War period. The war had demonstrated the value of secure raw material supply chains and the value of Fordist-style mass production of those natural resources. In the forest sector, postwar rebuilding, the baby boom, and the explosive growth of suburbanisation and single-family detached dwellings all helped fuel a demand for lumber and related wood products. The expansion of rural 'frontier' regions in Canada, the United States, Australia and New Zealand that had been tested during the war were joined by the rebuilding economies of places such as northern Sweden, Norway and Finland. The postwar forestry economy became one dominated by large firms – though often still at a national scale – that operated vertically integrated mass production manufacturing systems that were integrated into increasingly global lumber trading markets.

The production of natural resources for export has a long history in rural regions. Canadian political economist Harold Innis (1933) described the opportunities and the vulnerabilities inherent in natural resource production. His 'staples theory' (so named for the role that raw resources play as a staple or basic input into upstream manufacturing) helps to describe the social, political and economic implications of resource development. More specifically, it describes patterns of uneven development and the peripheral role that rural resource production plays within the global economy. While other economic theories predicted that staples extraction would propel the economy towards maturation through the development of higher order industries, Innis countered that diversification and maturity were neither automatic nor assured. Indeed, Innis's staples theory saw the institutional frameworks associated with staples production as posing long-term barriers to development.

Dependency

Staples theory scholars elucidated two key problems for a natural resource-based economy: 'dependency' and 'truncated development' (Drache, 1991; Haley, 2011). The dependency problem comes from the resource supply 'warehouse' orientation of the rural economy. As price-takers in the global economy, producing regions are dependent upon the demands of external markets and are thus vulnerable to sudden price and market shifts. The dependence problem is exacerbated by the challenge of truncated development. Resource development projects require world-scale firms and access to requisite levels of financing. Once in place, the region's natural resource production path becomes increasingly entrenched as industrial capital consolidates its control and management of the natural resource, needed services and regional labour. The implications of such foreign ownership 'relate to a loss of autonomy over strategic investments and technology decisions' (Hayter, 1982, p. 281).

Table 9.1 illustrates the increasing participation of multinational capital and the accelerating pace of corporate turnover. The example is from the forest-dependent community of Mackenzie in northern British Columbia (BC). The original BC Forest Products pulp and paper mill operated under its original ownership for approximately 24 years. It was then taken over by New Zealand-based Fletcher Challenge and ran under that corporate flag for 12 years. A series of short-term purchases and sales involving Norske Skog (Norway) and Pope & Talbot (USA) quickly turned over ownership. Once Pope & Talbot went bankrupt, the mill was bought by a Canadian-based holding company that then walked away from its investment. Since 2010 the mill has been operated by Indonesian-based Sinar Mas Group. In addition to the 'uncertainty' these ownership changes/bankruptcies created for the mill (which at one time constituted 25% of all jobs in the town), these changes in ownership dramatically impacted the workforce. Prolonged strikes with Fletcher Challenge, shutdowns with Pope & Talbot, the introduction of flexible labour contracts (read 'job losses'), and management layoffs by Norske Skog reduced the workforce, stressed families and the community and hampered the ability of the town to move beyond resource production since many continue to pin hopes on the 'faint hope' that the mill will come back to its glory years of full production and big employment numbers.

The 'path dependence' of natural resource production is significant as not only does industry provide the bulk of basic sector employment, but it also supports the bulk of secondary employment. The more local economies depend upon single industries, and even more with

Table 9.1 Ownership changes – original BC Forest Products pulp and paper mill in Mackenzie

1964	British Columbia Forest Products (BCFP) pulp and paper mill opens.
1988	Fletcher Challenge Canada Limited buys BCFP.
2000	Norske Skog ASA buys Fletcher Challenge Canada Limited.
2001	Pope & Talbot buys Norske Skog ASA's BC plants.
2008	Worthington Properties Inc. purchases Pope & Talbot mill.
2009	Worthington Properties Inc. abandons Mackenzie mill, forcing provincial government to manage the site.
2010	Paper Excellence, a subsidiary of Sinar Mas Group, purchases the shuttered mill.

single companies, the more the problem of unequal power and bargaining increased. Local government often had little to do except manage the delivery of basic residential services as all other key matters related to the survival of the community rested with industry. When stresses came to that industry, the local government and local community rallied behind its great benefactor to advocate for any type of change in policy or taxation that would help keep the industry operating and profitable.

Dependence is also much wider than just rural places and rural regions, however. Entire jurisdictions can become dependent on the wealth that natural resource production can generate – both from direct revenues and indirectly through taxation of workers and related spending. Freudenburg (1992) long ago described the rise of these 'addicted economies' and the barriers such addictions can have for effectively dealing with change at local, regional and national levels.

Challenges and responses

The global economic recession of the early 1980s has been labelled a watershed moment for industrial resource production. This is due, in part, to the impact of the recession on global commodity trade through a collapse in the demand for manufactured products, a loss of consumer confidence and a tightening of financial markets. But there was also an acceleration brought to a number of nascent pressures in and around these industries that had been building for some time. This section outlines two key transformations: international competition and environmentalism.

International competition

As the industrial forestry sector matured in the immediate postwar years, it came to dominate the marketplaces of developed economies. Increasing competition from low-cost production regions had been growing for years, bolstered in part by the decreasing cost of transportation due to containerisation. The recession of the early 1980s, however, provided an opening for low-cost producers to move into increasingly price-conscious marketplaces. Following that recession, there was also a dramatic increase in efforts to liberalise and globalise trading relationships such that tariff walls were reduced and opportunities were increased for the movement of lower priced goods. As well, some long-running trade disputes between consumer markets (the United States) and forest products producers (in Canada) provided further opportunity for other players to enter lucrative markets. As a result, the forest sector in OECD countries adopted aggressive cost-cutting approaches. This included reducing costs in payroll and increasing the pace and volume of production so as to lower their per-unit costs. Some firms also began shifting their own production to the 'global south' to take advantage of lower wages, lower regulatory and tax requirements and its faster growing forests.

There were other changes in production and markets along this timeline as well. One need only think of the newspaper industry – and the market opportunities for pulp and paper. After the Second World War, as suburbanisation and the growth of the middle class boomed, so did mass newspaper circulation. Television news negatively impacted circulation from the late 1960s onwards, but it was the rise of the Internet, and especially social media, that led to the demise of many large and small newspapers, a resulting dramatic collapse of the newsprint market, and the closure of newsprint mills in many rural and small town places dependent upon them for direct and indirect jobs as well as local taxation.

As part of its cost-cutting initiatives, the forest industry transitioned from a Fordist mode to a flexible mode of production. The impacts on rural places were significant. More natural resources were demanded to support the increasing scale of production, fewer workers were employed per unit volume of that production, and firms sought relief from 'expenses' such as taxation, fees and land management responsibilities. Natural resources can still be significant in rural economies, but they do not provide the employment or tax contributions that they did in the past (BC Ministry of Forests, 2014).

Environmentalism

A related significant change in developed economies is with shifting attitudes towards the environment and the use of natural landscapes for economic and industrial purposes. Awareness of human and economic impacts on natural environments had been growing since the 1950s and 1960s. Early on, the forest industry had been successful in adjusting to these concerns by including more complete utilisation of harvested trees, replanting and stewardship of those replanted forests, changes to the timing and the location of forest harvesting to reduce environmental impacts and efforts to increase the value of products from harvested wood.

As concerns about human impacts on the environment continued to grow, they could acted out in different ways. In some countries, much of the forested land is owned by the government and the forest industry gains access to that timber via a suite of tenure or lease arrangements. As these lands remain in 'public' ownership, an increasingly environmentally aware public began to want more input into what was happening on those lands. Protests in the woods, in urban areas, and in political, community and business spheres all impacted the industry (Hayter, 2003). In the 're-regulation' of public lands, some jurisdictions increased the amount of land devoted to parks or protected areas; in others there were reductions in cutting rights to protect sensitive habitat – both actions typically made with little compensation to forestry-dependent communities.

However, in other countries much of the forest industry harvesting work occurs on privately owned lands. In these cases, environmental protest had a more narrow geographic range of options. One common route was via political protest calling for dialogue around new forest governance and/or management regimes. In Finland, debate and conflict over forest use is nothing new, and various forms of collaborative planning frameworks (Raito, 2013), including 'Regional Forest Councils' (Saarikoski, Åkerman & Primmer, 2012), have been posited as options. On the industry side, Finnish firms have explored the use of environmental reporting as a way to include the public and to publicise their environmental performance (Koskela & Vehmas, 2012; Toppinen & Korhonen-Kurki, 2013).

Increasing environmental awareness has also fuelled competition over the land base from other types of uses and user groups. In terms of environmental impact concerns, perhaps one of the best known examples involved a small bird in Oregon – the Northern Spotted Owl

(Freudenburg, Wilson & O'Leary, 1998). The Northern Spotted Owl inhabits old-growth forests and has a range that stretches from southern Oregon to Canada. It is very sensitive to habitat disturbance and needs a large range for hunting and nesting. In 1990, it was listed as a 'threatened species' under the US Endangered Species Act of the federal Fish and Wildlife Service. Logging in the US National Forests of Oregon was stopped by court order in 1991 to protect the owl. Over the subsequent decades, actions under a suite of environmental and species protection legislation has significantly changed forest practices and reduced the industry (and related employment) in Oregon. At a larger scale, there has been a shift of forest industry production to southern US or global south jurisdictions that support non-union legislation and where forest harvesting occurs largely on private lands.

Finally, another critical venue for the expression of environmental concerns around natural resource products was the 'consumer'. Advertising, protests, political action and a host of other activities can be effective in raising the profile of particular issues. In some countries, protest movements (sometimes when accompanied by political parties) convinced governments to impose bans or restrictions on certain products, or products from perceived fragile ecosystems such as old-growth forests. In other cases, more general campaigns educated consumers about the types of questions they should be asking about the sourcing of the products they were considering buying. Consumers were going 'green', and the forest industry responded by seeking out environmental certifications for their activities and their products. One of the largest certification regimes now includes the Forest Stewardship Council, and its impacts are being studied in many countries (Espinoza, Buehlmann & Smith, 2012; Johansson, 2012; Buizer & Lawrence, 2014).

Special topic areas

Against the trends described above, there is also a range of topic areas whose own trajectories of change are impacting, and/or being impacted by, transitions in natural resource production. This section introduces and looks briefly at a few of these topic areas and traces some of their implications for rural transformation.

Social/political values

The immediate postwar period introduced three new dynamics into the mix of social and political values. The first involved the opportunities afforded by the new scope and scale of industrial production. Mass production techniques were now being applied to household (and housing) and consumer goods. The increases in production and consumption needed a concomitant increase in the supply of raw materials. This boom in demand drove massive new forest industry investments in many forest products exporting countries. The infusion of cash which raw material exports could bring was seen in many countries as a vital tool for postwar redevelopment.

The two other dynamics – the Cold War and the baby boom – complemented the almost insatiable need of Western industrial production for ever-increasing supplies of natural resources. Years of government-guided policy and programming to address the Depression and then to fight the war was now transformed into a government-driven suite of actions to create jobs and communities and fulfil the promise of a 'good life' after so many years of hardship.

Fifty years later, much has changed. A Keynesian public policy approach has transitioned into a neoliberal public policy approach. Investments in rural places are now viewed as expenses even in countries where natural resource wealth from rural regions still makes major contributions to the national economy. Government-led initiatives have been replaced by public scepticism as to government intentions and increasing demands for greater openness and public participation. The baby boom in most developed countries has been replaced by stagnant population growth and dramatic population ageing.

Land

In the immediate postwar period, the land, especially remote rural lands, were often seen as 'unused opportunities' for enhanced resource exploitation and candidate sites for the faster growth of productive forests through the application of scientific management. Rural resource lands were sold, or the tenure rights were allocated, and transportation infrastructure to move raw materials to market was constructed. All of this was done with little regard for the people, cultures and economies that may have existed in those rural spaces for centuries. Indigenous and Aboriginal populations were especially impacted (Gjertsen & Halseth, 2015).

Again, 50 years later a great deal has changed. Aboriginal rights and title have been affirmed in many jurisdictions, and these populations are now exercising their rights for not only a greater say in development, but also a greater share of the benefits from any development that does occur. Lands that were once allocated to single-use forest harvesting activity now must be multifunctional and allow access to a wider range of users and user groups. In concert with the rise of environmentalism there has been a diversification of the types of values that natural resource landscapes provide. This has supported the expansion of new resource-based industries such as outdoor recreation, tourism, ecotourism, experiential tourism and other variants. A wider range of intrusive and non-intrusive, as well as extractive and non-extractive, activities now vie for access to rural lands and landscapes. Forest lands, in particular, have been a key part of this re-evaluation of rural landscapes.

At one time, forest lands were looked at only in terms of their raw timber supply for lumber, pulp, paper and wood panel products. Today, in addition to these products, the debate now includes a wider range of timber-based products including biofuels, biopharmaceuticals and a host of inputs into upstream bioeconomy processing. Also of note are a host of non-timber forest products, as well as the economic contributions of forest lands via various types of recreation and outdoor living activities. Forests are also now recognised as contributing value through a range of ecosystem services such as the production of clean air, clean water, bird and wildlife habitat and, of course, carbon storage. Finally, competition over the economic values of forest lands is also challenged by those advocating for the intrinsic values of wild, natural, unspoiled, forested landscapes.

Firms

The immediate postwar period witnessed the rise of large national and multinational firms. The large firm spawned such social trends as the 'company man' and a burgeoning management middle class. Whether independently owned or traded on the stock market, the typical characteristics of forestry sector firms included that they were vertically integrated, had robust corporate planning and management structures and had a significant presence in the locales where they conducted their primary operations. In production they were models of 'Fordism', and in their relationships with forest-dependent communities they tended to be models of 'paternalism'.

The global economic recession of the early 1980s impacted commodity trade so much that the forest industry firms that remain today are almost unrecognisable from their earlier incarnations. Lean management has meant layoffs of 'white collar' staff – to the point where firms are often unable to effectively respond to opportunities or changes due to a lack of internal capacity. Lean production, and the substitution of capital for labour, has also meant 'blue collar' job losses. These have especially impacted the forest-dependent communities that long relied on these jobs. While technology change had always been part of industrial forestry, advancements from harvesting to marketing helped to quicken the pace of change and job losses. Computer-assisted flexible production was especially important as it replaced the older labour-intensive Fordist approach – even though some firms remain stuck in the commodity production 'box' (Edenhoffer & Hayter, 2013). Finally, firms have also withdrawn from many of the active ways they supported rural communities beyond the wages of production employees.

A corporate strategy that focuses upon traditional commodity production but also seeks to address trade barriers and costs of production is reflected in the Canadian firm West Fraser Timber. Starting as a family-owned sawmill company in the small town of Quesnel, British Columbia, today West Fraser is the largest lumber producer in North America (West Fraser, 2014). In 2014, it had about 7,000 employees, and annual sales of over $3 billion. Beginning in 2000, the company began a new strategy that included a major expansion into the United States – specifically the southeastern USA where southern pine grew fast and supported a significant lumber industry. The US expansion also allowed the company to bypass the ongoing Canada–US lumber trade disputes and remain a key supplier in the US market. West Fraser operates a total of 26 lumber mills: 12 in western Canada (British Columbia and Alberta) and 14 in the southeastern USA (North Carolina, South Carolina, Georgia, Tennessee, Alabama, Arkansas, Louisiana, Texas and Florida).

Products

Related to the transformation of firms, there have also been significant transformations in the types of forest industry products. Access to large-diameter old-growth timber meant easy production of lumber products. The improvements in pulp and paper production technologies meant that smaller diameter stands of slower growing northern forests could be utilised in an expansion of this 'value added' sector in the 1960s and 1970s.

Overcutting, and recognition that second-growth forests do not generate the same volume of biomass as old-growth forests, has led to production diversification and product innovation. Also contributing has been marketplace/public concerns about the efficient use of all harvested wood so as to reduce environmental impacts. Another comes from the long-term downward pressure on commodity prices, and profits, from the recursive relationships between global competition, the application of technology to support greater production efficiency, and the need to increase production levels to repay the capital required for that more efficient technology/equipment (which only puts more product into the marketplace thereby putting further downward pressure on prices). This means that firms have looked to previous production wastes as new sources of income, commodities and profit chains. Much of this innovation is concentrated around the general concept of engineered wood. Strips, chips, trim ends, sawdust and even finer grains of wood are now recombined with glues and subjected to heat and pressure to create particle boards, finger-jointed lumber, chipboards, oriented strand boards, glue-lam beams, para-lam beams, medium density fibreboard and a host of other new products that make use of previous industrial waste and create cheaper products and product substitutes in the marketplace.

Policy

Many developed economies used regulation, investment, public policy and even government-owned lands to support a massive expansion of natural resource production after 1950. Incentives, tax breaks, public spending on infrastructure, subsidies, cheap energy supply and other tools helped attract global industrial capital to rural hinterlands. In many countries, this helped establish the natural resource industries that supported the long boom of manufacturing economies into the 1970s. As noted above, this Keynesian public policy approach set the foundation for over 30 years of rural development.

The neoliberal response to post-1980 economic stagnation was to aggressively remove trade barriers and other impediments to the 'free functioning' of the marketplace. International trade agreements and modifications to global trading structures such as the General Agreement on Tariffs and Trade (GATT) opened new markets and introduced new competitors. Within these agreements there were also restrictions on what individual countries could do to manage or intervene in their own economies. As countries lost some of their power and authority to act, so too did they purposefully deconstruct their own capacity to act. Under a neoliberal policy agenda, efforts at tax reduction resulted in a reduction in the size and regulatory power of government. It has been left in a reduced position that affects its ability to plan and respond to change.

But policy impacts are wide reaching and span all of the topics raised in this chapter. At local and regional levels, for example, public policy actions became further limited by fiscal crises, deficits and debt. 'Addicted' local and regional government tax bases could not maintain earlier spending trajectories as resource rents and other revenues failed to keep pace. Older infrastructure (physical and human) was allowed to run its course and reinvestment has been severely limited. As noted, public policy (and public benefit) was often sacrificed to support industrial profitability and continued operation.

Communities

One of the keys behind a place-based approach to community development is recognition that it is the locality, in this case rural communities, where the impacts of change and transformation across the global economy, multinational firms, international trade agreements, national and regional public policy, infrastructure investment and a host of other external 'shocks' are felt (Markey, Halseth & Manson, 2012). Rural places have no influence or control over these shocks, but they feel their impact, and they must respond.

Since 1980 rural places have been impacted by all the pressures described above. In general, how they have responded has been problematic. To start, the trajectory of the past has a powerful momentum that is difficult to change. Local leaders, economies, labour, infrastructure and other trappings of power and authority were vested in the old economy. It has been difficult for many rural places and regions to change, difficult for them to see an alternative future. Further, against the economic, policy and political advantages sent out for industrial capital, communities have few options by which to respond, or even to organise to respond in ways that Galbraith (1956) would have called a 'countervailing power'.

There was also a key transformation in the way local government in forest-dependent communities was required to act. Previously, it had played a limited managerial role – concerned with the delivery of basic services to residents and property. But under economic decline, government reticence to intercede, and neoliberal approaches that put increasing demands on local government to divine its own social and economic destiny, rural local governments now had to transition (somewhat uncomfortably) into an entrepreneurial role. That is, they had to take responsibility for attracting industry, capital, labour and support sectors to their community. They increasingly had to market their own place and the opportunities it might afford to capital.

Future directions

It is always a speculative gamble to posit comments about the future. In the case of forestry, and its role in rural places and regions, this is especially challenging given the range of pressures and responses outlined above. Through the following examples, the themes of change and opportunity reflect how rural places have always had to adapt to the realities of the times. They also reflect some new ways to reimagine and re-bundle their development assets (natural resource and otherwise) to sustain the economy, employment and communities. In other cases, they identify troubling trends that may see rural areas transformed in ways that do not create local jobs or support local communities.

To pull out the environmental thread, it seems that increasing concern over climate change, the need to better manage our industrial 'carbon balance' and the competing values around forested landscapes as everything from economic drivers to being good for the human soul means that approaches to rural land management will increasingly reflect multifunctionality. Debate over 'carbon trading' and its short- and long-term impacts on rural places are especially pronounced in New Zealand where the government introduced an Emissions Trading Scheme in 2008 (Bullock, 2012). As with earlier staples theory concerns, much of the early evidence suggests that any positive benefits are precariously linked to rising carbon pricing (Adams & Turner, 2012; Manley & Maclaren, 2012).

In rural southwest England, such an approach has put down early roots. Forested areas that had long ago been cleared for agriculture are now being returned to forests. Under a complex schedule of fees and carbon credits, urban industries are funding the replanting and tending of new forests. In addition to carbon sequestration, and the greening of the landscape, the relatively open access that traditional use rights afford to the English countryside means that fresh air and exercise in nature is increasingly available to the general public. These reforested lands will also impact water quality and wildlife and bird habitat. Rural regions can expect pressure to support these forms of multifunctionality to increase. But will the survival of rural communities/economies be sacrificed to the sins of urban/industrial pollution?

To draw out the economic thread a bit further, there is the emergent role of the bioeconomy. With many environmental concerns linked to the petroleum economy, there is a chance that product substitution with greener/renewable commodities will provide a base for the retooling of older rural industry and the creation of new rural investments and jobs. Along this path, early innovation adopters will need to be subsidised until technologies are better tested and cost effective (typical of all new processes and technologies). As a nascent industry, partnerships appear to be a key element in the further development of biorefineries (Ekman et al., 2013; Näyhä & Pesonen, 2012, 2014).

A good start on the manufacturing side of the bioeconomy is already under way. In Sweden, a former pulp mill in Örnsköldsvik has been transformed into a biorefinery. Located in mid-Sweden, the original sulphite pulp mill opened in 1903 (Domsjö Fabriker – Aditya Birla Group, 2014). The transition to a 'green' biorefinery was based on a simple premise: 'Oil is a fossil biomass. Therefore, whatever is based on oil can also be based on wood … Skillfully utilising the various constituents of wood makes it possible to develop and manufacture many products to replace oil as raw material or energy source' (Domsjö Fabriker, 2010, p. 4). Today, products include specialty cellulose, lignin, biogas, bioethanol, bioresin and carbon acid. End products can range from fuel and energy to detergents to paints to toothpaste to automobile tires to food products. A current focus is textiles, especially after Domsjö Fabriker was acquired in 2011 by the Indian consortium Aditya Birla Group.

A more basic approach is expanded utilisation of forest harvest residuals to support a bioenergy industry. In Norway, where forested lands have been expanding as a result of farmland abandonment (Bryn, Dourojeanni, Hemsing & O'Donnell, 2013) and where forest industry production costs are high, domestic substitution of fossil fuels with 'green' bioenergy has received considerable attention (Forbord, Vik & Hillring, 2012; Brough, Rørstad, Breland & Trømborg, 2013; Trømborg et al., 2013) for its potential to protect land and also create some local employment.

And then there is the industrial production of basic lumber and pulp commodities from the forest. The increasing competition from low-cost production regions, and changes in demands due to recycling, electronic media and so on, is likely to increase. While much has been written about the clear-cutting of the Amazonian rainforest, less has been written about Siberia, where a new north–south rail link from the Trans-Siberian Railway now reaches to the city of Yakutsk in eastern Siberia. The line runs through the eastern heart of the largest boreal forest on the planet and one that has ready access to the two largest emergent markets for wood products – China and India.

Taken together, the environment and economy often collide in debates over climate change. Reconciling forest management policies with climate change obligations under agreements such as the Kyoto Protocol now occupies debate in many countries. In France, the 'green shift' in forest policy brings together issues ranging across ecological diversity, sustainable forest management, eco-certification, renewable energy transition and the impacts of postwar forest use and reforestation (González-García et al., 2013; Tissot & Kohler, 2013; Sergent, 2014). The challenge for rural places is how to navigate these pressures to create the opportunities for a local economy that will sustain jobs and communities.

Closing comments

Resource-based development, and the rural places that depend upon such development, will continue for the foreseeable future. Challenging markets, an increasing price squeeze, the need to stay cost competitive and an erosion of local benefits are part of a wider suite of transformations in the global economy that include public policy, Aboriginal/Indigenous rights and attitudes towards the environment. These transformations have replaced the now outdated 'overcoming the cost of distance' approach to getting rural resources to market. Today there is a more nuanced, complicated and interwoven web of economic, social, cultural, ethical and environmental considerations to not just whether we extract natural resources but even how we think about the relationship between people, places, environments and economies (locally and globally) over both the short- and long-term. Witness the debates around forestry in Oregon, oil drilling in Alaska, oil and gas fracking anywhere it occurs, the Northern Gateway pipelines in BC and the Keystone XL pipeline in the United States. Each includes multilayered and multifaceted arguments both for and against (and many that seem to simply swirl about in the middle between support and opposition) that range across issues (sometimes selectively chosen and sometimes all-encompassing) and spatial scales.

This chapter has sought to tell a broader story about the changing nature of resource economies through the example of transformations within the forest industries of developed economies. The challenges and transitions described herein will continue to shape and change rural places and rural regions, and they will continue to shape and change rural economies and rural livelihoods. The difficult choices ahead will involve investments in rural community development to support an economic platform that allows for a revaluing and re-bundling of local assets to allow for new and sustainable economic values to be mobilised.

Acknowledgement

This chapter was supported by the Canada Research Chairs program grants 950-222604 and 950-203491.

References

Adams, T & Turner, J (2012). An investigation into the effects of an emissions trading scheme on forest management and land use in New Zealand. *Forest Policy and Economics* 15, 78–90.

BC Ministry of Forests (2014). *Employment in the forest industry in BC*. Available at http://www.for.gov.bc.ca/hfp/publications/00001/3-2g-can-employ.htm (accessed 4 March 2014).

Brough, P, Rørstad, P, Breland, T & Trømborg, E (2013). Exploring Norwegian forest owner's intentions to provide harvest residues for bioenergy. *Biomass and Bioenergy* 57, 57–67.

Bryn, A, Dourojeanni, P, Hemsing, L & O'Donnell, S (2013). A high-resolution GIS null model of potential forest expansion following land use changes in Norway. *Scandinavian Journal of Forest Research* 28, 81–98.

Buizer, M & Lawrence, A (2014). The politics of numbers in forest and climate change in Australia and the UK. *Environmental Science & Policy* 35, 57–66.

Bullock, D (2012). Emissions trading in New Zealand: Development, challenges and design. *Environmental Politics* 21(4), 657–975.

Domsjö Fabriker (2010). *We are part of the green future*. [Brochure]. Örnsköldsvik, Sweden.

Domsjö Fabriker – Aditya Birla Group. (2014). http://www.domsjo.adityabirla.com/ (accessed 23 July 2014).

Drache, D (1991). Harold Innis and Canadian capitalist development. In G Laxer (Ed.), *Perspectives on Canadian economic development: Class, staples, gender, and elites* (pp. 22–49). Don Mills, ON: Oxford University Press Canada.

Edenhoffer, K & Hayter, R (2013). Organizational restructuring in British Columbia's forest industries 1980–2010: The survival of a dinosaur. *Applied Geography* 45, 375–384.

Ekman, A, Campos, M, Lindahl, S, Co, M, Börjesson, P, Karlsson, E & Turner, C (2013). Bioresource utilisation by sustainable technologies in new value-added biorefinery concepts – two case studies from food and forest industry. *Journal of Cleaner Production* 57, 46–58.

Espinoza, O, Buehlmann, U & Smith, B (2012). Forest certification and green building standards: Overview and use in the U.S. hardwood industry. *Journal of Cleaner Production* 33, 30–41.

Fitchen, J (1991). *Endangered spaces, enduring places: Change, identity, and survival in rural America*. Boulder, CO: Westview Press.

Forbord, M, Vik, J & Hillring, B (2012). Development of local and regional forest based bioenergy in Norway: Supply networks, financial support and political commitment. *Biomass and Bioenergy* 47, 164–176.

Freudenburg, WR (1992). Addictive economies: Extractive industries and vulnerable localities in a changing world economy. *Rural Sociology* 57(3), 305–332.

Freudenburg, WR, Wilson, LJ & O'Leary, DJ (1998). Forty years of spotted owls? A longitudinal analysis of logging industry job losses. *Sociological Perspectives* 41(1), 1–26.

Galbraith, JK (1956). *American capitalism: The concept of countervailing power*. Boston, MA: Houghton Mifflin.

Gjertsen, T & Halseth, G (Eds). (2015). *Sustainable development in the Circumpolar North – From Tana, Norway to Oktemtsy, Yakutia, Russia: The Gargia Conferences for local and regional development (2004–14)*. Prince George, BC: Publications Series of the UNBC. Community Development Institute and Tromso, Norway: University Library at UiT The Arctic University of Norway, Septentrio Conference Series, Number 1.

González-García, S, Bonnesoeur, V, Pizzi, A, Feijoo, G & Moreira, M (2013). The influence of forest management systems on the environmental impacts for Douglas-fir production in France. *Science of the Total Environment* 461–462, 681–692.

Haley, B (2011). From staples trap to carbon trap: Canada's peculiar form of carbon lock-in. *Studies in Political Economy* 88, 97–132.

Hayter, R (1982). Truncation, the international firm and regional policy. *Area* 14(4), 277–282.

Hayter, R (2003). The 'war in the woods': Post-Fordist restructuring, globalization and the contested remapping of British Columbia's forest economy. *Annals of the Association of American Geographers* 93(3), 706–729.

Innis, H (1933). *Problems of staple production in Canada*. Toronto: Ryerson Press.

Johansson, J (2012). Challenges to the legitimacy of private forest governance – The development of forest certification in Sweden. *Environmental Policy and Governance* 22, 424–436.

Koskela, M & Vehmas, J (2012). Defining eco-efficiency: A case study on the Finnish forest industry. *Business Strategy and the Environment* 21, 546–566.

Manley, B & Maclaren, P (2012). Potential impact of carbon trading on forest management in New Zealand. *Forest Policy and Economics* 24, 35–40.

Markey, S, Halseth, G & Manson, D (2012). *Investing in place: Economic renewal in northern British Columbia.* Vancouver: UBC Press.

Näyhä, A & Pesonen, H (2012). Diffusion of forest biorefineries in Scandinavia and North America. *Technological Forecasting & Social Change* 79, 1111–1120.

Näyhä, A & Pesonen, H (2014). Strategic change in the forest industry towards the biorefining business. *Technological Forecasting & Social Change* 81, 259–271.

Raitio, K (2013). Discursive institutionalist approach to conflict management analysis – The case of old-growth forest conflicts on state-owned land in Finland. *Forest Policy and Economics* 33, 97–103.

Saarikoski, H, Åkerman, M & Primmer, E (2012). The challenge of governance in regional forest planning: An analysis of participatory forest program processes in Finland. *Society and Natural Resources* 25, 667–682.

Sergent, A (2014). Sector-based political analysis of energy transition: Green shift in the forest policy regime in France. *Energy Policy* 73, 491–500.

Tissot, W & Kohler, Y (2013). *Integration of nature protection in forest policy in France.* EFICENT-OEF, Freiburg: INTEGRATE Country Report.

Toppinen, A & Korhonen-Kurki, K (2013). Global reporting initiative and social impact in managing corporate responsibility: A case study of three multinationals in the forest industry. *Business Ethics* 22(2), 202–217.

Trømborg, E, Ranta, T, Schweinle, J, Solberg, B, Skjevrak, G & Tiffany, D (2013) Economic sustainability for wood pellets production. A comparative study between Finland, Germany, Norway, Sweden and the US. *Biomass and Bioenergy* 57, 68–77.

West Fraser (2014). www.WestFraser.com (accessed 4 March 2014).

10

The Emerging Contours of Rural Manufacturing

Stuart A. Rosenfeld and Timothy R. Wojan

Preface

In most advanced national economies, a political consensus is forming that manufacturing is vital to growth. Not only does manufacturing affect direct and indirect employment, but it disproportionately contributes to exports, innovation, and research and development. In these advanced economies, manufacturing accounts for 70% of global trade, 77% of private sector R&D, and 37% of productivity growth (Manyika et al., 2012). Every dollar or euro of manufacturing output requires 19 cents in service inputs. But what is produced in these economies and how it is produced is in a state of flux. Increased competition for routine operations that rely on low-skilled labour has forced many manufacturers to either automate or outsource, reducing proportions of employment in manufacturing. In manufacturing sectors able to compete, labour has shifted towards more technical and creative competencies and higher proportions of service jobs.

How do these patterns affect rural regions where manufacturing has long been an important source of employment and wealth? How will they be able to competitively develop, attract and retain industry in the future? What comparative advantage do rural places have for making things and where will their opportunities for retaining and growing jobs from the production of goods lie?

This chapter explores: (1) the changing landscape of rural manufacturing; (2) issues influencing the potential of manufacturing in rural areas; (3) the potential for developing and sustaining manufacturing in rural areas; and (4) what it will take to make that happen.

The changing landscape of manufacturing

The heavy penetration of manufacturing into rural areas in the United States did not occur until the second half of the 20th century, spurred by a low-cost labour force made redundant by the mechanisation of agriculture. State and local governments, particularly in the South, used labour and land along with new investments in roads and utilities to attract industry. Together with generous financial incentives and favourable tax policies these factors provoked a massive migration of manufacturing from urban to rural areas (Summers et al., 1976).

Similar shifts to lower cost and remote rural areas occurred in some parts of Europe. But in more densely populated rural areas, locally owned producers were embedded in the social fabric and culture of their communities. Much of Europe's industrial strength was based on specialised, artisanal, locally owned manufacturing firms that collectively and collaboratively produced place-based goods. Proximity to those who designed and produced their equipment and to demanding customers spurred innovation, as exemplified by Sassuolo's ceramic tile district and Castel Goffredo's hosiery district in Italy, Ibi's toy district in Spain, and the Outer Hebrides' Harris tweed in Scotland.

The pattern of relative prosperity for rural manufacturing in the USA slowed measurably in the 1980s and 1990s, as advantages shifted from cost of goods to quality, precision and time to market. Western Europe and Japan, with greater emphasis on process innovation and collaboration, surged ahead. To catch up, the USA took steps to help SMEs (small and medium-sized enterprises) modernise, first through its rural community colleges (Rosenfeld, 1998), then, in the 1990s, through the federal and state-supported Manufacturing Extension Partnership (MEP).

The diffusion of technology and management practices that made rural manufacturers much more competitive (Gale, 1998; Gale, McGranahan, Teixeira & Greenberg, 1999), however, did not stop at the borders of the technologically advanced nations. Advanced and prosperous economies educated and trained technicians and scientists and facilitated the diffusion of knowledge and advanced production technologies to less-developed nations, where costs of doing business are significantly lower. In the USA, the normalisation of trade relations with China in 2000 marked a critical structural shift in the pattern of global manufacturing, demarcating the most relevant time period for examining rural manufacturing employment trends (Pierce & Schott, 2012).

The ubiquitousness of technology and skills affects urban and rural places differently. Rural parts of advanced economies are struggling more than urbanised areas with more diversified economies. To compete, rural manufacturers are either relocating, shifting routine operations to lower cost locations or automating. Overall, the proportion of the total workforce employed in manufacturing in the 24 OECD (Organisation for Economic Co-operation and Development) countries declined from 24.5% in 1970 to 17.8% in 1995 to 13.4% in 2009. Among all 30 OECD countries in 2009, manufacturing employment rose to 15.9% of total employment, indicating a higher manufacturing share in most accession countries. This aggregate, however, masks important differences across OECD countries, with Germany (18.5%) and Italy (19.3%) employing close to a fifth of all workers in manufacturing in 2009, while fewer than 1 in 10 work in manufacturing in the UK (9.8%) and the USA (8.9%).

The decline in manufacturing employment shares is nearly universal in predominantly urban, intermediate, rural adjacent, and rural remote regions (Figure 10.1). Comparing rural manufacturing employment shares with urban employment shares in OECD countries suggests that: in general, (1) rural manufacturing shares tend to be higher than urban shares; and (2) among rural areas, those that are adjacent to metro areas tend to support higher shares of manufacturing. The exception within OECD countries of declining trends are in Eastern European countries that tend to have lower labour costs, where manufacturing employment shares are higher and, at least for Hungary and Poland, have been more stable. Anecdotal evidence suggests that the relocation of some manufacturing activities from higher cost Western European economies is helping to reinforce the manufacturing economy in these countries.

Detailed industry and geographic data on manufacturing employment in the USA between 2001 and 2013 allow comparing trends between metropolitan, non-metropolitan adjacent to metro, and non-adjacent non-metropolitan areas by technology intensity. The industry classification developed by the OECD labels industries as low tech (e.g., food, wood, textiles), medium low tech (e.g., basic and fabricated metals, rubber), medium high tech (e.g., electrical machinery, motor vehicles, chemicals), or high tech (e.g., pharmaceuticals, computing and

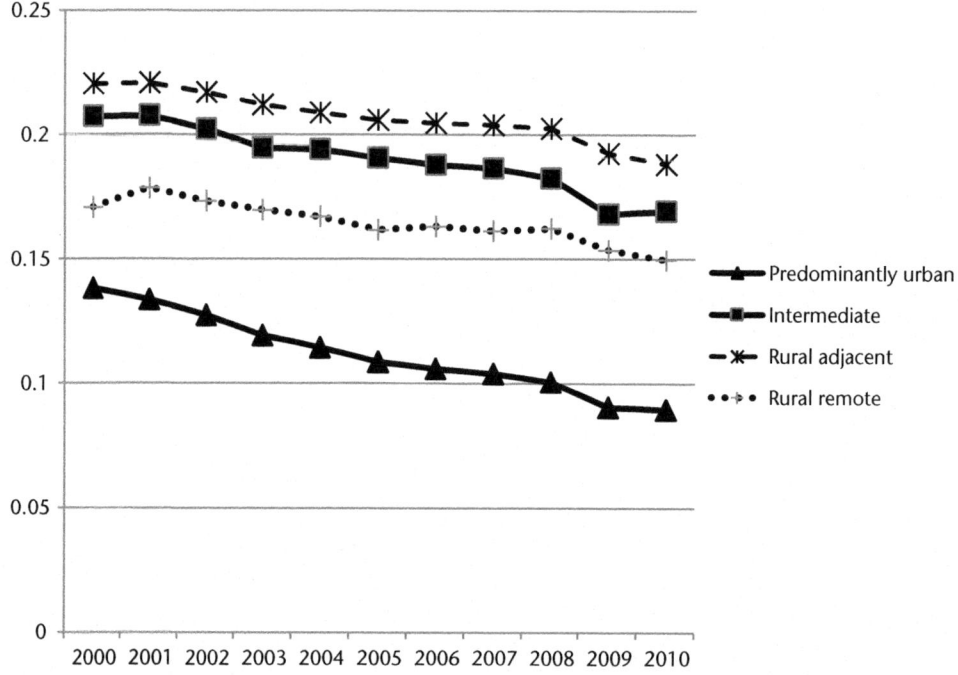

Figure 10.1 Manufacturing employment shares in collection of select OECD countries, by OECD regional typology

Note: The countries supplying manufacturing employment data to the OECD Regional Database over the time period include Austria, Denmark, Hungary, Ireland, Slovenia, Sweden and the United Kingdom.

Source: OECD Regional Database.

communications equipment, aerospace) based on industry technology intensity and technology intensity of principal input industries.

These are the salient points regarding trends of US manufacturing in the new millennium:

- Employment declined from 2001 to 2013 in all industry groups across all geographies.
- Declines in the low technology industries were continual throughout the period, and amounted to roughly 70% of their 2001 level for metro, non-metro adjacent, non-metro non-adjacent counties.
- Declines in medium low-tech industries were also surprisingly similar across all three. The main difference with low-technology industries has been very modest employment growth to roughly 80% of the 2001 level after hitting a trough of 73% during the great recession of 2008.
- The medium high-tech industries demonstrated different employment growth dynamics in recovery. Non-metro adjacent counties experienced the strongest recovery, going from 72% of their 2001 level in 2009 back to 85% in 2013. Non-adjacent counties recovered to 80% of their 2001 level in 2013 with metro counties returning to 76% of their 2001 level.
- Employment trends in the high-technology industries demonstrate a more modest non-metro adjacent advantage over metro areas – 85% versus 81% of 2001 levels, respectively – while employment in non-adjacent non-metro counties declined to 71% of their 2001 level as of 2013.

The results suggest that raising the level of technology has some benefits for rural areas, but is not a panacea. Non-adjacent non-metro counties appear to face the most serious challenges in retaining manufacturing employment as they share in the decline of low- and medium-low-technology industries but also experienced steeper declines in high-tech employment.

Factors reshaping manufacturing in rural areas

This section examines factors that contribute to the trends that can provide insights as to the types of companies that can best operate successfully in rural areas. Among the most important factors are automation, globalisation, education, innovation and location.

Automated production

The level of automation that was predicted half a century ago but was largely unrealised is now becoming a reality (Stiglitz, 2014). Mass production factories once teeming with human activity increasingly are populated by rows of automated production and materials-handling machines, approaching the futuristic full computer-controlled automation described by Kurt Vonnegut in *Player Piano* in 1952. 'Factories are becoming vastly more efficient, thanks to automated milling machines that can swap their own tools, cut in multiple directions and "feel" if something is going wrong, together with robots equipped with vision and other sensing systems … The days of huge factories full of lots of people are not there anymore' (*Economist*, 2012).

Global competition among advanced nations in the 1980s and 1990s led to policies and programs to encourage the deployment of digital technologies to rural factories, accelerating automation. Although increasing production efficiencies, this led to redundancies in shop and mid skilled production jobs, which had given rural areas an advantage. The demands for a much smaller but more highly skilled workforce are less easily met in rural areas, where so many of the most talented young people continue on to higher education, different career paths and migrate to the cities.

Global competition

Competition from abroad is among the strongest influences on rural manufacturing. The accessibility of production technologies, knowledge and skilled labour in lower cost less-developed and emerging economies has negated the cost advantages that brought and/or sustained rural manufacturing in OECD countries. Also, rapid advances in communications and transportation have created global supply chains that allow companies to outsource many aspects of production that once dominated rural economies of the United States and Europe.

The first and hardest hit by global competition were non-durable goods sectors. With the phase-out of the Multifiber Arrangement in 2004, trade quotas that had protected many apparel and textile industries in developed countries were eliminated, resulting in a steep decline of these sectors (USDA-ERS, 2012).

The dilemma that global supply chains create for rural manufacturing employment is that the production component in the chain that traditionally accounted for the bulk of jobs is increasingly adding the least value, while elements that are more likely to be found in urban areas are adding more value. The OECD uses 'the smiling curve' to graphically demonstrate changes in the distribution of value along the global value chain (OECD, 2013). The corners of the smile represent R&D and product-oriented services at the beginning and end of the chain, respectively, which are adding more value currently than was true in the 1970s. Increases in value of intermediate pre-production (design) and post-production (marketing) reinforce the turn-up at the corners. The only part of the value chain providing a smaller share of value is production, at the centre of the smile, with supply logistics and distribution holding steady.

Some rural places have managed to retain production by integrating specialised products with intangible functions in the supply chain such as design and cultural identity. Greenville, Mississippi is able to continue to make kitchen appliances and Tupelo, Mississippi motion furniture, through a combination of taking advantage of global value chains for some mass-produced parts and components, but mainly by establishing a regional identity. Others use globalisation to realise post-production intangibles. Hosiery companies in Italy's Castel Goffredo are opening new markets overseas, retaining high levels of production at home and outsourcing where necessary, primarily within Italy (Capasso, Cusmano & Morrison, 2013).

Increased skill requirements

The availability of labour has played a large part in the development of rural manufacturing over the past century. In the United States and remote rural areas of Europe, redundant agricultural labour attracted labour-intensive production. In more populated and already industrialised rural parts, particularly in Europe, the contextual skills and tacit knowledge of the local labour force have been the sustaining force. In both Europe and the United States, rural post-compulsory, pre-baccalaureate colleges have been leading sources of a skilled workforce. In Europe, a long tradition of apprenticeship-based vocational education governed by social partnerships among government, industry and labour meet workforce needs. In the USA, relationships between industry and community colleges help match education to rural workforce needs.

Manufacturers generally rank access to and retention of a skilled local workforce among the highest of all factors influencing location and expansion. For example, Gadsden State Community College's Bevill Technology Centre was instrumental in bringing an automotive cluster to northern Alabama, while Oulu South in Finland attributes much of the growth of its electronics cluster to a technical college (Virkkala, 2007).

Across both Europe and the USA, however, interest in vocational preparation for manufacturing among young people is waning (Mourshed, Patel & Suder, 2014). Youth in both urban and rural regions are choosing educational paths that lead either to baccalaureate degrees or towards careers in sectors that seem more attractive or offer better long-term opportunities. The still-prevalent image of labour-intensive, low-paying manufacturing, coupled with documented declines in production employment, diverts many of the brightest rural youth into other career paths that are more prevalent in cities.

Capacity to innovate

Innovation, often described as a predominantly urban research or technology-driven phenomenon in the literature (World Bank, 2009; Katz & Bradley, 2013; Carlino & Kerr, 2014), also is a powerful source of wealth creation in rural areas. Using hard statistics such as patents per capita, the largest US metro areas score six times higher than in non-metro counties. Science- and engineering-based innovation tends to co-locate with elite higher education in industrialised nations, which is nearly exclusively in cities. Rural areas have far less access to the concentration of knowledge and expertise that characterise urban pooled labour markets (Mahroum et al., 2007). However, when patenting rates are computed using that part of the population that might plausibly contribute to patenting, the large city patenting rate is only three times the rural rate (Wojan, Dotzel & Low, 2015).

The technology and innovation story (Figure 10.2) appears to play out differently for non-metro counties in the USA based on their proximity to a metropolitan area. Both non-metro areas fared better than metro counties in the first manufacturing crisis between 2001 and 2003, but non-metro non-adjacent counties did not demonstrate robust recovery as was true in non-metro adjacent counties. Non-adjacent counties also suffered the steepest employment declines in the recession. And despite promising trends in the first year of recovery, employment growth has since flatlined. The difference in the employment indices of the two non-metro types has increased from 5% in 2010 to 14% in 2013. Given the innovation–intensive characterisation, the anaemic recovery of metro employment is surprising. What the graph over two business cycles suggests is that increases in demand associated with recovery have increased employment mainly in proximate non-metro counties. The downside from the graph is that non-metro adjacent areas appear to be subject to more employment volatility through the business cycle, due perhaps to a spatial division of labour in these innovation-intensive industries.

If this type of innovation is critical to the economic success of manufacturing then the observed pattern of innovation-intensive industries recovering fastest in metro proximate rural areas may portend challenges for remote rural areas. However, innovation is not merely a product of R&D labs. Innovations that have substantive market impacts are more likely to come from the workforce, customers or suppliers than from researchers. Grassroots innovation in Europe is exemplified by small city industrial districts, often driven by the close relationships among makers, customers and machine/tool builders and by cultural, historical and environmental context.

Based on the EU's Community Innovation Survey (CIS), which has collected information on this type of innovation since 1992, supplemented by industry expert evaluations of reported innovations, North and Smallbone (2000) estimate that 24% of rural manufacturers in England are 'highly innovative'. Estimates from the Rural Establishment Innovation Survey in the USA that combine the CIS questions with auxiliary information to identify substantive innovators produce similar results: 23% of non-metro manufacturers are classified as substantive innovators, compared with 28% of metro manufacturers. For innovation-intensive manufacturing, the metro and non-metro shares of substantive innovators are nearly identical: 37.4% and 38.3%, respectively. Despite the urban advantages from formal innovation systems, rural firms in the United States do not appear to be thwarted in their pursuit of grassroots innovation.

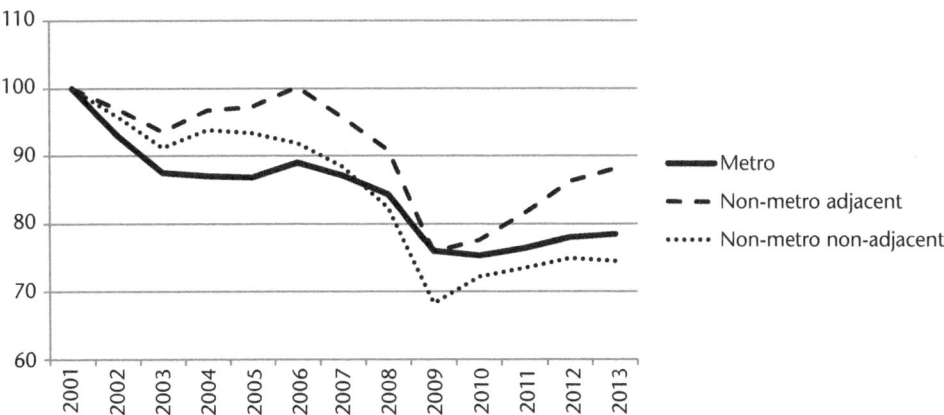

Figure 10.2 National Science Foundation innovation-intensive employment index for metro, non-metro adjacent, and non-metro non-adjacent counties, 2001–2013

Source: US Bureau of Labor Statistics, Quarterly Census of Employment and Wages.

Overcoming scale and distance

The revolution in digital communications, overnight deliveries and improved transportation, however, are changing the meaning of isolation. The explosion of high-speed broadband Internet access has given many small and remote areas a new lease on life. Scale and distance still constrain access to new ideas, knowledge and innovations that come through informal social interactions and networking, but the growth of web-based social networking and virtual meeting spaces has generated a new set of opportunities for workers and for locating businesses in smaller and more remote places. The Internet even opens up access to capital through crowdsourcing web portals such as kickstarter, indiegogo and equitynet.

Those rural areas able to keep up with rising demands of both advanced manufacturing and manufacturing services for digital and physical infrastructure to support the transfer of data and movement of goods and people are best able to compete for the contracting numbers of manufacturing jobs. To help SMEs meet these needs, many industrialised nations have established technical assistance programmes for small and isolated SMEs. In Germany's Baden Wurttemburg, the Steinbeis Foundation uses dispersed technology centres, the United Kingdom has Manufacturing Advisory Services, the US Manufacturing Extension Partnership has state-based centres.

These five factors suggest impediments for the establishment of successful manufacturing enterprises, particularly if a factor takes on particular attributes or characteristics, such as a strong association between the benefits of automation and the necessity of achieving large economies of scale, or if innovation is largely driven by science-based research systems that focus on generating patentable advances. However, each of the five factors can also be associated with characteristics that are more favourable for rural areas, such as the potential for advances in e-learning to provide advanced workforce training in small communities, or the possibility that globalisation can provide a much expanded market for a highly specialised niche product that is made by a small rural firm.

Preconditions for growing and sustaining manufacturing in rural areas

Assuming that the strength of many rural economies will continue to depend on sustaining a manufacturing base for many years, what will it take to keep that production alive and well? In much of the developed world, many predict that megacities will lead the revival and survival of manufacturing (Berube, 2007; Muro et al., 2015), despite the lack of confirming data.

What will it take to compete with both advanced urban regions and less developed but increasingly skilled countries? What are the preconditions for a competitive manufacturing base in the rural parts of advanced economies?

Among the most important of those preconditions are encouragement and support that accelerates innovation; cultural and creative amenities that attract businesses and talent; clustering of interdependent companies; a talented and skilled workforce; urban–rural market and supply chain connections; and access to technical and business assistance.

Accelerating innovation

The ability of rural communities to support and produce innovation is greatly underestimated, particularly with respect to technology and manufacturing. Rural innovation was addressed by the European Union during its Year of Creativity in 2009, but primarily with respect to food production, tourism, environmental industries and broadband access (Thuesen, 2009). The use of the word 'countryside' to define rural in Europe tends to align rural development with traditional rural sectors. In the USA, measures of innovation based on R&D investments, patents and levels of education also underestimate the potential for innovation in rural areas (Freshwater, 2012).

Whereas innovation may flow easily in a dense population of creative people, it also happens in rural areas, possibly to find a creative solution to a problem or need, retrofit existing equipment to improve a production process, or develop new higher value-added goods and find markets. In Florence, Alabama, Alabama Chanin grows and harvests organic cotton and with two internationally acclaimed designers and about 30 employees turns it into high-end sustainable clothing.

Perhaps the greatest barrier to rural innovation is isolation. Rural areas need more accessible pathways and pipelines to customers, competitors, researchers and suppliers around the globe, via, for example, study tours, international trade shows and professional meetings. 'Global pipelines' are as important as 'local buzz' to innovation (Bathelt, Malmberg & Maskell 2004).

Amenities to attract and keep talent-dependent manufacturers

The cultural capital of place is increasingly important to young people wanting to balance their lifestyle and quality of life with economic opportunities. This is especially important to millennials who express preferences for cities that can provide a wide selection of amenities (Moretti, 2012). But the escalating congestion and costs in large metro areas plus the appeal of the physical and social characteristics of rural areas to many – particularly in rural border regions where larger cities are accessible – are causing some migration to exurbia and beyond. The talent needed by advanced manufacturing is increasingly discriminating and may choose place first, job second (Wojan & McGranahan, 2007).

There is considerable diversity, however, in the ability of less populated places to attract and retain the talent needed by advanced manufacturing. Places with physical attractions such as coastlines, lakes, mountains, national parks, exceptional weather, or special cultural strengths in the arts, entertainment or specialty foods are more attractive to technology-dependent businesses seeking lower cost locations (Knox & Mayer, 2009). An increasing number of rural places that lack exceptional physical or cultural amenities in both Europe and North America are turning to historic preservation and 'creative placemaking' to emphasise distinctiveness and target niche businesses and talented young people.

Clustering industries and skills

Despite decades of diversification efforts, many rural economies are still specialised. In Europe, these small-town industrial districts are celebrated, supported and, where they represent locally authentic and historic features, may have brands protected by the EU. Industrial districts are still quite common in many sparsely populated regions where an industrial heritage – for example, skills, knowledge and reputation – has developed over decades and centuries. Employment in sparsely populated parts of Europe reveals a 'patchwork of local specialisation' (Dubois & Roto, 2012). These districts include electronics and, more recently, clean energy in Sønderborg, Denmark; eye glasses in Belluna, Italy; cutlery in Sheffield, England; and plastics in Oyonnax, France (Becattini, Bellandi & De Propis 2009).

In North America, where business and labour are more mobile and local traditions weaker, cluster strategies have focused more on mega-metro regions than communities. Yet many rural places in North America have been able to develop clusters (Rosenfeld, 2009) such as fibre optics in Bozeman, Montana, heavy lift helicopters in southern Oregon, and wine near Walla Walla, Washington. Most clusters develop organically due to serendipity, not policy. Branch plants, however, whose primary sources of knowledge and decision making lie elsewhere, are less likely to cluster in rural areas. They choose rural locations to monopolise labour markets, not to share (Wojan & Lackey, 2000). Where firms do cluster and are locally owned, manufacturing has proven somewhat more resilient and resistant to global competition.

Globalisation and the Internet are taking their toll on clusters, affecting what to outsource and what to keep. In Europe, many rural clusters choose to preserve core strengths in management, design, finance, marketing and high-value added production but outsource routine production and service functions. The result is lower employment among local artisan firms while keeping the knowledge base within the nucleus of the cluster. In Italy, where innovation has been highly dependent on interactions between engineers and designers and those using the machinery on a daily basis, the basic innovative structure of industrial districts is changing (Tattara, 2009). To retain the historical strength of industrial districts, firms will have to find innovative ways to use the Internet and foreign production capabilities to complement their strengths while protecting their knowledge, designs and brands.

Talented and skilled workforce

The dedicated but under-educated surplus labour force that sustained rural manufacturing in the USA in the past, or the informal learning systems and/or apprenticeship systems that sustained rural manufacturing in Europe in the past, are unlikely to be sufficient for more technologically advanced rural manufacturing in the future.

Rural schools – often smaller than urban schools – will need more resources to deliver the academic and vocational programmes to not only match local current and future demand but also produce the next generation of creative innovators and entrepreneurs. And they will have to find ways to induce the best and brightest to either stay in or return to the region. Advances in distance learning are already providing significant benefits to rural schools and can play an even greater role.

The responsibility for developing a highly skilled and creative workforce and encouraging youth to enrol in technical fields will rest with pre-baccalaureate post-secondary institutions – community/technical, further education and vocational-technical colleges. However, it is increasingly difficult to attract promising post-secondary students into career paths in manufacturing in either rural or urban schools despite documented skill shortages. Today, talented youth are looking for careers that offer flexibility, creativity and fulfilment based on their social and personal values. To attract today's youth, employers may have to make the workplace more flexible and interesting, and offer a greater variety of career paths including entrepreneurial possibilities.

Connections to nearby cities

The growth of many rural areas is dependent on transactions and interactions with nearby more highly populated areas. This is not a particularly new phenomenon. 'In the last twenty years, most successful rural areas have become prosperous because of some external urban based influence' (Freshwater, 2001). Rural manufacturers tend to rely more on suppliers, services, expertise and markets in nearby urban economic centres (Dabson, 2007). At the same time, manufacturers in urban places may look to nearby rural economies for suppliers, resources, food and recreation. These urban–rural relationships also serve as a counterweight to globalisation, with the interdependencies providing more strength and visibility and allowing small firms to pool resources and establish collaborative links.

Proximity-based economies also influence development patterns. 'Many major European cities have recently formed, or are in a process of forming, a new type of coalition with their neighbouring peri-urban and rural areas on an equal footing, so called Metropolitan Regions' (Kelling, 2013). Some 80% of Europe's rural population lives near cities. To enable stronger regional ties to benefit rural areas, the trend in the EU has been towards institutional structures that cross boundaries (Pezzini, 2000). For example, 'a string of small local manufacturing employment can be found along the existing railroad corridor' in Sweden (Dubois & Roto, 2012).

Opportunities for rural manufacturing

Although rural manufacturing is unlikely to ever reach the relative employment levels it realised in the second half of the 20th century, making things will remain vital to the identity and prosperity of small towns for some time to come. Manufacturing is still an important source of employment and wealth and a powerful incubator for innovation and creativity, but will depend on meeting the price-based challenges of rising low-cost competitor nations, the talent-based challenges of large cities and the technology-based challenges of automation and digitalisation.

To realise opportunities to develop and sustain an industrial base, rural places will have to be innovative. They will have to take advantage of place, overcome a lack of ability to achieve economies of scale and find niches to compete. They will have to find ways to attract the young and the talented that do not want an urban experience; promote the kind of innovation that thrives in rural settings; take advantage of growing demands for energy conservation and sustainability; access global knowledge, networks and markets; and generate scale from small-scale production.

Creative place-making can make places distinctive, interesting, active and attractive (Markusen & Gadwa, 2012). This is particularly important to the millennials that will form and produce the next generation of workers and to small businesses seeking less congested and/or lower cost environments. European cities largely have resisted the proliferation of homogenous big box retailers and malls that emptied main streets in so many US small towns. But in Europe, too, the status quo often is not enough for youth seeking new and different experiences and peers. The creative and cultural investments once aimed primarily at tourism are now equally important to the skilled and talented workers needed to create and operate technology-intensive and creative industries.

Alternative energy can provide advantages to manufacturers that find it advantageous to locate nearer the necessarily space-intensive alternative energy sources. Although future scenarios regarding the need for, conflicts with and location of alternative energy sources are numerous and difficult to predict, there are salient contrasts between alternative and fossil fuel energy sources that favour rural manufacturing locations. The very high energy density of fossil fuels that made large urban agglomerations economically feasible in the first place is not possible with renewable fuel sources reliant on solar or wind energy (Cruz & Taylor, 2012). The shift to a bio-based energy economy will require the location of processing facilities near where bulky feedstocks are produced (OECD, 2012). Energy-intensive activities such as manufacturing may find it advantageous to locate nearer the necessarily space-intensive alternative energy sources.

Customised, design-oriented manufacturing offers rural areas opportunities to tap into a growing market for place-based and design-oriented products. Affluent consumers are more selective, seeking experience over pure function. Mass customisation based on user-driven innovation is replacing mass production. It has been most obvious in rural areas with a proliferation of artisanal beverages, chocolates and other food products. But it also has been a major factor in a wide range of fashion products, particularly in Europe. The recent affordability and accessibility of 3D printing now is allowing many more entrepreneurs to customise complex products. Just as the laptop and handheld computer technologies changed the locational advantages of ICT-dependent businesses, affordable desktop computer-controlled production equipment has the potential for altering the locational advantages of production. Facilities converted to makerspaces, 'fab' labs and tech shops are growing in both crowded urban areas and remote rural areas. Even if the scale of the market for specialty goods may not generate the growth and wealth to warrant investment as a rural development strategy, the new technologies can have an affect where young people who once had hoped to be employed in a factory making things can become the makers and owners themselves.

Tailored technical assistance for rural and remote areas is necessary to improve workforce skills. The lower the population density, the less likely specialised services will be locally available and quickly accessible. Engineering and business consulting firms, transportation experts and equipment repair services, for example, are less likely to be nearby smaller, low density markets. These same problems of lacking the ability to achieve economies of scale make it more difficult for government agencies to adequately serve rural areas. Some of these scale issues can be overcome by broadband and web-based advice. However, digital connections do not replace the value of having someone familiar nearby to talk with and visit your facility.

Government programmes in the USA have largely bypassed user-driven innovation and focused almost exclusively on technology-driven innovation. Design-oriented manufacturing like Oriole Mills in western North Carolina, Peavy Electronics in Meridian, Mississippi, or Alabama Chanin in Florence, Alabama rely on design to stay in business. Most states have no baccalaureate programmes in industrial design. In contrast, most European nations have design programmes and emphasise design as a competitive advantage.

Digital and personal connections to global knowledge, networks and markets make rural areas more competitive. Recent OECD trends show that innovation-intensive companies have performed less well over the past decade in remote areas. The more remote and poorer a rural community is, the greater the need for connections to value chains, markets and ideas, but the more challenging it is to develop and maintain them. Broadband helps, but the Internet is no substitute for the informal exchange of ideas and tacit knowledge that comes from face-to-face interaction and visiting another place. The more isolated the community, the greater the need to develop and maintain external business, professional and collegial relationships through associational memberships, personnel/student exchanges, trade shows and market tours.

If these opportunities are available or can be developed, manufacturing may once again become a building block for rural areas in advanced economies, perhaps not as dominant as in the last century but part of a sustainable foundation that continues to provide well-paying jobs and spur innovation and entrepreneurial activity.

Sustaining manufacturing in rural areas

Despite the range of opinions on the future of making things in advanced economies, there is general agreement that: (1) the continued ability to design, manufacture and sell goods will continue to be vital to regional innovation and economic growth; (2) the structure of manufacturing and its value chains is undergoing a transformation; and (3) manufacturing, like agriculture, is not likely to reach its past proportionate levels of employment.

These changes are likely to have significant impacts on rural areas. Manufacturing will no longer be driven nearly as much by low costs, whether labour, land or energy, which had long advantaged rural areas. Manufacturing, however, can continue to flourish where it makes things that carry regional physical, cultural or historical attachments or brands. It will do well where it produces innovative things based on skills that have accumulated over time, or in proximity to local resources. Towns and small cities that have well-developed industrial districts or clusters with accumulated knowledge, that have entrepreneurial strength and local firms committed to place and that have the loyalty of their customer base, will be more sustainable.

Success in rural manufacturing will depend on sustaining a local culture of innovation, learning and entrepreneurship that depends on a very different kind of workforce, one with more formal education to complement the contextual skills and tacit knowledge that have developed over time. Successful rural communities must provide the environment and amenities that attract and retain the talented and skilled millennial and generation X young people necessary to support a modern manufacturing base. Rural manufacturers will have to be well connected to distant markets, suppliers, machine builders, innovators and sources of knowledge (see Weber and Freshwater, this volume). Some of this can be accomplished digitally but for the foreseeable future much will still depend on building and maintaining informal personal relationships. Rural areas that lack physical amenities, a desirable climate and proximity to urban centres will be particularly challenged to make their communities attractive to the companies and the workforce they need.

In summary, retaining a manufacturing base in rural parts of advanced economies, once sustained by low cost and/or experience, in the future will depend on creative place-making, continual innovation and global connections.

Acknowledgement

The views expressed here are those of the authors and may not be attributed to the Economic Research Service of the US Department of Agriculture.

References

Bathelt, H, Malmberg, A & Maskell, P (2004). Clusters and knowledge: Local buzz, global pipelines, and the process of knowledge creation. *Progress in Human Geography* 28(1), 31–56.

Becattini, G, Bellandi, M & De Propis, L (2009). *A handbook of industrial districts*. London: Edward Elgar.

Berube, A (2007). *MetroNation: How U.S. metropolitan areas are fueling American prosperity*. Washington, DC: Brookings Institution.

Capasso, M, Cusmano, L & Morrison, A (2013). The determinants of outsourcing and offshoring strategies in industrial districts: Evidence from Italy. *Regional Studies* 47(4), 465–479.

Carlino, G & Kerr, WR (2014). Agglomeration and innovation. NBER Working Paper w20367. Cambridge, MA: National Bureau of Economic Research.

Cruz, JM & Taylor, MS (2012). Back to the future of green powered economies. NBER Working Paper w18236. Cambridge, MA: National Bureau of Economic Research.

Dabson, B (2007). Rural–urban interdependence: Why metropolitan and rural America need each other. Background paper for The Blueprint for American Prosperity. Washington, DC: The Brookings Institution.

Dubois, A & Roto, J (2012). Making the best of Europe's sparsely populated areas. Nordregio Working Paper 2012:15. Stockholm, Sweden: Nordregio.

Economist, Special Report (2012). Manufacturing and innovation: A third industrial revolution. *The Economist*, 21 April.

Freshwater, D (2001). Delusions of grandeur: The search for a vibrant rural America. TVA Rural Studies Working Paper 01-07. Lexington: University of Kentucky.

Freshwater, D (2012). Rural innovation – Crucial, but rarely systemic. Agricultural Economic Research Report #139829. Lexington: University of Kentucky, Department of Agricultural Economics.

Gale, F, McGranahan, D, Teixeira, R & Greenberg, E (1999). Rural competitiveness: Results of the 1996 Rural Manufacturing Survey. Agricultural Economic Report No. (AER-776). Washington, DC: Economic Research Service.

Gale, HF (1998). Rural manufacturing on the crest of the wave: A count data analysis of technology use. *American Journal of Agricultural Economics* 80(2), 347–359.

Katz, B & Bradley, J (2013). *The metropolitan revolution: How cities and metros are fixing our broken politics and fragile economy.* Washington, DC: Brookings Institution.

Kelling, J (Ed.). (2013). *Urban–rural relationships in metropolitan–rural cooperation.* Hamburg: Ministry of Economy, Transport, and Innovation.

Knox, PL & Mayer, H (2009). *Small town sustainability: Economic, social, and environmental innovation.* Berlin: Birkhauser.

Mahroum, S et al. (2007). *Rural innovation.* London: National Endowment for Science, Technology, and the Arts.

Manyika, J et al. (2012). *Manufacturing the future: The next era of global growth and innovation.* San Francisco, CA: McKinsey Global Institute.

Markusen, A & Gadwa, A (2012). *Creative placemaking.* Washington, DC: National Endowment for the Arts.

Moretti, E. (2012). *The new geography of jobs.* New York: Houghton Mifflin.

Mourshed, M, Patel, J & Suder, K (2014). *Education to employment: Getting Europe's youth into work.* McKinsey Centre for Government.

Muro, M, Rothwell, J, Andes, S, Fikri, K & Kulkarni, S (2015). *Advanced industries: What they are, where they are and why they matter.* Washington, DC: Brookings Institution.

North, D & Smallbone, D (2000). The innovativeness and growth of rural SMEs during the 1990s. *Regional Studies* 34(2), 145–157.

OECD (2012). *Linking renewable energy to rural development.* Paris: OECD.

OECD (2013). Who's smiling now? *OECD Observer* 296(Q3). Available at http://www.oecdobserver. org/news/fullstory.php/aid/4227/Who_92s_smiling_now_.html (accessed 18 January 2016).

Pezzini, M (2000). Rural policy lessons from OECD countries. In *Beyond agriculture: New policies for rural America.* Kansas City: Centre for the Study of Rural America, Federal Reserve Bank of Kansas City.

Pierce, JR & Schott, PK (2012). The surprisingly swift decline of U.S. manufacturing employment. NBER Working Paper w18655. Cambridge, MA: National Bureau of Economic Research.

Rosenfeld, S. (1998). Technical college, technology deployment, and regional development. Stock-taking paper for International Conference on Building Competitive Regional Economies, Organisation for Economic Co-operation and Development, Modena, Italy, 28–29 May 1998.

Rosenfeld, S (2009). *A compendium of clusters in less populated places: Circumstances, interventions, and outcomes.* Carrboro, NC: Regional Technology Strategies.

Stiglitz, JE (2014). Unemployment and innovation. NBER Working Paper Series No. w20670. Cambridge, MA: National Bureau of Economic Research.

Summers, GF et al. (1976). *Industrial invasion of nonmetropolitan America.* New York: Praeger.

Tattara, G (2009). The internationalization of production activities of Italian industrial districts. In G Becattini, M Bellandi & L De Propis (Eds), *A handbook of industrial districts* (pp. 682–693). London: Edward Elgar.

Thuesen, AA (2009). Facilitation and dialogue leads to innovation: Creativity and Innovation in EU Rural Development. *EU Rural Review* 2, 30–31.

USDA-ERS (2012). U.S. textile and apparel industries and rural America. Available at http://www.ers. usda.gov/topics/crops/cotton-wool/background/us-textile-and-apparel-industries-and-rural-america.aspx (accessed 18 January 2016).

Virkkala, S (2007). Innovation and networking in peripheral regions – A case study of emergence and change in rural manufacturing. *European Planning Studies* 15(4), 511–529.

Wojan, TR, Dotzel, KR & Low, SA (2015). Decomposing regional patenting rates: How the composition factor confounds the rate factor. *Regional Studies Regional Science* 2(1), 535–551.

Wojan, TR & Lackey, SB (2000). Manufacturing specialisation in the southeast: Rural necessity, rural possibility, or rural vestige. *The Review of Regional Studies* 30(2), 167–187.

Wojan, TR & McGranahan, DA (2007). Ambient returns: Creative capital's contribution to local manufacturing competitiveness. *Agricultural and Resource Economics Review* 36(1), 133–148.

World Bank (2009). *World development report 2009: Reshaping economic geography.* Washington, DC: World Bank.

11

Rural–Urban in a Peri-Urban Context

Joan Noguera and David Freshwater

Introducing the rural–urban interface

In recent decades, the limits of the urban space have been fading as location patterns of economic activity and population have changed. If we look back at history for a moment to contextualise, we note that, until the mid-19th century, most towns were contained behind the protection of walls or similar elements, and this delimitation of the urban space had fundamental implications for life, government, protection, power and provision of services. Towns, 'wrapped' in their walled enclosures, were protected from many of the risks affecting the rural population and developed distinct identities.

By the late 19th century, population growth was responsible for extending the physical limits of towns beyond their protected enclosures. Depending on the dominant urban model, the city grew vertically or horizontally, in a more or less compact form around its nucleus by expanding into previously rural areas, although conditioned by the specific features of the local geography. Initially, the development of mechanised public transport – trains, buses and trams – allowed for the first urban-linked commuter developments, where people lived relatively far from cities with intervening green space, but continued to work in the core. Later, after multiple ruptures caused by the effects of two world wars, the spread of new transport technologies (automobiles) and changes in the social order, some of the most advanced societies and economies began an expansive period during which cities and towns grew beyond their previous limits.

Therefore, it is from the 1950s on that large parts of the Anglo-Saxon world record a striking transformation based on suburban formulas of low-density, single-family homes aimed at the middle class, that took place in territory that, until then, had never been regarded as 'urban'. These extensions, conceptualised as 'suburbs', referring to residential or mixed land uses, often distant from the original urban location, with autonomous governance, occupied large areas of the countryside. This new transition territory showed an intensification and quick path of change in the use of land as its major feature, while its economy, social mix, cultural background and environmental dynamics reflected new situations derived from a much broader and wider interaction between the previously separated urban and rural processes (McManus & Ethington, 2007). Thus, the concept of 'peri-urban' areas emerged as a way to describe territory that had attributes of both rural and urban but was neither.

In countries with different traditions cities also showed a similar pattern of growth and physical extension, but mostly not in the form of suburbs. For instance, in the Mediterranean culture, the urban momentum since the 1950s, due to a strong rural exodus driven by the mechanisation of farming, led to the development of new urban districts made of social housing that followed more traditional urban housing formulas. In the countries of northern and western Europe the evolution of urban areas soon registered two types of trend: on the one hand, the inertia of a soft centripetal movement started decades before from the most disadvantaged, remote rural areas; on the other, a much more intensive centrifugal move by urban population leaving central urban spaces to the immediate peri-urban areas. Along with North American cities, these are the first areas to coin such concepts as *counter-urbanisation* and *suburbanisation*. In the case of communist countries, a frequent phenomenon was the *ex novo* creation of towns in a pre-planned fashion to accommodate the workforce for large factories, but without the development of new suburban housing. In the developing countries of Latin America, South Asia and Africa, the growth of cities has been more intense and much less planned. Traditional urban space grew, first, both in terms of formal construction mode and 'quality'. Ultimately, this chaotic growth led to the rapid construction of informal, shoddy housing, with few services that literally 'piled' onto mountain slopes or any other unused land.

In recent times, the concept of 'suburb' has been used by other cultures and geographical settings. For example, in the Mediterranean, at least in the northern basin, the so-called urbanisations arise from the 1970s as development projects, composed of low building density and predominantly single family residence, targeting the middle and working classes. In other contexts, and more recently, these 'suburbs' have taken the form of condominiums geared to accommodate an upper middle class 'fleeing' from urban centres in search of more space and security. Both groups predominantly occupy the peri-urban areas of major cities, on predominantly rural territory that continues to support agriculture and forestry. The emergence of this peri-urban 'string' of territory between what could be clearly identifiable as 'urban' and 'rural' is the result of two long-term, centrifugal processes, one originating in rural areas, and the other 'blowing out' from urban centres.

From the urban side, the development and modernisation of the city brings about a double centrifugal trend. People and economic activity leave urban centres in search of better life and work conditions (i.e., premises, accessibility, price of land, etc.). This 'suburbanisation' involves not only the creation of the above-mentioned 'suburbs', but also the location of more and more urban cultured people in the nearby rural settlements, with the potential for conflicts of interest. In parallel, industrial activity begins to be 'expelled' from urban centres for various reasons and processes that involve relocation to specialised spaces that are also located in the suburban area.

In addition, the traditional monocentric city characterised by a single dominant urban core is now challenged by the development of polycentric urban areas that are made up of multiple cores and surrounding rural territory. These regional cities reflect multiple factors, but the shift from linear transport systems (canals, rail and bus) to individual automobile and truck transport is the most important. In addition, modern telecommunications has shifted retail and service functions from the city centre and increased the ability of people with different preferences in terms of lifestyle to find more remote locations that better suit them. The result is urban forms that are no longer dominated by a single downtown.

In many rural areas, there has been a persistent trend of population loss, due to a combination of factors that contribute to a spiral of decline, described as early as 1983 by Gilg. According to this process, low population means less viability for the provision of services, which in turn discourages and drives more people out, which in turn further reduces the viability of service provision. The trend of out-migration is exacerbated by modern communications media that show rural people a 'better' urban lifestyle than is available in the countryside, which increases the incentive to move. At the same time, changing technology in the natural resource industries replaces workers with machinery, which results in surplus labour that is pushed out of the countryside, often to cheap housing in the lower cost urban fringe.

Thus, throughout the territorial continuum, from the depths of remote rural areas to the more central business district, territorial dynamics point to the evolution of a rural–urban interface; a complex set of social, economic, political and environmental relationships that, over time, has resulted in complex flows of economic activity, commuting, infrastructure and resources.

The evolving context of rural–urban interactions

Academic analysis of rural and urban areas appears as one of the first and most traditional concerns in the search for models and forms of better regional development. Although theories on the evolution of the city, or on the role of agriculture and rural areas, can be traced back to the cultures of ancient China, Greece or Rome, among others, modern analysis starts during the first half of the 20th century with the postulates of Weber (1917), Park (1925) or Dewey (1927). However, most of this analysis dealt with only one part of the 'equation' – that is, either the 'rural' or the 'urban' territory. Studies of the existing interrelations between rural and urban were rare, implying the two processes and phenomena were independent of each other.

About 1980, an important shift in focus occurs in the examination of regional economic development. Authors suggest a change in how regional development happens, from considering the central role of sectoral development to focusing instead on the characteristics of the territorial context and its specific features. Thus, unprecedented importance is given to aspects such as business networks, individual and social capital, or institutional density when explaining differences among regions (Morgan, 1997; Keeble, Lawson, Moore & Wilkinson, 1999; Castells, 2000). This shift involves a new interest in determining and understanding the features that can identify 'winning' territories, and this focus makes it essential to identify those territories where most effort should be placed when defining and implementing public policies in order to maximise policy relevance and effectiveness. In this context, the rural–urban fringe emerges as a place of functional relationships, be they economic, social, cultural or political.

More recently, as systems theory was applied to the study of territory and the concept of a territorial system emerged, references appear to relationships of all kinds that link rural and urban areas. The complexity of the territorial changes affecting the interstitial space that separate and unite traditional urban and rural realities creates a new form of territory. However, the dual nature of this rural–urban fringe (Briquel & Collicard, 2002), which contains characteristics and activities of both types of space, hinders its consideration as a distinct separate space, different from both the 'rural' and the 'urban'. This fact, along with high evolutionary dynamism and regional peculiarities, causes difficulty in addressing the needs and opportunities offered by these 'fringe' territories. Proof of this is the scarcity of the concept of rural–urban fringe in regional legislation, and its frequent consideration as transitional or 'intermediate' areas, lacking a separate, meaningful identity.

Identifying a complex territory

Whitehand (1988) argues that the origins of the term 'rural–urban fringe' can be traced back to the writings of the German geographer Herbert Louis in 1936 (Hoggart, 2005). However, the clearest evidence of an early use of the concept belongs to a study by Martin (1953) in which this 'fringe' is defined as 'that area of interpenetrating rural and urban land use peripheral to the modern city' (p. iii). More recently, discussion of the nature and extent of the rural–urban fringe has become profuse. Although the specific physical and time distances vary from one tradition to another, there are commentators speaking of large areas under different names. For example, Lapping and Furuseth (1999) consider territory up to 60–80 km from large urban agglomerations as 'fringe'. As Hoggart (2005) points out, interestingly, these extensions, with some nuances, come to agree with the concept of a 'regional city' by Bryant and associates (1982), the concept of 'outer city' developed by Herrington (1984), and also the idea of travel-to-work-areas or commuting zones defined by Champion et al. (1987).

This latter concept has become the basis for defining 'metropolitan areas' that combine an urban core and an associated hinterland made up of nearby small urbanised areas (towns and small cities) and the surrounding rural territory. The bounds of metropolitan regions are defined by journey-to-work data that are used to construct a self-contained local labour market, where the vast majority of workers both live and work. The concept has been used by the United States, the United Kingdom and Canada, among others, to construct metropolitan regions, or regional cities, and has recently been adopted by the OECD for use in its urban programme. In all cases the vast majority of the territory of these conurbations is peri-urban, fringe or '(r)urban' (rural–urban).

There is no doubt that the rural–urban fringe appears, more and more, as a complex and evolutionary territory, where many processes linking urban and rural areas happen (Lichter & Brown, 2011). These interactions occur in a number of ways. Most obvious are worker commuting patterns that can involve either one-way flows – traditionally rural workers to urban jobs – or more recently, two flows – urban workers to rural jobs and rural workers to urban jobs. Obviously, the shift to two flows reflects two phenomena. The first is the dispersion of population from cities to the countryside in search of better housing options. Second is a parallel shift in firm location as the central business district becomes too congested, too expensive, too difficult to find a large enough space, or inhospitable to certain industries. Firms are dispersed through space but can still interact effectively through better transport that requires urban and rural coordination to be effective, and through telecommunication networks that also, by definition, can only be implemented through coordination. Finally, urban and rural are linked through environmental services and public services. Adjacent rural territory provides water, green space and space for solid waste. Urban areas allow nearby rural residents to have easy access to higher education, advanced medical care and a host of cultural opportunities, such as museums, professional sports, theatre and fine dining.

Understanding the evolution of spatial patterns in this new, complex territory is important. Urban growth typically takes the form of an 'oil slick' and, therefore, is not homogeneous or constant. Unlike the hard and regular boundaries of von Thunen models, the city 'stretches' along main roads, and mixes with traditional rural areas, creating blurred or fuzzy boundaries. As urban development continues, some urban classes, typically those in the medium/upper range, initiate a centrifugal move towards the nearby rural areas, in search of better living conditions within a suburban model. The process fills many of the interstitial spaces that remained empty during previous urban growth pulses. A set of communication infrastructures develops to serve these new functional spaces connecting the urban centre to its periphery and 'beyond'. The increasing distance between residence and workplace makes new individual or collective transport solutions necessary. This is also the time in which manufacturing, logistics and wholesale functions abandon urban centres to find new, more suitable locations, typically in the vicinity of cities.

Profound socioeconomic changes associated with rural decline and the reinforcement of urban areas as providers of services to nearby rural residents have created new types of relationships between urban and rural areas. The old model, characterised by distinct specialisations with rural areas only serving as sources of primary goods or natural resources, is less and less recognised. Although primary activities remain central to the multifunctional configuration of rural areas, they are increasingly embedded into higher value-added processes, where quality is often more important than quantity, and in which environmental conservation values and traditional culture are increasingly apparent. Along with this new economic role in many, but not all, countries we find public support for territorially based development, and a focus on innovation and new forms of governance at the metropolitan level (Brenner, 2003; Scott & Storper, 2003; OECD, 2014). This has transformed many adjacent rural regions into experimental laboratories that engage in public–private partnerships for development. Conversely, other adjacent rural areas have become trapped in intense conflicts between a growing presence of new, culturally urban, residents, who support development strategies based on principles of sustainability and protection of territorial resources that conflict with the traditional values and interests of long-time residents.

Overall, the relative advantage of rural areas largely depends on a lower (more advantage) or greater (less advantage) physical and time distance to a large urban centre. Rural advantage is also connected, although less strongly, to the unique elements that provide a positive differential advantage for that rural area (cultural or natural landmarks, for instance). This highlights a fundamental dual dependency of rural areas compared to urban areas. On the one hand, rural areas depend on nearby urban centres for the provision of many goods and services, as local rural markets are not able to meet these needs. On the other hand, new activities, like tourism, have become a cornerstone of the development strategies of rural districts but rely on nearby urban markets to provide customers. Here, improvements in accessibility and mobility may favour rural areas with short travel time.

A similar, but perhaps less powerful, duality exists for urban areas. Increased urbanisation provides benefits but also costs as density increases. Rural areas provide needed green space and other environmental services that cannot be produced in an urban core. Similarly, the decline of the monocentric city and the increase in two-way commuting flows has moved adjacent rural regions from an economic dependency situation to one where they may offer complementary economic benefits to an urban core in a symbiotic relationship.

The diversity of (r)urban territories

So far we have presented the rural–urban fringe as though it was a homogeneous territory. Nothing is further from the truth. Although there are shared features (functional definition of territories, transit between urban reality and remote rural, rapid transformations in land use and socioeconomic composition, etc.), these are different in each place, depending on factors such as the dominant type of urban settlement, the nature of the production system and the intensity of human occupation. We can speak, therefore, of a set of elements that give cohesion to the rural–urban fringe, and a number of specificities in terms of national contexts, regional and urban typologies, and factors of a geographical, economic, social, cultural, temporal and political nature.

It is relatively easy to highlight the common elements that give coherence to the whole territory of the rural–urban fringe. One of the main features of these regions is the fact that these are territories of 'accumulation'. The rural–urban fringe concentrates, as mentioned above, population, economic activity and infrastructure and equipment in ways similar to urban space, while maintaining a high level of agricultural and other 'rural' activity. This mixture of actions can easily lead to a lack of coherence if the rural–urban fringe lacks adequate planning and management tools.

On the other hand, spaces in the rural–urban fringe show rapid evolution due to their dynamism. Landscape, land use and economic function evolve much faster than in most pure urban or rural regions. Again, the existence of management tools – for instance, land use and landscape planning – are essential to maintain and even boost the appeal of these territories. They are also spaces of flows and reflecting: movements in and out from the urban space, movements associated with the provision of urban markets, and commuting between workplace and residence. Importantly these flows are not simply one way or single purpose. In many metropolitan regions some workers commute from urban residences to rural jobs, along with others from rural residences to urban jobs. Goods and services flow in both directions, and people combine multiple activities during their travels. For example, travel to a major medical facility by a rural resident may be combined with visiting a major sports event. And a weekend visit to the country for hiking by an urban dweller may be coupled with the purchase of local foods. The resulting functional spaces that are defined by these complex flows do not conform well to traditional administrative boundaries and require a new approach for management, organisation and governance.

From administrative management to integrated governance

There is sufficient academic literature and empirical evidence to state that functional territories do not fit well, in terms of government, within traditional administrative jurisdictions. The reasons are many, but the most relevant are the intensity of flows of all kinds (economic, social, cultural, environmental, political, etc.) for which administrative boundaries are only odd artificial divisions; and, a more or less evident lack of a tradition of institutionalised cooperation between the various administrative authorities that overlie the functional reality. It is in this context that theories such as new public management (NPM), or the concept of 'governance' arise. Although these theories are not a fundamental break with the traditional approaches to public administration, they do emphasise a set of features and functions that depend upon good governance. Aguilar (2006), summarising contributions from various authors (Stoker, 1998; Pierre, 2000; European Commission, 2001; Prats, 2004, among others), describes good governance as governance that meets a particular set of characteristics.

According to Aguilar (2006), in the framework of the most recent and innovative practices in government there are four characteristics of good governance:

- first, a set of institutions, and intra and extra-governmental actors that recognise the permeability between the public and private sector boundaries in addressing the problems of a community;
- second, an acknowledgement of the interdependencies of all kinds between institutions and actors to achieve their goals;
- third, the recognition of the existence of social networks of 'autonomous actors' capable of self-government in matters vital to their lives and coexistence;
- fourth, acceptance of the possibility of achieving common goals without resorting to authority and hierarchy. In this context, the public authority becomes *primus inter pares*, renouncing, most of the time, the strategy of coercion.

These characteristics of good governance are particularly important when talking about the rural–urban interface, where in many cases the history of cooperation, mutual understanding and shared management is riddled with bad practices and failures. Therefore, good governance of rural–urban areas calls for the existence of a governance system characterised by the elements described above. Moreover, the governance system in these areas must be able to promote cooperation and collaboration among local stakeholders by building meeting spaces. It also must draw the boundaries of the reference territory to adequately address the identification, planning and management of challenges. Finally, it must consider consensus as a natural form of decision making, the result of the consolidation of forms of participatory democracy that can build neutral institutional spaces.

Collaborative governance for a complex rural–urban territory: the partnership approach

According to the principles of good governance of the rural–urban fringe featured in the previous section, public–private partnerships (PPP) are optimal structures for the implementation of participative models of governance. A PPP constitutes an association between representatives of a local society that group together in order to boost efforts to achieve certain objectives. As long as a rural–urban partnership gets the recognition of the main authorities and representatives of a particular region (mainly through participation in the partnership composition and decision making), it can represent a rural–urban forum with wide scope of action. If the partnership remains legitimised by those involved, it may become more relevant with regard to the implementation of the regional development strategy. Some models (for instance the Local Action Groups approach in the framework of the LEADER programme philosophy) can certainly become a benchmark in rural–urban dialogue if some important conditions hold.

One of these conditions refers to the existence of an adequate integration of key stakeholders in the partnership. Addressing mutual needs comprehensively, and becoming the reference forum for the definition of the regional strategy, requires having 'on board' those that can make it possible. This, in turn, makes matching appropriate representatives and achieving mutual consensus about goals, objectives and implementation of procedures necessary. Important factors determining the adequate integration of local community in the partnership include the identification of appropriate representatives for each stakeholder, knowing the aims of each stakeholder in relation to their participation, and raising consensus on goals and objectives to be achieved.

Another condition is achieving legitimacy. One of the main advantages of partnerships when compared to other modes of governance organisation is their greater ability to legitimately represent the interests and concerns of local stakeholders. Partnerships have the benefit of being able to successfully integrate a greater number of viewpoints. Unfortunately, a sizeable proportion of partnerships do not capitalise on this potential because they have tended to mirror the existing local balance of power and, sometimes, to follow the same logic of partisanship. Moreover, members of decision-making bodies within the partnership tend to 'forget' their 'representing' role and end up not 'accounting' for the positions taken. Mechanisms for participation often do not work. A number of factors can help to overcome these problems. For instance, a high degree of heterogeneity and representation allows more legitimated decisions and greater integration of existing views into the development strategy. Also, bottom-up initiation of partnerships means shared concerns about problems and the need for common action, thus increasing legitimation. Sufficient local decision-making capacity is also fundamental to exploit the advantages afforded by knowledge and the joint action of local actors.

One more condition needed for rural–urban partnerships to be successful is the presence of a tailor-made strategy. Strategy constitutes a 'road map' for effective and legitimated action. However, it should be noted that the design of a development strategy is often tied to specific requirements of a funding programme that feeds the partnership. Therefore, only a small percentage of partnerships would undertake strategic thinking, grounded in local participation. This happens when there is a clear awareness that common action can bring long-term benefits. Then, the partnership is able to conduct the entire process, including design of strategy, and it is responsible for maintaining the involvement of local society.

The capacity to put in place tools for the permanent observation of the local context (the rural–urban fringe) is a fundamental contribution of PPP. A most valuable tool is the so-called local observatory. An observatory must be functionally and/or legally dependent upon the institution that leads the cooperation process, that is, usually a local council. The observatory must have a reporting and dissemination strategy. Results of the observation should be discussed in the frame of the partnership in order to integrate them in the form of lessons, guidelines or recommendations for the partnership's strategy.

The partnership must also have abilities for capacity building. The existence of a partnership frequently has led to the introduction of new administration, new ways of conducting relationships between local actors and even changes in attitudes and mentalities, all of which have many beneficial effects. Beyond the financial investment achieved by partnership actions, the implementation of these other processes is the real benefit for long-term, sustainable development of the rural–urban fringe. For this achievement it is fundamental to develop cooperation networks between the partnership and local society; and also adequate leadership skills by members of partnerships, allowing greater integration of existing views into the development strategy.

The last condition, probably the widest and more important, is the achievement of a path of local sustainable development. Rural–urban partnerships promote local endogenous development in two ways: first, by providing the most appropriate institutional framework for local cooperation and the use of local human resources; second, by closing the gaps between the skills available in the local context and the strategic needs of businesses and organisations.

Good practices for a more sustainable rural–urban fringe

Creating a governance framework for the rural–urban fringe means, primarily, taking into account some relevant processes that reflect the diversity of institutional contexts and cultures present in various countries and regions. In addition, urban–rural fringes are not well suited to traditional administrative boundaries, given a context of dynamic and growing functional flows that can overwhelm a traditional territorial structure. These needs must be taken into account when considering optimal forms of government in the rural–urban fringe.

So far we have described the main features of the rural–urban fringe, its cohesive elements and the characteristics that differentiate these spaces internally. In these last words we suggest some recommendations to help ensure that these complex territories acquire a more sustainable organisation.

A coordinated, multilevel strategy for the development of the rural–urban fringe

Even if allowing for a fundamental reference frame, spatial planning is not sufficient for good governance. There must also be a development strategy with adequate tools and resources for implementation. The territory can only be understood as a system. Consequently, it is meaningless carrying out uncoordinated actions that may be not only ineffective but counterproductive. Therefore, it must define not only development activities but also effective coordination mechanisms and an adequate budget to make a positive impact on sustainable development in rural areas.

Combining identity, functionality and sustainability in a new governance

The rural–urban fringe corresponds to the type of functional territories needing more rational spaces of government by promoting legislation that provides supra-local scales with skills and powers to the provision of services, the design of territorial development strategies, and so on. Another important issue relates to the need for optimisation of the structure and functioning of local governance. Inter-institutional cooperation, PPP and other forms of cooperative governance are paradoxical when local councils lack internal cohesion and communication. At the same time there is a need to establish methods and protocols for communication and coordination between the different areas of local government. The governance in the rural–urban fringe must be based in a process of strategic reflection and action agreed by local stakeholders. Although there are countries or regions in which this appears to be a 'truism', the reality of many other regions and countries is that territorial governance barely exists, there is little supra-municipal cooperation and there are no strategic processes of reflection–action that rationally direct development efforts. Consequently, the proposal goes through the definition of 'territorial model of the future' to be defined in a shared and agreed form with local stakeholders. This involves commitment at the political level, involvement of social and economic organisations, and working towards a real model of participatory democracy.

A good place to test participative democracy

Recent times tell us about a growing dissatisfaction of citizens with regard to their political representatives and, even worse, with respect to the democratic system. The continued misuse and perversion of the principles of representative democracy have led, in recent statistical barometers, to the fact that one of the main problems perceived by citizens are 'politicians'. This disaffection threatens to delegitimise the entire democratic system, with enormous associated risks. Recent public demonstrations of discontent are only an initial expression of the direction events may take if the 'divorce' between citizens and political representatives continues or increases. The reality is proving that the social sphere evolves much faster than the institutional sphere. As a result, responses to citizens' movements are between disqualification and ideological sympathy with no real implications. At the core of most of these movements lies the idea that representative democracy has been perverted in a way that primarily serves the interests of political groups and the associated social and economic lobbies. The proposals in this situation are also varied and range from quasi-anarchic visions to models of participatory democracy with an increased role for the local scales, greater concern for issues of sustainability and greater control of the citizenry. In this scenario, functional regions as rural–urban fringes may be adequate places for the promotion of participatory models of governance that come closer to the concept of participative democracy.

References

Aguilar Villanueva, L (2006). *Gobernanza y Gestión Pública*. Mexico: Fondo de Cultura Económica.

Brenner, N (2003). Metropolitan institutional reform and the rescaling of state space in contemporary Western Europe. *European Urban and Regional Studies* 10(4), 297–324.

Briquel, V & Collicard, J (2002). Introduction to a method for detecting and classifying peri-urban areas. NEWRUR Deliverable 2.2a-2.2b. Grenoble: CEMAGREF.

Bryant, CR, Russwurm, LH & McLellan, AG (1982). *The city's countryside: Land and its management in the rural–urban fringe*. London: Longman.

Castells, M (2000). *The rise of the network society*. Oxford: Blackwell.

Champion, AG, Green, AE, Owen, DW, Ellin, DJ & Coombes, MG (1987). *Changing places: Britain's demographic, economic and social complexion*. London: Edward Arnold.

Dewey, J (1988 [1927]). *The public and its problem*. Athens, OH: Swallow Press.

European Commission (2001). Governance in the European Union: a White Paper. Official Journal of the European Communities, 12-10-2001. Brussels: European Commission.

Herrington, J (1984). *The outer city*. London: Harper & Row.

Hoggart, K (Ed.). (2005). *The city's hinterland. Dynamism and divergence in Europe's peri-urban territories*. London: Ashgate.

Keeble, DE, Lawson, C, Moore, B & Wilkinson, F (1999). Collective learning processes, networking and 'institutional thickness' in the Cambridge region. *Regional Studies* 33, 319–332.

Lapping, MB & Furuseth, OJ (1999). Introduction and overview. In OJ Furuseth & MB Lapping (Eds), *Contested countryside: the rural urban fringe in North America* (pp. 1–5). Farnham: Ashgate.

Lichter, D & Brown, DL (2011). Rural America in an urban society: Changing social and spatial boundaries. *Annual Review of Sociology* 37, 565–592.

Martin, WT (1953). *The rural–urban fringe: A study of adjustment to residence location*. Eugene, OR: University of Oregon Press.

McManus, R & Ethington, P (2007). Suburbs in transition: New approaches to suburban history. *Urban History* 34(2), 317–337.

Morgan, K (1997). The learning region: Institutions, innovation and regional renewal. *Regional Studies* 31, 491–503.

OECD (2014). OECD regional outlook regions and cities: Where policies and people meet. Paris: OECD.

Park, R (1967 [1925]). The city: Suggestions for the investigation of human behaviour in the urban environment. In R Park & L Wirth (Eds), *The city* (pp. 124–139). Chicago: University of Chicago Press, 1967, orig. 1925.

Pierre, J (2000). *Debating governance*. Oxford: Oxford University Press.

Prats, J (2004). De la Burocracia al *Management* y del *Management* a la Gobernanza. *Instituciones y Desarrollo* 3.

Scott, AJ & Storper, M (2003). Regions, globalization, development. *Regional Studies* 3(6–7), 579–593.

Stoker, G (1998). Governance as theory: Five propositions. *International Social Science Journal* 155, 17–28.

Weber, M (1917). Suffrage and democracy in Germany. In P. Lassman & R Speirs (Eds), *Political writings* (pp. 80–129). Cambridge: Cambridge University Press.

Whitehand, JWR (1988). Urban fringe belts: Development of an idea. *Planning Perspectives* 3, 47–58.

12

Changing Dynamics of Rural Labour Markets

Anne Green

Theoretically, a local labour market is a functional area in which the majority of jobs are filled by local residents and in which the majority of local residents in employment have their workplaces. In practice, a local labour market is difficult to delineate: different population sub-groups and jobs are associated with variations in commuting patterns in accordance with individuals' occupations, earnings, transport mode, hours of work, and so on. Hence the boundaries of local labour markets are imprecise and fuzzy, and in circumstances where commuting can substitute for migration this is increasingly the case (Green, 2004). In this chapter 'rural labour markets' are interpreted broadly as local labour markets in rural areas. Given the differential commuting flows by sub-group mentioned above, it is important to note that workplace-based and residence-based statistics for some rural areas may yield rather different pictures.

This chapter is divided into eight sections. First, an introductory overview sets the context for the more detailed sections that follow. Second, the main features of the changing profile of jobs in rural areas are outlined, emphasising sectoral and occupational variations vis-à-vis urban areas. Third, the emphasis shifts to the supply side, focusing on implications of population ageing, out-migration (especially of young people) and international immigration. The fourth section looks at access to employment in rural areas and what the structure of rural labour markets means for in-work progression. Fifth, local demand-side and supply-side dynamics, and associated implications for policy, are considered. Sixth, the focus shifts to challenges in utilising and accessing skills and in delivering training in rural areas. In the seventh section the role of the Internet in changing access to, and opportunities for, employment and training is assessed. The concluding section considers the implications of likely future trends for the prospects for rural labour markets.

Introductory overview

Over time, the employment structures of rural areas in OECD countries have tended to become more similar to those of urban areas as employment in the primary sector (notably agriculture) has continued to decline. A key feature has been technological change and the substitution of capital for labour. Rural areas have tended to share in similar trends in the occupational structure of employment apparent in urban areas, including professionalisation (i.e., a shift towards a greater share of total employment in higher skilled jobs) and polarisation (i.e., a trend towards larger shares of employment in higher skilled and lower skilled occupations, coupled with a contraction of middle-level jobs). Nevertheless rural labour markets retain some distinctive features vis-à-vis urban ones, albeit there is diversity amongst rural labour markets.

Key demographic features include workforce ageing and selective out-migration of more qualified young people. These features pose challenges for rural economic development. An ageing workforce creates employment opportunities through 'replacement demand' (which takes into account the need to replace those who leave the employed workforce because of retirement or other reasons), meaning that there are job openings in declining sectors. Selective out-migration of the more highly qualified means that those employers seeking higher level skills may face labour and skill shortages and skills gaps. International migration to rural areas to address such shortages has become a distinctive feature of some rural labour markets, with implications for their operation.

Some rural employers use migrant labour to keep costs down. Those competing on the basis of low-skill and low-cost factors may be vulnerable to offshoring to lower cost locations, while at the same time rural areas do not offer the agglomeration economies that make large urban labour markets attractive to many high-value added growth sectors (Glaeser & Gottlieb, 2009). The conjunction of an establishment profile skewed towards small employers, sparsely distributed populations and transport difficulties pose particular problems in delivering training in rural areas to address skills deficiencies. However, over the last decade or so information and communications technologies (ICTs) have offered new opportunities for delivery of training, and for rural labour markets to attract some types of employment not traditionally associated with them.

Looking to the future, developments in local distributed manufacturing may lead to a growth in manufacturing in workplaces in urban and rural areas (Government Office for Science, 2013). Employment projections suggest continuing growth in professional and associate professional occupations (CEDEFOP, 2012; Wilson et al., 2014). It is possible that some of these people who are not necessarily tied to a specific workplace will choose to live and work in rural areas. It seems likely that the gains and losses in changing rural labour markets will be unevenly distributed across space.

A demand-side perspective: key features of the profile of employment in rural labour markets

Historically, a key feature of the employment structure of rural areas has been the importance of employment in land-based industries. Such industries have been associated with seasonal working, leading to a greater prevalence of pluriactivity. As employment in these industries has continued its long-term decline, employment in rural areas (as in urban areas) has been dominated by services, with a smaller proportion of employment in manufacturing (Atterton, Bryden & Johnson, 2012). Within the service sector, producer services tend to be under-represented relative to urban areas and those that exist tend to be general purpose rather than specialised in nature (OECD, 2014). Hence occupational structures tend to be less diverse in rural than in urban areas. In occupational terms, in remote rural labour markets particularly, the availability of higher skilled jobs (in professional and associate professional occupations) is limited, alongside over-representation of employment in intermediate occupations (such as skilled trades and plant, process and machine operatives) and in low-pay elementary occupations (Atherton, Price, Gray & Bosworth, 2010). Manufacturing remains an important, albeit minority source of employment in some rural areas, but it has been suggested that most rural manufacturing firms are not large enough to compete in specialised markets (OECD, 2014).

Nevertheless, employment structures in rural areas are much more diverse now than formerly (Shucksmith, Brown & Vergunst, 2012).

A further key feature of rural labour markets is the preponderance of small and medium-sized enterprises (SMEs). UK evidence suggests that rural businesses are more likely to be sole traders than those in urban areas, with many of these businesses in land-based, retail, construction or professional services sectors. Compared with some SMEs in urban areas, low population density, high commuting costs and small populations mean reduced competition, fewer information spillovers and reduced potential for developing specialised labour (OECD, 2014). Limited exposure to international markets and competitive pressure means that there is limited external impetus to drive up the demand for skills.

It is pertinent to consider the role of self-employment given that promotion of enterprising behaviour has risen up the local economic development agenda. Moreover, limited opportunities in the external labour market (particularly for residents of remote rural labour markets) may prompt some workers to consider self-employment. Research suggests that there are important differences in the nature of the relationship between self-employment and entrepreneurship in rural and urban labour markets. Analysis combining individual data and firm-level data at the travel-to-work area scale in Great Britain shows that a higher incidence of self-employment positively and strongly correlates with business creation and innovation in urban but not rural areas (Faggio & Silva, 2014). This is consistent with the idea that in urban areas with good labour market opportunities the self-employed become risk-taking, innovative entrepreneurs, whereas the fact that more rural than urban workers become self-employed in areas with comparatively poor labour market opportunities indicates that more residents in the former than the latter areas transit into self-employment as a last resort because of a lack of alternatives. Of course, some entrepreneurs decide to move from cities to rural areas, often for non-work related reasons. Research in Denmark examining entrepreneurs in knowledge-intensive sectors, based initially in urban areas and then moving to the countryside, shows that the businesses gradually tend to evolve into 'regional lifestyle businesses', operating in regional markets, with limited direct impacts on local employment in rural areas (Herslund, 2012).

A supply-side perspective: impacts of ageing and migration on rural labour markets

Many rural labour markets in OECD countries are characterised by an ageing population (both an increase in the average age of the population and an increase in the proportion of older people in the population) and a shrinking workforce, as a result of low birth rates and high out-migration of young people to urban areas, alongside in-migration of pre-retirement and retirement age persons (Champion & Brown, 2012). UK analyses of local population age profiles show that the highest median ages are found in the least densely populated parts of the UK (Philip, Brown & Stockdale, 2012). More qualified young people tend to be more migratory, whether to continue post-compulsory education or to take up employment opportunities in urban areas, where there are a greater range of more secure jobs. This skews the capacity of the labour force in rural areas towards those with lower skills levels. In comparison with urban areas with larger and more varied skills profiles, the likely greater incidence of missing elements in skills profiles in rural areas may preclude employment for some residents, because to deliver some products and services and enter new markets employers need a full complement of skills. Hence, weak skills and an ageing workforce have been cited as key attributes of the traditional rural economy (Freshwater, 2013).

Although agriculture in some countries has had a long-standing reliance on seasonal migrant labour (which has become increasingly international over time), traditionally, international immigrants have concentrated in large urban areas. In the 21st century the penetration of international migrants to rural areas has increased (Bauere, Densham, Millar & Salt, 2007; Green, de Hoyos, Jones & Owen, 2009). Many such areas have not been used to receiving international migrants on such a large scale and lack appropriate institutional infrastructure to deal with them (de Lima, Parra & Pfeffer, 2012). While many international migrants work in agriculture, their role extends to other sectors, such as hospitality, manufacturing and construction, which play an important role in rural labour markets.

Since 2004, following the enlargement of the European Union (EU) to include more member states from central and eastern Europe, there has been a sizeable migration to rural areas in northwestern Europe. Migrant labour has become a structural part of rural labour markets, and given that many such migrants in rural areas are working in jobs below their skills levels, questions have been raised regarding the ongoing availability of such labour – especially given the ease of labour circulation in the EU context (Pemberton & Stevens, 2010). International migrants to rural areas in the USA are less likely to be involved in such circulatory movement since militarisation of the US–Mexican border, and tend to be less well qualified than those in Europe (in the United States the vast majority of Mexican farmworkers lack a formal education). However, as in Europe, the range of rural destinations for international migrants to the USA has broadened since 1990 (Champion & Brown, 2012). Likewise, international migrants play an important role in rural labour markets in southern Europe. In a study of three different localities in northern Greece, where international migrants are mainly from the Balkans and Africa, Kasimis, Papadopoulos and Pappas (2010) found that migrants' contribution is fundamental to preserving the multifunctional character of rural areas, and so has an influential role on the economy and society there.

A second stream of international migrants to rural areas is in professional occupations, notably in the health sector (Shortall & Warner, 2012). In some rural areas such professional occupations are hard to fill, perhaps because of smaller internal labour markets or thin external labour markets. Moreover, remote rural areas are unattractive for nationals in dual career households, because of the difficulties in finding opportunities in two careers (Green, 1997).

Access to employment, prospects for in-work progression, and retention and recruitment issues

Challenges facing job seekers in rural areas include a relative lack of high-level jobs (as outlined above), limited opportunities for gaining and broadening work experience, and issues of limited transport and mobility (public transport services are often limited and may not be available temporally or spatially to link with employment and training opportunities) (de Hoyos & Green, 2011). Lack of appropriate skills and lack of transport, together with other potential barriers to employment, such as caring responsibilities, health problems and so on, are not unique to rural areas, but may be exacerbated by limited services and opportunities associated with low population density.

Excluding seasonal jobs, many rural labour markets tend to be characterised by lower staff turnover, which is in itself a function of limited alternative opportunities. This means that for employers retention may be less of an issue than recruitment (de Hoyos & Green, 2011), which in turn may mean there is less onus on employers to support in-work progression. For workers, the limited possibilities for career ladders in internal labour markets and thin external labour markets may in turn lead to limited worker interest in training and skills development.

In terms of recruitment, low population density in rural areas tends to mean that, *ceteris paribus*, employers have a smaller labour pool to select from. It may be especially challenging to find suitable candidates for more specialised positions. Analyses of the UK Employer Skills Survey 2011 found a slightly higher incidence of hard-to-fill vacancies in rural than in urban areas, but factors other than skills were a more important component in such vacancies in rural than in urban areas. A limited labour pool in rural areas, exacerbated by remote location and poor public transport, are factors that increase the incidence of both hard-to-fill and skill-shortage vacancies in rural relative to urban areas (Owen, Li & Green, 2013). The main consequence of hard-to-fill vacancies is an increased workload for other staff, which may in turn mean that less time is available to devote to training (if employers/employees were inclined to participate therein). Establishments in rural areas are more likely to have to outsource work or withdraw from markets than are urban establishments. They are also more likely to redefine existing jobs or increase training than establishments in rural areas.

There is a relatively limited literature on differences in the behaviour of job seekers in rural and urban areas and most studies pre-date recent increased use of the Internet for job searching (Green, Li, Owen & de Hoyos, 2012). A study of job search methods of unemployed job seekers in three local areas in Scotland (a sparsely populated remote rural area, a small rural town and a centrally located peri-urban area) found that those in rural areas were significantly more likely to use social networks to look for work than those in the peri-urban area, with social networks being seen as having practical value (Lindsay, Greig & McQuaid, 2005). Similarly, analyses of survey evidence and qualitative interviews in urban and rural areas in Canada (Matthews, Pendakur & Young, 2009) reveal that social networks (both strong and weak ties) are used more frequently by rural residents to find jobs than by city residents, with the latter relying more on formal job search methods. Those without strong social networks would seem to be especially disadvantaged in rural locations. These might include some incomers, who *ceteris paribus* are less likely than more established rural residents to have a support network to help with transport, childcare and access to informal information (Hodge, Dunn, Monk & Fitzgerald, 2002).

Local demand and supply dynamics and implications for economic development

The interaction of labour demand and supply dynamics at local level may be conceptualised using a framework formulated by Green, Hasluck, Hogarth and Reynolds (2003) and then promulgated by Froy and Giguère (2010) (see Figure 12.1). Four quadrants are identified:

- *Skills gaps and shortages* (top left-hand quadrant): Here the supply of skills is insufficient to meet the demand for skills, and this will be manifested in skills gaps (where an employee is not fully proficient – i.e., not able to do their job to the required level) and relatively high levels of skills shortage vacancies (where employers are unable to find sufficient applicants with appropriate skills, qualifications or experience). Shortcomings in local skills supply may be due to low levels of educational attainment and poor skills. It might be necessary to encourage in-migration of skilled workers to meet the demand for labour.
- *High skills equilibrium* (top right-hand quadrant): This is the desired destination of a high-performing local economy. In this situation the demand for high-level skills is met by the supply of high skills. Such areas are likely to be characterised by high levels of educational attainment, high employment rates and low unemployment rates.

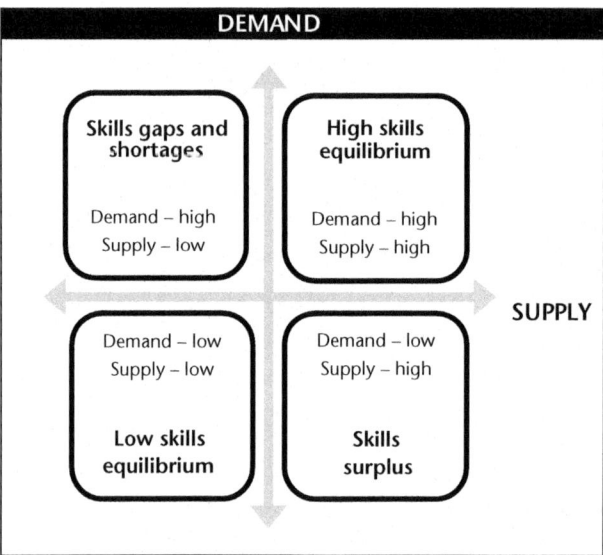

Figure 12.1   Conceptual framework for exploring demand and supply dynamics at local level
Source: Green, Hasluck, Hogarth & Reynolds (2003) and then promulgated by Froy and Giguère (2010).

- *Low skills equilibrium* (bottom left-hand quadrant): Here there is both a low demand for skills and a low supply of skills. Such a situation is characterised by low-wage and low-productivity jobs, and by low educational attainment and a high proportion of workers with low skills. There is likely to be out-migration of the highly skilled. In some areas with a low skills equilibrium employment rates may be relatively high.
- *Skills surplus* (bottom right-hand quadrant): Here the demand for skills is low but the supply of skills is high. Hence there is a mismatch between high levels of educational and skills attainment and a lack of high-skilled jobs. Such local labour markets are likely to be characterised by skills under-utilisation (perhaps leading to the attrition of human capital), relatively high unemployment rates and out-migration of the highly skilled. It is also possible that in circumstances of excess labour and downward pressure on wages, employers may be inclined to substitute labour for capital, with negative implications for productivity.

A particular focus of policy attention has been on the low skills equilibrium (LSEq). The LSEq hypothesis was formulated by Finegold and Soskice (1988) to account for low productivity in some labour markets. The key issue here is that local skills levels may be self-reinforcing: a LSEq occurs where employers face few skill shortages in a predominantly low-skilled workforce, and where there is little incentive to participate in education and training and raise qualifications and aspirations. A broad categorisation of local areas in Great Britain into each of the four quadrants specified above (OECD, 2015) shows that while there are rural areas in each of the four categories, they tend to be over-represented amongst the LSEq quadrant (particularly in the case of remote rural areas) and the skills surplus quadrant. Empirical analysis has identified the existence of a LSEq in rural areas: for Wales, Marsden, Franklin and Kitchen (2005) suggest that such dynamics are deeper and more profound in rural areas in west Wales (i.e., generally more remote rural areas) than in east Wales.

for reminding

Rural labour markets characterised by a LSEq have low skills levels amongst the indigenous population and a lack of high-value added businesses requiring higher level skills. Such areas are likely to find it difficult to attract in, or retain employers or workers with higher level skills. As employers demand relatively low skills from their workforce, there is little incentive for workers to improve their skills. Yet as noted by Owen, Hogarth and Green (2012), drawing on case study evidence from part of rural Lincolnshire in England, it is difficult for employers to move higher up the value chain because of local skills shortages, and yet at the same time employers are often loath to invest in training because of fears of losing skilled workers or because of difficulties in accessing relevant training opportunities. In such instances, it seems that the workforce has adjusted to available employment opportunities locally by not seeking to develop their skills or by migrating away if they are more ambitious. They will likely be in intense competition with workers in low-cost developing countries for routine work, unless markets are specifically local. Clearly, the limited size and spatial dispersion of labour in remote rural labour markets means that they do not benefit from the benefits of agglomeration that are apparent in urban labour markets, where greater specialisation within the workforce is associated with enhanced performance (Atherton, Price, Gray & Bosworth, 2010).

Blurkes - absence.

Tools and policies that have been identified for addressing the LSEq and improving skills utilisation include support for technology transfer (including setting up partnerships for sharing innovation in new technologies), providing holistic business support (in which skills development and attempts to raise productivity are incorporated in business development), encouraging participation in training for managers and workers, and ensuring that skills policies are embedded in local economic development policies. In the latter case, local partnership working plays an important role. This means that whereas historically much local economic development policy focused on creating jobs for unemployed and under-employed residents, with little attention devoted to whether such a policy approach contributed to low wages and low productivity, it is now increasingly important to focus policy on creating good jobs (Freshwater, Simms & Ward, 2014).

Inch of strategic economic development most areas.

Skills and training

Improving the supply and utilisation of workforce skills has become a key feature of rural economic development policy focusing on increasing productivity (OECD, 2014). This implies an enhanced focus on training and skills development. But typically it is more costly to provide training in rural areas due to low density and low critical mass. Transport is generally the main barrier to effective delivery of skills support in rural areas – given high travel costs of potential attendees (especially for more advanced/technical courses), such that training availability may be limited to more generalist courses/lower level qualifications. As noted in the following section, internet-based education and training has the potential to overcome some of the challenges of training delivery in remote rural areas.

Take-up of skills support (and also more general business support) is generally low in rural areas. Of course, not all businesses need support in taking up skills, but not all employers who do need help in developing skills know what support is available – this suggests a need for better tailored information (Hillage, 2013). Indeed, evidence suggests that personal approaches/ contact via trusted intermediaries is important in take-up of skills support. Analyses of data from the 2011 UK Employer Skills Survey showed that rural establishments tend to have a more informal approach to training than urban ones; they are less likely to have a training plan specifying in advance the level and type of training that employees will need, or a dedicated budget for training expenditure, and although they are more likely to make use of Further

149

Education colleges (supplying academic and vocational training at a variety of levels), they are less likely than urban establishments to undertake training for formal qualifications (Owen, Li & Green, 2013). A lack of relevant training courses and a lack of training providers locally are more frequently cited as reasons for not training in rural areas, by comparison with urban areas, and as noted above, travel to training may also pose more of a barrier to training in rural labour markets than in urban ones.

However, indicative of a relatively informal approach to training, rural establishments are more likely than urban ones to undertake training without having planned to do so. Analyses of 2011 UK Employer Skills Survey data also show that rural employers were less convinced about the benefits of providing training leading to vocational qualifications than employers in urban areas – with lack of interest amongst staff, insufficient knowledge of qualifications available and lack of government funding being amongst the reasons for not undertaking vocational training. In turn, rural establishments also placed less importance on formal qualifications (academic or vocational) in recruiting than urban establishments (Owen, Li & Green, 2013), perhaps indicating a greater onus on tacit knowledge in rural than in urban labour markets. This poses challenges to stakeholders seeking to advance the skills agenda in rural areas.

The role of ICTs and the Internet

Broadband access to the Internet can affect supply and demand in the labour market in at least three main ways (Atasoy, 2013). First, Internet job search methods can extend the reach and penetration of, and speed up, information flows about labour market vacancies, and (at least theoretically) improve the job-matching process (Autor, 2001). Second, employment opportunities may be created directly in ICT industries, and more broadly through e-commerce demand for goods, and services (in non-ICT related as well as in ICT-related industries) may extend into a larger geographical area. Third, broadband can affect work organisation and practices.

Hence, the Internet and ICTs have the potential to mitigate problems of geographical remoteness in rural areas, so overcoming handicaps of distance. Based on economic modelling of the expansion of broadband Internet access from 1999 to 2007 on labour market outcomes in the USA, Atasoy (2013) finds that gaining access to broadband services in a county is associated with approximately a 1.8 percentage point increase in the employment rate, with larger effects in rural and isolated areas. Shucksmith, Brown and Vergunst (2012) suggest that a narrowing of the urban–rural digital divide could mean that the employment structures of rural labour markets will be more diverse in future. However, the reality has been one of higher costs of installing broadband in rural areas than in urban ones, and rural areas also remain disadvantaged relative to urban areas in the face of synergies between electronic and face-to-face contact in the operation of labour markets and economies (OECD, 2014).

Importantly, the Internet may be thought of as extending the economic boundaries of rural areas. Through Internet-enabled working – for example, via crowdsourcing, where functions/ tasks are outsourced to a large pool of individuals using an open call over the Internet (Howe, 2008) – rural residents are not confined to opportunities in rural labour markets, but rather can participate in global labour markets (Green et al., 2014). Likewise, crowdsourcing platforms (where people can search for and access paid work, which is often, but not always, conducted remotely) enable some rural businesses to purchase services from way beyond the local labour market – offering rural businesses the opportunity to supplement the local skills pool with workers from elsewhere. This opens up prospects for shifting the sectoral mix in rural areas. It also affords the possibility for crowdsourced workers to work from home in a way that might fit around their non-work activities. It is likely that e-working and e-learning may be only a partial solution to challenges faced by rural residents in enhancing and utilising their skills, and for employers in addressing labour and skills needs. Not all work and learning can take place remotely: face-to-face interaction remains important in many circumstances for performing job tasks and for learning.

Conclusions

A key feature of rural labour markets is a limited labour pool (both quantitatively and qualitatively) for employers to draw on to meet their labour and skills requirements (Green & Hardill, 2003; Francis & Pillai, 2008). This means that employers in rural areas (and especially those in peripheral rural areas) face less choice than those in urban labour markets. Knowledge-intensive sectors and occupations tend to be under-represented in rural areas relative to urban areas. Also, in rural areas the preponderance of small establishments is greater than average and the size structure of establishments in rural areas means that there are fewer large establishments to play a leading role in driving up demand for skills locally. This highlights two key issues for rural labour markets: first, limited prospects for in-work progression in situ (in either internal or external labour markets); and second, the challenge of driving up demand for skills.

Looking ahead, it seems likely that there will continue to be differentiation in the fortunes of rural labour markets, reflecting the different opportunities and constraints in rural areas (OECD, 2014). The most advantaged rural labour markets may well be characterised by good accessibility to wider metropolitan labour markets. They may be in a high skills equilibrium with high pay and high value added. Conversely, other rural labour markets may find it difficult to break out of a situation of LSEq characterised by low pay and low value added or to drive up demand for skills to address a situation of skills surplus. This suggests that different local labour markets need different types of support. As noted in research on local labour markets of different sizes in Atlantic Canada, Freshwater, Simms and Ward (2014) suggest that this requires stakeholders, at a range of geographical scales (from the local to the regional/provincial to the national), to act collaboratively, taking account of the size and resources of different local labour market areas. It also means that a territorial approach is needed, going beyond local administrative boundaries to include other rural and urban areas with economic and spatial linkages. This highlights three further key issues for rural labour markets. The first is the need for intelligent, place-informed, local economic development policies taking account of the rural and urban settlement structure and the existing and possible future geography of economic opportunity. The second is, where possible, to strengthen and fashion urban–rural links to the advantage of rural areas. In England, longitudinal research suggests that long-distance commuting is not necessarily a transitory condition for rural in-migrants, but rather that the migration–commuting nexus contributes to rural economic and social relationships binding rural and urban areas (Brown, Champion, Coombes & Wymer, 2015). The third issue is to maximise the opportunity to use the Internet to extend the global reach of rural businesses and workers – through ensuring both infrastructure provision and business support to enable rural enterprises and entrepreneurs to service wider markets.

References

Atasoy, H (2013). The effects of broadband internet expansion on labor market outcomes. *Industrial and Labor Relations Review* 66(2), 315–345.

Atherton, A, Price, L, Gray, D & Bosworth, G (2010). *Rurality, productivity and skills in the East Midlands.* Lincoln: Lincoln Business School.

Anne Green

Atterton, J, Bryden, J & Johnson, TG (2012). Rural economic transformation in the UK and US. In M Shucksmith, DL Brown, S Shortall, J Vergunst & ME Warner (Eds), *Rural transformations and rural policies in the US and UK* (pp. 117–137). London: Routledge.

Autor, D (2001). Wiring the labor market. *Journal of Economic Perspectives* 15(1), 25–40.

Bauere, V, Densham, P, Millar, J & Salt, J (2007). Migrants from Central and Eastern Europe: Local geographies. *Population Trends* 129, 7–19.

Brown, DL, Champion, T, Coombes, M & Wymer, C (2015). Examining the migration-commuting nexus: Migration and commuting in rural England: a longitudinal analysis. *Journal of Rural Studies* 31, 118–128.

CEDEFOP (2012). Skills supply and demand in Europe. CEDEFOP Research Paper 25. Luxembourg: Publications Office of the European Union.

Champion, T & Brown, DL (2012). Migration and urban–rural population redistribution in the UK and US. In M Shucksmith, DL Brown, S Shortall, J Vergunst & ME Warner (Eds), *Rural transformations and rural policies in the US and UK* (pp. 39–57). London: Routledge.

de Hoyos, M & Green, A (2011). Recruitment and retention issues in rural labour markets. *Journal of Rural Studies* 27, 171–180.

de Lima, P, Parra, PA & Pfeffer, MJ (2012). Conceptualizing contemporary immigration integration in the rural United States and United Kingdom. In M Shucksmith, DL Brown, S Shortall, J Vergunst & ME Warner (Eds), *Rural transformations and rural policies in the US and UK* (pp. 79–99). London: Routledge.

Faggio, G & Silva, O (2014). Self-employment and entrepreneurship in urban and rural labour markets. *Journal of Urban Economics* 84, 67–85.

Finegold, D & Soskice, D (1988). The failure of training in Britain: Analysis and prescription. *Oxford Review of Economic Policy* 4(3), 21–53.

Francis, R & Pillai, R (2008). *Working in 21st century rural England: A scoping study*. Brighton: Institute of Employment Studies.

Freshwater, D (2013). Modernising rural economies: Strengthening economic growth in the 21st century. OECD Rural Development Policy Conference, Krasnoyarsk, Russian Federation, 4 October.

Freshwater, D, Simms, A & Ward, J (2014). *Local labour markets as a new way of organizing policies for stronger regional economic development in Atlantic Canada*. Canada: The Harris Centre, Memorial University.

Froy, F & Giguère, S (2010). Putting in place jobs that last: A guide to rebuilding quality employment at local level. OECD Local Economic and Employment Development (LEED) Working Papers, No. 2010/13. Paris: OECD.

Glaeser, R & Gottlieb, J (2009). The wealth of cities: Agglomeration economies and spatial equilibrium in the United States. *Journal of Economic Literature* 47(4), 983–1028.

Government Office for Science (2013). The future of manufacturing: A new era of challenge and opportunity for the UK. London: Government Office for Science.

Green, AE (1997). A question of compromise? Case study evidence on the location and mobility strategies of dual career households. *Regional Studies* 31(7), 641–657.

Green, A (2004). Is relocation redundant? Observations on the changing nature and impacts of employment-related geographical mobility in the UK. *Regional Studies* 38(6), 629–641.

Green, A (2012). Skills for competitiveness: Country report for the United Kingdom. OECD Local Economic and Employment Development (LEED) Working Papers 2012/05. Paris: OECD.

Green, A, de Hoyos, M, Barnes, S-A, Baldauf, B & Behle, H (2014). *Exploratory research on Internet-enabled work exchanges and employability*. JRC Scientific and Policy Reports. Luxembourg: European Commission Joint Research Centre IPTS.

Green, AE, de Hoyos, M, Jones, P & Owen, D (2009). Rural development and labour supply challenges in the UK: The role of non-UK migrants. *Regional Studies* 43(10), 1261–1273.

Green, AE & Hardill, I (2003). Rural labour markets skills and training. Coventry: Institute for Employment Research, University of Warwick.

Green, AE, Hasluck, C, Hogarth, T & Reynolds, C (2003). East Midlands FRESA targets project: Final report. Nottingham: emda. Available at http://irep.ntu.ac.uk/R/URQCKE5GA1M2EU12H7RIG74S2T3CK4XLMV2SJCDLL8R9SPXDNR-05571 (accessed 28 September 2014).

Green, AE, Li, Y, Owen, D & de Hoyos, M (2012). Inequalities in use of the Internet for job search: Similarities and contrasts by economic status in Great Britain. *Environment and Planning A* 44, 2344–2358.

Herslund, L (2012). The rural creative class: Counterurbanisation and entrepreneurship in the Danish countryside. *Sociologia Ruralis* 52(2), 235–255.

Hillage, J (2013). Access to national skills and business support programmes among rural businesses. Institute of Employment Studies, Brighton.

Hodge, I, Dunn, J, Monk, S & Fitzgerald, M (2002). Barriers to participation in residual rural labour markets. *Work, Employment and Society* 16(3), 457–476.

Howe, J (2008). *Crowdsourcing: How the power of the crowd is driving the future of business.* London: Random House Business.

Kasimis, C, Papadopoulos, AG & Pappas, C (2010). Gaining from rural migrants: Migrant employment strategies and socioeconomic implications for rural labour markets. *Sociologia Ruralis* 50(3), 258–276.

Lindsay, C, Greig, M & McQuaid, RW (2005). Alternative job search strategies in remote rural and peri-urban labour markets: The role of social networks. *Sociologia Ruralis* 45(1/2), 53–70.

Marsden, T, Franklin, A & Kitchen, L (2005). *Rural labour markets: Exploring the mismatches.* Wales Rural Observatory Research Report 7. Wales.

Matthews, R, Pendakur, R & Young, N (2009). Social capital, labour markets, and job-finding in urban and rural regions: Comparing paths to employment in prosperous cities and stressed rural communities in Canada. *The Sociological Review* 57(2), 306–330.

OECD (2014). *Innovation and modernising the rural economy.* Paris: OECD.

OECD (2015). *Employment and skills strategies in England.* Paris: OECD.

Owen, D, Hogarth, T & Green, A (2012). Skills, transport and economic development: Evidence from a rural area in England. *Journal of Transport Geography* 21, 80–92.

Owen, D, Li, Y & Green, A (2013). *Secondary analysis of employer surveys: Urban and rural differences in jobs, training and skills.* Evidence report 75. Wath-upon-Dearne: UK Commission for Employment and Skills.

Pemberton, S & Stevens, C (2010). The recruitment and retention of Central and Eastern European migrant workers in the United Kingdom: A panacea or a problem under the new policies of 'managed migration'. *Regional Studies* 44, 1289–1300.

Philip, L, Brown, DL & Stockdale, A (2012). Demographic ageing in rural areas: Insights from the UK and US. In M Shucksmith, DL Brown, S Shortall, J Vergunst & ME Warner (Eds), *Rural transformations and rural policies in the US and UK* (pp. 58–78). London: Routledge.

Shortall, S & Warner, ME (2012). Rural transformations: Conceptual and policy issues. In M Shucksmith, DL Brown, S Shortall, J Vergunst & ME Warner (Eds), *Rural transformations and rural policies in the US & UK* (pp. 3–17). London: Routledge.

Shucksmith, M, Brown, DL & Vergunst, J (2012). Constructing the rural–urban interface. In M Shucksmith, DL Brown, S Shortall, J Vergunst & ME Warner (Eds), *Rural transformations and rural policies in the US and UK* (pp. 287–303). London: Routledge.

Wilson, R, Beaven, R, May-Gillings, M, Hay, G & Stevens, J (2014). *Working futures 2012–2022.* Evidence report 83. Wath-upon-Dearne: UK Commission for Employment and Skills.

13

The Death of Distance?

Networks, the Costs of Distance and Urban–Rural Interdependence

Bruce A. Weber and David Freshwater

Remarkable advances in information and communications technologies (ICT) in recent decades have dramatically affected spatial economic relationships, including opportunities for development in rural areas. Two particularly important ways in which ICT has changed spatial economic relationships are through changes in the costs of distance and through the expansion of networks. The 'death of distance' hypothesis suggests that with falling transport and information costs rural areas may no longer be at a disadvantage when it comes to producing many goods and services because it is now relatively cheaper to get rural goods to urban markets domestically and internationally.[1] ICT has also led to improvements in the magnitude and scope of networks affecting the distribution of jobs and people across the entire settlement system. Indeed, it has been argued that the growth of networks has fundamentally changed societies (Castells & Cardoso, 2006) and economies (Shapiro & Varian, 1999). Both of these developments mean that rural and urban areas are more strongly connected now than in the past.

But does a reduction in distance, however measured, in conjunction with an increase in the density and scope of various networks enhance or impede rural development? The 'death of distance' hypothesis would seem to favour rural areas, while the emergence of denser networks associated with agglomeration effects could favour urban areas. In this chapter, we explore possible connections between regional economists' fascination with economic agglomerations and distance on the one hand, and economic and sociological research on the role of networks on the other. We attempt to sort out: (1) how reductions in the costs of distance may have affected the spatial distribution of economic activity; and (2) how the existence of denser networks – both within and across rural and urban places – might affect the location of economic activity.

The chapter has five parts. The first reviews external forces that have transformed the location of economic activity over the past half-century, leading rural areas to become more integrated with urban centres and blurring boundaries between 'rural' and 'urban'. The second section reviews studies of how distance from urban centres and rank in the urban hierarchy affect population/job growth and poverty/inequality. The next section, using the concepts of 'spread' and 'backwash', explores mechanisms by which urban growth can benefit or disadvantage the rural periphery of urban centres. It explores the strength of geographic spillovers from urban growth for rural areas and the impact of these spillovers on rural growth and rural poverty. A fourth section focuses on the concept of networks and how modern information and communications technology may have affected rural society and the spatial distribution of economic activity and population. The concluding section draws four lessons for policy.

Forces affecting the spatial transformation of urban and rural areas

Urban and rural places have been subject to enormous economic and social shocks over the past century, particularly the past quarter-century (OECD, 1993, 2012; Galston & Baehler, 1995; Marini & Mooney, 2006; Johnson, 2014). Changes have blurred the boundaries, and increased the links, between urban and rural areas as they have opened both to the competitive pressures of global investment and trade (also see Noguera and Freshwater, this volume). Changes in costs of distance and the formation of networks have been both caused by, and affected by, the blurring of boundaries, increased interdependence and globalisation.

Lichter and Brown (2011) identify technological change, globalisation and governmental devolution as drivers of the increased linkages between urban and rural places, and articulate the key role of technology: 'Technological advances have brought most aspects of rural life into the urban fold and linked rural people and communities directly to the global economy' (pp. 567–568).

Similarly, Barca, McCann and Rodríguez-Pose (2012, p. 136) emphasise how globalisation has increased the importance of space and distance in economic development:

> Globalization has made localities and their interaction more important for economic growth and prosperity ... Space is becoming increasingly "slippery," in the sense that capital, goods, people, and ideas travel more easily ..., but, at the same time, increasingly "sticky" and "thick" because capital, goods, people, and ideas, despite being constantly on the move, tend to remain stuck in large agglomerations ... Consequently, globalization has made space and place more rather than less important.

Irwin et al. (2009, p. 435) describe the new urban–rural interdependence as the 'emergence of urban-rural space ... characterized by the merging of a rural landscape form with urban economic function'. Based on their reading of recent research, they reached three conclusions about this new form of interdependence:

1 Urban function is no longer limited to cities and suburbs. In many regions of North America and Europe, an increasing proportion of the population in seemingly rural areas is economically and socially tied to urban areas.
2 Ongoing economic restructuring, caused by falling transportation costs, new communications technologies and increased global competition, has simultaneously strengthened urbanisation and spurred urban decentralisation.
3 Urban growth has penalised more remote rural areas in terms of lower job and population growth. The exceptions are amenity-rich rural areas, particularly those in the United States that have grown rapidly as a result of rising real incomes and changes in transportation and technology.

These three assessments each point out how connections between rural and urban places have been strengthened as a result of new technologies that have reduced the cost of moving goods and people and that have allowed new forms of communication that have enhanced connectivity. But, while rural regions are better connected to urban regions than in the past, it is not clear that improved connectivity is sufficient to lead to better rural economic outcomes.

The 'death of distance?' Effects of distance from urban centres on rural economies

When Frances Cairncross announced the 'death of distance' in 1995, she wondered how reductions in telecommunications costs would reshape the world's economy.

'Thanks to technology and competition in telecoms,' she asserted, 'distance will soon be no object ... The death of distance as a determinant of the cost of communications will probably be the single most important economic force shaping societies in the first half of the next century' (1995, p. 5). Others noted that technological advances and investments in information and transportation infrastructure had also reduced costs to businesses and consumers in ways that could affect relative costs in urban and remote rural areas. With lower communication, information and transportation costs, the costs of distance no longer represented a major barrier to access to inputs or product markets in remote locations.

Effects of distance on population and job growth

Glaeser and Kohlhase (2004), noting that the standard theories of urban and regional economics were built on the cost of transporting manufactured goods, argue that the steep decline in transport costs ('over 90% in real terms') in the 20th century requires a rethinking both of classic location theory, central place theory and monocentric urban models, and of the new economic geography models. 'These reduced costs, and the declining importance of the goods-producing sector of the economy, mean that in our view, it is better to assume that moving goods is essentially costless than to assume that moving goods is an important component of the production process' (2004, p. 199).

Urban economics has focused on the development of cities and the spatial evolution of the metropolitan areas surrounding cities. Several studies have estimated the geographic extent of urban agglomerations. Rosenthal and Strange (2003) find that 'agglomeration economies attenuate with distance. The initial attenuation is rapid, with the effect on own-industry employment in the first mile being up to 10 to 1000 times larger than the effect 2 to 5 miles away. Beyond 5 miles attenuation is much less' (p. 378). In a subsequent paper (2008), they found that 'most of the spillover effects of agglomeration occur within five miles although some spillovers extend out even as far as 50 miles' (p. 383). These results suggest that rural places in relatively close proximity to urban centres are in the best position to 'piggy-back' on urban agglomeration effects, but also these agglomeration effects extend some distance out.

Economists and regional scientists concerned with rural places have taken a larger view of the urban system, focusing not just on how the effect of urban agglomerations attenuate as one moves into hinterlands of large cities, but on the cumulative effect of distance for successive tiers in the urban hierarchy. They examine, for example, how the effect of distance from a metropolitan area on rural counties' population and employment growth depends on both the distance from the metro area and the metro area's rank size in the urban hierarchy.

The most extensive scholarship on this issue is by Partridge, Rickman, Olfert and colleagues who examined the effect of distance on both population growth and employment growth. Three studies looked at the relationship between distance and population growth. Partridge, Olfert and Alasia (2007) examined the effect of proximity to major cities on population growth in Canadian communities (Census Consolidated Subdivisions) between 1981 and 2001. Their results

> suggest that positive marginal effects from proximity to major centres [defined as metropolitan areas greater than 500,000] extend out about 830 km (516 mi) for other

urban centres, and 800 km (497 mi) for RST CCSs [Rural and Small Town Census Consolidated Subdivisions]. One implication is that the positive forces of urban agglomeration extend far beyond their major centre's boundaries – much further than the more localised effects often depicted by urban economists – so that virtually all residents outside the major centres benefit from closer proximity to them.

(2007, p. 58)

In a second study, Partridge, Rickman, Ali and Olfert (2008c) explored the effect of proximity to cities on population growth in hinterland US counties. They examined proximity as distance to higher tiered cities. 'Over the period 1950–2000, we find strong negative growth effects of distances to higher-tiered urban areas. Further, the costs of distance, if anything, appear to be increasing over time' (p. 727). In two other studies, the research team looked at the effect of distance from urban centres on employment growth. The general conclusions are the same as for population growth (Partridge, Rickman, Ali & Olfert, 2008a).

Using geographically weighted regression, Partridge, Rickman, Ali and Olfert (2008b) examined the relationship between proximity to urban centres and job growth for US non-metropolitan counties, allowing the effect of distance from successively higher ordered cities on county job growth to vary across regions. They hypothesise that the 'rural distance penalty' inhibiting job growth should be less for rural regions near densely populated areas because these regions have more points of access to agglomeration economies. They also considered the possibility that 'distance protection from spatial competition' might spur job growth in isolated rural areas. As in the earlier analysis, they find that there is a rural distance penalty, with this penalty being strongest for distance to the nearest urban place. County job growth does appear to be related to distance from urban centres and 'remoteness is a major deterrent to job growth for most counties outside a metro area'. However, the distance penalty is reduced somewhat if distance to a large metropolitan region is also included in the regression. That is, if a rural county has access to both a small urban centre and a more distant metropolitan agglomeration, it has a smaller distance penalty than a similar rural area that only has access to a small urban centre. Moreover, the larger the metropolitan region, the greater the reduction in the distance penalty facing the rural county.

To summarise: the best evidence available to us suggests that distance still matters, but it matters less than we might suppose for those rural places that are not truly remote. Research on the relationship between distance from urban agglomerations and growth and poverty consistently finds that distance is not dead, that proximity of rural places to urban centres is associated with them having higher population and job growth. Finally, it is important to recognise that distance penalties are not linear in nature but increase slowly after an initial spike.

Effects of distance on rural poverty

Partridge and Rickman (2008) examined the relationship between poverty in rural US counties and their proximity to successively higher tiered metropolitan areas. They find that 'poverty increases with greater distance from each successive tier of a Metropolitan Statistical Area (MSA), even when accounting for a host of county characteristics such as the area's amenity attractiveness and the demographic composition of the local population' (p. 287).

In a Canadian study, Chokie and Partridge (2008) investigated the relationship between low-income cut-off rates and distances from urban agglomerations, using two measures of distance.[2]

Consistent with positive agglomeration effects and better commuting linkages, a greater population base within 100 km is associated with less poverty in the 1996 model, supporting claims that thicker regional labour markets improve the prospects of disadvantaged workers. However, being located near a larger population that is 100–200 km away is associated with higher poverty rates, perhaps because of remoteness from larger population centers. (2008, p. 328)

The 'death of distance?' Spread and backwash effects of urban growth on peripheral rural economies

In the previous section, we explored the literature on whether *proximity* to cities affected the population growth and job growth in the rural hinterland. In this section, we turn to the dynamic question of whether *growth* in urban centres has spread or backwash effects on population, jobs and poverty in their rural peripheries. Barkley, Henry and Bao (1996) identified a number of mechanisms through which core metropolitan regions can have 'spread effects': (1) urban funds can be invested in rural communities; (2) urban growth can provide new markets for rural periphery products; (3) urban growth can provide jobs for rural commuters; (4) urban workers can move to rural communities and commute back to the core; (5) urban firms in mature industries can move to lower cost rural locations; (6) knowledge, technology and expansionist cultural attitudes originating in the core can spread to the rural periphery; (7) urban growth can generate funding and policies promoting decentralisation. Each of these flows can go in the opposite direction, of course, generating 'backwash effects'.

Spread and backwash effects on rural population and jobs

Gunnar Myrdal (1963) introduced the terms 'spread' and 'backwash' effects into the economic development literature to capture the positive and negative impacts of trade in less developed economies. The study of whether urban growth has spread or backwash effects in rural areas of developed countries grew out of the growth centre policy debates of the 1970s and 1980s. With the development of spatial analytic techniques in the 1990s, regional scientists gained more powerful tools to examine spatial patterns and spatial linkages.

Barkley, Henry and Bao (1996) conducted one of the earliest examinations of this type in North Carolina, South Carolina and Georgia. They found evidence of both spread and backwash effects, and that the pattern of effects was associated with particular characteristics of a region's metro core. They found that metro growth in the 1980s involved population decentralisation. 'This redistribution was limited, however, to rural tracts at the urban fringe. Population densities were stable or declined in tracts more distant from the nodal centre. Thus, backwash effects were evident in most rural areas in the economic regions' hinterlands' (p. 336).

Henry et al. (1999) used a similar approach to estimate population and employment spread and backwash effects for functional economic regions in Denmark, eastern France and the US state of South Carolina. Their findings supported the conclusion that spread effects of urban nodes are 'often significant and tend to dominate urban backwash impacts on rural communities' (p. 526). They generally found urban spread effects for rural places with average or large labour markets or population sizes, and that the spread effects increased with the size of the zone. They found backwash effects of urban growth on rural places in smaller zones.

More recent examinations of the spread and backwash effects have focused on the geographic extent of spread effects in Canada and the United States. Partridge, Bollman, Olfert and Alasia

(2007) developed a 'spread–backwash topography' in which the effect of distance from an urban centre on a rural community is a function of two independent forces: (1) an 'urban distance discount' (UDD) that captures the positive effect of *being close to an urban area* that declines with distance from the urban area; and (2) the 'spread effect' which captures the positive effect of *growth of the urban area* that declines with distance from the urban area and may become negative – in which case it is a 'backwash effect'. The total effect of distance from an urban core is the sum of these two effects, and it is important to distinguish the long-run equilibrium UDD from the shorter run or cyclical spread effect of urban growth.

Ganning, Baylis and Lee (2013) attempted to estimate the geographic extent and effect of growth spillovers in 276 US MSAs on population in 1,988 non-metropolitan communities for 2000–2007, comparing three methods of weighting a city's influence: the traditional approach that estimates distance to the nearest city only; an approach that weights relevant MSAs according to the inverse distance between an MSA and the non-metropolitan community; and an approach that uses commuting flows to weight MSAs. For all three measures, they find that larger MSAs have larger spread effects. They estimate the 'tipping points' for each size of city as the point at which spread effects diminish to zero. Their preferred model (the inverse distance approach) suggests that spread effects extend 67 miles from small cities (< 100,000 population), 78 miles for medium cities (100,000–500,000) and 89 miles for large cities (> 500,000). One implication of the preference for the inverse distance model is that 'nonmetropolitan places may develop their local economies around multiple cities rather than only the nearest city, suggesting a collaborative approach to regional and nonmetropolitan development' (Ganning, Baylis & Lee, 2013, p. 476).

Spread and backwash effects on rural poverty

The spread and backwash mechanisms that affect changes in population and economic activity will also affect the distribution of income and poverty across the settlement system. Noting that high poverty persisted in remote rural areas during the strong economic growth and overall declines in poverty rates of the 1990s, Partridge and Rickman (2008) explored the spread effect of urban job growth on rural poverty rates in the USA. They found that rural county poverty rates increase as distance to higher tiered metropolitan areas increases. But they also found that urban proximity may allow commuting to existing jobs. Hence, urban job growth in the nearest urban centre could create new job opportunities for the rural poor. They find that 'urban "spread" effects reduce rural poverty, in which one likely avenue is through creating job-commuting opportunities' (p. 302). In further analysis, they examined whether there was a protective effect of distance from metropolitan counties. 'We also found that local employment growth has greater poverty-reducing impacts in remote counties. This likely occurs because of smaller commuting and migration flows between remote areas and other areas; i.e., remote areas have a more inelastic labor supply' (pp. 306–307).

Partridge and Rickman (2007) have also examined this issue. They looked at the effect of distance from successively higher tiered metropolitan areas on 1999 poverty rates in *persistent poverty* rural counties (counties with poverty rates exceeding 20% in 1969, 1979 and 1989). They examined separately the effects of growth in successively higher tiered metropolitan areas on persistent-poverty and non-persistent-poverty counties. They found that in fact job growth in the nearest MAs (metropolitan areas) did reduce poverty in persistent-poverty counties, and that this effect attenuated as distance from the MA increased.

The research reviewed in this section suggests that distance is not dead; that proximity to urban agglomerations is increasingly important for rural communities, with a beneficial effect extending far into the hinterlands; and that the spread effects of population and employment growth in urban cores enhance employment and population growth and reduce poverty in the rural peripheries of cities.

Networks, agglomeration economies and distance

The notion of networks is found in all social sciences, but there are considerable differences among disciplines in the importance placed on the idea, and on the meanings that are attached to it (Gluckler, 2007). We focus on the role of networks as they affect rural economic development, in particular their potential to alleviate the rural challenges of long distance, low density and lack of critical mass. Following Murdoch (2000) we consider three broad types of networks: (1) physical networks (energy, transport and telecommunications); (2) social capital networks that link people, firms and organisations; and (3) value or supply chains that connect the production of firms.

The strength of the various networks has implications for local development, particularly in terms of the complexity of the networks in a rural place; the complexity of networks in other places, including urban and rural regions; and, of course, the degree to which the various local networks are interconnected. In terms of physical networks, rural places have stronger energy and transport connections than in earlier times, but in most instances they remain disadvantaged relative to urban regions. In particular, external connections from rural regions may be limited – one road, a single power line, slow Internet. Similarly, it is generally held that rural regions have strong internal ties – people are closely linked even when they have adversarial relationships, but often there are only weak social relationships that provide connections to other regions. Finally, local supply chains in rural regions tend to be short because the local economy is small and specialised and rural firms can face difficulty in connecting to global markets either as input suppliers or as purchasers. It is also important to distinguish between network relations that are market exchanges, such as supply chain linkages and energy transmission, and relations that are based on reciprocity, such as relationships among individuals or alliances among firms that fit within the rubric of social capital.

Gluckler sees geography affecting networks in two ways: first, proximity facilitates network formation – there is a distance penalty – and second, the attributes of each place make a difference, in terms of both opportunities and benefits (2007, pp. 621–622). Distance penalties can be in the form of monetary costs, time lags or insufficient bandwidth to allow complex knowledge flows. Similarly, nearby network opportunities may have low value or be redundant, while more distant ones are difficult to identify and establish.

In general, rural regions appear to be disadvantaged by most forms of network effects. In this vein, Marsden notes that in rural areas two forms of networks have to be considered: those that link actors within that specific region and those that connect the region to other regions (Marsden, 1998). While strong external linkages can offer opportunities to connect to new market opportunities and new sources of goods and services, this is a two-edged sword, because local firms may be displaced and residents may learn they have a better future elsewhere and leave. Murdoch identifies two distinct types of networks in rural areas that support economic development: vertical networks in the form of commodity chains that bind rural natural resources to national markets, and horizontal networks that foster joint learning and innovation within the rural region (Murdoch, 2000), He sees the possibility for both to coexist and notes that in many cases rural innovation is tied to natural resources and actually builds upon pre-existing supply chain linkages. On the other hand, there is a belief that electronic communication networks may be advantageous for rural development because they can offset weak rural social networks, allow access to goods and services not available locally, and reduce the penalty of distance.

A similar tension is found in Johansson and Quigley (2004) who suggest that in urban regions there is a public good aspect to the benefits of concentration of firms and households, which leads to agglomerations of people and businesses into dense settlements. However, networks based on information and communications technology may support either concentration or dispersion of economic activity:

> networks among economic actors dispersed over space may act as a substitute for agglomerations of actors at a single point, providing some or all of the utility gains and productivity increases derived from agglomeration … In the spatial context, networks play a role in facilitating exchange both within and between regional agglomerations ….
>
> … [E]conomic networks arise from a collective decision by group members, generating a private institution. Networks are clubs in which exclusion is possible and price discrimination is the norm. Agglomerations cannot exclude economic actors from receiving benefits nor can they price these benefits efficiently.
>
> *(Johansson & Quigley, 2004, p. 166)*

Thus, the benefit of proximity is a public good that can be enhanced by ICT and leads to agglomerations whose benefits spill over to proximate rural areas, but in a way that attenuates as distances from the centre increase. The costs of distance, however, are not a critical barrier to the formation of private networks that span vast distances in the current epoch of dizzying advances in information and communications technology. Emerging networks supported by ICT do in fact diminish the influence of spatial distance and can strengthen the economic opportunities in remote rural places. This, of course, depends critically on the extent of access to wireless communications and the Internet in rural areas. While access has improved greatly in recent years, access to the Internet is not yet universal across the landscape (Malecki, 2003; Warren, 2007).

Face-to-face communication is still, however, arguably a driver of urban agglomerations, and the localisation economies that are based on face-to-face contacts do not appear to be diminishing with the rise of ICT. In a review of controlled laboratory experiments on face-to-face communications, Frank (2014) found that 'face-to-face communication, compared to e-mail communication, increases trust and cooperation in most cases (except for pure coordination tasks)' (p. 423). Frank notes that, while trust and communication might also be able to be established through video conferencing, and thus diminish the importance of this reason for face-to-face contact, there are other potential benefits of face-to-face communication (increases efficiency of communication, serves as indicator of commitment, allows unplanned or random communication) about which we do not have experimental evidence. Calhoun (1998) suggests that the two mechanisms are in fact complementary and reinforce each other. Even so, advances in ICT may permit communication where face-to-face contacts are difficult and facilitate the creation of networks over greater distances. This could allow rural areas to experience some of the benefits of 'utility and productivity gains' that are currently available mostly in urban agglomerations.

On balance, it is difficult to conclude other than that network effects in general tend to favour urban regions, because the variety and density of networks is much greater there. Even when rural regions are connected to these networks there is typically some reduction in benefits caused by the cost of dealing with distance, as a cost in terms of either money, time or, increasingly, bandwidth. These costs are clearly smaller for ICT networks because the underlying infrastructure is relatively cheap and quick. However, ICT of itself is not a driver of economic activity.

Lessons for policy

Improvements in transport infrastructure and the rapid adoption of ICT by retailers, service providers and most other businesses have greatly expanded the linkages between urban and rural regions. However, proximity remains important and remote rural regions remain at a disadvantage. But distance is also not destiny. Public policies can enhance the links between urban and rural places, support the development of remote rural communities and support the evolution of local institutions by drawing on the unique strengths of individual places. Local policies can recognise the limits imposed by their location relative to urban centres and use the benefits of ICT to form networks that support the development of local assets in ways that link them better to urban and world markets.

In particular, we see four policy lessons from our consideration of how technological changes affecting transport and communication costs have altered connectivity among rural and urban regions:

1   For proximate rural regions and communities, development is largely driven by what happens in the nearby urban area. Understanding how spread and backwash effects impact rural territory is crucial in formulating effective development strategies.
2   Remote rural places may benefit from the protection from competition that distance provides, and remote places may find that place-based policies can create jobs for local unemployed workers and reduce poverty. In these regions natural resources and resource-based amenities are likely to be the main sources of economic growth but have to be utilised in new ways that increase local value-added by identifying new uses, new customers and new marketing approaches.
3   Good broadband connections are now a necessary platform for rural economic development. The Internet provides a way to reduce the penalty of distance by allowing rural firms to have a presence in urban markets either as purchasers or as sellers. But this presence is a two-edged sword, since it allows external competition for rural firms. Policies that support improvements in productivity, marketing and procurement for rural firms can help them to take advantage of niche markets that open with access to good broadband.
4   It is crucial to think about rural regions in a network context. Individual places are linked to other places through physical connections – roads, rail lines, the Internet and the power grid. Firms in rural regions are linked through supply chains that have a local component but also have external connections. People and firms are linked through a variety of strong and weak ties that provide contacts, information and context for decisions. Policies that simply target individual firms or individual places without recognising the interrelated nature of the development process are likely to be less effective than policies that see these linkages.

Notes

1   Of course, reduced transport costs also make it cheaper to transport rural inputs to urban areas to process, and to ship urban goods to rural places, so it is not clear, a priori, that rural areas will benefit from lower transport costs.
2   The first is the distance from the CCS to the nearest Census Agglomeration (CA) or Census Metropolitan Area (CMA). The second measure consists of two variables: the population within 100 km of the CCS (a measure of proximity to agglomerations), and the population between 100 km and 200 km of the CCS (indicating remoteness from population agglomerations).

References

Barca, F, McCann, P & Rodríguez-Pose, A (2012). The case for regional development intervention: Place-based versus place-neutral approaches. *Journal of Regional Science* 52(1), 134–152.

Barkley, DL, Henry, MS & Bao, S (1996). Identifying 'spread' versus 'backwash' effects in regional economic areas: A density functions approach. *Land Economics* 72(3), 336–357.

Cairncross, F (1995, 30 September). The death of distance. *The Economist* 336(7934), 5–6.

Calhoun, C (1998). Community without propinquity revisited: Communications technology and the transformation of the urban public space. *Sociological Inquiry* 68(3), 373–397.

Castells, M & Cardoso, G (Eds). (2006). *The network society: From knowledge to policy.* Centre for Transatlantic Relations. Baltimore, MD: Johns Hopkins University Press.

Chokie, M & Partridge, MD (2008). Poverty dynamics in Canadian communities: A place-based approach. *Growth and Change* 39(2), 313–340.

Frank, B (2014). Laboratory evidence on face-to-face: Why experimental economics is of interest to regional economists. *International Regional Science Review* 37(4), 411–435.

Galston, W & Baehler, K (1995). *Rural development in the United States: Connecting theory practice and policy.* Washington, DC: Island Press.

Ganning, JP, Baylis, K & Lee, B (2013). Spread and backwash effects for nonmetropolitan communities in the US. *Journal of Regional Science* 53(3), 464–480.

Glaeser, EL & Kohlhase, J (2004). Cities, regions and the decline of transport costs. *Papers in Regional Science* 83(1), 197–228.

Glückler, J (2007). Economic geography and the evolution of networks. *Journal of Economic Geography* 7(5), 619–634.

Henry, MS, Schmitt, B, Kristensen, K, Barkley, DL & Bao, S (1999). Extending Carlino–Mills models to examine urban size and growth impacts on proximate rural areas. *Growth and Change* 30, 526–548.

Irwin, EG, Bell, KP, Bockstael, NE, Newburn, DA, Partridge, MD & Wu, J (2009). The economics of urban–rural space. *Annual Review of Resource Economics* 1, 435–462.

Johansson, B & Quigley, J (2004). Agglomeration and networks in spatial economics. *Papers in Regional Science* 83, 165–176.

Johnson, T (2014). Rural policy. In G Green (Ed.), *Handbook of rural development* (pp. 42–55). Cheltenham: Edward Elgar.

Lichter, DT & Brown, DW (2011). Rural America in an urban society: Changing spatial and social boundaries. *Annual Review of Sociology* 37, 565–592.

Malecki, E (2003). Digital development in rural areas: Potentials and pitfalls. *Journal of Rural Studies* 19(2), 201–214.

Marini, M & Mooney, P (2006). Rural economies. In P Cloke, T Marsden & P Mooney (Eds), *Handbook of rural studies* (pp. 91–103). Thousand Oaks, CA: Sage.

Marsden, T (1998). New rural territories: Regulating the differential rural spaces. *Journal of Rural Studies* 14(1), 107–117.

Murdoch, J (2000). Networks – A new paradigm of rural development? *Journal of Rural Studies* 16, 407–419.

Myrdal, G (1963). *Economic theory and underdeveloped regions.* London: Methuen.

OECD (1993). *What future for our countryside?* Paris: OECD.

OECD (2012). *Promoting growth in all regions.* Paris: OECD.

Partridge, MD, Bollman, R, Olfert, MR & Alasia, A (2007). Riding the wave of urban growth in the countryside: Spread, backwash, or stagnation. *Land Economics* 83(2), 128–152.

Partridge, MD, Olfert, MR & Alasia A (2007). Agglomeration or amenities: Canadian cities as engines of growth. *Canadian Journal of Economics* 40, 39–68.

Partridge, MD & Rickman, DS (2007). Persistent rural poverty: Is it simply remoteness and scale? *Review of Agricultural Economics* 29(3), 430–436.

Partridge, MD & Rickman, DS (2008). Distance from urban agglomeration economies and rural poverty. *Journal of Regional Science* 48(2), 285–310.

Partridge, MD, Rickman, DS, Ali, K & Olfert, MR (2008a). Employment growth in the American urban hierarchy: Long live distance. *B.E Journal of Macroeconomics* 8(1) (Contributions), Article 10. Available at http://www.bepress.com/bejm/vol8/iss1/art10.

Partridge, MD, Rickman, DS, Ali, K & Olfert, MR (2008b). The geographic diversity of U.S. nonmetropolitan growth dynamics: A geographically weighted regression approach. *Land Economics* 84(2), 241–266.

Partridge, MD, Rickman, DS, Ali, K & Olfert, MR (2008c). Lost in space: Population dynamics in the American hinterlands and small cities. *Journal of Economic Geography* 8(6), 727–757.

Rosenthal, SS & Strange, WC (2003). Geography, industrial organization and agglomeration. *The Review of Economics and Statistics* 85(2), 377–393.

Rosenthal, SS & Strange, WC (2008). The attenuation of human capital spillovers. *Journal of Urban Economics* 64, 373–389.

Shapiro, C & Varian, H (1999). *Information rules: A strategic guide to the network economy.* Boston, MA: Harvard Business School Press.

Warren, M (2007). The digital vicious cycle: Links between social disadvantage and digital exclusion in rural areas. *Telecommunications Policy* 31(6–7), 374–388.

14

Invigorating the New Rural Economy

Entrepreneurship and Innovation

Jane Atterton

Introduction

Fundamental restructuring has occurred in many rural economies across OECD countries. This restructuring has resulted in an increasingly diversified, interdependent and outward-looking rural economy that interacts with adjacent urban areas, as well as with other regions nationally and internationally (Copus & de Lima, 2015, p. 3). These features are the result of an important shift in the economic characteristics of rural areas, whereby there has been a decline in traditional primary sector activities, and, to a certain extent, large-scale manufacturing sector activities, and a growth in service sector activities. Some of these changes have been prompted by national drivers, such as government investment in broadband, which has led to a more diverse range of local businesses, and the ability for people to work remotely and flexibly. Others are the result of global drivers – such as in the division of labour or in trade rules – which has seen a shift in the location of major manufacturing plants, for example. The outcomes of these complex regional, national and global processes have meant fundamental changes for those living and working in rural areas, opening up new opportunities and bringing new challenges.

With reference back to Freshwater (in the introduction to this section), this chapter briefly describes the main features of this 'new rural economy', focusing particularly on the key processes of entrepreneurship and innovation and the resultant outcomes for rural areas. These attributes have always been important features of rural economies but have not always been fully acknowledged, understood or measured. Importantly, in these processes, actors are not just regarded as passive recipients. Rather they have the resources, skills and capacity to shape the processes to their advantage, and to the advantage of their local economies, albeit to varying extents.

While the characteristics of the new rural economy may be becoming more deeply embedded across a larger number of rural regions, the chapter also explores whether 'new new rural economies' are emerging. This term is used to describe locations where current and projected future economic and social processes are leading to further changes in the characteristics of rural economies, such that local areas with different features are starting to emerge. The chapter concludes by briefly setting out policy priorities for boosting levels of entrepreneurship and innovation, and identifies a number of misleading assumptions underlying rural policy formulation which must be addressed to better support sustainable rural development.

What is the new rural economy?

David Freshwater, in the introduction to this section of the Handbook, outlines the key distinct, but strongly connected, attributes of the new or modern economy, including the importance of networks, the critical role of agglomeration effects in improving productivity, and the importance of innovation as a driver of growth. The modern economy is an open economy as a result of the reduction of trade barriers and transport costs and better information availability (facilitated by improved information technology); it is post-industrial (i.e., the service sector accounts for the largest share of output and employment as traditionally important primary and heavy manufacturing activities has declined); and it is characterised by a core workforce of highly skilled, well-paid individuals.

Importantly in the context of this chapter, the modern economy is generally seen as an urban economy with growth driven by large cities. As Freshwater notes, it is seen as being driven by science-based innovation, dependent on highly skilled workers, and mainly focused on the production of services. As a result, other (rural) places may benefit from spillover effects but they have a limited (if any) role in terms of generating their own – or wider regional or national – growth. Worse still, they may become more dependent on transfer income from urban places.

So are the features of the new economy different in rural areas compared to non-rural areas? As discussed by Freshwater above, some features are impossible or very difficult for rural regions to attain, such as agglomeration effects, face-to-face networks or high investment in research and development and significant numbers of patents – the traditional measures of innovative activity. However, others can be achieved, albeit perhaps in different ways from urban areas, such as through the use of electronic networks to improve connectivity and openness or the recognition of a broader range of innovations. Some areas may be advantaged while others are disadvantaged. Better links between urban and rural areas may emerge or the differences or similarities between the two may be enhanced. For example, observed at broad industry level, rural and urban areas have become more similar in terms of the dominance of the service sector. As a result, commentators in the United Kingdom have noted that the range of business activity in rural areas now mirrors that in more urban areas (Commission for Rural Communities, 2008; Taylor, 2008). There has been a shift away from the countryside's production role towards 'a countryside of consumption' (Slee, 2005) where the economy is shaped primarily by public and private consumption demands. At the same time, as Freshwater notes, digging more deeply below broad industrial sectors demonstrates that there are still important differences in the type of service sector activities in rural and urban locations, in terms of education, health and business and financial services, for example. This has knock-on impacts in terms of workforce skills, which are generally lower in rural areas, as employment in low-paid, low-skilled sectors, including tourism and retail, remains so important. It is true that some rural areas are becoming part of the network economy as broadband access has improved, but by no means all rural areas are well connected. Often these regions are left reliant on exogenous forces for their growth opportunities because they lack the capacity and resources, including human and social capital, to lead them by themselves. Moreover, they may suffer from challenges such as depopulation and out-migration, poverty and low wages, declining service provision and low business creation rates.

Certainly many rural areas have seen a decline in the importance of traditional primary sector activities (although they remain important in some areas) and there have been changes within the sector, including a rise in the number of small family farms producing high quality local food, alongside ever-larger farms using advanced technologies. Large-scale manufacturing has also declined in many rural areas. Recent evidence issued by the Department for the Environment, Food and Rural Affairs about rural England demonstrates some of the key features of the new rural economy, including a growth in population (often through in-migration of wealthy (pre)retirees), overall employment growth, an increasing number of knowledge-intensive businesses (including consultancy and computer programming) (Defra, 2014) and a substantial proportion of workers (33% in rural hamlets and dispersed areas) working from home helped by improving connectivity (Defra, 2015). (For a more detailed discussion of the new rural economy in different places, see Argent & Measham, 2014; Hill, 2005; Kilkenny, 2002; and the work of the Canadian Rural Revitalization Foundation's New Rural Economy national research and education project which started in 1997.)

The next sections of this chapter focus on entrepreneurship and innovation as two key, related processes through which rural actors can engage positively with long- and short-term changes. Through this activity they can engender positive outcomes for their localities, thereby proactively shaping the characteristics of the rural economies in which they operate.

Entrepreneurship in the new rural economy

Entrepreneurship has been widely studied using a variety of points of departure, including explanations based on personality theories, economic theory and ethnic background and culture (Greve, 1995). For Chell & Baines (2000), an entrepreneur must be alert to opportunities and have the desire or capabilities to act on them, either personally or through the help of friends and advisers. This may come through knowledge of the business environment or through having highly creative or innovative ideas and a willingness to take risks in acting upon them (Bosworth & Glasgow, 2012).

Economic growth in rural areas is closely associated with the entrepreneurial capacity of the local population (Labrianidis, 2004). Business density in rural areas can be compared to urban areas as a proxy for entrepreneurial activity. In Scotland, for example, per 10,000 adults, there were 490 businesses in remote rural Scotland, compared to 578 in accessible rural areas and a lower figure of 327 in urban Scotland in 2013 (Scottish Government, 2015). This suggests a higher level of business ownership amongst rural than urban dwellers, although, importantly, these data do not tell us whether people are setting up businesses through necessity or through choice.

For economic growth, it is therefore critical for rural areas to maintain an adequate supply of entrepreneurial individuals. However, in disadvantaged or remote rural areas, it is generally the case that these people are the first to leave in search of better opportunities elsewhere. In contrast, many more accessible rural areas across OECD countries have experienced waves of in-migration recently, leading to a rising proportion of the population in rural areas, a process referred to as counter-urbanisation (Berry, 1976; Champion, 2003).

While these migratory moves have tended not to be driven by the search for new employment opportunities but rather by the pursuit of a more desirable residential environment, evidence suggests that in-migrants become involved in entrepreneurial activities more often than locals, thus helping to expand the enterprise base of rural areas (Keeble, Tyler, Broom & Lewis, 1992; Stockdale, 2005; Kalantaridis & Bika, 2006a, 2006b; Atterton, 2007; Mitchell & Madden, 2014; see also Florida's work on the creative class and knowledge sector workers: Florida, 2000, 2002). In the UK, these moves to the countryside are often made by individuals of working age or in their 'pre-retirement' phase. In contrast, in parts of rural America, there has been an influx of older in-migrants who bring new sources of income and entrepreneurial activity, as well as a commitment to engage in community-related activities and provide informal care for family and friends (Reeder, 1998; Brown & Glasgow, 2008; Philip, MacLeod & Stockdale, 2013).

Entrepreneurs cannot be studied in isolation and they operate as part of a network of actors, whether those networks are many or few, strong or weak, or long or short term (Johannisson, 1987; Dubini & Aldrich, 1991; McQuaid, 1996; Chell & Baines, 2000; Huggins, 2000; Goudis & Skuras, 2001; Bosworth & Glasgow, 2012). Some researchers have focused their attention specifically on the networking relationships of rural business owners (see, for example, Murdoch, 2000; Kneafsey, Ilbery & Jenkins, 2001; Atterton, 2005). Some of this work has focused on the geography of networking relationships, emphasising the importance of local networks to overcoming the disadvantages of remoteness and limited markets faced by rural entrepreneurs, and the need for extra-local network relationships to give owners access to resources located outside the region (Gorton, 1999; Murdoch, 2000; Goudis & Skuras, 2001; Kneafsey, Ilbery & Jenkins, 2001).

This empirical work has informed conceptual work in economic and rural geography, in particular on the concept of neo-endogenous development (Murdoch, 2000; Ward et al., 2005). This recognises the importance of extra-local factors and networks in the development of a local area, but retains belief in the potential of local areas to shape their own future (Ray, 2001, p. 4). Linking directly back to the new rural economy, Skuras and Dubois (2015) discuss the 'rural business network paradigm' which emphasises the interconnectedness of the multiple socioeconomic spaces within which rural businesses are 'embedded' and the role of business networks in supporting additional linkages of knowledge, learning and innovation, beyond conventional flows of commodities.

Some of this work on the networking of entrepreneurs has built on Granovetter's (1985) idea of embeddedness, which he describes as the integration or enmeshing of economic action in social relations and institutions. It has been argued that the local scale overlap of economic or business and social or informal networking relationships in rural areas is particularly strong as a result of the strength of bonding social capital and trust (Gorton, 1999; Jack & Anderson, 1999; Ritsila, 1999). This strong overlap creates an environment in which entrepreneurs may be motivated by factors other than profit maximisation, sharing costs or achieving economies of scale, such as supporting the community in which they live (Atterton, 2007). As Shortall and Warner (2012) note, local entrepreneurship – perhaps more so in rural areas than urban – is about more than just economic benefits; it also contributes to place-making and civic and democratic impulses that help reinforce local communities. However, becoming over-embedded leaves rural business owners at risk of being locked in to overly strong local social relationships and unable to access new and different resources, including information and knowledge from outside the local area (Oinas, 1997; Atterton, 2007). Through their networks, therefore, rural business owners are critical actors in processes of neo-endogenous development, proactively helping to create a strong, diverse and dynamic new rural economy (Lee, Arnason, Nightingale & Shucksmith, 2005).

Innovation in the new rural economy

Studies of the innovative behaviour of rural firms in the last 30 to 40 years have uncovered a mixed picture (see, for example, Keeble, Tyler, Broom & Lewis, 1992; North & Smallbone, 2000; Raley & Moxey, 2000; Atterton & Affleck, 2010; Dabson, 2011; Freshwater, 2012). Some studies found that rural firms were more innovative than urban firms, or at least found evidence of considerable innovative activity in rural areas (see, for example, Keeble, Tyler,

Broom & Lewis, 1992; Atterton & Affleck, 2010; Freshwater, 2012). This was generally explained by arguing that rural firms are required to be more innovative as a result of the challenges they face, including remoteness and distance, the limited local market, and a shortage of proximate firms with which to collaborate. The converse argument is that size, low population density (and therefore limited face-to-face contact) and remoteness restrict the production of radical innovations that can transform local economies (Henderson, 2007).

Innovation is widely recognised as a key driver of economic growth at the heart of the knowledge economy (see, for example, OECD, 1996; Her Majesty's Treasury, 2000; European Commission, 2010), but recent innovation research has tended to take a somewhat narrow definition to the types of activity that 'qualify', a somewhat linear approach to explaining how the process occurs, and a limited geographical approach to where it happens. It is usually assumed that innovation refers to a new idea which has direct connections to a firm or other organisation being able to produce a better product or service (Dargan & Shucksmith, 2008). Thus, the motive for innovative activity is to improve economic conditions (Freshwater & Wojan, 2014). This process is usually regarded as being a linear one, in which basic research in universities, research centres and large firms in urban centres leads to applied research and development, innovation and then diffusion of the new idea. Patents generated and expenditure on formal R&D have become the key measures of innovation outcomes and effort and these tend to underplay innovative activities in rural areas.

There is very little, if any, room in this approach for individual creativity, inspiration and learning but in rural areas this is likely to be the most probable form of innovation, which is led by entrepreneurs. Entrepreneurial rural individuals frequently implement creative ideas in their work and/or home life in order to overcome problems or make the most of new opportunities (North & Smallbone, 2000; Copus, Skuras & Tsegenidi, 2007; Baumol, 2010; Freshwater & Wojan, 2014). As such, it is not always the case that profit drives the search for innovation (Freshwater & Wojan, 2014). Instead, innovations from entrepreneurs may be the result of an effort to resolve a personal problem, and only later (if ever) does the idea to market the innovation occur. Often this effort is based on tacit knowledge (see Labrianidis, 2004, p. 3) and strong social networks (Esparcia, 2014).

Granted, this rural 'user-innovation' may not be the formal, high-investment, science-based innovation that is the main focus of current research and policy attention. Nevertheless, it is very important for individuals seeking to find solutions to the particular problems they are facing (often because support is not available to them from elsewhere). A lack of recognition of this innovative activity has led to a damaging assumption that rural areas and people are not innovative or dynamic themselves and therefore must rely on urban centres for innovation and associated economic development to trickle down to them in a very passive way. Worse still, they may be completely excluded from their national innovation system (see, for example, Roper, Love, Cooke and Clifton's 2006 work on the Scottish innovation system).

This brief review of the literature demonstrates the strong link between entrepreneurship and innovation in rural areas (also see Dinis, 2007; North & Smallbone, 2007; Virklala, 2007). For the most part, innovative rural firms remain small, but their employment and income effects may be significant. Innovation may be the best opportunity for rural firms to increase economic growth as it has the potential to offset limitations in the number and skills of the local workforce and can play a role in opening access to external markets. Because innovation in rural areas is strongly coupled to entrepreneurship, a high rate of innovation can also be associated with new firm formation and a strengthening of existing firms (Freshwater, 2013).

It is also important to acknowledge that innovations in rural areas may take other forms than the individual entrepreneur-led actions described here. For example, the European Union's

LEADER programme,[1] established in 1991, has encouraged innovation in the form of bottom-up social or community-led activities (Moseley, 2000; Dargan & Shucksmith, 2008). While some have argued that innovation has been somewhat constrained by the programme's bureaucratic requirements, that local actions are often not understood as being innovative by those involved, and that external people were often critical to the process, it nevertheless represents a significant move to encourage community-led rural social and cultural innovation (Dargan & Shucksmith, 2008; Dax, Strahl, Kirwan & Maye, 2013). While this is different from the entrepreneur-led innovation described above, it may also be motivated by a need to solve a problem, such as tackling a gap in service provision.

Returning to the key concept of the new rural economy, this review of entrepreneurship and innovation has demonstrated the importance of these two highly interconnected processes in ensuring that rural economies and societies are proactively and positively responding to changes occurring in the regional, national and global economies around them. As Smallbone (2009) suggests, in rural regions it is difficult to separate entrepreneurship from innovation, since for many rural entrepreneurs, the impetus to start a business comes from having innovated as a result of being unable to find an existing product or process that resolved a problem they were experiencing. As the OECD notes, it is widely believed that the future prosperity of rural regions will be driven by enterprise, innovation and new technologies (OECD, 2014). However, what is challenging from a rural development point of view is ensuring that the operation of these processes in rural areas is fully acknowledged and supported by national policymakers, while allowing for local people to lead the shape of development responses based on their priorities and assets. This challenge is the focus of the final section of this chapter, which follows on from a discussion of the extent to which 'new new rural economies' might be emerging.

Are 'new new rural economies' emerging?

Introduction

By reviewing some of the most important current and future economic and social processes and how they are affecting rural economies and might affect them in future, the chapter now turns to discuss whether there is evidence of 'new new rural economies' emerging, and/or of the new rural economy becoming embedded more deeply across a larger number of rural regions. By *new new rural economies*, the suggestion is that some rural areas may be showing signs of further shifts in their key characteristics, such that new types of regions are emerging. This may be because of various current economic and social processes, including the 2008 global financial crisis; international conflicts and migration patterns; the tightening of public sector budgets; rapidly evolving information technology; concerns about climate change and the negative environmental and social impacts of the pursuit of growth; and the growing importance of a range of other objectives, including the pursuit of quality of life, happiness and sustainability, instead of, or alongside, economic growth.

First, the use of the term 'economies' in this section is deliberate and important. There is a huge amount of diversity across the rural regions of the OECD – indeed this is the case within countries and within regions in countries – and therefore we cannot assume that a single new rural economy exists. If the new rural economy is becoming more deeply embedded across a wider range of rural areas, then it will look very different in different locations, as a result of the varied range of processes involved and the different ways in which they are shaped by local activities.

Rural economic performance and characteristics

Reviewing statistical evidence from OECD countries shows that, on average, rural economies – at least those in accessible rural areas – are continuing to perform well (OECD, 2012).[2] Recent analysis by the UK government (Defra, 2014), for example, highlights that rural England is home to 26% of businesses, 16% of gross value added, 16% of total employment and 18% of the population. More rural areas are benefiting from investment in information technology, including broadband, meaning that they are in a position to participate in global economic processes and flows, and many areas are continuing their transition from primary sector to service sector dominated economies, perhaps the key feature of the new rural economy. Rural areas are maintaining, if not enhancing, their offer of a flexible labour market, including part-time, contract and seasonal employment options for those who find themselves unable or unwilling to take on permanent, long-term employment (see Green, 2006). On this basis, the productivity of rural England's economy, for example, and particularly knowledge-based activities such as IT and consultancy, could grow faster than in urban areas over the next decade (Defra, 2014). So, we can say that the new rural economy is becoming embedded in a larger number of rural areas. But can we say that economic and social processes are creating rural regions with different characteristics, perhaps building on new rural economy features? This section describes seven emerging features which might be leading to the creation of these different rural regions, focusing on employment and demographic changes, public sector shifts, the potential for natural resources to serve as a generator of growth, strengthening urban–rural links, and the potential for rural areas to be sites for pursuing alternatives to economic growth.

First, we can look at the employment characteristics of rural areas. Focusing on homeworking, for example, the proportion of homeworkers in remote rural Scotland increased from 20% in 2007 to 25% in 2011. The increase has been lower in accessible rural areas (17% in 2007 to 19% in 2011) while the level has remained relatively stable across the rest of Scotland (7% in 2007 and 8% in 2011) (Steiner & Atterton, 2014). Breaking these figures down further, in 2011, 27% of males in remote rural Scotland were homeworkers, compared to 21% in accessible rural areas and 11% in the rest of Scotland, for example (Scottish Government, 2015).

Homeworking is therefore becoming an important element of rural economies, bringing opportunities in terms of demand for local business and consumer services and, more broadly, the diversity and dynamism of local economies. While the reasons that people choose to work from home vary (Mason, Carter & Tagg, 2011; Wynarczyk & Graham, 2013), this trend is important at a time when there is growing interest amongst policymakers in how positive local growth processes can be generated as a counterweight to ever more prevalent global-scale links (see the recent report by Mason & Reuschke, 2015). Moreover, the environmental benefits from reduced commuting journeys as a result of people working from home provide a new sustainability agenda around which to shape rural economies. This would contrast with the traditional view of rural areas as being environmentally unsustainable which has tended to underlie planning policy in the UK, for example (see, for example, Sturzaker & Shucksmith, 2011; Shucksmith 2012a).

Rural demographic trends

Second, we can look at key demographic trends in rural areas. In-migration to (particularly accessible) rural locations looks set to continue for the foreseeable future as rural areas attract people for the high quality of life and amenities they can offer. In Scotland, for example, rural local authorities close to urban centres, such as Aberdeenshire and Perth and Kinross, are predicted to see 16.2% and 30.3% migrant-led population increases by 2035 (Skerratt et al., 2012, p. 10). Recent evidence from Greece suggests a 'crisis counter-urbanisation' move triggered by unemployment in the (urban) origin, rather than pro-rural motivations or idyllic constructions of rurality. In these moves, the availability of migrants' family networks and support is critical, especially in times of crisis (Gkartzios, 2013). This process may be observed elsewhere in southern Europe and beyond as austerity measures take further hold. While the outcome is the same as the traditionally understood process of counter-urbanisation, the activities of these individuals in their destinations may be somewhat different.

Third, and linked to migration, demographic ageing may have an important role to play in redefining rural economies. While this is seen as a 'pensions and care' challenge by many, particularly in rural areas where the trend is often most marked and services are more expensive to deliver, ageing may have more positive economic and social outcomes (Lowe & Speakman, 2006). Indeed, Champion and Shepherd (2006) suggest that rural areas are at the cutting edge of a major social transition catalysed by older people. It may result, for example, in a growth in the business stock as the 'young older' set up new ventures (Stockdale & MacLeod, 2013; Atterton & Thompson, 2014). Brown and Glasgow (2008) set out how the migration patterns of older people in the USA are leading to new economic opportunities for some rural retirement destinations. Opportunities also exist to serve growing demand for health and social care services from the 'older old'. As such, older residents should be viewed as a potential source of rural development rather than a 'problem' for rural communities (Bosworth & Glasgow, 2012, p. 154).

Innovations in service delivery and natural resource management

Fourth, as the public sector withdraws, there may be opportunities for the rural private and third sectors to drive innovations in service delivery, using the latest technology, or through social enterprise models, for example. Again these developments may bring new economic (and social) opportunities for entrepreneurship and innovation at local level, although the increased pressure this brings for the third sector and its volunteers needs to be acknowledged (see, for example, Woolvin & Rutherford, 2013).

Fifth, there is considerable potential for remote rural areas to build new new rural economies around their stock of natural resources (this is the 'amenity-based economy narrative' as outlined by Shucksmith & Brown, introduction in this volume). Further work has been undertaken on the role of rural (natural and built) amenities in attracting new residents in the United States, including in attracting 'lone eagles' (footloose entrepreneurs) and the 'creative class' (see, for example, Deller, Tsung-Hsiu, Marcouiller & English, 2001; McGranahan & Wojan, 2007). As Mahroum et al. (2007) note, there is an important link between natural resources and innovation, enhanced by the growing importance of sustainable technologies that rely on rural resources such as crop-based energy and wind and tidal power. Not only do these technologies bring new resources to (often remote) rural areas, they potentially tackle the fuel poverty challenge (by providing cheaper energy), generate community development (from community benefit funds, for example), increase the local skills base (for example, turbine technicians) and, more broadly, they also create renewed political interest in their role in the wider economy.

Rural–urban interactions

Sixth, there is evidence that rural and urban areas are becoming ever more closely integrated, through commuting for work and leisure activities, travel to the countryside for day trips and holidays, and the 'rural' coming to urban centres in the form of farmers' markets to take advantage of rising disposable incomes and the demand for high quality, healthy and local food products. Increasingly important flows also exist as essential resources such as clean water and renewable energy flow out of rural areas to sustain our cities. As Shucksmith and Brown (this volume) note, recent economic, social and technological processes transcend urban and rural boundaries. The rural–urban interface therefore becomes a zone of interdependence and connectivity, constructed through interactions, linkages and flows of people, money, ideas, information and materials. New new rural economies will be created in this zone, ever more closely tied in with urban centres and bringing both opportunities and challenges.

Rural areas as 'test beds' for alternatives to economic growth

Finally, rural areas could serve as important 'test beds' for exploring alternatives to pursuing economic growth as the key driver of individual and collective action, such as social justice, well-being or environmental sustainability. There has been an ever-increasing amount of evidence on the negative impacts of human activities on the world's climate and on growing inequalities between people and places at global, national, regional and local levels (Shucksmith, 2012b). These changes have prompted new thinking about the role of rural regions and people in relation to a variety of issues, including economic growth and prosperity, well-being and happiness, environmental degradation and social justice (see, for example, Scott, 2012). These issues are being tackled by individuals and groups who are taking on the ownership and management of assets, for example, through Transition Town initiatives, local currency unions and social finance projects, and local food-growing projects. While many of these projects result in economic outcomes, often these are not the primary motivation for their establishment. More important factors might be a desire to reduce the environmental footprint, achieve a more sustainable lifestyle or improve quality of life, well-being or happiness, or to simply create a place of shelter from, or even resistance to, dominant global economic trends. For many rural in-migrants, these might be the primary motivations to move to a rural area, which epitomises 'the good life', in keeping with nature rather than destroying it, and something which should be protected from negative external influences. As Shucksmith and Brown (this volume) argue, the zombie phase of neoliberalism which we are now in offers opportunities for 'the re-mobilisation, recognition and valuation of multiple, local forms of development, rooted in local cultures, values and movements'.

Conclusions

To conclude this section, the characteristics of the new rural economy are evident more deeply in some rural areas and are emerging in other rural areas as economic and employment transitions continue and information technology investment spreads. Equally, however, there are many rural areas which are not experiencing any of these positive trends, and still suffer from depopulation, a decline in service provision, a narrow economic base, poverty and disadvantage, poor connectivity and weak social cohesion and social capital. As Shucksmith (2012b) notes, these areas will not be in a position to take advantage of the opportunities available to them, particularly as the role of the state (an important provider of services and employment) contracts. Only those communities with capacity will be able to defend their interests and access the funding that remains.

But there are other changes which could be creating new new rural economies based around new forms of entrepreneurship and innovation – for example, homeworking; older entrepreneurs and/or new opportunities brought by demographic ageing; innovative service delivery; new economic sectors such as renewables; rural–urban interrelationships and flows; or the pursuit of different objectives such as equality, social justice, happiness and environmental improvement, in part to tackle emerging societal challenges. The shape, extent and impacts of these processes will vary across different localities, creating an ever more differentiated landscape of rural areas, but at least some rural areas could find themselves at the forefront of future economic and social change.

So what does this mean for rural policies?

The chapter concludes by briefly discussing the implications of these changes for rural policy.

First, in terms of entrepreneurship, there is a long history of public and private sector organisations seeking to encourage (rural) entrepreneurship in various different ways, including making grant or loan finance available, providing business start-up support and advice, organising networking and market development events, investing in premises, and encouraging entrepreneurship amongst specific groups, such as older or younger people. The critical message for policymakers from evaluations of these activities is that they need to recognise the specific challenges and opportunities facing entrepreneurs in rural locations, such as their distance to markets, the lower availability of capital and their tendency to access private rather than public sector sources of support (Atterton & Affleck, 2010). They also need to recognise the importance of small businesses, including microenterprises and sole traders in rural areas which, although they might not provide large numbers of jobs, may deliver essential services, help to diversify the local economy and support the economic and social sustainability and resilience of their local community (Bosworth & Glasgow, 2012; Freshwater, 2013; Sanchez-Zamora, Gallardo-Cobos & Cena-Delgado, 2014; Steiner & Atterton, 2014).

Some policy interventions to support business owners focus specifically on their networking relationships. Even here, though, we can see evidence that initiatives to establish or grow such networks in rural areas have tended to be mono-sectoral or geographically limited in their scope (Lee, Arnason, Nightingale & Shuckmith, 2005). Instead, what is needed are initiatives that are anchored in local stocks of social capital (Rosenfeld, 2002; Skuras & Dubois, 2015) but which support the greater integration of rural actors into inter-sectoral and interregional networks (Skuras & Dubois, 2015).

However, perhaps what is more critical than these examples of specific policy initiatives is to tackle a number of misleading underlying assumptions amongst policymakers (and often amongst the general population) to ensure that future rural policies are shaped appropriately. The remainder of this section outlines these assumptions.

The first misleading assumption is that 'rural = agriculture'. While this sector remains important in many rural areas, its contribution in terms of employment and income has declined recently. Researchers have long argued that a broad territorial, place-based policy approach is preferable to a more traditional agriculture-focused sectoral approach, as it better reflects the strengths and needs of the new rural economy (Saraceno, 2005; Ward & Brown, 2009; Copus & Dax, 2010; Strahl & Dax, 2010; Dax, 2015). But this sectoral approach remains evident in many OECD countries, not least in the EU's Common Agricultural Policy (CAP) (Atterton, Bryden & Johnson, 2012). For example, the limited funding which has traditionally been allocated to the EU's LEADER programme when compared to other items of expenditure in 'Pillar 2' of the CAP is testament to this continued emphasis on primary sector based activities. At the same time, it is important to recognise that the CAP is not the only place where support for rural areas is available. It is also available through the EU's Structural Funds and European

Social Fund, for example. Moreover, as Dax (2015) notes, the shift towards greater coordination at EU level between the five EU Structural and Investment Funds to be delivered through a Common Strategic Framework appears to be a step towards greater coherence in the new 2015–2020 programme.

The second misleading assumption is that rural areas cannot generate their own economic growth and therefore are not active in shaping their own destinies. Drawing on the evidence of others (such as OECD, 2012), this chapter demonstrates that rural areas are often more entrepreneurial than urban areas, and that they are proactive and dynamic, not passive actors. City region and other urban-focused policies that do not recognise the interdependencies between urban and rural areas put rural areas at a disadvantage. In reality, places outside city regions are more than capable of generating their own growth and making a substantial contribution to the regional and national economies of which they are a part (see, for example, Commission for Rural Communities, 2008). As Nardone, Sisto and Lopolito (2010) argue, the EU LEADER programme is built on the premise that all regions are expected to contribute to European growth aims. At the same time, however, policymakers need to take heed of the argument earlier in this chapter that rural areas may be at the forefront of actions pursuing drivers other than economic growth. While many national governments have re-emphasised economic growth outcomes during the recent period of austerity as we recover from global economic crisis, a shift in thinking is required to allow for alternative drivers to be acknowledged alongside economic growth.

The third misleading assumption is one that is held by the population in many developed nations generally, and not just policymakers, and that is that demographic ageing is a problem which is simply creating new demands and pressures (Lowe & Speakman, 2006). In reality, while the process will result in greater pressures on health and care services (especially in rural areas), it will also bring opportunities as many older people are healthy and keen to remain economically and socially active. Taking a more positive attitude to this process will enable rural areas to be at the cutting edge of responses to population ageing.

The fourth misleading assumption is that rural areas are not innovative. Popular definitions and measurements of innovation do not recognise the innovative activity that predominantly occurs in rural areas. While the LEADER initiative is somewhat of an exception, most national and supra-national policies have tended to emphasise the importance of core regions and places in generating innovation, leaving rural areas absent from these debates. A fundamental shift in approach is required which recognises that innovations can be small scale and led by an individual with a creative idea to tackle a problem; they need not involve huge R&D expenditure or large numbers of patent registrations.

The chapter concludes by focusing on one other shift that is required: the need to recognise that 'a one-size rural policy does not fit all'. As the new rural economy becomes embedded across more rural regions, and new new rural economies emerge, it will be even more important to encourage multiple sustainable development pathways. Some places will need extra or different policy support otherwise they are at risk of being left behind, while others with a stock of more or better assets (including social networks and relationships, institutional capacity, levels of entrepreneurship and innovation), and the capacity to exploit them, will be in a position to perform well, perhaps with minimal external support. Understanding the nature of these assets and how local actors use them to create more resilient and sustainable places is critical to ensure that policy and practice responses can be shaped appropriately. However, as many authors have argued, concepts such as neo-endogenous development, multilevel governance and related emphases on innovation, creativity, networking, cooperation, rural–urban interactions, and the positive exploitation of the full range of natural, material and less tangible (including human, social and cultural) assets in a region, have had little impact on policy implementation so far, unfortunately leaving the innovative potential and assets of rural regions untapped (see, for example, Copus & de Lima, 2015; Dax, 2015; Dwyer, Ward, Lowe & Baldock, 2007; OECD, 2006).

A more territorial approach to (rural) development requires a change in underlying presumptions such that, instead of a narrow sectoral approach or one which is focused on transferring resources from rich to poor regions, a place-based, multi-sectoral and neo-endogenous approach is taken, building on the assets and capacities of local actors, and providing a way of anchoring local economic transition in a long-term perspective. This will require inclusive local governance approaches that encourage actors to get involved, and trust on the part of policymakers to allow them to do so – or even to lead, sometimes with the involvement of key external actors and potentially in ways that can be difficult to measure and monitor.

This chapter has reviewed the features of the new rural economy, and discussed processes of entrepreneurship and innovation as two means by which rural actors can proactively shape the extent and impact of economic and social processes happening around them. It then discussed the extent to which we might see new new rural economies emerging which may encourage entrepreneurial and innovative behaviour to be demonstrated in new ways. While challenges undoubtedly remain for many rural areas, others could find themselves able to draw on their entrepreneurial and innovative populations to be at the forefront of emerging economic and social trends.

Notes

1 An acronym derived from French meaning 'liaison between actions for the development of the rural economy'.
2 For reasons of space, the chapter does not undertake a detailed review of the statistical evidence for these assertions.

References

Argent, N & Measham, T (2014). New rural economies: Introduction to the special themed issue. *Journal of Rural Studies* 36, 328–329.

Atterton, J (2005). Networking in the Highlands and Islands of Scotland: A case study of the embeddedness of firms in three small towns. Unpublished PhD thesis, University of Aberdeen.

Atterton, J (2007). The 'strength of weak ties': Social networking by business owners in the Highlands and Islands of Scotland. *Sociologia Ruralis* 47(3), 228–245.

Atterton, J & Affleck, A (2010). *Rural businesses in the north east of England: Final survey results 2010*. Centre for Rural Economy Research Report (June 2010). Available at http://www.ncl.ac.uk/cre/publish/researchreports/index.htm (accessed 30 January 2015).

Atterton, J, Bryden, J & Johnson, T (2012). Rural economic transformations in the UK and US. In M Shucksmith, D Brown, S Shortall, J Vergunst & M Warner (Eds), *Rural transformations and rural policies in the US and UK* (pp. 117–137). London: Routledge.

Atterton, J & Thompson, N (2014). *Demographic ageing and rural business: Issues for policy, research and practice*. Centre for Rural Economy Discussion Paper No. 33, University of Newcastle. Available at http://www.ncl.ac.uk/cre/publish/discussionpapers/index.htm (accessed 13 February 2015).

Baumol, W (2010). *The microtheory of innovative entrepreneurship*. Princeton, NJ: Princeton University Press.

Berry, B (1976). *Urbanization and counterurbanization*. Beverley Hills, CA: Sage.

Bosworth, G & Glasgow, N (2012). Entrepreneurial behaviour among rural in-migrants. In M Shucksmith, D Brown, S Shortall, J Vergunst & M Warner (Eds), *Rural transformations and rural policies in the US and UK* (pp. 138–155). London: Routledge.

Brown, D & Glasgow, N (2008). *Rural retirement migration*. Dordrecht: Springer.

Champion, A (2003). Testing the differential urbanization model in Great Britain, 1901–1991. *Tijdschrift voor Economische en Sociale Geografie* 94(1), 11–22.

Champion, A & Shepherd, J (2006). Demographic change in rural England. In P Lowe & L Speakman (Eds), *The ageing countryside: The growing older population of rural England* (pp. 29–50). London: Age Concern.

Chell, E & Baines, S (2000). Networking, entrepreneurship and microbusiness behaviour. *Entrepreneurship and Regional Development* 12, 195–215.

Commission for Rural Communities (2008). *England's rural areas: Steps to release their economic potential, advice from the rural advocate to the Prime Minister*. Cheltenham: Commission for Rural Communities.

Copus, A and Dax, T (2010). *Conceptual background and priorities of European rural development policy*. Deliverable 1.2, EU Project FP7 – 213034 'Assessing the impact of rural development policies' (RuDI). Stockholm. Available at www.rudi-europe.net/uploads/media/RuDI_Deliverable_1_2.pdf (accessed 13 February 2015).

Copus, A & de Lima, P (2015). *Territorial cohesion in rural Europe: The relational turn in rural development*. London and New York: Routledge.

Copus, A, Skuras D & Tsegenidi, K (2007). Innovation and peripherality: An empirical comparative study of SMEs in six European Union member countries. *Economic Geography* 84(1), 52–82.

Dabson, B (2011). Rural regional development: A response to metropolitan framed place-based thinking in the United States. *Australasian Journal of Regional Studies* 17(1), 7–21.

Dargan, L & Shucksmith, M (2008). LEADER and innovation. *Sociologia Ruralis* 48(3), 274–291.

Dax, T (2015). The evolution of European rural policy. In A Copus & P de Lima, *Territorial cohesion in rural Europe: The relational turn in rural development* (pp. 35–52). London: Routledge.

Dax, T, Strahl, W, Kirwan, J & Maye, D (2013). The LEADER programme 2007–2013: Enabling or disabling social innovation and neo-endogenous development? Insights from Austria and Ireland. *European Urban and Regional Studies*. Published online 26 July. doi: 10.1177/0969776413490425.

Defra (Department for the Environment, Food and Rural Affairs) (2014). *Productivity in rural and urban areas 2013 (provisional)*. Available at https://www.gov.uk/government/statistics/rural-productivity (accessed 13 February 2015).

Defra (Department for the Environment, Food and Rural Affairs) and Rogerson, D (2015). *Rural home working*. Available at https://www.gov.uk/government/statistics/rural-home-working (accessed 8 April 2015).

Deller, S, Tsung-Hsiu, T, Marcouiller, D & English, D (2001). The role of amenities and quality of life in rural economic growth. *American Journal of Agricultural Economics* 83(2), 352–365.

Dinis, A (2007). Marketing and innovation: Useful tools for competitiveness in rural and peripheral areas. *European Planning Studies* 14(1), 9–22.

Dubini, P & Aldrich, H (1991). Personal and extended networks are essential to the entrepreneurial process. *Journal of Business Venturing* 6, 305–313.

Dwyer, J, Ward, N, Lowe, P & Baldock, D (2007). European rural development under the Common Agricultural Policy's 'Second Pillar': Institutional conservatism and innovation. *Regional Studies* 41(7), 873–887.

Esparcia, J (2014). Innovation and networks in rural areas. An analysis from European innovative projects. *Journal of Rural Studies* 34, 1–14.

European Commission (2010). *A strategy for smart, sustainable and inclusive growth*. Brussels: European Commission.

Florida, R (2000). *Competing in the age of talent: Environment, amenities and the new economy*. A report prepared for the R K Mellon Foundation, Heinz Endowments and Sustainable Pittsburgh. Available at http://www.creativeclass.com/rfcgdb/articles/2000-Competing_In_The_Age_Of_Talent.pdf (accessed 28 January 2015).

Florida, R (2002). *Rise of the creative class: And how it's transforming work, leisure, community and everyday life*. New York: Basic Books.

Freshwater, D (2012). Rural innovation: Crucial but rarely systemic. University of Kentucky, Agricultural Economics Research Report. Available at http://ageconsearch.umn.edu/handle/139829 (accessed 13 February 2015).

Freshwater, D (2013). Modernizing rural economies: Strengthening economic growth in the 21st century. Paper based on presentation at the 8th OECD Rural Development Policy Conference, Krasnoyarsk, Russia, October.

Freshwater, D & Wojan, T (2014). User entrepreneurship: Defining and identifying an explicit type of innovation. Paper presented at the North American Regional Science Association Conference, Bethesda, Maryland, November.

Gkartzios, M (2013). 'Leaving Athens': Narratives of counterurbanisation in times of crisis. *Journal of Rural Studies* 32, 158–167.

Gorton, M (1999). Spatial variations in markets served by UK-based small and medium-sized enterprises. *Entrepreneurship and Regional Development* 11, 39–55.

Goudis, A & Skuras, D (2001). Conceptual paper: Business networks. ASPIRE (Aspatial Peripherality, Innovation and the Rural Economy), EU 5th Framework Programme, Contract Number QLK5-2000-00783. Available at http://www.academia.edu/2508164/Goudis_A_and_Skuras_D_2001_AsPIRE_Conceptual_Paper_Business_Networks_and_Innovation (accessed 13 February 2015).

Granovetter, M (1985). Economic action and social structure: The problem of embeddedness. *American Journal of Sociology* 91(3), 481–510.

Green, A (2006). Employment and the older person in the countryside. In P Lowe & L Speakman (Eds), *The ageing countryside: The growing older population of rural England* (pp. 94–118). London: Age Concern.

Greve, A (1995). Networks and entrepreneurship – an analysis of social relations, occupational background and use of contacts during the establishment process. *Scandinavian Journal of Management* 11, 1–24.

Henderson, J (2007). The power of technological innovation in rural America. *The Main Street Economist Regional and rural analysis*, 2(4).

Her Majesty's Treasury (2000). *Productivity in the UK: The evidence and the government's approach.* London: Her Majesty's Treasury.

Hill, B (Ed.). (2005). *The new rural economy: Change, dynamism and government policy.* London: The Institute of Economic Affairs. Available at www.iea.org.uk/publications/research/the-new-rural-economy-change-dynamism-and-government-policy (accessed 13 February 2015).

Huggins, R (2000). The success and failure of policy-implanted inter-firm network initiatives: Motivations, processes and structure. *Entrepreneurship and Regional Development* 12, 111–135.

Jack, S & Anderson, A (1999). The effects of embeddedness upon the entrepreneurial process. Paper presented at the 9th Annual Global Entrepreneurship Research Conference, New Orleans (April).

Johannisson, B (1987). Beyond process and structure: Social exchange networks. *International Studies of Management and Organisation* 17(4), 3–23.

Kalantaridis, C & Bika, Z (2006a). In-migrant entrepreneurship in rural England: Beyond local embeddedness. *Entrepreneurship and Regional Development* 18, 109–131.

Kalantaridis, C & Bika, Z (2006b). Local embeddedness and rural entrepreneurship: Case study evidence from Cumbria, England. *Environment and Planning A* 38, 1561–1579.

Keeble, D, Tyler, P, Broom, G & Lewis, J (1992). *Business success in the countryside: The performance of rural enterprise.* London: HMSO.

Kilkenny, M (2002). The new rural economy (discussion). *American Journal of Agricultural Economics* 84(5), 1253–1255.

Kneafsey, M, Ilbery, B & Jenkins, T (2001). Exploring the dimensions of culture economies in rural west Wales. *Sociologia Ruralis* 41(3), 296–310.

Labrianidis, L (2004). Introduction. In L Labrianidis (Ed.), *The future of Europe's rural peripheries* (pp. 1–30). Farnham: Ashgate.

Lee, J, Arnason, A, Nightingale, A & Shucksmith, M (2005). Networking, social capital and identities in European rural development. *Sociologia Ruralis* 45(4), 269–283.

Lowe, P & Speakman, L (2006). *The ageing countryside: The growing older population of rural England.* London: Age Concern.

Mahroum, S, Atterton, J, Ward, N, Williams, A, Naylor, R, Hindle, R & Rowe, F (2007). *Rural innovation.* London: NESTA Publications.

Mason, C, Carter, S & Tagg, S (2011). Invisible businesses: The characteristics of home-based businesses in the United Kingdom. *Regional Studies* 45(5), 625–639.

Mason, C & Reuschke, D (2015). *Home truths: The true value of home-based businesses.* Report prepared for the Federation of Small Businesses (February). Available at http://www.fsb.org.uk/LegacySitePath/policy/rpu/scotland/assets/home%20truths%20-%20final.pdf (accessed 22 January 2016).

McGranahan, D & Wojan, T (2007). Recasting the creative class to examine growth processes in rural and urban counties. *Regional Studies* 41(2), 197–216.

McQuaid, R (1996). Social networks, entrepreneurship and regional development. In M Danson (Ed.), *Small firm formation and regional economic development* (pp. 118–131). London: Routledge.

Mitchell, C & Madden, M (2014). Rethinking commercial counterurbanisation: Evidence from rural Nova Scotia, Canada. *Journal of Rural Studies* 36, 137–148.

Moseley, M (2000). Innovation and rural development: Some lessons from Britain and Western Europe. *Planning Practice and Research* 15(1/2), 95–115.

Murdoch, J (2000). Networks – a new paradigm of rural development? *Journal of Rural Studies* 16, 407–419.

Nardone, G, Sisto, R & Lopolito, A (2010). Social capital in the LEADER initiative: A methodological approach. *Journal of Rural Studies* 26(1), 63–72.

North, D & Smallbone, D (2000). The innovativeness and growth of rural SMEs during the 1990s. *Regional Studies* 34(2), 145–157.

North, D & Smallbone, D (2007). Development entrepreneurship and enterprise in Europe's peripheral rural areas: Some issues facing policy-makers. *European Planning Studies* 14(1), 41–60.

OECD (1996). *Territorial indicators of employment: Focusing on rural development.* Paris: OECD.

OECD (2006). *The new rural paradigm: Policies and governance.* Paris: OECD.

OECD (2012). *Promoting growth in all regions.* Paris: OECD.

OECD (2014). *Innovation and modernising the rural economy.* OECD Rural Policy Reviews. Paris: OECD.

Oinas, P (1997). On the socio-spatial embeddedness of business firms. *Erdkunde* 51, 23–32.

Philip, L, MacLeod, M & Stockdale, A (2013). Retirement transition, migration and remote rural communities: Evidence from the Isle of Bute. *Scottish Geographical Journal* 129(2), 122–136.

Raley, M & Moxey, A (2000). *Rural microbusinesses in North East England: Final survey results.* Centre for Rural Economy Research Report RR00/3, University of Newcastle.

Ray, C (2001). *Culture economies.* Newcastle: CRE Press.

Reeder, R (1998). *Retiree-attraction policies for rural development.* An Economic Research Service Report, United States Department of Agriculture, Agriculture Information Bulletin No. 741 New York: USDA.

Ritsila, J (1999). Regional differences in environments for enterprises. *Entrepreneurship and Regional Development* 11, 187–202.

Roper, S, Love, J, Cooke, P & Clifton, N (2006). *The Scottish innovation system: Actors, roles and actions.* Report prepared for the Scottish Executive (January). Available at http://www.scotland.gov.uk/Publications/2006/01/18151934/0 (accessed 28 January 2015).

Rosenfeld, S (2002). Networks and clusters: The yin and yang of rural development. Paper presented at a conference organised by the Centre for the Study of Rural America – Exploring Policy Options for a New Rural America, May 2001.

Sanchez-Zamora, P, Gallardo-Cobos, R & Cena-Delgado, F (2014). Rural areas face the economic crisis: Analyzing the determinants of successful territorial dynamics. *Journal of Rural Studies* 35, 11–25.

Saraceno, E (2005). Rural development policies and the Second Pillar of the Common Agricultural Policy: The way ahead. In K Ortner (Ed.), Assessing rural development policies of the Common Agricultural Policy. Selection of papers from the 87th Seminar of the European Association of Agricultural Economics (EAAE), 21–23 April, Vienna, Austria (pp. 25–47). Kiel: Wissenschaftsverlag Vauk.

Scott, KA (2012). 21st century sustainable community: Discourses of local well-being. In S Atkinson, S Fuller & J Painter (Eds), *Well-being and place* (pp. 185–200). Farnham: Ashgate.

Scottish Government (2015). *Rural Scotland key facts 2015.* Scottish Government Publications, Edinburgh. Available at http://www.gov.scot/Publications/2015/03/5411 (accessed 9 April 2015).

Shortall, S & Warner, M (2012). Rural transformations. In M Shucksmith, D Brown, S Shortall, J Vergunst & M Warner (Eds), *Rural transformations and rural policies in the US and UK* (pp. 3–17). New York and London: Routledge.

Shucksmith, M (2012a). Class, power and inequality in rural areas: Beyond social exclusion? *Sociologia Ruralis* 52(4), 377–397.

Shucksmith, M (2012b). *Future directions in rural development.* Dunfermline: Carnegie UK Trust. Available at http://www.carnegieuktrust.org.uk/publications/2012/future-directions-in-rural-development-(full-repor (accessed 13 February 2015).

Shucksmith, M, Brown, D, Shortall, S, Vergunst, J & Warner, M (Eds). (2012). *Rural transformations and rural policies in the US and UK.* New York and London: Routledge.

Skerratt, S, Atterton, J, Hall, C, McCracken, D, Renwick, A, Revoredo-Giha, C, Steinerowski, A, Thomson, S, Woolvin, M, Farrington, J & Heesen, F (2012). *Rural Scotland in focus 2012.* Edinburgh: Rural Policy Centre, Scottish Agricultural College.

Skuras, D & Dubois, A (2015). Business networks, translocal linkages and the way to the New Rural Economy. In A Copus & P de Lima (Eds), *Territorial cohesion in rural Europe: The relational turn in rural development* (pp. 151–172). Oxford: Routledge.

Slee, R (2005). From countrysides of production to countrysides of consumption? *Journal of Agricultural Science* 143, 255–265.

Smallbone, D (2009). Fostering entrepreneurship in rural areas. In OECD, *Strengthening entrepreneurship and economic development in East Germany: Lessons from local approaches* (pp. 161–188). Final Report, OECD Local Entrepreneurship Reviews, OECD Publications, Paris.

Steiner, A & Atterton, J (2014). Contribution of private sector enterprises to rural resilience. *Local Economy* 29(3), 219–235.

Stockdale, A (2005). Incomers: Offering economic potential in rural England. *Journal of the Royal Agricultural Society of England* 166, 1–5.

Stockdale, A & MacLeod, M (2013). Pre-retirement age migration to remote rural areas. *Journal of Rural Studies* 32(4), 80–92.

Strahl, W & Dax, T (2010). Das Programm zur Entwicklung des landlichen Raums der EU 2007 bis 2013 – ein integrativer Politikansatz? Analyse und Bewertung am Beispiel von osterreich. *Standort, Zeitschrift fur Angewandte Geographie* 32(4), 55–61. Available at http://link.springer.com/article/10.1007/s00548-010-0136-y#page-2 (accessed 22 January 2016).

Sturzaker, J & Shucksmith, M (2011). Planning for housing in rural England: Discursive power and spatial exclusion. *Town Planning Review* 82(2), 169–194.

Taylor, M (2008). *Living working countryside: The Taylor review of rural economy and affordable housing.* London: Department for Communities and Local Government.

Virkkala, S (2007). Innovation and networking in peripheral areas – A case study of emergence and change in rural manufacturing. *European Planning Studies* 15(4), 511–529.

Ward, N, Atterton, J, Kim, T-Y, Lowe, P, Phillipson, J & Thompson, N (2005). Universities, the knowledge economy and 'neo-endogenous rural development'. Centre for Rural Economy Discussion Paper No. 1, University of Newcastle.

Ward, N & Brown, D (2009). Placing the rural in regional development: Ruralities, mobilities and diversities. *Regional Studies* 43(10), 1237–1244.

Woolvin, M & Rutherford, A (2013). Volunteering and public sector reform in Scotland. Rural Policy Centre Research Report (June). Available at http://www.sruc.ac.uk/downloads/file/1466/volunteering_and_public_service_reform_in_rural_scotland (accessed 13 February 2015).

Wynarczyk, P & Graham, J (2013). The impact of connectivity technology on home-based business venturing: The case of women in the north east of England. *Local Economy* 28(5), 504–523.

Part III
Food Systems and Land

Section editor: Geoffrey Lawrence

15

Food Systems and Land

Connections and Contradictions

Geoffrey Lawrence

Introduction

As the physical base for agriculture, land-related resources are crucial to sustaining human life. Land, however, has much deeper meaning than the provision of food. The meanings attached to land include social, cultural and spiritual dimensions. For First World peoples, in particular, land and water are central to culture, part of their extended selves. Land reinforces cultural identity and its protection is paramount. A different, market-based, view is that land is a tradable resource whose real value can be discovered through price signals. While it may have social significance for those occupying the land, it also has an overriding economic value related to its particular characteristics (level of fertility, access to water, proximity to markets, and so forth) and its ability to generate profits for investors. The 'struggle' over the meaning/s of land is ongoing. But there has also been a more direct 'struggle' over physical access to, and ownership of, land. Conquest and dispossession in the colonial era occurred as European nations entered new territories and appropriated lands. Even today, agricultural lands – and associated resources – are being purchased and leased by nations and companies eager to grow food, fibre and biofuels. While seemingly not as pernicious as in colonial times, many of today's large-scale land acquisitions have been identified as illegal and unfair, denying people their customary and legal rights over lands providing food, water, clothing, energy and shelter.

Food systems have been associated with different forms of human occupation of lands. The large-scale transition from hunter-gatherer to farming societies occurred around 11,000 years ago and by 6,000 years ago farm animals were domesticated. That is, for some 6,000 years much of the globe was occupied by a rudimentary agricultural/grazing rural economy. Today, there are three recognisable food systems – *traditional*, *modernising* and *industrialised* – represented on the global stage. *Traditional* (peasant-based and subsistence) farming systems, although currently feeding some 50% of the global population, are not considered in detail in this section. Rather, we focus on *modernising* and *industrialised* systems – the ones most prevalent in the global north, and increasingly prevalent in the global south.

The changing contours of global farm and food systems

Farming and food systems are complex and their characteristics vary enormously over time and space. One attempt to provide a typology of contemporary food systems (McCullough, Pingali & Stamoulis 2008) identified three basic forms: traditional, modernising and industrialised (see Table 15.1).

Traditional food systems are dependent on small-scale and subsistence farmers growing foods for family consumption and for local markets. Foods are produced with limited use of artificial chemicals and fertilisers, are seasonal, and undergo partial, if any, processing. Organisationally, there is limited control by the state, with farmers relying upon local-level middle agents to procure inputs and sell their produce. The system is crucial in feeding rural and urban populations throughout the developing world. Food is rarely exported, although penetration by foreign agri-capital has provided opportunities for the niche marketing of some crops (such as out-of-season vegetables and fruits destined for the global north – see McMichael, 2014). As indicated above, this food system is not the main focus of chapters in this section.

Table 15.1 Forms and characteristics of global food systems

	Traditional	*Modernising*	*Industrialised*
Share of agriculture in GDP	High	Medium	Low
Consumption	Rising calorie intake; diversification of diets	Diversification of diets; move to processed foods	Higher value, processed foods
Retail	Small-scale and wet markets	Diversification of retail; spread of supermarkets	Supermarkets are widespread
Processing	Limited processing sector	Growing opportunities for processing/value adding	Large processing sector for domestic and export markets
Wholesale	Traditional wholesalers with domestic focus	Traditional and specialised wholesalers	Specialised wholesalers; retailers often by-pass these via own distribution centres
Procurement	From local farmers; small market trading	From local and national sources; markets are regulated	From national and international sources; via managed chains; advanced arrangements
Production systems	Diversified low-input systems	Semi-intensive farming; a mix of family and corporate farms	Specialised, intensive, 'productivist' farming – large family farms and corporate farms
Safety in food systems	No traceability	Traceability in some chains via private standards	GlobalGAP, Hazard Analysis and Critical Control Points (HACCP) analysis, private standards
Vertical coordination	Relationships	Relationships and rules	Binding agreements
Examples	Bhutan, Cambodia, Kenya, Laos	Brazil, China, India, Mexico	Australia, Canada, USA, many EU countries

Source: Adapted from McCullough, Pingali & Stamoulis (2008, pp. 10–12).

The so-called *modernising* food system is one characterised by an increased size and capitalisation of farms, allowing for the injection of many of the latest agri-technologies and the application of integrated management regimes. Production is for national and export markets, there are specialised roles for processors and wholesalers, and the state and private food companies set rules and regulations to help ensure foods are safe and produced in line with basic principles for environmental protection. This mixed family-farm/corporate-farm structure was typical of the United States, Canada and Australia from the 1950s to the 1980s, but has now been embraced by nation states (such as Brazil, China, India and Mexico) which are seeking to place farming on a more industrial footing, while overseeing quite profound nationally based moves towards urbanisation. Foods are available in an array of retail outlets, with supermarkets coming to play an increasingly important role in food distribution.

In today's *industrialised* food system, where farmers make up only 2–5% of the total national workforce, an increasing volume of food is produced by large-scale specialised farmers and corporations with strategic linkages to processors and wholesalers. The 'productivist' approach to farming – using enhanced seed varieties, agri-chemicals, artificial fertilisers, computerised equipment and precision-farming techniques – has encouraged intensification. In relation to cropping, large monocultures of wheat, soy and canola dominate the landscape while, for animal production, there is a growing presence of so-called CAFOs – concentrated animal feeding operations – housing thousands of birds and animals in carefully controlled environments (Weis, 2007, 2013; Weis, this volume). Input efficiency is the driver of agricultural production and – despite the environmental harm that has been associated with productivism – it is, as its name suggests, the basis of the drive for ever greater productivity outcomes in farming (Lawrence & Campbell, 2014). The industrial nature of the food industry is discernible from the farm to the supermarket, with the latter using sophisticated cool-storage technologies in the 'just-in-time' delivery of fresh foods to consumers. Supermarkets dominate food retailing and impose their own private standards on suppliers.

Globally, the rules for trade in food are set by the World Trade Organization (WTO), with food safety standards devised by the WTO's Sanitary and Phytosanitary Measures Agreement under the auspices of *Codex Alimentarius* (see *Codex Alimentarius*, 2015). Private standards are also generalised internationally via organisations such as GlobalGAP, and certification schemes such as ISO 14001 and HACCP (Hazard Analysis and Critical Control Point). The reason for the proliferation of private standards is that food is no longer locally embedded but, rather, is integrated into global food supply chains (Oosterveer & Sonnenfeld, 2012). While these long food supply chains deliver a variety of foods, in a generally reliable manner, to consumers in the global north, they have high energy needs and a propensity for wastage, leading critics to raise serious questions about long-food chain efficiency and sustainability (Carolan, 2011; Evans, Campbell & Murcott, 2013). In fact, there has been a noticeable re-emergence, in the face of the industrial food model, of short or 'alternative' food chains, characterised by many of the features present in *traditional* food systems (see Table 15.1). It is therefore important to view the three food systems described above as neither discrete nor impermeable to change. And, while there has been a historical trend from *traditional* through *modernising* to *industrialised*, this is not, in some evolutionary sense, ineluctable. The three systems coexist, with national sentiment, global geopolitics, food security imperatives and social movements – among a host of other factors – helping to shape their contours (McCullough, Pingali & Stamoulis, 2008; Ingram, Ericksen & Liverman, 2010). Importantly, what has been demonstrated by social scientists is that various 'macro' processes are at work influencing all three food systems. These are described, below and receive prominence in many of the chapters that follow.

Globalisation, neoliberalism and financialisation

Three common underlying trends which have had, and continue to have, significance in the shape and performance of food systems are globalisation, neoliberalism and financialisation. Globalisation is often described as time/space 'compression', which fosters interdependence (and strong interconnectedness) between the global and the local (Held, McGrew, Goldblatt & Perraton, 1999; Martell, 2010). Transnational and transcultural integration has been promoted through technology – the personal computer, the Internet, the smartphone, modern transportation, biotechnology, nanotechnology and scientific innovation, in general. Such technologies, themselves, are created and distributed by transnational corporations with global reach. In relation to food and farming, globalisation has altered the nature of food production, transportation, marketing and sales. Agricultural practices throughout the global north (and parts of the south) have been transformed as technical innovations have been reproduced on a global scale, with crops and animals being 'tailored' according to food chain demands. The transportation of food has been revolutionised via containerisation which provides food traders with both spatial flexibility and efficiencies of scale (Rodrigue & Notteboom, 2013). In terms of profit-making strategies, globalisation allows lead firms in developed countries to outsource their low-value, bulk production functions to countries with base-level wages, yet retain control of value-creating activities in their home nation (Neilson, Pritchard & Yeung, 2014). Globalisation has promoted the movement of cheap farm labour throughout the world, keeping the cost of foods down for consumers, while providing profit-making opportunities for employers and contractors (Gertel & Sippel, 2014).

Neoliberalism has fostered the process of globalisation by promulgating an influential and widespread discourse of the benefits associated with free markets, by endorsing policy settings that give rise to deregulation, and by promoting governance arrangements that favour global economic integration. In agriculture, deregulation has been represented in the removal of tariffs, subsidies, buffer-stock schemes, and other government interventions once designed to stabilise small-scale capital – that is, to help protect the 'family farm' sector (Gray & Lawrence, 2001; Guptill & Welsh, 2014). State-run activities including research and extension have been privatised and – especially in the case of extension – must now be purchased by farmers in the marketplace, consistent with the principle of 'user pays'. There is a self-help ideology in agrarianism that resonates with the claims of neoliberalism, and farmers – especially in nations like the United States, Australia and Canada – have abandoned earlier, collective ('farmer union'), approaches to solving economic problems such as the cost-price squeeze and are adopting individual solutions, including becoming larger, more specialised, and signing one-on-one contracts with large food retailers (Higgins & Lawrence, 2005). At the global level, WTO rules favour corporate agro-exporters, promote market-based solutions to problems of food scarcity and environmental degradation, extend intellectual property rights to agribusiness companies creating seed/chemical 'packages', and impose penalties on nations which balk at trade liberalisation (McMichael, 2013, 2014). The result is that global governance of agriculture by the WTO encourages the consolidation of more concentrated and powerful lead firms, suppliers and intermediaries in food supply chains (Rosset, 2006; Gereffi, 2014). Yet, for the WTO and many governments and economists throughout the world, neoliberal settings are viewed as having the greatest likelihood, via the unfettered price mechanism and less-distorted trade relations, of delivering the best long-term outcomes for global food security (WTO, 2015).

The third concept of considerable significance for the agri-food sector is that of financialisation, a term used to denote the increasing presence and influence of financial entities in aspects of contemporary economic life (Lawrence, Sippel, Larder & DesFours, 2014; Lawrence, Sippel & Burch, 2015). In seeking reliable returns on investments, firms in the finance sector – including merchant banks, hedge funds, private equity firms and state-owned sovereign wealth funds – have traditionally favoured technology, energy stocks, bullion and real estate. In recent times where dot-com bubbles have burst and swathes of real estate have become 'toxic', the finance sector has turned its attention to food and farming. There are strong reasons for doing so: land is a scarce commodity and its price is rising, globally; newly generated middle-class wealth in nations like China, India and Indonesia is creating considerable demand for animal protein; land ownership allows profits to be gained from carbon sequestration, as part of carbon trading; and, concerned with oil price and availability, governments are legislating for, and promoting, crop biofuel production (Lawrence, Sippel, Larder & DesFours, 2014). Financialisation is being facilitated by the presence of financial deregulation (as a product of neoliberal globalisation) and the subsequent emergence of new investment products. Food has become 'just another tradeable commodity [extracting value] from the food chain in order to carve new spaces for corporate profit' (Russi, 2013, p. 30). As will be discussed below, financialisation has also encouraged large-scale land acquisitions and, in some cases, the unfair removal of people from their farms (the 'land grab') (see Margulis, McKeon & Borras, 2014; Gertel & Sippel, this volume).

It is important to recognise that globalisation, neoliberalism and financialisation are not inevitable processes but are uneven, indeterminate and 'fluid', as well as being open to contestation. Two good examples of the latter are the food riots that were generated by the food price hike of 2008, and the extent of both peaceful and violent social protest about large-scale land purchases by foreign governments and companies (Margulis, McKeon & Borras, 2014).

Impacts of current trends

'Family farms' are those relying primarily on family members for both labour and management in the running of the farm. According to the Food and Agriculture Organization (FAO, 2014), there are over 500 million family farms worldwide, comprising some 98% of all farm holdings. They are responsible for the creation of some 56% of agricultural production on 56% of Earth's surface. Even in the EU and USA where pressure for property consolidation has been intense, family farms comprise some 98% of all farms (Moreno-Perez & Lobley, 2015). What has been observed in the *modernising* and *industrialised* food production systems has been a reduction in the actual number of farms, leading some to predict the long-term demise of family farming (see Brookfield & Parsons, 2007). There has been a 'hollowing out' of medium-sized farmers, referred to in the USA as the 'declining middle' of small commercial farms (Guptill & Welsh, 2014). Yet, as Brunori and Bartolini (this volume) argue, in some regions of the world, policy changes, population pressures and subdivisions have resulted in family farms increasing in number – particularly in former socialist nations and in Asia.

The concentration and centralisation of capital in the agri-food industries is readily demonstrated by the growth of CAFOs, the growing presence of finance firms, and by supermarkets. According to Weis (this volume) the industrial production of poultry and animals for human consumption represents the narrowing of agricultural production and the creation of a more unsustainable global food production system. The 'meatification' of diets is facilitated by some of the world's largest TNCs (transnational corporations), with scant regard for longer term environmental degradation, climate change impacts or animal welfare. 'Meatification' is bound to the industrial grain–oilseed–livestock complex in a manner that creates and perpetuates 'expansive ecological violence'.

Financialisation is being facilitated by the presence of financial deregulation (as a product of neoliberal globalisation) and the subsequent emergence of new investment products. Central amongst these are 'derivatives' which bundle agricultural commodities with minerals, cars, mortgages and an array of other products, in the creation of liquid securities which are traded on futures, and over-the-counter markets (see Gertel & Sippel, this volume). They are a mechanism to hedge against risk, but they can also be used in speculative trading, often to the detriment of farmers (who want stability over volatility) and consumers (disadvantaged by food price increases) (Breger Bush, 2012; Barthwal-Datta, 2014). As Gertel and Sippel (this volume) argue, while finance capital might have appeal for some farm operations, for others livelihoods are compromised and some are banished from the land.

Supermarkets are playing an increasingly significant role in global food production and retailing. As Dixon and Banwell (this volume) have highlighted, there are numerous strategies employed by the supermarkets to strengthen their presence in food supply chains. They undercut smaller retailers who find it difficult to compete, creating oligopsony conditions of a few buyers able to choose from many competing suppliers. While the presence of supermarkets in nations with *traditional* food systems is currently low (with a share of about 10% of sales) growth is accelerating (McCullough, Pingali & Stamoulis, 2008). In relation to the *modernising* and *industrialised* food systems, the domination of supermarkets has become entrenched (Lawrence & Dixon, 2015). When the top four firms in any commodity market hold 40% of market share, the market is considered to be 'highly concentrated'. When this increases to 60% and over, the market is viewed as 'significantly distorted'. Yet, as Carolan (2013, pp. 102, 112) has demonstrated, the level of concentration of the top four supermarkets in many nations sits on or above the 'significantly distorted' level – 99% in Australia, 91% in Sweden, 71% in France and the UK, and 60% in the USA. Not surprisingly, questions continue to be raised about the real level of competition in the industry and socioeconomic impacts of supermarket expansion (Richards, Lawrence, Loong & Burch, 2012; Carolan, 2013; Dixon & Banwell, this volume).

The seminal work of Leland Glenna and co-researchers has investigated the political economy of agricultural science and technology. Investigations reveal that a neoliberal calculus has been increasingly applied to state-funded research in the United States, with an assessment by governments that such public investment is 'useless' if it is not commercialised (Glenna, Lacy, Welsh & Biscotti, 2007; Glenna & Henke, 2014). A 'technological fix' mentality has also become widespread as administrators and scientists come to view progress in terms of technological applications, often with little consideration of the socioeconomic and environmental contexts into which those technologies are embedded (Glenna & Henke, 2014; Glenna, Brandl & Jones, 2015). The assumption? Technical progress equals social progress (Beck, 1992, p. 201). Glenna and Ransom (this volume) posit that, under neoliberalism, there is a concerted effort to convert R&D in public universities into privately owned goods from which profits can be exacted, skewing research away from non-commercial but publicly beneficial areas of investigation.

As Smith (this volume) and others (Lawrence, Lyons & Wallington, 2010; Rosin, Stock & Campbell, 2012) have argued, there are identifiable symptoms of crisis in global food systems. We live in a world of food insecurity and malnutrition. Rural poverty is rife, particularly in the global south. Environmental degradation is taking its toll on agricultural output (Cribb, 2010; Lawrence, Lyons & Wallington, 2010). Increases in temperature associated with climate change will severely compromise farming systems (IPCC, 2014). Biodiversity – essential in guaranteeing ecosystem health through nutrient recycling, water cleansing and soil formation – is declining at a rate deemed unacceptable: humans are said to have initiated the sixth great mass extinction in Earth's history (Mittermeier et al., 2011). Is there hope of reversing the present, unsustainable, trajectory? Smith (this volume) argues that there are recognisable discursive and political changes being driven by grassroots peasant farmer movements as well as by enlightened leaders in peak food policy organisations. She argues that through emerging civic–intergovernmental pacts and multi-stakeholder deals, key players are identifying new ways of creating a more just global food system.

Conclusion

As argued throughout this chapter, and the chapters in this section of the Handbook, globalisation is viewed as having encouraged horizontal and vertical integration favouring corporate agribusiness expansion. Neoliberal policies have justified removal of the state from support of family farming and have promoted market-based 'solutions' to problems of agricultural development and food security. Financialisation has fostered corporate-based mergers and acquisitions, driven large-scale land acquisitions that have displaced family farmers, and has encouraged speculative activities in futures markets. The overall outcomes have been the entrenchment of productivist agriculture, as part of *modernising* and *industrialised* food production systems, and the constant pressure on *traditional* food systems to 'modernise', moving quickly to embrace the neoliberal trade regime and its corporate agribusiness future.

It has been projected that to feed a global population of some 9 billion people by 2050 will require an increase of about 70% above 2007 food production levels (FAO, 2009). How might this be achieved? The corporate-based model of *modernising* and *industrialised* farming appears to be the preferred choice of governments in the global north. But another option is that of agro-ecology, with the UN's Special Rapporteur on the Right to Food predicting that world food supply could be doubled in some globally significant farming regions within a 10-year period by strategic investment in agro-ecological methods and technological innovations targeting smallholder producers (De Schutter, 2010). Clearly, different 'visions' will produce different outcomes.

Acknowledgement

Emeritus Professor Lawrence receives part-funding from the Australian Research Council (Project Nos DP 110102299, DP 120101949 and DP 160101318) and from the National Research Foundation of Korea (NRF-2010-330-00159) and the Norwegian Research Council (FORFOOD Project No 220691).

References

Barthwal-Datta, M (2014). *Food security in Asia: Challenges, policies and implications*. London: International Institute for Strategic Studies.

Beck, U (1992). *Risk society: Towards a new modernity*. London: Sage.

Breger Bush, S (2012). *Derivatives and development: A political economy of global finance, farming and poverty*. New York: Palgrave Macmillan.

Brookfield, H & Parsons, H (Eds). (2007). *Family farms: Survival and prospect*. London: Routledge.

Carolan, M (2011). *The real cost of cheap food*. London: Earthscan.

Carolan, M (2013). *Reclaiming food security*. London: Earthscan.

Codex Alimentarius (2015). About codex. Available at http://www.codexalimentarius.org/about-codex/en/ (accessed 8 May 2015).

Cribb, J (2010). *The coming famine: The global food crisis and what we can do to avoid it*. Berkeley: University of California Press.

De Schutter, O (2010). Report submitted by the Special Rapporteur on the Right to Food, Olivier De Schutter. Available at http://www.srfood.org/images/stories/pdf/officialreports/20110308_a-hrc-16-49_agroecology_en.pdf (accessed 21 May 2015).

Evans, D, Campbell, H & Murcott, A (Eds). (2013). *Waste matters: New perspectives on food and society.* Chichester: Wiley-Blackwell.

FAO (2009). *How to feed the world in 2050.* Available at http://www.fao.org/fileadmin/templates/wsfs/docs/expert_paper/How_to_Feed_the_World_in_2050.pdf (accessed 22 May 2015).

FAO (2014). Family farming. Available at http://www.fao.org/family-farming/en/ (accessed 12 May 2015).

Gereffi, G (2014). Global value chains in a post-Washington Consensus world. *Review of International Political Economy* 21(1), 9–37.

Gertel, J & Sippel, SR (Eds). (2014). *Seasonal workers in Mediterranean agriculture: The social costs of eating fresh.* London: Routledge.

Glenna, L, Brandl, B & Jones, K (2015). International political economy of agricultural research and development. In A Bonanno & L Busch (Eds), *Handbook of the international political economy of agriculture and food* (pp. 322–343). Cheltenham: Edward Elgar.

Glenna, L & Henke, C (2014). Agricultural technologies and the structure of the North American agrifood system. In C Bailey, L Jensen & E Ransom (Eds), *Rural America in a globalizing world: Problems and prospects for the 2010s* (pp. 85–102). Morgantown: West Virginia University Press.

Glenna, L, Lacy, W, Welsh, R & Biscotti, D (2007). University administrators, agricultural biotechnology, and academic capitalism: Defining the public good to promote university–industry relationships. *Sociological Quarterly* 48(1), 141–164.

Gray, I & Lawrence, G (2001). *A future for regional Australia: Escaping global misfortune.* Cambridge: Cambridge University Press.

Guptill, A & Welsh, R (2014). The declining middle of American agriculture: A spatial phenomenon. In C Bailey, L Jensen & E Ransom (Eds), *Rural America in a globalizing world: Problems and prospects for the 2010s* (pp. 36–50). Morgantown: West Virginia University Press.

Held, D, McGrew, A, Goldblatt, A and Perraton, J (1999). *Global transformations: Politics, economics and culture.* Cambridge: Polity.

Higgins, V & Lawrence, G (Eds). (2005). *Agricultural governance: Globalization and the new politics of regulation.* London: Routledge.

Ingram, J, Ericksen, P & Liverman, D (Eds). (2010). *Food security and global environmental change.* London: Earthscan.

IPCC (2014). *Climate change for 2014: Impacts, adaptation and vulnerability.* Cambridge: Cambridge University Press.

Lawrence, G & Campbell, H (2014). Neoliberalism in the antipodes: Understanding the influence and limits of the neoliberal political project. In S Wolf & A Bonanno (Eds), *The neoliberal regime in the agri-food sector: Crisis, resilience and restructuring* (pp. 263–283). London: Routledge.

Lawrence, G & Dixon, J (2015). The political economy of agri-food: Supermarkets. In A Bonanno & L Busch (Eds), *Handbook of international political economy of agriculture and food* (pp. 213–231). Cheltenham: Edward Elgar.

Lawrence, G, Lyons, K & Wallington, T (Eds). (2010). *Food security, nutrition and sustainability.* London: Earthscan.

Lawrence, G, Sippel, S & Burch, D (2015). Financialisation of food and farming. In G Robinson & D Carson (Eds), *Handbook on the globalisation of agriculture* (pp. 309–327). Cheltenham: Edward Elgar.

Lawrence, G, Sippel, S, Larder, N & DesFours, L (2014). Will the financialisation of food and farming provide the basis for a prosperous future for rural Asia? *Proceedings of the fifth international conference of the Asian Rural Sociology Association.* Available at http://www.arsa1996.org/html/downloads/5tharsa_proceedings_vol1.pdf (accessed 9 May 2015).

Margulis, M, McKeon, N & Borras, S (Eds). (2014). *Land grabbing and global governance.* London: Routledge.

Martell, L (2010). *The sociology of globalization.* Cambridge: Polity.

McCullough, E, Pingali, P & Stamoulis, K (2008). Small farms and the transformation of food systems: An overview. In E McCullough, P Pingali & K Stamoulis (Eds), *The transformation of agri-food systems: Globalization, supply chains and smallholder farmers* (pp. 3–46). London: Earthscan.

McMichael, P (2013). *Food regimes and agrarian questions.* Halifax: Fernwood Publishing.

McMichael, P (2014). Land grabbing as security mercantilism in international relations. In M Margulis, N McKeon & S Borras (Eds), *Land grabbing and global governance* (pp. 47–64). London: Routledge.

Mittermeier, R, Turner, W, Larsen, F, Brooks, T & Gascon, C (2011). Global biodiversity conservation: The critical role of hotspots. In F Zachos & J Habel (Eds), *Biodiversity hotspots: Distribution and protection of conservation priority areas* (pp. 3–22). New York: Springer.

Moreno-Perez, O & Lobley, M (2015). The morphology of multiple household family farms. *Sociologia Ruralis* 55(2), 125–149.

Neilson, J, Pritchard, B & Yeung, H (2014). Global value chains and global production networks in the changing international political economy: An introduction. *Review of International Political Economy* 21(1), 1–8.

Oosterveer, P & Sonnenfeld, D (2012). *Food, globalization and sustainability*. London: Earthscan.

Richards, C, Lawrence, G, Loong, M & Burch, D (2012). A toothless chihuahua? The Australian Competition and Consumer Commission, neoliberalism and supermarket power in Australia. *Rural Society* 21(3), 250–263.

Rodrigue, J-P & Notteboom, T (2013). The containerization of commodities. Available at http://people. hofstra.edu/geotrans/eng/ch3en/appl3en/ch3a2en.html# (accessed 8 May 2015).

Rosin, C, Stock, P & Campbell, H (Eds). (2012). *Food systems failure: The global food crisis and the future of agriculture*. London: Earthscan.

Rosset, P (2006). *Food is different: Why we must get the WTO out of agriculture*. Halifax: Fernwood Publishing.

Russi, L (2013). *Hungry capital: The financialization of food*. Alresford, UK: Zero Books.

Weis, T (2007). *The global food economy: The battle for the future of farming*. London: Zed Books.

Weis, T (2013). *The ecological hoofprint: The global burden of industrial livestock*. London: Zed Books.

WTO (2015). Agriculture: Explanation. Available at https://www.wto.org/english/tratop_e/agric_e/ag_intro01_intro_e.htm (accessed 9 May 2015).

16

The Family Farm

Model for the Future or Relic of the Past?

Gianluca Brunori and Fabio Bartolini

Introduction

> Family farming produces most of the food in the world. But this family farming is about much more than just production. It is about transmitting knowledge from generation to generation benefitting families and communities. It is about respecting and valuing local tradition, customs and culture. It is about improving nutrition and providing healthier diets based on fresh food, fruits and vegetables. It is about linking production to families, to schools, to communities. It is about territorial development. And it is about sustainability. Nothing comes closer to the sustainable development paradigm in food systems than family farming.
>
> *(Da Silva, 2014)*

In his opening statement to the Global Dialogue on Family Farming, FAO Director-General José Graziano da Silva (2014) argued that family farming is not only a peculiar production unit, but also a complex socio-ecological entity crucial to food security, the viability of rural areas and environmental integrity. The centrality of family farming is now part of an emerging 'consensus frame' (Mooney & Hunt, 2009) – one general enough to involve a wide set of positions and interests but ambiguous enough to allow different, and often conflicting, interpretations. In declaring 2014 the Year of Family Farming, the United Nations consolidated a global consensus about the need to prioritise family farms in policies for development and for food and nutrition security (FNS). This position has emerged from a long debate that has divided generations of scholars and policy makers. This debate had a turning point in 2007–2008, when the food price spikes made food security a global priority. In fact, the structural adjustment that occurred in developing countries during the 1980s reduced subsidies to agriculture while also liberalising trade. Yet, as the World Bank (2008) recognised, private investments did not replace public ones, and lack of investment had exposed food systems, and family farms, to global drivers such as climate change, price volatility, and corporate domination of global value chains. When the prices of some food commodities grew by more than 200% and food riots spread all over the globe, policy makers acknowledged the level of vulnerability of national food systems and its dramatic implications.

The Food and Agriculture Organization has revealed that: (a) more than 90% of farms are run by an individual or a family and rely primarily on family labour; (b) family farms occupy around 70–80% of farmland; and (c) family farms produce about 80% of the world's food (FAO, 2014). These figures show that family farming is the dominant form of agricultural production in the world, and in some countries farm numbers have increased. What happened to disprove the thesis of several generations of scholars predicting the disappearance of family farming?

This chapter details how the perception of family farming has changed in rural studies and how this perception has affected empirical research and policies. Family farming is intimately linked to key global challenges, and the importance of bridging a theoretical divide appears particularly urgent in this field.

What is a family farm?

In a background paper for the State of Food and Agriculture in 2014, Lowder, Skoet and Singh (2014) reviewed definitions of family farming across the world, arguing that, to be a meaningful term, 'family' needs to be considered in the context of 'labour' and 'size'. Different definitions of 'family farm' result in different interpretations. For example, the think-tank GRAIN (2014) – using definitions of 'small' farms (ranging from less than 200 ha in Argentina and less than 1 ha in Vietnam) – calculated that 90% of farms in the world are small farms, but occupy only 25% of agricultural land.

Existing definitions of 'family farm' range from the very inclusive US-based one, where family members manage, and provide some labour, to the farm, to more restrictive ones, such as the Brazilian definition, where a maximum economic size is set as a threshold. The US definition allows 97.7% of farms to be classified as family farms, with 87.7% of total land occupied. Such a broad definition risks being meaningless, as it can encompass a huge range of forms (Lowder, Skoet & Singh, 2014). According to Hoppe, Korb and Banker (2008), about 80% of farms with a turnover above US$1 million are family farms if the US definition is applied. In practice, non-family farms that take the form of what are termed 'C-corporations' (taxed separately from its owner) and 'S-corporations' (small business corporations, having the benefits of incorporation but being taxed like a sole proprietorship) prevail only in the category above US$5 million.

To have analytical and policy significance, a more restrictive definition is required. Lowder, Skoet and Singh (2014) found that most definitions specify that a member of the household must own, operate and/or manage the farm either in part or fully. When these criteria are applied, 87.1% of US farms (accounting for 57.6% of US farm production) are family farms (MacDonald, 2014); in the European Union 75% of the total number of holdings and less than 40% of utilised agricultural area fall into this category (Davidova & Thompson, 2014). According to the FAO, a family farm is 'an agricultural holding which is managed and operated by a household and where farm labour is largely supplied by that household' (Lowder, Skoet & Singh, 2014). This definition brings family farming closer to that of a 'peasant farm' – relating to ownership or tenure of land and means of production, to a strong component of household labour, to a relative autonomy from conventional markets and technologies (Ellis, 1993; Van der Ploeg, 2013) and to the concept of 'simple commodity production' (see Friedmann, 1978).

Why does family farming survive?

Debates on family farming have centred upon the 'disappearance thesis', arguing for 'the necessary dissolution of the peasantry as a logical consequence of the advancing process of class differentiation in the rural areas of (European) nations' (Araghi, 1995, p. 340). The relevance of this prediction relates to the historical interpretation of the role of capitalist agriculture and of its political implications, known as the 'agrarian question' (Goodman & Redclift, 1981). For Marx and many neo-Marxists, capitalism had the historical role of liberating productive forces and preparing the ground for the next, 'socialist', phase of development. Without a capitalist transition, socialism would be premature. Agrarian capitalism was therefore considered a necessary step to allow the transition to socialism. Within this framework, agriculture played a pivotal role, as the generation of surplus would constitute the material basis for industrial accumulation. Capitalist agriculture, replacing the peasantry, would introduce technological advancement and therefore liberate labour for industrial activities. The prediction was that petty bourgeois relations in agriculture were transitional – the small-scale family farm would either die or become a much larger, capitalist, entity.

However, family farms have not disappeared. In some countries, as indicated earlier, the total number has increased, as in former socialist countries and in many Asian countries – an effect of land reforms or population pressure. In other countries, the total number of farms has decreased, but not the proportion of family farms. Between 1960 and 2000 the average size of farm in high-income countries increased, while in low-income countries the average size decreased at the expense of middle-sized farms, often accentuating a bimodal distribution (that is, a large number of small farms, together with an increasing number of large-scale farms) (Hazell, 2011).

These trends are caused by a multiplicity of drivers. When considering drivers of agrarian change, we should distinguish between 'root causes' and 'dynamic pressures' (Blaikie, Cannon, Davis & Wisner, 2004). Root causes affect conditions of development in the long term, while dynamic pressures have a lower intensity and are generally reversible.

Tenure regimes, together with population pressure, are considered the main 'root causes' of family farming development. Enclosures in the pre-industrial era, depriving rural families of their right to cultivate and to use common land, constituted the basis of capitalist development and – through the removal of farm labour – the formation of a proletarian class. Collectivisation in socialist countries resulted in a fast and painful de-peasantisation. After the Second World War, land reforms in Japan, South Korea, Italy and Germany transformed tenants into smallholders, increasing substantially the presence and impact of family farming within rural economies. In recent times, land reforms in China, Latin America, Southeast Asia, South Africa, Zimbabwe, and former socialist countries have occurred with varying outcomes. As access to land is the necessary condition for farmers to create a farm resource base, changes in tenure regimes can be considered as turning points, on which further evolution depends.

When considering dynamic pressures, it is important to assess the conditions of economic development. An earlier pattern of change observed in the post-Second World War period was based on a clear urban–rural divide that coincided with 'traditional' and 'modern' economic sectors (Lewis, 1954). Finding employment in the 'modern' sector would be contingent upon urbanisation and rural out-migration. More recent patterns of change show that, as transport and communication infrastructures improve, and industrialisation is spread more widely than in urban areas, rural households have the possibility of reallocating their labour in a flexible way between farm and outside jobs. In this case, de-agrarianisation (Bryceson, 1996) – reduction of the importance of agriculture on total household income – does not necessarily mean de-ruralisation (Araghi, 2012), that is, reduction of the number of people living in rural areas.

Agrarian change is, in most cases, based on a strong policy component. Agricultural trade and support policies have contributed, for industrialised countries, up to 30% of farmers' incomes (OECD, 2014). In high-income countries, where governments were aware of the importance of agriculture for the political stability of their countries, support was intended to give farmers stability of income and encourage them to 'modernise' – that is, to invest and grow. In developing countries, the 'Green Revolution' assumed that productivity growth would be enhanced among smallholders. It was a programme heavily involving international organisations as well as national states. In Asia, government expenditure in agriculture in 1972 totalled 15.4% of total government expenditure, reaching some 23.2% in Bangladesh and 22.1% in India (Hazell, 2009).

Technological change is a further dynamic pressure in most cases of farm differentiation. Since the 1960s the Green Revolution has allowed increases in land productivity, albeit with negative consequences for the environment (McIntyre, Herren, Wakhungu & Watson, 2009) and for social equality. Mechanisation and genetically modified seeds have encouraged family farms to push specialisation and increase the ratio of land to labour. Feeding and breeding technologies have changed the optimal economic size of farms, especially in the livestock sector (MacDonald, 2014). Precision farming, with its use of satellite data, ICTs and more recently drones, has generated new economies of scale by reducing the cost of control of operations. Other labour-saving technology such as robotisation in harvesting and automation of milking activities are examples of further intensification and have increased the flexibility of household labour. Where a lively labour market has 'pulled' people from the land, the above processes have resulted in consolidation of remaining farms. Importantly, where off-farm employment opportunities have not emerged, new technologies have resulted in economic marginalisation and increasing poverty (Li, 2010).

The changing shape of family farming

As indicated above, the root causes and dynamic pressures in each context have generated a multiplicity of differentiation patterns (Whatmore, Munton, Little & Marsden, 1987; Kasimis & Papadopoulos, 2013). Davidova and Thompson (2014) have recently classified European family farms into *livelihood*, *semi-subsistence*, and *commercial*, each of these further articulated into full-time and part-time, diversified and non-diversified. In high-level income countries, stability provided by agricultural policies has encouraged farms to invest, allowing them to grow in size and acquire entrepreneurial attitudes without losing their 'family farm' characteristics. However, when transport and communication infrastructures have improved, household members have had the possibility of choosing between leaving the land and moving to the city, or reallocating their labour in a flexible way between farm and outside jobs. An expanding urban labour market, and its increasing flexibility, in high-level income countries have widened the range of strategies that family farms adopt (Shucksmith & Hermann, 1992). Young people can leave the farm to follow their aspirations; older farmers can develop 'exit' strategies; farmers with expected turnover can invest for new generations; and households can combine off-farm and on-farm activities and incomes. Integration of farming into labour markets allows farmers the opportunity to hire salaried workers. Availability of cheap unskilled labour, often irregular, which has increased strongly in the last two decades, has allowed family farms in developed countries to take advantage of labour-intensive pathways. Lifestyle motivations and the search for alternatives, encouraged by rural development policies, have combined to generate new models of business based on diversification of farm products and services, short supply chains, quality development and embeddedness with local territories (Van der Ploeg et al., 2000). A renewed interest in the values of the countryside has generated back-to-land movements – something that has gained momentum since the global financial crisis of 2008 (Kasimis & Papadopoulos, 2013; Wilbur, 2013).

The changes outlined above have proceeded alongside the transformation of the family in society, and have opened another field of investigation related to internal, rather than external, drivers. Family farming is traditionally considered to be a seat of patriarchal relations, but new on-farm/off-farm relations can bring about a change in the relations of power between genders (Bock & Shortall, 2006). Whatmore (1991) argued that to overcome the dualism between family and business, and reproduction and production, it would be necessary to focus on the interplay between the productive and the reproductive aspects of work on the farm. Shortall (2002) showed how women's off-farm income in Northern Ireland in times of crisis provided an opportunity for a renegotiation of domestic responsibilities and gender role expectations. In developing countries, women's involvement in farming has deepened (Lastarria-Cornhiel, 2008) as a response to the need for diversification for rural households (Deere, 2005). Today, on average, women constitute 43% of the agricultural labour force, ranging from 20% in Latin America to 50% in eastern Asia and sub-Saharan Africa (FAO, 2011). 'Closing the gap' in access to resources between men and women has become a priority of international organisations.

From disappearance to re-emergence?

Empirical evidence on the persistence of family farming has helped to dismantle the 'grand narrative' of disappearance. At the same time, a new 'grand narrative' has emerged. Scholars of different disciplines have focused on specificities of family farms, rediscovering Chayanov's legacy. Chayanov (1966 [1925]) explained that the farm household had the capacity to reduce consumption in order to cope with adversities. Household life cycles can explain different work capacity, attitudes to risk, to investments, to intensification, and can explain entry and exit from agriculture.

Agricultural economists (Singh, Squire & Strauss, 1986) have turned Chayanov's ideas into agricultural household models that consider the household as a decision-making unit in a market economy. According to these models, households allocate their time to on-farm, off-farm and leisure according to their utility function which, in turn, is influenced by salaries, conditions of work, price of consumer goods and technological progress (mainly referring to labour-saving innovation). Given the utility function, which is the 'subjective' component of household behaviour, relative prices determine the allocation of labour. Some of these models are dynamic, as they not only measure changes in farm patterns in relation to changes in prices and preferences, but capture the effects of aging and of intergenerational investments (Viaggi et al., 2011). When farm labour is integrated into labour markets, diversification with off-farm work is explained in terms of decreasing marginal utility of off-farm and on-farm labour.

From a sociological perspective, the focus has shifted to the interaction of the farm household with its social, natural, administrative and technical environments. Drawing upon Chayanov, Friedmann (1978) showed that global competition activated by American wheat imported into Europe in the 1870s put European capitalist farms (namely in the UK and in Germany) into stress because of declining product prices and decreasing land values, while family-farm households survived by reducing family consumption to a minimum. Mann and Dickinson (1978) focused on the difference between labour time (i.e., the time dedicated by workers to production) and production time (e.g., the time from sowing to harvesting), during which labour is not necessary. The gap between labour time and production time, which depends on the natural component of agricultural production, is viewed as making farming 'unattractive to capitalist penetration' (Mann & Dickinson, 1978, p. 471). Reinhard and Bartlett (1989), analysing the development of US agriculture, claimed that family farms enjoy a natural competitive advantage for 'subjective' reasons, such as commitment to a lifestyle that implies a different economic calculus, long-term considerations about family members' welfare, and lifecycle-related strategies in terms of attitude to risk (where risk relates to farm investment, innovation and level of indebtedness). Mooney (1988) built upon Weberian categories of substantial and formal rationality to explain family farmers' different pathways. More recently, Calus and Van Huylenbroeck (2010) have linked economic and sociological analysis by developing an approach based on transaction costs: family life allows more frequent interactions, and loyalty to the family reduces the need for monitoring and surveillance.

Unlike neoclassical theories that consider utility functions as given, sociologists have developed actor-oriented interpretations based on the earlier writings of Chayanov. Van der Ploeg (2000) follows Giddens's (1971) approach that views structure and agency as being mutually constituted in arguing that 'styles of farming' – principles of farm organisation and patterns of behaviour – are at the same time socially constructed and individually adapted. On a similar basis, 'livelihood frameworks' (Scoones, 1998; Ellis, 2000) have progressively gained consensus in development studies and in international institutions such as the World Bank. According to these frameworks, and inspired by Amartya Sen's theory of capabilities (Sen, 1999), well-being depends on the capacity of households and individuals to mobilise their assets and to turn them into livelihood outcomes (Bebbington, 1999). Some of these assets – such as natural and human capital – are produced and reproduced through the coordination of activities of different types within the household (on-farm/off-farm, agriculture/other activities), while others – social, institutional and cultural capital – are reproduced through interaction of the farm with the outside world.

The development of these approaches opens new perspectives for the study of family farming and for the role of policies. All the approaches mentioned in this section put stress on the environment where family farms operate, and advocate a territorial, rather than a sectorial, approach to agricultural policies (Van der Ploeg et al., 2000). This means considering farms not only as part of agricultural supply chains, but as components of broader local economies and societies, in which farmers are embedded (Bowen, 2011; Morris & Kirwan, 2011).

Who is more progressive?

For more than a century since the writings of Marx and Lenin, the key challenges in the public and scientific debates around agriculture have been how to generate agricultural surplus and how to ensure that agricultural surplus contributes to wider economic growth. Today, the issue of sustainability – a highly contested concept but one which has generated a new academic discipline within the past few decades – has set the terms for a 'new agrarian question' (Van der Ploeg, 1993). Science has revealed the hidden costs of agricultural production and there are emerging debates about the public goods – such as ecosystem services – that agriculture can produce. In this regard the question 'which forms of production have a progressive role?' may have different answers than in the past, calling into question the role of agricultural science, along with previous and current agricultural policies.

Today, one of the benchmarks to measure the progressive role of farming is sustainability. It is now largely agreed that 'industrial agriculture', a technological paradigm associated with capital-intensive, large-scale, monocultural and 'factory farming' agriculture, is largely unsustainable (McIntyre, Herren, Wakhungu & Watson, 2009; Clunies-Ross & Hildyard, 2013; Lawrence & McMichael, 2014). Environmental impacts of this model include soil compaction, contamination of soil and groundwater with fertiliser and pesticide residues, reduction in plant and animal biodiversity, and high rates of carbon emission (McIntyre, Herren, Wakhungu & Watson, 2009; Woodhouse, 2010). Small-scale family farming is also capable of harming the environment – particularly where it employs highly intensive farming methods based on irrigation, fertilisation and pesticide use (Wilson & Tisdell, 2001). Yet, there is evidence that traditional agro-ecosystems, mainly managed by smallholders, have high levels of biodiversity and environmentally friendly systems of land and water resource management and conservation (Altieri, Funes-Monzote & Petersen, 2012). Importantly, most agro-ecological principles best fit with labour-intensive, risk-averse, diversified, locally embedded, multifunctional patterns of production, which tend to correspond to small-scale family farms (Pretty, Toulmin & Williams, 2011).

According to Van der Ploeg (2013), the peasant mode of farming is based upon co-production. Exchange with nature, together with non-market labour relations, are the keys to understanding their relative autonomy from market relations. This autonomy is built, step by step, through the maintenance and improvement, over time, of the family-farm resource base. A vast literature, centring upon the concept of public goods (Cooper, Hart & Baldock, 2009), has clarified what should be expected from agriculture in addition to commercial output. Accordingly, the concept of multifunctional agriculture, initially used as an argument for justifying support to agriculture in trade negotiations (Potter & Burney, 2002), is now a guiding principle for more sustainable and economically successful models of farming (Huylenbroeck & Durand, 2003). The concept is now accepted both in a neoliberal framing (the OECD, 2001, now recognises that farming produces non-commercial public goods) and in more critical framings (Renting et al., 2009, for example, focus on non-agricultural goods produced for private markets – food quality, care services and education). More recently, multifunctionality has been framed in a transitional manner (Hassink, Grin & Hulsink, 2013), anticipating eventual regime change. Multifunctional models, be they applied to small- or larger scale farming, have blossomed in Europe, in large part due to an enabling regulatory environment (Huylenbroeck & Durand, 2003).

Another benchmark against which to assess the progressive role of family farming is food security. Although food security is often considered to be a production problem, there is now wide – and growing – agreement that achieving food security depends upon acting on a combination of variables that influence how food is procured and its nutritional value (FAO, 2014). Since farming represents an important source of income for many rural households, and many small farms are net buyers of food, rural households are both units of consumption and business units. When looking at them as units of consumption, it can be considered that farming is a fundamental component of livelihood strategies of rural households. However, the size of most farms and their resource endowment are not sufficient to let families achieve adequate levels of food security. According to Nagayets (2005), half the malnourished people in the developing world live on small farms. Hazell (2011) argues that governments should consider measures that help subsistence farmers reduce household vulnerability. For 'commercial' farms that are net sellers of food, policies should create a business environment which allows them to better integrate with markets. In this regard, the World Bank (2008) considers the development of modern value chains as an opportunity. However, this approach fails to address the most important driver of food insecurity, that of dispossession. This is discussed in the next section.

Is family farming under threat?

Recent economic concerns have brought discussions about food and agriculture to the centre of international debates about the future of farming, with discussions about family farming having intensified once again. The 2007–2008 food crisis shows the limits of the current system of food production, delivery, procurement and consumption (see, for example, Lang & Barling, 2012; McMichael, 2012; Rosin, Stock & Campbell, 2012). The crisis has highlighted the structural incapacity of food systems to address fundamental societal challenges. Issues such as obesity, food price inflation, oil and other resource 'peaks', climate change, pollution, biodiversity loss, food safety concerns and food insecurity (even in high-income countries) are symptoms of an incumbent regime crisis.

The impact of globalisation on family farms has been analysed in the literature through interconnected processes including the creation of monopolies of input production and sale, development of global value chains, and the financialisation of agriculture.

Creation of monopolies, especially in the seed sector, is one of the most studied effects of the globalisation of agriculture (Higgins & Lawrence, 2005; Clapp & Fuchs, 2009; Lappé & Bailey, 2014). Monopolies have developed as a result of significant financial investments in research and development by corporations. In return, corporations have sought intellectual property protection via regulations that allow seed developers to obtain royalties on seeds and which forbid producers from saving, and replanting, proprietary seeds. According to many scholars and activists, this is a threat to food security, as the control over seeds means control over the basis of subsistence of millions of people. Patents on seeds are considered amongst the 'new enclosures' (May, 2013). Companies developing and selling genetically engineered (GE) seeds have been accused of bringing many family farmers to bankruptcy (Gruere, Mehta-Bhatt & Sengupta, 2008). In other words, there is a long but clear chain of impacts relating to seed monopolies with a monopoly of seeds equating to a monopoly of knowledge. As Kloppenburg (2010) states, the issue of monopolies created by the existing intellectual property regimes is more relevant to small farming than the issue of GE technologies per se, which in a different institutional framework could play a positive role in development.

Another important driver of agrarian change is the development of global value chains (Neilson, Pritchard & Yeung, 2014), which provide a wide range of products for urban consumers' markets. There is contrasting evidence relating to their impact on family farming (Seville, Buxton & Vorley, 2011; Gereffi & Luo, 2014). However, when the impact is negative, the reproduction of inequality is not related to direct labour exploitation but to the marginalisation that small farmers face as a result of their inability to comply with quality standards that food retailers impose. High costs of compliance with these standards have favoured larger farms. When small farmers are involved in these chains, it is usually through middle agents whose bargaining power allows them to appropriate a great deal of the final value of farm products.

A third trend that has emerged in recent years is the financialisation of agriculture (McMichael, 2012; Lawrence & McMichael, 2014). 'New investors' have entered into this market: private equity funds, start-up companies, state-owned funds, pension funds and large cross-industry entrants (Heumesser & Schmid, 2012; *The Economist*, 2015). Capital mobility and ICT technologies provide the ground for a new interest in farming. They see optimistic prospects for profit-making in countries such as Brazil, Ukraine and Zambia 'where farming techniques are often still underdeveloped and potential productivity gains [are] immense' (*The Economist*, 2014). Financialisation is normally associated with the establishment of large corporate farms. These farms are established when the existing production structures are not able to produce the quantity and quality required, or the instability of the output is too high (UNCTAD, 2009). In this case, investors build the necessary infrastructures, control production, and integrate agricultural production with the next processing stages, using state-of-the-art technologies and technologically sophisticated management regimes. Palm oil, livestock, aquaculture and sugar cane are being added to more traditional plantation activities. Operational units of these corporate farms exceed 10,000 ha, and some of them are bigger than 500,000 ha (Deininger & Byerlee, 2012). Governments of many countries are supportive of such development, even if this compromises the rights to land of local people and may compromise food security (De Schutter, 2011).

Relic of the future?

There are different ways to interpret the future of family farming. One view stresses the resilience of family farming, and links support for family farming to the struggle against rural poverty. But when considering global food security, a dual economy is envisaged, as commercial farms are more suited to satisfy a growing food demand from an urbanizing society. This is the position endorsed by the World Bank, among others (World Bank, 2008). An alternative perspective, inspired by the food sovereignty movement, is that small-scale family farming is the backbone of agricultural development, but is under threat and needs urgent support. What is happening? Despite their resilience and their contribution to sustainability and food security, family farms are losing ground against corporate farms, not as a consequence of fair competition, but in relation to an unbalanced power distribution and – especially in the global south – poor governance that undermines the resource base of family farms and does not respect fundamental human rights (GRAIN, 2014). Land reform, territorial approaches, family farms' tailored agriculture knowledge systems, support to farmers' organisations, public support for family farms and specific programmes for women are viewed as the necessary measures to remove the imbalance (FAO, 2014).

Diverging trends have affected family farms in low-income and high-income countries, mainly related to economic growth and policy support. But in the future we might see more convergence than divergence. Will the present interest in farming by new (finance-related) investors continue in European countries? What will happen to middle-sized farms? According to one report, 'the agricultural sector went in the last decades through an enormous structural transformation – [away] from the small scale family farms towards large, capital intensive, fully mechanised and specialised industrialised farms. Corporate agricultural business thrives while small and middle sized agricultural companies vanish' (quoted by Matthews, 2013).

One prediction is that, while small-size diversified farms will survive as they have done in the past, middle-size capitalised farms will suffer the most. Is an aging farm population able to respond to the new societal challenges? How will it be possible to guarantee access to land for new generations of family farmers? And, given the transformation families are undergoing in society, to what extent will family farms of the future resemble those of the past? Another important question is 'What will happen to family farming when support levels are reduced or even abolished?' After all, in neoliberal settings, subsidies are viewed as distorting markets and supporting inefficient producers (Shucksmith & Rønningen, 2011). Today, family farms are not necessarily small farms, and small farms can have very different characteristics. Is it the highly capitalised, specialised commercial family-farm model that will be sustained? Or should the diversified, high value-added farm be prioritised? Should hobby or lifestyle farms, run by wealthy retired professionals, be a cornerstone of the future? Will small farms in marginal areas of Eastern Europe, where farming is key to household food security, continue to exist? And what about pluriactive farms in rural marginal areas? The problem with agriculture is that farms, be they small or large, are supposed to produce public goods, and in this case support is aimed not only at guaranteeing a decent income, but also at providing incentives to the production of public goods that otherwise, under market competition, would not be produced. As we have seen, family farms are better suited to these tasks, but this is not a guarantee that – under current market philosophies – their role in the production of public goods will continue.

Family farming – is it part of our global future, or a relic of the past? It is likely that family farming will continue to be part of our future and of future generations. Its growth or decline, its centrality or its marginality, will depend upon public support and regulatory frameworks. If our societies want equitable food security, sustainable rural places and food diversity, family farms will continue to play a pivotal role. This is likely to require a policy move away from neoliberalism to the promotion of a regulatory environment that enables family farming to survive and thrive.

References

Altieri, M, Funes-Monzote, F & Petersen, P (2012). Agroecologically efficient agricultural systems for smallholder farmers: Contributions to food sovereignty. *Agronomy for Sustainable Development* 32(1), 1–13.

Araghi, F (1995). Global depeasantization, 1945–1990. *The Sociological Quarterly* 36(2), 337–368.

Araghi, F (2012). The invisible hand and the visible foot. Peasants and globalization. In A Akram-Lodhi & C Kay (Eds), *Peasants and globalization: Political economy, agrarian transformation and development* (pp. 111–147). London: Routledge.

Bebbington, A (1999). Capitals and capabilities: A framework for analyzing peasant viability, rural livelihoods and poverty. *World Development* 27(12), 2021–2044.

Blaikie, P, Cannon, T, Davis, I & Wisner, B (2004). *At risk: Natural hazards, people's vulnerability and disasters*. London: Routledge.

Bock, B & Shortall, S (Eds). (2006). *Rural gender relations: Issues and case studies*. Cambridge, MA: CABI Publishing.

Bowen, S (2011). The importance of place: Re-territorialising embeddedness. *Sociologia Ruralis* 51(4), 325–348.

Bryceson, D (1996). Deagrarianization and rural employment in sub-Saharan Africa: A sectoral perspective. *World Development* 24(1), 97–111.

Calus, M & Van Huylenbroeck, G (2010). The persistence of family farming: A review of explanatory socio-economic and historical factors. *Journal of Comparative Family Studies* 41(5), 639–660.

Chayanov, A (1925/1966). *The theory of peasant economy*. Ed. D Thorner, B Kerblay & R Smith. Madison: University of Wisconsin Press.

Clapp, J & Fuchs, D (Eds). (2009). *Corporate power in global agrifood governance*. Cambridge, MA: MIT Press.

Clunies-Ross, T & Hildyard, N (2013). *The politics of industrial agriculture*. London: Routledge.

Cooper, T, Hart, K & Baldock, D (2009). *Provision of public goods through agriculture in the European Union*. Available at http://simple.europe.bg/upload/docs/report_en.pdf (accessed January 14, 2016).

da Silva, J (2014). Dialogue on family farming: Opening statement. Available at http://www.fao.org/about/who-we-are/director-gen/faodg-statements/detail/en/c/262782/ (accessed 16 June 2015).

Davidova, E & Thompson, D (2014). *Family farming in Europe: Challenges and prospects*. Brussels: European Parliament.

De Schutter, O (2011). How not to think of land-grabbing: Three critiques of large-scale investments in farmland. *The Journal of Peasant Studies* 38(2), 249–279.

Deere, C (2005). *The feminization of agriculture? Economic restructuring in rural Latin America*. Available at http://kms1.isn.ethz.ch/serviceengine/Files/ISN/38739/ipublicationdocument_singledocument/0e02da66-430c-4841-9950-a14bfaa90d8c/en/OP+001.pdf (accessed 14 January 2016).

Deininger, K & Byerlee, D (2012). The rise of large farms in land abundant countries: Do they have a future? *World Development* 40(4), 701–714.

Ellis, F (1993). *Peasant economics: Farm households in agrarian development*. Cambridge: Cambridge University Press.

Ellis, F (2000). The determinants of rural livelihood diversification in developing countries. *Journal of Agricultural Economics* 51(2), 289–302.

FAO (2011). *The state of food and agriculture 2011*. Rome: FAO.

FAO (2014). *Towards stronger family farms. Voices in the International Year of Family Farming*. Rome: FAO.

Friedmann, H (1978). World market, state, and family farm: Social bases of household production in the era of wage labour. *Comparative Studies in Society and History* 20(4), 545–586.

Gereffi, G & Luo, X (2014). Risks and opportunities of participation in global value chains. World Bank Policy Research Working Paper. Available at http://papers.ssrn.com/sol3/papers.cfm?abstract_id=2430541 (accessed 14 January 2016).

Giddens, A (1971). *Capitalism and modern society*. Cambridge: Cambridge University Press.

Goodman, D & Redclift, M (1981). *From peasant to proletarian: Capitalist development and agrarian transitions.* Oxford: Basil Blackwell.

GRAIN (2014). Hungry for land: Small farmers feed the world with less than a quarter of all farmland. Available at http://www.grain.org/article/entries/4929-hungry-for-land-small-farmers-feed-the-world-with-less-than-a-quarter-of-all-farmland (accessed 14 January 2016).

Gruere, G, Mehta-Bhatt, P & Sengupta, D (2008). Bt cotton and farmers suicides in India: Reviewing the evidence. Available at http://www.ifpri.org/sites/default/files/publications/ifpridp00808.pdf (accessed 18 June 2015).

Hassink, J, Grin, J & Hulsink, W (2013). Multifunctional agriculture meets health care: Applying the multi-level transition sciences perspective to care farming in the Netherlands. *Sociologia Ruralis* 53 (2), 223–245.

Hazell, P (2009). *The Asian green revolution. IFPRI Discussion Paper.* Washington: IFPRI.

Hazell, P (2011). *Is small farm led development still a relevant strategy for Africa and Asia? A festschrift in honour of Per Pinstrup Andersen.* Available at http://ppafest.nutrition.cornell.edu/authors/hazell.html (accessed 14 January 2016).

Heumesser, C & Schmid, E (2012). *Trends in foreign direct investment in the agricultural sector of developing and transition countries – A review.* Available at http://www.trademarksa.org/sites/default/files/publications/2012-07%20Paper_Trends%20in%20Foreign%20Direct%20Investment%20in%20the%20Agricultural%20Sector%20of%20Developing%20and%20Transition%20Countries%20-%20A%20Review.pdf (accessed 14 January 2016).

Higgins, V & Lawrence, G (Eds). (2005). *Agricultural governance: Globalization and the new politics of regulation.* London: Routledge.

Hoppe, R, Korb, P & Banker, D (2008). *Million-dollar farms in the new century.* Available at http://future.aae.wisc.edu/publications/million_dollar_farms.pdf (accessed 27 January 2015).

Huylenbroeck, G & Durand, G (Eds). (2003). *Multifunctional agriculture: A new paradigm for European agriculture and rural development.* London: Ashgate.

Kasimis, C & Papadopoulos, A (2013). Rural transformations and family farming in contemporary Greece. In D Ortiz-Miranda, A Moragues-Faus & E Arnalte-Alegre (Eds), *Agriculture in Mediterranean Europe: Between old and new paradigms* (pp. 263–293). Bingley, UK: Emerald.

Kloppenburg, J (2010). Impeding dispossession, enabling repossession: Biological open source and the recovery of seed sovereignty. *Journal of Agrarian Change* 10(3), 367–388.

Lang, T & Barling, D (2012). Food security and food sustainability: Reformulating the debate. *The Geographical Journal* 178(4), 313–326.

Lappé, M & Bailey, B (2014). *Against the grain: Genetic transformation of global agriculture.* London: Routledge.

Lastarria-Cornhiel, S. (2008). *Feminization of agriculture: Trends and driving forces.* Washington, DC: World Bank.

Lawrence, G & McMichael, P (2014). Global change and food security. In B Freedman (Ed.), *Handbook of global environmental pollution: Global environmental change* (pp. 667–676). New York: Springer.

Lewis, W (1954). Economic development with unlimited supplies of labour. *The Manchester School* 22(2), 139–191.

Li, T (2010). To make live or let die? Rural dispossession and the protection of surplus populations. *Antipode* 41(s1), 66–93.

Lowder, S, Skoet, J & Singh, S (2014). What do we really know about the number and distribution of farms and family farms worldwide? Background paper for The State of Food and Agriculture 2014. ESA Working Paper No. 14-02. Rome: FAO.

MacDonald, J (2014). *Family farming in the United States.* Available at http://www.ers.usda.gov/amber-waves/2014-march/family-farming-in-the-united-states.aspx#.VJ5tNsAdg (accessed 14 January 2016).

Mann, S & Dickinson, J (1978). Obstacles to the development of a capitalist agriculture. *The Journal of Peasant Studies* 5(4), 466–481.

Matthews, A (2013). Family farming and the role of policy in the EU. Available at http://capreform.eu/family-farming-and-the-role-of-policy-in-the-eu/ (accessed 16 June 2015).

May, C (2013). *The global political economy of intellectual property rights: The new enclosures?* New York: Routledge.

McIntyre, B, Herren, H, Wakhungu, J & Watson, R (2009). *Agriculture at a crossroads. Global report: international assessment of agricultural knowledge, science and technology for development (IAASTD).* Washington, DC: Island Press.

McMichael, P (2012). Food regime crisis and revaluing the agrarian question. In R Almås & H Campbell (Eds), *Rethinking agricultural policy regimes: Food security, climate change and the future resilience of global agriculture* (pp. 99–122). Bingley, UK: Emerald.

Mooney, P (1988). *My own boss? Class, rationality, and the family farm.* Boulder, CO: Westview Press.

Mooney, P & Hunt, S (2009). Food security: The elaboration of contested claims to a consensus frame. *Rural Sociology* 74(4), 469–497.

Morris, C & Kirwan, J (2011). Ecological embeddedness: An interrogation and refinement of the concept within the context of alternative food networks in the UK. *Journal of Rural Studies* 27(3), 322–330.

Nagayets, O (2005). Small farms: Current status and key trends. In International Food Policy Research Institute (Ed.), *The future of small farms: Proceedings of a research workshop.* Washington, DC: IFPRI.

Neilson, J, Pritchard, B & Yeung, H (2014). Global value chains and global production networks in the changing international political economy: An introduction. *Review of International Political Economy* 21(1), 1–8.

OECD (2001). *Multifunctionality: Towards an analytical framework.* Paris: OECD.

OECD.(2014). *Agricultural policy monitoring and evaluation 2014.* Paris: OECD.

Pinstrup-Andersen, P. (2009). Food security: Definition and measurement. *Food Security* 1(1), 5–7.

Potter, C & Burney, J (2002). Agricultural multifunctionality in the WTO – legitimate non-trade concern or disguised protectionism? *Journal of Rural Studies* 18(1), 35–47.

Pretty, J, Toulmin, C & Williams, S (2011). Sustainable intensification in African agriculture. *International Journal of Agricultural Sustainability* 9(1), 5–24.

Reinhardt, N & Barlett, P (1989). The persistence of family farms in United States agriculture. *Sociologia Ruralis* 29(3–4), 203–225.

Renting, H, Rossing, W, Groot, J, Van der Ploeg, J, Laurent, C, Perraud, D … & Van Ittersum, M (2009). Exploring multifunctional agriculture. A review of conceptual approaches and prospects for an integrative transitional framework. *Journal of Environmental Management* 90(2), S112–S123.

Rosin, C, Stock, P & Campbell, H (Eds). (2012). *Food systems failure: The global food crisis and the future of agriculture.* London: Routledge.

Scoones, I (1998). *Sustainable rural livelihoods: A framework for analysis.* Working Paper 72. Brighton, UK: Institute for Development Studies.

Sen, A (1999). *Development as freedom.* New York: Oxford University Press.

Seville, D, Buxton, A & Vorley, B (2011). *Under what conditions are value chains effective tools for pro-poor development?* Available at http://pubs.iied.org/pdfs/16029IIED.pdf (accessed 21 August 2014).

Shortall, S (2002). Gendered agricultural and rural restructuring: A case study of Northern Ireland. *Sociologia Ruralis* 42(2), 160–175.

Shucksmith, M & Hermann, V (1992). Future changes in British agriculture: Projecting divergent farm household behaviour. *Journal of Agricultural Economics* 53(1), 37–50.

Shucksmith, M & Rønningen, K (2011). The uplands after neoliberalism? – The role of the small farm in rural sustainability. *Journal of Rural Studies* 27(3), 275–287.

Singh, I, Squire, L & Strauss, J (1986). *Agricultural household models: Extensions, applications, and policy.* Baltimore, MD: Johns Hopkins University Press.

The Economist (2015). Investing in agriculture: Barbarians at the farm gate. *The Economist* (printed edition), 2 January 2015.

UNCTAD (2009). *World investment report 2009: Transnational corporations, agricultural production and development.* New York: United Nations.

Van der Ploeg, J (1993). Rural sociology and the new agrarian question: A perspective from the Netherlands. *Sociologia Ruralis* 33(2), 240–260.

Van der Ploeg, J (2000). Revitalizing agriculture: Farming economically as starting ground for rural development. *Sociologia Ruralis* 40(4), 497–511.

Van der Ploeg, J (2013). *Peasants and the art of farming: A chayanovian manifesto.* Winnipeg, MB: Fernwood.

Van der Ploeg, JD, Renting, H, Brunori, G, Knickel, K, Mannion, J, Marsden, T, De Roest, K, Sevilla-Guzmán, E & Ventura, F (2000). Rural development: From practices and policies towards theory. *Sociologia Ruralis* 40(4), 391–408.

Viaggi, D, Bartolini, F, Raggi, M, Sardonini, L, Sammeth, F & Gomez y Paloma, S (2011). *Farm investment behaviour under the CAP reform process.* Brussels: Publications Office.

Whatmore, S (1991). Life cycle or patriarchy? Gender divisions in family farming. *Journal of Rural Studies* 7(1/2), 71–76.

Whatmore, S, Munton, R, Little, J & Marsden, T (1987). Towards a typology of farm businesses in contemporary British agriculture. *Sociologia Ruralis* 27(1), 21–37.

Wilbur, A (2013). Growing a radical ruralism: Back-to-the-land as practice and ideal. *Geography Compass* 7(2), 149–160.

Wilson, C & Tisdell, C (2001). Why farmers continue to use pesticides despite environmental, health and sustainability costs. *Ecological Economics* 39(3), 449–462.

Woodhouse, P (2010). Beyond industrial agriculture? Some questions about farm size, productivity and sustainability. *Journal of Agrarian Change* 10(3), 437–453.

World Bank (2008). *World development report 2008: Agriculture for development.* Washington, DC: World Bank.

17

Industrial Livestock and the Ecological Hoofprint

Inequality, Degradation and Violence

Tony Weis

Introduction: the fast-changing place of animals in agricultural landscapes and diets

The interconnected practices of growing, preparing and eating food have always been central to human social relations and to the diversity of cultures. Agriculture is also humanity's most fundamental ecological relationship, involving the organisation of photosynthetic activity and the management (and usually reduction) of plant and animal diversity over a given landscape. For roughly 10,000 years, agriculture and permanent pasture have been the biggest human land uses, displacing self-organizing ecosystems and, with this, reducing the habitats of non-domesticated animals while increasing the direct control exerted over the lives of domesticated animals. In short, agriculture comprises an inextricably interwoven set of social, ecological and inter-species relations (Duncan, 1996; Friedmann, 2000).

A heavy friction of distance prevailed for most of the history of agriculture, meaning that it was hard to move things (especially perishable foodstuffs) very far across space, even in comparatively large and complex pre-industrial societies. Put simply, until extremely recently, agriculture and food systems had to be relatively localised. Concurrent with this was pressure to manage cycles of biological and physical materials in regenerative ways in order for agricultural landscapes to be productive and durable over long periods. Of course, some biological and physical materials inevitably moved beyond agricultural landscapes, and farming communities drew some materials from surrounding ecosystems, but on the whole farming practices had to maintain or enhance the health of soils with limited external inputs, and where this failed to happen the long-term deterioration of soils led to many civilizational crises (Montgomery, 2007).

Small, mixed livestock, populations related to these broad organising imperatives in a range of ways, holding multifunctional roles (encapsulated in Figure 17.1). One of the primary roles of domesticated animals in pre-industrial agricultural systems was to supply on-farm labour and off-farm transport, marshalling photosynthesised energy in plants and turning it into sources of effective power for agricultural tasks and for helping move people, food, fuel and other items across space – with the large exception of the Americas prior to European conquest, where there were no 'beasts of burden'. Lappé (1991) described the nutritional role of livestock as

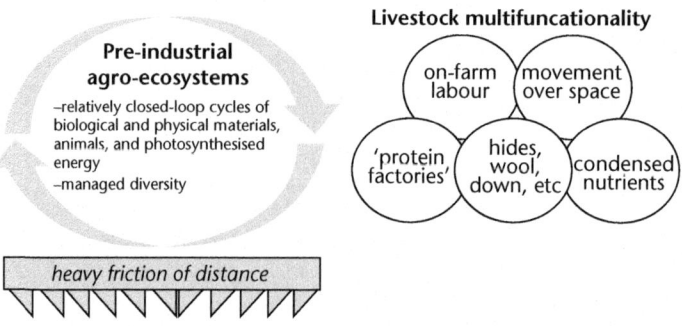

Figure 17.1 Agro-ecological imperatives and the historic multifunctionality of livestock
Source: Author

'protein factories' to highlight two key points: first, that protein was the most important contribution that milk, eggs and flesh made to human diets; and, second – the 'factory' part – that this was produced by animals largely on their own, that is, animals fed mainly from crop stubble and parts of plants not edible for humans, household wastes, fallowed land in rotations, and poorer quality farmland used as pasture, *without* directly consuming the nutrition in crops that was useable by humans (apart from what was needed for overwintering in temperate regions). The nutritional role of livestock was complemented both by the use of hides, wool and down for clothing and other needs, the use of dry manure as a fuel source in some places, and the role of animals returning condensed nitrogen, phosphates and other soil nutrients to the land.

The nutritional role of livestock varied considerably across time and place but, in general, livestock products tended to be peripheral in the diets of most agricultural societies. There was also an intimacy to this consumption, in that almost everyone would have had at least a reasonable sense of how the animals whose milk, eggs and flesh they consumed lived (and died), and many people would have directly known the individual animals. To reflect on how pervasively people have been exposed to livestock animals through most of agrarian history, it is worth remembering that the world's human population was still overwhelmingly rural and livestock populations were still overwhelmingly reared outdoors until well into the 20th century.[1] This should not romanticise how animals were treated, as there was a large spectrum of inter-species relations that varied with human use-values and cultures. Yet, the variety of use-values, along with limits of technology and agricultural surpluses, ensured that animals had some mobility and autonomy within agricultural landscapes and increased the concern paid to animal health, welfare and longevity, as compared to when the sole use-value of animals is defined as producing food outputs.

In 2013, about 70 billion animals were killed for food, a nearly *ninefold* increase in a mere half-century. This explosive growth in the annual population of slaughtered animals pivots on the growth and industrialisation of poultry and pig production, especially chickens, as their smaller bodies means that many more individuals are needed to produce the same volume of meat as compared with most other animals. For decades, industrial pig and poultry production has been the primary force enabling the 'meatification' of diets on a world scale, a term that marks the shift of meat from the periphery of human diets to the centre. In 2013, the average person on Earth consumed nearly twice as much meat as a half-century prior (from roughly 23 to 43 kg per year), over a period when the human population increased from roughly 3 to 7 billion. If the current trajectory holds, the average person will be consuming over 50 kg of meat per year in 2050 in a world with more than 9 billion people. While growth is occurring almost everywhere, on a world scale meatification starkly reflects global disparities: people living in rich countries consume vastly more meat per capita than do people in poor countries, and increasing affluence in fast-industrialising countries is the biggest force in the rising demand for livestock products (Weis, 2013).

At the same time as humans are on average, though very unevenly, consuming more animal products than ever before, farmed animals are vanishing from sight and mind across large parts of the world. With rising urbanisation and complex, long-distance corporate networks influencing and linking an ever-growing share of production and consumption, it is increasingly difficult for a growing share of the world's population to have any sense of the social, ecological or inter-species relations in agriculture. The basic goal of this chapter is to examine the fast-changing place of animals in agricultural systems and food consumption patterns, and explain why this is a momentous aspect of how industrial capitalism is reconfiguring rural landscapes and contributing to a more unequal, unsustainable and violent world. To do this, it presents the *ecological hoofprint*, a conceptual framework for understanding the system of agriculture at the heart of these changes: the *industrial grain–oilseed–livestock complex*.

In pursuit of scale: oceans of monocultures and islands of concentrated animals

An elemental imperative in historical capitalism is the endless pursuit of capital accumulation, which is entwined with the need for continual economic growth, the creation of ever more commodities (including the commodification of ever more parts of the world), and the competitive pressure to reduce the relative cost of labour and seek economies of scale in production (Foster, 2009; Wallerstein, 2011; Moore, 2015). The pursuit of economies of scale in agriculture entails a radical transformation in the basis of farming, casting aside localised ecological knowledge, managed diversity and attention to biophysical cycles, and replacing these with a new organizing imperative: *biological simplification* and *standardisation* (Weis, 2010).

As this transformation unfolds, agricultural practices and dynamics of innovation are detached from diverse bioregions and cultures and are, instead, centred in high-tech labs, test plots and animal breeding sites – and heavily based upon patentable traits. This leads to increasingly uniform genetics that are designed and owned by a handful of exceptionally powerful agro-input corporations (Goodman, Sorj & Wilkinson, 1987; Kloppenberg, 2004). Agro-food corporations then take homogenised inputs and couple them with artificial flavours, colours, fillers and coagulants, constantly innovating in order to replace lost tastes, textures and nutritional content, to enhance durability, and to seek to boost demand in a competitive marketplace. The net result is that agriculture and food, once fulcrums of cultural diversity, are increasingly reduced to generic processes and de-spatialised commodities. Production is governed first and foremost by profitability and access is governed first and foremost by money, which determines 'effective demand' (Friedmann, 2000; Weis, 2007).

The biological narrowing of the world's food supply is reflected in the fact that a mere ten crops occupy over 90% of the world's arable land, while the 'big three' livestock species – pigs, chickens and cattle – are responsible for over 90% of world meat production by volume. The spread of the industrial grain–oilseed–livestock complex on a world scale is central to this narrowing. The landscapes of the industrial grain–oilseed–livestock complex can be likened to 'oceans' of monocultures and 'islands' of factory farms and feedlots, which are both fundamentally disarticulated and intertwined, with the multifunctional roles of animals obliterated by the sole objective of accelerating the turnover time of commodity production – in other words, speeding up animal weight gain, laying and lactation (Weis, 2013).

With the expansion of factory farms, a growing share of the world's pigs and poultry birds (and a much smaller but growing share of dairy cattle) does not touch the earth, breathe fresh air, experience natural seasonal and diurnal rhythms, or have anything resembling normal social interactions with fellow members of their own species, while beef cattle feedlots are somewhat less dense and regulated environments. Both factory farms and feedlots are then attached to coarse grain and oilseed monocultures through great flows of feed, led by corn and soybeans, through which they effectively occupy roughly 30% of the world's arable land. Chickens and pigs already account for roughly 70% of world meat by volume, and rising factory farm production of the 'soaring two' species is expected to meet virtually all further increases in demand, with growth in chicken production at the forefront. As a result, there will be around 120 billion animals slaughtered in 2050 if the meatification of diets continues as projected (Steinfeld et al., 2006; D'Silva & Webster, 2010; Imhoff, 2011; Weis, 2013; Lymbery, 2014).[2]

Biophysical contradictions: overriding barriers to scale

The ecological hoofprint stems in part from the well-established conceptual framework of the ecological footprint, which provided an innovative way of approaching the environmental relations of complex modern societies. More specifically, the ecological footprint considers the resource budgets and pollution loads associated with different levels of consumption, and the ensuing physical area (the 'footprint') needed for the associated production and waste absorption (Wackernagel & Rees, 1996; York, Rosa & Dietz, 2003). In a similar vein, the ecological hoofprint provides a way of approaching the resource budgets and pollution loads associated with the industrial grain–oilseed–livestock complex, which is a big part of uneven ecological footprints on a world scale (Weis, 2013).

A key starting point in this framework is to recognise that there are inescapable biophysical barriers to the pursuit of economies of scale in agriculture. Whereas farming that gives attention to diversity, crop complementarity and regenerative cycles is necessarily labour (and ecological knowledge) intensive, reducing the relative cost of labour through mechanisation necessarily entails biological simplification and standardisation over large areas. This establishes or exacerbates a series of biological and physical problems which are never resolved but instead are continually overridden through a range of external inputs, again amidst the pressure to reduce labour costs. Biophysical barriers to scale and 'overrides' are therefore dialectically related, engrained in the logic of how both industrial monocultures and livestock production are organised (Kimbrell, 2002; McIntyre, Herren, Wakhungu & Watson, 2009; Weis, 2010).

Oceans of monocultures

One of the most fundamental barriers to scale in agriculture is degradation of soil health arising from the elimination of complementary intercrops and reduction in ground cover (to enable rapid planting and harvesting), the damage from large machinery repeatedly compacting and tilling the soil, the proliferation of chemical pesticides, and the loss of soil organisms. Soil degradation is principally overridden by the massive application of external fertilisers, in particular nitrogen, phosphorous and potassium – which entail significant energy budgets in production and movement, sometimes over very long distances (Pimentel, 2006; Montgomery, 2007; McIntyre, Herren, Wakhungu & Watson, 2009; Sage, 2012).

The long-term decline of soil health both contributes to, and is affected by, another major barrier to scale: the proliferation of pests. The definition of pests necessarily widens in monocultures, as attention to complementarity is cast aside and natural controls on undesirable species are reduced. Vast, homogenised landscapes and impoverished soils create conditions conducive to the rapid spread of certain insects, weeds and fungus. As with soils, pest problems are never resolved but overridden with more inputs, and long-term rates of agro-input consumption have dwarfed the rates of yield gains over the past half-century (Moore, 2002; McIntyre, Herren, Wakhungu & Watson, 2009; Sage, 2012).

The diminished ground cover and biological diversity of soils makes them drier and, along with the nature of high-yielding seed varieties, serves to heighten the demand for irrigation. Industrial monocultures have therefore been tied to great freshwater diversions and massive groundwater pumping schemes (including from some very important aquifers that are not regenerating), with energy needed to pump water against gravity (Briscoe, 2002; McIntyre, Herren, Wakhungu & Watson, 2009; Hoekstra, 2013). The fact that agricultural landscapes are standardised across such large areas means that food must move over greater distances[3] – extreme illustrations being the Corn Belt in the US Midwest, and the so-called 'Republic of Soy' that straddles a number of countries in southern South America – increasing energy costs in transport and processing.

Islands of concentrated animals

As with the oceans of monocultures, considering the biophysical barriers to scale and the ensuing 'overrides' within islands of concentrated animals enables an understanding of their resource intensity. This starts with a primary contradiction: while mechanisation and density greatly reduce labour costs, they do so while greatly enlarging the costs of feed, resulting in a basic competitive pressure to contain this expense by increasing the rates at which feed is converted to flesh, eggs and milk. Related to this is an increased demand by birds and animals for drinking water: they can no longer find water themselves and plant moisture is lost in concentrated feed. The pressure to enhance feed conversion ratios has driven a spectrum of innovations such as developing artificial insemination techniques and specialised breeding sites; changing the genetics of animals over time; confining animals into smaller spaces and controlling temperatures to reduce the energy animals expend moving or regulating body temperatures; augmenting hormones; and manipulating lighting regimes to stimulate desired metabolic processes or mitigate undesired ones (Mason & Singer, 1990; Pew Commission, 2008; D'Silva & Webster, 2010; Imhoff, 2011; Weis, 2013; Lymbery, 2014). This is also a central reason that poultry is the biggest source of overall growth, as birds convert feed to flesh and reproductive outputs better (or, more aptly, less inefficiently) than mammals.

Another great barrier to scale with livestock production stems from the fact that animals are sentient beings which can suffer pain and misery. Intensive confinement induces a range of psychosocial health problems in animals, which are interrelated to a range of behavioural pathologies. These are overridden with a combination of pharmaceuticals and blunt force, which includes un-anaesthetised mutilations like 'beak-trimming' and 'tail docking'. Animal health problems also stem from the unnatural densities and the great volumes of faeces and urine that are generated, conditions prone to pathogens thriving, spreading quickly and mutating. Filth, bacterial growth, contagion and unhealthy ambient environments are met with a combination of overrides including water and disinfectants to clean out animal enclosures, antibiotics[4] and ventilation fans, which mitigate – but never resolve – omnipresent disease risks. The scale and nature of factory farms also fundamentally transforms the fertilisation role of livestock; instead of animals returning concentrated nutrients to fields and largely spreading it around themselves, biowastes must be treated for chemical and antibiotic residues, transported for application to fields, and stored in nauseating lagoons, since not all of the processed slurry is capable of being absorbed on surrounding landscapes (Mason & Singer, 1990; Pew Commission, 2008; D'Silva & Webster, 2010; Imhoff, 2011; Weis, 2013; Lymbery, 2014).

As with monocultures, the pursuit of scale ties to the large-scale specialisation of landscapes and necessarily means that, in addition to increased inputs needed to override problems, outputs must move across much greater distances than in the past. In livestock production, transportation requirements are augmented by the movement of animals from specialised breeding sites to factory farms and feedlots and ultimately to large-scale industrial slaughterhouses, which together might be seen to constitute a spatially disaggregated assembly line. The energy budget in transport (overwhelmingly oil) adds to the energy already used in heating, cooling, venting, pumping and monitoring factory farm production. Added to this is the energy and water intensity of industrial slaughterhouses, and the energy budget beyond this, as flesh, eggs and milk have much greater refrigeration demands than plant-based nutrition in processing plants, transport, retail and household storage.

Burning useable nutrition

While the resource-intensive nature of industrial monocultures and factory farms can be seen in parallel, it is also crucial to recognise the inherent inefficiency in how they are rearticulated, as much useable nutrition is lost cycling grains and oilseeds through animals to produce food (Lappé, 1991; Goodland, 1997; Gilland, 2002; Pimentel & Pimentel, 2003). Whatever nutritional value milk, eggs, and meat may once have had (or still have) in contexts of protein scarcity, they were usually part of integrated farming systems. Meatification, however, hinges on an entirely different relationship, with livestock appropriating a massive share of the world's arable land. Meatification on a world scale relates to unequal effective demand and taste preferences rather than human necessity, and appears to be making human health worse, not better. Excessive consumption of animal foods is widely recognised as a major contributing factor in rising levels of obesity and many non-communicable diseases such as cardiovascular disease, type 2 diabetes, hypertension, fatty liver disease and some cancers – epidemiological patterns often tellingly described as 'diseases of affluence' (Campbell & Campbell, 2006; Popkin, 2009; Lim et al. 2012).

The essence of the material inefficiency stems from the fact that much of the useable nutrition contained in crops gets burned in animal metabolic processes before being converted to flesh, eggs and milk. So in place of the historic protein factory role, concentrated animals are transformed into large and growing '*reverse* protein factories' in the sense that they reduce the protein that could have otherwise been available to humans if consumed directly from plants (Lappé, 1991). This wastage of plant nutrition has the effect of magnifying the resource intensity of industrial monocultures, and means that people who are consuming a lot of animal flesh are effectively commanding a great deal more arable land than people who gain their nutrition directly from plant-based sources (Lappé, 1991; Goodland, 1997; Gilland, 2002; Pimentel & Pimentel, 2003).

A destructive and violent course

Understanding the biophysical contradictions of industrial monocultures and factory farms in parallel, and the wastage of useable nutrition at their nexus, opens up a way of appreciating the resource intensity of the system as a whole and, in turn, the multidimensional pollution loads (see

Figure 17.2). A glaring aspect of this is the energy budget involved in the running of huge machinery, the production, movement and application of fertilisers and pesticides, irrigation pumping, the powering of factory farms and slaughterhouses, and the expanded transportation and refrigeration demands – much of which derives from the combustion of fossil fuels and results in carbon dioxide (CO_2) emissions. Greenhouse gas (GHG) emissions rise further as a result of the nitrous oxide emissions from industrial fertilisers and livestock production, the methane emissions from ruminant flatulence (which ties more to extensive grazing than factory farms) and the CO_2 emissions embedded in constructing environments of concrete and steel.

Another important way that the industrial grain–oilseed–livestock complex impacts climate change stems from the inefficiency of land use: first, through the 'reserve protein factory' effect, and second, through the fact that nutritional output per land area could be increased through more dense and diverse (and labour-intensive) cropping patterns – while simultaneously reducing external inputs to farms (Altieri, 1995; McIntyre, Herren, Wakhungu & Watson, 2009; Koohafkan, Altieri & Holt Gimenez, 2012). The fact that much more self-organizing ecosystems have been converted to agriculture than is needed to meet human nutritional needs implicates the system in both historic CO_2 emissions from past ecological transformations and ongoing CO_2 emissions from soil degradation, while constraining the potential to conserve and restore ecosystems and improve carbon sequestration. In sum, the industrial grain–oilseed–livestock complex and the uneven meatification of diets are tied to grossly disproportionate atmospheric footprints (in addition to gross disparities in the world's food supply), which are exacerbating global inequalities, with climate change expected to hurt agricultural productivity most immediately and adversely in many of the world's poorest regions (Steinfeld et al., 2006; McMichael, Powles, Butler & Uauy, 2007; McIntyre, Herren, Wakhungu & Watson, 2009; Hertel, Burke & Lobell, 2010; IPCC, 2013).

The industrial grain–oilseed–livestock complex is also a major consumer and polluter of water. The wastage of useable nutrition, the increased irrigation needed for 'thirstier' seeds and drier soils in monocultures, and the increased water needed for thirstier animals and washing enclosures and facilities in factory farms and slaughterhouses together amplify water consumption far beyond what would be necessary in more diversely cropped landscapes. Residues from

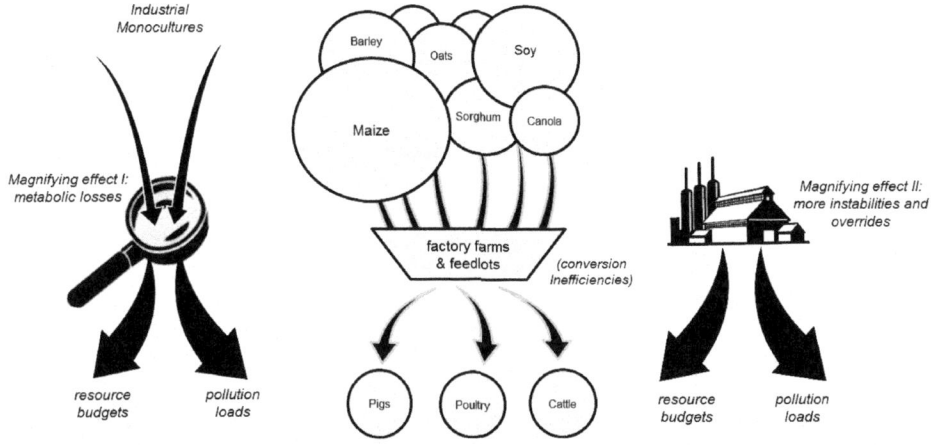

Figure 17.2 The environmental burden of the industrial grain–oilseed–livestock complex
Source: Weis (2013). Used with permission from Zed Books.

fertilisers, pesticides, pharmaceuticals, treated slurries, untreated faeces and urine seepage, and corporal wastes contribute to a range of problems in aquatic environments, with the eutrophication caused by excess nitrates and phosphates an especially large-scale and widespread concern in both freshwater and coastal marine environments (Pew Commission, 2008; McIntyre, Herren, Wakhungu & Watson, 2009; Imhoff, 2011; Sage, 2012). These pollutant loads serve to expand challenges for water treatment facilities, though the long-term public health risks from the proliferation of pesticides and pharmaceuticals can never be entirely contained, mitigated or predicted. Two well-established threats stem from the bioaccumulation of persistent toxins and the danger that chronic usage of pesticides and pharmaceuticals will erode their effectiveness and give rise to stronger, chemically resistant, pests and drug-resistant diseases over time (Moore, 2002; McIntyre, Herren, Wakhungu & Watson, 2009).

While the uneven responsibility for environmental problems is more often presented in terms of *injustice*, especially in light of the differential vulnerability to the burden of degradation, *violence* also inheres in the despoliation of habitats, the suffering and dislocation of people and animal species, and the extinction spasm which is now unfolding – though often in distant and indistinct ways. One of the goals of the ecological hoofprint is to help illuminate how the industrial grain–oilseed–livestock complex and the meatification of diets are implicated in this expansive ecological violence. At the same time, it seeks to problematise another, more direct sort of violence that, while soaring in scale, is increasingly hidden within modern societies.[5]

By examining how factory farms are organised and the ways that barriers to scale are overridden, it fixes attention on the extreme ways that animals' lives are dominated and the routinised violence they endure. Billions of animals have been reduced to the status of nearly pure commodities, and as humans consume them more than ever there is less and less understanding about where and how these animals live. And, as physical and cognitive distances grow, the sense of responsibility fades. Together scale, commodification and invisibility in the everyday lives and consciousness of human beings constitute a revolution in inter-species relations (Weis, 2013). This revolution in inter-species relations is also connected to exceptionally degraded forms of labour, from artificial inseminators at breeding sites to positions on fast-moving slaughter and disassembly lines, where workers face high rates of injury and job turnover and an immeasurable toll from contributing to, and being constantly immersed in, conditions of intense physical and psychosocial suffering. This is another reason why, in addition to their environmental burden, the expansion of factory farms and feedlots is despoiling rural communities in a much deeper way than simply hollowing them out (Eisnitz, 2006; Pew Commission, 2008; Imhoff, 2011; Pachirat, 2011).

Conclusion: unconsciousness and awakening

It is very hard to appreciate most of the relations that are embedded in commodities. This can have a naturalising effect, in the sense that it can lead many to take the economic system and its 'laws of motion' for granted, to fixate on illusory dimensions of commodities, and to pay little attention to the real nature of production and its implications. The ecological hoofprint takes aim at the widespread unconsciousness that surrounds a critical aspect of modern agro-food systems, the industrial grain–oilseed–livestock complex, which involves relations that are simultaneously sprawling (occupying nearly one-third of the world's arable land) yet extremely intimate (in the regulation of animal lives and the bodily encounter with food).

The conceptual framework of the ecological hoofprint focuses on the biophysical barriers to scale and how they are overridden in both oceans of monocultures and islands of concentrated animals, along with the wasteful flows of nutrition that connect them. This provides a way of understanding the resource budgets and pollution loads of the industrial grain–oilseed–livestock complex, and in turn how this system – and the dietary change it supports – bears on worsening human inequality, environmental degradation and the expansion of violence. Ultimately, it points to the need to deindustrialise livestock and rethink the place of animals in agricultural landscapes, and to reconsider diets, as essential steps in any efforts to construct more equitable, sustainable and humane agro-food systems.

The abiding intimacy of food, however commodified it is or might become, is even more intense with meat since it binds people to the lives and deaths of other animals. In this sense, to view meatification through the lens of the ecological hoofprint might also help to awaken people to the destructive course of industrial capitalism and the need for fundamentally different social, ecological and inter-species relations (Foster, 2009; Moore, 2015).

Notes

1   Some intensive confinement occurred long before the onset of industrial capitalism (Johnson, 1991) but the rise of large-scale slaughterhouses in the US Midwest in the late 19th century and the rise of large-scale poultry sheds on the US mid-Atlantic coast in the early 20th century mark key innovations in the expansion of factory farming (Weis, 2013).

2   This is without counting fish, the production of which is rapidly industrialising as open-ocean fisheries decline, with potentially highly regressive dynamics (Anticamara, Watson, Gelchu & Pauly, 2011). There are also significant parallels and growing linkages between industrial agriculture and aquaculture that are beyond the scope of discussion here.

3   The process of standardisation is also entwined with the increasing consolidation of landholding, as the highly mechanised winners who can thrive at low margins are able to get bigger while many of the losers get driven out of agriculture (Weis, 2007).

4   Antibiotics were found to have a beneficial role in enhancing feed conversion ratios, which led to their application at sub-therapeutic levels.

5   In this, it is posed as a very direct challenge to most environmentalism, which has overwhelmingly focused on wild spaces and wild species, and not the human-dominated landscapes that are driving wild animals to ever smaller spaces, and certainly not the growing populations of animals living in those spaces and the conditions they endure.

References

Altieri, M (1995). *Agroecology: The science of sustainable agriculture*. Boulder, CO: Westview.

Anticamara, JA, Watson, R, Gelchu A & Pauly, D (2011). Global fishing effort (1950–2010): Trends, gaps, and implications. *Fisheries Research* 107, 131–136.

Briscoe, M (2002). Water: The overtapped resource. In A Kimbrell (Ed.), *The fatal harvest reader: The tragedy of industrial agriculture* (pp. 181–190). Washington, DC: Island Press.

Campbell, TC & Campbell, TM (2006). *The China study: The most comprehensive study of nutrition ever conducted and the startling implications for diet, weight loss and long-term health*. Dallas: BenBella Books.

D'Silva, J & Webster, J (Eds). (2010). *The meat crisis: Developing more sustainable production and consumption*. London: Earthscan.

Duncan, C (1996). *The centrality of agriculture: Between humankind and the rest of nature*. Montreal/Kingston: McGill-Queen's University Press.

Eisnitz, G (2006 [1997]). *Slaughterhouse: The shocking story of greed, neglect, and inhuman treatment inside the US meat industry* (2nd edn). Amherst, NY: Prometheus.

Foster, J (2009). *The ecological revolution: Making peace with the planet*. New York: Monthly Review.

Friedmann, H (2000). What on earth is the modern world-system? Foodgetting and territory in the modern era and beyond. *Journal of World Systems Research* 6(2), 480–515.

Gilland, B (2002). World population and food supply: Can food production keep pace with population growth in the next half-century? *Food Policy* 27(1), 47–63.

Goodland, R (1997). Environmental sustainability in agriculture: Diet matters. *Ecological Economics* 23(3), 189–200.

Goodman, D, Sorj, B & Wilkinson, J (1987). *From farming to biotechnology: A theory of agro-industrial development*. Oxford: Blackwell.

Hertel, TW, Burke, MB & Lobell, DB (2010). The poverty implications of climate-induced crop yield changes by 2030. *Global Environmental Change* 20(4), 577–585.

Hoekstra, AY (2013). *The water footprint of modern consumer society*. London: Routledge.

Imhoff, D. (Ed.). (2011). *The CAFO reader: The tragedy of industrial animal factories*. Berkeley: University of California Press.

IPCC (Intergovernmental Panel on Climate Change). (2013). *Climate change 2013: The physical science basis*. Contribution of working group I to the fifth assessment report of the Intergovernmental Panel on Climate Change. Cambridge: Cambridge University Press.

Johnson, A (1991). *Factory farming*. Oxford: Basil Blackwell.

Kimbrell, A (Ed.). (2002). *The fatal harvest reader: The tragedy of industrial agriculture*. Washington, DC: Island Press.

Kloppenburg, JR (2004 [1988]). *First the seed: The political economy of plant biotechnology*. Madison: University of Wisconsin Press.

Koohafkan, P, Altieri, MA & Holt Gimenez, E (2012). Green agriculture: Foundations for biodiverse, resilient and productive agricultural systems. *International Journal of Agricultural Sustainability* 10(1), 61–67.

Lappé, FM (1991 [1971]). *Diet for a small planet*. New York: Ballantine.

Lim, SS et al. (2012). A comparative risk assessment of burden of disease and injury attributable to 67 risk factors and risk factor clusters in 21 regions, 1990–2010: A systematic analysis for the Global Burden of Disease Study 2010. *The Lancet* 380(9859), 2224–2260.

Lymbery, P (2014). *Farmageddon: The true cost of cheap meat*. New York: Bloomsbury.

Mason, J & Singer, P (1990 [1980]). *Animal factories: What agribusiness is doing to the family farm, the environment and your health* (2nd edn). New York: Harmony Books.

McIntyre, B, Herren, H, Wakhungu, J & Watson, R (2009). *International assessment of agricultural knowledge, science and technology for development: Agriculture at a crossroads*. Washington, DC: Island Press.

McMichael, AJ, Powles, JW, Butler, CD & Uauy, R (2007). Food, livestock production, energy, climate change, and health. *The Lancet* 370(9594), 1253–1263.

Montgomery, DR (2007). *Dirt: The erosion of civilizations*. Berkeley: University of California Press.

Moore, JW (2015). *Capitalism in the web of life: Ecology and the accumulation of capital*. London: Verso.

Moore, M (2002). Hidden dimensions of damage: pesticides and health. In A Kimbrell (Ed.), *The fatal harvest reader: The tragedy of industrial agriculture* (pp. 130–147). Washington, DC: Island Press.

Pachirat, T (2011). *Every twelve seconds: Industrialized slaughter and the politics of sight*. New Haven, CT: Yale University Press.

Pew Commission on Industrial Farm Animal Production (2008). *Putting meat on the table: Industrial farm animal production in America*. Washington: The Pew Charitable Trusts and The John Hopkins Bloomberg School of Public Health.

Pimentel, D (2006). Soil erosion: A food and environmental threat. *Environment, Development and Sustainability* 8(1), 119–137.

Pimentel, D & Pimentel, MH (2003). Sustainability of meat-based and plant-based diets and the environment. *American Journal of Clinical Nutrition* 78(3S), S605–633.

Popkin, B (2009). Reducing meat consumption has multiple benefits for the world's health. *Archives of Internal Medicine* 169(6), 543–545.

Sage, C (2012). *Environment and food*. New York: Routledge.

Steinfeld, H, Gerber, P, Wassenaar, T, Castel, V, Rosales, M & de Haan, C (2006). *Livestock's long shadow: Environmental issues and options*. Rome: FAO.

Wackernagel, M & Rees, WE (1996). *Our ecological footprint: Reducing human impact on the earth*. Gabriola Island, BC: New Society Publishers.

Wallerstein, I (2011 [1983]). *Historical capitalism with capitalist civilization*. London: Verso.

Weis, T (2007). *The global food economy: The battle for the future of farming*. London: Zed Books.

Weis, T (2010). The accelerating biophysical contradictions of industrial capitalist agriculture. *Journal of Agrarian Change* 10(3), 315–341.

Weis, T (2013). *The ecological hoofprint: The global burden of industrial livestock*. London: Zed Books.

York, R, Rosa, EA & Dietz, T (2003). Footprints on the earth. *American Sociological Review* 68(2), 279–300.

18

The Financialisation of Agriculture and Food

Jörg Gertel and Sarah Ruth Sippel

Introduction

The concept of financialisation has emerged as a meta-narrative for global socioeconomic change. It is intrinsically associated with the ambivalent power of financial markets, their simultaneous importance and fragility, and an international financial system of increasingly fragmented responsibilities. Financialisation has been used as a 'descriptor of a wider transformation in economy and society' (French, Leyshon & Wainwright, 2011, p. 799), understood as a 'host of structural changes in advanced political economies' (Van der Zwan, 2014, p. 99). It has become a 'focal point of a burgeoning research programme' (Nölke, Heires & Bieling, 2013, p. 209), drawing on contributions from economics, geography, sociology, anthropology and political science. Financialisation is becoming a 'schema', a meta-narrative that increasingly orders and explains knowledge and experience (Lyotard, 1984; Stephens & McCallum, 1998). In this chapter, we consider financialisation as a process in which expanding and volatile financial capital is increasingly penetrating and shaping the 'real economy'; restructuring accumulation strategies, altering the roles of both nation states and private corporations; and impacting more directly upon the livelihood systems of citizens than in previous times (Epstein, 2005; Froud, Johal, Leaver & Williams, 2006; Krippner, 2011). Financial capital and affiliated actors have also become involved in agriculture and in food production and marketing thereby impacting upon, and altering, contemporary ruralities.

Given that financialisation is still an emerging field of research, the challenge for scholars studying rural areas, agriculture and food is fourfold, as described below.

1   Financialisation has not appeared from 'nowhere'. It is a process that relies upon certain techniques and metrics which have been created over several centuries. Financialisation is rooted in colonialism as well as in the post-Second World War development era, which paved the way for its emergence and current form.
2   While financialisation has been driven by the strong post-Second World War position of the USA, it is necessary to explain how it has become increasingly polycentric, as financial hubs – embodied in specific states, cities and corporations – have emerged around the globe. This also reshapes the various articulations between finance, agriculture and food.
3   It is important to understand to what extent financialisation, although expanding on a global scale, unequally affects groups and subjects. It needs to be questioned whether some

parts of society – such as those involved in agricultural subsistence production or in marginally integrated regional market systems – are less exposed to international financial crises than financial cores.

4   Financial exchange processes and their inscribed, increasingly techno-governed, temporalities need to be captured as emerging risks. Facilitated by technological innovations, ever greater volumes of capital tied to complex regulations (algorithms) are handled at an accelerating pace. The growing speed of financial transactions increasingly exceeds human agency while producing unintended consequences in a new form.

In this chapter three periods of financialisation (European colonialism, the post-Second World War development era, and the new millennium) are identified, along with the territoriality and governmentability of shifting power centres. This is followed by a discussion of the more recent dynamics of expanding financialisation, focusing on the consequences for agribusiness, agricultural derivatives trading and land.

European colonialism

European colonialism prepared the way for the age of financialisation as it established and spread practices of measurement, standardisation and centralisation of information as part of a colonial reordering of the world. European colonialism was characterised by conquest, large-scale territorial expansion and violent confrontations with local communities. It relied on exploitation and the asymmetrical transfer of (agricultural) resources into the colonial homelands and thus established and furthered the political and economic dominance of European powers, particularly in the 19th and 20th centuries. This has been identified as the first 'food regime' (Friedmann & McMichael, 1989; McMichael, 2009). Parallel to integrated export-oriented agricultural projects, local subsistence economies and regional economic circuits prevailed (Wallerstein, 1974, 1980; Wolf, 1982).

Of crucial importance were metrologies that travelled as models along the lines of cross-continental commodity chains and hegemonic cultural exchange processes within and between colonial empires, leaving their imprints on the postcolonial heritage. These models involved practices of measurement and of standardisation and were applied, tested, adjusted as well as redeveloped, in the colonies. Statistics, as a science, developed in a world of colonial framing and was, for example, applied for insuring ships as well as in tropical medicine and town planning, 'creating the world of modern power' (Asad, 1994, p. 55). These calculations entailed processes of commensuration, such as the surveying, mapping and pricing of land, the conversion of currencies and the standardisation of the measurement of time as a prerequisite for remunerating wage labour (Blomley, 2003). Measuring, recording and centralising information thus became the bedrock of an emerging financial system. At the same time, temporalities bifurcated: embodied transactions increasingly developed into a long-distance 'network market' enabled, for example, by the opening of a transatlantic telegraph line in 1865 and the invention of the 'stock ticker' in New York in 1867 (Knorr Cetina & Preda, 2007), while agricultural calendars were still based on 'slow' seasonal growing and work cycles.

Postcolonial development and US hegemony

In the era of postcolonial development and after the Second World War, globalisation takes on pace, becomes omnipresent, unfolds as disembedding mechanisms, and is rearranging time and space – as time–space distanciation (Giddens, 1990) or time–space compression (Harvey, 1989). While the United States became the driver of the international financial system, transactions accelerated and became more and more polycentric.

After a postwar phase of two decades of industrial development and state regulation, US firms increasingly withdrew from productive investment and, instead, started to channel capital towards financial markets. Two policy shifts caused this turn to finance (Krippner, 2011, pp. 15, 52): the deregulation of financial markets over the course of the 1970s, resulting in a dramatic expansion of credit; and higher interest rates introduced in the early 1980s in response to deregulation and the loose fiscal policy of the Reagan administration. As a consequence, foreign capital was drawn into the US economy, making the US dependent on this capital to finance deficits. Together, these changes fostered an increased uncertainty in the cost of credit. For the majority of US firms facing high costs of capital, company takeovers appeared to be the only economically viable strategy. Simultaneously, new financial instruments such as interest rate swaps and derivative contracts were developed, further empowering the financial industry. Shareholder value became 'the privileged metric for assessing corporate success (or failure) in the 1980s and 1990s' (Krippner, 2011, p. 7).

These changes inside the USA were related to large-scale transformations. With the end of Bretton Woods (the collapse of the gold standard) and as an outcome of the so-called oil crisis in 1973, capital moved from Europe and the United States to oil-producing nations and from there into xeno-dollar markets (that is, US dollars circulating outside the US) and newly emerging private banks, often with Western backgrounds but increasingly located in Asia. Cheap money with low interest rates became available for young postcolonial nations. Lending with low securities, compounded by mechanisms of 'herding' and the (false) assumption that nation states could not become bankrupt, prepared the way for the international debt crises of the 1980s (El Masry, 1994). Triggered by increasing interest rates due to the unfolding European recession, most developing countries that had borrowed money and had subscribed to credit lines with variable interest rates were hit severely (Walton & Seddon, 1994). The dynamics and consequences of this global redistribution of capital cannot be reduced to a single cause – they were not linear and they were far from being planned. While the USA, with New York and Chicago as financial marketplaces, remained the pulse relay for financial and agricultural markets, London, Tokyo, Hong Kong and other global cities became the new nodes of the international – and increasingly polycentric – financial web (Sassen, 1998; Harvey, 2005).

Meanwhile, agricultural development was characterised by mechanisation, commercialisation and technological innovation. Combined with the overall shift towards a finance-driven economy, capital-intensive businesses, mergers and business concentrations increasingly shaped agricultural development in the USA and western Europe (Friedland, Busch, Buttel & Rudy, 1991; Kimbrell, 2002). Three processes were crucial. First, the dissolution of family farms and the emergence of industrial agriculture based on the expansion of large-scale, capital-intensive production caused tremendous environmental problems (Clay, 2004). Second, emerging from the Reagan administration, the US government promoted deregulation and enabled the 'merger mania' of the 1980s, resulting in highly concentrated and vertically integrated corporations (such as Bunge, Mitsui, Louis Dreyfus, Cargill and Continental Grain), which went on to become key actors in the financialisation of agriculture and food (Heffernan & Constance, 1994; Kneen, 1995; Clapp & Fuchs, 2009). Third, some of these corporations were also actively involved in shaping international trade agreements such as the Uruguay Round of the General Agreement on Tariffs and Trade (GATT) leading to the establishment of the World Trade Organization (WTO) in 1994 as well as the deregulation of financial markets (Nader & Taylor, 1986; Murphy, Burch & Clapp, 2012). Deregulation prompted re-regulation: a new governance of the global agri-food systems emerged that was dominated by trade blocks such as NAFTA (North American Free Trade Agreement) and the European Union in combination with Western-centric international organisations and private corporations, including banks. However, the agri-food sector was not global in any simple sense, with multinationals such as Cargill applying 'multi-domestic' strategies rather than sourcing through centralised global intra-firm production systems (Watts & Goodman, 1997, p. 14). Nonetheless, the power of corporations structured the move from competitive to oligopolistic structures, which also entailed a shift from government to governance, privatising the responsibility for food security and food safety (Higgins & Lawrence, 2005).

From the perspective of the global south, the debt crisis was largely responsible for the implementation of structural adjustment measures and the profound restructuring of national economies. Boosted by the Washington Consensus and the collapse of the Soviet Union, the neoliberal project unfolded at an even greater pace. Veiled behind the rhetorical commitment to universal liberalisation and privatisation, the 'development space' of low-income countries increasingly shrank, as international agreements from the Uruguay Round, such as the TRIPS (Trade Related Intellectual Property Rights) agreement, unleashed uneven regulations about investment measures and property rights (Wade, 2003). The new regimes of intellectual property rights for commons such as seeds (cotton, rice) disenfranchised farmers from their means of reproduction (Shiva, 2000). Processes of de- and re-territorialisation shaped postcolonial agri-food systems that became increasingly polarised. On the one hand, sites of industrial and irrigated agriculture with centres for export production emerged, following a Californian model. This was driven by assumptions about comparative advantages and facilitated by improved supply management (Gertel & Sippel, 2014). On the other hand, given the oligopolistic structures of rent-seeking by transnational corporations (TNCs), family farms, smallholders and agricultural tenants experienced social hardship (Sippel, 2014). Old dependencies were reframed, as in the context of contract farming, when buyers directly shaped production decisions through contractually specifying market obligations and exercising control over inputs and capital (Little & Watts 1994; Gibbon & Ponte 2005).

At the turn of the millennium, the scope of financialisation remains asymmetric and the world economic system is far from being unified. Some parts, such as major sections of world cities and of leading capitalist economies, are integrated into real-time transactions of particular currency trade, while others are not. According to Castells (2003), the core components of the global economy now have the capacity to work as a unit in real time – or in a chosen time – on a planetary scale. At the turn of the century, financial flows have 'increased dramatically in their volume, in their velocity, in their complexity and in their connectedness' (Castells, 2003, p. 312). Other parts of the world, such as Western Africa, remain shallowly integrated. While Western currency is now 'hard currency' and 'fast money', African currencies remain 'soft currencies' and 'slow money' (Guyer, 2004). While the first are monitored daily by the banking system and are infinitely convertible, large parts of the latter, once issued, never go back through the banking system. This observation does not intend to repeat a dualistic narrative of an integrated progressing centre (i.e., the global north) and a traditional backward periphery (i.e., the global south), but rather to stress that financial transactions are articulated in complex ways. They are built, extended and reproduced from above and below, as well as from different parts within the global agri-food system. Unilateral top-down perspectives would misrepresent the financialisation of agriculture and food. Indeed, shallowly integrated agricultural subsistence activities might, in some cases, work as a buffer against financial volatilities.

To sum up, at the turn of the millennium, the US financial system remains in a driving position at the same time as financial transactions are becoming increasingly polycentric, with established and newly emerging hubs. Simultaneously, material transactions are becoming increasingly superimposed by virtual transactions. Far from being disconnected from one another, virtual monetary transactions are unfolding at higher paces and are able to carry substantially larger financial volumes, enabling a shift from (public) government to (private) governance, thereby furthering the fragmentation of social responsibilities.

Post-millennium intersections between food and finance

Post-millennium dynamics in agriculture and food are characterised by an increasing nexus between finance and the agri-food system making the boundaries between the two areas blurry and fluid. While banks and financial players are assuming a more direct engagement with agriculture and food – commanding dramatically expanding volumes of financial capital – 'traditional' actors of the agri-food sector are also making use of new opportunities offered by financial instruments. Markets are changing; they are moving from involving the direct interaction of human beings to becoming algorithms that interact in virtual spaces at high frequencies (MacKenzie, 2014, pp. 2–3). The financial system is now driven by a 'capitalisation of almost everything' (Leyshon & Thrift, 2007), while the scale, speed and complexity of speculative activities renders transactions opaque and produces large-scale unintended consequences. The temporality of financialisation and the production of risks reach new forms and dimensions. Three areas of the finance–agri-food nexus have received most attention so far: agri-food businesses (shareholder value versus labour rights); agricultural derivatives (speculative gains versus the right to food); and land (investment versus the right to subsistence).

Agri-business

The financialisation of agri-food businesses is part of the wider process of the financialisation of non-financial companies (cf. Krippner, 2005; Lazonick, 2013). As such, it relies on the rise of 'shareholder capitalism', on the legal frameworks enabling certain activities (particularly of private equity capital), as well as on decades of consolidation and corporatisation that resulted in a high level of power concentration in the agri-food industry. This renders agri-food companies attractive for financial takeovers while some transnational corporations become powerful financial players themselves. So far, intersections with finance have been observed for agri-business companies that are involved in food trading, retailing and processing, the provision of agricultural inputs, storage and logistics as well as offering inspection and certification (Burch & Lawrence, 2009; Isakson, 2014).

Two studies have addressed the financialisation of retailing. Baud and Durand's (2012) study underlines the increasing importance of profits from financial activities for non-financial firms and the shifts of power involved. Starting in the early 1990s, the ten leading global retailers not only became international players but their internationalisation strategies were further coupled with financialisation in regard to three dimensions. First, their objectives turned to the implementation of shareholder value norms, resulting in an increase of financial flows from non-financial corporations to the financial sector. Second, their investments included an increasing share of financial assets; this, in combination with their improved position towards their suppliers and workers within the context of the globalisation of their operations, allowed them to provide continuously high returns to their shareholders. Third, they changed their operations towards offering financial products (e.g., credit cards, savings/checking accounts) to their customers while simultaneously imposing financial relationships on workers and suppliers (e.g., by taking advantage of payment differences). Together, these have fuelled a shift of power towards financial capital while financial costs and risks are being transferred to weaker actors. Burch and Lawrence (2013) analyse the private equity takeover of the UK supermarket chain Somerfield, thereby shedding light on the implications of short-term private equity interests to capitalise from a temporal engagement in the food sector. As a 'typical case' of a private equity company seeking to realise shareholder value as quickly as possible, three strategies were applied: divesting existing assets to repay debt; introducing 'efficiencies' in the company taken over; and leveraging existing assets so as to generate new income streams. The implemented measures included the streamlining of sourcing, the reduction of costs (such as cutting the number of suppliers and employees), and the introduction of an 'opco/propco' model (splitting the company into two parts, an operating and a property component) to de-bundle and repackage assets. These kinds of takeovers are thus not interested in the core business of food retailing, but rather aim at realising short-term financial gains.

Similar to large retailers, the four largest grain traders – Archer Daniels Midland (ADM), Bunge, Cargill, and Louis Dreyfus – are also increasingly engaged in financial activities. They have been actively involved in the financialisation of commodity markets and in lobbying to influence financial regulatory reforms in the USA and the EU (Murphy, Burch & Clapp, 2012). The nature of the global grain trade, the capital and infrastructure required, and the size these firms have achieved over many decades has placed them in a particularly good position to capitalise on their knowledge and power in branching out into financial activities. These include financial speculation on agricultural commodity markets and index funds, transportation and storage, developing financial subsidiaries that offer asset management services to third-party investors as well as investing in primary production and land. In-depth studies on the financialisation of large grain traders – in this case focusing on Cargill – further underline the various alliances between finance and the agricultural system, in large part facilitated by the corporatisation of agriculture (Salerno, 2014).

In sum, the financialisation of agri-business companies means shareholder value has often been realised at the expense of the rights of suppliers, workers and customers while, at the same time, undermining employment security.

Agricultural derivatives

Food prices are a critical element in moral economies and their control is a crucial means to prevent social unrest and upheaval. The recent food crises revealed the new dimensions of complexity that are governing food insecurity in the new millennium. Food prices have been 'financialised' as agricultural derivatives (financial instruments based on the value of agricultural commodities) have become subject to financial speculation.

After two decades of volatile but overall declining food prices, the prices of key staple foods increased sharply between 2007 and 2008, and again in 2011, provoking 'food riots', largely in urban centres of the global south. The explanations provided for the recent food crises are diverse and include short- and mid-term factors (such as the decline of agricultural production and food stocks, rising demand, export restrictions and new agro-fuel policies) as well as long-term influences (including declining investment, and the reduced regulatory role of the state). These factors, however, were coupled with one further driver: the financialisation of agricultural commodity derivatives markets. Three overlapping developments have been identified as having contributed to, and enabled, the financialisation of commodity derivatives markets: the changing regulatory framework in the USA where the majority of investors as well as trading are concentrated; the weak performance of 'traditional' asset classes; and the impact of financial studies on risk-return characteristics of commodity derivatives.

To prevent speculation, market manipulation and sharp price shifts, agricultural futures markets in the United States were tightly regulated from the early 19th century by the Grain Futures Act of 1922, the Commodity Exchange Act of 1936 and, since 1974, oversight by the Commodity Futures Trading Commission (CFTC). Since the 1980s, this regulatory framework has been relaxed while new ways of off-exchange trading – such as swaps or 'over-the-counter' (OTC) transactions – as well as vehicles for speculation, in particular Commodity Index Funds (entailing the bundling of futures contracts), have been developed (see Zaloom, 2006; Ho, 2009). Most importantly, two revisions of statute occurred under the pressure of the US financial lobby in 2000. First, the Gramm-Leach-Bliley Act dissolved old boundaries in financial markets and allowed banks to unify all sorts of financial business within one company. Second, the Commodity Futures Modernisation Act exempted OTC-derivative-transactions from CFTC oversight and, as a result, withdrew most instruments of regulatory control (Berg, 2011; Clapp, 2014). Investment banks such as Goldman Sachs appeared as both the main drivers as well as the main beneficiaries of this deregulation. The influx of capital into agricultural derivatives, and especially commodity indices, was further triggered by the 'bursting' of other bubbles, such as the dot-com bubble in late 2001 and the US housing market in 2007. Consequently, investors searched for new 'alternative' asset classes providing returns uncorrelated with the 'traditional' ones (such as equities and bonds) already existing in their portfolios (Masters & White, 2008). At the same time, commodity derivatives were touted as offering the desired non- or even negative-correlation, an assumption mainly based on a study by Gorton and Rouwenhorst (2006) claiming that they served as ideal means to balance portfolios (Schumann, 2011). One new group in particular, the so-called 'index speculators', has been identified as driving food price increases (Bass, 2013). These are mainly institutional investors (especially pension funds) which are administering enormous amounts of money – an estimated US$29 trillion – and which have started to speculate on commodity futures indices to diversify their portfolios, hedge against inflation or bet against the dollar. In addition to the sheer amount of money, the 'long-only' investment strategy ('virtual hording') of institutional investors has been seen as driving up prices. They continuously swap agreements and thus extract liquidity from the market.

Three consequences of these developments need further analysis: the implications of index fund speculation (contributing up to one-third to food commodity futures) on price building processes of food in the spot market; the consequences of the large concentration of swap agreements in the hands of only a few investment banks; and the effects of high-frequency trading in derivatives and interaction between technology platforms.

Here, and elsewhere, knowledge production is at stake and remains a highly contested field with regard to the availability of data, their interpretation, and the performativity of financial models. First, data on commodity futures transactions are not easily accessible; they are often incomplete, incoherent or undisclosed with privately organised (transnational) corporations, which, protected by legal systems, primarily seek to comply with their own interests and profits. Second, even if data are available, their interpretation is far from being neutral and remains contested as their use largely depends on professional interests. Some studies neglect the impact of commodity indices development on spot market prices of food (Irwin & Sanders, 2012; Will, Prehn, Pies & Glauben, 2013), others argue in favour of a correlation (Bass, 2013), while still others emphasise a strong articulation between commodity speculation and food price hikes (Schumann, 2011; Russi, 2013). Third, financial models (as all models) are 'performative' as they impact on, and shape, financial practices (MacKenzie, Muniesa & Siu, 2007). In this vein, Gorton and Rouwenhorst's (2006) study functioned as a 'self-destroying prophecy' (Bass, 2013, p. 22). By generating a common pattern of investment across a basket of previously unrelated commodity futures markets, index investment led to cross-commodity price correlation and thereby prompted a convergence with other asset prices (Gibbon, 2013, p. 13).

To conclude, food security is becoming complex: livelihoods in the global north (seeking long-term financial gains by pension schemes) and livelihoods in the global south (the risk of food insecurity) are connected via speculative financial activities. These interconnections are increasingly taking place at enormous speed beyond human capability and with limited opportunities for intervention.

Land

The conjunction of the financial, food and energy crises that peaked in 2008 has also provoked the acceleration and globalisation of investments in land. The recent rediscovery and engagement with land has been largely spurred by the 'land grab' debate, identifying new financial actors such as sovereign wealth funds and private equity funds as driving large-scale land acquisitions in foreign countries. Initial concerns were originally raised by non-governmental organisations (GRAIN, 2008). They then quickly entered the public media and were also identified by a wide range of academics (e.g., White et al., 2012; Edelman, Oya & Borras, 2013). However, the notion of 'land grabbing' entails value judgements and is not, per se, equivalent to the financialisation of land. Here the focus is on land, conceptualised as property, which is turned into a financial asset class.

Four main and interrelated drivers of the financialisation of land, partly overlapping with commodity futures investment, have been identified (see Painter & Eves, 2008; Fairbairn, 2014). First, the rise of the interest in land has equally been seen as a response to the poor performance of 'traditional' asset classes. Second, land is considered as offering a low or negative correlation with traditional assets and positive risk-return characteristics both adding to the overall performance of financial portfolios. Third, the finite availability of land combined with a rising demand for food has been emphasised. Fourth, and contrary to other asset classes, both appreciation and its productive capacity (i.e., the value of its products) constitute the financial value of land. Further to that, however, land is different: it serves as a reference point for the formation of identity and constitutes a crucial means of livelihood security for millions of people. It has a complex history of shifting, and often contested, forms of governance regulating the rights to access or use it (Gertel, Calkins & Rottenburg, 2014). Thirty years of neoliberal policies promoting foreign direct investment and fostering the privatisation, commodification and consolidation of land have provided the basis for the current financialisation of land aiming at profiting from its capacity as an asset class.

After 2000, numerous specialised real-asset investment vehicles have been established that can take various legal forms (including private equity funds, hedge funds, real estate management trusts, and private and public companies) and which are pursuing different farm ownership and management strategies. The different sources of 'finance capital' involve fundamentally different investment interests and strategies. Capital invested by sovereign wealth funds stemming from one national source such as Saudi Arabia, Qatar or Norway will normally entail substantially different timelines and interests (such as long-term national food security goals – see Sippel, 2015). Private equity-backed investments usually represent a melting pot of capital in-flows, generally have a five- to seven-year time horizon, and – based on the ability to quickly increase the value of their target investment – tend to be speculative in nature (Daniel, 2012). Apart from direct purchase or lease, other strategies to access land are being pursued. For example, securitisation turns land into a highly liquid, tradable, asset – similar to a stock – to open it up for more speculative purposes (Fairbairn, 2014).

In 2012, the estimated amount of financial capital invested in primary agriculture globally varied between US$5 billion and $40 billion (Luyt, Santos & Carita, 2013, p. 32). While much of the reporting has addressed the global south, the bulk of investment – that is, more than 80% of its global value – has taken place in five countries (USA, Canada, Australia, New Zealand and Brazil), four of which are located in the global north (Luyt, Santos & Carita, 2013, p. 32). Although this figure might be contested, these countries obviously offer favourable investment conditions given their vast tracts of consolidated land properties and existing land markets (Gunnoe, 2014; Larder, Sippel & Lawrence, 2015; Sommerville & Magnan, 2015). At the same time, new areas – so-called 'emerging' or 'frontier markets' – are targeted, especially by private equity investments, which are often facilitated by international development organisations. The World Bank Group, in particular, has advanced the conditions for private sector investment in the global south via its investment promotion strategy and directly supported the influx of private equity capital (Daniel, 2012). Also, Dixon (2014) concludes that, in relation to Egypt, private equity funds have been jointly created by private co-investors and institutional investors like the World Bank's International Finance Group, serving as major guarantors of leveraged buyouts in emerging markets. Private equity capital has not only played a critical role in restructuring the Egyptian agri-food sector but has also become an important vehicle used by companies and multinational corporations to invest in agricultural production and to gain (indirect) control over land. Examples for this are Citadel Capital's investment in Sudan (Dixon, 2014) and Cargill's role in land investments in the Philippines (Salerno, 2014).

Financialisation of land thus represents a new challenge for the future of rural communities. For some, financial capital might provide new opportunities (for example, providing capital to expand farm operations or fund retirement). For others, the selling of land or forced expulsion from the land threatens livelihoods and the ability to feed their families.

Conclusion

Financialisation is increasingly used as a concept to frame and explain empirical observations about activities in the finance sector. As a meta-narrative ordering and explaining knowledge and experience it risks becoming a catch-all concept, exceeding its analytical scope. A continuous effort to further delineate the dynamic properties of financial capital and to trace its flows is thus required. In regard to the financialisation of agriculture and food, three insights are crucial. First, financialisation is based on changing relations of technological innovations, standardisation of metrics, and the expansion of private property rights which have built up over a long time; it has done so in the context of overlapping phases of governance, where old patterns and discourses are still working and impacting on current agri-food systems. Second, financialisation creates unequal spatial outcomes. The configurations of power centres are shifting from Europe and the United States to a polycentric financial system with various hubs while expanding into everyday life. The scope of penetration is uneven and the deepness of integration varies, pushing and unlocking new frontiers. In this sense, financialisation appears as antagonistic to 'the commons' and to alternative agri-food movements which are challenging private property, scarcity discourses and the dissolution of sociability. Third, financialisation is characterised by unequal temporalities of agricultural exchange processes. Within these exchange processes material transactions are superimposed by virtual monetary transactions, while simultaneously, seasonal produce and biographical time continue to shape agriculture and food.

References

Asad, T (1994). Ethnographic representation, statistics and modern power. *Social Research* 61(1), 55–89.

Bass, H-H (2013). *Finanzspekulation und Nahrungspreise: Anmerkungen zum Stand der Forschung*. Institut für Weltwirtschaft und Internationales Management, Universität Bremen: Studie für foodwatch.

Baud, C & Durand, C (2012). Financialization, globalization and the making of profits by leading retailers. *Socio-Economic Review* 10(2), 241–266.

Berg, A (2011). The rise of commodity speculation: From villainous to venerable. In A Prakash (Ed.), *Safeguarding food security in volatile global markets* (pp. 253–278). Rome: FAO.

Blomley, N (2003). Law, property, and the geography of violence: The frontier, the survey, and the grid. *Annals of the Association of American Geographers* 93(1), 121–141.

Burch, D & Lawrence, G (2009). Towards a third food regime: Behind the transformation. *Agriculture and Human Values* 26(4), 267–279.

Burch, D & Lawrence, G (2013). Financialization in agri-food supply chains: Private equity and the transformation of the retail sector. *Agriculture and Human Values* 30(2), 247–258.

Castells, M (2003). Global informational capitalism. In D Held & A McGrew (Eds), *The global transformation reader: An introduction to the globalization debate* (pp. 311–333). Malden, MA: Blackwell.

Clapp, J (2014). Financialization, distance and global food politics. *The Journal of Peasant Studies* 41(5), 797–814.

Clapp, J & Fuchs, D (Eds). (2009). *Corporate power in global agrifood governance*. Cambridge, MA: MIT Press.

Clay, J (2004). *World agriculture and the environment*. Washington, DC: Island Press.

Daniel, S (2012). Situating private equity capital in the land grab debate. *The Journal of Peasant Studies* 39(3–4), 703–729.

Dixon, M (2014). The land grab, finance capital, and food regime restructuring: The case of Egypt. *Review of African Political Economy* 41(140), 232–248.

Edelman, M, Oya, C & Borras, SM (2013). Global land grabs: Historical processes, theoretical and methodological implications and current trajectories. *Third World Quarterly* 34(9), 1517–1531.

El Masry, GZ (1994). *Die afrikanische Auslandsverschuldung*. Berlin: Haupt Verlag.

Epstein, G (Ed.). (2005). *Financialization and the world economy*. Cheltenham: Edward Elgar.

Fairbairn, M (2014). 'Like gold with yield': Evolving intersections between farmland and finance. *The Journal of Peasant Studies* 41(5), 777–795.

French, S, Leyshon, A & Wainwright, T (2011). Financializing space, spacing financialization. *Progress in Human Geography* 35(6), 798–819.

Friedland, WF, Busch, L, Buttel, FH & Rudy, AP (Eds). (1991). *Towards a new political economy of agriculture*. Boulder, CO: Westview.

Friedmann, H & McMichael, P (1989). Agriculture and the state system: The rise and decline of national agricultures, 1870 to the present. *Sociologia Ruralis* 29(2), 93–117.

Froud, J, Johal, S, Leaver, A & Williams, K (2006). *Financialization and strategy: Narrative and numbers*. London: Routledge.

Gertel, J, Calkins, S & Rottenburg, R (2014). Disrupting territories: Commodification and its consequences. In J Gertel, R Rottenburg & S Calkins (Eds), *Disrupting territories: Land, commodification and conflict in Sudan* (pp. 1–30). Woodbridge: James Currey.

Gertel, J & Sippel, SR (2014). Seasonality and temporality in intensive agriculture. In J Gertel, & SR Sippel (Eds), *Seasonal workers in Mediterranean agriculture: The social costs of eating fresh* (pp. 3–22). New York: Routledge.

Gibbon, P (2013). *Commodity derivatives: Financialization and regulatory reform*. Copenhagen: DIIS.

Gibbon, P & Ponte, S (2005). *Trading down: Africa, value chains, and the global economy*. Philadelphia, PA: Temple University Press.

Giddens, A (1990). *The consequences of modernity*. Stanford, CA: Stanford University Press.

Gorton, G & Rouwenhorst, KG (2006). Facts and fantasies about commodity futures. *Financial Analysts Journal* 62(2), 47–68.

GRAIN (2008). *Seized: The 2008 land grab for food and financial security*. Barcelona: GRAIN.

Gunnoe, A (2014). The political economy of institutional landownership: Neorentier society and the financialization of land. *Rural Sociology* 79(4), 478–504.

Guyer, JI (2004). *Marginal gains: Monetary transactions in Atlantic Africa*. Chicago: University of Chicago Press.

Harvey, D (1989). *The condition of postmodernity: An enquiry into the origins of cultural change*. Cambridge, MA: Blackwell.

Harvey, D (2005). *A brief history of neoliberalism*. Oxford: Oxford University Press.

Heffernan, WD & Constance, DH (1994). Transnational corporations and the globalization of the food system. In A Bonanno, L Busch, W Friedland, L Gouveia & E Mingione (Eds), *From Colombus to ConAgra: The globalization of agriculture and food* (pp. 29–51). Lawrence, KS: University Press of Kansas.

Higgins, V & Lawrence, G (Eds). (2005). *Agricultural governance: Globalization and the new politics of regulation*. London: Routledge.

Ho, K (2009). *Liquidated: An ethnography of Wall Street*. Durham, NC: Duke University Press.

Irwin, SH & Sanders, SR (2012). Testing the masters hypothesis in commodity futures markets. *Energy Economics* 34(1), 256–269.

Isakson, SR (2014). Food and finance: The financial transformation of agro-food supply chains. *The Journal of Peasant Studies* 41(5), 749–775.

Kimbrell, A (Ed.). (2002). *The fatal harvest reader: The tragedy of industrial agriculture*. Washington, DC: Island Press.

Kneen, B (1995). *Invisible giant: Cargill and its transnational strategies*. London: Pluto Press.

Knorr Cetina, K & Preda, A (2007). The temporalization of financial markets: From network to flow. *Theory, Culture and Society* 24(7–8), 116–138.

Krippner, G (2005). The financialization of the American economy. *Socio-Economic Review* 3(2), 173–208.

Krippner, GR (2011). *Capitalizing on crisis: The political origins of the rise of finance*. Boston, MA: Harvard University Press.

Larder, N, Sippel, SR & Lawrence, G (2015). Finance capital, food security narratives and Australian agricultural land. *Journal of Agrarian Change* 15(4), 592–603. doi: 10.1111/joac.12108.

Lazonick, W (2013). From innovation to financialization: How shareholder value ideology is destroying the US economy. In MH Wolfson & GA Epstein (Eds), *The handbook of the political economy of financial crises* (pp. 491–511). New York: Oxford University Press.

Leyshon, A & Thrift, N (2007). The capitalization of almost everything: The future of finance and capitalism *Theory, Culture and Society* 24(7–8), 97–115.

Little, PD & Watts, MJ (Eds). (1994). *Living under contract: Contract farming and agrarian transformation in sub-Saharan Africa*. Madison: University of Wisconsin Press.

Luyt, I, Santos, N & Carita, A (2013). *Emerging investment trends in primary agriculture: A review of equity funds and other foreign-led investments in the CEE and CIS region*. Rome. FAO.

Lyotard, J-F (1984). *The postmodern condition: A report on knowledge*. Minneapolis: University of Minnesota Press.

MacKenzie, D (2014). A sociology of algorithms: High-frequency trading and the shaping of markets. Available at www.maxpo.eu/Downloads/Paper_DonaldMacKenzie.pdf (accessed 25 May 2015).

MacKenzie, D, Muniesa, F & Siu, L (Eds). (2007). *Do economists make markets? On the performativity of economics*. Princeton, NJ: Princeton University Press.

Masters, MW & White, AK (2008). The accidental hunt brothers: How institutional investors are driving up food and energy prices. Available at https://loe.org/images/content/080919/Act1.pdf (accessed 25 May 2015).

McMichael, P (2009). A food regime analysis of the 'world food crisis'. *Agriculture and Human Values* 26, 281–295.

Murphy, S, Burch, D & Clapp, J (2012). *Cereal secrets: The world's largest grain traders and global agriculture*. Oxfam Research Report. Oxford: Oxfam International.

Nader, R & Taylor, W (1986). *The big boys: Power and position in American business*. New York: Pantheon Books.

Nölke, A, Heires, M & Bieling, H-J (2013). Editorial: The politics of financialization. *Competition and Change* 17(3), 209–218.

Painter, M & Eves, C (2008). The financial gains from adding farmland to an international investment portfolio. *Journal of Real Estate Portfolio Management* 14(1), 63–73.

Russi, L (2013). *Hungry capital: The financialization of food*. Winchester/Washington: Zero Books.

Salerno, T (2014). Capitalising on the financialisation of agriculture: Cargill's land investment techniques in the Philippines. *Third World Quarterly* 35(9), 1709–1727.

Sassen, S (1998). *Globalization and its discontents*. New York: New Press.

Schumann, H (2011). *Die Hungermacher: Wie Deutsche Bank, Goldman Sachs & Co. auf Kosten der Ärmsten mit Lebensmitteln spekulieren*. Berlin: foodwatch.

Shiva, V (2000). *Stolen harvest: The hijacking of the global food supply.* London: Zed Books.

Sippel, SR (2014). Disrupted livelihoods? Intensive agriculture and labour markets in the Moroccan Souss. In J Gertel & SR Sippel (Eds), *Seasonal workers in Mediterranean agriculture: The social costs of eating fresh* (pp. 186–198). New York: Routledge.

Sippel, SR (2015). Food security or commercial business? Gulf state investments in Australian agriculture. *The Journal of Peasant Studies* 42(5), 981–1001.

Sommerville, M & Magnan, A (2015). 'Pinstripes on the prairies': Examining the financialization of farming systems in the Canadian prairie provinces. *The Journal of Peasant Studies* 42(1), 119–144.

Stephens, J & McCallum, R (1998). *Retelling stories, framing culture: Traditional story and metanarratives in children's literature.* New York: Garland.

Van der Zwan, N (2014). Making sense of financialization. *Socio-Economic Review* 12, 99–129.

Wade, RH (2003). What strategies are viable for developing countries today? The world trade organization and the shrinking of 'development space'. *Review of International Political Economy* 10(4), 621–644.

Wallerstein, I (1974). *The modern world-system I: Capitalist agriculture and the origins of the European world-economy in the sixteenth century.* New York: Academic Press.

Wallerstein, I (1980). *The modern world-system II: Mercantilism and the consolidation of the European world-economy, 1600–1750.* New York: Academic Press.

Walton, J & Seddon, D (1994). *Free markets and food riots: The politics of global adjustment.* Oxford: Blackwell.

Watts, M & Goodman, D (1997). Agrarian questions: Global appetite, local metabolism: nature, culture, and industry in *fin-de-siècle* agro-food systems. In D Goodman & MJ Watts (Eds), *Globalising food: Agrarian questions and global restructuring* (pp. 1–32). New York: Routledge.

Wolf, E (1982). *Europe and the people without history.* Berkeley: University of California Press.

White, B, Borras, SM, Hall, R, Scoones, I & Wolford, W (2012). The new enclosures: Critical perspectives on corporate land deals. *The Journal of Peasant Studies* 39(3–4), 619–664.

Will, MG, Prehn, S, Pies, I & Glauben, T (2013). Schadet oder nützt die Finanzspekulation mit Agrarrohstoffen? – Ein Literaturüberblick zum aktuellen Stand der empirischen Forschung. *List Forum für Finanz- und Wirtschaftspolitik* 39(1), 16–45.

Zaloom, C (2006). *Out of the pits: Traders and technology from Chicago to London.* Chicago: University of Chicago Press.

19

Supermarketisation and Rural Society Futures

Jane Dixon and Cathy Banwell

Introduction

Over two decades ago corporate food retailers were crowned the 'new masters of the food system' (Flynn & Marsden, 1992, p. 34). In this and subsequent work the rise of supermarket chains in the United Kingdom was attributed to regulatory powers shifting from governments and farmer organisations to retail corporations between the 1960s and the 1980s (Marsden & Wrigley, 1996). A similar trajectory towards corporate food retailer dominance over agri-food systems was under way in the United States several decades earlier (Seth & Randall, 1999). This 'supermarket revolution' has penetrated most countries in the developed and developing world in the last half-century (Burch & Lawrence, 2007; Coe & Wrigley, 2007; Humphrey, 2007; Reardon & Gulati, 2008; Mei & Shao, 2011; Reardon, Timmer & Minten, 2012). The impacts of this revolution on urban ways of living, transportation systems, culinary cultures, trade rules, food-quality standard setting, and agri-food systems – along with rural societies – have been profound. While this chapter focuses on rural societies, it is impossible to disentangle the behaviours of urban consumers from the fortunes of rural communities. At its most simple, the supermarket revolution is the outcome of two revolutions: an urban food provisioning revolution and an agri-food supply chain revolution. Supermarket chains have been central to both. In order to reveal how supermarkets have escaped strong state regulation – and, consequently, how well positioned they are to control much of what happens in national and local food systems – the contours of the demand- and supply-side revolutions are outlined below.

Supermarketisation: the unfolding of a cultural economy process

Supermarketisation refers to a process of domination, rather than an outcome. This domination takes both cultural and economic forms and exerts a presence across numerous spheres of social life. The precise nature of the domination is contingent on sociopolitical histories of state regulation, agricultural policies, urban and town planning, labour relations and culinary cultures. As a result, the process plays out unevenly from nation to nation despite the major actors being global corporations operating across borders by harmonising regulations that they themselves have arranged. Despite the variegated role that supermarkets play worldwide, their initial establishment and penetration appears to follow a common pattern.

A century ago within industrialising nations, household food provisioning (consisting of sourcing foods and food preparation) involved a relatively simple set of steps. Farmers (and to a lesser extent households) grew, harvested and processed agricultural products, physically took the produce to city and town markets and received cash from the wholesaler/trader. Small-scale food retailers who often specialised in one or two food items – bacon, butter, coffee – sold their products to citizens for whom food purchasing was a ritualised activity. The highly personalised and expert food provisioning approach continues across tens of thousands of Asia's towns and villages, but has become unusual for most urban households in North America, the UK, Australia, and in many parts of Europe.

Today's basic supermarket format – high volumes of an enormous variety of imported and domestically sourced goods sold each day at low margins; consumer self-service in terms of selecting and bagging produce, often paying at a machine; the provision of a physical retail environment experienced as clean and offering consistent food safety and other basic food quality attributes; and, the twin promise of consumer convenience and control – originated in the USA in the 1930s, followed by England in the 1940s. The early outlets employed distributional efficiencies, obviating the need for numerous shop-floor employees – that is, customers served themselves. Scale efficiencies were then introduced through adopting the chain store model (Seth & Randall, 1999) which was premised on the notion that one store was not sufficient to generate profits but multiple stores were, due to their bulk buying and vertical integration with suppliers (Bowlby, 1997).

While most US food chains were content to coexist with specialist grocers on high streets, Wal-Mart set out to eliminate all competition through a philosophy of 'We Sell for Less'. Opening its first store in 1962, it quickly asserted itself by locating stores away from high streets in huge purpose-built warehouses or out-of-town shopping centres, accessible by car, leaving high street shops without customers (Satterthwaite, 2001). Wal-Mart oriented food shopping towards economic transactions and away from personalised interactions, to use a typology developed by Stone (see Hewer & Campbell, 1997). Against a common backdrop of steadily growing populations, deriving relatively stable livelihoods from factory work and other occupations dependent on mechanised technologies, the early UK chains determined that there would be a demand for a more convenient, market-based, approach to accessing the food supply. At the same time, they knew they could capitalise on the very same mechanisation to deliver standardised food products at low prices (Seth & Randall, 1999). By transforming agri-food systems from producer-driven systems to buyer-driven systems (Konefal, Bain, Mascarenhas & Busch, 2007) Wal-Mart, along with UK counterparts, led the way in disembedding food provisioning from all contexts but the household budget.

The symbiosis between mass production technologies and the profits derived from lowering wage bills via low food prices has been explored by Goodman and Redclift (1991), who describe how an economic system based on industrialisation came to rely on an industrialising agri-food system which kept food prices – and subsequently wages – low. They have linked industrial-food system developments to the later stages of the 'passing of rural society' in the United Kingdom. Between 1955 and 1975, with encouragement from government, the proportion of land farmed in England and Wales grew from 27% to 43%, but at the same time the number of farm holdings declined by half and the number of full-time farmers declined by a third. Thousands of small farms were being replaced by a growing number of large farm holdings, as these businesses were able to capitalise on newly available technological inputs. The resulting exponential growth in food yields kept lowering the market price of food, making small farms even less viable and resulting in a decline in the number of farmers and farm workers (see, for Australia, Lawrence, 1987).

As supermarkets emerged during the 1950s, agricultural restructuring was independently under way. While land ownership and tenure arrangements differed between nations, giving rise to unique class structure formations, key common features of the agri-food system were evolving across the industrialised world. These included: a move away from low-input and on-farm inputs to externally provided inputs supplied by agribusiness corporations; the growth in the size of farms; increased specialisation of production; mechanisation to reduce human labour-power costs; a focus on yields and markets as opposed to what the farm's natural environment could more readily tolerate; the rise of food manufacturers as the major customers for farm produce; and price-setting commodity boards coming under sustained pressure by governments in line with an emerging neoliberal ideology (Lawrence, 1987; Lawrence & Campbell, 2014; Bonanno & Busch, 2015).

Mechanised labour exacted a heavy toll on waged agricultural labourers, who were forced to move from rural areas to towns and cities in search of work. Farm unit viability, as an outcome of broad public policy and capitalist supply and demand dynamics, was inextricably connected to the entrenched interests of landowners in conflict with the political power of industrialists (in the UK and other parts of Europe, landowner-industrialists constituted an important class which used farm income streams to support their industrial investments). The fortunes of rural society waxed and waned as these dynamics played out in combination with the steady growth in size and political clout of urban populations. This situation has been encapsulated in the theory of 'urban bias' – the skewing of policies towards improving the living standards of the urban population (Lipton, 1984; Kay, 2009; Dixon & McMichael, 2015).

In short, as supermarkets began to institute supply chain arrangements with preferred and reliable suppliers, they encountered farm sectors and rural societies which had been already marginalised within national polities. Since the 1960s, supermarkets, along with the global free trade architecture forged after the Second World War, have been the major force shaping agriculture. How supermarket chains have been changing the face of farming via their power in agri-food chains has been the subject of numerous analyses (Humphrey, 2007; Reardon & Gulati, 2008; Burch, Dixon & Lawrence, 2013). These works reveal a number of key strategies which have provided the underlying basis of the strength of supermarkets.

Six strategies underpinning the supermarketisation process

The first strategy involves the growing concentration of a handful of supermarket chains within the food retail sector. A few supermarket firms arise as a result of displacing the livelihood options of small and independent food retailers (in Asia this extends to the traditional wet or fresh markets). This process of displacement narrows the field of potential buyers, leading to what is known as monopsony conditions: many suppliers vying to supply a few buyers.

The second strategy enables and sediments the first. Over time, supermarket chains come to control the majority of the purchasing power of a nation's consumers because smaller alternative retail formats find it difficult to provide: the lowest prices due to their lack of economies of scale; a similar range of fresh, packaged and processed foods allowing for one-stop shopping; an open-all-hours model because they are generally family-run businesses; and a sound reputation for the quality control of food.

The third strategy is part economic and part cultural. From their inception, supermarkets have used advertising and other symbolic means (for example, by integrating the role of the motor car in household daily life) to position themselves to be in the vanguard of modernisation. They have always placed themselves as service providers rather than as traders, promising to meet the financial and time-pressured needs of modern citizens. Supermarkets no longer simply sell food and household items. They provide easy access to household lines of credit and car insurance, cooking demonstrations and wine tasting opportunities, and nutritional information, among a host of other attractions. In the UK, Tesco, which has long offered multiple services – such as dry cleaning and crèches – adopts a by-line which goes well beyond household budgeting in regards to cheap food: 'Every little helps'. This illustrates how chains become identified as key participants in the moral economy of households and, as such, position themselves as valued authorities, sitting alongside governments and religious bodies in times of need (Dixon, 2008).

A fourth strategy – again both cultural and economic – involves the supermarkets' regulatory or standard-setting role (Marsden & Wrigley, 1996; Richards, Lawrence & Burch, 2011). Beginning with the International Standards Organisation's HACCP guidelines – adopted internationally by firms to audit, address and monitor hazards to human health – supermarkets have been enthusiastic adopters of self-governing regulatory tools. They have also developed their own supply chain audit tools, which become integral to the contractual relationships they enter into with suppliers (Campbell & Le Heron, 2007; Dixon & Banwell, 2012). The safety priority applied to food production standards has had two direct impacts: it has consolidated supermarket chain reputations as safe and dependable quality food providers, and it has provided incentives for small farms and processing firms to become larger in order to have the capital to invest in the technological requirements to meet supermarket-led audit specifications.

The quality audit systems enacted by supermarkets have had another benefit for supermarkets. Through it, they have learned about production techniques, meal formulations and other paddock-to-shelf considerations allowing them to move upstream into production. Their production activities can be direct – when they own farms or food processing companies – or indirect, through entering into contracts with farmers and processors to deliver products according to production stipulations. The resulting home brand or own brand strategic development, the fifth strategy to be described here, has had a negative impact on the economic viability of local and even esteemed global brand makers of cereals, tinned and frozen fruit and vegetables, not to mention raw-ingredient producers (milk in particular). The home/own brand category operates as a profitable brand-switching device. By the early 1990s, one-third of grocery sales in Britain were own labels (Doel, 1996).

A recent assessment of the world's major supermarkets shows that four of the top five – Wal-Mart, Tesco, Carrefour and Costco – have global reach (Winson, 2013). In effect, they can readily tap their international supply chain networks to import fresh and processed products and – through switching suppliers – can have a devastating impact on existing production sites (Hattersley, Isaacs & Burch, 2013). The loss and gain of supermarket supply contracts affects whole rural communities which support, and rely upon, a commodity's production (Dixon & Isaacs, 2013). The search for alternative sites of production is often described in terms of the need to find locales featuring low wages and benign regulatory regimes. This is one reason that food processors give for shutting existing plants. Less remarked upon is the fact that sites of production are suffering either biophysical exhaustion or are increasingly subject to climate change pressures, meaning that the supplies from those areas are potentially no longer viable. Thus the global supply chain strategy, or sixth strategy, is becoming imperative, in part as a result of the damage that industrial agriculture has been unleashing on agri-environments.

Built upon the six foregoing strategies, supermarketisation exerts significant influence over the terms of food and agricultural trade and hence over food producer livelihoods and food producer environments and communities. At the same time that supermarkets have been exercising ever greater control over farmers and manufacturers, the value of agriculture to national economies in the OECD has been declining relative to other sectors. This has led to the downgrading of agricultural ministries and a wider marginalisation of rural affairs in many nations (Marsden & Wrigley, 1996; Pretty, 2002). In countries like Australia, where the rural was singularly synonymous with agriculture and associated export revenues (Brett, 2011), rural populations are now considered marginal to the economy and it is in rural areas where one finds sub-populations which are the poorest, the sickest, least educated and the most government-benefit dependent (Hogan & Young, 2014).

Inferior rural socioeconomic and health outcomes have not been caused by supermarket corporations, but supermarket supply and demand-led dynamics compound political economies which favour urban populations and cultural economies which skew societal values towards a new calculus of efficiency – of low-price goods based on the most efficient production methods; food as a 'quick' energy source; and appreciation of ease of effort in food provisioning. The successful delivery of this particular value set legitimises the hands-off approach exhibited by governments in the USA and Australia towards farmer livelihoods. The more supportive EU directives on farming and farm livelihoods reflect an affiliation for food/culture values, along with recognition of the multifunctional nature of farming (Renting et al., 2009).

While acknowledging the downsides of supermarket supply chains, some researchers have also been identifying the opportunities which they can bring to rural communities. This line of reasoning is explored in the final section.

Case studies

How the process of supermarketisation has been unfolding and impacting on rural producers and communities is illustrated by two case studies, Australia and Thailand. While this section highlights a similar diffusion in retail power over agri-food systems, it also reveals different sources of contestation depending on politico-cultural history.

Australia

Within agri-food studies circles, Australia is known as one of a handful of 'settler states' along with Canada, New Zealand and Rhodesia (now Zimbabwe). These states arose, in part, as a result of the migration of labour forced by the decline under way in English rural society (McMichael, 1984). As a colony of the British Empire from 1788 to the early decades of the 20th century, Australia's major role was to supply raw materials – mainly wool, wheat, sheep meat and beef – to Britain and, in turn, to use resulting revenues to purchase the mass-processed goods coming from the metal, machinery and textile factories of Britain. Based on pastoral practices transferred from Britain, Australia's interior was opened up from the 1820s onwards to sheep and cattle and to cereal grain production, allowing a settler hegemony to be established. However, the pastoral activity, in particular, had a devastating impact on the environment through the clearing of native vegetation and over-grazing (Lawrence, 1987; Lawrence & Vanclay, 1994).

Yet, such was the importance of pastoral activities to national revenues that governments ignored the ongoing environmental damage and, up until the 1970s, put in place a succession of incentives to continue production of farm commodities. State support came in numerous forms including price supports, taxation concessions, statutory marketing, and rural research and extension services (Lawrence, 1987). Investments were made also in infrastructures to service agriculture – railways, irrigation schemes, telecommunications – along with government services to rural populations, including police stations, law courts, schools and post offices (Brett, 2011). The flow of public monies was not one way, however, and farmers subsidised manufacturing industries for decades through the government imposition of tariffs on machinery, chemicals and equipment to protect the steel and car industries (Gray & Lawrence, 2001). Rural policy was largely an amalgam of monetary, trade, agricultural and manufacturing industry policy, despite there being a political party to represent rural population interests. On the occasions when rural policy has been concerned with rural population well being, it has typically come in the form of rural reconstruction initiatives, the heart of which has been agri-industry adjustment programmes designed to help struggling farmers sell to larger farmers in order to accelerate productivist agriculture (Lawrence, 1987; Gray & Lawrence, 2001).

Imitating the retail revolutions under way in the USA and UK, corporate supermarket chains emerged in Australia in the 1960s as the one-stop shop for dry groceries and minimally processed farm produce. Their early consolidation took shape against a backdrop of marked transitions in the political economic conditions governing agricultural production and food consumption. Under an Australian Labor Party government in the 1980s, farm protection measures were wound back through the deregulation of tariffs, removal of import quotas and the floating of the dollar. Instead of government-regulated commodity boards setting prices, producers of all sizes were expected to compete on world and domestic markets with periodic assistance (drought programmes, ease of credit programmes, sectoral restructuring) being available when economic and environmental conditions faltered. On the consumption side, a labour-industry accord tied wages and social benefits to productivity gains, rather than pegging them to changing household needs as had been the case for the previous 70 years (Brett, 2011). This shift in industrial relations policy made the promise of cheap food even more appealing.

Currently, Australia produces more food than its population of 25 million can eat and successive governments boast that it feeds a further 40 million people abroad (Commonwealth of Australia, 2014). These impressive figures result from an agricultural workforce of 2.5% of all employed people, almost half the number of 20 years ago (ABS, 2012). However, food imports are steadily growing and half of all food export earnings goes to pay for food imports (AU$18 billion as against AU$9 billion; see PMSEIC, 2010, p. 34). Once successful agricultural exporters now face considerable competition from Asian neighbours who have made rapid productivity gains. In an effort to compete, Australian farms have had to borrow money to increase their landholdings and invest in technology, and farm debt across the dairy and the broadacre sectors – the nation's two major agri-export sectors – has doubled in a decade, averaging AU$546,000 per farm in 2009–2010 (ABARES, 2014, p. 42). For agriculture as a whole, farm debt in Australia has increased from AU$40.3 billion in 2004 to AU$70 billion in 2014 – an increase of almost 75% over the past decade (Garnett, 2014).

Food retail is now by far the most dominant part of the agri-food system in terms of value to the Australian economy. In 2007–2008, primary production of food and fish was worth AU$37 billion, food processing AU$79 billion and retail food sales amounted to AU$123 billion (PMSEIC, 2010, p. 33). Combined, the supermarket chains Coles and Woolworths employ more than 400,000 Australians, with only state governments employing more (Knox, 2014, p. 30). There are five main (or 'full service') supermarket chains in Australia and three limited-range supermarket chains, along with more than 3,000 limited-range single supermarket outlets. Together, they accounted for 67% of the AU$130 billion spent by Australians on food and non-alcohol beverages in 2010–2011. Such is their dominance that the two major chains – Coles and Woolworths with 2,300 outlets – commanded more than two-thirds of that amount, or AU$61 billion (Spencer & Kneebone, 2012).

As monopsony conditions have evolved between rural producers and the two major supermarket chains, so too has the penetration of global supermarkets, particularly ALDI and wholesaler Metcash. These corporations are well placed to use their international supply chains to replace or augment domestic production. This global competition for supply has further contributed to a reduction in farmer numbers and incomes, and while it is not possible to attribute this decline to any particular actor, supermarkets are largely responsible for the hard times besetting several agri-industrial sectors: dairy, processed fruit, vegetables and pigmeat (NSW DPI, 2006; Spencer & Kneebone, 2012).

To date, the major resistance to the relentless supermarketisation of supply chains has come from consumers, not governments. A nascent 'alternative food system', coming from within civil society and supported by affluent urbanites, has been offering an income stream lifeline to small producers for the past decade (Burton et al., 2013; Lyons, Richards, DesFours & Amati, 2013). The alternative supply chains are typically farmers' markets and other schemes for direct selling between producers and consumers, like community-supported agriculture and food box schemes. Of more recent note has been growing consumer pressure on supermarkets to recommit to using domestically grown food in their home-branded products (Richards, Lawrence & Burch, 2011). This pressure follows waves of consumer discontent at supermarkets not supporting local producers (Dixon & Isaacs, 2013; Knox, 2014; Neal, 2014).

Arguably of greater significance to larger numbers of rural producers is yet another government inquiry into the supply chain conduct of the supermarket chains. What is new about the most recent inquiry is the proven charges of misconduct of one of the chains, with the other major chain coming before the courts for similar behaviour. In late 2014, Coles accepted a AU$10 million fine from the Federal Court for 'serious, deliberate and repeated' misconduct towards suppliers. In a case brought by the Australian Competition and Consumer Commission, Coles's conduct was found to be 'deliberate, orchestrated and relentless', involving hounding suppliers for payments which they might not owe or threatening to withhold payments that were owed. As part of the court settlement, Coles has agreed to compensate 200 suppliers for some AU$26 million. Woolworths, too, has been subject to damaging page-one newspaper headlines, including: 'Woolies hounds suppliers' (Hawthorne, 2014). In both cases, suppliers have been asked to fund the shortfalls that supermarkets face when they transfer products into their discount ranges, similar to behaviour that has been reported of Tesco (Armitage, 2015). The retrospective claw-back is in addition to charging suppliers for shelf space and promotional materials that the supermarkets use as part of their sales strategies.

Thailand

In 2011 Thailand was upgraded by the World Bank from a Lower to an Upper Middle Income Country (UMIC) on the basis of its gross national income (GNI), which at US$4,210 is at the low end of the UMIC bracket. A senior World Bank economist attributed the improvement to Thailand's economic achievements and decreasing levels of poverty. He added: 'Thailand has a friendly business environment and has been successful in attracting foreign direct investments and achieving greater diversification in manufacturing production, both in terms of higher value-added production and expansion into new emerging export markets' (World Bank, 2011). The growth of agri-food industries has played a large part in this success. The country has evolved from being dependent on rice as the primary source of export earnings to having diverse food processing, export and food technology industries that are part of its strategy to be identified as 'the kitchen to the world'.

The rapid growth of the modern food retail sector in Thailand is integral to this economic policy mix. Thailand has been identified as a member of the 'second wave' of the supermarket revolution, along with China, Indonesia and Malaysia (Reardon, Timmer & Minten, 2012). Traditionally, Thais have purchased fresh food from floating markets on canals (*talad nam*) and on land-based markets (*talad din*), but around the 1960s the retail environment began to change. In 1963, a dozen supermarkets were present in Bangkok (Wigglesworth & Brotan, 1996), with supermarkets spreading to outer urban areas and then to rural centres as the Thai economy grew – a process which accelerated in the 1990s. The growth in supermarkets was accompanied by the arrival of 7-Eleven convenience stores in 1989, located near commuter stops and coinciding with rapidly growing wealth and a greater desire for Western lifestyles (Tokrisna, 2007). As part of the 1997 financial crisis, the government dissolved the requirement that international companies have a Thai partner, leaving foreign firms free to purchase joint-partnered chains and expand.

The major companies that took advantage of this opportunity were Tesco (UK), Carrefour (French) and Big C (French) (Kanchoochat, 2008). Foreign firms were not the single modernising force in food retailing; Thailand's own CP group was – and continues to be – at the forefront of introducing global innovations. This conglomerate owns the Thai-based 7-Eleven chain (the world's third or fourth largest 7-Eleven chain) as well as Siam Makkro, another major food retailer (Gen, 2013). In late 2014 Tesco's problems in the UK sparked discussions with the CP group (which originally partnered with Tesco in the establishment of Tesco Lotus) about buying back ownership of the company.

Modern retail formats have rapidly taken hold in Thailand for the same reasons as elsewhere. These include: the entry of women into the workforce and the increased opportunity cost of women's time providing incentives to seek shopping convenience and processed foods to save meal preparation time; real per capita income growth, along with the rise of a middle class primed for the offerings of the supermarket; and growth in refrigeration, increasing the ability to shift from daily shopping to weekly or monthly shopping – aided by access to cars and public transport. The major supermarket chains operating in Thailand have applied similar strategies to those described earlier to assist in their expansion. They have employed attractive marketing and promotion tactics, provided air-conditioned, clean environments, customer service add-ons, food safety standardisation and labels, as well as novel Western-style products. Another factor contributing to their success has been the willingness of transnational food corporations (TFCs) to adapt their businesses to local conditions. This has included stocking traditional Thai, and particularly regional speciality, foods alongside the imported products and setting up market stall areas around hypermarkets and shopping malls in order to more closely approximate a traditional Thai shopping experience (Kanchoochat, 2008). Through visual markers of Thai-ness and other processes of imitation (Isaacs, 2009; Isaacs et al., 2010) they have attempted to forge connections with Thai consumers who clearly value personal and trust-based relationships with fresh market vendors (Banwell et al., 2013).

The impact of the last decade of changes in the retail sector is already being felt by traditional retailers and fresh markets. A backlash has begun with political pressure being brought to bear to restrict the levels of TFC investment in Thailand by legislating against foreign ownership, and local community campaigns against the opening of new stores (Kanchoochat, 2008). These measures have not yet met with great success although there has been government debate over the issue in recent years, particularly under the military government which was in place in 2006–2007. More success has been achieved in community campaigns in local areas where, for example, in Chumphon province Tesco was pressured into not opening a new store, and also in Phrae province (Kanchoochat, 2008). However, the Thai government is expected to welcome foreign direct investment as part of global liberalisation promoted by the World Trade Organization and International Monetary Fund, and there are fears that increasing restrictions on TFCs may cause a general drop in foreign investor confidence which, in turn, may cause the economy to stagnate.

It is unclear whether the 'supermarket revolution' in Thailand will have the deleterious effect on rural incomes and communities that it has in Australia or if it will provide a pathway out of the poverty that many small Thai farmers experience. At the outset, there are contradictory projections for the growth and progress of the supermarket revolution. Reardon, Timmer and Minten (2012) and others have described the rapidity and intensity of supermarket growth from urban to rural areas in Southeast Asian countries, including Thailand, as 'precocious' while at the same time observing that there are still some impediments to growth. Supermarkets in Thailand and elsewhere in Southeast Asia have been less successful than these authors have expected in selling fresh, rather than processed, produce. One of the impediments to the supermarket growth in fresh produce is the need for more modern procurement systems and supply chain modernisation (Reardon, Timmer & Minten, 2012), with each major chain adopting a different approach to the problem (Gen, 2013). Gen (2013) argues that the supermarkets will continue to struggle to win the loyalty of Thai consumers for fresh produce sales due to their comparative expense and the lack of cars and refrigerators required for those involved in weekly shopping. They struggle to compete with fresh markets that cater to a culturally embedded practice of daily shopping for small quantities of food (Banwell et al., 2013).

The growth of agri-business has impacted on Thai rural communities. Thailand, of any Asian country, now has one of the largest populations of producers working under contract, a trend that was initiated by the CP group in the 1970s (Goss, Burch & Rickson, 2000). Yet, poor farmers in Thailand are still at risk of food insecurity due to low productivity and falling commodity prices (Buch-Hansen, 2001; Walker, 2012). They may gain economically from supplying under contract to supermarket chains (Sriboonchitta & Wiboonpoongse, 2008), but smaller, less resourced producers can be economically excluded from supermarket growth (Timmer, 2009; Gomez & Ricketts, 2013). Evidence from other countries suggests that they may benefit from increased employment opportunities as nearby larger commercial farmers supply to modern food retail outlets (Gomez & Ricketts, 2013), although the effects of involvement with modern retail on the welfare and health of small producers is often not considered (Sriboonchitta & Wiboonpoongse, 2008). Some propose that structural efforts should be made to help small farmers become enmeshed with modern food retail (Schipmann & Qaim, 2011; Reardon, Timmer & Minten, 2012); but evidence from Australia suggests that over the long term, as supermarkets gain market share and monopsony conditions come into play, their contracted rural suppliers could experience lower economic returns.

Conclusion: what is the likely future of supermarkets and their impacts on rural societies?

As they embed themselves within high- and middle-income nations, supermarkets consolidate a 'cheap food regime' which threatens the livelihoods of rural food producers. At the same time, with growing poverty in rural Thailand and across urban and rural Australia – the two settings for our case studies – cheap food is needed more than ever. This chapter has argued that supermarketisation plays a major role in this dialectic: on the one hand, supermarket supply chains have reinforced other structural forces in reducing the numbers of farms and rural community income streams while, on the other hand, they have made food more affordable, including to households affected by loss of farm livelihoods.

Within development economics and agri-food studies, debates are ongoing regarding the merits of what appears to be an inevitable move to de-agrarianisation and a general decline in rural societies, given the macroeconomic realities of globalisation, including supermarketisation.

For some, the answer lies in European Union-style protection of rural populations, based on re-peasantisation through land reforms, pluri-activity and income streams to pay for the conservation of natural environments (Van der Ploeg, 2009). Others propose a burgeoning alternative food system where producers engage directly with consumers, bypassing corporatised supply chains altogether. This second option can include investments in the modernisation of fresh or produce markets to better compete against the supermarket retail format (Reardon & Gulati, 2008). In part, supermarkets themselves are responsible for the growth in alternative supply chains because they have energised citizen-consumers to take the food supply seriously, including questioning retailer activities (Konefal, Bain, Mascarenhas & Busch, 2007).

In contrast to the non-corporate pathway of rural development, some who have been studying supermarket penetration in low- and middle-income nations argue that the best prospects for small producers lies in public–private partnerships to enhance linkages between single farm units and modern retailers. On the basis of extensive research in Asia and South America, Reardon and colleagues (2012) have provided a catalogue of approaches that 'bring modern markets to farmers'. Typically the model here is a food hub, park or platform which allows small farmers to access a host of co-located services to facilitate their produce moving from the farm and onto supermarket shelves. In any one setting there may be physical spaces (warehouses, collection centres, processing plants), agri-food support services (logistics companies, technical assistance, infrastructure providers) and possibly retailers. To date, hubs have been initiated by governments, supermarket chains, international and domestic NGOs and farmer associations. This sociotechnical innovation can operate to transform 'smallholding peasants into budding commercially-oriented entrepreneurs able to compete in global markets by linking them more effectively into the agro-industrial commodity chains in which supermarkets are gaining increasing influence' (Kay, 2009, p. 127).

From a rural livelihoods perspective, as presently articulated, neither the entrepreneurial nor the alternative supply chain scenario is seen as adequate. Scoones (2009), for example, argues that livelihood debates which are couched in 'bottom-up, locally-led, participatory development' ignore struggles for rights, justice and equality. Like Kay (2009), he reminds us that livelihoods are structured by class relations and that the state is central to the structuration process. Both Scoones and Kay note the impact that global capitalism has on local conditions, imperilling worthwhile local initiatives that lack government policy support. Additionally they argue that agriculture alone cannot lift rural communities out of poverty. For Kay, a developmental state is required to establish the industrial–agricultural–service sector arrangements that can stimulate growth and equity while eradicating poverty (Kay, 2009, p. 128). For Scoones (2009), a singular response to insert farmers into modern supply chains ignores the rural livelihoods opportunities that can follow from policies to make it easier for households to engage in cross-sectoral (on-farm and off-farm) livelihood strategies created by urban–rural economic zones or 'city regions'. By focusing only on supermarketisation or its alternatives without acknowledging the dynamics unleashed by the world capitalist system, and the corporate–state nexus which perpetuates that system, rural development will not be well served.

Acknowledgement

Jane Dixon is grateful to research support from an Australian Research Council Discovery Project Grant DP150100504.

References

ABARES (2014). *Australian farm survey results 2011–2012 to 2013–2014*. Canberra: Australian Bureau of Agricultural and Resource Economics and Sciences.

ABS (2012). *Year book Australia, 2012: Farming in Australia*. Canberra: Australian Bureau of Statistics.

Armitage, J (2015). Tesco crisis: 'They say every little helps, but supermarket demands are never little'. *The Independent*, 14 January 2015.

Banwell, C, Dixon, J, Seubsman, S-A, Pangsap, S & Kelly, M (2013). Evolving food retail environments in Thailand and implications for the health and nutrition transition. *Public Health Nutrition* 16(4), 608–615.

Bonanno, A & Busch, L (Eds). (2015). *Handbook of the international political economy of agriculture and food*. Cheltenham: Edward Elgar.

Bowlby, R (1997). Supermarket futures. In P Falk & C Campbell (Eds), *The shopping experience* (pp. 92–110). London: Sage.

Brett, J (2011). Fair share: Country and city in Australia. *Quarterly Essay* 42. Available at https://www.quarterlyessay.com/essay/2011/06/fair-share (accessed 16 June 2015).

Buch-Hansen, M (2001) Is sustainable agriculture in Thailand feasible? *Journal of Sustainable Agriculture* 18(2–3), 137–160.

Burch, D, Dixon, J & Lawrence, G (2013). Introduction to the changing role of supermarkets in global supply chains: From seedling to supermarket: Agri-food supply chains in transition. *Agriculture and Human Values* 30(2), 215–224.

Burch, D & Lawrence, G (Eds). (2007). *Supermarkets and agri-food supply chains*. Cheltenham: Edward Elgar.

Burton, P, Lyons, K, Richards, C, Amati, M, Rose, N, DesFours, L, Pires, V & Barclay, R (2013). *Urban food security, urban resilience and climate change*. Gold Coast: National Climate Change Adaptation Research Facility.

Campbell, H & Le Heron, R (2007). Supermarkets, producers and audit technologies: The constitutive micro-politics of food, legitimacy and governance. In D Burch & G Lawrence (Eds), *Supermarkets and agri-food supply chains* (pp. 131–153). Cheltenham: Edward Elgar.

Coe, N & Wrigley, N (2007). Host economy impacts of transnational retail: The research agenda. *Journal of Economic Geography* 7, 341–371.

Commonwealth of Australia (2014). *Agricultural competitiveness issues paper*. Canberra: Commonwealth of Australia.

Dixon, J (2008). Operating upstream and downstream: How supermarkets exercise power in the food system. In J Germov & L Williams (Eds), *A sociology of food and nutrition: The social appetite* (pp. 100–124). London: Oxford University Press.

Dixon, J & Banwell, C (2012). Choice editing for the environment: Managing corporate risks. In T Measham & S Lockie (Eds), *Risk and social theory in environmental management* (pp. 175–184). Collingwood, Australia: CSIRO Publishing.

Dixon, J & Isaacs, B (2013). There is certainly a lot of hurting out there: Navigating the trolley of progress down the supermarket aisle. *Agriculture and Human Values* 30(2), 83–297.

Dixon, J & McMichael, P (2015). The urban bias revisited. In C Butler, J Dixon & A Capon (Eds), *Health of people, places and planet: Reflections based on Tony McMichael's four decades of contribution to epidemiological understanding* (pp. 313–330). Canberra: ANU Press.

Doel, C (1996). Market development and organisational change: The case of the food industry. In N Wrigley & M Lowe (Eds), *Retailing, consumption and capital* (pp. 48–67). Harlow: Longman.

Flynn, A & Marsden, T (1992). Food regulation in a period of agricultural retreat: The British experience. *Geoforum* 23, 85–93.

Garnett, A (2014). Farmers are in debt and more debt won't help. Available at http://theconversation.com/farmers-are-in-debt-and-more-debt-wont-help-22698 (accessed 16 June 2015).

Gen, E (2013). *Diversifying retail and distribution in Thailand*. Chiang Mai: Silkworm Books.

Gomez, M & Ricketts, K (2013). Food value chain transformations in developing countries: Selected hypotheses on nutritional implications. *Food Policy* 42, 129–138.

Goodman, D & Redclift, M (1991). *Refashioning nature, food, ecology and culture*. London: Routledge.

Goss, J, Burch, D & Rickson, R (2000). Agri-food restructuring and third world transnationals: Thailand, the CP group and the global shrimp industry. *World Development* 30, 513–530.

Gray, I & Lawrence, G (2001). *A future for regional Australia: Escaping global misfortune*. Cambridge: Cambridge University Press.

Hattersley, L, Isaacs, B & Burch, D (2013). Supermarket power, own-labels, and manufacturer counterstrategies: International relations of cooperation and competition in the fruit canning industry. *Agriculture and Human Values* 30(2), 225–253.

Hawthorne, M (2014). Woolies hounds suppliers. *The Age*, 26 December 2014, pp. 1, 12.

Hewer, P & Campbell, C (1997). Research on shopping – a brief history and selected literature. In P Falk & C Campbell (Eds), *The shopping experience* (pp. 186–206). London: Sage.

Hogan, A & Young, M (2014). *Rural and regional futures*. London: Routledge.

Humphrey, J (2007). The supermarket revolution in developing countries: Tidal wave or tough competitive struggle? *Journal of Economic Geography* 7, 433–450.

Isaacs, B (2009). Imagining Thailand in European hypermarkets: New class-based consumption in Chiang Mai's 'cruise ships'. *The Asia Pacific Journal of Anthropology* 10(4), 348–363.

Isaacs, B, Dixon, J, Banwell, C, Seubsman, S-A, Kelly, M & Pangsap, S (2010). Imitation, adaptation and substitution: Fresh market and supermarket conventions in Thailand. *Journal of Sociology* 46(4), 413–436.

Kanchoochat, V (2008). Services, servility and survival: The accommodation of big retail. In P Phongpaichit & C Baker (Eds), *Thai capital after the 1997 crisis* (pp. 85–104). Singapore: ISEAS Publishers.

Kay, C (2009). Development strategies and rural development: Exploring synergies, eradicating poverty. *The Journal of Peasant Studies* 36, 103–137.

Knox, M (2014). Duopoly money. Coles, Woolworths and the price we pay for their domination. *The Monthly*, August, pp. 20–31.

Konefal, J, Bain, C, Mascarenhas, M & Busch, L (2007). Supermarkets and supply chains in North America. In D Burch & G Lawrence (Eds), *Supermarkets and agri-food supply chains* (pp. 268–288), Cheltenham: Edward Elgar.

Lawrence, G (1987). *Capitalism and the countryside*. Sydney: Pluto Press.

Lawrence, G & Campbell, H (2014). Neoliberalism in the Antipodes: Understanding the influence and limits of the neoliberal political project. In S Wolf & A Bonanno (Eds), *The neoliberal regime in the agri-food sector: Crisis, resilience and restructuring* (pp. 263–283). London: Routledge.

Lawrence, G & Vanclay, F (1994). Agricultural change in the semiperiphery: The Murray–Darling Basin, Australia. In P McMichael (Ed.), *The global restructuring of agro-food systems* (pp. 76–103). Ithaca, NY: Cornell University Press.

Lipton, M (1984). Urban bias revisited. *Journal of Development Studies* 20(3), 139–166.

Lyons, K, Richards, C, DesFours, L & Amati, M (2013). Food in the city: Urban food movements and the (re)imagining of urban spaces. *Australian Planner* 50(2), 157–163.

McMichael, P (1984). *Settlers and the agrarian question: Foundations of capitalism in colonial Australia*. Cambridge: Cambridge University Press.

Marsden, T & Wrigley, N (1996). Retailing, the food system and the regulatory state. In N Wrigley & M Lowe (Eds), *Retailing, consumption and capital* (pp. 33–47). Harlow: Longman.

Mei, L & Shao, D (2011). Too cheap hurt farmers, too expensive hurt customers: The changing impacts of supermarkets on Chinese agro-food markets. *Millenial Asia* 2(1), 43–64.

Neal, S (2014). Thousands rally for grapes of wrath farmers. *The Australian Newspaper*, 10 December 2014, p. 5.

NSW DPI (2006). *Understanding the pork industry. Prime fact 105*. Sydney: New South Wales Department of Primary Industry.

PMSEIC (2010). *Australia and food security in a changing world*. Canberra: The Prime Minister's Science, Engineering and Innovation Council.

Pretty, J (2002). *Agri-culture: Reconnecting people, land and nature*. London: Earthscan.

Reardon, T & Gulati, A (2008). *The supermarket revolution in developing countries. Policies for 'competitiveness with inclusiveness'*. IFPRI Policy Brief 2. Washington, DC: IFPRI.

Reardon, T, Timmer, C & Minten, B (2012). Supermarket revolution in Asia and emerging development strategies to include small farmers. *Proceedings of the National Academy of Sciences of the United States of America* 109(31), 12332–12337.

Renting, H, Rossing, W, Groot, J, Van der Ploeg, J, Laurent, C, Perraud, D … Van Ittersum, M (2009). Exploring multifunctional agriculture: A review of conceptual approaches and prospects for an integrative transitional framework. *Journal of Environmental Management* 90(2), S112–S123.

Richards, C, Lawrence, G & Burch, D (2011). Supermarkets and agro-industrial foods. *Food, Culture and Society* 14(1), 29–47.

Satterthwaite, A (2001). *Going shopping: Consumer choices and community consequences.* New Haven, CT: Yale University Press.

Schipmann, C & Qaim, M (2011). Modern food retailers and traditional markets in developing countries: Comparing quality, prices and competition strategies in Thailand. *Applied Economic Perspectives and Policy* 33(3), 345–362.

Scoones, I (2009). Livelihoods perspectives and rural development. *Journal of Peasant Studies* 36(1), 171–196.

Seth, A & Randall, G (1999). *The grocers: The rise and rise of the supermarket chains.* London: Kogan Page.

Spencer, S & Kneebone, M (2012). *Foodmap. An analysis of the Australian food supply chain.* Canberra: Department of Agriculture, Fisheries and Forestry.

Sriboonchitta, S & Wiboonpoongse, A (2008). *Overview of contract farming in Thailand: Lessons learned.* Tokyo: Asian Development Bank Institute.

The World Bank (2011). Thailand now an upper middle income country. Press Release. 2 August. Bangkok: World Bank.

Timmer, C (2009). Do supermarkets change the food policy agenda? *World Development* 37(11), 1812–1819.

Tokrisna, R (2007). Thailand's changing retail food sector: Consequences for consumers, producers, and trade. *PECC - Pacific Food System Outlook Meeting.* Kunming, China: Pacific Economic Cooperation Council.

Van der Ploeg, J (2009). *The new peasantries: Struggles for autonomy and sustainability in an era of empire and globalization.* London: Earthscan.

Walker, A (2012). *Thailand's political peasants: Power in the modern rural economy.* Madison: University of Wisconsin Press.

Wigglesworth, E & Brotan, J (1996). Retailing trends in Thailand. *Journal of Retailing* Summer, 41–51.

Winson, A (2013). *The industrial diet.* Vancouver: University of British Columbia.

World Bank (2011). Thailand now a middle income country. Press release, 2 August 2011. http://www.worldbank.org/en/news/press-release/2011/08/02/thailand-now-upper-middle-income-economy.

20

Agricultural Science and Technology
Tensions and Contradictions

Leland Glenna and Elizabeth P. Ransom

Introduction

Agricultural science and farm-based technologies have been important forces behind the dramatic rise in agricultural production in the industrial world during the 20th century, as well as in large portions of the developing world (Stanton, 1998). In the United States, mechanisation, improved seeds and breeds, chemical inputs, and other scientifically inspired production technologies and techniques are often credited with productivity gains (Dimitri, Effland & Concklin, 2005). After the Second World War, the Marshall Plan exported many of these technologies and techniques to Europe, along with aspects of the political economy of agricultural science and technology. The Green Revolution in the 1960s and 1970s diffused new crop and animal husbandry technologies and techniques to developing nations. Between 1950 and 1990, irrigated cropland around the world expanded from 94 million hectares to 271 million hectares, grain production expanded from 618 million metric tons to 1,938 million metric tons, numbers of tractors in use expanded from 6 million to 26 million, commercial fertiliser use expanded from just under 5 million metric tons to nearly 27 million metric tons, and livestock production also saw dramatic increases (Stanton, 1998). More recently, agricultural research and development has turned towards even more sophisticated high-technology approaches, including computer- and satellite-monitored precision agriculture and genetically engineered (GE) crops and livestock. However, the shift to expensive, high-tech solutions raises questions concerning the affordability and appropriateness for smallholder agricultural producers who make up the vast majority of producers in the world.

One pitfall when discussing how agricultural science and technology fosters productivity gains is that it is easy to treat science and technology as determining outcomes. Moreover, narratives about agricultural science and technology tend to perpetuate ideological agendas and fail to capture the conflicts and competing processes that have been present at important moments in the historical trajectory (Glenna & Henke, 2014). It is important not to overlook the role that institutions and structures play in shaping people's decisions and actions, as well as the distribution of beneficial and negative consequences.

In industrialised countries, science- and technology-driven agricultural industrialisation is associated with declines in farm numbers, expansion in farm size and specialisation in production.

In the case of the United States, farm policies were often directed at limiting farm number decline, but some of those same policies also contributed to agricultural specialisation and expansion (Dimitri, Effland & Concklin, 2005). Other industrialised nations have adopted similar policies, such as price supports for farmers and regulations directed at reducing negative environmental consequences, including soil erosion, water pollution and deforestation (Stanton, 1998; Potter & Burney, 2002).

In developing nations, the Green Revolution had similar impacts. The introduction of improved crop technologies enhanced production, but it also tended to favour larger and more prosperous farmers (Evenson & Gollin, 2003). It is important to recognise that there are debates about how science and technology lead to these negative outcomes. For example, Birner and Resnick (2010) contend that Green Revolution technologies were scale neutral. Indeed, agricultural science and technology do not carry with them any inherent qualities that determine outcomes. Yet, it is also important to recognise that political-economic contexts influence the agricultural research and development agendas, as well as the adoption and diffusion of the products of that agenda. Griliches's (1957) research on the diffusion and adoption of hybrid maize in the United States found that private firms strove to promote the new technology to the largest farmers, first. It is common sense that a firm could sell as much hybrid maize seed in one transaction to a 100-hectare farmer as it could in ten transactions with 10-hectare farmers. The same logic would hold for an agricultural extension agent charged with promoting the diffusion of seeds or other technologies. Birner and Resnick (2010) concede that agricultural political-economic conditions and ideologies shaped outcomes that disadvantaged smallholders.

The Green Revolution has also been linked to environmental problems (Pretty, Toulmin & Williams, 2011) and to mass migrations of rural people to major urban areas in developing nations (Araghi, 2000). It has long been assumed by many development proponents that rural–urban migration is an effective poverty reduction strategy. However, following migration from poor rural areas to urban areas that do not have employment opportunities, as was the case with the Green Revolution, poverty is transferred, but not reduced (Pingali, 2012). Despite the failure of policies to benefit smallholder agriculture, smallholder producers remain prominent in many regions of the world, particularly in parts of Asia and Africa. Moreover, in recent years, there has been an expansion of smallholders (or what some refer to as peasants), even in many industrialised countries (Van der Ploeg, 2009).

Simultaneously, there has been an emphasis on high-technology approaches to address agrifood challenges, combined with a reliance on the private sector to generate these high-technology solutions. The approach has been pursued in both developed and developing nations. The rationale for the political-economic shift seems to be premised on two basic ideas. The first is that private firms have substantial resources and capabilities that could be harnessed to meet social welfare needs (Fuglie & Toole, 2014). The second is that private goods generated in the private sector are effectively and efficiently diffused through markets and, indeed, are more effective and efficient than are public goods generated by the public sector and distributed through educational and government agencies (Block, 2011). Furthermore, in the cases where public institutions, like agricultural universities, do generate public goods of potential value, the assumption is that this value is not fully realised until those public goods are converted into private goods and licensed to private firms (Glenna, Lacy, Welsh & Biscotti, 2007).

In past decades, agricultural science and technology have contributed to the productivist goals of maximising production while seeking the greatest efficiency from inputs. However, there have always been tensions and contradictions because the distribution of risks and benefits has not been even. Despite these insights, recent shifts in the political economy of agricultural science and technology indicate a trend that favours the private sector and global markets, a move that tends to exacerbate some of those underlying and persistent tensions and contradictions. We explore these issues by examining how these political-economic shifts are affecting agricultural science and technology in industrialised and developing nations.

Political economy of agricultural research in industrial nations

Perhaps one of the earliest examples of focusing on high-technology, private sector approaches was the development of hybrid corn in the United States in the middle of the 20th century. Between the early 1900s and the early 2000s, corn yields increased from an average of 25 bushels per acre to over 160 bushels per acre (that is, from 17 metric tons per hectare to 108 metric tons per hectare) (Ramey, 2010). Although it is often hailed as a great scientific and technological breakthrough, Kloppenburg (2004) and Berlan and Lewontin (1986) argue that hybridisation was chosen less for its contribution to yield than for providing a kind of biological patent that would attract the private sector's investment in plant breeding. Because it is not possible to achieve the same yields each year from saved hybrid corn seed, farmers needed to purchase seed each year. Berlan and Lewontin (1986) argue that the same yields could have been achieved without hybridisation. To support their claim, they note that corn was not bred for yield prior to the emergence of hybridisation. They also observe that wheat yields increased even faster than corn, but without hybridisation, between 1937 and 1945. They further note that increased corn yields coincided with mechanisation, crop rotation, fertilisers and public subsidies for production. The key point is that an ideological shift towards favouring the private sector's investment in agricultural science and technology development emerged in the middle of the 20th century, and that an ideology of privatisation contributed to the development of hybrid corn because of its built-in intellectual property protection, as distinct from the public availability of open-pollinated corn.

A series of policies in the USA led to more rigorous intellectual property protections for US crops. For example, the 1930 Plant Patent Act provided patent-like protection to asexually propagated plants, the 1970 Plant Variety Protection Act gave patent-like protection to sexually propagated plants, and the 1980 Supreme Court decision, *Diamond v. Chakrabarty*, allowed the patenting of novel life forms (Busch, Lacy, Burkhardt & Lacy, 1991; Kloppenburg, 2004). Furthermore, since the adoption of the Bayh-Dole Act in the United States, many other industrial countries have adopted similar policies (OECD, 2003; Lacy et al., 2014). This has been an important development in agriculture because farmers had always been able to save a portion of their crop to replant the next season. Patent protection changed that. However, the political-economic reasoning is that this transformation is justified because the private sector will have a greater incentive to invest in agricultural research and development if it can secure patent protection.

Private sector investments in agricultural science and technology research did increase between 1981 and 2000. In 1981, in OECD nations, the public sector contributed US$8,339.8 million and the private sector invested US$6,478.4 million, which amounts to 44% of the total. By 2000, the private share of agricultural science and technology research had risen to 54%, US$12,184.5 million from private sources and US$10,267.6 million from public sources. Information relating to the private investments in agricultural science and technology was not available for all nations in 1981. By 2000, the private share of agricultural science and technology research investments amounted to 39% (Alston, Andersen, James & Pardey, 2010, p. 144).

It appears, at first glance, that higher private sector investments are positive. Private agri-food businesses have substantial scientific expertise and resources that can be mobilised to improve agricultural production, which may contribute to more food availability and lower food costs. However, greater investments from the private sector have not yielded the same levels of agricultural innovation across nations (Fuglie et al., 2012), and the impacts have not been the same across all crops. To explain the variation in impacts, Glenna, Shortall and Brandl (2015) compared crop yields in the United States, the United Kingdom, Germany and Ireland. They point out that the private sector tends to invest in crops that have intellectual property protections, such as patents or hybridisation, which enable the holder to exclude others from using those private goods. These crops include maize, canola, rice and soybeans. Public goods, by contrast, can reasonably be accessed by anyone. Before hybridisation, and before it became possible to patent genetically engineered (GE) crops, seeds were predominantly treated as public goods. Today, GE crops and hybrid crops are treated as private property, while open-pollinated crops that are not GE or hybrid, such as wheat and barley, continue to be treated as public goods.

One of Glenna, Shortall and Brandl's (2015) findings is that hybrid crops and GE crops had yield increases in the USA over the last three decades. However, open-pollinated crops, like wheat, saw a decline in yield growth over the same time period. They argue that this outcome is likely because intellectual property protections enticed private sector investments in improving GE crops and hybrid crops, whereas the private sector considered open-pollinated crops to be a risky investment. By contrast, Germany has banned GE crops, even though it does have hybrid maize. Germany had modest increases in multiple crops, including wheat. They argue that this is likely because Germany emphasises the enhancement of public goods, even from research that is conducted in the private sector.

This outcome raises concerns because it indicates that, in the absence of strong government policies to promote public-goods research, the private sector tends to invest in research that yields private goods. However, there are many food and agricultural problems, including concerns over water management and environmental protection, for which privatisation is not conducive to generating a solution. Glenna, Shortall and Brandl (2015) conclude, therefore, that many agri-food challenges require public-goods research and that the increasing emphasis on private goods may inhibit the broad innovations needed to address global agricultural and food problems.

A second problem related to the increasing reliance on private sector research funding and the trend in generating more private goods is that intellectual property protections may restrict agricultural research at universities and, therefore, may be stifling agricultural innovations (Glenna, Tooker, Welsh and Ervin, 2015). In the USA, where GE crops are widespread, a group of public sector entomologists submitted two letters in 2009 to the Environmental Protection Agency claiming that intellectual property restrictions were preventing them from doing research on the efficacy and environmental impacts of GE crops. Glenna, Tooker, Welsh and Ervin (2015) conducted a survey of those entomologists and found that 31% claimed that their research had been hindered by an industry partner; and nearly 59% said that there is research on the efficacy or environmental impacts on GE crops that they would like to conduct, if it were not for the intellectual property restrictions that prevented such research. One respondent reported that research findings were suppressed. The authors conclude that there is conflict between public and private sector scientists, that current policy arrangements have not removed obstacles to undertaking important research, and that the integrity of the regulatory review process may even be in question. Moreover, they claim that these findings support arguments that strict intellectual property protections are hindering innovation (Glenna, Tooker, Welsh and Ervin, 2015).

There are limits to the generalisability of the entomologist study. First, it was a small sample. Second, the sample focused exclusively on entomologists who do applied research.

However, their findings support those from other research. For example, Lei, Juneja and Wright (2009, p. 36) found in a survey of agricultural biologists in the University of California system that a majority of the scientists concluded 'that patenting impedes the progress of research'. In the same vein, Schimmelpfennig, Pray and Brennan (2004) found that concentration in the seed industry has been linked to a reduction in research intensity in the agricultural biotechnology field.

Glenna and Cahoy (2009) explain that, since GE crop research expanded in the 1980s, 37 companies have secured patents on GE corn and 118 companies have secured patents on non-corn GE crops. However, through buyouts and strategic alliances, just three companies now control 85% of patents on GE corn, and just three companies control nearly 70% of patents on non-corn GE crops (Glenna & Cahoy, 2009, p. 122). These findings raise questions about how competitive the market is for agricultural seeds. The findings also lend support to the claims that strict intellectual property protections are inhibiting innovation, since concentration in the seed industry is likely to enhance the power of the large seed companies, which they can use to control the types of research that university scientists are able to conduct.

Political economy of agricultural research in developing nations

As noted at the beginning of this chapter, promoting increases in agricultural production has been a preoccupation of many agricultural science and technology programmes. Specifically, the emphasis on agricultural productivity in developing countries at the international level came by way of the Consultative Group on International Agricultural Research (CGIAR), which evolved into several commodity-specific affiliated research programmes, including the International Rice Research Institute (IRRI), International Centre for the Improvement of Maize and Wheat (CIMMYT) and later the International Livestock Research Institute (ILRI). From the outset CGIAR grew out of the partnerships created during the development of the Green Revolution, particularly between the Mexican Ministry of Agriculture, the Rockefeller Foundation and the Ford Foundation (Shaw, 2009).

Officially founded in 1971, CGIAR's focus was on increasing production of staple foods, with an implicit goal of focusing on the production of international public goods that 'are non-exclusive in access and non-rival in use, and have widespread applicability beyond national boundaries' (Shaw, 2009, p. 88). A large part of CGIAR's work has focused on improved crop varieties. The mandate has shifted noticeably over the past 40 years, moving from solely focusing on food production to focusing on the environment, biodiversity and policy improvement. Shaw (2009, p. 93) also maintains that funding to CGIAR is increasingly restricted, meaning donors limit how and where the money can be spent, a situation that 'threatens the integrity and functioning' of CGIAR as a system for coordinating research and funding. CGIAR funding continues to be dominated by the industrialised countries. The developing nations that stand to gain the most from CGIAR research contribute only 5% of the budget, which in its entirety stood at approximately US$430 billion in 2006 (Shaw, 2009, p. 92). Thus, despite being the intended target of agricultural research, CGIAR is not financed or managed primarily by these countries. In addition, CGIAR recognises the limited pace and scale at which the outcomes of their research have been adopted by farmers. They are now working with private foundations, including Gates and Rockefeller, to increase the dissemination of their work. However, the influence of private philanthropists is not without its downsides. The Gates Foundation is third only to the USA and the World Bank in financial contributions to the CGIAR. By emphasising high-technology and private sector solutions, Glenna, Brandl and Jones (2015) argue, the Gates Foundation's impact on the

CGIAR research agenda is similar to the impact that private firms are having on public sector research organisations in OECD nations.

At the national level, with heavy influence from development programmes emanating from industrialised countries, especially the United States, most developing countries have some type of National Agricultural Research Institute (NARI). However, these publicly funded agricultural research and development institutions, along with agricultural extension and investment in production systems, have experienced a general weakening since the 1970s (Collinson, 2001; Pretty, Toulmin & Williams, 2011). NARIs, like the CGIAR consortium, have historically been commodity focused and discipline based in their research agendas (Collinson, 2001). In addition, much of the university agricultural curriculum and education and, by association, agricultural extension services, has been based on a Western curriculum which, many argue, fails to be relevant to the context of developing countries, particularly for smallholder farmers. This is because smallholders tend to operate multi-enterprise systems, with no one commodity being the primary focus (Collinson, 2001). When agricultural research and extension focus solely upon one commodity (such as rice or wheat or milk), the real needs of smallholders – to manage a variety of commodities – is largely ignored.

Smallholders and agricultural science and technology

Focusing on smallholder farmers, whether in industrialised or developing nations, is important because they continue to represent the vast majority of farm producers. According to an analysis by the United States Census of Agriculture, around 12% of large farms (annual sales exceeding US$250,000) account for 84% of the value of agricultural production (Hoppe & Banker, 2010, p. iv). However, that means that there are still approximately 1.5 million small and medium-sized farmers in the USA. Although these farmers may not be making substantial contributions to overall production, Lobao and Meyer (2004) contend that, for these smaller operators, farming still accounts for a substantial portion of their household livelihood strategy. In other words, when agricultural research and development focuses on high-technology and market-based approaches to increasing productivity, it may be ignoring the specific needs of farmers who still provide important social and economic contributions.

Smallholders are located throughout the world and, in fact, smallholders have actually increased in the past few decades in both industrialised and developing nations (Van der Ploeg, 2008). Van der Ploeg (2008) admonishes much of the existing literature for separating peasants into two geographical categories – industrialised and developing countries – and then applying different theories and concepts to these two groups. Despite this rebuke, much of the recent literature focuses on Asia and the Pacific, or Africa. In part, this is because some 90% of the world's one billion global poor live on small farms (Birner & Resnick, 2010, p. 1442) and are largely located in developing countries. For example, it is estimated that about 87% of the world's 500 million small farms (less than 2 ha) are in Asia and the Pacific region (Thapa, 2009, p. 1). In Africa, agriculture accounts for 65% of full-time employment, 25–30% of GDP and over half of total export earnings (IFPRI, 2004, p. 2), and it underpins the livelihoods of over two-thirds of Africa's poor (Pretty, Toulmin & Williams, 2011). Thus, when discussing the tensions and contradictions surrounding smallholders and agricultural science and technology, much, though not all, of our discussion is limited to smallholders in developing countries.

While the conventional definition of 'smallholder' in developing nations is farming less than 2 hectares of land (Hazell, Poulton, Wiggins & Dorward, 2007), other definitions of smallholders extend to farmers with limited resources, including capital, labour and skills. This is important to bear in mind in terms of thinking about the relevance of agricultural science and technology. Smallholders generally feed their households and, to varying degrees, may sell a portion of their production in the marketplace. Despite the broad application of the label, smallholders represent a diverse group, with some evidence of growing disparities between smallholders in terms of land and asset holdings (Jayne, Mather & Mghenyi, 2010; Ransom, 2015).

Smallholder is, of course, a contested category. Many view smallholders as an obstacle to change and predict they will disappear as economic development accelerates (see Collier & Dercon, 2014). Others view smallholders as providing abundant opportunities, particularly in terms of environmental sustainability and economic opportunity (Van der Ploeg, 2008; Pretty, Toulmin & Williams, 2011). Our interests are less in debating the role of smallholders and more in recognising how the new trends in agricultural research and development are failing to meet the needs of a large number of farmers in the world. Generally, high-technology solutions being developed in the private sector, such as new biotechnologies, are unlikely to benefit smallholders. Thapa (2009) observes that the development of private GE crops is generally disadvantageous to small farmers because private research companies lack incentives to address small farmers' concerns. Similarly, Muzari, Gatsi and Muvhunzi (2012) argue that some of the most important crop improvements that need to happen for smallholders are 'in situ' (i.e., in the field) where interbreeding of traditional crops with varieties that have improved characteristics would be beneficial. But the authors observe there is little to no interest from commercial seed enterprises in such research and development, because the profits are too low, even though this could improve productivity for smallholders (Muzari, Gatsi & Muvhunzi, 2012, p. 75).

Of those interested in the role smallholders could play in creating a more sustainable agri-food system, there are several who believe in the opportunity to create sustainable or agro-ecological intensification (Pretty, Toulmin & Williams, 2011; Nelson & Coe, 2014). For example, in a study of rice production in northern Ghana, Glenna et al. (2012) found that, given the right policies to provide inputs and guaranteed markets, smallholder rice farmers were able to dramatically improve rice yields using conventionally improved rice varieties. They also note that such efforts to enhance productivity of smallholders were being hampered by World Bank policies that discourage public investments aimed at supporting smallholder farms.

Gender and agricultural science and technology

Alongside the continuing presence of smallholders has been the so-called feminisation of agriculture. Women in low-income countries have typically been involved in a range of livelihood strategies that include growing, processing and preparing food (Ransom, Wright & Bain, forthcoming). However, these roles are also changing as social and economic forces transform the agricultural sector in many places. Agriculture is becoming feminised, especially in sub-Saharan Africa, where women are increasingly responsible for the farm as men exit from the sector to migrate to urban areas in search of paid work, or as a result of involvement in civil wars and conflicts, or deaths and illnesses from HIV/AIDS. Meinzen-Dick et al. (2011) have highlighted that, despite the fact that women play a central role in food production in most developing countries, only one in four agricultural researchers in sub-Saharan Africa and one in three in Latin America are female. The authors elaborate that, although male researchers can address the needs of women farmers, 'the lack of gender balance among agricultural scientists diminishes the likelihood that the specific needs of rural women will be met' (Meinzen-Dick et al., 2011, p. 49). This lack also means that 'women's voices are less heard in critical, often male-dominated, policy debates and decision making processes' (p. 50).

The feminisation of agriculture is also relevant to the topic of technology adoption. Agricultural technologies that were created, but never adopted, litter the agricultural development landscape. There is a long line of technologies that were either not perceived as appropriate by smallholders and/or the policies that were needed to support adoption were never implemented (Birner & Resnick, 2010; Muzari, Gatsi & Muvhunzi, 2012). There has been a renewed focus on agricultural development in the past decade, and with this focus has come renewed attention to the factors that facilitate technology adoption among smallholders. Factors affecting technology adoption include assets, vulnerability and institutions. Generally, smallholders with limited material and non-material (e.g., education) assets will be less likely to adopt asset-intensive technologies. So, for the poorest farmers, technologies with low-asset requirements are more likely to be adopted (Muzari, Gatsi & Muvhunzi, 2012). A high degree of vulnerability is identified among smallholders because they have very little protection from climatic or market fluctuations. Generally, this means technologies should be perceived by smallholders as low risk (Collison, 2001; Muzari, Gatsi & Muvhunzi, 2012). Finally, an assortment of institutions, including financial, insurance and information dissemination, are viewed as important, but historically absent or ineffectual at working with smallholders in developing countries. Many of these institutions also have a history of gender bias, primarily only willing to work with men, which is problematic as more and more women can be identified as smallholders (Doss, 2001). Moreover, government policies and investment, particularly in Africa, have increasingly come under scrutiny. On average, African countries spend 4–5% of national budgets on agriculture, compared to 8–14% in Asia (Fan, Johnson, Saurkar & Makombo, 2008, p. 2).

Conclusion

Scientific research and technology have made great contributions to agricultural productivity gains over the last century. Yet, these gains have come with costs, most notably social and economic inequality and ecological problems. These outcomes have led some commentators to highlight the contradictions and tensions of relying on scientific research and new technologies to solve productivity problems while paying too little attention to questions of equity and ecological sustainability. Although the productivist approach has never been free of challenges, recent shifts in the political economy of agricultural science have served to exacerbate some of those underlying and persistent tensions and contradictions.

In general, the share of private funding for agri-food research and development in industrialised and developing nations has grown in relation to public funding. Although there are benefits to having more investments from firms and private philanthropists in research, these investments tend to be directed at securing private goods at the expense of public goods and favour larger commodity producers and market-based approaches over smallholders and collective agro-ecological approaches. As a result, research agendas directed at generating scientific knowledge and technologies more appropriate to smallholder farmers in industrialised and developing nations tend to be underfunded. These missed opportunities may be undermining smallholders' abilities to meet their own needs and to produce a sufficient and sustainable food supply for their nations and the world.

References

Alston, JM, Andersen, MA, James, JS & Pardey, P (2010). *Persistence pays: US agricultural productivity growth and the benefits from public R&D spending*. New York: Springer.

Araghi, F (2000). The great global enclosure of our times: Peasants and the agrarian question at the end of the twentieth century. In F Magdoff, JB Foster & FH Buttel (Eds), *Hungry for profit* (pp. 145–160). New York: Monthly Review.

Berlan, JP & Lewontin, R (1986). The political economy of hybrid corn. *Monthly Review* 38, 35–47.

Birner, R & Resnick, D (2010). The political economy of policies for smallholder agriculture. *World Development* 38(10), 1442–1452.

Block, F (2011). Innovation and the invisible hand of government. In F Block & MR Keller (Eds), *State of innovation: The US government's role in technology development* (pp. 1–26). Boulder, CO: Paradigm.

Busch, L, Lacy, WB, Burkhardt, J & Lacy, LR (1991). *Plants, power and profit: Social economic, and ethical consequences of the new biotechnologies.* Oxford: Basil Blackwell.

Collier, P & Dercon, S (2014). African agriculture in 50 years: Smallholders in a rapidly changing world? *World Development* 63, 92–101.

Collinson, M (2001). Institutional and professional obstacles to a more effective research process for smallholder agriculture. *Agricultural Systems* 69, 27–36.

Dimitri, C, Effland, A & Concklin, N (2005). *The 20th century transformation of US agriculture and farm policy.* Washington, DC: USDA/ERS.

Doss, C (2001). Designing agricultural technology for African women farmers: Lessons from 25 years of experience. *World Development* 29, 2075–2092.

Evenson, RE & Gollin, D (2003). Assessing the impact of the Green Revolution. *Science* 300(5620), 758–762.

Fan, S, Johnson, M, Saurkar, A & Makombo, T (2008). *Investing in Africa to halve poverty by 2015.* IFPRI Discussion Paper 751. Washington: International Food Policy Research Institute.

Fuglie, K, Heisey, P, King, J, Pray, CE & Schimmelpfennig, D (2012). The contribution of private industry to agricultural innovation. *Science* 338(6110), 1031–1032.

Fuglie, KO & Toole, AA (2014). The evolving institutional structure of public and private agricultural research. *American Journal of Agricultural Economics* 96(3), 862–883.

Glenna, L, Ader, D, Bauchspies, W, Traoré, A & Agboh-Noameshie, RA (2012). The efficacy of a program promoting rice self-sufficiency in Ghana during a period of neoliberalism. *Rural Sociology* 77(4), 520–546.

Glenna, L, Brandl, B & Jones, K (2015). International political economy of agricultural research and development. In A Bonanno & L Busch (Eds), *Handbook of international political economy of agriculture and food* (pp. 322–343). Cheltenham: Edward Elgar.

Glenna, L & Cahoy, DR (2009). Agribusiness concentration, intellectual property, and the prospects for rural economic benefits from the emerging biofuel economy. *Southern Rural Sociology* 24(2), 111–129.

Glenna, L & Henke, CR (2014). Agricultural technologies and the structure of the North American agrifood system. In C Bailey, L Jensen & E Ransom (Eds), *Rural America in a globalizing world: Problems and prospects for the 2010s* (pp. 85–102). Morgantown, WV: West Virginia University Press.

Glenna, L, Lacy, LB, Welsh, R & Biscotti, D (2007). University administrators, agricultural biotechnology, and academic capitalism: Defining the public good to promote university–industry relationships. *Sociological Quarterly* 48(1), 141–164.

Glenna, L, Shortall, S & Brandl, B (2015). The university, public goods, and food and agricultural innovation. *Sociologia Ruralis* 55(4).

Glenna, L, Tooker, J, Welsh, R & Ervin, D (2015). Intellectual property, scientific independence, and the efficacy and environmental impacts of genetically engineered crops. *Rural Sociology* 80(2), 147–172.

Griliches, Z (1957). Hybrid corn: An exploration in the economics of technological change. *Econometrica* 25, 501–522.

Hazell, P, Poulton, C, Wiggins, S & Dorward, A (2007). *The future of small farms for poverty reduction and growth.* Washington, DC: International Food Policy Research Institute.

Hoppe, RA & Banker, DE (2010). *Structure and finances of US farms: Family farm report, 2010 edition.* Washington, DC: United States Department of Agriculture Economic Research Service.

IFPRI (2004). *Ending hunger in Africa: Prospects for the small farmer.* Washington, DC: International Food Policy Research Institute.

Jayne, TS, Mather, D & Mghenyi, E (2010). Principal challenges confronting smallholder agriculture in sub-Saharan Africa. *World Development* 38(10), 1384–1398.

Kloppenburg, Jr, JR (2004). *First the seed: The political economy of plant biotechnology: 1942 to 2000.* Madison: University of Wisconsin Press.

Lacy, W, Glenna, L, Biscotti, D, Welsh, R & Clancy, K (2014). The two cultures of science: Implications for university–industry relationships in US agriculture biotechnology. *Journal of Integrative Agriculture* 12(1), 60345–60347.

Lei, Z, Juneja, R & Wright, BD (2009). Patents versus patenting: Implications of Intellectual property protection for biological research. *Nature Biotechnology* 27(1), 36–40.

Lobao, L & Meyer, K (2004). The power of farming without the farmers. *Contexts* 3(Fall), 12–21.

Meinzen-Dick, RQ, Quisumbing, A, Behrman, J, Biermayer-Jenzano, P, Noordeloos, M, Ragasa, C & Beintema, N (2011). *Engendering agricultural research, development, and extension*. Washington, DC: International Food Policy Research Institute.

Muzari, W, Gatsi, W & Muvhunzi, S (2012). The impacts of technology adoption on smallholder agricultural productivity in sub-Saharan Africa: A review. *Journal of Sustainable Development* 5(8), 69–77.

Nelson, R & Coe, R (2014). Transforming research and development practice to support agroecological intensification of smallholder farming. *Journal of International Affairs* 67.

OECD (2003). *Turning science into business: Patenting and licensing at public research organisations*. Paris: OECD.

Pingali, P (2012). Green Revolution: Impacts, limits, and the path ahead. *Proceedings of the National Academy of Sciences* 109(31): 12302–12308.

Potter, C & Burney, J (2002). Agricultural multifunctionality in the WTO: Legitimate non-trade concern or disguised protectionism? *Journal of Rural Studies* 18(1), 35–47.

Pretty, J, Toulmin, C & Williams, S (2011). Sustainable intensification in African agriculture. *International Journal of Agricultural Sustainability* 9(1), 5–24.

Ramey, EA (2010). Seeds of change: Hybrid corn, monopoly, and the hunt for superprofits. *Review of Radical Political Economics* 42(3), 381–386.

Ransom, E (2015). The political economy of agriculture in southern Africa. In A Bonanno & L Busch (Eds), *The handbook of international political economy of agriculture and food* (pp. 19–39). Cheltenham: Edward Elgar.

Ransom, E, Wright, W & Bain, C (forthcoming). Female farming systems. In N Naples (Ed.), *The Wiley-Blackwell encyclopedia of gender and sexuality studies*. Hoboken, NJ: Wiley-Blackwell.

Schimmelpfennig, D, Pray, C & Brennan, M (2004). The impact of seed industry concentration on innovation: A study of US biotech market leaders. *Agricultural Economics* 30(2), 157–167.

Shaw, J (2009). *Global food and agricultural institutions*. New York: Routledge.

Stanton, BF (1998). Agriculture: Crops, livestock, and farmers. In R Bulliet (Ed.), *The Columbia history of the 20th Century* (pp. 345–380). New York: Columbia University Press.

Thapa, G (2009). *Smallholder farming in transforming economies of Asia and the Pacific: Challenges and opportunities*. Thirty-third session of IFAD's Governing Council. Rome: International Fund for Agricultural Development.

Van der Ploeg, JD (2009). *The new peasantries: Struggles for autonomy and sustainability in an era of empire and globalization*. London: Earthscan.

Van der Ploeg, JD J& Douwe, J (2008). *The new peasantries: Struggles for autonomy and sustainability in an era of empire and globalization*. London: Earthscan.

21

Food Systems Failure
Can We Avert Future Crises?

Kiah Smith

Introduction

This chapter charts the growing awareness – within academia, policy making and wider society – of the systemic failures and structural inequalities of the current global food system, and of the potential for a fundamental shift towards a more just and secure food future for all. The food crisis of 2008 is understood here as a defining moment in the coalescence of multiple social, environmental and political failures of a global food system based on industrial agriculture, neoliberal economic and trade policy regimes, and a host of new (and not-so-new) global structural conditions (globalisation, industrialisation/productivism, corporatisation, marketisation and financialisation). Instead of 'feeding the world' as promised, producing *more* food through Green Revolution technologies and Green Growth policies has not solved the underlying problems of inequitable access, rising costs, over-reliance on fossil fuels, poor labour conditions, insufficient nutrition, and distorted trade relations. Food insecurity, hunger and malnutrition have increased; rural poverty persists; livelihood options for the rural poor have decreased; and environmental degradation linked to unsustainable food production and consumption practices shows few signs of slowing. These problems are exacerbated in the context of increasing global population growth, decreasing productivity levels in many key agricultural regions, and the uneven distribution of climate change impacts. In contrast to the continued emphasis on increasing food production (itself a contested assessment of the food security dilemma), more critical analyses of power and agency, participation, rights, democracy and governance have highlighted the complex relationships between food system inequalities and the failure to solve the problem of global hunger.

The global food crisis of 2008 has also provided a catalyst for dissent and convergence. Global policy makers at the highest level are beginning to recognise the possibility that multiple, interconnected *crises* are symptomatic of our failure to shift towards a more holistic food model in which small-scale farmers and agro-ecological systems are supported, and where the negative health, poverty and justice implications of continuing with 'business as usual' are addressed. Parallel to this is an unprecedented upsurge of civic mobilisation and resistance to entrenched food politics, worldwide, leading the push for alternatives. Rural peasant movements for food sovereignty and agrarian reform in the global south (and increasingly in the north), ethical production and consumption models (such as fair trade), civic food networks, agro-ecology and 'climate smart' agriculture, and advances in the 'right to food' have not only raised the profile of food justice as a key component of food security discourse, but have also raised questions about the incipient processes of social and political transformation needed to avert future food crises. What solutions do these emergent trends present for reimagining our socio-ecological relationships with food, and what challenges do they present for food system governance?

The chapter explores the contours of current food system failure yet concludes, optimistically, that despite persistent structural challenges inherent in the corporate food regime, creative proposals exist for reorienting the global food system towards justice (and food security) for people and for the restoration of balance in ecological systems. These provide strong foundations upon which a more 'just' food system might be built.

Food systems in crisis

The food price crisis of 2008 has been variously described as a temporary 'blip', a reflection of structural conditions or as a 'harbinger' of greater challenges to come (Rosin, Campbell & Stock, 2012, p. 2). The die-hard supporters of corporate neoliberalism nothwithstanding, the 2008 crisis demonstrated the vulnerability, uncertainty and lack of resilience of a global food system that is failing both humanity and the environment.

Evidence of inequality

The UN Food and Agriculture Organization (FAO) defines food security as existing 'when all people at all times have physical or economic access to sufficient safe and nutritious food to meet their dietary needs and food preferences for an active and healthy life' (FAO, 2009, p. 8). Food security is commonly broken down into five components: *availability*, *accessibility*, *acceptability*, *adequacy* and *stability*. Food insecurity occurs when any of the five aspects is threatened. for example, if food is unavailable, unaffordable or if people are not healthy enough to make use of it. But despite six decades of explicit 'food security' agendas, approximately one in nine people (that is, some 805 million) remain food insecure globally (FAO, IFAD & WFP, 2014). Although the actual proportion of food insecure people has fallen since 1990, experiences are uneven both across and within countries, and particular groups (such as women, children, the poor and refugees) remain disproportionately vulnerable. The Millennium Development Goal to halve the proportion of people who suffer from hunger globally was not met by 2015. This is despite the fact that the global food system produced 17% more calories per person at the turn of the century than it did 30 years earlier (and in spite of a 70% increase in population) (Carolan, 2013).

The food crisis (followed almost immediately by the global financial crisis of 2009) was indicative of deep structural inequalities in the way food is produced, traded, financed, governed and consumed. Evidence of injustice within the current food system abounds:

- The overwhelming majority of the world's hungry – some 95% – live in the global south, with three-quarters living in rural areas.
- In some countries, up to 70% of the adult population is either obese or overweight.
- Women farmers provide 40–80% of agricultural labour, but only 10–20% of landholders are women, only 5% of women have access to agricultural extension services, and they receive just 7% of the investment provided for farming.
- Of the global grain supply, 40%, or 650 million tonnes, feeds livestock. This is enough grain to feed over 3.5 billion people.

- Agribusinesses Monsanto, DuPont and Syngenta control half the world's commercial seed and pesticide supply.
- Roughly one-third of food produced – 1.3 billion tonnes per year – is lost or wasted globally.
- In 2008, an estimated 20 million people were displaced or evacuated because of climate-related disasters; over the last 30 years, more than 2 billion people have been affected by droughts and storms.

(ETC Group, 2009; FAO, 2013; FAO/MICCA, 2014; UN General Assembly, 2014)

Concerns have also emerged around the social impacts of transgenic crops and biofuels, migrant and women's labour issues, violence and oppression, farmer suicides, indigenous rights, and unequal access to land, food, water and biodiversity which further exacerbate discrimination, unemployment, malnutrition and poverty. The gendered nature of food system inequalities is substantial (Agarwal, 2011). Injustice in the global food system is especially obvious when considering shifting patterns of: (a) malnutrition; (b) de-peasantisation; and (c) environmental degradation.

As food prices have increased, a general trend has been for consumers to turn to cheaper foods – often processed foods high in oil, sugar, fat and salt. This has occurred alongside a 'nutrition transition' from staple grains to meat- and dairy-based diets, particularly in countries with growing middle classes, such as India and China. The health implications of heavily meat-based diets have come under increased scrutiny, and high oil/fat/sugar/salt foods have been found to be associated with excessive weight gain, obesity, diabetes, cancer, allergies, poisoning and death. Today, 70% of North Americans are either overweight or obese, compared to the world average of 34% (FAO, 2013, p. 17). Such 'over-nutrition' contrasts starkly with the experiences of malnutrition, under-nutrition and 'hidden hunger' in other places and for other social groups. For example, in the global north, 'food deserts' have emerged where people with low incomes cannot access fresh foods, as these have been replaced by the 'empty calories' provided by supermarket ready-meals and fast-food restaurants (Wrigley, 2002). Hidden hunger – deficiencies in essential micronutrients, such as iron, vitamin A and zinc – affected more than 2 billion people globally in 2013, including 162 million children (or 25% of all children under 5 years old). This proportion rises to 38% of children under 5 in sub-Saharan Africa and South Asia (IFPRI, 2014). When data on hunger, micronutrient deficiency and obesity are combined, at least half of the world's population (that is, some 3.3 billion people) are poorly served by the current food system, in comparison to the 3.3 billion who are adequately nourished (ETC Group, 2009, p. 3).

A second major driver of inequality is de-peasantisation (or de-agrarianisation). This occurs when smallholder or family farmers are displaced from their farms as a consequence of accumulated debts incurred as they have attempted to shift into a more 'advanced' (read: Green Revolution) form of agriculture (Lawrence, Lyons & Wallington, 2010, p. 4). Producers who were once self-sufficient have become net importers of food. This has led to extensive rural–urban migration, increased off-farm income generation, growing export-oriented agriculture and diversification into high-value horticulture at the expense of local food security. This is confounded by other livelihood pressures on rural food producers, such as declining yields, increasing costs of agricultural inputs, exclusionary 'good agricultural practice' standards, rising household expenditures (health care, education etc.), ageing rural populations and precarious rural livelihoods in general. It has been predicted that by 2050, at least 1.3 billion people will migrate (by choice or by force) from country to city, resulting in two-thirds of the world's population being urban (ETC Group, 2009). In the global north, household food security tends to take a back seat to national food self-sufficiency goals. The importance of access to land as the main source of rural livelihood declines, and family farming becomes peripheral to large-scale, corporate agriculture. In the global south, rural food producers are replacing traditional crops such as sorghum and millet to grow wheat, rice, soy or corn (staples for the food manufacturing industry) or high-value horticultural products (such as baby vegetables or flowers) for export to rich countries. While some rural peasants benefit economically (they may have increased incomes from their participation in international markets), others do not fare so well (Smith, 2014). They suffer as national agricultures weaken and household debts increase (Neilsen & Arifin, 2012) and as agriculture and trade policy become more oriented towards meeting the demands of already well-fed consumers in other parts of the world (Lawrence, Lyons & Wallington, 2010).

This 'agrarian transition' may be seen as a natural structural consequence associated with the consolidation of small farms into larger, more labour-efficient and more productive ones: part of the broader trend towards decentralisation under neoliberal 'structural adjustment' trade policies that 'delink' rural livelihoods and poverty alleviation from agriculture (Neilson & Arifin, 2012). It can also be viewed as the centralisation of corporate agribusiness and private entrepreneurs linked in global value chains (McMichael, 2012, p. 72). A 'new rurality' has emerged in which rural households and agrarian livelihoods have not disappeared, but have 'hybridised' and diversified, blurring traditional boundaries between urban and rural (Fairbairn et al., 2014, p. 659). A more critical perspective is that global value chains increasingly draw farmers into competitive markets, contract labour arrangements, increasing debt and dependence on agri-industrial inputs, which is a catalyst in the displacement of small-scale, diversified agricultural systems and the rural communities they traditionally support.

Finally, there is mounting scientific and civic consensus that the food system is failing the environment. For Lang (2010), climate change, water, biodiversity and ecosystems support, energy and non-renewable fossil fuels have combined with population growth, waste, land, soil, labour and public health issues to represent a set of 'new fundamentals' affecting food policy making. The urgency of addressing climate change undercuts many of these; there is widespread consensus that more frequent climate-related disasters, changing weather patterns and new levels of pests and diseases will dramatically impact upon food production, human health, livelihoods and food security, especially for those already most vulnerable. Other indicators of environmental stress with implications for both rural communities and food systems include:

- desertification, salinity, and depleting water tables linked to over-irrigation;
- declining capacity of soils to provide essential ecosystem services;
- decline of coral reefs linked to excessive fertiliser run-off;
- rapid loss of native forest cover to biofuels and/or beef farming;
- loss of agricultural and dietary biodiversity resulting from industrial monocultures;
- overfishing, depleting fish stocks and loss of ocean biodiversity;
- pollution, health risks and animal rights concerns arising from factory farming;
- peak oil, peak phosphorus, peak nitrogen;
- risks to genetic and ecological diversity associated with GMOs and transgenic crops;
- high carbon emissions from agricultural reliance on non-renewable fossil fuels;
- land use competition between biofuels, food crops and renewable energies.

(FAO, 2009; Cribb, 2010; Ingram, Ericksen & Liverman, 2010;
Lawrence, Lyons & Wallington, 2010; UN General Assembly, 2014)

The structural basis of food system inequality

The drivers of these structural inequalities are widely debated. Dominant food crisis discourses often place blame on the demand-side of the global food system including the growing demand for grain for biofuel production in response to depleting fossil fuel resources, rapid population growth, changing middle-class diets, accelerating urbanisation, and increased imports into countries of the global south. These represent production-centric challenges that are largely surmountable by improving technological efficiency. Others argue that supply-side effects – such as the impact of climate change and extreme weather events on reducing food production capacity, the lack of investment in agricultural science, diminishing productivity gains, distorted food and labour markets, increasing costs of fossil fuel-based agricultural inputs, and increased environmental degradation – can be mitigated by increasing investment in agricultural infrastructure, mainly by established corporate, financial and agri-food institutions (Rosin, Campbell & Stock, 2012). Both supply and demand challenges can be also addressed through the 'greening' of agricultural and trade policy (such as the OECD's Strategy for Green Growth) and regulatory infrastructure to support green and ethical production–consumption shifts (such as the UN's Global Compact). International food aid also continues as a key food security strategy, despite governance inconsistencies between the global institutions responsible for its regulation (Pritchard, 2012).

Underpinning each of these suggestions, however, is: (a) framing food security as an issue of calories, and thus, production; (b) continued emphasis on industrial and export-oriented agriculture as the solution to food security; (c) the expectation that market signals will push corporate or financial involvement in food and labour markets in a more sustainable direction; and (d) belief in the 'technological fix'. This is in line with the paradigm of productivism that has underpinned global agriculture since at least the beginning of the second food regime (1940s), when the market vision of food security became thoroughly entwined with Green Revolution technologies, the deregulation of agricultural commodities, and food aid (McMichael, 2013). It is also thoroughly entrenched in the key tenets of neoliberal globalisation – getting prices 'right' via the market, private property rights, trade liberalisation, government deregulation, dismantling tariff barriers and reduced public investment (Rao, 2009, p. 1280). One outcome has been the rapid financialisation of the global food system, as new markets have emerged where none existed previously (i.e., biofuels such as ethanol and bio-diesel, to replace fossil fuels). Defined as the increasing power of financial markets, financial motives, financial institutions and financial elites in global governance, this has increased the number and type of actors involved in global agricultural commodity chains and has abstracted food into highly complex agricultural commodity derivatives (Clapp, 2014). This has been understood, by critical scholars, as being an outcome of an inherently unjust corporate food regime, and a consequence of neoliberal globalisation and the accumulation crisis of capitalism (McMichael, 2013).

Unfortunately, neoliberal trade policy and industrial agriculture have not succeeded in feeding the world. Instead, they have contributed to the corporatisation, privatisation, monopolisation, consolidation, concentration and 'supermarketisation' of the food system (Burch & Lawrence, 2007; Dixon & Banwell, this volume), with detrimental effects on people and the environment. Market solutions have been widely criticised for their potential to mask broader socioeconomic contexts and the imbalance of power between corporations, global regulatory bodies, rural producers and urban consumers whose livelihoods and food security outcomes are impacted. For example, food price spikes have been attributed to 'speculative land appropriation' for food and fuel by new financial actors external to agriculture (Fairbairn et al., 2014, p. 656), which both: (a) reduced the amount of land available for food and livestock production, and increased costs of food and fuel; and (b) further concentrated profit in the hands of agribusiness, investors, governments and other finance actors. Critically termed 'land grabbing', these diverse forms of dispossession and 'commodification of the commons' have rapidly displaced peasants, indigenous peoples, pastoralists, fisherfolk and whole rural communities from land, forests and rivers in favour of consolidated corporate ownership (see Rosset, 2011; McMichael, 2012, 2013; Fairbairn et al., 2014).

For beneficiaries of neoliberalism, corporatisation and financialisation, the interconnected crises described above (of food, climate, fuel and finance) have strengthened the belief that the food system might recover using the same political and financial institutions that lie at the very root of the crisis. But for a rapidly growing minority, the 'business as usual' model appears to be breaking down. The disruptive structural forces of global capitalism are leading to the growing agency of rural food producers (and their supporters) to define new visions for the future of agriculture and rural communities. This is the focus of the rest of this chapter.

From crises to opportunity?

Political and civic recognition of the kinds of food system injustices described above is growing, with major implications for food system restructuring. As Lang (2010) has strongly argued, food system failure is no longer confined to agriculture, but is everywhere in the food system. Important discursive and political shifts can thus be observed from the grassroots expansion of rural peasant movements to the highest levels of food policy governance.

Oppositional movements

Opposition to food system failure takes numerous forms. The first is the emergence and consolidation of global food movements, whereby what were once marginal ideas inform new visions and practices for a more just agricultural future. The 'food riots' in over 30 countries which followed the food price spike of 2008 drew political focus to the activities and demands of more organised forms of civic mobilisations, such as peasant movements for 'food sovereignty' in the global south, and middle-class 'alter-globalisation' and 'food justice' movements in the global north (Holt-Gimenez, Patel & Shattuck, 2009). A key shift has been the participation of family farmers and consumers in the north in solidarity with southern farmers. Many of these movements combine traditionally rural concerns (such as land reform) with a broader appeal to the governance, values and ethics that connect food politics to key human development challenges (rights, empowerment, equity, fairness, knowledge and accountability, for example). That is, 'they are driven by beliefs about how food economies should function and the sense that governing authorities are not meeting their responsibilities' (Fairbairn et al., 2014, p. 658). Their arguments are strengthened by connecting food with other issues, such as climate change, debt reduction, energy, intellectual property rights, minority rights, gender equity, poverty reduction and environmental justice.

Central to many of these movements is a reassertion of smallholder or family farming as more efficient, more environmentally friendly and more socially just than productivist agriculture (Altieri, 2009; Rosset, 2011). Many movements have been instrumental in reorienting the concept of food security towards 'food sovereignty'; challenging the notion of food security divorced from where food comes from or how it is produced and, instead, emphasising the need for collective approaches, democratic control and local choice (Carolan, 2013, p. 100). As 'a movement informed by a peasant perspective underlining the importance of revaluing farming for domestic food provisioning and for addressing social inequalities', food sovereignty bridges the rural–urban divide (McMichael, 2014, p. 935). Such movements strongly reject neoliberal solutions to world hunger, and prioritise structural reform based upon:

- right to food;
- gender equity;
- redistributive land reform;
- local market access over export markets;
- relocalisation and regionalisation of food production and consumption;
- de-privatisation and de-corporatisation;
- agro-ecology and organics, ecological 'stewardship';
- fair trade;
- solidarity;
- self-sufficiency and local autonomy;
- participation and empowerment;
- collective and cooperative organisational forms;
- democratic decision making.

(Pimbert, 2009; Schanbacher, 2010; Holt-Gimenez & Shattuck, 2011)

The growing influence of these (mostly) rural food movements is both ideological and political. In contestation of neoliberalism, traditional agrarian movements have either localised their struggles in response to partial decentralisation, privatised their activities to substitute states' withdrawal from social service delivery, or internationalised in response to global restructuring (Borras, Edelman & Kay, 2008). Some movements are involved in dramatic anti-corporate actions, while others negotiate with the FAO, IFAD (International Fund for Agricultural Development) and UNHCR (UN High Commissioner for Refugees). La Via Campesina – a global alliance of family farmers, peasants, the landless, rural youth and rural women – has been especially successful in this regard, although numerous challenges remain (see McMichael, 2014). Thus, both the increasing uptake of rural concerns by key political actors in the north and the formation of new coalitions between civic and other (e.g., government, intergovernmental, business) actors (both north and south) constitute a central element shaping the dynamics of food regime restructuring today.

A second key shift has been towards 'progressive' food networks, which are 'possibly the largest and fastest growing grassroots expression of the food movement' (Holt-Gimenez & Shattuck, 2011, p. 115). These include initiatives focused on: (a) restructuring global trade relations, via Fair Trade; (b) improving corporate social responsibility and accountability, such as addressing labour rights via the UK's Ethical Trading Initiative; (c) improving ecological aspects of food production, via organics, agro-ecology and, more recently, 'climate-smart agriculture'; (d) promoting rural–urban links, via urban gardens and community-supported agriculture; and (e) enhancing pleasure or place, via Slow Food and local food networks. These initiatives are largely driven by the rise of ethical consumption in the north (reflecting the 'quality' turn in mainstream food systems) and they are mostly middle class and youth oriented (Goodman, DuPuis & Goodman, 2014). Nutrition and food safety concerns are central and distinct middle-class concerns; this is reflected in the willingness of consumers to pay the higher costs of food produced 'ethically' under such initiatives, and in the highly regulated (albeit voluntary) nature of their institutional forms. In urban settings, their focus is often on local or regional inequalities attributed to the interplay of race, ethnicity, location, social exclusion and poverty. Rural producers are brought into such networks largely to reduce 'food miles' from long-distance food transport, and urban citizens become producers themselves. This contrasts with the processes of distancing (between producer/consumer, commodity/food) associated with financialisation (Clapp, 2014). Like their radical (and more rural) counterparts, these movements reflect the host of new values of 'ethicality' permeating mainstream and alternative food networks today, including improved livelihoods, social justice, environmental sustainability, fairness and well-being (Smith, 2014).

Such consumer-driven movements seek to advance practical alternatives to industrial food systems largely within the framework of existing capitalist food systems, however. In general (with perhaps the exception of fair trade and agro-ecology), they are less concerned with the deeper challenge of addressing power imbalances between southern food producers and northern consumers, and more concerned with creating economically viable, multi-stakeholder business models, or 'markets for the poor'. Fair and ethical trade, for example, have been criticised for prioritising the ethical values of northern consumers over southern producers (and especially smallholders), who are often either excluded from ethical markets due to the high costs of accreditation or excluded from governance processes that do little to ensure their meaningful participation in decision making (Smith, 2014). This further consolidates the power of food retailers/supermarkets through increasing the vertical integration of global value chains, and by blending normative power (to define social and ecological values) with the institutional power to embed particular visions into market arrangements (Raynolds, 2012). Goodman and colleagues (2014) have thus warned against the tendency to romanticise local/civic food networks based on a predefined (and often, rather narrow) set of norms and values, as this can negate the diversity of local food politics/activism and open up spaces for corporate co-optation.

Despite their limits, both the radical and progressive food movements 'directly and indirectly challenge the legitimacy and hegemony of the corporate food regime' (Holt-Gimenez & Shattuck, 2011, p. 109). They deepen democracy and decrease inequality by expanding notions and practices of citizenship, and by creating more inclusive settings for multiple stakeholders to voice their concerns and to demand accountability. For example, at the Rio Conference on Sustainable Development in 2012 ('Rio+20'), the UN proposed the 'green economy' (read: the 'greening' of technology, markets and finance) as a solution to the stagnation of global progress on sustainable development and the Millennium Development Goals. The notion was so heavily contested by civic actors (as well as by some governments, especially in the south) that contestation itself became a central factor challenging the legitimacy of the green economy concept, solutions and its proponents. The People's Summit, running parallel to official UN proceedings, was one of the largest civil society gatherings to date.

Global governance

The second indication that a major paradigm shift is in progress can be seen in the elevation of 'right to food' discourse as a significant opponent to productivist interpretations of food security. The former UN Special Rapporteur on the Right to Food explains that:

> The right to food has more to do with modes of production and issues of distribution than with levels of food production alone. It primarily aims to guarantee to each person, individually or as part of a group, permanent and secure access to diets that are adequate from the nutritional point of view, sustainably produced and culturally acceptable.
>
> *(UN General Assembly, 2013, p. 4)*

The concept increasingly has 'teeth'. It has shifted from implementation in charity-based schemes to conferring legal entitlements, whereby states have legal obligations to respect,

257

protect and fulfil the right to food of their citizens. This is to be achieved through state support for self-production, access to income-generating activities for rural food producers, and state-administered or community-generated social protection mechanisms. The Right to Food has been included explicitly in the constitution of over 26 countries, with many others either in the process of doing so or including it implicitly in other policies or processes. Framework laws and national strategies in support of the progressive realisation of the right to food have also emerged – particularly in Latin America, but also in Africa (Malawi, Uganda, Senegal and Mali), Thailand and in India's recent Food Security Bill. These include mechanisms to address barriers to participation, accountability, non-discrimination, transparency, human dignity, empowerment and the rule of law which have proved major hurdles to reducing hunger and malnutrition (UN General Assembly, 2013, p. 13).

Rights-based approaches to food security necessitate major ideological and institutional change. For example, considering the discrepancy between actual food produced and the continued prevalence of hunger worldwide, Carolan (2013, pp. 2–5) has argued for expanding our definitions and measurements of food security to encompass objective and subjective measures that better reflect 'food security's original spirit' – inclusive of issues of sustainability, and individual, societal and nutritional well-being and prosperity. Evidence that a change of consciousness may be leading to political reconfigurations includes the following:

- In recognition of the crucial contribution of smallholder farming to food and nutrition security, 2014 was named the International Year of Family Farming by the FAO, highlighting the need for improved support, investment and empowerment within the smallholder sector.
- Participation by civil society organisations in agriculture, food security and nutrition policy development was formalised in 2010 within the newly formed Civil Society Mechanism (CSM) within the FAO's Committee on World Food Security (CFS). This was due in part to successful negotiations by the International Planning Committee (IPC) for Food Sovereignty (which includes civic organisations such as La Via Campesina).
- The FAO has rebranded food security as 'food and nutrition security', while 'food sovereignty' figures in key United Nations documents.
- Addressing interconnections between crisis in agriculture and food security and other global 'crises' (such as climate change, energy, poverty) informs the structure and content of emerging Sustainable Development Goals, as does the need for people-centred approaches based on principles of human rights, inclusion and accountability. The UN FAO's Right to Food unit and the Special Rapporteur on the Right to Food have been instrumental in this regard.
- New metrics for measuring progress on food security that appeal to rights, ethics and values are emerging, within the broader project of developing subjective measures of well-being beyond GDP.

Conclusion: towards a more just global food system?

Climate scientists increasingly use the metaphor of 'tipping points' to predict indicators of certain ecological demise – the point of no return – associated with climate change. This usually involves scenarios whereby an ecological process (either natural or human-made) accelerates, a critical threshold is reached, and a rapid shift in form or function proceeds with little likelihood of returning to its original state. Considering the systemic injustice within the global food system today – and the subsequent growth of concrete proposals for alternative ways of thinking, organising and governing food – is the food system on the verge of its very own tipping point?

As this chapter has described, although the contradictions of a world 'stuffed and starved' (Patel, 2007) have been relatively absent from mainstream discussions of the food crisis, this itself has influenced a strong counter-movement. Industrial, corporate, market-driven, export-oriented, high-tech approaches to feeding the world are increasingly delegitimised when 'externalities' such as malnutrition, rural dispossession from land and livelihoods, growing resource conflict, environmental unsustainability and failing corporate accountability are considered. Food justice perspectives and approaches, by contrast, acknowledge the interconnected nature of crises (food–climate–fuel–finance) and in doing so, bring questions of rights, livelihoods, entitlements, well-being, redistribution, participation and accountability centrally into dialogue with traditional concerns about agricultural production, trade and consumption. These represent competing visions for the future of food and agriculture, providing fertile ground for the contestation that defines contemporary food politics.

The food crisis of 2008 was not a temporary 'blip', but was symptomatic of system-wide structural crises indicating a need for radical transformation. This transformation needs to be structural, institutional and normative (Bello, 2013, p. 95). It is certainly under way when we consider the growing civic discontent expressed in recent social movement mobilisation, and the instances where civic actors and their demands have led to major shifts in food system governance. Still, any transformation will necessarily come with gaps, contradictions, unintended social consequences and a host of strategies that are more or less successful.

The task of creating a more just global food system remains fraught with persistent structures of state and corporate power that resist and restrict food system transformation. Despite growing social opposition to current food system dynamics, the global forces of neoliberalism, productivism, marketisation and financialisation show little signs of slowing down. The same global policy architecture that has contributed to structural inequalities in the past (that of the World Bank, IMF, WTO) continues to drive food policy-making and shape the markets-versus-rights debate, particularly in the areas of climate-smart agriculture and the green economy. Rural farmers currently manage over half of the world's arable land and mostly feed themselves, but their diverse grassroots movements struggle in contexts devoid of overarching agrarian policies. Northern consumption-based movements affect only niche segments of global food production and consumption. Still, emergent multi-stakeholder alliances, global research platforms and civic–intergovernmental coalitions indicate the potential for more equal partnerships to emerge. Whether the shift to rights-based discourse and policy is the answer remains to be seen.

Many lessons have emerged from the food crisis and food systems failure, the most significant of which may simply be found in the expansive imagination and creativity that flourishes within and around civic food movements. The challenge is to elevate the diverse understandings of 'ethicality' and 'justice' in food systems to become key drivers of fairer institutional forms and processes. This will require rural constituents and their supporters to continue to envisage and experiment with creative solutions to hunger, along with a commitment on the part of governments, international organisations, business, industry and civil society to challenge those in power who serve their own interests over those of the poor, hungry and vulnerable.

References

Agarwal, B (2011). *Food crises and gender inequality*. DESA Working Paper 107. New York: UNDESA.
Altieri, M (2009). Agroecology, small farms and food sovereignty. *Monthly Review* 61(3), 102–113.

Bello, W (2013). Post-2015 development assessment: Proposed goals and indicators. *Development* 56(1), 93–102.

Borras, Jnr, S, Edelman, M & Kay, C (2008). Transnational agrarian movements: Origins and politics, campaigns and impact. *Journal of Agrarian Change* 8(2), 169–204.

Burch, D & Lawrence, G (Eds). (2007). *Supermarkets and agri-food supply chains: Transformations in the production and consumption of foods.* Cheltenham: Edward Elgar.

Carolan, M (2013). *Reclaiming food security.* London and New York: Earthscan/Routledge.

Clapp, J (2014). Financialisation, distance and global food politics. *The Journal of Peasant Studies* 41(5), 797–814.

Cribb, J (2010). *The coming famine: The global food crisis and what we can do to avoid it.* Berkeley: University of California Press.

ETC Group (2009). Who will feed us? Questions for the food and climate crises. Available at http://www.etcgroup.org/content/who-will-feed-us (accessed 21 June 2015).

Fairbairn, M, Fox, J, Isakson, R, Levien, M, Peluso, N, Razavi, S, Scoones, I & Sivaramakrishnan, K (2014). Introduction: New directions in agrarian political economy. *The Journal of Peasant Studies* 41(5), 653–666.

FAO (2009). *Agriculture and the environmental challenges of the twenty-first century: A strategic approach for FAO.* Available at ftp://ftp.fao.org/docrep/fao/meeting/016/k4554e.pdf (accessed 10 February 2011).

FAO (2013). *State of the world food and agriculture report: Food systems for better nutrition.* Rome: FAO.

FAO, IFAD & WFP (2014). *The state of food insecurity in the world 2014: Strengthening the enabling environment for food security and nutrition.* Rome: FAO.

FAO/MICCA (2014). Equal access to resources and power for food security in the face of climate change. Available at http://www.fao.org/climatechange/38080-0e86363b233f2bd2c8dd37574ff90cc86.pdf (accessed 21 January 2015).

Goodman, D, DuPuis, M & Goodman, M (2014). *Alternative food networks: Knowledge, practice and politics.* London and New York: Routledge.

Holt-Gimenez, E, Patel, R & Shattuck, A (2009). *Food rebellions! Crisis and the hunger for justice.* Oakland, CA and Oxford: Food First and Pambazuka.

Holt-Gimenez, E & Shattuck, A (2011). Food crises, food regimes and food movements: Rumblings of reform or tides of transformation? *Journal of Peasant Studies* 38(1), 109–144.

IFPRI (2014). *2013 Global food policy report.* Washington, DC: IFPRI.

Ingram, J, Ericksen, P & Liverman, D (Eds). (2010). *Food security and global environmental change.* London: Earthscan.

Lang, T (2010). Crisis, what crisis? *Journal of Agrarian Change* 10(1), 87–97.

Lawrence, G, Lyons, K & Wallington, T (Eds). (2010). *Food security, nutrition and sustainability.* London: Earthscan.

McMichael, P (2012). Biofuels and the financialisation of the global food system. In C Rosin, H Campbell & P Stock (Eds), *Food system failure: The global food crisis and the future of agriculture* (pp. 60–82). London: Earthscan.

McMichael, P (2013). Rethinking land grab ontology. *Rural Sociology* 79(1), 34–55.

McMichael, P (2014). Historicizing food sovereignty. *Journal of Peasant Studies* 41(6), 933–957.

Neilson, J & Arifin, B (2012). Food security and the de-agrarianisation of the Indonesian economy. In C Rosin, H Campbell & P Stock (Eds), *Food system failure: The global food crisis and the future of agriculture* (pp. 147–165). London: Earthscan.

Patel, R (2007). *Stuffed and starved: Markets, power and the hidden battle over the world's food system.* London: Portobello Books.

Pimbert, M (2009). *Towards food sovereignty.* London: IIED.

Pritchard, B (2012). Trading into hunger? Trading out of hunger? International food aid and the debate on food security. In C Rosin, H Campbell & P Stock (Eds), *Food system failure: The global food crisis and the future of agriculture* (pp. 46–59). London: Earthscan.

Rao, JM (2009). Challenges facing world agriculture: A political economy perspective. *Development and Change* 40(6), 1279–1292.

Raynolds, L (2012). Fair Trade: Social regulation in global food markets. *Journal of Rural Studies* 28, 276–287.

Rosin, C, Campbell, H & Stock, P (2012). Introduction: Shocking the global food system. In C Rosin, H Campbell & P Stock (Eds), *Food system failure: The global food crisis and the future of agriculture* (pp. 1–14). London: Earthscan.

Rosset, P. (2011). Food sovereignty and alternative paradigms to confront land grabbing and the food and climate crises. *Development* 54(1), 21–30.

Schanbacher, W (2010). *The politics of food*. Santa Barbara, CA: Praeger.

Smith, K (2014). *Ethical trade, gender and sustainable livelihoods*. London: Earthscan.

UN General Assembly (2013). *Right to food: Note by the Secretary-General*. Interim Report of the Special Rapporteur on the Right to Food, Sixty-eighth session (item 69b of the provisional agenda), A/68/288, 7 August 2013.

UN General Assembly (2014). *Report of the Special Rapporteur on the right to food, Olivier de Schutter, final report: The transformative potential of the Right to Food*. Twenty-fifth session of the Human Rights Council (item 3), A/HRC/25/57, 24 January 2014.

Wrigley, N (2002). Food deserts in British cities: Policy context and research priorities. *Urban Studies* 39(11), 2029–2040.

Part IV
Environment and Resources

Section editor: Katrina Rønningen

22

Environment and Resources

New and Old Questions for Rural Landscapes

Katrina Rønningen

In this chapter, issues of environment and resource use in rural areas are examined in the light of a set of dramatic shifts in the place of the rural in the global north. These shifts are partly the result of short-term shocks arising from multiple crises accumulating since 2008 and yet are also triggered by wider shifts and challenges in the relationship between society and the environment on a planetary scale.

In arguing that we are partly turning away from a strong focus on the 'social countryside' of post-productivism and back towards what can be termed a more material countryside, this is neither a totalising nor a trivial claim. Rather, the chapter will examine three sets of dynamics that reveal the kinds of new challenges and interventions disrupting the post-productivist countryside (and its academic framings):

1   Within frameworks of policy and economic development, the secondary sector is reorienting and reframing the rural in the form of a renewed interest in the considerable economic potential locked in the bedrock and in various types of renewable energy developments. Visions of a fossil fuel-free future and climate change adaptations are partly driving the latter, interlinked with economic potentials and incentives, while the geopolitical situation is also an important driver for (shale) oil and gas extraction, mineral extraction and related developments. Within these frameworks, the rural is reoriented away from being portrayed as primarily a site of social and cultural dynamics and is being 'rematerialised' within concrete social and resource relationships.

2   There is a reconfiguring of urban–rural relationships and power (asymmetries) linked to conservation/consumption/production discourses, the role of the rural as production landscapes and worked environments, the protection of worthy cultural landscape or wilderness landscapes, particularly in light of for whom these things are designed and directed by. The situation of contested wind power developments and the re-entry of large carnivores into farmed landscapes reveal these kinds of tensions.

3   Finally, the neo-productivist turn within agriculture has been linked to responses to the 2007/2008 world food crisis, with a new focus on climate change, food security and food sovereignty issues, and the re-emergence of farmland as an asset for investment and 'land grabbing'. The chapter will touch upon the expectations for new 'bioeconomies',

particularly the way they anchor to and revalorise materials (both socioeconomic and biophysical) within ecologies and economies. The new bioeconomies have the potential to radically reframe development trajectories in rural spaces.

Each of these topics reveals both the contested politics and inequalities of rural development as well as some of the emerging environmental challenges of the 21st century.

Through these topics, the direct effects of the recent crises in the world economy can be clearly seen. In examining the recent tensions in the global north around policy paradigms of productivism, neoliberalism and multifunctionality, Almås and Campbell (2012) suggested that each of these policy paradigms is differentially confronted by new challenges to the future sustainability of agricultural policy regimes – in particular, the three recent shocks to world food production: the global food crisis of 2008 and beyond; climate change and related issues around energy and biofuels; and the emergence of 'neo-productivist' claims for agriculture seeking to re-establish productivism as the central policy rationale for agriculture (Almås & Campbell, 2012, p. 5). However, some wider challenges are emerging that cannot be entirely understood as the specific products of a period of crisis in the global north since 2008. First is the challenge of inexorably rising inequality. Piketty's (2014) analysis of capital in the 21st century details the rise of inequality: the exploding wealth of the richest and the increasing disparity in the proportion of income earned from work – labour income – with that inherited through capital accumulation. The implications are that we are entering an era socially and politically dominated by these very rich. The rural–urban implications related to property (including second homes), ownership, technology (including digital) developments, jobs and income are compelling.

On an even wider canvas, the idea of the anthropocene (Steffen, Crutzen & McNeill, 2007) radically resituates environmental challenges within all elements of social existence. The anthropocene demands that we reframe our scholarly work to address new kinds of challenges to those which previously shaped social scientific research into rural land use. Such changes in focus are congruent with Cloke (2006) who previously criticised rural research for not addressing sufficiently the subject of power, with many scholars having withdrawn from studying social practices, relations and struggles. Halfacree (2006) responds to these concerns with his threefold architecture of rural space: (a) as based on rural localities inscribed through relatively distinctive spatial practices; (b) as formal representations of the rural; and (c) as everyday lives of the rural. A further development of this concern about rural power grounded in everyday practices and through which entangled power is analytically discernible has been suggested (Frisvoll, 2012). Such approaches require analytical sensitivity towards social actors, agency and power, as these will be crucial for understanding the conflicts, the actors, their agencies and the resources – knowledge, networks, money, juridical and personal faculties – activated in contested use of land and resources. This kind of focus on power is consistent with a wider shift in frameworks towards inequality, partly inspired by the work of Piketty, but also taking into account the varying effects of neoliberalisation within different rural landscapes.

Back to bedrocks? The revival of mining

The new challenges and contradictions of rural landscapes and resource use are amply demonstrated through a brief consideration of the tension between new mining developments and the valuing of cultural landscapes. The closedown of many mines and other industries, from the 1970s on, was to some extent followed up by programmes, incentives and initiatives linked to new economic development measures, in which culturally based activities were positioned as being central to the economic and social reinvention of many cities and regions. Also, a number of nature restoration projects have led to a legacy of environmentally, recreationally and also culturally significant areas: previous sites of industrial waste have in some cases ended up on UNESCO's World Heritage list. Those areas that were reinvented as heritage landscapes are often now of great significance both culturally and economically for tourism through the commodification of cultural heritage, or 'heritagisation'.

A return to mining significantly challenges this kind of economic development framework. While concerns about the rate of global economic growth over the next decade will potentially have a major impact on the mining industry in the short term, the cyclical mineral booms will almost invariably be ongoing. The EU consumes about 20% of global metal resources, but only produces 3% of the raw materials themselves. The EU has launched a raw materials initiative (European Commission, 2008, 2013) and has put up a list of materials considered critical for industry and development.

In the last mining boom in the 2000s, one of the key influences on mining development internationally was the paradigm shift in governance towards the political philosophy of market liberalism. In neoliberal countries such as New Zealand, Canada and Australia this involved greater responsibility being handed to the mining companies for self-regulation of sustainability objectives as well as the speeding up of resource consenting processes.

At the same time, within Europe, the 2000s have seen significantly stricter environmental regulation, including the growing importance of NATURA 2000 within the EU. A related challenge is the situation of indigenous peoples: to what extent are mine developers and their government supporters required to actually relate to international laws such as the International Covenant on Civil and Political Rights, the International Labour Organization (ILO) Convention No. 169 concerning Indigenous and Tribal Peoples in Independent Countries, and the United Nations (UN) Declaration on the Rights of Indigenous Peoples?

With renewed interest in mineral extraction we can see contours of the return of 'high impact' resource use into societies where 'low impact' norms in rural spaces and economies are valued; currently partly geared towards cultural consumption and the tertiary sector, positioning themselves as postmodern, clean and hi-tech. Oil economy-based Norway serves as a case illustrating the many paradoxes linked to environment: increasing pressures of neoliberalisation, contradictory opportunities with natural resources but also high levels of commitment to welfare and jobs. Civil disobedience and actions are planned in response to a decision by the government to permit mining of deposits of rutile within the Førde fjord on the west coast. Also, permission for the reopening of a copper mine in northern Norway has been given, despite both of these cases involving fjords of great importance for fish stocks. The tourism industry fears for the image of the country as it relies on clean fjords and cultural landscapes of small farms; the seafood industry – the country's second biggest industry after oil – is concerned about impacts on fisheries; and the Sámi parliament representing indigenous Norwegians is concerned due to the blocking of important reindeer migration routes. Only four other countries worldwide are practising the mining of seabed deposits, and environmental organisations have filed a complaint against the government to the European Surveillance Authority for breaking EU water regulations. (Although not a member of the EU, Norway is required to comply with a number of agreements that involve EU regulations.)

The government's decision was partly based on contested scientific analyses that maintain the fjords will ecologically restore themselves after mineral extraction is over, although it will take many decades. Other arguments are that, besides locally needed work opportunities, the strict Norwegian regime of regulations will ensure sound mining practices. There is also the sense of a reverse NIMBY-effect: that the global north must be willing to take on its share of high-impact production, as well as being the site for consumption of such resources. Further, with the ongoing (albeit slow) phasing out of the oil sector, Norway needs to look for alternatives to secure future economic prosperity and these are the kinds of resource challenges that will increasingly face the global north (and south) as the ecological challenges of the 21st century unfold.

The emerging contradictions of renewable energy

In spite of its 'cleanness', wind energy also reveals some of the significant contradictions and tensions of the current moment (Haggett & Futak-Campbell, 2011; Devine-Wright, 2013). An EU COST Action on renewable energy and landscape is studying how to increase acceptability of wind farms throughout Europe:

> While objectives to boost renewable energy and trans-European energy networks are ambitious, it is increasingly understood that public acceptance becomes a constraining factor, and general support for green energy does not always translate into local support for specific projects. Perceived landscape change and loss of landscape quality have featured heavily in opposition campaigns in many European countries, even though renewable energy can facilitate sustainable development, especially in disadvantaged regions rich in wind, water, biomass, geothermal or solar energy.
>
> *(COST, 2014)*

One critical question social scientists ought to ask is whether and how climate change as a moral claim trumps other environmental approaches and concerns in decision making. The complexity of the energy market and the (as yet) insufficient grid systems are leading to a number of paradoxical situations. Energy surpluses exist while more windmills are being constructed within more or less pristine nature, and the maintenance of existing infrastructure and installations are accorded less priority due to economic and political interests, which includes subsidies being invested into wind energy developments. However, we cannot sit down and wait for the perfect solution – which may be solar, in combination with other energy forms and technologies, notwithstanding that solar energy may also generate land use debates and conflicts.

Climate change is acknowledged as the highest priority environmental challenge. Market and technology will not themselves drive a green shift, thus the public sector through incentives and regulations needs to take an active role. While the role of climate science is central to these responses, scientific knowledge must increasingly be assembled alongside more social and economic questions around new energy developments, not least of which is where and how social and economic power is implicated in new initiatives. Renewable energy has no climate effect unless it replaces fossil energy. Prices in energy decide how economically viable development of windmills will be. And while subsidies are often crucial to promote new technology and build market infrastructures, we still need to analyse the economic returns deriving from green certificates, subsidies and tax incentives and the kinds of new industries that form around these new sources of value. Accordingly, in the same way that we have been addressing agriculturally related policies, we need to ask the same questions of land-based renewable energy developments: what are the responses, adaptations and consequences on the land and for people?

The complex outcomes of biodiversity and rewilding policies

In spite of the many agri-environmental schemes in existence, the EU's *State of Nature* report (European Environment Agency, 2015) details massive deterioration of grassland habitats and declining populations and biomass of farmland birds, bee species, butterflies and other insects. Land use changes related to agricultural ecosystems, including intensification, abandonment, and pollution and changes in hydrology, are some major causes. But another issue is the extent to which the design of policy instruments, along with constant changes in policies and schemes, has reduced the potential benefits of the agri-environmental schemes. Other contradictions are also evident. While the loss of pollinators, partly due to land use changes, is a global problem, so are the increasingly devastating effects of wildfires. The abandonment of traditional land uses and increased land cover by scrub etc. has, in combination with longer and drier periods, increased the risk of wildfires getting out of control (see Moreira & Russo, 2007; Soliva et al., 2008). However, 'rewilding' has also been introduced as an alternative, sustainable development option (Navarro & Pereira, 2015).

Rural landscapes, inhabitants and animals are also caught in narratives and discourses between wilderness and cultural landscapes, between urban, educated middle-class values and cultural resistance, nature management and rural livelihoods/lifestyles and policies, which does have some very material effects. The strong return of carnivores in Europe (Chapron et al., 2014), and in particular in Scandinavia (bear, wolf, lynx, wolverine and also eagles), coincides with increased economic, structural, political and societal marginalisation of agriculture and rural areas, and carnivore resistance partly serves as a cultural resistance towards the urban elite and dominance (Krange & Skogen, 2011). However, protected species and landscapes that are dependent upon low-intensity farming systems, it could be argued, are just as threatened as the carnivores – as farmers give up due to high losses and psychological pressures (Blekesaune & Rønningen, 2010). Carnivore numbers are also increasing in other parts of Europe, and the French prime minister's plan for French agriculture (released in July 2015) includes measures for carnivore management. From a situation in which sheep farmers have been seen as irresponsible owners hunting compensation for carnivore damages and lacking the 'correct' environmental values, the material and sometimes contradictory effects of conservation policies may be about to be more widely recognised.

These kinds of wildlife management challenges have implications for how we understand the production of scientific knowledge. Knowledge is both interwoven in rural power relations, and has tended to privilege a narrow set of scientific disciplines and approaches in the framing of wildlife management policies. Wider, complex environmental perspectives must help reframe the premises upon which carnivore management, and ecosystems and nature in general, are based.

Bioeconomy – redefining rural resources

Much hope has been invested in the economic potential of a 'new bioeconomy', both in terms of providing new jobs, development and growth, and in terms of representing a transition from an oil-based to a renewable-based energy economy. Bioeconomy is defined by the OECD (2009, p. 8) as 'a world where biotechnology contributes to a significant share of economic input … using … renewable biomass and efficient bioprocesses to support sustainable production'. The term 'sociotechnical regime' is relevant here, defined as a stable, well-developed alignment of technologies, regulations, institutions, and cultural discourses that hold them together (Geels, 2005; Bollinger et al., 2014).

Zilberman and colleagues (2013) describe the desired bioeconomic transition as 'a continuing evolutionary process of transition from systems of mining non-renewable resources to farming renewable ones'.

A critical component of this transition is the application of transformative biotechnology – much of which has yet to be developed – to enable the conversion of biomass into clothes, pharmaceuticals, housing materials, food, fuel and so on (Arancibia, 2013). The implications for rural areas are potentially profound. For example, should an effective process/enzyme for converting cellulose to edible starch be discovered, formerly marginal agricultural regions could become key areas of global food production. Economically, socially, environmentally and at all scales, the long-term impact of such a fundamental transformation would be to make many of the world's rural areas unrecognisable. Kitchen and Marsden (2011) suggest a more human-centred 'eco-economic' approach involving the realignment of production–consumption chains to capture local and regional value, while others contend a combined 'pluralistic' approach is possible (Levidow, Birch & Papaioannou, 2012).

However, radical transitions and reframing may be exactly what will be required if we are to survive the anthropocene.

Conclusions – new questions for new challenges

Starting with the global meta-challenges of inequality and the anthropocene, this chapter has traced the kinds of new sites of conflict and generation of new potential futures that we will need in order to transition to more sustainable rural futures. It is by reconnecting with the social and the material that we are able to trace crucial issues like the morality of resource valuations, activation of knowledge systems and the related power geometries, which are all vital factors in delineating who has control and ownership of resources, and further, how this affects the various claims, and how interests are articulated in relation to rural land and landscapes.

Along with the new attention to the resource 'bedrocks' of the global north, new bioeconomic thinking is pointing to a turn towards strengthened primary- and secondary-sector interests in rural areas, challenging many of the ideas and notions linked to (post-) modernisation of agriculture and rural areas. The growing emphasis on bioeconomy, with a cross-sectorial and life-cycle approach to natural and agricultural resources as bioresources (even reduced to 'biomass') will challenge and possibly also transform how rural resources are used and perceived, thus also potentially transforming the rural as space, place, home and construct.

Technological advances and cross-sectorial approaches are rolled out in an increasingly neoliberal political environment, and partly in a context of a financial crisis hitting both urban and rural areas. Land use development in the global north; abandonment and intensification; and various types of land investments and the effects of these processes at various levels and scale need urgent consideration. There is a strong need for national institutions to back up sustainable processes; at the same time, confronting international institutions and globalising processes will be equally important.

At this point, it is arguable that we are not experiencing the end of a long trajectory of rural development that culminated in the multifunctional project in agriculture and rural land management. Rather, we seem to be at the start of a series of transitions, partly triggered by specific crises since 2008 and partly driven by wider crises of intensifying inequality and climate change (and the mutual effects they will have on each other). In this context, we are not consolidating past approaches, epistemologies and theories, rather we are searching for new, critical, social scientific approaches to new, planetary-scale, problems.

References

Almås, R & Campbell, H (2012). *Rethinking agricultural policy regimes: Food security, climate change and the future resilience of global agriculture*. Bingley, UK: Emerald.

Arancibia, F (2013). Challenging the bioeconomy: The dynamics of collective action in Argentina. *Technology in Society* 35, 79–92.

Blekesaune, A & Rønningen, K (2010). Bears and fears: Cultural capital, geography and attitudes towards large carnivores in Norway. *Norwegian Journal of Geography* 64(4), 185–198.

Bollinger, LA, Bogmans, CWJ, Chappin, EJL, Dijkema, GPJ, Huibregtse, JN, Maas, N, Schenk, T, Snelder, M, Thienen, P. van, Wit, S de, Wols, B & Tavazzy, LA (2014). Climate adaptation of interconnected infrastructures: A framework for supporting governance. *Regional Environmental Change* 14(3), 919–931.

Chapron, G, Kaczensky, P, Linnell, J et al. (2014). Recovery of large carnivores in Europe's modern human-dominated landscape. *Science* (19 December 2014) 346(6216), 1517–1519.

Cloke, P (2006). Conceptualizing rurality. In P Cloke, T Marsden & PH Mooney (Eds), *Handbook of rural studies* (pp. 18–28). London: Sage.

COST 2014. TUD COST Action TU1401: Renewable energy and landscape quality. Available at http://www.cost.eu/COST_Actions/tud/Actions/TU1401 (accessed January 15, 2016).

Devine-Wright, P (2013). Explaining 'nimby' objections to a power line: The role of personal, place attachment and project-related factors. *Environment and Behavior* 45, 761–781.

European Commission (2008). Communication from the Commission to the European Parliament and the Council – The raw materials initiative: meeting our critical needs for growth and jobs in Europe. [SEC(2008) 2741] / COM/2008/0699 final.

European Commission (2013). Non-energy raw materials. http://ec.europa.eu/enterprise/policies/raw-materials/index_en.htm.

European Environment Agency (2015). *State of nature in the EU. Results from reporting under the nature directives 2007–2012*. Technical report No. 2/2015.

Frisvoll, S. (2012). Power in the production of spaces transformed by rural tourism. *Journal of Rural Studies* 28, 447–457.

Geels, FW (2005). *Technological transitions and system innovations: A co-evolutionary and socio-technical analysis*. Cheltenham: Edward Elgar.

Haggett, C & Futak-Campbell, B (2011). Tilting at windmills? Using discourse analysis to understand the attitude-behaviour gap in renewable energy conflicts. *Journal of Mechanisms of Economic Regulation* 1(2), 207–220.

Halfacree, K (2006). Rural space: Constructing a three-fold architecture. In P Cloke, T Marsden & PH Mooney (Eds), *Handbook of rural studies* (pp. 44–62). London: Sage.

Kitchen, L & Marsden, T (2011). Constructing sustainable communities: A theoretical exploration of the bioeconomy and eco-economy paradigms. *Local Environment: The International Journal of Justice and Sustainability* 16(8), 753–769.

Krange, O & Skogen, K (2011). When the lads go hunting: The 'hammertown mechanism' and the conflict over wolves in Norway. *Ethnography* 12(4), 466–489.

Levidow, L, Birch, K & Papaioannou, T (2012). EU agri-innovation policy: Two contending visions of the bio-economy. *Critical Policy Studies* 6(1), 40–65.

Moreira, F & Russo, D (2007). Modelling the impact of agricultural abandonment and wildfires on vertebrate diversity in Mediterranean Europe. *Landscape Ecology* 22(10), 1461–1476.

Navarro, LM & Pereira, HM (2015). Rewilding abandoned landscapes in Europe. In HM Pereira & LM Navarro (Eds), *Rewilding European landscapes* (pp. 3–23). Springer International.

OECD (2009). *The bioeconomy to 2030: Designing a policy agenda*. Paris: OECD.

Piketty, T (2014). *Capital in the twenty-first century*. Cambridge, MA: Harvard University Press.

Soliva, R, Rønningen, K, Bella, I, Bezak, P, Flø, BE, Marty, P & Potter, C (2008). Envisioning upland futures: Stakeholder responses to scenarios for Europe's mountain landscapes. *Journal of Rural Studies* 24, 56–71.

Steffen, W, Crutzen, PJ & McNeill, JR (2007). The anthropocene: Are humans now overwhelming the great forces of nature? *Ambio* 36(8), 614–621.

Zilberman, D, Kim, E, Kirschner, S, Kaplan, S & Reeves, J (2013). Technology and the future bioeconomy. *Agricultural Economics* 44, 1–8.

23

Transformations of Rural Society and Environments by Extraction of Mineral and Energy Resources

Jo-Anne Everingham

Introduction

With various trends unfolding at different spatial and temporal scales, the extractive industries are increasingly influential in changing patterns of land use, social relationships, local economies and community identities in rural regions. While agriculture has been seen as the essence of rural areas and changes in that sector have been integral to structural change in northern economies and societies, suitably endowed rural areas could be the emerging industrial heartlands and sites of readjustment. This is because of their prominence as sites of extraction of subsurface resources, notably construction materials such as sand, aggregates and stone; industrial minerals such as salts, rare earth elements and phosphate; metals such as iron ore, gold, copper and zinc; and energy sources such as coal, oil, uranium and gas. This chapter focuses on the rural transformations associated with extraction of metals, minerals, coal, oil and gas (collectively termed 'mining') and emerging issues for rural studies.

Over recent decades, changing market forces, patterns of regulation, investment strategies and trade have driven major structural change in the global mining industry. As well, the industry has had to adjust to diminishing primary resource stocks, changing economics of extraction and competition from recycling, reuse and renewable alternatives. Hence, in many countries in Western Europe, and in the USA, the transition from agrarian to industrial to post-industrial societies is well under way; mining has reduced in relative importance and is emblematic of the old economy even where it remains a large industry in absolute terms (Upstill & Hall, 2006). In contrast, a handful of nations – Australia and Canada amongst them – have not undergone this transition and continue to actively expand exploitation of their rich mineral resources as a significant part of their national economies. For instance, Australia's mining and energy sectors have recently experienced a massive escalation such that their production constituted over half the value of Australia's total exports and, at 8%, the industry was the fourth largest contributor to the nation's total gross domestic product in 2010–2011 (ABS, 2012, p. 567).

This resurgence and increased economic significance of mining is not universally evident. Though it is found in countries at the periphery of Europe such as the Nordic and Baltic states, by and large the nations of the global north experiencing most radical change in the industry are Canada, the USA and Australia. Hence this chapter concentrates on North America and

Australia, where 46% of global exploration for metals and one-third of investment in metal mining projects are concentrated, even without considering hydrocarbons or industrial minerals (Ericsson, 2004). The resource-rich rural regions of these nations are subject to converging politico-economic processes such as shortages of raw materials, currency fluctuations, speculative investments, technological innovations, resource nationalism, and especially the commodity-intensive growth in China and other BRIC nations (Brazil, Russia, India) that drove prices for metal and mineral commodities higher in the early 21st century.

As a consequence of these global forces there has been a dramatic change in the rate, scale and scope of extractive activity in recent decades with larger quantities of more varied commodities being removed from more extensive, less readily accessible deposits in more varied environments. These broad-scale changes impact on local landscapes and have produced, in rural regions rich in resources, configurations of rural populations, economies and space aligned with familiar 'boom' and 'bust' scenarios but increasingly also sites of clashing land uses and values. These developments have rendered the rural a site of contested identities, uncertainties, ambivalences, contradictions and the all-pervasive risks associated with human activities that typify late modernity (Beck, 1992).

The competition and risks from these changes in land use and populations include opposing demands on limited supplies of skilled labour, water and land. Hence they typically bring new opportunities and also pose numerous challenges for rural localities. The challenges include population growth that outstrips the capacity of available services and infrastructure including housing; exacerbation of a two-speed economy; environmental degradation; and changes to the character of sparsely populated rural areas rich in natural amenity.

The chapter discusses these changes in terms of new mining technologies and industry structures, changed demographics and social relationships, reshaped economies and cumulative impacts on rural environments.

New technologies and industry structures

Global resource companies have responded to increased demand, rising commodity prices and new markets by boosting production of fuels, metals and minerals significantly. In 2005 the ores and minerals extracted were 27 times what were mined in 1900; and annual extraction of fossil fuels increased by a factor of 12 over the same period with the bulk of the growth occurring after the Second World War (Fischer-Kowalski et al., 2011). However, this exponential growth occurs in a context of both social and production challenges. Given higher expectations about the environmental and social performance of companies, mineral production has become more difficult and expensive. In addition, cheap and accessible sources and major known reserves of many metals, minerals and energy resources are depleting and ore grades are declining, so extraction involves substantially more mine waste, rising energy and water consumption, and falling productivity (Prior et al., 2012). The greater expertise, capital and risk-taking required to find and extract the resources has driven technological advancement in exploration, production and processing.

More sophisticated technology has, in turn, opened up new locations of production, with mining of asteroids and arctic locations being investigated as well as deep offshore exploration and mining. There is also ocean-floor mining of sedimentary nodules, for example of manganese and phosphorus, and of sulphide deposits near hydrothermal vents containing metals such as silver, gold, copper, manganese, cobalt and zinc (Halfar & Fujita, 2007). The remotely operated vehicles used in this ocean mining, and other forms of automation, are also being introduced to onshore mining to allow round-the-clock, consistent operation in sometimes inhospitable environments (like the life-threateningly hot and humid tunnels of the Mexican Naica lead, zinc and silver mine 300 metres underground). Not only do companies now venture into more challenging geographical contexts but also more challenging political territories, such as many African and Central Asian nations.

Perhaps the technological advances making the greatest changes to rural landscapes in the countries focused on in this chapter are those that make onshore exploitation of lower grade ores and new commodities feasible. New technological capabilities, such as hydraulic fracturing ('fracking') and horizontal drilling, have facilitated the rapid expansion of unconventional development in the oil and gas industries, thereby drawing rural spaces of North America and Australia into new circuits of capital, labour and global commodity chains and transforming rural landscapes (Bridge, 2008). Examples include heavy oil and oil/tar sands in Canada and shale oil and coal-bed methane in the USA and Australia (Hein, 2006; Jacobs, 2011).

New techniques are also employed to access conventional resources, with mountaintop removal, and mega-size open-cast or open-cut pits imposing sizeable scars on rural landscapes (Lindberg et al., 2011; Wickham et al., 2013). The Bingham Canyon mine in Utah and the 'super-pit' in Kalgoorlie, Western Australia are not only hundreds of metres deep but each is around four kilometres long. Such huge operations continue production even as a transition from surface mining to deep underground mines is heralded (Latimer, 2014). Deep underground operations, which include Canada's Kidd Creek copper mine, the Aitik mine in Sweden, and the Ernest Henry mine in Australia, also employ new mass mining methods such as block caving and decline mining to reach deeper deposits more economically.

Much of this activity, rather than being confined to remote and sparsely populated areas, is infringing on settled areas with established agricultural and also recreational industries. In numerous cases, economies of scale and other market considerations mean these developments proceed as mega projects extending over a vast spatial area and involving the integration of disparate activities such as a port, rail or pipeline infrastructure and multiple mines operating simultaneously. However, the new methods and increased mechanisation of production result in reduced employment and the pace of innovation leaves many uncertainties, potentially incurring greater environmental and social costs and exposing rural communities and environments to ill-defined risks and cumulative impacts, as discussed below (Bell & York, 2010; Franks, Brereton & Moran, 2010; Cottle & Keys, 2014).

The ramifications of shifts in production techniques suggest that, rather than a transition away from primary production, productivism and extractivism continue to govern the dynamics of rural change and the diversification of land uses that is occurring in resource-rich regions (Pinto-Correia & Kristensen, 2013). The changes and associated workforce demands are reflected in reshaped demographic patterns and social relationships.

Changed demographic patterns and social relationships

Mining alters, diversifies, disrupts and even displaces rural populations. The Californian and Australian gold rushes of the 19th century illustrated this, but, as identified in the previous section, this is now occurring on a bigger scale and often in different rural contexts. In an era when big corporations dominate mining in these countries, spontaneous population movements of prospectors are less dramatic. However, two practices of modern mining companies that radically reshape demographies are displacement and long-distance commuting workforces. When mineral deposits lie underneath farms and villages – whether small communities like Acland in Queensland, Australia (Felton-Taylor, 2011) or villages of several thousand, as are being impacted by the Roşia Montană project in Romania (Alexandrescu, 2011), relocation or resettlement is the fate of many former residents. More often, plans for new or increased mining activity stimulate demand for labour in new locations and historically it was common for purpose-built company towns to be established for miners and their families (Alanen, 1979; Lea & Zehner, 1986).

Nowadays, some resource sector workers reside locally but the industry also brings an influx of transient workers to established towns near their operations. In Australia, up to half of the present-day mining workforce commutes long distances to and from work for a roster block of multiple shifts. As they usually commute by plane, they are colloquially known as fly-in-fly-out (FIFO) workers. In Australia and other mining nations, notably Canada, the fly-in-fly-out practice has been observed to bring substantial demographic and economic changes, especially to the rural communities close to the work sites of these non-resident workers (Newhook et al., 2011; Petrova & Marinova, 2013; Rolfe, 2013).

A number of studies have identified the mining workforce, both commuters and local residents, as very prominent in communities and contrasting with other rural workers because they customarily dress in high visibility clothing, drive distinctively marked vehicles and are overwhelmingly male (Langton, 2010; Everingham, Devenin & Collins, 2015). In other words, these workers boost population numbers (at least temporarily), but, more significantly, as urban, industrial workers (albeit not exactly cosmopolitan and gentrified) they differ in many respects from the established population, leading one Australian study to colloquially identify the well-paid, white, working-class newcomers as 'cashed up bogans' (Pini, McDonald & Mayes, 2012).

The long-recognised diversity *among* rural towns (McManus et al., 2012) is now becoming diversity *within* towns, which is greater than the previous status differentiation between the agri-elite and farm workers (Tonts, 2005; Bryant & Pini, 2009; Cassidy & McGrath, 2015). This is regarded by many as eroding the distinctive character of localities functioning as economic enclaves with an identity based on their dominant industry – for example, grazing and ranching, grain-growing, grape-growing or mining. In particular, notions of rurality and traditional agrarian identities (Lockie, 2000; McManus & Connor, 2013) compete with the more industrial identity of the extractive industry workers (de Rijke, 2013; Everingham, Devenin & Collins, 2015).

The more heterogeneous rural populations with more fluid alignments are manifestations of the transition from an agrarian to an urban-industrial society (Lichter & Brown, 2011) and much literature associates resource development, and especially resource boom towns, with typically negative changes of urban-related growth (Lichter & Brown, 2011). These include not only threats to rural identities and social-psychological disruption but also community conflict and social divisions (Albrecht et al., 2007; Moffatt & Baker, 2013; Jacquet, 2014). The more diverse and often conflicting identities and values emerging in communities affected by mining lead to a range of relationships encompassing conflict, collaboration, coexistence and other interactions, though arguably conflictual relationships between mining companies and other segments of the community are most studied.

McManus and Connor's (2013, p. 166) study of the social marginalisation of communities in the coal mining district of the Upper Hunter region of New South Wales, for example, demonstrated how communities use 'new and reflexive constructions of "the rural" that integrate traditional identity, discourses of sustainability and the re-centring of rural life'. Other studies too have identified competing claims to 'stewardship', 'place attachment' and even nationalism underpinning new alignments and new divisions and the emergence of 'unlikely bedfellows' as former foes – environmentalists and farmers – join forces to oppose mining development (de Rijke, 2013). In the 1980s Australia's Indigenous people invoked birthright and heritage to assert their claim to vast areas of agricultural land amidst considerable opposition;

now farmers are asserting their right to deny resource companies land access on the same grounds (Lloyd, Luke & Boyd, 2013).

However, positions with respect to mining are not fixed and unambiguous. It is common to find ambivalent corporate–community relationships, with mining positioned as both a threat and an opportunity. Epitomising this is a recent Australian report on long-distance commuting which dubbed FIFO the 'Cancer of the bush or salvation for our cities' (House of Representatives Standing Committee on Regional Australia, 2013). Anti-mining protests in the global north may not often reach the scale of those in the global south – such as the 2011 demonstration by 25,000 protesters in Puno, Peru against the Canadian Bear Creek Mining Company's plans to construct a 5,400 hectare open-pit silver mine in the southern highlands of Puno, adjacent to Lake Titicaca and the border with Bolivia (McDonell, 2015). Nevertheless, from the industrial sand mines of Wisconsin (Pearson, 2013) and the tar sands of Alberta (Preston, 2013) to Europe's largest gold mine proposed for Roşia Montană (Alexandrescu, 2011), and the fertile Liverpool Plains of northern NSW facing coal seam gas development and mining by the Chinese coal company, Shenhua (Boyd, 2013), vocal public activism, protests and legal battles are waged to try to halt mining. Although threats to identity, such as those discussed above, commonly underlie such conflicts (Boyd, 2013), research into 'costs of conflict' identified the top causes of conflict between companies and communities as: pollution; distribution of benefits; and competition over access to resources (Davis & Franks, 2014). These issues are discussed in the following sections.

A particular mining–community conflict evident in Canada, the USA and Australia, as nations with settler populations, is the clash of interests between Indigenous people and mining corporations. In this case the expansion of the mining industry, alongside greater recognition of native title rights, has led to the forging of new relationships between Aboriginal communities and mining companies centred on rural territories that, it has been suggested, may offer a model for greater economic empowerment of Indigenous people (Wall & Pelon, 2011; Langton, 2012; O'Faircheallaigh, 2012, 2013; Martin, Trigger & Parmenter, 2014). These relationships are often enshrined in formal Impact and Benefit Agreements or Indigenous Land-Use Agreements that express mutual interdependence and a commitment by companies to provide compensation and benefits to those with traditional ties or native title to the lands from which they extract resources. Besides financial payments, the arrangements usually include undertakings about Indigenous employment and training, contracts for Indigenous businesses as well as cultural heritage protection and environmental management. As the situation with regard to Indigenous people demonstrates, the changing sociopolitical divisions often have an economic dimension as well.

(Re)shaped economies

Whether formalised in agreements, projected in socioeconomic impact assessments or touted by government development enthusiasts, resource extraction projects promise many benefits – including job creation, supplier contracts and regional economic growth – for rural communities that may otherwise be stagnant or declining (Wildman, Moore, Baker & Wadley, 1990; McManus et al., 2012; Hogan & Lockie, 2013; Measham & Fleming, 2013). The seminal work of Richard Auty (1993) spawned a significant literature exploring the paradox of the resource curse whereby countries rich in natural resources experience conflict and limited economic growth, and there are related phenomena like the apparent negative impact of resource sector development on other sectors of the economy known as Dutch disease. Nevertheless, developed countries such as Canada and Australia have been regarded as avoiding this 'curse' since mining has long played an important role in their national economies, and it can be argued that the sector has recently gained greater significance, particularly in Australia (Measham, McKenzie, Moffat & Franks, 2013).

The recent mining boom in Australia is estimated to have boosted average household incomes by 13% over the decade to 2013 and contributed to a significant appreciation of the Australian dollar which assisted importers but hampered other industries exposed to trade, such as manufacturing and agriculture (Tulip, 2014). However, at a subnational level the trade-offs for economic benefits and the distribution of benefits reveal a more complex picture. Michaels (2011) studied the long-term effects of resource abundance at a county level in southern USA. He found that counties specialising in producing oil from plentiful reserves increased their population and experienced higher incomes, higher employment (in mining but also in other sectors) and enhancement of local infrastructure such as roads and airports, which in turn increased output in the agriculture and manufacturing sectors. Research on other mining commodities in other parts of the nation, however, found that coal mining regions have comparatively lower incomes and higher unemployment (Perdue & Pavela, 2012).

Some observers identifying a surge in economic activity and opportunities associated with resource production note that these flow to urban and metropolitan centres rather than concentrating in the proximate rural localities (Langton, 2010; Rolfe et al., 2011). For example, in one Australian iron-ore mining region, the Pilbara, only $80 million of the estimated $30 billion generated by the industry was captured locally. This leakage of economic benefits has been attributed to fiscal arrangements and also to fly-in-fly-out employment (Haslam McKenzie, 2011), multinational ownership of corporations (Cottle & Keys, 2014) and other practices of mining, oil and gas companies.

Booming mining development then, results in contrasting fortunes for various sectors of the economy, and different localities depending on their role in the mining supply chain (Rolfe et al., 2011). The industry has also been diagnosed as inducing a 'two-speed economy' *within* communities that is characterised by big disparities between the personal income and economic well-being of those working in the industry and those not directly associated with the mining sector. Hence the situation in mining-affected communities frequently reveals a sharp distinction between 'haves and have-nots' (Langton, 2010; Everingham et al., 2013; Cottle & Keys, 2014). One other contrast is between locals eligible for compensation and those located close to the project but not deemed eligible because they are less directly affected (Alexandrescu, 2011).

Not only are the economic benefits unevenly distributed across segments of the population but they are often short-lived, producing a temporal imbalance as well (Haggerty, Gude, Delorey & Rasker, 2014). Since they result from production of a finite resource whose value fluctuates on commodity markets, local economic benefits are very often temporary and associated with isolated 'booms' and subsequent 'busts' that involve painful readjustment for affected communities. Because of the interplay of these various factors, resource booms have been shown to expose rural communities to uneven distribution of costs and benefits and new risks of rapid industrialisation, with population growth outstripping the capacity of available services and infrastructure, and unintended consequences including reduced affordability of accommodation and higher costs of living (Langton, 2010; Jacquet, 2014).

The disproportionate emphasis on short-term returns to the state and national economies is particularly contentious since mining and onshore oil and gas extraction are expanding into highly productive rural regions of many countries. In these locations, where the disparities between 'haves' and 'have-nots' are most acute, clashes are also evident between different sectors of the economy.

While conflict over alternative land uses and between neighbouring industries is not new (Duus, 2013), new circumstances mean that areas where subsurface resources were previously unprofitable to exploit have now opened to mining. In the case of unconventional oil and gas this requires (non-exclusive) use of vast areas of land connected by a grid of pipelines and pumping stations and often in land already fully dedicated to other productive uses.

The notion of resource regions as distinct from agricultural regions and as places where mining is the leading economic activity and source of employment (Franks, Brereton, & Moran, 2013) may no longer capture those rural regions most affected by extraction of metals, minerals, oil and gas. With a juxtaposition of industries – farming, grazing, tourism, mining and gas extraction – interacting with each other and competing for similar resources as production inputs – including land, water, employees, infrastructure and support services – these areas have become a locus of land use conflict. Where mining occurs on and near productive agricultural land, it raises the spectre of undermining food security and threats to the foundations of vital agricultural industries, such as soil and water, provoking fears of negative economic, social and environmental consequences (de Rijke, 2013; Everingham et al., 2013). This risk perception is linked to irreconcilable values and confounded by a lack of mutually acceptable, comprehensive, salient and credible data to guide decisions about regional planning and development (Everingham et al., 2013). Thus the intensification of land use to meet human needs for food and energy disrupts communities' economic base (Hogan & Lockie, 2013), generates clashes between different sectors of the economy (McManus & Connor, 2013) and provokes disparities between the economic fortunes of mining regions and other localities and between those working in, or compensated by, the sector and others in society (Langton, 2010; Rolfe et al., 2011). The challenge is to identify complementarities and synergies that might build resilience of rural communities and provide a buffer against the fluctuations and uncertainties that have plagued rural economies already subject to the vagaries of climate and international markets.

The characterisation of the farming–mining opposition as 'colliding treadmills' of production (Gasteyer & Carrera, 2013, p. 24) has much salience when considering the present-day economic dimensions of the situation of rural communities and their 'economic identity' (Bell & York, 2010). However, this recognition of competing identities ignores many of the issues that scholars and policy makers have attempted to highlight with the concept of multifunctionality – notably the importance of ecosystem services as well as economic production. By maintaining extractivist and productivist values it puts industries on a 'collision course' not only with each other but also with ecological goals (Sayer et al., 2013).

Cumulative impacts on rural landscapes and environments

Despite the potential for economic returns, there is an increasingly contested nexus between productive activities and the conditions for sustainable food production and healthy environments in rural areas (Estrada-Carmona et al., 2014). In this respect, the use and management of rural land for mining, as for agriculture, involves decisions, trade-offs, risks and impacts and has ramifications for the multiple functions rural landscapes serve, including the production of metals, minerals, energy, food and fibre; the maintenance of ecosystem services, biodiversity and habitats; and the provision of recreation and amenity.

The effects of each industry have been separately investigated and there has been recent research interest in the impacts of resource extraction on agriculture both in terms of the possibility of rehabilitating mined land for agricultural use post-mining, and in terms of simultaneous production of agricultural commodities and oil or gas from the same land holdings. As a result, both of these productive activities have been subject to pressure to adopt more environmentally sustainable practices to gain the social licence they need to operate if they are to successfully produce in-demand commodities. Further, it has been suggested that countries where economic growth is founded on primary production and extractive industries face a major challenge to 'decouple national growth from increased pressures on our environment' (State of the Environment 2011 Committee, 2011, p. 11).

While more than 20% of Australia's land is under conservation management and another 20%-plus is managed by Indigenous Australians, livestock grazing is the most extensive use, extending over 55% of the land area (State of the Environment 2011 Committee, 2011). Mining occupies a much smaller proportion of the nation's land area although it increasingly overlaps with or encroaches on these other land uses. This situation is not unique to Australia. If not a large footprint industry, on the relatively small proportion of land it occupies resource extraction is usually a heavy footprint industry that has adverse effects on rural environments. Mine waste dumps, dust particles, air pollution, water contamination and destruction of flora and habitats are among the localised ecological impacts of highly mechanised industrial mega-mines which (especially in areas of concentrated open-cut or mountaintop removal mining) remove landscape features, and leave major, often irreversible scars on landscapes (Bridge, 2004; Cottle & Keys, 2014).

In these localised respects, and sometimes on a more extensive scale such as whole river basins, many places face unwelcome legacies of decades, and in some cases a century or more, of mining. However, the recent increase in the scale, scope and pace of mining in many rural regions means that over time there has been a multiplication of the extent, magnitude and dimensions of the impacts and pressures that mining places on the environment. Not only do the impacts of overlapping and contiguous mines combine and interact with each other, they also interact with other land uses in diversified regions, to create often unpredictable cumulative impacts. Cumulative impacts are defined as 'the successive, incremental and combined impacts (both positive and negative) of one or more activities on society and the environment ... [that] ... result from the aggregation and interaction of impacts on a receptor and may be the product of past, present or future activities' (Franks, Brereton & Moran, 2013, p. 641).

In the Laciana Valley, near Leon, Spain, which is an environmentally protected area under the EU Habitats Directive, 30 years of mountaintop-removal coal mining on five mountains, without adequate environmental regulation, have had dire environmental as well as social impacts. In that case, it took the removal of government subsidies for coal mining, and regional government clampdowns, to bring a halt to expansion that concerted local opposition and legal action failed to achieve (Cabrejas, 2012). This exemplifies how management of rural areas at the vortex of contest involves a wide range of private, civil society and government actors at the local, regional and national levels of governance.

The interaction of actors at various levels and between local and exogenous factors, such as government policies, are among the confounding factors when it comes to assessing and managing cumulative impacts of mining. Uncertainty is another. Uncertainty about impacts on a range of valued ecosystem components, including water, is of particular concern to mining-affected agricultural communities (McManus & Connor, 2013).

Notwithstanding the challenges and the side effects of new technologies, the impact of outside forces and the problems in calculating the likelihood and extent of negative consequences with any certainty, considerable attention has been directed to understanding and improving the assessment and management of these impacts (Canter & Ross, 2010; Franks, Brereton & Moran, 2011, 2013; Gunn & Noble, 2011; Hegmann & Yarranton, 2011; Johnson et al., 2011; Weber, Krogman & Antoniuk, 2012; Moran, Franks & Sonter, 2013).

Some of the practices advocated for assessing and managing cumulative impacts are: adopting a systems approach, engaging in regional and strategic planning and participatory monitoring as well as joint advocacy (Franks et al., 2010). In general, there is a suggestion that issues that arise as a result of multiple activities are best tackled collectively by multiple actors and at multiple levels. Hence the emphasis is on networking, cooperation, multi-sector collaboration and facilitation of synergies which involve varying degrees of sharing of resources, risks, responsibilities, rewards and information (even where information is incomplete and contested) (Franks et al., 2010; Porter, Franks & Everingham, 2013). Such multilevel, multidisciplinary governance of the impacts of mining reflects the approaches being adopted for natural resource management in general in many nations, but is a relatively new way of operating for mining companies.

Conclusion

There is a radically different industrial landscape of metals, minerals and energy production disrupting rural Australia, Canada and the USA with pursuit of subsurface resources reshaping the surface activities of humans and contrasting with the taken-for-granted agricultural character and activities of rural regions. The mining–agriculture conflict and many of the tensions outlined above are likely rooted in a more powerful cultural clash. Because the alternatives are considered by decision makers in the technical and scientific terms of industrial development and environmental management, there is little consideration of feelings of social anxiety, of attachment to country, of belonging in the community, of tradition, of threats to existing community values or to community identity (Boyd, 2013, p. 25).

Many of the basic assumptions about extraction of finite, spatially concentrated mineral resources being focused on very rural and isolated towns with marginal agricultural value while more densely settled areas are devoted exclusively to various complementary agricultural endeavours are being challenged (Jacquet & Kay, 2014). Mining expansion has placed enormous pressures on land and water resources, local businesses and social relationships in some rural communities. This is partly the result of institutional conditions that prioritise large-scale investment and short-term returns over livelihoods, local socioeconomic systems and environment. A reframing of rural landscapes as 'lifescapes' (Cassidy & McGrath, 2015) may shift the priorities.

In this vein, the influential concept of multifunctionality in policy and rural sociology has gained recognition of the value of ecosystem services and a balanced view of the supporting, provisioning and regulating functions of the environment. However, it falls short of providing understanding of the material and social consequences of the juxtaposition of industries on local ecosystems and the economies and social relations in rural towns. For example, differential impacts for different groups of people with different values and the consequences for aquifers over time are not highlighted by this framing. Nor is the understanding of risks and contingencies – and the role of uncertainty in these – accommodated (Millennium Ecosystem Assessment, 2005).

The nature and drivers of structural changes in agriculture, including impacts of technological change and corporate farming, have been widely canvassed in rural studies. However, there has also been what could be considered an industrial transformation of rural territories. This involves a more diversified industry mix since economies of scale and reduced costs of transport and communication led to centralisation and the loss of traditional agriculture-related value-adding and processing businesses. Counterbalancing gains have included examples of rare, major infrastructure projects that give a one-off boost to rural locations. Notable drivers of this transformation have been changes in extraction of minerals, oil and gas. The resultant rural landscapes are characterised as much by contention, flux, risks and contradictions as late modern urban spaces. The emergence of a new equilibrium appears less likely than more diverse and constantly changing rural lifescapes with ever-shifting relationships between people and between humans and their environments.

References

ABS (2012). *2012 Yearbook of Australia* (No. 92). Canberra: Retrieved from http://www.abs.gov.au/ausstats/abs@.nsf/Lookup/by%20Subject/1301.0~2012~Main%20Features~Downloads~96.

Alanen, AR (1979). The planning of company communities in the Lake Superior Mining Region. *Journal of the American Planning Association* 45(3), 256–278. doi: 10.1080/01944367908976966.

Albrecht, G, Sartore, G-M, Connor, L, Higginbotham, N, Freeman, S, Kelly, B, … Pollard, G (2007). Solastalgia: The distress caused by environmental change. *Australasian Psychiatry* 15(s1), S95–S98. doi: 10.1080/10398560701701288.

Alexandrescu, F (2011). Gold and displacement in Eastern Europe: Risks and uncertainty at Roşia Montană. *Revista Română de Sociologie* 22(1–2), 78–107.

Auty, R (1993). *Sustaining development in mineral economies: The resource curse thesis*. London: Routledge.

Beck, U (1992). *Risk society: Towards a new modernity*. Trans. M Ritter. London: Sage.

Bell, SE & York, R (2010). Community economic identity: The coal industry and ideology construction in West Virginia. *Rural Sociology* 75(1), 111–143. doi: 10.1111/j.1549-0831.2009.00004.x.

Boyd, WE (2013). Postcolonial times: Lock the gate or pull down the fences? *Coolabah* 12, 1–31.

Bridge, G (2004). Contested terrain: Mining and the environment. *Annual Review of Environment and Resources* 29(1), 205–259. doi: 10.1146/annurev.energy.28.011503.163434.

Bridge, G (2008). Global production networks and the extractive sector: Governing resource-based development. *Journal of Economic Geography* 8(3), 389–419.

Bryant, L & Pini, B (2009). Gender, class and rurality: Australian case studies. *Journal of Rural Studies* 25(1), 48–57. doi: http://dx.doi.org/10.1016/j.jrurstud.2008.05.003.

Cabrejas, AH (2012). 'Laciana is black. Greens go away!' Environmentalists as scapegoats in a mountaintop removal conflict in Laciana Valley, Spain. *Organization and Environment* 25(4), 419–436. doi: 10.1177/1086026612464973.

Canter, L & Ross, B (2010). State of practice of cumulative effects assessment and management: The good, the bad and the ugly. *Impact Assessment and Project Appraisal* 28(4), 261–268. doi: 10.3152/146155110x12838715793200.

Cassidy, A & McGrath, B (2015). Farm, place and identity construction among Irish farm youth who migrate. *Journal of Rural Studies* 37, 20–28. doi: http://dx.doi.org/10.1016/j.jrurstud.2014.11.006.

Cottle, D & Keys, A (2014). Open-cut coal mining in Australia's Hunter Valley: Sustainability and the industry's economic, ecological and social implications. *International Journal of Rural Law and Policy* (1). Retrieved from http://epress.lib.uts.edu.au/journals/index.php/ijrlp/article/view/3844.

Davis, R & Franks, DM (2014). Costs of company–community conflict in the extractive sector. Report No. 66 *Corporate social responsibility initiative*. Cambridge, MA: Harvard Kenney School.

de Rijke, K (2013). The agri-gas fields of Australia: Black soil, food, and unconventional gas. *Culture, Agriculture, Food and Environment* 35(1), 41–53. doi: 10.1111/cuag.12004.

Duus, S (2013). Coal contestations: Learning from a long, broad view. *Rural Society* 22(2), 96–110.

Ericsson, M (2004). Global mining restructuring and EU25 – Consequences for European miners. *Řada hornicko-geologická* L (2), 73–82.

Estrada-Carmona, N, Hart, AK, DeClerck, FAJ, Harvey, CA & Milder, JC (2014). Integrated landscape management for agriculture, rural livelihoods, and ecosystem conservation: An assessment of experience from Latin America and the Caribbean. *Landscape and Urban Planning* 129, 1–11. doi: http://dx.doi.org/10.1016/j.landurbplan.2014.05.001.

Everingham, J-A, Collins, N, Rodriguez, D, Cavaye, J, Vink, S, Rifkin, W & Baumgartl, T (2013). Energy resources from the food bowl: An uneasy co-existence. Identifying and managing cumulative impacts of mining and agriculture. Project report. Brisbane, QLD: Centre for Social Responsibility in Mining, University of Queensland.

Everingham, J-A, Devenin, V & Collins, N (2015). 'The beast doesn't stop': The resource boom and changes in the social space of the Darling Downs. *Rural Society* 24(1), 42–64. doi: 10.1080/10371656.2014.1001480.

Felton-Taylor, A (2011). Cattle to graze on former mine site. *Australian Broadcasting Corporation (ABC) News*, 9 December.

Fischer-Kowalski, M, Swilling, M, Von Weizsäcker, EU, Ren, Y, Moriguchi, Y, Crane, W, … Siriban Manalang, A (2011). *Decoupling natural resource use and environmental impacts of growth.* A report of the Working Group on Decoupling to the International Resource Panel. Paris: United Nations Environment Programme.

Franks, DM, Brereton, D & Moran, CJ (2010). Managing the cumulative impacts of coal mining on regional communities and environments in Australia. *Impact Assessment and Project Appraisal* 28(4), 299–312.

Franks, DM, Brereton, D & Moran, CJ (2011). Cumulative social impacts. In F Vanclay & A M Esteves (Eds), *New directions in social impact assessment: Conceptual and methodological advances* (pp. 202–220). Cheltenham: Edward Elgar.

Franks, DM, Brereton, D & Moran, CJ (2013). The cumulative dimensions of impact in resource regions. *Resources Policy* 38(4), 640–647. doi: http://dx.doi.org/10.1016/j.resourpol.2013.07.002.

Franks, DM, Brereton, D, Moran, CJ, Sarker, T & Cohen, T (2010). *Cumulative impacts – A good practice guide for the Australian coal mining industry.* Brisbane: Centre for Social Responsibility in Mining & Centre for Water in the Minerals Industry, Sustainable Minerals Institute, University of Queensland, Australian Coal Association Research Program.

Gasteyer, S & Carrera, J (2013). The coal–corn divide: Colliding treadmills in rural community energy development. *Rural Sociology* 78(3), 290–317. doi: 10.1111/ruso.12013.

Gunn, J & Noble, BF (2011). Conceptual and methodological challenges to integrating SEA and cumulative effects assessment. *Environmental Impact Assessment Review* 31(2), 154–160. doi: http://dx.doi.org/10.1016/j.eiar.2009.12.003.

Haggerty, J, Gude, PH, Delorey, M & Rasker, R (2014). Long-term effects of income specialization in oil and gas extraction: The U.S. West, 1980–2011. *Energy Economics* 45(0), 186–195. doi: http://dx.doi.org/10.1016/j.eneco.2014.06.020.

Halfar, J & Fujita, RM (2007). Danger of deep-sea mining. *Science* 316(5827), 987. doi: 10.2307/20036268.

Haslam McKenzie, F (2011). Resource boom times: Building better towns and cities in remote places. Paper presented at the Fifth State of Australian Cities, University of Melbourne. http://soac.fbe.unsw.edu.au/2011/papers/SOAC2011_0070_final.pdf.

Hegmann, G & Yarranton, GA (2011). Alchemy to reason: Effective use of Cumulative Effects Assessment in resource management. *Environmental Impact Assessment Review* 31(5), 484–490. doi: http://dx.doi.org/10.1016/j.eiar.2011.01.011.

Hein, F (2006). Heavy oil and oil (tar) sands in North America: An overview & summary of contributions. *Natural Resources Research* 15(2), 67–84. doi: 10.1007/s11053-006-9016-3.

Hogan, A & Lockie, S (2013). The coupling of rural communities with their economic base: Agriculture, localism and the discourse of self-sufficiency. *Policy Studies* 34(4), 441–454. doi: 10.1080/01442872.2013.822702.

House of Representatives Standing Committee on Regional Australia (2013). Cancer of the bush or salvation for our cities? Canberra, ACT: Parliament of the Commonwealth of Australia.

Jacobs, D (2011). The global market for liquefied natural gas. *RBA Bulletin*, September quarter, pp. 17–27.

Jacquet, JB (2014). Review of risks to communities from shale energy development. *Environmental Science & Technology* 48(15), 8321–8333. doi: 10.1021/es404647x.

Jacquet, JB & Kay, D (2014). The unconventional boomtown: Updating the impact model to fit new spatial and temporal scales. *Journal of Rural and Community Development* [Online] 9(1), 1–23.

Johnson, D, Lalonde, K, McEachern, M, Kenney, J, Mendoza, G, Buffin, A & Rich, K (2011). Improving cumulative effects assessment in Alberta: Regional strategic assessment. *Environmental Impact Assessment Review* 31(5), 481–483. doi: http://dx.doi.org/10.1016/j.eiar.2011.01.010.

Langton, M (2010). The resource curse: New outback principalities and the paradox of plenty. Ed. J Schultz. *Griffith Review* 28, 47–63.

Langton, M (2012). The quiet revolution: Indigenous People and the resources boom. *ABC Boyer Lectures* – 5 part series (18 November 2012–2 December 2012).

Latimer, C (2014). The next age of mining? *Australian Mining*, 21 March. Retrieved 4 January 2015 from http://www.miningaustralia.com.au/features/the-next-age-of-mining.

Lea, JP & Zehner, RB (1986). *Yellowcake and crocodiles: Town planning, government and society in Northern Australia.* Sydney: Allen & Unwin.

Lichter, DT & Brown, DL (2011). Rural America in an urban society: Changing spatial and social boundaries. *Annual Review of Sociology* 37, 565–592. doi: 10.2307/41288622.

Lindberg, TT, Bernhardt, ES, Bier, R, Helton, AM, Merola, RB, Vengosh, A & Di Giulio, RT (2011). Cumulative impacts of mountaintop mining on an Appalachian watershed. *Proceedings of the National Academy of Sciences* 108(52), 20929–20934. doi: 10.1073/pnas.1112381108.

Lloyd, D, Luke, H & Boyd, WE (2013). Community perspectives of natural resource extraction: Coal-seam gas mining and social identity in Eastern Australia. *Coolabah* 10, 144–164.

Lockie, S (2000). Crisis and conflict: Shifting discourses of rural and regional Australia. In B Pritchard & P McManus (Eds), *Land of discontent. The dynamics of change in rural and regional Australia* (pp. 14–32). Sydney: University of New South Wales Press.

Martin, D, Trigger, D & Parmenter, J (2014). Mining in Aboriginal Australia: Economic impacts, sustainable livelihoods and cultural difference at Century Mine, northwest Queensland. In E Gilberthorpe & G Hilson (Eds), *Natural resource extraction and Indigenous livelihoods: Development challenges in an era of globalisation* (pp. 37–56). Farnham, UK: Ashgate.

McDonell, E (2015). The co-constitution of neoliberalism, extractive industries, and indigeneity: Anti-mining protests in Puno, Peru. *The Extractive Industries and Society* 2(1), 112–123. doi: http://dx.doi.org/10.1016/j.exis.2014.10.002.

McManus, P & Connor, LH (2013). What's mine is mine(d): Contests over marginalisation of rural life in the Upper Hunter, NSW. *Rural Society* 22(2), 166–183.

McManus, P, Walmsley, J, Argent, N, Baum, S, Bourke, L, Martin, J, … Sorensen, T (2012). Rural community and rural resilience: What is important to farmers in keeping their country towns alive? *Journal of Rural Studies* 28(1), 20–29. doi: http://dx.doi.org/10.1016/j.jrurstud.2011.09.003.

Measham, TG & Fleming, DA (2013). Impacts of unconventional gas development on rural community decline. Working Paper. Australia: CSIRO.

Measham, TG, McKenzie, FH, Moffat, K & Franks, DM (2013). An expanded role for the mining sector in Australian society? *Rural Society* 22(2), 184–194.

Michaels, G (2011). The long term consequences of resource-based specialisation. *The Economic Journal* 121(551), 31–57. doi: 10.1111/j.1468-0297.2010.02402.x.

Millennium Ecosystem Assessment (2005). Ecosystems and human well-being. Synthesis. Washington, DC: World Resources Institute.

Moffatt, J & Baker, P (2013). Farmers, mining and mental health: The impact on a farming community when a mine is proposed. *Rural Society* 23(1), 60–74. doi: dx.org/10.1080/00141840903202132.

Moran, CJ, Franks, DM & Sonter, LJ (2013). Using the multiple capitals framework to connect indicators of regional cumulative impacts of mining and pastoralism in the Murray Darling Basin, Australia. *Resources Policy* 38(4), 733–744. doi: http://dx.doi.org/10.1016/j.resourpol.2013.01.002.

Newhook, JT, Neis, B, Jackson, L, Roseman, SR, Romanow, P & Vincent, C (2011). Employment-related mobility and the health of workers, families and communities: The Canadian context. *Labour/Le Travail* 67 (Spring), 121–156.

O'Faircheallaigh, C (2012). Community development agreements in the mining industry: An emerging global phenomenon. *Community Development* 44(2), 222–238. doi: 10.1080/15575330.2012.705872.

O'Faircheallaigh, C (2013). Extractive industries and Indigenous peoples: A changing dynamic? *Journal of Rural Studies* 30, 20–30. doi: http://dx.doi.org/10.1016/j.jrurstud.2012.11.003.

Pearson, TW (2013). Frac sand mining in Wisconsin: Understanding emerging conflicts and community organizing. *Culture, Agriculture, Food and Environment* 35(1), 30–40. doi: 10.1111/cuag.12003.

Perdue, RT & Pavela, G (2012). Addictive economies and coal dependency: Methods of extraction and socioeconomic outcomes in West Virginia, 1997–2009. *Organization & Environment* 25(4), 368–384. doi: 10.1177/1086026612464767.

Petrova, S & Marinova, D (2013). Social impacts of mining: Changes within the local social landscape. *Rural Society* 22(2), 153–165.

Pini, B, McDonald, P & Mayes, R (2012). Class contestations and Australia's resource boom: The emergence of the 'cashed-up bogan'. *Sociology* 46(1), 142–158. doi: 10.1177/0038038511419194.

Pinto-Correia, T & Kristensen, L (2013). Linking research to practice: The landscape as the basis for integrating social and ecological perspectives of the rural. *Landscape and Urban Planning* 120, 248–256. doi: http://dx.doi.org/10.1016/j.landurbplan.2013.07.005.

Porter, M, Franks, DM & Everingham, J-A (2013). Cultivating collaboration: Lessons from initiatives to understand and manage cumulative impacts in Australian resource regions. *Resources Policy* 38(4), 657–669. doi: http://dx.doi.org/10.1016/j.resourpol.2013.03.005.

Preston, J (2013). Neoliberal settler colonialism, Canada and the tar sands. *Race & Class* 55(2), 42–59. doi: 10.1177/0306396813497877.

Prior, T, Giurco, D, Mudd, G, Mason, L & Behrisch, J (2012). Resource depletion, peak minerals and the implications for sustainable resource management. *Global Environmental Change* 22(3), 577–587. doi: http://dx.doi.org/10.1016/j.gloenvcha.2011.08.009.

Rolfe, J (2013). Predicting the economic and demographic impacts of long distance commuting in the resources sector: A Surat basin case study. *Resources Policy* 38(4), 723–732. doi: http://dx.doi.org/10.1016/j.resourpol.2013.03.002.

Rolfe, J, Gregg, D, Ivanova, G, Lawrence, R & Rynne, D (2011). The economic contribution of the resources sector by regional areas in Queensland. *Economic Analysis and Policy* 41(1), 15–36.

Sayer, J, Sunderland, T, Ghazoul, J, Pfund, J-L, Sheil, D, Meijaard, E, … Buck, LE (2013). Ten principles for a landscape approach to reconciling agriculture, conservation, and other competing land uses. *Proceedings of the National Academy of Sciences* 110(21), 8349–8356. doi: 10.1073/pnas.1210595110.

State of the Environment 2011 Committee (2011). Australia state of the environment 2011. Independent report to the Australian Government Minister for Sustainability, Environment, Water, Population and Communities. Canberra, ACT: Department of Sustainability, Environment, Water, Population and Communities.

Tonts, M (2005). Government policy and rural sustainability. In C Cocklin & J Dibden (Eds), *Sustainability and change in rural Australia*. Sydney: University of New South Wales Press.

Tulip, P. (2014). The effect of the mining boom on the Australian economy. *RBA Bulletin* December quarter, pp. 17–22.

Upstill, G & Hall, P (2006). Innovation in the minerals industry: Australia in a global context. *Resources Policy* 31(3), 137–145. doi: http://dx.doi.org/10.1016/j.resourpol.2006.12.002.

Wall, E & Pelon, R (2011). Sharing mining benefits in developing countries. *Extractive industries and development series* (Vol. 21). Washington, DC: World Bank.

Weber, M, Krogman, N & Antoniuk, T (2012). Cumulative effects assessment: Linking social, ecological, and governance dimensions. *Ecology and Society* 17(2), Article 22. doi: 10.5751/es-04597-170222.

Wickham, J, Wood, PB, Nicholson, MC, Jenkins, W, Druckenbrod, D, Suter, GW, … Amos, J (2013). The overlooked terrestrial impacts of mountaintop mining. *BioScience* 63(5), 335–348. doi: 10.1525/bio.2013.63.5.7.

Wildman, P, Moore, R, Baker, G & Wadley, D (1990). Push from the bush: Revitalisation strategies for smaller rural towns. *Urban Policy and Research* 8(2), 51–59. doi: 10.1080/08111149008551428.

24

Changing Environmental Values
Beyond Production and Consumption

Jo Vergunst

This chapter explores the range of values that currently underpin relationships with rural environments, and those that might do so in the future. Rural areas have long been subject to diverse and sometimes contradictory discourses, ranging from development to dependency, and from repositories of traditional culture to nodes of globalisation. When we consider the environment, we find that tensions in land use, ownership, nature conservation and productivity all play out according to notions of what is appropriate and what is possible in rural places. Here I discuss the kind of values that both underpin these processes and emerge from them. The focus on landscape and environment not only refers to the basis for some of the most fundamental values of rurality, but also allows often dichotomous values – production and consumption, traditional and modern, local and non-local – to be analysed within the same frame of reference.

Notions of value have been described, asserted and contested in different ways in social science, and there is no single synthesis of a theory of value. One starting point is to distinguish between an exchange-value – for example, where monetary value is attached to a commodity – and cultural and ethical values in the sense of shared norms attitudes, beliefs and morals. The primary concern of this chapter is to explore the informal and often implicit ways in which values are embedded in the environments and the social forms of everyday rural life. It is important to recognise this social aspect of value, asserting that value is not intrinsic but rather created, shared and exchanged through society.

One influential formulation is the idea of a 'regime of value', part of Appadurai's theory of commodities and exchange (1988). Drawing on Marx and Engels, Appadurai argues that categories of objects gain value through the cultural contexts in which they are embedded and exchanged. A regime of value refers to the ways in which value is created and shared socially beyond a local system of meaning, or how it can be generalised and made commensurate across domains in space and time. Yet within a regime of value, 'the degree of value coherence may be highly variable from situation to situation' (1988, p. 15). So values may fragment, shift and cut across boundaries as well as contribute to the creation of boundaries.

Developing this notion beyond a focus on objects and commodities, Otto and Willerslev debate senses of value that occur, on the one hand, through exchange and, on the other, through 'different worldviews or cultural systems, where the emphasis is … on how people express their religious and social attitudes and how this informs their actions' (Otto & Willerslev, 2013, p. 3). Marxist concepts of value derived from material production and exchange can be contrasted with the 'ethical' value of action (Lambek, 2013). These are the kind of values we might learn as part of our habitus (in Bourdieu's terms), but that also emerge through relationships with people and places. Indeed we could contend that values 'sit in places' (as does wisdom, according to Basso (1996)), as well as enabling exchange and movement. In reaching for a synthesis between exchange theories and cultural theories, we need to see 'how action is informed by values and simultaneously creates value' (Otto & Willerslev, 2013, p. 3) – that values and action or behaviour are mutually constituting, rather than causal. A third approach to theorising value is identified by David Graeber (2001, p. 3), referring to the linguistic sense of the term as the 'meaningful difference' between the alternatives in an expression. It is through an iterative process between value and action, situated in and across specific regimes, that we can seek to analyse the meaningful differences of culture and social life.

By locating value not in universalising economic or ethical principles, but turning instead to the sociocultural contexts of ordinary life, researchers can gain insights into relations with environments and landscapes. However, the challenge of a focus on value is to respond to Graeber's claim that it has been easier to describe forms of social and cultural life than it has been to find ways of valuing them meaningfully – such as in ways that lead to action (2001, p. x; 2009). Rural social science should not simply represent diverse cultural opinion, or document forms of exchange that create value, but find ways of clarifying how rural life and rural landscapes are themselves valued and, crucially, could yet be valued in the future.

Production and consumption as values

Exploring production and consumption as values entails looking at their meaning for people involved rather than just describing more abstract economic processes. Debates have been kept up around the nature of productivism, post-productivism and other variants through which rural social scientists have attempted to interpret rural economies and rural space. The question that emerges from much of this literature is how the identified changes are being experienced 'on the ground', according to those involved, and this is where a focus on values can be helpful. Farmers and other rural inhabitants may produce economic value in commodities that is commensurable across different realms, but at the same time they may create ethical value, which often resides in places and landscapes and may not transfer so easily.

The shift from productivism has been recognised, and contested, in different ways. Based on fieldwork in southern England from 1989 to 1992, Murdoch and Marsden outlined a move simply from production to consumption in the countryside (Murdoch & Marsden, 1994, ch. 6). Golf courses were also an example of farm diversification as a response to increased market and regulatory uncertainty. 'Under the old regime of "productivism" land could be regarded as firmly tied to agriculture and this tie stretched back into the past and forward into the future. Now, however, such certainty has gone and land must play its part in the new flexible order' (Murdoch & Marsden, 1994, p. 144). The 'regime' and 'order' are not merely political or economic structures, but regimes of value, in Appadurai's terms, as they shape notions of what is appropriate and worthwhile action.

The other key 'consumptive' uses of space contributing to post-productivist rurality are tourism along with other service industries, and nature conservation along with environmental interest in general (Ilbery, 1998). They signal a move from productivist, intensive agriculture based on support for food production – even though, as Gray (2000) noted, in Europe the Common Agricultural Policy (CAP) has always had a twin value discourse of supporting systems of high-production agriculture (valuing food security) as well as the socially constructed ideal of the small family farm (valuing a kind of rural idyll). Demographic shifts through counter-urbanisation have served to shift this association of rurality with the archetypal family farm, while recognising the spatial unevenness of these processes (Ilbery, 1998, p. 5).

Locating senses of value in these accounts of a shift away from productivism is not straightforward. The identification of post-productivism and its variants have sometimes been seen as an economic or spatial process and sometimes as a set of values in the cultural sense outlined above. In both cases other scholars have challenged the ways in which the changes are identified and their ubiquity, and in doing so have subjected productivism and post-productivism as regimes of value to further scrutiny. Hoggart and Paniagua (2001), for example, challenged the notion that 'rural restructuring' had been under way in England in the forms described by Murdoch and Marsden amongst others, based in part on the values of those involved as well as the actions. In this case farmers are identified as centrally important agents in the productivist/post-productivist shift: 'The much touted shift towards a more consumerist and environmentally friendly farm sector is contradicted by evidence that farmers are not passive agents, but resist change or creatively recreate themselves in a manner of their own choosing' (Hoggart & Paniagua 2001, p. 48).

Further work describes the complexity of these relations. Various kinds of rural productivist values have continued to be identified, both amongst rural dwellers and in surveys of public policies that have driven agricultural production through the 20th century and into the 21st. Wilson noted how rural social science literature had tended to reify productivism and post-productivism as a mutually exclusive dichotomy: 'post-productivism is seen as a move away from the agricultural fundamentalism and exceptionalism that characterized productivism, with a loss of the ideological and economic sense of security for farmers, the latter now branded as "destroyers" of the countryside rather than "stewards of the land"' (Wilson, 2001, p. 82). The shift in values here is stark. Wilson, however, argued that rather than separating the two terms, they should be conceived of as a spectrum (ibid.). By drawing on actor-oriented and behaviourally grounded approaches, a much more spatially and economically variable situation emerges – also noted by others (Evans, Morris & Winter, 2002; Mather, Hill & Nijnik, 2006) – which Wilson characterises as a 'multifunctional agriculture regime' (Wilson, 2001, p. 94).

Farmers' perceptions of their own activities and environments also play into the construction of a regime of values. The notion of farmers as archetypal rational economic actors seeking to maximise their profits has long been recognised as too simplistic, not least through the value-driven nature of agricultural subsidy regimes such as the CAP noted above, but also in how farmers have reacted differently to the new circumstances. Shucksmith and Herrmann for example, found that while family farmers might have 'an orientation towards exchange values and a form of possessive individualism', '[a]t the same time, farmers have tried to maintain a belief in their work which has its roots in a traditional rural/agricultural culture, represented by the tie to the land, the work ethic, expressive rationality itself and other localised aspects' (2002, p. 41).

From the latter perspective, the 'productivity' of a farm can also refer to the significance of keeping the land within appropriate forms of farming as a cultural good in itself. Focusing on farmers themselves, Burton explores the cultural aspects of farming value systems and demonstrates the distinctive aesthetic values and cultural norms amongst 'productivist' farmers that may not be shared with the wider population (Burton, 2004). While the wider public's preferences for the appearance of landscape usually involve those which are 'natural, verdant, forested, traditionally cultural, mixed order/disorder, half-open, and contain water', farmers often prefer tidy and often intensive agricultural landscapes (Burton, 2012, p. 52). Burton continues: 'It is because farmers understand the everyday practices involved in shaping farm landscapes that they are able to interpret and appreciate fully what they are seeing' (2012, p. 53).

The farmers develop cultural capital amongst their peers through adhering to these norms, yet also expressed a personal well-being in maintaining the 'good' appearance of the land – or indeed discomfort from seeing the land not as it should be. Their way of valuing the land is closely tied with their actions in relation to it.

Values in agri-environment, environmentalism and ecosystem services

Understanding productivist values in farming also enables counterpoints to be drawn in other kinds of farm and landscape practices. Sutherland and Darnhofer (2012) focus on the changing idea of 'good farmer', through new 'rules of the game' such as direct payments in the CAP, cross-compliance of environmental practice on the farm, and demand for organic food. They found that organic farmers more commonly recognised environmental conservation as an aspect of 'good farming', but there was significant overlap in attitudes amongst groups. Farmers had also begun to value their own practice in other ways. One of Sutherland and Darnhofer's recent converts to organic farming told them: 'I guess I saw farming as being more than food production and so agriculture with the emphasis on the culture. I see the land as a resource and so one output resource is edible food but there are other outputs you can be achieving from the land (2012, p. 236).'

Studies of participation in voluntary agri-environment schemes have also shown a range of motivations. Morris and Potter (1995) presented a typology from active to passive adopters and outright opponents of such schemes, while arguing that the schemes themselves should operate 'to bring about a shift in the attitudes of farmers towards countryside management which will outlast the schemes themselves and to establish conservation as a legitimate use of land and resources which, for some at least, can earn them a living' (1995, p. 61). More recent work in this field has moved towards recognising regional perspectives that allow for differing value systems and local negotiation of priorities (Morris, 2006; Sutherland, 2010). In Orkney, for example, a strong local sense of proprietorship of the land, based in udal land tenure, was identified by farmers as the basis for valuing so-called 'active management schemes' for participative agri-environmental work rather than being required to simply comply with lists of regulations (Vergunst, 2012). This is not to suggest that tenant farmers are necessarily more inclined to follow prescriptions, but rather, as Krauss (2010) argues, to recognise the significance of regional landscapes in shaping environmental values.

Emergent in this research is a value of 'the environment' not simply as an obstacle for agriculture, to be overcome in becoming a good producer of economic value. The environment is instead recognised as the source of growth and productivity upon which all its inhabitants depend. Farmers are often very appreciative of the 'small' aspects of the living landscape – songbirds, wildflowers and so on – in contrast to the grand scenic visions and backdrops of rural nature (Vergunst, 2012, p. 179). Value in this sense is created through the action of working the land as well as the production taken 'off' it (Lambek, 2013). Nature conservation designations, meanwhile, may be mistrusted often because they seem to fix and attempt to preserve the landscape (Anderson & Berglund, 2003).

This view from local perspectives by no means discounts the need to better protect the environment. In the context of the 'anthropocene' (Crutzen, 2002; Sayre, 2012; Irvine, 2014) – a naming that itself values the significance of human influence on the environment – the release of greenhouse gases, rising temperatures, higher sea levels and changing weather patterns, together with deforestation, the impoverishment of soils and destruction of other natural habitats and biodiversity are all empirically verified by the Intergovernmental Panel on Climate Change (IPCC) and a wide swathe of research in the natural sciences. There is little doubt that such work has played into greater public awareness of and sympathy for environmental issues, while recognising that environmentalism itself has a much longer and diverse history (Milton, 1993; Evans, 1997; Rootes, 1999). Research into the communication of climate change science, however, traces the difficulties of making seemingly universal scientific knowledge commensurable with values held in relation to specific environments. From the Inuit notion of *sila* as the animating force of life that runs through ice as much as it does through people (Hastrup in Diemberger et al., 2012), to farmers' awareness of deep time in the peaty Fenlands of eastern England (Irvine and Evans in Diemberger et al., 2012), it is clear that there is no single narrative of climate and environmental change that can be told from an objectivist standpoint. Climate science emerges from this situation as a 'post-normal science … charged with high degrees of uncertainty; values are in dispute, stakes are high and decisions are—more or less—urgent' (Krauss & von Storch, 2012, p. 214). This points towards a much more flexible and open-ended view of what environmental values could or should be.

At the same time however, the Payments for Ecosystem Services (PES) paradigm has become widespread in the EU and beyond, attempting to provide a generalisable value to natural environments. PES is an administrative tool that attaches monetary value to aspects of the environment which are hard to otherwise quantify a value for, such as biodiversity, the provision and control of water, or carbon storage, along with other ecological processes from which society can be said to gain benefit (DEFRA, 2007). PES has in turn been subject to critique as a tool of neoliberal environmental governance, in that it enables market-style calculations to be made on nature (Wynne-Jones, 2013; Higgins, Potter, Dibden & Cocklin, 2014). In this sense PES is not merely the attribution of financial value to an aspect of an ecosystem, but the creation of a broader regime of value amongst human and non-human actors that transfers meaning from one realm to another.

Kenter et al. (2015, p. 87) describe the useful distinction between 'valuation' and 'valuing' in the context of ecosystem services as follows:

> We consider the latter as an informal, largely implicit process not bound to any particular setting, while the former relates to formal research, analysis or decision-making processes where values (of various types) are explicitly expressed (e.g., in surveys or workshops) or deduced (e.g., through content analysis of media). The purpose of valuation … is to provide knowledge about the value of ecosystems and their services as a contribution to environmental decision-making, monitoring and management processes.

In other words, where valuation is ultimately a technique of governance, valuing is a process of ordinary life in which environments come to have meaning and significance. Kenter and colleagues go on to describe the important ways in which values are not merely held by individuals, as in the PES model, but are also social and shared. For example, in 2011 the UK government attempted to 'sell off' public forests managed by Forestry Enterprise England, but changed course in the face of concerns articulated through direct action groups, national NGOs and the media. This was a collective response to a collective concern, and Kenter et al.'s point is that these shared values need to be incorporated into environmental valuation for policy.

Recognising alternative values in rural environments

It seeems that productivist values have come to exist not independently but in a dichotomy with the conservation or preservation of nature in rural environments. Land can often be recognised as *either* productivist *or* for nature conservation, even within the same landholding.

More broadly, rural environments appear as either to be exploited primarily for private economic gain in a neoliberal mode or to be kept in a state of nature that does not allow for development and change. But this leads to a challenge for rural social science. Both sides of the dichotomy seem unsustainable as sources of values in the face of the challenges of climate change and human-induced environmental change more broadly. Moreover, in circumstances where we might seek to sustain both the diversity of rural ways of life and a broader common-good public interest, what alternatives are on offer? Values around production and consumption (or preservation, consumption etc) are by no means the only possibilities upon which to base action. It is here that we might begin to argue and stake moral claims around values for rural environments. As Otto and Willerslev (2013, p. 15) write, 'All questions of value are also questions of ethics. In this sense, looking at *value as theory* cannot avoid questions of *value as morality*.'

This section pursues environmental values apparent in rural areas where different kinds of people act and interact. The two research monographs discussed next provide sustained accounts of the interaction between values and action in rural environments. It is in such in-depth accounts that we can best explore how productivist and other sorts of values are formed and play out in relation to each other, especially on a regional scale.

Valuing water: Veronica Strang's Gardening the World

The research for *Gardening the World: Agency, Identity and the Ownership of Water* (Strang, 2009) is based in ethnographic techniques of participant observation, interviews and archival research in two river catchments in Queensland, Australia. Building on her previous work on the 'meaning of water' along a river in southwest England in the context of utility privatisation (Strang, 2004) and on cultural landscapes in Australia (Strang, 1997), Strang rejects an a priori distinction between nature and culture in explaining ecological processes. 'Material environments are far more than ecological or "natural" surroundings: they are the product of cultural practices, a repository for memory and cultural knowledge' (2009, p. 29). And while investigating the meaning and use of water involves recognising processes of production and consumption, the key question is slightly different: 'When the costs of overproduction and consumption are "externalised", where do they go?' In this case, intensive water use for farming, industry and domestic use affects the whole ecosystem on a regional scale and all those beings, including people, who live in it.

Productivist values are, unsurprisingly, readily apparent amongst the farming community in Queensland, as they are in the European examples described above. Strang finds that, 'For some, any fresh water that reaches the sea is simply wasted', and one informant described land given back to Indigenous groups or national parks as 'not being used' (p. 123). Another spoke about an irrigation scheme: 'Water means life ... Without it [the irrigation scheme] this area would not have developed to the stage it has now ... It'd be a desert ...Water made this area' (p. 122). The environment is framed by these communities in terms of its ability to produce (p. 123).

The costs of this intensive use are apparent elsewhere in the region, however. An Aboriginal informant from Brisbane Council of Elders is quoted on his concern about irrigation: 'There used to be all these creeks and now there's nothing, it's all gone ... You could drink it before' (p. 108). Such disruption is not just an environmental problem (indeed an environmental injustice), but a much more fundamental challenge to Aboriginal cultural values. They share a sense of water's relation to life with some in the farming community, but the value is not in its economic productive capacity but in the more basic generation of life itself. Strang writes: 'According to traditional beliefs, the ancestral forces concentrated in water sources generate "spirit children" that "jump up" from the water to enliven the foetus in a woman's body. ...

When individuals die, their spirit is "sung" back to its original water place, to be reunited with a totemic ancestor' (pp. 89–90). Water does not just 'mean' life. As another Aboriginal informant says, 'Water is life' (p. 91).

Despite these divergences in values, there are attempts at co-management of water resources, for example in national parks where some Aboriginal communities are beginning to regain rights in fishing and camping (p. 101). Yet where groups of 'stakeholders' are involved, Aboriginal representatives end up in a small minority. Strang provides an example of a river watershed co-management group that started locally and successfully but became dominated by outside environmental organisations (p. 104). Land claims through the Native Title Act are being pursued instead.

Valuing land: Fiona Mackenzie's Places of Possibility

Mackenzie's book, *Places of Possibility: Property, Nature and Community Land Ownership* (2013), shares a concern with the status of collective and communal values in relation to environmental resources (Mackenzie, 2013). Based in long-term qualitative research in the Outer Hebrides island chain to the west of Scotland, it describes and evaluates the process of community land reform under way in Scotland since the late 1990s. Since 2003, crofting communities (crofting is small-scale tenant landholding) in the Highlands and Islands of Scotland have had the right to buy land regardless of the owner's consent to sell, as long as both community and land come within the terms of the bill (2013, p. 47). As Mackenzie writes, this was a radical political step by the new Scottish parliament, partly because of its redistributive effect in a setting of concentrated land ownership, where feudal land tenure and legislation from the 17th century onwards 'supported the movement towards enclosure and privatization, which led, in turn, to the forced removal of vast numbers of people in the interest of large-scale sheep rearing and, later, the establishment of sporting estates' (p. 42). But the land reform legislation also connects with a much older idea in Gaelic culture, that of *dùthchas* – 'a term that might be conceived as both an inherited right and an evolving right to the land … It calls into being collective rights and a collective identity rather than an individual right and identity; it suggests that these collective rights are open and changing rather than fixed, essentialist and exclusionary' (p. 38). A crofter from Mackenzie's study says: 'There is no sense of ownership; it is a sense of belonging. You are part of the land. … It is your heritage. … In Gaelic, you never think about the land belonging to you, it is you that belongs to the land' (p. 40).

The community right to buy 'conjures a politics of the possible' (p. 47). At the same time as reworking the ownership and governance of land, it also revalues alternatives to neoliberalisation and the private and exclusive ownership of land. While land reform has affected the means by which the exchange value of land is calculated, it has asserted the land's cultural value, creating a regime of value that connects political will on different scales from the local to the national. Mackenzie describes the new kinds of 'work' done in relation to property, nature and the wind (renewable energy), together with concepts of place and finally 'possibility' itself.

Mackenzie's case study, the North Harris Trust, was formed as a company to buy, with the help of grants, land totalling over 25,000 hectares from two private owners in 2003 and 2006 (pp. 6, 63). Membership of the Trust is based on residence rather than interest, which means that the crofters have to share ownership with others (p. 65). The founding objectives of the Trust, quoted by Mackenzie, reflect the broad base from which it conceives and values the potential of rural space. In summary form, they are: to conserve the natural heritage for the benefit of the community and public; to promote trade and industry; to relieve poverty and help the infirm; to provide housing for those in need; and to develop infrastructure and communications (p. 66). These are all tasks made newly possible by 'troubling the norms of private property and, through a commoning of the land, making visible an alternative optic to that of commodification' (pp. 70–71).

Towards renewed values for rural environments

The research of Strang and Mackenzie demonstrates the contested nature of rural space, in which 'regimes' of economic and cultural value vary between groups and provide the grounds for different kinds of action. One conclusion is that by listening to rural people's own accounts of their places and ways of life, other ways of valuing environments can come to the fore. It seems clear that seeking to comprehend people's relations and attachments to the environment in their own terms, rather than translating them to a different register, remains an important task for rural social science. Exploring values – and different senses of value – is one way in which this can be done. If values create, as Graeber (2001, p. 3) puts it, 'meaningful difference' between entities (people, other living things, places, objects), it is the generation of value in different objects and places, how it comes to be transferred or exchanged across different spheres, and how it relates to different actions that will be significant to research.

This review has argued that the values of rural environments in modernity – farming and otherwise – have often been constructed around ideas of production and consumption. But such values come up against alternatives, especially on a regional scale that Strang and Mackenzie's work develops. It is often the alternatives that suggest the most fruitful directions for research and for rural environments themselves. It may be possible to suggest some 'renewed' values of rural environment – with cultural depth but contemporary significance – that could usefully play into rural social science research.

Continuity and change: Much of the research considered here shows no easy relationship between rural environments and values of continuity and change. Where productivism involves the constant development or improvement of the land, preservationist discourses attempt to fix the land in an idealised state of nature or culture. In reality, people and communities often seem to pivot around desires to maintain valued ways of rural life at the same time as seeking certain kinds of change: to confront injustice, improve quality of life and so on (Árnason, Shucksmith & Vergunst, 2009). Exploring ideas of continuity and change in relation to rural environments will remain significant in rural social science.

Viability: 'Viability' is often used in the rural social science literature, but the concern to 'keep things going' in often difficult circumstances is also sometimes expressed by farmers and other rural dwellers. Farmers in Orkney often talk about diversification projects or agri-environment schemes in terms of their contribution to the viability of the farm, for example (Lee, 2007), often using the word to mark a difference from the 'environmentalist' notion of sustainability. Focusing on the value of viability in rural society and environments more broadly would mean ensuring that existing ways of living with and on the land can be pursued into the future.

Balance: In relation to the environment, a value of balance would involve respecting divergent viewpoints, but also recognising that economic productivity (in whatever form) and nature conservation can exist together. 'Balance' can also be asserted as a value in land use conflict. Fischer and Marshall (2010) found most stakeholders identifying themselves as having a balanced view on woodland restoration, even if their professional affiliations would incline them to one side or the other. How can values of balance play out as a kind of bridge between opposing positions, and how can positive values of conflict – those that lead to positive transformation – be sustained through it?

Creativity: Rural space is not just the periphery to urban cores but is a source of growth, innovation and inspiration in its own terms, all of which could be underpinned by a value of rural creativity. Rural environments themselves create life through organic growth and ecological-cultural processes, while artistic responses to rurality can include assertions of belonging and the powerful presence of landscapes in rural lives (Mackenzie, 2004). Mitchell (2013) offers 'creative enhancement' as a multifunctional aspect of rural space in contrast to the production–consumption dichotomy, thus emphasising the creativity of rural life and rural responses to diverse forms of change.

References

Anderson, D & Berglund, E (Eds). (2003). *Ethnographies of conservation: Environmentalism and the distribution of privilege*. Oxford: Berghahn.

Appadurai, A (1988). Introduction. In A Appadurai (Ed.), *The social life of things* (pp. 1–57). Cambridge: Cambridge University Press.

Árnason, A, Shucksmith, M & Vergunst, J (Eds). (2009). *Comparing rural development: Continuity and change in the countryside of western Europe*. Farnham: Ashgate.

Basso, K (1996). *Wisdom sits in places: Landscape and language among the Western Apache*. Sante Fe: University of New Mexico Press.

Burton, R (2004). Seeing through the 'good farmer's' eyes: Towards developing an understanding of the social symbolic value of 'productivist' behaviour. *Sociologia Ruralis* 44, 195–215.

Burton, R (2012). Understanding farmers' aesthetic preference for tidy agricultural landscapes: A Bourdieusian perspective. *Landscape Research* 37(1), 51–71.

Crutzen, PJ (2002). Geology of mankind: The Anthropocene. *Nature* 415, 23.

DEFRA (Department for Environment, Food and Rural Affairs) (2007). *An introductory guide to valuing ecosystem services*. London: DEFRA.

Diemberger, H, Hastrup, K, Schaffer, S, Kennel, C, Sneath, D, Bravo, M, Graf, H-F, Hobbs, J, … Bodenhorn, B (2012). Communicating climate knowledge: Proxies, processes, politics. *Current Anthropology* 53(2), 226–244.

Evans, D (1997). *A history of nature conservation in Britain*. London: Routledge.

Evans, N, Morris, C & Winter, M (2002). Conceptualizing agriculture. A critique of post-productivism as the new orthodoxy. *Progress in Human Geography* 26(3), 313–332.

Fischer, A & Marshall, K (2010). Framing the landscape: Discourses of woodland restoration and moorland management in Scotland. *Journal of Rural Studies* 26, 185–195.

Graeber, D (2001). *Toward an anthropological theory of value: The false coin of our own dreams*. New York: Palgrave Macmillan.

Graeber, D (2009). *Direct action. An ethnography*. Edinburgh: AK Press.

Gray, J (2000). The Common Agricultural Policy and the re-invention of the rural in the European Community. *Sociologia Ruralis* 40(1), 30–52.

Higgins, V, Potter, C, Dibden, J & Cocklin, C (2014). Neoliberalising rural environments. *Journal of Rural Studies* 36, 386–390.

Hoggart, K & Paniagua, A (2001). What rural restructuring? *Journal of Rural Studies* 17, 41–62.

Ilbery, B (Ed.). (1998). *The geography of rural social change*. Harlow: Longman.

Irvine, R (2014) Deep time: An anthropological problem. *Social Anthropology* 22(2), 157–172.

Kenter, J, O'Brien, L, Hockley, N, Ravenscroft, N, Fazeyf, I, Irvine, K, Reed, M, Christie, M, … Williams, S (2015). What are shared and social values of ecosystems? *Ecological Economics* 111, 86–99.

Krauss, W (2010). The 'dingpolitik' of wind energy in northern German landscapes: An ethnographic case study. *Landscape Research* 35(2), 195–208.

Krauss, W & Von Storch, H (2012). Post-normal practices between regional climate services and local knowledge. *Nature and Culture* 7(2), 213–230.

Lambek, M (2013). The value of performative acts. *Hau Journal of Ethnographic Theory* 3(2), 141–160.

Lee, J (2007). Experiencing landscape: Orkney hill land and farming. *Journal of Rural Studies* 23(1), 88–100.

Mackenzie, AFD (2004). Place and the art of belonging. *Cultural Geographies* 11(2), 115–137.

Mackenzie, AFD (2013). *Places of possibility: Property, nature and community land ownership*. Chichester: Wiley Blackwell.

Mather, A, Hill, G & Nijnik, M (2006). Post-productivism and rural land use: Cul de sac or challenge for theorization? *Journal of Rural Studies* 22, 441–455.

Milton, K (Ed.). (1993). *Environmentalism: The view from anthropology.* London: Routledge.

Mitchell, C (2013). Creative destruction or creative enhancement? Understanding the transformation of rural spaces. *Journal of Rural Studies* 32, 375–387.

Morris, C (2006). Negotiating the boundary between state-led and farmer approaches to knowing nature: An analysis of UK agri-environmental schemes. *Geoforum* 37, 113–127.

Morris, C & Potter, C (1995). Recruiting the new conservationists: Farmers' adoption of agrienvironmental schemes in the UK. *Journal of Rural Studies* 11, 51–63.

Murdoch, J & Marsden, T (1994). *Reconstituting rurality. Class, power and community in the development process.* London: UCL Press.

Otto, T & Willerslev, R (2013). Introduction: 'Value as theory'. Comparison, cultural critique, and guerrilla ethnographic theory. *HAU: Journal of Ethnographic Theory* 3(1), 1–20.

Rootes, C (Ed.). (1999). *Environmental movements: Local, national and global.* London: Frank Cass.

Sayre, N (2012). The politics of the anthropogenic. *Annual Review of Anthropology* 41, 57–70.

Shucksmith, M & Herrmann, V (2002). Future changes in British agriculture: Projecting divergent farm household behaviour. *Journal of Agricultural Economics* 53(1), 37–50.

Strang, V. (1997). *Uncommon ground: Cultural landscapes and environmental values.* Oxford: Berg.

Strang, V. (2004). *The meaning of water.* Oxford: Berg.

Strang, V. (2009). *Gardening the world: Agency, identity and the ownership of water.* Oxford: Berghahn.

Sutherland, L (2010). Environmental grants and regulations in strategic farm business decision-making: A case study of attitudinal behaviour in Scotland. *Land Use Policy* 27 (Special Issue), 415–423.

Sutherland, L & Darnhofer, I (2012). Of organic farmers and 'good farmers': Changing habitus in rural England. *Journal of Rural Studies* 28, 232–240.

Vergunst, J (2012). Farming and the nature of landscape: Stasis and movement in a regional landscape tradition. *Landscape Research* 37(2), 173–190.

Wilson, G (2001). From productivism to post-productivism … and back again? Exploring the (un)changed natural and mental landscapes of European agriculture. *Transactions of the Institute of British Geographers* 26(1), 77–102.

Wynne-Jones, S (2013). Connecting payments for ecosystem services and agri-environment regulation: An analysis of the Welsh Glastir Scheme. *Journal of Rural Studies* 31, 77–86.

25

Land Use Planning in an Era of Hyper-Security

Charles Geisler and David Kay

Introduction

As the environmental movement gained ground in the 1960s and 1970s, the land use planning powers vested in state and federal government agencies in the United States ballooned. Environmentalists welcomed this 'quiet revolution' in land use controls, heretofore reserved to state and local governments as a police power under the Tenth Amendment of the US Constitution. Even by the early 1970s, however, this trend faltered somewhat (Plotkin, 1980; Sabatier, 1988), and by the 1980s and 1990s conservatives trumped conservationists with a rising tide of neoliberal regulation roll-backs, land use controls among them. Property rights groups, Republican-dominated state legislatures, and state and federal courts successfully hamstrung the quiet revolution (Kayden, 2004; Adler, 2005; Heynen, McCarthy, Prudham & Robbins, 2007). In its place appeared a broad 'devolution revolution' (Soss, Schram, Vartanian & O'Brian, 2001).

On the eve of the new millennium, however, something unforeseen occurred. Novel societal threats erupted, challenging the assumptions of minimalist government and neoliberalism. Hyper-security became a new vernacular in the face of social precarities and a worldwide web of wicked problems, such as unrelieved global warming, rip-tides of economic calamity, dysfunction among nation states as viable ruling units, and a torrent of international terrorism – what Robb (2007) called the 'brave new war'. Heightened government resolve to tighten security bore a resemblance to the quiet revolution. But something more profound was occurring. The new federalisation of land use planning in America had a decidedly military cast.

In advance of the evidence, the argument of the present chapter is as follows. Crisis, conflict and emergency are touchstones of the new millennium in the United States and globally (Boin, Hart & McConnell, 2009; Smith, 2014), and together are a breeding ground for a reinvigorated regulatory state. In the face of homeland securitisation in the USA and elsewhere, liberalism is becoming increasingly illiberal, in keeping with what Kienscherf (2013a, 2013b) calls 'liberal governmentalities of security'. Amid this illiberalism, land use regulation consistent with Agamben's (2005) 'state of exception' reasoning is emerging that is both centralised and, at least in de facto ways, more militarised.

States of exception (sometimes called 'laws of necessity' or, in extreme cases, 'martial law') have their roots in the French Revolution and became 'paradigmatic' in the 20th century (Humphreys, 2006). By 1986 some 70 countries were in states of emergency and 147 had some sort of state-of-exception law by 1996. In these periods, civilian functions – including policing and certain police powers of the state – assume military overtones and resort to war imagery (e.g., the war on drugs, on crime, on poverty, on terrorism, etc.). 'War' salience justifies pre-emptive action by central governments for political ends, as Carl Schmitt (1922/1985) explained in the abstract and Agamben (2005) demonstrated more concretely in recent European and US history.

Put simply, the long-standing rationale for land use planning and regulation – maintaining the health, safety and welfare of local jurisdictions (particularly in the US case) – is giving way to a more encompassing logic of national security. As this occurs and the campaign against terrorism becomes open-ended, a soft form of martial law over land and space is emerging. Though this chapter spotlights the United States' 'homeland', where decentralised and market-driven land use planning have been deeply entrenched, we make reference as well to other societies where land use planning is moulting in a military direction.

Past militarisation of land use

The United States has previously used military land policy in the name of national security and nation building on its borderlands and rural interiors. The army pacified Indian homelands, consolidated the Northwest Territories, and incorporated the vast Mormon state of Deseret as well as the northern half of Mexico into the Union. After the American Revolution and several other wars, Washington settled 'empty' areas with soldiers paid with homestead plots (Sakolski, 1957). The first national parks were governed by the US Army (Runte, 1979), and Forest Service Rangers mimicked military rangers in dress and deed (Pratt, 2014). Since 1802 the Army Corps of Engineers has guided land use by surveying, mapping and building the nation's infrastructure (Tegler, 2013).

This military 'easement'[1] on domestic lands continues to evolve. Some 29,000 acres of land in the United States are dedicated to military bases, test sites and strategic zones (Schilling, n.d.). Surrounding jurisdictions often receive federal 'hosting' funds for their compliance. Omaha, Jacksonville, Tucson, Salt Lake City, Colorado Springs, San Jose, San Franciso, Los Angeles, San Diego, Tampa, Amarillo and Albuquerque (and dozens more) include military officials in their land use decisions (Kirby, 1992). Houston and Las Vegas became major Sunbelt cities thanks to heavy military investment, and Nevada's Nellis Air Force Base has long been a military 'company town' and southern Nevada's largest employer (Parker & Feagin, 1992). The demography, employment, tax base and land use of whole regions wax and wane according to military presence (Markusen, Hall, Campbell & Dietrick, 1991; Lutz, 2001), sometimes referred to as 'military Keynesianism' (Melman, 1988).

The Cold War had its own brand of homeland securitisation and alterations for rural landscapes. Most readers will know that the 41,000-mile US Interstate Highway System was authorised and strategically renamed the National System of Interstate and Defense Highways during the Cold War (Weingroff, 1996). Fewer may recall that urban sprawl onto America's farmlands was in part planned, a 'defensive dispersal' of land and population in response to Cold War nuclear fears (Dudley, 2001; Ziegler, 2005). To a lesser degree, 9/11 threats to urban centres have influenced population dispersals (Kay, Geisler & Bills, 2010), land values and local government land use plans. Yet these examples, though diverse, form a small fraction of the landscape ultimately subject to military decision making across the continent in the course of homeland securitisation.

Post-Posse Comitatus

The military content of domestic land use planning intensified, in several ways and for a variety of reasons, following the 2001 attacks on the United States. A core US military doctrine in the war theatres of Iraq and Afghanistan was the integration of police and military, modelled after the French Gendarmerie and the Italian Carabineiri. This 'security continuum' logic, as explained by Bayley and Perito (2010), drew on the seminal work of Oakley, Dziedzie and Goldberg's *Policing the New World's Disorder: Peace Operations and Public Security* (1998) and recalled precedents for the US military performing law enforcement before and after the Cold War.

The terrorist attacks on the United States in 2011 broadened this role yet again. As Mayer (2006, p. 55) noted, 'The attacks of 9-11 … raised the issue of the role the military will play in America's domestic security. Since 1878, the Posse Comitatus Act has prevented active duty military personnel from making domestic arrests or conducting searches on American citizens … If another large-scale terrorist attack occurs, the government's power could grow yet again.' And grow it did, with a spate of emergency statutes closely simulating Agamben's (2005) 'state of exception' and de facto martial law. The new 'Age of Terror' (Croft, 2007) registered in public opinion (Lustick, 2006), in the bi-partisan '9/11 Report' by Lee Hamilton and Thomas Kean (2005), and in the National Intelligence Estimate of 2007 (NIE, 2007), all of which saw further terrorist attacks on the United States as near certainties.

Authorisations for militarised land use planning were formalised anew in the Patriot Act (2001), the Homeland Security Act (2002), the Military Commissions Act (2006), the National Defense Authorization Act (2012), and various secret laws and executive security directives. The Military Commissions Act, signed by President George W. Bush on October 17, 2006, authorised trial by military commissions and denied habeas corpus. The National Defense Authorization Act of 2012 mandates that anyone 'suspected' of terrorism be held indefinitely in military custody without trial, and revokes citizenship. More secretive legislation, not directly relevant to this chapter though similarly born of emergency conditions, is summarised in the Cato Institute's 2009 Handbook for Congress, 7th edition, and in White (2014). Though these laws appear to abridge civil liberties and not pertain to land use, they entail broad search warrants, with the police and military 'trespassing on property without regard for the rights of owners and the blurring of distinctions – for purposes of searches and seizures – between what is private and public property' (Whitehead, 2013).

In 2002 Defense Secretary Donald Rumsfeld announced the establishment of US Northern Command as part of the Unified Command Plan, calling it the most sweeping change in the unified command system since 1946. NORTHCOM's mission was redrawn to prioritise 'the preparation for, prevention of, deterrence of, preemption of, defense against, and response to threats and aggression directed towards U.S. territory, sovereignty, domestic population, and infrastructure; as well as crisis management, consequence management, and other domestic civil support' (Scott, 2006). The Northern Command is today in charge of homeland defence; its domain covers the continental United States, Alaska, Canada, Mexico and surrounding 500 miles of water (Global Security Organization, 2014a).[2]

On any given day, more than 5,000 troops conduct law enforcement operations within the United States, not including the even larger number of National Guard troops routinely involved in law enforcement (Kopel, 2000). In 2001 lawyers for George W. Bush asserted that the President could arrest anyone in the world so long as he had issued an 'enemy combatant' order with the Secretary of Defense. The same lawyers argued that the courts should not 'second-guess' the President's 'battlefield' decisions in the war on terror. They defined the entire world and every inch of US territory as 'battlefield', from Florida to Hawaii and all towns in-between (Cato Institute, 2009, p. 296). Little wonder, then, that a senior fellow for National Security and Homeland Security, James Carafano (2006), predicted that the military could be summoned for domestic duty with virtually no changes to the Constitution or the Posse Comitatus Act. Related mission creep assumed many forms. The Department of Defense's Law Enforcement Support Office (LESO) supplies surplus military equipment to 17,000 federal and state law enforcement agencies in the USA under the motto 'from warfighter to crimefighter'. These agencies received nearly US$450 million in 2013 in military equipment, up from US$1 million in 1990 (Dansky, 2014).[3] In addition, some 22 states now have internal state defence forces (SDF), legalised militias, to protect infrastructure (e.g., the Alaskan pipeline after 9/11) or assist recovery efforts after natural disasters (Zuckerman, Hershkowitz, Smalkin & Carafano, 2012).

Homeland securitisation

What does the blending of police, the ultimate enforcers of land use regulation, and a military unencumbered by posse comitatus legislation mean for land use planning? The Patriot Act of 2001 became law less than two months after the attacks of 9/11 and enjoyed renewal in 2006 and again in 2011 and 2015, a crowning case of 'state of exception' government behaviour. The Act and its amendments abridge both civil rights and property rights (Bovard, 2003). It allows the President to confiscate the property of foreign persons, organisations or countries believed to be involved in hostilities toward the United States (Title I, §106); it authorises the government to confiscate all property of persons, entities or organisations engaged in domestic or international terrorism against the country, its people, or their property (Title VIII, §806); and, by defining terrorism broadly (Title VIII, §808), it enables sweeping government forfeiture (property confiscation) powers (Ball, 2004; Abele, 2005).

The Homeland Security Act, passed the following year, produced a cabinet-level Department of Homeland Security (DHS) and a national command centre for coordinating intergovernmental implementation of the National Strategy for Homeland Security set forth in 2003; its fusion of 22 agencies was the largest reorganisation of the federal government since the creation of the US Department of Defense in 1947. In his 2003 speech, 'Securing the Homeland, Strengthening the Nation', President Bush directed a $37.7 billion allocation for DHS purposes, up from $19.5 billion the year before (Bush, 2003). Such levels of annual funding have continued since (2015 Fiscal Year Budget Request for DHS is $38.2 billion). Substantively, and astutely for a president who would make the 'Ownership Society' a leading plank in his 2004 re-election campaign, the speech unveiled a road map for future homeland security involving a partnership with state and local governments – the constitutional locus of land use planning.

But in an updated version of the National Strategy in 2007, the President expanded the partnership to include the military:

> Our Nation's armed forces are crucial partners in homeland security. Our active, reserve, and National Guard forces are integrated into communities throughout our country, and they bring to bear the largest and most diverse workforce and capabilities in government to protect the United States from direct attacks and conduct missions to deter, prevent, and defeat threats against our Nation. Over the past several years, our armed forces have been preparing to meet a wider range of challenges to our Nation by restructuring their capabilities, rearranging their global force posture, and adapting forces to better fight the War on Terror.

The homeland securitisation of land use planning ensued in many forms. And because the global war on terrorism persisted abroad and at home, few local land use advocates, urban or rural, challenged the federalising or militarising of their domain.[4] In the remainder of this chapter, we review three principal DHS initiatives with land use planning implications: regulatory reform; the protection of critical infrastructure; and the securing of national borders.

Regulatory reform

In the same year the National Strategy appeared, the American Law Institute and the American Bar Association offered their annual Land Use Institute and included a paper entitled: 'Homeland Security Begins at Home: Local Planning and Regulatory Review to Improve Security'. Published in *Land Use Law & Zoning Digest* (Young & Merriam, 2003; Young, 2008), it proposed ways in which land use planning could play a role in mitigating terrorist threats to the nation. The authors reassured local officials that national security benefits follow from normal applications of property law (ownership, control and continuing property rights) but warned that local land use planners and others who fail to take proactive homeland security measures (e.g., revise ordinances and codes, comply with inspections by law enforcement personnel and amend plans to incorporate 'homeland security' elements) do so at 'considerable risk' and possible liability (2003, p. 10).[5]

Two years later, the American Bar Association (ABA) drafted a guide for state and local governments engaged in homeland security and emergency management. Its authors, Abbot and Hetzel (2006), again concurred that inaction would incur considerable liability risks and added a strong 'use it or lose it' proviso; local officials charged with planning must be proactive or face prospects of federal override. Local partners were encouraged, for example, to use conditional use permits that impose clean-up responsibility on property owners in the event of attacks resulting in the release of hazardous substances. Failure to respond was serious and could result in federal pre-emption (Abbot & Hetzel, 2006, p. 93). A precedent existed in the Comprehensive Environmental Response, Compensation, and Liability Act (CERCLA), commonly known as the Superfund law and enacted by Congress in 1980. Local governments were instructed to undertake comprehensive studies of their development review and permitting processes so as to incorporate Homeland Security considerations; they were urged to revise ordinances, codes and site inspections to comply with the DHS's 'defensive steps'; and they were directed to perform due diligence in planning, purchasing and remodelling buildings to conform with DHS security guidelines – especially those facilities designated 'terrorist sensitive' (Abbot & Hetzel, 2006, p. 95).

But the ABA guide went even further, offering spatial and territorial directives. They proposed buffer zones, moats and bollards to stem terrorist attacks by vehicles (Abbot & Hetzel, 2006, p. 90). Whereas in the past, adjoining land uses considered incompatible according to health, welfare and safety standards were separated by lines on zoning maps, physical impediments would now separate land uses based on security concerns. Subsequent work by Nemeth and Hollander (2009) investigated the spatial consequences of these recommendations in three urban centres (Los Angeles, San Francisco and New York); an average of 17% of the study sites were closed or severely limited to public access. The authors consider these zones 'militarised' and suggest the emergence of a new land use category, saying:

> Even before these terror attacks (9/11), owners and managers of high-profile public and private buildings had begun to militarise space by outfitting surrounding streets and sidewalks with rotating surveillance cameras, metal fences and concrete bollards. In emergency situations, such features may be reasonable impositions, but as threat levels fall these larger security zones fail to incorporate a diversity of uses and users.

Similar land use restrictions are organic to the urban militarism in other countries, some with the encouragement and active partnering with the United States and others not (Reveron, 2010). Better known cases are England (Graham, 2011; Minton, 2012; Graham & Kaker, 2014) and Israel (Weizman, 2006). In the *Planet of Slums*, Mike Davis (2006) cites research from the US Army War College journal asserting that,

> The future of warfare lies in the streets, sewers, high-rise buildings, industrial parks, and the sprawl of houses, shacks, and shelters that form the broken cities of our world ... Our recent military history is punctuated with city names – Tuzla, Mogadishu, Los Angeles, Beirut, Panama City, Hue, Saigon, Santo Domingo – but these encounters have been but a prologue, with the real drama still to come.

To this list could be added Mexico City, São Paulo, Kuala Lumpur, Singapore, Beijing, Seoul, Karachi, Baghdad, Moscow, Soma and Detroit and numerous other global cities hosting paramilitary policing and spatial management (Graham, 2011).

Security-based, militarised land use planning extends beyond these major urban sites. In the United States, DHS offices in all 50 states routinely promote security zones around critical infrastructure and military facilities.[6] California, the state with the most military installations and operations areas in the nation, offers a leading example. In a 2006 Handbook prepared by the California governor's Office of Planning and Research (OPR), concern was expressed that the state's urban growth was encroaching into military zones. The Handbook notes that by 2001 more than half of the California military installations were adjacent to or within metropolitan areas and that the state was projecting a population increase of over 50% by 2050. Not surprisingly, the threat of civilian–military land use incompatibility is 'one of the military's greatest concerns' under any circumstances, but especially in a time of national emergency (OPR, 2006, pp. 1–2).

A close reading of the California Handbook and its updates (e.g., Bryant, 2013) shows encouragement for regulatory reform backed with overtones of state or federal override if local officials are uncooperative or unresponsive. Its authors say land use compatibility will be achieved when communities and military installations balance their competing interests. This congenial assertion is overshadowed by state laws passed in 2002 requiring cities and counties to consider the impact of further growth on military readiness in their general plans for property adjacent to military facilities or under military aviation routes. The same Act amends the state's Environmental Quality Act to ensure that the military is notified of project proposals within two miles of their installations or special use airspace. These notification requirements expanded again in 2004 and since. They override the police power of local jurisdictions, preventing amendment of general land use plans without military review.[7] Though seemingly about partnerships, the Handbook (2006, pp. 1–3) sends a clear message as to where ultimate planning authority rests: 'Local governments must recognize the needs of military installations and operation areas to determine what planning tools local communities should use to promote compatibility.' This language is grounded more in the soft authority of planning than in the hard authority of regulation; the legislation 'requires' notification, consideration of and consultation with military interests but fails to explicitly require local government deference to those interests.

Protection of critical infrastructure

Closely related to security partnerships with local governments is the multi-jurisdictional protection of Critical Infrastructure and Key Resources (CIKR). In selling the Department of Homeland Security to the nation, President Bush (2003, p. 5) stated that his administration was going to great lengths to identify and protect critical sea and water ports, airports, nuclear facilities, dams, water and sewer plants, electric power plants, gas pipelines, bridges, biological and chemical facilities, military installations and government facilities. Special technologies would be deployed (such as Intelligent Transportation Systems) for highways and mass transit systems relied upon by parcel delivery companies, pipeline operators, police, fire, ambulance services and others.[8] Several times since 2003, and for every state, the DHS has assessed 18 infrastructural types and resource sectors in terms of terrorist threats in its National Infrastructure Protection Plan (NIPP) of 2006. States, local governments and Indian Tribes across the nation partner in this effort, as described above. The resulting information is entered into national geospatial databases for security planning (Allen, 2008, p. 3). The Federal Emergency Management Administration offers retrofitting grants to local governments to modify their land use plans in conformance with national security goals (NIPP, 2014).

Among the nation's critical infrastructure are its electric, hydroelectric and hydrocarbon extraction and transmission technologies spanning vast rural expanses. Where they run between states, they are arguably a domain of federal regulation and planning, and have important land use implications. The Energy Policy Act of 2005 (Public Law 109-58) directs the Secretary of Energy to conduct electric transmission congestion studies every three years in consultation with affected states and regional organisations. Based on these studies in 2006, 2009 and 2013, the Secretary could designate any geographical area experiencing electric transmission capacity constraints or congestion as a national interest electric transmission corridor (NIETC) (US Office of Electricity Delivery and Energy Reliability, 2014). At the same time Congress empowered the Federal Energy Regulatory Commission (FERC) with backstop authority to use 'eminent domain' to site transmission lines within the NIETCs under certain circumstances – for example, where hosting states were slow to act or where they impeded the economic viability of such projects. Historically, states held the authority to site electrical transmission lines. After the Energy Policy Act of 2005, the FERC rolled out national security narratives to assume these powers and shift regulatory prerogatives to Washington (Swanstrom & Jolivert, 2009).

This power shift was contested by states and landowners. At least on procedural grounds, it was challenged in the courts with its scope narrowly construed (Kay, 2012; Hoeckner & Smith, 2014). After 9/11, the Department of Energy's (DOE) Infrastructure Security and Energy Restoration (ISER) division worked with Homeland Security to formulate laws authorising the DOE to use eminent domain under interstate circumstances or within states where cooperation was lacking. These proposed NEITC were vast and extended over sweeping geographies: the Mid-Atlantic Area National Corridor covered parts of Ohio, West Virginia, Pennsylvania, New York, Maryland, Virginia, New Jersey, Delaware and the District of Columbia, and the Southwest Area National Corridor included counties in California, Arizona and Nevada. Within these NIETCs, the FERC had the authority to issue permits to build or modify transmission infrastructures over state objections (DOE, 2007; Hempling, 2007; US Office of Electricity Delivery and Energy Reliability, 2014). Lawsuits eventually put the NIETC strategy on hold and, for the present, reduced their pre-emptive potential.[9] The 2005 Energy Policy Act also forged an extensive set of energy right-of-ways (ROWs) across federal (mostly rural) lands.

Spatial planning refers to airspace and cyberspace as well as land. The threat of cyber attacks has added momentum to federal interventions in securing electric infrastructure. The proposed Electric Grid Cyber Security Bill of 2009, had it become law, contained provision to give the FERC authority to issue broad 'emergency rules' when cyber threats were imminent (APPA, 2013). The appearance of the Stuxnet computer worm in 2010 threatened power generation and led the North American Electric Reliability Corporation (NERC) to develop Critical Infrastructure Protection (CIP) standards on cyber security. Version 4 of these standards is now operative, making 15–20% of electrical utilities compliant with CIP, and version 5 will commence in 2016, raising compliance requirement still further (MacElroy, n.d.).

Secure Borders Initiative

The Secure Borders Initiative (SBI) is a partnership by DHS, DOD and the US Customs and Border Protection (CBP) covering all coastal ports of entry and the land between ports, coastal and inland, that constitute US borders. Its ambit is the perimeter of the United States, urban and rural, as well as 400–500 domestic airport zones protected by air marshals and 47,000 Transportation Security Administration (TSA) officers who are also part of the DHS (GAO, 2008).[10] The SBI merges terrorist prevention with immigration control, as directed by Title IV of the Patriot Act. As of 2015, it had over 240,000 employees, eight times its number in 2003 and the largest federal law enforcement agency in the country (Vitiello & Vaughan, 2012). It operates on land ('boots on the ground') and with drones, satellites and aircraft overhead ('boots in the air'), and is referred to as a 'daunting domestic army' (Miller, 2014).

What are its implications for land use planning and federal pre-emption? The CBP partnership secures approximately 4,000 miles of border with Canada, 2,000 miles of border with Mexico and 2,600 miles of additional shoreline, a sprawling zone of exception. DHS descriptive materials underscore its partnership approach with state and local jurisdictions, but federal agencies are the senior decision makers. Much has been written, for example, about federal eminent domain in creating effective *cordons sanitaires* along the US–Mexican border, a third of which the United States has secured with walls, roads, cameras and a 300-foot wide buffer zone (Archibold, 2007; Sammartino, 2013). The DHS issued waivers suspending over 30 laws that could interfere with the 'expeditious construction of barriers' within the zone (Liptak, 2008), and immigration law authorises the DHS Secretary to purchase any interest in land adjacent to or in the vicinity of the international border. Condemnation is used if a mutually agreed upon price cannot be found.[11]

However, the spatial implications of the SBI go much further and potentially affect both civil and property rights of over half the nation's population. After 9/11, Congress authorised the Customs and Border Patrol within the DHS to operate within 100 miles of the actual border (Figure 25.1). Using data provided by the US Census Bureau, the ACLU has determined that nearly two-thirds of the 2007 US population (197.4 million people) live within this 100-mile zone of exception (Table 25.1). The American Civil Liberties Union refers to this as a 'Constitution-Free Zone' because, within it, Border Patrol agents have extra-constitutional powers of stop and search (ACLU, 2008a), as well as to seize property (Geisler, 2011). This pertains to the personal property of travellers – legal or illegal – within the zone and to any real property of its residents deemed necessary for national security via eminent domain or forfeiture.

The maritime portion of SBI offers its own zone of exception in and around 300 US seaports, along US coasts, and over expansive offshore territories. It extends inland from coasts to rivers, bridges, tunnels, ports, waterside industries, as well as boats and ships (e.g., on the Great Lakes) that may be terrorists' suppliers or targets. Temporary quarantines extend to millions of shipping containers seen as potential 'Trojan horses' housing weapons of mass destruction under the DHS's Container Security Initiative (Lipton & Wald, 2005; Global Security Organization, 2014b). The CBP's 2006 strategic plan announced a 'Secure Environment' goal, stating its intentions to intensively manage seaports: 'Every port of entry is a physical locale shaped by a number of complex environmental factors … [t]he physical design plays a large role in CBP's day-to-day operations within the ports' (2006, p. 36).

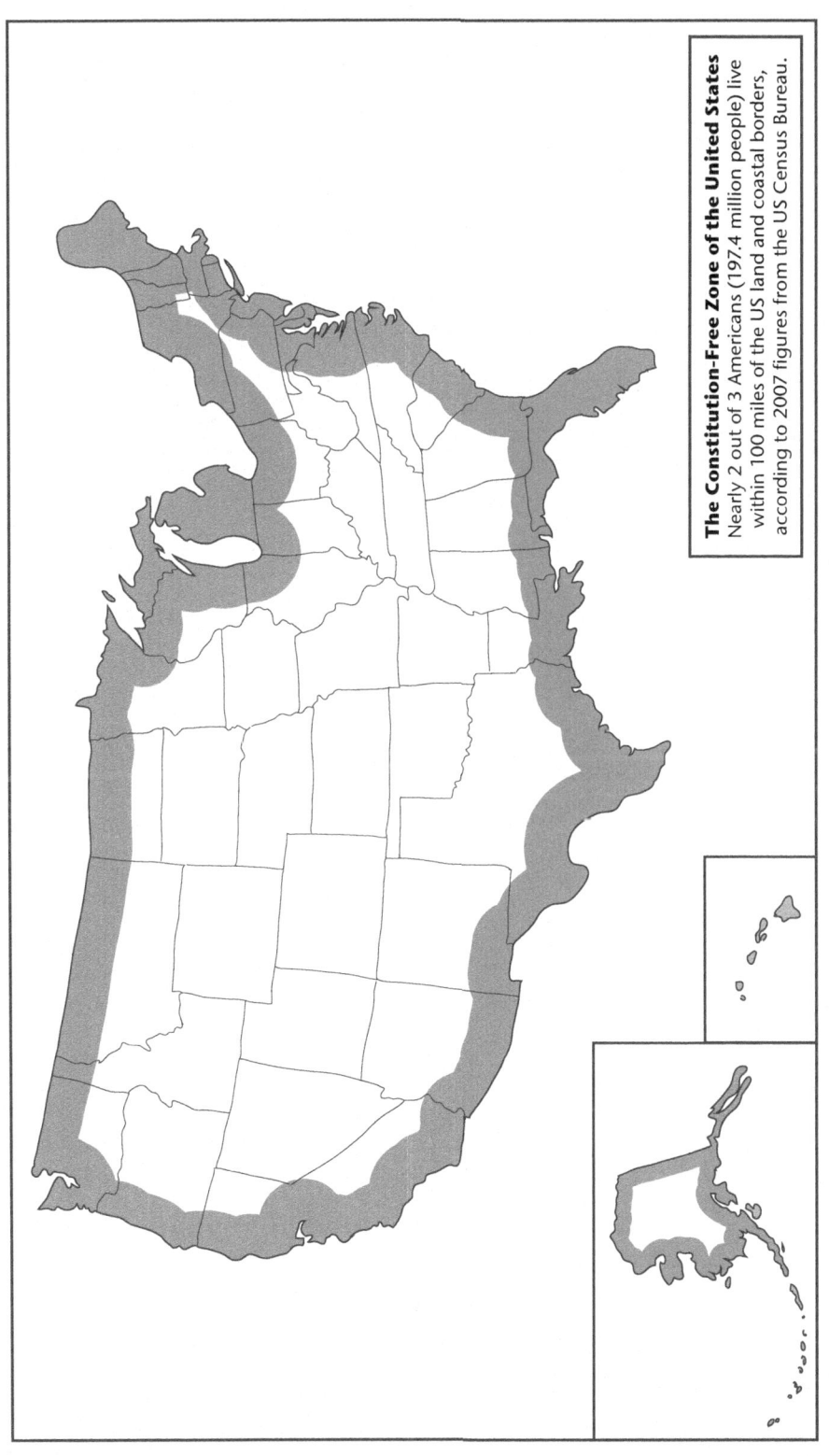

The Constitution-Free Zone of the United States
Nearly 2 out of 3 Americans (197.4 million people) live within 100 miles of the US land and coastal borders, according to 2007 figures from the US Census Bureau.

Figure 25.1 The 100-mile zone of constitutional exception

Source: Original figurre from ACLU (2008a) and redrawn with urban centres deleted by Routledge at author's request.

Charles Geisler and David Kay

Table 25.1 US population in the 100-mile 'Constitution-free zone'

State	Estimated 2007 border population	Estimated 2007 state population	Percentage of population in Constitution-free zone
Alabama	1,104,926	4,627,851	23.88
Alaska	584,156	683,478	85.47
Arizona	5,570,479	6,338,755	87.88
California	36,453,649	36,553,215	99.73
Connecticut	3,502,309	3,502,309	100.00
Delaware	864,764	864,764	100.00
District of Columbia	588,292	588,292	100.00
Florida	18,251,243	18,251,243	100.00
Georgia	1,512,950	9,544,750	15.85
Hawaii	1,283,388	1,283,388	100.00
Idaho	199,202	1,499,402	13.29
Illinois	9,847,235	12,852,548	76.62
Indiana	2,607,575	6,345,289	41.09
Louisiana	3,388,334	4,293,204	78.92
Maine	1,317,207	1,317,207	100.00
Maryland	5,516,123	5,618,344	98.18
Massachusetts	6,449,755	6,449,755	100.00
Michigan	10,071,822	10,071,822	100.00
Minnesota	623,477	5,197,621	12.00
Mississippi	976,345	2,918,785	33.45
Montana	518,717	957,861	54.15
New Hampshire	1,315,828	1,315,828	100.00
New Jersey	8,685,920	8,685,920	100.00
New Mexico	452,904	1,969,915	22.99
New York	18,795,187	19,297,729	97.40
North Carolina	2,795,661	9,061,032	30.85
North Dakota	279,695	639,715	43.72
Ohio	7,885,365	11,466,917	68.77
Oregon	3,249,327	3,747,455	86.71
Pennsylvania	10,890,623	12,432,792	87.60
Rhode Island	1,057,832	1,057,832	100.00
South Carolina	2,603,946	4,407,709	59.08
Texas	10,301,403	23,904,380	43.09
Vermont	584,802	621,254	94.13
Virginia	6,282,997	7,712,091	81.47
Washington	6,076,268	6,468,424	93.94
West Virginia	233,344	1,812,035	12.88
Wisconsin	4,716,621	5,601,640	84.20

Note: The population numbers are taken from the 2007 US Census. States not listed have zero population within the 100-mile zone.

Source: ACLU (2008b).

One thus sees the police power of local jurisdictions migrating to ever-larger coastal zones that previously attracted federal regulation as part of the quiet revolution in land use planning noted earlier (the Coastal Zone Management Act of 1972). Regulating such areas and defending them from attacks necessitates unusual interventions at the state and federal level. For example, the powerful Port Authorities of New York and New Jersey (known together as PANYN) oversee or act as landlord to 20 major cargo terminals and have another 167 privately owned terminals in their joint jurisdiction. Before 9/11, the docks in these facilities were accessible to the public. As requested by the 9/11 Commission, all individual berths are now off-limits to the public. All area terminals within PANYN must today have security plans that are overseen by the US Coast Guard, and the DHS restricts access to the expanding domain secured by the Coast Guard (Viana, 2009).

The Coast Guard is emerging as an important repository of newly assumed federal police powers thanks to its performance during Hurricane Katrina in 2005. The potential for a shift in police power from local governments to the Coast Guard seems open-ended. Today its Atlantic Area Command extends from the East Coast to the Rocky Mountains and it is the lead agency in protecting the coasts of the Great Lakes and the water bodies of the interior, not to mention the vast (11,351,000 km^2) offshore Exclusive Economic Zone of the United States.[12] In the words of a senior Coast Guard authority, 'Today, the Coast Guard is a military, multi-mission, maritime force within the Department of Homeland Security … [whose] missions are executed by shore-based multi-mission forces assigned to 35 sectors in 9 Coast Guard Districts' (US Coast Guard, 2006 p. 2).

Pre-emption precedents

The gradual militarisation of land use planning under homeland securitisation has civilian sector precedents beyond those noted early in this chapter. Again, many are of paramount importance in rural areas. The land use regulations embedded in the Clean Air, Section 404 of the Clean Water Act, the habitat protections of the Endangered Species Act, the Coastal Zone Management Act, the Mining Control and Reclamation Act, the Superfund Law, and of course many laws pertaining to the federal lands themselves are all relevant. As early as 1879, Congress established the Mississippi River Commission within the War Department to draw up standard plans for flood control and supervise the disbursement of federal funds (White, 1945). Ongoing floods brought the Army Corps of Engineers into the picture in 1917, and, during the Great Depression, Washington became more aggressive. By the mid-1930s, local flood control problems were reinterpreted as regional and national challenges, resulting in the 1936 National Flood Control Act.

The Tennessee Valley Authority of the same era, created by Congress for flood control, national defence and energy generation, all but obliterated local land use planning in parts of seven states. According to Meinig (1995), 'The TVA was a geopolitical entity imposed upon the states by the central government … [without] elected officials; its directors were appointed by the president and confirmed by Congress and were accountable only to the same.' On the urban front, federally directed urban renewal began in 1949 with the Federal Housing Act, an extension of wartime housing planning (Mandelker, 2008) and a prototype for the nationwide urban renewal of the 1960s. In numerous national emergencies and natural disasters Washington assumed responsibility for local and regional land use planning (Buell, 2003; Nolan & Rodriguez, 2007).

Nor are these precedents limited to the United States. Numerous countries have mobilised military, police and security personnel to take charge of space, resources and borderlands during 'permanent' emergencies. A British case study (Coaffee & Wood 2006), for example, argues that neoliberal forces commodifying security have blurred the significance of boundaries between national borders and those of local/personal security. This opens the door to tropes of security and embeds them in local and regional land use policies under the banner of 'resilience'. Elsewhere, homeland securitisation against extremist threats to states themselves brings lethal force to bear on land policies, turning parks, forests and frontiers into security and pacification zones (e.g., Peluso, 2001; Keller, 2007; Peluso & Vandergeest, 2011). In some societies, military bodies have a long history of indirect land use planning through cartography, boundary maintenance, base expansion and infrastructure control. The ordering of space by the military is reported in Britain (Minton, 2012), France (Luke & O Tuathail, 2000), Israel (Weizmann, 2006), Iraq (Walther, 2011), India and Bangladesh (Dunn & Cons, 2014), South Africa (Abrahemsen & Williams, 2007), and in the now-familiar militarised geographies of Egypt, Guatemala, Myanmar, Colombia, Nigeria, Thailand, Indonesia, North Korea, Russia and Pakistan.

In point of fact, the US 'security regime' not infrequently alters rural landscapes globally as its homeland security objectives reach offshore, fostering new military bases, exercises and operations (e.g., policing land with drones) (Kienscherf, 2013a). Close US allies such as Saudi Arabia and Israel secure their homelands with US-supplied hardware and equipment. Regarding the latter, Oren and Newman (2006, p. 561) write: 'There is virtually no region within Israel where competition between civilian and military land uses and priorities does not take place', and the latter tends to have supremacy. On a global scale, Woodward (2004, p. 3) makes a similar point: 'Military geographies are everywhere: every corner of every place in every land in every part of this world of ours is touched, shaped, viewed and represented in some way by military forces and military activities – a soldier's footprint, a landowner's custody, an invader's force, and occupier's presence.'

Conclusion

As the global war on terrorism narrative proliferates, land use planning in different societies has centralised, contributing to the impotency of small jurisdictions and rural places. In the United States, a bastion of private ownership and localised police powers over land use control, hyper-security concerns are inviting ever-stronger non-local land use planning infused with military thinking. As the de facto military easement spreads over the landscape, land use planning is shifting to the hands of non-elected personnel from within the Department of Defense's Northern Command, the Coast Guard, the Border Patrol, the Transportation Security Administration, the National Guard and private security firms (Altman, 2014; Hagedorn, 2014). Land use planning, responding to the security threat of a 'perpetual war on terrorism', is undergoing a quiet revolution unlikely to be easily overturned.

Is, as alleged at the outset of this chapter, homeland securitisation driving illiberalism in the United States and elsewhere, and creating a climate in which ever more regulation is imperative? The answer would seem self-evidently affirmative: militarised land use planning by definition means regulatory intervention from above and a more *dirigiste* political economy overall. This is antithetical to neoliberalism, deregulation and market-defined social relations. Militarised land use planning appears to reshape the soft power of market-led decisions into ever-harder power using fiat, martial law, eminent domain, forfeiture and other non-voluntary means of space-making.

Yet to imply that militarised land use planning is a pendulum swing away from neoliberalism is to misconstrue neoliberalism and the paternalistic statecraft that can accompany it (Wacquant, 2009). Although neoliberalism provides economic freedom for capital, it has geostrategic planning needs that require state intervention. It turns to government for subsidies and a long list of public goods – infrastructure, market safeguards, and domestic and international protection. At least some aspects of the UN's Security Sector Reform and the World Trade Organization's free trade initiatives can be seen in this light. Neoliberalism rolls back certain government functions even as it rolls out others (Peck & Tickell, 2002).

Kienscherf (2013b) is quite clear that the war on terror is part of a larger pacification and spatial control effort aiding and abetting neoliberalism in a highly nuanced fashion. The militarisation of land use planning is a neoliberal tourniquet on the landscape that keeps the social body alive and well for the beneficiaries of free enterprise. Draconian planning measures such as this are requisite to controlling the movement and containment of population, the access and use of vital resources by these populations, and the rules of ultimate ownership and control over rural and other landscapes.

Acknowledgements

We acknowledge funding support from the Land Project of the Institute of Social Studies at Cornell University. Thanks to Professor Manny Teodoro, Department of Political Science, Colgate University for useful criticisms and comments.

Notes

1 An easement is a use right by one entity over the property of another, often permanent, in recognition of a payment or other benefit (e.g., tax relief) to the owner-seller or donor. Military easements can be explicit, as in flowage easements on private land by the Corps of Engineers, or liminal, as in the present case. In providing military security against extremist threats, the government extinguishes selected property rights in exchange for protection, in the name of an 'overriding public interest', and often without material compensation.

2 Although the Posse Comitatus Act of 1878, as amended, makes it a felony to use any part of the armed forces other than the Coast Guard as a posse comitatus in domestic law enforcement except as authorised by the Constitution or act of Congress (18 U.S.C. § 1385), the Global Security Organization cites numerous historical examples of the US Army performing domestic policing functions since 1878.

3 The Excess Property (1033) Program within the Department of Defense is managed through LESO to provide surplus military equipment to state and local civilian law enforcement agencies for use in counter-narcotics and counter-terrorism operations. Dansky et al. (2014) summarise police force 'militarization' across the USA.

4 There are approximately 90,000 local governments in the United States, ranging from counties to municipalities and special-purpose districts. Many of these are 'rural' with regard to location, population density or cultural identity. Since the 1920s, states have transferred land use planning 'police powers' to some local governments; other rural places have no local land use controls other than those of their parent counties.

5 The 2003, 2006 and 2008 reports that followed provide an overview of selected publications, GAO reports, and a NEPA finding germane to security since 2003 (Young, 2008).

6 Homeland Security's National Infrastructure Protection Plan (NIPP), discussed below, emphasises a buffer zone approach to keeping enemy surveillance and attacks at bay (NIPP, 2006, p. 183). Physical access management requires barriers, state-of-the-art intrusion detection, and evolving 'special security zones' around air and maritime ports (Fessler, 2003), along with police and military regulation of cyberspace.

7 In compliance with state law, the military has provided electronic maps of critical land and air information on the Internet to assist planners, and the state has done the same with its California Military Land Use Compatibility Analyst (CMLUCA) (see Byrant, 2013).

8 Critical infrastructure is defined in the US Patriot Act of 2001 (Section 1016(e)).

9 Based on the 2006 Study, two National Interest Electric Transmission Corridors were designated in 2007. In 2008, the Pennsylvania Land Trust Association and Piedmont Environmental Council, along with other organisations and jurisdictions, filed a suit against the US Department of Energy's final designation of the Mid-Atlantic National Interest Electric Transmission Corridors (NIETC). The 9th Circuit Court ruled in 2011 that the DOE failed to conduct an environmental review as required by the National Environmental Policy Act and failed to consult with affected states.

10 TSA officers are armed but cannot legally make arrests.

11 The DHS's resolve to make the border secure using eminent domain was emphasised by Michael Chertoff (2007), DHS Secretary under President Bush. In late 2013 a Federal Court upheld the right of the federal government to use eminent domain to secure the border.
12 This United States' Exclusive Economic Zone (EEZ) is the largest in the world and covers both the eastern and western seaboards, the Gulf of Mexico, the Northwest Pacific, Northeast Pacific, Micronesia, Polynesia and the Arctic Ocean. A map of the EEZ for the USA can be found at http://www.nauticalcharts.noaa.gov/csdl/mbound.htm (accessed 29 January 2016).

References

Abbot, EB & Hetzel, O (Eds). (2006). *Homeland security and emergency management for state and local governments: A legal guide*. Washington, DC: ABA Press.
Abele, RP (2005). *A user's guide to the USA Patriot Act and beyond*. New York: University Press of America.
Abrahamsen, R & Williams, MC (2007). Securing the city: Private security companies and non-state authority. *Global Governance* 21(2), 237–253.
ACLU (2008a). Know your rights: The government's 100-mile 'border' zone – map. Available at https://www.aclu.org/know-your-rights-governments-100-mile-border-zone-map (accessed 30 October 2014).
ACLU (2008b). Constitution free zone: The numbers. Available at https://www.aclu.org/technology-and-liberty/constitution-free-zone-numbers (accessed 27 October 2014).
Adler, JH (2005). Back to the future of conservation; changing perceptions of property rights and environmental protection. *NYU Journal of Law and Liberty* 1(3), 987–1022.
Agamben, G (2005). *State of exception*. Chicago: University of Chicago Press.
Allen, CE (2008). Keynote address at GEOINT conference by Charles E. Allen, Under Secretary for Intelligence and Analysis. GEOINT Conference, Nashville, Tennessee (May).
Altman, A (2014). The pot raiders: Private security pulls weed in an economy no longer quite underground. *Time* (September) 184(12), 15.
APPA (2013). *Bulk power system cyber security*. American Public Power Association Issue Brief (February).
Archibold, RC (2007). 28-Mile virtual fence is rising along the border. *New York Times* Late Edition, 26 June 2007, A-12.
Ball, H (2004). *The USDA Patriot Act of 2001*. New York, NY: ABC-CLIO.
Bayley, DH & Perito, RM (2010). *The police in war: Fighting insurgency, terrorism, and violent crime*. London: Lynne Rienner.
Boin, A, Hart, P & McConnell, A (2009). Crisis exploitation: Political and policy impacts of framing contests. *Journal of European Public Policy* 16(1), 81–106.
Bovard, J (2003). *Terrorism and tyranny: Trampling freedom, justice, and peace to rid the world of evil*. New York: Palgrave Macmillan.
Bryant, C (2013). *Community and military compatibility planning*. Sacramento, CA: Governor's Office of Planning and Research.
Buell, F (2003). *From apocalypse to way of life*. New York: Routledge.
Bush, GW (2003). *Securing the homeland, strengthening the nation*. Washington, DC: The White House.
Carafano, JJ (2006). Catastrophic disaster and the future of military response. *Disaster Preparedness* 1 (Summer), 6–10. Cato Institute (2009). *Cato handbook for policymakers* (7th edn). Washington, DC: Cato Institute.
Chertoff, M (2007). Remarks by homeland security director Michael Chertoff and commerce secretary Gutierrez at a press conference on border security and administrative immigration reforms. Retrieved 20 September 2007 from http://www.dhs.gov/xnews/releases/pr_1186781502047.shtm.
Coaffee, J & Wood, DM (2006). Security is coming home: Rethinking scale and constructing resilience in the global urban response to terrorist risk. *International relations* 20(4), 503–517.
Croft, S (2007). Introduction. *Government and Opposition* 42, 1–9.
Dansky, K (2014). *War comes home: Excessive militarization of American policing*. New York: American Civil Liberties Union.
Dansky, K, Solon, S, Bohm, A, Anderson, E & McCurdy, J (2014). *War comes home: The excessive militarization of American policing*. New York: American Civil Liberties Union.
Davis, M (2006). *Planet of slums*. London: Verso.

DOE (2007). DOE issues two draft national interest electric transmission corridor designations. April 26. Retrieved 10 September 2009 from http://www.doe.gov/news/4997.htm.

Dudley, MQ (2001). Sprawl as strategy: City planners face the bomb. *Journal of Planning Education and Research* (21), 52–63.

Dunn, E & Cons, J (2014). Aleatory sovereignty and the rule of sensitive space. *Antipode* 46(1), 92–109.

Fessler, P (2003). Interview with Stephen Flynn (Senior Fellow, Council on Foreign Relations), Vulnerability of US ports 18 months following the 9/11 attacks. All Things Considered broadcast on National Public Radio, 12 March.

GAO (2008). *Aviation security: Transportation security administration has strengthened planning to guide investments in key aviation security programs, but more work remains.* Washington, DC: GAO-08-456T.

Geisler, C (2011). Accumulating insecurity: Dispossessing migrants. In S Feldman, C Geisler & G Menon (Eds), *Accumulating insecurity: Violence and dispossession in the making of everyday life* (pp. 240–260). Athens, GA: University of Georgia Press.

Global Security Organization (2014a). U.S. Northern Command Department of Defense. Global security organization. Available at http://www.globalsecurity.org/military/agency/dod/northcom.htm (accessed 8 October 2014).

Global Security Organization (2014b). Container security initiative. Homeland security. Available at http://www.globalsecurity.org/security/ops/csi.htm (accessed 30 October 2014).

Graham, S (2011). *Cities under siege: The new military urbanism.* London: Verso.

Graham, S & Kaker, SA (2014). Living the security city: Karachi's archipelago of enclaves. *Harvard Design Magazine* 37, 12–16.

Hagedorn, A (2014). *The invisible soldiers: How America outsourced our security.* New York: Simon & Schuster.

Hamilton, L & Keane, T (2005). National commission on terrorist attacks upon the United States. Available at http://www.9-11commission.gov/ (accessed 17 February 2014).

Hempling, S (2007). Will FERC's transmission siting rule create more jurisdictional conflict? *Power: Business and Technology for the Global Generation Industry*, 15 February. Available at http://www.powermag.com/issues/departments/speaking_of_power/Will-FERCs-transmission-siting-rule-create-more-jurisdictional-conflict_258.html (accessed 11 May 2009).

Heynen, N, McCarthy, J, Prudham, S & Robbins, P (Eds). (2007). *Neoliberal environments: False promises and unnatural consequences.* New York: Routledge.

Hoecker, J & Smith, D (2014). Regulatory federalism and development of electric transmission: A brewing storm? *Energy Law Journal* (35), 71–99.

Humphreys, S (2006). Legalizing lawlessness: On Giorgio Agamben's state of exception. *The European Journal of International Law* 17(3), 677–687.

Kay, DL (2012). Energy federalism: Who decides? Available at http://cardi.cals.cornell.edu/sites/cardi.cals.cornell.edu/files/shared/documents/Community-Energy/Energy-Federalism.pdf (accessed 29 January 2015).

Kay, DL, Geisler, C & Bills, NL (2010). Terrorism and residential preferences: Evidence in New York state. *Rural Sociology* 75(3), 426–454.

Kayden, JS (2004). Charting the constitutional course of private property: Learning from the 20th century. In HM Jacobs (Ed.), *Private property in the 21st century* (pp. 31–49). Northampton, MA: Edward Elgar.

Keller, P (2007). Transboundary protected area proposals along the southern Andes of Chile and Argentina: Status of current efforts. *USDA Forest Service Proceedings RMRS-P-49*, 244–248.

Kienscherf, M (2013a). *US domestic and international regimes of security: Pacifying the globe, securing the homeland.* London: Routledge.

Kienscherf, M (2013b). A programme of global pacification: US counterinsurgency doctrine and the biopolitics of human (in)security. *Security Dialogue* 42(6), 517–535.

Kirby, A (1992). The Pentagon versus the cities? In A Kirby (Ed.), *The Pentagon and the cities* (pp. 1–22). London: Sage.

Kopel, D (2000). Militarized law enforcement: The drug war's deadly fruit. In *After prohibition: An adult approach to drug policies in the 21st century* (pp. 61–88). Washington, DC: Cato Institute.

Liptak, A (2008). Power to build border fence is above U.S. law. *New York Times*, 8 April 2008. Available at http://www.nytimes.com/2008/04/08/us/08bar.html?_r=0 (accessed 27 October 2014).

Lipton, E & Wald, M (2005). U.S. to spend billions more to alter security systems. *New York Times*, 8 May 2005.

Luke, T & O Tuathail, G (2000). Thinking geopolitical space: The spatiality of war, speed, and vision in the work of Paul Virilio. In M Craig & N Thrift (Eds), *Thinking space* (pp. 360–379). London: Routledge.

Lustick, I (2006). *Trapped in the war on terror*. Philadelphia, PA: University of Pennsylvania Press.

Lutz, C (2001). *Homefront: A military city and the American twentieth century*. Boston, MA: Beacon Press.

MacElroy, P (2015). Cyber security to move from headline to bottom line. Telecommunications issues, *Black & Veatch*. Available at http://bv.com/Home/news/solutions/Smart-Cities-Telecom/cyber-security-to-move-from-the-headline-to-the-bottom-line (accessed July 22 2015).

Mandelker, D (2008). Kelo's lessons for urban redevelopment: History forgotten. Washington University Law Review slip opinions, 24 November. Retrieved 30 October 2014 from http://lawreview.wustl.edu/slip-opinions/kelos-lessons-for-urban-redevelopment-history-forgotten.

Markusen, A, Hall, P, Campbell, S & Dietrick, S (1991). *The rise of the gunbelt: The military remapping of industrial America*. Oxford: Oxford University Press.

Mayer, JD (2006). *9-11: Aftershocks of the attack*. Belmont, CA: Thomson Wadsworth.

Meinig, DW (1995). *The shaping of America*. New Haven, CT: Yale University Press.

Melman, S (1988). Economic consequences of the arms race: The second rate economy. *Papers and Proceedings of the American Economics Association* 78(2), 55–59.

Miller, T (2014). Border patrol agents train for war on the US–Mexico border. *Border Wars: NACLA Update*, 12 March. Available at https://nacla.org/blog/2014/3/12/border-patrol-agents-train-war-us-mexico-border (accessed 27 October 2014).

Minton, A (2012). We are returning to an undemocratic model of land ownership. *The Guardian*, 11 June 2012. Available at http://www.theguardian.com/commentisfree/2012/jun/11/public-spaces-undemocratic-land-ownership (accessed 20 November 2014).

Nemeth, J & Hollander, J (2009). Lost space: Security zones and New York City's shrinking public space. *International Journal of Urban and Regional Research* 34(1), 20–34.

NIE (National Intelligence Estimate) (2007). *Today's terrorist threat: National intelligence estimate*. Washington, DC: FBI.

NIPP (2006). *National infrastructure protection plan*. Washington, DC: Department of Homeland Security.

NIPP (2014). *National infrastructure protection plan – 2013*. Washington, DC: Department of Homeland Security.

Nolon, JR & Rodriguez, D (Eds). (2007). *Losing ground: A nation on edge*. Washington, DC: Environmental Law Institute.

Oakley, R, Dziedzie, M & Goldberg, E (1998). *Policing the new world's disorder: Peace operations and public security*. Washington, DC: National Defense University Press.

OPR (2006). *California governor's office of planning and research handbook*. Sacramento, CA.

Oren, A & Newman, D (2006). Competing land uses: The territorial dimension of civil–military relations in Israel. *Israel Affairs* 12(13), 561–577.

Parker, RE & Feagin, JR (1992). Military spending in free enterprise cities: The military industrial complex in Houston and Las Vegas. In A Kirby (Ed.), *The Pentagon and the cities* (pp. 100–125). London: Sage.

Peck, J & Tickell, A (2002). Neoliberalizing space. *Antipode* 34(3), 380–404.

Peluso, NL (2001). *Violent environments*. Ithaca, NY: Cornell University Press.

Peluso, NL & Vandergeest, P (2011). Political ecologies of war and forests: Counterinsurgencies and the making of national natures. *Annals of the Association of American Geographers* 101(3), 1–21.

Plotkin, S (1980). Policy fragmentation and capitalist reform: The defeat of national land-use policy. *Politics & Society* 9(4), 409–445.

Pratt, J (2014). Forest ranger job requirements. *Chron: Work by Demand Media*. Retrieved 4 October 2014 from http://work.chron.com/forest-ranger-job-requirements-13287.html.

Reveron, DS (2010). *Exporting security: International engagement, security cooperation, and the changing face of the U.S. military*. Washington, DC: Georgetown University Press.

Robb, J (2007). *Brave new war: The next stage of terrorism and the end of globalization*. Hoboken, NJ: John Wiley & Sons.

Runte, A (1992). *National parks: The American experience*. Lincoln, NE: Smithsonian Institution Press.

Sabatier, P (1988). An advocacy coalition framework of policy change and the role of policy-oriented learning therein. *Policy Sciences* 21(2–3), 129–168.

Sakolski, A (1957). *Land tenure and land taxation in America*. New York: Robert Schalenbach Foundation.

Sammartino, C (2013). Border patrol taking land through eminent domain for border surveillance. *KGUN9 On Your Side*, 30 August.

Schilling, J (n.d.). *Collaborative land use planning: A guide for military installations and local government.* International City/County Management Association. Alexandria, VA Metropolitan Institute at Virginia Tech.

Schmitt, C (1922/1985). *Political theology: Four chapters on the concept of sovereignty.* Cambridge, MA: MIT Press.

Scott, PD (2006). Preparing for martial law? *Pacific News,* 2 March 2006. Retrieved 22 July 2014 from http://educationforum.ipbhost.com/index.php?showtopic=6116.

Smith, D (2014). Consume, screw, kill: The origins of today's mass extinction. *Harper's Magazine* 328 (May), 84–89.

Soss, J, Schram, S, Vartanian, T & O'Brian, E (2001). Setting the terms of relief: Explaining state policy choices in the devolution revolution. *American Journal of Political Science* 45(2), 378–395.

Swanstrom, D & Jolivert, MM (2009). DOW transmission corridor designation & FERC backstop siting authority: Has the energy policy act of 2005 succeeded in stimulating the development of new transmission facilities? *Energy Law Journal* 30, 415–466.

Tegler, E (2013). History of Army Corps of Engineers projects: Missile and space programs to the American Recovery and Reinvestment Act part II. *Defense Media Network.* Available at http://www.defensemedianetwork.com/stories/history-of-army-corps-of-engineers-projects-part-ii/ (accessed 10 August 2014).

US Coast Guard (2006). *Report of the Judge Advocate General of the United States Coast Guard.* Presented to the American Bar Association, New York.

US Office of Electricity Delivery & Energy Reliability (2014). *National electric transmission congestion studies.* Available at http://energy.gov/oe/services/electricity-policy-coordination-and-implementation/transmission-planning/national (accessed 27 October 2014).

Viana, LP (2009). Best practices half a world away. *HSToday Magazine* 6(3), 20–24.

Vitiello, R & Vaughan, M (2012). Boots on the ground or eyes in the sky: How best to utilize the National Guard to achieve operational control. House Committee on Homeland Security, Subcommittee on Border and Maritime Security hearing 17 April. Available at http://www.dhs.gov/news/2012/04/17/written-testimony-us-customs-and-border-protection-house-homeland-security (accessed 27 October 2014).

Wacquant, L (2009). *Punishing the poor: The neoliberal government of social insecurity.* Durham, NC: Duke University Press.

Walther, C (2011). *Managing change in the wetlands: Iraq's critical choices. United Nations Integrated Water Task Force for Iraq.* New York: United Nations.

Weingroff, RF (1996). Federal-aid highway act of 1956: Creating the interstate. *Public Roads* (Summer) 60(1). Available at http://www.fhwa.dot.gov/publications/publicroads/96summer/p96su10.cfm (accessed 31 October 2014).

Weizman, E (2006). The art of war. *Frieze Magazine* 99 (May). Available at http://www.frieze.com/issue/article/the_art_of_war/ (accessed 15 July 2015).

White, G (1945). Human adjustment to floods. University of Chicago Department of Geography, Research paper No. 29.

White, JR (2014). *Terrorism and homeland security.* Belmont, CA: Thomson-Wadsworth.

Whitehead, JW (2013). *A government of wolves: The emerging American police state.* New York: Selectbook.

Woodward, R (2004). *Military geographies.* Oxford: Blackwell.

Young, RC, Jr. (2008). *2008 Update: Homeland Security consideration in land use.* Land Use Institute: Planning, regulation, litigation, eminent domain, and compensation. ALI-ABA course of study. Cosponsored by the Center for Urban and Environmental Solutions, Florida Atlantic University, 13–16 August.

Young, RC, Jr. & Merriam, D (2003). Homeland security begins at home: Local planning and regulatory review to improve security. *Land Use Law & Zoning Digest* 55(11), 1102–1115.

Zeigler, EH (2005). American cities and sustainable development in an age of global terrorism: Some thoughts on fortress America and the potential for defensive dispersal II. *William and Mary Environmental Law & Policy Review* 30, 95–151.

Zuckerman, J, Hershkowitz, M, Smalkin, F & Carafano, JJ (2012). *Why more states should establish state defense forces.* Backgrounder 2655, National Security and Defense. Washington, DC: The Heritage Foundation.

26

Multifunctionality, Rural Diversification and the Unsettlement of Rural Land Use Systems

Katrina Rønningen and Frode Flemsæter

Introduction

Modernisation processes in rural areas are taking on different shapes, and with contradictory and paradoxical effects in the global north. In this chapter we explore the commodification of rural resources, focusing on ways the revaluation of the material values of rural areas are unsettling land use and land use rights. The exercise of land use rights – customary rights linked to commons and rural areas – is under pressure within the prevailing economic, political and structural ideologies and developments. Consequently, a key question is whether existing multifunctional agricultural policies and land use planning systems are willing or able to control the commodifying modernisation processes in agricultural and rural economies and, consequently, safeguard long-term environmentally and culturally sustainable land use systems. Is the further 'enclosure' of rights inevitable? Is it naive to suggest that the many competing or parallel interests may coexist through improved 'choreography' of activities in these landscapes?

Two decades of political focus on multifunctionality of agriculture in Europe and diversification of farm and rural income was premised upon strong notions of post-productivism. The collective goods of natural and cultural heritage were intended to provide a basis for new income and rural development as a necessary counterbalance to the fact that agricultural income and profitability has been continuously declining. The emphasis of agricultural and rural policies on commodifying natural and cultural heritage resources was paralleled by an increase in conservation designations, and former primary sectors and rural areas increasingly became a tertiary recreational and consumption provider. The shift from productivism to post-productivism linked rural economies to wider national and global trends – entailing a change from production to consumption of both material and immaterial resources – and triggered profound changes in sociocultural arrangements and related land uses.

It is worth considering whether this may be seen as a part of the polarisation of agricultural and rural areas, 'conforming to an embedded neo-liberal mode of governance' (Tilzey & Potter, 2008). Geographical bifurcation into post-productivist and productivist areas may be one result, although it is important to note that one may find both approaches locally and even at farm level.

A range of studies have demonstrated that farmers' adaptations reflect not only 'economic man', nor value and idealistic positions, but also pragmatism and overall farm household strategies as well as what is seen as acceptable practices within the given social contexts.

To explore some interrelations between multifunctionality, rural diversification and the unsettlement of rural land use systems, we will examine issues related to the commodification of the commons and outfields ('outback', unfenced areas of rough grazing land, forest, moorland and mountains), in particular how interventions such as second home developments, developments for energy production and conservation designations and policies have major influences on rights systems and land fragmentation crucial for land use practices dependent upon seasonality, nomadism and land use rights.

Multifunctionality and diversification of agriculture

Increasing production, efficiency and food security were the overarching policy objectives after the Second World War, and powerful political measures such as tariff barriers, agricultural subsidies and market regulations stimulated agricultural production in the industrialised world (Friedman & McMichael, 1989). However, avoiding rural exodus and an uncontrolled growth of the cities was also an objective of the EU's Common Agricultural Policy (CAP). During the 1980s overproduction and environmental degradation and high budgetary costs became pressing issues, along with World Trade Organization negotiations on liberalisation of agricultural trade. While agricultural export-oriented countries like New Zealand chose full deregulation as a response, European agricultural policies avoided deregulation and started 'greening' parts of their subsidies into agri-environmental payments, diversification and 'multifunctionality'. These developments took place both within the EU (European Union) as well as in non-EU member states such as Norway and Switzerland (Rønningen, Burton & Renwick, 2012; see also Burton & Wilson, 2012 on various forms of agricultural regimes).

Addressing the need for maintaining agriculture's production of collective goods, related to environment, landscape, rural community sustainability, cultural heritage and values, as well as animal welfare and health, the success of these strategies has been mixed, but has nevertheless been important. We will argue that what is often overlooked is the *infrastructure* these landscapes and communities hold for resilience and potential for new developments, while critics may see agri-environmental payments and other incentives as interventions hampering radical, needed changes. The various critics of these multifunctional policies and regimes overseas have referred to them as 'protection in green disguise' (see Tilzey & Potter, 2008). It is worth mentioning that multifunctionality can also be identified in Japanese and South Korean policies (Sakamoto, Choi & Burmeister, 2007; Wilson 2007), and the approach is also receiving increasing attention in North America (e.g., Jordan & Warner, 2010; Brummel & Nelson, 2014).

Agricultural policy rhetoric connected to the multifunctionality concept was heavily related to agriculture as a producer and maintainer of well-kept cultural landscapes, carrier of cultural heritage, and as a part of agriculture's legitimacy in this post-productivist period (Daugstad, Rønningen & Skar, 2006). The many less favoured areas (both within and outside the EU's terminology of Less Favoured Areas) and areas of High Nature Value farmland rely on high support levels to maintain biodiversity, landscapes and cultural heritage. The concept of multifunctionality has been gradually reinterpreted and transformed into an issue of diversification and rural entrepreneurship, thus also contributing to a movement of the critical focus away from economic and structural pressures on agriculture.

The basis for commodification and consumption are the more or less collective values connected to the natural and cultural heritage of farmed landscapes and traditions and of rural areas more generally, including land that is actual or perceived commons. However, the continued reproduction of these values may not be upheld due to changes in or cessation of land use and the culture of the old economy that developed what is now seen as valuable within the new economy. Currently, these landscapes are to some extent mimicked under new economic, technological and social framework conditions, such as agri-environmental payments, strategies of the tourism sector and 'heritageisation' processes.

Commodification of the commons – unsettling rights and practices

Commodification denotes processes where resources such as goods and services, but also ideas, are transformed into a commodity, and thus made marketable and open to commercialisation (Best, 1989). Commodification processes are significant parts of contemporary rural change, challenging and modifying established economic, cultural, social and legal arrangements (e.g., Perkins, 2006).

Land use rights are adapted from historic resource use, and interactions between formal law, customary rights and institutions and the physical environment can help explain both change and continuity in the landscape (Jones, 2005). Olwig (2003, p. 15) points out 'the commons' enormous symbolic importance to society as an epitome of shared abstract values and democracy'. Environmental and social justice have been brought to the foreground within a number of international conventions signed by many countries. For example, the European landscape convention promotes the protection, management and planning of European landscapes; it came into force in 2004, partly as a result of, and further influencing, a debate on issues such as participation and landscape democracy (Jones, 2015).

How rural resources and landscapes are valorised is dependent on the purposes different stakeholders see in them, and these purposes are changing along with wider societal changes (Macpherson, 1978). A number of works on moral landscapes, detailing the co-constitution of morality and different spaces, places and landscapes (e.g., Philo, 1991; Matless, 1998; Flemsæter, Setten & Brown, 2014), draw attention to the way morality underpins the fundamental relationship people have with land and how landscape is used to both inhibit and enable certain behaviour. Rural landscapes are continuously re- and devalued according to wider changes in society and, subsequently, land rights are enacted in accordance with these kinds of valuations. Within a functioning democracy, rights to land can only be successfully enacted by particular individuals, groups or economic sectors if there is moral as well as legal backing for their claims (Blomley, 2004). The ongoing commodification processes in rural areas are activating moral assessments and bringing established land rights into play, both formally and informally.

Land rights encompass the capacity to exclude other groups or individuals also wishing to use or utilise the same resources, and those who have power over this delineation of property boundaries often try to stabilise property to enhance its potential for capital accumulation (Blomley, 2004). The commodification of rural resources where natural and cultural resources are valued and utilised in new ways unsettles the relations that link people to the resources. Norms and practices of land use, land ownership and rights systems in rural areas are thus destabilised and challenged with consequences for land use based on user rights and seasonal and migrating land use patterns.

Some important aspects of these manifestations of rural change – such as second home developments and new energy initiatives – have complex and contradictory outcomes: on one hand demonstrating a growing interdependence of rural and urban societies and environments, and on the other a rise in inequality and power asymmetries.

South Sámi reindeer herding – lost in rural diversification, enclosure and environmental policies?

Nomadic and indigenous ways of life all over the world have suffered under land acquisition, new 'land grabs', colonialism, neocolonialism, even due to nature conservation regimes (Adams & Mulligan, 2012). The situation of South Sámi reindeer herding in Scandinavia provides a very useful illustration of some overlooked consequences of multifunctionality, diversification, commodification and conservation policies in the highly developed global north. It also serves to illustrate some neoliberal characteristics of new ways of addressing (common) land issues.

The multifunctionality discourse has partly developed into a diversification discourse, emphasising the need to develop a more robust farm and rural economy by taking more of the resources connected to agricultural property into use. Most Norwegian farms are small and the amount of fertile farmland is very limited, but farms also entail land or land use rights, such as grazing, hunting and angling rights, in the outfields. These areas are either state or rural community commons or are private land but perceived and partly used as commons as they contain a number of different user rights, including the Public Right of Access to all land that is not in-bye land. The access to various rights of use has often been more crucial than ownership (Sevatdal, 1998). Although many types of rights are not exercised any longer, grazing rights are still crucial for animal husbandry, especially sheep farming and reindeer herding, which utilise large, unfenced areas.

Sámi reindeer herding takes place in Sweden, Finland, Norway and Russia. Norwegian Sámis have land use rights, but not fixed property ownership.

About 3,100 persons are registered as reindeer herders/owners in Norway, of whom fewer than 500 persons are within the South Sámi area; of those, only 150 are defined as having this as their occupation. There are an estimated 2,000 South Sámis in total in Central Norway and Sweden, and South Sámi is spoken by an estimated 500 persons in Norway and is on the UN list of threatened languages. South Sámis are thus a minority within a minority, a fact that makes reindeer herding as a cultural activity even more imperative. This vulnerability of Sámi communities was demonstrated in 1986 when the reindeer industry and the Sámi way of life, including diet, was severely harmed by nuclear fallout in the aftermath of the Chernobyl disaster. Animals, people and food are still regularly tested for radioactivity (Skuterud & Thørring, 2012).

Sámi reindeer herding rights are based on the legal principle of 'use from time immemorial', and in Norway these rights are also covered by the Reindeer herding Act and the ILO convention No. 169 concerning indigenous and tribal peoples in independent countries, as well as the United Nations' covenant concerning civil and political rights. However, a requirement for herding rights is that the use of that particular land must have been 'sufficiently strong', and the idea that reindeer herding and Sámi presence are only a 'tolerated use' which then has to give way to other interests whenever required has been dominant (Bull, 2004), and still prevails. An underlying conviction held by the Norwegian authorities and society for a long time was that reindeer herding would inevitably disappear as a result of modernisation.

Having gradually been pushed back, losing land to colonisation and agricultural expansion, South Sámis have been involved in conflicts over land and grazing rights for several hundred years, and have been described as 'a people at court' (see Fjellheim, 2012). While constantly losing land to farming and other interests, their counterparts also experience losses, as reindeer herds can cause significant damage to farmland. Fencing is a troublesome issue here.

In Norway, the Ministry of Agriculture and Food is responsible for reindeer herding, along with agriculture and forestry. As a part of the cooperative state system, Sámi organisations annually negotiate with the state regarding prices, regulations and subsidies. A main responsibility of the reindeer herding sector, as part of a social contract with society, is to maintain its role as a vital carrier of Sámi cultural heritage. South Sámi reindeer herding has adapted to state-imposed regulations and agronomic ideals, and more so than reindeer herding in the north of the country; there are no problems with overgrazing and calf weights have been high. Yet, South Sámi reindeer herding may be on the brink of collapse, mainly due to the combined or cumulative effects of a number of land use pressures, including those from within the agricultural sector, land losses, land fragmentation and increasing carnivore numbers.

Second home developments

Strong urbanisation culturally situates the rural as recreational space. Counter-urbanisation has not been a strong trend in Scandinavia, apart from migrant workers in the primary industries and especially Dutch rural in-migrants (see Grimsrud, 2011; Eimerman, Lundmark & Müller, 2012; and also Halfacree, 2012). Relatively late centralisation and urbanisation, relatively small and green cities, and the widespread ownership of cabins, summer houses or second homes may be important reasons. With a population of five million, there are approximately 420,000 cabins and second homes in Norway. While these traditionally were simple buildings, there has been a remarkable increase in quality, standard and infrastructure in recent years. Low property taxes make multiple second homes economically feasible for many. Further, low interest rates over a long period have also contributed to a debt-financed consumption of second homes. The growth in cabins and second home developments has been very much encouraged by many rural municipalities looking for ways to increase activity and income. Along with the cabins, second homes follow the development of more infrastructure and more diversified activities, which combine to increase land fragmentation and pressure.

Among other stakeholders, reindeer herders are often seen as holding considerable power in planning processes, leading to delays, although not often entirely stopping developments. This, however, earns them a reputation for 'preventing rural development':

> I see five reindeer on that piece of land every three years. A cabin area development would save my farm and secure my family's future. (Farmer, potential cabin area developer)

> The planning application was for five cabin development areas. We think we can't say no all the time, so we agreed on three. And of course, three was what they actually wanted. (Local reindeer herding authority representative)[1]

Recreational home development raises numerous issues, of which three that particularly materialise are those of planning, legislation and taxation. Although legislation and planning procedures are in place and potentially effective, land use plans for cabin developments are in many cases poorly coordinated between the local municipalities, and thus contribute to land fragmentation. Recently, farmers with grazing animals have been confronted with some of the same pressures resulting from changed views of property and land use, typically through conflicts with cabin owners over grazing rights.

Energy

Renewable energy developments are becoming increasingly important for rural diversification and economic development. Between the 1950s and the 1980s major landscape-altering hydropower dam developments and infrastructure developments cut off large areas and severed reindeer migration routes. From the 1990s it was widely assumed that the large and highly controversial landscape interventions had come to an end in Norway. However, it has become evident in recent years that the combined cumulative effects of numerous smaller developments are also having a significant impact. Micro hydropower plants have been encouraged and have been popular among farmers and other rural small-scale investors. However, even micro hydropower plants can alter river conditions, changing biodiversity and leading reindeer to change their migratory routes. Both micro hydropower plants and windfarms are rewarded with green certificates and subsidies for their contribution to reducing climate change. Contemporary, extensive development plans for windfarm developments are being contested in part because of concerns for nature and landscape conservation and fragmentation, but also because of their effects on reindeer.

Municipalities are the principal body governing Norway's development, socially, environmentally, industrially, and not least its land use through land use planning and the capacity to grant development permits. The principle of local autonomy is thus important, although the regional county level has an important function for control and may overrule local decisions. The state also possesses tools for ensuring overall guidelines for land use and for vetoing local decisions. While a national plan for management of the waterways and hydropower developments was established during the 1980s, there is currently little political will to implement more centralised and stricter coordination of land use for large developments such as windfarms. Local municipalities' high degree of autonomy and planning authority is strengthened with the rollback of the state, and increasingly more neoliberal governments. Further, commentators have pointed out insufficiently transparent planning and decision-making processes linked to large windfarm developments, in which investors and developers can dominate. While the planning and legislative systems are, in principle, in place, in practice the legal measures and the use of impact assessments to prevent clearly problematic developments are not particularly effective (Winge, 2013). Ultimately, it is poor returns on the development projects due to low prices for energy and green certificates, along with a surplus of energy, that may halt some of the developments (see Statkraft, 2015).

Conservation and green colonisation

Rural diversification and commodification processes influence nomadic land use in a number of ways. The need for a flexible and significant land area for reindeer grazing, and the changing of their migration routes dependent on factors such as weather and climate mean that existing loss of habitat is already having a major impact on reindeer herding. The increased pressure on the land has resulted in escalating tensions and conflicts over use and rights.

This raises questions about access to rural landscapes and rights to utilise its resources. Various regulations and customs determining levels of more or less restricted access within rural areas exist in most countries. The recent land reforms in Scotland that began with the Land Reform Act of 2003 have significantly widened rights of access. A number of community land or land-based development initiatives have followed (see Bryden & Geisler, 2007; Shucksmith, 2010). A global increase in conservation designations implies that centralised control is being strengthened for many rural landscapes. At the same time, these designations may also represent a form of enclosure in terms of cutting off locals and indigenous people from previous practices, while providing the general public and other user groups with much wider and better access than was previously available.

Another aspect of conservation is the successful increase in numbers of great carnivores in Scandinavia. Norway has stated its aim to increase the numbers (defined by litters or breeding pairs) of wolves, bears, wolverines, lynx and eagles, as well as designating specific geographical priority areas for carnivores. When these desired levels are reached, management in terms of culling – hunting – can take place in order to stabilise numbers and cull out individuals which have been identified as causing high losses. To some herders, reindeer calf losses to carnivores have been extremely high, sometimes at over 70%. Important calving areas may overlap with prioritised areas for carnivores, meaning that permission to cull carnivores will be restricted.

As for sheep, the provision of monetary compensation by the state is not reducing the psychological stress for herders. Reindeer herders have defined the great carnivores as a significant new land use pressure, and, in an effort to avoid predation, previously good grazing land and migration routes are being avoided, thus leading to new conflicts with other land users. On the positive side, the carnivore issue is one area that brings farmers and reindeer herders together.

While it may appear logical that the reindeer herding sector and conservation agencies have common interests in keeping open lands intact from fragmentation, there has, until very recently, been a remarkable lack of collaboration. Conservation designations have in many cases restricted reindeer herding. Riseth (2005) shows how nature conservation policies and outdoor recreation interests are intimately ideologically connected, linked to ideas of pristine nature and wilderness. Furthermore, outdoor recreation interests are being promoted by authorities due to their important contribution to health and well-being. The cultural and value aspects and differences become clear here; modern Sámis' use of all-terrain vehicles and snowmobiles conflict with more urban, elite-based moral imperatives and perceptions of the appropriate use of nature. Further, reindeer herders' opposition to increased carnivore stocks has also made it difficult for any alliance between herders and recreational users to solidify. This derives from fundamental cultural framings of human–nature relations (Riseth, 2005). The conflicting views between harvesting, cultural or 'worked' landscapes and what are perceived as wild, natural landscapes and their inherent ideologies is hampering otherwise logical alliances. Cultural capital is obviously one issue here (see Skogen & Krange, 2003). Recent initiatives, however, indicate potential for change.

Diversification and commodification the answer to land use pressures?

Cultural and natural heritage provides some economic opportunities for entrepreneurship and job creation and potentially opens up new economic opportunities for rural development. Sweden provides a recent example of how bear populations can be turned into a resource for wildlife safari tourism. This is nothing new in the global south, but is a relatively new approach in the north. Such measures, in utilising knowledge about carnivores and carnivore management, raise the importance of carnivore-related cultural capital (skills and knowledge) and can potentially strengthen social networks (generating both bridging and bonding capital) and the status of these communities.

Within many Sámi communities there has been an inherent scepticism towards commodification, as it is widely associated with souvenir kiosks and putting their culture on display. However, a number of recent high quality 'product' developments have been seen as both positive and successful. This represents possibilities too for non-reindeer owners to maintain and develop their links, heritage and economy linked to the Sámi community, and could also provide a valuable opportunity for communication and dialogue with society more broadly. Not neglecting the continued existence of racism and discrimination, our observation is that, partly as a response from an increasingly multicultural society, there has been a 'rediscovery' of Sámi-ness as an exotic but nevertheless familiar and increasingly integrated aspect of Scandinavian-ness.

Yet, without maintenance of the land and upholding the nomadic character of Sámi reindeer herding, one may argue that what is left are only the physical artifacts – the animals and the costumes. The fact that reindeer herding has a somewhat less nomadic character in Finland and parts of Sweden, with stationary management and feeding more common practices, should not be used as an argument for further limiting land use rights. Further, to most reindeer herders as well as sheep farmers, giving up is probably more realistic than entering the tourism business.

Managing the rural landscapes of commons and outfields

It is by reconnecting with the social and the material that we are able to trace crucial issues like the morality of resource valuations, activation of knowledge systems and the related power geometries, how this affects the various claims, and how interests related to rural land and landscapes are articulated.

The utilization of many rural resources relies on various forms of land use rights or property rights established over a long period of time. It is, however, not clear whether the institutional system they constitute is able to adapt to and sustainably manage the kinds of innovations in resource use implied in the envisioned role of the future rural economy – an economy that is based on both recreational consumption and neo-productivism in which minerals, energy and biomass in the emerging 'bioeconomy' are central. Consequently, a particular interest is the interrelationship between commodification processes and the disruption of established formal and informal systems of land rights and use.

Local autonomy and governance play a crucial role in concepts of democracy in many countries of the global north. One major issue is the (lack of) willingness of state authorities to implement state guidelines in land use developments, deferring instead to local authorities. The policy instruments exist at a national level, but there is a clear trend for local autonomy to be favoured as the state draws back from potentially unpopular decisions. While the state may intervene on behalf of national or regional interests when seen as 'necessary', a crucial issue is how power relations between local, regional and national authorities unfold when major new economic or political interests emerge.

The potential for local or even national democracy to handle large-scale land development processes in the future may be further challenged by new international trade agreements. Increased deregulation, and its consequences in democratic societies, deserves scrutiny and transparent debates.

Is there any future for long-term, conservative land use management? Reindeer herding Sámi describe themselves as 'the people of eight seasons', reflecting the various use of different areas throughout the year. Such mobility and flow provide a profound challenge within land use and planning practices that are delivering a world of increasing enclosure and privatisation of land. Brown (2012) explores the concept of choreography in land use and 'the dilemma of when to accept or extend the limits of attunement in facilitating coexistence in public space' (p. 801). Although relating to outdoor access and recreation, we believe her analysis may have wider relevance in managing commons and outfields as competing needs and purposes clash. A way to successfully manage old and new users and uses of the outfields when resources are utilized in new ways – and a better alternative to enclosing land areas as private and segregating different activities – may be to attend to choreographies of co-presence.

Certain trends within, for example, tourism, where the seasonal variations of certain 'products' increase their exclusiveness and/or attractiveness; within architecture, towards higher flexibility of buildings, and within the 'sharing economy' – could this indicate a trend towards reduced prominence of fixed property as investments, leading to a decreasing need for enclosures and privatisation? A powerful instrument would be changes in tax systems that encourage more sustainable investments, less in land and resource-consuming property investments.

What we do know is that modernisation processes are once again changing the face of rurality in the global north. Following the well-known shift from productivist policies to multifunctional policies, the world is once again changing and, while multifunctionality continues to be important, the small family farms it once supported are diminishing at a rapid rate (see Fischer & Burton, 2015), and, as we have seen, nomadic land use is struggling. Challenging it, we are witnessing the emergence of an increasingly commodified and materialised countryside, governments stridently advocating the development of technologically oriented and globalised bioeconomies (OECD, 2009). At the same time, there is a growing rhetoric that future technologies will transform these areas into biomass production sites, while the diminishment of easily reachable mineral resources elsewhere puts pressure on the re-emergence of mining in rural areas.

Climate change and land pressures challenge policy makers, planners, land users and developers to implement approaches to land use in which the wider access to land and land use rights for our common survival and well-being will inevitably find itself in some escalating challenges to the prevailing processes of rural diversification and unsettlements of land rights. The move towards a more neo-productivist and market-driven rurality raises many important issues for the commodification of rural resources. In particular, whereas under multifunctionality the focus was on the small and local, the new regional role in addressing the global issues of resource depletion, climate change and food insecurity is reconstituting rural areas as sites of global consumption/production. Within this frame, there is a tension between the moralities of using rural areas for local communities and the moralities of rural areas as a global resource. Paradoxically, the deployment of market forces as a moderator means that many of the economic benefits accruing from neo-productivist policies will be provided to large corporations and globalised companies, and not to the local communities that were the very core of multifunctionality. We argue that maintaining the flexibility and robustness of open, non-enclosed spaces with the co-presence of a wide range of user groups presents us with the best approach to meet current and future challenges of rural diversification. This is, in our view, an important argument for defending systems of diverse land use rights and their enactments.

Acknowledgement

This chapter was supported by the Norwegian Research Council's BIONÆR research programme, grant project no. 199365, administered by the Centre for Rural Research.

Note

1   A reorganisation has now moved the responsibility from decentralised Reindeer Herding Authority offices to the Regional County Governor.

References

Adams, WM & Mulligan, M (2012). *Decolonizing nature: Strategies for conservation in a post-colonial era*. London: Earthscan.

Best, S (1989). The commodification of reality and the reality of commodification: Jean Baudrillard and post-modernism. *Current Perspectives in Social Theory* 19, 23–51.

Blomley, N (2004). *Unsettling the city: Urban land and the politics of property*. New York: Routledge.

Brown, KM (2012). Sharing public space across difference: Attunement and the contested burdens of choreographing encounter. *Social & Cultural Geography* 13(7), 801–820.

Brummel, RF & Nelson, KC (2014). Does multifunctionality matter to US farmers? Farmer motivations and conceptions of multifunctionality in dairy systems. *Journal of Environmental Management* 146, 451–462.

Bryden, J & Geisler, C (2007). Community-based land reform: Lessons from Scotland. *Land Use Policy* 24(1), 24–34.

Bull, KS (2004). Saami customary law and the proposals of the Saami Rights Committee. *Diedut / Sámi instituhtta* 3, 163–171.

Burton, R & Wilson, GA (2012). The rejuvenation of productivist agriculture: The case for 'cooperative neo-productivism'. In R Almås & H Campbell (Eds), *Rethinking agricultural policy regimes: Food security, climate change and the future resilience of global agriculture* (pp. 51–72). Bingley, UK: Emerald Publishing.

Daugstad, K, Rønningen, K & Skar, B (2006). Agriculture as an upholder of cultural heritage? Conceptualisations and value judgements – A Norwegian perspective in international context. *Journal of Rural Studies* 22, 67–81.

Eimerman, M, Lundmark, M & Müller, DK (2012). Exploring Dutch migration to rural Sweden: International counter urbanisation in the EU. *Tijdschrift voor Economische en Sociale Geografie* 103(3), 330–346.

Fischer, H & Burton, RF (2015). Understanding farm succession as socially constructed endogenous cycles. *Sociologia Ruralis* 54(1), 417–438.

Fjellheim, S (2012). *Gåebrien sijte – en sameby i Rørostraktene*. [Gåebrien Sijte – a Sámi village in the Røros area]. Tallinn: Tallinn Book Press.

Flemsæter, F, Setten, G & Brown, K (2014). Morality, mobility and citizenship: Legitimising mobile subjectivities in a contested outdoors. *Geoforum* 64, 342–350.

Friedman, H & McMichael, P (1989). Agriculture and the state system: The rise and decline of national agricultures, 1870 to the present. *Sociologica Ruralis* 29(2), 93–117.

Grimsrud, GM (2011). How well does the 'counter-urbanisation story' travel to other countries? The case of Norway. *Population, Space and Place* 17(5), 642–655.

Halfacree, K (2012). Heterolocal identities? Counter-urbanisation, second homes, and rural consumption in the era of mobilities. *Population, Space and Place*. Special Issue: Re-Making Migration Theory: Transitions, Intersections and Cross-Fertilisations 18(2), 209–224.

Jones, M (2005). Law and landscape – some historical-geographical studies from northern Europe. In T Peil & M Jones (Eds), *Landscape, Law and Justice* (pp. 95–109). Oslo: Novis.

Jones, M (2015). Landscape democracy and participation in a European perspective. In KK Jørgensen et al. (Eds), *Mainstreaming landscape through the European landscape convention*. Abingdon: Routledge.

Jordan, N & Warner, KD (2010). Enhancing the multifunctionality of US agriculture. *BioScience* 60(1), 60–66.

Macpherson, CB (1978). *Property, mainstream and critical positions*. Toronto: University of Toronto Press.

Matless, D (1998). *Landscape and Englishness*. London: Reaktion.

OECD (2009). *The bioeconomy to 2030: Designing a policy agenda*. Paris: OECD.

Olwig, K (2003). Commons and landscape, landscape, law & justice. Proceedings of a workshop on old and new commons, Centre for Advanced Study, Oslo 11–13 March 2003.

Perkins, HC (2006). Commodification: Re-resourcing rural areas. In P Cloke, T Marsden & P Mooney (Eds), *Handbook of rural studies* (pp. 243–257). London: Sage.

Philo, C (1991). *New words, new worlds: Reconceptualising social and cultural geography*. Department of Geography, St David's University College, Lampeter.

Riseth, JA (2005). Nature protection and the colonial legacy – Sámi reindeer management versus urban recreation: The case of Junkerdal-Balvatn, northern Norway. In T Peil & M Jones (Eds), *Landscape, Law and Justice* (pp. 173–186). Oslo: Novis.

Rønningen, K, Burton, R & Renwick, A (2012). Western European approaches to and interpretations of multifunctional agriculture – and some implications of a possible neo-productivist turn. In R Almås & H Campbell (Eds), *Rethinking agricultural policy regimes: Food security, climate change and the future resilience of global agriculture* (pp. 73–97). Research in Rural Sociology and Development, Vol. 18. Bingley, UK: Emerald Publishing.

Sakamoto, K, Choi, Y & Burmeister, LL (2007). Framing multifunctionality: Agricultural policy paradigm change in South Korea and Japan? *International Journal of Sociology of Agriculture and Food* 15(1), 24–45.

Sevatdal, H (1998). Common property in Norway's rural areas. In E Berge & G Stenseth (Eds), *Law and the governance of renewable resources. Studies from Northern Europe and Africa* (pp. 141–161). International Centre for Self-Governance. ICS Press. Institute for Contemporary Studies, Oakland, California.

Shucksmith, M (2010). Disintegrated rural development? Neo-endogenous rural development, planning and place-shaping in diffused power contexts. *Sociologia Ruralis* 50(1), 1–14.

Skogen, K & Krange, O (2003). A wolf at the gate: The anti-carnivore alliance and the symbolic construction of community. *Sociologia Ruralis* 43(3), 309–325.

Skuterud, L & Thørring, H (2012). Averted doses to Norwegian Sámi reindeer herders after the Chernobyl accident. *Health Physics* 102(2), 208–216.

Statkraft (2015). [Statkraft halts wind power planning in Central Norway]. Press release, 4 June 2015. http://www.statkraft.no/media/Nyheter/2015/statkraft-halts-wind-power-planning-in-central-norway/#sthash.o30fSQ6M.dpuf (accessed 15 July 2015).

Tilzey, M & Potter, C (2008). Productivism versus post-productivism? Modes of agri-environmental governance in post-Fordist agricultural transitions. In GM Robinson (Ed.), *Sustainable rural systems – sustainable agriculture and rural communities* (pp. 41–66). Aldershot: Ashgate.

Wilson, G (2007). *Multifunctional agriculture: A transition theory perspective.* CABI.

Winge, N (2013). *Kampen om arealene.* [The battle about the land]. Oslo: Universitetsforlaget.

27

Industrialising the Marine Commons

Adapting to Change in Europe's Coastal Fisheries

David Symes and Jeremy Phillipson

Rise and fall of distant water fishing

Fishing is widely recognised as one of the most dangerous and physically demanding occupations; it may require crews to work up to 18 hours a day for several days on end in appalling conditions in return for uncertain and sometimes quite meagre returns. Such unsocial working arrangements require major adjustments to family life (Williams, 2008), sometimes putting unbearable pressure on marital relations (Vervaele, 2014). Governed by vicissitudes of the weather, rhythms of the seasons and the variability of complex, dynamic ecosystems, no economic activity is so directly influenced by environmental conditions. Fishing remains, in practice, a hunting economy – albeit one that has been technologically enhanced. It is also a peripheral activity commonly associated with less developed rural areas. Highly fragmented and widely dispersed, the fishing industry is characterised by small-scale enterprises mainly in family ownership. Poorly organised at national and regional levels and often weakly integrated into the wider business community, it usually commands little political influence.

The world's capture fisheries are a finite resource, renewable under precautionary management but limited by the carrying capacities of ocean ecosystems. Modernisation and expansion of the fishing industry, which began in the second half of the 19th century in the northeast Atlantic, spread throughout the rest of the world during the 20th century. A remarkable surge in global fishing capacity between circa 1960 and 1995 led to the world's capture fisheries becoming fully exploited. Stocks fished within biologically sustainable limits fell from 90% in 1974 to 71% in 2011, by which date roughly 30% of global fish stocks were 'overfished', 60% 'fully fished' and only 10% 'underfished' (FAO, 2014).

The following analysis of key issues confronting capture fisheries as a consequence of 'industrialising the commons' is framed by the northeast Atlantic, historically the most heavily exploited of the world's fishing regions, bordered by countries that formed the heartland of the Industrial Revolution in the 18th and 19th centuries. Its present political geography is striking – it is dominated by the European Union (EU) of 28 nation states, with four much smaller coastal or island states (Norway, Iceland, Greenland and the Faeroe Islands) and a fragment of the Russian Federation coastline on the Baltic shore. Overall, fishing makes only a small contribution to the regional economy in terms of output, gross domestic product (GDP) or employment, accounting for around 0.3% of GDP in the EU, though significantly higher levels in the smaller independent states where fishing-related issues can take on national political significance.

Traditionally forming part of a pluriactive coastal economy, the inclusion of fishing within the rural world is becoming tenuous. Fishing takes place in marine rather than terrestrial space, with an increasing urbanisation of land-based, fishing-related activities. Nevertheless fishing shares many cultural, social and economic features associated with the utilisation of other natural resources (in particular farming) and many of the issues affecting marginal rural areas.

Industrialising the commons

'Industrialising the commons' is a term more readily associated with the development of marine hydrocarbon and renewable energy industries around the coasts of northwest Europe over the last 40 years. It sits much less easily with the structures and practices of the fishing industry. Yet, in a very real sense, industrialisation of the fishing industry did occur on a relatively limited scale in the late 19th and the first half of the 20th centuries, following the introduction of steam-powered fishing vessels and adoption of the otter trawl, with the development of Europe's distant water fleets engaged in the relentless pursuit of the ubiquitous and iconic cod throughout the North Atlantic (Kurlansky, 1997). The exploitation of distant water fishing grounds off Iceland, north Norway and later Greenland amounted to a 'colonisation' of their coastal waters by the more developed industrial nations of Western Europe (United Kingdom, Germany, Belgium and France). Successive waves of technological innovation affecting vessel and gear design, culminating in the development of on-board refrigeration and the creation of factory trawlers in the 1950s and 1960s, completed the process of industrialisation.[1] Production peaked in 1974 when over a thousand distant water vessels operating out of Western and Eastern European ports landed circa 2.2 million tonnes (Warner, 1977). Already the warning signs of a depleted fishery – falling catch per unit of effort and increasing numbers of small fish in the catch – were evident.

In the context of fishing, industrialisation describes a combination of features associated with distant water fishing similar to those associated with the Industrial Revolution in 18th- and early 19th-century Europe. These include increasing levels of resource exploitation; specialisation, economies of scale and concentration of production; substitution of capital for labour; company ownership; partial involvement in a wage economy and the casualisation of labour (Tunstall, 1962); and the emergence of hierarchical social relations. Distant water fishing was essentially urban based, typically forming 'encapsulated' working-class communities of deckhands close to the fish dock, with the ships' officers (skippers, engineers and wireless operators) dispersed into the 'leafy' middle-class suburbs (Horobin, 1957). Such features were, however, atypical of the North Atlantic fishing industry as a whole, where over 80% of fishing enterprises were involved in simple commodity production mainly within local inshore fisheries. But the economic footprint of the large-scale 'industrial' sector was profound, accounting for a rapidly expanding share of total output and dominating a market in which volume of production was judged more important than quality of the product.

The most significant long-term impact of industrialising the commons – depletion of commercial fish stocks and growing evidence of fishing down the food chain – was not confined to distant water fishing grounds. Economies of scale, technological innovation and increasing fishing effort had diffused throughout near and middle water fisheries, so that overfishing had become endemic throughout much of the North Atlantic. In the North Sea, for example, although overall biomass remained relatively constant throughout the 20th century and the level of total catches high, the composition of the catch had altered, with declines in major food fish species and increases in landings of lower value 'industrial' species for reduction to fishmeal and oil, though the boom in these industrial fisheries was to prove short lived.

Enclosing the commons

The colonisation of distant water fishing grounds and industrialisation of the commons owed much to the principle of freedom of the high seas and the ungoverned and ungovernable nature of the ocean commons. Belated attempts to fill the institutional vacuum with the establishment of the North East Atlantic Fisheries Commission in 1959 (Sen, 1997) met with limited success. Solving what Hardin (1968) called the 'tragedy of the commons' would require two separate actions: enclosure and privatisation of the commons. Enclosing the commons was achieved from the late 1970s onwards through the contagious spread of 200-mile exclusive economic zones (EEZs), initially promulgated in the North Atlantic by Iceland to provide protection for commercial fish stocks in its coastal waters, and subsequently endorsed in the UN Convention on the Law of the Sea (UNCLOS III) in 1982.

The impact of enclosure was dramatic, with winners and losers easily identified. Within a few years little remained of the distant water fishing industry: a handful of trawlers from countries like the UK, Germany and Belgium were licensed to fish for limited quota in the newly enclosed northern waters. The only significant survivors of industrial-scale fishing were the relatively small numbers of large, technologically sophisticated pelagic trawlers and purse seiners in pursuit of the highly migratory herring and mackerel. The fishing seasons are short but intensive: in 2008 the average pelagic vessel in Scotland spent only 54 days at sea (Scottish Government, 2010). The winners were the coastal fishing industries of Iceland, Faeroes and Norway, free to exploit their own rich fishing grounds and no longer outmuscled by more powerful foreign fleets. The losers were countries like the UK that had relied heavily on distant water landings to supply their domestic markets. The ports of Hull and Grimsby, that together boasted the greatest concentration of distant water fishing capacity, witnessed the dispersal of their fleets of modern freezer trawlers and the decimation of their function as major fishing ports. The balance of power within the northeast Atlantic had shifted.

New management regimes

Realising the benefits of improved fisheries management within the enclosed commons has proved difficult. 'Privatising the commons' – Hardin's favoured action – through allocation of transferable fishing rights to individual fishing enterprises was intended to let the market find an efficient solution to excess capacity in the fishing industry. Despite vigorous endorsement by some fisheries economists (Munro & Pitcher, 1996) privatisation has proved politically contentious and slow to take root in the North Atlantic. Only Iceland and more recently Denmark (in 2007) have legislated for the formal introduction of ITQs (individual transferable quotas) although quota management systems in certain EU member states have informally adopted the principle of transferability. Most coastal states opted to contain the rising pressure on fish stocks through regulatory frameworks based on output controls (total allowable catches and vessel quotas) supported by effort restrictions (days at sea) and technical conservation measures.[2] Such systems achieved limited success: the politicisation of decision making meant that output limits were often set too high; policing of regulations tended to be patchy; and, worst of all, the policy instrument (quota) became a major part of the problem when vessels routinely discarded over-quota fish at sea (Johnsen & Eliasen, 2011). Only in the last decade or so has the northeast Atlantic witnessed a sustained recovery of its most important demersal species.

Weaknesses in management had arguably more to do with institutional failings than with ineffective regulation. In the EU the decision was taken to merge the EEZs of coastal member states to create a single 'common pond' managed from Brussels through the Common Fisheries Policy (CFP). The rationale for a unified approach made good sense – at least while the focus of interest was limited to the North Sea – but became increasingly implausible with successive enlargements of the Union. In a centrally driven and science-based system of fisheries management, the EU Commission became directly responsible[3] for micro-managing the world's most complex and diverse fishing zone, extending through 40 degrees of latitude. Involvement of the fishing industry in the policy process has been restricted to participation in advisory committees that exercise only a limited influence on policy decisions, leading Sissenwine and Symes (2007, p. 51) to conclude that 'the CFP has lost the confidence of its client group (the fishing industry) and the public at large. The very legitimacy of the CFP is being challenged'. The narrow focus on conserving commercial stocks and the technocratic approach to management implied an abstraction from the reality of dynamic marine ecosystems, rejection of the principles of common resource management (Ostrom, 1990) and a denial of the basic truth that managing coastal fisheries is a much more complex 'wicked problem' (Jentoft & Chuenpagdee, 2009). It had the effect of disembedding fishing and fisheries from the environmental, economic and social contexts that shape their existence.

Fundamental reform of the CFP's centralised, top-down approach and its narrow terms of reference has so far proved almost impossible. The reasons for the apparent stalemate are clear: the institutional lock-down imposed by the immutability of the Treaties that define the principles and procedures of the European Union; the reluctance of some member states to embrace radical reform for fear it would erode the principle of relative stability;[4] and the inevitability of compromise resulting from negotiations between different fishing interests and between the Council of Ministers and European Parliament, jointly responsible for signing off the final agreement. As a result, reforms of the CFP are set to follow a path-dependent route (Hegland & Raakjaer, 2008) that limits their scope to incremental changes to existing practices rather than transformational change.

Not all responsibility for management rests with the EU institutions. Significant areas, including quota management and inshore fisheries, remain in the hands of the member states. Their decisions, mediated through negotiations with stakeholder organisations, reflect not only customary preferences relating to target species and fishing methods but also the structure of the industry and its organisation. As a result, national fishing industries tend to retain their distinctive identities and are subject to contrasting patterns of fisheries governance.

A different set of circumstances faced the smaller, independent northeast Atlantic states that rely on fisheries as a source of wealth creation and employment. Partly because of their small populations and the greater relative importance of the fisheries, a closer and more productive relationship exists between industry and government. In Norway, for example, in a system described by Hersoug and Rånes (1997, p. 157) as 'centrally directed consultation', fisheries representatives are present on several organisations that exert influence on fisheries policy. The Norwegian Fishermen's Association is consulted formally and informally on a range of policy issues, emerging as 'the government's fisheries partner' (Gezelius, 2008, p. 43).

Enclosure of the commons, intended to protect the small-scale fisheries of Iceland, Norway and the Faeroes from overfishing by distant water fleets, exposed these fisheries to the demands of the Nordic welfare model (Andersen et al., 2007) that seeks to combine private prosperity with public wealth through high taxation. As a result, market-based solutions, sometimes in the form of ITQs that ensure the fishing sector's profitability and productivity, have tended to prevail over policies designed to secure social sustainability of small-scale fisheries (Holm, Raakjaer, Jacobsen & Henriksen, 2015).

From co-management to interactive governance

Co-management

Two broad themes – governance and sustainability – have come to dominate the social science literature on fisheries. In the first of these, studies of co-management, where responsibility for the implementation of policy is shared between state and fishing industry, provided an early entry point (Jentoft, 1989). Ostensibly, the involvement of user groups assists in the adaptation of universal regulations to local circumstances. Co-management assumes many forms (Sen & Raakjaer Nielsen, 1996) and is more widely associated with coastal and especially inshore fisheries where in some instances pre-modern organisations have been adapted to meet modern conditions.

A recent example of deploying user groups in management is the network of self-governing producer organisations (POs) across the EU. Initially concerned with ensuring favourable conditions for the sale of their members' catches, POs in some member states have become directly involved in collective forms of quota management (Goodlad, 1998). Under the 2013 CFP reforms, POs will also assume responsibility for annual management plans linking production and marketing.

Co-management is credited with introducing a range of attributes relating to good governance. In addition to increased rationality and legitimacy for the policy process and the regulatory system, it implies greater transparency, a broader basis of knowledge, lower transaction costs and enhanced levels of commitment and compliance from industry (Symes & Phillipson, 1999). National studies (Phillipson, 2002; Piriz, 2004) can expose contextual and institutional factors that inhibit the efficacy of co-management. Of particular concern is ensuring the appropriate balance of representation between different interest groups and their incorporation within the institutional design (Jentoft & McCay, 1995). Such issues are intensified where the management remit is widened to include the interface between fisheries and the marine environment.

Participative governance

Whereas co-management usually involves stakeholders in the implementation of policy, participative governance seeks to engage them in the full range of policy formulation and implementation through user group representation at all stages of the policy process. Such developments are more strongly evident in Norway's corporative system of governance and at member state level (Hegland & Raakjaer, 2008) than at EU level where participation is limited to a range of advisory committees, one step removed from decision making. A useful source of information and opinion, advisory committees have the ability to bring policy makers in Brussels more closely in touch with the realities of fishing across the strikingly different regional seas that make up the EU's 'common pond'.

The EU has been reluctant to contemplate devolving any of its responsibilities in relation to resource conservation. The one exception has been the 1982 derogation in respect of the 12 nautical miles of territorial waters that left their management largely in the hands of the coastal state. Only in parts of the UK, however, do we find a fully devolved system of inshore fisheries management (Phillipson & Symes, 2010).

During negotiations leading to the 2013 CFP reforms, a major area of debate was the suggestion in the Green Paper (Commission of the European Communities, 2009) of introducing some form of regional management (see Symes, 2009; Hegland, Ounanian & Raakjaer, 2012). Despite support from many member states, the proposition eventually fell victim to legal arguments that the EU treaties were unable to countenance an intermediate level of policy making that might challenge the status and authority of EU institutions. All that survived in the revised CFP were provisions for member states to collaborate in the implementation of common policy.

Alternative approaches to governance

Towards the end of the 20th century there was considerable academic and policy interest in moving away from narrowly defined and mechanistic forms of sectoral management and towards holistic, integrated approaches that could re-embed fisheries management in the wider context of the marine environment. Of particular interest was the ecosystem-based approach that, according to Schramm and Hubert (1996, p. 6), represents 'an evolution of management philosophy that focuses on local and large geographic scales, considers long term temporal scales and preserves biotic and abiotic components of ecosystems when making natural resource management decisions'. Although the approach is a guiding principle of the CFP, little effort has been made to develop operational objectives as a basis for its implementation. Significantly, one of the principal advantages to be gained from regionalising the CFP is the opportunity to develop management strategies around the specific ecosystems of the EU's regional seas.

One impediment to an integrated approach to fisheries policy and management has been the absence of a robust theoretical framework capable of embracing the underlying environmental, economic and sociocultural systems. Interactive governance theory (Kooiman, Jentof, Pullin & Bavinck, 2005) offers a comprehensive reconceptualisation of the governing system as a private–public partnership, involving public authorities, the market, fishing industry and civil society. Central to its approach is recognising the diversity, complexity, scale and dynamics of fisheries and the need for flexibility within the governing system in order to maintain the essential diversity of the system to be governed. In contrast to the image of co-management as a pragmatic response to a crisis in state–industry relations, interactive governance requires a new approach, building upwards from foundations in ethical values, carefully articulated governing principles and the incorporation of inclusivity, partnership and interactive learning among its principal characteristics (Symes, 2006).

It is hard to envisage interactive governance providing a template for reform of fisheries policy in the northeast Atlantic in the foreseeable future. Its purpose might be better served in guiding the development of governing institutions in the global south (Bavinck et al., 2005). What interactive governance theory offers the developed world of the North Atlantic is a more powerful lens for analysing governing systems and a diagnostic tool for assessing how far the systems to be governed are in fact governable (Bavinck, Chuenpagdee, Jentoft & Kooiman, 2013).

Social sustainability

The challenge

Throughout the northeast Atlantic, fishing currently faces a concatenation of problems that pose an existential threat to coastal fisheries and their fishing communities. Resource depletion

– a legacy of industrialising the commons and sustained by ineffective policy – and inadequate quota and rising costs of production set against unstable quayside prices, raise questions in the minds of younger generations over the benefits to be derived from a lifetime in fishing, especially in circumstances where an increasing burden of regulation eats away at the fishers' ability to deploy their skills, knowledge and experience in bringing home a good catch and providing a steady income (Williams, 2008). The impacts of demographic transition, culminating in smaller household size and ageing coastal populations, and increasing spatial and social mobility have been to dilute and disperse local kin-based networks that formerly provided the basis for crew selection (Symes & Frangoudes, 2001). Recruitment of new entrants has become a problem in many fishing-dependent areas – employment of non-local, sometimes immigrant, labour and the replacement of traditional share systems of remuneration by wage agreements are becoming more widespread.

Possibly the biggest threat to social sustainability comes from privatisation of the commons and the adoption of ITQs, allowing the market to determine the size and structure of fishing fleets. An inconclusive debate over ITQs has pitted economists against other social scientists. There is little doubt that introducing ITQs helps create a more efficient industry with capacity closely aligned to available resources (Arnason, 1993), but it comes at a very high cost in terms of employment, social equity and the sustainability of smaller coastal settlements (Eythorsson, 1996). In Iceland, difficulties and high costs of acquiring quota are forcing younger fishers to pursue their ambitions abroad, notably in Norway. Not only do privatised fishing rights become financial assets in their own right and their ownership concentrated in fewer hands – in some cases non-fishing interests – but the structure of the industry tends to shift away from smaller family enterprises towards larger, possibly company owned, vessels. In one sense, therefore, the introduction of ITQs could usher in a second phase of 'industrialising the commons'.

Competition for marine space from wildlife and water-based recreation interests, as well as from new industrial uses including hydrocarbon and renewable sources of energy, threaten access to established fishing grounds. Onshore, there is further disruption through 'urbanisation' of the waterfront, where premium real estate values have led to the conversion of fishers' cottages into retirement and second home ownership. Similarly, larger commercial properties formerly associated with fishing have been converted into hotels, restaurants and retail outlets (Williams, 2014). The absence of affordable housing in areas previously occupied by the fishing community has added to the problem of social renewal and the dispersal of the fishing community. As a result the cohesion of fishing communities is undermined and their identity challenged: functional working communities are replaced by 'communities of the mind' (Ross, 2015) sharing memories of a time when fishing was the centre of their universe. Throughout certain areas of the northeast Atlantic we are witnessing the translation of 'real' fishing communities into 'virtual' fishing communities (Brookfield, Gray & Hatchard, 2005), serving as a suitable backdrop to the burgeoning tourism industries.

The nature and intensity of the existential threat varies throughout the northeast Atlantic; it is at its most intense in the North Sea bordering some of Europe's old established industrial areas where coastal population densities are high and the range of competing uses are greatest. Intensity declines as one moves north or south and the challenge assumes more specific identities: second home ownership and recreational fishing interests in the Baltic, and sun-seeking, tourism-related pressures along Britain's south coast and France's Atlantic coastline. Although the pressures are arguably weaker in the mid-Atlantic states of Iceland and the Faeroe Islands and in north Norway, their impact is more pronounced simply because of the stronger role of fishing-related activities in the national or regional economy.

Such developments provide fertile ground for social analysis at the level of the fisheries dependent region, the fishing community and the fisher household. Overall the content of the social science literature has seen a shift towards a more structured analysis of fishers' livelihoods and greater attention to fisher households as the organising framework for coastal fishing and their crucial roles as the agencies for mediating the industry's response to its changing fortunes.

Living the fishing: sustaining livelihoods and quality of life

Guaranteeing access to fishing opportunities for all who fish is no longer feasible. Arguably more important and certainly more challenging is the task of ensuring the identity, dignity and well-being of those able to pursue the distinctive way of life associated with fishing. While some involved in coastal fishing are guided by instrumental values with ambitions to earn a reputation based upon conspicuous financial success, for the majority the motivation is a combination of intrinsic, social and individual values. In an industry where the risks are high, the work demanding and the financial rewards uncertain, the identity, status and satisfaction of being a fisher is defined rather less by material achievement and more by their independence, self-employment and reliance on personal skills, knowledge and experience. However, the skipper is not an autonomous agent but dependent on the skills, experience and reliability of a crew with whom he must develop a close-knit, trust-based relationship and share the risks and rewards (Pálsson, 1994). While these attributes are ascribed to the fishers, they are reflected, mediated and ultimately supported from within the family household and more widely throughout the fishing community.

Whatever the time scale – the next fishing trip, the next year or the next generation – the future in fishing is always uncertain and to a large degree unpredictable. Fishers and their families must live essentially adaptive lives, responding to the rhythm of the seasons, the unpredictability of conditions at sea – and therefore of catch and income – and the changing expectations of policy makers. In contrast to specialised large-scale enterprises operating in offshore waters, coastal fishers usually rely upon diversity and flexibility of their operations. Small-scale fishers are in essence multi-skilled and their boats designed to accommodate a variety of métiers. At the heart of the adaptability of the coastal fishing enterprise is the largely undervalued and often invisible roles of fisher wives active in managing the family household, servicing the needs of the fishing enterprise and often providing an invaluable source of additional household income (Nadel-Klein, 2003). Fisher households today display a much less rigid set of roles and relationships; less centred upon the fishing enterprise *per se*. In the longer term, as women become distanced from the fisheries occupationally and emotionally and more sceptical about socialising their children with a view to a future in fishing, the transmission of a traditional coastal culture will be weakened, putting its future in some doubt (Pettersen, 2001).

Faced with disruption to the normal pattern of fishing activity caused by unpredicted environmental, economic or policy-related events, the response of individual fishing enterprises will vary. Among the factors influencing the response are the structure of the family household, its financial circumstances, latent sources of labour and/or skill and how its members evaluate the importance of living by fishing; the availability of alternative employment opportunities locally; and the ability and willingness of family members to move elsewhere. Pettersen (1996), examining the response of coastal fishers in the Lofoten Islands in north Norway to the collapse of northern cod stocks, identified four alternative strategies: expansion and diversification, favoured by younger, more flexible households, and retrenchment and withdrawal affecting older households, close to retirement and with increased dependence on welfare payments.

Being adaptive incurs both financial and emotional costs (Britton, 2014). Few options are neutral in terms of their implications for different household members. For men, withdrawal is difficult: the accumulated assets (vessel, gears) and fishing skills are largely non-transferable and a move into non-fishing employment or premature retirement implies some loss of identity and status within the community. For women, expansion or diversification is likely to add to their workloads and to the stress of managing the family household. The impacts of adaptive change will be distributed unevenly across the fishing community, between fishing enterprises and within fisher households. The sustainability of coastal fisheries and living by fishing depends to a significant extent on the overall balance of decisions taken within a large number of fisher households (Broch, 2013).

Squaring the circle

Recently two different but complementary developments have occurred that could help to give greater structure and direction to adaptive strategies designed to promote sustainability of coastal fisheries and fishing dependent areas by reconnecting them with their environmental, economic and sociocultural roots. The first of these is theoretical and involves the application of 'resilience thinking' to coastal fisheries. Resilience thinking had its origins in ecosystem resilience (Holling, 1973) and was later adapted (Berkes & Folke, 1998) to suit the circumstances surrounding coastal and more especially inshore fisheries. It is based on the integration of local ecological and social systems so as to maintain the rich diversity of local ecosystems – vulnerable to disturbance from environmental changes and overfishing – and the integrity of local social systems through management approaches that safeguard the flexibility and adaptability of small-scale, low-impact fishing.

A resilience-based approach involves a deeper understanding of the functioning of both systems, avoidance of simplistic quantitative management approaches and their replacement by more sensitive, parametric measures (Wilson & Dickie, 1995) that relate more closely to life cycle behaviours of the target species, thus embracing a genuine ecosystem-based approach. It requires fishing effort to vary in line with natural fluctuations of fish and shellfish stocks and to be maintained at levels set below the ecosystem's carrying capacity. Above all, 'living the fishing' means living with uncertainty rather than constantly battling against it. Resilience-building strategies should focus not only on securing the sustainability of individual fishing enterprises but also on the overall integrity, flexibility and dynamics of the ecological and social systems.

The theme of creating a new symbiosis between coastal fisheries, the marine environment and the wider local economy is continued in a more recent development related to the funding arrangements to support the implementation of the EU's common policy. Axis 4 of the European Fisheries Fund (2007–2013) makes provision for a separate funding stream to assist the sustainable development of fishing-dependent areas in an approach that is modelled on the earlier LEADER programme for rural areas. Axis 4 funding is available to support both marine and inland fisheries development. It establishes a means of delivering local potentials for increased resilience by charting a 'middle way' between the frequently divergent sectoral and territorial approaches to development (Phillipson & Symes, 2015), in which diversification is interpreted not as providing alternatives to fishing but as a way of complementing fishing activity.

Implementing Axis 4 objectives involves a network of self-governing Fisheries Local Action Groups (FLAGs) – partnerships between fishing, local business interests and community interest groups. Their tasks include the preparation of a development strategy articulating the needs of the local fishing industry and the subsequent selection, nurturing and part funding of projects initiated by individuals or groups of fishers that would add value to the local catch, generate additional employment within or outwith the fisher household or improve the area's environmental quality. Projects range from new product development, direct sales of catch within and beyond the local area, through ecotourism, fishing heritage and educational initiatives, to water quality improvement and wildlife conservation *inter alia*. Although Axis 4 has still to be fully evaluated, early results (see FARNET, 2015; van de Walle, Gomes da Silva, O'Hara & Soto, 2015) are encouraging, both in relation to employment generation and closer integration with the local business community. Its rapid diffusion throughout the EU – with over 300 FLAGs established and more than 9,000 projects at some stage of implementation at the end of 2014 – and its retention within the next funding programme (2014–2020) provide further indications of its perceived potential in strengthening the resilience of fishing communities and securing sustainable development for coastal fishing in the EU.

Conclusion

Many of the issues concerning the governance and social sustainability of capture fisheries discussed above will be played out on a global stage over the next two decades. In the northeast Atlantic there is evidence of improving systems of fisheries governance based in part on increasing stakeholder participation and recognition of the need to re-embed fisheries in their distinctive social, cultural and environmental contexts. A number of residual battles, especially in relation to small-scale fisheries, still have to be won.

In the global south outcomes will vary markedly, shaped by intrinsic regional conditions, resilience of local institutions and the power play between indigenous coastal interests, emerging political elites and global pressures for market-based solutions to the distribution of fishing rights. The struggle to retain fishing opportunities in the hands of local fishing interests as a basis for local employment, economic development and food security will be crucial; and the success of the UN project to embed small-scale, indigenous fishing rights in a robust system of human rights could be vital.

Notes

1   The huge Russian fleet of mother ships and factory trawlers, based mainly in Murmansk, operated primarily in the northwest Atlantic off the coasts of the USA, Canada and Greenland.
2   In 1996, following a brief dalliance with ITQs, the Faeroe Islands switched to a system of input restrictions involving the allocation of a specific number of fishing days to different classes of fishing vessels.
3   Unusually, the EU Commission was granted 'sole competence' for formulating policy proposals in respect of fisheries conservation; the decisions, approved by the Council of Ministers and European Parliament, are issued in the form of Regulations rather than the softer, more pliable Directives.
4   Relative stability is based on fixed keys for allocating quota.

References

Andersen, TM, Holmström, B, Houkapoja, S, Korkman, S, Söderström, HT et al. (2007). *The Nordic model: Embracing globalisation and sharing risks*. Research Institute of Finnish Economy (ETA). Helsinki: Taloustieto Oy.

Arnason, R (1993). Ocean fisheries management – recent international developments. *Marine Policy* 17(5), 334–339.

Bavinck, M, Chuenpagdee, R, Diallo, M, van der Heijden, P & Kooiman, J et al. (2005). *Interactive fisheries governance: A guide to better practice*. Delft: Eburon.

Bavinck, M, Chuenpagdee, R, Jentoft, S & Kooiman, J (Eds). (2013) *Governability of fisheries and aquaculture: Theory and applications*. Dordrecht: Springer.

Berkes, F & Folke, C (Eds). (1998). *Linking social and ecological systems*. Cambridge: Cambridge University Press.

Britton, E (2014). The social wellbeing impacts of the salmon ban on Lough Foyle's fishing communities. In J Urquhart, TG Acott, D Symes & M Zhao (Eds), *Social issues in sustainable fisheries management* (pp. 143–164). Dordrecht: Springer.

Broch, HB (2013). Social resilience – Local responses to changes in social and natural environments. *Maritime Studies* 12(6).

Brookfield, K, Gray, T & Hatchard, J (2005). The concept of fisheries-dependent communities. A comparative analysis of four UK case studies: Shetland, Peterhead, North Shields and Lowestoft. *Fisheries Research* 72, 55–69.

Commission of the European Communities (2009). Green paper: Reform of the Common Fisheries Policy. COM(2009) final. Brussels: CEC.

Eythorsson, E (1996). Coastal communities and ITQ management: The case of Icelandic fisheries. *Sociologia Ruralis* 36(2), 212–223.

FAO (Food and Agriculture Organization) (2014). *The state of fisheries and aquaculture*. Rome: United Nations.

FARNET (2015). *Sailing towards 2020: Axis 4 in action*. Brussels: European Union.

Gezelius, SS (2008). Implementation of resource conservation policies in the Norwegian fisheries: A historical outline. In SS Gezelius & J Raakjaer (Eds), *Making fisheries management work: Implementation of policies for sustainable fishing* (pp. 41–98). Dordrecht: Springer.

Goodlad, J (1998). Sectoral quota management – Fisheries management by fish producer organisations. In T Gray (Ed.), *The politics of fishing* (pp. 146–160). London: Macmillan.

Hardin, G (1968). The tragedy of the commons. *Science* 162, 1243–1248.

Hegland, TJ, Ounanian, K & Raakjaer, J (2012). Why and how to regionalise the Common Fisheries Policy. *Maritime Studies* 11(7).

Hegland, TJ & Raakjær, J (2008). Recovery plans and the balancing of fishing capacity and fishing possibilities: Path dependence in the Common Fisheries Policy. In SS Gezelius & J Raakjaer (Eds), *Making fisheries management work: Implementation of policies for sustainable fishing* (pp. 131–159). Dordrecht: Springer.

Hersoug, B & Rånes, SA (1997). What is good for the fisherman is good for the nation: Co-management in the Norwegian fishing industry in the 1990s. *Ocean and Coastal Management* 35(2–3), 157–173.

Holling, CS (1973). Resilience and stability of ecological systems. *Annual Review of Ecology and Systematics* 4, 1–23.

Holm, P, Raakjaer J, Jacobsen RE & Henriksen E (2015). Contesting the social contracts underpinning fisheries – Lessons from Norway, Iceland and Greenland. *Marine Policy* 55, 64–72.

Horobin, GW (1957). Community and occupation in the Hull fishing industry. *The British Journal of Sociology* 8(4), 343–356.

Jentoft, S (1989). Fisheries co-management: Delegating government responsibility to fishermen's organisations. *Marine Policy* 13(2), 137–154.

Jentoft, S & Chuenpagdee, R (2009). Fisheries and coastal governance as a wicked problem. *Marine Policy* 33, 553–560.

Jentoft, S & McCay, B (1995). User participation in fisheries management: Lessons drawn from international experiences. *Marine Policy* 22(4–5), 423–436.

Johnsen, JP & Eliasen, SQ (2011). Solving complex fisheries management problems: What the EU can learn from the Nordic experiences of reduction of discard. *Marine Policy* 35(2), 130–139.

Kooiman, J, Jentoft, S, Pullin, R & Bavinck, M (Eds). (2005). *Fish for life: Interactive governance for fisheries*. Amsterdam: Amsterdam University Press.

Kurlansky, M (1997). *Cod: A biography of the fish that changed the world*. London: Jonathan Cape.

Munro, GR & Pitcher, TJ (Eds). (1996). Individual transferable quotas. Special Issue, *Reviews in Fish Biology and Fisheries* 6(1).

Nadel-Klein, J (2003). *Fishing for heritage: Modernity and loss along the Scottish coast*. Oxford: Berg.

Ostrom, E (1990). *Governing the commons: The evolution of institutions for collective action*. Cambridge: Cambridge University Press.

Pálsson, G (1994). Enskilment at sea. *Man* 29, 901–927.

Pettersen, LT (1996). Crisis management and household strategy in Lofoten: A question of sustainable development. *Sociologia Ruralis* 36(2), 236–248.

Pettersen, LT (2001). Household adaptations and gender differences in inshore fishing communities in northern Norway. In D Symes (Ed.), *Fisheries dependent regions* (pp. 82–91). Oxford: Blackwell Science.

Phillipson, J (2002). *Widening the net: Prospects for fisheries co-management*. Newcastle: CRE Press.

Phillipson, J & Symes, D (2010). Recontextualising inshore fisheries: The changing face of British inshore fisheries management. *Marine Policy* 34(6), 1207–1214.

Phillipson, J & Symes, D (2015). Finding a middle way to develop Europe's fishing dependent regions: The role of Axis 4. *Sociologia Ruralis* 35(3), 343–359.

Piriz, L (2004). *Hauling home the co-management of coastal fisheries*. Göteborg: Göteborg University Press.

Ross, N (2015). Understanding the fishing community: The role of communities of the mind. *Sociologia Ruralis* 35(3), 309–324.

Schramm, HL Jr. & Hubert, WA (1996). Ecosystem management: Implications for fisheries management. *Fisheries* 21(12), 6–11.

Scottish Government (2010). *The future of fisheries management in Scotland: Report of an independent panel*. Edinburgh: The Scottish Government.

Sen, S (1997). The evolution of high seas fisheries management in the north-east Atlantic. *Ocean and Coastal Management* 36(2–3), 85–100.

Sen, S & Raakjaer Nielsen, J (1996). Fisheries co-management: A comparative analysis. *Marine Policy* 20(5), 405–418.

Sissenwine, M & Symes, D (2007). *Reflections on the Common Fisheries Policy*. Report to the General Directorate for Fisheries and Maritime Affairs of the European Union. Brussels: European Commission.

Symes, D (2006). Fisheries governance: A coming of age for fisheries social science? *Fisheries Research* 81, 113–117.

Symes, D (2009). *Regionalising the Common Fisheries Policy: What kind of solution?* Nordic Council of Ministers Seminar, Copenhagen. http://www.norden.org/en/publications/2009-579.

Symes, D & Frangoudes, K (2001). The social organisation and reproduction of inshore fishing. In D Symes & J Phillipson (Eds), *Inshore fisheries management* (pp. 159–175). Dordrecht: Kluwer.

Symes, D & Phillipson, J (1999). Co-governance in EU fisheries: The complexity and diversity of fishermen's organisations in Denmark, Spain and the UK. In J Kooiman, M van Vliet & S Jentoft (Eds), *Creative governance: Opportunities for fisheries in Europe* (pp. 59–93). Aldershot: Ashgate.

Tunstall, J (1962). *The fishermen: The sociology of an extreme occupation*. London: MacGibbon & Kee.

van de Walle, G, Gomes da Silva, S, O'Hara, E & Soto, P (2015). Achieving sustainable development of local fishing interests: The case of the Pays d'Auray. *Sociologia Ruralis* 35(3), 360–377.

Vervaele, K (2014). Flemish fishermen's wives: Their lives and roles in fisheries. In J Urquhart, TG Acott, D Symes & M Zhao (Eds), *Social issues in sustainable fisheries management* (pp. 201–213). Dordrecht: Springer.

Warner, WW (1977). *Distant water: The fate of the North Atlantic fisherman*. Boston, MA: Atlantic-Little, Brown.

Williams, R (2008). Changing constructions of identity: Fisher households and industry restructuring. Unpublished PhD thesis, Newcastle University.

Williams, R (2014). The socio-cultural impact of industry restructuring: Fishing identities in north east Scotland. In J Urquhart, TG Acott, D Symes & M Zhao (Eds), *Social issues in sustainable fisheries management* (pp. 301–318). Dordrecht: Springer.

Wilson, JA & Dickie, LM (1995). Parametric management in fisheries: An ecosystem-social approach. In S Hanna & M Minasingha (Eds), *Property rights in a social and ecological context* (pp. 156–167). Washington, DC: The Beijer International Institute of Ecological Economics and The World Bank.

28

Climate Change, Environment Hazards and Community Sustainability

Michelle A. Meyer

Rural communities have a cultural and historical legacy of an intimate connection to the physical environment. Farming, animal herding, resource extraction and recreation are still prominent in many rural areas today. These environmental spaces and activities also offer a sense of place and identity for many rural people. Globalisation and neoliberalism have brought changes to rural areas in recent decades, creating pressures and opportunities for economic and social activity across rural areas. As climate change impacts increase and droughts, floods, storms and heatwaves become more frequent and intense, rural populations' connections to the environment are again being altered. In this chapter I provide a brief overview of climate change and hazard vulnerability and resilience for rural communities in the 21st century

A disaster is defined as 'a serious disruption in the functioning of a community or society involving widespread human, material, economic or environmental losses and impacts, which exceeds the ability of the affected community or society to cope using its own resources' (UNISDR, 2014). Disasters can cause death, injury, disease and adverse effects on mental health and social connections along with damage to property, destruction of assets, loss of services, economic disruption and environmental degradation. Physical disaster risk depends upon geographic location, such as along coastlines, earthquake fault lines, in floodplains, or near hazardous facilities. Yet, the actualised impact of a disaster on individuals and communities is conditioned by social processes – processes that can vary by rural or urban context. Particularly, rural areas' hazard risk and impacts differ from those in urban areas due to variation in social and economic composition (Cutter, Boruff & Shirley, 2003), especially related to types of economic activity, household incomes, and access to organisational and governmental resources for mitigation and adaptation. Variation in disaster impacts for rural areas has been mostly discussed at the international level, where it is noted that developing countries are especially vulnerable to climate change because of their geographic exposure, low incomes and greater reliance on climate-sensitive economic activities. At the national level, though, many rural areas are more vulnerable to climate change and certain disaster impacts than their neighbouring urban counterparts. At the community level, income, age, gender and race all create differential effects of disaster and climate change within a rural community.

Connecting the disaster and climate change literature, I provide a brief review of potential impacts, which may be common across many, though not all, rural areas. One important argument within this literature is to avoid viewing rural areas as monolithic in either physical risk, disaster resilience or vulnerability. Thus, I discuss patterns that may be more prevalent in rural areas than in urban areas. Then, I focus on social vulnerability to describe how social processes result in unequal environmental risks for some rural communities. Finally, I close with a discussion of opportunities and efforts to promote equitable adaptation and resilience.

Disaster and climate vulnerability in rural areas

From 1983 to 2012, the average annual financial losses from disasters worldwide totalled US$128 billion, and only $32 billion of that was insured. Average disaster-related fatalities worldwide over the same time period topped 56,000 annually. In comparison to average losses in the last 30 years, financial and death tolls from disaster in the last 10 years were higher, at $184 billion and 106,000 deaths annually (Table 28.1) (III, 2014). These increasing averages point to a trend due in part to population growth and development in physically risky areas, but also increasing risk due to climate change. While no specific disaster event can be attributed to climate change, disaster frequency and intensity are rising across the world as a result of changes in temperature and precipitation patterns. For example, the number of areas affected by heatwaves is expected to double by 2020.

Disaster impacts and capacity to mitigate or recover are not equitably spread across the world. The International Federation of Red Cross and Red Crescent Societies compares yearly disaster losses and deaths using the United Nations Development Programme's Human Development Index (HDI). Table 28.2 shows the total number of disasters, disaster losses and fatalities by HDI for the past 10 years. As shown, countries that are among the most highly developed have the most dollar losses in disasters, while those with the lowest human development experienced the most deaths from disasters. Based on these numbers, the global north, as a whole, has greater capacity to prepare and recover from disasters than other parts of the world.

Based on these measures of impacts – fatalities and financial losses – rural areas are considered to be at less physical risk because they have smaller populations, less infrastructure and fewer assets to be affected (Cross, 2001). Most research and attention to disaster vulnerability and resilience focuses on large disasters in urban areas, such as New Orleans, Louisiana following Hurricane Katrina, or Kobe, Japan following the 1995 earthquake. For example, the World Bank and the International Federation of Red Cross and Red Crescent Societies, among others, have urban-specific disaster risk reduction initiatives.

Table 28.1 Natural catastrophes worldwide, 2003–2012

	Number of events	Fatalities	Overall losses US$ billion	Insured losses US$ billion	Insured losses 10-year average US$ billion
Earthquake/tsunami	657	678,400	489	77.0	7.7
Heatwave/drought (excludes famine)	207	132,600	118	22.0	2.2
Tropical cyclone	424	65,500	539	234.0	23.4
River flood/flash flood	2,458	54,600	274	48.0	4.8
Winter events	401	13,000	101	44.0	4.4
Severe thunderstorm	2,375	6,310	206	126.0	12.6
Wildfire	524	1,270	27	11.0	1.1

Source: 2013 Munich Reinsurance Company, Geo Risks Research, NatCatSERVICE.

Table 28.2 Disaster impact by Human Development Index (HDI) level, 2004–2013

HDI	Number of disasters	Damage (US$)	Fatalities
Very high	1,119	1,119,023	41,947
High	1,288	95,138	120,886
Medium	2,207	404,090	395,545
Low	1,811	51,374	500,694
Total	6,525	1,669,626	1,059,072

Source: International Federation of Red Cross and Red Crescent Societies World Disasters Report 2014: Focus on Culture and Risk (https://www.ifrc.org/Global/Documents/Secretariat/201410/WDR%202014.pdf).

Rural scholars have argued that this focus on total dollars and lives lost oversimplifies risk, and that especially under climate change, disaster risk in rural areas needs more study (Dunlap, 2010). Further, this research needs to be linked to poverty reduction and livelihood research as well as cross-national comparisons to understand patterns across rural areas. Understanding the uniqueness of climate changes in rural areas, especially rural areas of developed countries, is only recently gaining academic and policy attention.

To begin to understand disaster and climate change in rural areas, an understanding of the physical and social risk is necessary. Physical risk is the geographical risk and risk to industries directly tied to the environment or area. Rural areas, more commonly that urban areas, use the environment for economic resources – from agriculture to energy resource extraction to tourism to manufacturing (Abel, Gabe & Stolarick, 2012). The environmental-based industries are highly dependent on weather, climate and water availability, and are thus affected by weather- and climate-related patterns and natural disasters, more so than the knowledge-based economic sectors that are more common in urban areas. For example, agriculture can be affected by contamination of water bodies, loss of harvest or livestock, increased susceptibility to disease, increased pest activity, and destruction of irrigation systems or other agricultural infrastructure during a disaster or climate change impact (Piao et al., 2010). Beyond agriculture, natural amenities most connected to precipitation and temperature will be affected by changes in the environment. For example, mountain ski resort areas are expected to face reduced natural snowfall and rising temperatures, which will increase pressure on water resources for snowmaking and shorten the winter tourist season as temperatures stay warmer longer and spring arrives sooner (Gilaberte-Burdalo, Lopez-Martin, Pino-Otin & Lopez-Moreno, 2014). While many rural areas do not rely solely on these environmental services, climate change effects on these resources can have wide-ranging effects across the industries they support, including processing and transportation, and may be consequential for rural populations that have fewer alternative economic options.

Rural social vulnerability to disaster and climate impacts

As noted above, discussion of physical environmental change is directly linked to economic and social structures. Moving beyond physical risk, researchers focus on social factors that determine how physical risk manifests into unequal impacts across a population. This social vulnerability to disaster paradigm describes 'the characteristics of a person or group and their situation that influence their capacity to anticipate, cope with, resist and recover from the impact of a natural hazard' (Wisner, Blaikie, Cannon & Davis, 2004). This perspective highlights how social relations across different nations and within a given society create

337

differential impacts of disaster for different populations (Cutter, Boruff & Shirley, 2003; Phillips, Thomas, Fothergill & Blinn-Pik, 2010), and focuses on social relationships within and between populations that result in certain people being more or less able to bounce back from a hazardous event. Thus, physical risk cannot be isolated from social processes that both increase and decrease environmental risk and foster or constrain adaptive action.

Rural and urban disparities is one area of research on social vulnerability to disaster. Scholars attempting to quantify social vulnerability to disaster and potential disaster resilience highlight that populations within rural areas differ from urban areas in social risk to various impacts; and across rural areas, risk varies based on community and population features. To more deeply understand how climate and disaster affect rural populations specifically, we need to look at factors that are more common across rural communities than urban areas: less economic diversity; high percentage of populations considered socially vulnerable such as those living in poverty, the elderly, women and ethnic minorities; decaying or lacking infrastructure; and limited institutional capacity.

Rural economics and vulnerability

Economic diversity across various sectors is viewed as a positive for community-level resilience (Adger et al., 2005; Norris et al., 2008). In a nation or community with multiple productive economic activities, when one sector is affected by a disaster, others continue and may be able to absorb the losses in the affected sector. In contrast, nations or communities that are dependent on one or a limited number of economic sectors are more vulnerable if those particular sectors are affected by disaster and environmental change.

This issue of economic diversity is a particular concern for those rural areas whose economies depend at least somewhat on environmental services. Though many rural economies are diversifying in the 21st century, some, even in high-income countries, are still dominated by environmentally based employment and incomes that are at greater risk to environmental change than are knowledge-based, professional or financial businesses. These rural economic sectors at risk in times of disaster and climate change include agriculture (farming, manufacturing and processing of farm and food products), timber, mining, energy extraction and recreation (parks, mountains, beaches) (USDA, 2014). Rural resilience studies have commonly focused on the effect of disaster and climate change on agriculture as a central economic and cultural institution for rural areas (Cheshire, Esparcia & Shucksmith, 2015). For example, disasters and climate change can have short- and long-term negative effects on the resource itself, such as drought affecting crops or lakes popular for tourism; and on infrastructure tied to the resource, such as flooded timber or animal processing facilities or hurricane-destroyed tourist accommodations. For example, drought can truncate or eliminate an entire agricultural season, meaning landowners and farm labours are out of income for an entire year. In 1973, the Buffalo Creek flood occurred in rural Appalachian mountains of the United States when an industrial dam was unable to hold during a large rainfall. Most men in the community were employed by this company, and the community had trusted the company to protect and serve those who had served it for so long (Erikson, 1976). Following the flood, the entire town was displaced. This displacement severed community relationships and, along with a lack of recovery support from the company, mental and financial stress ensued. As environmental changes and disasters affect limited employment and economic opportunities in rural areas, increased conflict, out-migration, service withdrawal and social stress may be expected, as has been witnessed following technological disasters such as the Exxon Mobil or Deepwater Horizon oil spills (Gill & Picou, 1998; Warner, 2010; Cheshire, Esparcia & Shucksmith, 2015).

Demographic factors and vulnerability

Across the world, economic inequality is rising, poverty rates are stagnant, lifespans and thus elderly populations are increasing, and gender and racial disparities in access to resources continue. Women, racial and ethnic minorities, persons with disabilities, persons living in poverty and the elderly are more likely to face greater impacts from climate change because of this social stratification of resources.

Poverty is one of the greatest risk factors for disaster impacts – the poor are more likely to die, be injured, be displaced, have higher rates of mental health impacts, lose employment, lose housing, and have slower recovery times than higher income populations (Fothergill & Peek, 2004; Hartman & Squires, 2006; Molnar, 2010). Rural areas have a higher proportion of the global poor than urban areas, with 75% of the world's poor living in rural areas, many of which are at high risk of climate change (Davies et al., 2009). But within the global north, the rate of rural poverty varies, with some areas still facing concentrated poverty, while others, such as those within the European Union, show similar poverty rates as urban areas. For example, in the United States, rural poverty continues to outpace urban poverty (18.2% versus 15.4%), rural median incomes are markedly lower than urban incomes ($41,000 versus $53,000), and many rural areas have continued to lose jobs or have slow employment growth since the great recession of 2008 (USDA, 2014). Northern and western Europe may be an exception to this trend, while southern and eastern Europe still have areas of concentrated rural poverty (IFAD, 2015).

Even when poverty rates are similar, poor people living in rural areas are more likely than their urban counterparts to live in substandard housing located in hazardous areas (such as hillsides prone to landslides or floodplains), which place them at greater risk of disaster and climate impacts than urban poor. Further, poor and low-income labourers are more likely to lose employment, especially service-sector jobs or those related to environment resources affected by the disaster (Abramson et al., 2010; Weber & Peek, 2012). Global rural poor who rely on environmental services can be impacted by hazards through price fluctuation, resource loss and job loss (Davies et al., 2009). For example, rural areas in the USA have higher rates of low-skill jobs, which have the slowest return rates following major disasters (Abramson et al., 2010). Disaster and climate change impacts, especially those related to job loss, can increase temporary or permanent migration of at least part of rural populations (Warner, 2010). While rural individuals continue to seek employment in urban areas, climate change is expected to increase the pace of rural population decline.

A variety of age-related factors are important to consider for disaster resilience such as physical and cognitive ability, social networks or cultural family relationships, and socioeconomic status. The elderly are among those most likely to perish in disasters (Peek, 2010). For example, the elderly are more likely to die from heatwaves and have increased mortality after evacuation due to transportation-related trauma. Decreased physical and mental capacity affect the elderly's ability to understand warnings and take necessary protective action. Also, limited social integration and isolation, lower incomes or living within a fixed income, and dependence on community or private support systems for livelihoods put the elderly at increased vulnerability to impacts (Peek, 2010). During disaster recovery, the elderly are least likely to seek public aid and, depending on the culture they live in, may receive less social support from family and friends.

These vulnerability factors are compounded for elderly people who reside in rural communities. The rural elderly are more likely to live in substandard housing and more likely to own their homes than urban elderly (HAC, 2003). Thus, elderly populations have more of their financial assets at risk and face higher proportional dollar losses in disaster than urban elderly (Bolin & Klenow, 1983). Rural elderly are also more likely than urban elderly to lack transportation, which limits their capacity to gather disaster preparation supplies or evacuate when necessary.

Gender stratification also affects access to resources and power relationships across the world. In disaster, the consequences of gender relations can be fatal, often more fatal for women than men (Tobin-Gurley & Enarson, 2013). The responsibilities of women to provide for their families and social networks in rural communities are increasing with environmental pressures (Terry, 2009). But there are also opportunities based on changing gender dynamics in response to changing agriculture patterns, such as increased female labour outside the home as a mechanism for adapting to changing agriculture production systems (Bock & Shortall, 2006). Yet in disaster, men are more likely to be in decision-making positions, which may result in women's needs being overlooked. Men are also more likely to do immediate clean-up and debris removal across the community, increasing their risk of injury, while women are more likely to take on caregiving for their household and other community members and express greater emotional and psychological stress from disasters (Morrow & Phillips, 1999).

Climate change-induced conflict is a hot topic in policy and academic circles as some theory indicates that pressure for dwindling resources will increase violence (Raleigh, Jordan & Salehyan, 2008). While this thesis has yet to be proved, violence against women is one known outcome of disasters and environmental stress. Studies have shown an increase in domestic violence against women by male family members due to the increased familial stress over loss of resources caused by the environmental event (Anastario, Shehab & Lawry, 2009). Also, when male household members migrate for work, women are more likely to remain in environmentally stressed communities and the lack of male family members puts women at increased risk of victimisation, such as sexual assault and robbery. Lack of social services and domestic violence shelters in rural communities makes it more difficult for rural women to find protection.

Across disasters, racial and ethnic minorities fare worse during a disaster (Norris et al., 2002). This result is again related to social stratification since resources and power depend on race or ethnicity. Thus, race and ethnicity commonly correlate with income and poverty, making racial and ethnic minorities disproportionately affected by the income-related resilience issues discussed above – such as living in more environmentally risky areas in substandard housing (Van Zandt et al., 2012). Beyond economic differences, racial and ethnic minorities often have separate social networks and may speak different languages than the majority population, which affects their ability to receive preparedness and warning information. For example, in rural areas where warning systems and communication networks are limited, racially segregated social networks can affect the ability of these populations to receive life-saving disaster information. Minorities also face outright discrimination and violence during disasters. For example, evacuation assistance may not be provided to certain groups (Rivera & Miller, 2007). Even without outright discrimination, minorities are less likely to hold positions of power in communities and nations, lessening their ability to determine mitigation, preparedness and recovery strategies and direct resources to their needs.

Infrastructure, institutional capacity and vulnerability

Sufficient and well-maintained infrastructure can provide protection to assets and lives during environmental impacts. For example, levees reduce flooding, bridges and roads provide access for evacuation, storm-water drainage removes excess water from roads and away from homes. Infrastructure capacity will become more important as climate change affects precipitation frequency and intensity in particular.

Across the world, rural areas are more likely than urban areas to have inadequate infrastructure – or completely lack these types of infrastructure. Further, disasters can destroy or damage the minimal infrastructure in a rural area, effectively cutting off these regions from vital services. As environmental impacts increase migration and rural areas lose population, public investment further decreases and rural areas face the compounded risk of environmental change, loss of investment and infrastructure decay. Effects include lack of safe drinking water, lack of proper sanitary facilities for disposal of sewage and garbage, lack of electricity and food stores, and rising malnutrition and poor and badly maintained roads (Fox & Porca, 2001).

Organisational, social, political and economic resources can be used to adapt and counteract disaster and climate change impacts. Currently, indicators of disaster and climate resilience show that rural areas may be less resilient than urban areas due to fewer of these resources and less ability to access external resources (Cutter, Burton & Emrich, 2010). As Norris et al. (2002) show, rural areas – and especially those within low-income countries across the world – experienced greater impairment from disaster and slower recovery than urban areas and high-income countries.

The adaptive capacity of the rural poor to emerging environmental threats depends on the success of formal and informal rural institutions (Agrawal, 2010). Emergency management response mechanisms can reduce the lives lost and protect property from damage if they are initiated quickly. Rural areas are also less likely to have critical emergency management infrastructure such as tornado sirens, evacuation shelters, trained and paid emergency personnel such as firefighters or paramedics, or hospitals. Rural areas' public or governmental health departments also tend to have fewer staff and resources compared to urban areas (HRSA, 2002). This lack of resources and staff mean rural areas may rely more heavily on volunteers or external agencies for assistance in disaster.

Non-governmental organisations supply aid, connect rural poor households to external resources, and implement national and international policies that can mitigate or support preparedness to climate and disaster vulnerability. In comparison to urban areas, formal institutions are limited in rural areas, and those that operate may oversee a variety of population needs, such as food, shelter, clothing for the impoverished as well as risk communication and cultural practices. In the United States, rural areas have dramatically fewer non-governmental organisations located within the area and most rural areas must share institutional services with several other communities in the region (Cutter, Burton & Emrich, 2010). The lack of non-governmental actors can affect the amount of social capital – trust, norms and social networks – that contributes to capacity for collective action (Aldrich & Meyer, 2014). Because of the lack of many services in rural areas or limited numbers of organisations, these organisations can be overwhelmed and have limited capacity themselves to incorporate climate and disaster planning into their mission.

The limited number of formal organisations within rural areas does not preclude the existence of informal norms and governance systems. Informal norms of exchange and social support also affect the vulnerability of rural populations whose networks and norms may change as actors attempt to adapt rules to new environmental stress and resource constraints. For example, pastoralists and fishers have coordinated collective responsibility for many resources and adapted to environmental stress over time (Ostrom, Gardner & Walker, 1994). These informal arrangements are often overlooked in research and practice on disaster and climate resilience, and little is known about these mechanisms in rural areas of developed countries.

As disasters and climate change impacts increase, rural areas can expect an increased influx of public, civic and private institutions, in which external organisations enter communities without prior understanding of current environmental practices or needs. These institutions may operate in conflict with local established institutions and then also may leave before the adaptive strategies have been fully implemented – both of which limit their impact on resilience. External support for mitigation, preparedness and adaptation are best implemented through local coordination and understanding of the existing formal and informal institutions. More research is needed on how local institutions in rural areas use internal and external resources to address social and environmental vulnerability.

Rural adaptation and resilience

Climate change and disasters present economic and social risks, but rural areas have adaptive capacity that can be supported to address these risks. Thus, the Millennium Development Goals, poverty reduction targets, disaster risk reduction and climate change adaptation are interwoven enterprises that to date are often undertaken separately (Schipper & Pelling, 2006). As Davies et al. (2009, p. 7) state, 'Adapting to the impacts of climate change has grown from a minor environmental concern to a major challenge for human development and is a crucial element in eradicating poverty and achieving the Millennium Development Goals.'

Disaster risk reduction as defined by the United Nations Office for Disaster Risk Reduction is built on the understanding that there are only natural hazards, whereas natural disasters result from human action or inaction. Disaster Risk Reduction activities aim to reduce the damage and fatalities due to natural hazards, through reducing physical risk and exposure to hazards, reducing social vulnerability of people and assets, preventative management of land and environment, and incorporating preparedness and early warning mechanisms (UNISDR, 2014).

The literature focused on adaptation to climate change also describes the importance of adjusting human activities related to ecological, social and economic systems to reduce predicted impacts of changes. Similar to disaster risk reduction strategies, Adger, Arnell and Tompkins (2005) describe the three cornerstones of adaptation to climate change:

- reduce sensitivity to risk;
- alter exposure to risk; and
- increase resilience of the social system to handle the risk.

Overall, these three cornerstones correspond to Disaster Risk Reduction targets of reducing exposure, reducing social vulnerability to risk, and affecting resilience through land management and preparedness programmes.

Adaptive capacity for disasters and climate change is context specific to the household, community, region and nation, but it is not independent of scale. Just as risk from climate change and disasters have impacts at various scales, adaptation and resilience also can be described and effected at individual, organisational and governmental – from local to national and international – scales, and often involve interconnected programmes ranging from government to household. For example, agricultural resilience mechanisms include weather-indexed crop insurance, asset restocking (including direct livestock provision) and cash transfers that incorporate individual purchasing decisions, organisational programmes and governmental policy and economic support (Davies et al. 2009, p. 8).

Equity at the international level is often discussed in the climate change literature. The power dynamics around international agreements and aid programmes that transfer assistance from high-income countries (who have contributed most to the causes of climate change) to low-income countries (who will experience the most consequences) are equity issues well known in policy and research circles (Thomas & Twyman, 2005). Yet, beyond equity and justice between countries, there are power issues between urban and rural areas within specific countries and within rural areas. Rural and urban areas are interconnected, yet many resilience programmes are based on assumptions of endogenous resilience and self-help (Cheshire, Esparcia & Shucksmith, 2015). For example, areas along the Louisiana coast are rapidly disappearing with sea level rise, and coastal adaptation plans include large infrastructure investment to protect New Orleans, while small communities and those inhabited by indigenous populations are fighting to receive any support to protect their communities (Melker, 2012). The plans for mitigation of sea level rise and storm surge in this area use population density to determine level of flood protection, with dense urban areas planned for 500-year flood events (i.e., a large flood that happens only once every 500 years) and rural areas, including Native American populations, planned for protection from only a 50-year flood event (i.e., the smaller flood more likely to happen at least once every 50 years) (Dalbom, Hemmerling & Lewis, 2014). Urban areas often have more resources and more political attention to garner resources and support for adaptation, and the greater populations as well as the greater number of assets at risk provide reasons for regional and national governments to support greater protection for these areas.

Moving forward in rural resilience

To address the needs of rural populations in climate change and disaster resilience, Davies et al. (2009, p. 16) offer a framework for adaptive social protection that integrates the above concerns of environmental risk and equity. Key goals of this adaptive social protection include protecting, adapting and transforming livelihoods beyond basic coping mechanisms; targeting the root causes of poverty and focusing on vulnerability to multiple, not individual, environmental risks; focusing on a rights based rationale for equity and justice; and developing longer term perspectives for social policies to address the increase of environmental risks that climate change and disasters create.

These broad goals call for best practices and increased research on participatory planning processes that include stakeholders from government, organisations and affected households; capacity building and training opportunities at all scales to enhance understanding of drivers and obstacles to adaptive action; and application of risk assessment tools that integrate social, environmental and economic risks at multiple scales.

Moving forward on climate and disaster resilience requires more research on strategies that support rural populations to become more resilient; greater understanding of the complex interaction between rural resources, livelihoods, formal and informal institutions, and adaptation strategies; and improved policy discussion to focus not just on rural economics and agriculture but on the broader social and cultural vulnerability and capacity of rural populations.

References

Abel, JR, Gabe, TM & Stolarick, K (2012). *Workforce skills across the urban–rural hierarchy.* Staff Report No. 552. Federal Resource Bank of New York.

Abramson, D, Stehling-Ariza, T, Park, YS, Walsh, L & Culp, D (2010). Measuring individual disaster recovery: A socioecological framework. *Disaster Medicine and Public Health Preparedness* 4, S46–S54.

Adger, WN, Arnell, NW & Tompkins, EL (2005). Successful adaptation to climate change across scales. *Global Environmental Change* 15(2), 77–86.

Adger, WN, Hughes, TP, Folke, C, Carpenter, SR & Rockstrom, J (2005). Social-ecological resilience to coastal disasters. *Science* 309 (5737), 1036–1039.

Agrawal, A (2010). Local institutions and adaptation to climate change. In R Mearns & A Norton (Ed.), *Social dimensions of climate change: Equity and vulnerability in a warming world* (pp. 173–198). Washington, DC: World Bank.

Aldrich, DP & Meyer, MA (2014). Social capital and community resilience. *American Behavioral Scientist* 59(2), 254–269.

Anastario, M, Shehab, N & Lawry, L (2009). Increased gender-based violence among women internally displaced in Mississippi 2 years post-Hurricane Katrina. *Disaster Medicine and Public Health Preparedness* 3(1), 18–26.

Bock, BB & Shortall, S (Eds). (2006). *Rural gender relations: Issues and case studies.* Oxfordshire, UK: CABI.

Bolin, R. & Klenow, DJ (1983). Response of the elderly to disaster – an age-stratified analysis. *International Journal of Aging & Human Development* 16(4), 283–296.

Cheshire, L, Esparcia, J & Shucksmith, M (2015). Community resilience, social capital, and territorial governance. *Journal of Depopulation and Rural Development Studies*, 7–38.

Cross, JA (2001). Megacities and small towns: Different perspectives on hazard vulnerability. *Global Environmental Change Part B: Environmental Hazards* 3(2), 63–80.

Cutter, SL, Boruff, BJ & Shirley, WL (2003). Social vulnerability to environmental hazards. *Social Science Quarterly* 84(2), 242–261.

Cutter, SL, Burton, C & Emrich, C (2010). Disaster resilience indicators for benchmarking baseline conditions. *Journal of Homeland Security and Emergency Management* 7(1), 1–22.

Dalbom, C, Hemmerling, SA & Lewis, JA (2014). *Community resettlement prospects in coastal Louisiana.* New Orleans, LA: Tulane Institute of Water Resources Law and Policy.

Davies, M, Guenther, B, Leavy, J, Mitchell, T & Tanner, T (2009). Climate change adaptation, disaster risk reduction and social protection: Complementary roles in agriculture and rural growth? *IDS Working Papers* (320), 1–37.

Dunlap, RE (2010). Climate change and rural sociology: Broadening the research agenda. *Rural Sociology* 75(1), 17–27.

Erikson, K (1976). *Everything in its path: Destruction of community in the Buffalo Creek flood.* New York: Simon & Schuster.

Fothergill, A & Peek, L (2004). Poverty and disasters in the United States: A review of recent sociological findings. *Natural Hazards* 32(1), 89–110.

Fox, WF & Porca, S (2001). Investing in rural infrastructure. *International Regional Science Review* 24(1), 103–133.

Gilaberte-Burdalo, M, Lopez-Martin, F, Pino-Otin, MR & Lopez-Moreno, JI (2014). Impacts of climate change on ski industry. *Environmental Science & Policy* 44, 51–61.

Gill, DA & Picou, JS (1998). Technological disaster and chronic community stress. *Society & Natural Resources: An International Journal* 11(8), 795–815.

HAC (2003). *Rural seniors and their homes.* Washington, DC: Housing Assistance Council. Retrieved 5 February 2016 from http://www.ruralhome.org/storage/documents/ruralseniors.pdf.

Hartman, CW & Squires, GD (2006). *There is no such thing as a natural disaster: Race, class, and Hurricane Katrina.* New York: Routledge.

HRSA (2002). *Rural communities and emergency preparedness.* Washington, DC: Office of Rural Health Policy, Health Resources and Services Administration. Retrieved 15 July 2015 from ftp://ftp.hrsa.gov/ruralhealth/RuralPreparedness.pdf.

IFAD (2015). Rural poverty portal. International Fund for Agricultural Development. Retrieved 15 July 2015 from http://www.ruralpovertyportal.org/home.

III (Insurance Information Institute) (2014). Catastrophes: Global. Retrieved 20 January 2015 from http://www.iii.org/fact-statistic/catastrophes-global.

Melker, SD (2012). Native lands wash away as sea levels rise. Retrieved 12 January 2015 from http://www.pbs.org/newshour/updates/climate-change-jan-june12-louisianacoast_05-30/.

Molnar, JJ (2010). Climate change and societal response: Livelihoods, communities, and the environment. *Rural Sociology* 75(1), 1–16.

Morrow, BH & Phillips, B (1999). What's gender 'got to do with it'? *International Journal of Mass Emergencies and Disasters* 17(1), 5–11.

Norris, FH, Friedman, MJ, Watson, PJ, Byrne, CM, Diaz, E & Kaniasty, K (2002). 60,000 disaster victims speak: Part I. An empirical review of the empirical literature, 1981–2001. *Psychiatry* 65(3), 207–260.

Norris, F, Stevens, S, Pfefferbaum, B, Wyche, K & Pfefferbaum, R (2008). Community resilience as a metaphor, theory, set of capacities, and strategy for disaster readiness. *American Journal of Community Psychology* 41(1), 127–150.

Ostrom, E, Gardner, R & Walker, J (1994). *Rules, games, and common-pool resources.* Ann Arbor, MI: University of Michigan Press.

Peek, L (2010). Age. In BD Phillips, DSK Thomas, A Fothergill & L Blinn-Pike (Eds), *Social vulnerability to disasters* (pp. 155–185). Boca Raton, FL: CRC Press.

Phillips, BD, Thomas, DSK, Fothergill, A & Blinn-Pike, L (Eds). (2010). *Social vulnerability to disasters.* Boca Raton, FL: CRC Press.

Piao, S, Ciais, P, Huang, Y, Shen, Z, Peng, S, Li, J, Zhou, L, Liu, H, … Fang, J (2010). The impacts of climate change on water resources and agriculture in China. *Nature* 467(7311), 43–51.

Raleigh, C, Jordan, L & Salehyan, I (2008). *Assessing the impact of climate change on migration and conflict.* Washington, DC: World Bank Group.

Rivera, JD & Miller, DS (2007). Continually neglected: Situating natural disasters in the African American experience. *Journal of Black Studies* 37(4), 502–522.

Schipper, L & Pelling, M (2006). Disaster risk, climate change and international development: Scope for, and challenges to, integration. *Disasters* 30(1), 19–38.

Terry, G (Ed.). (2009). *Climate change and gender justice.* Oxford: Oxfam GB.

Thomas, DS & Twyman, C (2005). Equity and justice in climate change adaptation amongst natural-resource-dependent societies. *Global Environmental Change* 15(2), 115–124.

Tobin-Gurley, J & Enarson, E (2013). Gender. In DSK Thomas, B Phillips, W Lovekamp & A Fothergill (Eds), *Social vulnerability to disasters* (pp. 139–166). Boca Raton, FL: CRC Press.

UNISDR (2014). What is disaster risk reduction? Retrieved 1 December 2014 from http://www.unisdr.org/who-we-are/what-is-drr.

USDA (2014). *Rural America at a glance.* Economic brief number 26. Washington, DC: United States Department of Agriculture.

Van Zandt, S, Peacock, WG, Henry, DW, Grover, H, Highfield, WE & Brody, SD (2012). Mapping social vulnerability to enhance housing and neighborhood resilience. *Housing Policy Debate* 22(1), 29–55.

Warner, K (2010). Global environmental change and migration: Governance challenges. *Global Environmental Change* 20(3), 402–413.

Weber, L & Peek, L (Eds). (2012). *Displaced: Life in the Katrina diaspora.* Austin, TX: University of Texas Press.

Wisner, B, Blaikie, P, Cannon, T & Davis, I (2004). *At risk: Natural hazards, people's vulnerability and disasters.* New York: Routledge.

Part V

Changing Configurations of Gender and Rural Society

Section editor: Sally Shortall

29

Changing Configurations of Gender and Rural Society

Future Directions for Research

Sally Shortall

Ridgeway (2009) argues that if we want to understand social behaviour and organisational structures, we have to understand gender and how it interacts with social processes. Ridgeway believes gender is a primary frame for organising social relations, hence the wonderful title of her article, 'Framed Before We Know It: How Gender Shapes Social Relations'.

Rural gender research has been an embedded topic of rural research for over 40 years. It has followed general trends in the wider disciplines to which scholars belong and has considered issues of power, symbolic interaction and the performance of gender, and culturally hegemonic beliefs about gender that become entrenched in social structures such as the media, law and taken-for-granted organisational practice.

Any section on gender in rural society has to be partial, but the following chapters offer an excellent overview of the key debates in the area and provide a wealth of literature for scholars interested in this topic. More importantly, they offer a useful and imaginative agenda for research in the future. This part of the overview identifies some of the common themes that emerge from the various chapters.

Themes of continuity and change frequently emerge. While women's labour market position has changed dramatically in the recent decades, it does not necessarily change women's representation in governance structures (Thuesen) or leadership roles (McVay), and women entrepreneurs are often judged as bad mothers (Little). The hegemonic discourse of the masculine prevails despite changing gender roles (Brandth and Haugen). At the same time, change occurs. Masculinities are recreated to incorporate the parenting father identity. Women's changed identities can impact on men's well-being. Roles on and off farms change. Views on gender equality change between generations and leadership roles are different in a changing world where connections between urban and rural places increase. Several chapters raise the concern that some research can tend to present the rural as backward and static, and overlook dynamic processes of change that are occurring.

The usefulness of urban/rural comparisons is a common theme across all of the chapters. Thuesen notes that country variance on equality, gender and governance is more significant than urban/rural differences. Shortall reviews research that cautions against putting 'rural' in front of masculinity, because it suggests a greater spatial difference than might actually exist. But Charatsari and Černič Istenič make the most biting observation when they state that much of rural research presumes the uniqueness of rural as a category without any reference or comparison with the urban.

Numerous chapters note the lack of gender-disaggregated data about farm work and rural governance structures. It is vexingly poor. This hampers large-scale quantitative analysis, and comparative analysis.

The need to examine the construction of identities through social interaction, and look at how changes in one identity affect others, are points raised by several of the authors. How the identities change or whether they are reinforced – and the power plays inherent in this process – are raised as questions to examine going forward.

The chapters cover these themes, but much more, and it is to these we now turn.

The chapters

In her chapter on social enterprise, Little considers the social construction of entrepreneurial activity, and in so doing draws attention to broader theoretical discussions surrounding the relationship between enterprise and gender. Entrepreneurs are often heralded as 'innovators' and seen as playing a central role in economic prosperity. Little considers how much of the social construction of entrepreneurialism rests on typically masculine attributes: power, control and competitiveness. She then considers how debates about rural entrepreneurial activities focus on the spatial context of space and place and what a particularly rural entrepreneurship might look like. She argues that two distinguishing features of rural enterprise relate to the specific raw materials of rural areas, in particular land and food. Second, she argues that in some parts of the world, particularly Britain and parts of the USA, the influx of migrants who bring social, cultural and economic capital with them can lead to a surge in entrepreneurial activity, although the importance of local talent should not be underestimated.

When she turns to consider the question of gender and rural entrepreneurship, like most chapters in this section Little identifies different types of questions that emerged in early literature compared to more recent scholarship. Early research tended to focus on the limited labour market opportunities for women, and these labour market constraints were a key motivation for women to establish an entrepreneurial activity, usually on the farm, and in Europe, generally inspired by the availability of European funding. Many of women's on-farm diversification activities involved the existing resources of the agricultural business, and supported the survival of the farm. She details the studies that found women's entrepreneurial activities to be an extension of their family roles and responsibilities. Their enterprises were usually small scale and allowed women to combine family and work duties.

More recent research has turned to feminist theories to consider how the social construction of 'enterprise' is inherently masculine. Women's activities tend to be smaller in scale for many reasons: managing other gender-constructed responsibilities such as domestic and childcare responsibilities; less access to capital; and different motivations. The decision not to undertake larger scale enterprises can result in women being judged as failed entrepreneurs, because the definition is constructed according to the discourse and knowledge of the prevailing heteronormativity. Understanding women's enterprises requires a different analytical framework, which in particular needs to consider different gender motivations for undertaking entrepreneurial activities. Going forward, Little argues that structures of policy and support need careful scrutiny to examine whether the masculine norm has become embedded in these institutional structures. She identifies networks as an important component of successful entrepreneurial activities, and suggests a good critical feminist analysis of differences in gendered networks in this context would be very beneficial.

McVay's chapter on leadership and gender is an important contribution that introduces a wider debate than the one usually used when considering leadership roles in rural organisations. McVay introduces mainstream leadership theory and debates and argues that the concept of leadership is as contested and complex as 'rural' or 'gender'. She discusses what leadership means, noting that there is no widely agreed definition. Sometimes it is seen as a visionary, or as an accomplishment, where performance is an effort to establish it. She reviews rural development structures, as Thuesen and Shortall do, noting that all male organisations are perceived as gender neutral.

She discusses the social construction of leadership and how bodies serve as markers of acceptable and unacceptable leadership candidates. Normalising discourses about who is an appropriate leader based on physical appearance hide the power structures that regularise gender barriers to leadership roles. McVay reviews concepts such as the glass ceiling, or as Alston (2000) famously coined it, the 'grass ceiling'; the 'glass cliff', when organisations in trouble appoint women leaders because they are perceived to have better relational skills; and 'glass walls', when women-only organisations place women in the constraints of an organisation outside the gender-neutral male norm. She examines the complexities of rural women-only organisations which offer support and opportunities to women leaders, but also reinforce the perception that their correct sphere is outside of the mainstream norm. Much of the research reviewed focused on obstacles to women leaders. Despite these obstacles, McVay reviews studies, including her own very important contribution, which examines rural women leaders and the means by which they surmounted obstacles. While women often lack leadership training, it is the practice and experience of leadership which is key for them. Leadership training can, at any rate, reinforce the presumption of a male norm and can stimulate deference from women.

McVay's own research found that many rural women leaders simply do not self-identify as leaders, but rather define themselves as team players, even when they are in elected roles with considerable responsibility. Successful women leaders recount their support structures of family, colleagues and mentors who encouraged them to be leaders. Much European and US research has examined the reluctance of successful rural women's organisations to identify as challenging norms or as feminist, and they equally find women's reluctance to identify as leaders. McVay notes that self-identity is complicated by prevailing concepts of appropriate leadership and leaders for all genders.

She argues for more research on the benefits for all genders of a release from gender stereotypes about who most appropriately should occupy leadership roles or caring roles. She describes Norwegian research which shows the freedom for men who are no longer locked into the breadwinner role and can undertake more of a caring role with their children, and the reduced pressure on young boys to be the farm leader and follow in their father's footsteps. Like Thuesen, she suggests that there is value in quotas, but she calls for a wider policy analysis of how leadership roles are decided; for instance, European rural policy prescribes the membership of devolved rural development groups. They must contain representatives from particular organisations, but often these organisations are male dominated. Interestingly, she recommends focusing on leadership activities with young boys and girls, as women leaders reported early opportunities as a key factor overcoming obstacles. A great deal of research has recounted the fewer sport and socially acceptable outdoor activities for girls in rural areas. Paying attention to this might reduce the gendered gap in rural leadership roles.

In her chapter on rural governance, Thuesen begins with a very helpful overview of the general literature on governance. She explains how governance is seen as a change in the meaning of government, and suggests a new process of governing. In theory it is more inclusive, including public, private and voluntary sectors alongside traditional government. She goes on to examine rural governance structures and notes the explosion of such forms of organisation in the 1990s in the European Union, Scandinavia, the USA, Canada and Australia. Thuesen gives a good overview of the questions asked and addressed by scholars in each place. The main body of the chapter examines how, despite claims of greater inclusivity, rural governance structures are exclusive, and she focuses on gender in this respect. She structures her chapter around Young's (2000) dichotomy of external and internal exclusion, and the literature reviewed is coherently organised around these two themes. External exclusion is somewhat similar to Dahl's (1957) concept of power, which Lukes (1974) called the first dimension of power.

The studies reviewed in this section offer a quantitative numerical analysis of the number of women participating in various forms of governance, assuming, rightly, that if women are not there they cannot participate. These studies are predominantly macro level and quantitative in nature. Thuesen reports that cross-country analyses find women generally less active in all areas of political activism, although this is different for membership of civic activism organisations. She notes that country variance is more significant than rural/urban variations within countries. Her second section looks at internal exclusion, which is reminiscent of Bachrach and Baratz (1962), what Lukes (1974) described as the second face of power, which argues that it is not just about being present, but also about who gets to make the decisions and the internal processes that occur within the meeting place. Thuesen reports numerous studies that have examined the differences between involving women and gender equality. Often a jargon that excludes women prevails at meetings. Other research has found that women are rarely involved in the agenda-setting processes of rural development. Again she notes regional variations in these practices. In her concluding section, Thuesen looks to the future directions needed for research in this area. She considers some of the policy questions which need to be considered, such as quotas and equality measures, and how they might be targeted.

In terms of research she calls for much more critical and deeper analyses of the key questions, reminiscent of what Lukes identified as the third face of power – the unobserved and taken-for-granted exercise of power. Thuesen calls for meta-analysis research which examines laws and regulations that may inadvertently cause exclusion, and micro-level analyses that explore gendered patterns of interaction which presume masculine patterns to be the norm and in this way exclude women, or make their participation more difficult. Interestingly, Thuesen calls for perspective when examining gender inequalities in the global north, arguing they are much more severe in the global south and more immediately demanding of scholarly attention.

Charatsari and Černič Istenič focus specifically on farming and gender identity. They provide an excellent critical overview of research in this area and identify a coherent programme of research that needs to be addressed in the future. They begin with a review of what they see as the four key areas that have interested researchers to date. They start with entitlement, and consider how men are predominantly farmers. They review research that has attributed this to patterns of inheritance, and research that has considered cultural belief systems. Even when women are given the title of 'farmer', some research has found that women still have less access to agricultural services than men as they are not seen as farmers. Next, they review research that has considered how women's gender identity on farms is created and recreated. In particular, they consider the formation of gender identities in childhood. In the following section they review literature that considers 'participation', and here they review literature that looks at women's participation in the labour market, in off-farm employment, and on-farm work. They review the literature of policy initiatives that have considered gender inequalities in agriculture, and also review European, US and Canadian literature. Then they turn to look at future research questions, and this part of their chapter is first rate. They reflect that most research on gender in farming has focused on women, without commensurate research on men. They argue that while Brandth and Haugen (this volume) argue that there has been an increase in masculinity studies, much of this has not specifically focused on men farmers. Some research suggests that men take considerable risks on farms, and this is an under-researched area. In general, they call for increased research that studies both men and women.

Next, they suggest that a wider lens needs to be taken to understand what women's marginalisation in farming structures means, although the first step should be to ascertain if women do actually feel marginalised. They say that examining welfare and psychological well-being are questions that need more attention, and argue that some research shows that marginalisation can have negative or positive effects depending on whether marginalisation means belonging to a strong sub-group of marginalised people. They point out that too much of the focus to date has been on men and women as the primary categories of research, and argue that we need to move beyond this to look at disabled farmers, and sexual minorities. Ageing farm couples is another area that needs research although Riley's (2012, 2016) work is a very important contribution to this topic. Charatsari and Černič Istenič note that while there has been lesbian, gay and bisexual (LGB) research in rural studies, very little of this has considered the farming community. They point out that a considerable amount of research has focused on how macho masculinities are constructed around dangerous farming activities and farming machinery, but very little has considered what this might mean for gay farm men. Like Shortall, they argue that more quantitative analysis is needed, which would allow for greater cross-regional and longitudinal analysis.

Shortall takes on the unenviable task of generally trying to provide an overview of research on gender and identity formation. She argues that identity is central to most research in rural studies even if it is not specifically stated. She begins with a general overview of the sociological and psychosocial literature on identity that helps frame the analysis of the literature reviewed. She notes that identity is individual and collective. We need to categorise and make assumptions about people to manage everyday social interaction, although this is also the basis of stereotypes and discrimination. Central to identity is social interaction. It is a continuous process rather than an individual trait. West and Zimmerman (1987) famously referred to it as 'doing' gender. Identity is performed, reaffirmed and reinforced through social interaction. When signs and symbols in any situation reinforce our identity, positive emotions result. When it is threatened it leads to negative feelings and distress, and this increases depending on the significance of the person or people not reinforcing our identity.

Discourse is central to social interaction and identity formation. Power is central to all processes involved in identity creation, including discourse, where Foucault (1975) argued that some people have more power than others to construct their discourse and make it the dominant one. Following this overview Shortall goes on to review the literature on identity and begins with agriculture and work. She begins with early research that looked at the gendered identities within farm families, and in particular the invisibility of women's farm work. She refers back to the identity literature to show that gendered identities about what agricultural work is counted and recognised are embedded in social structures such as the media, government policies and law. While on the one hand it can be argued that gendered identities around farming and farm work have remained stubbornly in place, on the other hand she argues that women's increased participation in off-farm employment represents considerable change, and it is to this she turns next. Here she reviews research that has pondered why women's off-farm work has not resulted in greater identity renegotiation. She reviews literature that suggests this is because identity is a performance and women and men are 'doing' gender through social interaction. Brandth and Haugen (2010) argue that even when work situations change, men and women can do and undo gender identities in ways that reinforce traditional understandings of masculine and feminine areas of work. Other research reviewed finds the same types of processes occurring between farm couples.

Next Shortall turns to consider how space is gendered and reinforces identities by suggesting one space is appropriate for one gender and not the other. She reviews the literature that considers the outdoors to be coded masculine and the indoors to be coded feminine. Agricultural training courses, farming organisations and women's organisations are all gendered spaces reinforcing identities. Next, she notes that most literature on rural gender identities has focused on rural occupations such as farming, forestry, hunting, mining and fisheries. Some other research, though, has considered how the rural shapes gendered identities or social patterns of behaviour. She reviews research that has considered how the EU Rural Development Programme has been implemented across Europe in ways that reinforce gender identities. She also reviews research that cautions against using the rural as an explanatory variable. The distinction between urban and rural is seen as less useful than before industrialisation, and boundaries are increasingly blurred. Some scholars of rural masculinity studies have argued against the term 'rural masculinity' because it suggests there is a rural phenomenon different to an urban one.

Going forward, she suggests, like Charatsari and Černič Istenič, that identity formation research needs to consider the iterative and interactive nature of identity formation and how identities of one group influence those of others. Again like Charatsari and Černič Istenič, she argues for more quantitative and mixed-methods research. She also suggests that more comparative research would allow us to better understand how cultural differences and institutional frameworks shape the processes of 'doing' gender. She argues, too, that future research needs to focus on the changes in identities that have occurred, rather than presenting *rural, gender* and *identity* as static categories.

Brandth and Haugen present an overview of the literature on rural masculinity. Rural masculinity study has developed since the mid-1990s and is now a large and well-established area of research that has strengthened our knowledge of (gendered) rural culture, practices, realities and representations. They identify two contradictory descriptions of rural masculinity in the literature. One is of the privileged man, the strong, powerful, heroic man battling with nature and in this performing his masculinity. The other is the socially inept, vulnerable man, trapped inside his socially constructed masculinity. They begin with an overview of theoretical perspectives of masculinity as socially constructed, dynamic, changing and multiple. They note that masculinities are temporal and situational. They are different in particular contexts, and throughout different periods of history. They review literature that shows how masculinity is performed; it is not a fixed identity. They demonstrate how masculinity is historically situated and has to be recreated and renegotiated over time. They give examples of men redefining masculinity as office business performance as more traditional physical industries decline. They also show how outsiders can seek to present and construct particular occupations as masculine to engage men; for example, when dairying was industrialised there were strategic attempts to change its representation from a feminine occupation to a masculine occupation because the expansion depended on access to male-controlled resources. As part of this strategy, the milking machine was presented as masculine and requiring men to understand how it operated.

Brandth and Haugen discuss how masculinity is constructed and how it changes as women's practices and positions change. They review some research that demonstrates how men's well-being is threatened when the farm is in crisis and their masculinity is questioned by the decline of the farm. They also discuss research that shows how younger rural men have added parenting responsibilities to their identity in a way that does not threaten the dominant norms of rural masculinity. Other research has shown that through interactional processes identities are negotiated and if women feel their changing identities are threatening the masculine identity to the extent that it may damage well-being, identities are negotiated to mitigate this impact. One very interesting observation Brandth and Haugen make is that in good times the hegemonic masculine norm serves men well, but in times of crises it threatens their sense of identity and well-being. They discuss how traditional masculinity can prevent men seeking help during natural disasters, or discussing upset and distress after divorce. Next, they review literature that advocates an intersectional perspective to explore how gender and rurality interact with other forms of identification. They consider class, age and sexuality. Rural masculinity is usually associated with primary low-skilled industries, and the typical social construction is one of blue-collar workers employed in tough physical jobs. They argue that rural youth resonates with masculinity and it is performed in rural areas through drinking and sports that exclude women.

Like Charatsari and Černič Istenič, they note that there is a limited amount of research on older rural masculinity. Regarding sexuality, they note that the norm of heterosexuality is presumed, and has been the one that is primarily researched. They quite rightly argue that research that deviates from the norm sheds light on the social construction of the dominant narrative. So, for example, the absence of wives supports a representation of rural men as socially helpless and inept. Divorce threatens the masculine breadwinner norm and men's position as head of household, and men suffer a huge emotional blow linked to the risk to their masculine identity. Turning to sexuality, they argue that research shows gay masculinities are disguised and marginalised, although they note that the literature on whether rural areas are more or less tolerant towards homosexuality is disputed. They reflect on the patchiness of research on rural masculinity and suggest there is a need for more comparative and systematic research on different themes. They recommend that research needs to consider whether the agricultural crisis and economic change leads to greater flexibility and gender equality, or the reinforcement of threatened aspects of masculinity.

Conclusion

There is a wide breadth of research reviewed in this section. It provides an excellent overview of key theoretical debates that inform particular aspects of rural gender research. The contributors provide state-of-the-art reviews and critically analyse key debates. Insightful suggestions are made to shape our research agendas in the future. We hope this section informs scholars and students and we look forward to participating in the debates that will no doubt emerge.

References

Alston, M (2000). *Breaking through the grass ceiling: Women, power and leadership in agricultural organisations.* London: Routledge.

Bachrach, P & Baratz, M (1962). The two faces of power. *American Political Science Review* 56, 947–952.

Brandth, B & Haugen, M (2010). Doing farm tourism: The intertwining practices of gender and work. *Signs* 35(2), 425–446.

Dahl, R (1957). The concept of power. *Behavioural Science* 2, 201–215.

Foucault, M (1975). *Abnormal: Lectures at the Collège de France 1974–1975.* London: Verso.

Lukes, S (1974). *Power: A radical view.* London: Macmillan.

Ridgeway, C (2009). Framed before we know it: How gender shapes social relations. *Gender and Society* 23(2), 145–160.

Riley, M (2012). 'Moving on'? Exploring the geographies of retirement adjustment amongst farming couples. *Social and Cultural Geography* 13(7), 759–781.

Riley, M (2016). Farming masculinities and the lifecourse. In S Shortall & B Bock (Eds), *Gender and rural globalisation: International perspectives on gender and rural development*. Oxford: CAB International.

Young, IM (2000). *Inclusion and democracy*. Oxford: Oxford University Press.

West, C & Zimmerman, D (1987). Doing gender. *Gender and Society* 1(2), 125–151.

30

Gender and Entrepreneurship

Jo Little

Introduction

Studies of the rural economy and society have, over many years, highlighted the key role played by entrepreneurial activity and evaluated the particular contributions made by entrepreneurs to the economic characteristics and prosperity of the countryside. Early research on entrepreneurship tended to focus on the economic issues facing rural areas as a result of agricultural transformation and the decline in primary industry and examined the role and potential of new business activity for creating jobs and supporting existing rural enterprises (Davis, Mack & Kirke, 1997; Ilbery, Healy & Higginbottom, 1997). A particular interest was the growth of entrepreneurial activity on farms and the opportunities afforded by the (need for the) diversification of agricultural businesses. Such activity was identified in some cases as central to the survival of individual farm enterprises and hence to the viability and sustainability of agriculture more broadly. Entrepreneurial activity on farms was also recognised to have important implications for the organisation of the farm business and, in many cases, to the economic activity and division of labour within the farm family household.

As work on rural entrepreneurial activity developed, studies began to pay greater attention to the nature of the businesses themselves and to their social characteristics. As a result, gender emerged as a key component of rural entrepreneurship and a focus for research. Links were made to the gendered composition of the rural labour market and to the issues surrounding the problems that women in particular experienced in gaining access to employment opportunities in rural areas (Bock, 2004a). But as well as recognising entrepreneurship as potentially gendered in terms of job availability and employment opportunity, research began to examine other aspects of its social construction including, crucially, its relationship to gender identity and to constructions of masculinity and femininity.

It is on this more detailed examination of the social construction of entrepreneurial activity that this chapter on rural gender and enterprise will largely concentrate. In so doing it will draw attention not only to different aspects of women's involvement in rural entrepreneurship but also to broader theoretical discussions surrounding the relationship between enterprise and gender. In particular the chapter will examine how entrepreneurship shapes and is shaped by popular constructions of work and household activity in rural areas as well as the meaning of entrepreneurship to individuals' sense of self and achievement. The chapter starts by situating rural enterprise and the study of entrepreneurial activity in the countryside within a more conventional economic framework and understanding of rural employment. It then goes on to focus much more specifically on the detail of gender divisions and the relationship between entrepreneurship and constructions of rural gendered identity.

Entrepreneurship and the rural economy

According to the literature, there is no disputing the place of entrepreneurs in influencing the economic prosperity of countries and regions. As Faggio and Silva (2014, p. 68) observe, '(e)ntrepreneurs are thought to be purveyors of innovation, engines for job creation and sparks for economic growth.'

In rural areas of Western countries the decline in agricultural employment and incomes over recent decades together with the limited nature of alternative economic activity has provided additional stimulus for entrepreneurial activity as farming families seek out new sources of income both on and off the farm. As Bock (2004b) observes, those farmers who have developed alternative economic activity to support their ailing agricultural businesses are no longer treated with suspicion (or even as failures) but are more likely to be seen as innovators with vision and creativity. Such a view indeed reflects a more general shift in the value and potential of entrepreneurship that has accompanied, according to Ahl and Marlow (2012, p. 544), a greater neoliberal individualism enabling the 'realization of the human potential for creativity'.

Efforts to understand the nature and importance of entrepreneurship in scholarly and applied research have included a range of perspectives beyond the direct economic contribution of businesses. Studies have explored, for example, the skills, characteristics and behaviour of entrepreneurs in examining the issue of creativity (see Bruni, Gheradi & Poggio, 2004). They have also considered institutional and policy contexts of entrepreneurial activity (Kalantaridis & Bika, 2006). Significantly, in terms of understanding entrepreneurship in rural areas, have been the debates around the importance of space and place in the development of new businesses and entrepreneurial activity. This focus on geography and the recognition of spatial context has led to the development and application of the concept of embeddedness as a way of thinking about the relationship between entrepreneurial activity and the characteristics of the region. As Kalantaridis and Bika (2006, p. 1564) argue, embeddedness is a highly valuable concept as it 'enables us to understand economic agents as individuals with a purpose, who exist and function within concrete socio-economic milieu. Local embeddedness can, thus, be described as the nature, depth and extent of an entrepreneur's ties into the local environment.' The concept of embeddedness has been examined through (and utilised by) a variety of empirical studies exploring the specific characteristics and contribution of entrepreneurial activity in rural areas. While there is some debate about the exact contribution of 'the local', there is strong evidence that certain qualities of rural areas are central factors in the nature and success of rural entrepreneurship.

While it is not the purpose of this chapter to discuss in detail the characteristics of rurality that have been identified as important, in terms of local embeddedness it is relevant to briefly mention some of the key attributes that have contributed to the development of rural entrepreneurial activity. For example, several studies have considered the particular contribution of raw materials (particularly food but also large areas of land) to the success of some forms of enterprise in rural areas – Murdoch (2000), for example, talks about the competitive advantage afforded by access to high quality sources of food. In other studies the presence of in-migrants (including those from the creative classes – see Herslund, 2012) within rural communities is noted as initiating and supporting new businesses. Such people, it is suggested, can bring not only resources of capital but also new skills and experiences into rural areas. In such cases, emphasis is placed on the 'pull factors' of rural areas and on the importance of quality of life to attract new entrepreneurs. Other studies have, however, identified existing rural residents as a factor in the success of rural entrepreneurialism, suggesting that the resourcefulness and commitment of local people (particularly those that have worked hard to develop local, often agricultural, businesses) should not be underestimated. Again, the relevance of a 'place-based' analysis is argued by such studies.

The focus on social characteristics of entrepreneurialism in rural areas in studies of embeddedness has highlighted the role of household relations and, in particular, the issue of gender. The different experiences and contributions of men and women to entrepreneurial activities have developed into a key area of research. Initially, studies tended to focus on the differing opportunities that entrepreneurial activity offered men and women and how such opportunities fitted into traditional economic activity (Merrett & Gruidl, 2000). This focus drew on a broader area of research and writing that explored the nature of rural employment, the pressures on rural households and labour relations within both the workplace and the home. It drew on traditional gender theory which sought to understand the constraints on women's economic activity as part of the gendered power relations within the labour market and the operation of patriarchy within the home. More recently, studies have developed understanding of gender and entrepreneurialism in the application of more varied theoretical perspectives on the construction of identity and the performance of masculinity and femininity. In the remaining part of the chapter I elaborate on both the traditional theoretical approaches to gender and entrepreneurialism and the more innovative work. I draw on a range of empirical studies from the UK and Europe which have documented the gendered nature of entrepreneurial activity in rural areas as well as the detail of women's particular contribution.

Rural entrepreneurship, gender and the household

In their article on women's involvement in 'side activities' on farms in the Netherlands, Markantoni and van Hoven (2012) outline the nature and importance of rural women's entrepreneurial activity as documented in a range of different studies. They suggest that a variety of kinds of businesses initiated by women can be identified, reflecting the different motivations for establishing the businesses and also the varying role of those businesses in the household and the local economies. Like other authors (see, for example, Bock 2004a), Markantoni and van Hoven identify one of the key areas of entrepreneurial activity amongst rural women as the establishment of businesses on the farm. Such businesses are often driven by (at least initially) the economic necessity to diversify away from the main agricultural activities due to falling incomes. As many studies have acknowledged, women's on-farm diversification businesses are generally orientated towards the existing resources of the agricultural business and include, for example, agro-food production, agro-tourism and artisanal products. The often critical role of these on-farm businesses in supporting the 'main' agricultural activities on the farm has been widely reported as having implications for women's status and the gender division of labour within the farm household (see Oberhauser, 1995; O'Toole & Macgarvey, 2003).

In addition to businesses developed in connection with farm diversification, other examples of rural women's entrepreneurial activities exist away from farms. Again, such businesses include a range of sizes and types of business. They also vary in terms of their significance to the wider household income and in their relationship to the 'main' household business or employment. While it is risky to generalise from the array of specific studies on rural women's entrepreneurial activities, it has been suggested that certain patterns can be observed – particularly in the scale and 'importance' of such businesses. Women's entrepreneurial activity in rural areas thus tends to be small scale and often located in the home. Although some businesses are highly significant to the wider household income, many remain peripheral and are regarded, as Markantoni and van Hoven (2012) note, as 'side activities' and do not develop in terms of size and importance. Some researchers have attempted to identify the common characteristics of women's entrepreneurial activity through the development of typologies relating to the size and profitability of the business and also the personal qualities of the entrepreneur. For example, Iakovidou, Koutsou and Partalidou (2009, p. 176) produce a typology of women entrepreneurs in rural Greece, concluding that the majority are:

> middle aged, of low educational level and without any relevant training in the type of their business activity. They are usually married and come from and live permanently in rural areas that they have chosen as the location for their business activity … Their enterprises are very small, with low turnover supplementing the women's family income, providing only self employment and no other job places.

These authors also conclude, as do others, that rural women's entrepreneurial activities are often an extension of their family roles and responsibilities. They are thus designed around childcare, both in terms of the location and the scale of the activities. Research on the motivation for rural women's involvement in entrepreneurial activity has concluded that, for many, the decision to start a business is related to their desire to make use of existing skills and experiences (especially for those migrating into a rural area as a part of a 'lifestyle choice' – see Kalantaridis, 2010) but in a way that fits into their family commitments. The constraints operating on rural women's involvement in 'regular' employment, including the scarcity of jobs, poor transport and a lack of accessible childcare, have been well documented (see Little, 2002) and often such constraints make the apparent flexibility of self-employment very attractive. In addition, as Iakovidou and colleagues (2009) observe, as well as the importance of combining their (self) employment with childcare, some women entrepreneurs claim that an important motivation for starting a business is to be able to pass on not only money but also a possible job, to their children as they get older.

Recognition of the importance of fitting entrepreneurial activity into family life for rural women has helped to broaden the scope of research on gender and entrepreneurialism. Rather than simply looking at the economic characteristics of rural businesses and entrepreneurial activities, studies began to situate analysis in a wider understanding of the 'place-based' nature of rural entrepreneurship and its social context. In relation to gender, this has meant looking not only at the ways in which gender roles constrain (and/or facilitate) economic activity but also at issues such as connections with rural institutions and the operation of networks. Studies of rural women and entrepreneurialism have thus explored how women use contacts and networks to develop businesses and, importantly, how their involvement in new businesses may serve to empower them both within the household and the community. As Bock (2004a) has observed, as woman-owned businesses become more familiar within rural areas so it is possible to detect a shift in the ways in which women are regarded and ultimately how they are accepted as legitimate entrepreneurs in their own right.

Greater attention to issues of empowerment, knowledge, networks and so on illustrate some of the weaknesses of much of the existing research on gender and entrepreneurship. While important progress has been made in turning attention to the gendered nature of business ownership and development, this progress has been fairly limited in terms of its theoretical understanding. In other words, we may know a lot more about rural women's entrepreneurial activity (the kinds of businesses they run, how these contribute to household income and why some women choose to develop new businesses), but such work has yet to place analysis within an explicitly feminist theoretical framework. Such a framework would recognise the beliefs underpinning normative entrepreneurial discourse and seek to deconstruct this through feminist critiques of issues such as self-identity and institutional assumptions. The following section of the chapter will introduce in more detail the ways in which the application of a post-structural feminist perspective would provide new understandings of the gendered nature of rural entrepreneurship. While, as recognised, studies adopting such approaches are relatively few, by drawing on existing research I hope to demonstrate the kinds of areas where insights could be offered by a more explicitly feminist theoretical perspective.

Rural entrepreneurship and post-structural feminist theory

Constructions of entrepreneurialism

A key concern of feminist analyses of entrepreneurialism is the construction of enterprise and business leadership as inherently masculine. Those working on the adoption of feminist perspectives in the study of entrepreneurship stress that any attempt to understand its gendered assumptions must acknowledge the prevailing heteronormativity which positions women as failed or reluctant entrepreneurial subjects. Ahl and Marlow (2012, p. 544) argue that despite a growing culture of liberal individualism (as noted above and which supposedly recognises human potential when freed from institutional and organisational regulation), there are 'limitations upon the possibilities of who can claim the subject position of "entrepreneur"'. According to these authors, the characteristics which define the entrepreneur are essentially those that define masculinity – power, control, aggressiveness, competitiveness – and so it is inevitable that women will be seen as less able to perform as entrepreneurs. Further, they stress that acknowledging the gender bias in notions of entrepreneurialism is not just about recognising men's superior status as entrepreneurs but also the ways in which this leaves women as *deficient* in terms of the skills and characteristics needed to succeed as an entrepreneur.

Ahl and Marlow (2012), along with other researchers, call for an explicitly feminist perspective in order to deconstruct the assumptions underpinning the normative discourse of entrepreneurialism. In advocating such a perspective, however, they note the ways in which some existing attempts to understand the gendering of entrepreneurialism have tended to essentialise gender characteristics and in so doing not only oversimplify the issues but also end up blaming women for their subordination. Thus rather than seeing gender as constructed through homogeneous biological identity and socioeconomic positioning, they articulate a post-structuralist perspective in which gender as constructed through discourse is 'framed as a fluid, contextualised diverse performance' (Ahl & Marlow, 2012, p. 548). When aligned, moreover, with Foucauldian post-structuralist feminism, recognition is given to the ways in which knowledge and discourse produce power and, as such, have material effects that go beyond language.

More in-depth study of the gendered nature of entrepreneurial discourse from a post-structural feminist perspective has explored many aspects of entrepreneurship and policy in their privileging of masculinity. Research has identified the ways in which expectations and assumptions about the characteristics of entrepreneurs are reproduced in decisions around funding and support, analyses of the 'success' of the business and priorities attached to the business. While initial research had frequently argued for women to be acknowledged as equal in 'competing' with men for resources and recognition, more recent work seeks to go beyond the idea that women entrepreneurs should be judged according to male norms. Thus research on gender and entrepreneurialism now argues that women be seen as subjects worthy of attention in their own right and recognised for bringing different skills and qualities to entrepreneurial practice. As Ahl and Marlow (2012, p. 556) conclude,

> Essential feminine qualities are identified such as female empathy, focus on service quality and more caring employment conditions for instance, such traits can bring a softer element to the hard edged image of entrepreneurship which defines popular representations. This stance… celebrate[s] female distinctiveness and so, challenge[s] the devaluation of the feminine and ultimately seek[s] to contest the patriarchal gender order.

While research in rural areas has not explicitly developed post-structuralist feminist approaches, or indeed work highlighting more nuanced issues concerning gender identity and entrepreneurship, some discussion of the different qualities women bring to entrepreneurial activity has emerged. For example, research by Markantoni and van Hoven (2012) on Dutch women's involvement in 'side activities' (additional businesses) talk about the wider 'intangible benefits' that characterise their entrepreneurial activities. Such benefits are perhaps not the traditional ones associated with entrepreneurship but instead relate to the ways in which the side activities provide self-fulfilment and social goals. The authors argue that the entrepreneurship of rural women may serve to keep households 'in their place' and also to generate a greater sense of creativity in the region that will help to improve quality of life and well-being in declining rural regions.

In her study of farm women, also in the Netherlands, Bettina Bock (2004a) goes further in arguing the need for an analysis of entrepreneurship that takes an explicitly feminist perspective and prioritises different issues and characteristics of women's business development. Bock notes the generally smaller scale of rural women's enterprises but suggests any analysis of their entrepreneurial activity needs to consider not only their more limited access to finance and other resources and their greater aversion to risk, but also the fact that they generally attach more importance to self-fulfilment and the flexibility to combine family and work duties. Citing work by Cliff (1998), Bock claims that female entrepreneurs 'not only start in a different way compared to men but also, in the longer run, follow a different approach to business management, in which non-economic goals, such as product quality, self-fulfilment and a balance of professional and private life are of great importance'. As such, the success and performance of women as entrepreneurs, she argues, should be 'evaluated in a different way' (Bock, 2004a, p. 447).

Further exploration of Bock's arguments (in research undertaken between 1995 and 2001) clarifies the different ways in which she sought to understand and evaluate farm women's entrepreneurial activities. Importantly, Bock's research found that in starting their new activities women were extremely conscious of the effect they might have on the rest of the household and were careful not to risk denying their children in particular the care and attention they needed. As Bock explains, 'they [the farm women] therefore tried to limit the working time by starting activities on a very small scale or by choosing seasonal activities' (2004a, p. 248). This finding is not surprising in the light of other studies of women's entrepreneurial activity, but what is important here is the extent to which it calls for a different understanding of women's entrepreneurship. While many of the ventures studied by Bock and others were successful in terms of economic viability and development, opportunities to grow the business were always evaluated, it seems, in the context of the same issues concerning the effects it had (or might have) on the family and existing farm business. Bock argues that from the start women had 'constructed a specific entrance' to entrepreneurship and one which already consciously limited the range of alternative enterprises.

Traditional evaluations of entrepreneurship would, as she recognises, see women limiting the size of their businesses (maybe setting aside the opportunity for expansion) as indicating a lack of success in comparison to men. As the businesses develop, however, and women become more self-confident so their behaviour becomes, according to Bock, more masculine, complying with a more usual model of entrepreneurship. She argues that business advice and policy needs to recognise this initial caution (particularly in countries where more traditional gender relations continue to dominate) and to adapt to be able to assist women entrepreneurs at a point when their self-belief and experience allow them to think about expanding their business. This highlights two related areas that need developing in terms of the adoption of feminist approaches to entrepreneurship: namely, the importance of identity and empowerment, and the role of emotions in women's entrepreneurial activity. These will be examined in the following section.

Gender identity, empowerment and emotion in rural entrepreneurship

Feminist analyses of gender and entrepreneurialism stress the ways in which women's motivation to start a new business and their subsequent relationship to that business link to constructions of identity. Studies have identified decisions around entrepreneurship as highly influenced by women's life cycle stage, often reflecting a period of transition. Markantoni and van Hoven (2012), for example, in research on rural women entrepreneurs, found that major life transitions such as changes in marital status (i.e., divorce), a period of poor health or the diagnosis of infertility were important motivations for starting a new business. Their respondents talked of entrepreneurial activity as a way of changing their identities and finding positive outcomes from what were negative life events. Other respondents in this study also spoke of life transition as a motivating factor for starting a new business but generally linked this to changes in family and household size as a result of having children. Again, however, such a shift was often about a change in rural women's identities, and the new business represented a way of redefining their sense of self.

Another study of rural women entrepreneurs by Sattler Weber (2007) also examines the development of new business activity in relation to rural identity. This study suggests that the motivation for entrepreneurial activity is very firmly embedded in social structure and in women's identities as community actors. Sattler Weber's research explores the (re)building of rural businesses in order to resurrect the community of St James, Cedar County, Nebraska, following the closure of the local church and meeting place. She charts the ways in which local women drew on their farming skills and experiences to develop a new micro enterprise. In this case women were not independent economic actors but worked together as rural farm women, reflecting, according to Sattler Weber, their cultural norms and social embeddedness. She argues that the characteristics demonstrated by the women in developing the business were a reflection of their gendered identities and included 'value found in helping others, self-fulfilment more than profit, responding to a social issue, creating incomes, providing flexibility and cooperative and informal planning' (2007, p. 432). They also drew on women's network of relationships and reflected their strong associations as relatives, friends and members of the community.

The relationship between rural women's gender identity and entrepreneurial activity also reflects, feminist research suggests, the empowerment that can be gained from starting a business. Many studies of rural women as entrepreneurs (especially farm women) suggest that the opportunity to redefine themselves through running a business can give women a strong sense of empowerment (Tigges & Green, 1994). Markantoni and van Hoven (2012) claim that the sense of achievement and empowerment gained by their Dutch respondents from running their side activities was not limited to the financial rewards but included rewards such as personal happiness, personal growth, time for relaxation and the opportunity to do something of their own. While, as these authors point out, many of the women in the study seemingly did not challenge traditional gender roles through their businesses – in that they remained the main carer and domestic worker in the household – their entrepreneurial activity did offer them the opportunity to do something on their own terms. This, in itself, was for some a means of empowerment.

As these studies have shown, feminist analyses of rural entrepreneurship also recognise and value the emotional investment surrounding the start-up and running of new businesses. Again, it is argued that conventional analyses of entrepreneurial activity tend to overlook both the emotions underlying the motivation for starting a new business and also the potential contribution of such businesses to the emotional well-being of the entrepreneur and their family. As already noted, studies have shown how for rural women the decision to start a business is often driven by a need to do something for themselves – something that they feel strongly about and care about (for example, using locally produced food) – and hence they often feel an emotional connection to their business. As Iakoviou, Koutsou and Partalidou. (2009) identified in their study of Greek women entrepreneurs, the feelings of self-worth and independence were an important motivator for certain groups. For many rural women, however, guilt is a key emotion surrounding their entrepreneurial activity. As Bock (2004a) notes, spending time away from household and childcare 'duties' was, for many women, a difficult decision and one which they feared would mean they were seen as bad mothers. This is a finding replicated in many studies of rural women's employment generally and has frequently been linked to a more conservative culture and expectation of gender roles. While some research suggests that such attitudes towards rural women's involvement in the labour market are changing, some parts of the economy and society of rural areas remain stubbornly traditional in terms of what it means to be a 'good mother' (Sattler Weber, 2007). Interestingly, Markantoni and van Hoven (2012) argue that while some rural women experience negative responses to their involvement in entrepreneurship, others suggest that such involvement is crucial in providing the 'emotional glue' required to hold farm families together in times of economic strain. Clearly the relationship between entrepreneurship and emotions is a complicated one and, as feminist analysis demonstrates, needs to be taken seriously in the evaluation of rural women's economic, social and cultural identities.

Concluding remarks

In presenting a review of gender and rural entrepreneurship this chapter has chosen to focus, at least in its empirical detail, on women's entrepreneurial activity. It has argued for the need to look differently at not only the motivation behind decisions to get involved in new businesses but also the wider experience of working in such businesses. Further, the chapter has argued that feminist analyses which emphasise the importance of issues such as identity, empowerment and emotions provide a richer and more nuanced understanding of the nature and value of entrepreneurship from a gender perspective. The chapter has tried to illustrate the greater richness provided by such an analysis through reference to a number of in-depth studies of rural women's entrepreneurial activity. It recognises, however, the limitations of relying on existing work, some of which was not undertaken primarily in order to advance feminist perspectives.

Finally, one area of academic writing on rural entrepreneurship that has not been looked at closely in this chapter is that of policy and support. A number of studies have focused specifically on entrepreneurialism as a development strategy in rural economies and, for example, evaluated the potential of entrepreneurship to stimulate endogenous development (see Baumgartner, Schultz & Seidl, 2013). Many of these studies recognise the changing policy context of rural business development (especially that shaped by shifts in agricultural support) but also focus on the specificity of local economic influences and the role of local histories in determining entrepreneurial activity (Kalantaridis, 2010). Few of these studies make reference specifically to gender in the detail of policy (exceptions include Scholten, 2004) but some do look at the broader context of rural governance in relation to entrepreneurialism and at how this frequently encourages a 'masculine' approach to rural business and economic development. Pini (2006), for example, in her study of local economic development and governance in Australia, notes the gendered nature of subject positions in discussions around support for entrepreneurs as well as the continuing power of the 'old guard'. Particularly important is the gendered nature of networks and contacts – it was noted above that women often benefit from different kinds of support networks, although these may not always be helpful in accessing business funding or advice. While other studies of gender and entrepreneurialism have mentioned the different attitudes towards women's businesses amongst local policy makers – especially in the context of agricultural enterprises – there still remain important gaps in understanding and the need for a more sustained feminist analysis of policy and implementation around rural entrepreneurialism.

References

Ahl, H & Marlow, S (2012). Exploring the dynamics of gender, feminism and entrepreneurship: Advancing debate to escape a dead end? *Organization* 19, 543–562.

Baumgartner, D, Schultz, T & Seidl, I (2013). Quantifying entrepreneurship and its impact on local economic performance: A spatial assessment in rural Switzerland. *Entrepreneurship and Regional Development* 25, 222–250.

Bock, B (2004a). Fitting in and multi-tasking: Dutch farm women's strategies in rural entrepreneurship. *Sociologia Ruralis* 44, 245–260.

Bock, B (2004b). It still matters where you live: Rural women's employment throughout Europe. In H Buller & K Hoggart (Eds), *Women in the European countryside* (pp. 14–41). Aldershot: Ashgate.

Bruni, A, Gheradi, S & Poggio, B (2004). *Gender and entrepreneurship: An ethnographic approach*. New York: Routledge.

Cliff, J (1998). Does one size fit all? Exploring the relationship between attitudes towards growth, gender and business size. *Journal of Business Venturing* 13, 523–542.

Davis, J, Mack, N & Kirke, A (1997). New perspectives on farm household incomes. *Journal of Rural Studies* 13, 57–64.

Faggio, G & Silva, O (2014). Self-employment and entrepreneurship in urban and rural labour markets. *Journal of Urban Economics* 84, 67–85.

Herslund, L (2012). The rural creative class: Counterurbanisation and entrepreneurship in the Danish countryside. *Sociologia Ruralis* 52, 235–255.

Iakovidou, O, Koutsou, S & Partalidou, M (2009). Women entrepreneurs in the Greek countryside: A typology according to motives and business characteristics. *Journal of Development Entrepreneurship* 14, 165–179.

Ilbery, B, Healy, M & Higginbottom, J (1997). On and off farm business diversification but farm households in England. In B Ilbery, Q Chiotti & T Richard (Eds), *Agricultural restructuring and sustainability: A geographical perspective* (pp. 135–152). Oxford: CAB.

Kalantaridis, C (2010). Inmigration, entrepreneurship and rural-urban interdependencies: The case of East Cleveland, North East England. *Journal of Rural Studies* 26, 418–427.

Kalantaridis, C & Bika, Z (2006). Local embeddedness and rural entrepreneurship: Case study evidence from Cumbria, England. *Environment and Planning A* 38, 1561–1579.

Little, J (2002). *Gender and rural geography: Identity, sexuality and power in the countryside*. London: Pearson.

Markantoni, M & van Hoven, B (2012). Bringing 'invisible' side activities to light: A case of female entrepreneurs in the Veenkolonien, NL. *Journal of Rural Studies* 28, 507–516.

Merrett, C & Gruidl, J (2000). Small business ownership in Illinois: The effect of gender and location on entrepreneurial success. *Professional Geographer* 52, 425–436.

Murdoch, J (2000). Networks – a new paradigm for rural development. *Journal of Rural Studies* 16, 407–419.

Oberhauser, A (1995). Gender and household economic strategies in rural Appalachia. *Gender, Place and Culture* 2, 51–70.

O'Toole, K & Macgarvey, A (2003). Rural women and local economic development in SW Victoria. *Journal of Rural Studies* 19, 173–176.

Pini, B (2006). A critique of 'new' rural governance: The case of gender in a rural Australian setting. *Journal of Rural Studies* 22, 396–408.

Sattler Weber, S (2007). Saving St James: A case study of farm women entrepreneurs. *Agriculture and Human Values* 24, 425–434.

Scholten, C (2004). Partnerships for regional development and the question of gender equality. In H Buller & K Hoggart (Eds), *Women in the European countryside* (pp. 83–122). Aldershot: Ashgate.

Tigges, L & Green, G (1994). Small business success among men- and women-owned firms in rural areas. *Rural Sociology* 59, 289–310.

31

Leadership and Gender

Lori McVay

Introduction

Leadership and gender may well be two of the most complex and contested concepts of our time. It is no surprise, then, that the ways in which they intersect and are studied and written about are also complicated. In this chapter I have attempted to gather and synthesise the most recent thinking on the convergence of gender and leadership in rural areas across the developed world, beginning with how leadership is generally conceptualised, defined and enacted. It will become quickly apparent that theorising around rural leadership cannot be completely disentangled from the broader body of leadership literature; nor, as Skerratt (2011) argues, should it be, if we are to be faithful to the value and importance of rural communities in an increasingly connected world.

From this opening discussion of the ways in which leadership functions and is perceived emerges one of the most consistent facets with which leadership studies have been concerned over time: the role of gender in leadership. As Marshall (2013, p 267) wrote in her article on leadership and sustainability, 'Male domination of a field is a cue for critical questioning rather than a simple stereotyped explanation' – and leadership, with but a few rare exceptions, is certainly a male-dominated field. Martin's (2011) claim that nearly all gender research is shaped around issues of gender inequality is proven here by the depth and breadth of research focused on differences in how females and males develop leadership skills, access leadership positions and gain approval as effective or successful leaders.

Predominant throughout the studies cited below is the theme of socially constructed and shifting gender roles, and the subtlety with which traditional gender roles are reproduced in organisations and groups. The approaches to this theme present a fascinating panoply. For example, Acker (2012) and Bryant and Garnham (2014) focus on how bodies serve as markers of acceptable – and unacceptable – leadership candidates; Bruckmüller and Branscombe (2010) show that women's perceived capacity for empathy (and men's lack thereof) is the source of the 'glass cliff'; and Liebowitz and Zwingel (2014) point out the limitations of data gathering to capture and explain multifaceted gendered practices, and the ability of measurements to help create realities as well as reflect them.

At this particular moment in time, the percentage of women in leadership in rural organisations is of concern for a number of organisations and for a number of reasons. Michelle Bachelet's 30-30-30 call[1] at the July 2012 Convention to Eliminate all forms of Discrimination Against Women (CEDAW) meeting is but one instance of a large and ongoing movement toward gender equity in leadership. With this in mind, the chapter closes by examining how the development of future rural leaders can be facilitated, and whether gender will continue to be a factor in leadership selection in rural areas.

How leadership is conceptualised, defined and enacted among rural organisations

Any discussion of leadership must begin from the complex point that there is no widely agreed-upon definition of *leadership* as a concept. In contrast to past ideologies, leadership is no longer limited to the fulfilment of the role of visionary, but rather is described as a 'much more complex and contested role, or set of roles' (Beer, 2014, p. 260). Sinclair (2011, p. 124) describes it as being 'not a stable set of objective skills, but a dynamic accomplishment where the very performance of it is understood as an effort to establish it'. Further, Skerratt (2011, p. 91) postulates that rural leadership may be even more elusive a concept 'due to the embeddedness of leadership in social situations'.

In the context of gender and rural leadership, this description becomes doubly apt, with *masculinity* and *femininity* being firmly entrenched in confining definitions that tend toward the marginalisation of women – particularly women in rural areas (Heggem, 2014). From this perspective, it would appear that little has changed in the last decade with regard to gender and the conceptualisation of leadership in rural organisations. Research has consistently shown that stereotypical gender roles are embedded in the culture of rural organisations and have a moderating effect on who has access to leadership within those organisations (Bryant & Garnham, 2014; Cassidy & McGrath, 2014). Acker (2012, p. 215) attributes much of this to 'gendered substructures' produced by 'invisible processes in the ordinary lives of organizations'. These substructures reinforce gender stereotypes and maintain segregation via organisational culture and processes, both of which reflect the particular social milieu within which the organisation exists (Acker, 2012). In one striking example, Sheridan, Haslam, Mckenzie and Still (2011) decry systems of appointment to regional development boards for their lack of transparency and commitment to explicitly address diversity, as well as the presumption of all-male boards as gender neutral (and thus the equating of *gender* with *women*). Female participants in both McVay's (2013) research on rural women leaders and in Bryant and Garnham's (2014) study of the Australian wine industry did not feel that they faced barriers because of their gender, in spite of the gender inequalities and masculine norms present in their narratives of work. Bryant and Garnham (2014) attribute this to the ways in which power structures are disguised by normalising discourses regarding male and female bodies. It could be argued that this is one way in which 'rurality itself' reproduces systems of inequality and provides for their 'intergenerational transmission' (Shucksmith, 2012, p. 377).

Despite the European Union's legislative reforms regarding gender-neutral leadership selection criteria for organisations, the hoped-for increase in women in organisational leadership in the EU has not taken place (Claus, Callahan & Sandlin, 2013). Women continue to fill a higher percentage of low-level jobs compared to men, and women who do fill more prestigious posts may be limited in their ability to transform organisational structures by virtue of the position of their post (e.g., outside the upper levels of decision making) (Bryant & Garnham, 2014). Organisations with a long history of males in leadership positions continue to be much more likely to elect or appoint males to leadership positions, and rural organisations are no exception (see Alston & Wilkinson, 1998; Brandth & Haugen, 1998; Shortall, 2001; Pini, 2003, 2005). Most recently, Sheridan, Haslam McKenzie and Still (2011) showed that appointment to regional development boards has demonstrated a male-centric pattern over the last two decades in the United States, the United Kingdom, Canada and Australia.

As an alternative to male-centric organisations, in which women may feel that they are not welcome or not heard (Barbercheck et al., 2009), many rural women have formed women-only organisations. These groups help to offset participants' frustration with their treatment by – or exclusion from – male-dominated associations and to mediate isolation by offering a 'sense of collective identity' (Pini, Brown & Ryan, 2004, p. 290) and a place to support farm women's multiple identities and roles (Brasier et al., 2014; see also Shortall et al., forthcoming). In some cases they also serve as a place to support work that connects members' livelihoods with the broader community (Trauger et al., 2010). Women's organisations play a vital role in many rural communities, particularly among women farmers who look to them for training and connection (Trauger et al., 2008). They also tend to have less bureaucratic structures (Edwards, Dillard & Juska, 2008), and serve as excellent sources of leadership experience for rural women (McVay, 2013). A number of these women's organisations focus primarily on women and 'women's issues' – a trend reflected in female political representatives' much higher likelihood of standing as proponents of legislation concerning 'women's issues' than male representatives (Wittmer & Bouché, 2013). Critically, it has been noted that women-only groups may also serve to perpetuate the perception of rural women and women farmers as outsiders to male-dominated industries and institutions (Shortall, 2001; Pini, Brown & Ryan, 2004).

Notwithstanding the continued dearth of women in high levels of leadership in institutions that are not primarily identified as 'women's organisations', there are signs of improvement; and, as McVay (2013) highlights, rural women have repeatedly shown themselves capable of overcoming even firmly entrenched obstacles to leadership attainment. Liebowitz and Zwingel (2014) found that incorporating gender equality as a goal in organisations that had not previously considered it important raised critical awareness and opened the possibility of change in the organisations' gender relations. The potential to create change was also an important theme for Skerratt (2011), who asserts that leadership can be learned, despite the shortcomings of much leadership training.

Role of gender in development of leadership skills and attainment of leadership positions

Recognising that opportunities to develop and practise leadership skills are often shaped by gender, McVay (2013) also found that for rural women leading in a broad range of organisations, leadership training was one of several common factors that had supported their development of leadership skills. In line with Skerratt's (2011) discussion, participants in McVay's study noted the lack of practical application in some leadership courses, and therefore emphasised the necessity of combining training with experience in order to develop leadership more fully. Beer (2014, p. 257) notes that the actual *practice* of leadership is critical, and that it 'implies some form of mobilisation or exercise of power'. Programmes that have incorporated experiential components into their leadership training have found it valuable in giving students a greater awareness of their personal leadership potential (Velez, Moore, Bruce & Stephens, 2014).

Coder and Spiller (2013) maintain that leadership training is hampered by the predominance of leadership textbooks written by white males, and that many such texts simultaneously promote both diversity and gender role stereotypes that encourage women to defer to men. For Bryant and Garnham (2014), such deflection of women away from top leadership posts is, in part, a result of organisational language that utilises male experience as the gender-neutral norm. A lack of clear, unified concepts of gender equality may contribute to this quandary as well, placing responsibility for 'women's agency or empowerment' on individual women rather than addressing broader social structures (Liebowitz & Zwingel, 2014, p. 377). At the national level, cultures that are resistant to change in any area may be particularly unwilling to move towards gender equality in leadership; however, once practices begin to change, the same tendency towards resistance may help maintain movement in the direction of equality (Toh & Leonardelli, 2012).

Although there are many instances of women attaining leadership within male-dominated organisations, without intentional practices of gender equality, glass ceilings often re-form after being broken (Haack, 2014); and as with the broader literature, rural literature has also demonstrated the effect of various 'glass' structures on women in organisational leadership. The term *glass cliff* refers to the disproportionate number of female leaders elected or appointed when organisations are in crisis (Rink, Ryan & Stoker, 2013) – a phenomenon Bruckmüller and Branscombe (2010, p. 435) attribute to 'stereotypes about gender and leadership', saying: 'If men have manoeuvred the organisation into trouble, appointing a female leader will appear as one way to achieve the transformation needed to turn things around.' The double-edged stereotype of women's superior relational ability positions them as desirable leaders for organisations in times of crisis because it is a trait that men are perceived as lacking (Bruckmüller & Branscombe, 2010).

In contrast to such stereotyping, rural women leaders who operate from a relational mentality articulate it as a positive act, and may view it as merely being a 'team player' (McVay, 2013, p. 111). Of equal importance to education, therefore, McVay's participants articulated self-confidence and the ability to set goals as fundamental aspects of rural women's leadership development – both of which were dependent in large part upon access to supportive people such as family, colleagues and mentors. In exploring US rural community college leadership, Eddy (2013, p. 28) states that 'relationships and mentoring provided a central role in the development of the leaders in this research'. Relationships continue to be central throughout both male and female leaders' careers. As Skerratt (2011) has noted, leadership is relational in nature, and its effectiveness depends on the leader's ability to create meaningful *interactions* rather than direct *transactions* with followers.

In contrast with this more gender-neutral perspective, Haack (2014, p. 47) maintains that the United Nations' leadership structure demonstrates a second glass structure – glass walls – through its placement of women into 'gender-appropriate' work portfolios that differ from the portfolios of men within the UN. Of particular interest is the Food and Agriculture Organization (FAO) of the UN, which is dominated by men (Haack, 2014), in spite of the recent emphasis on women as agents of agricultural change (FAO, 2014). Similar 'glass walls' were shown in O'Toole and Macgarvey's (2003, p. 173) Australian research, where the portrayal of rural women's gender identity has been that of 'auxiliaries playing a supporting or "invisible" role'. And within the European Union, women are less likely to attain leadership positions in for-profit organisations than in non-profit organisations (Claus, Callahan & Sandlin, 2013).

The glass ceiling – or, in rural settings, the 'grass ceiling' as Alston (2003) names it – is an all too familiar concept in leadership literature. Many variables have been credited with contributing to the 'glass ceiling' phenomenon, in which women find their upward mobility within an organisation obstructed by gender-related barriers. As noted above, Coder and Spiller (2013) connect this to leadership and management training and the lack of focus on female experience. Bryant and Garnham (2014, pp. 422–423) attribute the glass ceiling directly to divergent career paths produced by organisations' essentialist, heteronormative view of women's bodies as 'reproducing bodies' that require experience-minimising career breaks for childbearing/care and men's as 'unencumbered work bodies' that do not. Women who are perceived as overly sexually attractive may also find their body to be an encumbrance in leadership advancement (Kelan, 2013). Conversely, women who are too masculine may also be passed over for leadership selection (Sheridan, Haslam McKenzie & Still, 2011). Simply put, ideal bodies are portrayed differently for men and women in leadership (Sinclair, 2011).

Sheridan and colleagues (2011) also raise the issue of difference in perception between male and female leadership candidates, and reinforce the importance of education for females by noting that it may mediate the higher degree of scrutiny given to their competence as compared to men's. Participants in McVay's (2013) study also correlated general educational attainment and school activity involvement (such as sport and extracurricular clubs) with successful leadership development. And while much of the education gap between men and women has been bridged in 'developed' countries (in many of these cases women now lead men in educational achievements; Ganguli, Hausman & Viarengo, 2014), higher female participation in school clubs does not necessarily reflect a higher level of school leadership participation (Ludden, 2011).

Effect of gender on individuals' self-identification as leaders

With strong gender role traditions in rural communities and agricultural organisations, glass ceilings, walls and cliffs are not the primary concern of many rural women leaders, present though they may be. The ways in which gender shapes ideas of leadership are powerful, and rural women have long operated within a social system that prioritises tasks associated with males over tasks associated with females (Heggem, 2014). Gender role stereotypes may also contribute to differing concepts of power and power motivation between men and women, resulting in women's reluctance to identify as *leader* when that role is perceived as limited to the framework of aggressive masculinity (Schuh et al., 2014). This can lead to another dimension of disconnect between women *acting* as leaders and *self-identifying* as leaders (McVay, 2013), as well as to rural women framing leadership activities as service to their families and communities rather than as exercises of political or organisational power (Sheridan, Haslam McKenzie & Still, 2011).

In light of these perspectives, the importance of family in shaping rural leaders – and particularly rural women leaders – cannot be overestimated. Brandth (2002), Saugeres (2002) and McNay (2004) all firmly ground rural women's development in the experiences of relationships, the most impactful of which is the family. Gender roles in rural families have long placed women in the positions of nurturers and caretakers, with responsibility for others (and the farm, for farm women) given priority over self-care (Heather, Skillen, Young & Vladicka, 2005; Heggem, 2014). Additional pressure comes from the community, as acceptance depends on properly carrying out gendered identities and duties (Saugeres, 2002; Little & Austin, 1996). The internalisation of these expectations normalises them for rural women, creating a dynamic in which gender roles are assumed as a natural part of belonging to a family rather than as prescribed ways of functioning (Heather, Skillen, Young & Vladicka, 2005). This milieu of responsibility to others plays a key role in the self-concepts of rural women, and, when combined with the lack of clarity around the title *leader* (as discussed above), can create reluctance for them to identify as leaders. Instead, leadership duties may be downplayed as simply doing what is expected or accomplishing what needs to be done, even when those duties include elected or appointed leadership positions (McVay, 2013).

Twenty years ago, in her book *Gendered Fields: Rural Women, Agriculture and Environment*, Carolyn Sachs stated: 'In comparison to urban women, rural women remain reluctant to form feminist organizations that focus specifically on actively challenging male authority and privilege' (1996, p. 9). Such feminist action was advocated by Alston and Wilkinson in 1998, but among rural women who do self-identify as leaders, many remain keen to distance themselves from being perceived as masculine or being labelled as feminist, in spite of operating in line with feminist ideals (McVay, 2013). Much of this desire is as reflective of broader cultural expectations (Claus, Callahan & Sandlin, 2013) as it is of local ones. However, it may also exemplify Shortall's (2008, p. 452) view of non-participation (with the feminist movement, in this case) as a 'valid and legitimate choice … made from a position of power', as rural women leaders enact gender role-defying practices without the hindrance of the disconnect that is at times perceived between rural ways of life and feminist ideals/identities. Horlings and Padt (2013, p. 418) concur, recognising that in politics the personal and political may not be perfectly aligned.

In several realms, however, involvement of women in leadership has been seen as a catalyst for other women to become involved or accepted in leadership. Coalitions and partnerships of women leaders in politics and rural activism have been found to greatly enhance women's perceptions of themselves as successful leaders (Bjørnå, 2012; Wittmer & Bouché, 2013). Politically, increased participation by and representation of women is symbolic of changing public opinion around women's roles as well as men's dominion of the field (Haack, 2014). Non-profit organisations have witnessed like phenomena, with the empowerment of women being linked to higher rates of involvement (Claus, Callahan & Sandlin, 2013); and rural women's engagement in agri-tourism is helping to shape gender dynamics by changing the perception of women from 'farm help' to 'agricultural authority' (Wright & Annes, 2014, p. 494). Research in the OECD DAC[2] has demonstrated that gender mainstreaming is a more effective means of building equality within both recipient groups and development organisations than gender-focused programmes (Jones & Swiss, 2014). Shortall (2015) has criticised the Common Agricultural Policy for failing to recognise this and for ignoring the causes of gender inequality while seeking to treat its symptoms. In a similar vein, Bock (2015) has called for gender development to be reintroduced to political agendas as a means of making gendered practices visible and of ensuring material systemic adherence to gender-inclusive requirements.

'Feminine', 'masculine' and 'androgynous' leadership: labels that reflect actual leadership practices?

For people of all genders, self-identification as *leader* is complicated by prevailing theories of leadership, which conflict in their assertions regarding whether 'masculine', 'feminine' or 'androgynous' leadership is most effective (Coder & Spiller, 2013). Data around this topic can be flattened by forms of measurement that have limited scope to capture the 'complex and fluid' social constructions of gender (Liebowitz & Zwingel, 2014, p. 365). Stereotypes around masculine and feminine behaviours have varying influence on perceptions of leadership effectiveness, dependent upon social context and the success of the organisation (Bruckmüller & Branscombe, 2010). Toh and Leonardelli (2012) add that the emergence of leaders is dependent upon followers' conceptions of leadership, as well as upon the prospective leader's willingness to lead and be seen as leader – especially for women. In part, gendered access to leadership roles is attributable to semantics: being a leader is often equated with being a white, straight male (Bruckmüller & Branscombe, 2010) or acting in ways that are perceived as masculine – which Sinclair (2011) posits is reinforced through the language used to talk about leaders and leadership.

As Acker (2012) and Bryant and Garnham (2014) have affirmed, the exclusive association of women with reproduction and men with work carries over into organisational cultures' vision of the ideal leader. Even women who are seen as successful leaders and/or experts in their fields may find themselves physically placed at conferences and gatherings in ways that are different from men and signify the women as outsiders (Marshall, 2013). Rural areas continue to see a reinforcement of this ideation through practices such as male succession in farming, regardless of females' level of involvement (Koutsou, Partalidou & Petrou, 2011; Cassidy & McGrath, 2014) and through the prevalence of 'othering' rural women in male-dominated professions (Mundy, 2013). The desire to work among peers with shared perspectives thus contributes to a lack of leadership diversity (Sheridan, Haslam McKenzie & Still, 2011) and to a distinct power differential in favour of organisations led by males over those led by females (Andersson & Lehtola, 2011). This ideation of leadership as a male domain produces fascinating dynamics when male-dominated boards are forced into 'the feminized experience of not having direct agency over resources' (Sheridan, Haslam, Mackenzie & Still, 2011, p. 290). It has also created a lower likelihood that males will follow female leadership than vice versa (Edwards, Dillard & Juska, 2008), prompting Jones and Swiss (2014) to hypothesise that while women in leadership look for opportunities to support other women, male leaders seek to maintain patriarchal structures.

To O'Shaughnessy and Krogman (2011), however, the idea that male leaders and female leaders behave in strictly gendered ways is an incomplete one. 'Masculine' and 'feminine' characteristics have been recognised among leaders of all genders (Coder & Spiller, 2013). While there is a strong sense among rural women leaders that the primary purpose of their work should be to positively influence the lives of others (McVay, 2013), research has also revealed that both female and male leaders who demonstrate 'androgynous' and/or 'feminine' characteristics are perceived as more successful (Kark, Waismel-Manor & Shamir, 2012). However, Kark and colleagues go on to suggest that male leaders may require more training in the area of 'androgynous' leadership, and caution that females risk losing status if they move too far towards 'masculine' leadership behaviours. Conversely, in her article on farm diversification and re-feminisation, Heggem (2014) points out that perceptions of innate gender differences are not always limiting, and may in fact open a door for the inclusion of women in agriculture. In terms of local representation, gender is often not the key concern of communities, but rather how the community will benefit from the candidate's selection (Bjørnå, 2012).

Rural leadership research emphasises the leader's ability to connect with others and to build local and extra-local networks over leaders' gender identity and roles (Skerratt, 2011; Horlings & Padt, 2013). The conceptualisation of leadership as a team process is characteristic of rural women leaders (McVay, 2013), but it is not limited to females. Eddy (2013) identified the tendency of rural community college leaders to exercise collaborative leadership, even when promotion to leadership changed the nature of their peer relationships. In all cases, effective leaders recognised the individual responsibility and agency associated with their position, but valued the opinions and perspectives of those supporting them (Kark, Waismel-Manor & Shamir, 2012; Eddy, 2013; McVay, 2013).

The future: will gender continue to be seen as significant to leadership development and potential in rural organisations?

Although the importance of understanding the situational requirements of rural leadership have been highlighted as important (Eddy, 2013), and rural women serving in leadership have emphasised the need for leadership opportunities and training among younger people – regardless of gender (McVay, 2013) – the development of future rural leaders does indeed appear to have a gendered component that will need to be addressed in order to achieve greater inclusivity among leadership candidates. As reflected in broader leadership literature, rural leadership suffers from the lack of a clear definition, and this may be complicated by inflexibility in gender role conceptions, limiting definitions of leadership to specific functions (Skerratt, 2011). Coder and Spiller (2013) maintain that leadership training often includes discordant messages that leave students questioning whether their leadership style should be 'masculine', 'feminine' or 'androgynous' – questions that may lead to the loss of potential candidates who are concerned that they must act in ways that are contrary to their everyday selves.

Schuh et al. (2014, pp. 363–364) recognise that discrimination against women in power still exists, and that it was reinforced among the women in their study by 'lower power motivation' than men, creating a link 'between gender and leadership role occupancy'. They are not alone in recognising the multiple facets of gendered access to leadership. For example, appointments to local governing bodies continue to be plagued by the presence of differing/higher criteria for women than for men (Sheridan, Haslam, Mackenzie & Still, 2011). Practices that go against gender-equitable policies have been shown to be directly connected to the particular dynamics of a community, including the intersection of changes in many social structures (O'Shaughnessy & Krogman, 2011) and to the agency of individual actors (Bjørnå, 2012). In their article on measuring gender equality, Liebowitz and Zwingel (2014) show that isolating indicators from each other and from social processes and agency may give an overly positive or overly negative view of an organisation's incorporation of gender-equitable practices.

Proposed solutions to these gendered disparities are many, and have met with varying degrees of acceptance, implementation and success. Andersson and Lehtola (2011) call for a hybridisation of legal requirements (such as gender quotas) and collaborative democratic processes that empower women and organisations run by women. 'Quota women', as Allen, Cutts and Campbell (2014) have labelled women who attain leadership in the United Kingdom through these legal requirements, were perceived to be as acceptable to voters as non-quota candidates, as fully qualified to take office, and as not being discriminated against by executive office gatekeepers. However, this is tempered by reminders that organisations may reject gender quota systems (Bjørnå, 2012), and that attempts to overlay a gender perspective on policy fields with strict gender role stereotypes may simply lead to the perpetuation of those stereotypes (Liebowitz & Zwingel, 2014).

Though Acker (2012) recognises that limiting forms of gender role socialisation are still occurring – albeit in less visible ways – there are signs that attitudes towards women in agricultural and community leadership are changing significantly. Economic, political and social developments in the last decade have begun to erode the long-standing and entrenched gender role binaries in rural communities, creating space for women to enter leadership in new ways. In rural Australia, increasing numbers of women are parlaying their experiences in 'auxiliary roles' into leadership, creatively blending their expertise of 'previously hidden concerns' with traditional decision-making processes to challenge patriarchal leadership practices (O'Toole & Macgarvey, 2003, p. 184). The Lithuanian post-Soviet service economy is facilitating the entrance of rural women into leadership in community organisations due to their higher educational levels and skill sets in relation to men (Edwards, Dillard & Juska, 2008).

Rural men have also benefited from these shifts in gender role perception and adherence. According to Bryant and Garnham (2014), changing organisational practices and policies to recognise that both men's and women's bodies are involved in economic *and* social reproduction will allow for broader conceptualisations of leadership. Brandth and Overrein (2012, p. 96) note that there is already a generational change among farmers who are fathers, postulating that they are no longer limited to being seen as breadwinners to the exclusion of caring, and 'that children and childcare have been a fairly invisible practice for men living in the countryside'. For the children of these farm families, there is a recognition that males and females are capable of having an equal attachment to farming and the family farm (Cassidy & McGrath, 2014), and a lessened pressure for young males to perform farm work or to adhere to the tradition of following in their farmer fathers' footsteps (Brandth & Overrein, 2012).

With less time spent on farm tasks, rural children are more likely to participate in school and sport activities (Brandth & Overrein, 2012). Participants in McVay's (2013) study demonstrated the importance of such activities in leadership development, furthering Ludden's (2011) assertion that communities and young people reap great mutual benefit from students' civic engagement. In these cases, leadership is demonstrated to be a skill that may be learned rather than an innate and unobtainable gift, which is key for the opening of leadership opportunities for rural women (Heggem, 2014). Velez, Moore, Bruce and Stephens (2014) observe that leadership training has been recognised as a necessity in the United States among agricultural educators for more than 20 years, with the last decade seeing significant growth in leadership education among agricultural schools. Further, education and mentoring have been described as 'critical' for rural entrepreneurship by Figueroa-Armijos and Johnson (2013, p. 31), and included in the Center for Rural Pennsylvania's list of important facets for developing rural leaders (Williams & Lindsey, 2011).

Conclusion

As rural areas experience the shifts and changes of social structures, the need for diversity in leadership has become increasingly clear, even with the risk of conflict involved in diversification (Sheridan, Haslam, Mckenzie & Still, 2011; Alston & Whittenbury, 2013). 'Masculine' and 'feminine' behaviours are continuously being shaped by social processes, and the recognition that leaders may demonstrate multiple types of leadership (Kark, Waismel-Manor & Shamir, 2012) opens valuable possibilities for rural organisations. Further research is needed to examine how rural organisations' practices are influenced by the participation of women in leadership, and to highlight the successes and developmental processes of rural women leaders as a means of providing exemplars for young rural women aspiring to leadership in rural organisations. Reconceptualising leadership to include positions of influence outside traditionally validated 'masculine', project-focused leadership facilitates the incorporation of a wider array of members of the rural community into conversations and decisions about the future of rural people, organisations and places (Skerratt, 2011; Horlings & Padt, 2013; Beer, 2014).

Notes

1 'At the 30th anniversary of the CEDAW committee, more than 30 countries have 30 percent or more parliamentarians, and we are joining forces to achieve gender parity by 2030'. (Bachelet quoted in Haack, 2014, p. 38).
2 Organisation for Economic Co-operation and Development (OECD) Development Assistance Committee (DAC).

References

Acker, J (2012). Gendered organisations and intersectionality: Problems and possibilities. *Equality, Diversity and Inclusion: An International Journal* 31(3), 214–224.

Allen, P, Cutts, D & Campbell, R (2014). Measuring the quality of politicians elected by gender quotas – are they any different? *Political Studies*. doi: 10.1111/1467-9248.12161.

Alston, M (2003). Women's representation in an Australian rural context. *Sociologia Ruralis* 43(4), 474–487.

Alston, M & Whittenbury, K (2013). Does climatic crisis in Australia's food bowl create a basis for change in agricultural gender relations? *Agriculture and Human Values* 30, 115–128.

Alston, M & Wilkinson, J (1998). Australian farm women – shut out or fenced in the lack of women in agricultural leadership. *Sociologia Ruralis* 38(3), 391–408.

Andersson, K & Lehtola, M (2011). Regulating the new equine industry in Finland. Wicked problems, governance models, and gendered power structures. *Sociologia Ruralis* 51(4), 387–403.

Barbercheck, M, Brasier, KJ, Kiernan, NE, Sachs, C, Trauger, A, Findeis, J, Stone, A & Moist, LS (2009). Meeting the extension needs of women farmers: A perspective from Pennsylvania. *Journal of Extension* 47(3), article no. 3FEA8.

Beer, A (2014). Leadership and the governance of rural communities. *Journal of Rural Studies* 34, 254–262.

Bjørnå, H (2012). Gender balance and institutions in local government – examples from rural Norway. *Lex Localis – Journal of Local Self-Government* 10(2), 129–152.

Bock, B (2015). Gender mainstreaming and rural development policy: The trivialisation of rural gender issues. *Gender, Place & Culture* 22(5), 731–745.

Brandth, B (2002). Gender identity in European family farming: A literature review. *Sociologia Ruralis* 42(3), 325–344.

Brandth, B & Haugen, MS (1998). Breaking into a masculine discourse: Women and farm forestry. *Sociologia Ruralis* 38(3), 427–442.

Brandth, B & Overrein, G (2012). Resourcing children in a changing rural context: Fathering and farm succession in two generations of farmers. *Sociologia Ruralis* 53(1), 95–111.

Brasier, KJ, Sachs, C, Kiernan, NE, Trauger, A & Barbercheck, ME (2014). Capturing the multiple and shifting identities of farm women in the northeastern United States. *Rural Sociology* 79(3), 283–309.

Bruckmüller, S & Branscombe, NR (2010). The glass cliff: Why women are selected as leaders in crisis contexts. *British Journal of Psychology* 49, 433–451.

Bryant, L & Garnham, B (2014). The embodiment of women in wine: Gender inequality and gendered inscriptions of the working body in a corporate wine organization. *Gender, Work and Organization* 21(5), 411–426.

Cassidy, A & McGrath, B (2014). The relationship between 'non-successor' farm offspring and the continuity of the Irish family farm. *Sociologia Ruralis* 54(4), 399–416.

Claus, VA, Callahan, J & Sandlin, JR (2013). Culture and leadership: Women in non-profit and for–profit institutions in the European Union. *Human Resource Development International* 16(3), 330–345.

Coder, L & Spiller, MS (2013). Leadership education and gender roles: Think manager, think '?'. *Academy of Educational Leadership Journal* 17(3), 21–51.

Eddy, PL (2013). Developing leaders: The role of competencies in rural community colleges. *Community College Review* 41(1), 20–43.

Edwards, B, Dillard, M & Juska, A (2008). Gender and leadership in the Lithuanian rural community movement: Issues, activities, and impacts. *Transitions* 49(1), 107–131.

FAO (Food and Agriculture Organization of the United Nations) (2014). Why gender? Available at http://www.fao.org/gender/gender-home/gender-why/why-gender/en/ (accessed 20 December 2014).

Figueroa-Armijos, M & Johnson, TG (2013). Entrepreneurship in rural America across typologies, gender and motivation. *Journal of Developmental Entrepreneurship* 18(2), 1350014-1–1350014-37.

Ganguli, I, Hausman, R & Viarengo, M (2014). Closing the gender gap in education: What is the state of gaps in labour force participation for women, wives and mothers? *International Labour Review* 153(2), 173–207.

Haack, K (2014). Breaking barriers? Women's representation and leadership at the United Nations. *Global Governance* (20), 37–54.

Heather, B, Skillen, L, Young, J & Vladicka, T (2005). Women's gendered identities and the restructuring of rural Alberta. *Sociologia Ruralis* 45(10), 86–97.

Heggem, R (2014). Diversification and re-feminisation of Norwegian farm properties. *Sociologia Ruralis* 54(4), 439–459.

Horlings, I & Padt, F (2013). Leadership for sustainable regional development in rural areas: Bridging personal and institutional aspects. *Sustainable Development* 21(6), 413–424.

Jones, RC & Swiss, L (2014). Gendered leadership: The effects of female development agency leaders on foreign aid spending. *Sociological Forum* 29(3), 571–586.

Kark, R, Waismel-Manor, R & Shamir, B (2012). Does valuing androgyny and femininity lead to a female advantage? The relationship between gender-role, transformational leadership and identification. *The Leadership Quarterly* 23(3), 620–640.

Kelan, EK (2013). The becoming of business bodies: Gender, appearance, and leadership development. *Management Learning* 44(1), 45–61.

Koutsou, S, Partalidou, M & Petrou, M (2011). Present or absent farm heads? A contemporary reading of family farming in Greece. *Sociologia Ruralis* 51(4), 404–419.

Liebowitz, DJ & Zwingel, S (2014). Gender equality oversimplified: Using CEDAW to counter measurement obsession. *International Studies Review* 16, 362–389.

Little, J & Austin, P (1996). Women and the rural idyll. *Journal of Rural Studies* 12(2) 101–111.

Ludden, AB (2011). Engagement in school and community civic activities among rural adolescents. *Journal of Youth and Adolescence* 40, 1254–1270.

Marshall, J (2013). En-gendering notions of leadership for sustainability. *Gender, Work and Organization* 18(3), 263–281.

Martin, J (2011). Does gender inequality ever disappear? In EA Jeanes, D Knights & PY Martin (Eds), *Handbook of gender, work, and organization* (pp. 213–230). Chichester: John Wiley & Sons.

McNay, L (2004). Agency and experience: Gender as a lived relation. *The Sociological Review* 52, 173–190.

McVay, LA (2013). *Rural women in leadership: Positive factors in leadership development*. Oxford: CABI.

Mundy, T (2013). Engendering 'rural' practice: Women's lived experience of legal practice in regional, rural and remote communities in Queensland. *Griffith Law Review* 22(2), 481–503.

O'Shaughnessy, S & Krogman, NT (2011). Gender as contradiction: From dichotomies to diversity in natural resource extraction. *Journal of Rural Studies* 27(2), 134–143.

O'Toole, K & Macgarvey, A (2003). Rural women and local economic development in south-west Victoria. *Journal of Rural Studies* 19(2), 173–186.

Pini, B (2003). The question of 'the Italians' and women's representation in leadership in the Australian sugar industry. *Australian Geographer* 34(2), 211–222.

Pini, B (2005). The third sex: Women leaders in Australian agriculture. *Gender, Work and Organization* 12(1), 73–88.

Pini, B, Brown, K & Ryan, C (2004). Women-only networks as a strategy for change? A case study from local government. *Women in Management Review* 19(6), 286–292.

Rink, F, Ryan, MK & Stoker, JI (2013). Social resources at a time of crisis: How gender stereotypes inform gendered leader evaluations. *European Journal of Social Psychology* 43, 381–392.

Sachs, C (1996). *Gendered Fields: Rural Women, Agriculture and Environment*. Boulder, CO: Westview Press.

Saugeres, L (2002) The cultural representation of the farming landscape: Masculinity, power and nature. *Journal of Rural Studies* 18(4), 373–384.

Schuh, SC, Hernandez Bark, AS, Van Quakquebeke, N, Hossiep, R, Frieg, P & Van Dick, R (2014). Gender differences in leadership role occupancy: The mediating role of power motivation. *Journal of Business Ethics* 120(3), 363–379.

Sheridan, A, Haslam McKenzie, F & Still, L (2011). Complex and contradictory: The doing of gender on regional development boards. *Gender, Work and Organization* 18(3), 282–297.

Shortall, S (2001). Women in the field: Women, farming and organizations. *Gender, Work and Organization* 8(2), 164–181.

Shortall, S (2008). Are rural development programmes socially inclusive? Social inclusion, civic engagement, participation, and social capital: Exploring the differences. *Journal of Rural Studies* 24(4), 450–457.

Shortall, S (2015). Gender mainstreaming and the Common Agricultural Policy. *Gender, Place and Culture* 22(5), 717–730.

Shortall, S, Braiser, K, McVay, L, Sachs, C & Tickamyer, A (forthcoming). Empowering farm women's identity – the role of the collective.

Shucksmith, M (2012). Class, power, and inequality in rural areas: Beyond social exclusion? *Sociologia Ruralis* 52(4), 377–397.

Sinclair, A (2011). Leading with body. In EA Jeanes, D Knights & PY Martin (Eds), *Handbook of gender, work, and organization* (pp. 117–130). Chichester: John Wiley & Sons.

Skerratt, S (2011). A critical analysis of rural community leadership: Towards systematised understanding and dialogue across leadership domains. *The Journal of Contemporary Issues in Business and Government* 17(1), 87–107.

Toh, SM & Leonardelli, GJ (2012). Cultural constraints on the emergence of women as leaders. *Journal of World Business* 47, 604–611.

Trauger, A, Sachs, C, Barbercheck, M, Kiernan, NE, Brasier, K & Findeis, J (2008). Agricultural education: Gender identity and knowledge exchange. *Journal of Rural Studies*, 24(4), 432–439.

Trauger, A, Sachs, C, Barbercheck, M, Brasier, K & Kiernan, NE (2010). 'Our market is our community': Women farmers and civic agriculture in Pennsylvania, USA. *Agriculture and Human Values* 27, 43–55.

Velez, JJ, Moore, LL, Bruce, JA & Stephens, CA (2014). Agricultural leadership education: Past history, present reality, and future directions. *Journal of Leadership Studies* 7(4), 65–70.

Williams, LL & Lindsey, MJ (2011). *Report: Rural leaders and leadership development in Pennsylvania.* Harrisburg, PA: The Center for Rural Pennsylvania.

Wittmer, DE & Bouché, V (2013). The limits of gendered leadership: Policy implications of female leadership on 'women's issues'. *Politics & Gender* 9, 245–275.

Wright, W & Annes, A (2014). Farm women and agritourism: Representing a new rurality. *Sociologia Ruralis* 54(4), 477–499.

32

Gender and Rural Governance

Annette Aagaard Thuesen

Introduction

Rates of employment among women are high in an increasing number of Western countries, which has caused service institutions and welfare schemes to assume tasks that were previously considered women's tasks (EC, 2011). Esping-Andersen (2009) refers to this change as a 'revolution'. Inglehart and Norris (2003) describe the change as a 'rising tide', in which gender equality is more advanced in post-industrial countries than industrial and agrarian countries. Despite major changes in the conditions of women in the labour market, the high rate of female participation in the labour force in many Western countries is not reflected in participation in governance institutions, particularly rural governance institutions, despite gender mainstreaming policies. The objective of this chapter is to critically assess the state of gender in Western rural governance locations.

The empirical unit of analysis in this chapter is rural governance networks and partnerships at the local scale. The majority of the feminist literature on gender and rural areas has been concerned with topics other than gender and cross-sectoral rural governance, such as women's situations on farms and in workplaces, which are beyond the cross-sectoral governance realm approached here. This chapter provides examples of local rural governance networks, such as the European local action groups (LAGs) that have been established at an increasing rate since the 1990s as part of the new rural governance in the community initiative – LEADER – and the LEADER part of the Rural Development Programme (RDP). Similar nationally initiated local governance networks have been established in parallel in other countries, such as Finland (Pomo groups), Germany (Regionen Aktiv), the USA (Empowerment Zones and Enterprise Communities Program), Canada (Community Futures Development Corporations) and Portugal (Proder groups). Local governance actors in these constellations frequently originate from the public, private and voluntary sectors.

As gender and rural governance are both concerned with concrete participation and the ability to affect decision making, the main part of the chapter is structured according to the conceptual framework of external and internal inclusion/exclusion discussed by Young (2000). Young is concerned with the inequalities in society that contribute to the exclusion of people from political processes because they constitute minorities and are socially or economically disadvantaged or because the political discourse is controlled by other perspectives. She finds that everybody's resources must be included to ensure a just democracy. Many people are excluded from the decision-making process via external and/or internal exclusion. External exclusion occurs when persons who should participate in decision-making processes are absent because decisions about representation are made by appointment and self-selection or for more concrete reasons such as the timing of a meeting. Conversely, internal exclusion involves situations in which people do not succeed in gaining influence despite their actual presence in decision-making forums because their arguments are not considered mainstream or conventional, and therefore they 'lack effective opportunity to influence the thinking of others' (Young, 2000, p. 55). This review of gender and rural governance includes literature addressing whether men and women equally *gain access to* the governance network, that is, their actual numerical presence, and whether the persons that gain access are allowed to *have a say* in the content of discussions within networks and partnerships.

The chapter describes the concepts of governance and rural governance. A review of the literature about the state of gender in rural governance settings is also presented. The last section concludes the review and suggests future research directions.

Governance and rural governance

Governance

The discussion of governance in rural studies has followed the general governance discussions by Rhodes (1996) and Stoker (1998) 20 years ago. Stoker stated that Anglo-American political theory used the term 'government' to refer to the formal institutions of the state and their monopoly of legitimate coercive power (Stoker, 1998, p. 17). He further specified, when referring to Rhodes, that the traditional use of the word 'governance' had been as a synonym for 'government'. Still, according to Stoker, the focus had shifted more and more in the direction of understanding governance as Rhodes defined the concept in 1996, as 'a change in the meaning of government, referring to a new process of governing; or a changed condition of ordered rule; or the new method by which society is governed' (Rhodes, 1996, pp. 652–653). More explicitly, Rhodes described the shared characteristics of governance as interdependencies between authorities and organisations from the public, private and voluntary sectors, continuing interactions between network members, game-like interactions and a significant degree of autonomy from the state. As part of five propositions for governance, Stoker (1998) subsequently emphasised that the boundaries and responsibilities for addressing social and economic issues have become blurred; many self-governing networks have arisen and – similar to Rhodes's position – there is power dependence among institutions involved in governance. It is thus not only the role of organisations and associations – now acting as self-governing networks – that has changed. The role of public authorities has changed, too, and public authorities must use 'new tools and techniques to steer and guide' (Stoker, 1998, p. 18). Governance networks can be seen as expressions of self-regulation in the 'shadow of hierarchy' (Scharpf, 1994), which entails that public authorities still have a role with regard to self-governing networks even though the role has transformed into a meta-governor role with authorities being organisers of self-organisation (Jessop, 1998) or governors of self-governance (Sørensen, 2006). Recent trends in governance research point towards addressing the complexities of governance (Klijn & Koppenjan, 2014) and towards addressing the potential for partnerships and governance networks to contribute to innovation.

Rural governance

Goodwin (1998) assessed the governance term in relation to rural communities, building upon Stoker's five propositions for governance. He stated that partnerships and networks are proposed in official policy statements at all levels as important governance mechanisms, although this conclusion had not been extensively considered in academic debates or rural studies literature. He emphasised a range of orientations that rural research could employ to investigate mechanisms of governance, one of which concerned the question of the identities of the agencies, institutions and individuals involved in the new rural governance. Goodwin questioned whether the same parties would participate in the new rural governance constellations. Goodwin's paper was part of a special issue of the *Journal of Rural Studies* that addressed 'The Shifting Nature of Rural Governance and Community Participation'. Similar to Goodwin, Marsden and Murdoch (1998) emphasised the importance of investigating community participation in processes of rural governance. However, the articles in that special issue examined rural community participation broadly and did not focus on specific groups or minorities and gender issues.

Subsequent to Goodwin's 1998 paper, various studies have investigated topics concerning the identities of the participants in networks established under rural governance. Many studies state that there is nothing 'new' about the new rural governance with respect to gender and rural governance (Little & Jones, 2000; Pini, 2006; Bock, 2010). These studies reference Rhodes's 1996 definition, which specifically emphasises *newness*, and conclude that both external and internal exclusion of women continues to occur in rural governance constellations. In a gender proofing study of the situation in Northern Ireland, Shortall (2002) emphasises that ideological and cultural barriers exist despite the new governance discourse on inclusion, representativeness and transparency, and thus rural development initiatives are continually gendered. Shortall argues that presenting the issue as a numerical problem is inadequate because it reduces the actual gendered aspects of the problem. She notes that 'Involving women and addressing gender are two very different matters' (Shortall, 2002, p. 168) since it does not necessarily mean that gender inequalities are regarded. This argument makes Young's extended view of participation, with a simultaneous focus on both external and internal exclusion, relevant.

Gender and rural governance in the literature

External exclusion?

The majority of the studies included in this section employ quantitative data. Data on the numerical representation of women are employed, although many feminist writers argue that this approach is unproductive for determining whether gender equality standards have been satisfied.

Rising Tide by Inglehart and Norris (2003) is an example of a gender study that investigates actual participation – that is, who participates in the decision-making arenas and who is absent from these arenas. Inglehart and Norris use systematic quantitative survey evidence from the World Values Survey to identify total trends; however, they admit that surveys may be unsuccessful in exploring some of the more nuanced facets of social affairs. Inglehart and Norris's study (2003) does not have a rural dimension, although they distinguish between groups of societies at different levels of societal modernisation – agrarian, industrial and post-industrial societies – when making their conclusions. A gender gap persists in civic/political activism, the most governance-related aspect of their study; women are less active than men in nearly all areas of political activism. The memberships of civic organisations differ: men are more active in sports clubs and professional associations, whereas women dominate religious, health and social welfare groups. The gender gap is greatest in agrarian societies but also persists in post-industrial societies. An important point for this chapter on gender and rural governance is that differences in views *between* generations on gender equality are greater in post-industrial societies than in traditional agrarian societies, which indicates that in post-industrial societies equalities will develop further in the future. This point may prompt an assessment of whether a similar tendency can be transferred to rural–urban relations within post-industrial societies in the global north. A final result from Inglehart and Norris's study is that egalitarian countries are more likely to believe that women and men are equally able to be good political leaders. Inglehart and Norris note that these countries may also be more positive towards the introduction of institutional changes and affirmative action strategies, such as quotas, that can prevent external exclusion.

In some of her studies, Bock (2010, 2015) investigates gender participation patterns in politics and LAG rural governance networks. Regarding external exclusion and rural development policies, Bock notes that the 'analysis of rural development policies reveals that women seldom participate in the formation of rural development plans or decision making on the distribution of funds' (Bock, 2010, p. 9). Bock demonstrates that women are externally excluded from decision making on LAG boards in the majority of the EU-15 countries. The exceptions are Luxembourg, Portugal and, to a certain extent, Finland, the United Kingdom and Ireland. Thuesen and Derkzen (2015) have distinctly noted this point in their study of gender distribution on Danish LAG and FLAG[1] boards. As one explanation of the low participation of women on the boards, Bock notes the rules that define the composition of the LAG boards. These rules require representation of local/regional administrations and agricultural organisations on the boards; these entities are usually male-dominated, which results in a greater number of male representatives on the boards (Bock, 2015). Another explanation by Bock is self-exclusion. Women indicate that their time and experience is insufficient to contribute to the boards. Bock (2010) also notes a geographical distinction when analysing gender equality and suggests that inequalities continue to prevail primarily in peripheral rural regions, particularly Central/Eastern European areas. However, she does not employ data on the gender composition of LAG boards in these countries.

As previously mentioned, empirical data from Denmark also reveal external exclusion. The average percentage of women on Danish LAG boards in the RDP and the coastal areas that are part of the Fisheries Programme (FP) from 2007 to 2013 was 29% (Thuesen & Sørensen 2009; Thuesen & Derkzen, 2015), suggesting external exclusion. The percentage of women decreases as the association of the LAGs with the FP increases. The boards of LAGs that only serve within the FP are 13% women. The percentage of women on boards increases in more urbanised and centrally located municipalities. Women are elected more frequently to serve as non-organised, independent citizens than in nominated positions via organisational representation. According to Bock, organisations such as farmers' unions, chambers of commerce and fisheries organisations (as also indicated by Thuesen and Derkzen's data) are more male dominated. Thuesen and Derkzen's data also indicate that compared to men women have a low number of acquaintances on LAG boards when they enter the boards. However, no advanced statistical tests of the data were conducted.

Another Danish study of the gender distribution of the main participants in Danish rural policy forms the following general conclusion:

> Generally, we see that especially men account for project activities, both in terms of amount of funding and the number of projects. This does not of course mean that women do not work 'behind the scenes'. There is nonetheless a very clear tendency for men to come first, corresponding to the gender distribution in the positional hierarchy at ministerial

level and to the predominance of men among presenters and panelists in the national rural conferences.

(Busck, Jensen, Svendsen & Tanvig, 2004, p. 36, trans. Thuesen)

Oedl-Wieser's (2015) paper also investigated the gender equality effect of the RDP. She focuses on the period since 1995 and discusses topics of external exclusion from an Austrian perspective. Her study demonstrates that gender mainstreaming is a challenge to politicians and administrators and reveals the institutional, political and social barriers to gender mainstreaming of a male-dominated programme; these barriers maintain and extend gender roles instead of enabling less patriarchal structures. According to Oedl-Wieser (2015), the lack of awareness of the needs and interests of rural women by central meta-governors of the RDP is problematic. Both individual and institutional resistance to the gender issue and a lack of awareness and competence with regard to gender exist. At the European level, the programme monitoring system includes few gender-disaggregated indicators. When referring to Hafner-Burton and Pollack (2009), Oedl-Wieser (2015) notes that the European Commission seems to be more competent at formulating policies than at implementing policies. Shortall (2015) also forms this conclusion in her analysis of gender mainstreaming and the Common Agricultural Policy. In addition, Bock (2010) notes that gender is not systematically addressed and is primarily handled 'en passant' and sporadically in individual projects within the male-dominated governance structures of the RDP.

In relation to the local governance part of the RDP, Oedl-Wieser indicates a large under-representation of women on Austrian LAG boards and significant external exclusion; only 3.5% of the chairs and 12.4% of the board members were women during the 2007–2013 programming period. As a result, at the end of the programming period, the Austrian Federal Ministry of Agriculture, Forestry, Environment and Water Management set quotas for women on the LAG project-selection committees. Oedl-Wieser notes that the quotas have generally been satisfied, despite large differences among the LAGs (from 7% to 55% women). In cases in which women have been included, she notes that greater steps towards equal opportunity were taken. According to Oedl-Wieser, this notion is as important as the numerical representation of women. She places herself in the group of researchers that emphasise that the new rural governance is not 'new': 'There are substantial path dependencies in the Austrian regional policy setting and newly emerging structures remain highly influenced by "old" structures of policy-making and administration' (Oedl-Wieser, 2015, p. 6). Oedl-Wieser concludes that the introduction of affirmative actions such as gender- and equality-specific measures, including quotas for board and steering committees, are necessary to improve the monitoring systems; the inclusion of gender-disaggregated indicators is also needed.

Prugl (2011) discusses LEADER in Germany and gender mainstreaming in relation to this initiative. The Land is highly influential in Germany with regard to gender issues. Thus, very different German approaches to gender mainstreaming exist, and she investigates two Länder as examples. She examines how EU gender mainstreaming requirements are interpreted at the local level of the LEADER initiative and demonstrates that, in both examples, gender mainstreaming strategies evaporated as they approached the local level. According to Prugl, the gender equality topic lacks political will and suffers from bureaucratic proceduralism. Gender equality has advanced in the Bavarian LEADER area due to the action of individual women and not as a result of planned, systematic actions of the state. In the Saxony-Anhalt LEADER area, LEADER was implemented in a more gender-equal manner, and gender-disaggregated data were employed due to historically freer gender relations. Prugl explains: 'Unlike in Bavaria, where individual women could benefit when they put their demands before an unmotivated state, the more-egalitarian gender rules institutionalized in the state in Saxony-Anhalt enabled a form of rural development that included women and their needs. … Gender mainstreaming appeared redundant in this context where women had a forceful voice in the local state' (Prugl, 2011, p. 128).

In a comparison of two partnerships based on territorial development programmes in Ontario, Canada and Sweden, Fuller and Larsson note a difference between the two countries in the gender composition of partnership boards. Boards in Ontario primarily comprise middle-aged men, whereas the boards in Sweden are composed of younger women (Fuller & Larsson, 2009, p. 31) because the rules for gender composition are upheld in Sweden.

Regarding external exclusion, the general picture is that representation of women is numerically worse in rural governance institutions, with minor exceptions, and external exclusion exists. Only a few of the reviewed studies have performed an initial overview and analysed and predicted locations of potential openings. Thus, a comprehensive quantitative analysis of the topic is needed in the future. The next section of this chapter considers the dimensions of internal exclusion with regard to gender and rural governance.

Internal exclusion?

Imagine a golf match in which one player employs a fully equipped bag and a caddy and the other player only employs 50% of the irons and has no caddy. This example illustrates the position presented in this area of the literature on gender and rural governance and corresponds with the concept of internal exclusion. Several authors have suggested that body/head counting is not sufficient for addressing whether women and men participate on equal terms in rural governance institutions (Little & Jones, 2000; Pini, 2006). These authors emphasise the need to investigate the roles in which women actually participate and their responsibilities due to internal exclusion rather than external inclusion. Qualitative methods are primarily employed in the studies included in this section.

Little and Jones (2000) and Pini (2006) refer to an article by Tickell and Peck from 1996 although the latter addresses gender and *urban* governance. The Tickell and Peck article demonstrates that there is *not much new* with respect to gender equality in the *new* urban governance. The following quote indicates their focus on internal exclusion: 'Regendering local governance is not just about packing committees with men, it is also about privileging masculinist forms of decision-making and agenda-setting' (Tickell & Peck, 1996, p. 596).

Tickell and Peck discuss the occurrence of systematic internal exclusion and the peripheralisation of women. These authors characterise some interests and decision-making approaches, such as social interests and consensus building, as feminine and economic interests and elite networking as masculine. Tickell and Peck suggest that some countries, such as the Scandinavian countries, are more women friendly although they generally present the state as a patriarchal structure because 'different gender interests are articulated through the state in ways that systematically favor men' (Tickell & Peck, 1996, p. 600).

Little and Jones (2000) extend the rural governance focus introduced by Goodwin and others in 1998 and by Tickell and Peck (1996) in their work on masculinity, gender and rural policy. Little and Jones review the literature on the topic and incorporate examples from the English Rural Challenge Policy, finding both external and internal exclusion due to masculine values in policy. Little and Jones characterise certain interests in the Rural Regeneration Policy as masculine and other interests as feminine, for example, 'they privilege economic over social interests, and in doing so they favor men's interests over those of women' (p. 627). In addition, they identify several masculine tendencies in rural policy making that exclude women, such as the insertion of competition and partnerships with an emphasis on the private sector and the very nature of the regeneration projects, which are often dealing with bricks and mortar and substantial economic investments. Little and Jones indicate that they take a rather simplistic approach and that additional studies are needed. Bock, however, also discusses self-exclusion due to factors aligning with the arguments by Little and Jones. According to Bock, women 'often prefer to engage in informal political activities that are perceived as less difficult and less competitive, dealing with issues that are more closely related to their daily life' (Bock, 2015, p. 7).

In her study of the new rural local governance in Australia, Pini (2006) also extends the discussion by Tickell and Peck (1996) by highlighting the importance of not limiting the focus to body count – that is, external exclusion – in the new *rural* governance. She emphasises: 'To limit our focus to the body is inadequate, as the body is just one of many ways in which gender may be socially, culturally and symbolically produced' (Pini, 2006, p. 406). Pini employs a single case study about the 'new' rural local governance in the Villa shire and analyses interviews with 40 men and women involved in leadership. She demonstrates that women are marginalised by a hegemonic discourse on business and entrepreneurship. Fraternal networks and coalitions are important for the selection of committee members in the new rural governance in Australia, and women risk being 'reviled rather than rewarded' if they align themselves with the masculine discourse (Pini, 2006, p. 405). When women do gain leadership positions, Pini argues that this may be because power is vested elsewhere. According to the studies by Tickell and Peck (1996) and Little and Jones (2000), women's roles occur at the local, everyday level, whereas men's influence occurs at the level of the district and exhibits a more strategic character.

Bock and Derkzen (2006) investigate whether specific Dutch reconstruction projects focus on gender issues. They note: 'Because of the official recognition of quality of life as a political problem that needs to be solved, and because of women's possibly increased participation in decision making, reconstruction policies and programmes might also become more responsive to women's needs and interests compared to previous rural development policies' (Bock & Derkzen, 2006, p. 225). Their main conclusion is, however, that gender budget analysis shows that specific rural women's needs are not addressed despite women's higher unemployment rates and lower rates of participation in decision making. Their research considers a case in which women actually enter the scene. They indicate that women generally have less opportunity to succeed in concrete rural policy settings and are less self-evident coalition partners. They refer to Little and Jones (2000) when suggesting that policies and programmes often employ a masculinist approach and that women frequently have a lower probability of receiving governmental rural development subsidies. Internal exclusion due to a competitive attitude is evident from the following quote: 'The newcomers find themselves in an arena which is still dominated by the established players and whose formal and competitive culture has not changed, despite the attempts to design Reconstruction policy in a participatory and interactive way' (Bock & Derkzen, 2006, p. 229). They also note that 'officially, negotiations were consensus driven, but just below the surface the culture was still competitive and conflict-driven' (Bock & Derkzen, 2006, p. 236).

According to Bock and Derkzen (2006), equal participation is required for high legitimacy, and a lack of equal participation can lead to the exclusion of quality-of-life issues, which are not very clearly defined, but relate to daily living conditions. When day-to-day living conditions are declining, it is experienced more severely by women than men, according to Bock and Derkzen. They discuss quality of life as a women's issue and investigate whether women participate to promote quality-of-life issues and are successful in this endeavour. Quality of life *is* used to legitimise the presence of women on boards. However, representing women's issues can be problematic and may place the women on boards in a potential conflict: 'they are caught in the crossfire – the women support organizations who want them to act as women representatives, and the committee members who demand proof of their neutrality' (Bock & Derkzen, 2006, p. 229). They note that 'defining more clearly what quality of life means and which aspects may be important in the context of Reconstruction policy would enhance rural women's ability to participate in policy making in an effective and efficient way' (Bock & Derkzen, 2006, p. 230). Bock and Derkzen also demonstrate that internal exclusion and inequalities exist due to differing degrees of support from mother organisations, even though the committee members sit on the committee in a personal capacity. They suggest that 'in comparison to other committee members, rural women have a serious lack of support' (Bock & Derkzen, 2006, p. 228). This finding is also evident in a study by Derkzen and Bock (2007) of professionalism in partnerships, which shows that woman have no direct connection to organisations and therefore no direct access to technical knowledge, organising capacity and so forth.

In a study of local governance at the village level in Poland, Matysiak (2015) does not refer to cross-sectoral governance but instead focuses on the village representative side of the existing governance. The results of the study indicate an increase in the number of women who function as village representatives and greater involvement of women as village representatives compared to other government levels in Poland. Matysiak, however, also relates that the role as village representative has changed from addressing 'masculine' heavy investment activities to more 'feminine' concerns involving 'soft activities'. In a study of the characteristics of women's voluntary work in England, Little (1997, p. 204) also suggests that women are automatic candidates for ordinary and monotonous tasks.

Conclusion

The review has demonstrated that the cross-sectoral networks established as part of the new rural governance are characterised by external exclusion because the partnerships do not include women to a large extent. In some cases, quota-like rules succeed in improving the situation. Inequalities in representation may be due to recruitment via male-dominated networks and appointments, but self-exclusion may also play a role. Additional extensive quantitative studies and subsequent in-depth analysis are required to identify the true factors underlying the minority status of women in the partnerships of the new rural governance and motivators for women's participation. Future studies of broader meta-governance via laws and regulations from the EU and the ministries are important to identify structural opportunities to reduce external exclusion. The literature indicates that internal exclusion also occurs. The meeting styles and jargon employed are competitive and conflict oriented and thematically focused on economic development. The literature suggests that women are more concerned with quality-of-life issues and are attracted to a more consensual form of meeting. Young notes that the form of communication is important because the degree of internal exclusion is determined by how individuals talk to each other and listen to each other's views. According to Young, everyone's resources must be included to ensure the development of a just democracy. Comprehensive, quantitative studies of gender equality are needed to complement qualitative studies of internal exclusion.

The focus on the new rural governance and gender are also important because the stage is set for the use of additional partnerships in new policy areas. For example, in the European political landscape between 2014 and 2020, LAG partnerships will be obligatory within the Agricultural Fund for Rural Development and may be an option within the European Regional Development Fund, the European Social Fund and the European Maritime and Fisheries Fund. Comparative studies of the experience obtained with gendered external and internal exclusion in policy areas other than rural policy and in urban-oriented policy areas would be appropriate to determine if these policies will succeed in engaging both sexes more equally.

However, we must not disregard the notion that the gendered inequalities discussed in the literature are minor in scope compared with inequalities encountered in other parts of the world, where unequal gender stratification is significantly widespread. Inglehart and Norris's study (2003) notes that the post-industrial egalitarian values influence development in the Western part of the world. Here, the differences between generations are substantial, which indicates that changes might occur in the future. Real problems exist in traditional countries, where gender continues to serve as an example of social stratification to a much larger extent than demonstrated in this chapter.

Note

1   FLAGs are fisheries local action groups established as part of the European Maritime and Fisheries Fund and they work towards the sustainable development of coastal areas.

References

Bock, BB (2010). *Personal and social development of women in rural areas of Europe.* Directorate-General for internal policies, Policy department B Structural and cohesion policies.

Bock, B (2015). Gender mainstreaming and rural development policy: The trivialisation of rural gender issues. *Gender, Place & Culture* 22(5), 731–745.

Bock, B & Derkzen, P (2006). Gender and rural development budgets. In BB Bock & S Shortall (Eds), *Rural gender relations: Issues and case studies* (pp. 218–223). Oxford: CABI.

Busck, AG, Jensen, MV, Svendsen, GLH & Tanvig, HW (2004). *Ligestilling i dansk landdistriktspolitik er ikke lige meget.* 9/04. Esbjerg: Danish Centre for Rural Research and Development.

Derkzen, P & Bock, BB (2007). The construction of professional identity: Symbolic power in rural partnerships in The Netherlands. *Sociologia Ruralis* 47(3), 189–204.

EC (2011). *Strategy for equality between women and men 2010–2015.* Luxembourg: European Commission.

Esping-Andersen, G (2009). *The incomplete revolution – Adapting to women's new roles.* Cambridge: Polity.

Fuller, T & Larsson, L (2009). *Insights from comparing community futures in Ontario with Leader in Sweden – A qualitative assessment of policy and practice in two government sponsored rural development programmes.* FedNor: Industry Canada.

Goodwin, M (1998). The governance of rural areas: Some emerging research issues and agendas. *Journal of Rural Studies* 14(1), 5–12.

Hafner-Burton, EM & Pollack, MA (2009). Mainstreaming gender in the European Union: Getting the incentives right. *Comparative European Politics* 7(1), 114–138.

Inglehart, R & Norris, P (2003). *Rising tide: Gender equality and cultural change around the world.* Cambridge: Cambridge University Press.

Jessop, B (1998). The rise of governance and the risk of failure: The case of economic development. *International Social Science Journal* 155(1), 29–45.

Klijn, EH & Koppenjan, JFM (2014). Complexity in governance network theory. *Complexity Governance & Networks* 1(1), 61–70.

Little, J (1997). Constructions of rural women's voluntary work. *Gender, Place & Culture: A Journal of Feminist Geography* 4(2), 197–210.

Little, J & Jones, O (2000). Masculinity, gender and rural policy. *Rural Sociology* 65(4), 621–639.

Marsden, T & Murdoch, J (1998). Editorial: The shifting nature of rural governance and community participation. *Journal of Rural Studies* 14(1), 1–4.

Matysiak, I (2015). The feminization of governance in rural communities in Poland: The case of village representatives. *Gender, Place & Culture* 22(5), 700–716.

Oedl-Wieser, T (2015). Gender equality: A core dimension in Rural Development Programmes in Austria? *Gender, Place & Culture* 22(5), 685–699.

Pini, B (2006). A critique of 'new' rural local governance: The case of gender in a rural Australian setting. *Journal of Rural Studies* 22, 396–408.

Prugl, EM (2011). *Transforming masculine rule: Agricultural and rural development in the European Union.* Ann Arbor, MI: University of Michigan Press.

Rhodes, RAW (1996). The new governance: Governing without government. *Political Studies* 44(4), 652–667.

Scharpf, F (1994). Games real actors could play – Positive and negative coordination in embedded negotiations. *Journal of Theoretical Politics* 6(1), 27–53.

Shortall, S (2002). Gendered agricultural and rural restructuring: A case study of Northern Ireland. *Sociologia Ruralis* 42(2), 160–175.

Shortall, S (2015). Gender mainstreaming and the Common Agricultural Policy. *Gender, Place & Culture* 22(5), 717–730.

Sørensen, E (2006). Metagovernance: The changing role of politicians in processes of democratic governance. *The American Review of Public Administration* 36(1), 98–114.

Stoker, G (1998). Governance as theory: Five propositions. *International Social Science Journal*, UNESCO, 155(1), 17–28.

Thuesen, AA & Derkzen, P (2015). Questioning the gender distribution in Danish LEADER LAGs. In K Andersen, L Granberg & I Kovacs (Eds), *Evaluating the European approach to rural development grass-roots experiences of the LEADER programme.* Aldershot: Ashgate.

Thuesen, AA & Sørensen, JFL (2009). *Danish local action groups in rural and fishing areas 2008: Composition, activities and cooperation in the start-up phase.* Esbjerg: Danish Centre for Rural Research.

Tickell, A & Peck, J (1996). The return of the Manchester men: Men's words and men's deeds in the remaking of the local state. *Transactions of the Institute of British Geographers* 21(4), 595–616.

Young, IM (2000). *Inclusion and democracy.* Oxford: Oxford University Press.

33

Gender, Farming and Rural Social Research

A Relationship in Flux

Chrysanthi Charatsari and Majda Černič Istenič

Introduction

Gender in agriculture, as a topic of research, has attracted a considerable amount of interest among scholars from diverse fields, leading to a wide array of studies focused on the ways gender is constructed (and reconstructed) within farm spaces. Dominated by qualitative enquiries – and mainly focused on the sociological aspects of gender relations, divisions, distinctions and inequalities – the literature of gender in farming provides a rich body of findings on power relations, representational codes, gender boundaries and gender identities. However, a number of critical issues remain to be explored. The aim of this chapter is to bring together the major streams of research dedicated to the intersection of gender and farming and to highlight some under-researched issues in this area.

Portrayal of gender in rural studies

Rural sociological research has come a long way, from Fortmann's (1981) and Sachs's (1983) early works on women farmers' invisibility in agriculture to more recent studies (e.g., Shortall, 2014) addressing the social construction of both men's and women's identities in relation to profound changes in agriculture. Nevertheless, despite the positive developments in women's access to land and capital, findings from both the developing and developed world continue to raise many concerns about the achievement of gender equality in rural settings. Evidence supporting this contention comes from fields as diverse as rural sociology, geography, medicine, psychology and agricultural economics, to name just a few. Among the many topics addressed by this literature, there are arguably four that have attracted the greatest interest from researchers: entitlement, gender identity, participation and targeted actions for gender equality. In the following sections, we present the key findings of, and raise some questions in connection with, research published in these areas to date.

Entitlement

The first of these strands refers to the compatibility of the roles of woman and farmer. Although the modernisation of agriculture has paved the way for a more active involvement of women in on-farm work (Haugen & Brandth, 1994), traditional cultural belief systems still impose distinctive roles for male and female farmers (O'Brien & Wegren, 2015). However, research in this area offers conflicting results. Some studies conclude that women who acquire the label 'farmer' become more widely accepted as active participants in the work process of the farm (Ball, 2014), and that the importance of their role – as equal partners – for the sustainability of the family farm is more likely to be acknowledged (Beach, 2013). Furthermore, the patrilineal transfer of farms from fathers to sons – which is favoured by both traditional (Silvasti, 2003; Shortall, 2006) and legal practices (Voyce, 2014) – although it remains a common pattern in some countries, is in decline in others (Otomo & Oedl-Wieser, 2009).

At the other end of the spectrum, findings show that women are still less actively involved in on-farm decision making than men (Gidarakou, Kazakopoulos & Koutsouris, 2008; Černič Istenič, 2015). Even when the title 'farmer' is socially attributed to women, female farmers enjoy limited privileges compared to their male counterparts (Dufour, Courdin & Dedieu, 2010), a situation that pushes women to adopt a more 'masculine' way of life in order to succeed (Pilgeram, 2007). Furthermore, although Tutor-Marcom, Bruce and Greer (2014) found that women show a strong affiliation with farming and an affective attachment to the farm, farming communities treat them as marginal farmers because of the popular imagery that describes only men farmers as having an innate and robust conception of nature (Saugeres, 2002b). This marginalisation is visible not only in family and intra-community relationships, but also in the mindset of rural services, which often view only male farmers as having a protagonistic role in agriculture – a finding that has been repeatedly demonstrated in the case of extension/education services (Shortall, 1996; Charatsari, Černič Istenič & Lioutas, 2013).

Gender identity

Gender identity is one of the most dominant topics in the literature on the intersection of gender and farming, and has strong ties with the issue of entitlement. Farming, with its traditional, strict division of gender-specific roles, evokes a particularly salient sex-categorisation. A number of studies have focused their interest on what Person and Ovesey (1983) call 'gender role identity' and the ways it is affected by social patterns and norms. For example, Pini (2005a) examined the way women's gender identities are (re)constructed when they are involved in on-farm physical work, and Silvasti (2003) focused on the correlation between farm succession and gender identity. In both works, farm women who take the role of farmer and engage in masculine-identified activities seem to challenge traditional perceptions of sex roles.

Given that – as Deaux and Major's (1987) seminal model of gender-related behaviour suggests – a person's behaviour is affected by perceivers' expectations, farm women tend to provide confirming evidence of traditional stereotypes by adopting a socially approved behaviour or, in other words, by trying to adapt their goals to the expectations of others within the farming communities. Conversely, the suggestion that women who farm transgress traditional gender role identities needs a very cautious approach, since, as work on social psychology indicates, women (or men) engaged in non-traditional gender roles do not necessarily take a critical stance towards the legitimacy of gender disparities (Swim, Aikin, Hall & Hunter, 1995). In any case, the conceptualisation of gender identity provided by Gurin and

Townsend (1986) – which recognises three dimensions of women's gender identities (perceived similarity to other females, a sense of common fate, and centrality of gender to the self) – could shed more light on the issue of farmers' gender identities, as well as on the interrelation between gender identity and social identity (Cameron & Lalonde, 2001). Such a conceptualisation could offer insights on farm women's collective identities and/or gender consciousness.

In addition, as Tyson (1986) and Spence (1985) have noted, childhood is the most critical stage in an individual's construction of gender identity. For that reason, in order to better understand how farmers' gender identities are developed, it is important first to understand their developmental origins. Halim and Ruble (2010) argue that family is the first field in which gender identity is cultivated. As Bronstein (2006) explains, gender appropriateness is conveyed from parents to children not only through direct means, but also through modelling of prototypical gender-typed behaviour – a mechanism which operates below the level of awareness.

In a recent study on changes of women's position within the farm family in Thessaly, Greece, it was found that mother–daughter bonds are important precursors of daughters' gender identities, and that sociohistorical changes variously affect the (re)construction of gender identities (Charatsari, 2014). Studies on personality also suggest that gender roles are heavily affected by social and cultural changes (Twenge, 1997; Costa, Terracciano & McCrae, 2001). These findings call for more research on how (and to what extent) gender identities change over time and under the influence of different political, institutional, sociocultural and economic transformations which take place in rural areas.

Although early works on gender identity emphasised its inherited nature (Stoller, 1964), most recent theories agree that gender identity is shaped (or re-formed) through a gradual process which encompasses cognitive and psychological mechanisms (Bussey & Bandura, 1999). In rural spaces, recent evidence suggests that this (re)construction of gender identities is achieved through a continuous process of social interaction (Shortall, 2014). Nonetheless, although the social dimension of farm women's gender identity is a central issue in the relevant literature, its complex and multidimensional psychological nature remains under-investigated.

Participation

The third strand – literature on participation – refers to women's opportunities to participate in off-farm work or in the public realm. According to this set of literature, women's participation in off-farm income-generating activities is increasing (Bjørkhaug & Blekesaune, 2008). Farm women enter into paid work not only because of their willingness to contribute to family income, but also to gain employee benefits and to expand their social environment (Bharadwaj, Findeis & Chintawar, 2013). Nevertheless, women who work simultaneously on- and off-farm often face a psychological conflict, emerging from the many different and – at times – incompatible values and roles. As Kelly and Shortall (2002) note, in spite of their significant contribution to the financial sustainability of the family farm, these women have to correspond to traditional gender roles within the farm. Although there are indications that the distribution of household tasks gradually takes a more balanced shape (Benjamin & Kimhi, 2006), farm women are still primarily responsible for household chores (Wegren et al., 2015) and are viewed as housekeepers and child-carers rather than as professionals (Charatsari, 2014).

In addition, women continue to be under-represented in agri-political organisations (Bock & Derkzen, 2008; Oedl-Wieser, 2008; Sheridan, McKenzie & Still, 2011), and have a limited share of agri-political leadership (Pini, 2002), which results in limited opportunities to direct rural policy making. However, the influence of this under-representation on farm women's actual social and psychological well-being is assumed rather than demonstrated. For example, Pini (2005b) discovered that women's involvement in agricultural leadership in Australia had no direct impact on the development of a more equitable farm sector, since women are still considered as having just a supporting role in farming. Moreover, as Shortall (2001) argues, women's participation in agricultural organisations may sharpen rather than minimise gender differences.

Gendered policies

Concerning policy initiatives towards gender equality in rural spaces, there is a clear consensus among researchers that these interventions have not yet reached the desired outcomes in terms of – for example – equal opportunities for participation in paid work (Berry et al., 2008), rural governance schemes (Pini, 2006) and farm management (Kazakopoulos & Gidarakou, 2003). In the European Union, rural development policies have failed to sufficiently address gender issues due to a lack of systematic consideration of the interaction between gender and development (Bock, 2015) and an emphasis on the consequences of, rather than the antecedents to, gender inequalities (Shortall, 2015). In addition, these policies are often built upon traditional, male-oriented ideologies (Little & Jones, 2000).

Thus, in many cases, instead of facilitating the conditions within which farm women can gain strength, such initiatives maintain rigid gender dichotomies (Černič Istenič, 2015) and sustain gender stratification (Oedl-Wieser, 2015). In research outside the European Union, Keller (2014) notes that US agricultural policy follows a similar line, restricting women's access to capital and other inputs; and Price (2012) argues that agricultural organisations in Canada operate in a mindset which favours traditional patrilineal structures.

It takes two to tango

As we have already mentioned, farming communities – and rural spaces in general – are mirrored in the literature as gendered spaces characterised by a series of prejudices and discriminations against farm women. This premise has inevitably led rural sociological research to a particular 'subjectivity' (referring to researchers' beliefs, thoughts, positions and – sometimes – assumptions on rural gender), which has driven scholars to focus their interest on farm women. Accordingly, although women farmers have received a fair amount of attention from researchers, men farmers remain under-represented in the literature. While Brandth and Haugen (this volume) argue that there has been an increase in masculinity studies, there are few specific studies that focus on men farmers. This complicates and curtails our understanding of the relationship between gender and farming. As Price (2010) notes, men's integration into gender research may lead to a more complete picture of the issues under study. Nevertheless, in many studies male farmers are considered as a stable reference standard against which gender differences are evaluated, often without being included in the study sample.

Most contemporary efforts to depict men farmers in the literature are focused on the issue of masculinities produced by agricultural occupations. As a highly sex-segregated occupation, farming is considered a proving ground for masculinity (Saugeres, 2002a; Ferrell, 2012). In this vein, male farmers shape and sustain their masculine identities through behaviours and symbolic practices akin to socially constructed masculine ideals, which impose a strong (and socially obvious through visible manifestations) connection to land (Peter, Bell, Jarnagin & Bauer, 2000) and farm machinery (Brandth, 2006).

However, men farmers – and especially homosexuals (Fellows, 1998) – often experience a coercion to conform to the pervasive standards of hegemonic masculinity, which may have a negative impact on their psychological well-being. Indeed, several indications confirm that masculinity is associated with higher occupational risk-taking (Courtenay, 2000), increased rates of occupational accidents (Harrell, 1986), greater tendency to internalise violence (Carrington, McIntosh, Hogg & Scott, 2013), higher levels of depression and emotional burden (Barlett & Conger, 2004; Alston & Kent, 2008) and higher rates of mental illness and suicides (Alston, 2012; Garnham & Bryant, 2014).

Nevertheless, as with femininity, the social construct of masculinity is sensitive to political, economic and cultural changes. However, research on the changing nature of farmers' masculinity has arrived at contradictory conclusions. Specifically, while studies from different parts of the developed world converge to show that as the nature of agriculture changes so does the prevailing notion of masculinity, taking a less pressing form for men farmers and especially for the younger cohorts (Brandth, 1995; Laoire, 2002; Coldwell, 2007), other research suggests that male farmers continue to encounter – and be negatively affected by – the stress of masculinity (Bryant & Garnham, 2015).

Forgotten groups and hidden relationships

Although rural sociological literature has addressed a variety of topics, relatively little is known about the impact of the intersection of gender and farming on farmers' well-being. In general, the discussion of women as 'farm heads' has focused on women's entrepreneurial skills and competencies, overlooking the issue of welfare. On the other hand, while several studies focused on the participation of women in off-farm employment, the influences that such a transition may bring to women's psychological status remains unexplored. In one of the few exceptions, Haugen and Blekesaune (2005), investigating the influence of off-farm employment on satisfaction with life, found that women who have an off-farm job express higher life satisfaction than those who work solely on farm.

However, the question remains: what is the influence of women's marginalisation from agricultural production on their actual well-being? Marginalisation as a form of personal discrimination can generate a particular 'invisibility syndrome' similar to that manifested by racial minorities (Franklin & Boyd-Franklin, 2000), which erodes self-esteem and engenders inner conflicts and personal stress. Nevertheless, when viewed as a form of group discrimination (discrimination towards women, in general), it may – surprisingly – lead to some positive attitudes towards the self. For instance, work in social psychology provides evidence that this kind of discrimination may offer the basis for higher levels of an individual's self-esteem in some groups, including women (Bourguignon, Seron, Yzerbyt & Herman, 2006) and gay men (Doyle & Molix, 2014). Of course, to examine such an effect it is important to integrate new concepts (psychological well-being, life satisfaction, group identification) into research on the intersection between gender and farming.

On the other hand, women who assume the role of farmer are exposed to occupational risks more than male farmers (Zhang et al., 2011). Furthermore, a longitudinal study in the USA (Rayens & Reed, 2014) and two surveys in the UK (Booth & Lloyd, 2000; Gregoire, 2002) revealed that female farmers suffer from higher levels of stress compared to men. According to Fraser et al. (2005), this can be attributed to the heavy workloads farm women have to carry and the multiplicity of the roles they perform, since, apart from their on-farm work, female farmers continue to undertake the bulk of household chores (Gallagher & Delworth, 1993; Allen & Sachs, 2007). Another possible explanation is that women who are farm operators, being a minority, are more visible than their male counterparts. As such, they face a higher (actual or perceived) social pressure to succeed, which leads to higher levels of risk-taking behaviour and psychological distress.

Overall, in order to effectively address the issue of well-being there is a need to incorporate new concepts into the research on gender–farming interrelation. Moreover, examining the mediating and combined effects of other variables in this relationship can provide a more complete picture of how farming and farm life affects both male and female farmers. The segmentation of farmers into two general categories – men and women – offers limited opportunities for drawing conclusions for specific sub-groups within farming populations, such as older farmers or sexual minorities. For instance, little is known about the way gender affects elder farmers' everyday lives. In one of the very few attempts to deal with this issue, Riley (2012), studying the passage of farming couples into retirement, found that adjustment to the new conditions of life are easier for women because of their previous engagement in a variety of off-farm activities.

Another under-investigated group includes lesbians, gay and bisexuals (LGB). Despite the difficulty of approaching such populations in farming communities, and in spite of the fact that LGB research has focused on rural rather than farming populations (see, for example, Bell & Valentine, 1995; Little, 2003; Bryant & Pini, 2011), recently there has been an increasing volume of studies which clearly indicate some differences between rural and urban settings and provide some very interesting findings on the everyday lives of sexual minorities in the rural. For instance, Eldridge, Mack and Swank (2006) found that homophobia still prevails in rural Appalachia (USA); and Lee and Quam (2013) discovered that older LGB adults have lower levels of outness and higher levels of guardedness with other people. Kazyak (2015, p. 843) found that rural areas are more open to (masculine) lesbians than to (effeminate) gay men, since 'constructions of female masculinity align with those of rurality and lesbian sexuality', while constructions of male femininity are not compatible with rurality.

Conclusion

In the extant literature farm spaces are represented as masculine spaces in which farm women are marginalised by the production and reproduction of power and privilege. Within this framework, several studies converge to show that farm women are marginalised from some public (agricultural leadership, rural policy making) and/or private (on-farm decision making) aspects of life because of their gender. However, the impact of women's (under)representation in leadership roles on their actual (social and/or psychological) well-being remains elusive. Further, the distinction between 'private spheres' (housekeeping, caregiving) and 'public spheres' (taking on the role of farmer, working off-farm, participating in agricultural organisations) – as Gerson and Peiss (1985) argue – is problematic, since it cannot conceptualise the overlap between the two realms. Accordingly, a more holistic, multifocal view of women's roles is required to study farm women's positions and statuses within farm families and societies.

As we proposed earlier in this chapter, the discussion around women's invisibility in agricultural production offers conflicting conclusions. Whilst a number of studies suggest that women's role in farming is currently more widely acknowledged, other indications confirm that farming communities continue to treat women as second-order farmers, and that official services (especially agricultural education and extension services) do not favour the development of entrepreneurial skills among farm women. In addition, the robustness of traditional gender identities in farm spaces complicates and/or prevents women's economic activity.

Interestingly, although there is a common agreement that gender identities are socially constructed, their fluid and contingent nature is often disregarded by scholars. In order to better conceptualise and understand the construction of farm women's gender identities, we argue that the focus of conceptualisation should turn to cultural and sociohistorical influences on the way women's identities are formed (or re-formed) and activated through a process of self-categorisation within farming communities. In addition, the link between farm women's gender identities and their social identities (a term which refers to an individual's definition and sense of self arising from his or her identification with different social groups) is still unclear. Moreover, since a woman's position in the family determines both her gender and social identity, the way gender identity is developed within the farm family remains to be uncovered.

On the whole, we conclude that in order to better depict the intersections between gender and farming we need to compare women's (or men's) actual situation with a reference standard. Hence, we propose a 'relativity hypothesis', according to which neither a farm woman's position within her family, community and farm operation, nor her gender identity, can be fully understood without considering how these parameters have been changed over time or without evaluating the corresponding position or identity of men farmers within a given society. Moreover, one cannot draw safe conclusions on the current social status of women farmers without comparing it with their prior status or the corresponding status of male farmers, other (non-farmer) rural women, urban women or women from other regions or countries.

For example, comparing attitudes and behaviour towards gender roles of men and women from urban, rural and farm settings, Černič Istenič (2007) demonstrated that farm women's occupational choices are significantly determined by the fact that they live on a farm. In this vein, it is expected that similar comparative research can contribute to uncovering some new aspects of the intersection of gender and farming, and can provide deeper insight into cause–effect relationships between social and cultural contexts as catalysts of gender in farming. Since the fruitfulness of comparative research using different theoretical frameworks in gender rural studies is demonstrated elsewhere (e.g., Bock & Shortall, 2006; Asztalos Morell & Bock, 2008), the future research on gender and farming should build on this approach.

Of course, the dominance of qualitative methods in the field of rural gender studies and the lack of well-validated quantitative instruments which permit comparisons across different sociocultural contexts and across time complicate any attempts at cross-regional or longitudinal research designs. In addition, the application of retrospective considerations of women's role in agriculture could offer an alternative view on these issues. For example, Richardson (2014) provided a 150-year historical overview of women's status in Welsh agriculture, while other studies used autobiographical memories of Greek women farmers to examine life and gender role transitions over a period of 60 years (Charatsari 2013, 2014). Inhetveen (1990) argues that such biographical research approaches can offer a wealth of information on women farmers' changing status.

Moreover, apart from the need for more longitudinal and comparative research designs, there is also a need for a more active incorporation of new concepts and a focus on less researched groups within the study of the intersections of farming and gender. So far, (heterosexual) farm women have received the lion's share of attention by researchers, followed by (heterosexual) farm men. Concerning other sub-groups, rural LGB literature shows a growing trend; however, cohorts such as disabled or elder farmers have attracted only minor research interest. Finally, in order to better depict gender negotiation in farm (and/or rural) spaces, it will be important for future research to incorporate concepts related not only to the social but also to the psychological precursors of gender identities and gender-related behaviours.

References

Allen, P & Sachs, C (2007). Women and food chains: The gendered politics of food. *International Journal of Sociology of Agriculture and Food* 15(1), 1–23.

Alston, M (2012). Rural male suicide in Australia. *Social Science and Medicine* 74(4), 515–522.

Alston, M & Kent, J (2008). The Big Dry: The link between rural masculinities and poor health outcomes for farming men. *Journal of Sociology* 44(2), 133–147.

Asztalos Morell, I & Bock, BB (2008). Rural gender regimes: The development of rural gender research and design of comparative approach. In I Asztalos Morell & BB Bock (Eds), *Gender regimes, citizen participation and rural restructuring* (pp. 3–30). Research in Rural Sociology and Development, Vol. 13. Oxford: Elsevier.

Ball, JA (2014). She works hard for the money: Women in Kansas agriculture. *Agriculture and Human Values* 31(4), 593–605.

Barlett, PF & Conger, KJ (2004). Three visions of masculine success on American farms. *Men and Masculinities* 2, 205–227.

Beach, SS (2013). 'Tractorettes' or partners? Farmers' views on women in Kansas farming households. *Rural Sociology*, 78(2), 210–228.

Bell, D & Valentine, G (1995). Queer country: Rural lesbian and gay lives. *Journal of Rural Studies* 11(2), 113–122.

Benjamin, C & Kimhi, A (2006). Farm work, off-farm work, and hired farm labour: Estimating a discrete-choice model of French farm couples' labour decisions. *European Review of Agricultural Economics* 33(2), 149–171.

Berry, AA, Katras, MJ, Sano, Y, Lee, J & Bauer, JW (2008). Job volatility of rural, low-income mothers: A mixed methods approach. *Journal of Family and Economic Issues* 29(1), 5–22.

Bharadwaj, L, Findeis, JL & Chintawar, S (2013). Motivations to work off-farm among US farm women. *The Journal of Socio-Economics* 45, 71–77.

Bjørkhaug, H & Blekesaune, A (2008). Gender and work in Norwegian family farm businesses. *Sociologia Ruralis* 48(2), 152–165.

Bock, B (2015). Gender mainstreaming and rural development policy: The trivialisation of rural gender issues. *Gender, Place & Culture* 22(5), 731–745.

Bock, BB & Derkzen, P (2008). Barriers to women's participation in rural policy making. In I Asztalos Morell & BB Bock (Eds), *Gender regimes, citizen participation and rural restructuring* (pp. 263–281). Research in Rural Sociology and Development, Vol. 13. Oxford: Elsevier.

Bock BB & Shortall, S (Eds). (2006). *Rural gender relations: Issues and case-studies* Oxford: CABI.

Booth, NJ & Lloyd, K (2000). Stress in farmers. *International Journal of Social Psychiatry* 46(1), 67–73.

Bourguignon, D, Seron, E, Yzerbyt, V & Herman, G (2006). Perceived group and personal discrimination: Differential effects on personal self-esteem. *European Journal of Social Psychology* 36(5), 773–789.

Brandth, B (1995). Rural masculinity in transition: Gender images in tractor advertisements. *Journal of Rural Studies* 11(2), 123–133.

Brandth, B (2006). Embodying family farm work. In BB Bock & S Shortall (Eds), *Rural gender relations: Issues and case studies* (pp. 329–344). Oxford: CABI.

Bronstein, P (2006). The family environment: Where gender role socialization begins. In J Worell & CD Goodheart (Eds), *Handbook of girls' and women's psychological health: Gender and well-being across the lifespan* (pp. 262–271). New York: Oxford University Press.

Bryant, L & Garnham, B (2015). The fallen hero: Masculinity, shame and farmer suicide in Australia. *Gender, Place and Culture* 22(1), 67–82.

Bryant, L & Pini, B (2011). *Gender and rurality*. New York: Routledge.

Bussey, K & Bandura, A (1999). Social cognitive theory of gender development and differentiation. *Psychological Review* 106(4), 676–713.

Cameron, JE & Lalonde, RN (2001). Social identification and gender-related ideology in women and men. *British Journal of Social Psychology* 40(1), 59–77.

Carrington, K, McIntosh, A, Hogg, R & Scott, J (2013). Rural masculinities and the internalisation of violence in agricultural communities. *International Journal of Rural Criminology* 2(1), 3–24.

Černič Istenič, M (2007). Attitudes towards gender roles and gender role behaviour among urban, rural, and farm populations in Slovenia. *Journal of Comparative Family Studies* 3(37), 477–496.

Černič Istenič, M (2015). Do rural development programmes promote gender equality on farms? The case of Slovenia. *Gender, Place and Culture* 22(5), 670–684.

Charatsari, C (2013). Woman's position in rural society from 1950 onwards: A study based on women's autobiographical memories. Thesis, Aristotle University, Thessaloniki.

Charatsari, C (2014). Is this a man's world? Woman in the farm family of Thessaly, Greece from the 1950s onwards. *Gender Issues* 31(3–4), 238–266.

Charatsari, C, Černič Istenič, M & Lioutas, ED (2013). 'I'd like to participate, but …': Women farmers' scepticism towards agricultural extension/education programmes. *Development in Practice* 23(4), 489–502.

Coldwell, I (2007). New farming masculinities 'More than just shit-kickers', we're 'switched-on' farmers wanting to 'balance lifestyle, sustainability and coin'. *Journal of Sociology* 43(1), 87–103.

Costa, P, Terracciano, A & McCrae, RR (2001). Gender differences in personality traits across cultures: Robust and surprising findings. *Journal of Personality and Social Psychology* 81(2), 322–331.

Courtenay, WH (2000). Constructions of masculinity and their influence on men's well-being: A theory of gender and health. *Social Science and Medicine* 50(10), 1385–1401.

Deaux, K & Major, B (1987). Putting gender into context: An interactive model of gender-related behavior. *Psychological Review* 94(3), 369–389.

Doyle, DM & Molix, L (2014). Perceived discrimination and well-being in gay men: The protective role of behavioural identification. *Psychology and Sexuality* 5(2), 117–130.

Dufour, A, Courdin, V & Dedieu, B (2010). Femmes et travail en couple: pratiques et représentations en élevage laitier en Uruguay et en France. *Cahiers Agricultures* 19(5), 371–376.

Eldridge, VL, Mack, L & Swank, E (2006). Explaining comfort with homosexuality in rural America. *Journal of Homosexuality* 51(2), 39–56.

Fellows, W (1998). *Farm boys: Lives of gay men from the rural Midwest*. Wisconsin: University of Wisconsin Press.

Ferrell, AK (2012). Doing masculinity: Gendered challenges to replacing burley tobacco in central Kentucky. *Agriculture and Human Values* 29(2), 137–149.

Fortmann, L (1981). The plight of the invisible farmer: The effect of national agricultural policy of women in Africa. In R Dauber & ML Cain (Eds), *Women and technological change in developing countries* (pp. 205–214). Boulder, CO: Westview.

Franklin, AJ & Boyd-Franklin, N (2000). Invisibility syndrome: A clinical model of the effects of racism on African-American males. *American Journal of Orthopsychiatry* 70(1), 33–41.

Fraser, CE, Smith, KB, Judd, F, Humphreys, JS, Fragar, LJ & Henderson, A (2005). Farming and mental health problems and mental illness. *International Journal of Social Psychiatry* 51(4), 340–349.

Gallagher, E & Delworth, U (1993). The third shift: Juggling employment, family, and the farm. *Journal of Rural Community Psychology* 12(2), 21–36.

Garnham, B & Bryant, L (2014). Problematising the suicides of older male farmers: Subjective, social and cultural considerations. *Sociologia Ruralis* 54(2), 227–240.

Gerson, JM & Peiss, K (1985). Boundaries, negotiation, consciousness: Reconceptualizing gender relations. *Social Problems* 32(4), 317–331.

Gidarakou, I, Kazakopoulos, L & Koutsouris, A (2008). Tracking empowerment and participation of young women farmers in Greece. *Research in Rural Sociology and Development* 13, 143–165.

Gregoire, A (2002). The mental health of farmers. *Occupational Medicine* 52(8), 471–476.

Gurin, P & Townsend, A (1986). Properties of gender identity and their implications for gender consciousness. *British Journal of Social Psychology* 25(2), 139–148.

Halim, ML & Ruble, D (2010). Gender identity and stereotyping in early and middle childhood. In JC Chrisler & DR McCreary (Eds), *Handbook of gender research in psychology* (pp. 495–525). Gender research in general and experimental psychology, Vol. 1. New York: Springer.

Harrell, WA (1986). Masculinity and farming-related accidents. *Sex Roles* 15(9–10), 467–478.

Haugen, MS & Blekesaune, A (2005). Farm and off-farm work and life satisfaction among Norwegian farm women. *Sociologia Ruralis* 45(1–2), 71–85.

Haugen, MS & Brandth, B (1994). Gender differences in modern agriculture: The case of female farmers in Norway. *Gender and Society* 8(2), 206–229.

Inhetveen, H (1990). Biographical approaches to research on women farmers. *Sociologia Ruralis* 30(1), 100–114.

Kazakopoulos, L & Gidarakou, I (2003). Young women farm heads in Greek agriculture: Entering farming through policy incentives. *Journal of Rural Studies* 19(4), 397–410.

Kazyak, E (2015). Midwest or lesbian? Gender, rurality, and sexuality. *Gender and Society*. doi: 10.1177/0891243212458361.

Keller, JC (2014). 'I wanna have my own damn dairy farm!': Women farmers, legibility, and femininities in rural Wisconsin, US. *Journal of Rural Social Sciences* 29(1), 75–102.

Kelly, R & Shortall, S (2002). 'Farmers' wives': Women who are off-farm breadwinners and the implications for on-farm gender relations. *Journal of Sociology* 38(4), 327–343.

Laoire, CN (2002). Young farmers, masculinities and change in rural Ireland. *Irish Geography* 3(1), 16–27.

Lee, MG & Quam, JK (2013). Comparing supports for LGBT aging in rural versus urban areas. *Journal of Gerontological Social Work* 56(2), 112–126.

Little, J (2003). 'Riding the rural love train': Heterosexuality and the rural community. *Sociologia Ruralis* 43(4), 401–417.

Little, J & Jones, O (2000). Masculinity, gender, and rural policy. *Rural Sociology* 65(4), 621–639.

O'Brien, DJ & Wegren, SK (2015). The underrepresentation of women in leadership positions in rural Russia. *Rural Sociology* 80(1), 86–107.

Oedl-Wieser, T (2008). The rural gender regime: The Austrian case. In I Asztalos Morell & BB Bock (Eds), *Gender regimes, citizen participation and rural restructuring* (pp. 283–297). Research in Rural Sociology and Development, Vol. 13. Oxford: Elsevier.

Oedl-Wieser, T (2015). Gender equality: A core dimension in Rural Development Programmes in Austria? *Gender, Place and Culture* 22(5), 685–699.

Otomo, Y & Oedl-Wieser, T (2009). Comparative analysis of patterns in farm succession in Austria and Japan from a gender perspective. *Jahrbuch der Österreichischen Gesellschaft für Agrarökonomie* 18(2), 79–92.

Person, ES & Ovesey, L (1983). Psychoanalytic theories of gender identity. *Journal of the American Academy of Psychoanalysis* 11(2), 203–226.

Peter, G, Bell, MM, Jarnagin, S & Bauer, D (2000). Coming back across the fence: Masculinity and the transition to sustainable agriculture. *Rural Sociology* 65(2), 215–233.

Pilgeram, R (2007). 'Ass-kicking' women: Doing and undoing gender in a US livestock auction. *Gender, Work and Organization* 14(6), 572–595.

Pini, B (2002). The exclusion of women from agri-political leadership: A case study of the Australian sugar industry. *Sociologia Ruralis* 42(1), 65–76.

Pini, B (2005a). Farm women: Driving tractors and negotiating gender. *International Journal of Sociology of Agriculture and Food* 13(1), 1–12.

Pini, B (2005b). The third sex: Women leaders in Australian agriculture. *Gender, Work and Organization* 12(1), 73–88.

Pini, B (2006). A critique of 'new' rural local governance: The case of gender in a rural Australian setting. *Journal of Rural Studies* 22(4), 396–408.

Price, L (2010). 'Doing it with men': Feminist research practice and patriarchal inheritance practices in Welsh family farming. *Gender, Place and Culture* 17(1), 81–97.

Price, L (2012). The emergence of rural support organisations in the UK and Canada: Providing support for patrilineal family farming. *Sociologia Ruralis* 52(3), 353–376.

Rayens, MK & Reed, DB (2014). Predictors of depressive symptoms in older rural couples: The impact of work, stress and health. *The Journal of Rural Health* 30(1), 59–68.

Richardson, F (2014). Women farmers of Snowdonia, 1750–1900. *Rural History* 25(2), 161–181.

Riley, M (2012). 'Moving on'? Exploring the geographies of retirement adjustment amongst farming couples. *Social and Cultural Geography* 13(7), 759–781.

Sachs, CE (1983). *The invisible farmer: Women in agricultural production.* Totowa: Rowman & Allanheld.

Saugeres, L (2002a). Of tractors and men: Masculinity, technology and power in a French farming community. *Sociologia Ruralis* 42(2), 143–159.

Saugeres, L (2002b). The cultural representation of the farming landscape: Masculinity, power and nature. *Journal of Rural Studies* 18(4), 373–384.

Sheridan, A, McKenzie, FH & Still, L (2011). Making visible the 'space of betweenness': Understanding women's limited access to leadership in regional Australia. *Gender, Place and Culture* 18(6), 732–748.

Shortall, S. (1996). Training to be farmers or wives? Agricultural training for women in Northern Ireland. *Sociologia Ruralis* 36(3), 269–285.

Shortall, S (2001). Women in the field: Women, farming and organizations. *Gender, Work and Organization* 8(2), 164–181.

Shortall, S (2006). Gender and farming: An overview. In BB Bock & S Shortall (Eds), *Rural gender relations: Issues and case studies* (pp. 19–26). Oxford: CABI.

Shortall, S (2014). Farming, identity and well-being: Managing changing gender roles within Western European farm families. *Anthropological Notebooks* 20(3), 67–81.

Shortall, S. (2015). Gender mainstreaming and the Common Agricultural Policy. *Gender, Place and Culture* 22(5), 717–730.

Silvasti, T (2003). Bending borders of gendered labour division on farms: The case of Finland. *Sociologia Ruralis* 43(2), 154–166.

Spence, JT (1985). Gender identity and its implications for concepts of masculinity and femininity. In T Sondregger (Ed.), *Nebraska symposium on motivation* (pp. 59–95). Lincoln: University of Nebraska Press.

Stoller, RJ (1964). A contribution to the study of gender identity. *The International Journal of Psychoanalysis* 45(2–3), 220–226.

Swim, JK, Aikin, KJ, Hall, WS & Hunter, BA (1995). Sexism and racism: Old-fashioned and modern prejudices. *Journal of Personality and Social Psychology* 68(2), 199–214.

Tutor-Marcom, R, Bruce, J & Greer, A (2014). North Carolina farm women: Opportunities for support and farm-related education. *Journal of Agromedicine* 19(2), 191–200.

Twenge, JM (1997). Changes in masculine and feminine traits over time: A meta-analysis. *Sex Roles* 36(5–6), 305–325.

Tyson, P (1986). Male gender identity: Early developmental roots. *Psychoanalytic Review* 73(4), 405–425.

Voyce, M (2014). Family provision, the family farm and rural patriarchy: Three actors in search of a play? *Deakin Law Review* 19(2), 349–372.

Wegren, SK, Nikulin, A, Trotsuk, I, Golovina, S & Pugacheva, M (2015). Gender inequality in Russia's rural formal economy. *Post-Soviet Affairs* 31(5), 367–396.

Zhang, X, Zhao, W, Jing, R, Wheeler, K, Smith, GA, Stallones, L & Xiang, H (2011). Work-related pesticide poisoning among farmers in two villages of Southern China: A cross-sectional survey. *BMC Public Health* 11(1), article number 429.

34

Gender and Identity Formation

Sally Shortall

Introduction

Gender and identity formation is a central question in rural studies. Much of the literature has focused on gender roles in agriculture. Farming is an occupation that has continued to be shaped by differential gender relations in most of the Western world despite far-reaching changes in gender roles in the last century. It is a persistent social pattern that farmers are predominantly men. More recently, scholarship has turned to consider whether living in rural areas shapes gender identity. In this chapter, this body of work on agriculture and rural areas more generally will be reviewed.

The literature on identity is vast and spans a number of disciplines. Identity has been at the heart of most sociology; it is the basis of Goffman's (1959) ideas about presentation of self and symbolic interactionism, and Becker's (1963) work on labelling theory and how it shapes social interaction based on perceived identities. Although there are some exceptions (see, for instance, Brandth, 2002; Bock, 2006; Brasier et al., 2014; Shortall, 2014a), research on gender and identity in rural studies does not directly refer back to this more general literature. Explicating and elaborating these links is, however, important to assess what has been done and identify which important questions still need to be considered. This chapter therefore begins with an overview of the sociology of identity literature which informs rural studies of gender identity. As Hall (1996) notes, while there has been an explosion in research on identity, it has also been subject to a searching critique. Identity studies mirror all of the usual debates and dilemmas in sociological research: the relationship between structure and agency, the role of social interaction, the importance of power and the construction of social narratives. All of these questions are reflected in debates on gender and identity in rural studies and are used to organise the review of rural gender identity research.

After the general overview on identity theory, the ways in which it has been used in rural studies to understand gender and identity is reviewed. First, institutional means of creating gender identities are examined, focusing on agriculture and work. Early feminist scholars tried to move beyond these structurally created gender identities to examine the unaccounted farm work women were doing. Following this section is one which examines how men and women 'do' gender and perform gender identities when changes in on- and off-farm work patterns occur. Next, I consider the way in which symbolic interactionism is used to shape gender appropriate space, focusing on agricultural training, the outdoors and farming organisations. Finally, the literature examining the interaction between rurality and gendered identities is considered. Throughout the chapter, it is clear that gendered identities are embedded in institutions and performed by individuals. There is evidence of persistence and change. The discourse of organisations and individuals displays and creates gendered identities. In the concluding discussion section, I consider some research questions that need attention as we go forward with our scholarship on gender and identity formation in rural studies.

The sociological importance of identity

Jenkins (2008, p. 1) puts it simply: many of us, much of the time, are able to take identity for granted. We know who we are, we know who the others in our lives are, and they appear to know us in the way we know ourselves. Identity is individual and collective. To function, we need shared common knowledge for social relations and social interaction. We need categories of people, and assumptions about collective identities (Cerulo, 1997; Ridgeway, 2009). While this is necessary to manage social interaction, it also leads to debates that question the essentialism of collective attributes and identities (Cerulo, 1997; MacInnes, 2004). Foucault (1975) disputed this idea of an inner essence and argued instead that our identity is constructed through discourse, and some people have more power than others to construct their discourse and make it the dominant one. Power relations and gender identities are constructed through spoken interaction (Baxter, 2003). Like gender, identity formation is a process of 'doing'. Identity is a continuous process rather than a trait of an individual and it is verified or questioned through social relations and social interaction (Burke, 1991; Burke & Harrod, 2005; Stets & Burke, 2005; Jenkins, 2008). While identity is continuously constructed through social interaction, a personal sense of coherence over time is essential to well-being (MacInnes, 2004; Shortall, 2014a). There are many types of research on identity. Here I will focus on two key strands that best illuminate gender and identity formation in rural studies. The first strand focuses on the linkages of social structures with identities, and examines the importance of symbolic interaction in this process (Stryker, 1968, 1973, 1980; Turner, 2013). Here people have particular roles in social structures, and identity is formed around these roles. Social interaction symbolically reinforces the identity of people in their roles. West and Zimmerman (1987, 2009) famously referred to it as 'doing gender'. People 'do' gender through social interaction in particular situations. This interactional process is related to but also distinct from institutional constructions of gender. They argue that conversation and discourse analysis is an excellent methodology to examine the performance of gender through social interaction. The other key strand focuses on internal processes of self-verification (Burke, 1991, 2015; Burke & Harrod, 2005; Stets & Burke, 2005). When the signs and symbols in any situation reinforce identity, identity is then confirmed and positive emotions result. However, when our identity is threatened, it leads to negative feelings and distress (Burke, 1991; Burke & Harrod, 2005; Stets & Burke, 2005; Jenkins, 2008). Identity loss threatens the continuity of our sense of self. Burke (1991, p. 841) describes it as 'the broken loop'. This occurs when our sense of self is not verified by those with whom we socially interact. The impact of non-identity verification depends on who it is. Greater distress is caused when the source of the feedback is a significant other. Spouses are highly significant sources of identity verification. Families are also crucial sources of identity verification. They have an archival function, and retain symbols of events and performances relevant to each member's identity (Weigert & Hastings, 1977; Shortall, 2014a).

Ridgeway (2009) argues that gender is one of the primary frames used to transmit information. She argues that gender as a primary frame is a belief system that privileges men over women, and means that men have an interest in enacting and maintaining that system. Gender as a primary frame interacts and shapes social relations in institutional frames, such as the family and workplace. Ridgeway (2009) considers how change occurs and notes that it can be a slow and gradual process. People tend to reinterpret the meaning of change through the lens of their existing more conservative gender beliefs (p. 157). Schneider (2012) argues that when men and women deviate from normative expectations about gender in one area of social life, they may seek to neutralise or compensate for this deviance in another sphere of social interaction. While he does not specifically discuss identity, his basic argument is that gender identity can be done and undone in different identity spheres. He further argues that threats to masculinity are more 'severe' in terms of their impact on men than threats to femininity are for women. Engagement in gender-atypical occupations is a less serious threat to women's gender identity than men's (p. 1066).

This brief overview of the literature on the sociology of identity will help inform scholarship going forward. It also allows a coherent interpretation of the wealth of research on gender and identity formation in rural studies, to which we now turn.

Institutionally embedded gender identities: agriculture and farm work

A considerable amount of early literature has considered the peculiarities of the occupation of farming, and how social practices shape gender identities. A persistent social pattern across most of Western society is that, in the main, men inherit farms. Much early research on farm families did not explicitly discuss gender, but the characteristics of gendered identities can easily be extracted (Brandth, 2002). This research was trying to make visible the world of women within the family farm (Gasson, 1980; Bartlett, 1983; Sachs, 1983; Haugen, 1990; Shortall, 1991, 1992, 1999; Whatmore, 1991; Alston, 1995, 1998; O'Hara, 1998; Overbeek, Efstatouglou, Haugen & Saraceno, 1998; Brandth, 2002; Pini, 2002; Silvasti, 2003; Černič Istenič, 2006). Research considered how men's identity as farmers is tied to their land ownership. Their role identity as farmer comes from owning the means of production. They occupy the occupational position of 'farmer' and they are seen to do the productive agricultural work. This was a prestigious occupation (Hannan & Commins, 1992) and defined the man's identity as head of the farm and the family. Women's identity on the farm was strongly tied to their marital status and much early research refers to 'farmers' wives' – underlining women's identity as spouse of the farmer. The institutional sphere embedded gender identities: agricultural statistics tended to report the activities of women as spouses. Early research sought to move beyond the dominant structural understanding of gender identities and make visible the gendered definitions of farm labour and farming, and in this way illuminate women's work on the farm, and indeed the importance of their work role to their identity. These studies considered women's participation in decision making, the types of work they undertook and the tasks performed, and noted that considerable amounts of this work was not recorded in official statistics. Women's work was private, unpaid and not publicly recognised. Ridgeway (2009) argues that gender stereotypes are not just individual beliefs. They are culturally hegemonic beliefs because they become embedded in social structures such as the media, the law and taken-for-granted organisational practices. This is very clear for the hegemonic beliefs about gendered farming identities. Men predominantly continue to inherit land, despite national variations in how the legal transfer of agricultural land is regulated (Shortall, 2010). Agricultural media mainly feature men and extension training services are still predominantly oriented towards men (Trauger et al., 2008, 2010; McGowan, 2011). On the one hand, gendered identities around farming and farm work have remained stubbornly in place. On the other hand, the increased on-farm and off-farm employment of farm women has meant a considerable change in their work status and identities. How this has led to renegotiation of gender identities is now considered.

'Doing' and performing gender: on-farm and off-farm work

Many farms, particularly in Europe, because of the funds available through the EU Rural Development Programme, have undertaken farm diversification activities. While the data available are vexingly poor, there are many national case studies that show that women are active in farm diversification activities (Bock, 2004, 2010; Gorman, 2006; Brandth & Haugen, 2010, 2011). Interestingly, the way in which farm diversification develops often reinforces gender identities on the farm. Bock (2004) argues that women undertake smaller scale diversification activities. This is reflective of their more restricted access to capital, but also to their desire to fit diversification activities around their other caring commitments and their wish to multi-task other domestic gender identity roles. Research has shown instances of men and women performing gender to reinforce traditional gender identities in the face of change. Brandth and Haugen (2010, 2011) argue that when farming couples diversify into tourism activities, gender and work identities are done and undone in ways that can reinforce traditional understandings of masculine and feminine areas of work. Men become responsible for outdoor activities, women for indoor activities. Spouses praise each other for their prowess in their particular gender sphere, for doing gender distinctive work well, thus engaging in positive identity reification. The authors also note that many tourists come expecting these types of gender roles and identities, recognising them as symbolic of authentic farming life. Their recreation and maintenance, then, becomes a component of the farm tourism business.

Women's off-farm employment has changed significantly in recent decades due to increased educational levels and labour market participation for women generally and to the lifting of a marriage bar preventing women working after marriage that was in place in many parts of the Western world until the 1960s and 1970s. Brandth (2002) argues that with the increase in off-farm work, one would have expected new identities to emerge in a way which did not happen. It moves women's employment into the public sphere, and in many instances women are often the primary breadwinner, or at least significantly contribute to the survival of the farm (Moss, Jack, Wallace & McErlean, 2000; Kelly & Shortall, 2002; Shortall, 2014a). Kelly and Shortall (2002) argue that farm women's increased resources from off-farm work do not contribute to significant renegotiation of domestic responsibilities and gender role expectations. They say that much of the literature on income and gender identities presumes that people behave as maximising individuals. Farm households, however, require analysis at the level of the household to explore what off-farm employment by women means for gender role expectations and the division of labour within the farm family. The farm household behaves as a collective and tries to ensure the well-being of family members by verifying key identities (Wheelock & Oughton, 1996). Shortall (2014a) has argued that despite their elevated economic status as breadwinner, women on farms continue to do gender identities such that they reinforce men's work identity as a farmer, as the decision maker, and in this way reinforce his masculinity. Here we see the interactional construction of gender identity as defined by West and Zimmerman (1987). The changed economic and status position of farming means then men's work and gender identity is threatened. Women engage in identity verification for the well-being of their spouses. Other research has focused on the detrimental effect on men's health and well-being when their identity as the breadwinner and farming head of household is threatened. Schneider (2012, p. 1033) maintains that the construct of the male breadwinner has proved to be exceptionally durable and continues to structure the expectation that men will be the primary earners in married couples and that masculinity is produced in part through fulfilling that expectation. This seems to be particularly the case for men on farms, whose identity is not only linked to their position as the breadwinner, but also to the power and privilege that has been associated with being a landowner. When the economic and social standing of their position is threatened, it has significant implications for men's mental health (Ní Laoire, 2002; Alston, 2006, 2012; Barlett, 2006; Alston & Kent, 2008; Price & Evans, 2009).

Socially constructed gender appropriate space

Space is gendered. This, of course, has a cultural and temporal context; some cultures and religions have more gendered space than others, and in general, the rigidities of gendered space have dissipated. This is true for rural areas as well as urban areas. Nonetheless, rural space continues to be used to signify and maintain distinctive gender identities. The outdoors is coded as masculine, while indoor activities are coded as feminine (Campbell & Bell, 2000; Little & Panelli, 2003; Pini, 2004; Campbell, Bell & Finney, 2006; Brandth & Haugen, 2010, 2014; Little, 2014). In the outdoors, men undertake hard, physical and sometimes dangerous work such as handling heavy machinery, being foresters and dealing with chemicals. The tractor, for example, is argued to have become a symbol of male power and spatial domination by men of the outdoors. Men have appropriated agricultural technology to underline their identity as farmers (Brandth & Haugen, 1998; Saugeres, 2002; Pini, 2005). Specific activities such as hunting and mining are seen as outdoor male activities (Campbell & Bell, 2000). Women who breach this male space and work with heavy machinery often seek other ways to reconfirm their feminine identity (Brandth, 1994). Women's indoor work is predominantly seen as domestic or as socially reproductive work. It is seen as sustaining the household (Whatmore, 1991; Trauger et al., 2010). This significantly contributes to the invisibility of components of women's work such as management of accounts, and decision making, because the indoor nature of this work means it is not seen as authentic farm work and thus reduces women's identity as farm workers or tourism managers (Sachs, 1983; Alston, 1995; Bock & Shortall, 2006).

Further gender-segregated space is evident in the provision of agricultural training. Most agricultural training is structured in a vocational way for those that will enter the occupation, so in many ways it is not surprising that most agricultural programmes have a majority of male students. However, the socially constructed identities of women as home makers and farmers' wives means that they do not obtain a knowledge transfer appropriate to their farming roles. Women farmers are under-served in agricultural education and technical assistance (Shortall, 1996; Alston, 1998; Liepins & Schick, 1998; Trauger et al., 2008). Women often view training groups and programmes as being for men and feel unwelcome and conspicuous in this space. Agriculture extension workers do not always see women as 'authentic' farmers, because they do not occupy outdoor space, and the extension workers hence do not invite them to training initiatives or address programmes to their work (Teather, 1994; Barbercheck et al., 2009; Trauger et al., 2010). Here we see women's self-verification of not being the farmer being institutionally reinforced by agricultural extension workers. It is remarkable that this gender-divided space persists. It is problematic because, increasingly, off-farm employment to support the farm is decided between the couple, and educational levels and life cycle issues determine who will work on the farm and who will work off the farm (Benjamin & Kimhi, 2006; El-Osta, Mishra & Morehart, 2008). Seeing men as the authentic farmer means the relevant person on the farm may not receive appropriate training. For decades now, research has shown that agricultural extension workers often do not see the implicit gender barriers to women's participation, and instead claim that agricultural training is open to everyone (Shortall, 1999; Trauger et al., 2010). In some instances, where the exclusive gendered space of agricultural training has been recognised, agricultural advisers have established provisions specifically targeted at women (Sachs, 1988; Shortall, 1996). In these instances, there is sometimes an exact reproduction of what is provided to the men's groups, and additional provisions that deal with women's caring roles, such as safety of children on farms. Women appreciate the opportunity to avail themselves of this training where it is provided, and state that it legitimates the knowledge they have obtained experientially. The social construction of a specific space for women's education and training is double-edge. It reinforces the social unacceptability of women attending mainstream training and underlines their identity distinctive to that of male farmers. Here we see in action how some people have more power than others to construct their discourse and make it the dominant one: men's agricultural training groups do not have to state their gender; it is implicitly understood that the farming identity is owned by men.

Similar to education initiatives for women, women's organisations occupy a shared space based on a collective identity. It is interesting to consider the many varied ways in which women's farming organisations emerge. In some cases farm women's organisations have developed organically, such as the Canadian Farm Women's Movement and Norwegian Women in Forestry (Shortall, 1994; Teather, 1994; Brandth, Follo & Haugen, 2014; Leach, 2014), or as a combination of a bottom-up response to state funding as in Australia (Panelli & Pini, 2005), or as a top-down initiative as in Northern Ireland (Shortall, 1996), or as a partnership between women, extension workers and a university as in Pennsylvania (Trauger et al., 2008). The strength of the identity of the group, depending on whether it is self-formed or whether it is established by people outside of the group, is disputed; Jenkins (2008) suggests that membership of a group is sufficient to develop a particular identity and collective sense of belonging to the group. Once again, the gender is always stated in women's groups: Women in Forestry, North Antrim Farm Ladies Group or Pennsylvania Women's Agricultural Network. The gendered identity of women has to be stated in the title because they are invisible in the mainstream norm. A number of theoretical explanations of this exercise of power have been offered in rural studies. It has been described as 'the third face of power': gender and power relations are so shaped by the structure of agriculture that those involved do not see them anymore (Shortall, 1992, 1999). Others have used Bourdieu's concept of *habitus* to describe the same powerful way in which the institution of farming is understood as masculine and embodying male work, rendering women invisible (Shucksmith, 1993).

Rural and gendered identity

Most literature on rural gender identities – and this is true for rural masculinities studies too – have focused on gender identities related to rural occupations and the associated social structures: farming, farm families, farming organisations, forestry, hunting, mining and fisheries. Some studies have also looked more generally to see if rural space shapes gendered identities or social patterns of behaviour (Bryant & Pini, 2011). While identity necessarily includes some understanding of similarity and difference (Jenkins, 2008), rural gendered identities lead to a double use of binaries: it compares rural men and rural women, and also compares rural men/women, with urban men/women. Some researchers have suggested that rural areas are generally more conservative than urban places and enforce and enact more rigid gender identities (Little & Panelli, 2003).

The European Rural Development Programme (RDP), established in the early 1990s, sought to provide support more generally to rural areas beyond agriculture. This is delivered through a number of measures, including one which established local action groups (LAGs) to deliver rural development at the local level. Given that land ownership is not necessary to participate in LAGs, there was speculation that this could lead to greater equality in rural areas, and many people have studied the gender roles and identities of those involved in the Rural

Development Programme (Little, 1994; Bock & Derkzen, 2008; Thuesen & Sørensen, 2009; Bock, 2010, 2015; Prugl, 2010; Černič Istenič, 2015; Oedl-Wieser, 2015). Invariably, the RDP did not generate equality. Research found that the RDP is adopted in ways that reflect existing gender inequalities. In other words, gendered identities, cultural norms and established patterns of practice shape how the programme is implemented, and the gendered identity of rural outdoor, visible space as masculine persists in this context. Women continue to be under-represented in monitoring boards and implementing bodies, and in the general design and implementation of initiatives. German research has suggested that the rural programme denies that gender is a problem, and gender divisions are reinforced through the way programmes are implemented (Prugl, 2010). A macro analysis of rural development programmes across the EU shows that women seldom participate in the formation of rural development plans or decision making on the distribution of funds (Bock, 2010, 2015). This research also shows the huge variation across Europe. Most projects that attempt to address gender inequality are fragmented attempts to solve some problems for some women. A coherent plan to address gender equality does not exist. There is a need for further research to understand the interaction of gender issues with rural development and rural decline (Little & Morris, 2005; Bock, 2010).

Some research has cautioned against using 'rural' as an explanatory variable. There is often an understanding of rural that is nostalgic, with a positive view of rural places (Brown & Cromartie, 2004; Shucksmith, 2012) and an attempt by rural elites to maintain this image of the rural idyll (Shucksmith, 2012). Nonetheless, the distinction between urban and rural is seen as less useful than it was in the era of industrialisation (Brown & Cromartie, 2004). Brown and Cromartie (and many others) are highly critical of traditional approaches that treat rural (and urban) as a single undifferentiated entity. Boundaries have become blurred, spatial flows are different, and people often live in one place and work in the other. Yet place matters for identity, and it also matters in shaping life chances. Place is still important to individual identity, and remains so, despite (or perhaps because of) increased travel, telecommunication and mobility (Savage, 2010; Shucksmith, 2012). Brown and Cromartie (2004) present it nicely: place does not have causal power, but it acts in a contingent manner. They note that education is positively related to income in all locations, but the strength of that relationship varies across labour markets depending on their industrial and occupational structure. Campbell and Bell (2000) cautioned researchers over using the term 'rural masculinities' to suggest there is a rural phenomenon separate to an urban one. Over-deterministic and singular images of femininity and masculinity have been constructed and reified (Little, 2014). Bock (2010) has argued that, in Europe, the situation of rural women varies considerably between and within member states and there is no evidence of a general rural disadvantage. Problems are experienced in peripheral rural regions and in Central and Eastern Europe relating to employment and services, but these relate to men as much as women. Equality varies across member states depending on cultural norms and values, but the cultural norms and values of a society impact on the constraints of identities for urban and rural people. Henderson and Hoggart (2003) acknowledge there are significant processes at play that limit the ability of women as a group to reach their full potential in the workplace. However, they take issue with 'the sentiment that drifts from the pages of the rural literature that the position of rural women is somehow special; that the forces of socialisation, opportunity and constraint in some way bear more heavily on women in rural areas than in cities' (Henderson & Hoggart, 2003, p. 371). Their research did not support such a view of rural gender relations. More recently, Shortall (2014b) has argued that there is an incentive for European-funded rural gender organisations, funded to address gender disadvantage to maintain an outdated understanding of the position of women in rural areas. She suggests that while it can be argued that it is important for rural women's lobby groups to engage in strategic essentialism to advance their political objectives, this runs the risk of creating static essentialism, which naturalises differences that may be historically variant and socially created. This question is returned to in the next section, which considers some future directions for research on identity formation.

Future directions for research

It is impossible to review all of the literature on gender and identity formation in rural studies, but this chapter gives a good flavour of the wealth of literature available. It examines structure and agency, choice, power constraints, essentialism, similarity and difference, discourse and social interaction, and how all of these social processes shape identity formation. All of the research reviewed illuminates various aspects of the mainstream theory of identity. It demonstrates the gendered identities institutionally embedded in farming organisations and rural structures. Discourse analysis provides an understanding of the power differentials in rural gendered identities. Interactional studies demonstrate the way in which people 'do' and perform genders. Now, some ideas to consider going forward are suggested.

While much of the literature acknowledges and discusses the iterative and interactive nature of identity formation, empirical research still has a tendency to focus on the identity formation processes for one group rather than the interactions between different identity groups and how the identities of one influence the identities of the others. Who decides which gendered identity takes precedence or which one is more important to protect? Do women perform particular gendered identities to protect men? This is a methodological and theoretical issue to consider. While this question related to identity, there is a more general insight that we could reflect on for rural studies. In our research we tend to either look at agriculture/farming or rural space/ rural population and not how the two are interrelated. It is the interaction between different groups within a rural space that creates particular identities and structures.

Another methodological issue to consider in the future is that much research on identity formation is based on small qualitative studies, dependent on in-depth interviews, participant observation and focus groups. In some respects, the nature of the question begs for a qualitative approach. Some consideration of the potential benefits of combining this research with quantitative analysis, and what a quantitative approach might bring, would be helpful. Henderson and Hoggart (2003) suggest that one of the reasons their findings are contrary to essentialised views of rural women's labour market participation is because they used census data to explore gender differences and spatial differences. Brasier et al. (2014) offer a very interesting quantitative analysis of gendered identities, and there is scope to further develop quantitative analyses in this area.

An issue that has been discussed for the last couple of decades but which remains unresolved is the lack of comparative data on gender issues across countries, particularly in the European Union (see Bock, 2010; Shortall, 2010). While many claims are made about the rate of gendered participation in rural development and community activities, little robust quantitative data exists. There is much more data about men in farming in general. The lack of comprehensive data on women in farming across the EU is disappointing. Information that is available tends to be case studies and national studies. Much more comprehensive data is necessary to allow for comparative research. It would be useful to be informed about the different ways in which the European Common Agricultural Policy (CAP) impacts on women spouses and women farmers, and how the CAP could be better tailored to meet their needs. Comparative analysis will allow a much more comprehensive examination of cultural differences in 'doing' gender and the different ways in which institutional frameworks embed gendered identities.

It is hard to escape binaries in the social sciences, and to some extent they are an important component of social analysis. However, they must be used with caution. As much of the scholarly work reviewed here notes, there is no such thing as a uniform rural femininity or rural masculinity. They intersect with many of the other social processes reviewed in this volume, such as class, ethnicity and national and cultural location.

Over 20 years ago, Whatmore, Marsden and Lowe (1994) noted that both *rural* and *gender* are socially constructed and dynamic. It is to be expected, then, that rural and gender identities, and how they intersect, will change over time. Further critical analysis of how we use notions of identity formation, and presumptions we make about the impact of rural on gender identity, would be very welcome. It is interesting here to consider Burawoy's (2013) reflections on his ethnographic fallacies. He reflects that he ignored the world, reified the world and homogenised the world. This came about because of a lack of theoretical reflection. Theoretical reflections on rural, gender and identity – how they interact, and how change has occurred – are central to our future research. I have argued that we need greater reflexivity about the assumptions we make about gendered identities (Shortall, 2013). Gender identities are socially constructed and performed. How they change over time is critical to our scholarship.

Finally, one of the strengths of rural studies is the interdisciplinary nature of the research which informs the subject. Gender and identity formation analysis is informed by historians, planners, geographers, sociologists, social workers, feminist studies and more. It is always useful and informative for scholars from other disciplines to read research situated within the theoretical literature of the discipline from which the author has emerged. This will contribute to the richness of our analysis, and lead to more informed interdisciplinary research in the future.

References

Alston, M (1995). *Women on the land: The hidden heart of Australia*. Australia: UNSW Press.

Alston, M (1998). Farm women and their work: Why is it not recognised? *Journal of Sociology* 34(1), 23–34.

Alston, M (2006). The gendered impact of drought. In BB Bock & S Shortall (Eds), *Rural gender relations: Issues and case studies* (pp. 204–220). Oxford: CABI.

Alston, M (2012). Rural male suicide in Australia. *Social Science and Medicine* 74(4), 515–522.

Alston, M & Kent, J (2008). The Big Dry: The link between rural masculinities and poor health outcomes for farming men. *Journal of Sociology* 44(2), 133–147.

Barbercheck, M, Brasier, K, Kiernan, N, Sachs, C, Trauger, J, Fiendeis, J & Moist, L (2009). Meeting the extension needs of women farmers. *Journal of Extension* 47(3), 1–11.

Barlett, P (2006). Three visions of masculine success on American farms. In H Campbell, M Bell & M Finney (Eds), *Country boys: Masculinity and rural life*. Pennsylvania: Pennsylvania State University Press.

Bartlett, P (1983). *American dreams, rural realities: Family farms in crisis*. Chapel Hill, NC: North Carolina Press.

Baxter, J (2003). Positioning gender in discourse: A feminist research methodology. Paper presented at the British Education Research Association Annual Conference, Heriot-Watt University, Edinburgh, 11–13 September.

Becker, H (1963). *Outsiders*. New York: Free Press.

Benjamin, C & Kimhi, A (2006). Farm work, off-farm work, and hired farm labour: Estimating a discrete-choice model of French farm couples' labour decisions. *European Review of Agricultural Economics* 33(2), 149–171.

Bock, B (2004). Fitting in and multi-tasking: Dutch farm women's strategies in rural entrepreneurship. *Sociologia Ruralis* 44(3), 245–260.

Bock, BB (2006). Rurality and gender identity: An overview. In BB Bock & S Shortall (Eds), *Rural gender relations: Issues and case studies* (pp. 279–287). Oxfordshire: CABI.

Bock, B (2010). European parliament 2010. Social situation of women in rural areas. Brussels: European Parliament. IP/B/AGRI/IC/2010_089.

Bock, B (2015). Gender mainstreaming and rural development policy: The trivialisation of rural gender issues. *Gender, Place & Culture* 22(5), 731–745.

Bock, BB & Derkzen, P (2008). Barriers to women's participation in rural policy making. In I Asztalos Morell & BB Bock (Eds), *Gender regimes, citizen participation and rural restructuring* (pp. 265–283). Elsevier: Rural Sociology and Development Series.

Bock, B & Shortall, S (Eds). (2006). *Rural gender relations: Issues and case studies*. London: CABI.

Brandth, B (1994). Changing femininity: The social construction of women farmers in Norway. *Sociologia Ruralis* 34(1), 27–49.

Brandth, B (2002). Gender identity in European family farming: A literature review. *Sociologia Ruralis* 42(3), 181–197.

Brandth, B & Haugen, M (1998). Breaking into a masculine discourse. Women and farm forestry. *Sociologia Ruralis* 38, 427–442.

Brandth, B & Haugen, M (2010). Doing farm tourism: The intertwining practices of gender and work. *Signs* 35(2), 425–446.

Brandth, B & Haugen, M (2011). Farm diversification into tourism – Implications for social identity? *Journal of Rural Studies* 27(1), 35–44.

Brandth, B, Follo, G & Haugen, M (2014). Paradoxes of a women's organisation in the forestry industry. In B Pini, B Brandth & L Little (Eds), *Feminisms and ruralities* (pp. 57–69). London: Lexington Books.

Brasier, K, Sachs, C, Kiernan, NE, Trauger, A & Barbercheck, M (2014). Capturing the multiple and shifting identities of farm women in the northeastern United States. *Rural Sociology* 79(3), 283–309.

Brown, D & Cromartie, J (2004). The nature of rurality in postindustrial society. In T Champion & G Hugo (Eds), *New forms of urbanization: Beyond the urban-rural* (pp. 269–283). Farnham: Ashgate.

Bryant, L & Pini, B (2011). *Gender and rurality*. Oxford: Routledge.

Burawoy, M (2013). Ethnographic fallacies: Reflections on labour studies in the era of market fundamentalism. *Work, Employment & Society* 27(3), 526–536.

Burke, P (1991). Identity processes and social stress. *American Sociological Review* 56, 836–849.

Burke, P (2015). Identity control theory. In G Ritzer (Ed.), *Blackwell encyclopaedia of sociology* (pp. 1–8). Oxford: Blackwell.

Burke, P & Harrod, M (2005). Too much of a good thing? *Social Psychology Quarterly* 68(4), 359–374.

Campbell, H & Bell, M (2000). The question of masculinities. *Rural Sociology* 65(4), 532–546.

Campbell, H, Bell, MM & Finney, M (Eds). (2006). *Country boys: Masculinity and rural life*. Pennsylvania: Pennsylvania State University Press.

Černič Istenič, M (2006). Farm women in Slovenia. In B Bock & S Shortall (Eds), *Rural gender relations: Issues and case studies* (pp. 63–96). Oxford: CABI.

Černič Istenič, M (2015). Do rural development programmes promote gender equality on farms? The case of Slovenia. *Gender, Place and Culture* 22(5), 670–684.

Cerulo, KA (1997). Identity construction: New issues, new directions. *Annual Review of Sociology* 23, 385–409.

El-Osta, H, Mishra, A & Morehart, M (2008). Off-farm labor participation decisions of married farm couples and the role of government payments. *Applied Economic Perspectives and Policy* 30(2), 311–332.

Foucault, M (1995). *Madness and civilization: A history of insanity in the age of reason*. London: Routledge.

Gasson, R (1980). Roles of farm women in England. *Sociologia Ruralis* 20, 165–180.

Goffman, E (1959). *The presentation of self in everyday life*. New York: The Overlook Press.

Gorman, M (2006). Gender relations and livelihood strategies. In B Bock & S Shortall (Eds), *Rural gender relations: Issues and case studies* (pp. 27–47). London: CAB International.

Hall, S (1996). Introduction: Who needs 'identity'? In S Hall, & P du Guy (Eds), *Questions of cultural identity* (pp. 1–17). London: Sage.

Hannan, D & Commins, P (1992). The significance of small-scale landholders in Ireland's socio-economic transformation. In J Goldthorpe & C Whelan (Eds), *The development of industrial society in Ireland* (pp. 79–104). Oxford: Oxford University Press.

Haugen, MS (1990). Female farmers in Norwegian agriculture. From traditional farm women to professional farmers. *Sociologia Ruralis* 30, 197–209.

Henderson, S & Hoggart, K (2003). Ruralities and gender divisions of labour in Eastern England. *Sociologia Ruralis* 43(4), 349–378.

Jenkins, R (2008). *Social identity* (3rd edn). Oxford: Routledge.

Kelly, R & Shortall, S (2002). 'Farmers' wives': Women who are off-farm breadwinners & the implications for on-farm gender relations. *Journal of Sociology* 38(4), 327–343.

Leach, B (2014). Feminist connections in and beyond the rural. In B Pini, B Brandth & L Little (Eds), *Feminisms and ruralities* (pp. 81–95). London: Lexington Books.

Liepins, R & Schick, R (1998). Gender and education: Towards a framework for a critical analysis of agricultural training. *Sociologia Ruralis* 38(3), 286–302.

Little, J (1994). Gender relations and the rural labour process. In S Whatmore, T Marsden & P Lowe (Eds), *Gender and rurality* (pp. 11–31). London: David Fulton Publishers.

Little, J (2014). The development of feminist perspectives in rural gender studies. In B Pini, B Brandth & L Little (Eds), *Feminisms and ruralities* (pp. 107–119). London: Lexington Books.

Little, J & Morris, C (2005). *Critical perspectives in rural gender studies.* Aldershot: Ashgate.

Little, J & Panelli, R (2003). Gender research in rural geography. *Gender, Place and Culture* 10(3), 281–289.

MacInnes, J (2004). The sociology of identity: Social science or social comment? *The British Journal of Sociology* 55(4), 531–543.

McGowan, C (2011). Women in agriculture. In D Pannell & F Vanclay (Eds), *Changing land management: Adoption of new practices by rural landowners* (pp. 141–153). Australia: CSIRO Publishing.

Moss, JE, Jack, CJ, Wallace, M & McErlean, SA (2000). Securing the future of small family farms: The off-farm solution. Paper presented at the European Rural Policy at the Crossroads, The Arkleton Research Centre, University of Aberdeen, 29 June to 1 July 2000.

Ní Laoire, C (2002). Young farmers, masculinities and change in rural Ireland. *Irish Geography* 35(1), 16–27.

Oedl-Wieser, T (2015). Gender equality? A core dimension in Rural Development Programmes in Austria? *Gender, Place & Culture* 22(5), 670–684.

O'Hara, P (1998). *Partners in production? Women, farm and family in Ireland.* New York: Berghahn.

Overbeek, G, Efstatouglou, S, Haugen, M & Saraceno, E (1998) *Labour situation and strategies of farm women in diversified rural areas of Europe.* Luxembourg: Office for Official Publications of the European Communities.

Panelli, R & Pini, B (2005). 'This beats a cake stall!': Farm women's shifting encounters with the Australian state. *Policy and Politics* 33(3), 489–503.

Pini, B (2002). Constraints to women's involvement in agricultural leadership. *Women in Management Review* 17(6), 276–284.

Pini, B (2004). Managerial masculinities in the Australian sugar industry. *Rural Society* 14(1), 22–35.

Pini, B (2005). Farm women: Driving tractors and negotiating gender. *International Journal of Sociology and Food* 13(1), 1–12.

Price, L & Evans, N (2009). From stress to distress: Conceptualizing the British family farming patriarchal way of life. *Journal of Rural Studies* 25(1), 1–11.

Prugl, E (2010). Feminism and the postmodern state: Gender mainstreaming in European rural development. *Signs* 35, 447–475.

Ridgeway, CL (2009). Framed before we know it: How gender shapes social relations. *Gender and Society* 23(2), 145–160.

Sachs, CE (1983). *The invisible farmers: Women in agricultural production.* Totowa, NJ: Rowman and Allanheld.

Sachs, C (1988). The participation of women and girls in market and non-market activities in Pennsylvania. In W Haney & J Knowles (Eds), *Women and farming: Changing roles, changing structures* (pp. 123–134). Boulder, CO: Westview.

Saugeres, L (2002). Of tractors and men: Masculinity, technology and power in a French farming community. *Sociologia Ruralis* 42(2), 143–159.

Savage, M (2010). *Identities and social change in Britain since 1940: The politics of method.* Oxford: Clarendon.

Schneider, D (2012). Gender deviance and household work: The role of occupations. *American Journal of Sociology* 117(4), 1029–1072.

Shortall, S (1991). The dearth of data on Irish farm wives: A critical review of the literature. *The Economic and Social Review* 22(4), 311–322.

Shortall, S (1992). Power analysis and farm wives – An empirical study of the power relationships affecting women on Irish farms. *Sociologia Ruralis* 32(4), 431–452.

Shortall, S (1994). Farm women's groups: Farming or feminist or community groups, or new social movements? *Sociology* 28(1), 279–292.

Shortall, S (1996). Training to be farmers or wives? Agricultural training for women in Northern Ireland. *Sociologia Ruralis* 36(3), 269–286.

Shortall, S (1999). *Gender and power – Women and farming.* London: Macmillan.

Shortall, S (2010). Women working on the farm: How to promote their contribution to the development of agriculture and rural areas in Europe. European Parliament, Brussels. IP/B/AGRI/IC/2010_090.

Shortall, S (2013). Does putting 'rural' in front of 'women' tell us anything? Paper presentation. XXIII Congress – European Society for Rural Sociology (Florence, Italy).

Shortall, S (2014a). Farming, identity and well-being: Managing changing gender roles within Western European farm families. *Anthropological Notebooks* 20(3), 67–81.

Shortall, S (2014b). A rural feminist perspective on gender mainstreaming: Can it work if it is blind to gendered spaces and gendered occupations? In B Pini, B Brandth & L Little (Eds), *Feminisms and ruralities* (pp. 69–81). London: Lexington Books.

Shucksmith, M (1993). Farm household behaviour and the transition to post-productivism. *Journal of Agricultural Economics* 44(3), 466–478.

Shucksmith, M (2012). Class, power and inequality in rural areas: Beyond social exclusion? *Sociologia Ruralis* 52(4), 377–397.

Silvasti, T (2003). Bending borders of gendered labour division on farms: The case of Finland. *Sociologia Ruralis* 43(2), 154–166.

Stets, J & Burke, P (2005). New directions in identity control theory. *Advances in Group Processes* 22, 43–64.

Stryker, S (1968). Identity salience and role performance: The relevance of symbolic interaction theory for family research. *Journal of Marriage and the Family* 30(4), 558–564.

Stryker, S (1973). Fundamental principles of social interaction in sociology. In Neil J. Smelser (Ed.), *Sociology* (2nd edn) (pp. 495–547). New York: Wiley.

Stryker, S (1980). *Symbolic interactionism: A structural version.* Menlo Park, CA: Benjamin/Cummings.

Teather, E (1994). Contesting rurality: Country women's social and political networks. In S Whatmore, T Marsden & P Lowe (Eds), *Gender and rurality* (pp. 31–50). London: David Fulton Publishers.

Thuesen, AA & Sørensen, JFL (2009). *Danish local action groups in rural and fishing areas 2008: Composition, activities and cooperation in the start-up phase.* Esbjerg: Danish Centre for Rural Research.

Trauger, A, Sachs, C, Barbercheck, M, Kiernan, N, Brasier, K & Findeis, J (2008). Agricultural education: Gender identity and knowledge exchange. *Journal of Rural Studies* 24(4), 432–439.

Trauger, A, Sachs, C, Barbercheck, M, Kiernan, N, Brasier, K & Schwartzberg, A (2010) The object of extension: Agricultural education and authentic farmers in Pennsylvania. *Sociologia Ruralis* 50(2), 85–103.

Turner, J (2013). *Contemporary social theory* (8th edn). Newbury Park: Sage.

Weigert, A & Hastings, R (1977). Identity, loss, family and social change. *American Journal of Sociology* 82(6), 1171–1185.

West, C & Zimmerman, D (1987). Doing gender. *Gender and Society* 1(2), 125–151.

West, C & Zimmerman, D (2009). Accounting for doing gender. *Gender and Society* 23(1), 112–122.

Whatmore, S (1991). *Farming women: Gender, work and family enterprise.* London: Macmillan.

Whatmore, S, Marsden, T & Lowe, P (1994). Introduction. In S Whatmore, T Marsden & P Lowe (Eds), *Gender and rurality* (pp. 1–11). London: David Fulton Publishers.

Wheelock, J & Oughton, E (1996). The household as a focus for research. *Journal of Economic Issues* 3(1), 143–159.

35

Rural Masculinity

Berit Brandth and Marit S. Haugen

Introduction

In the mid-1990s scholars began to examine the gendered character of rural men's lives and experiences. The study of men and masculinities grew out of feminist approaches to research on rural society and has over the years adapted to the changing theoretical orientation of gender studies in the social sciences more generally. In the two decades since the field emerged, studies of rural masculinity have produced a rich body of literature. As a result, there is an abundance of perspectives and topics to be explored.

Initially, the study of men and masculinities in rural societies started from the recognition that rural men have traditionally held power in relation to women because of their ownership of land and their position as heads of household who exercise authority over the allocation of family labour. Several authors (Sachs, 1983; Whatmore, 1991; Shortall, 1999) point to the significance of property relations, as women who 'marry in' to landowning families are structurally in a weaker position despite their responsibility for a significant share of productive labour and their centrality to the intergenerational reproduction of the farm. As this review will show, not all of the more recent literature proceeds from this recognition of fundamental gender inequality and men's position of relative privilege.

This chapter considers literature from across the social sciences. Major contributions to the study of rural masculinities have come from sociology and geography, particularly because space and place are central to rurality. Indeed, rurality is not uniform; different places shape the performance of masculinity and femininity differently. As Datta (2008, p. 202) has recognised, rurality is 'a fragmented collection of multiple places' that reinforce, transgress and redefine gender identities.

Previous reviews by Little (2002) and Cloke (2005) underlined the fundamental connections between rurality and masculinity. This relationship has been analysed through a distinction between 'the masculine in the rural' and 'the rural in the masculine' (Campbell & Bell, 2000, p. 540). The *masculine in the rural* refers to the ways in which masculinities are constituted in different kinds of rural spaces, while the *rural in the masculine* refers to the manner in which the rural symbolically constitutes ideas of masculinities regardless of location. While these distinctions are not mutually exclusive and often tend to collapse, discourses of rurality and masculinity feed off each other (Pini, 2008, p. 18).

Two earlier reviews (Brandth, 2002; Pini, 2008) emphasised gendered practices of agricultural work and their implications for rural masculinities. Pini's review demonstrates that scholars recognised the plurality of farming masculinities by exploring shifting farm technologies, sustainable farming practices, agricultural crises, the privileging of heterosexuality, and agricultural organisations. It offers a solid demonstration of the practices of farm-based masculinity and its multiple and shifting characteristics within a primary sector of the rural economy. Sociology and geography have both incorporated a cultural approach that emphasises subjectivity and identity and the discursive construction of masculinity, as well as a 'strategic approach' (Hopkins & Noble, 2009) that explores masculinities as performances in particular contexts. Brandth and Haugen (2014), for instance, analysed how farm tourist hosting implies gendered performances of the rural idyll to satisfy customers' expectations.

This review identifies key topics in the literature on rural masculinities. It aims to present a comprehensive review of the literature from the past decade, but it is impossible to do justice to all the theoretical approaches represented and empirical knowledge produced.

Theorising masculinity: change, variation and hegemony

Studies of rural masculinity have drawn inspiration from Connell's (1995) work. Her conceptual framework has three central dimensions. First, masculinity is dynamic and changes over time; no form of manliness remains fixed. When economic shifts transform rural communities, the construction of masculinities also changes. This understanding of gender as embedded in other social relations has meant that processes of change have received much attention.

Second, Connell theorises that masculinity has a diverse set of configurations. The meaning of masculinity varies across settings and spaces. Complexities, ambivalences and contradictions are central to its very definition. This approach is consistent with feminist theorising of gender difference that interprets femininities and masculinities as practices and discourses in different contexts and places, rather than as stable roles or identities. Rural masculinities have, for instance, been conceptualised by a distinction between monologic and dialogic masculinities (Peter, Bell, Jarnagin & Bauer, 2000). Monologic masculinity is tradition-bound and limited, while dialogic masculinity entails more openness and a broader understanding of what it is to be a man (p. 216).

The third dimension concerns power. While sharing the feminist recognition of the asymmetrical power involved in relations between women and men, Connell has also problematised power relations among men. The concept of 'hegemonic masculinity' (Connell, 1995; Connell & Messerschmidt, 2005) has been the single most utilised theoretical contribution to masculinity research in general. Hegemonic masculinity was initially conceptualised as the form of masculinity that structures hierarchical gender relations among men as well as between men and women. This relational concept has two dimensions: men's patriarchal domination over women, and the dominance of some masculinities over other, alternative or subordinated masculinities. Hegemonic masculinity has attracted a wide range of critiques. Scholars have, for instance, pointed out that it is problematic to include these two hierarchies in one unified concept or a single social-structural framework (Christensen & Jensen, 2014). They might not always work together, but rather act separately in some domains of life. To assume that the most legitimate form of masculinity in any society and at any point in time necessarily legitimates patriarchy is highly deterministic, when gender is dynamic and its actual formations are a subject for open, empirical investigation. Only some men exercise power both over women and over other men. Less powerful men may, however, still express many characteristics of hegemonic masculinity. Critics of notions of hegemonic masculinity have sought to expand this concept and connect it with individual experiences (Lusher & Robins, 2009).

This review examines how these three theoretical dimensions of masculinity have gained empirical attention in work on rural masculinities during the last decade. While change and variation are treated in separate sections, the issue of power is inherent in these two sections.

Rural masculinities: stability and change

A significant body of work has recognised that certain gendered practices and discourses are legitimised while others are marginalised. Hegemonic discourses of rural masculinity have originated from primary industries such as agriculture, forestry and fishing and emphasised physical strength, stamina and hard work. The domination of nature, which is imagined as wild, dangerous and hostile, and the mastery of demanding and dirty manual labour outdoors are important signifiers of manliness. Moreover, command of machinery and other forms of technical control have reinforced this hegemonic discourse. Indeed, the tractor has become so central to current understandings of agrarian masculinity (Brandth, 1995; Saugeres, 2002) that it seems to have been naturalised (Heggem, 2014). The tractor functions as a symbol of masculine power, as well as figuring in ideologies that exclude women from the performance of highly valued farm tasks. The obvious contradiction between earlier notions of manual labour and current levels of mechanisation, that makes brute brawn largely irrelevant to the performance of many farm tasks, cannot be ignored.

Liepins (1998; 2000) identified two prominent discourses of rural masculinities: 'strong men farm' and 'powerful men lead'. Pini's (2008) seminal study of managerial masculinities in agricultural organisations documents the paternalistic character of these groups, showing how members of the Australian Farmers' Union conflate discourses of farming and business management by referring to the need for the supposedly masculine qualities of 'aggression, toughness, tenacity and strength' (p. 120). Likewise, Brandth and Haugen (2000) found that managerial masculinity in a forestry organisation gains legitimacy from the men's experience as practical forestry workers. There is a mutual dependency between the 'tough' and the 'powerful' men, but they also compete for hegemony. Hegemony may persist by incorporating new elements. As Bye (2009) observed, it may be easier to add new elements than to remove older ones. In her study of young hunters in rural Norway, she found that men continued to express monologic characteristics while at the same time incorporating more emotional openness and family involvement.

Drivers of change

While this rich literature has confirmed the salience of discourses of hegemonic rural masculinity, it has also demonstrated processes of change. Three drivers of change are especially prominent in the scholarship: economic change and the transformation of rural industries; social change in rural communities; and changes in women's activities and positions in the economy and society.

When masculinities are defined primarily in terms of work-based characteristics, restructuring may challenge the established masculine order. The work that supports these masculinities may disappear or be replaced. It has, for example, been documented that shifting to organic farming creates space for more dialogic masculinities (Peter, Bell, Jarnagin & Bauer, 2000) and that changes in rural work regimes open up the possibility of more flexible masculinities. Ferrell's (2012) study of tobacco growers in Kentucky shows that growers are 'doing a particular locally valued masculinity at the same time as they do tobacco work'. Replacing tobacco with another crop, which they are urged to do, implies a change in masculinity, for their farming is strongly tied to 'tobacco as a crop, a craft, and a source of occupational identity' (p.147). Diversification may have similarly unsettling effects on masculinity. Farm tourism, for example, necessitates the incorporation of new elements, particularly emotional work. Farm men guiding visitors in the wilderness have to combine traditional attributes of masculinity, such as managing nature, with social skills associated more with service sector work (Brandth & Haugen, 2005a, 2010). In this way, a change in production may imply a gendered transition as well.

Moreover, researchers have found that technological changes in rural industries influence which masculine qualities are valued. When tractors replaced horses, new masculine ideals based on efficiency and mechanical expertise became more important (Wilson, 2014). The milking machine, for instance, was deliberately presented as a masculine technology to overcome the previous cultural identification of milking with femininity (Sommestad, 1992). When computerisation made operating a tractor more like working in an office, displays of manly strength gave way to performances of a more white-collar, business-oriented image (Brandth, 1995). Similarly, when mastering expert information and financial matters became more central in the forestry sector, the masculine image of the forester as 'tough' was challenged by the masculine image of the 'powerful' businessman who works, not alone, but in a large organisation (Brandth & Haugen, 2005b). Regardless of tasks there seems to be an identification of manliness with technology.

Rural social change has significantly challenged hegemonic masculinity. As farming, forestry and other male-dominated occupations have declined, rural economies have become more heterogeneous. Globalisation, increased mobility, in-migration by people from different educational and ethnic backgrounds, and increasing emphasis on the rural as a site of leisure and consumption have all affected rural masculinities. When work in extractive industries disappears, the basis for the construction of masculine identities also shifts. Examining the impact of long-term unemployment and deindustrialisation in the rural United States, Sherman (2011) found that after the closure of a sawmill some of the men embraced a broader and more flexible understanding of masculinity as encompassing involved fatherhood, the sharing of domestic labour, and other sources of life satisfaction beyond work. Crisis may stimulate the construction of alternative masculinities, particularly as men take jobs in the service sector. At the same time, crisis may spark a revival of interest in activities that reaffirm traditional 'manly' pursuits. Rural men construct different masculinities according to available physical and social resources in rural spaces. Trell, van Hoven and Huigen (2014), for example, have shown how variable and contradictory aspects of masculinities are expressed depending on the context in rural Estonia. Activities may reflect dominant characteristics of rural masculinity but also include elements associated with femininity and urbanity. As rural societies are changing, new and more flexible representations of rural masculinities are emerging. Stenbacka (2011) has pointed out, however, that new constructions of rural masculinity are not always recognised from an urban point of view. In television programmes, rural masculinities continue to be described as unequal, traditional, 'backward' and deviant (p. 235).

Since masculinity is relationally constructed, it is profoundly influenced by changes in women's practices and positions. Alston and Kent (2008) found that changes in the status of the 'farm wife' threatened long-established hierarchies of gender that figured men as breadwinners in Australia. When women's off-farm income-generating work becomes central to family farm survival, men's patriarchal position is destabilised. As agriculture assumes a less central role in rural areas, men's pre-eminence is weakened and gender identities must be renegotiated. For example, when women are employed off the farm, men are expected to be more involved in housework and childcare. A study of Norwegian farm fathers shows that fathering practices have changed over a generation to include greater involvement in childcare indoors, such as changing diapers, feeding, bathing and comforting babies (Brandth, 2016). Younger fathers' involvement does not, however, clash with dominant norms of rural masculinity; rather, new fathering practices are added to and combined with stable features of rural masculinity. Men can gain new competences as a result of women's employment and contribute to remaking masculinity in ways that do not involve patriarchal domination. However, research from England and Ireland has demonstrated that women's off-farm employment may not have any significant effects on power relations between husbands and wives. Indeed, Kelly and Shortall (2002) argue that when women's income subsidises the continued existence of a family farm it serves to support gender inequality and men's identities as farmers, which they would otherwise be forced to forfeit.

Problems linked to theories of rural hegemonic masculinity

Recent research has considered the negative consequences of hegemonic rural masculinity. Despite current changes in the performance of masculinity, studies of economic crises and natural disasters show what can happen when 'traditional masculinity' is put to the test (Alston & Kent, 2008; Sherman, 2011; Tyler & Fairbrother, 2013). When men confront circumstances beyond their control, the threat of status loss or their felt inability to fulfil internalised masculine ideals can result in depression and suicide (Ní Laoire, 2005; Alston, 2012; Roy, Tremblay & Robertson, 2014; Bryant & Garnham, 2015). The idealised character of rural masculinity, which assumes, if not invulnerability, at least a high degree of stoicism, tends to undermine men's mental health (Courtenay, 2006) and prevent them from expressing their emotional distress before it overwhelms them (Coen, Oliffe, Johnson & Kelly, 2013; Haugen & Brandth, 2015).

Alston and Kent (2008), who examined the mental health implications of the long-term crisis in Australian agriculture, concluded that men's identification with normative rural masculinity reduces their 'ability to seek help during times of extreme stress' (p. 144). Similarly, Tyler and Fairbrother (2013) showed how the cultural and structural construction of hegemonic masculinities in rural Australia affected the ways men prepared for and responded to disastrous bushfires. 'Real men' were expected to stay and battle nature, defending their family and homes like 'warriors', taking risks and neglecting their own health and safety (p. 114). The decision to stand and fight was socially accepted as strong and manly, while evacuating for the sake of personal safety was seen as weak and feminine. Bryant and Garnham (2015) use the metaphor of the 'fallen hero' to capture men's sense of shame and the 'undoing' of masculine subjectivity when they gave up the struggle to survive as farmers. They argue that Australia's environmental, social and economic crises have destroyed the viability of farming and consequently eroded farmers' pride, self-worth and masculine identity. Suicide is understood in terms of a masculine subjectivity that is shamed by the loss of power. Roy, Tremblay and Robertson (2014), who investigated how masculinities influenced help-seeking, found that farm men adopted a variety of coping strategies, demonstrating that traditional norms of masculinity are under pressure to change. Help-seeking for psychosocial problems was not considered solely as a sign of weakness but could also be viewed positively, as having the 'guts' to seek help (p. 470).

Divorce has been shown to challenge farmers' masculine self-identity, as it jeopardises their position and may result in a loss of meaning in their life. They are vulnerable to situational depression, as asking for help is difficult, and perhaps even more difficult in personal crises than in situations of shared economic or environmental crises. The divorced men whom Haugen and Brandth (2015) studied adopted avoidance strategies, not admitting their personal problems until a farm crisis materialised. Perhaps, as Alston and Kent (2008, p. 144) suggest, in good times hegemonic masculinity serves men well, but, because it locks them into fairly rigid subject positions, a rural crisis they cannot control also threatens their sense of masculinity. On the other hand, a crisis is also an opportunity to remake masculinities.

While internalisation of violence in terms of inflicting harm upon themselves seems to be a response to threatened rural masculinities, there are also other problems of violence linked with hegemonic masculinity, such as physical and sexual abuse of women. Carrington, McIntosh, Hogg and Scott (2013), who compared violence in agricultural and mining communities in rural Australia, found that male-on-male assaults in public places dominated violence in mining communities, whereas violence in agricultural communities was characterised by individualised and privatised violence such as self-harm and domestic violence. As reported by Carrington and Scott (2008, p. 661), in some contexts violence is about exerting male domination and in other contexts it is an expression of the fragility of patriarchal power.

Diversity and rural masculinities

Masculine identities interact with other forms of identification in rural societies, generating considerable diversity. Bryant and Pini (2011) advocate an intersectional perspective in order to explore how gender and rurality coalesce with other social positions and produce heterogeneity in the lives of men and women. An intersectional perspective conveys the flexibility and localism of power relations. Differences generate multiple subjectivities and relational positions on a variety of axes. Our review of the literature on how masculine identities are intertwined with class, age and sexual identities demonstrates that in specific circumstances one category may become salient while another recedes.

Class

While class has not been given much attention in rural gender research in the past, recent work by Pini and her colleagues has begun to illuminate it (Bryant & Pini, 2009, 2011; Pini & Leach, 2011; Pini & Mayes, 2011). Taking a qualitative approach, they view class as a lived reality 'represented through symbolic signifiers and cultural narratives' (Bryant & Pini, 2009, p. 48), contending that class differentiation is defined not only by property ownership but also by prevailing notions of 'good farming' over generations that generate status and respect for men (though not for women).

Another material basis for the interrelation of rurality, class and gender is the fact that many rural communities are dominated by natural resource extraction, such as mining, forestry and fisheries, which have almost exclusively employed men. In these places masculinity has carried blue-collar connotations of toughness, hardiness, physically active work, and recreation that men enjoy together (Campbell, Bell & Finney 2006). Endurance and hands-on skills are valued. As Coen, Oliffe, Johnson and Kelly (2013) have shown for northern Canada, norms of rural working-class masculinity stigmatise any sign of bodily or emotional weakness. Alternative, potentially dialogic masculinities are represented by the unemployed or men in white-collar occupations, but they tend to recalibrate masculinity within monologic frames, for instance through sexual prowess (Coen, Oliffe, Johnson & Kelly, 2013). The ways in which class and gender are interconnected often emanate from their rural location.

Age

The working-class masculinity embodied in toughness and manual labour also resonates with rural youth. Morris (2008, 2011), who studied school performance among rural high school students, demonstrated how the intersection of class, gender and rurality could be seen in individual efforts to represent particular statuses and identities. Boys' academic underachievement has often been interpreted from a disadvantage perspective, but Morris argued that their hostility towards school is central to boys' performance of gender. Similarly, Keddie (2007) pointed to the significance of power hierarchies among rural adolescent boys in legitimating masculinities. There are two ways to acquire power, either through academic achievement or through rebelling against the values of the school, and these are connected to middle- and working-class status respectively. Keddie has shown that rurality amplifies these class differences. Rural boys who fail to gain academic or occupational skills but rely on physical strength and toughness in order to demonstrate their masculinity face limited futures.

Drawing on ethnographic research with young people from fishing communities in western Ireland, Donkersloot (2012) explored the gendered dimensions of rural youth experience in leisure pursuits. The production of hegemonic masculinity through drinking and sports by local young men works to exclude women and marginalise men who do not fit in. Declining fisheries, however, changes the gendered nature of this 'male periphery' and upsets 'old hierarchies' of rural gender relations through new markers of power (p. 591).

Generational change may be a precursor to a departure from traditional rural gender practices and discourses. Younger farmers, for instance, value alternative masculine practices rather than those based on relentless work (Roy, Tremblay & Robertson, 2014; Brandth, 2016). A Norwegian study characterises young hunters in a forest community as carriers of a new type of masculine culture (Krange & Skogen, 2007). These country boys did not leave for education but remained in the community, established families, and found jobs in the service sector. Krange and Skogen describe a typical representative of the group:

> He wears tattered jeans and heavy boots, a dirty old baseball cap, a green hunting jacket, a fleece sweater and a checkered shirt. He has not shaved for a while. He is a local patriot with a working-class background and a strong interest in hunting, dogs and weapons. He has not got much education himself, although he may be a skilled worker, and he readily accepts temporary work if nothing else is available. And he hates wolves.
>
> *(2007, p. 216)*

This description can easily be understood as a stereotypical portrait of rural working-class men, but because these young men were unable to acquire rural working-class jobs they had to find other ways to express their class and gender identity, especially through their shared leisure pursuits. They refute the common impression that young men who stay behind in the rural represent marginalised masculinities. Another Norwegian study (Bye, 2009) confirms that young rural men enact more flexible masculinities, expressed through new occupations in the service sector coupled with masculine leisure activities such as hunting and motorsports.

Rural research has been less concerned with older men than with the young, despite the fact that rural communities in Western societies are characterised by an ageing population. Even less attention has been paid to how ageing affects the subjective meanings of men's gender identities. In a recent special issue of the *Journal of Rural Studies* (2012) on ageing, none of the articles focused explicitly on intersections with gender. Bryant and Pini (2011), who explored the literature to find what is uniquely rural, pointed to older people's memories, social belonging and historical connection to the community. Men and women both value experiences of social connectivity, but the signifiers are gendered. The authors described men as valuing family history and sport events, while women participate in clubs and voluntary work. Experiences of growing old in rural places depend on their economic viability and provision of essential services, and place-based change may have damaging effects on older people.

Research on ageing farmers has demonstrated that belonging to the land, family heritage, and a lifetime of hard work are central elements in men's self-perception (Gullifer & Thompson, 2006). Loss of working capacity with old age may be negatively experienced as a loss of masculinity. A Swedish study (Nilsson, Hagberg & Grassman, 2013) has analysed how age and gender intersect in the self-presentations of older unmarried and childless men in a small rural community. Others' familiarity with these men's history is essential to their masculine sense of self. Their lingering identity as strong and capable working men, not their age, is important, and the harsh conditions in which they grew up and their capacity to work were often used to explain their lack of long-term heterosexual relationships (p. 68).

Sexuality

Heterosexuality has been an invisible but taken-for-granted presence in scholarship, as it has been in rural societies. The major site in which heterosexuality has been examined is agriculture, where identities and practices have been highly patriarchal. Little (2007) has demonstrated that rural space is heterosexually ordered through the power of farming men. Because heterosexuality is a central organising principle of agricultural societies and marriage customarily provides an heir to the family farm, heterosexual masculinities are naturalised as hegemonic. Little contends that these practices extend beyond farm households and become characteristic of rural society. Other scholars agree: 'Heteronormativity, which naturalises heterosexuality and essentialises women, remains woven into understandings of community and thereby relationships in rural spaces' (Bryant, 2013, p. 61).

By illustrating the importance of heterosexual marriage within rural communities, several studies have demonstrated the stratification of rural masculinities between those who had a partner and those who were still looking for one. The absence of wives supports a narrative of rural men as socially helpless and inept. Bachelor farmers, living alone or with their mothers, are often described as 'shambolic, hopeless and wayward', which contradicts the dominant understanding of rural masculinity as powerful, strong and fit (Little, 2003, p. 414). Exploring how farmers met prospective partners through involvement in rural dating programmes, Little and Panelli (2007) highlight the hegemonic model of heterosexuality but reveal that rural men, in order to increase their appeal/attractiveness, accommodate changing notions of femininity and patterns of women's employment.

The disintegration of relationships (as well as their foundation) is an interesting point of departure for studying discourses and practices of rural masculinity. Haugen and Brandth (2015) explored what a farm break-up reveals about rural ideals of masculinity and femininity. Analysing the efforts of both men and women to measure up to the expectations of gendered agricultural moralities, they found that the agrarian definition of masculine success that values family life, partnership and continuity on the land suffers a deep blow. As a consequence of the divorce, some men did not manage to stay physically and mentally fit enough to manage the farm work; their emotional paralysis created a greater risk of the loss of status that comes from forfeiting their position as farmers than the divorce itself did. Since hegemonic masculine ideals define men as the patriarchal heads of farming families, losing their wives (and often children) to divorce undermines their sense of self as well. Their reactions suggest the existence of an 'authentic' version of masculinity to which rural men subscribe and feel compelled to fulfil.

An abundance of scholarship has shown the unequal allocation of domestic labour and caring in heterosexual relationships. Examining intimacy in heterosexual marriages among Australian farmers, Bryant (2013) found that men used a discourse of mutuality and equality when describing how they and their wives shared farm work, but inequality continued to prevail in domestic labour. As it is the community that regulates and sanctions their gendered behaviour and work–family practices, the constraints of the moral community may reinforce gender inequity.

Rural scholarship has increasingly acknowledged the sexualised character of rurality (Gorman-Murray, Pini & Bryant, 2013) by showing interest in non-hegemonic masculinities. Gay masculinities have been disguised and marginalised in rural societies (Bell, 2006). Preston and D'Augelli (2013) show that rurality has distinctive effects on how gay men cope with the stigma of homosexuality in the United States. In most counties, rural communities are reputed to be more homophobic and prejudiced than cities. Nevertheless, some scholars see signs that the situation may be changing (Little, 2015). Dasper (2012), who studied gay masculinity in relation to equestrian sports, which remain tied to rurality, observed a move towards greater recognition and tolerance. Dasper advocates paying more attention to 'inclusive masculinity theory' and interprets her results to mean that masculinities may be ordered horizontally as well as hierarchically.

Concluding observations

The main focus of early studies of rural masculinities was to demonstrate the fundamental relationship between rurality and masculinity and to describe the characteristics of hegemonic masculinity. Some scholars came to this research almost by default: aspiring to explore discrimination against women in a male-dominated place, they discovered that there were no women to study and ending up focusing on masculinity instead (Brandth, 1995). All-male arenas were well suited for the study of hegemonic masculinities. This scholarship tended to overemphasise the spaces and times when 'men are mostly male' (Bull, 2009, p. 446), however, ignoring many other social spaces and moments in which strength, stamina and power are less essential.

Our observations may be summed up according to Connell's three theoretical rubrics described in the introduction: variation, change and power. Studies in the last decade have been very much concerned to show variability and change in masculine practices and discourses in different contexts. Although most take hegemonic rural masculinity as a point of departure, they often draw attention to the contradictory nature of hegemonic masculinity as 'it is constituted by an amalgam of practices, values and meanings and realised in particular places and contexts' (Van Hoven & Hörschelmann, 2005, p. 18). Emerging topics include men's efforts to preserve or change masculinity in times of economic transformation and environmental disaster and in response to women's shifting economic and social positions. These changes have played out differently in specific places, either reinforcing patriarchy or facilitating new forms of masculinity that are more compatible with gender equality. Scholars concur that research on masculinity must seek to 'grasp changes, complexities, ambivalences, ruptures and resistance' (Christensen & Jensen, 2014, p. 71). As researchers have become more attentive to variations, rural masculinities are presented as more diffuse and flexible.

In line with the challenges facing hegemonic ideals of rural masculinity in times of crises, studies have been concerned with men's psychosocial problems and reluctance to seek help. Hegemonic masculinity has proven counterproductive when it comes to men's health. Working too much, suppressing their responses to stress, and silencing their emotions are deleterious results of men's tendency to measure their subjectivity against dominant discourses of rural masculinity. Perhaps we can say that situations change, but discourses are more resistant.

Broadly speaking, the last decade has seen less concern about power in rural masculinity studies although the concern with the detrimental effects of rural masculine ideals can be interpreted as a loss of status. Despite there often being a clear divide between men's and women's responsibilities and activities in rural settings, men's power over women or efforts to distance themselves from femininity have not been a prominent topic. Rather, concern with gender inequality seems to be linked to feminist women's studies (Pini, Brandth & Little, 2015).

Moreover, studies on rural masculinities have demonstrated differences among masculinities without necessarily seeing them as ordered hierarchically. Perhaps this view has arisen through efforts to describe how men negotiate their masculinities in local, everyday social practices and interactions. Most significantly, hegemonic and subordinate masculinities can exist as contradictions within male subjectivities; one man can express several different masculinities depending on the situation.

What seems striking after 20 years of research on rural masculinities is the patchiness of the research; there are often only a few studies of each topic in widely separated places. However, two debates seem to have been studied across a range of settings: the status of hegemonic masculinity and the effects of agricultural crisis and economic change. Results suggest a shift in gender relations towards greater flexibility and equality or, at least in the short run, towards the reinforcement of threatened aspects of rural masculinity. We believe that further research is needed to observe the situation on a global basis.

References

Alston, M (2012). Rural male suicide in Australia. *Social Science & Medicine* 74(4), 515–522.

Alston, M & Kent, J (2008). The big dry: The link between rural masculinities and poor health outcomes for farming men. *Journal of Sociology* 44(2), 133–147.

Bell, D (2006). Cowboy love. In H Campbell, MM Bell & M Finney (Eds), *Country boys: Masculinity and rural life* (pp. 163–180). Philadelphia, PA: Pennsylvania University Press.

Brandth, B (1995). Gender images in tractor advertisements. *Journal of Rural Studies* 11(2), 127–149.

Brandth, B (2002). Gender identity in European family farming: A review of literature. *Sociologia Ruralis* 42(3), 181–200.

Brandth, B (2016). Rural masculinities and fathering practices. *Gender, Place and Culture* 26(3), 435–450.

Brandth, B & Haugen, MS (2000). From lumberjack to business manager: Masculinity in the Norwegian forestry press. *Journal of Rural Studies* 16(3), 343–355.

Brandth, B & Haugen, MS (2005a). Doing rural masculinity – from logging to outfield tourism. *Journal of Gender Studies* 14(1), 13–22.

Brandth, B & Haugen, MS (2005b). Text, body and tools: Changing mediations of rural masculinity. *Men and Masculinities* 8(2), 148–163.

Brandth, B & Haugen, MS (2010). Doing farm tourism: The intertwining practices of gender and work. *Signs: Journal of Women in Culture and Society* 35(2), 426–446.

Brandth, B & Haugen, MS (2014). Embodying the rural idyll in farm tourist hosting. *Scandinavian Journal of Hospitality and Tourism* 14(2), 101–115.

Bryant, L (2013). Heterosexual marriage, intimacy and farming. In A Gorman-Murray, B Pini & L Bryant (Eds), *Sexuality, rurality, and geography* (pp. 51–64). Lanham, MD: Lexington.

Bryant, L & Garnham, B (2015). The fallen hero: Masculinity, shame and farmer suicide in Australia. *Gender, Place & Culture* 22(1), 67–82.

Bryant, L & Pini, B (2009). Gender, class and rurality: Australian case studies. *Journal of Rural Studies* 25(1), 48–57.

Bryant, L & Pini, B (Eds). (2011). *Gender and rurality*. London: Routledge.

Bull, J (2009). Watery masculinities: Fly-fishing and the angling male in the South West of England. *Gender, Place and Culture* 16(4), 445–465.

Bye, LM (2009). 'How to be a rural man': Young men's performances and negotiations of rural masculinities. *Journal of Rural Studies* 25(3), 278–288.

Campbell, H & Bell, MM (2000). The question of rural masculinities. *Rural Sociology* 65(5), 532–546.

Campbell, H, Bell, MM & Finney, M (2006). Masculinity and rural life: An introduction. In H Campbell, MM Bell & M Finney (Eds), *Country boys: Masculinity and rural life* (pp. 1–22). University Park, PA: Pennsylvania State University Press.

Carrington, K, McIntosh, A, Hogg, R & Scott, J (2013). Rural masculinities and the internalization of violence in agricultural communities. *International Journal of Rural Criminology* 2(1), 3–24.

Carrington, K & Scott, J (2008). Masculinity, rurality and violence. *British Journal of Criminology* 48, 641–666.

Christensen, AD & Jensen, SQ (2014). Combining hegemonic masculinity and intersectionality. *NORMA: International Journal for Masculinity Studies* 9(1), 60–75.

Cloke, P (2005). Masculinity and rurality. In B van Hoven & K Hörschelman (Eds), *Spaces of masculinities* (pp. 45–62). London: Routledge.

Coen, SE, Oliffe, JL, Johnson, JL & Kelly, MT (2013). Looking for Mr. PG: Masculinities and men's depression in a northern resource-based Canadian community. *Health & Place* 21, 94–101.

Connell, RW (1995). *Masculinities*. Cambridge: Polity.

Connell, RW & Messerschmidt, JW (2005). Hegemonic masculinity: Rethinking the concept. *Gender & Society* 19(6), 829–859.

Courtenay, WH (2006). Rural men's health: Situating risk in the negotiation of masculinity. In H Campbell, MM Bell & M Finney (Eds), *Country boys: Masculinity and rural life* (pp. 139–158). University Park, PA: Pennsylvania State University Press.

Dasper, K (2012). 'Dressage is full of queens!' Masculinity, sexuality and equestrian sport. *Sociology* 46(6), 1109–1124.

Datta, A (2008). Spatialising performance: Masculinities and femininities in a 'fragmented' field. *Gender, Place and Culture* 15(2), 189–204.

Donkersloot, R (2012). Gendered and generational experiences of place and power in the rural Irish landscape. *Gender, Place and Culture* 19(5), 578–599.

Ferrell, AK (2012). Doing masculinity: Gendered challenges to replacing burley tobacco in central Kentucky. *Agriculture and Human Values* 29(2), 137–149.

Gorman-Murray, A, Pini, P & Bryant, L (Eds). (2013). *Sexuality, rurality, and geography*. Lanham, MD: Lexington.

Gullifer, J & Thompson, T (2006). Subjective realities of older male farmers: Self-perceptions of ageing and work. *Rural Society* 16(1), 80–97.

Haugen, MS & Brandth, B (2015). When farm couples break up: Gendered moralities, gossip and the fear of stigmatisation in rural communities. *Sociologia Ruralis* 55(2), 227–242.

Heggem, R (2014). Exclusion and inclusion of women in Norwegian agriculture: Exploring different outcomes of the 'tractor gene'. *Journal of Rural Studies* 34, 263–271.

Hopkins, P & Noble, G (2009). Masculinities in place: Situated identities, relations and intersectionality. *Social and Cultural Geography* 10(8), 811–819.

Keddie, A (2007). Games of subversion and sabotage: Issues of power, masculinity, class, rurality and schooling. *British Journal of Sociology of Education* 28(2), 181–194.

Kelly, R & Shortall, S (2002). 'Farmers' wives': Women who are off-farm breadwinners and the implication for on-farm gender relations. *Journal of Sociology* 38(4), 327–343.

Krange, O & Skogen, K (2007). Reflexive tradition: Young working-class hunters between wolves and modernity. *Young: Nordic Journal of Youth Studies* 15(3), 215–233.

Liepins, R (1998). The gendering of farming and agricultural politics: A matter of discourse and power. *Australian Geographer* 29(3), 371–388.

Liepins, R (2000). Making men: The construction and representation of agriculture-based masculinities in Australia and New Zealand. *Rural Sociology* 65(4), 605–620.

Little, J (2002). Rural geography: Rural gender identity and the performance of masculinity and femininity in the countryside. *Progress in Human Geography* 26(5), 665–670.

Little, J (2003). Riding the rural love train: Heterosexuality and the rural community. *Sociologia Ruralis* 47(4), 401–417.

Little, J (2007). Constructing nature in the performance of rural heterosexualities. *Environment and Planning D: Society and Space* 25(5), 851–866.

Little, J (2015). The development of feminist perspectives in rural gender studies. In B Pini, B Brandth & J Little (Eds), *Feminisms and ruralities* (pp. 107–118). Farnham: Lexington.

Little, J & Panelli, R (2007). 'Outback' romance: A reading of nature and heterosexuality in rural Australia. *Sociologia Ruralis* 47(3), 174–188.

Lusher, D & Robins, G (2009). Hegemonic and other masculinities in local social contexts. *Men and Masculinities* 11(4), 387–423.

Morris, EW (2008). 'Rednecks', 'rutters', and 'rithmetic': Social class, masculinity, and schooling in a rural context. *Gender and Society* 22(6), 728–751.

Morris, EW (2011). The 'hidden injuries' of class and gender among rural teenagers. In B Pini & B Leach (Eds), *Reshaping gender and class in rural spaces* (pp. 221–238). Farnham: Ashgate.

Ní Laoire, C (2005). 'You are not a man at all!' Masculinity, responsibility and staying on the land in contemporary Ireland. *Irish Journal of Sociology* 14(2), 94–114.

Nilsson, M, Hagberg, J-E & Grassman, EJ (2013). To age as a man: Ageing and masculinity in a small rural community in Sweden. *Norma. Nordic Journal for Masculinity Studies* 8(1), 58–76.

Peter, G, Bell, MM, Jarnagin, S & Bauer, D (2000). Coming back across the fence: Masculinity and the transition to sustainable agriculture. *Rural Sociology* 65(2), 215–233.

Pini, B (2008). *Masculinities and management in agricultural organizations worldwide.* Aldershot: Ashgate.

Pini, B, Brandth, B & Little, J (2015). *Feminisms and ruralities.* Farnham: Lexington.

Pini, B & Leach, B (Eds). (2011). *Reshaping gender and class in rural spaces.* Farnham: Ashgate.

Pini, B & Mayes, R (2011). Configurations of gender, class and rurality in resource affected rural Australia. In B Pini & B Leach (Eds), *Reshaping gender and class in rural spaces* (pp. 113–129). Farnham: Ashgate.

Preston, DB & D'Augelli, AR (2013). *The challenges of being a rural gay man: Coping with stigma.* New York: Routledge.

Roy, P, Tremblay, G & Robertson, S (2014). Help-seeking among male farmers: Connecting masculinities and mental health. *Sociologia Ruralis* 54(4), 460–476.

Sachs, CE (1983). *The invisible farmers: Women in agricultural production.* Totowa, NJ: Roman and Allenheld.

Saugeres, L (2002). Of tractors and men: Masculinity, technology and power in a French farming community. *Sociologia Ruralis* 42(2) 143–159.

Sherman, J (2011). Men without sawmills: Job loss and gender identity in rural America. In KE Smith & AR Tickamyer (Eds), *Economic restructuring and family well-being in rural America* (pp. 82–102). University Park, PA: Pennsylvania State University Press.

Shortall, S (1999). *Women and farming: Property and power.* London: Macmillan.

Sommestad, L (1992). *Från mejerska till mejerist: En studie av mejeriyrkets masculiniseringsprocess.* Lund: Arkiv förlag.

Stenbacka, S (2011). Othering the rural: About the construction of rural masculinities and the unspoken urban hegemonic ideal in Swedish media. *Journal of Rural Studies* 27(3), 235–244.

Trell, E-M, van Hoven, B & Huigen, PPP (2014). Youth negotiation and performance of masculine identities in rural Estonia. *Journal of Rural Studies* 34, 15–25.

Tyler, M & Fairbrother, P (2013). Bushfires are 'men's business': The importance of gender and rural hegemonic masculinity. *Journal of Rural Studies* 30, 110–119.

van Hoven, B & Hörschelman, K (Eds). (2005). *Spaces of masculinities.* London: Routledge.

Whatmore, S (1991). *Farming women: Gender, work and family enterprise.* London: Macmillan.

Wilson, CA (2014). A manly art: Plowing, plowing matches, and rural masculinity in Ontario, 1800–1930. *Canadian Historical Review* 95(2), 157–186.

Part VI
Social and Economic Equality

Section editor: Bettina B. Bock

36

Social and Economic Equality

A Territorial and Relational Perspective

Bettina B. Bock

Introduction

Rural areas have never escaped poverty and social exclusion. Social inequality is of all times and all places. Unequal access to land perpetuated traditional relations of dependency and domination between peasants and large estate holders well into the 20th century, and may still be found in novel forms in many parts of the world. Of course, the scenery has substantially changed and, generally speaking, the quality of life in rural areas of the global north has improved considerably since the Second World War. Substantial governmental investments in agriculture and rural development played an important role here as well as changes in society at large – such as the rolling out of the welfare state in some nations, and improvement of (technological) infrastructure that substantially improved the connectivity of rural areas. While rural disadvantage and deprivation never disappeared, scenes of extreme rural inequality portrayed in numerous movies and novels, such as *Novecento* and *Grapes of Wrath*, seem to be irrevocably part of the past, at least in the global north. In recent years, however, images of the exploitation of migrant agricultural workers in the United States and southern Europe and the desperate living conditions of minority groups, such as refugees, Roma and Native Americans in the USA, make one wonder if that is not changing again.

More generally, there are clear indications that social and economic inequalities are again increasing within and across countries and between social groups (OECD, 2008, 2011; Stiglitz, 2012; Kremer, Bovens, Schrijvers, & Went, 2014; Picketty, 2014). The global financial crisis of 2008 plays an important role here, producing so-called 'new poor' among middle-class groups – and especially the self-employed – struggling to keep up their standard of living while facing unemployment and increasing costs of living (MacInnes et al., 2014). In addition, groups that were already vulnerable have been driven into poverty because of the loss of public support. The crisis and cut-back in public spending goes along with a rethinking of governmental responsibility for social equality. Reducing financial support to community services and withdrawing financial contributions to costs of, for example, higher education and health care, not only increases costs for individual households; it also questions the long-time responsibility of states to support social equality and to temper disparity through economic redistribution and welfare programmes that assure equal access to development and well-being. Of course, this situation is felt more so in some nations than in others, depending on the generosity of the assistance package prior to the recession and the depth of programme cuts. This development fits a long-standing turn towards neoliberal ideas that has legitimated a shift towards individual responsibility in many countries in the last decades (Peck & Tickell, 2002; Bauman, 2005). The global financial crisis gave it another push in that direction as it undermined the prosperity of states in a formerly unimaginable fashion, and with it states' capability to fulfil their social responsibilities. As a result, achieved levels of social equality and general welfare are seriously at risk. This is very dramatically felt in southern Europe. To give just a few examples: the percentage of (youth) unemployment in 2014 reached 26.5% (52.4% for youth) in Greece and 24.5% (53.2% for youth) in Spain (Eurostat, 2015a); at the same time the percentage of citizens under the poverty line was at 35.7% in Greece and 27.3% in Spain (Eurostat, 2015b). The crisis has also substantially reordered the interrelation, interdependence and hierarchy of states. In Europe, this is reflected in the discussions about the extent to which the rising inequality within and between member states is a common or national responsibility.

It is not yet clear how the crisis affects rural areas. A study by the Economic Commission suggests that rural areas have been hit by the closure of plants, loss of employment in industry and construction, and the cuts in public budgets and resulting loss of services, although agriculture has been relatively protected through the Common Agricultural Policy (CAP) (European Commission, 2011). In the USA, rural areas appear to have been somewhat shielded from the worst impacts partly because house lending was more responsible and fewer households were faced with unpayable mortgages. In addition, the situation may differ considerably between rural areas, depending on factors such as geographical location, institutional capacity and civic engagement. In 2003 the remote rural areas in the east and south of Europe were clearly disadvantaged compared to urban areas and rural areas elsewhere in Europe in their material level of welfare and perceived quality of life. This is reflected in objectively measured indicators of material disadvantage such as lower average income, higher levels of unemployment, limited access to the Internet and worse housing conditions (e.g., damp and lack of inside toilet). It is also echoed in the rural residents' perceived deprivation in terms of prosperity and sense of security, and their relatively low rate of life satisfaction and happiness compared to urban residents (Shucksmith, Cameron, Pichler & Merridew, 2009).

Increasing figures of rural out-migration tell a similar story. Many rural areas across Europe and the USA are struggling with depopulation and extreme ageing (Copus et al., 2006; Goll, 2010). In Central and Eastern Europe (circular) migration has been one of the main livelihood strategies ever since European enlargement (Horváth, 2008; White, 2010; Eurostat, 2011). With the global financial crisis these figures went down a bit but in agriculture and rural domestic services there is still a high demand for migrant labour (see Bock, Osti & Ventura, this volume). In the meantime, rural youth out-migration has substantially increased in southern Europe as a result of the high levels of youth unemployment. Yet some rural areas seem to attract new residents who, in search of a refuge from the crisis, build up new communities and new economic systems (Gkartzios, 2013; Kasimis & Papadopoulos, 2013). In addition, throughout Europe citizens in rural areas take up the initiative to maintain services despite budget cuts through collaboration with business, non-profit and governmental organisations and the development of new business and service delivery models. Here, the rural areas are not victims of the crisis but sites of resistance and social innovation.

Review and synthesis of major scholarship in this area

So far there is hardly any comparative research looking into rural social inequality. As a result there is little systematic knowledge of inequality in rural areas and little insight into the pattern and factors of rural marginalisation. Comparative research is hampered by the lack of statistics that allow the precise localisation of poverty and deprivation. Generally, data are collected at a level of scale that hides the existence of poorer places and groups within relatively rich areas (Bock, Kovacs & Shucksmith, 2015). Another question is whether indicators such as income and employment, used to assess inequality in both rural and urban areas, allow us to understand the particular features of rural inequality. Access to land, for instance, may be an important marker of inequality within rural areas as land offers opportunities for food production and entrepreneurial activities to some and not to other rural inhabitants. The proximity or distance of public services is another potentially useful indicator that reflects the variable extent of welfare state inclusion of citizens in more or less remote or central rural (and urban) areas. The same question may be posed for what may be understood as rural inequality across regions, countries and continents. The evidence presented above points at an important divergence in the nature and extent of social inequality in rural areas. What matters most for identifying vulnerable groups and understanding the process of their (relative) deprivation may, hence, differ across regions and countries. This is not just a question of statistics, but points at the difficulty of conceptualising social inequality in a way that takes account of its context dependency.

In the USA, social inequality is predominantly conceptualised in terms of poverty with research focusing on the material dimension of inequality (Lichter & Schafft, 2015; see Milbourne, this volume). Longitudinal research into poverty demonstrates its intergenerational and spatial features and points to the fact that inequality is continuously (re)produced in the in situ interaction between economic structure and institutional arrangements. Such research underscores the spatially bound and systemic character of poverty which helps to explain why the inhabitants of those places that have a long history of material deprivation are so persistently marginalised (see Hooks, Lobao & Tickamyer, this volume).

In Europe, social inequality is usually addressed through the concept of social exclusion that replaced the exclusive focus on income poverty from the 1990s on (see Shucksmith, this volume, for an in-depth discussion). Social exclusion highlights the multidimensionality of inequality and its embeddedness in a dynamic social process. It is the variable integration in different social systems and relations which produces exclusion. Following Reimer (2004), the following types of relations are most important in this respect: market relations, bureaucratic relations, associative relations and communal relations. Social exclusion is, hence, a result of the functioning of society, and its production and expression may differ in time and place, depending on the organisation of social relations. In so doing, the context dependency of social exclusion may be accounted for as well as its interrelatedness with specific places. It is not only people who are socially excluded in certain places; places themselves may become blemished, stigmatised and excluded (see Bock, Kovacs & Shucksmith, 2015). We may find poor people in rich places, and rich people living in poor places. In both cases their position is defined in relation to the status of their co-residents yet also in interaction with the status of the place itself. Or in other words, the exclusion of 'places of abandonment' is one of the factors contributing to the exclusion of people. Hence, rural social exclusion – or social inequality for that matter – may only be understood if approached from a relational and a territorial perspective.

Approach chosen and questions raised in this section of the Handbook

This section of the Handbook aims at better understanding rural inequality by approaching equality from a territorial and relational perspective, which takes the interrelation between territories, nation states as well as social groups or classes into account. As these processes are neither fixed nor irreversible, the section also gives room to rural areas as sites of resistance and social innovation. In doing so, it intends to further elucidate the interrelation between the inequality of (rural and urban) territories, macro regions and nation states, and social groups. As a result, this section contributes in particular to the first two of the Handbook's cross-cutting themes, but also touches upon the third and fourth.

In the first chapter, Mark Shucksmith reviews the different concepts used for describing and analysing social and economic inequalities, while focusing on Europe and the USA. He discusses how concepts such as poverty, social inequality and social exclusion elucidate the underlying processes that produce and reproduce social divisions, obstruct the empowerment of so-called vulnerable groups and (re)generate new vulnerabilities. He unravels the differences in how social inequality is usually approached in North America (poverty) and Europe (social exclusion), and underscores the context dependency of social inequality. He points at the rural features of social inequality and particularities of the rural context, and calls for more research to elucidate how social constructions of rurality contribute to the formation of particular class relations in specific areas or territories. At the same time, he points to the important role that macro-structural processes, such as the global financial crisis, play in local expressions of social inequality. This chapter, hence, contributes in particular to the first and second cross-cutting themes.

The following chapter by Paul Milbourne focuses on the presence of poverty in rural places, its variable definition and categorisation such as reflected in the different approaches used in research across countries, as well as its relative invisibility in comparison with poverty in urban contexts. He elaborates on how our understanding of the causes of rural poverty has changed over time. Whereas research initially focused on the role of economic structures in producing poverty everywhere, there is now more understanding of the role of local cultures, and how poverty is shaped by the complex relations between people and places. He then discusses the role of welfare politics and welfare reforms in the (re)production of poverty and welfare in rural areas. Based on initial research findings in the UK, he reports on a two-sided development: on the one hand, austerity measures perpetuate the invisibility of rural poverty and increase the vulnerability of certain groups; on the other, budget cuts stimulate the development of new modes of service provision. Milbourne's chapter contributes to the first, second and third cross-cutting themes.

The chapter by Gregory Hooks, Linda M. Lobao and Ann R. Tickamyer provides an overview of the literature on spatial inequality and its application to the rural context. They focus on the United States for empirical examples with some references to Europe, where significant differences arise. Their combination of sociological and geographical approaches brings to the fore how places themselves become markers and makers of inequality, and why lack of well-being and inequalities of race, class and gender differ and intersect across geographic entities. They describe how interest in uneven development promoted the development of political economic theory and with it attention for inequality in access to valued resources and power. Current research points to the importance of explaining differences in stratification processes across space; studying inequality at subnational levels of spatial scale and within specific territories; and understanding how social inequality is (re)produced in specific places. While considering the role of economic structure, institutional arrangements and spatial context in producing social inequality, they also discuss the impact of neoliberal reforms of the welfare state for rural areas. This chapter, hence, contributes in particular to the first, second and third cross-cutting themes.

Ruth McAreavey focuses on the role ethnicity plays in the production of social inequality in rural areas. This becomes more and more important, she argues, as rising international migration increases the heterogeneity of rural areas. Taking account of ethnic inequality is, however, also important to better understand the production of inequality in those rural areas that have always been ethnically diverse or home to ethnic 'minorities', such as Native Americans in the United States. McAreavey discusses the conceptualisation of ethnicity and the production of inequality at multiple levels through social practices, representation and in macro structures, and in the intersection of ethnicity with other dimensions of inequality (such as gender and class). She points to the invisibility of ethnic groups who because of their 'otherness' fall outside the scope of mainstream interest, or because of their unofficial status never appear in official records. She unravels the production of ethnic inequality in the context of the rural economy, and looks into the role place and space play in the creation of social boundaries and relational divisions, or in other words spatial 'ghettoisation' of non-migrant ethnic minorities. McAreavey's chapter contributes in particular to the second intersecting theme.

In the final chapter of this section Menelaos Gkartzios and Ann Ziebarth look into rural housing in Europe and the USA, arguing that rural housing may serve as a symbol of inequalities. Rural housing is a research topic that received little attention prior to the current financial crisis, among other reasons because of the predominant association of rural localities with private home ownership. Recently, demographic changes have raised awareness about rural housing issues. Counter-urbanisation and gentrification create problems through increasing demand for (age-specific) rural housing, raising price levels and the outbidding of locals by commuters, retirees, second-home owners and tourists. At the same time there is a lack of affordable social housing as a result of limited public investment in rural social housing. Hence one finds residential segregation in rural areas, with high concentrations of ethnic minorities living in poor housing conditions. Last but not least, Gkartzios and Ziebarth discuss the effects of the global financial crisis and in particular the 'foreclosure crisis' around mortgage debts in the USA. This chapter contributes in particular to the second and third intersecting themes.

While each of the chapters deals with a specific aspect of inequality in rural areas, the five chapters altogether take up some of the issues identified above as pertinent to better understanding the development of social inequality in rural areas. The discussion of different conceptualisations of social inequality in the first three chapters elucidates the context dependency of social inequality in structural and cultural terms and explains why we need to understand social inequality both socially and spatially. This is elaborated upon in the other two chapters, which discuss the social construction of ethnic minorities as 'others' in specific places, and consider a specific living condition (housing) as a reflection of unequal social relations. Therefore, all the chapters contribute to the development of a relational and territorial approach to social inequality. They all demonstrate that inequality is socially and spatially constructed and a product and reflection of territorial social relations.

References

Bauman, Z (2005). *Work, consumerism and the new poor*. Maidenhead: Open University Press.

Bock, B, Kovacs, K & Shucksmith, M (2015). Changing social characteristics, patterns of inequality and exclusion. In AK Copus & P de Lima (Eds), *Territorial cohesion in rural Europe* (pp. 193–211). London: Routledge.

Copus, A, Hall, C, Barnes, A, Dalton, H, Cook, P, Weingarten, P, Baum, S, Stange, H, Johansson, M (2006). *Study on Employment in Rural Areas (SERA)*, Final deliverable. Brussels: DG Agriculture.

European Commission (2011). *Poverty in rural areas of the EU*. EU Agricultural and Economic brief no. 1.EC DG Agriculture and Rural Development.

Eurostat (2011). *Migrants in Europe*. Luxembourg: European Union.

Eurostat (2015a). Unemployment statistics. eurostat: statistics explained. Available at http://ec.europa.eu/eurostat/statistics-explained/index.php/Unemployment_statistics (accessed 24 June 2015).

Eurostat (2015b). People at risk of poverty or social exclusion. eurostat: statistics explained: Available at http://ec.europa.eu/eurostat/statistics-explained/index.php/People_at_risk_of_poverty_or_social_exclusion (accessed 25 June 2014).

Gkartzios, M (2013). 'Leaving Athens': Narratives of counterurbanisation in times of crisis. *Journal of Rural Studies* 32, 158–167.

Goll, M (2010). Ageing in the European Union: Where exactly? Eurostat statistics in focus. Brussels: Eurostat. Available at http://www.trf.sll.se/Global/Dokument/Statistik/externa_rapporter/2010_6_ageing_in_the_european_union.pdf (accessed 27 January 2016).

Horváth, I (2008). The culture of migration among Romanian youth. *Journal of Ethnic and Migration Studies* 34(5), 771–786.

Kasimis, C & Papadopoulos, AG (2005). The multifunctional role of migrants in Greek countryside: Implications for the rural economy and society. *Journal of Ethnic and Migration Studies* 31(1), 99–127.

Kasimis, C & Papadopoulos, AG (2013). Rural transformations and family farming in contemporary Greece. In D Ortiz-Miranda, A Moragues-Faus & E Arnalte-Alegre (Eds), *Agriculture in Mediterranean Europe: Between old and new paradigms* (pp. 263–293). Research in Rural Sociology and Development, 19. Bingley, UK: Emerald Publishing.

Kremer, M, Bovens, M, Schrijvers, E & Went, R (Eds). (2014). *Hoe ongelijk is Nederland? Een verkenning van de ontwikkeling en gevolgen van economische ongelijkheid.* WRR verkenning no. 28. Amsterdam: Amsterdam University Press.

Lichter, DT & Schafft, KA (2015). People and places left behind: Rural poverty in the new century. In D Brady & L Burton (Eds), *Oxford handbook of poverty and society.* Oxford: Oxford University Press.

MacInnes, T, Aldridge, H, Bushe, S, Tinson, A & Born, TB (2014). *The changing picture of poverty in the UK.* York: Joseph Rowntree Foundation & New Policy Institute.

OECD (2008). *Growing unequal?: Income distribution and poverty in OECD countries.* Paris: OECD.

OECD (2011). *Divided we stand: Why inequality keeps rising.* Paris: OECD.

Peck, J & Tickell, A (2002). Neoliberalizing space. *Antipode* 34(3), 380–301.

Piketty, T (2014). *Capital in the twenty-first century.* Cambridge, MA: Harvard University Press.

Reimer, B (2004). Social exclusion in a comparative context. *Sociologia Ruralis* 44(1), 76–94.

Shucksmith, M, Cameron, S, Pichler, F & Merridew, T (2009). Urban–rural differences in quality of life across the EU. *Regional Studies* 43(10), 1275–1289.

Stiglitz, J (2012). *The price of inequality: How today's divided society endangers our future.* New York & London: Norton.

White, A (2010). Young people and migration from contemporary Poland. *Journal of Youth Studies* 13(5), 565–580.

37

Social Exclusion in Rural Places

Mark Shucksmith

Introduction

This chapter reviews conceptualisations of poverty, social exclusion and inequality and the ways in which these concepts have been applied in rural studies in different parts of the world, focusing especially on Europe and North America. The chapter begins with concepts of absolute and relative poverty and the ways in which these have been deployed in the global north, before reviewing the concept of social exclusion, now prominent in Europe. The chapter then goes on to consider the various ways in which these concepts have been applied in rural studies, and summarises some of the insights that have emerged, especially in relation to the processes underlying poverty, inequality and exclusion.

These are always important issues for rural studies, as they are for humanity, but there is a particular need to research these issues at a time of growing inequalities of wealth and income across much of the world. In most of the global north, a neoliberal hegemony of marketisation and rising inequalities has displaced the progressive postwar settlement, and since 2007 the global economic crisis has intensified these disparities further. Many countries have imposed austerity policies which reduce demand, targeting poorer and more vulnerable groups with cuts in public spending, so creating further hardships. How can rural studies contribute to an understanding of these complex, multidimensional and multiscalar processes?

Poverty, inequality and social exclusion

Reviewing studies of lay discourses of poverty, Veit-Wilson (2006, p. 318) reports the everyday meaning of the word 'poverty' as 'the enforced lack of resources demonstrably needed for respect and inclusion'; meanwhile, the United Nations uses a different, but also commonly accepted, definition of poverty in terms of inability to fulfil basic human needs (UN, 1995). This nuanced distinction may mask substantial differences in application, and illustrates the necessity of recognising poverty research as 'inescapably political' (O'Connor, 2001, p. 12).

Social scientists have sought to understand poverty and inequality in various ways. One approach, exemplified by the UN, is to conceive of poverty in absolute terms as a failure to fulfil basic human needs. Thus, the UN defines poverty as 'a condition characterized by severe deprivation of basic human needs, including food, safe drinking water, sanitation facilities, health, shelter, education and information. It depends not only on income but also on access to social services' (UN, 1995, p. 57). Rowntree, a pioneer of social research (1901), similarly defined poverty in terms of nutritional requirements, a logic echoed today in work on Minimum

Income Standards and a Living Wage (JRF, 2015). The poverty line in the USA, set at three times the cost of what is thought to be a minimally adequate diet, has also echoed this logic since it was adopted in the 1960s as part of the President's 'war on poverty'.

However, the EU and most European countries understand poverty as a relative, not as an absolute, concept. Following Townsend (1979), people or households are defined as poor if they cannot enjoy the every lifestyles of the majority in that society. This relative concept of poverty is operationalised in official statistics across Europe as an 'at-risk-of-poverty rate', defined as an income below 60% of the national median income. The OECD also adopts a relative approach, measuring poverty as below 50% of median household income. The widespread use of a relative approach in the global north highlights within-country inequality, rather than the potentially life-threatening consequences of absolute poverty (Madanipour, Shucksmith & Talbot, 2015).

The emphasis on income common to most of these definitions is contested. For some commentators, this reflects a mistaken belief that the cure for poverty is simply a higher income or income transfers (Veit-Wilson, 2006); while for others the emphasis on income is thought to be driven by pragmatism, since income data are regularly collected and thus widely available as a proxy for wider aspects of welfare and poverty (Ruggeri Laderchi, Saith & Stewart, 2003). An alternative approach giving less emphasis to income is Sen's capabilities approach which focuses instead on 'the freedom of individuals to live lives that are valued' (ibid., p. 253). This underpins the UNDP's national 'human development index', which includes life expectancy, level of education and gross national income per capita. In something of a hybrid approach, the EU aims to lift 20 million people out of poverty or exclusion by 2020, defining this target in terms of a combination of three indicators: at-risk-of-poverty, material deprivation and very low work intensity (European Commission, 2010).

In the last two decades, the concept of *social exclusion* has gained ascendancy in Europe as a means of exploring the dynamic, multidimensional and systemic processes underlying inequality (Silver, 1994; Room, 1995; Levitas, 1999, 2006; Hills, 2002). The concept developed out of the EU anti-poverty programme (Room, 1995), when the term 'poverty' was unacceptable to the governments of the UK and Germany, but also reflects the Delors presidency's concern for social inclusion (Ferrera, Matsaganis & Sacchi, 2002). The concept was attractive too to many policy makers and academics because of its focus on the multidimensional, dynamic processes underlying inequality and poverty, and its association with Durkheim's ideas on social integration and cohesion. It is interesting to reflect on the way in which the concept of social exclusion was institutionalised in its adoption and promotion by the EU. Armstrong (2010, p. 18) argues that

> this 'institutionalization' of the language was also advanced by the establishment of the European Observatory on Policies to Combat Social Exclusion … the combined effect of funding action programmes and of establishing the Observatory was to create a means by which the very language of social exclusion might be diffused through a European academic research community and gradually taken up by political actors. It is difficult to imagine that the language of 'social exclusion' could have made the direct leap from French social policy into domestic policy contexts without the mediation of European structures and European programmes.

Burchardt, Le Grand and Piachaud (2002) confirm that the term originated in France as a reference to those who slipped through the social insurance system. At first, the term referred to those (primarily immigrants in the *banlieues*) administratively excluded by the state, but later

French and European thinking moved the focus towards a concern with unemployment and labour market exclusion, and especially to the impacts of globalisation and neoliberalism on individuals and social groups. Byrne (1999, p. 128) indeed portrays social exclusion as 'a necessary and inherent characteristic of unequal post-industrial capitalism founded around a flexible labour market'. To him, the socially excluded are a reserve army of labour in the Marxist sense. These ideas have been elaborated by a number of authors, including Silver (1994), Berghman (1995), Philip and Shucksmith (2003) and Commins (1993, 2004). Reimer (2004), reformulating Polanyi's (1944) three 'modes of economic integration', argued that social exclusion should be studied in terms of market, bureaucratic, associative and communal relations. Philip and Shucksmith (2003) and Reimer see these four systems not only as underlying dimensions of social exclusion but also as relational means of enhancing or diminishing individuals' and communities' capacity to act. Meanwhile, Silver (1994) proposed three paradigms of social exclusion: solidarity, specialisation and monopoly. The first, the solidarity paradigm, sees exclusion as a breakdown of a social bond between the individual and society that is cultural and moral, not economic. Under the specialisation paradigm, exclusion derives from relationships between individuals, notably discrimination. The monopoly paradigm highlights how powerful groups, often displaying distinctive cultural identities, restrict the access to resources of outsiders (Silver, 1994, p. 570). A wide literature has developed (see, for example, Levitas, 1999), critiquing, refining and applying this contested concept, primarily in Europe.

In terms of policy, social exclusion is written into the core of the EU's Maastricht and Lisbon treaties, and in its implementation it is pursued largely in terms of an 'active welfare policy', emphasising employment, in contrast to a passive, redistributive welfare policy. In the UK, the concept was adopted by the 'New Labour' government in 1997, who established a Social Exclusion Unit in the Cabinet Office, although this was discontinued by the Conservative-led coalition after 2010. This UK/EU approach to welfare reform drew from the US model of 'welfare to work' but placed its emphasis on helping people into work, with rather less emphasis on 'individual failings' (such as fecklessness or laziness) that might hinder labour-market integration (Hirsch & Millar, 2004). In the UK, until 2010, it sought to help young people, older unemployed men in areas of industrial restructuring, and deprived urban neighbourhoods through a series of 'New Deals', with employment seen as the key integrating force which would bring income, identity, self-worth and networks. However, Philip and Shucksmith (2003) and Copus et al. (2015a) argue that a broader approach is needed since the processes extend far beyond the labour market and indeed are multidimensional and multiscalar.

Social exclusion remains a contested term. Some regard it as merely a euphemism, diverting attention from necessary redistribution or, worse, code for cultural explanations of poverty and a US-derived 'underclass' discourse (Murray, 1990; Levitas, 1999). The concept's advocates resist such criticisms, arguing that such a relational understanding of poverty and inequality would allow policy to address the causes rather than merely the symptoms. Even so, substantive criticisms of the concept of social exclusion remain, notably that it unduly emphasises boundary formation and carries an implicit notion that all but a few are included in a cohesive society undifferentiated by class or social division (Savage, 2000). The EU continues to seek to tackle social exclusion, as part of the pursuit of 'smart, sustainable, inclusive growth' (European Commission, 2010), even though some of its policies create severe poverty and exclusion, as discussed below. Meanwhile, the UK Conservative-led governments since 2010 no longer refer to social exclusion, emphasising instead individual-cultural explanations of poverty, redefining 'fairness' in terms of 'strivers' and 'shirkers', and arguing that selectivity, sanctions and disincentives to welfare dependency represent the truly 'progressive' approach. In this vein, for example, in July 2015 the government announced it would repeal the statutory commitment to reduce child poverty, and amend the definition of child poverty so that it refers to a broad range of household deficiencies (worklessness, low education, family breakdown, debt and addiction) instead of relative income poverty (DWP, 2015).

Studying poverty and social exclusion in rural places

People live in – and experience poverty, inequality and social exclusion in – places both urban and rural, and this section reviews the various ways in which these concepts have been applied in rural studies in the global north.[1] Among US rural researchers, and in eastern and southern Europe, there has been a long-standing consensus that poverty is at least as much a rural problem as an urban problem, in contrast to the UK where poverty is perceived primarily as an urban issue: in each case, however, the study of rural poverty has been relatively neglected. 'In common with the US, UK research on rural poverty has similarly been overshadowed by research on urban poverty – partly because rural areas are seen as idyllic and rural poverty is hidden and diffuse – and policy has shown little interest in rural poverty' (Shucksmith & Schafft, 2012, p. 115). Milbourne (2004, p. ix) agrees that in Britain and the US 'poverty in rural areas is less well recognised than its urban counterpart in terms of research inputs, academic publications, media representations and policy interventions'.

North American approaches

Despite this under-recognition, over the last 20 years there have been several studies of rural poverty in the United States, reviewed by Shucksmith and Schafft (2012) and earlier by Milbourne (2004), as well as in Canada (Reimer, 2004). Especially notable was the 1993 publication of *Persistent Poverty in Rural America*, assembled by the Rural Sociological Society Task Force on Rural Poverty to 'provide conceptual clarification regarding the factors and dynamics of society which precipitate and perpetuate rural poverty' (RSS Task Force, 1993, p. 3). The Task Force argued that three predominant theoretical approaches had been used to explain persistent rural poverty: human capital theories (insufficient skills), economic organisation theories (inadequate employment opportunities) and culture of poverty theories (economically irrational lifestyle preferences) (Shucksmith & Schafft, 2012).

The Task Force argued that each of these approaches is insufficient and, instead, it proposed a number of alternative perspectives emphasising factors such as the way in which work and gendered relations are embedded within particular social contexts; the effects of historically embedded formal and informal institutions that reproduce inequality across social groups; and *under*-investment in human capital. At macro levels the Task Force suggested the utility of dependency theories, particularly for resource extraction dependent areas; the effects of global economic restructuring; and the failure of national policy to respond to rural needs or develop effective, comprehensive rural policies extending beyond agricultural policy.

Subsequently, rural poverty research in the USA has developed along several avenues (Shucksmith & Schafft, 2012, pp. 109–111). First, research on the relationship between spatial inequality and social inequality has provided a more nuanced examination of the dynamics by which poverty is distributed and redistributed over space. Prior to the early 1990s, 'attention has been divided between studies of poor people, most commonly households, and studies of poor places, usually counties or regions. The relationship between poor people and poor places, however, often remains unspecified' (Fitchen, 1995, p. 181).

Studies inspired by Fitchen's work began to examine more seriously the complex relationships between the geographies of poverty and place, often raising new theoretical and policy questions about differential migration patterns of poor movers, 'geographies of exclusion' and the dynamics of rural poverty concentration. Some of this work, directly inspired by Fitchen's research on rural poverty, housing insecurity and residential mobility (Fitchen, 1994) has challenged human capital theories of migration and mobility by examining the dynamics of residential mobility of disadvantaged households within and across poor places. A related policy issue on which there has been less work concerns why poor people stay in poor places, and the degree to which this might be due to 'sticky' labour markets and/or housing markets, to a reliance on social networks, or to poverty itself. Other studies have looked at the geography of racial and ethnic exclusion (Lobao & Saenz, 2002), such as Lichter and colleagues' (2007) examination of racial and socioeconomic segregation and municipal annexation patterns in the non-metropolitan South, and Lichter and Johnson's (2007) study of poverty concentrations among rural minorities in the context of overall decreasing spatial inequality in non-metropolitan America (Lobao, Hooks & Tickamyer, 2007).

Second, Shucksmith and Schafft (2012) note that rural researchers have paid increasing attention to the in-migration of foreign-born ethnic and racial minorities into 'non-traditional' rural destinations. This work implicitly focuses on the relationship between demographic change and the shifting economic and social status of rural people, newcomers and longer term residents alike, and the communities in which they reside. During the 1990s, and particularly with the release of the 2000 US Census data, demographers began to detect marked shifts in the patterns of immigrant settlement, in particular noting movement to 'non-traditional' migration locations, often in rural areas that had not previously attracted many migrants (Kandel & Cromartie, 2004; Barcus, 2006; Kandel & Parrado, 2006; Farmer & Moon, 2009). These were found to be linked to changes in the organisation of the meat processing industry, the siting of new meat processing facilities in economically declining rural areas, and the active recruitment of immigrant (and often undocumented) labour (Stull, Broadway & Griffith, 1995; Broadway, 2007; Massey, 2008). Hence, demographic analyses were quickly aligned with political economic examinations of rural disadvantage, industrial organisation and structural changes in food processing (especially meat and poultry) all in the context of shifting labour market conditions and international trade and immigration policies.

At the same time, these demographic and political economic analyses were coupled with research at the community level, some of which analysed community economic and demographic change in the context of rapid natural resource development (see, for example, Broadway, 2007; McConnell & Miraftab, 2009). Other research in this area examined what these new migration patterns have meant for local culture, community and identity, the social and economic integration of new immigrants within and beyond the ethnic enclave, and community responses and reactions to new immigrant-related diversity in rural America (Salamon, 2003; Gimpel & Lay, 2008; Crowley & Lichter, 2009; Pfeffer & Parra, 2009).

Third, Shucksmith and Schafft (2012) point to several notable examples of US rural poverty research that explicitly examined the relationship between local culture, poverty discourses, and how those discourses, often with specific racial and/or gendered dimensions, are embedded within broader cultural constructions of poverty, race and rurality. This work is largely qualitative and often informed by multiple disciplinary and theoretical orientations, as for example in Sherman's work (2006, 2009) on poverty, gendered identity and constructions of morality in the context of logging industry collapse in rural California. Devine (2006, p. 953) similarly looks at the social construction of poverty 'along markers of difference, such as race, class, gender, and generation' to examine the ways in which local understandings in the rural northwest United States differentially position first-generation 'hardworking' Hispanic immigrants as either (deserving) 'working poor' or (undeserving poor) who 'choose' poverty as a way of life.

Taken together, argue Shucksmith and Schafft (2012), these three strands of US rural poverty research are consistent with the recommendations of the 1993 RSS Task Force Report through their multilevel foci and their examinations of how local social, cultural and economic processes are embedded within and reflect (and in some cases resist) macro-structural processes. Duncan's *Worlds Apart* (1999) is notable in this context for its synthesis of structural and cultural explanations of persistent poverty, drawing on Wilson's approach to studying inner-city poverty.

Additionally, the rural poverty research reviewed here has contributed to better understandings of the various relationships and processes that connect the poverty of people to the poverty of place. While social exclusion as a conceptual or discursive device has seldom been used in US contexts (Parent & Lewis, 2003), much US rural poverty research, with its emphasis on the relationship between social and spatial inequality, contains strong foci on relational and historically embedded patterns of disadvantage at multiple micro and macro levels. However, consistent with the broader body of US poverty research, this work has similarly been challenged in its ability to coherently and substantively influence public policy.

European approaches

In Europe these are also important issues for rural poverty research, but the focus of effort has been rather different, and these issues have been approached to varying degrees and from different perspectives and academic traditions, to some extent reflecting differing welfare regimes and levels of national prosperity. In the UK, for example, from 1945 until 1990 researchers such as Newby, Bell, Rose and Saunders (1978), Newby (1979, 1980, 1987), McLaughlin (1986), Walker (1978) and Shaw (1979) tended towards three intertwined explanations for rural poverty: the role of the state; the role of class relations; and the role of broader economic and social processes. Of these, the role of class relations was more deeply rooted in social theory.

In the 1990s, rural studies in the UK, and particularly rural geography, switched their focus from poverty and inequality to cultural identities and differences under the influence of the 'cultural turn' in human geography (Cloke & Little, 1997). Philo's (1992) seminal paper on 'the rural other' showed how people in rural areas may be marginalised through cultural practices in everyday life, and particularly through the social construction of identity and symbolic capital in social and lay discourses (Cloke & Little, 1997; Milbourne, 1997; Hughes, Morris & Seymour, 2000). Many studies in this style are relational and revealing, but they have been criticised for failing to speak to policy and practice (Milbourne, 2000) or to assist practical action (Cloke, 1997). Accordingly, Milbourne (2004, p. 34) called for a resurgence of interest in poverty among rural geographers and specifically for a greater interest in the local contexts of rural poverty, investigating 'the linkages between poverty and people in particular places'. He points out that the concept of social exclusion emphasises the importance of local context, and argues that research should be 'concerned with the productions, representations, materialities and experiences of poverty in particular spaces, as well as the specific mixes of welfare facilities and welfare policy contexts in these spaces' (Milbourne, 2004, p. 123). In proposing this place-based approach to rural poverty studies, Milbourne emphasises its antecedents in the USA, and specifically the work of Duncan and Lambourghini (1994) and Duncan (1996, 1999, and now 2015).

While rural geographers have emphasised cultural differences and identities, the concept of social exclusion was taken as the basis for multidisciplinary, mixed-method research under the

Joseph Rowntree Foundation's Action in Rural Areas programme from 1997 to 2000[2] (Shucksmith, 2000). The research drew attention to the rural effects of market processes, and the rolling back of state systems, as a neoliberal hegemony promoted deregulation, privatisation, cuts in public spending and global capital's penetration of labour and product markets (Shucksmith, 2002). The programme found that both labour markets and housing markets were instrumental in generating inequality and exclusion, with many respondents perceiving very restricted opportunities for well-paid, secure employment or for affordable housing, while at the same time these markets facilitated in-migration of affluent households and displacement of other social groups. These impediments to inclusion were closely bound up with failings of private and public services, notably transport, social housing and childcare. Moreover, the welfare state was failing to reach potential recipients through selective benefits, and the take-up of welfare entitlements was lower than in urban areas (Bramley, Lancaster & Gordon, 2000). To mitigate these failings of markets and state, there was a greater reliance on the voluntary sector and on friends and family, although migration and the loss of young people had meanwhile ruptured informal support networks and left elderly people in rural areas socially isolated. The research concluded that the risk of poverty was not confined to a small minority but touched many rural dwellers, especially in old age. The findings pointed strongly towards structural causes of rural poverty, finding no evidence of 'cultures of poverty' nor benefit dependency. On the contrary, while elderly people and lone parents faced long-term poverty, others faced short spells of poverty during which the support of the welfare state was crucial (Chapman et al., 1998; Shucksmith & Chapman, 1998; Phimister, Shucksmith & Vera-Toscano, 2000; Shucksmith, 2000; Shucksmith, Shucksmith & Watt, 2006). It should be noted that all these studies precede the 2008 banking crisis and subsequent austerity policies, leaving us poorly informed about the ways in which these affected rural citizens. In the UK generally, we know that both child poverty and poverty in old age diminished markedly under the Labour government of 1997–2010, while 'poverty in work', associated with low pay, flexible hours and insecurity, is now the main challenge. Since 2010, inequality is rising again while welfare benefits are being reduced.

These studies suggest that multidimensional conceptualisations of social exclusion and inclusion are helpful in researching the interconnectedness of the many different dimensions of service provision, transport, childcare, labour market participation and community engagement which characterise the experience of low-income groups in rural areas. Specifically, this allows us to consider the complex interactions between bureaucratic, associative, communal and market relations within particular social contexts which give rise to exclusion. This is pursued further below.

Across Europe, similarly, a small number of studies have sought to investigate processes of social exclusion in rural areas (see Bock, Kovacs & Shucksmith, 2015; Bertolini & Peragine, 2009 for an overview). For example, Jentsch and Shucksmith (2004), Dax and Machold (2002) and Shucksmith (2004) investigated how social exclusion affects young people across rural Europe, a situation that has become much worse since the economic crisis. Table 37.1 presents unpublished analysis of data from the EU Labour Force Survey showing changes in youth unemployment from 2009 to 2012 according to the degree of urbanisation: huge increases in rural youth unemployment can be seen in Greece, Bulgaria, Cyprus, Spain and Portugal, in particular, over these three years, contrasting markedly with the youth unemployment rates in rural Germany, Austria and the Netherlands (updated from Shucksmith, 2010a).

Other studies looked into gender difference and the vulnerability of rural women (Bock, 2010). Rural women are more at risk of social exclusion compared to men, especially in the remote rural areas in the south and east of Europe, where employment depends heavily on

Table 37.1 Youth unemployment (15–24 years), 2009 and 2012 by degree of urbanisation

| | Youth unemployment rate, 2009 and 2012 | | | | | | | |
	Densely populated		Intermediate		Thinly populated		All	
EU27	20.3	24	17.9	21	20.8	22	19.8	23
Austria	13.9	15	10.4	9	6.7	5	10.0	9
Belgium	26.1	28	16.8	16	22.5	19	21.9	20
Bulgaria	12.7	22	22.4[b]	32	18.6	34	16.2	28
Cyprus	14.1	27	13.1[b]	27	13.5[b]	31	13.8	28
Czech Republic	15.9	18	18.2	22	16.2	19	16.6	20
Germany	12.4	10	10.3	8	9.6	6	11.2	8
Denmark	11.8	15	10.8	16	10.9	13	11.2	14
Estonia	29.6	20	27.2[a]	21	25.4	22	27.5	21
Spain	37.0	51	39.2	57	38.2	53	37.8	53
Finland	17.7	17	22.4	21	23.5	19	21.5	19
France	24.2	25	21.4	26	20.0	20	22.6	24
Greece	23.2	55	31.7	57	26.5	54	25.8	55
Hungary	21.8	27	23.5	28	30.5	29	26.5	28
Ireland	20.4	26		31	26.7	34	24.2	30
Italy	27.6	41	23.6	33	25.1	33	25.4	35
Lithuania	26.2	20			31.6	33	29.2	26
Luxembourg	17.5[b]	22	16.7[b]	21	17.4[b]	15	17.2	18
Latvia	33.5	27	21.0[a]	28	34.1	30	33.6	28
Malta	14.4	15	17.8[a]	15		10.2[a]	14.4	14
Netherlands	7.4	11	5.2	8	5.6[b]	7	6.6	10
Poland	19.0	24	20.3	28	21.9	27	20.6	27
Portugal	23.3	44	16.8	32	19.3	35	20.0	38
Romania	25.7	30	14.4[a]	31	18.7	15	20.8	23
Sweden	22.1	23	24.1	24	26.2	23	25.0	24
Slovenia	16.8[b]	21	12.1	20	13.5	21	13.6	21
Slovakia	15.3	24	26.9	31	31.5	39	27.3	34
UK	20.5	23	17.0	19	14.5	15	19.1	21

Notes: [a] [b] indicate that the figures may be unreliable due to small sample sizes. Further details are given in notes accompanying the Labour Force Survey.

Source: Eurostat (2012).

agriculture and women's employment is low (Copus et al., 2006; Bock, 2010). The rural exodus of young women may be one response (Bock, 2010), and indeed there are still many areas of rural Europe which suffer from continuous youth out-migration and a vicious circle of ongoing decline (Copus et al., 2006).

In Eastern Europe, rural social exclusion became a topical issue during the accession period after the turn of the millennium. The collapse of rural economies, land privatisation, the dismantling of large-scale agriculture and its inevitable consequences – emerging mass joblessness, insecure livelihoods and deepening rural poverty – dominated political and academic discourses. According to Alanen (2004, p. 49), rural poverty inevitably appeared across the Baltic countries when collective farms were relinquished on the advice of the World Bank. In Estonia large-scale farming survived, with lower capacity for employment than previously, but in Latvia and especially in Lithuania family farms that were too small to secure people's livelihoods became dominant. Even more destruction and emerging poverty were reported from the poorest countries of East–Central Europe, Bulgaria and Romania, where millions became dependent on subsistence farming for their sheer survival (Vincze & Swain, 1998;

Kostov & Lingard, 2002). The relational character of rural poverty is apparent, as illustrated by Shubin (2007, p. 594) in relation to rural Russia: 'Poverty is loneliness and isolation, but it is also involvement in the systems of help because of people's knowledge of local symbolic practices such as collecting firewood or swapping agricultural products. Poverty is not neatly categorised simply on the basis of income or remoteness, but it is constructed within complex webs of relationships in the village.'

A review of research on poverty and social exclusion in rural areas of the EU by Bertolini and Peragine (2009) made an important distinction between *poor places* and *poor people*, and the relationship between social and spatial inequality is as significant in Europe as it is in North America. Across the EU the incidence of rural and urban poverty varies markedly between places, at many scales of analysis, with rural poverty systematically more characteristic of poorer EU countries, as indicated in Figure 37.1 (reproduced from Copus et al., 2015a) which shows rural and urban poverty in each EU member state (see also Copus et al., 2015b).

Some further insights may be gained from an analysis by Shucksmith, Cameron, Pichler and Merridew (2009) of urban–rural differences across the EU using data from the European Quality of Life Survey (EQLS) for 2003. In richer EU countries, urban–rural differences within the domains considered were minimal, but differences between urban and rural areas were much greater in the poorer countries of eastern and southern Europe, where rural households experienced a markedly lower level of material welfare and quality of life. This was reflected in lower levels of income, lack of basic household items, poor housing conditions and lack of basic amenities. There were also significant differences in level of education, IT literacy and Internet access, unemployment and primary sector employment. Within this general pattern, the 'accession' countries stood out as having particularly high levels of urban–rural disparity and high levels of reported disadvantage in rural areas. The obvious implication is that in relation to the cohesion and convergence objectives of EU policy it is the rural areas of the new member states, accession and candidate countries that are most in need of support.

The quality-of-life approach also allowed examination of the widely held view that the intrinsic, non-material qualities of rural life compensate for material poverty. The results revealed little evidence that such aspects of lifestyle, social network and community are better in rural areas than urban. The EQLS data do not therefore support the myth of a rural idyll which compensates for objective, material disadvantages and thereby might lessen the need to address the cohesion issues affecting rural areas in the poorer countries.

Spatial inequality and social inequality – issues of scale

In thinking about spatial aspects of social inequality it is necessary to think about the scales at which different processes operate, and the appropriateness of responses at different scales from place-based endogenous or neo-endogenous rural development to regional and supra-national instruments and policies. Neither should be overlooked.

Several European studies have examined the factors which operate at the micro scale to explain the economic or demographic trajectories of rural areas (Terluin, 2003; Bryden & Hart, 2004; Arnason, Shucksmith & Vergunst, 2009; Copus & Hörnström, 2011; Copus & Van Well, 2014). These confirm the importance of networks and social capital, institutions and governance, social cohesion, entrepreneurship and education as factors operating at the micro scale. This combination of knowledge resources, network resources and mobilisation capabilities has been termed 'institutional capacity' (Healey, 2005; Shucksmith, 2010, 2012b). There is also evidence of the stigmatisation of places at the micro scale, which adds to the place-based exclusion of people (Bock, Kovacs & Shucksmith, 2015). Thus Wacquant (2007) shows how territorial

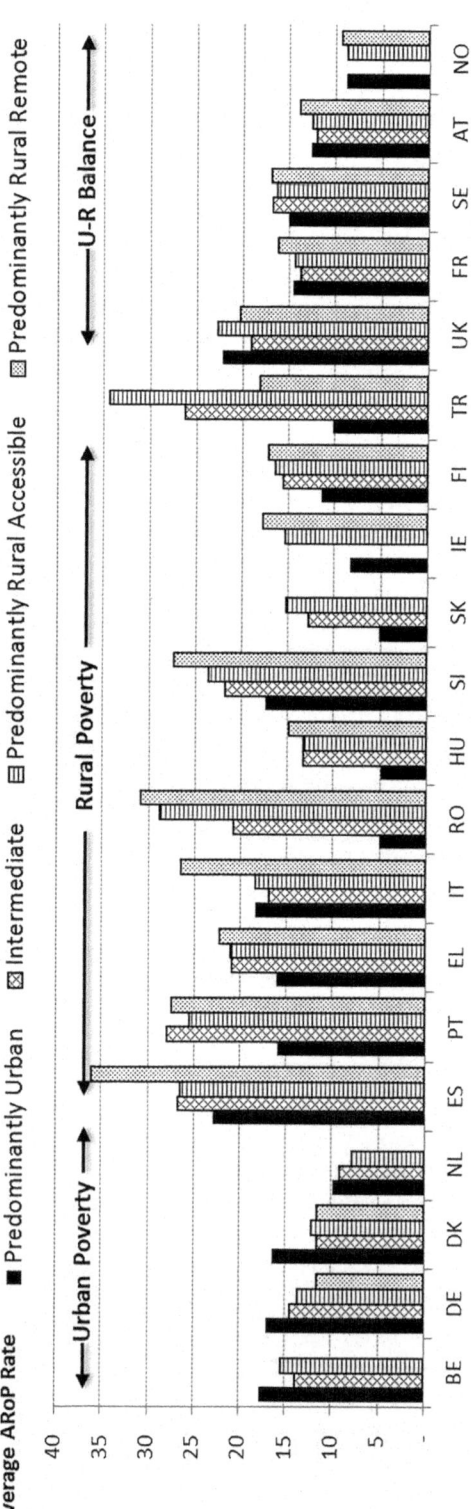

Figure 37.1 At-risk-of-poverty rate by OECD rural/urban definition in each EU member state, 2011

Source: Copus et al. (2015a)

stigmatisation contributes to the dissolution of places, by undermining feelings of belonging and encouraging disengagement, de-solidarisation and ultimately out-migration.

Research also highlights a vital role for enhanced governance in the form of the 'enabling state', without which inequalities between places will widen (Cheshire, 2006; Shucksmith, 2010, 2012b). The highly uneven capacity of different communities of place to bring forward 'development from within' has been a consistent finding of studies in Britain and abroad. For example, Shortall and Warner (2010, p. 7) report that 'lagging regions in the US are viewed as needing more market, not more government (Brown & Warner, 1991). Instead of policies that make the reversal of declining rural areas a priority, the US market-focused 'sink or swim' attitude assumes individual relocation is a natural and acceptable response to changed economic opportunities (Brown & Swanson, 2003). In Australia, similarly, governmental strategies to address rural vulnerability have fed on narratives of community self-help to pass responsibility for mediating and negotiating change on to local citizens (Cheshire, 2006; Cheshire, Esparcia & Shucksmith, 2015). This involves both a *rescaling* of responsibility and a *shifting* of responsibility from state to market and civil society. Shucksmith (2012b) has argued that there is instead a need for capacity building in two respects. First, this is necessary to enable the most marginalised individuals to gain the confidence, competencies and skills they need to participate as active citizens in local civil societies. Second, this is necessary to allow new institutions and groups to emerge in less active places, enabling them to foster and articulate a collective view on the form and content of regeneration for their locality and on how best to realise this vision.

Of course, many of the processes driving spatial inequality operate at scales far beyond the locality. A recent study of processes of differentiation across rural areas of Europe (Copus & Hörnström, 2011) found that these operate at many scales (global, national, regional, local) to influence rural change. At the European scale, there are clear and persistent patterns of structural differentiation, closely associated with disparities in economic performance – for example, between core and periphery; between the consumption countryside and agricultural and ex-industrial rural areas; and between western and eastern and southern Europe. In an especially penetrating analysis of the contemporary crisis across southern Europe, Hadjimichalis and Hudson (2014) show the need to go beyond the endogenous development paradigm to understand places 'as open to and in large part constituted through global flows and international relations, albeit they are unique and locally embedded places' (p. 215). A focus only on the micro scale (innovation, networking, learning regions, clusters, social capital, etc.) and a neglect of macro-scale processes of deregulation, globalisation, financialisation and monetary union, they argue, have constituted (perhaps inadvertently) a gradual slide towards the dominant neoliberal discourse and its exacerbation of sociospatial inequality.

Discussion and conclusion

As inequalities widen across the global north, one might argue that it is incumbent upon rural scholars to return to researching the causes and experiences of inequality, poverty and injustice encountered in rural areas. Since 2007 the global financial crisis has spread across rural and urban places, from its origins in the sub-prime mortgage markets of the USA and the irresponsible practices of the financial sector to become a fiscal crisis of nations, regions and municipalities visited unevenly as a human crisis upon the most vulnerable people (Harvey, 2010). Periodic crises may be integral to capitalist development 'but at considerable human and socio-spatial cost' (Hadjimichalis & Hudson, 2014, p. 216). Rural studies have a responsibility to investigate these processes and their effects, both in the immediate aftermath of the crisis and over the longer term. But to what extent this is a research priority for rural scholars is less certain.

In researching poverty and disadvantage, scholars in Europe have often employed the concept of social exclusion to focus their efforts on studying, in local context, the multidimensional, dynamic processes that underlie poverty and the reproduction of inequality. Class analysis has also been refreshed by new developments in social theory. I have argued elsewhere (Shucksmith, 2012a) that we can move beyond the limiting aspects of the concept of social exclusion while retaining a focus on multidimensional dynamic processes, rooted in localities, by returning to class analysis in its new reinvigorated Bourdieuvian formulation. Bourdieu rejects earlier ideas of classes as exogenous and fixed, seeing these instead as contested and socially constructed, as a stake in symbolic struggles that are themselves part of the class struggle. Class formation is therefore a continuous, contested and fluid process of discursive construction, identity formation, mobilisation and struggle based around habitus, field and capital. Moreover, class formation is inextricably bound up with place, in that the social construction of place (and rural places) is necessarily class infused, in Bourdieu's sense, and these place-identities are themselves a source of advantage to dominant classes and conversely also a source of inequality and exclusion. Much UK research has viewed rural areas as a site of middle-class colonisation but, as Murdoch (1995) argued, this has tended to see rural areas as simply a stage on which the exogenous, national class structure was played out. Following Bourdieu's approach to class analysis would allow us instead to investigate the reflexive and localised nature of class formation, and the associated role of class-infused constructions of place and rurality in the accumulation and storing of assets and in relations of exploitation, which together lead to persistent inequality.

Researchers in the USA appear more active in exploring rural poverty than other rural scholars. They have developed new insights, broadly following the recommendations of the seminal 1993 RSS Task Force Report through their multilevel foci and their examinations of how local social, cultural and economic processes are embedded within and reflect (and in some cases resist) macro-structural processes. Additionally, this work has contributed to better understandings of the various relationships and processes that connect the poverty of people to the poverty of place.

It is instructive to reflect on the roles played by the RSS Task Force and by the EU Observatory on Policies to Combat Social Exclusion in formulating, promoting and disseminating these two approaches to poverty research and policy. The EU Observatory was highly influential not only in promoting adoption of the concept of social exclusion through academic networks but also within formal and informal policy networks, and ultimately in policies themselves (Armstrong, 2010). The RSS Task Force primarily shows how scholars took stock and influenced the direction of future research (Shucksmith & Schafft, 2012).

The ideas of the RSS Task Force are still relevant to research agendas for investigating rural poverty and disadvantage in the 21st century in North America and beyond. It is evident that explanations of poverty, inequality and social exclusion in rural areas must examine processes at multiple scales, from the local to the global; that they must connect the social and the spatial; that they must synthesise structural and cultural explanations; and that they must be relational. Insights may be derived from various research methods, from analysis of large and complex sets of household panel data to detailed ethnographic work in specific localities or fields, interrogating cultural and symbolic markers as well as the material. Our research should elaborate the causal pathways through which macro-structural transformations (global financial crisis; collapse of socialism; global inequality and political instability, etc.) are transmitted to rural localities. In other words, it should link history to biography, connecting individual experiences and everyday lives to political economy and the macro processes which we must seek to mediate and negotiate at multiple scales through our agency.

Most of all, we must analyse poverty and inequality in relation to power, whether conceived as a matter of social production (groups' capacity to act) or of social control (by government or elites) – that is, 'power to' or 'power over'. But that is the subject of another section of this handbook.

Notes

1   This section draws heavily on Shucksmith and Schafft (2012) and Bock, Kovacs and Shucksmith (2015).
2   Since identification of this as a research priority by Shucksmith et al. (1997), research in the UK began to be conducted on dynamic processes, and the identification of 'bridges and barriers' to exclusion and integration, through a combination of longitudinal analysis of rural households in the British Household Panel Survey (BHPS), following the same randomly selected 7,164 individuals each year between 1991 and 1996 (Chapman et al., 1998), alongside a suite of nine qualitative, place-based studies conducted by several universities. Similar studies have been undertaken in the USA (e.g., Rank & Hirschl, 1999, 2001, 2005; Rank, Hirschl & Foster, 2014). No such studies have been undertaken in the UK since 2010, to the author's knowledge.

References

Alanen, I (2004). The transformation of agricultural systems in the Baltic countries – A critique of the World Bank concept. In I Alanen (Ed.), *Mapping the rural problem in the Baltic countryside* (pp. 5–580). Aldershot: Ashgate.

Armstrong, K (2010). *Governing social inclusion. Europeanisation through policy coordination.* Oxford: Oxford University Press.

Arnason, A, Shucksmith, M & Vergunst, J (2009). *Comparing rural development: Continuity and change in the countryside of Western Europe.* Aldershot: Ashgate.

Barcus, HR (2006). New destinations for Hispanic migrants: An analysis of rural Kentucky. In HA Smith & OJ Furuseth (Eds), *Latinos in the new South* (pp. 89–109). Burlington, VT: Ashgate.

Berghman, J (1995). Social exclusion in Europe: Policy context and analytical framework. In G Room (Ed.), *Beyond the threshold: The measurement and analysis of social exclusion* (pp. 10–28). Bristol: Policy Press.

Bertolini, P & Peragine, V (2009). *Poverty and social exclusion in rural areas.* Report to CEC Directorate General for Employment, Social Affairs and Equal Opportunities.

Bock, BB (2010). *Personal and social development of women in rural areas of Europe.* Brussels: European Parliament, Committee on Agriculture and Rural Development.

Bock, B, Kovacs, K & Shucksmith, M (2015). Changing social characteristics: Patterns of inequality and social exclusion. In A Copus & P De Lima (Eds), *Territorial cohesion in rural Europe: The relational turn in rural development* (pp. 193–211). London: Routledge.

Bramley, G, Lancaster, S & Gordon, D (2000). Benefit take-up and the geography of poverty in Scotland. *Regional Studies* 34(6), 507–520.

Broadway, M (2007). Meatpacking and the transformation of rural communities: A comparison of Brooks, Alberta and Garden City, Kansas. *Rural Sociology* 72(4), 560–582.

Brown, D & Swanson, L (2003). *Challenges for rural America in the 21st century.* Philadelphia, PA: Penn State Press.

Brown, D & Warner, M (1991). Persistent low income non-metropolitan areas in the US: Some conceptual challenges for policy development. *Policy Studies Journal* 19(2), 22–41.

Bryden, J & Hart, K (2004). *Why local economies differ? The dynamics of rural areas in the European Union.* New York: Edwin Mellen Press.

Burchardt, T, Le Grand, J & Piachaud, D (2002). Introduction. In J Hills, J Le Grand & D Piachaud (Eds), *Understanding social exclusion* (pp. 1–12). Oxford: Oxford University Press.

Byrne, D (1999). *Social exclusion.* Milton Keynes: Open University Press.

Chapman, P, Phimister, E, Shucksmith, M, Upward, R & Vera-Toscano, E (1998). *Poverty and exclusion in rural Britain: The dynamics of low income and employment.* York: York Publishing Services.

Cheshire, L (2006). *Governing rural development.* Farnham: Ashgate.

Cheshire L, Esparcia J & Shucksmith M (2015). Community resilience, social capital and territorial governance. *ager Revista de Estudios Sobre Despoblacion Y Desarrollo Rural*, 18, 7–38.

Cloke, P & Little, J (Eds). (1997). *Contested countryside cultures*. London: Routledge.

Commins, P (Ed.). (1993). *Combating exclusion in Ireland, 1990–94: A midway report*. Brussels: European Commission.

Commins, P (2004). Poverty and social exclusion in rural areas: Characteristics, processes and research issues. *Sociologia Ruralis* 44(1), 60–75.

Copus, A, Hall, C, Barnes, A, Dalton, H, Cook, P, Weingarten, P, Baum, S, Stange, H, ... & Johansson, M (2006). *Study on employment in rural areas (SERA)*. Final report. Brussels: DG Agriculture.

Copus, A & Hörnström, L (Eds). (2011). *The new rural Europe: Towards rural cohesion policy*. Nordregio.

Copus, A & Van Well, L (2014). Parallel worlds? Comparing perspectives and rationales of EU rural development and cohesion policy. In A Copus & P de Lima (Eds), *Territorial cohesion in rural Europe* (pp. 53–78). London: Routledge.

Copus, A et al. (2015a). *Territorial indicators of poverty and social exclusion in Europe* (TIPSE). Final Report to ESPON. Aberdeen: James Hutton Institute.

Copus, A, Melo, P, Kaup, S, Tagai, G & Artelaris, P (2015b). Regional poverty mapping in Europe – Challenges, advances, benefits and limitations. *Local Economy* 30(7), 742–764.

Crowley, M & Lichter, DT (2009). Social disorganization in new Latino destinations? *Rural Sociology* 74(4), 573–604.

Dax, T & Machold, I (Eds). (2002). *Voices of rural youth: A break with traditional patterns?* Vienna: Bundesanstalt für Bergbauernfragen.

Devine, J (2006). Hardworking newcomers and generations of poverty: Poverty discourse in Central Washington. *Antipode* 38(5), 953–976.

Duncan, CM (1996). Understanding persistent poverty: Social class context in rural communities. *Rural Sociology* 61(1), 103–124.

Duncan CM (1999). *Worlds apart: Why poverty persists in rural America*. New Haven, CT: Yale University Press.

Duncan CM (2015). *Worlds apart: Why poverty persists in rural America* (2nd edn). New Haven, CT: Yale University Press.

Duncan, C & Lambourghini, N (1994). Poverty and social context in remote rural communities. *Rural Sociology* 59(3), 437–461.

DWP (2015). Government to strengthen child poverty measure. Press release. Department of Work and Pensions. https://www.gov.uk/government/news/government-to-strengthen-child-poverty-measure.

European Commission (2010). *Europe 2020: A strategy for smart, sustainable and inclusive growth* (COM (2010) 2020 final). Brussels: European Commission.

Eurostat (2012). *Labour force survey: Youth unemployment 2009 and 2012 by degree of urbanization*. Brussels: Eurostat.

Farmer, F & Moon, ZK (2009). An empirical examination of characteristics of Mexican migrants to metropolitan and nonmetropolitan areas of the United States. *Rural Sociology* 74(2), 220–240.

Ferrera, M, Matsaganis, M & Sacchi, S (2002). Open coordination against poverty: The new EU 'Social Inclusion Process'. *Journal of European Social Policy* 12(3), 223–239.

Fitchen, JM (1994). Residential mobility among the rural poor. *Rural Sociology* 5(3), 416–436.

Fitchen, JM (1995). Spatial redistribution of poverty through migration of poor people to depressed rural communities. *Rural Sociology* 60(2), 181–201.

Gimpel, JG & Lay, JC (2008). Political socialization and reactions to immigration-related diversity in rural America. *Rural Sociology* 73(2), 180–204.

Hadjimichalis, C & Hudson, R (2014). Contemporary crisis across Europe and the crisis of regional development theories. *Regional Studies* 48(1), 208–218.

Harvey, D (2010). *The enigma of capital and the crises of capitalism*. London: Profile Books.

Healey, P (2005). *Collaborative planning: Shaping places in fragmented societies*. London: Macmillan.

Hills, J (2002). Does a focus on social exclusion change the policy response? In J Hills, J Le Grand & D Piachaud (Eds), *Understanding social exclusion* (pp. 226–243). Oxford: Oxford University Press.

Hirsch, D & Millar, J (2004). *Labour's welfare reform: Progress to date*. York: Joseph Rowntree Foundation.

Hughes, A, Morris, C & Seymour, S (2000). *Ethnography and rural research*. Cheltenham: Countryside and Community Press.

Jentsch, B & Shucksmith, M (Eds). (2004). *Young people in rural areas of Europe*. Aldershot: Ashgate.

JRF (2015). *A minimum income standard for the UK in 2015.* York: Joseph Rowntree Foundation. Available at http://www.jrf.org.uk/publications/minimum-income-standard-uk-2015 (accessed 27 January 2016).

Kandel, W & Cromartie, J (2004). *New patterns of Hispanic settlement in rural America.* USDA Rural Development Research Report No. 99. Washington, DC: USDA.

Kandel, W & Parrrado, E (2006). Rural Hispanic population growth: Public policy impacts in nonmetro counties. In W Kandel & DL Brown (Eds), *Population change and rural society* (pp. 155–176). Dordrecht: Springer.

Kostov, P & Lingard, J (2002). Subsistence farming in transitional economies. Lessons from Bulgaria. *Journal of Rural Studies* 18, 83–94.

Levitas, R (1999). *The inclusive society? Social exclusion and New Labour.* London: Macmillan.

Levitas, R (2006). The concept and measurement of social exclusion. In C Pantazis, D Gordon & R Levitas (Eds), *Poverty and social exclusion in Britain* (pp. 123–160). Bristol: Policy Press.

Lichter, DT & Johnson, KM (2007). The changing spatial concentration of America's rural poor population. *Rural Sociology* 72(3), 331–358.

Lichter, DT, Parisi, D, Grice, SM & Taquino, M (2007). Municipal unbounding: Annexation and racial exclusion in small southern towns. *Rural Sociology* 72(1), 47–68.

Lobao, L & Saenz, R (2002). Spatial inequality and diversity as an emerging research area. *Rural Sociology* 6(4), 497–511.

Lobao, L, Hooks, G & Tickamyer, AR (Eds). (2007). *The sociology of spatial inequality.* Albany: State University of New York Press.

Madanipour, A, Shucksmith, M & Talbot, H (2015). Concepts of poverty and social exclusion in Europe. *Local Economy* 30(7), 721–741.

Massey, D (Ed.). (2008). *New faces in new places: The changing geography of American immigration.* New York: Russell Sage.

McConnell, ED & Miraftab, F (2009). Sundown town to 'Little Mexico': Old-timers and newcomers in an American small town. *Rural Sociology* 74(4), 605–629.

McLaughlin, B (1986). The rhetoric and the reality of rural deprivation. *Journal of Rural Studies* 2, 291–307.

Milbourne, P (Ed.). (1997). *Revealing rural 'others': Representation, power and identity in the British countryside.* London: Pinter

Milbourne, P. (2000). Exporting 'other' rurals: New audiences for qualitative research. In A Hughes, C Morris & S Seymour (Eds), *Ethnography and rural research* (pp. 179–197). Cheltenham: Countryside and Community Press.

Milbourne, P (2004). *Rural poverty: Marginalisation and exclusion in Britain and the US.* London: Routledge.

Murdoch, J (1995). Middle-class territory? Some remarks on the use of class analysis in rural studies. *Environment and Planning A* 27, 1213–1230.

Murray, C (1990). *The emerging British underclass.* London: IEA.

Newby, H (1979). Urbanisation and the rural class structure: Reflections on a case study. *British Journal of Sociology* 30(4), 475–498.

Newby, H (1980). *Green and pleasant land?* London: Penguin.

Newby, H (1987). *Country life.* London: Weidenfeld & Nicholson.

Newby, H, Bell, C, Rose, D & Saunders, P (1978). *Property, paternalism and power: Class and control in rural England.* London: Hutchinson.

O'Connor, A (2001). *Poverty knowledge.* Princeton, NJ: Princeton University Press.

Parent, FD & Lewis, BL (2003). The concept of social exclusion and rural development policy. *Southern Rural Sociology* 19(2), 153–175.

Pfeffer, MJ & Parra, PA (2009). Strong ties, weak ties, and human capital: Latino immigration employment outside the enclave. *Rural Sociology* 74(2), 241–269.

Philip, L & Shucksmith, M (2003). Conceptualising social exclusion. *European Planning Studies* 11(4), 461–480.

Philo, C (1992). Neglected rural geographies: A review. *Journal of Rural Studies* 8, 193–207.

Phimister, E, Shucksmith, M & Vera-Toscano, E (2000). The dynamics of low pay in rural households: Exploratory analysis using the British Household Panel Survey. *Journal of Agricultural Economics* 51(1), 61–76.

Rank, MR & Hirschl, TA (1999). The likelihood of poverty across the American life span. *Social Work* 44, 201–216.

Rank, MR & Hirschl, TA (2001). The occurrence of poverty across the life cycle: Evidence from the PSID. *Journal of Policy Analysis and Management* 20, 737–755.

Rank, MR & Hirschl, TA (2005). Likelihood of using food stamps during the adulthood years. *Journal of Nutrition Education and Behavior* 37(3), 137–146.

Rank, MR, Hirschl, TA & Foster, KA (2014). *Chasing the American dream: Understanding what shapes our fortunes.* New York: Oxford University Press.

Reimer, W (2004). Social exclusion in a comparative context. *Sociologia Ruralis* 44(1), 76–94.

Room, G (1995). Poverty and social exclusion: The new European agenda for policy and research. In G Room (Ed.), *Beyond the threshold: The measurement and analysis of social exclusion* (pp. 1–9). Bristol: Policy Press.

Rowntree, BS (1901). *Poverty: A study of town life.* London: Macmillan.

RSS Task Force (1993). *Persistent poverty in rural America.* Boulder, CO: Westview Press.

Ruggeri Laderchi, C, Saith, R & Stewart, F (2003). Does it matter that we do not agree on the definition of poverty? A comparison of four approaches. *Oxford Development Studies* 31(3), 243–274.

Salamon, S. (2003). *Newcomers to old towns: Suburbanization of the heartland.* Chicago: University of Chicago Press.

Savage, M (2000). *Class analysis and social transformation.* Buckingham: Open University Press.

Shaw, JM (1979). *Rural deprivation and planning.* Norwich: Geobooks.

Sherman, J (2006). Coping with rural poverty: Economic survival and moral capital in rural America. *Social Forces* 8 (2), 891–913.

Sherman, J (2009). *Those who work, those who don't: Poverty, morality, and family in rural America.* Minneapolis: University of Minneapolis Press.

Shortall, S & Warner, M (2010). Social inclusion or market competitiveness? A comparison of EU and US rural development policies. *Social Policy and Administration* 44(5), 575–597.

Shubin, S (2007). Networked poverty in rural Russia. *Europe–Asia Studies* 59, 591–620.

Shucksmith, M (2000). *Exclusive countryside? Social inclusion and regeneration in rural Britain.* York: Joseph Rowntree Foundation.

Shucksmith, M (2002). Social exclusion and poverty in rural areas. *Belgeo: the Belgian Journal of Geography,* 2001–3, 165–184.

Shucksmith, M (2004). Young people and social exclusion in rural areas. *Sociologia Ruralis* 44(1), 43–59.

Shucksmith, M (2010). Dis-integrated rural development: Neo-endogenous rural development, planning and place-shaping in diffused power contexts. *Sociologia Ruralis* 50, 1–15.

Shucksmith, M (2010a). *How to promote the role of youth in rural areas.* Report to the Agriculture Committee of the European Parliament.

Shucksmith, M (2012a). Class, power and inequality in rural areas: Beyond social exclusion? *Sociologia Ruralis* 52(4), 377–397.

Shucksmith, M (2012b). *Future directions in rural development?* Dunfermline: Carnegie UK Trust.

Shucksmith, M & Chapman, P (1998). Rural development and social exclusion. *Sociologia Ruralis* 38(2), 225–242.

Shucksmith, M & Schafft, K (2012). Poverty and social exclusion in the UK and US. In M Shucksmith, D Brown, S Shortall, J Vergunst & M Warner (Eds), *Rural policies and rural transformations in the UK and US* (pp. 100–116). New York: Routledge.

Shucksmith, M, Cameron, S, Pichler, F & Merridew, T (2009). Urban–rural differences in quality of life across the EU. *Regional Studies* 43(10), 1275–1289.

Shucksmith, M, Roberts, D, Scott, D, Chapman, P & Conway, E (1997). *Disadvantage in rural areas.* Rural Development Commission, Rural research report No. 29. London.

Shucksmith, M, Shucksmith, J & Watt, J (2006). Rurality and social inclusion: A case of preschool education. *Social Policy and Administration* 40(6), 678–691.

Silver, H (1994). Social exclusion and social solidarity: Three paradigms. *International Labour Review* 133(5–6), 531–578.

Stull, DD, Broadway, MJ & Griffith, D (1995). *Any way you cut it: Meat processing and small town America.* Lawrence, KS: University Press of Kansas.

Terluin, IJ (2003). Differences in economic development in rural regions of advanced countries: An overview and critical analysis of theories. *Journal of Rural Studies* 19(3), 327–344.

Townsend, P (1979). *Poverty in the United Kingdom.* Harmondsworth: Penguin.

UN (1995). *The Copenhagen Declaration and Programme of Action: World Summit for Social Development 6–12 March 1995.* New York: United Nations Department of Publications.

Veit-Wilson, J (2006). No rights without remedies: Necessary conditions for abolishing child poverty. *European Journal of Social Security* 8(3), 317–337.

Vincze, M & Swain, N (1998). Agricultural transformation and the rural labour market in Romania. In K Kovács (Ed.), Restructuring post socialist agriculture. *Replika* 9, 191–206.

Wacquant, L (2007). Territorial stigmatization in the age of advance marginality. *Thesis Eleven* 91, 66–77.

Walker, A (1978). *Rural Poverty: Poverty, deprivation and planning in rural areas.* London: Child Poverty Action Group.

38

Poverty and Welfare in Rural Places

Paul Milbourne

Introduction

Academic, policy and media discussions of poverty are characterised by certain sociospatial assumptions. Across most countries of the global north these discussions have come to be associated with specific forms of poverty occurring in particular spaces in the city, with the presence of other types of poverty in small town and rural places often understated and sometimes denied altogether. Given that poverty represents a social (policy) issue, impacting on particular social groups regardless of their place of residence, the spatialised nature of these discussions raises key questions for welfare researchers. The most important of these is: why should the city have generated so much of the coverage of poverty and welfare? Perhaps the most obvious response to this question lies in the significance of sociospatial visibility within understandings of poverty.

For more than a century, poverty researchers and commentators have been attracted to the most obvious and most visible spaces and forms of poverty and welfare provision. The dominant sights and sites of poverty are constructed in terms of spatial concentrations of poor people in the inner and outer spaces of the city, often associated with large social housing estates, degraded urban environments and high levels of immigration. In short, 'the urban' has emerged as the taken-for-granted space of poverty in many countries. This focus on concentrated poverty in the city has also led to attention being directed towards specific *forms* of poverty, most notably unemployment and public welfare dependency. A picture has emerged of poverty being experienced in socially dysfunctional spaces, which are characterised by a lack of community cohesion, high crime rates and widespread dissatisfaction with place. However, poverty involves a broader range of social groups, situations and experiences, including people in low-paid employment, those living in other types of housing, and low-income groups who are detached from the welfare state. It also involves senses of belonging as well as exclusion, and different relationships with place. When approached in these terms, it is possible to construct poverty as a feature of a broader range of places.

This chapter provides a critical overview of research on poverty and welfare in rural places, with a particular focus on countries in the global north. The chapter is structured around seven sections. The first provides an account of the definition and categorisation of poverty as well as of the ways in which poverty and welfare have been researched in the rural context. In the second section, attention is directed to the importance of physical, political and sociocultural invisibilities to understandings of rural poverty. An important means by which some of these invisibilities have been overcome has been through spatial analyses of official statistics and data from household surveys. Key findings from these analyses are presented in section three to provide an account of the statistical scale and profiles of rural poverty in different countries. Section four explores the sociocultural dynamics of rural poverty, highlighting how the relations between people and place shape everyday understandings of poverty. In the fifth section consideration is given to the scalar politics of welfare and, more specifically, the impacts of national programmes of welfare restructuring on local welfare systems in rural areas. With austerity increasingly reshaping the welfare agenda in many countries of the global north, the penultimate section of the chapter explores the rural impacts of recent public sector cuts and welfare reform associated with the austerity agenda. The chapter concludes with a discussion of some future directions for rural welfare research.

Researching poverty and welfare in rural places

It is now widely recognised that poverty needs to be understood in relative terms in countries of the global north. This is not to deny the presence of absolute poverty – people's inability to secure basic goods in order to sustain everyday life, such as shelter, food and clothing – but poverty is generally recognised in relation to particular levels of income. In countries of the European Union, for example, the official poverty line is defined as 60% of median household income, adjusted for by housing costs. In other countries, such as the United States, the official poverty threshold is set in relation to a minimum income level that enables people to secure basic goods, including housing and food. Other approaches have sought to capture the non-material dimensions of poverty, with attention given to social, cultural and political forms of deprivation, disadvantage and exclusion that accrue from living on a low income. Important here has been work exploring the relations between material, sociocultural and moral/symbolic aspects of poverty, where attention has been given to the lived experiences of poverty and poor people's own constructions of their situations.

Although it is possible to find passing references to rural poverty in historical accounts of rural social life in different countries (see, for example, Newby, 1985), it has only been since the 1990s that a critical mass of academic research on poverty and welfare in rural places has been developed. It is also the case that this research has been largely undertaken in a couple of countries – the United States and the United Kingdom. Notwithstanding this late start and geographical specificity, researchers have done much to reveal the scale, nature and experiences of rural poverty, as well as highlight the particular impacts of national programmes of welfare reform in rural places. The seminal research on rural poverty took place in the 1980s. In the United States, spatial analyses of official income data began to be undertaken that enabled researchers to set out the statistical significance, social profile and geographies of poverty in non-metropolitan areas. Across the Atlantic, the first research evidence on rural poverty emerged in the mid-1980s based on a household survey in five areas of rural England (Bradley, 1986; McLaughlin, 1986).

The 1990s witnessed both a broadening and a deepening of research on rural poverty in these two countries. In the USA, further attention was given to the construction of statistical profiles of the rural poor population, again making use of official income statistics, while a small number of researchers began to conduct ethnographic studies of poverty within rural places (see Fitchen, 1995; Sherman, 2006; Duncan, 2014). In the UK, new surveys of households in a wider range of rural localities were undertaken in the early 1990s that provided more comprehensive accounts of the scale, geographies and social profile of rural poverty (see Cloke, Goodwin &

451

Milbourne, 1997; Cloke, Milbourne & Thomas, 1997). These were later supplemented with qualitative forms of research that allowed deeper understandings to be developed of the experiences of life on low income in rural areas.

From the late 1990s, rural poverty researchers in the UK began to engage with emerging (continental) European policy discourses of social exclusion. Critiquing poverty research for its narrow focus on materiality and outcomes of problems, the social exclusion concept sought to broaden understandings of poverty and other social problems by adopting a processual, multidimensional and dynamic framework. At the core of the concept is the detachment of individuals and groups from mainstream social, economic, political and cultural systems that enable integration within contemporary society (Walker & Walker, 1997). Although social exclusion involves consideration of poverty, it casts its net much wider to encompass issues of rights and access to adequate housing, education and health services. In this sense, its focus is on the ways in which social infrastructure can prevent or create a two-tier society of included and excluded groups.

In the UK, research began to explore the rural dimensions of social exclusion. Initial efforts focused on longitudinal analyses of official household surveys to examine the dynamics of low income in rural and urban areas. This work highlighted a higher incidence of persistent poverty in rural places, and remoter rural areas in particular. Following on from these statistical analyses of income dynamics, attention began to be given to the experiences of different dimensions of social exclusion in rural places. Through a programme of research funded by a third sector organisation, studies were undertaken on the constraints imposed by employment, housing and transport systems in rural areas, with a particular focus on the difficulties encountered by young people. A key finding to emerge from this research was that social exclusion amongst different social groups was resulting from the failings of public and private systems, and the less developed nature of the welfare state in rural areas, with calls made for new forms of policy intervention to address the rural dimensions of exclusion (see Shucksmith, 2000; Shucksmith, this volume).

Critical attention has also been given to rural welfare themes and more particularly to the impacts of national programmes of welfare reform in rural places. It has been in the USA that this work has been most pronounced, reflecting both the country's tradition of rural poverty research and the significance of recent rounds of national welfare reform within it, although more limited research has been undertaken in the UK, Finland, Canada and Australia (see Milbourne, 2010a). Research on rural welfare has involved spatial analyses of official welfare caseload data together with in-depth accounts of the rural impacts of welfare reform on particular social groups and places. Recently, efforts have been made to explore the impacts of new policy discourses of austerity on the provision of welfare services to vulnerable groups in rural places.

The invisibilities of rural poverty

Poverty remains largely hidden within the physical, political and sociocultural fabric of rural space. Not only are the poor scattered across the rural landscape, but some of the taken-for-granted sites and sights of poverty, such as social housing estates and welfare support centres, are largely absent in rural places. One important outcome of these restricted visibilities is that the rural poor are denied the legitimacy accorded to their counterparts in the city. Another is that it is more problematic to research poverty in rural settings. Rural poverty does not lend itself to conventional statistical mapping techniques, whereby particular bounded spaces with significant concentrations of poor people can be identified. Nor does the dispersed nature of rural poverty allow for place-based in-depth enquiry. Notwithstanding these methodological difficulties, the neglect of rural poverty as a research theme also reflects the rather conservative traditions of rural studies. It was not just the increased visibilities of poverty in the city that resulted in urban scholars researching poverty earlier and with greater intensity than their rural colleagues, but their increased willingness to engage with critical theoretical literatures on sociospatial inequalities and injustices.

Although researchers have developed an impressive evidence base on rural poverty during the last three decades, the policy and media focus on poverty has remained fixed on the city for a number of reasons. First, the visibility of urban poverty has increased in recent years as 'new' forms of poverty, associated with rough sleeping and begging, have emerged in the prime and public spaces of many cities. A second reason is that the diverse composition of the rural poor – in terms of ethnicity, age and economic activity – makes it more difficult for media commentators to construct rural poverty as a single social problem. Third, the significance of rural poverty continues to be downplayed by sociocultural processes. Within the dominant national imagination, rural places have come to be associated with notions of close-knit and harmonious forms of community living that construct poverty and poor people as 'out of place' in rural spaces. In some countries, these discourses of rurality have been actively imposed on to rural social space by ex-urban middle-class migrants, accentuating feelings of relative deprivation amongst low-income groups and further reducing the physical and statistical presence of poverty in rural places (see Milbourne, 2004).

Finally, the limited provision of welfare support services for low-income groups in rural places compounds the 'out of place' nature of poverty. For much of the 20th century, local political and economic elites in many rural areas actively resisted attempts by the national state to develop welfare assistance programmes for low-income and vulnerable groups in an effort to protect their vested interests. Consequently, local cultures of 'making do', self-sufficiency and informal support have come to dominate ideas of welfare assistance in rural places, which has led to the internalisation and individualisation of poverty. What also follows from these processes is that the visibilities accorded to the presence of state-based welfare institutions in the city remain largely absent from rural areas.

The scale and profile of poverty in rural places

It has been the production of statistical data on rural poverty that has been important in raising its profile within the mainstream poverty literature. In the UK, commissioned household surveys and, more recently, spatial analyses of official statistics have been utilised to indicate the scale and geography of poverty in rural areas. The seminal research, undertaken in 1980–1981, revealed that one-quarter of households in five rural areas in England were living in, or on the margins of, poverty (Bradley, 1986; McLaughlin, 1986). Ten years later, a repeat survey in these and 11 other rural areas in England and Wales highlighted a similar level of poverty in the original areas, and at least one-fifth of households living in or on the edge of poverty in 13 of the 16 areas (Cloke, Goodwin & Milbourne, 1997; Cloke, Milbourne & Thomas, 1997). This persistent nature of rural poverty has been confirmed by more recent analyses of government data on low-income households, with 19% of households in rural England shown to be living in poverty in 2006–2007 (Palmer, 2009), although it should be noted that the most recent data (for 2011–2012) indicate that the rural poverty rate has reduced to 15% (Defra, 2015). These official statistics also permit comparisons to be made of poverty rates in rural and urban England. What these reveal is a consistent differential between rural and urban poverty rates, with levels of rural poverty lower than those recorded in urban areas and some evidence that this gap has widened during the last three years.

Poverty researchers in the United States have been able to make use of official local income statistics for several decades, which has allowed both spatial and temporal analyses of the incidence of poverty to be undertaken. In the mid-1960s it was shown that 20% of households in rural America were living below the official poverty line, a rate that was double that recorded in metropolitan areas. Moving forward in time, the rural poverty rate has declined somewhat and in 1999 stood at about 14%. The differential between rural and urban levels of poverty has also reduced since the 1960s, although the rural poverty rate has remained higher across the whole of this period. Unlike in the UK, this gradual reduction in levels of poverty came to an abrupt end with the economic downturn in the mid-2000s and the rural poverty rate had risen to 18% in 2012 compared with 16% in metropolitan areas (USDA, 2015).

In other countries it is more difficult to locate information on rural poverty rates, but where data do exist they tend to point to levels of poverty similar to those revealed in the USA and UK. Consistent with the situation in the United States, they also demonstrate (marginally) higher poverty rates in rural areas. Examples from three countries illustrate these points. In Australia, 13.1% of households in 'rural, regional and remote' areas were living below the official poverty line in 2010 compared with 12.6% in 'capital cities' (National Rural Health Alliance, 2013). The poverty rate for rural districts in France was 25% in 2002, compared with 24% in large cities and 13% in small cities (Behaghel, 2008). Evidence from Ireland also indicates a higher rate of poverty in rural areas, with the proportion of households 'at risk of poverty' in 2013 standing at 19.3% in rural areas and 12.6% in urban areas (European Anti Poverty Network Ireland, 2015).

In terms of geography, although rural poverty exhibits a rather dispersed spatial patterning at the local level, it is possible to identify some distinct regional disparities and concentrations. In the UK, for example, analyses of household survey and official income data indicate that poverty rates are highest in remote rural areas (Cloke, Goodwin & Milbourne, 1997; Cloke, Milbourne & Thomas, 1997; Palmer, 2009). Spatial analyses of official income data in the USA reveal strong regional concentrations of poverty in the South (Lower Mississippi Delta and southern Black Belt areas), the ex-industrial spaces of central Appalachia, southern border colonial areas and Native American lands (see USDA, 2015). Indeed, there has been considerable academic and policy concern about the persistent nature of high levels of poverty in these areas across a number of decades (see Hooks, Lobao & Tickamyer, this volume).

The social profile of the rural poor tends not to conform to dominant (urban) discourses of poverty in three important respects. First, research in the USA and the UK highlights how the vast majority of the working-age poor in rural areas are in paid work rather than unemployment, an indication of both the low-wage nature of many rural labour markets and cultures of anti-welfarism present in rural places (see later section). Second, in relation to household composition, the rural poor largely comprise two-parent family households and there exists an over-representation of older people compared with metropolitan areas. Third, and reflecting the ethnic makeup of many rural areas, the rural poor are more likely to be composed of majority white groups, although it is recognised that there exist regional disparities and the risks of entering poverty are higher amongst minority ethnic groups. It is also the case that recent processes of 'minority white' migration to rural areas, particularly in the USA, are beginning to alter the ethnic composition of the rural poor. Finally, the limited provision of public goods in rural areas requires poor households to place increased reliance on private or informal forms of provision in relation to housing and transport, which cuts against conventional societal discourses of public sector dependency amongst the poor.

Structural and sociocultural understandings of rural poverty

Discussions of the causes of rural poverty have involved structural and sociocultural factors. Early explanations were based on political economy approaches, viewing poverty in rural places as a symptom of broader sets of economic processes and inequalities. As such, it was argued that while it was possible to identify *rural manifestations* of poverty, it was unhelpful to seek out *rural explanations* for the presence of poverty in rural places. In terms of some of the structural specificities of rural poverty, attention was, and continues to be, given to the economic structures of (remote) rural areas, and particularly their increased reliance on declining primary industries; remoteness and the problems this creates for promoting economic investment and new employment opportunities; limited infrastructural provision; and the restricted availability of subsidised or social housing and other public services.

More recently, attempts have been made to blend these structural explanations with cultural understandings of rural poverty through what has become known as the social context approach (Duncan, 2014). Although earlier work had developed cultural explanations of (rural) poverty, it was criticised for its tendency to see poor people as being trapped within local cultures of poverty and to place blame on the poor for their situations. At the core of the social context approach is the idea of the socialisation of culture, whereby experiences of poverty are shaped by both structures of opportunity and the mixes of social groups, community institutions and cultural norms present in particular places. For Duncan (2014), it is the interactions between people and place – the local social context – that are critical to understandings of rural poverty. More particularly, she identifies the significance of local political structures, the actions of local institutions and elites, and the nature of local community in influencing everyday experiences of poverty in rural places.

Other studies have highlighted the importance of local sociocultural structures and processes to understandings of rural poverty. Newby's (1985) study of English rural society in the 19th and early 20th centuries, for example, shows how local systems of paternalism, unequal power relations and a weakly developed local welfare system resulted in the normalisation of poverty and reliance on informal welfare support mechanisms amongst the rural poor. Within more recent rural research in the UK, the long shadow of these previous political and cultural norms is very much evident with widespread denials of the presence of local poverty, even amongst those people officially categorised as living in poor households (see Cloke, Goodwin & Milbourne, 1997; Cloke, Milbourne & Thomas, 1997; Milbourne, 2004).

What is also clear is that the rural poor tend to discuss their situations more in relation to their immediate sociocultural worlds than in terms of low income and material deprivation (Milbourne, 2014). The sociocultural contexts of place are constructed as compensatory factors capable of offsetting many of the material problems associated with life on a low income. Indeed, the poor in rural areas often express high levels of satisfaction with place and strong senses of belonging to local community. These senses of social and cultural inclusion, though, can also be interpreted in more critical terms. Community can promote particular moral discourses of rurality and welfare that often downplay the significance of poverty and sometimes deny its existence altogether. In addition, people's senses of community inclusion can act to localise advice and support networks, given that it is based on bonding rather than bridging forms of social capital. These types of local community context can also promote particular cultural norms – what Sherman (2006) refers to as moral discourses of rurality – that prioritise informal work and self-sufficiency over welfare dependency, and construct coping strategies employed by the poor in urban areas as both economically irrational and socially unacceptable in rural places (Sherman, 2006; see also Shubin, 2010).

Rural welfare

The welfare state in most developed countries came into being in the middle years of the 20th century and involved a radical transition from the market towards the universal provision of rights to minimum income and job security. Following an initial period of relative stability lasting until the 1970s, global economic crises, neoliberal critiques of welfare and concerns about the long-term welfare consequences of population ageing have led to periodic programmes of welfare restructuring (Esping-Anderson, 1996). For some commentators, the scale of this restructuring has created a crisis of the welfare state; others suggest that we are witnessing the end of the welfare state; and others still point to the resilience and stability of the welfare state in the face of significant external pressure. Notwithstanding these different interpretations, it is generally agreed that, across many countries, the principle of universal welfare support has been gradually undermined through a shift from a *welfare state to a welfare society*, whereby state responsibilities for welfare provision have been devolved to a broader range of non-state organisations, local communities and individuals, and through a transition from a *welfare to a workfare state*, involving a move from universal welfare entitlement towards labour market inclusion as the central plank of welfare policy (Peck, 2001).

Much of the research undertaken on these forms of welfare restructuring has either been concerned with the national scale, involving assessments of the impacts of welfare reform on different social groups, or at the pan-national level, comparing changing national systems of welfare across different countries. Less attention has been given to the geographies of welfare reform within particular countries – how welfare is developed and delivered in different regions and places, and how national programmes of welfare restructuring impact (differently) at the sub-national level. Furthermore, within this work it is claimed that there has been an inherent bias towards the city, with workfare underpinned by an urbanised discourse of welfare and the academic research agenda largely following policy initiatives in the city (Cope & Gilbert, 2006).

It has been in the USA that research on the rural impacts of national welfare policy is most developed (see Pickering, Harvey, Summers & Mushinski, 2006; Harvey & Pickering, 2010; Tickamyer & Henderson, 2010). In part, this reflects long-standing policy recognition of the rural dimensions of poverty within national anti-poverty policy that dates back to the New Deal of the 1930s. It also relates to the scale of welfare reform programmes introduced by national governments during the last three decades. From the 1980s the nature of welfare began to shift under consecutive Republican administrations as key dimensions of the welfare system were dismantled and welfare policy reconfigured to meet the changing needs of the national economy. This transition towards what became known as workfare was accelerated by the Clinton administrations of the 1990s. In 1996 the Personal Responsibility and Work Opportunity Reconciliation Act (PRWORA) was introduced. This Act placed more emphasis on labour market inclusion and overcoming barriers to work faced by the long-term unemployed; removed universal entitlement to certain types of benefit; introduced the notion of conditionality reinforced by sanctions; and decentralised elements of welfare power and responsibility.

The significance of this programme of welfare reform, together with its claimed spatial bias towards dealing with deep-seated problems of the inner cities, led to calls for a programme of research examining its impacts in rural areas. During the 2000s an impressive body of research material began to emerge on the rural dimensions of national welfare reform in the United States (see Pickering, Harvey, Summers & Mushinski, 2006; Tickamyer, 2006; Tickamyer & Henderson, 2010). Three themes from this research are worthy of highlight. First, the particularities of rural labour markets and the structural underpinnings of rural poverty were seen to be undermining the key policy goal of labour market integration. Various studies highlighted how lower wages, increased distances to places of employment and the limited availability of job training, public transport and childcare in rural areas were creating significant barriers to work. Second, although PRWORA produced significant reductions in welfare caseloads, it was shown that welfare recipients were largely moving to low-paid jobs and levels of rural poverty had remained constant. Third, the devolution of welfare powers and responsibilities had encouraged the development of new place-based approaches to labour market inclusion that were better able to deal with local obstacles to work. However, the localisation of welfare provision had been accompanied by the centralisation of key aspects of welfare governance, most notably in relation to the financial resourcing of the local welfare state, which had constrained key elements of local autonomy (see Hooks, Lobao & Tickamyer, this volume). In addition, some of the case study research indicated that welfare devolution had been utilised by local elites to reinforce local anti-welfare discourse and maintain unequal power relations in rural places (see Harvey & Pickering, 2010).

Welfare reform in the UK has closely resembled that initiated in the USA, with a workfare regime now clearly evident. Current welfare policies are now aligned with labour market inclusion and training programmes, and these are being enforced by the use of sanctions. Similarities also exist in relation to the privatisation and devolution of welfare responsibilities, with employment agencies now actively involved in securing work for welfare recipients and a broader range of local agencies awarded increased powers to formulate local and individualised packages of support to overcome barriers to employment. As in the USA, recent research on the implementation of workfare in rural parts of the UK has pointed to particular tensions between national policy objectives and local implementation (Milbourne, 2010a, 2010b). Workfare would appear to represent a blunter policy instrument in rural places given that low-paid work represents a more significant problem than unemployment. Another tension concerns the additional costs of providing training and securing employment for welfare recipients in rural areas linked to greater home–work distances and the domination of low quality employment within the SME (small and medium-sized enterprise) sector. With employment agencies paid by results, some have suggested that there is a risk of 'cherry picking' not only 'work ready' groups but also those places where employment opportunities are more readily available. Others have countered by arguing that work-focused cultures of rurality will mean that unemployed people in rural places will be more 'work ready' (see Milbourne, 2010b).

There is some evidence that the UK government's workfare initiatives have been more effective in rural areas than in cities. Between 1999 and 2006, the number of recipients of Jobseeker's Allowance, a key unemployment benefit, in rural districts of England fell by 46% compared with 27% in urban areas. Similarly, the New Deal for Young People resulted in 48% of rural participants securing employment against 41% in urban areas (see Milbourne, 2010b). However, Watkin (2010) warns that it is the quality of the destination employment that should be used to assess the success or otherwise of these workfare initiatives. Drawing on findings from research with young employed groups in rural Wales, she argues that workfare has largely been successful in stigmatising unemployment so that work, even at low rates of pay, represents a more preferable option for many young people. Indeed, it has been claimed that job centre personal advisers sometimes disregard people's skills and qualifications in order to move people from welfare to work, perpetuating the issue of underemployment in rural areas (Milbourne, 2010b)

More limited discussion of rural welfare in other countries has pointed to similar themes to those emerging from research in the USA and UK. Reimer (2010) suggests that the roll-out of a neoliberal regime of welfare in Canada has been complicated by the particular conditions of rural areas, including their increased reliance on seasonal labour, larger distances between poor people and welfare services, the lack of concentrated poverty to justify welfare provision, and misunderstandings about the nature of rural poverty on the part of national policy makers. Writing about rural welfare in rural Australia, Alston (2010) similarly argues that the national workfare policy's prime focus on labour market integration has remained insensitive to rural circumstances. Focusing on remote rural regions that have been doubly hit by droughts and economic decline, she highlights how high rates of employment and low levels of income in the agricultural sector, together with a lack of alternative employment, work against the principles of workfare. Dufty and Gibson (2010) argue that neoliberalism has also been associated with a re-spatialisation of welfare policy in Australia. Within recent national policy discourse, large parts of rural Australia have been constructed as problematic spaces – characterised by high levels of unemployment, out-migration, needy older people and unviable industries. Rather than seeking to fix these problems in situ, they suggest that the goal of the new welfare regime is to relocate rural welfare recipients to places where employment and welfare services can be accessed more efficiently.

The rural impacts of austerity

These accounts of the rural impacts of national welfare reform were largely written prior to the global banking crisis and subsequent economic downturn that occurred in the mid-2000s. Since then, many countries of the global north have witnessed the emergence of austerity as a key policy discourse, with national governments seeking to deal with increased levels of national debt resulting from the bailing out of key financial institutions. For some countries, austerity policy has been introduced unilaterally by national governments; for others, including the largely rural countries of Ireland, Greece, Spain and Portugal, austerity has been imposed on governments by the European Commission. Far from the banking crisis leading to new forms of state regulation of the financial sector or increased taxation contributions from high earning groups, the focus of various governments has been on reducing spending on public services, and welfare programmes in particular.

Although there has been little written about the rural impacts of austerity, it is clear that it has the potential to reshape the ways in which welfare and other public services are provided in rural areas for decades to come. There exist two contrasting viewpoints on the rural ramifications of this austerity agenda. The first contends that austerity provides new opportunities for rural places. Austerity has long been a feature of welfare provision in rural regions, with their local welfare state less developed and increased reliance placed on informal welfare support provided by the third sector and local communities. As such, it is claimed that rural places are well placed not only to withstand the financial pressures associated with the new politics of austerity, but also to develop new forms of community-based welfare services that may be better able to meet the needs of local groups. A second viewpoint is more pessimistic in its reading of the rural impacts of austerity. Rural areas are particularly vulnerable to public sector cuts given lower levels of existing welfare service provision and the increased costs of delivering these services. As such, there is the potential for austerity to *remove* rather than just *reduce* the provision of key welfare services in rural places, producing potentially damaging impacts on rural community cohesion.

A recent study of the rural impacts of austerity in the UK reveals evidence of both of these perspectives. Based on research on the provision of welfare services for older people in rural Wales, Milbourne (2015) argues that national austerity policy is reinforcing long-standing local politics and cultures of anti-welfarism in rural places, perpetuating the invisibilities of rural poverty and making vulnerable groups more reluctant to seek the welfare advice, support and services to which they are entitled. It is also possible to identify more positive outcomes of the national austerity agenda, with public sector funding cuts forcing local authorities to develop new modes of service provision, some of which have drawn on community assets to deliver support that better meets the needs of local groups. It is perhaps too early to assess the real impacts of austerity on these and other rural communities. What is clear, though, is that while third sector and community-based forms of welfare provision are more developed in rural areas – and so potentially more resilient to national austerity policy – they remain reliant, to varying degrees, on public funding, which means that their futures remain in considerable doubt. Indeed, this is one of the paradoxes of the austerity agenda: it claims to award more power and responsibility to voluntary and community groups to provide local welfare while reducing their funding (Milbourne, 2015). It will be interesting to see how the austerity agenda impacts on different vulnerable groups, welfare services in rural places in the UK and other countries in future years.

Conclusion: new directions for rural welfare research

Recent decades have witnessed a growing body of academic work on the themes of rural poverty and rural welfare, and the outputs from this work are now broadly recognised within rural studies and social science more generally. Key texts in rural studies, including this one, now provide space for the discussion of welfare issues, while mainstream accounts of poverty generally acknowledge that poverty extends beyond the boundaries of the city. Such recognition should not breed any degree of complacency amongst rural welfare researchers though, for rural welfare continues to remain a marginalised theme within both rural studies and the academic poverty literature. The same remains true within the policy domain where key initiatives on welfare reform, workfare and austerity continue to be developed largely in response to crises in and of the city.

It is also the case that the nature of poverty and welfare in rural places will continue to twist and turn in response to external and internal processes of change, prompting new forms of investigation by rural scholars. The rural impacts – actual and potential – of national programmes of welfare reform and austerity will require critical scrutiny from researchers to ensure that these programmes are meeting the needs of, rather than stigmatising and penalising, those on low incomes in rural areas. The increased flow of economic migrants to rural labour markets – largely involving Hispanics in the USA and Poles in the UK – will not only perpetuate the low-skill and low-pay characteristics of peripheral rural economies but reshape the social composition of the rural poor, and will raise some interesting research questions for rural welfare researchers. The welfare impacts of the ageing rural population will also demand research attention. In one sense, the presence of larger numbers of more active older people will boost the capacity of the voluntary sector in rural areas. In another, rising numbers of immobile and vulnerable elders living in places stripped of their key public services by the austerity agenda will create major welfare policy challenges. Finally, there exists a need to expand the geographic scope of rural welfare research. As is apparent from this chapter, almost all of the academic work on rural poverty and welfare has emerged from the USA and UK. Research in other countries in the global north will no doubt provide additional significance to these themes; it may also throw up new questions on the relations between poverty, welfare and rural place.

References

Alston, M (2010). Australia's rural welfare policy: Overlooked and demoralised. In P Milbourne (Ed.), *Welfare reform in rural places: Comparative perspectives* (pp. 199–218). Bingley, UK: Emerald Publishing.

Behaghel, L (2008). *Poverty and social exclusion in rural areas: France.* Brussels: European Communities. Available at http://www.parisschoolofeconomics.com/behaghel-luc/rural_poverty_annex_fr_en.pdf (accessed 1 July 2015).

Bradley, T (1986). Poverty and dependency in village England. In P Lowe, T Bradley & S Wright (Eds), *Deprivation and welfare in rural areas* (pp. 151–178). Norwich: GeoBooks.

Cloke, P, Goodwin, M & Milbourne, P (1997). *Rural Wales: Community and marginalization.* Cardiff: University of Wales Press.

Cloke, P, Milbourne, P & Thomas, C (1997). Living lives in different ways? Deprivation, marginalisation in rural lifestyles. *Transactions of the Institute of British Geographers* 22(2), 210–230.

Cope, M & Gilbert, M (2006). Geographies of welfare reform. *Urban Geography* 22(5), 385–390.

Defra (Department for Environment, Food and Rural Affairs) (2015). *Statistics: Rural poverty.* Available at https://www.gov.uk/government/uploads/system/uploads/attachment_data/file/428604/Rural PovertyStats_May2015.pdf (accessed 29 June 2015).

Dufty, R & Gibson, C (2010). Shifting welfare, shifting people: Rural development, housing and population mobility in Australia. In P Milbourne (Ed.), *Welfare reform in rural places: Comparative perspectives* (pp. 173–198). Bingley, UK: Emerald Publishing.

Duncan, C (2014). *Worlds apart: Poverty and politics in rural America.* New Haven, CT: Yale University Press.

Esping-Anderson, G (Ed.). (1996). *Welfare states in transition: National adaptations in global economies.* London: Sage.

European Anti Poverty Network Ireland (2015). Relative poverty rates. Available at http://www.eapn.ie/eapn/training/poverty-in-ireland (accessed 1 July 2015).

Fitchen, J (1995). *Poverty in rural America: A case study.* Boulder, CO: Westview Press.

Harvey, M & Pickering, K (2010). Color-blind welfare reform or new cultural racism? Evidence from rural Mexican- and Native-American communities. In P Milbourne (Ed.), *Welfare reform in rural places: Comparative perspectives* (pp. 61–80). Bingley, UK: Emerald Publishing.

McLaughlin, B (1986). The rhetoric and reality of rural deprivation. *Journal of Rural Studies* 2, 291–307.

Milbourne, P (2004). *Rural poverty: Marginalization and exclusion in Britain and the United States.* London: Routledge.

Milbourne, P (2010a). *Welfare reform in rural places: Comparative perspectives.* Bingley, UK: Emerald Publishing.

Milbourne, P (2010b). Placing welfare in rural England. In P Milbourne (Ed.), *Welfare reform in rural places: Comparative perspectives* (pp. 111–130). Bingley, UK: Emerald Publishing.

Milbourne, P (2014). Poverty, place and rurality: Material and socio-cultural disconnections. *Environment and Planning A* 46(3), 566–580.

Milbourne, P (2015). Austerity, welfare reform and older people in rural places: Competing discourses of voluntarism and community? In N Hanlon & M Skinner (Eds), *Growing old in resource communities: New frontiers of rural aging.* New York: Routledge.

National Rural Health Alliance (2013). *A snapshot of poverty in rural and regional Australia.* Available at http://ruralhealth.org.au/documents/publicseminars/2013_Sep/Joint-report.pdf (accessed 1 July 2015).

Newby, H (1985). *Country life.* London: Weidenfeld & Nicholson.

Palmer, G (2009). *Indications of poverty and social exclusion in rural England: 2009.* Cheltenham: Commission for Rural Communities.

Peck, J (2001). *Workfare states.* London: Guilford Press.

Pickering, K, Harvey, M, Summers, G & Mushinski, D (2006). *Welfare reform in persistent rural poverty: The new political economy of welfare.* University Park, PA: Pennsylvania State University Press.

Reimer, B (2010). Social welfare policies and rural Canada. In P Milbourne (Ed.), *Welfare reform in rural places: Comparative perspectives* (pp. 81–110). Bingley, UK: Emerald Publishing.

Sherman, J (2006). Coping with rural poverty: Economic survival and moral capital in rural America. *Social Forces* 85(2), 891–913.

Shubin, S (2010). Cultural dimension of poverty in Ireland and Russia. *Transactions of the Institute of British Geographers* 35, 555–570.

Shucksmith, M (2000). *Exclusive countryside? Social inclusion and regeneration in rural areas.* York: Joseph Rowntree Foundation.

Tickamyer, A (2006). Rural poverty. In P Cloke, T Marsden & P Mooney (Eds), *Handbook of rural studies* (pp. 411–426). London: Sage.

Tickamyer, A & Henderson, D (2010). Devolution, social exclusion and spatial inequality in US welfare provision. In P Milbourne (Ed.), *Welfare reform in rural places: Comparative perspectives* (pp. 41–60). Bingley, UK: Emerald Publishing.

USDA (United States Department of Agriculture) (2015). Rural poverty & well-being. Available at http://www.ers.usda.gov/topics/rural-economy-population/rural-poverty-well-being.aspx (accessed 29 June 2015).

Walker, A & Walker, C (Eds). (1997). *Britain divided: The growth of social exclusion in the 1980s and 1990s.* London: Child Poverty Action Group.

Watkin, S (2010). Rural welfare to work in Wales: Young people's experiences. In P Milbourne (Ed.), *Welfare reform in rural places: Comparative perspectives* (pp. 131–150). Bingley, UK: Emerald Publishing.

39

Spatial Inequality and Rural Areas

Gregory Hooks, Linda M. Lobao and Ann R. Tickamyer

As global economic, social and environmental changes alter the fortunes of populations differently across geographic settings, social science attention to spatial disparities has become critical. In this chapter, we provide an overview of the literature on spatial inequality and how it applies to the study of rural populations. By spatial inequality, we refer to a thematic body of work that cross-cuts the social sciences and is relevant to nations across the globe. Spatial inequality addresses how and why valued resources vary across places, and how places themselves become markers and makers of inequality. This tradition bridges the geographic and non-geographic social sciences, combining sociology's and other disciplines' interest in social inequality with a concern for uneven development. Researchers ask, 'Who gets what, where and why?' They seek to answer, for example, how and why economic, social, health and other forms of well-being and inequalities of race, class and gender vary and intersect across geographic entities (e.g., localities, states, provinces, regions). And conversely, researchers are interested in how geographic context itself contributes to the reproduction (or potential alleviation) of inequalities among individuals, households and community populations. This tradition thus overall recognises both the importance of where actors are located in geographic space and that geographic entities themselves are moulded by stratification processes of uneven development and in turn mould stratification among their populations.

This chapter proceeds as follows. First, we explain the contours of spatial inequality as research tradition. Here we address its development, how its lens has been applied to the study of rural areas, and the specific substantive literatures that comprise it. Second, we move to a core question raised by this research tradition: what factors give rise to spatial inequalities across places? Here we consider the role of three factors implicated in studies of rural areas – economic structure, institutional arrangements and spatial/geographic context. We highlight this discussion by providing examples from recent research into rural areas that present a more holistic understanding of the welfare state and the challenges posed by neoliberalism. The literature on spatial inequality is extensive but diffuse. It spans studies from different social science disciplines, subfields within disciplines, and national contexts. We take a synthetic approach in pulling together disparate studies, but in a succinct review our discussion is necessarily limited in detail. To provide a more coherent account of how rural researchers have engaged this tradition, we draw particularly from empirical examples using the case of the United States. Ultimately, to do justice to the subject, it will be important to conduct cross-national comparative research to better understand individual national cases and to extend and refine a common theoretical framework.

Spatial inequality as a research tradition: turning the lens to rural places and populations

Inequality – the differential allocation of valued resources across social groups – has been a foundational social science concern. Yet, until almost the last decade of the 20th century, social scientists studied stratification and class disparities primarily at the national level and widely neglected the consideration of geographic territory. Soja (1988) documents how classical theory and events of the early 20th century gave rise to a view that attention to stratification was incompatible with attention to geographic space. Thus with notable exceptions (e.g., Wallerstein, 1974), theorising about stratification developed largely aspatially over the last century. Even in human geography, while interest in spatial variation across places was always of interest, attention to power and inequality came rather recently with the rise of political economic theorising, ushered into the discipline by David Harvey (1989), Neil Smith (1984), and others.

From the 1980s onward, owing to disciplinary shifts such as the rise of political economic theory in geography and urban studies, the diffusion of this work to sociology, and social scientists' observations about globalisation and deindustrialisation (seen to have regional/local impacts), spatial inequality grew as a general social science concern (Lobao, Hooks & Tickamyer, 2007). Economics too became transformed with Krugman's (1991) influential extension of the neoclassical model that recognised the potential for geographic uneven development. An empirical and theoretical turnaround occurred when social scientists recognised that the study of inequality needed to be critically informed by bringing in space.

But for social science fields engaged in studying rural areas, interest in spatial inequality occurred differently: attention to space was inherent while attention to power and inequality came later. Over most of the last century, rural sociology, like human geography, had given extensive attention to variation across places and to describing the unique qualities of specific communities and regions. This approach was seen in the study of the urban–rural continuum and the work of the US regionalists (Odum & Moore, 1938). But until the 1980s, as Newby (1983) documented, attention to rural places proceeded from structural-functionalist theory and the related human ecology framework that neglected power and inequality. The study of rural areas was transformed first with the infusion of political economic theorising into the analysis of agricultural change with the development of the sociology of agriculture. The rural economies of most advanced societies were undergoing dramatic changes in the 1980s, manifested most vividly in the farm sector. Political economic theorising then diffused to other substantive concerns of rural scholars, notably the study of poverty, industrial restructuring, and labour markets (Rural Sociological Task Force on Persistent Rural Poverty, 1993; Lyson & Falk, 1993; Falk, Schulman, & Tickamyer, 2002; Falk & Lobao, 2003). A broader critical tradition arose which also turned attention to the inequalities faced by distinct rural populations based on race, ethnicity, class, gender and later sexuality and their intersections (Sachs, 2014).

Especially in European studies, the concept of social exclusion gained ascendancy in analysing the multidimensionality of rural disparity and disadvantage, particularly in the analysis of rural poverty. As Shucksmith (this volume) explains, attention to social exclusion emerged for both theoretical and ideological reasons. Many of the variants of the theoretical development of social exclusion are aspatial. Nevertheless, in its application to rural localities, the emphasis on the relative and relational aspects of poverty adds a distinct theoretically grounded cultural dimension to rural spatial inequalities. This contrasts sharply with US analyses of poverty that are grounded in measures of absolute deprivation while evoking cultural dimensions in a pejorative manner. Poverty in a social exclusion approach is characterised by lack of participation and integration in social life which by necessity is grounded in particular locales.

This trajectory of a widespread concern with inequality continues today and is seen within various thematic areas (denoted below) that span rural sociology and rural studies more generally. It yields a distinct rural sociological/rural studies approach to studying spatial inequality that differs from that of other social sciences. Lobao (1996) characterised rural sociology itself as 'a sociology of the periphery' – fundamentally concerned with uneven development and the most disadvantaged areas globally, while simultaneously referencing the frequent relegation of the study of rural society to the sidelines of sociology.

Space, spatial scale and place: rural scholars' unique approach to spatial inequality

To explain the manner by which scholars in different fields address spatial inequality, Lobao, Hooks and Tickamyer (2007) call attention to three concepts: space, spatial scale and place. We bring in these concepts to provide a synopsis of how rural researchers have offered a distinct lens on spatial inequality.

Space and place are fundamental social science concepts about which much has been written. For reviews of conceptualisations of space, see Friedland and Boden (1994), Lefebvre (1991) and Tickamyer (2000), and for place see Agnew (1987) and Entrikin (1991). *Space* is regarded as the more abstract, broader concept, similar in ontological status as time, while *place* can be considered a particularistic aspect of space, that is, a distinct spatial setting. But across the social sciences, space and place are not treated as singular, binary concepts in opposition to each other. Massey (2004), for example, influentially argues for emphasising a relational understanding of places and spaces. In this framework, relational aspects of both places and spaces are complementary, socially constructed, the site of a multiplicity of interrelationships, and always in process. Thus space and place are fluid, mutually constituted, and both the product and the source of social inequalities, power relations and changing divisions of labour (Massey, 1993, 1999). Amin (2004) goes so far as to substitute the notion of topological for territorial, emphasising the fluidity of spatial relations composed of networks and 'transnational flows' that transcend standard locality-based geography. While these conceptualisations have been influential beyond geography, across the social sciences, we believe that it is useful to consider the types of spaces and places conceptualised in different bodies of literatures relevant to rural spatial inequalities.

In studying inequality, social scientists tend to treat space in three different ways. The first is simply not to take geographic space into account – which, as noted, typified much stratification research conducted in the 20th century. The second is to treat space as a confounding influence that needs to be bracketed out in order to study true relationships of interest. For example, geographic space may be treated as 'noise', as is often the case in quantitative regression-type studies on inequality. Here social scientists seek to control for the influence of spatial processes: they may correct for spatial spillovers in the dependent variable or unmeasured spatial factors in the error term because without such corrections statistical inference may be unreliable. A third way to consider space is to elevate it into a concept of intrinsic interest. In this vein, the insertion of geography into the study of social relationships differentiates rural sociology/rural studies as distinct from most other fields.[1]

Rural researchers employ space as an intrinsic component of the study of stratification in ways that depend upon the specific research question at hand. First, for example, rurality or rural spatial location is observed to channel inequality processes, amplifying or diminishing their effects (Weber et al., 2005). Thus, while education is a marker of human capital known to increase earnings, returns to a college degree are usually found to be lower in US non-metropolitan areas, rural location depressing the earnings effects of schooling. Rurality also reflects compositional differences among populations, seen in race, class, gender, age and other statuses as well as differences along an array of social, economic, health, environmental, government and other well-being indicators. Explaining how and why life chances and societal resources vary spatially are questions long addressed in rural inequality research. Researchers also question how rural spaces themselves are produced by inequality processes under capitalism. Uneven development within nations and persistent poverty in traditional rural regions such as the Appalachian USA (Billings & Blee, 2000) and the Brazilian Amazon (Bunker, 1985) are examples. Similarly, the regional politics found in the uneven development experienced by numerous European Union nations (Amin, 2004) may also correspond to rural–urban inequalities, although they are rarely framed in this manner.

Another unique contribution of rural inequality research is its spatial scale of focus. A large literature on spatial scale has emerged across the social sciences. As Brenner (2004) explains, this literature stresses the importance of moving downward from the nation state to scrutinise subnational processes of development and inequality. By the subnational scale, we refer to regional territory below the nation state level and beyond the limits of individual cities or communities. In the European Union there is extensive interest in subnational inequality in light of policy efforts to ensure social cohesion (Alber, Fahey, & Saraceno, 2008; Copus & Hörnström, 2011) and decentralise government within nations (Kazepov, 2010). But although the subnational scale should be central to the study of inequality, Lobao, Hooks and Tickamyer (2007, p. 4) characterise it as sociology's 'missing middle' because it represents a far less scrutinised territorial arena for theory and research when compared to the more voluminous work centred on the nation state and the city.

Rural research fills an important gap in the social sciences because the regional or subnational scale always has been of intrinsic interest. Researchers focus on a continuum of urban–rural places within nations (Partridge & Rickman, 2006; Brown, Greskovits & Kulcsar, 2007; Brown & Schafft, 2011; Almeida 2014). Even when rural researchers study individual communities, they tend to take a comparative subnational lens (Salamon, 2003). That is, to explain inequality processes in single communities, rural researchers typically look to the broader regional context in which such communities are embedded and seek to draw contrasts with communities elsewhere. Rural researchers also integrate the study of inequality across geographic scales – addressing multilevel processes spanning individuals/households, communities and regions (Brown, 2002; Peters, 2012).

Finally, rural spatial inequality research is characterised by its distinct approach to studying 'places'. Social science literatures tend to be divided along two traditions for analysing places (Lobao, Hooks & Tickamyer, 2007). The *place-in-society* tradition pursues research questions through the examination of specific places. The purpose is to illuminate the distinct character of a given place, and potentially generalise outward. This approach infuses urban sociology, leading to its near-reification of cities as the only worthy territorial unit of study. A second tradition, the *society-in-place* approach, tackles place from the opposite angle: interest in the societal level and how social processes work out across places. For example, interest may be in causal forces that generate inequality, such as economic restructuring and institutional shifts such as cutbacks in the welfare state, and how these are manifested across places.

How places are conceptualised affects research design. Researchers working from the place-in-society tradition tend to focus on a limited number of places, collecting detailed data about them as in case studies of cities or communities. The society-in-place approach is more place-extensive, lending itself to a larger number of cases and use of various territorial units of analysis (e.g., city, county, village, labour markets and so forth). Rather than conceptualising these as binary opposites, however, they can be viewed as a continuum, with case-comparative designs forming a middle and overlapping ground that calls on both traditions. Thus rural research is characterised by both traditions – providing an inherently richer view of spatial inequality than some other fields. To understand inequality across places, recognition of place-distinctiveness is necessary. At the same time, the ability to compare the experiences of many different places has generated a legacy of generalisable work on rural areas.

Rural substantive literatures with spatial inequality traditions

We turn now to a brief overview of the different bodies of rural literatures that have most directly carved out the study of spatial inequality. These are not comprehensive reviews; many are the subject of extensive review in other chapters in this volume, but rather they serve to highlight areas where spatial inequality theory and research have solid grounding. Except where otherwise noted, the US research tradition provides the main examples with the understanding that systematic comparative work would greatly enhance our knowledge.

The general rural inequality tradition

Researchers working from three bodies of literature, rural poverty, labour markets, and demography, have tended to shape the study of spatial inequality. These literatures overlap substantively and conceptually and can be seen to comprise a general rural inequality tradition. Most attention is given to how and why poverty, income or other economic well-being indicators vary across geographic territory. In terms of causal determinants, focus has tended to be on economic structure, such as manufacturing and service employment, although institutional arrangements and the role of the state are increasingly given attention. Population aggregates such as communities, counties and labour market areas are typically used as units of analysis directly or as contexts surrounding households and individuals in multilevel analyses. Comparative urban–rural relationships are often a focus. While each literature below is distinct, individual scholars' work often spans all three areas.

The literature on rural poverty is one of the most well-developed and debated areas of rural social inequalities research. It has tended to focus on the characteristics of the rural poor, urban–rural differences in poverty, and historically disadvantaged regions and their populations. In the US case, the Rural Sociological Society Task Force on Persistent Rural Poverty gave impetus to this literature in their classic 1993 volume. It has continued to generate a long line of work across disciplines. For notable reviews see Blank (2005), Tickamyer (2006) and Weber et al. (2005) and related chapters in this volume.

Research on rural poverty is one area of clear divergence in theoretical perspectives employed by US scholars and those in other countries of the global north. The biggest difference is that US poverty researchers emphasise absolute deprivation and European researchers take a relative approach. While the field of poverty research generally is noteworthy for its variety of (and ideologically tinged) theoretical traditions in explaining causes and consequences of poverty, especially in contentious debates over individual versus structural factors, rural poverty research in the United States tends to conceptualise it as absolute deprivation arising from structural-level sources of inequality even when the interest is in individual outcomes (Tickamyer & Duncan, 1990; Tickamyer, 2006). Partly this conceptualisation reflects a rejection of popular cultural explanations that 'blame the victim' through an emphasis on individual and family disorganisation and dysfunction as causes of poverty. Partly, it is inherent in the larger traditions of spatial inequality noted here.

The aversion to cultural and individual explanation among poverty analysts diverges from European traditions that conceptualise and measure poverty in relative terms that heavily emphasise social exclusion and inequalities across a spectrum of material and more abstract resources (see chapters by Milbourne and Shucksmith, this volume). Social exclusion perspectives emphasise the relational components of the causes and impacts of poverty but they also carry some of the same ideological baggage as US cultural explanations (Shucksmith, this volume; Moffat & Glasgow, 2009). In this approach, emphasis is on the multidimensionality of poverty, its relative nature in comparison to other members of society, and the degree to which individuals and groups face barriers to social participation and integration (Shucksmith, 2012). Recently, US scholars have attempted to incorporate more nuanced understanding of cultural factors in their studies of rural poverty (Duncan, 1999; Sherman, 2009), yet few incorporate the concept of social exclusion directly.

Rural labour market research tends to focus on the demand-side of poverty creation with attention to rural economic structure, particularly the quantity and quality of jobs (Falk & Lyson, 1988; Singelmann & Deseran, 1993), and more recently to the role of the state (Falk, Schulman, & Tickamyer, 2003). By attending to the structural determinants of inequality, labour market sociologists have demonstrated the inadequacy of neoclassical economic explanations and shown how returns to individuals' human capital attributes vary by urban–rural structural context (Cotter, 2002).

Rural demographers have long addressed inequality. In comparison to the two traditions above, demographic research moves beyond economic inequalities to a variety of well-being indicators such as migration, fertility, mortality, family formation, and health status and access (Brown, 2002; McLaughlin, Stokes, Smith & Nonoyama, 2007; Lichter & Cimaluk, 2012). Most recently, the discipline of demography has embraced the goal of spatialising analysis of population processes, and some of the most sophisticated spatial analyses can be found in demographic publications.

Rural racial/ethnic segregation literature and rural gender research

A rich tradition of rural studies on racial and ethnic segregation exists in the case of the United States (Saenz, 1997; Wimberley, 2008; Pruitt, 2009; Lichter, Parisi & Taquino, 2012). Regional patterns of race/ethnic segregation and concentration are examined through attention to Native American reservations, the Southern Black Belt, Mexican–American border enclaves, and communities with newer ethnic immigration. This research varies somewhat from the 'rural inequality' tradition above by giving greater attention to high-poverty regions. It also goes beyond the conventional urban segregation literature in its breadth of territorial scale and depth of historical analysis. Researchers consider how distinct regions are produced and constrain subsequent development, such as through past political-economic changes and public policies.

Gender researchers also address spatial inequality. Research on rural women considers subnational variations in patterns of women's work (in both the farm and non-farm sectors) and earnings and other indicators of women's well-being (Tickamyer, 2006; Sachs, 2014; Struthers, 2014). In the USA focus tends to be on individual women and their households, with rurality addressed through considering community context. Urban–rural differences are often studied through multilevel, contextual models. Rural women are typically found to fare poorer in terms of earnings relative to their urban counterparts – a rural penalty found for women who otherwise have similar human capital attributes. These studies have extensive counterparts in other parts of the global north. This topic would particularly benefit from systematic cross-national comparisons that examine both the status of rural women (as in US studies) and how gender identities are constructed from rural social policies (as in EU work) (Shortall & Bock, 2015).

Agriculture and spatial inequality

The sociology of agriculture has longed addressed spatial inequality through research analysing agricultural change and community well-being (Lobao & Meyer, 2001; Constance, Hendrickson, Howard & Heffernan, 2014). While this body of work developed independently from the traditions above, it shares commonalities with them. Attention is given to the impact of economic structure, in this case farming and non-farm agribusiness, on various well-being indicators. Four types of changes have been of interest: the loss of farms and farm population historically; farm structural changes, such as the relative growth of industrialised farms and decline of traditional family farming; agro-food system changes, as seen in the commodity chains literature that connects different stages of the production process to geographic regions; and, more recently, local food systems and their ability to generate economic growth and provide for the needs of less affluent populations. Studies addressing these changes all share the insight that places are differentiated by agricultural production, which influences quality of life within and between them.

Environment/natural resources sociology

Too frequently, the sociological study of environmental inequality has focused on the 'end of the pipe' (Pellow, 2000, p. 595), resulting in a focus on urban areas and overlooking rural dynamics. Instead of looking at the 'end of the pipe', rural researchers have long been concerned with the impacts of extractive industries, particularly mining and forestry, in resource-dependent regions globally (Bunker, 1985; Freudenburg & Gramling, 1994; Rudel, Katan & Horowitz, 2013). They are also concerned with spatial inequalities arising from environmental and social impacts of hazardous waste and other pollution (Hooks & Smith, 2004). Rural researchers stress that modes of extraction are connected to life chances of the population within and across places (Bunker, 1985). Development processes involving extractive industries work out in different ways than in manufacturing or services, with boom and bust cycles generating greater swings in regional fortunes (Bunker, 1985; Freudenburg & Gramling, 1994). Research on the environment and natural resources uniquely informs social science by focusing on economic sectors that are often neglected, particularly in developed societies. Recent shifts in the energy industry – particularly the move towards shale gas/oil production – will continue to have important implications for subnational variations in well-being across developed nations (Kinchy et al., 2014). The rise and fall of boom towns, that is, energy-driven accelerated and even explosive development primarily in rural locations, is once again a topic of intense interest globally and one that could benefit from cross-national as well as subnational comparative research.

Inequality across rural areas: economic structure, institutional arrangements and space

Spatial inequality brings a valuable lens to the study of rural areas. More than this, the study of spatial inequality in rural areas informs broader social science theorising. To highlight this potential and how it is being realised, we first outline the conceptual factors that help explain the rise of inequalities across rural and subnational space. Then, we describe how researchers employ spatial units empirically to study spatial inequality. Finally, we examine research (focused on the United States) into the welfare state and neoliberalism and its connection to rural spatial inequality. In so doing, we make the case that studying spatial inequality in rural areas can help us to better understand policy contexts and transformations that are changing the nation and world.

Conceptualising factors that contribute to spatial inequality

Inequalities arise from and are mediated by the institutionalised relationships emerging from struggles among actors such as capital, labour, the state and citizens. These insights, staples of stratification, political sociology and economic sociology, are applicable on the ground to explaining subnational rural inequality. We (Lobao, Hooks & Tickamyer, 2007) conceptualise subnational variations in poverty and prosperity as related to:

1   *Economic structure or the ways in which surplus is accumulated from economic activities.* Different types of industries, firms and jobs result in different levels of economic growth and also affect the degree to which benefits of growth are distributed.
2   *Institutional arrangements between key social actors.* By institutional arrangements, we refer to the relationships established between social actors via customary social practices, laws and organisations regulating economic growth and distribution of social benefits. Employers have differential stakes in supporting and capacity to support the workforce at certain material levels. Workers possess different resources, such as education, skill levels, professional associations and unions to press for material demands from employers. Citizens, too, possess different resources, including a vibrant civic society and social climate empowering of women and racial/ethnic groups that enable them to press for concessions from the state or capital. Finally, the state varies in intensity of support for its own interests and the interests of capitalists vis-à-vis the interests of workers and citizens.
3   *Spatial situation and site factors.* The location and relative position of places in the national and global political economy varies, affecting populations' well-being. 'Glocalisation' – the interaction of global with local forces – also creates place variations. In turn, places have distinct site or internal characteristics, such as natural amenities, infrastructure, population attributes and other ecological features which confer differential advantages.
4   *Past history of economic structure, institutional arrangements, spatial factors.* The history of social forces and other attributes above is embedded in place. This history sets in motion the potential for path dependency in development processes and to cumulative, uneven development across places.

In sum, the interplay of economic structure, institutional arrangements, spatial factors and past history create current inequalities across subnational rural space.

(Subnational) spatial scale and units of analysis

The ability to analyse spatial inequalities is only as good as the available data, and rural spaces and places are particularly subject to inadequate data sources. In the United States, there are numerous sources of information but relatively few that provide consistent data at a scale that captures rural socioeconomic structure and process. The county (and its equivalent) is a unique and valuable subnational unit of analysis because it provides stable and meaningful geographic and administrative data and parameters. This unit of analysis not only provides comprehensive coverage of rural areas, but counties also provide governance and data collection for suburban and urban areas as well. Moreover, counties are well suited for studying labour market processes (Partridge & Rickman, 2006, p. 128) and their boundaries are relatively fixed over time (Isserman, Feser & Warren, 2009). But the advantages go beyond data collection. The county government provides a range of services and exercises significant discretion over how and if these services are made available to residents (Benton, 2002). Counties are also a taxing entity – they raise and allocate significant revenues (Benton, 2002; Craw, 2006). Further, county governments also act as the regional development coordinator of local governments within them (Lobao, Jeanty, Partridge & Kraybill, 2012). The county is by no means the only unit of analysis for studying rural areas. In particular, counties are embedded in and overlap with a variety of other administrative jurisdictions, most notably the states in the United States. However, this uniquely comprehensive and stable unit of analysis is often the best source of data that facilitates theory-testing and comparative analyses, especially within rural places, populations and processes and across the rural–urban continuum.

In the complex federal system that characterises the USA, as noted above, counties are embedded in and subject to state jurisdiction. States are larger geopolitical units that function both locally and nationally and that are the site of experimentation and implementation of welfare policies that promote or reduce social and spatial disparities. Thus to fully understand the welfare state and the threats posed by neoliberalism, it is important to move beyond a national-level focus – for both urban and rural areas – and, particularly, in the US case, to understand the relationship of the state to the states (Lobao & Hooks, 2007; Lobao, 2016). The United States offers a clear example of how the study of rural areas provides unique opportunities to test and extend theories of the welfare state at different spatial scales and units of analysis.

The welfare state and neoliberalism

'Many states, including the American one, now devote themselves mainly to the maintenance of incomes, the treating of the ill, and the provision of services to citizens … In short, they have become welfare states' (Amenta, Bonastia & Caren, 2001, p. 213). There is a rich literature on comparative welfare states, especially across the global north. For details on theoretical and empirical research into the welfare state, see Alesina and Glaeser (2004), Esping-Andersen (1990), Heclo (1974), Hicks (1999), Huber and Stephens (2001), Quadagno (1994). Typically the nation state is the unit of analysis and there is little attention to subnational structures and processes. Yet the state at the subnational scale is an important factor that sets the USA apart from its European counterparts. Among affluent democracies, the United States is distinctive for its decentralised federal system, and as a result, for the large and growing role of state and local government in its social safety net (Peck, 2001). Although subnational and rural dynamics have not been ignored, the extant literature has focused on variation in support for the welfare state and/or neoliberalism, often associated with distinctive historic racial and ethnic relations. Quadagno (1994, p. 196) argues that 'anti-government ideology has generated most antagonism to the welfare state when it has been associated with racial issues' that vary subnationally (see also Alston & Ferrie, 1999). Amenta and collaborators (Amenta, 1998; Amenta & Halfmann, 2000; Amenta, Bonastia & Caren, 2001) have examined variation in political support for social welfare policies among the 50 states, emphasising the importance of institutions, politics and social movements. Although many of these studies find or imply significant rural–urban differences, this is not typically the focus of the research.

When the focus is restricted to social insurance programmes managed by the central government – as is common in the comparative welfare state literature – the USA is notable for the 'stinginess and backwardness' of its welfare state (Amenta, Bonastia & Caren, 2001, p. 215). But if the focus expands to consider public health, education, housing, employment assistance and other public services – as Amenta, Bonastia and Caren (2001) recommend – a more complex pattern emerges. The United States looks somewhat (but only somewhat) more generous with this broader conceptualisation. Given its federal structure and ongoing devolution, coming to terms with subnational dimensions of social equity in the United States constitutes a valuable contribution and raises methodological challenges.

To develop a comprehensive understanding of the welfare state, research must look beyond nation-level debates and trends. The size of a nation's public bureaucracy is a key measure of state capacity. In the United States, for example, 64% of public (civilian) employment is local; state governments account for 23% and federal government only 12% (US Bureau of the Census, 2008). Local governments range from some that are highly professionalised, offering a range of services, to others with weak bureaucracies and minimal services. Capacity differences coincide but certainly are not completely correlated with rural–urban location. Similarly, they are closely linked with wealth and poverty, but they are not the same.

Thus while sociologists have long studied economic disparities across US localities, variations in capacity among local governments and their relationship (if any) with socioeconomic well-being is little studied or understood. Yet the evidence that exists, especially of policy that is explicitly designed to be devolutionary such as PRWORA, the Personal Responsibility and Work Opportunity Reconciliation Act of 1996 (PRWORA), otherwise known as welfare reform, suggests an enormous impact of local capacity and institutional arrangements in both the form and impact of its implementation. Rural areas, although little studied, are particularly vulnerable to capacity issues that influence policy implementation and effectiveness. In a state such as Ohio, where responsibility for design and implementation was initially assigned to the counties, major differences in rural county administrative capacity and social capital influenced their ability to effectively design and administer new programmes, even when they shared similar levels of chronic poverty and deindustrialisation (Tickamyer, White, Tadlock, & Henderson, 2007, Tickamyer & Henderson, 2010). Case comparative examples such as this study of rural Appalachian Ohio counties, while illustrative and informative, are limited in scope and generalisability, underscoring the need for more comprehensive, systematic subnational research, especially as the push for decentralisation continues to dominate public policy. These issues are particularly important to address in the US case of a geographically diverse and politically fragmented system (Lobao, Adua & Hooks, 2014).

Just as research into the welfare state has over-emphasised national trends, this same focus has compromised our understanding of neoliberalism (Leicht & Jenkins, 2007). Neoliberalism as a theory stresses the limited role of government and the advantages of market-based policies (Goode & Maskovsky, 2001). This theory can be readily extended to subnational units of government and to rural areas. In fact, specific to the United States, neoliberalism prefers the devolution of policy and responsibility from federal to state and local governments. The preferred balance between the public and private sectors is more likely when subnational governments bear heavy responsibility for and enjoy greater autonomy in policy formation and implementation (Morrill, 1999; Ruben, 2001; Peck & Tickell, 2002). Neoliberalism highlights the private sector's role in sustaining growth and relies on non-governmental processes and institutions for material goods to trickle down to citizens (Mitchell & Simmons, 1994).

A decentralised state is compatible with neoliberal thinking because local and state governments, in concert with the private sector, can form a bulwark against the encroachment of the federal government. Thus, preserving the functions and privileges of the subnational state is essential (Robin, 2008). Moreover, decentralisation likely constrains the overall scope of government. The inherent trade-off between growth and distribution (Okun, 1975) as well as the immediacy of taxpayer resistance forces local officials to minimise government size and tax burden (Peterson & Rom, 1990). Social services in particular are less likely to expand when funding and service delivery are controlled locally. Decentralisation also encourages competition between states and localities both for central government resources and for global capital. Subnational governments are motivated to promote business-friendly policies and become engines of economic development.

Recent research into the subnational spread of neoliberal policies provides evidence of the importance of internal institutional attributes in setting policy (Lobao, Adua & Hooks, 2014). Variation in local state bureaucracies and capacity – urban and rural – means that there is also substantial variation in their adoption of neoliberal policies. This variation is *not* first and foremost urban versus rural; rather, the most important factors are institutional. County governments with greater administrative capacity, including size, centralised leadership and professional staff, are more likely to make policy choices that support the local social safety net. Studying spatial inequality – more specifically studying subnational variation and rural inequality – makes possible an innovative line of research that challenges the conventional view that neoliberalism is spreading inexorably and uniformly across policy domains and jurisdictions. In rural areas – as is the case in urban areas – local variation in governmental capacity, economic structure and institutional variation influence the degree to which the extant welfare state persists or is being transformed by neoliberal policy dictates.

Conclusion

This chapter has addressed the importance of studying spatial inequality in rural areas. In so doing, we have identified the many challenges and the rich opportunities when pursuing this line of research. Spatial inequality is concerned with how and why valued resources vary across places; and how places themselves become markers and makers of inequality: who gets what, *where* and why? For rural areas, the questions and answers provided by the spatial inequality literature can be quite valuable. Spatial inequality results in sharp variation in economic, social, health and other forms of well-being across rural areas. Inequalities of race, class and gender vary and intersect across urban and rural areas. It is noteworthy that spatial inequality researchers have highlighted how the geographic context itself contributes to the reproduction (or potential alleviation) of inequalities among individuals, households and community populations. In terms of theory, the study of spatial inequality in rural areas has informed the sociological study of inequality more generally. In this theoretical stance, economic structure, institutional arrangements and spatial/geographic factors figure prominently.

This chapter also highlighted ways in which the study of social inequality in rural areas contributes to larger theories of politics, social change and social inequality. Specifically, by studying rural areas it will be possible to develop a richer and more comprehensive understanding of the welfare state and challenges to the welfare state posed by neoliberalism. Particularly important will be systematic comparative research at different spatial scales that include rural places and spaces. Thus empirical work comparing the contours of US spatial inequalities and their influence on social welfare policies and politics with other advanced industrial and post-industrial nations of the global north as they unfold in rural regions needs to be conducted. The comparative studies will need to recognise and work through variation in policy emphasis across nations. For example, as Shucksmith (this volume) discusses, emphasis in Europe has been on social exclusion. In the United States, however, the policy emphasis has been on poverty.

There are a number of compelling questions for comparative researchers to ask. To what extent are variations the result of different historical experiences and trajectories? For example, how does difference in population dynamics, particularly related to the history of slavery, racial politics and ethnic migration, influence US inequalities compared to other affluent nations? Has size and influence of the military-industrial complex and US exceptionalism more generally influenced the complexity and decentralisation of the US welfare state (Hooks & McQueen, 2010)? Thus systematic comparative investigation of subnational units within and across nations, although an ambitious project, needs to be placed on a future research agenda. Devolution and decentralisation have often accompanied the neoliberal agenda. What is the impact on spatial inequalities where they have been implemented? Given the decentralised and fragmented social safety net in the United States, understanding the influence of local governments on socioeconomic well-being is critical. The extent that this can be replicated in other parts of the global north remains to be investigated. These issues are of even greater importance when attempting to understand dynamics at work in the context of both global and local ongoing economic development and more cataclysmic economic shocks such as the great recession, the global banking crisis and their aftermath.

Beyond these specific policies, the study of spatial inequality in rural areas can contribute to a still larger project: developing a better understanding of the spatial dynamics of inequality and, more progressively, a sociologically cast geography of social justice. This will entail expanding the focus beyond an emphasis on poverty and deprivation to comparative analysis of wealth and advantage, especially in a world where gains at the top have accelerated and increasingly exacerbate historical inequalities. Most notably, it requires greater recognition of the theoretical and empirical commonalities among sociology's spatial inequality traditions, as well as moving beyond fixing the study of inequality at any particular scale. As inequality and all the social disparities it entails become a pressing issue at every spatial scale, sociology is uniquely positioned to contribute to the understanding of continuing spatial inequalities and the social justice responses they entail. The study of spatial inequality in rural areas must be central to these debates.

Note

1   It should be noted that scholars engaged in quantitative studies of rural inequality, while having a primary interest in space, further recognise that some spatial processes need to be statistically controlled for the purpose of analysing rurality or other causal variables of interest.

References

Agnew, J (1987). *Place and politics: The geographical mediation of state and society.* Boston, MA: Allen & Unwin.

Alber, J, Fahey, T & Saraceno, C (2008). *Handbook of quality of life in the enlarged European Union.* London: Routledge.

Alesina, A & Glaeser, E (2004). *Fighting poverty in the US and Europe: A world of difference.* New York: Oxford University Press.

Almeida, P (2014). *Mobilizing democracy: Globalization and citizen protest.* Baltimore, MD: Johns Hopkins University Press.

Alston, L & Ferrie, J (1999). *Southern paternalism and the American welfare state: Economics, politics, and institutions in the South 1865–1965.* New York: Cambridge University Press.

Amenta, E, Bonastia, C & Caren, N (2001). US social policy in comparative and historical perspective: Concepts, images, arguments, and research strategies. *Annual Review of Sociology* 27, 213–234.

Amenta, E (1998). *Bold relief: Institutional politics and the origins of modern American social policy*. Princeton, NJ: Princeton University Press.

Amenta, E & Halfmann, D (2000). Wage wars: Institutional politics, WPA wages, and the struggle for U.S. social policy. *American Sociological Review* 65, 506–528.

Amin, A (2004). Regions unbound: Towards a new politics of place. *Geografiska Annaler* 86 B (1), 33–44.

Benton, JE (2002). *Counties as service delivery agents*. Westport, CN: Praeger.

Billings, DB & Blee, KM (2000). *The road to poverty: The making of wealth and hardship in Appalachian America*. New York: Cambridge University Press.

Blank, RM (2005). Poverty, policy, and place: How poverty and policies to alleviate poverty are shaped by local characteristics. *International Regional Science Review* 28, 441–464.

Brenner, N (2004). *New state spaces: Urban governance and the rescaling of statehood*. New York: Oxford University Press.

Brown, DL (2002). Migration and community: Social networks in a multilevel world. *Rural Sociology* 67(1), 1–23.

Brown, DL, Greskovits, G & Kulcsar, LJ (2007). Leading sectors and leading regions: Economic restructuring and regional inequality in Hungary since 1990. *International Journal of Urban and Regional Research* 31(3), 522–542.

Brown, DL & Schafft, A (2011). *Rural people and communities in the 21st century*. Malden, MA: Polity.

Bunker, S (1985). *Underdeveloping the Amazon*. Chicago, IL: University of Illinois Press.

Constance, DH, Hendrickson, M, Howard, P & Heffernan, WD (2014). Economic concentration in the agrifood system: Impacts on rural communities and emerging response. In C Bailey, L Jensen, & E Ransom (Eds), *Rural America in a globalizing world: Problems and prospects for the 2010s* (pp. 16–35). Morgantown, WV: West Virginia University Press.

Copus, A & Hörnström, L (Eds). (2011). *The new rural Europe: Towards rural cohesion policy*. Stockholm, Sweden: Nordregio. Available at http://www.nordregio.se/en/Publications/Publications-2011/The-New-Rural-Europe-Towards-Rural-Cohesion-Policy/ (accessed 28 January 2016).

Cotter, DA (2002). Poor people in poor places: Local opportunity structure and household poverty. *Rural Sociology* 67(2), 534–555.

Craw, M (2006). Overcoming city limits: Vertical and horizontal models of local redistributive policy making. *Social Science Quarterly* 87(2), 361–379.

Duncan, C (1999). *Worlds apart*. New Haven, CT: Yale University Press.

Entrikin, JN (1991). *The betweenness of place*. Baltimore, MD: Johns Hopkins University Press.

Esping-Andersen, G (1990). *The three worlds of welfare capitalism*. Princeton, NJ: Princeton University Press.

Falk, W & Lobao, LM (2003). Who benefits from economic restructuring? Who is worse off?: Lessons from the past and challenges for the future. In D Brown & L Swanson (Eds), *Rural areas and policies in the new millennium* (pp. 152–165). Philadelphia, PA: Pennsylvania State University Press.

Falk, W & Lyson, TA (1988). *High tech, low tech, no tech: Recent industrial and occupational change in the South*. Albany: State University of New York Press.

Falk, W, Schulman, M & Tickamyer, A (Eds). (2003). *Communities of work: Rural restructuring in local and global context*. Athens, OH: Ohio University Press.

Freudenburg, WR & Gramling, R (1994). Natural resources and rural poverty: A closer look. *Society and Natural Resources* 7, 5–22.

Friedland, R & Boden, D (1994). *NowHere: space, time, and modernity*. Berkeley, CA: University of California Press.

Goode, J & Maskovsky, J (2001). Introduction. In J Goode & J Maskovsky, *The new poverty studies: The ethnography of power, politics, and impoverished people in the United States* (pp. 1–34). New York: New York University Press.

Harvey, D (1989). *The urban experience*. Oxford: Blackwell.

Heclo, H (1974). *Modern social politics in Britain and Sweden*. New Haven, CT: Yale University Press.

Hicks, A (1999). *Social democracy and welfare capitalism: A century of income security politics*. Ithaca, NY: Cornell University Press.

Hooks, G & McQueen, B (2010). American exceptionalism revisited: The role of racial tensions and defense employment on the decline of the New Deal. *American Sociological Review* 75, 185–204.

Hooks, G & Smith, CL (2004). The treadmill of destruction: National sacrifice areas and Native Americans. *American Sociological Review* 69, 558–575.

Huber, E & Stephens, J (2001). *Development and crisis of the welfare state*. Chicago, IL: University of Chicago Press.

Isserman, AM, Feser, E & Warren, DE (2009). Why some rural places prosper and others do not. *International Regional Science Review* 32(3), 300–342.

Kazepov, Y (Ed.). (2010). *Rescaling social policies: Towards multilevel governance in Europe*. Farnham: Ashgate.

Kinchy, A, Perry, S, Rhubart, D, Stedman, R, Brasier, K & Jacquet, J (2014). Natural gas development and rural communities: Key issues and research priorities. In C Bailey, L Jensen & E Ransom (Eds), *Rural America in a globalizing world: Problems and prospects for the 2010s* (pp. 260–278). Morgantown, WV: West Virginia University Press.

Krugman, P (1991). *Geography and trade*. Cambridge, MA: MIT Press.

Lefebvre, H (1991). *The production of space*. Cambridge, MA: Basil Blackwell.

Leicht, K & Jenkins, C (2007). New and unexplored opportunities: Developing a spatial perspective for political sociology. In L Lobao, G Hooks & A Tickamyer (Eds), *The sociology of spatial inequality*. Albany: State University of New York Press.

Lichter, DT & Cimaluk, LA (2012). Family change and poverty in Appalachia. In JP Zilliak (Ed.), *Appalachian legacy: Economic opportunity after the war on poverty* (pp. 81–105). Washington, DC: Brookings.

Lichter, DT, Parisi, D & Taquino, MC (2012). The geography of exclusion: Race, segregation, and concentrated poverty. *Social Problems* 59(3), 364–388.

Lobao, L (1996). A sociology of the periphery versus a peripheral sociology: Rural sociology and the dimension of space. *Rural Sociology* 61(1), 77–102.

Lobao, L (2016). The sociology of subnational development: Conceptual and empirical foundations. In G Hooks (Ed.), *Development sociology: A handbook*. Los Angeles, CA: University of California Press.

Lobao, L, Adua, L & Hooks, G (2014). Privatization, business attraction, and social services across the United States: Local governments' use of market-oriented, neoliberal policies in the post-2000 period. *Social Problems* 61, 644–672.

state to the states Lobao, L & Hooks, G (2007). Advancing the sociology of spatial inequality: Spaces, places, and the subnational scale. In L Lobao, G Hooks & A Tickamyer (Eds), *The sociology of spatial inequality* (pp. 29–68). Albany, NY: State University of New York Press.

Lobao, L, Hooks, G & Tickamyer, A (2007). Introduction: Advancing the sociology of spatial inequality. In L Lobao, G Hooks & A Tickamyer (Eds), *The sociology of spatial inequality* (pp. 1–25). Albany, NY: State University of New York Press.

Lobao, L, Jeanty, PW, Partridge, M & Kraybill, D (2012). Poverty and place across the United States: Do county governments matter to the distribution of economic disparities? *International Regional Science Review* 35(2), 158–187.

Lobao, L & Meyer, K (2001). The great agricultural transition: Crisis, change, and social consequences of twentieth century farming. *Annual Review of Sociology* 27, 103–124.

Lyson, T & Falk, W (1993). *Forgotten places: Uneven development and the underclass in rural America*. Lawrence, KS: University of Kansas Press.

Massey, D (1993). Questions of locality. *Geography* 78(2), 142–149.

Massey, D (1999). Philosophy and politics of spatiality: Some considerations. The Hettner-Lecture in human geography. *Geographische Zeitschrift* 87(1), 1–12.

Massey, D (2004). Geographies of responsibility. *Geografiska Annaler* 86 Series B (1), 5–18.

McLaughlin, DK, Stokes, CS, Smith, PJ & Nonoyama, A (2007). Differential mortality across the United States: The influence of place-based inequality. In L Lobao, G Hooks & A Tickamyer (Eds), *The sociology of spatial inequality* (pp. 141–162). Albany, NY: State University of New York Press.

Mitchell, WC & Simmons, RT (1994). *Beyond politics: Markets, welfare, and the failure of bureaucracy*. Boulder, CO: Westview Press.

Moffat, S & Glasgow, N (2009). How useful is the concept of social exclusion when applied to rural older people in the United Kingdom and the United States? *Regional Studies* 43(10), 1291–1303.

Morrill, R (1999). Inequalities of power, costs, and benefits across geographic scales: The future uses of the Hanford Reservation. *Political Geography* 18, 1–23.

Newby, H (1983). The sociology of agriculture: Toward a new rural sociology. *Annual Review of Sociology* 9, 67–81.

Odum, HE & Moore, HE (1938). *American regionalism: A cultural historical approach to national integration*. New York: Henry Holt.

Okun, AM (1975). *Equality and efficiency: The big tradeoff*. Washington, DC: Brookings Institution.

Partridge, M & Rickman, D (2006). *The geography of American poverty*. Kalamazoo, MI: W.E. Upjohn Institute.

Peck, J (2001). *Workfare states*. New York: Guilford Press.

Peck, J & Tickell, A (2002). Neoliberalizing space. *Antipode* 34(3), 380–404.

Pellow, DN (2000). Environmental inequality formation: Toward a theory of environmental injustice. *American Behavioral Scientist* 43(4), 581–601.

Peters, DJ (2012). Income inequality across micro and meso geographic scales in the Midwestern United States, 1979–2009. *Rural Sociology* 77(2), 171–120.

Peterson, PE & Rom, MC (1990). *Welfare magnets: A new case for a national standard.* Washington, DC: Brookings Institution.

Pruitt, LR (2009). Latina/os, locality, and law in the rural south. *Harvard Latino Law Review* 12, 140–169.

Quadagno, J (1994). *The color of welfare: How race undermined the war on poverty.* New York: Oxford University Press.

Robin, C (2008). Out of place. *The Nation* 286(24), 25–26, 28–32.

Ruben, M (2001). Suburbanization and poverty under neoliberalism. In J Goode & J Maskovsky (Eds), *The new poverty studies: The ethnography of power, politics, and impoverished people in the United States* (pp. 435–469). New York: New York University Press.

Rudel, T, Katan, T & Horowitz, B (2013). Amerindian livelihoods, outside interventions, and poverty traps in the Ecuadorian Amazon. *Rural Sociology* 78(2), 167–185.

Rural Sociological Society Task Force on Persistent Rural Poverty (1993). *Persistent poverty in rural America.* Boulder, CO: Westview Press.

Sachs, C (2014). Gender, race, ethnicity, class, and sexuality in rural America. In C Bailey, L Jensen & E Ransom (Eds), *Rural America in a globalizing world* (pp. 421–434). Morgantown, WV: West Virginia University Press.

Saenz, R (1997). Ethnic concentration and Chicano poverty: A comparative approach. *Social Science Research* 26, 205–228.

Salamon, S (2003). *Newcomers to old towns: Suburbanization of the heartland.* Chicago, IL: University of Chicago Press.

Sherman, J (2009). *Those who work, those who don't: Poverty, morality, and family in rural America.* Minneapolis, MN: University of Minnesota Press.

Shortall, S & Bock, B (2015). Introduction: Rural women in Europe: The impact of place and culture on gender mainstreaming the European Rural Development Programme. *Gender, Place and Culture* 22(5), 662–669.

Shucksmith, M (2012). Class, power, and inequality in rural areas: Beyond social exclusion. *Sociologia Ruralis* 54 (October), 377–397.

Singelmann, J & Deseran, FA (Eds.) (1993). *Inequalities in labor market areas.* Boulder, CO: Westview.

Smith, N (1984). *Uneven development: Nature, capital, and the production of space.* Oxford: Basil Blackwell.

Soja, E (1989). *Post-modern geographies: The reassertion of space in critical social theory.* London: Verso.

Struthers, C (2014). The past is the present: Gender and the status of rural women. In C Bailey, L Jensen & E Ransom (Eds), *Rural America in a globalizing world: Problems and prospects for the 2010s* (pp. 489–505). Morgantown, WV: West Virginia University Press.

Tickamyer, AR (2000). Space matters! Spatial inequality in the future of sociology. *Contemporary Sociology* 29, 805–813.

Tickamyer, AR (2006). Rural poverty. In T Marsden, P Cloke & P Mooney (Eds), *Handbook of rural studies* (pp. 407–422). London: Sage.

Tickamyer, AR & Duncan, CM (1990). Poverty in rural America. *Annual Review of Sociology* 16, 67–86.

Tickamyer, AR & Henderson, DA (2010). Devolution, social exclusion, and spatial inequality in U.S. welfare provision. In P Milbourne (Ed.), *Welfare reform in rural places: Comparative perspectives, Research in rural sociology and development* (pp. 41–60). Bingley, UK: Emerald Publishing.

Tickamyer, AR, White, J, Tadlock, B & Henderson, D (2007). Spatial politics of public policy. In L Lobao, G Hooks & A Tickamyer (Eds), *The sociology of spatial inequality* (pp. 113–39). New York: SUNY Press.

US Bureau of the Census (2008). *Annual survey of state and local government employment and census of governments (1982–2008).* Washington, DC.

Wallerstein, I (1974). *The modern world-system* (Vol 1.). New York: Academic Press.

Weber, B, Jensen, L, Miller, K, Mosely, J & Fisher, M (2005). A critical review of rural poverty literature: Is there truly a rural effect? *International Regional Science Review* 28(4), 381–414.

Wimberley, RC (2008). Sociology with a Southern Face: Why are we sociologists and what are we doing about it in the South? *Social Forces* 86, 881–909.

40

Understanding the Association between Rural Ethnicity and Inequalities

Ruth McAreavey

This chapter examines inequalities arising from ethnicity in a rural context. It identifies how different factors, including recent patterns of international migration and historical legacies of ethnic diversity, intertwine to produce multicultural rural areas. First of all, an overview of the significance of the 'ethnic' label is presented, recognising its limitations and also its usefulness. Having established this context the review proceeds by highlighting the way in which rural ethnic inequalities are measured. The processes that produce inequalities among ethnic groups are examined, with particular attention to migration and space and place but mindful of historical legacies along with economic transformations and associated recent migration patterns.

The significance of ethnicity

One of the problems in classifying social groups by ethnicity, gender, migration status and so forth is that it can leave individuals in certain groups open to manipulation by more dominant groups (Massey, 1994; Waters & Eschbach, 1995; Eide, 2010). This overlooks important nuances within and between groups and fails to pay attention to the way different aspects of identity intersect, but perhaps more importantly it ignores the fact that ethnicity, like other aspects of identity, is socially constructed (Jenkins, 2014). It is formed through ever changing, social interaction (Bauman, 2004), shifting according to many other factors including culture along with individual experiences, expectations, qualifications and socioeconomic status (Barnard & Turner, 2011). Thus different groups continue to 'change shape', altering their social identity according to particular circumstances (Waters & Eschbach, 1995, p. 420). For example, migrants wish to belong rather than remain solely within a static social group, often with essentialised identity (Probyn, 1996). This desire can give rise to hybrid identities and in certain circumstances migrants may use double frames of reference as they position themselves in a new destination (Nowicka, 2012 in Nowicka, 2014). Ethnicity is therefore one aspect of 'identity as transition' (Fortier, 2000, p. 8) with symbolic representations produced, reproduced and transformed over time (Waters & Eschbach, 1995).

Considered as a social construct, embedded in a particular context and with peculiar circumstances, ethnicity allows us to consider the way in which the category is constructed and deployed in respect to exclusion and inequalities. Ethnicity thus represents an important demarcation within society. It allows us to examine the mechanisms whereby ethnic boundaries are blurred, sharpened, shifted or traversed as a means of reinforcing, or indeed overcoming, structural inequalities (Barth, 1969; Bauböck, 1994; Zolberg & Woon, 1999; Alba, 2005; Wimmer, 2008; McAreavey & Swindal, 2014; Special Issue Ethnic and Racial Studies, 2014). Put simply, the way in which social groups are treated differently due to ethnicity allows us to examine opportunities across society.

Multicultural rural areas

In many rural places in the developed world, 'whiteness' has for a long time been a symbol of rurality (see, for example, Philo, 1992; Cloke, 2004; Lichter, 2012). It can lead to misconceptions about certain places, such as the 'popular view ... that the [Australian] countryside is by and large not multi-cultural' (Missingham, Dibden & Cocklin, 2006, p. 133). While much of the literature has underplayed or simply ignored the importance of rural ethnic heterogeneity (de Lima, 2012), some attempts have been made to shed light on the matter (Snipp et al., 1993). It is the case that many rural areas have a predominantly white ethnic population, but so too has racial diversity long been the norm in some places. Historical factors, coupled with recent increased levels of voluntary international migration, means that ethnic heterogeneity has become the norm in many rural places. Before I review recent patterns of immigration, I consider some of the other factors contributing to rural ethnic diversity, including the prevalence of established heterogeneous rural communities in certain locations.

Many rural areas have been shaped by historical patterns of migration. Ethnic diversity is a recognised feature of rural communities in Australia (Burnley, 2001) and Canada (Reimer, Burns & Gareau, 2007). In Canada, targeted immigration is an established economic policy employed to bolster flagging rural economies (Preibisch, 2007; Jentsch & Simard, 2009), and this strategy is commonly used in Australia (Hugo & Morén-Alégret, 2008). Meanwhile rural America has a rich legacy of immigration, voluntary and forced: in the mid-19th century different European migrants in the Midwest, including Scandinavian and German families, established farmsteads; Scots and Irish arrived in the Appalachia to work in coal mines and the timber sector (Lichter, 2012). Rather less positively, a 'legacy of slavery, conquest, and racial subjugation (and genocide)' (Lichter, 2012, p. 4) explains current ethnic residential patterns that include the 'black belt' of the southern states and unregulated housing in rural Texas.

As already identified, one of the major impacts of globalisation has been the reliance on mobile labour and capital – people move across borders to secure employment opportunities thereby contributing to a wider neoliberal aspiration of economic growth and development. Consequently many rural regions across Europe[1] including Ireland, Scotland, Greece, Italy, Spain, all of which had a limited history of international migration, are now experiencing the arrival of significant numbers of international migrants from Central and Eastern Europe as well as from South America, Asia, Africa and the Middle East (see, for instance, Kasimis, Papadopoulos & Zacopoulou, 2003; Jentsch & Simard, 2009; see also Chapters 2, 6 and 7 in this volume).[2] Even countries with histories of immigration have experienced recent accelerated immigration beyond traditional gateways. Scholars in the US point to the new phenomenon of ethnic migration to many parts of rural and small town America that is transforming communities in the process (see, for instance, Kandel & Cromartie, 2004; Jensen, 2006; Broadway, 2007; Lichter & Johnson, 2007; McConnell & Miraftab, 2009; Lichter & Brown, 2011; Marrow, 2011; Lichter, 2012; Crowley, Lichter & Turner, 2015).

Although absolute migrant numbers may remain small in many of these so-called 'new destinations', the proportion of the foreign-born population has increased rapidly. In the United

States, the Midwest and Southeast regions of the country have seen the most rapid increase in newcomers; in some places more than a third of the foreign-born population arrived only in the past 15 years (Batalova & Lee, 2012). In Jefferson County, Alabama, the foreign-born population increased by 65% between 2000 and 2007 (Singer, 2009). As late as 2012, only 4% of Alabama residents were born outside the USA; remarkably, 70% of Alabama residents were born in the state itself. In Mississippi and Louisiana the figures are 72% and 79% respectively (Aisch, Gebeloff & Quealy, 2014). The particular demographies emerging within the USA and the shifting majority–minority ratio point to Coleman's (2006) third demographic transition (Lichter, 2012). This implies a general movement from a low-fertility, native-born majority to a high-fertility, racial and ethnic immigrant population, something that Coleman argues is also more widely discernible in the UK. Lichter makes it clear: 'Immigration and the new ethnoracial diversity will be at the leading edge of major changes in rural community life as the nation moves toward becoming a majority–minority society by 2042' (2012, p. 3). However, some research disputes the emergence of an absolute majority–minority American society due to 'mixed unions' and more fluid contemporary understandings of race and ethnicity (see, for example, Pew Research Centre, 2015; Alba, 2015).

In a European context, country-of-birth figures for Northern Ireland show that in 2001 1.5% of the population was born outside the UK and Ireland. This figure rises to 4.5% in 2011.[3] But it is more locally nuanced than this; geographic pockets have emerged with growth rates as high as 21% recorded in the Dungannon District Council area of Northern Ireland. Moreover, within this council boundary, particular areas have experienced dramatic increase in heterogeneity: for instance, the Ballysaggart ward includes 825 people – or 30% of the population – who are EU and other migrants. Meanwhile, across Spain the foreign-born rural population has steadily risen by 15.8% between 2000 and 2008 (Collantes, Pinilla, Sáez & Silvestre, 2014). Collantes and colleagues also found that the pace of Spanish immigration countered economic decline and/or depopulation due to youth emigration, falling fertility rates and an ageing society. This is similar for many other rural areas within southern Europe, including Portugal and Greece (see for example Fonesca, 2008 and Kasimis, Papadopoulos & Zacopoulou, 2003; respectively) and for some rural localities within northern European countries including Sweden (see, for example, Rye & Andrzejewska, 2010).

In addition to the arrival of economic migrants, rising numbers of refugees, especially from North Africa and the Middle East, are settling in rural areas, often spurred to locate in rural locations because many governments choose to put asylum centres here. This is evident in the UK with so-called 'detention centres' sprinkled across the region. Meanwhile localities in non-metropolitan Australia, often with depopulating and declining communities, actively attract refugees to settle by highlighting employment opportunities (Hugo, 2008).

Following these transformations, international migration is no longer an urban experience. The arrival of new residents has changed, and is changing, the social structure of local areas forever. The way in which these different ethnic (majority and minority) communities interact is of interest to rural scholars. It begs the question: what does a multicultural rural society look like? In light of this backdrop, the review proceeds by identifying the association between rural ethnicity and inequalities.

The specificity of rural ethnic inequalities

A lens of diversity is useful for understanding facets of an individual's identity, but it is not sufficient. Increasingly the literature stresses the need to examine the relational and temporal dimensions of inequalities (see, for instance, Bürkner, 2012; Nowicka, 2014), showing how, over time, circumstances and outcomes for individuals and social groups may change. This is further complicated by the way in which certain places present different opportunities for individuals, something that is revisited later in this chapter. The wider social and cultural context thus requires attention if we are to understand how social groups are identified as different in terms of ethnic identity and the implications of these categories (Jenkins, 2000, 2014). This is important because certain groups have been found to have relatively poorer prospects than other groups in the same area. Moreover, particular places suffer unwaveringly from inequalities. For instance, in areas with historical legacies of ethnic minority communities in the USA, wider political and economic processes have been found to drive persistent poverty among minority populations (see, for example, Lyson & Falk, 1993; Parisi, Lichter & Taquino, 2011; Lichter, Parisi & Taquino, 2012).

Drawing on intersectionality debates for understanding inequalities, Bürkner (2012) provides ideas for moving forward in migration research[4] that have relevance to debates on rural ethnic inequalities, helping to take account of specificity. He offers a multilevel view of institutional inequality at the micro (i.e., social practices), meso (representation) and macro (social structures) levels. Additionally Bürkner stresses the importance of understanding the 'episodic nodes of exclusion, which have a complex (i.e. intersectional) origin' (2012, p. 186). Thus Bürkner's multilevel perspective is not necessarily nested, but the different levels are socially constructed, dependent on uneven power relations and with intersecting trajectories (Glick Schiller & Çağlar, 2015). This means that social interaction, while occurring at a very local level, is set within wider social structures, a point that is acknowledged within rural poverty debates (see, for instance, Dudenhefer, 1994; Cloke, Goodwin, Milbourne & Thomas, 1995; Milbourne, 2004; Shucksmith & Schafft, 2012). Social structures could be global in nature such as those associated with neoliberal aspirations and associated policies promoting labour market deregulation, but they provide variable opportunities (or obstacles) for individuals within particular places (Popke, 2011). Here context is important for understanding an individual's micro-social action and corresponding coping strategies, as are the wider macro structures. This emphasises 'the dynamic modes of exclusion, which are triggered by the practice of specific milieus or by other context-driven micro-social embeddings of the individual' (Bürkner, 2012, p. 188). Paying attention to particular circumstances and, paraphrasing Harvey (1990), to the specificity of time and place is important (in capital accumulation).

Unravelling multilevel structures and identifying nodes of exclusion are challenging tasks, but ultimately they allow us to better comprehend symbolic representations and relations between minority groups and mainstream society. Nowicka's 'migrating skills' (2014, p. 182) is a good example. She shows how migrants are able to overcome institutional boundaries that potentially undermine their employment options due to different recognition of education and skills in the UK and Poland. Accordingly, Nowicka's study finds that Polish migrants adapt their skills while seeking employment in the UK. This shows how, as 'stable behavioral patterns of association' (Lamont & Molnár, 2002, p. 168), skills validation processes represent social boundaries that delineate unequal access to and distribution of resources. They combine with symbolic boundaries that are based on cultural norms and traditions (Lamont & Molnár, 2002). Ultimately both types of boundaries exist through social interaction and both are used strategically, such as when groups compete to acquire status or to gain access to certain resources. This allows them to permeate, if not move across boundaries, eventually contributing to collective mobility strategies.

Focusing like this on particular situations and contexts rather than uniform structures pays attention to the fluidity of space and place (Lefebvre, 1991; Massey, 2005) and overcomes challenges of structure and agency (Giddens, 1986). Concentrating on scale and context also responds to the need to move towards interdisciplinary and context-attentive perspectives (Levitt & Nyberg-Sørensen, 2004; Favell, Feldblum & Smith, 2006; Bauböck & Faist, 2010; Miraftab, 2012). Before examining the multiplicity of issues that give rise to rural ethnic inequalities, some of the particular challenges of measuring rural poverty are identified.

Rural ethnic inequalities and challenges of measurement

Existing problems of encapsulating inequalities within general studies of rural poverty have a bearing on measuring rural ethnic inequalities. Historically, at least in the USA, the rural population has faced disproportionately high and persistent poverty (Cotter, 2002; Lichter & Johnson, 2007; Lichter, Parisi Taquino, 2012), and this is not a priority for policy makers (Weber et al., 2005). Even if there is a desire to identify vulnerable communities, large-scale patterns can mask local specificities, overlooking the existence of pockets of communities and creating places that are 'statistically invisible' in that they are not easily identified through statistical analyses (Wheeler & La Jeunesse, 2008, p. 175; see also Lichter & Johnson, 2007; Foulkes & Schafft, 2010). This has been further complicated because the poor population became less concentrated from the 1990s (Lichter, Parisi, Taquino & Beaulieu, 2008). Examining income inequality in the Midwest, Peters (2012) argues that at a micro scale, neighbourhoods that are skewed by extremes of wealth and poverty will present an overall impression free of very real inequalities that are experienced at the micro level. Meanwhile, in other rural places the prevalence of 'poverty among affluence' has been identified (see, for instance, Milbourne, 2004; Shucksmith & Schafft, 2012, p. 111). One of the problems of measuring rural ethnic inequalities arises because ethnic minorities often remain invisible, hidden through isolation or because of their location in a depressed region. This can happen if ethnic minorities are confined to particular spaces within a locality because of their designation as 'other' (Miraftab & McConnell, 2008; Doyle & McAreavey, 2015). Larger scale invisibility can also arise for rural ethnic minorities due to wider structural forces and political agendas, as indicated earlier in the chapter. This is evident in the 'black belt' where poor socioeconomic conditions are highly concentrated (Allen-Smith, Wimberley & Morris, 1993; Lyson & Falk, 1993; Lichter, Parisi & Taquino, 2012).

In some rural places ethnic groups may not be sufficiently large to be 'statistically significant'. Other problems of reporting accuracy and under-reporting can result in imprecise figures; all of which can conceal the real picture. Even in scenarios where small numbers are recorded, further problems include undocumented individuals who may not 'officially' exist (Maher & Cawley, 2014) and therefore fall outside of official records and formal support mechanisms.

Unravelling the processes that produce rural ethnic inequalities

According to Waters and Eschbach (1995), there are many ways to measure inequalities among ethnic and racial groups including 'health and demographic measures such as infant mortality rates, life expectancy, morbidity, and disability'. They continue by explaining that '[E]thnic and racial groups also differ in rates of homeownership, residential segregation, overall wealth, exposure to crime and toxic pollutants, and in access to power in the upper reaches of our society' (Waters & Eschbach, 1995, p. 425). Indicators across a range of domains are thus frequently used by researchers to evaluate inequalities – including income, but also housing, access to amenities, social and family networks, health, life expectancy and well-being, along with individual perceptions of these categories (see, for instance, Mathieson et al. 2008; Shucksmith, Cameron, Merridew & Pilcher , 2009).

Clearly there are many factors that require consideration if rural ethnic inequalities are to be fully explored. This review cannot cover all domains – education, housing, welfare, social networks and relations, social income, employment. It does, however, focus on the role of the rural economy and on the significance of historical legacies and political ideologies across space and place. The way in which these create particular dynamics that give rise to rural ethnic inequalities will be examined below.

The rural economy

In the face of increasing mobility of capital and correspondingly competitive markets, substantial rural industrial and agricultural restructuring has created demand for low-wage, low-skilled workers. Many of the employment positions that have arisen due to these economic transformations have little security and social status. They are typically filled by migrants or by the relocation of ethnic minority communities, and both of these broad groups are over-represented in this type of rural employment (see Hoggart & Mendoza, 1999; Kandel & Parrado, 2005; Preibisch, 2007; Anderson & Ruhs, 2012; Nelson, Trautman & Nelson, in press). Studies reveal labour market segmentation in terms of the types of jobs available and also regarding the type of industries employing ethnic groups (Jensen, 1994). Understanding features of 'employment adequacy' and ultimately of employment hardships are central to economic well-being (Slack & Jensen, 2002, p. 212). The availability of employment opportunities in different sectors, the conditions of the workplace – such as the extent to which employees may work the hours and employee–employer relations – are all bounded within the labour market. This section explores those labour-related rural ethnic inequalities.

There is a predominance of migrants in agriculture, horticulture, food processing, construction, small industries and social care (Kasimis, Papadopoulos & Zacopoulou, 2003; Kandel & Cromartie, 2004; Kritzinger, Barrientos & Rossouw, 2004; Missingham, Dibden & Cocklin, 2006; Broadway, 2007; McConnell & Miraftab, 2009; Findlay, Geddes & McCollum, 2010; Lichter, 2012). Labour market segmentation can result from the predominance of certain ethnic groups in particular sectors. For instance, Filipinos tend to fill social care posts across the globe; within Europe, Eastern European migrants predominate in the construction and the meat- and food-processing sectors (Fonesca, 2008; Findlay et al., 2013). Differences exist within countries and regions: Fonesca shows how Eastern Europeans are under-represented in the Portuguese service sector, probably due to lack of Portuguese language proficiency. Meanwhile, this sector is dominated by migrants from Portuguese-speaking African countries. Employment in agriculture in Spain is over-represented by African workers. In the Midwest and southern USA, meatpacking is reliant on Hispanics, creating something akin to the 'boom towns' of the 19th century (Kandel & Cromartie, 2004; Broadway, 2007). All of these sectors are characterised by low pay, flexible working, low skills and little security (Hoggart & Mendoza, 1999; Anderson & Ruhs, 2012).

It is hardly surprising that broad questions of equality have been raised in connection to migrants' experiences and their marginalisation within the labour market. They often face discrimination and unequal access to employment rights, thereby existing in a precarious position in the rural economy (Standing, 2011). This is well illustrated for modern migrants working as farmworkers (see *International Journal of Sociology of Agriculture and Food* Special Section: Migrants in the Global Food System, 2014). There is evidence of migrants being paid less to undertake the same work (Anderson & Ruhs, 2010; Rye & Andrzejewska, 2010; Maher & Crawley, 2014), migrants working below their qualification levels (Fonesca, 2008; Irwin, McAreavey & Murphy, 2014) and migrants living in accommodation tied to their employment.

This renders them particularly vulnerable since they face destitution if they lose their job and so are more likely to 'put up with' exploitation. Visible boundaries such as these highlight difference and entrench inequalities.

More generally, small and medium-sized enterprises (SMEs) have been shown to be more discriminatory than larger employers towards ethnic groups (Green, Owen & Wilson, 2005; Irwin, McAreavey & Murphy, 2014). Low-wage traps affect ethnic minorities disproportionately (Barnard, 2014).

All sorts of strategies for coping are employed within minority households, including risky behaviour relating to poor health, increased reliance on informal networks and more generally increased pressure to generate social income[5] beyond salary and wages (Standing, 2011). Rural ethnic groups' equal treatment in the workplace can be hampered because of the lack of recognition of overseas qualifications, thereby curtailing the opportunities available to them (European Commission, 2009). Migrants have been shown to circumvent these barriers by making their skills and qualifications a better 'fit' to local contexts (Nowicka, 2012), but individual strategies are not always successful (Irwin, McAreavey & Murphy, 2014). Employers can therefore exploit vulnerable workers through a range of mechanisms including discouraging unionisation or worker solidarity (Gorodzeisky & Richards, 2013), acting with impunity or instilling fear among rural ethnic workers who have few alternative employment options. Specific regulations can outlaw migrant unionisation, such as for farmworkers in Canada (Tucker, 2012 in Preibisch & Otero, 2014). The politics of labour markets and the extent to which they are regulated shape outcomes for rural ethnic employees.

Demand for workers in low-wage, insecure sectors as described above is socially constructed by the various actions of the state and wider society and of employers and employees, all of which can limit labour market opportunities. The bottom line is that many local people refuse to do this type of 'unworthy' work (see Kandel & Parrado, 2004; Broadway, 2007; Preibisch, 2007), often despite high levels of unemployment (Findlay, Geddes & McCollum, 2010). Employers, and recruitment agencies operating on their behalf, target particular localities where they know a pool of labour exists, often selecting so that productivity is maximised and worker solidarity is minimised (Kandel & Parrado, 2004; Broadway, 2007; Preibisch, 2007; Findlay et al., 2013). Employers' actions help to shape the 'good' and desirable worker, particularly around institutional recruitment and selection processes, helping to cull workers who do not conform to particular standards and targeting particular ethnic communities (Johnson-Webb, 2002; Findlay et al., 2013). It has been found that migrants themselves can also cultivate this perception simply because they have no choice (McAreavey, 2015).

In the EU (Awad, 2009; Findlay et al., 2013) and the USA (Hanson, 2009) firms influence the actions of the state by actively lobbying for larger immigration flows. The state provides the structure that helps to sufficiently meet demand for labour (Castles, de Haas & Miller, 2014) using mechanisms such as work permit schemes (Hoggart & Mendoza, 2000; Preibisch & Otero, 2014) and regulating via equality legislation. During times of recession or stagnation, opportunities for migrant labour decrease as state regulation becomes more stringent. The creation of quota systems and other means of channelling migrants to particular sectors generate boundaries that in turn reproduce economic difference and vulnerabilities for certain groups. This raises all types of questions of inclusion and exclusion and of the rights of individuals. For instance, seasonal worker schemes often mean that individuals, rather than families, are able to migrate and when they do move they are more likely to agree to work longer hours simply because they are in an unfamiliar place (Preibisch, 2007). Legal systems in Spain and Italy were found to institutionalise exclusion through the creation of quota systems for immigrant workers that are limited to sectors 'shunned' by the indigenous population and where low wages and poor working conditions prevail (Calavita, 2005, p. 156; 2007). In the longer term these types of schemes counter any progressive immigrant integration policies that might exist, demonstrating inherent contradictions in the political economy (Calavita, 2005). Additionally, designating other individuals such as those who are economically active but lacking certain legal documents as 'illegal' raises questions about the legal system, how it is devised and interpreted and for whom it affords protection (Cohen, 2003; see also Massey, Durand & Malone, 2002).

Ethnic communities are not homogenous; there are differences between and within different groups. In some circumstances conflict between and within different groups of workers can emerge. Competition between minorities has been illustrated in the south of the USA with a perception among African American workers that at the very least Latinos increase the competition for low-wage jobs (Marrow, 2011; Parisi, Lichter, & Taquino, 2011). Preibisch uncovered tension between newcomers and natives within Canadian agriculture because the latter group perceived that migrants were 'taking' their jobs (Preibisch, 2007). Conversely, some studies suggest a shielding effect as labour market segmentation in a sufficiently expanding economy buffers certain groups from wider competition while also creating multiplier growth effects (Turner, 2014; Crowley, Lichter & Turner, 2015).

The workplace is clearly political in nature, but national context influences inherent workplace systems and opportunities (Burawoy, 1985). By creating distinctions between migrants and non-migrants and between different ethnic communities, it involves symbolic boundaries that determine who constitutes a 'good' worker and culminates in differential access to resources. These matters are important in understanding the symbolic construction of ethnic minorities within the rural economy.

The significance of space, place and context

Slack and Jensen (2002) use the phrase 'double jeopardy' to describe the plight of non-metropolitan minorities, because their membership of a racial/ethnic minority group combines with their geographical residency to increase their odds of unemployment. In fact the debate on whether people or places are poor is abundant, but there is consensus in the literature that place and space matters when considering rural ethnic inequalities (Lichter, 1989; Snipp et al., 1993; Jensen, 1994; Tickamyer, 2000; Slack & Jensen, 2002; Milbourne, 2004; Shucksmith, Cameron, Merridew & Pilcher , 2009; Peters, 2012; Ledwith & Reilly, 2014). Within this debate it has been shown that certain groups fare worse than others (Parisi, Lichter, & Taquino, 2011; Crowley, Lichter & Turner, 2015). Research shows persistently higher levels of poverty in certain areas that are predominantly populated by minority ethnics, such as the Dakotas (Native American reservations) (Lichter & Johnston 2007; Peters 2012) or areas of Texas (African American) (Saenz & Thomas, 1991). In certain regions this can cause further inequalities and Gray suggests that high concentrations of African Americans in the Mississippi Belt may have negatively influenced high-skilled industries' location decisions. This reflects the intersectoral nature of rural ethnic inequalities discussed at the beginning of this chapter. Further, it supports what Lichter and Johnson (2007, p. 334) describe as a 'ghettoization' of minorities and it is similar to Bock et al.'s 'blemishing places' (Bock, Kovács & Shucksmith, 2014, p. 205, after Wacquant, 2008) when areas become socially and territorially stigmatised. Thus we see evidence of poor people in poor places. In other places, where there are concentrations of minorities, research from the USA shows how employment and education options are similarly curtailed (see, for instance, Lyson & Falk, 1993; Jensen, McLaughlin & Slack, 2003; Lichter, Qian & Crowley, 2005). Ledwith and Reilly argue that educational inequalities are so critical that they could lead to 'socio-demographic balkanisation' (2014, p. 224), demonstrating how some places are quickly stigmatised.

Neighbourhood dynamics: local attitudes, politics and services

While persistent poverty among rural minority populations is driven by 'local political and economic processes rather than narrowly defined neighborhood dynamics' (Lichter, Parisi & Taquino, 2012, p. 368), those neighbourhood dynamics can influence prospects for minorities. For instance, attitudes are important factors in curbing perpetuating inequalities and, like many aspects of migration, attitudes are not static; and they depend on a range of factors.

Jones-Correa (2012) shows that American society falls into the category of an ageing society and those 'older' citizens have a disproportionate effect on the political system. They also have fairly conservative views of American society and culture. He argues that they feel threatened by massive change within their community and will resist such change. This may be manifested in negative attitudes, but also through measures such as the creation of anti-immigrant ordinances or legal barriers to employment that can nurture inequalities (Pruitt, 2009; Pruitt & O'Neil, 2010). Media reporting of migration is powerful and it increases during economic depression (Chavez 2001 in Wilkes, Guppy & Farris, 2008, p. 325).

Historically many 'new' migration destinations are ethnically homogenous with little or limited experience of immigration (Broadway, 2007; Gimpel & Lay, 2008; Hugo & Morén-Alegret, 2008; McAreavey, 2012). In noting the prevailing ethnic 'stability' within agricultural communities, Salamon (2002) shows how the shared history, identity and norms of a place can be shattered by the arrival of newcomers. Local rural political processes, often conservative in nature, influence the interpretation of the rights of new social groups, causing challenges, and opportunities, for group relations within receiving societies (see, for instance, Missingham, Dibden & Cocklin, 2006; Parra & Pfeffer, 2006; Preibisch & Otero, 2014). In some areas like Marshalltown, Iowa (Jensen, 2006) or Armagh in Northern Ireland (McAreavey, 2012) a relatively warm reception prevailed and this has brought the potential for social transformation. Negative responses can also ensue. Negative actions are closely connected to macro-political ideologies – pro-immigration opinions tend to be held for ideological reasons, typically among those on the left (Wilkes, Guppy & Farris, 2008, p. 305).

Conflict and competition within the labour market has been identified above. Other challenges may arise because receiving communities struggle to meet the demand for additional services such as health, housing and interpretation (Krannich & Greider, 1990 in Broadway, 2007; Waters & Jiménez, 2005; Jentsch & Simard, 2009; McConnell & Miraftab, 2009). They may also lack the skills and expertise to effectively and appropriately deliver services in the wake of increased ethnic diversity, such as the need for cultural sensitivity in relation to health and social care (see, for example, Parra & Pfeffer, 2006; Martin & Phelan, 2010; McAreavey, 2010). Equality legislation can afford protection to vulnerable groups, but there is often a mismatch between policy aspirations and the impact on the ground (see, for example, Rye & Andrzejewska, 2010; Irwin, McAreavey & Murphy, 2014). Additionally, for societies in transition, state action can lag behind immediate requirements, such as evidenced in Ireland, causing particular challenges around integration such as the adequacy of service provision, much of this impacting on rural ethnic groups disproportionately (Wallace, McAreavey, Atkin & Bradshaw, 2013; Maher & Cawley, 2014).

Heterogeneity

Place certainly matters in understanding rural inequalities: rural poverty rates among some ethnic groups in certain locations remain persistently higher than for their urban counterparts (Jensen, McLaughlin & Slack, 2003). This changes over time. For example, during the 1990s, there was evidence that new rural migrant destinations fared better than traditional migrant gateways for Latinos where poverty rates among families with children were found to be lower than rates observed in traditional migrant communities in the Southwest (Crowley, Lichter & Qian, 2006; Jensen, 2006). But this has not remained constant over time: since then, Crowley, Lichter and Turner (2015) show that higher rates of Latino poverty were experienced in the 2000s across the USA and this decline was more accentuated in new destination areas compared to established gateways. Their study further suggests that new Latino destinations may point to the creation of rural ethnic enclaves as their geographic mobility has not been accompanied by socioeconomic progress. This was perhaps obscured during the economic boom and now there is evidence of these migrants moving back to established gateways following the recession (Parrado & Kandel, 2011). Clearly this is not an option available to everyone.

Meanwhile the outlook for different ethnic groups differs. Some well-established ethnic minority groups such as Native Americans (Peters, 2012) and Roma in Europe (Kovács, 2015) endure persistent poverty and educational inequalities. Compared to African Americans, Latinos in new rural destinations face higher individual and family poverty rates; they earn lower wages and they have access to fewer safety nets (Crowley, Lichter & Turner, 2015). Crowley and Lichter (2009) argue that higher poverty levels are due in part to high fertility rates and the relatively high numbers of children in families that reduces proportionate income per family member. Similar conclusions cannot be reached for ethnic groups in other rural areas, particularly within Europe, where ethnic diversity is a relatively recent development. However, comparisons between pathways for urban and rural ethnic groups and between different ethnic groups within a locality could shed some light on prospects for different ethnic minorities within a rural area. This would highlight how outcomes differ for rural ethnic groups compared to their urban counterparts and for different ethnicities within a particular locality. For instance, analysis of educational attainment for minority groups in urban and rural settings would highlight inequalities between groups and it would identify urban and rural difference. The way in which urban areas (as established destination gateways) have overcome inequalities could provide lessons for rural areas. Additionally, the migration pattern of ethnic groups across rural space warrants attention. Elsewhere it has been found that African American and Latino migration not only reinforces existing concentrations of poverty, but it severely exacerbates poverty in rural areas (Foulkes & Schafft, 2010).

Gender, families and fertility

As an aspect of segmented assimilation (Curran, Shafer, Donato & Garip, 2006) and being important determinants of rural ethnic inequalities, it is imperative that gender differences and household relations are completely understood. Inequalities arise due to heavy reliance on family and social networks because of limited access to support structures (see, for instance, Cloke, 2004; Panelli, Hubbard, Coombes & Suchet-Pearson, 2009; Forrest & Dunn, 2013). It is known that non-metro minority families headed by females are among those experiencing the highest poverty rates (McLaughlin & Sachs, 1988; Snyder & McLaughlin, 2006). For female migrants context presents different outcomes regarding their position as potential employees and particularly regarding access to childcare, but also regarding their role as mothers and the corresponding educational attainment of their children (Crul & Mollenkopt, 2012). The literature shows that male migrants tend to experience downward mobility whereas women are more likely to be entering the labour market for the first time (Fernandez-Kelly & Garcia, 1990). Meanwhile other research shows how, possibly due to a shift in the control of resources, for many women the migration process is empowering (Röder & Mühlau, 2014). It is apparent that the gender implications of emerging inequalities merits closer scrutiny, as do household strategies for managing these evolving positions within the family.

Demographic factors will play an increasing role in sustaining rural diversity. Lichter (2013) shows how minority fertility and white natural decrease will result in high levels of inequalities. Understanding outcomes for the children of ethnic minorities will provide a key to overcoming inequalities. Research on outcomes for second-generation migrants in established migrant gateways and for regions with a legacy of diversity is an established research area (see, for instance, Portes, 1996; Kasinitz, Mollenkopf, Waters & Holdaway, 2008; Portes, Femández-Kelly & Haller, 2009), but the outcomes for second-generation migrants in 'new rural destinations' are not fully understood (Röder, 2014). This surely represents an area ripe for future research.

Moving forward: areas for future research

This review does not purport to examine all facets of rural ethnic inequalities – that task would be impossible. Instead it provides an indication of the complexity of the issues facing rural researchers. The literature clearly shows how in some rural places shifting minority–majority ratios (arising mainly from increased minority fertility and decreases in the majority population) will transform the rural landscape. Other rural localities will continue to experience significant levels of immigration – internal and international – both of which warrant further investigation. The bottom line is that rural societies are highly likely to become increasingly diverse.

While macro policies are important, context and the specificities of a locality influence opportunities for different social groups. Bürkner contends that 'social inequality and fragmented social spaces have not received the analytical attention they deserve' (2012, p. 190). They are fragmented because they are multifaceted. Applying some of the conceptual framings explored in this chapter will help us to understand the multidimensional nature of rural ethnic inequalities and also how everyday social practices are enacted through space and within a place. This cannot be achieved through a single disciplinary approach as an array of factors typically culminates to produce rural ethnic inequalities. This is illustrated through several examples presented below.

First, the return of urban Greeks to the countryside (Kasimis & Zografakis, 2012; Gkartzios, 2013) presents the possibility of displacement of certain groups within the rural labour market, likely to be ethnic minorities due to their lowly status and minimal legal and regulatory protection. Meanwhile Nelson, Trautman and Nelson (in press) illustrate the link between amenity migration and Latino migration, showing how the former is driving the latter. The process raises a whole set of unknown and underexplored issues relating to these seemingly distinct migration processes. In both these instances connections between different streams of migration are likely to emerge as growing areas of interest. Perhaps more provocatively, Nelson's study reminds us of a call from Lichter and Brown (2011) for rural scholarship to recognise boundary changes, particularly relating to emerging urban and rural social and economic dependencies.

The need for an interdisciplinary approach is further exemplified through Standing's (2011) analysis of the labour market. He shows how it is closely connected to wider flows of (secure and less secure) social income that transcend traditional economic models. Thus the mechanisms by which ethnic minority employees generate income from employment, family networks and through other sources supports their involvement in the labour market. One example might be tied housing from an employer that also provides basic shelter. This transaction represents a paternalistic relationship that raises certain vulnerabilities including risks associated with possible job loss due to the strong connection between employment and housing. Equally, the impact of individuals remitting home while taking up seasonal employment opportunities requires analysis beyond family income as it affects relationships and roles within the family. More widely, by providing cheap and flexible labour, seasonal workers bolster certain businesses that might not otherwise survive in a globalised food market. In this way different geographical areas and different sectors face diverse challenges, all of which have implications for relations between and within ethnic groups as the status quo becomes undermined. The literature shows that we need to understand specific contexts if we are to unravel the complex web of factors that influence outcomes for ethnic minorities.

This chapter underlines the importance of the labour market in creating rural ethnic inequalities. In an emerging landscape, the 'migrant labour' label symbolises a certain type of employment that entails labour market segmentation, job insecurity and employment vulnerabilities such as significant wage differentials. These all distinguish migrants from the mainstream. In areas with a history of ethnic diversity, the labour market remains important for understanding outcomes as entrenched unequal practices, and negative attitudes can significantly curtail employment opportunities and mobility outcomes for certain groups. Boundaries can create a sense of belonging and inclusion, but equally they can emphasise difference between groups. Lamont and Molnár's boundary model (2002) is a promising tool for understanding how such divisions between ethnic minorities and 'others' are created and maintained and thus the spaces that rural ethnic minorities inhabit. Boundaries cannot be considered in the absence of wider politics such as the extent to which different political ideologies influence boundary creation and maintenance.

Space is important for understanding the manifestation of inequalities. Physical space is one component of this and in a rural context existing research highlights how this encompasses very particular questions of how visibility and containment produce ethnic inequalities. Thus the workplace, neighbourhood and community zones should all receive attention in terms of how migrants inhabit these areas, but also relating to the way in which these spaces are created and ultimately how these spaces are used by more powerful groups. Space is clearly not just physical; it refers to social relations, all set within wider social structures, all within a political context. The politics of rural diversity as we move through the 21st century is surely an area for fruitful enquiry. To what extent do political ideologies influence the creation of boundaries that serve to emphasise difference between minority and majority groups? Additional questions about childcare, gender and family relations, coercion and dominance need to be posed. Fundamentally, we should be asking why it is that some areas provide 'strategic holes' (Marrow, 2011, p. 241) that support rural migrants' incorporation, *as equal citizens*, while others do not?

Notes

1 The expansion of the Europe Union in 2004 witnessed the removal of working restrictions in certain member states including Ireland, UK and Sweden. These countries experienced more significant increases in migrants from Eastern Europe.

2 But it is also true that many of these countries have a long tradition of more slow-paced patterns of migration involving fewer numbers (Hoggart & Mendoza, 1999; Wallace, McAreavey, Atkin & Bradshaw, 2013).

3 Worker Registration Scheme (WRS) figures reveals large numbers of Accession 8 citizens, particularly from Poland and Lithuania. Accession 8 or A8 countries refer to the eight European countries from Eastern Europe who joined the EU in 2004. They are the Czech Republic, Estonia, Hungary, Latvia, Lithuania, Poland, Slovakia and Slovenia. Between 2004 and 2011 the Worker Registration Scheme required A8 nationals to register with the UK government (Home Office) if they wished to take up employment for more than one month's duration.

4   Traditional migration research has received criticism because it is under-theorised and it tends to reduce analyses to one of either structures or individual micro-practices (Bakewell, 2010; Portes, 2010; Iosifides, 2011; Levitt, 2012; O'Reilly, 2012).

5   Standing (2011) uses the concept of social income to encapsulate direct income from employers through wages or salary alongside private income (such as from investments) and the value of benefits from the employer (such as health insurance), family and community (such as child minding and caring tasks) and the state (such as welfare benefits, tax credits etc.).

References

Alba, R (2005). Bright vs. blurred boundaries: Second-generation assimilation and exclusion in France, Germany, and the United States. *Ethnic and Racial Studies* 128(1), 20–49.

Alba, R (2015). The myth of the white minority. *New York Times*, 11 June 2015. Available at http://www.nytimes.com/2015/06/11/opinion/the-myth-of-a-white-minority.html?_r=0 (accessed 19 June 2015).

Aisch, G, Gebeloff, R & Quealy, K (2014). Where we came from and where we went, state by state. *New York Times*, August 19, 2014. Available at http://www.nytimes.com/interactive/2014/08/13/upshot/where-people-in-each-state-were-born.html?abt=0002&abg=1&_r=1 (accessed 19 June 2015).

Allen-Smith, JE, Wimberley, RC & Morris, LV (1993). America's forgotten people and places: Ending the legacy of poverty in the rural south. In TA Lyson & WW Falk (Eds), *Forgotten places: Uneven development in rural America*. Lawrence, KS: University Press of Kansas.

Anderson, B & Ruhs, M (2010). Migrant workers: Who needs them? A framework for the analysis of shortages, immigration, and public policy. In B Anderson & M Ruhs (Eds), *Who needs migrant workers? Labour shortages, immigration, and public policy* (pp. 15–52). Oxford: Oxford University Press.

Anderson, B & Ruhs, M (2012). Reliance on migrant labour: Inevitability or policy choice? *Journal of Poverty and Social Justice* 20(1), 23–30.

Awad, I (2009). *The global economic crisis and migrant workers: Impact and response*. Geneva: International Labour Office.

Bakewell, O (2010). Some reflections on structure and agency in migration theory. *Journal of Ethnic and Migration Studies* 36(10), 1689–1708.

Barnard, H (2014). *Tackling poverty across all ethnicities in the UK*. York: Joseph Rowntree Foundation.

Barnard, H & Turner, C (2011). *Poverty and ethnicity: A review of evidence*. York: Joseph Rowntree Foundation.

Barth, F (1969). Introduction. In F Barth (Ed.), *Ethnic groups and boundaries: The social organization of cultural difference* (pp. 9–38). London: George Allen & Unwin.

Batalova, J & Lee, A (2012). Frequently requested statistics on immigrants and immigration in the United States. MPI Spotlight (3/21/12). Washington, DC: Migration Policy Institute.

Bauböck, R (1994). *The integration of immigrants*. Report for the Council of Europe, CMDG (94). 25E, Strasbourg.

Bauböck, R & Faist, T (Eds). (2010). *Transnationalism and diaspora: Concepts, theories and methods*. Amsterdam: Amsterdam University Press.

Bauman, Z (2004). *Identity: Conversations with Benedetto Vecchi*. Cambridge: Polity.

Bock, B, Kovács, K & Shucksmith, M (2014). Changing social inequalities, patterns of inequality and exclusion. In AK Copus & P de Lima (Eds), *Territorial cohesion in rural Europe: The relational turn on development* (pp. 193–211). Abingdon: Routledge.

Broadway, M (2007). Meatpacking and the transformation of rural communities: A comparison of Brooks, Alberta & Garden City, Kansas. *Rural Sociology* 72(4), 560–582.

Burawoy, M (1985). *The politics of production*. London: Verso.

Bürkner, HJ (2012). Intersectionality: How gender studies might inspire the analysis of social inequality among migrants. *Population, Space and Place* 18, 181–195.

Burnley, IH (2001). *The impact of immigration on Australia. A demographic approach*. Melbourne: Oxford University Press.

Calavita, K (2005). *Immigrants at the margins: Law, race, and exclusion in southern Europe*. Cambridge: Cambridge University Press.

Calavita, K (2007). *Law, immigration and exclusion in Italy and Spain* Papers 8. (pp. 95–108). Irvine, CA: University of California.

Castles, S, de Haas, H & Miller, MJ (2014). *The age of migration* (4th edn). Basingstoke: Palgrave Macmillan.

Cloke, P (2004). Rurality and racialised others: Out of place in the countryside? In P Chakraborti & J Garland (Eds), *Rural racism* (pp. 17–35). Cullompton: William Publishing.

Cloke, PJ, Goodwin, M, Milbourne, P & Thomas, C (1995). Deprivation, poverty and marginalisation in rural lifestyle in England and Wales. *Journal of Rural Studies* 11(4), 351–365.

Cohen, S (2003). *No-one is illegal*. Stoke-on-Trent: Trentham Books.

Coleman, D (2006). Immigration and ethnic change in low-fertility countries: A third demographic transition. *Population and Development Review* 32(3), 401–446.

Collantes, F, Pinilla, V, Sáez, LA & Silvestre, J (2014). Reducing depopulation in rural Spain: The impact of immigration. *Population, Space and Place* 20, 606–662.

Cotter, DA (2002). Poor people in poor places: Local opportunity structures and household poverty. *Rural Sociology* 67(4), 534–555.

Crowley, M & Lichter, DT (2009). Social disorganization in new Latino destinations? *Rural Sociology* 74(4), 573–604.

Crowley, M, Lichter, DT & Qian, Z (2006). Beyond gateway cities: Economic restructuring and poverty among Mexican immigrant families and children. *Family Relations* 55, 345–360.

Crowley, M, Lichter, DT & Turner, RN (2015). Diverging fortunes? Economic well-being of Latinos and African Americans in new rural destinations. *Social Science Research* 51, 77–92.

Crul, M & Mollenkopt, J (2012). *The changing face of world cities. Young adult children of immigrants in Europe and the United States*. New York: Russell Sage Foundation.

Curran, SR, Shafer, S, Donato, KM & Garip, F (2006). Mapping gender and migration in sociological scholarship: Is it segregation or integration? *International Migration Review* 40(1), 199–223.

De Lima, P (2102). Moving beyond class and status – Intersectionality and place/space as a framework for understanding social divisions? Paper presented to QUCAN/TARRN annual meeting, Inverness, Scotland.

Doyle, C & McAreavey, R (2015). Patterns and processes of recent migration to Northern Ireland. *Irish Geography*.

Dudenhefer, P (1994). Poverty in the rural United States. *Rural Sociologist* 14(1), 4–25.

Eide, E (2010). Strategic essentialism and ethnification hand in glove? *Nordicom Review* 31(2), 63–78.

European Commission (2009). *Employment in Europe 2008*. DG for Employment, Social Affairs and Inclusion. Brussels: European Commission.

Favell, A, Feldblum, M & Smith, MP (2006). The human face of global mobility: A research agenda. In MP Smith & A Favell (Eds), *The human face of global mobility* (pp. 1–25). New Brunswick, NJ: Transaction.

Fernández-Kelly, P & Garcia, A (1990). Power surrendered, power restored: The politics of home and work among Hispanic women in Southern California and Southern Florida. In LF Tilly & P Guerin (Eds), *Women in politics in America* (pp. 215–228). New York: Russell Sage Foundation.

Findlay AM, Geddes, A & McCollum, D (2010). International migration and recession. *Scottish Geographical Journal* 126, 299–320.

Findlay, AM, McCollum, D, Shubin, S, Apsite, E & Krisjane, Z (2013). The role of recruitment agencies in imagining and producing the 'good' migrant. *Social and Cultural Geography* 14(2), 145–167.

Fonseca, ML (2008). New waves of immigration to small towns and rural areas in Portugal. *Population, Space and Place* 14(6), 525–535.

Forrest, J & Dunn, K (2013). Cultural diversity, racialisation and the experience of racism in rural Australia: The South Australian case. *Journal of Rural Studies* 30, 1–9.

Fortier, AM (2000). *Migrant belongings: Memory, space, identity*. Oxford: Berg.

Foulkes, M & Schafft, KA (2010). The impact of migration on poverty concentrations in the United States, 1995–2000. *Rural Sociology* 75(1), 90–110.

Giddens, A (1986). *The constitution of society*. Berkeley, CA: University of California Press.

Gimpel, JG & Lay, JC (2008). Political socialization and reactions to immigration-related diversity in rural America. *Rural Sociology* 73(2), 180–204.

Gkartzios, M (2013). 'Leaving Athens': Narratives of counterurbanisation in times of crisis. *Journal of Rural Studies* 32, 158–167.

Glick Schiller, N & Çağlar, A (2015). Displacement, emplacement and migrant newcomers: Rethinking urban sociabilities within multiscalar power. *Identities: Global Studies in Culture and Power*. doi: 10.1080/1070289X.2015.1016520.

Gorodzeisky, A & Richards, A (2013). Trade unions and migrant workers in Western Europe. *European Journal of Industrial Relations* 19(3), 239–254.

Green, A, Owen, D & Wilson, R (2005). *Changing patterns of employment by ethnic group and for migrant workers.* Warwick: Institute of Employment Research, University of Warwick.

Hanson, G (2009). *The economics and politics of illegal immigration in the United States.* Washington, DC: Migration Policy Institute.

Harvey, D (1990). Between space and time: Reflections on the geographical imagination. *Annals of the Association of American Geographers* 80(3), 418–434.

Hoggart, K & Mendoza, C (1999). African immigrant workers in Spanish agriculture. *Sociologia Ruralis* 37(4), 538–563.

Hugo, G (2008). Immigrant settlement outside of Australia's capital cities. *Population, Space and Place* 14(6), 553–571.

Hugo, G & Morén-Alégret, R (2008). International migration to non-metropolitan areas of high income countries: Editorial introduction. *Population, Space and Place* 14(6), 473–477.

Iosifides, T (2011). *Qualitative methods in migration studies: A critical realist perspective.* Farnham: Ashgate.

Irwin, J, McAreavey, R & Murphy, N (2014). *Economic and social mobility among ethnic minority communities in Northern Ireland.* York: Joseph Rowntree Foundation.

Jenkins, R (2000). The limits of identity: Ethnicity, conflict, and politics. ShOP Issue 2: November 2000, Sheffield University, UK. Available at https://www.sheffield.ac.uk/polopoly_fs/1.71447!/file/2 jenkins.pdf (accessed 5 May 2015).

Jenkins, R (2014). *Social identity* (4th edn). Abingdon: Routledge.

Jensen, L (1994). Employment hardship and rural minorities: Theory, research and policy. *The Review of Black Political Economy* 22(4), 125–144.

Jensen, L (2006). New immigrant settlements in Rural America: Problems, prospects and policies. *Reports on Rural America* 1(3).

Jensen, L, McLaughlin, DK & Slack, T (2003). Rural poverty: The persisting challenge. In DL Brown & LE Swanson (Eds), *Challenges for rural America in the twenty-first century* (pp. 118–131). University Park, PA: Penn State University Press.

Jentsch, B & Simard, M (Eds). (2009). *International migration and rural areas, cross-national comparative perspectives.* Farnham: Ashgate.

Johnson-Webb, KD (2002). Employer recruitment and Hispanic labor migration: North Carolina urban areas at the end of the millennium. *Professional Geographer* 54, 406–421.

Jones-Correa, M (2012). *Contested ground: Immigration in the United States.* Washington, DC: Migration Policy Institute.

Kandel, W & Cromartie, J (2004). *New patterns of Hispanic settlement in rural America.* Rural Development Research report No. 99. Washington, DC: United States Department of Agriculture.

Kandel, W & Parrado, E (2005). Restructuring of the US meat processing industry and new Hispanic migrant destinations. *Population Development Review* 31, 447–471.

Kasimis, CA, Papadopoulos, AG & Zacopoulou, E (2003). Migrants in rural Greece. *Sociologia Ruralis* 43(2), 167–184.

Kasimis, C & Zografakis, S (2012). 'Return to the land': Rural Greece as refuge to crisis. Paper Presented at the XIII World Congress of Rural Sociology, 29 July to 4 August 2012, Lisbon, Portugal.

Kasinitz, P, Mollenkopf, J, Waters, M & Holdaway, J (2008). *Inheriting the city: The children of immigrants come of age.* Cambridge, MA: Harvard University Press and Russell Sage Foundation.

Kovács, K (2015). *Exploring impacts of the crisis on macro-regions of rural Europe.* Research Report, Centre for Economic and Regional Studies, Hungarian Academy of Sciences.

Kritzinger, A, Barrientos, S & Rossouw, HM (2004). Global production and flexible employment in South African horticulture: Experiences of contract workers in fruit exports. *Sociologia Ruralis* 44, 17–39.

Lamont, M & Molnár, V (2002). The study of boundaries in the social sciences. *Annual Review of Sociology* 28, 167–195.

Ledwith, V & Reilly, K (2014). Fringe benefits? Educational experiences of migrant and non-migrant youth in the urban-rural fringe of Galway City, Ireland. *Journal of Rural Studies* 36, 219–225.

Lefebvre, H (1991). *The production of space.* Oxford: Wiley-Blackwell.

Levitt, P (2012). What's wrong with migration scholarship? A critique and a way forward. *Identities: Global Studies in Culture and Power* 19(4), 493–500.

Levitt, P & Nyberg-Sørensen, N (2004). The transnational turn in migration studies. *Global Migration Perspectives* No. 6. Geneva, Switzerland: Global Commission on International Migration.

Lichter, DT (1989). Race, employment hardship, and inequality in the American nonmetropolitan South. *American Sociological Review* 54(3), 436–446.

Lichter, D (2012). Immigration and the new racial diversity in rural America. *Rural Sociology* 77(1), 3–35.

Lichter, D (2013). Integration or fragmentation? Racial diversity and the American future. *Demography* 50, 359–391.

Lichter, DT & Brown, DL (2011). Rural America in an urban society: Changing spatial and social boundaries. *Annual Review of Sociology* 37, 1–27.

Lichter, DT & Johnson, KM (2007). The changing spatial concentration of America's rural poor population. *Rural Sociology* 72(3), 331–358.

Lichter, DT, Parisi, D & Taquino, M (2012). The geography of exclusion: Race, segregation, and concentrated poverty. *Social Problems* 59(3), 364–388.

Lichter, DT, Parisi, D, Taquino, M & Beaulieu, B (2008). Race and the micro-scale concentration of poverty. *Cambridge J. Reg. Econ. Soc.* 1(1), 51–67.

Lichter, DT, Qian, Z & Crowley, MI (2005). Child poverty among racial minorities and immigrants: Explaining trends and differentials. *Social Science Quarterly* 86, 1037–1059.

Lyson, TA & Falk, WW (Eds). (1993). *Forgotten places: Uneven development in rural America.* Lawrence, KS: University Press of Kansas.

Maher, G & Cawley, M (2014). Short-term labour migration: Brazilian migrants in Ireland. *Population, Space and Place.* doi: 10.1002/psp.1859.

Marrow, HB (2011). *New destination dreaming: Immigration, race and legal status in the rural American South.* Stanford, CA: Stanford University Press.

Martin, MC & Phelan, M (2010). Interpreters and cultural mediators – Different but complementary roles. *Translocations: Migration and Social Change* 6(1).

Massey, D (1994). *Space, place and gender.* Minneapolis: University of Minnesota Press.

Massey, D (2005). *For space.* London: Sage.

Massey, DS, Durand, J & Malone, NJ (2002). *Beyond smoke and mirrors: Mexican immigration in an era of economic integration.* New York: Russell Sage Foundation.

Mathieson, J, Popay, J, Enoch, E, Escorel, S, Hernandez, M, Johnston, H & Rispel, L (2008). *Social exclusion: Meaning, measurement and experience and links to health inequalities. A review of literature.* WHO Social Exclusion Knowledge Network Background Paper 1. Lancaster, UK: Institute for Health Research Lancaster University.

McAreavey, R (2010). Transcending cultural differences: The role of language in social integration. *Translocations: Migration and Social Change* 6(2), 596–601.

McAreavey, R (2012). Resistance or resilience? Tracking the pathway of recent arrivals to a 'new' rural destination. *Sociologia Ruralis* 52(4), 488–507.

McAreavey, R (2015). 'New' migrant identities: A burden or benefit? Paper presented at TARRN (Trans-Atlantic Rural Research) annual meeting, May 2015, Penn State, PA.

McAreavey, R & Swindal, M (2014). The uneven geography of mobility: Comparative research on migrants and their host communities in the United States and United Kingdom. Paper presented at TARRN (Trans-Atlantic Rural Research) annual meeting, March 2014, Newcastle, UK.

McConnell, ED & Miraftab, F (2009). Sundown town to 'Mexican town': Newcomers, old timers, and housing in small town America. *Rural Sociology* 74(4), 605–629.

McLaughlin, DK & Sachs, C (1988). Poverty in female-headed households: Residential differences. *Rural Sociology* 5, 287–306.

Milbourne, P (2004). *Rural poverty: Marginalisation and exclusion in Britain and the United States.* London: Routledge.

Miraftab, F (2012). Emergent transnational spaces: Meat, sweat and global (re)production in the heartland. *International Journal of Urban and Regional Research* 36(6), 1204–1222.

Miraftab, F & McConnell, ED (2008). Multiculturalizing rural towns insights for inclusive planning. *International Planning Studies* 13(4), 343–360.

Missingham, B, Dibden, J & Cocklin, C (2006). A multicultural countryside? Ethnic minorities in rural Australia. *Rural Society* 16(2), 131–151.

Nelson, L, Trautman, L & Nelson, PB (in press). Latino immigrants and rural gentrification: Race, 'illegality' and precarious labor regimes in U.S. rural amenity destinations. *Annals of the Association of American Geographers.*

Nowicka, M (2012). Deskilling in migration in transnational perspective: The case of recent Polish migration to the UK. Working Paper 112/2012. Bielefeld: Centre on Migration, Citizenship and Development.

Nowicka, M (2014). Migrating skills, skilled migrants and migration skills: The influence of contexts on the validation of migrants' skills. *Migration Letters* 11(2), 171–186.

O'Reilly, K (2012). *International migration and social theory*. London: Palgrave Macmillan.

Panelli, R, Hubbard, P, Coombes, B & Suchet-Pearson, S (2009). De-centring white ruralities: Ethnicity and indigeneity. *Journal of Rural Studies* 25(4), 355–364.

Parisi, D, Lichter, DT & Taquino, M (2011). Multi-scale residential segregation: Black exceptionalism and America's changing color line. *Social Forces* 89, 829–852.

Parra, P & Pfeffer, MJ (2006). New immigrants in rural communities: The challenge of integration. *Social Text* 24(3), 81–98.

Parrado, EA & Kandel, WA (2011). Industrial change, Hispanic immigration, and the internal migration of low-skilled native male workers in the United States, 1995–2000. *Social Science Research* 40, 626–640.

Peters, DJ (2012). Income inequality across micro and meso geographic scales in the Midwestern United States, 1979–2009. *Rural Sociology* 77(2), 171–202.

Pew Research Center (2015). *Multiracial in America: Proud, diverse and growing in numbers*. Washington, DC: Pew Research Center.

Philo, C (1992). Neglected rural geographies: A review. *Journal of Rural Studies* 8(2), 193–207.

Popke, J (2011). Latino migration and neoliberalism in the U.S. South: Notes toward a rural cosmopolitanism. *Southeastern Geographer* 51(2), 242–259.

Portes, A (1996). *The new second generation*. New York: Russell Sage Foundation.

Portes, A (2010). Migration and social change: Some conceptual reflections. *Journal of Ethnic and Migration Studies* 36(10), 1537–1563.

Portes, A, Fernández-Kelly, P & Haller, W (2009). The adaptation of the immigrant second generation in America: Theoretical overview and recent evidence. *Journal of Ethnic and Migration Studies* 35(7), 1077–1104.

Preibisch, K (2007). Local produce, foreign labor: Labor mobility programs and global trade competitiveness in Canada. *Rural Sociology* 72(3), 418–449.

Preibisch, K & Otero, G (2014). Does citizenship status matter in Canadian Agriculture? Workplace health and safety for migrant and immigrant laborers. *Rural Sociology* 79(2), 174–199.

Probyn, E (1996). *Outside belongings*. New York; London: Routledge.

Pruitt, L (2009). Migration, development, and the promise of CEDAW for rural women. *Michigan Journal of International Law* 30, 707. UC Davis Legal Studies Research Paper No. 182.

Pruitt, L & O'Neil, K (2010). Hazleton and beyond: Why communities try to restrict immigration. Migration Information Source, November. (http://www.migrationpolicy.org/article/hazleton-and-beyond-why-communities-try-restrict-immigration (accessed 30 January 2016).

Reimer, B, Burns, M & Gareau, P (2007). Ethnic and cultural diversity in rural Canada: Its relationship to immigration. *Rural Communities: Our Diverse Cities* 3, 30–35. Montreal: Concordia University.

Röder, A (2014). The emergence of a second generation in Ireland: Some trends and open questions. *Irish Journal of Sociology* 22(1), 155–158.

Röder, A & Mühlau, P (2014). Europe's immigrants and gender egalitarianism. Are they acculturating? Europe's immigrants and gender egalitarianism. *Social Forces* 92(3), 899–928.

Rye, JF & Andrzejewska, J (2010). The structural disempowerment of Eastern European migrant farm workers in Norwegian agriculture. *Journal of Rural Studies* 26(1), 41–51.

Saenz, R & Thomas, JK (1991). Minority population in nonmetropolitan Texas. *Rural Sociology* 56(2), 204–223.

Salamon, S (2002). *Newcomers to old towns: Suburbanisation of the heartland*. Chicago, IL: Chicago University Press.

Shucksmith, M, Cameron, S, Merridew, T & Pilcher, F (2009). Urban–rural differences in quality of life across the European Union. *Regional Studies* 43(10), 1275–1289.

Shucksmith, M & Schafft, K (2012). Rural Poverty and social exclusion in the United States and the United Kingdom. In M Shucksmith, D Brown, S Shortall, J Vergunst & M Warner (Eds), *Rural transformations and rural policies in the US and UK* (pp. 100–116). New York: Routledge.

Singer, A (2009). *The new geography of United States immigration*. Brookings Immigration Series No. 3, July 2009. Washington, DC: Brookings Institution.

Slack, T & Jensen, L (2002). Race, ethnicity, and underemployment in nonmetropolitan America: A 30-Year profile. *Rural Sociology* 67, 208–233.

Snipp, CM, Horton, HD, Jensen, L, Nagel, J & Rochin, R (1993). Persistent rural poverty and racial and ethnic minorities. In the Rural Sociological Society Task Force on Persistent Rural Poverty (Ed.), *Persistent poverty in rural America* (pp. 173–199). Boulder, CO: Westview.

Snyder, AR & McLaughlin, DK (2006). Economic well-being and cohabitation: Another nonmetro disadvantage? *Journal of Family and Economic Issues* 27, 562–582.

Special Issue *Ethnic and Racial Studies* (2014). Symposium: Ethnic boundary making: institutions, power, networks 37(5), 804–842.

Standing, G (2011). *The precariat: The new dangerous class.* London: Bloomsbury.

Tickamyer, AR (2000). Space matters! Spatial inequality in future sociology. *Contemporary Sociology* 29(6), 805–813.

Turner, RN (2014). Occupational stratification of Hispanics, whites, and Blacks in southern rural destinations: A quantitative analysis. *Population Research and Policy Review* 33(5), 717–746.

Wacquant, L (2008). *Urban outcasts: A comparative sociology of advanced marginality.* Cambridge: Polity.

Wallace, A, McAreavey, R, Atkin, K & Bradshaw, J (2013). *Poverty and ethnicity in Northern Ireland: An evidence review.* York, UK: Joseph Rowntree Foundation.

Waters, MC & Kschbach, K (1995). Immigration and ethnic and racial inequality in the United States. *Annual Review of Sociology* 21, 419–446.

Waters, M & Jiménez, TR (2005). Assessing immigrant assimilation: New empirical and theoretical challenges. *Annual Review of Sociology* 31, 105–125.

Weber, B A, Jensen L, Miller K, Mosley J & Fisher M (2005). A critical review of rural poverty literature: Is there truly a rural effect? Institute for Research on Poverty. *International Regional Science Review* 28(4), 381–414.

Wheeler, C & La Jeunesse, E (2008). Trends in neighborhood income inequality in the U.S.: 1980–2000. *Journal of Regional Science* 48, 879–891.

Wilkes, R, Guppy, N & Farris, L (2008). 'No thanks, we're full': Individual characteristics, national context, and changing attitudes toward immigration. *International Migration Review* 42(2), 302–329.

Wimmer, A (2008). The making and unmaking of ethnic boundaries: A multilevel process theory. *American Journal of Sociology* 113(4), 970–1022.

Zolberg, AR & Woon, LL (1999). Why Islam is like Spanish: Cultural incorporation in Europe and the United States. *Politics and Society* 27(1), 5–38.

41

Housing

A Lens to Rural Inequalities

Menelaos Gkartzios and Ann C. Ziebarth

Introduction: rural housing as a symbol of inequalities

It is impossible to think of rural communities without envisaging the people and their housing conditions. Rural housing research matters because housing is critical for the well-being of individuals, of families and of communities (MacTavish, Ziebarth & George, 2014). For many people home ownership represents a life aspiration and the largest asset they will ever own. Across the global north, rural localities are primarily associated with private home ownership, for example in Canada, southern Europe and Ireland (CMHC, 2003; Gallent, Shucksmith & Tewdwr-Jones, 2003). Eastern and Central European countries also have extraordinarily high home ownership levels, attributed to large rural populations who typically either built their own homes or inherited them, and the rapid privatization of public rental housing following the collapse of state socialism (Edgar, Filipovic & Dandolova, 2007). Despite stagnant and declining home values, asset and investment accumulation through home ownership is still a considerable economic factor for many rural residents.

A high level of home ownership in rural contexts does not mean that there are no problems attached to rural house provision. On the contrary, such conditions might actually mask processes of exclusion and inequality. Common global trends are impacting rural housing in unique and specific ways with a diverse set of outcomes providing both opportunities and challenges for rural studies. We argue in this chapter that housing constitutes a useful and critical lens for researching inequalities. In particular we ask: How are these inequalities demonstrated from a housing perspective? What research has been done in the global north? And what other research areas need to be further developed? Inequalities can result from mobility processes, affecting the social fabric of rural areas, as well as macroeconomic processes including the global financial crisis and its local impacts on rural areas. Housing serves as a physical indicator of rural restructuring, involving increasingly consumerist uses of rural land. Housing can be viewed as a symbol of social change: housing construction, renovation or change of owners and occupants demonstrates new and sometimes contested representations of rurality. Much work on rural gentrification points to increasingly exclusive countrysides and middle-class rural enclaves, while other rural areas are depopulating, confronted by policy apathy and faced with insufficient social housing. Such characteristics point to social and economic inequalities in rural areas.

The aim of this chapter therefore is to review the literature of contemporary rural housing research, highlighting inequalities, and suggest new avenues for research. The chapter is structured as follows. First, we explore comparative approaches to housing studies and the role of housing in wider rural development research. Second, we focus on the context of rural economies and observed inequalities associated with residential mobilities. Third, we consider territorial exclusion based on poverty, race and ethnicity. We then turn to a discussion of structural causes of these inequalities, focusing on mortgage finance and the global recession's impact on rural housing. We conclude with suggestions for further research directions.

Housing research in the rural global north

With few exceptions (see special issue of *Housing and Society*, 2014; *Planning Practice and Research*, 2009), most housing research focuses on urban areas. This section aims to place housing research in an international, and ambitiously comparative, context within existing rural development literature.

Comparative rural housing research is important because it creates opportunities for policy transfer and 'lesson learning' (Hantrais, 2009), while demonstrating the potency and limitations of knowledge itself (Lowe, 2012). Comparative research is challenging because different contexts demonstrate contrasting and complex rural housing issues (Gallent, 2009). Furthermore, rural areas are characterised by high levels of differentiation (Murdoch, Lowe, Ward & Marsden, 2003), including the socioeconomic structure of rural areas from agriculture-dominated to consumerist area types, multiple community stakeholders with unequal power relations guiding the development narratives, and contrasting policy interventions regarding housing, from tight regulation to absence of intervention. Another difficulty in comparative analyses is identifying what is 'rural'. Definitions of rural, especially with regard to housing policies, vary widely across the global north (Bertolini, Montanari & Peragine, 2008). This highlights the need for interpretive comparative approaches that look beyond efforts to homogenise ruralities in the research design, focusing instead on local context and culture in the production of housing-related social phenomena (Lowe, 2012).

Rural housing concerns in the global north also reflect conflicts and power struggles about the construction of rural in policy discourses (i.e., prioritising economic development vs. environmental preservation or mediating conflicts regarding housing developments). Much of the rural housing literature is presented in Anglo-American contexts. Elsewhere, rural housing literature is less developed, although there has been an increased interest in exploring diverse rural housing issues internationally (in Australia: Jones & Tonts, 2003; in the Netherlands: de Groot, Daalhuizen, van Dam & Mulderd, 2012; in Italy: Gallent, 2015). Despite these developments, comparative perspectives, while less common, are worth highlighting in this review. Gallent and Allen (2003) critically classify ten European cases across three regimes based on cultural conditions and power regimes that inform rural housing policies and politics. The authors distinguish between contexts characterised by strong policy intervention that does not necessarily favour environmental conservation over housing development (Scandinavian countries), weak state intervention sometimes associated with tolerated illegal housing construction (southern Europe) and strong rural planning restrictions and market distortions (UK). In another example, Gkartzios and Shucksmith (2015) provided a case for comparative interpretive analysis between Ireland and England. The authors point to selective constructions of rurality dominating policy discourses, contrasting a 'republican rurality' favouring home ownership in the Irish case, with an 'environmental rurality' favouring conservation in the UK. Furthermore, Gkartzios and Shucksmith (2015) draw attention to comparative approaches as opportunities for promoting a culture of reflexivity, among both academics and practitioners, which is critical for unveiling normative assumptions about regulating rural housing developments. Such approaches promote a pluralistic universalism (Lowe, 2012), in which comparative analysis, as a reflective 'mirroring exercise', moves beyond issues of identifying differences and similarities to challenging taken-for-granted thinking about housing development.

Within the rural studies literature, scant attention has been paid to the connection between housing debates and the wider rural development policy direction (Scott & Murray, 2009). This is rather surprising for two reasons: first, because of the level of social change and economic restructuring that has taken place in rural areas associated with increased residential mobility and, subsequently, increased (or decreased) housing demand; and second, because rural development policy itself has witnessed a shift from a sectoral focus to a territorial one, with plenty of rural development theorists and practitioners arguing for integrated explorations of rural policies involving local participation and prioritising local needs (Ray, 2000; OECD, 2006; Shucksmith, 2009). Despite these approaches, housing remains missing from wider rural development narratives and subsequent projects. While the European Union has actively supported rural development measures promoting economic diversification, combating social exclusion and improving rural livelihoods, housing-related activities are rarely among the rural development programmes and activities (ENRD, 2015). Gkartzios and Scott (2014), from a neo-endogenous rural development perspective, argue that housing policy needs to be part of a territorial strategy that connects housing development with rural economic and social development strategies.

Rural development policies can take a preservationist view of the countryside, hindering housing construction (de Groot, Daalhuizen, van Dam & Mulderd, 2012). In the UK, for example, policy priorities include urban containment and environmental preservation (Satsangi, Gallent & Bevan, 2010). Such preoccupations have been linked with romanticised constructions of rurality (the 'rural idyll') prioritising environmental conservation, serving the interests of rural elites and downplaying the role of housing in sustaining thriving rural communities (Murdoch & Lowe, 2003; Sturzaker & Shucksmith, 2011). The seminal study of Peter Hall and colleagues (1973) draws attention to the rural middle classes who had to gain from preserving their natural environment by enhancing their own property values. Conversely, Newby (1985) has argued that the rural poor were socially excluded, pointing to planning as an instrument of social exclusion. According to Shucksmith (2000, 2012), this remains the case today: limited rural housing supply, coupled with increased rural residential demand, has created acute affordability problems for local residents.

Despite formal policy disconnects between housing and rural development, housing construction in some contexts is seen as an indicator of community health (Scott, 2012) and governmental policies have promoted rural house construction, but outside an integrated rural development framework (Gkartzios & Norris, 2011). Similarly, 'local need' criteria are used in planning practices to ensure rural house provision for local people. These, however, have been criticised for having adverse effects, favouring only certain social groups (Satsangi, Gallent & Bevan, 2010). Shucksmith (1981) argued, for example, that 'local need' criteria can make existing rural housing stock even more competitive, benefiting those with already existing housing. Gallent and Robinson (2012) warn how powerful groups might frame constructions of localism on their own terms to resist unwanted housing development. The resulting housing shortage is further ensured by strong anti-development attitudes amongst rural residents towards new house building (Gallent, Juntti, Kidd & Shaw, 2008). In Ireland, local need criteria drawing on bloodline, residency, language requirements and so on facilitated access to private rural house building, but in many cases such distinctions in policy have been associated with a culture of clientelism in the planning system (Gkartzios & Scott, 2014).

The disconnect between housing and rural development can be partly explained because of the role of self-developed (or self-build) housing as a response to meeting rural housing needs (see also Donovan & Gkartzios, 2014). Such pathways to rural home ownership are common in the global north, but not in the UK (NaCSBA, 2011). Murphy and Scott (2013) argue that self-build housing has reduced the exposure of rural households to the economic crisis in Ireland by enabling households to reduce overall their housing costs. However, such opportunities are undermined for those who have no access to land or in planning systems with very controlling rural house regulations (such as in the UK and the Netherlands). Addressing that concern, an innovative state grant in Scotland operated to subsidise costs of new housing for rural residents in specific areas. Morgan and Satsangi (2011) argue that the scheme was successful (albeit with a small contribution to housing output) because it dealt with major supply constraints in rural areas, especially land access, and because it involved community members in self-build housing.

In the USA, the prevailing policy objectives for rural communities are to promote economic development as measured by job growth while, at the same time, maintaining the rural character of the community. These two objectives are often in conflict: successful rural economic development results in increased housing demand, but proposals to develop housing are frequently met with an anti-development 'not in my backyard' (NIMBY) response based on the desire to maintain the status quo rural character of the community. Work by Roe, Irwin and Morrow-Jones (2004) indicates that land preservation policies can have mixed results in that preservation of farmland may be counterproductive, increasing housing demand and the cost of housing development. This highlights a need to move beyond policies that reproduce a rural idyll, acknowledge housing needs and allow rural areas to grow and diversify.

Mobility and housing inequalities

Population migration into and out of rural areas has resulted in major demographic changes for the global north. Mobilities are extremely important as they can offer both an opportunity for regeneration, housing construction and economic development (Stockdale, Findlay & Short, 2000; Bosworth & Atterton, 2012), but can also lead to processes of depopulation and marginalisation, gentrification and exclusion (Nelson & Nelson, 2010). In this section we highlight two key population shifts – counter-urbanism and ageing – that are impacting rural communities.

Counter-urbanism and amenity development

A key driver of rural mobilities in the global north has been counter-urbanisation (see reviews in Mitchell 2004; Chi & Marcouiller, 2012). Irrespective of whether counter-urbanisation refers to aggregate population turnovers or selective geographical processes, much research has associated counter-urbanisation with the perception of rural areas as better areas to live, a pattern usually discussed as amenity-led or lifestyle-led migration (Benson & O'Reilly, 2009; Gosnell & Abrams, 2009). Such influx of urban migrants into rural areas involves, almost without fail, new rural planning challenges and housing development (Paquette & Domon, 2003). While these processes contribute to the development of rural areas, the same processes can also create inequalities (Shucksmith, 2000).

Rural areas in the UK have been growing faster than urban areas continuously for the past four decades (Champion & Brown, 2012) and while this trend has slowed, it has not yet been reversed (Defra, 2015). Rural policies that target environmental conservation results in housing supply being outstripped by increased demand from commuters, retirees, second-home owners, and those buying properties as holiday homes (Best & Shucksmith, 2006). In Scotland, Liu and Roberts (2012) confirm that rural in-migrants originating from urban environments outbid local buyers in rural areas. Gentrification and displacement processes in rural England are commonly discussed in the literature (i.e., Smith & Phillips, 2001). Milbourne (2004) suggests that housing is the most significant issue facing rural residents. Private housing is consumed by middle-class in-migrant groups, while opportunities for social housing remain very limited, giving rise to a new form of social exclusion. England's 'affordability gap' is widely acknowledged as one of the most important issues currently facing rural areas (Satsangi, Gallent & Bevan, 2010; Rural Housing Policy Review, 2015).

Differentiated patterns of counter-urbanisation have been described in other global north countries with implications regarding housing affordability (van Dam, Heins & Elbersen, 2002; Freeman & Cheyne, 2008). However, cases of rural gentrification are not clearly evidenced everywhere (Argent, Tonts, Jones, & Holmes, 2014). For example, in Ireland the lack of gentrification has been attributed to the relaxed rural planning system that facilitates housing construction for locals (Gkartzios & Scott, 2013).

Amenity-driven rural development focused on promoting tourism and second homes has led to substantial housing inequalities in the USA (Pellow & Park, 2011). MacTavish, Ziebarth and George (2014) point to selective counter-urbanisation processes that have important implications for housing including the loss of affordable housing, displacement and gentrification. Second home development often creates tensions around rural development priorities (Overvag & Berg, 2011), although Gallent (2014) has argued that it can also contribute to social capital accumulation for some rural communities.

Retiree relocation and ageing-in-place

Another key characteristic of amenity-driven mobility patterns is the age of rural in-migrants, including retirement migration, although Brown and Glasgow (2008) have demonstrated that the major determinant of rural population ageing is the chronic out-migration of young adults. Furthermore, many older rural in-migrants are at a working age and research has demonstrated the changing migration patterns of pre-retirement groups (Stockdale, 2006). Retiree migrants are more likely to be of higher socioeconomic status and live in homes with higher values than long-time rural residents. They can also offer new skills to their communities and time for volunteering activities. As such, they can be viewed as a resource for rural areas and part of an overall rural economic development strategy (Glasgow & Brown, 2012).

While retiree in-migration is occurring in high-amenity rural areas, other rural communities face economic declines. Older rural residents, regardless of whether they are long-time residents or new in-migrants, typically have much higher rates of home ownership, often without mortgages, than other households (Bevan, 2009; HAC, July 2012). Yet, the equity benefits of home ownership can be limited due to the relatively high utility and maintenance costs of older housing stock and the lack of housing markets resulting in declining property values. This situation can result in what Satsangi, Gallent and Bevan (2010) describe as ageist views of rural areas as 'ghettos of the elderly' (p. 74).

The profile of older rural residents creates a set of inequalities in relation to rural housing provision. First, it draws attention to the provision of age-specific housing and community service needs for an increasing number of elders living in rural areas (Bevan, 2009). In the UK policies have been developed to encourage house design inclusive of the needs of older populations, but these have been criticised as focusing too narrowly on physical access while ignoring wider housing quality issues (Milner & Madigan, 2004). Second, although homeowners have property assets, incomes may be quite low, pointing to processes of social exclusion (Bevan, 2009). Older adults with low incomes living in older homes with stagnant or declining values characterise the proportion of rural elders who are ageing-in-place. This contrasts with those retiree migrants who relocate to high-amenity rural areas; these elderly households tend generally to have higher socioeconomic status than long-time residents in rural communities (Nash Jr et al., 2011).

Territories of exclusion: poverty, race and ethnicity in rural housing disparities

According to the European Commission, 'rural areas are characterized by a higher degree of income poverty with respect to urban areas in all countries for which such distinction is possible' (Bertolini, Montanari & Peragine, 2008, p. 14). While a systematic and complete analysis of rural–urban patterns of income poverty in the global north is not available, country-specific surveys indicate that poverty rates are consistently higher in rural places. In spite of the high rates of poverty, provisions for affordable and social housing are less common in rural areas than in urban areas (see, for example, Satsangi & Dunmore, 2003). In the USA the federal government's investment in affordable housing is a complex patchwork of grants, loans, loan guarantees, subsidies and tax incentives administered by a number of different agencies at the federal, state and local levels (HAC, 2012). It is estimated that more than six million units of affordable housing are supported by federal funding; however only about one-quarter of households eligible for housing programmes actually receives any assistance.

In contexts where private home ownership dominates, public investment in rural social housing is nearly non-existent (see Allen et al., 2004; Edgar, Filipovic & Dandolova, 2007). Neoliberal policies worldwide have converted subsidised social rental housing into home ownership units and reduced investments in new social housing (Desilver, 2013). In the UK, for example, the 'right to buy' social rental housing shifted the responsibility for affordable housing provision from the government to other agencies, led by private/voluntary arrangements. As a consequence, the volume of social housing in the countryside has been substantially reduced (Satsangi, Gallent & Bevan, 2010). It is estimated that 7,500 new affordable homes per annum are required in settlements of less than 3,000 people in the UK (Rural Housing Policy Review, 2015).

Arguably the most extreme indicator of poverty-linked housing problems is the risk and reality of rural homelessness. Unlike urban homelessness, in rural areas homelessness tends to be hidden. Rather than literally 'living on the street' or in temporary emergency shelters, rural homeless individuals and families find themselves in positions of precarious housing, living in temporary campsites or staying in barns, sheds or other structures not meant for human habitation. Those at risk of homelessness double up with others sharing unaffordable, substandard and overcrowded accommodations (see Milbourne, this volume). Causes of rural homelessness tend to be structural, such as economic changes beyond the control of the individual, poverty and a lack of affordable housing (Cloke, Milbourne & Widdowfield, 2001; CMHC, 2003). In many rural communities across the global north there has been increasing competition for a relatively static housing stock. The combination of higher housing prices and lower household incomes relative to urban places, and a planning system that tends to limit new housing construction in an effort to preserve open space and reduce energy consumption, has led to a rise in the level of rural homelessness (OECD, 2011). While reported homelessness rates are lower in rural areas than in urban centres (e.g., Defra, 2015), in many cases homeless people from rural places end up in urban areas (Robinson, 2004). Rural areas that have witnessed greater levels of middle-class counter-urbanisation demonstrated higher levels of homelessness (Cloke, Milbourne & Widdowfield, 2001). The failure of rural local authorities to recognise the housing insecurities of rural people is exacerbated by the hidden nature of rural homelessness and further compounded by the social and cultural construction of rural areas as idyllic places to live, undermining the discussion about rural homelessness internationally (Satsangi, Gallent & Bevan, 2010).

Concentrations of poverty and the impact of residential segregation by race and ethnicity on the well-being of individuals and families has been a focus of significant research on neighbourhood influences on urban poverty (Tigges, Browne & Green, 1998). Evidence indicates that inequality based on race and ethnicity is substantial in rural places as well (Bock, Kovacs & Shucksmith, 2015). Many areas where concentration of poverty has persisted over decades are also areas with concentrations of minority populations. In the USA, for example, Latino residents of Colonia communities along the US–Mexico border and African Americans in the lower Mississippi Delta face serious housing stress including high housing costs and substandard living conditions (HAC, 2012). In Eastern and Central Europe high percentages of Roma live in rural areas in poor and inhuman housing conditions (Somogyi & Teller, 2011).

Globalisation, especially in the agri-industrial food sector, has triggered increased international mobilities of guest workers, immigrants and illegal 'aliens', leading to further diversity and increasing minority populations in rural areas. Agriculture remains a significant rural employer where low incomes and seasonality of work represent important risks of poverty and social exclusion. Linked to agricultural activity in Western countries are the large numbers of immigrants employed as seasonal workers associated with illegal immigration, low incomes and often very poor living conditions (see also Bock, Osti & Ventura, this volume). Activities of criminal organisations controlling the labour market in Italy, Spain and France increases the risk of poverty and exclusion for these workers (Bertolini, Montanari and Peragine, 2008). These international migrants have become a 'reserve workforce' and the 'shadow economy' for globalised industrialised nations (Schinkel, 2009).

For international migrants, housing is often tied to their employment, making them particularly beholden to their employers; issues of exploitation and overcrowded house conditions are reported in the literature (i.e., McAreavey, 2012). In rural Wales the growth of migrants added further pressures to the local housing market due to the lack of good quality housing stock, resulting in inflated rental house prices (Jones & Lever, 2014). Similarly in the United States, the vast majority of farmworkers are members of racial or ethnic minority populations and almost three-quarters of all farmworkers were born outside the country. The housing conditions of these workers are particularly dire; while traditionally farmworkers were accommodated in employer-owned housing, there has been a significant decline in the provision of this employee benefit and most farmworkers now have to obtain their housing through the highly competitive private rental market (HAC, 2011).

However, positive implications of international migration have been discussed as well, particularly in countries with permissive housing planning regimes. In Greece, for example, international migrants have provided the labour force for house construction and renovation in rural areas, bringing traditional house-building skills to rural areas and contributing to wider demographic and social development (Kasimis, Papadopoulos & Zacopoulou, 2002). In Ireland, too, rural local investment through building new houses is reported by Maher and Cawley (2014) in relation to Brazilian migrants in the rural west of the country. These examples hardly typify the plethora of experiences associated with migrant groups, reflecting diverse mobility forces, employment conditions and engagement with rural communities (Woods, 2011).

Mortgage lending and global finance

Structural and macroeconomic forces compound rural housing concerns with globalisation in the financial sector, impacting rural housing across the global north. In the USA, for example, the banking industry deregulation that occurred in the 1980s and 1990s led to an urban concentration and centralisation of local financial institutions. Rural areas with declining populations, places with lower per capita incomes and those farther from urban areas were often left without banks. Larger urban institutions with ties to the global financial markets led to increased capital mobility. During the 1990s and early 2000s economic growth occurred based on low-cost consumer credit (Murphy & Scott, 2014). Housing demand rose rapidly as mortgage financing was readily available. Private mortgage lenders and US bankers were able to issue home loans and sell them on the secondary market at low risk and in a highly profitable manner. Global investment fuelled demand as mortgage loans were securitised and sold across Europe, Asia and the USA (Sassen, 2009). The financial sector globalisation coupled with deregulation of the US banking industry resulted in a substantial increase in subprime and predatory mortgage lending, inflating housing prices well above their values. By 2006, the housing market collapsed and prices fell sharply, leaving many US borrowers in foreclosure or 'underwater' with mortgage debt exceeding the value of their homes (Feldstein, 2009). This situation triggered a 'foreclosure crisis' where the level of defaults and foreclosures more than doubled previous record highs (US Department of Housing and Urban Development, 2010) leaving individual borrowers, communities and the global financial sector in an economic crisis (Aalbers, 2009; Martin, 2011; Murphy, 2011).

Recent research demonstrates that the global recession following the foreclosure crisis increased risk of poverty and severe deprivation in many rural areas, while other rural areas act as spaces of refuge due to lower costs of living and cheaper housing (Bock, Kovacs & Shucksmith, 2015). In Ireland, a period of housing expansion and price inflation with a subsequent housing 'bust' had significant implications, including vacant and empty housing in the countryside (Kitchin, O'Callaghan & Gleeson, 2014). Murphy and Scott (2013, 2014) point to the extreme hardship and stress faced by rural households since the onset of the housing crash in relation to mortgage repayments. The authors argue that the greatest financial vulnerability is observed in rural households in areas that experienced housing overdevelopment.

In US rural locations, access to credit, especially mortgage financing remains difficult, with rural areas and minority or low-income borrowers receiving a disproportionate level of high-cost home loans (CMHC, 2003; HAC, 2012, 2013). The high proportion of manufactured homes also impacts rural mortgage lending. Typically, manufactured homes are financed with high-cost personal property loans with shorter loan terms than standard mortgage financing (HAC July, 2012). While manufactured housing provides a source of unsubsidised, low-cost home ownership (MacTavish, Eley & Salamon, 2006), these homes have about one-fourth the value of otherwise comparable site-built rural homes (Mimura, Love-Myers, Sweaney & Leigh, 2013). Furthermore, half these homes are clustered in 'trailer parks' or manufactured home communities (MacTavish, Eley & Salamon, 2006) where ownership fails to provide the expected benefits of equity in both the building and land (MacTavish & Salamon, 2001).

Conclusions and further questions

Housing research is central to understanding and addressing rural inequalities. Global trends surrounding key rural housing issues include counter-urban and international mobilities, amenity-driven development, economic restructuring, as well as greater racial and ethnic diversity. These trends have direct impacts on housing in rural areas, although the lack of adequate housing data and analysis (Bertolini, Montanari and Peragine, 2008) has resulted in a relatively underdeveloped research field. In response to the need for a better understanding of rural housing that addresses current inequalities, we suggest that further empirical and public policy research is needed.

Empirically, rural housing research tends to be either applied descriptive reports of national housing conditions or case studies at the community level. We have argued that there are three principal areas of current rural housing research: (1) the context of rural economies and the observed inequalities associated with residential mobilities; (2) the concerns regarding territorial exclusion, areas of persistent poverty and issues of race and ethnicity; (3) structural causes of rural inequalities, such as housing finance for home ownership. For each of these areas the review of literature illuminates further research questions and suggestions for additional study. In order to address the complex and situational aspects of housing and the intersection with rural inequality, we must go beyond descriptive analyses towards providing potential explanations and predicting future outcomes for policy directions (see an example by Lowe & Ward, 2009, in which housing policy and preferences for rural residential environments are central to scenario planning). We suggest that additional research address the intersection of global macroeconomic conditions and local rural housing outcomes. Areas of persistent poverty and residential exclusion have been neglected in rural studies and demand attention, especially regarding international migrants and their housing experiences. In terms of structural causes of rural inequalities and housing disparities, research is needed to address more clearly the social and cultural constraints on housing as well as a more in-depth analysis of residential financing and the impacts of neoliberalism on rural communities and housing development.

Central to these issues are questions about resilience, inclusion and social justice. Is there an ideal rural housing policy? What values should regulate rural housing policy and who is responsible for articulating those? Whose housing expertise matters? How is power exercised to frame housing development interests, and by whom? What is the role of housing tenure in relation to the resilience of rural communities (drawing on Scott & Gkartzios, 2014)? Do, for example, different housing types (such as self-built or manufactured housing) and tenures (cooperatively owned or leased housing) result in more socially inclusive rural communities (see also MacTavis & Salamon, 2001; Skobba & Ziebarth, 2002; Mimura, Love-Myers, Sweaney & Leigh, 2013)? Useful policy reports have appeared in the literature addressing housing issues highlighted in this chapter (e.g., Rural Housing Policy Review, 2015), but how far do these policy recommendations travel in different cultural contexts? The Anglo-centric literature as well as the limited cases of international comparative rural housing research demonstrate the need for such comparative approaches. Critically, the development of symmetrical comparative research frameworks needs to ensure in-depth discussions of cultural conditions and values about housing development as well as linguistic and definitional barriers, avoiding the homogenisation of those (drawing on Lowe, 2012).

Furthermore, more research needs to be done in the context of global challenges, particularly in relation to climate change, natural disasters and conflicts. What are the rural housing impacts of climate change? What are the responses to natural disasters in rural areas and how does disaster recovery impact housing and rural inequalities over time (see Murakami & Wood,

2014)? In what way does war and internal conflict evolve into 'domicide' or the politically sanctioned demolition of housing as a strategy of violence?

We also observe that while class, race and ethnicity are discussed to some extent in rural housing literatures, other identities and inequalities remain relatively invisible from academic scrutiny. What is, for example, the role of gender in rural housing provision and research? Is there an embedded androcentric bias in exploring social relations and power struggles in relation to rural housing inequalities (see also Ziebarth, 2009; Satsangi, 2011)? We also call for more queer perspectives in relation to rural housing need and provision. There has been a growth of discussions on the housing needs of lesbian, gay, bisexual and transgender people, criticising heteronormative assumptions within urban planning and development practices (see Doan, 2011), yet such critical explorations on rural housing (and wider rural planning practices) have remained starkly underdeveloped. Similarly, the literature around disability and rural housing requires development. More importantly, we point to the need for research on the intersection of inequalities, instead of focusing on single 'competitive' categories, accepting that inequalities are multiple, fluid and overlapping (drawing on McCall, 2005; Nash, 2011).

From a policy analysis perspective, public investment in housing is critical in addressing needs across the global north. A main obstacle to addressing rural housing concerns, at least when this does not involve the rural middle classes opposing new rural housing development, is a general political irrelevance. Rural issues are less visible, thus less urgent. An 'out of sight, out of mind' attitude makes rural housing issues appear less relevant than urban housing. Inertia and resistance are common barriers to addressing rural social housing concerns (Satsangi, Gallent & Bevan, 2010). Compared to urban populations, the rural poor are less organised, more dispersed and remote from political and economic centres (Bertolini, Montanari & Peragine, 2008). While the housing stock itself might serve as a symbol of crisis and financial burden, referring to unfinished and vacant houses, foreclosures, poor quality housing, depopulation and poverty, powerful groups typically frame policy interventions on their terms. And, while researchers in the field question whose housing needs matter, rural housing policy can be analysed to unveil selective values and interests embedded in planning regimes regarding the social construction and regulation of the countryside.

References

Aalbers, MB (2009). Geographies of the financial crisis. *Area* 41, 34–42.

Allen, J, Barlow, J, Leal, J, Maloutas, T. & Padovani, L (2004). *Housing and welfare in Southern Europe.* Oxford: Blackwell.

Argent, N, Tonts, M, Jones, R, & Holmes, J (2014). The amenity principle, internal migration and rural development in Australia. *Annals of the Association of American Geographers* 104(2), 305–318.

Benson, M & O'Reilly, K (2009). Migration and the search for a better way of life: A critical exploration of lifestyle migration. *The Sociological Review* 57, 608–625.

Bertolini, P, Montanari, M & Peragine, V (2008). Poverty and social exclusion in rural areas. Final Study Report. European Commission, Directorate-General for Employment, Social Affairs and Equal Opportunities.

Best, R & Shucksmith, M (2006). *Homes for rural communities.* Report of the Joseph Rowntree Foundation Rural Housing Policy Forum. York: Joseph Rowntree Foundation.

Bevan, M (2009). Planning for an ageing population in rural England: The place of housing design. *Planning, Practice and Research* 24(2), 233–249.

Bock, B, Kovacs, K & Shucksmith, M (2015). Changing social characteristics, patterns of inequality and exclusion. In AK Copus & P de Lima (Eds), *Territorial cohesion in rural Europe: The relational turn in rural development* (pp. 193–211). Abingdon: Routledge.

Bosworth, G & Atterton, J (2012). Entrepreneurial in-migration and neoendogenous rural development. *Rural Sociology* 77(2), 254–279.

Brown, DL & Glasgow, N (2008). *Rural retirement migration*. Dordrecht: Springer.

Champion, T & Brown, DL (2012). Migration and urban–rural population redistribution in the UK and US. In M Shucksmith, DL Brown, S Shortall, J Vergunst & ME Mildred (Eds), *Rural transformations and rural policies in the US and UK* (pp. 39–57). New York: Routledge.

Chi, G & Marcouiller, DW (2012). Recreational homes and migration to remote amenity-rich areas. *Journal of Regional Analysis & Policy* 42(1), 47–60.

Cloke, P, Milbourne, P & Widdowfield, R (2001). Homelessness and rurality: Exploring connections in local spaces of rural England. *Sociologia Ruralis* 41(4), 438–453.

CMHC (Canada Mortgage and Housing Corporation) (November 2003). Housing needs of low-income people living in rural areas: Literature review. Research Highlight Socio-Economic Series 03-023. Available online at www.cmhc.ca (accessed 23 June 2015).

Defra (2015). Statistical digest for rural England. Department for Environment, Food and Rural Affairs. Available at www.defra.gov.uk/statistics/rural/publications (accessed 23 June 2015).

de Groot, C, Daalhuizen, FBC, van Dam, F & Mulderd, CH (2012). Once an outsider, always an outsider? The accessibility of the Dutch rural housing market among locals and non-locals. *Journal of Rural Studies* 28(3), 302–313.

Desilver, D (2013, August 6). Around the world, governments promote home ownership. Pew Research Center. Available at http://www.pewresearch.org/author/ddesilver (accessed 23 June 2015).

Doan, PL (2011). *Queering planning: Challenging heteronormative assumptions and reframing planning practice*. Farnham: Ashgate.

Donovan, K & Gkartzios, M (2014). Architecture and rural planning: 'Claiming the vernacular'. *Land Use Policy* 41, 334–343.

Edgar, B, Filipovic, M & Dandolova, I (2007). Home ownership and marginalization. *European Journal of Homelessness* 1, 141–160.

ENRD (European Network of Rural Development) (2015). Rural development gateway 2014–2020. Available at www.enrd.ec.europa.eu (accessed 23 June 2015).

Feldstein, M (2009). How to save an 'underwater' mortgage. *The Wall Street Journal*, 7 August.

Freeman, C & Cheyne, C (2008). Coasts for sale: Gentrification in New Zealand. *Planning Theory & Practice* 9(1), 33–56.

Gallent, N (2009). New agendas in planning and rural housing. *Planning, Practice and Research* 24(2), 153–159.

Gallent, N (2014). The social value of second homes in rural communities. *Housing, Theory and Society* 31(2), 174–191.

Gallent, N (2015). Bridging social capital and the resource potential of second homes: The case of Stintino, Sardinia. *Journal of Rural Studies* 38, 99–108.

Gallent, N & Allen, C (2003). Housing pressure and policy in Europe: A power regime perspective. In N Gallent, M Shucksmith & M Tewdwr-Jones (Eds), *Housing in the European countryside: Rural pressure and policy in Western Europe* (pp. 208–225). London: Routledge.

Gallent, N, Juntti, M, Kidd, S & Shaw, D (2008). *Introduction to rural planning*. London: Routledge.

Gallent, N & Robinson, S (2012). Community perspectives on localness and 'priority' housing policies in rural England. *Housing Studies* 27(3), 360–380.

Gallent, N, Shucksmith, M & Tewdwr-Jones, M (2003). *Housing in the European countryside: Rural pressure and policy in Western Europe*. London: Routledge.

Gkartzios, M & Norris, M (2011) 'If you build it, they will come': Governing property-led rural regeneration in Ireland. *Land Use Policy* 28(3), 486–494.

Gkartzios, M & Scott, M (2013). Attitudes to housing and planning policy in rural localities: Disparities between long-term and mobile rural populations in Ireland. *Land Use Policy* 31, 347–357.

Gkartzios, M & Scott, M (2014). Placing housing in rural development: Exogenous, endogenous and neo-endogenous approaches. *Sociologia Ruralis* 54(3), 241–265.

Gkartzios, M & Shucksmith, M (2015). 'Spatial anarchy' versus 'spatial apartheid': Rural housing ironies in Ireland and England. *Town Planning Review* 86(1), 53–72.

Glasgow, N & Brown, DL (2012). Rural ageing in the United States: Trends and contexts. *Journal of Rural Studies* 28(4), 422–431.

Gosnell, H & Abrams, J (2009). Amenity migration: Diverse conceptualizations of drivers, socioeconomic dimensions, and emerging challenges. *GeoJournal* 76(4), 303–322.

HAC (Housing Assistance Council) (2011). *Migrant and farmworker housing*. Washington, DC: HAC.

HAC (Housing Assistance Council) (2012). *Taking stock: Rural people, poverty, and housing in the 21st century.* Washington, DC: HAC.

HAC (Housing Assistance Council) (2012, July). *Homeownership in rural America.* Rural Research Brief. Washington, DC: HAC.

HAC (Housing Assistance Council) (2013). Rural mortgage activity increases, but high cost loans and denials are still problematic. Rural Research Note. Washington, DC: HAC.

Hall, P, Thomas, R, Gracey, H & Drewett, R (1973). *The containment of urban England.* Hemel Hempstead: Allen & Unwin.

Hantrais, L (2009). *International comparative research: Theory, methods and practice.* Basingstoke: Palgrave Macmillan.

Housing and Society (2014). Special issue: Housing in the countryside. *Housing and Society* 41(2), 105–348.

Jones, L & Lever, J (2014). Migrant workers in rural Wales and the South Wales valleys. Wales Rural Observatory Report. Available at http://www.walesruralobservatory.org.uk/ (accessed 23 June 2015).

Jones, R & Tonts, M (2003). Transition and diversity in rural housing provision: The case of Narrogin, Western Australia. *Australian Geographer* 34(1), 47–59.

Kasimis, C, Papadopoulos, AG & Zacopoulou, E (2002). Migrants in rural Greece. *Sociologia Ruralis* 43(2), 167–184.

Kitchin, R, O'Callaghan, C & Gleeson, J (2014). The new ruins of Ireland? Unfinished estates in the post-celtic tiger era. *International Journal of Urban and Regional Research* 38(3), 1069–1080.

Liu, N & Roberts, D (2013). Counter-urbanisation, planning and house prices: An analysis of the Aberdeen Housing Market Area, 1984–2010. *Town Planning Review* 84(1), 81–105.

Lowe, P (2012). The agency of rural research in comparative context. In M Shucksmith, DL Brown, S Shortall, J Vergunst & ME Warner (Eds), *Rural transformations and rural policies in the US & UK* (pp. 18–38). New York: Routledge.

Lowe, P & Ward, N (2009). England's rural futures: A socio-geographical approach to scenarios analysis. *Regional Studies* 43(10), 1319–1332.

MacTavish, K, Eley, M & Salamon, S (2006). Housing vulnerability among rural trailer-park households. *Georgetown Journal on Poverty Law & Policy* 13(1), 95–117.

MacTavish, K & Salamon, S (2001). Mobile home park on the prairie: A new rural community form. *Rural Sociology* 66(4), 487–506.

MacTavish, KA, Ziebarth, A & George, L (2014). Housing in rural America. In C Bailey, L Jensen & E Ransom (Eds), *Rural America in a globalizing world* (pp. 177–192). Morgantown, WV: West Virginia Press.

Maher, G & Cawley, M (2014). Short-term labour migration: Brazilian migrants in Ireland. *Population, Space and Place.* doi: 10.1002/psp.1859.

Martin, R (2011). The local geographies of the financial crisis: From the housing bubble to economic recession and beyond. *Journal of Economic Geography* 11, 587–618.

McAreavey, R (2012). Resistance or resilience? Tracking the pathway of recent arrivals to a 'new' rural destination. *Sociologia Ruralis* 52(4), 488–507.

McCall, L (2005). The complexity of intersectionality. *Signs* 30(3), 1771–1800.

Milbourne, P (2004). The local geographies of poverty: A rural case-study. *Geoforum* 35(5), 559–575.

Milner, J & Madigan, R (2004). Regulation and innovation: Rethinking inclusive housing design. *Housing Studies* 19, 727–744.

Mimura, Y, Love-Myers, K, Sweaney, AL & Leigh, M (2013). Comparing values of manufactured and equivalent site-built homes in the rural United States. *Housing and Society* 40(2), 150–169.

Mitchell, CJA (2004). Making sense of counterurbanization. *Journal of Rural Studies* 20, 15–34.

Morgan, J & Satsangi, M (2011) 'Reaching the parts other grants don't go?' Supporting self-provided housing in rural Scotland. *Housing Studies* 26(4), 615–628.

Murakami, K & Wood, DM (2014). Planning innovation and post-disaster reconstruction: The case of Tohoku, Japan. *Planning Theory and Practice* 15(2), 237–265.

Murdoch, J & Lowe, P (2003). The preservationist paradox: Modernism, environmentalism and the politics of spatial division. *Transactions of the Institute of British Geographers* 28, 318–322.

Murdoch, J, Lowe, P, Ward, N & Marsden, T (2003). *The differentiated countryside.* London: Routledge.

Murphy, E & Scott, M (2013). Mortgage-related issues in a crisis economy: Evidence from rural households in Ireland. *Geoforum* 46, 34–44.

Murphy, E & Scott, M (2014). 'After the crash': Life satisfaction, everyday financial practices and rural households in post Celtic Tiger Ireland. *Journal of Rural Studies* 34, 37–49.

Murphy, L (2011). The global financial crisis and the Australian and New Zealand housing markets. *Journal of Housing and the Built Environment* 26, 335–351.

NaCSBA (National Custom and Self Build Association) (2011). An Action Plan to promote the growth of self build housing. The report of the Self Build National Self Build Association. Government-Industry Working Group. Available at http://www.nasba.org.uk/reports (accessed 23 June 2015).

Nash Jr, B, Folts, WE, Muir, KB, Peacock, J & Jones, K (2011). Elderly population and the rural housing continuum. In D Marcouiller, M Lapping & O Furuseth (Eds), *Rural Housing, exurbanization, and amenity-driven development contrasting and 'haves' and the 'have nots'* (pp. 75–91). Burlington, VT: Ashgate.

Nash, JC (2011) 'Home truths' on intersectionality. *Yale Journal of Law and Feminism* 23(2), 445–470.

Nelson, L & Nelson, PB (2010). The global rural: Gentrification and linked migration in the rural USA. *Progress in Human Geography* 35(4), 441–459.

Newby, H (1985). *Green and pleasant land? Social change in rural England.* London: Penguin.

OECD (Organization for Economic Co-operation and Development) (2006). *The new rural paradigm – Policies and governance.* Paris: OECD.

OECD (Organization for Economic Cooperation and Development) (2011). *Profile of rural England in OECD Rural Policy Reviews: England, United Kingdom.* Paris: OECD.

Overvag, K & Berg, NG (2011). Second homes, rurality and contested space in Eastern Norway. *Tourism Geographies* 13(3), 417–442.

Paquette, S & Domon, G (2003). Changing ruralities, changing landscapes: Exploring social recomposition using a multi-scale approach. *Journal of Rural Studies* 19, 425–444.

Pellow, DN & Park, LS (2011). *Slums of Aspen: Immigrants vs. the environment in America's Eden.* New York: New York University Press.

Planning, Practice and Research (2009). Special issue: New agendas in planning and rural housing. *Planning, Practice and Research* 24(2), 153–326.

Ray, C (2000). The EU LEADER programme: Rural development laboratory. *Sociologia Ruralis* 40(2), 163–171.

Robinson, D (2004). The hidden and neglected experiences of homelessness in rural England. In P Milbourne & P Cloke (Eds), *International perspectives on rural homelessness* (pp. 25–44). Abingdon: Routledge.

Roe, B, Irwin, EG & Morrow-Jones, HA (2004). The effects of farmland, farmland preservation and other neighbourhood amenities on housing values and residential growth. *Land Economics* 80(1), 55–75.

Rural Housing Policy Review (2015). Affordable housing. A fair deal for rural communities. Available at http://www.acre.org.uk/cms/resources/afairdealforruralcommunitiesmainreport3-1.pdf (accessed 23 June 2015).

Sassen, IS (2009). When local housing becomes an electronic instrument: The global circulation of mortgages – A research note. *International Journal of Urban and Regional Research* 33(2), 411–426.

Satsangi, M (2011). Feminist epistemologies and the social relations of housing provision. *Housing, Theory and Society* 28(4), 398–409.

Satsangi, M & Dunmore, K (2003). The planning system and the provision of affordable housing in rural Britain: A comparison of the Scottish and English experience. *Housing Studies* 18(2), 201–217.

Satsangi, M, Gallent, N & Bevan, M (2010). *The rural housing question: Communities and planning in Britain's countrysides.* Bristol: Policy Press.

Schinkel, W (2009). 'Illegal aliens' and the state, or: bare bodies vs. the zombie. *International Sociology* 24(6), 779–806.

Scott, M (2012). Housing conflicts in the Irish countryside: Uses and abuses of post-colonial narratives. *Landscape Research* 37(1), 91–114.

Scott, M & Gkartzios, M (2014). Rural housing: Questions of resilience. *Housing and Society* 41(2), 247–276.

Scott, M & Murray, M (2009). Housing rural communities: Connecting rural dwellings to rural development in Ireland. *Housing Studies* 24(6), 755–774.

Shucksmith, M (1981). *No Homes for Locals?* Surrey: Gower.

Shucksmith, M (2000). *Exclusive countryside? Social inclusion and regeneration in rural areas.* York: Joseph Rowntree Foundation.

Shucksmith, M (2009). Disintegrated rural development? Neo-endogenous rural development, planning and place-shaping in diffused power contexts. *Sociologia Ruralis* 50(1), 1–14.

Shucksmith, M (2012). Interface: Exclusive rurality: planners as agents of rural gentrification. *Planning Theory and Practice* 12, 605–611.

Skobba, K & Ziebarth, A (2002). Empowerment in leasehold cooperatives and its influence on the member/management relationship. *Housing and Society* 29(1&2), 13–22.

Smith, D & Phillips, D (2001). Socio-cultural representations of greenified pennine rurality. *Journal of Rural Studies* 17(4), 457–469.

Somogyi, E & Teller, N (2011). *Vademecum: Improving housing conditions for marginalized communities, including Roma in Bulgaria, Czech Republic, Hungary, Romania and Slovakia through the absorption of ERDF.* Available at http://www.euromanet.eu/upload/84/25/vademecum_OSI_2011.pdf (accessed 23 June 2015).

Stockdale, A (2006). The role of a 'retirement transition' in the repopulation of rural areas. *Population, Space and Place* 12(1), 1–13.

Stockdale, A, Findlay, A & Short, D (2000). The repopulation of rural Scotland: Population and threat. *Journal of Rural Studies* 16(2), 243–257.

Sturzaker, J & Shucksmith, M (2011). Planning for housing in rural England: Discursive power & spatial exclusion. *Town Planning Review* 82, 169–193.

Tigges, L, Browne, I & Green, GP (1998). Social isolation of the urban poor: Race, class, and neighbourhood effects on social resources. *The Sociological Quarterly* 39(1), 53–77.

US Department of Housing and Urban Development (2010). *A report to Congress on the root causes of the foreclosure crisis.* Washington, DC: HUD Office of Policy Development and Research.

van Dam, F, Heins, S & Elbersen, BS (2002). Lay discourses of the rural and stated and revealed preferences for rural living: Some evidence of the existence of a rural idyll in the Netherlands. *Journal of Rural Studies* 18, 461–476.

Woods, M (2011). *Rural.* London: Routledge.

Ziebarth, A (2009). Housing heroines: A tradition of social action research. *Housing and Society* 36(1), 53–74.

Part VII

Social Dynamics and Institutional Capacity

Section editor: Kai A. Schafft

42

Social Dynamics and Institutional Capacity

Structures, Mobilities and Identities beyond the Periphery of the Global Metropolis

Kai A. Schafft

Introduction

The well-being of rural people and places is shaped in part by the ways in which local communities and areas where people live are organised, and the ways in which these local places, identities and institutions are embedded within interactive shifting economic, cultural and social spaces that are simultaneously local, regional, national and global in nature (McMichael, 2010; Barrett, 2014; Higgins, Potter, Dibden & Cocklin, 2014). The organisation and well-being of rural places can therefore be understood, in part, in institutional terms, including the structure of economies and the organisation of local institutional and governmental bodies. Rural areas with less diversified economies and weak institutional structures are less able to withstand economic shocks (Lobao, 2014), raising basic structural questions about community capacity, resilience and adaptation in the face of adversity (Freshwater, 2015). Policy trends promoting decentralisation and privatisation of governance and public services since the 1980s have further forced localities to increase their reliance upon market forces for public goods provision, throwing many rural areas, already challenged by poverty concentrations and limited fiscal resources, into further structural disadvantage. As Shortall and Warner note, 'although the view that decentralisation, privatisation and participation make for better government is contested for failing to meet efficiency, social redistribution or democratic objectives, it remains a primary ideological drive behind rural policy' (2012, p. 16), a theme also taken up by Gorlach and Starosta's chapter within this section. Further, some institutions, such as education, may work at cross purposes to rural community well-being if the role of schooling is primarily framed by policy makers and local stakeholders in terms of its economic function, and specifically the production of mobile human capital responsive to the shifting workforce demands of a global economy (Corbett, 2007; Nichols & Berliner, 2007). Under these circumstances, and with limited use-value in rural home communities, education may paradoxically contribute to rural youth out-migration, and ageing and under-skilled remaining local populations, reinforcing already existing structural disadvantages within rural areas (Corbett, 2007; Nelson, 2014; Petrin, Schafft & Meece, 2014).

The organisation of rural places, however, is also shaped by the multiple and contested symbolic constructions and social narratives of rurality, place, history and community. While rurality is often understood as an idealised landscape or a repository of traditional values and self-reliance, or a recreational space for urban dwellers, within sociospatial hierarchies it is also framed as second rate, backwards or 'anti-modern' (Corbett, 2007; Wagner, 2014). These varied and conflicting constructions of what rural is and what it means to *be* rural raise important questions not only about the self-efficacy of rural people and places, but also about the sociocultural practices and discourses that both reflect and reproduce the economic, social and political marginalities of places and spaces that lie beyond the peripheries of the global metropolis.

Furthermore, rural studies have increasingly focused on place and rurality not as signifiers of stable and static productivist space, but rather in terms of mobilities and relationalities (Urry, 2000; Bell & Osti, 2010; Woods, 2011; Heley & Jones, 2012; Goodwin-Hawkins, 2014) – the 'intersection of flows and objects' across space that both constitute and continuously remake place, resulting, in part, in a 'complicated interplay between mobility and fixity' (Milbourne & Kitchen, 2014, pp. 326, 327). Foregrounding mobilities, then, not only 'challenges the concept of community as a spatially localised center of usual residence' (Brown, 2002, p. 17), emphasising the *physical* mobilities of people (e.g., migration and demographic movements across and through space), but calls attention as well to flows of information, capital, symbols, technology and literacies (Walsh, 2012; Corbett & Vibert, 2013). This collection of chapters examines these interactivities at both the intra-locality level and as flows between and across geographies and scales, incorporating transdisciplinary, international-comparative, and multiple theoretical perspectives to better understand rural agencies, vulnerabilities and institutional capacity.

Resilience, adaptive capacity and rural sustainability

Krzysztof Gorlach and Paweł Starosta focus their chapter on farming families as rural social institutions, and the ways in which macro-level changes in the structure of agriculture have shaped rural social and institutional reorganisation. They argue that local social institutions have taken on ever-greater roles as the nation-state institutions have withdrawn, consistent with neoliberal restructuring. The result, argue the authors, is that many rural places resemble 'limited liability structures' in which local community institutions, while increasingly critical, are unable to satisfy the needs of local residents. With regard to farming families, the authors describe the instance of a pushback away from more corporatist farming models. This involves movement towards re-embedding agriculture within local social structures while renewing engagement with multiple institutional sectors as a means of 'neo-endogenous development', and reducing risk of food insecurity. However, the extent to which this is occurring, and the conditions which are most favourable for giving rise to agricultural relocalisation, remain unanswered.

In the following chapter, Joseph Campbell, Ajay Singh and Jeff Sharp use the 'press–pulse dynamic' framework (Collins et al., 2011; Morten & Rudel, 2014) to discuss the impacts of climate change on rural communities and the determinants that shape the capacity rural areas have to proactively and retroactively respond to climate change events that are both pervasive and incremental ('press' events), as well as those that are sudden and significant ('pulse' events). In the 21st century, climate change will likely pose one of the most significant sets of challenges for rural people and communities, a 'natural disaster evolving in slow motion on a global scale' (Molnar, 2010, p. 1). These challenges are currently, and are projected to be, most severe for regions of the global south[1] (Hertel, Burke & Lobell, 2010; Hurrell & Sengupta, 2012) including water shortages, violent conflict, displacement, and threats to food security (Barnett & Adger, 2007). Even so, Morten and Rudel (2014) note that in 2011 the United States experienced

14 extreme weather events, each costing over US$1 billion. And yet, despite the severity and impacts of these weather events, they are increasingly interpreted as the 'new normal'. For rural areas press and pulse climate change events may hold particular significance given rural poverty concentrations (and hence increased vulnerabilities), the disproportionate likelihood of rural communities to be economically dependent upon sectors such as recreation, agriculture, forestry, fisheries or other natural resources put at direct risk by climate change (Brown & Schafft, 2011), and reduced rural access to political resources and power.

Campbell and colleagues argue that 'a community's ability to react to or anticipate shocks will be conditioned by its ability to access and mobilise resources and relationships'. They propose the 'community capitals' framework (Flora & Flora, 2013) as a means of assessing the 'relative stocks and flows of community resources to mobilise for the common good' (Flora & Flora, 2014, p. 609). Community capitals therefore function as a theoretical heuristic for considering the stocks of social and institutional resources available to localities, including social capital, political capital, human capital, cultural capital, physical capital, financial capital and natural capital.[2] The authors suggest that greater stocks of these multiple resource dimensions translate into higher community adaptive capacity and the ability to mitigate or respond to climate change events. As such, the framework offers a conceptual strategy for both better understanding community social and institutional structure and thereby proving a theoretical approach for assessing rural community preparedness, needs and vulnerabilities.

While there are important reasons to work towards more complete theoretical and practical understandings of the different dimensions of community adaptive capacity, Campbell and colleagues provide both conceptual and methodological caveats. First, with regard to climate change rural people and places are in many respects at the mercy of political forces beyond their control. This is only underscored by the daunting logistical and political challenges confronting national and international actors to reach mutually agreed-upon accords aimed at significantly reducing greenhouse gas emissions and addressing climate change impacts. Second, the diversity of social-ecological contexts of rural communities vastly complicates efforts to develop the means of determining local resilience and vulnerability factors and what these factors mean for mitigating climate change impacts. Third, in focusing on relative stocks of resources available to localities, the community capitals framework may be less intrinsically suited to providing insights regarding the ways in which localities are embedded within multilevel social processes that create and reproduce spatial inequalities and structural disadvantage (Brown, 2002; Schafft & Brown, 2003), and how that in turn shapes the resources available to communities.

In the following chapter, Michael Corbett and Unn-Doris Bæck take up these multilevel processes and provide a comparative discussion of rural resource production in Canada and Scandinavia, focusing in particular on the knowledge and competencies of workers for rural industrial employment characterised by uncertainty, mobility and demand for an elite mobile labour force, largely unattached to place and responsive to labour markets on a global scale (Corbett, 2013). How are these workers imagined with regard to their skills and inclinations, and how in turn is this reflected in public policy discourse, and in particular, educational discourse? As Hayes-Conroy and Hayes-Conroy (in a later chapter) argue that 'embodied well-being' is reciprocally constructed by social difference, so too do Corbett and Bæck argue that the perception of opportunity structures for young people are shaped by (and help reproduce) social geographies of difference. Perception of opportunity is thus conditioned by the social, human and financial capital possessed by individuals, but also by the social and economic peripheralities of place, as well as the operative discourses of media, schools, government and other structures of authority.

In both Nova Scotia and Norway, the authors argue, rural people and places, having historically served as reserve armies of labour for capital expansion, find themselves discursively framed as backwards, 'outside modernity', and in critical need of acquiring 'the cultural sensibilities and knowledge required for prosperity in a neoliberal world'. This is starkly underscored in circumstances under which rural areas become central to national development agendas because of particular exploitable resources. They argue that in both national contexts educational policies and interventions based around entrepreneurship, innovation, science, technology, engineering and mathematics (STEM) education and standardised curricula are structured to prepare rural residents for industries that, while requiring increased technical skills and knowledge, are also inherently precarious and unpredictable. Rural underdevelopment is discursively constructed as an *inevitability* within national development processes rather than the result of particular political economic decision making, and Corbett and Bæck note that those rural residents who are not able (or willing) to acquire the qualifications and competencies to take advantage of these labour market opportunities are thus consigned to the cadre of un/underemployed, low-wage labour subsequently framed as a central *problem* of rural (under)development, rather than a necessary by-product of development decision making.

Kim Donehower and Bill Green extend these themes with the concept of 'rural literacies', specifically the multiple and context-specific textual mediations of social life within rural areas in the context of the symbolic, physical, informational and demographic mobilities associated with globalisation and economic restructuring. The rural literacies approach thus provides a conceptual counterpoint to 'community capital frameworks' as advocated by Campbell and colleagues given the fundamental relational framing of rural space. Instead, a reconception of rural literacies destabilises the fixity of both (rural) place and text, with each understood as relational, dynamic *in*stabilities and simultaneously as a critical resource in social renewal and sustaining rural life. 'Fixity,' the authors argue, 'has been a quality all too often ascribed to rural communities, in the sense of being "stuck in the past", conservative (if not reactionary) in politics and values. This interpretive frame has made it difficult to acknowledge rural diversity and has led to such policy proposals as the abandonment of rural places'. Indeed, their view directly challenges the state-sponsored literacies described by Corbett and Bæck that both reflect and further entrench neoliberal visions of development historically contributing to rural structural disadvantage.

Susan Faircloth and Anne Hynds, in their chapter, while not explicitly employing a 'rural literacies' frame, nonetheless discuss indigenous education and self-determination in US and New Zealand contexts that foreground not only demographic, informational and symbolic mobilities, but also the capacity of local communities to engage in practices leading to community sustainability and well-being. These authors discuss the parallels between American Indian and Māori historical experiences of globalisation, colonisation and domination, cultural resiliencies and resistance, as well as indigenous educational and practices strategies that link tribal sovereignty with educational sovereignty. 'Through this lens,' they argue, 'education becomes an inherently political act of interrogating and demanding change within the governmental, educational, societal, and other structures that have worked to promote and sustain economic and educational underdevelopment for tribal groups'.

From the aggregate levels of community and place, Allison Hayes-Conroy and Jessica Hayes-Conroy shift the focus to bodily well-being and what they term *visceral geography*, an approach to theory and scholarship within human geography that 'takes seriously the biosocial complexity of the body and, in so doing, invites deeper understanding of the material body's role in the unfolding of social, political and ecological processes' (cf. Hayes-Conroy, 2014). As such, they advance other thinking on *embodied* experiences of the rural (e.g., Carolan, 2008, 2011; Farrugia, Smyth & Harrison, 2015) not by (re)embedding the body within social and ecological contexts, but rather by (re)embedding social and ecological contexts within the *body*, positing bodily well-being as not only biosocially hybrid, but reflective of social-structural inequality. In this respect, their project is explicitly focused on bridging body-centred scholarship with scholarship that is centred on social difference, in which bodily well-being and social difference are not only interrelated but 'co-develop and co-define each other'.

Originally stemming from work focused on classism and the 'slow food' movement, in their chapter Hayes-Conroy and Hayes-Conroy discuss recent work in both Fukushima, Japan, and Antioquia, Colombia. In both places they closely examine how attempts to lead healthy lives, and indeed the immediate experience of bodily well-being, are directly shaped by social difference. In the aftermath of the earthquake that resulted in radioactive contamination from the damaged Fukushima Daiichi nuclear power plant, they discuss the ways in which local residents navigated risk and well-being, balancing radiation exposure against their embodied and visceral relations to family, community, locality and way of life – navigations shaped by the contours of social difference. Similarly for Colombia they discuss the experiences of participants with the Legion del Afecto, an initiative addressing youth well-being in communities wracked by violence, which includes the journeying of urban youth to rural areas of the country. The journeys are structured not around the assumption of the inherently 'therapeutic' qualities of the rural environment, but rather around the strategic production of a collective embodied experience in which young people are confronted with new sensory (bodily) experiences that provide a common space for imagining and enacting social change.

Institutional structure, rural well-being and relational ontologies of space

Rural studies, as these chapters in various ways suggest, have increasingly challenged 'fixed' spatial imaginaries by paying close attention to the ways in which rural people, places and spaces are reciprocally constituted by global–local flows of not only people, but information, culture, symbols and power. These approaches challenge earlier (more static) conceptions of the rural but at the same time yield new possibilities in understanding not only the everyday lived experiences of rural people, but the relationship between social and spatial inequalities. This, as Heley and Jones argue, amounts to *a relational ontology of space* in which 'our understandings of spatiality have become less constrained by bounded (territory) or hierarchical (scalar) structural forms, and our spatial analyses have become more attentive to connectivity in all its forms' (2012, p. 208). By extension then, these chapters suggest how recent scholarship on rural well-being, institutions and social dynamics have increasingly employed rural epistemologies attuned to the structural features of localities and yet fully attentive to the highly differentiated and heterogeneous rural spaces which are nonetheless themselves simultaneously constituent of globalised interrelationships, processes, power structures and dependencies.

Notes

1   This is of particular concern given that about 80% of rural households in the global south depend on some form of agriculture for household provisioning, paid labour and/or market production (IFAD, 2010). On a global scale as many as 49 million additional people may be placed at risk of hunger due to climate change (IFAD, 2008).
2   These 'capitals' are explained in greater detail in Campbell, Singh and Sharp's chapter.

Kai A. Schafft

References

Barnett, J & Adger, WN (2007). Climate change, human security and violent conflict. *Political Geography* 26, 639–655.

Barrett, G (2014). Deconstructing community. *Sociologia Ruralis* 55(2), 182–204.

Bell, M & Osti, G (2010). Mobilities and ruralities: An introduction. *Sociologia Ruralis* 50(3), 199–204.

Brown, DL (2002). Migration and community: Social networks in a multilevel world. *Rural Sociology* 67(1), 1–23.

Brown, DL & Schafft, KA (2011). *Rural people & communities in the 21st century: Resilience and transformation.* Malden, MA: Polity.

Carolan, MS (2008). More-than-representational knowledge/s of the countryside: How we think as bodies. *Sociologia Ruralis* 48(4), 408–422.

Carolan, MS (2011). *Embodied food politics.* Farnham: Ashgate.

Collins, SL, Carpenter, SR, Swinton, SM, Orenstein, DE, Childers, DL, Gragson, TL, Grimm, JM, Harlan, SL, Kaye, JP et al. (2011). An integrated conceptual framework for long-term social-ecological research. *Frontiers in Ecology and the Environment* 9(6), 351–357.

Corbett, M (2007). *Learning to leave.* Halifax, NS: Fernwood.

Corbett, M (2013). Improvisation as a curricular metaphor: Imagining education for a rural creative class. *Journal of Research in Rural Education* 28(10), 1–11.

Corbett, M & Vibert, A (2013). Mediating plastic literacies and placeless governmentalities: Returning to a corporeal rurality. In B Green & M Corbett (Eds), *Rethinking rural literacies* (pp. 257–274). New York: Palgrave Macmillan.

Farrugia, D, Smyth, J & Harrison, T (2015). Affective topologies of rural youth embodiment. Online first publication. *Sociologia Ruralis.* doi: 10.1111/soru.12077.

Flora, CB & Flora, JL (2013). *Rural communities: Legacy and change* (4th edn). Boulder, CO: Westview.

Flora, CB & Flora, JL (2014). Community organization and mobilization in rural America. In C Bailey, L Jensen & E Ransom (Eds), *Rural America in a globalizing world* (pp. 609–625). Morgantown: West Virginia University Press.

Freshwater, D (2015). Vulnerability and resilience: Two dimensions of rurality. *Sociologia Ruralis* 55(4), 497–515.

Goodwin-Hawkins, B (2014). Mobilities and the English village: Moving beyond fixity in rural West Yorkshire. *Sociologia Ruralis* 55(2), 167–181.

Hayes-Conroy, J (2014). *Savoring alternative food: School gardens, healthy eating and visceral difference.* New York: Routledge.

Heley, J & Jones, L (2012). Relational rurals: Some thoughts on relating things and theory in rural studies. *Journal of Rural Studies* 28, 208–217.

Hertel, T, Burke, MB & Lobell, DB (2010). The poverty implications of climate-induced crop yield change by 2030. *Global Environmental Change* 20, 577–585.

Higgins, V, Potter, C, Dibden, J & Cocklin, C (2014). Neoliberalizing rural environments. *Journal of Rural Studies* 36, 386–390.

Hurrell, A & Sengupta, S (2012). Emerging powers, north–south relations and global climate politics. *International Affairs* 88(3), 463–484.

IFAD (International Fund for Agricultural Development). (2008). *Climate change: Building the resilience of poor rural communities.* Rome: IFAD.

IFAD (International Fund for Agricultural Development). (2010). *Rural poverty report 2011.* Rome: IFAD.

Lobao, L (2014). Economic change, structural forces, and rural America: Shifting fortunes across communities. In C Bailey, L Jensen & E Ransom (Eds), *Rural America in a globalizing world* (pp. 543–555). Morgantown: West Virginia University Press.

McMichael, P (Ed.). (2010). *Contesting development: Critical struggles for social change.* New York: Routledge.

Milbourne, P & Kitchen, L (2014). Rural mobilities: Connecting movement and fixity in rural places. *Journal of Rural Studies* 34, 326–336.

Molnar, JJ (2010). Climate change and societal response: Livelihoods, communities, and the environment. *Rural Sociology* 75(1), 1–16.

Morten, LW & Rudel, T (2014). Impacts of climate change on people and communities of rural America. In C Bailey, L Jensen & E Ransom (Eds), *Rural America in a globalizing world* (pp. 172–189). Morgantown: West Virginia University Press.

Nelson, PB (2014). Concentrations of the elderly in rural America: Patterns, processes, and outcomes in a neoliberal world. In C Bailey, L Jensen & E Ransom (Eds), *Rural America in a globalizing world* (pp. 383–400). Morgantown: West Virginia University Press.

Nichols, SL & Berliner, DC (2007). *Collateral damage.* Cambridge, MA: Harvard Education Press.

Petrin, R, Schafft, KA & Meece, J (2014). Educational sorting and residential aspirations among rural high school students: What are the contributions of schools and educators to the rural brain drain? *American Educational Research Journal* 51(2), 294–326.

Schafft, KA & Brown, DL (2003). Social capital, social networks, and social power. *Social Epistemology* 17(4), 329–342.

Shortall, S & Warner, M (2012). Rural transformations: Conceptual and policy issues. In M Shucksmith, DL Brown, S Shortall, J Vergunst & M Warner (Eds), *Rural transformations and rural policies in the US and UK* (pp. 3–17). New York: Routledge.

Urry, J (2000). *Sociology beyond society: Mobilities for the twenty-first century.* London: Routledge.

Wagner, A (2014). Re-imagining the (un)familiar: Feminist pedagogy in rural spaces. *Gender & Education* 26(5), 553–567.

Walsh, D (2012). Using mobility to gain stability: Rural household strategies and outcomes in long-distance labor mobility. *Journal of Rural and Community Development* 7(3), 123–143.

Woods, M (2011). *Rural.* Abingdon: Routledge.

43

Farming Families in Rural Communities

Changing Rural Social Organisation in a Modern and Postmodern World

Krzysztof Gorlach & Paweł Starosta

Introduction

In attempting to create a comprehensive analytical framework for changes in rural areas Bogusław Gałęski (1972) proposed a three-level scheme involving farming families (micro), local communities (meso) and the social category of farmers embedded in the structure of the national society (macro). However, given the processes of globalisation in recent years, such a perspective requires some reconsideration. First of all, thanks to the processes of globalisation, the three layers mentioned above cannot be treated as separate levels of social organisation but rather as integrated parts of rural social networks (Murdoch, 2006; Pakulski, 2009). Moreover, we would argue that the transformation of rural communities with significant agricultural activities (meso layer) seems to be, on the one hand, a result of the pressures of global forces, and on the other, the context of changing family farming situations. Therefore, our chapter has been designed as a two-part argument. The first part examines major aspects of rural community transformations. The second examines problems faced by farming families in the context of the changing communities in which they are embedded. We focus on farming family issues for two important reasons: (a) family farms constitute the major component of pre-modern rural areas both in Europe and in North America; and (b) changes in family farms are a basic dimension of rural social reorganisation in this part of the world under the processes of modernisation and post-modernisation. We first sketch important dimensions of rural community change in the global north, and then consider how these changes have affected farming families living in rural space.

Main dimensions of rural community transformation

Fragmentation and persistence: an ironic dualism

The contemporary pattern of globalising development, based on information technologies, advanced and rapid means of transportation, a high degree of specialisation, and a liberal economic vision of the world have produced conditions that deepen the fragmentation of social bonds. This has occurred on a large scale in both rural and urban communities. In light of communications technology, and the growth of social and spatial mobility, this fragmentation contributes to the weakening of 'place attachment' as a factor organising social life in the countryside (Lewicka, 2011).[1] However, the weakening of the local aspect of social life in the global north does not mean its complete invalidation, as suggested by some community theorists (Delanty, 2003). The thesis of the de-territorialisation of social life seems much too one-sided (Clarke & Miller, 1990). Rather, the local dimension of rural life is not so much lost as *transformed* (Brown & Schafft, 2011). In the post-industrial period, the increasing intensification of agricultural production has resulted in a significant decline in the number of farmers in rural areas. Other rural industries such as manufacturing have also declined in importance while recreation and tourism have prospered, and long-distance commuting to urban workplaces has increased. These economic changes have resulted in a broad-scale change in the nature of rural social and economic relationships, and in many rural regions, a decline in population. However, the large-scale decline in rural populations, and of their share of total population, does not mean that rural spaces are empty. In fact, statistics indicate that in 2011 approximately 22.3% of the European population still lived in predominantly rural regions, and 35.3% in intermediary rural–urban regions (Statistics in focus, 2013). Thus, in contemporary rural areas we can identify two parallel processes moving in opposite directions. The first leads to the fragmentation of bonds with local social and economic structures, and the second to maintaining the significance of rural communities as places to live and work.

There are several reasons why rural communities persist in the contemporary world. The first encompasses environmental-aesthetic reasons related to the growing appreciation of living in accord with nature. The second is related to the increasing importance of rural areas as places of social recreation. A third reason, a negative one, is that the twin processes of pauperisation and proletarianisation of the rural population continues in many countries, especially those at the socioeconomic periphery of the global north. In these cases, rural communities are a refuge for those who, because of economic displacement, lack of relevant skills and competences or weak labour markets in nearby cities are unable to commute to urban jobs or migrate there altogether.

Changed state–local relations

Rural communities are linked at different levels with other places, regional and national entities, and globally. In particular, rural areas are affected by changes in the relations between local and state power. Ironically, in ever more highly urbanised societies, local institutions have become more and more important in inhabitants' everyday lives. This is because of the withdrawal of national-level state institutions from the regulation of many areas of public life. Similarly, local action groups and voluntary associations, in which membership is a matter of individual choice and not necessarily group pressure, have taken on increasing importance in community life (Tolbert, Irwin & Lyson, 2002). Legal regulations in North America and across the European Union have significantly expanded the scope of autonomy of local structures in relation to national state institutions. Local self-government has taken over responsibility for meeting needs in many public spheres, such as in primary health care, social welfare, primary education, housing, land management, and many other areas.[2] However, in many cases this extension of the scope of responsibilities of local authorities at the primary level has not been accompanied by the provision of adequate financial resources for the implementation of their proposed solutions (Warner, 2003). In these cases, lack of local government capacity often leads to the privatisation of service provision, and resulting social exclusion since some people lack the resources to purchase services in the market. Warner (2003) has also shown that privatisation contributes to further underdevelopment of peripheral places since they tend to be seen as weak places for capital investment, and/or easy targets for global offshoring of jobs.

Increased specialisation and weakened social relations

Increased specialisation of the process of meeting everyday needs in rural communities leads to the formation of increasingly diverse social roles. This phenomenon, in turn, leads to the increasing heterogeneity of rural communities, and may contribute to increasingly superficial and dispersed human interactions. In situations characterised by an increasing sense of insecurity, the extreme expansion of individual rights and freedoms, and the weakening role of the national-level state institutions and social security, efforts to rebuild local communities as relational structures which could mitigate the severity of the perceived 'eclipse of community' have been proposed. As Castells (1998, p. 66) has observed, 'When the world becomes too large to be controlled, social actors aim at shrinking it back to their size and reach, and … people affirm the transcendent value of the family and local community as God's will.' Hence, the irony is that as the pace of social and economic change increases and rural populations and economies become more specialised, dispersed and set adrift by the national state, rural communities tend to be seen as stable refuges and valued places. This perception often stems more from urbanites than from rural people and communities themselves. In the EU in particular, rural development is accorded significant priority in public policy – a priority that far exceeds its size and economic scope in post-industrial society (European Network for Rural Development, 2015).

Reconstructing rural communities

In the context of the macro-structural changes described above, scholars have proposed strategies to restructure rural communities in a manner that will sustain them in contemporary society. Attempts to reconstruct the local community can be understood as defensive reactions to the progressing pace of fragmentation of social life (Bauman, 2001). Social revitalisation projects in rural communities take place substantially in three dimensions, involving three interrelated approaches. This means that involvement in one dimension does not necessarily lead to an equally high level of integration in another. Rural localism thus becomes a selective process.

The symbolic dimension

The first dimension is the symbolic. From this perspective, the community offers a source of social identity. The more people experience a sense of security, the more strongly they identify with a given collective. In such cases, the sense of connectedness is not the consequence of a common economic interest or dependence, but rather a product of collective imagination, fears, sentiments or psychological desires. Local symbols, stored in the collective memory, constitute and support the cognitive and social boundaries of the community. By contrasting and comparing the 'self' of the community members with 'others', their social identity is determined (Cohen, 1985). The function of such a sense of community (or 'place') is more to reduce stress than to support real cooperation between individuals. This type of bond can have a 'dark side'. It does not necessarily produce mutual obligations and ethical responsibility (Bauman, 2001). In addition, the symbolic world, expressed in gestures, words, images and collective representations, replaces the real world, and can be rather closed to 'others'. This can lead to intolerance towards other communities, or what has been characterised as 'amoral familism' (Putnam, 1993).

Thus, community reconstruction based on symbolic resources leads to maintaining the psychological impulses of the community.[3] The more we are uprooted from our long-lasting social relationships by rapid social and economic change, the greater the emphasis we place on rebuilding the symbolic community. This spatial sense of identity does not, therefore, have to be so thoroughly decontextualised as theorists of late modernity sometimes assume (Giddens, 1997; Beck, 2001). People still identify with the place and community (Altman & Low, 1992). World Values Surveys conducted in the 1990s showed that local identity is the lowest in the Middle East (39%) and Africa (49%), and highest (64%, 62% and 58% respectively) in the southwest, northwest and eastern Europe (Norris, 2002, p. 292). This means that local identification in the global north, and in Europe in particular, is much higher than elsewhere in the world.

The network dimension

Another dimension reflecting a different approach to reconstructing a rural community is networking. This applies to the sphere of direct interactions and constructing a system of real support, such as social networks – also called the personal community (Wilkinson, 1991; Wellman, 1999; Sharp, 2001; Brown & Schafft, 2011). In this perspective, the concept of a local society is different than that of a local community in terms of the prevailing social interactions. The former means non-integrated population groups inhabiting a defined territory, while the latter means a network of intense relationships of entities that act together at a given time as a result of using the defined territory. The bounds of community are defined by the social interactions that occur within it (Wilkinson, 1991). Communities based on social networks are constructed by 'relational reach' rather than by physical propinquity. Hence, the bounds of network-based community may be quite extensive compared with more conventional visions of small, compact, place-based communities.

Network-based communities are comprised of actions undertaken to solve local problems and needs. This is a labile structure which changes its social composition according to the share/ contribution of individuals and groups within a given network or cooperation framework. A given person or entity is a component of a local community only when he/she/it participates in the interacting network during a given time. Viewed in such a perspective, the locality depends on the degree to which defined activities engage local symbols, structures, inhabitants or financial resources, and also on the degree to which the local population is engaged in collective action. Examples of local activities and endogenous social relationships would be the various initiatives undertaken at the grassroots level, as well as by distant structures stimulating activities of the local population (Duncan, 2001; Westlund & Kobayashi, 2013). Neighbourhoods, recognised in terms of personal communities, also belong to this category (Wellman, 1999).

Unlike traditional communities in which a small number of residents undertook activities, modern networks can be large and specialised. As Wellman (1999, p. 24) puts it, 'people must maintain differentiated portfolios of ties to obtain a variety of resources. They can no longer assume that any or all of their network members will help them, no matter what the problem'.

In developed countries (Canada, Japan and the USA) these social networks exceed the borders of neighbourhoods and administrative units. Via advanced technical means of communication and transportation, social associations are becoming spatially more scattered in these countries. On the other hand, in developing countries like Chile (Espinoza, 1999) or in middle-income countries like Poland (Gorlach & Starosta, 2001), the role of proximate spatial neighbouring and locality as a nexus for rural networks of social relationships is still high.

The 'community field' which integrates the community's issue-specific domains (Wilkinson, 1991) is being replaced by private organisations in today's neoliberal society. Some critics worry that this is placing individual interest over collective well-being (Selznick, 1992; Etzioni, 1996). Private networks of relationships are, increasingly, replacing the public sphere of social life, carrying out 'public activities' in a private mode (privatised education, health care, etc.). Research conducted on Hungarian agricultural co-ops (Sik & Wellman, 1999) confirms this trend. The authors emphasised the significance of companies functioning in a system of common exchanges and transactions between leaders of individual enterprises. According to this research, the most frequent providers of transactions were members of local authorities, representatives of local businesses, as well as of educational institutions, while the most frequent recipients were representatives of local agricultural and non-agricultural business. These kinds of mutual connections and relations, which are becoming a common structural and formative phenomenon in the postmodern era, are also subject to severe criticism, both for their manifestation of an 'immoral familism' (e.g., exceedingly closed networks, clientelism, etc.), and for their denial of an enlightened and civically engaged pattern of citizenship.

The institutional dimension

The third approach to the reconstruction of the modern rural community is an institutional one. Inhabitants of a given place are seen as 'clients', satisfying their needs through the purchase and sale of products and services from local institutions (O'Brien, Wegren & Patsiorkovsky, 2005). Institutions such as shopping centres, churches and culture centres located in a given locality are spots of temporary social contacts, and hubs of interactions connected to common interests, consumer needs and the acquisition of public goods. However, as discussed above, privatisation of institutional spheres can lead to social exclusion and further underdevelopment of peripheral areas. At the same time, institutions not formally under the control of local government, such as associations, foundations and specially tailored and limited companies, are becoming more meaningful entities in the system governing the distribution of public goods at the local level.

Contemporary rural localities are often extremely dynamic. In some ways they can be thought of as 'potential' communities, the functioning of which is related to mobilisation in response to a perceived social problem, need (or opportunity). Many of these perceived problems are associated with inadequate provision of services and incapable public management in diverse functional realms including economic development, public safety and environmental management. Since these structures emerge in response to particular needs or opportunities, they are not fixed in time, nor do they present a stabilised system of social roles.

Due to the increasing process of social differentiation as well as the progression of the privatisation of social life, rural local communities are becoming 'limited liability structures'. They are not structures within which the inhabitants' needs can be fully satisfied; they offer only limited degrees of fulfilment of such needs. Guarantees of safety are limited to given spheres of social life, and to a large extent health and security is a matter of individual choice. Nevertheless, data from the European Social Survey (ESS) show that in European countries the percentage of persons who declare that they feel secure is 10 to 14% higher in rural areas than among city inhabitants. These figures have remained constant over time, and have not changed during the first decade of the 21st century.

Farming families in the context of changing rural communities

In the following section, we consider how the macro-structural trends and adaptations at the rural community level discussed above have affected farming families in the global north. Hence, we examine the periphery of the post-industrial economy (farming), in peripheral spatial space (rural communities). While this may not be the primary vantage point for exploring social change in contemporary society, it provides an important window on how social change affects people and communities in contemporary society. As Lobao (1996) has observed, the sociology of the periphery is *not* peripheral sociology. In other words, we believe this vantage point – family farming – reveals how important aspects of macro-structural changes in the organisation of rural society are experienced in communities where people live and work.

Modernisation processes in the global north

The starting point of the European modernisation process was, on the one hand, peasant farms (Central and Eastern Europe), and on the other, family farms (Western Europe and North America). As a result of the economic development processes both of these types of farms have lost their family character and have been converted into farms operating in a manner characteristic of industrial companies. This standardisation of production, as one of the manifestations of industrial agriculture, is also associated with the specialisation of production. The other process connected with the industrialisation of agriculture is the emergence of the industrial culture or mentality in the farming/farmers' social environment. The attitude towards farmers and towards becoming a farmer is changing, along with changes in the attitude towards farm work itself. Farming no longer tends be treated as a way of life, but has become a profession and a business venture. The goal is not to maintain the farm at any cost, but to make a profit at any cost. The farm is no longer a separate universe in which the whole life of the farmer and his family takes place, but has become a company, a tool of expansion, with a focus on increasing and intensifying production. This brings with it an increased inclination to openness and risk, which are personality traits associated with 'modernity'. This affects the tendency to introduce technical and managerial innovations, but also to take out loans to finance the rising costs of industrial-scale agricultural production (van der Ploeg, 2013).

The agricultural transformations described above are the result of the 'technological treadmill'. This mechanism is based primarily on a well-known process referred to as 'adaptation of innovation' (Mooney & Tanaka, 2015). The key to its understanding is grasping the relationship between the inputs and outputs of the production process. When we introduce a new, more expensive, more complicated type of production technology, at the same time we should be aware that its effects are organisational as well as economic. The emphasis on efficiency over other values is contingent on an increase in the scale of the economic enterprise that is the farm (in accordance with the principle of economy of scale) and transformed relationships between the farm and other aspects of both rural and urban economy and society. The essence of the technological treadmill mechanism is stiff economic competition in a market over which no single farmer is able to exercise control, and which leads to a continuous absorption of innovation, replacing human labour with technology in order to maintain agricultural production and enterprise profitability.

The assumption of the universality of the technological treadmill has become the basis for the construction of universal models of agricultural development. An important element of all these changes is the process of 'commoditisation of agriculture', which has acquired particular momentum in the post-modernisation era. Nearly all farms begin to allocate most of their production to the market, thus changing the character of their social organisation. Gradually, they lose their family character, increasingly becoming typical companies which expand labour force employment. There are fewer and fewer farming households, while the average land area and production level of individual farms is steadily increasing. As part of the process of modernisation and post-modernisation, farms increasingly lose their social and economic autonomy. Their fate is ever more linked not only to the skills of their workers, but also to the condition of the companies supplying capital, the means of production, and the consumers of products who are mostly located at a distance. In other words, farms have become increasingly integrated within a 'farming system' that extends far in both directions, from agricultural research through marketing to consumers.

Regardless of the neoliberal discourse, most contemporary industrial-scale farms do not operate in a free market. Rather, they are increasingly dependent on state policy which stimulates increases in food purchases (consumption) by the society; provides foreign markets for agricultural goods by subsidising exports; and defends the domestic market from foreign competition through a system of tariffs, customs, import quotas and the like. The processes of modernisation and post-modernisation of agriculture are an expression of the fundamental transformation processes taking place in capitalist society. At the same time, these fundamental economic changes bring about transformation of rural communities (Almas & Campbell, 2012). As a result, one can distinguish three different types of farm and food supply systems, which may be referred to as 'competitive productivism', 'market productivism' and 'neo-productivism'. The first two form the basic elements of the 'super-productivism' system, in which the emphasis is on the profit resulting from the intensification and concentration of agricultural production – for example, with agribusiness operating on a global scale. However, this economic environment has not completely depleted opportunities for smaller, more localised agriculture. The third form of farm and food supply system, 'neo-productivism', utilises elements of multifunctional and sustainable rural development to adapt to macroeconomic transformations in the agricultural economy.

Family farms and their transformations have been the object of numerous social science studies (Gorlach, 2004). Intensification of this discussion is associated with the 1990s, which was the period when the visible effects of the 'neoliberal' project had already appeared. Among the American concepts, the idea of *simple good production* can be distinguished as well as the idea of *working time and production time*. Moreover, the dialectical approach to a family farm and the concept of a family farm in a system of contradictory class positions seems to be considered. In all of these concepts attention is paid to those factors that, within the family form of production, constitute specific areas of resistance to the ongoing expansion of the industrial-market capitalist economy. In the thinking of researchers from continental Europe, the tradition of peasant agriculture comes to the fore, according to which farms operate in a way subordinate to the cycle of development and transformations of the operating family (van der Ploeg, 2013). This resistance to the neoliberal agricultural system affects and is effected by organisational changes in the rural communities where family farming is located.

Three concepts of family farm in the global north

The question of the relationship between the family and the farm is an essential element of diversified perspectives on agriculture in Europe and elsewhere in the global north. These arrangements can be classified into three concepts: (a) economic microorganism; (b) dynamic farm–farm family interaction; and (c) a model which incorporates the 'family character' of farms. 'Economic microorganism' representatives are primarily Scandinavian researchers, who indicate that the family farm is a production unit which does not have its own capital, and is not capable of capital accumulation. It is, in fact, a household entirely dependent on external capital (Djurfeld, Aryeetey & Isinika, 2010).

The second concept is referred to as 'a model of dynamic interaction' between the family and its farm. French researchers primarily emphasise the role of other family members (other than the person who is normally fully focused on the farm) who, through diverse off-farm activity, networking and creating farm partnerships, facilitate the process of embedding the farm into the local economic and social environment. The same line of thinking is characteristic of German and Dutch sociologists, preferring to search for additional sources of income which support the functioning of the farm in accordance with a substantial type of rationality. The third concept of the family farm in the capitalist system has been suggested by the British and American scholars, which may be reflective of the English and American experience, where the elimination of peasantry took place much earlier than in continental Europe. Therefore, the discussion of issues relating to family farms in Britain is comparable to the discussion in the United States, where the tradition of peasantry does not play an important role. For British researchers (Gasson & Errington, 1993), the family character of rural farms subjected to the processes of modernisation is best reflected as a continuum, the extreme poles of which are the traditional peasant farm and the modern industrial enterprise. Therefore, in order to grasp the nature of the farms studied, Gasson and Errington construct an ideal type of family farm, where: (a) the farmer is at the same time its sole owner; (b) persons who play an important role in farm management are bonded with the farmer by ties of kinship and affinity (i.e., family ties); (c) all of the above-mentioned persons ensure the supply of capital which is used on the farm; (d) all of the above-mentioned persons constitute the workforce used on the farm; (e) ownership rights referring to the farm and related resources of all kinds are transmitted within the family through intergenerational transfer; and (f) the family lives on the farm (1993, p. 18).

By thus constructing a model which incorporates the 'family character' of farms, we are able to point out various types of farms which are exceptions to the above three patterns. At the same time, these deviations can be treated as evidence, in one way or another, of the advancement of development processes. It is thus possible to imagine an ideal type of institution typical of a modern industrial society – that is, a farm whose owner/user is only its manager; the people working with him are unrelated to him by any ties of kinship or affinity; the supply of capital is based on external sources; the workforce is typically hired; the farm may be transferred to a new owner according to market rules; and finally, the farm managers and workers do not live on the premises. This analytical framework might be used to evaluate the direction of rural social organisation change at the family level as well as the scope of family farm phenomena in recent North American and European reality. While this type of enterprise still forms the majority of productive organisational units in the northern hemisphere, they only produce a minority of food and fibre. In the United States, farms selling products for less than US$50,000 still account for more than 75% of the whole farming community (see, for example, Mooney & Tanaka, 2015, p. 47). In the European Union in 2010, family farms accounted for 97% of all productive units (11,653,960 of 12,014,760; Poczta, Szuba-Barańska, Beba & Czubak, 2015, p. 67). Using some other measures (concerning, for example, the amount of work performed by family members), roughly 30% of farms might be treated as family enterprises. However, such a number differs significantly between countries, from 97.5% in Belgium to —% in Slovakia (Poczta, Szuba-Barańska, Beba & Czubak, 2015, pp. 70–71).

The question arises whether the transition to the post-modern era in family farming is based on the same mechanisms across nation states. We believe it is, consistent with the theory of post-modernisation developed by Pakulski (2009). This process involves the intensification and deepening of the processes involved in the modernisation of farms, and comprises four main dimensions: (a) hyper-rationalisation, indicating the spread of economic calculations and reflective thinking to all spheres of social life and the emergence of the so-called expert cultures; (b) hyper-commodification, involving the recognition of all products as goods, including (going beyond the traditional market economy) intellectual property rights, market valuation of cultural goods, etc.; (c) hyper-differentiation, indicating the progressive fragmentation and multi-path operation of both community and social processes, manifested in specialisations and lifestyles forming specific hybrids such as super-disciplinary science, syncretic lifestyles, or multi-media, etc.; and (d) hyper-individualisation, indicating on the one hand the increasing autonomy of the individual, and on the other the need for conscious construction of their own biographies at every stage of life.

The processes described above are also reflected in changes in the character of family farms and the families working them. In the 'Green Ring' project, Granberg, Kovach and Tovey (2001) analysed these changes in Scandinavia, Ireland, the Mediterranean and East–Central Europe. In the last group of countries, particular attention was paid to the roles of tradition and culture as essential post-modernisation factors. As far as the Scandinavian societies and Ireland were concerned, the importance of state institutions and non-governmental organisations was primarily emphasised. In this environment, farmers' actions, taken in different institutional contexts, play an important role, for example, as spontaneous actions blocking state policy or attempts to actively achieve planned objectives (Foryś & Gorlach, 2015). It turns out, however, that such actions have a more general character. They can be observed not only in the highly developed countries in Europe, but also in, for example, Latin America. In all of these cases there emerges a fundamental trend in responses based on ecological, social and cultural capital principles. In the first case, the response to global industrialisation is expressed in the form of organic farming; in the second instance it involves the strengthening of ties between the farming operation and the rural community, creating cooperatives and other local institutions, and in the third instance it involves local food production (van der Ploeg, 2008, pp. 278–282).

Rural communities and farming families

Farming remains a critical part of the functioning of rural communities in the contemporary globalised world. On the one hand, the specialisation of farming as well as the increase of the average area of farms and the decline of the number of farms would seem to result in the elimination of rural communities in the global north. Specialisation of farming and other tendencies mentioned above would seem to contribute to the creation of farm networks that are only loosely tied to the meso–rural communities. As Goldschmidt (1947) stressed, the rapid modernisation in farming results in the disappearance of rural communities. However, in more recent literature the role of rural community as a context of the modernised farm has been reconceptualised. Terry Marsden (2003), among others, has argued that a post-productivist dynamic is emerging in some rural areas. Such a dynamic contains at least three main tendencies: (a) a change of farms and farming families from sectoral agricultural corporatism to farms and farming families as elements of agro-food networks; (b) changes in local sociopolitical organisations involving a reconstitution of the sectoral and regional state; and (c) some changes leading to reintegrating of agriculture into the rural economy. As Marsden (2003, p. 139) stresses, 'agricultural production interrelates and integrates with other types of development process which becomes important in conditioning rural development more generally'.

Such a perspective has also been framed as a road towards sustainable rural development (Marsden, 2003, 2006). Close connections between farming families and rural communities have been conceptualised as one of the most important conditions for the processes of agro-ecological and ecological modernisations overcoming the crisis of modernity. Some important elements of this frame involve local farmers' knowledge systems, endogenous potential, collective forms of social action, systemic strategies, ecological and cultural diversities as well as sustainable societies (see Marsden, 2006, pp. 205–207).

This new union between farming and the rural community – if we may use the phrase 'union' – seems to be both the precondition as well as one of the most important characteristics of rural sustainable development addressed earlier by Marsden. Moreover, it also requires a new mechanism of using resources, the formulation of developmental goals and ideas as well as their implementation. Such a mechanism has been called 'neo-endogenous development' (see, for example, Ray, 2006). According to the author, such a mechanism has to be based on important theoretical principles. Ray points out in this context the idea of social economy and the necessary need for economic coordination. As he says, 'the mix of economic integration/social organisation triad occurs along the three interconnecting planes: intra-territorial, vertical politico-administrative and inter-territorial (inter-local)' (Ray, 2006, p. 281). In this perspective, he especially stresses the role of change from sectors to territories in both production and social activity resulting in the development of partnerships and – as he calls it – local decision-making bodies. Therefore what has been lost, according to Goldschmidt, appears to be regained through neo-endogenous development. The rural community seems to have recovered with strong connections with other partners, including farms and farming families as well as cooperative credit unions, extension services, schools, health clinics and also some other extra-local actors.

Relations between communities and family farms can also be considered in a more specific way in terms of social capital and smaller and less intensive businesses. The infrastructure built in the context of neo-endogenous developmental processes seems to be a vital point in the processes of building social capital used by local farms as well as other social institutions forming partnerships. Communities can provide human and institutional resources that enhance the performance of family farms. In turn, family farms can improve community standards of living by providing tax contributions to local budgets, being parts of partnerships as well as the base of various social activities in local development processes. However, to achieve this interdependency it is necessary to develop not only the so-called network component of social capital but also a normative one expressed by social rules – for example, trust and reciprocity – forming the context of developmental processes (Markenson & Deller, 2015). This particular aspect has been stressed by Lyson (2006) in his examination of changing rural communities facing an impact of global capital. He introduces the concept of civic community based on several factors in opposition to processes of modernisation and corporatisation. Such a community has been based on several characteristics, namely, sustainability and re(localisation) development model concerned with economic and social equity, emphasis on household and community welfare, local craft production and consumption, smaller and locally controlled enterprises, democracy, civic engagement, associations, social movements and so on (Lyson, 2006, pp. 298–300). In this framework, a strong connection between local farms and local communities has been perceived as a precondition of food security in the contemporary globalised and risky world (see Mooney & Hunt, 2009). The authors argue that strengthening social bonds and relations among various local actors, including farming families, local authorities, local food processors and so on might result in better protection of local consumers seeking healthy foods. At the same time, these forms of social relationships strengthen rural community.

Conclusions

At the community level, the increasing process of globalisation and devolution within nation states leads to many changes in the structure and functioning of rural local societies. Owing to the rapid development of mass communication, localness has become a global phenomenon which may be experienced by the transmission of local events in the global communication network. Rural community social structure, hence, is undergoing a fundamental transformation. The increase in heterogeneity among communities spans the gamut from those inhabited by the landless rural proletariat to other areas inhabited by higher/privileged social classes who have migrated from the city to the countryside and have isolated themselves from the local community, including farming.

Rural societies are also coming to consist of ever more 'limited liability communities', that provide benefits and security only in selected areas of the social life of the residents, but leave them excluded in others. The internal social integration processes are undergoing an evolution away from the previously dominant task-oriented structures, connected with meeting the real social needs of the inhabitants, towards the establishment of symbolic connections, appealing to the historical memory and level of consciousness of the local inhabitants. In addition, many rural communities in the global north have taken on non-agricultural and other non-productivist roles. Many serve as residential commuter sheds providing labour to nearby (and not so nearby) urban labour markets, while others have been transformed into sites of amenity-based recreation and leisure. At the same time, agriculture has not disappeared from the rural economy. Rather it has become bifurcated into multiple forms. The dominant form concentrates production into large industrial units that employ few persons and have few if any links with local society. In contrast, a family and community-oriented form also persists in many nations of the global north, where production is directly marketed to consumers through farmers' markets, community-supported agriculture and other community-based mechanisms. These small and medium-sized farms are family businesses, which tend to be located at the rural–urban interface, are often organic or at least limit chemical inputs, and are motivated both by profit and civic engagement. These units appear to be increasingly sustainable as consumer preferences change and an increasing share of population is concentrated at the rural–urban interface. Hence, while the dominant transformation of agriculture and the rural economy is associated with globalisation and neoliberalism, and devolution within nations tends to undermine rural community viability, farmers and their families appear to be resisting this totalising process and figuring out strategies to persist as an economic and social form in the future.

Both components of the processes of social change – that is, rural communities and farming families – seem to show this particular pattern. The first one changes from a rather homogeneous community-type reality to a plurality of communities interacting at the same time with each other as well as with some other social actors (farming families, organisations, states and supra-national actors). In turn, farming families change from rather homogeneous-type families with all members involved in farming activities to multi-occupational families with some members having off-farm jobs. Such changing contexts form important frames for changing the nature and the reality of farming families and rural communities. As some empirical evidence from North America and Europe shows, such farm changes present a kind of contradictory image. On the one hand, they became the icons of modern enterprises playing in a market economy, while on the other, they still form a significant majority of agricultural productive units in the area of our interest.

Acknowledgement

The authors are very grateful to David L. Brown for his helpful and inspiring comments on earlier drafts of this chapter.

Notes

1 Place attachment is the emotional bond between person and place (Steadman, 2002).
2 This is more the case in some countries (e.g., the USA) than others (e.g., France).
3 Or, as environmental sociologists and cultural geographers would say, 'place identity' (Steadman, 2002; Lewicka, 2011).

References

Almas, R & Campbell, H (Eds). (2012). *Rethinking agricultural policy regimes. Food security, climate change and the future resilience of global agriculture.* Bingley, UK: Emerald Publishing.

Altman, I & Low, S (1992). *Place attachment.* New York: Plenum.

Bauman, Z (2001). *Community: Seeking safety in an insecure world.* Cambridge: Polity.

Beck, U (2001). Living your own life in a runaway world. In W Hutton & A Giddens (Eds), *On the edge* (pp. 164–174). London: Jonathan Cape.

Brown, DL & Schafft, KA (2011). *Rural people & communities.* Cambridge: Polity.

Castells, M (1998). *The power of identity.* Oxford: Blackwell.

Clarke, LL & Miller, MK (1990). The character and prospects of rural community health and medical care. In AE Luloff & LE Swanson (Eds), *American rural communities* (pp. 74–105). Boulder, CO: Westview.

Cohen, A (1985). *The symbolic construction of community.* London: Tavistock.

Delanty, G (2003). *Community.* London: Routledge.

Djurfeld, G, Aryeetey, E & Isinika, A (2010). *African smallholders: Food crops, markets and policy.* Wallingford: CABI.

Duncan, CM (2001). Social capital in America's poor rural communities. In S Saegert, JP Thompson & MK Warren (Eds), *Social capital and poor communities* (pp. 60–86). New York: Russell Sage Foundation.

Espinoza, V (1999). Social network among urban poor. Inequality and integration in American city. In B Wellman (Ed.), *Networks in the global village. Life in contemporary communities* (pp. 147–184). Boulder, CO: Westview.

Etzioni, A (1996). The responsive community: A communitarian perspective. *American Sociological Review* 61(1), 1–11.

European Network for Rural Development (2015). Rural development gateway, 2014–2020. European Commission. Available at http://enrd.ec.europa.eu/en/policy-in-action/cap-towards-2020/rdp-programming-2014-2020 (accessed 4 October 2015).

Foryś, G & Gorlach, K (2015). Defending interests. Polish farmer's protests under post-communism. In B Klandermans & C van Stralen (Eds), *Movements in times of democratic transition* (pp. 316–340). Philadelphia, PA: Temple University Press.

Gałęski, B (1972). *Rural sociology: Basic concepts.* Manchester: Manchester University Press.

Gasson, R & Errington, A (1993). *The family farm business.* Wallingford: CABI.

Giddens, A (1997). *The consequences of modernity.* Cambridge: Polity.

Goldschmidt, W (1947). *As you sow.* Glencoe, IL: Free Press.

Gorlach, K (2004). *Socjologia obszarów wiejskich. Problemy i perspektywy* [*Sociology of Rural Areas. Problems and Perspectives*]. Warsaw: Wydawnictwo Naukowe SCHOLAR.

Gorlach, K & Starosta, P (2001). De-peasantisation or Re-peasantisation? Changing rural structures in Poland after World War II. In L Granberg, I Kovach & H Tovey (Eds), *Europe's green ring* (pp. 41–65). Aldershot: Ashgate.

Granberg, L, Kovach, I & Tovey, H (Eds). (2001). *Europe's green ring.* Aldershot: Ashgate.

Lewicka, M (2011). Place attachment: How far have we come in the last 40 years? *Journal of Environmental Psychology* 31(3), 207–230.

Lobao, L (1996). A sociology of the periphery versus a peripheral sociology: A rural sociology and the dimension of space. *Rural Sociology* 61(1), 77–102.

Lyson, T (2006). Global capital and the transformation of rural communities. In P Cloke, T Marsden & P Mooney (Eds), *Handbook of rural studies* (pp. 292–303). Thousand Oaks, CA: Sage.

Markenson, B & Deller, SC (2015). Social capital, communities, and the firm. In J Halstead & SC Deller (Eds), *Social capital at the community level: An applied interdisciplinary perspective* (pp. 44–80). New York and London: Routledge.

Marsden, T (2003). *The condition of rural sustainability.* Assen: Van Gorcum.

Marsden, T (2006). The road towards sustainable rural development: Issues of theory, policy and practice in a European context. In P Cloke, T Marsden & P Mooney (Eds), *Handbook of rural studies* (pp. 201–212). Thousand Oaks, CA: Sage.

Mooney, PH & Hunt, SA (2009). Food security: The elaboration of contested claims to a consensus frame. *Rural Sociology* 74(4), 469–497.

Mooney, PH & Tanaka, K (2015). The family farm in the United States: Social relations, scale and region. *Wieś i Rolnictwo* 1(166), 45–58.

Murdoch, J (2006). Networking rurality: Emergent complexity in the countryside. In P Cloke, T Marsden & P Mooney (Eds), *Handbook of rural studies* (pp. 171–184). Thousand Oaks, CA: Sage.

Norris, P (2002). Global governance and cosmopolitan citizens. In D Held & A McGrew (Eds), *The global transformations reader. An introduction to the globalization debate* (pp. 287–297). Cambridge: Polity.

O'Brien, DJ, Wegren, SK & Patsiorkovsky, VV (2005). Marketization and community in post-Soviet Russian villages. *Rural Sociology* 70(2), 188–207.

Pakulski, J (2009). Postmodern social theory. In BS Turner (Ed.), *The New Blackwell companion to social theory* (pp. 251–280). Malden, MA: Blackwell.

Poczta, W, Szuba-Barańska, E, Beba, P & Czubak, W (2015). Family farms in the EU – Their structural and economic diversity and opportunities of growth. *Wieś i Rolnictwo* 1(166), 59–78.

Putnam, R (1993). *Making democracy work.* Princeton, NJ: Princeton University Press.

Ray, C (2006). Neo-endogenous rural development in the EU. In P Cloke, T Marsden & P Mooney (Eds), *Handbook of rural studies* (pp. 278–291). Thousand Oaks, CA: Sage.

Selznick, P (1992). *The moral commonwealth: Social theory and the promise of community.* Berkeley, CA: University of California Press.

Sharp, JS (2001). Locating the community field: A study of interorganizational network structure and capacity for community action. *Rural Sociology* 66(3), 403–424.

Sik, E & Wellman, B (1999). Network capital in capitalist, communist and postcommunist countries. In B Wellman (Ed.), *Networks in the global village: Life in contemporary communities* (pp. 225–253). Boulder, CO: Westview.

Statistics in focus (16/2013). EUROSTAT. Catalogue number:KS-SF-13-016-EN-N.

Steadman, R (2002). Toward a social psychology of place: Predicting behaviour from place-based cognitions, attitude, and identity. *Environment and Behaviour* 34(5), 405–425.

Tolbert, C, Irwin, M & Lyson, T (2002). Civic community in small town America: How civic welfare is influenced by local capitalism, and civic engagement. *Rural Sociology* 67(1), 90–113.

van der Ploeg, JD (2008). *The new peasantries: Struggles for autonomy and sustainability in an era of empire and globalization.* London: Earthscan.

van der Ploeg, JD (2013). *Peasants and the art of farming: A Chayanovian manifesto.* Halifax, NS: Fernwood Publishing.

Warner, M (2003). Competition, cooperation, and local governance. In DL Brown & L Swanson (Eds), *Challenges for rural America in the twenty-first century* (pp. 252–261). University Park, PA: Penn State Press.

Wellman, B (1999). The network community: An introduction. In B Wellman (Ed.), *Networks in the global village: Life in contemporary communities* (pp. 1–47). Boulder, CO: Westview.

Westlund, H & Kobayashi, K (Eds). (2013). *Social capital and rural development in the knowledge society.* Cheltenham: Edward Elgar.

Wilkinson, KP (1991). *The community in rural America.* New York: Greenwood Press.

44

Rural Communities and Responses to Climate Change

Joseph T. Campbell, Ajay S. Singh and Jeff Sharp

Introduction

Among climate scientists there is a consensus that we are experiencing the effects of global climate change which is in large part the direct result of human activity (International Panel on Climate Change [IPCC], 2014). Changes to temperatures and climate patterns around the globe are already threatening agricultural systems and coastal settlements, as evidenced by greater frequency of hot weather days, increased variation in precipitation, severe weather events and rising sea levels (IPCC, 2014).

Collins et al. (2011) use a 'press–pulse dynamic' framework to describe two different types of climate change processes that drive social and natural system change. Press processes 'alter the structure of a system in small increments' (Morton & Rudel, 2014, p. 175), through 'extensive, pervasive, and subtle change' (Collins et al., 2011, p. 352). Rising temperatures associated with climate change are an example of a press process. Pulse events, occurring as shocks or sudden events, are less predictable and may affect communities in very short periods of time. Climate change induced pulse events (e.g., floods, severe storms) present an immediate threat to both infrastructure (such as failure of levees, roads, bridges or sewer systems) and public health.

We approach this chapter assuming that human behaviours and the social outcomes of those behaviours can influence the scale or impact of press and pulse dynamics on rural communities. To help appreciate the options available to societies and communities (particularly rural communities) in response to climate change, some have sketched out at least three, non-mutually exclusive response options: seek to mitigate the drivers of climate change; adapt to the consequences of climate change; or do nothing (Thompson, 2010). Non-action might arise when international, national or regional actors opt out of mitigating the causes or facilitating adaptation to the effects of climate change. This option, however, may well result in great harm to human and natural systems with ecologically sensitive regions, especially those located in rural areas along coastal lands, mountainous systems and desert areas, being the locations most vulnerable to climate change events (Thompson, 2010).

The response option understood to most effectively address negative climate change events is the mitigation of the causes of climate change (National Research Council, 2010).

Through mitigation humans act proactively to reduce the frequency and magnitude of climate change impacts by limiting the volume of greenhouse gas emissions (GHGs). While mitigation may be the most effective means of reducing unwanted changes to the climate, select industries, private interests and public officials that profit significantly through the production of GHGs are resistant to change because of the potentially negative economic effects of a strong regulatory environment.

The inability of nation states or international bodies to reach a consensus on regulating GHGs is well documented and presents a significant impasse to climate change mitigation. To overcome these barriers, effective mitigation strategies may require significant social movement action by citizens, non-governmental organisations and key state actors to establish and enforce restrictions or reductions in GHGs by industries and consumers. The papal encyclical released by the Roman Catholic Church in summer 2015 is one example of a growing international countermovement against unconstrained fossil fuel consumption and GHG emissions, as well as a recognition of the threat of climate impacts on poor communities (Francis, 2015).

Rural communities may be in the unfortunate position of being especially vulnerable to both the press and pulse impacts of climate change, but mitigating the source of GHGs is largely beyond their control. Due to structural forces that exist beyond the local scale, rural communities are limited in their ability to affect climate change mitigation when operating in isolation (Molnar, 2010). To be effective in achieving mitigation, it might be necessary for rural communities and institutions to participate in broader resistance movements to seek reductions in GHG emissions.

However, another, more locally immediate response to climate change is seeking to adapt to and prepare for the potential adverse effects of climate change (e.g., improving levees, shifting agricultural practices). Through this scenario rural institutions and actors create both individual and collective-level decisions to adjust as well as possible to the direct consequences of climate change and build capacity to respond to future changes. An approach that simply seeks to adapt to the impacts of climate change concedes any rural community agency aimed at reducing the forces driving climate change. While not minimising or dismissing the potential influences of rural communities in shaping broader policy debates, in this chapter we primarily focus on community agency directed towards adaptation, seeking to synthesise prior literature on community-level adaptive capacity, and drawing upon a variety of rural sociological traditions, including the community capitals framework (Flora & Flora, 2013), to illustrate the factors that are critical to rural community adaptation in light of a changing climate.

There is some evidence to support the ability of social movements to meaningfully resist direct corporate influence over state actors (Bonnano & Constance, 2006). But, practically speaking, an argument can be made that even if GHG emissions are substantially reduced to levels pledged in 2010 at the United Nations' Framework Convention on Climate Change, the consequences of the existing climatic changes would persist and necessitate some response (see IPCC, 2014). So, while we focus on climate change adaptation and leave more elaborate discussions of the political and economic forces and resistance strategies to these forces to other, more expert scholars in this field, we do acknowledge the importance of rural places to be attentive to the historic economic inequalities and political forces that limit local-level adaptation and require local-level movements to mobilise and solicit higher level resources for improved adaptation capacity. Furthermore, it is increasingly important to understand not only the ways in which communities may respond, adapt and exhibit resiliencies, but also the ways in which certain communities – and especially those in rural areas – may be systematically and disproportionately more vulnerable to climate change events. This will be critically important to public policy if we take seriously the responsibility of ensuring that our most vulnerable people and places are not further thrust into disadvantage by climate change press and pulse events.

Rural communities, agency and institutions in the 21st century

Communities emerge through local, social interaction and the formation of common interests into associations and organisations (Wilkinson, 1991). Individuals are able to express their interests through these social institutions and relationships (Brown, 2002). These relationships cross beyond the boundaries of the local political unit and can significantly increase the access that rural communities have to national and global resources and information. The ability of communities to respond to events is enhanced when there is an external threat (Tilly, 1973), through internal conflicts (Luloff & Swanson, 1995), and when they have the social, political and economic capacity to do so (Flint & Luloff, 2005). In a similar vein, Flora, Sharp, Flora and Newton (1997) describe a community's ability to convert social capital into organisational forms for collective action as 'social entrepreneurial infrastructure'. The communities with the greatest ability to mobilise for collective action could be more likely to positively adapt local behaviours to reduce potential climate change suffering.

At the same time, conflict is inherent within interpersonal and group-level community interactions, and through the distribution of resources within social units (Flora & Flora, 2013). Social and political elites within communities have disproportionate access to, or influence over, decisions to allocate scarce resources due to historically embedded political, economic and social structures. The disparities that exist between residents affect a community's ability to adapt to exogenous shocks and to achieve long-term community development (Duncan, 1999). In the global north, local influence, decision making and the allocation of resources can be unevenly distributed along the lines of class, race and gender. In some instances, increasing extra local ties between rural communities and the globalised world can create greater financial and human capital mobility, while at times it can also reinforce pre-existing power dynamics and further social exclusion of historically marginalised groups (Flora & Flora, 2014).

Community-level adaptive capacity

A changing climate may motivate human communities to invest in measures that increase their adaptive capacity and reduce vulnerabilities to climate impacts (Smit & Wandel, 2006). Climate change adaptation can be described as adjusting to actual or expected changes to climate and associated disturbances (IPCC, 2007). Adjustments can occur by either moderating or avoiding a disturbance (e.g., increasing elevation of flood walls) or by increasing society's ability to respond to a disturbance by increasing resilience or exploiting beneficial opportunities due to climate change (e.g., diversifying cropping systems to prepare for a warmer, wetter climate) (IPCC, 2014). The rural community literature suggests that the ability of communities to adapt to socioeconomic 'shocks' is shaped by a community's social institutions and agency prior to, during and following the shock event(s). The emergency response and natural disaster literature reports similar findings as communities adapt to catastrophic events differently based upon their social and physical infrastructure.

Given variable geographic circumstances, rural communities across the world will differ in the climate change press and pulse dynamics that they experience (e.g., rate of change in temperature and precipitation), and these experiences will likely affect a community's ability to invest in adaptive behaviours. Press processes, such as rising temperatures evidenced over the last several decades, may allow communities to wait for disturbances (i.e., pulse events) to occur and not require major investment in or restructuring of existing natural, social, political, cultural or economic conditions. Press events may also allow for communities to experiment with different adaptive strategies, collaboratively learn from other communities, and make adjustments slowly thus reducing social, political and economic conflict. Pulse events (e.g., a hurricane), however, may require communities to mobilise resources and restructure how they address disturbances in order to protect life and property in the immediate term. Pulse events may motivate communities to either prepare for future events by reducing vulnerabilities, or invest in emergency response to catastrophic disturbances.

The literature recognises that a community's ability to react to or anticipate shocks will be conditioned by its ability to access and mobilise resources and relationships (Besser, Recker & Agnitsch, 2008). However, tracking and evaluating community response to these processes is problematic given that climate change involves multiple, often unpredictable circumstances occurring over time and with great variance depending upon geographic and locational context. Despite these inherent complications, it is critical to analyse community-level response because of the inability of national and international power actors to reach consensus on mitigation, forcing local communities to act or suffer the consequences of others' inaction (Molnar, 2010).

Urban areas in the global north are generally better suited to protecting themselves from climate hazards due to higher individual and neighbourhood assets (i.e., income, education, housing stock and municipal resources) and scale; however, urban areas can face greater complexities of management due to overlapping jurisdictions and population densities (IPCC, 2014). Low population density can impede a rural community's ability to mobilise resources for infrastructural development and to access resources for development such as education, health care, cultural activities and employment (Green & Zinda, 2013). Rural communities are often closely linked to industries that may be affected by changes in climate (i.e., agriculture, timber, fishing, natural amenities and recreation) and are potentially more vulnerable than urban areas due to this dependency and lack of economic and social resources to address weather-related disasters (Morton & Rudel, 2014). In addition, Homsy and Warner (2015) find that larger cities with greater numbers of municipal staff and an educated populace are likely to adopt a greater number of sustainability policies.

The spatial disparities of rural communities in the global north will likely produce dramatically different climate change adaptation capacities depending on a community's geographic isolation, ability to provide certain public services, vulnerability to weather-related events, and reliance upon the agricultural and some natural resource extraction sectors (e.g., forestry) (IPCC, 2014). In addition, these spatial characteristics exist within evolving governance structures due to effects of globalisation and the spread of neoliberal development policies, which includes favouritism for majority-owned foreign companies, shifting the nature of exports, and an increasing demand for immigrant workers (Lobao, 2014). This shift is underpinned by assumptions that traditional state structures are inadequate or, to some neoliberal advocates, directly interfere with economic and societal growth. Through state fiscal crises and expanded neoliberal ideologies, traditional political systems are forced to become more engaged with the private sector and civil society to continue to govern and provide basic social services. This process has opened up opportunities for networks of state and non-state actors, mobilised through shared rural governing projects, to emerge at the local level (Cheshire, Higgins & Lawrence, 2007). These local governing regimes differ from community to community. Last, there is spatial differentiation across communities in how residents interpret climatic changes both as individuals and as groups (Morton & Rudel, 2014).

Community capitals framework

How communities will react to climate change press and pulse dynamics – and a method for assessing at which point they are prepared for climate impacts – is still unknown. However, there is the potential for rural communities to differ greatly in their adaptation to climate change. These differences at the local level stem from differentiation in: (a) their experienced climatic changes through press and pulse dynamics; (b) governance systems; and (c) social and individual interaction and interpretation of these processes. A comprehensive framework is needed to encompass the broad range of factors that affect rural communities' adaptive capacity and to gauge this anticipated differentiation.

According to Molnar (2010) there are no clear measures of adaptive capacity at the community, regional, national or international level at present, so one must determine the relevance of an adaptive capacity research framework based upon the scale of analysis, the sectors under consideration and data availability. We propose that, given these barriers, a community-level framework for adaptive capacity is possible by assessing political, economic, environmental and social variables at the community level. While limited, one starting point is to assume that every community is endowed with a certain set of resources. The realisation of those resources can take the form of 'capitals' – that is, the stock (or wealth) of one resource that is invested to create greater wealth in that or another form of resource (Flora & Flora, 2013). The community capitals framework categorises these resources into material or 'foundational' (i.e., physical/built, natural and financial) and human or 'mobilising' (i.e., social, human, cultural and political) forms (Jacobs, 2011). Theoretically, the proper endowment, allocation, access and usage of these resources across the community increases the ability of residents to lead sustainable, healthy and safe lives (Flora & Flora, 2014).

Flora and Flora (2014, p. 160) recognise that 'these capitals are heuristic devices that allow identification of the entire range of community assets, which, when invested to create new resources, become capital'. The definitions of capital adopted here refer both to the stock of a particular asset and to the ability of members of the community to access and mobilise them to improve other community capitals. The loss, degradation or depletion of one capital may influence the quality or quantity of another capital, compromising the sustainability, livelihood, health and well-being of communities dependent on those capitals (Emery & Flora, 2006). Investment in one or more capital will allow for communities to address shocks that threaten or endanger levels of capital (Gutierrez-Montes, Emery & Fernandez-Baca, 2009).

Drawing on the community capitals framework allows researchers to measure how communities will mobilise accessible resources to prepare for expected climate impacts and enhance resilience by increasing levels of one or more capital to be accessible if catastrophic transformations occur. Looking at the community-level distribution of capitals during and/or following press or pulse events is one tool among many to assess a community's adaptive capacity to adjust to climate change.

A definition of each of the community capitals is derived from Jacobs (2011):

- *Social capital* can be broadly conceptualised as the networks within and outside of the community, which can take the forms of bonding, bridging and linking social capital between individuals and groups of individuals. Social capital can be measured in the form of the trust and relationships between individuals, voluntary associations and professional organisations. In response to climate change press and pulse events, social capital can be a key variable in mobilising human, financial and natural capitals to organise collective actions in response to environmental change.
- *Political capital* concerns the connections between community residents and the local governing structures, including citizen access to decision making. Within the capitals framework, political capital allows for the examination of power and the access that citizens have to the decision-making process determining how local resources are distributed within

a community. There are several ways that political capital can contribute to community adaptation to climate change press and pulse events. Some adaptive behaviours may require political authorisation or policy solutions in order to be effective. The ability for the community to engage in positive adaptation behaviour, while having ties to the resources and other capacities of higher levels of government, will be critical to navigating through press and pulse events. Governing bodies need to create consensus and have the trust of local constituents to positively adjust to climate change. However, these efforts may be difficult in communities with long histories of structural inequality and unequal access to decision making and distribution of resources. Understanding the relationship between political capital within a community and adaptive capacity to climate change may help to design adaptation behaviours and policies that consequently decrease inequality and lack of access to decision making and resources.

- *Human capital* is the set of skills (e.g., education) and personality characteristics (e.g., leadership) that allow individuals to access resources. Human capital is observed at the individual-level unit of analysis and frequently aggregated to social groups and communities (Flora & Flora, 2013). Human capital will help individuals and communities adapt to change by providing people with the means to create and implement solutions that address both immediate and long-term risks associated with climate change. Human capital also develops economic diversity, which can increase financial capital and mobilise resources towards infrastructural upgrades and improvements in community resilience to climate change press and pulse events.

- *Cultural capital* refers to the symbols, languages, ethnicities and activities (e.g., festivals) that represent residents' symbolic identity. Some communities will possess cultural assets that provide systems for organising collective action prior to, during and following press and pulse events (Stofferahn, 2012). As the natural environment shifts, it will be important for communities to modify their identities and patterns of behaviour (e.g., consumption models) towards better alignment with climate press and pulse events and through the socialisation process (i.e., the transmission of values from one generation to the next). Climate change effects will likely require the coordination of large groups of people through emergency responses and migration patterns.

- *Physical capital* (also referred to as built capital) is the community's basic infrastructure such as buildings, roads, and water and sewer systems. A community's quality and quantity of physical infrastructure will vary, as will its ability to accommodate changes brought about through shifting press and pulse dynamics. As the local environment is affected through press and pulse processes, local infrastructure should be developed to adequately address risks associated with climatic changes and positively adapt to these changes. Constructing or upgrading physical capital (e.g., flood control) can assist communities in reducing the harm caused by climate change events.

- *Financial capital* is the money used for investment (rather than consumption) within the community (e.g., taxes, foundation grants, wealth transfers). Mitigation strategies at the national and international level include massive investments in renewable or other long-term energy solutions that reduce greenhouse gas emissions (GHG), as opposed to GHG-intensive options. It is important that rural communities mobilise social, cultural, political and human capital to pressure these national- and international-level institutions to provide funding for these investments at a local level. In terms of adaptive behaviour, rural communities should align their local financial capital with higher government resources to make physical capital decisions to best adapt to press and pulse dynamics. However, many rural communities that are expected to be most affected by significant climatic swings are likely going to have the least ability to access and mobilise financial capital.

- *Natural capital* is the quality and quantity of environmental characteristics, such as biological, air, land (e.g., soils, minerals, nutrients) and water conditions and ecological processes. Natural capital will allow a community to reduce risks (e.g., mangroves buffering hurricane storm surges) as well as provide a community with natural resources that can increase community financial capital or help rebuild the community's physical capital. At the same time, some stocks of natural capital will be particularly vulnerable to depletion through climate change press and pulse events. For example, communities reliant upon cold-water fish species in lakes and rivers could be particularly vulnerable under warming temperatures.

In addition, the community capitals framework is based upon an understanding that large structural forces (e.g., global economic shifts, climate change) have significant influence on the health of rural communities, but local governments and civil society can play a limited role in stemming the negative consequences of larger structural forces, such as regulating local private markets and redistributing resources (Flora & Flora, 2014). Strong local institutions and the ability to mobilise social, human, cultural and political capitals are critical for rural community well-being in light of broader structural changes.

Community capitals and adaptive capacity

Several of the community capitals have individually been examined in relation to climate change, natural disaster and economic shocks. For instance, Besser, Recker and Agnitsch (2008) find that economic shocks can produce increased within-group (bonding) social capital. Safford (2009) found that bridging organisations that include voluntary input from the local business sector are important for moving community organisations through periods of economic crisis. Neighbourhoods with high levels of voter turnout and political gatherings (measures of social and political capital) more quickly rebounded from the devastating 1923 Tokyo earthquake (Aldrich, 2012). Aldrich (2012) found that social and political capital were stronger predictors of community-level recovery than levels of earthquake damage, population density, and human and financial capital factors.

Community access to financial resources, and the ability to mobilise them, constitute critical aspects of climate change adaptation. Homsy and Warner (2015) find that municipal revenue per capita among local governments is associated with a greater adoption of sustainability policies. Sustainability staff also contributed to the adoption of these policies in larger cities, but the role of citizen commissions helped make up for a lack of technical staff in smaller communities. There are several components of adaptation that have financial implications for communities, including requiring construction restrictions in disaster-prone areas, the construction of mitigation systems (e.g., levees along river systems) and the purchasing of insurance in the case of a pulse event (Randolph, 2004). Due to economies of scale, concentrations of poverty and diminished economic and political power, it is likely that many rural communities will possess lower individual and neighbourhood assets (i.e., income, education, housing stock and municipal resources) in comparison to urban areas.

Social capital can be limited in its ability to account for power and governance structures that selectively benefit some community members to the detriment of others. A framework that draws on social capital assumptions but discounts embedded power dynamics within social networks, as well as the historical context and potential long-term disparities in access to resources surrounding these linkages, can be highly problematic (Schafft & Brown, 2003). The inclusion of political capital assumes that relationships between civil society, local government and the private sector can be beneficial or exploitative if power is used to extract public goods for private purposes and benefit without adequate compensation or redistribution (Flora & Flora, 2013). The community's redistribution of resources is a critical aspect of the social and political capital nexus. For example, under certain local political apparatuses, such as the 'growth machine' (Logan & Molotch, 1987), local elites disproportionately prioritise the 'exchange' value of land (the sale and commercialisation of natural capital) through investments in physical and financial capital over the 'use' value of land (for non-commercial uses of natural capital). Local governance managed through this system could produce maladaptive behaviours (e.g., destruction of natural capital 'buffers' to climatic pulse events) if the available physical capital is not equipped to cope with climate change press and pulse processes.

Social capital at the neighbourhood level following pulse events can reduce broader regional redevelopment efforts. Aldrich and Crook (2008) found that communities in New Orleans with an active civil society (with higher rates of social capital and political capital) were more likely to deny the siting of trailer housing following Hurricane Katrina when affordable housing provision was considered a citywide priority endorsed and administered by a federal government agency. There is the potential that unwanted and unsightly aspects of the pulse event reconstruction process could be sited in areas with low social and political capital (Homsy & Warner, 2015).

In terms of improving adaptive capacity, Flint and Haynes (2006) found that rural communities in Alaska with high levels of community participation and involvement engaged in greater responsiveness and adaptations to manage massive tree mortality issues (caused, in part, by climate change through warmer summer temperatures) in coordination with public officials. In comparison, government officials and individuals were motivated to act outside of institutional structures to implement adaptation measures in communities with low political capital (lower participation and engagement). By working outside political and institutional structures, those communities were slower to adopt new management plans that may have allowed for broader community involvement. Trusted leadership can also contribute to adaptation, for instance Green and Haines's (2012) review of the Greensburg, Kansas tornado disaster recovery found that trusted and visionary community leadership was critical to positive adaption to the disaster.

Attention to political capital or the structures of governance that enhance or limit adaptive capacity are particularly salient in an era of neoliberalism due to the significant variability of how local communities interact with national and international governments and corporate interests (Cheshire, Higgins & Lawrence, 2007). While the power and mobility of financial capital and corporate interests are strong, their influence can be moderated by strong local political capital (Bonanno & Constance, 2006). Predictably, where the state recognises the threats of climate change, local political units can be more positively inclined to passing pro-adaptation policies. Homsy and Warner (2015) find large and small US municipalities are more likely to adopt pro-climate change adaptation policies when they are located in a state with renewable energy and greenhouse gas emission reduction standards (Homsy & Warner, 2015). Stofferahn's (2012) work demonstrates that one rural community in the USA was able to access some community capitals (i.e., social, cultural and human) to mobilise local political capital to receive the proper financial capital needed to recover from a massive tornado strike (i.e., depletion of some built and natural capital).

While climatic changes continue to unfold, and international and national institutions fail to develop comprehensive mitigation strategies, it is critical that rural communities assess their stock of human capital to determine how prepared their population is to respond to press and pulse dynamics and whether certain adaptation strategies are needed. With decades of population loss, and higher proportions of poverty and unemployment, it is expected that rural communities are likely to be comparatively less able, due to human capital shortcomings, to positively adjust to climate change impacts (IPCC, 2014). Reliance upon natural capital exports, coupled with limited economic diversity, makes rural communities more susceptible to global, macroeconomic changes (Lobao, 2014) accompanying climate change (IPCC, 2014).

Migration of residents during press and pulse processes will also influence community-level adaptive capacity. Fussell, Curtis and DeWaard (2014) found that in- and out-migration patterns from the city of New Orleans became more spatially concentrated to specific regional rural and non-regional urban communities. They found greater population in-flows to the city from surrounding rural parishes. At the same time, they identified very clear increased out-flows to urban communities located outside of the region. Migration patterns will be affected by climate change press and pulse dynamics. It will be important to examine how rural communities experience changes in their migration patterns, and how this in turn affects local human capital resources.

Also, some rural scholars express concern that rural individuals and communities, with lower incomes and less overall financial capital, will be burdened more greatly by GHG mitigation strategies, such as purchasing clean energy solutions (Morton & Rudel, 2014). Homsy and Warner (2015) find a rural lag in the adoption of sustainable municipal practices due to human and financial capital factors – mainly a lack of local government fiscal resources and the technical expertise available to adopt climate change mitigation policies.

Little research has explored the connection between cultural capital and climate change. Green and Haines (2012) argue that the forms of cultural capital that reside in community residents are not lost during a disaster or through climate change, unless large populations leave. However, adapting to climate change might require a shift in some socially constructed value systems, and some physical forms of cultural capital may be lost or threatened and might need to be rebuilt (e.g., art museum, cultural neighbourhood or concert hall built in a floodplain). Following a significant pulse event (a massive tornado) in North Dakota, and in the absence of immediate state- or federal-level intervention, cultural capital embedded in the community (i.e., internalised values of hard work, discipline and ethnic pride) allowed for the mobilisation of other capitals, such as social (e.g., post-disaster, clean-up volunteerism and social support) and physical capitals (e.g., through reconstruction of damaged buildings and community facilities) (Stofferahn, 2012). If communities are not able to retain their population and higher level units of government cannot mobilise the resources to recover to a pre-existing state following a pulse climatic event, then the stock of local knowledge and cultural capital, such as unique cultural identities, could be lost.

Of course physical and natural capitals are also critical to community adaptive capacity. During disaster events, physical capital (i.e., the infrastructure of community) is often given the most attention (Green & Haines, 2012). Rural geographic isolation may allow for access to natural capital, while it can also inhibit provision of public services, which can make it difficult to gain access to reinvestment in physical/built capital, therefore making recovery from pulse events more expensive (IPCC, 2014). Large metropolitan areas that are not spatially concentrated create added maintenance burden costs and can lead to incoherent policy measures across the region (Norris, 2001).

Much of the research on natural capital is based in ecological economics, which addresses the need to assess the value of natural capital and ecosystem services and measures the quantity of natural capital and community well-being (e.g., Costanza et al., 1998). Communities and institutions invest in natural capital by preserving, restoring or conserving those environmental characteristics. Investment in natural capital allows for communities to access this capital (or the ecosystem services derived from it) to maintain current conditions or facilitate changes leading to desirable community outcomes. Natural capital creates a foundation from which communities can build, develop and sustain human, social, physical and financial capital. The quality and quantity of natural capital will be necessary to address systemic shocks caused by either pulse or press shocks.

At its core, the relationship between climate change and society will occur with shocks to natural capital (and their ecosystem services), which may lead to degradation of natural capital and to decreases in financial, physical or social capital (Gutierrez, Emery & Fernandez-Baca, 2009). A fundamental question is whether communities that do not have sufficient quantity, quality or access to natural capital will be able to sustain levels of other capitals. For example, Morton and Rudel (2014) explain that climate change will require US farmers to adjust their routinised cropping systems due to changes in precipitation, heat, humidity and seasonality. These changes to cropping systems can either improve or further degrade their local stock of natural capital. Bailey and Majumdar (2014) show how absentee ownership of forest land in Alabama makes it difficult for local governments to gather and mobilise the financial resources necessary to respond to climate change. Currently there is insufficient evidence to show what levels of quality or quantity of natural capital – or level of access – is needed to determine whether the community has sufficient capacity to adjust to changing environmental conditions or whether other forms of capital can offset the degradation of natural capital.

Although there is a growing body of literature explaining how each capital allows for communities to address disturbances, there are challenges that impede using the community capitals framework to assess adaptive capacity. One challenge relates to the unit of analysis. Because this framework focuses on community and the qualities of that community, the external factors influencing levels, access and mobility of capitals could be ignored and overlook adaptive capacity arising from movement of capitals (such as financial) between communities or levels of governance.

Another challenge is the multidisciplinarity of the framework – sociologists focus on social capital, economists on financial, environmental scientists on natural capital, engineers on built capital, and so on. While disciplinary specialisation can provide systematic testing of certain variables, this single-track research approach can create an overemphasis on one capital in particular and does not allow for a better understanding of the relationships between capitals. The community capitals framework represents an institutional framework that presents an opportunity for multiple disciplines to work together across the sciences. This leads to a final challenge of note. There are problems in establishing consistent measurements of each capital, especially when multiple capitals are taken into account, due to the disciplinary, and often fragmented, nature of prior capitals research. This limits the ability to make generalisations and build theory using existing literature. However, existing literature creates a foundation for developing hypotheses and direction for new research.

Conclusion

Climate change is occurring and evidence of its effects on social and natural systems are documented globally (IPCC, 2014). International, national and regional leaders are presented with three, non-mutually exclusive options: mitigate the causes of climate change, adapt to the effects and symptoms of climate change, or do not take steps to address the causes or the effects of climate change. Given the current impasse on international and national levels to create mitigation strategies, it is imperative that rural sociologists identify what characteristics exist at a local level to enhance the ability of communities to adapt to climate change impacts, including soliciting resources from higher level institutions to make local-level changes.

The community capitals framework literature provides a rich body of research from which future rural community studies assessing adaptive capacity to address climate change can draw upon. Community-level climate change research should take into account the effect of both press and pulse processes on community well-being. Future research should draw upon longitudinal data over multiple time periods to help measure, and distinguish between, press and pulse processes on communities. Research that applies the capitals framework (or similar asset-oriented frameworks) should determine the existence, access to and mobilisation of capitals, extending beyond reporting pre-existing levels (or 'stocks') of each capital. In addition, longitudinal application of a capitals-oriented framework allows for identification of maladaptive conditions, such as low stocks of political capital impeding community-level mobilisation of natural or financial capitals.

In addition, community-level studies should take into account challenges of external influences on the community and measurement. Macroeconomic forces, such as the expansion of neoliberal governance regimes, have the ability to strongly influence adaptive capacity and resilience of rural communities as well. It is critical that community leaders, academics and policy makers are aware of what types of adaptive policies and programmes they can effect and implement at the local level in comparison to those issues that rest largely at higher political scales. Researchers should consider examining linking social capital between local governments, community organisations and citizens to higher levels of government and the distribution of political capital with multiple scales of government.

Meanwhile, sustainability metrics and indicators are at the cutting edge of many scientific fields. Our effort to build a framework that incorporates sustainability measures across seven thematic areas is a useful work in progress in this field. Rural sociologists, as leaders in developing community-level metrics at the rural/non-metropolitan scale, have a significant cross-disciplinary role to play in developing reliable measures. The community capitals framework provides a theoretical and empirical foundation that builds towards a common theory between the social sciences and the natural sciences. Additional work is necessary to create quantitative, reliable measures that can be applied at the rural and urban community scale, coupling these efforts with grounded, local case studies that can help to strengthen our understandings of community resilience and adaptation in the context of climate change challenges.

References

Aldrich, DP (2012). Social, not physical, infrastructure: The critical role of civil society after the 1923 Tokyo earthquake. *Disasters* 36(2), 398–419.

Aldrich, DP & Crook, K (2008). Strong civil society as a double-edged sword: Siting trailers in post-Katrina New Orleans. *Political Research Quarterly* 61(3), 379–389.

Bailey, C & Majumdar, M (2014). Absentee forest and farmland ownership in Alabama: Capturing benefits from natural capital controlled by non-residents. In J Pender, TG Johnson, B Weber & JM Fannin (Eds), *Rural wealth creation*. London: Routledge.

Besser, TL, Recker, N & Agnitsch, K (2008). The impact of economic shocks on quality of life and social capital in small towns. *Rural Sociology* 73(4), 580–604.

Bonanno, A & Constance, DH (2006). Corporations and the state in the global era: The case of seaboard farms and Texas. *Rural Sociology* 71(1), 59–84.

Brown, DL (2002). Migration and community: Social networks in a multilevel world. *Rural Sociology* 67(1), 1–23.

Cheshire, L, Higgins, V & Lawrence, G (2007). The complexity of state–citizen interactions. In L Cheshire, V Higgins & G Lawrence (Eds), *Rural governance: International perspectives* (pp. 291–303). London: Routledge.

Collins, SL, Carpenter, SR, Swinton, SM, Orenstein, DE, Childers, DL, Gragson, TL, Grimm, NB et al. (2011). An integrated conceptual framework for long-term social-ecological research. *Frontiers in Ecology and the Environment* 9(6), 351–357.

Costanza, R, d'Arge, R, De Groot, R, Farber, S, Grasso, M, Hannon, B & Van Den Belt, M (1998). The value of ecosystem services: Putting the issues in perspective. *Ecological Economics* 25(1), 67–72.

Duncan, CM (1999). *Worlds apart: Why poverty persists in rural America*. New Haven, CT: Yale University Press.

Emery, M & Flora, C (2006). Spiraling-up: Mapping community transformation with community capitals framework. *Community Development* 37(1), 19–35.

Flint, CG & Haynes, R (2006). Managing forest disturbances and community responses: Lessons from the Kenai Peninsula, Alaska. *Journal of Forestry* 104(5), 269–275.

Flint, CG & Luloff, AE (2005). Natural resource-based communities, risk, and disaster: An intersection of theories. *Society and Natural Resources* 18, 399–412.

Flora, CB & Flora, JL (2013). *Rural communities: Legacy and change* (4th edn). Boulder, CO: Westview.

Flora, CB & Flora, JL (2014). Community organization and mobilization in rural America. In C Bailey, L Jensen & E Ransom (Eds), *Rural America in a globalizing world: Problems and prospects for the 2010s* (pp. 609–625). Morgantown: West Virginia Press.

Flora, JL, Sharp, J, Flora, C & Newlon, B (1997). Entrepreneurial social infrastructure and locally initiated economic development in the nonmetropolitan United States. *The Sociological Quarterly* 38(4), 623–645.

Francis (2015). *Encyclical letter Laudato si' of the Holy Father Francis on care for our common home*. Vatican City: Libreria Editrice Vaticana.

Fussell, E, Curtis, K & DeWaard, J (2014). Recovery migration to the city of New Orleans after Hurricane Katrina: A migration systems approach. *Population and Environment* 35, 305–322.

Green, GP & Haines, A (2012). *Asset building and community development* (3rd edn). Thousand Oaks, CA: Sage.

Green, GP & Zinda, JA (2013). Rural development theory. In GP Green (Ed.), *Handbook of rural development* (pp. 3–20). Cheltenham: Edward Elgar Publishing.

Gutierrez-Montes, I, Emery, M & Fernandez-Baca, E (2009). The sustainable livelihoods approach and the community capitals framework: The importance of system-level approaches to community change efforts. *Community Development* 40(2), 106–113.

Homsy, GC & Warner, ME (2015). Cities and sustainability: Polycentric action and multilevel governance. *Urban Affairs Review* 51(1), 46–73.

IPCC (International Panel on Climate Change) (2007). Climate change 2007: Impacts, adaptation and vulnerability. Contribution of working group II to the fourth assessment report of the Intergovernmental Panel On Climate Change (IPCC).

IPCC (International Panel on Climate Change) (2014). Fifth Assessment Report: working group II impacts, adaptation, and vulnerability (IPCC).

Jacobs, C (2011). *Measuring success in communities: Understanding the community capitals framework*. Extension extra, ExEx 16005. Community capital series #1. South Dakota State University Cooperative Extension Service.

Lobao, L (2014). Economic change, structural forces, and rural America: Shifting fortunes across communities. In C Bailey, L Jensen & E Ransom (Eds), *Rural America in a globalizing world: Problems and prospects for the 2010s* (pp. 543–555). Morgantown: West Virginia Press.

Logan, JR & Molotch, HL (1987). *Urban fortunes: The political economy of place*. Berkeley, CA: University of California Press.

Luloff, AE & Swanson, LE (1995). Community agency and disaffection: Enhancing collective resources. In LJ Beaulieu & D Mulkey (Eds), *Investing in people: The human capital needs of rural America* (pp. 351–372). Boulder, CO: Westview.

Molnar, J (2010). Climate change and societal response: Livelihoods, communities, and the environment. *Rural Sociology* 75(1), 1–16.

Morton, LW & Rudel, T (2014). Impacts of climate change on people and communities of rural America. In C Bailey, L Jensen & E Ransom (Eds), *Rural America in a globalizing world: Problems and prospects for the 2010s* (pp. 543–555). Morgantown: West Virginia Press.

National Research Council (2010). *Limiting the magnitude of future climate change: Report in brief*. Washington, DC: National Academies Press.

Norris, DF (2001). Whither metropolitan governance? *Urban Affairs Review* 36(4), 532–550.

Randolph, J (2004). *Environmental land use planning and management.* Washington, DC: Island Press.

Safford, S (2009). *Why the garden club couldn't save Youngstown: The transformation of the Rust Belt.* Cambridge, MA: Harvard University Press.

Schafft, KA & Brown, DL (2003). Social capital, social networks, and social power. *Social Epistemology* 17(4), 329–342.

Smit, B & Wandel, J (2006). Adaptation, adaptive capacity and vulnerability. *Global Environmental Change* 16(3), 282–292.

Stofferahn, C (2012). Community capitals and disaster recovery: Northwood, ND recovers from an EF 4 tornado. *Community Development* 43(5), 581–598.

Tilly, C (1973). Do communities act? *Sociological Inquiry* 43(3–4), 209–238.

Thompson, L (2010). Climate change: The evidence and our options. *Behavioral Analysis* 33(2), 153–170.

Wilkinson, KP (1991). *The community in rural America.* Westport, CT: Greenwood Press.

45

Emerging Educational Subjectivities in the Global Periphery

New Worker Identities for New Times

Michael Corbett and Unn-Doris K. Bæck

Introduction

In the global north the idea of rurality takes on a particular inflection. Northern places, which are often considered to be rural and 'isolated', have often been marginalized in metrocentric discourses of development. Associated with these peripheral places are equally marginal backward, rough and uneducated identity stereotypes that have been well explored in the rural studies literature. But things are changing. In this chapter, focusing on the Canadian and Scandinavian contexts, we argue that contemporary resource development has complicated established discourses of modernity and that places outside the metropolis are increasingly central to national development agendas. We investigate how contemporary forms of resource production, and the identity structures that they facilitate, integrate into emerging national cultural imaginaries and educational policy narratives in and about northern and rural regions as either utopian or dystopian constructions. This in turn leads to discursive emphasis on retooling education systems in rural and remote areas. This reassertion and reconfiguration of the rural signals a need for a policy shift that recognises the centrality of modern rural regions to national development strategies. At the same time we interrogate the consequences of the entanglement of traditional primary industries such as fishing and farming with emerging associations with mining and oil and gas development.

In Canada and in Scandinavia the conflation of historic national identity with rural resource production are key metaphors in the cultural imaginary. Simultaneously, places outside the metropolis are increasingly central to national economic development strategy. This has led to new concerns about education in rural and remote regions aimed at creating new worker/subjects for emerging forms of technologically enhanced and increasingly globalised resource development requiring different knowledge and competencies. Drawing on research in Atlantic Canada and in Northern Norway, we interrogate the educational and identity consequences of current policy discourse to find that contemporary change forces a reimagining of the educated subject and a respatialising of the field in which s/he is imagined to work.

In 2011, the Canadian federal government announced that a major C$25+ billion contract for the construction of warships had been awarded to Halifax and the shipyards owned by the Irving family. The response was something akin to rejoicing in the streets and the CBC headlines on 19 October 2011 read: 'Jubilation as Halifax shipyard awarded contract' (CBC News, 2011). Premier Darrel Dexter gleefully intoned that this day would go down as one of the proudest in the history of the province and that thousands of people who had left Nova Scotia for work in western and central Canada could return home to stable employment. By early 2015 no steel was being cut, a brief real estate boom in Halifax had long fizzled out, and the Bank of Montreal (BMO) reported the province's continuing 'demographic drain', the weakest home sales in 16 years, decreasing labour force participation rates, and the continuing lure of high wages in other provinces (Bank of Montreal, 2014).

In Norway a similar story has to do with the emerging oil and gas industry in the northern part of the country – regarding how the global oil industry affects life in geographically remote areas. The northern part of Norway has traditionally had a peripheral position in relation to the national centre located in the south, and has been regarded as an outpost. Fisheries used to be the most important industry in the region, and structural changes in resource management as well as the cyclical nature of the availability of fish have led to recurring crises for small-scale fisheries (Jentoft, 1993). A population scattered across harsh and inhospitable landscapes, an industrial structure related to resource-based industries such as fishing and farming, and a lower educational level than the rest of the national population were all qualities that have served to give this part of the country status as somewhat inferior, backward and even primitive and underdeveloped. Against this backdrop, the petroleum industry created new optimism in Northern Norway.

In this chapter we focus primarily on how development, as described above, affects young people growing up in these regions, especially in relation to education. What happens when small, local communities are transformed into booming industrial sites or hubs for the oil and gas industry with global significance? One major impact in both Northern Norway and Nova Scotia is related to changes in the structure and dynamics of the labour markets.

Today, labour mobility in the context of mobile modernity (Forsey, 2015) results in what Corbett (2010) calls 'deployment' in and out of areas of capital expansion. This is now a multigenerational way of life in some peripheral regions. What is new in both Nova Scotia and in Northern Norway is the increasingly sharp call for a new kind of worker who is simultaneously mobile and stable, tough and educated. Apart from the hype of oil and ships, we are interested here in the kind of educated subject imagined for the emerging industrial machinery of contemporary development in rural and remote parts of the global north. Accompanying these development initiatives are new educational imaginaries that focus on STEM subject areas (science, technology, engineering and mathematics) and technical skills. At the same time, a parallel discourse that focuses on the need for appropriately educated labour that will remain in 'peripheral' areas has complicated contemporary educational discussions both in Canada and in Norway.

The population implosion and the chronic economic crisis

Most of the early reportage on the shipbuilding contract in Nova Scotia was rife with the emotionally laden idea that Nova Scotia's iconic migrant labour force would finally be able to return home to find good work in the province and not have to leave for Alberta, Ontario and British Columbia, as they have done for generations. Now the tone has shifted radically. A recent government-sponsored analysis of the province's economic prospects, apocalyptically entitled *Now or Never* (Government of Nova Scotia, 2014), opened with a description of a population ageing so rapidly that it will soon be unable to maintain basic services and infrastructure: 'Given low birth rates, we cannot grow the population unless the economy is generating more jobs to stem out-migration and attract immigrants. We cannot sustain economic growth over time unless renewed population growth provides more workers, more entrepreneurs and more consumers' (Government of Nova Scotia, 2014, p. 18).

Now or Never opens with the prediction of provincial population loss by the third decade of the 21st century. Today, the image of the population implosion is on the lips of virtually every politician. In Nova Scotia, only Halifax and the Annapolis Valley regions gained population between the census years of 2001 and 2011. In the most mobile cohort, those between the ages of 20 and 34 years of age, all regions other than Halifax lost population (Government of Nova Scotia, 2015).

In Norway similar tendencies can be found. Traditionally, Northern Norway had a limited labour market with a higher unemployment rate than the rest of the country. In the developmental phase of the petroleum and mining industries, but also after, the new industries generated increased employment, decreased unemployment, increased commuting into the region, and increased labour immigration in the north. This contributed to slowing down a negative depopulation trend and, in some places, even increasing the population (Aure, Abelsen & Nilsen, 2012). This development is, however, highly place specific. Overall, there was a 4.4% increase in the population 16–66 years of age in the northernmost county of Finnmark between 2001 and 2015. At the same time, only four out of the 19 municipalities in Finnmark showed a population increase during this period. One of these is Hammerfest, with a 17% increase for men and a 13% increase for women. This compares to a 33% decrease in one of the other coastal municipalities, Loppa. The population decrease is greatest amongst the younger generations due to low birth rates and high out-migration.

Both in Norway and in Atlantic Canada it seems as though all of the forces of modernity are arrayed in support of a great emptying of young people from most rural areas, new opportunities notwithstanding. There is the lure of high-wage work in the Alberta oil patch, or in the Snow White field in Hammerfest. For mobile, elite industrial workers, these opportunities are now global in scope. There are also the bright lights of Montreal and Oslo with the enticements of what Baeck (2004) calls the 'urban ethos'. There is also an established 'learning to leave' educational culture (Corbett, 2004, 2005, 2007) where many youth living in rural and remote places who experience success in the formal education system, leave their home places, often for good. Indeed, *Now or Never* identifies and connects a triangular population strategy that simultaneously addresses out-migration, immigration and low educational attainment as key focal points for social policy (Government of Nova Scotia, 2014, p. 6).

Changing opportunity structures: re-educating the new worker

Local labour markets constitute an important opportunity structure for young people in the sense that the possibilities they see at their places of residence will affect the choices they make for the future. Different places constitute different opportunity structures since they provide different conditions and barriers that directly and indirectly provide opportunities for individuals (Baeck, 2015). Local or regional labour markets constitute a structure within which the young evaluate their educational and occupational choices. There are, for example, other alternatives to school in areas with less knowledge-demanding labour markets than in areas where the majority of work places demand formal qualifications. It must also be said that established interests continue to benefit from informally educated labour, which is effectively trapped in local labour markets.

Actors' interpretations of the available opportunity structures are also affected by their own positions, the capital they possess, and also by input they receive from different sources. Discourses in the media, in school, in local communities, through national and regional policy and authority structures, and through the oil or the shipyard companies themselves, all 'tell stories' to the young. These stories in turn colour young people's perceptions of the opportunity structures and give direction to their actions.

An ageing population is a particular feature of regions peripheral to political economic power in contemporary Western societies. Today, many peripheral rural regions have more or less successfully transitioned from spaces of production to spaces of consumption (Woods, 2010; Brown & Schafft, 2011). In the post-productivist countryside, a different view of community emerges and it is one that focuses more on service industries, connections and relationships between near and distant places, and complex symbolic practices (Peters & Bulut, 2011). It is now well understood how spatial production now features consumption more than production (Bauman, 2000; Castells, 2009; Barrett, 2015) and productive work is increasingly mechanised and organised through information technologies. As young people leave 'declining' communities, the population has changed character. In the case of Nova Scotia, the population is not only older, but those parts of rural Nova Scotia which feature relatively accessible coastline, attract a wide variety of economically privileged in-migrants.

These regions have shed some of their singular attachments to particular productive activities like farming, fishing and logging; but still, these elements of rural communities and economies are never completely gone. Rather they become part of a rural economy that has other dimensions. The transformed primary resource and secondary industry labour market do require elements of industrial productivity of the kind imagined, for example, in the shipbuilding project that many Nova Scotians dream will lure back the industrial workforce that regularly makes the 'long commute' to the western oil fields. Whether this comes to pass is uncertain; the informally educated migrant labourer may not be the ideal modern worker imagined in contemporary policy discourse that has positioned formal education as an important mechanism of subject formation and cultural change. Not surprisingly, education policy documents in both countries are largely silent about culture and the arts but bullish regarding vocational education and STEM subjects.

The new opportunities for the young are emphasised, and in Norway new educational programmes, especially designed for (and sponsored by) the oil and gas industry, have been launched. Most of these seem quite specifically focused on the employment needs of the industry. The Norwegian government is also in sync with the oil and gas industry when they communicate to young people from the north about the importance of choosing educational and occupational paths that are right for the northern region. For example, the Norwegian minister of petroleum and energy has taken an active part in conveying this message in public statements, news articles and through partaking in education fairs for the promotion of the petroleum sector at schools, colleges and universities. The Norwegian Oil and Gas Association is deeply engaged in questions concerning competence and recruitment to the industry, emphasising that in the coming years there will be a special need for people (including women) with a science and technology education or a trade certificate.

The new worker of the future does not appear in the form of the informally educated, tough and robust, deployable northern worker who is by now a mythical character in Atlantic Canada and in rural Norway. He or she drives a top-of-the-line pickup truck purchased in the oil patch. He may live in Alberta or Saskatchewan or take part in the 'long commute', shuttling back and forth fortnightly or monthly for work stints (Walsh, 2012). Nearly 40,000 people, or about one-third of the population of Fort MacMurray Alberta (the principal site of oil sands production), is what is designated by the municipal census as 'non-permanent population' living mainly in project accommodations (Regional Municipality of Wood Buffalo, 2012).

Still, many northern workers continue to dismiss education, as did their forebears who worked on farms, in factories, on fishing boats and in the mines. They have been a problem for education systems for generations. But this rural identity construction is under attack for a number of reasons including the need for labour back home in the periphery, a declining population base, and fluctuations in commodity prices that lead to job shedding in mining and gas.

New 'ideal worker' identity narratives found in recruitment materials for Irving and the Norwegian oil company, Statoil, contain key corporate framing around environmentalism, linguistic and gender diversity and the importance of community in an attempt to simultaneously brand resource extraction companies as responsible corporate citizens and the region as an attractive place to live. Many of the available positions in fields require university education. As of January 2015, Irving was recruiting the following university degrees in its 'career track' programme: Engineering, Computer Science, Human Resources, Marketing, Public Relations, Commerce, Accounting, Finance and Supply Chain. The Statoil recruitment situation is very similar.

New educational narratives and the spatialisation of educational performance

All of these changes influence educational discourse in rural areas in many ways, not least of which is a respatialisation of educational geography made possible by national and international comparative metrics (Luke, 2011; Ball, 2012; Rizvi & Lingard, 2013; Sellar & Lingard, 2014). The local effects of the scaling up of educational data are felt in the micro-geographies of regional school boards and even local schools where educational performance is drawn into global matrices and to the current focus on STEM-related education (Schafft & Biddle, 2015).

In current policy discussions the scaling up and scaling down of standardised educational achievement analysis is combined with the discourse of the population implosion to generate an intensified focus on educational reform. Much like the heated and even alarmist rhetoric in *Now or Never*, a recent report on educational reform from the Nova Scotia Department of Education (DOE) employs similar language to rationalise major and immediate change (Government of Nova Scotia, 2015). The Minister's prologue puts it starkly: 'Time and again, test results show our students are falling behind in math and literacy, nationally and internationally. Over the years, there have been several different reports and public consultations that reached similar conclusions' (Government of Nova Scotia, 2015, p. 5).

The county of Finnmark illustrates the same phenomenon. National standardised tests show that students there perform below other Norwegian students. Also, dropout rates from vocational education and training (VET) in Finnmark are alarmingly high. In 2009 only 31% of VET students in Finnmark graduated with formal qualifications five years after starting secondary education compared to 58% in the top county of Sogn og Fjordane in the south of Norway. The policy analytic frame is one of rural and regional education systems that are backward and underperforming.

In Nova Scotia the story is much the same, with the rural school boards generally lagging behind urban jurisdictions in terms of measured educational achievement. On the basis of a provincial consultation in Nova Scotia that solicited input from the public, the DOE concludes that a major reorientation of the curriculum (particularly in maths and literacy), administrative structures, teacher education, leadership, inclusion, and a new focus on entrepreneurialism and

STEM subjects is necessary. Regardless of whether or not this vision of system reform actually reflects the deeply problematic nature of the existing system (Corbett, 2014a, 2014b), the vision is one of a reorientation of the culture of schooling.

The Minister's construction of reality addresses a clear and present danger, one that aligns with population decline and the general tone of the *Now or Never* report. The twin sources of panic – low educational achievement and the population implosion – come together to fill in some of the analytic and policy details in *Now or Never* and apply the logic to the province's education system. In the following section we will outline some of this material and explore the kind of worker it imagines.

Changing rural images and dreams: place-specific development

Important characteristics of the new natural resource-based industries in the periphery is that they are considerably more knowledge intensive and more heavily industrialised than the traditional industries, which means that the road to success in the petroleum industry goes through a specific kind of education, and particularly through STEM education. In order to be able to fully benefit from the oil adventure or to return to build ships, young people need the right admission ticket, which can be achieved through education.

The Norwegian oil companies claim that they are interested in youth (Eni Norge) with stable, local attachments. Irving Shipyards make the same claims about luring people home from the western Canadian oil patch. However, the majority of the workers required appear to be highly specialised and highly mobile elite workers who operate globally. The oil and gas sector is a notoriously unstable labour market largely based on short-term contracts designed for flexible workers. In Finnmark, the majority of design and developmental solutions and prefabrication in the high-activity initial phase of oil production took place in Germany, Italy, Belgium, the Netherlands, Spain, and Sweden (Eikeland, 2014). Most of the companies engaged in Finnmark in this phase brought their own staff, primarily male long-distance commuters flown in and housed during the construction period. Their task in Hammerfest was specific and required a minimal degree of contact and interaction with the regional business environment (Eikeland, 2014). After the initial developmental phase, the petroleum sector has relied heavily on outside labour and employers seem to search for qualified workers outside the region. A survey from NAV Eures in 2010 showed that 38% of the employers in Finnmark were planning to recruit workers from the EU in the upcoming year (Aure, Abelsen & Nilsen, 2012).

It is likely that a similar pattern could play out in Nova Scotia with the shipbuilding contract, where much of the design and development work appears to have been contracted out to European firms (CBC, 2013). It seems that access to the petroleum sector and the good jobs may not be automatic for local youth. Indeed, the escalation of the discourse around the need for a better educated workforce may be seen as a victim-blaming defensive position (see the section on 'shock doctrine' below) on the part of both government and industry when these new industries do not transform local labour markets in the way that was imagined.

Over time, the northern parts of Norway and Nova Scotia have also become more similar to the rest of their respective countries, developing services associated with modern society. At the same time, internal differences within these regions have increased due to the new presence of industry in certain communities and not in others. The results of this presence may take very concrete and visible forms. In the Hammerfest region, for example, increased activity provided a new waterfront promenade, renovated city streets/road networks, and kindergartens and schools were modernised and beautified (Eikeland, 2014). It is likely that these upgrades have an effect on how the locals view their communities, which may be why a 2008 Hammerfest youth survey showed that more young people wanted to live in Hammerfest than in 2004 (Aure, Abelsen & Nilsen, 2012). The survey did not, however, say anything about whether young people living in the small, rural communities surrounding Hammerfest had also changed their views about their own home places, which might look different in the shadow of the bright lights of the new and upgraded city of Hammerfest.

In Atlantic Canada, family incomes in some rural communities have been increased by mobile work and there are a variety of forms of evidence to support the transition effected by remittance money. The impact of contemporary forms of mobile work – its multiple effects on social, economic and cultural development in Canada – is not as yet well understood. What is clear, though, is that both population and wealth associated with development have tended to concentrate in urban centres like Halifax and Hammerfest. In Atlantic Canada, part of the workforce is highly mobile while other parts are not. Overall, the centralisation (urbanisation) tendencies continue, within the northern regions, but at the same time migration to resource boom areas concentrates population, at least temporarily, in select non-metropolitan locations. As the BMO report illustrates, there is little to suggest that this pattern of concentrated wealth and population will change. In Finnmark more than 90% of the petroleum-based revenue in 2010 came from the Hammerfest region.

With out-migration comes stagnating birth rates and an ageing population. Other places do, on the other hand, enjoy the benefits of the booming oil and gas industry, and the positive trends have a tendency to be self-perpetuating. Developmental differences between geographical places in the Norwegian north and in Atlantic Canada have always existed, because of differences in possibilities for landing fish, building the best harbours for fishing vessels and so on. Places have developed differently and unevenly (Harvey, 2006). Therefore, it has always been problematic to speak of the relationship between the north and the south in Norway, or the east and the west in Canada, in simple centre–periphery terms. However, new industrial developments seem to have enhanced these mechanisms, and the driving forces behind inter-regional and intra-regional disparities seem to have become stronger, faster and more insistent.

Not a moment to lose: educational shock doctrine and managing cultural change

Some years ago Naomi Klein (2008) coined the term 'shock doctrine' to describe the way that panic is sown in populations to keep people off balance and unsettled. This is done in two ways. First of all, the actual panics and disasters are exploited by leaders to promote neoliberal social and economic policies. Secondly, immediate and desperate problem situations are manufactured in various ways by leaders in order to consolidate their power. Today it is undeniable that there are many pressing and dangerous problems that we face collectively, which results in a general feeling of what Anthony Giddens (1991) has called 'ontological insecurity'. He refers here to the unpredictable consequences of modernity where the technologies we invent to solve problems actually create new sets of unintended and unforeseen trouble. Climate change is the quintessential example. The framing of the twin problems of population implosion and a 'discredited' pre-modern education system fits into well-established problem scenarios such as the massive out-migration of educated youth, the restructuring and even collapse of established resource industries, and places that have not urbanised in the way that other parts of the country have.

The key problem identified in Nova Scotia in the *Now or Never* report is to arrest the social and economic collapse imminent in the population implosion through culture change, and particularly the adoption of a neoliberal shift towards a focus on entrepreneurialism and the self-reliance required to shrink the role of the state. The shipbuilding contract is expected to lure people back from the Canadian west and from other places. But will the population have the skills for the leap into modernity? Will returning out-migrant 'leavers' from previous generations be enough to fill the jobs gap and, indeed, will they even want to return?[1] *Now or Never* argues that other strategies are needed, including immigration, more inclusive social attitudes and the inculcation of significant cultural change and entrepreneurialism.

Like *Now or Never*, which focuses substantially on cultural deficiencies and entrenched, complacent attitudes of the population, a recent publication from the provincial Department of Education, *The 3 Rs*, goes on to claim that cultural change in education is urgent:

> There is not a moment to lose: our students are in school now, awaiting better learning opportunities to prepare them for the challenges that lie ahead. Their future depends on having the knowledge and skills necessary to succeed in a quickly changing economy. Nova Scotia's future depends on healthy, well-educated and socially responsible citizens to build the economy.
>
> *(Government of Nova Scotia, 2015, p. 34)*

In Norway the educational issue that has received most attention recently is completion of upper secondary education. From the perspective of educational authorities, completion rates are too low, especially in vocational education and training, and especially in the north.[2] This analysis relates to national and regional policy documents emphasising changes and challenges faced by national and regional business interests. In the north, the importance of producing and maintaining a sufficient and well-qualified workforce is considered crucial. Due to structural change related to local economy and working life, such as the downsizing of primary industries including fisheries, other more knowledge-based industries such as marine biotechnology, petroleum, the maritime sector and tourism become increasingly important. Also, the traditional industries are themselves changing in terms of increased demands related to formal competence. In a knowledge-driven economy, formal competence becomes one of the most important national, regional and individual assets, and in policy documents this is seen as an important driver for increased innovation and worker competence.

A prerequisite for ensuring a competitive regional business life is that the young people complete formal education. Against this background, the government has launched a number of costly measures designed to improve throughput in secondary education, and even though the political discourse in Norway may have a softer tone than in Canada, there is no doubt how seriously the government views the situation. In a government white paper entitled *Students in Tomorrow's School*, the main goal of the education system is described as enabling students to keep up with changes in society and in knowledge development that are taking place at an increasing speed. These processes pose new demands on individuals, society, working life and the educational system. In Norway, regional differences in completion rates in secondary education and in national standardized test scores in primary education suggest that young people in the high north relate differently to the educational system than their counterparts further south (Bæck & Paulgaard, 2012; Bæck, 2015). Compared to young people in other places in Norway, northern youth therefore lag behind in the government-appointed race towards a knowledge society. From a government perspective, this situation needs to be corrected for the good of the individual and for strength of the society as a whole.

This cultural change mandated for Nova Scotia and Northern Norway includes the promotion of a specific construction of social responsibility aimed at changing how youth see themselves and others. This of course assumes that the opposite currently exists and that Nova

Scotians and North Norwegians have not adapted to a socially responsible and inclusive way of living, a contention that, again, is interesting and worthy of debate. If we understand policy as an authoritative allocation of values (Easton, 1953), the Nova Scotian and North Norwegian populations are being positioned in this discourse outside the cultural sensibilities and knowledge practices required for prosperity in a neoliberal world. This is a question of the extent to which youth who face multiple layers of ontological insecurity are prepared for globalized modernity. In these discourses they are assumed to require and desire a place in a globalized economy. Thus, it is the responsibility of the system to prepare them, primarily through a basic literacy and numeracy curriculum, a focus on science and technologies education, tighter controls on teachers and administrators, more surveillance, the promotion of entrepreneurship, and through a vague focus on inclusive education. The Government of Nova Scotia states the following: 'In reality, our public education system has lost credibility in the eyes of many Nova Scotians over the past couple of decades. We have not done enough for our students, teachers, or parents to deliver a modern education system that puts us at the top of the class' (Government of Nova Scotia, 2015, p. 6).

Through this form of discourse, people in Nova Scotia and in Northern Norway are framed as populations outside modernity. Indeed, statements such as these can be seen as an indictment of the failure to modernize, an old and familiar charge that can be read in many ways. For instance, historically, Nova Scotia has served to provide a reserve army of labour that can be deployed into areas of capital expansion when needed. Atlantic Canadians have then been criticised and defined as hopeless rustics and itinerants for fulfilling these roles. When this labour is not needed it is returned to the periphery where people are minimally maintained on social assistance, low-wage labour and a convivial culture of kinship, DIY, self-provisioning, barter and mutual aid (Sacouman & Brym, 1979). Even though the population in Northern Norway has not played the same role as reserve labour in a Norwegian context, the image of the northerner, as seen from the central south, has been much the same.

The irony is that this, in important respects, is the very mythic rural folk culture that is celebrated in tourism promotion for Nova Scotia (Mckay, 1994; Mckay & Bates, 2010) and for Northern Norway (Karlsen, 1998). To change this culture, then, is to change a deeply established way of being that despite its ontological ambivalence, is today very much a part of an Atlantic Canadian and a North Norwegian identity. It is also an image that has stamped the region as a therapeutic, slow-paced, relaxing tourist destination for generations (Kelly, 2013). The deeply ironic and somewhat confounding result of this analysis is that ongoing policies that strip infrastructure from multiply challenged rural communities not only continues, but is accelerated. The ultimate goal appears to be a thoroughgoing reconstitution of the modern rural subject, largely through education (Bennett, 2013; Howley, Howley & Kuemmel, 2014).

There are two fundamental features missing from this analysis (or lack of analysis), from our perspective. The first is the foundational assumption that contemporary change is an inevitable result of uncontrollable forces rather than political economic decisions. This discourse is essentially silent about the way that contemporary capitalism is systematically grabbing and despoiling land and moving people where it needs them for the ultimate benefit of a very small number of very rich and powerful people (Stiglitz, 2013; Fraser, 2014; Sassen, 2014). Contemporary economic thought has been caught in what Thomas Piketty (2014) has described as a massive exercise that denies the fundamental injustice built into the ordinary functioning of the economy. The analyses in the policy documents described above effectively accept that rural depopulation and community disintegration are inevitable results of economic development.

The second related feature in the analysis is the failure to confront the way that 'business as usual' actually requires large numbers of marginally educated precarious labour. The iconic northern worker, whom we find in different forms in both Northern Norway and Atlantic Canada, is one face of this 'precariat' (Standing, 2014), one which is relatively well paid when times are 'good' (i.e., when oil prices are high). The northern worker rides the waves of commodity prices, working when they are high and returning home when they are low. The work is hard and dangerous and the money is good when it is there. But work is not always available and eventually bodies can break down.

Another face of the precariat is the low-wage cadres of baristas and wait staff, store clerks, data workers, the low-wage service industry, as well as the other forms of 'unskilled' labour which relies on physical acumen, speed and automaticity rather than symbolic competence. Much of this labour force requires little formal education, and youth growing up in precarious families can drift rather easily into the same kinds of work their parents do, reproducing familiar patterns of unstable employment across generations. While some of it has been globalized and shifted to more or less permanent migrant, guest or immigrant workers, large amounts of this kind of labour continue to be necessary within advanced capitalist societies. This is entirely unacknowledged in the contemporary economic development rhetoric and there is no acknowledgement that it might be possible to improve the working conditions of ordinary but necessary workers who are essentially blamed for not joining the programme of modernity. This is the powerful and ironic paradox beneath the rhetoric of educational change, entrepreneurialism and innovation. Those who fail to heed its call and 'fall into' the service economy are not filling an important place in a contemporary labour market. They are constructed instead in reports like *Now or Never* and *The 3 Rs* as individual failures and a problem for society.

Conclusion: mixed messages for rural youth

As we have seen from Northern Norway, some rural and remote areas find themselves increasingly central to national development agendas because of the resources that suddenly show up there. In Nova Scotia the historic reserve army of labour ready to be deployed where it is needed is receiving new orders and being invited to participate in state-sponsored industry. What distinguishes these places from others is not connected to the place per se or to any qualities that these particular places exhibit. Rather, it has to do with the resources that happen to be at that particular place and what these resources can provide when it comes to economic growth, prosperity, development, urbanization and what can be described as 'modern' values. A flexible, educated/educable worker is needed, one that sometimes should be loyal to place and in other times ready to move depending on the requirements of capital. Apparently, not just any kind of (rural and remote) place or person is interesting and useful in terms of national labour and development agendas. As Zygmunt Bauman reminds us, in late modernity, no matter where we are born, there is no national, regional or even local community to protect and nourish. We are our own problem (Bauman, 1999).

Notes

1   Much of the answer to this kind of question lies in the vicissitudes of commodity prices, and particularly oil. As we write, oil prices are hovering between $40 and $50 per barrel. Economic growth is slowing down and Alberta lost population in the third quarter of 2014 when the slide was just beginning. Pull factors like the stabilising potential of the shipbuilding contract notwithstanding, inter-provincial

migration trends and the availability of workers in Nova Scotia depend to a considerable extent on global markets.

2 The average national completion rate five years after entering secondary education is 57% (83% in academic study programmes). In the northernmost county, for example, the completion rate in VET for those starting secondary education in 2008 was 42% among men and 48% among women.

References

Aure, M, Abelsen, B & Nilsen, T (2012). *Ungdom og Goliat. Unge i Hammerfest, Alta og Honningsvåg om petroleumssektoren som framtidig arbeidsmarked.* Alta, Norway: NORUT.

Bæck, UD (2004). The urban ethos: Locality and youth in north Norway. *YOUNG. Nordic Journal of Youth Research* 12, 99–115.

Bæck, U-DK (2015). Rural location and academic success. Remarks on research, contextualisation and methodology. *Scandinavian Journal of Educational Research.* doi: 10.1080/00313831.2015.1024163.

Bæck, U-DK & Paulgaard, G (2012). Introduction: Choices, opportunities and coping in the face of unemployment. In U-DK Bæck & G Paulgaard (Eds), *Rural futures? Finding one's place within changing labour markets* (pp. 9–21). Stamsund, Norway: Orkana Akademisk.

Ball, SJ (2012). *Global Education Inc.: New policy networks and the neoliberal imaginary.* Abingdon: Routledge.

Bank of Montreal (2014). *Provincial Monitor.* October.

Barrett, G (2015). Deconstructing community. *Sociologia Ruralis* 55(2), 182–204.

Bauman, Z (1999). *In search of politics.* Stanford, CA: Stanford University Press.

Bauman, Z (2000). *Liquid modernity.* Cambridge: Polity.

Bennett, PW (2013). *The last stand.* Halifax, NS: Fernwood Publishing.

Brown, DL & Schafft, KA (2011). *Rural people and communities in the 21st century: Resilience and transformation.* Cambridge: Polity.

Castells, M (2009). *The power of identity: The information age. Economy, Society, and Culture Vol. II* (2nd edn.). Malden, MA: Wiley-Blackwell.

CBC News (2011, 19 October). Jubilation as Halifax shipyard awarded contract. Available at http://www.cbc.ca/1.1059989 (accessed 26 January 2015).

CBC News (2013, 2 May). Shipbuilding contract holds $250M mystery. Available at http://www.cbc.ca/news/politics/shipbuilding-contract-holds-250m-mystery-1.1300816 (accessed 26 January 2015).

Corbett, M (2004). 'It was fine, if you wanted to leave': Educational ambivalence in a Nova Scotian coastal community 1963–1998. *Anthropology & Education Quarterly* 35(4), 451–471.

Corbett, M (2005). Rural education and out-migration: The case of a coastal community. *Canadian Journal of Education / Revue Canadienne de L'éducation* 28(1/2), 52–72.

Corbett, M (2007). *Learning to leave: The irony of schooling in a coastal community.* Black Point, NS: Fernwood Publishing.

Corbett, M (2010). Standardized individuality: Cosmopolitanism and educational decision-making in an Atlantic Canadian rural community. *Compare: A Journal of International and Comparative Education* 40(2), 193–207.

Corbett, M (2014a). We have never been urban: Modernization, small schools, and resilient rurality in Atlantic Canada. *The Journal of Rural and Community Development* 9(3), 186–202.

Corbett, M (2014b). Toward a geography of rural education in Canada. *Canadian Journal of Education* 37(3), 1–22.

Easton, D (1953). *The political system, an inquiry into the state of political science.* New York: Knopf.

Eikeland, S (2014). Building a high north growth pole: The northern Norwegian city of Hammerfest in the wake of developing the 'Snow White' Barents Sea gas field. *Journal of Rural and Community Development* 9, 57–71.

Forsey, M (2015). Learning to stay? Mobile modernity and the sociology of choice. *Mobilities* 10(5), 764–783.

Giddens, A (1991). *The consequences of modernity.* Stanford, CA: Stanford University Press.

Government of Nova Scotia. (2014). *Now or never: An urgent call to action for Nova Scotians.* Available at http://onens.ca/wp-content/uploads/Now_or_never_short.pdf (accessed 21 January 2015).

Government of Nova Scotia (2015). *The 3 Rs: Renew, Refocus, Rebuild: Nova Scotia's action plan for education 2015.*

Harvey, D (2006). *Spaces of global capitalism: A theory of uneven geographical development.* London: Verso.

Howley, C, Howley, C & Kuemmel, W (2014). Mining the schoolhouse: Neoliberal education policy in Appalachia. *ASA Annual Conference*. Available at http://mds.marshall.edu/asa_conference/2014/Full/362 (accessed 4 February 2016).

Jentoft, S (1993). *Dangling lines: The fisheries crisis and the future of the coastal communities: The Norwegian experience*. Memorial University of Newfoundland, St. Johns: Institute of Social and Economic Research.

Karlsen, UD (1998). Til forsvar for den moderniserte nordlending. In RA Nilsen & P Veiden (Eds), *Sosiologisk fantasi: Essays (Sociological phantasy: Essays)* (pp. 132–146). Oslo: Ad Notam Gyldendal.

Kelly, U (2013). Find yourself in Newfoundland and Labrador: Reading rurality as reparation. In B Green & M Corbett (Eds), *Rethinking rural literacies: Transnational perspectives* (pp. 53–74). New York: Palgrave Macmillan.

Klein, N (2008). *The shock doctrine: The rise of disaster capitalism*. New York: Picador.

Luke, A (2011). Generalizing across borders policy and the limits of educational science. *Educational Researcher* 4(8), 367–377.

McKay, I (1994). *The quest of the folk: Antimodernism and cultural selection in twentieth-century Nova Scotia*. Montreal: McGill-Queen's University Press.

McKay, I & Bates, R (2010). *In the province of history: The making of the public past in twentieth-century Nova Scotia*. Montreal: McGill-Queen's University Press.

Peters, MA & Bulut, E (Eds). (2011). *Cognitive capitalism, education and digital labor*. New York: Peter Lang.

Piketty, T (2014). *Capital in the twenty-first century*. Trans. A Goldhammer. Cambridge, MA: Belknap Press.

Regional Municipality of Wood Buffalo (2012). *Municipal census 2012*. Available at http://www.woodbuffalo.ab.ca/Assets/Corporate/Census+Reports/Census+reports+Part+1.pdf (accessed 3 February 2015).

Rizvi, F & Lingard, B (2013). *Globalizing education policy*. London: Routledge.

Sacouman, RJB & Brym, RJ (1979). *Underdevelopment and social movements in Atlantic Canada*. Toronto: New Hogtown Press.

Sassen, S (2014). *Expulsions: Brutality and complexity in the global economy*. Cambridge, MA: Belknap Press.

Schafft, K & Biddle, C (2015). Opportunity, ambivalence, and youth perspectives on community change in Pennsylvania's Marcellus Shale region. *Human Organization* 74(1), 74–85.

Sellar, S & Lingard, B (2014). The OECD and the expansion of PISA: New global modes of governance in education. *British Educational Research Journal* 40(6), 917–936.

Standing, G (2014). *The precariat: The new dangerous class*. London: Bloomsbury Academic.

Stiglitz, JE (2013). *The price of inequality: How today's divided society endangers our future*. New York: WW Norton.

Walsh, D (2012). Using mobility to gain stability: Rural household strategies and outcomes in long-distance labour mobility. *Journal of Rural and Community Development* 7(3), 123–143.

Woods, M (2010). *Rural: Key ideas in geography*. New York: Routledge.

46

Indigenous Education and Self-Determination in a Global Context

The Case of New Zealand and the United States

Susan C. Faircloth and Anne S. Hynds

Introduction

In this chapter, we discuss the importance of education and self-determination among the Indigenous peoples of New Zealand (Aotearoa) and the United States. Although these two countries are separated by thousands of miles of land and water, there are multiple historical, social and political parallels with regard to their histories and treatments of their Indigenous peoples. This shared history and treatment is rooted and grounded in these nations' settler colonialist histories, which Wolfe (2006, cited in Hoxie, 2008) describes as being intent 'on the elimination of native societies' (p. 1160). In both cases, 'the coloniser [came] to stay' (ibid., p. 1160). With the arrival of these colonising forces, the Indigenous Māori peoples of New Zealand and the American Indian and Alaska Native tribes of the Americas have endured the intentional and forceful taking of their lands, as well as the loss of cultures, languages and important social, economic and cultural capitals (Bourdieu, 1986). As a result, the Indigenous peoples of both New Zealand and the United States find themselves in the minority within their own lands – with Māoris constituting approximately 15% of the population of New Zealand (Statistics New Zealand, 2013) and American Indians and Alaska Natives constituting less than 1% of the population of the United States (Norris, Vines & Hoeffel, 2012). In both countries, Indigenous peoples experience disproportionate levels of unemployment, reduced educational attainment, poor health conditions and other indicators of social and economic well-being that place them at risk.

In their ongoing fight against the colonising forces that have helped to create and sustain these risks, many Indigenous peoples view education (and self-education) as a powerful tool for social and political change, and ultimately for the maintenance and/or reclamation of their Native languages, cultures and ways of knowing, doing and being. As scholars and educators, we work to support and engage individuals and communities as they assert their right to determine the overall scope and shape of their education and to use this education as a form of empowerment. Much of our work is with Indigenous and other historically marginalised groups and is grounded in a deep and abiding belief that all Indigenous peoples have the right, both legally and politically, to be educated in ways that affirm rather than weaken the role of Indigenous language and culture in the development and implementation of educational practices and experiences. In order to fully enjoy this right, we both believe that Indigenous peoples must exert a strong sense of self-determination and local control over the education of their children and youth. Thus, in this chapter, we discuss the role of self-determination in promoting education – and ultimately increased agency – among two historically marginalised groups: American Indians and Alaska Natives in the United States and Māoris in New Zealand. In addressing these issues, we draw on the work of Linda Tuhiwai Smith (2005), who cautions us that as researchers we are walking on 'tricky ground' when we attempt to tell the stories of Indigenous peoples and their communities.

As we navigate this tricky ground, it is important to acknowledge that Indigenous communities are diverse and are resistant to monocultural generalisations and stereotypes (Bishop & Glynn, 1999; Penetito, 2010). "Identities, then, by their very nature, are in a state of flux yet there is a tendency [by many non-Indigenous peoples and organisations] to try to apply rigid labels" (McIntosh, 2005, p. 39). The politics of identity make our own analysis work "tricky" in that we are speaking for others and interpretation is always filled with uncertainty (Smith, 2005, 2013). In speaking about Indigenous communities, Smith (2005) warns that localised knowledge cannot be separated from history, place and power relationships. Who gets to speak, who gets heard and who benefits are central questions, given that issues of privilege and marginalisation exist across all communities (Smith, 2005). Issues of voice, representation and legitimation are political within all communities (Bishop & Glynn, 1999; McIntosh, 2005; Smith, 2005) regardless of their classification as rural, urban, Indigenous, non-Indigenous or other similarly imposed labels. McIntosh (2005) argues, "Māori can experience marginalisation in a Pākehā [New Zealand European]-dominated society but can also experience it in Māori social arenas" (p. 43). McIntosh also says: "That some identities are more clearly marked than others signals that identity formation is a political process, meaning that while some identities are more clearly insider self-expressions, others are imposed by outsiders or created in conditions of scarcity or constraint and become expressions of resistance or desperation" (2005, p. 39).

A similar argument can be made for American Indians, Alaska Natives and other Indigenous peoples who are grappling with questions of who is Native or who is Native *enough* – questions that, in many cases, are related to the rural–urban divide that exists among many Indigenous peoples across the world. As Sissons (2004) points out, "Issues surrounding tribal and [I]ndigenous authenticity are, of course, by no means confined to New Zealand. They are a concern for all [I]ndigenous peoples within post-settler states" (p. 30).

Drawing upon our individual experiences as citizens of the nations of New Zealand and the United States, as Pākehā (New Zealand European) and American Indian, and as educators and scholars of Indigenous education, we attempt to discuss the ways in which we view these two nations engaging with Indigenous peoples, as they grapple to come to terms with their histories of hegemonic practices, colonisation, forced assimilation and resistance to these acts on the part of their Indigenous peoples. In doing so, we focus on the role of education as both a tool of the coloniser and a tool for promoting decolonisation and self-determination.

Although this Handbook focuses on rural peoples and communities, it is important to point out that the majority of American Indians, Alaska Natives (e.g., Urban Indian Health Institute, 2013) and Māoris (e.g., Ministry of Social Development, 2010) do not currently reside in rural areas. This rural out-migration stands in stark contract to demographics found in both countries until the first half of the 20th century (e.g., Fixico, 1986; Hill, 2010) when Indigenous peoples were encouraged by the governments of these two countries to relocate to urban areas. In the United States, these movements, although marketed as attempts to increase access to education, jobs and improved social and economic conditions, were in fact, part of a larger movement to decrease the number of Indigenous peoples residing in rural, reservation-based communities and to end or terminate the federal government's relationship with tribes (e.g., Burt, 1986; Nagel, 1995; Fixico, 2000). In New Zealand, urban relocation was similarly fuelled in large part by 'economic necessity' (Keiha & Moon, 2008); however, some (e.g. Hill, 2012) argue that urban relocation was utilised by the government as a means of hastening assimilation. Regardless of the motives behind the migration from rural to urban areas, such migration played an important role in the mobilisation of Indigenous peoples towards increased calls for iwi (tribal) control and the right for Indigenous peoples to determine their own economic, social, cultural and educational futures for themselves rather than having these futures imposed upon them.

Self-determination: the fight to reclaim identity, space and place

Viatori and Ushigua (2007, p. 7) define self-determination as the "ability of [I]ndigenous nations to make decisions about their identity, religion, culture, economy, and legal system without interference from external actors". Bishop (2012, p. 39) describes self-determination as 'the right to determine one's own destiny, to define what that destiny will be, and to define and pursue means of attaining that destiny'. For the "[I]ndigenous peoples of New Zealand, calls for self-determination represent the critical dimension of kaupapa Māori [philosophies and beliefs], that is, a critique of ongoing power imbalances that maintain a pattern of domination and subordination" (Bishop, 2012, p. 39). While the concept of self-determination (tino rangatiratanga) is fundamental to the rights of Indigenous peoples of New Zealand, the United States and elsewhere around the world, it is also important to note, as McCarty and Lee (2014) point out, the heterogeneous nature of Indigenous peoples. This is reflected in the wide range of cultures and languages practised and spoken. For example, in the United States, there are more than 600 federally and state-recognised tribes (National Council of State Legislatures, 2014; US Department of the Interior, Indian Affairs, Bureau of Indian Affairs, 2014), each with their own culture, and many with their own languages still spoken or in the process of being revitalised and relearned (e.g., Romero-Little et al., 2007; Hermes, 2012). This situation is similar in New Zealand, where there are more than 70 iwi (Statistics New Zealand, n.d.) and at least three distinct dialectical variations of te reo (Māori) spoken today (*The Encyclopedia of New Zealand*, n.d.a). Such diversity must be taken into account when attempting to understand Indigenous peoples and communities and the ways in which they pursue and enact principles of self-determination.

The education of Indigenous peoples in New Zealand and the United States – calls for increased local control and self-determination

For Indigenous communities in colonised countries, such as the United States and New Zealand, self-determination and tribal sovereignty are at the forefront of community revitalisation and sustainability efforts (Brayboy & Deyhle, 2000; Penetito, 2010; Bishop, 2012; McCarty & Lee, 2014). According to the National Congress of American Indians (n.d., p. 16), sovereignty "is a legal word for an ordinary concept – the authority to self-govern". Inherent in this principle of self-governance comes the call for tribal peoples to band together to establish and direct the priorities and goals of the tribes, tribal nations and their citizens. This requires the collective agency or "capacity to exercise control over the nature and quality of one's life"

(Bandura, 2001, p. 1). This principle, coupled with the individual and collective determination of Indigenous peoples, has been instrumental in efforts to reclaim and sustain 'linguistic and cultural' identity and self-expression 'according to local languages and norms' (McCarty & Lee, 2014, p. 101). In many cases, the pursuit of self-determination has been evidenced at the local level by attempts to implement and sustain tribally/locally controlled systems of education through which Indigenous languages and cultures are also supported. As Schimmel (2007) argues,

> the right to an education that is consonant with and draws upon the culture and language of [I]ndigenous peoples is a human right which is too often overlooked by governments when they develop and implement programmes whose purported goals are to improve the social, economic and political status of these peoples. Educational programs for [I]ndigenous peoples must fully respect and integrate human rights protections, rights to cultural continuity and integrity.
>
> *(p. 425)*

In New Zealand, collective agency can be seen through kaupapa Māori, an essential Indigenous strategy underpinning Māori medium institutions (where the Māori language/te reo is the primary mode of instructional delivery) and place-based education (Smith, 2007; Penetito, 2010). Since the 1970s, Māori medium schools have served as a leading force in decolonising and asserting control of the education of Māori children and youth in New Zealand. The first bilingual Māori medium school was established in New Zealand in 1977 in Ruatoki. This led to the opening of more than 20 schools by the end of the 1980s (Schimmel, 2007).

Indigenous strategies, such as kaupapa Māori (based on Māori thought, principles and beliefs) (Smith, 1990, as cited in Pihama & Penehira, 2005), seek to revitalise the linguistic and cultural knowledge bases and operationalise tribal aspirations to restructure power relationships with state or crown (governmental) entities (Penetito, 2010). According to Smith (1992, 1997, cited in Bishop, 2012), kaupapa Māori calls for "conscientisation, resistance and transformative praxis" (p. 42). Kaupapa Māori has both educational and political dimensions because it recognises the importance of community or place-based accountability (Penetito, 2010). Through this lens, education becomes an inherently political act of interrogating and demanding change within the governmental, educational, societal and other structures that have worked to promote and sustain economic and educational underdevelopment for tribal groups (Smith, 2015).

The Indigenous peoples of the United States have also engaged in their own fight for self-determination and increased local control of education. Acts of collective resistance have resulted in the enactment of the Indian Self-Determination and Educational Assistance Act of 1975 (Public Law 93-638[2]), the establishment of tribally controlled schools such as Rough Rock Demonstration School on the Navajo Reservation in New Mexico (e.g., Lomawaima & McCarty, 2002), and through the Tribally Controlled Colleges and Universities movement which created more than 30 colleges and universities across the United States (e.g., Tippeconnic & Faircloth, 2011). New Zealand differs from the United States in that it has developed and adopted a national strategy for addressing educational disparities between Māori and non-Māori students. This strategy, commonly referred to as Ka Hikitia (Ministry of Education, n.d.), calls for 'Māori enjoying and achieving education success as Māori', based on the following strategies:

- designing the future for Māori education at your school;
- being accountable for the performance of your school in relation to Māori student achievement;

- ensuring Māori stakeholders in your community are represented in governance, planning, and decision making; [and]
- ensuring your school is a good employer by supporting school staff to teach and support Māori students effectively.

(Ministry of Education, 2013, p. 3)

In theory, schools in New Zealand are tasked with engaging in productive partnerships with whānau (family), hapū (sub-tribe or clan) and iwi (tribe) to ensure Māori students achieve their potential. The New Zealand curriculum also identifies the Treaty of Waitangi as one of eight essential foundations of curriculum decision making that affect all schools (Ministry of Education, 2012). Despite such national policy statements, however, there is sufficient evidence to suggest that this is not happening in practice. For example, the Education Review Office's 2010 report found that a large number of schools did not review their performance around Māori student achievement and did not make use of the evidence about 'what works' to promote success for Māori students. School boards would require such information to make informed decisions and set clear directions for Māori education success. School boards, however, like school communities, can consist of diverse groups and schools are not immune to resistance from non-Indigenous parents/caregivers to culturally responsive programmes intended to serve the needs of local tribal communities (Hynds & Sheehan, 2011).

Another tension in New Zealand has emerged from the debate around biculturalism, in which Māori culture and language are recognised and on the surface appear to be incorporated into policies and practices at the national, regional and local levels (O'Sullivan, 2001). This issue of biculturalism raises questions regarding 'what it means for Māori students to be successful as Māori' within the confines of Western/Pākehā-dominated systems of schooling. According to O'Sullivan, "If self-determination is to be maximised within New Zealand's contemporary political, social, and educational context, then Māori communities must have the opportunity to establish clear educational goals for themselves" (2001, p. 163). A similar argument can be made for the Indigenous peoples of the United States where there is no official national strategy regarding the success of Indigenous students, beyond the efforts of states like Montana where legislation such as the Indian Education for All Act[3] has been adopted. While this act mandates the inclusion of American Indian history and culture into the curriculum, its impact is felt primarily at the state level given the separation of state and federal responsibilities for education, with education being a function of individual states rather than the federal government.

Although education has played a key role in the movement towards increased self-determination in both New Zealand and the United States, McCarty and Lee (2014) note both the contradictions and complexities of reforming educational systems as a result of the "colonial influences" that are deeply "embedded in curriculum, pedagogy, standards, policies, and Indigenous communities themselves" (p. 104). As such, efforts to Indigenise or decolonise educational systems and practices is complicated by the fact that the majority of Indigenous students in both New Zealand and the United States are educated in mainstream public schools where English is the primary mode of instruction; there is limited emphasis on or inclusion of Indigenous cultures, traditions and practices; and Indigenous teachers and administrators remain in the minority (e.g., Ministry of Education, 2010; National Center for Education Statistics, 2012).

Persistent challenges in actualising truly self-determined education for the Indigenous peoples of New Zealand and the United States

Some have argued that efforts to achieve true self-determination have been stymied by the fact that tribal nations still fall under the auspices of larger national governments, which constrain tribal nations' ability to self-govern (e.g., O'Sullivan, 2001). This limited self-governance extends into the educational arena where even tribally (iwi) controlled schools find themselves accountable to dictates of the national governments of the countries in which they operate. According to Tully (2000, pp. 41–42, cited in O'Sullivan, 2001),

> the aim of the system [the governments of New Zealand and the United States] is to ensure that the territory on which the settler societies is built is effectively and legitimately under their exclusive jurisdiction and open to settlement and capitalist development. The means to this end are twofold, the ongoing usurpation, dispossession, incorporation and infringement of the rights of [I]ndigenous peoples coupled with various long-term strategies of extinguishment and accommodation that would eventually capture their rights, dissolve the contradiction and legitimate the settlement.
>
> *(p. 158)*

In many cases, education has been used as a primary tool to accomplish this goal of legitimation.

The diversity of Indigenous peoples and their communities and their aspirations for self-determination also requires continued resistance towards standardising (homogenising) policies and neoliberal education reforms (Olssen & Peters, 2005; Luke, 2011). Neoliberalism as an economic strategy is linked with globalisation, enhanced consumerism and free markets and is influencing new modes of schooling regulation across the world (Olssen & Peters, 2005; Luke, 2011; Sleeter, 2012). These forms of regulation include an intense international focus on measuring student achievement through standardised tests and teacher performance within and across schools, to ensure competitive advantage. Standardisation also perpetuates stereotypes and generalisations of Māori communities and their knowledge bases since they are often described as one people (Smith, 2007). Decolonisation continues to be an essential Indigenous strategy for tribal communities both in Aotearoa and the United States, as 'knowing … the colonizer' means being prepared to fight for local control and authority (Smith, 2013, p. 8).

On a more personal and local level, the act of decolonisation requires Indigenous peoples to move "from an awareness of being in struggle, to actively engaging in everyday practices of resurgence" (Corntassel, 2012, p. 89). This requires actively addressing the lingering effects of mis-education on the parents and families of many of today's Indigenous youth. This is cited in the work of Schimmel (2007) who speaks to the potentially devastating effects of Westernised approaches to education on Indigenous peoples and their communities. Schimmel notes that much of the resistance to education today is related to parents' and grandparents' remembrance of their own education at the hands of the oppressor.

What lessons can we learn from the Indigenous peoples of New Zealand and the United States regarding working with and engaging Indigenous serving schools and communities?

Building on this notion of decolonising educational systems and practices, McCarty and Lee (2014) argue that tribal sovereignty is not possible unless it includes educational sovereignty – the right to determine ways in which Indigenous students are educated and to choose the curricular content that is privileged in schools educating Indigenous students. Although there is certainly room for improvement, New Zealand has much to offer the United States and other settler colonialist nations in terms of acknowledging and incorporating Indigenous knowledge and culture into the classroom. For example, in 2008, the New Zealand Ministry of Education implemented an educational strategy, Ka Hikitia ("to step up", "lift up" or "'lengthen one's stride") (Ministry of Education, 2013, p. 5), whose motto was "Māori achieving success as Māori" (Ministry of Education, 2013). According to Professor Mason Durie (as cited in Ministry of Education, 2013), this strategy means that Māori students have the right to be

> able to have access to te ao Māori, the Māori world – access to language, culture, marae [meeting house], … tikanga [customs and traditions]… and resources … If after twelve or so years of formal education, Māori youth were totally unprepared to interact within te ao Māori, then, no matter what else had been learned, education would have been incomplete.
>
> *(p. 5)*

In other words, a successful education programme for Indigenous children and youth is one that equips them to be successful in both their tribal communities/worlds and the world at large, rather than acculturating and assimilating them. Although the United States has adopted its own policies for the education of American Indian and Alaska Native students, these policies have failed to yield marked improvement in the academic outcomes of Native students (e.g., US Department of Education, 2011). Further, these policies have not been effective in promoting the inclusion of Indigenous languages and cultures into the classroom as a key element of instructional practice (e.g., Cohen & Allen, 2013). Lessons learned from New Zealand's work with Māori student success, as defined, in part, by local tribal communities, is a model the United States should be encouraged to pursue. According to Smith (2015),

> The real revolution that has occurred in Māori education was not the wonderful alternative schooling models … the real revolution was in our heads … it was a shift of mind-set of not waiting for education to be changed for us to getting up and doing it for ourselves.

This notion of being actively involved in the process of change is also echoed by Schimmel (2007) who writes that individuals and organisations working with Indigenous communities must develop "curricula, pedagogical methodologies and school environments that foster rather than undermine respect for indigenous culture – whilst simultaneously offering a rigorous educational programme in literacy, numeracy and other intellectual and vocational skills needed to succeed socially and economically in a broader national context" (p. 426). Examples of this active involvement are found in the successful efforts of Māoris in teaching language and culture, as well as the success of the Alaska Rural Systemic Initiative, which has conducted groundbreaking work in the area of culturally responsive pedagogies for Indigenous children and youth. According to Barnhardt and Kawagley (cited in Schimmel, 2007, p. 441), in Alaska,

> Students are spending more time out in the community with elders, parents, and local experts. The school curricula are reflecting the knowledge, values, and practices that have been a traditional part of the life in the local communities, and teachers are incorporating a more place-based pedagogy that is engaging students in studies associated with the surrounding physical and cultural environment.

This is an example of locally controlled, self-determined education.

Implications for policy, practice and future research

In the years to come, it will be important for Indigenous communities in New Zealand and the United States to respond to the shifting demographics of these groups, particularly as relates to geographical dispersion and increasing out-migration from rural to urban areas. Today, approximately 84% of Māoris live in urban areas compared with more than 80% who lived in rural areas prior to the Second World War. Similar to the USA, New Zealand implemented a 'social reform' in the 1960s, as a result of the Hunn Report of 1961, which recommended that Māori be moved to urban areas with the government providing housing, employment and other forms of government assistance. For many, this separation from home and community resulted in the loss or lessening of their Indigenous language and cultural identity. This has been combated to some extent by the emergence of tribal and political action groups in the urban areas. Today, this urban migration continues, due in large part to increased opportunities to work available in urban areas (*The Encyclopedia of New Zealand*, n.d.b).

The impact of continued out-migration from rural areas to urban areas is important as it has long-lasting implications for the futures of Indigenous peoples in their countries of origin. In the case of New Zealand, it will be particularly important to address the out-migration of Māori from New Zealand to other countries. According to one estimate, in 2006 at least one in every six Māori resided in Australia (Hamer, 2008). While urban and international destinations may offer much-needed opportunities for work and economic gain, this loss of Indigenous peoples will have a tremendous effect on New Zealand's ability to maintain its sense of Indigenous culture and identity. While out-migration of American Indians and Alaska Natives from the United States to other international areas is less of an issue than is found in New Zealand, the fact that many American Indians and Alaska Natives move from rural to urban areas each year is potentially an issue of concern. As was noted in a 2013 article in the *New York Times* (Williams, 2013, n.p.), "the migration [from rural to urban areas] goes to the heart of the question of whether the more than 300 reservations in the United States are an imperative or a hindrance to Native Americans, a debate that dates to the 19th century, when the reservation system was created by the federal government". Not only does this out-migration result in a loss of population in rural areas, it also creates an intense drain on the social, cultural and economic capitals critically important to the continued survival and growth of rural peoples and communities (e.g., Cooke & O'Sullivan, 2015).

In the years to come, it will also be important for Indigenous tribes/iwis and organisations to continue to advocate for the development and implementation of culturally responsive pedagogies and leadership practices for children and youth (e.g., Brayboy & Castagno, 2009). While many Indigenous students will have the opportunity to attend immersion or bilingual schools operated and/or funded by tribal organisations, the majority will most likely continue to attend public schools in the mainstream. In this case, it will be imperative that tribes assert their right to appropriate educational services as mandated by governmental agreements such as the Treaty of Waitangi in New Zealand and the federal trust responsible for American Indians resulting from treaties signed between tribes and the federal government in the United States. As history will show, tribes must hold national governments accountable to these treaty responsibilities in order for them to be fully enforced. As Schimmel (2007, p. 452) writes, "Unless governments develop educational programming in a manner that is sensitive and responsive to the needs, wishes and unique vulnerabilities of indigenous children and indigenous peoples, there is little likelihood that the goals of development and human rights can be reconciled." If this is to occur, governments must be sensitive to the historically tenuous relationship between tribes and governmental agencies. According to Manuelito (2005), the relationship between American Indians and Alaska Natives and the federal government of the United States has created a situation in which many American Indians and Alaska Natives are reluctant to trust the government and other agencies they perceive as being agents of the government – in this case, schools. If Indigenous peoples do not trust the very agencies and organisations that are charged with ensuring their health and well-being, their future is at risk.

In terms of research, scholars are encouraged to consider the following:

- the extent to which culturally relevant teaching, learning and leadership practices in schools have contributed to measurable improvements in the educational conditions and subsequent life outcomes of Indigenous students in both the United States and New Zealand; specifically, comparisons should be made between Indigenous students residing in rural areas and those residing in suburban and urban areas;
- the extent to which increased Indigenous control of education has resulted in increased or improved efforts to self-govern, or at least, to more effectively engage in governance processes at the local, regional and national levels; and
- the extent to which acts of self-determination in the educational arena, within the United States and New Zealand, have affected the efforts of other Indigenous peoples across the world to engage in truly self-determined education.

Conclusion

Around the world, Indigenous tribal communities (Penetito, 2010; Smith, 2013; McCarty & Lee, 2014) have expressed concerns regarding the survival of Indigenous languages, cultures and identities. These concerns are particularly relevant in colonised countries, such as New Zealand and the United States, where cultural and linguistic annihilation persists through assimilationist practices, despite treaty promises (Penetito, 2010). According to Alfred and Corntassel (2005, p. 597),

> The communities, clans, nations and tribes we call *Indigenous peoples* are just that: Indigenous to the lands they inhabit, in contrast to and in contention with the colonial societies and states that have spread out from Europe and other centres of empire. It is this oppositional, place-based existence, along with the consciousness of being in struggle against the dispossessing and demeaning fact of colonization by foreign peoples, that fundamentally distinguishes Indigenous peoples from other peoples of the world.

This fight to maintain language, culture, land and place are inextricably linked to the historical power imbalance between the Indigenous peoples of the United States and New Zealand and the policies and practices that have prevented Indigenous peoples from being fully engaged in the day-to-day operations of the governments of the two nations in which they reside (e.g., Wolfley, 1991). This hegemonic relationship between the governments of these two nations and their Indigenous peoples has made it difficult for those working to maintain, sustain and grow tribal languages and cultures, as well as those working to maintain or reclaim their traditional homelands, many of which are located in rural areas. Historically, education has been used as a primary tool to thwart attempts by Indigenous peoples to regain political and economic power. Rather than empowering or liberating them, education has been used in many cases to acculturate and assimilate. Fighting back against these practices, the Indigenous peoples of the United States and New Zealand are working to repatriate the Westernised educational system and to mould it into a system that incorporates, embraces and respects Indigenous languages and cultures both as instructional tools and as ways of strengthening language and culture. Much of this work is founded upon principles of self-determination, local control and, ultimately, self-governance. In rural areas where Indigenous peoples tended to be clustered, they engaged in their cultures and languages through deep-seated community connections, practices and traditions; however, when they moved from these rural communities and relocated to urban areas, they were forced to be more mindful and intentional about maintaining these cultural funds of knowledge (e.g., Moll, Amanti, Neff & Gonzalez 1992) if they were to survive with their cultures and languages somewhat intact. For some, economic and social demands overshadowed their attempts to maintain their connections to their rural roots and their Indigenous cultures; however, for others, the land from which they came grounded them and gave them a lasting sense of who they were and are, as culturally located individuals – 'having cultural understandings and experiences that are different from those of other people' (Bishop & Berryman, 2006, p. 270). This sense of cultural location is inherently linked to the places and spaces from which one comes – be it rural or urban. Having a sense of one's genealogy of place is critical to achieving true self-determination as it "provides the glue of community cohesion", "through value systems and practices that ensure reciprocal relationships are honoured over time and over succeeding generations" (Smith, 2007, p. 344).

In closing, we paraphrase the work of Lomawaima and McCarty (2002, pp. 281–282) who ask, if a

> nation cannot tolerate [its Indigenous peoples] … living as they might choose, both as Native people and as … citizens [of the nation], what does that mean for the democratic ideals of equality and freedom? If the nation-state cannot forge itself as a healthy, productive, and diverse society in its relations with [Indigenous peoples], what hope can other citizens hold that their rights, beliefs, practices, and values will be respected and protected?

While the fight for self-determination is a battle often associated with Indigenous peoples, it is at the very core of the founding of our two nation states – a laying of claims on lands and peoples in what were once rural, remote lands for the sake of the larger "colonialist project" (e.g., Grande, 2004), one of expansion, settlement and empire building at the expense of the Indigenous peoples of these lands. Thus, the pursuit of self-determination crosses the boundaries from rural to urban, Indigenous to non-Indigenous – boundaries that must be traversed if these nations' Indigenous peoples are to enjoy the rights that were taken from them in the founding of these two nations. Education is one means of achieving this right, but it requires Indigenous peoples be afforded the opportunity to develop and implement educational policies and practices that affirm rather than weaken Indigenous knowledges, practices and beliefs and that views cultural knowledge as equally important to academic knowledge. As Faircloth (2009, p. 3) writes,

> a return to local control of education will not ensure that all Native youth will be academically successful nor does it ensure they will remain in their communities of origin. However, it does provide a vehicle by which children and youth have the social, cultural, and economic capital necessary to be successful wherever they choose to reside – both in the physical and philosophical sense.

There are many lessons to be learned from the collective agency of Indigenous tribes across the world and their struggle to ensure that treaty obligations are upheld. An important first step is recognising education as a vehicle by which Indigenous cultures and languages can be embraced rather than erased.

Notes

1   The word Indigenous is capitalised throughout this chapter in honour of the original people of these lands. Selected quotes have been edited to conform with this practice.
2   For additional information regarding this law, see http://www.tribal-institute.org/lists/pl93-638.htm.
3   For more information on the Indian Education for All Act, see http://www.opi.mt.gov/programs/indianed/.

References

Alfred, T & Corntassel, J (2005). Being Indigenous: Resurgences against contemporary colonialism. *Government and Opposition Ltd*, 597–614. Available at http://web.uvic.ca/igov/uploads/pdf/Being%20 Indigenous%20GOOP.pdf.
Bandura, A (2001). Social cognitive theory: An agentic perspective. *Annual Review of Psychology* 52, 1–26.
Bishop, R (2012). Pretty difficult: Implementing kaupapa Māori theory in English medium secondary schools. *New Zealand Journal of Educational Studies* 47(2), 38–50.
Bishop, R & Berryman, M (2006). *Culture speaks: Cultural relationships and classroom Learning*. Wellington, New Zealand: Huia Publishers.
Bishop, R & Glynn, T (1999). *Culture counts: Changing power relations in education*. Palmerston North, New Zealand: Dunmore Press.
Bourdieu, P (1986). The forms of capital. In J Richardson (Ed.), *Handbook of theory and research for the sociology of education* (pp. 241–258). New York: Greenwood.
Brayboy, BMJ & Castagno, AE (2009). Self-determination through self-education: Culturally responsive schooling for Indigenous students in the USA. *Teaching Education* 20(1), 31–53.
Brayboy, BM & Deyhle, D (2000). Insider-outsider: Researchers in American Indian communities. *Theory into Practice* 39(3), 163–169.
Burt, LW (1986). Roots of the Native American urban experience: Relocation policy in the 1950s. *American Indian Quarterly* 10(2), 85–99.
Cohen, E & Allen, A (2013). Toward an ideal democracy: The impact of standardization policies on the American Indian/Alaska Native community and language revitalization efforts. *Educational Policy* 27(5), 743–769.
Cooke, M & O'Sullivan, E (2015). The impact of migration on the First Nations community well-being index. *Social Indicators Research* 122(2), 371–389.
Corntassel, J (2012). Re-envisioning resurgence: Indigenous pathways to decolonization and sustainable self-determination. *Decolonization: Indigeneity, Education & Society* 1(1), 86–101.
Education Review Office (2010, June). *Promoting success for Māori students: Schools' progress*. Wellington, New Zealand: Author. Retrieved from http://www.ero.govt.nz/National-Reports/Promoting-Success-for-Māori-Students-Schools-Progress-June-2010/Overview.
Faircloth, SC (2009). Re-visioning the future of education for Native youth in rural schools and communities. *Journal of Research in Rural Education* 2(9), 1–4.
Fixico, DL (1986). *Termination and relocation: Federal Indian policy, 1945–1960*. Albuquerque, NM: University of New Mexico Press.
Fixico, DL (2000). *The urban Indian experience in America*. Albuquerque, NM: University of New Mexico Press.
Grande, S (2004). *Red pedagogy: Native American social and political thought*. Lanham, MD: Rowman & Littlefield.
Hamer, P (2008). One in six? The rapid growth of the Māori population in Australia. *New Zealand Population Review* 33/34, 153–176.
Hermes, M (2012). Indigenous language revitalization and documentation in the United States: Collaboration despite colonialism. *Language and Linguistics Compass* 6(3), 131–142.
Hill, RS (2010). *Māori and the state: Crown–Māori relations in New Zealand/Aotearoa, 1950–2000*. Wellington, New Zealand: Victoria University Press.
Hill, RS (2012). Māori urban migration and the assertion of indigeneity in Aotearoa/New Zealand, 1945–1975. *Interventions: International Journal of Postcolonial Studies* 14(2), 256–278.
Hoxie, FW (2008). Discussion article. Retrieving the red continent: Settler colonialism and the history of American Indians in the US. *Ethnic and Racial Studies* 31(6), 11523e–1167.

Hynds, A & Sheehan, M (2011). Iwi versus Kiwi: Racism, race relationships and the experience of controversial political debates within a context of culturally responsive school reform. *New Zealand Annual Review of Education* 20(2010), 102–121.

Keiha, P & Moon, P (2008). The emergence and evolution of urban Māori authorities: A response to Māori urbanisation. *Te Kaharoa* 1, 1–17.

Lomawaima, KT & McCarty, TL (2002). When tribal sovereignty challenges democracy: American Indian education and the democratic ideal. *American Educational Research Journal* 39(2), 279–305.

Luke, A (2011). Generalizing across borders: Policy and the limits of educational science. *Educational Researcher* 40(8), 367–377.

Manuelito, K (2005, March). The role of education in American Indian self-determination: Lessons from the Ramah Navajo Community School. *Anthropology and Education Quarterly* 36(1), 73–87.

McCarty, TL & Lee, TS (2014). Critical culturally sustaining/revitalizing pedagogy and Indigenous education sovereignty. *Harvard Educational Review* 84(1), 101–124.

McIntosh, T (2005). Māori identities: Fixed, fluid, forced. *New Zealand Identities: Departures and Destinations*, 38–51.

Ministry of Education (2010). Ngā Haeata Mātauranga - The annual report on Māori education, 2008/09. Accessed at http://www.educationcounts.govt.nz/publications/series/5851/75954/introduction#nhmReportContents

Ministry of Education (2012). The New Zealand curriculum online. Treaty of Waitangi. Available at http://nzcurriculum.tki.org.nz/Principles/Treaty-of-Waitangi (accessed 4 February 2016).

Ministry of Education (2013). *Effective governance: Supporting education successes as Māori. Information for school boards of trustees.* Wellington, New Zealand: Ministry of Education. Available at http://www.minedu.govt.nz/~/media/MinEdu/Files/Boards/EffectiveGovernance/SupportingEducationSuccessAsMāori.pdf.

Ministry of Education (n.d.). The Māori education strategy: Ka Hikitia – accelerating success 2013–2017. Available at http://www.minedu.govt.nz/theMinistry/PolicyandStrategy/KaHikitia.aspx.

Ministry of Social Development (2010). *The social report 2010.* Wellington, New Zealand: Author. Available at http://www.socialreport.msd.govt.nz/people/distribution-population.html (accessed 4 February 2016).

Moll, L, Amanti, C, Neff, D & Gonzalez, N (1992). Funds of knowledge for teaching: Using a qualitative approach to connect homes and classrooms. *Theory Into Practice* 31(2), 132–141.

Nagel, J (1995). American Indian ethnic renewal: Politics and the resurgence of identity. *American Sociological Review* 60(6), 947–965.

National Center for Education Statistics (2012). *National Indian Education Study 2011* (NCES 2012–466). Institute of Education Sciences, US Department of Education, Washington, DC. Available at http://nces.ed.gov/nationsreportcard/pdf/studies/2012466.pdf (accessed 4 February 2016).

National Congress of American Indians (n.d.). *Tribal nations and the United States: An introduction.* Available at http://www.ncai.org/tribalnations/introduction/Tribal_Nations_and_the_United_States_An_Introduction-web-.pdf.

National Council of State Legislatures (2014). *Federal and state recognized tribes.* Available at http://www.ncsl.org/research/state-tribal-institute/list-of-federal-and-state-recognized-tribes.aspx#State.

Norris, T, Vines, PL & Hoeffel, EM (2012). *The American Indian and Alaska Native population: 2010 Census Briefs.* Washington, DC: United States Census Bureau. Available at http://www.census.gov/prod/cen2010/briefs/c2010br-10.pdf (accessed 4 February 2016).

Olssen, M & Peters, MA (2005). Neoliberalism, higher education and the knowledge economy: From the free market to knowledge capitalism. *Journal of Educational Policy* 20(3), 313–345.

O'Sullivan, D (2001). Māori education and principles of self-determination in the twenty-first century. *Waikato Journal of Education* 7, 157–170.

Penetito, W (2010). *What's Māori about Māori education?* Wellington, New Zealand: Victoria University of Wellington Press.

Pihama, L & Penehira, M (2005). *Literature review: Facilitating engagement.* Final Report. The University of Auckland. Available at http://www.kaupapaMāori.com/assets//te_puna_kokiri/facilitating_engagement.pdf.

Romero-Little, ME, McCarty, TL, Warhol, L, Zepeda, O, Ramanathan, V & Morgan, B (2007). Language policies in practice: Preliminary findings from a large-scale national study of Native American language shift. *TESOL Quarterly, Language Policies and TESOL: Perspectives from Practice* 41(3), 607–618.

Schimmel, N (2007). Indigenous education and human rights. *International Journal of Minority and Group Rights* 14, 425–453.

Sissons, J (2004). Māori tribalism and post-settler nationhood in New Zealand. *Oceania* 75(1), 19–31.

Sleeter, CE (2012). Confronting the marginalization of culturally responsive pedagogy. *Urban Education* 47(3), 562–584.

Smith, GH (2015). Transforming research: The indigenous struggle for social, cultural, and economic justice within and through education. Featured Presidential Session. Paper presented at 'Toward Justice. Culture, Language and Heritage in Education, Research and Praxis'. American Educational Research Association Annual Meeting, 16–20 April. Chicago.

Smith, LT (2005). On tricky ground: Researching the Native in the age of uncertainty. In NK Denzin & YS Lincoln (Eds), *Handbook of critical and Indigenous methodologies* (pp. 85–107). Thousand Oaks, CA: Sage.

Smith, L (2007). The Native and the neoliberal down under: Neoliberalism and endangered authenticities. In M de la Cadena & O Stam (Eds), *Indigenous experiences today* (pp. 333–351). New York: Berg.

Smith, LT (2013). *Decolonising methodologies: Research and Indigenous peoples* (2nd ed.). London: Zed Books.

Statistics New Zealand. (n.d.). 2013 Census iwi individual profiles. Available at http://www.stats.govt.nz/Census/2013-census/profile-and-summary-reports/iwi-profiles-individual.aspx.

Statistics New Zealand. (2013). 2013 Census quickstats about Māori. Available at www.stats.govt.nz.

The Encyclopedia of New Zealand. (n.d.a.). Te reo Māori – the Māori language. Available at http://www.teara.govt.nz/en/te-reo-Māori-the-Māori-language.

The Encyclopedia of New Zealand. (n.d.b.). Urban Māori. Available at http://www.teara.govt.nz/en/urban-Māori.

Tippeconnic, III, J & Faircloth, S (2011). Native American tribal colleges and universities: Utilizing Indigenous knowledges and ways of knowing to prepare Native peoples to meet the demands of an increasingly globalized community. In B Lindsay & WJ Blanchett (Eds), *Universities and global diversity: Preparing educators for tomorrow* (pp. 127–141). New York and London: Routledge.

Urban Indian Health Institute (2013). US Census marks increase in urban American Indians and Alaska Natives. Available at http://www.uihi.org/wp-content/uploads/2013/09/Broadcast_Census-Number_FINAL_v2.pdf.

US Department of Education (2011). *Tribal leaders speak: The state of Indian education, 2010*. Report of the consultations with tribal leaders in Indian country. Available at http://www.ed.gov/edblogs/whiaiane/files/2012/04/Tribal-Leaders-Speak-2010.pdf.

US Department of the Interior, Indian Affairs, Bureau of Indian Affairs (2014). Tribal leaders directory. 2014 Fall/Winter Edition. Available at http://www.bia.gov/cs/groups/webteam/documents/document/idc1-028053.pdf.

Viatori, MS & Ushigua, G (2007, Fall). Speaking sovereignty: Indigenous languages and self-determination. *Wicazo Sa Review* 22(2), 7–21.

Williams, T (2013). Quietly, Indians reshape cities and reservations. *The New York Times*. Available at http://www.nytimes.com/2013/04/14/us/as-american-indians-move-to-cities-old-and-new-challenges-follow.html?pagewanted=all&_r=0.

Wolfley, J (1991). Jim Crow, Indian style: The disenfranchisement of Native Americans. *American Indian Law Review* 16(1), 167–202.

47

Rural Literacies and Rural Mobilities

Textual Practice, Relational Space and Social Capital in a Globalised World

Kim Donehower and Bill Green

Literacy has long featured in social policy as a crucial resource with regard to the maintenance and renewal of modern society, and the emergence of abstraction and differentiation as organising principles for production and sensibility. Literacy in this view is most commonly conceived as a distinctive form of human capital, deeply implicated in social dynamics, institutional capacity, and political and economic order (Coulombe & Tremblay, 2004). It can be argued, however, that a human capital perspective is a limited frame for understanding literacy, at least in its fullest, most generative sense. Indeed, it may be far more appropriate to work with an expanded notion of 'capitals', and more specifically with certain understandings of *social capital*, particularly with regard to how literacy figures in rural social development.[1]

These points are usefully extended to consideration of rural society and its (re)contextualisation within a larger, more inclusive, critical understanding of the contemporary global-social condition. In this chapter we develop an account of what has been termed 'rural literacies' (Donehower, Hogg & Schell, 2007; Green & Corbett, 2013a), with reference to the role and significance of literacy for 'the organisation and transformation of rural society', more specifically in the context of the 'more developed regions of the world' (Introduction, this volume). The relatively recent emergence of rural literacies as a new formation in Literacy Studies, as a scholarly field, has resulted in the shaping of a distinctive, expanded view of literacy as a form of textual practice deeply implicated in the discourse practice of rurality and place (Donehower, Hogg & Schell, 2007, 2012; Green & Corbett, 2013b; Corbett, 2015).

This chapter considers the implications of global social change for a variety of institutions that serve as 'sponsors of literacy' (Brandt, 2001) in rural spaces. Such sponsors include schools and universities, but also religious organisations, social clubs and activist groups. The complex nature of contemporary rural migration has led to redefinitions of the rural as 'relational space' (Hedberg & do Carmo, 2012b), rather than as distinctly bounded, isolated, geographical space. At the same time, digitisation has enabled texts to be produced, consumed and shared across local, regional and national borders. Literacies and their sponsors, then, are key components structuring rural relational spaces.

New Literacy Studies and rural literacies

Our argument is principally organised within the framework of the New Literacy Studies (NLS), a term coined by James Paul Gee (1991) and Brian Street (1995). Street describes NLS in this way: 'What has come to be termed the New Literacy Studies ... posits that literacy is a social practice, not simply a technical and neutral skill; that it is always embedded in socially constructed epistemological principles. ... [and] in social practices, such as those of a particular job market' (Street, 2003, pp. 77–78). For this reason, NLS scholars speak of 'literacies', in the plural, since different social contexts produce distinct conceptualisations of what readers and writers are supposed to do with texts, the kinds of texts that should be produced and consumed, and why those texts and activities are valued.

Importantly, literacy is not to be identified as, or reduced to, education, certainly in its formal institutional aspect. Rather, literacy is not only associated with the whole educational spectrum, formal to informal, but also extends to domains outside education altogether, registering in social life more generally. This can be understood partly with reference to Dorothy Smith's notion of textually mediated social organisation (Smith, 1999), and partly as an instrumental feature of modernity, in its characteristic forms of abstraction and extended relationality. Hence rural literacies, rather than being simply one aspect of rural education, are to be understood as deeply embedded in contemporary rural life, including its 'trans-localism' (Hedberg & do Carmo, 2012b). Gee (1989, p. 23) argues that an individual's literacy might be measured by the number of different social contexts in which that person can do the things with texts (and with language in general) that count in that particular social milieu. In this way, literacy and social mobility are inextricably linked, as movement between diverse social contexts will demand new and different ways of producing and consuming language in a range of textual forms.

Literacy, then, can be seen as a resource for social mobility. US literacy scholar Deborah Brandt notes in her study of literacy in American lives:

> literacy skill [can be] treated primarily as a resource – economic, political, intellectual, spiritual – which, like wealth or education, or trade skill or social connections, is pursued for the opportunities and protections that it potentially grants its seekers. ... As a resource, literacy has potential payoff in gaining power or pleasure, in accruing information, civil rights, education, spirituality, status, money.
>
> *(Brandt, 2001, p. 5)*

This notion of literacy as a resource informs the definition of 'rural literacies' offered by Donehower, Hogg and Schell (2007, p. 4): '"Rural literacies" refers to the particular kinds of literate skills needed to achieve the goals of sustaining life in rural areas – or, to use Brandt's terms, to pursue the opportunities and create the public policies and economic opportunities needed to sustain rural communities.'

This vision, however, seems to presume a community in place – rural residents dedicated to deploying literacies to sustain the place in which they are rooted. But rurality in the 21st century often means mobility – not just of rural residents to cities and suburban areas, but of rural people migrating among rural communities, or moving to cities and then returning to rural areas, or residing part of the year in rural spaces and the remaining time in urban areas, as well as the sorts of 'everyday' and virtual mobilities that Milbourne and Kitchen describe (2014). In this chapter, we take on, and take seriously, the standpoint of the rural at a time of new intensities of globalisation, urbanisation and environmental pressure – and the resulting mobilities that these pressures create.

Rural mobilities and the new mobilities paradigm

Mobility has become a generative theme in contemporary enquiry, with significant implications for rural studies. As Hedberg and do Carmo (2012a, p. 1) note, 'mobilities' are now at 'the core of social science research'. They reference this to 'new forms of spatial mobility', in association with what are now acknowledged as widely prevailing '[p]rocesses of globalisation, economic restructuring and continuing urbanisation' (p. 1). This line of argument traces back to the seminal work of John Urry (2000, 2007), for whom mobility must be seen as the new organising principle for a reconstituted social theory in and for a global age.[2] The radical reorientation that this represents has been described as 'a new paradigm or way of framing research in the social sciences revolving around the study of the interdependent *movements* of people, information, images and objects' (Caletrio, 2012).

'All the world seems to be on the move', as Sheller and Urry (2006) observe – although this idea is more aptly formulated now in terms of a world in perpetual, restless motion, and indeed speeding up. This is due in large part to new developments in digital culture and technology, and associated global networks; but it must also take into account new forms and intensities of migration and diaspora, and other manifestations of what has usefully been called 'accelerated modernity' (Redhead, 2011). Within the 'new mobilities paradigm' (Sheller & Urry, 2006), work across a range of fields, although increasingly of a marked transdisciplinary nature, is addressed to 'the spatial mobility of humans, nonhumans and objects; the circulation of information, images and capital; as well as the study of the physical means for movement such as infrastructures, vehicles and software systems that enable travel and communication to take place' (Sheller, 2011, pp. 1–2). Space is a critical reference point here – or rather, *spatiality* – understood as dynamic and processual, and deeply implicated in power and the social (Massey, 2005). Thinking about space, moreover, is inextricable from considerations of place and scale, as well as time. Places are events, happening in space and time, at multiple and shifting scales. Moreover, 'spatial mobility [is] a basic variable in contemporary social life' (Bell & Osti, 2010, p. 200). Attention is drawn therefore to trajectories and itineraries, tracks and 'routes' – movements in and through space-time. As Sheller (2011, p. 1) writes, '[m]obilities research combines social and spatial theory in new ways'. This connects readily to thinking productively about rural literacies and rural education (Green, 2013; Corbett, 2015), despite the fact that mobilities may well still be largely 'a neglected phenomenon in rural studies' (Bell & Osti, 2010, p. 203).

Nonetheless, work is beginning to emerge on the conceptual relationship between rurality and mobility. Indeed, as Bell and Osti (2010, p. 109) claim, 'mobility is central to the enactment of the rural'. One significance of distance, for instance – in some contexts (e.g., Australia) at least, a significant marker of rurality – is that rural places are located differently in geospatial fields, and therefore travelling between them (literally and virtually) is required for transactions of various kinds. Moving between places, in space, takes time, and appropriate resources, and a distinctive economy. Similarly, many relations between the city and the country, and between nations, involve physical mobility in one way or another, as in migration and diaspora, or tourism and other forms of travel.[3] Accordingly Hedberg and do Carmo (2012a, p. 3) consider 'mobility as a way of connecting and transforming places', and point to 'an intensification and diversification of circulation between rural and urban areas, but also between distinct rural spaces situated in different regional, national or international geographies' (p. 2). In this context, Milbourne and Kitchen (2014, p. 327) discuss 'three forms of rural mobility: first, the complex movements of people to, from and through rural places; second, the everyday experiences of being on the move in rural places; and third, the problematics and potentialities of virtual forms of rural mobility'. All this indicates the changing nature of the rural and of rural place in contemporary social existence.

The implications of rethinking literacy through new understandings of mobility are considerable. Whereas social mobility is a theme relatively familiar in literacies research – see, for example, Deborah Hicks's powerful account of literacy and young Appalachian girls' restricted life opportunity (Hicks, 2013) – less attention has been given to spatial mobility, or indeed to the manner in which social and spatial mobility might usefully be thought of together. The challenge is to bring literacy, rurality and mobility organically into relation, in ways that move beyond current views and understandings. This requires rethinking literacy and rurality alike, and in this regard it is worth considering how both are commonly seen in terms of objects or 'fixings' – literacy-as-text and rurality-as-place – with 'text' and 'place' to be conceived now more dynamically, as productive (in)stabilities.

'In rural studies … there has long been a bias towards imagining the rural as stable' (Hedberg & do Carmo, 2012b, p. 199). Taking mobility into account, *as a first-order principle*, changes both literacy and the rural. 'The task here then is how to understand new forms and conditions of both literacy and rurality, and their intersection, in and for an increasingly complex and mobile world – a new global space of flows and places' (Corbett, 2015, p. 6). This is not to say that spatial states or fixities are no longer viable, or possible; rather, it indicates the importance of taking due account of 'the relations between mobilities and immobilities, scapes and moorings, movement and stillness', and 'the frictions of differential mobilities' (Sheller, 2011, p. 3). This formulation offers new perspectives on the complex contemporary relationship between literacy and rurality. Rural literacies in such a view are better regarded from the outset as 'multiple, mutable, and mobile, and ever relational' (Green & Corbett, 2013a, p. 12).

Relational spaces and literacy sponsors

If 'rural areas are relational and interconnected spaces', as Hedberg and do Carmo (2012a, p. 3) describe, how do literacies operate in those spaces? Hedberg and do Carmo note that the 'contradictory processes of depopulation and ageing, processes of modernisation or reinvention of tradition and or marginalisation … [of] functional reconfiguration' that exist in rural spaces 'are in part underpinned by an information economy' (p. 2). In such an information economy, literacies, as Brandt argues, become key resources, access to which is deeply affected by the networks of power that shape rural relational spaces.

Brandt coins the term 'literacy sponsor' to describe 'any agents, local or distant, concrete or abstract, who enable, support, teach, model, as well as recruit, regulate, suppress, or withhold literacy – and gain advantage by it in some way' (1998, p. 166).[4] Sponsors promote particular ideas about what, how and why to read and write. Such sponsors include, but are not limited to, schools and universities, employers, religious organisations, social clubs and political groups. Many different sponsors might be interacting with individuals in a particular rural space.

For example, in the US town of Hammond (a pseudonym), North Dakota, a single resident reported being heavily influenced in her ideas and practices about reading and writing from three different literacy sponsors: a regional university, a national churchwomen's group and the Farmers Union. The university, through distance education, had (unsurprisingly) provided an academic literacy, with an emphasis on research and methods of critical reading. The churchwomen's group, organised by the Evangelical Lutheran Church of America, had offered workshops for writing lay sermons, and promoted reading and writing for spiritual contemplation and evangelism. The North Dakota chapter of the Farmers Union, a national political advocacy organisation, had run a programme to create 'humanities couples', of which this interviewee and her spouse were one. The goal was to link the reading of artistic, historic and philosophical texts to advocacy for farmers and farm communities.

This community, of 500 people, has connections to other literacy sponsors, as well. The state historical society has an active local chapter that produced an 835-page centennial history of the town. Three different Christian denominations sponsor study groups, each of which espouses a method of reading scriptural and other religious texts that aligns with that particular denomination's values. The local chapter of a women's charitable club sponsors a reading incentive programme for schoolchildren, because they were unhappy with the ways the local K–12 school – another literacy sponsor – promoted reading. The local chapter of 4-H, a national youth organisation sponsored by the US Department of Agriculture, includes training in speechwriting and declamation as part of its programming.[5] The Hammond Economic Development Corporation manages a community business facility, with technological infrastructure for teleconferencing and other business needs, and free classes for area residents in a variety of digital literacies.

All these sponsors operate in this seemingly small and geographically isolated place: Hammond lies 175 kilometres from the nearest small city, across open plains subject to blizzards six months of the year. While money flows globally in and out of Hammond – global information systems technology for farmers developed by a Hammond company, which has clients in Germany and Brazil – literacy flows in and out of Hammond as well. The latter is aided by a technological infrastructure organised and funded through the efforts of a local economic development group, which opened the Hammond Business and Technology Center in part to provide high-speed Internet access to the community. Literacies in Hammond, then, can only be seen and fully scrutinised when they are considered as the product of multiple, overlapping literacy sponsors, many of them geographically remote from the town itself, whose many ways of valuing and practising literacy must be accepted, rejected, altered and combined by Hammond residents for their own purposes.

The choices rural residents make about what, how and why to read and write can, as Brandt (2001, p. 5) writes, have 'potential payoff in gaining power or pleasure, in accruing information, civil rights, education, spirituality, status, money'. But reading and writing can also work to shape individuals' relationships with other individuals and groups, and thus have a role in building social capital, in one of its earliest definitions: 'good will, fellowship, sympathy, and social intercourse' (Hanifan, 1916, p. 130). Reading and writing are rhetorical transactions: readers must consider their relationships to authors' purposes and imagined audiences, and writers must consider their relationships to their (often multiple) audiences (Brandt, 1990; Donehower, 2014). Rural residents' pleasure in reading, for example, might let them confirm or explore their relationships with entities both local and distant. Writing, particularly in online environments, lets rural people establish their connections to, and distinctions from, rural, urban and suburban people in other places. And for rural migrants, reading and writing offer tools to shape their relationship with their rural community of origin. Literacy, then, is integral in managing rural relational spaces.

This role for literacy is often overlooked, as research on rural sustainability tends to focus on economic development, and the types of literacies that manage social relationships may not be of the sort that create jobs in a knowledge economy. But benefits to a rural community do accrue from such activities, including the choices of individuals to migrate to or from those communities. It is important, then, to work with an understanding of social capital that goes beyond strict economic definitions. And as Linda Naughton (2014, p. 1) points out, social capital theories that rely on neoclassical economic assumptions (such as those of James Coleman and Robert Putnam) 'erase context and reduce space to a static form'. Specifically, Naughton argues that 'Coleman's stories of strong families and strong communities foreground economic self-interest and obligation at the micro-level, while excluding the wider economic context and non-economic motives. Putnam's story of "civicness" homogenises society and aggregates space into a singular analysable unit, separate from political power, and devoid of all other context, flow, and difference' (p. 12).

Such models, then, are a poor fit for understanding social capital within the complex flows of rural relational spaces. Such spaces are not strictly bounded, and thus amenable to analysis only at the micro level, nor are they so unbounded and homogenised that a generalised theory of 'civicness' could be applied to them. Instead, any understanding of social capital in rural relational spaces must be rooted in a conception of social capital that captures human networks both within and across distinct locations.

Naughton asserts that we must 'conceptualise social capital as an emergent effect of mediated relations rather than a pre-existing or added-to fund' (2014, p. 13). Furthermore, she asserts that 'the social capital of a group is always in the making, the outcomes will be unpredictable, but the crucial constitutive processes may be observed in play on the ground' (p. 13). We argue that literacy can be seen as one of these 'crucial constitutive processes'. The choices rural residents make about what, how and why to read and write can also, as Brandt writes, have 'potential payoff in gaining power or pleasure, in accruing information, civil rights, education, spirituality, status, money' (Brandt, 2001, p. 5) within and beyond their communities. But these acts of reading and writing must also be understood as embedded in larger networks of literacy sponsorship that emerge out of the particular historical, political, economic and cultural contexts that shape literacy in specific communities.

Naughton writes of Putnam that we must replace his 'singular and sentimental "civic" … with the multiple voices of interconnected "civics" situated in the particular historical, economic, cultural and political contexts' (2014, p. 15). Similarly, to understand how literacy functions in rural relational spaces, we must examine specific reading and writing practices, heeding Naughton's call for 'the observation of everyday practices where individuals and groups resolve their issues in messy and unanticipated ways, often using improvisations that are rarely captured by grand theory or abstract measures' (pp. 17–18). It is also important to document the larger contexts of literacy sponsorship that shape individuals' practices of, access to, and relationships with different forms of literacy – specifically, those pertaining to new and emergent forms of global restructuring and social inequality.

Rural literacies and the digital world

One feature of the growing literature on rural literacies is its engagement with a profound media shift, arguably the most far-reaching and significant since Gutenberg: put simply, from 'print' to 'digital electronics'. This is emphatically a paradigmatic shift, often associated with the emergence of what has been called the 'network society' (Castells, 1996). It is widely recognised as heralding in a new world order, a new global(ised) social logic, predicated on the proliferation of digital networks of information and communication, extending ostensibly across the entire world.

With work on rural literacies increasingly taking account of digital culture and technology, the emergence over the past decades of new formations and practices of techno-textuality,[6] image-based production and social media has decisively and irrevocably changed the manner in which literacy *and* rurality (and indeed mobility) are understood and articulated. This raises various challenges, not the least of which is a questioning of 'text' itself, as a stand-alone, fixed, more or less stable entity. This challenge has been mounted before the emergence of digital texts: in literacy studies, Brandt's earlier work, *Literacy as Involvement* (1990), calls into question a 'strong-text view of literacy', which, as she argues, emphasises the 'logical, literal, message-focused conventions of language-on-its-own' while ignoring, or at least underestimating, the roles that writers, readers and contexts play in making meaning from and with texts (Brandt, 1990, p. 13). Nonetheless there can be little doubt that digital-electronic networking has greatly enhanced interactivity, while further destabilising the 'fixed' character of texts and other objectivities.

When the roles of readers in constructing and reconstructing texts are emphasised, what comes into greater focus, of necessity, is the notion of literacy as a *practice*, and hence on the activities associated with literacy more generally – that is, 'reading' and 'writing', broadly conceived (Donehower, 2014). Moreover, it is important to acknowledge that this practice is now organised by principles of *mutability*, *multiplicity* and *mobility*, in ways distinctive to communication in a digital world (Green & Corbett, 2013a, p. 12). '[T]raditional ways of understanding rural space are no longer adequate as ruralities are transformed, sometimes radically by globalisation, the spread of mobile communication technologies, and the same contemporary change forces that have transformed literacy' (Corbett, 2015, p. 4). Here, our focus is on new understandings of mobility as a principle in and for rural literacies.

Understanding (rural) literacy as a practice opens up the possibility of asking what it is directed towards. What is its object or goal? What is at issue in its core activities of communication and exchange? What is it *doing*? What is it *for*? Brandt argues that outside the strong-text view, literacy may be seen as a means 'to sustain the processes of intersubjective life' (Brandt, 1990, p. 103) – in other words, to manage relationships and relational spaces. Drawing on Brandt, Donehower (2014) suggests that this kind of literacy-as-involvement is a key consideration in rural sustainability. This latter focus is supported by Butler and Edmondson's (2012, p. 226) endorsement of the need for 'a rural literacy that contributes to the sustainability of rural education and rural communities'. The critical point is that rural-regional sustainability is never simply a rural (or 'local') issue, since there are significant interdependencies among rural, urban and suburban constituencies that must be continually negotiated, and increasingly so in a globalised world. It is with this mind that we turn more directly to considering such matters in specific relation to rural mobilities.

New mobilities for rural literacies

It is now a relative commonplace of rural studies research that technological developments have decisively impacted the rural condition. This phenomenon ranges from transport technologies – roads, cars, etc. – to more recent communication technologies, themselves shifting over the last century from being largely print-based to digital-electronic as their primary mode. The latter refers not simply to email but to social media more generally, and includes the rise and consolidation of new entertainment and information media, with important and far-reaching ramifications for education and work alike.

Along with networked computing, perhaps the most significant development in this regard has been the Internet. Literacies research has clearly been energised by the Internet (Leander, Phillips & Taylor, 2010), as one among a range of new resources for social networking, across now extensive fields of relational space (Prinsloo & Rowsell, 2012). 'How … might we reconceive of the relations between physical mobility, virtual mobility, and educational mobility as social phenomena?' (Leander, Phillips & Taylor, 2010, p. 330). Originally posed with regard to children, this is a question with a much wider social and educational relevance, particularly with regard to rural studies and especially where physical location matters. What are the possibilities of the Internet, and digital information and communication technologies more generally, for the rural social world?

Immediately pertinent here is what was previously noted as one of 'three rural mobilities': 'the problematics and potentialities of virtual forms of rural mobility' (Milbourne & Kitchen, 2014, p. 327). As Milbourne and Kitchen (2014) found in their research in rural Wales, Internet-based literacies help rural residents maintain contact with family and friends out of the local area, renew or maintain relationships with out-migrants, and create connections with other local people (Milbourne & Kitchen, 2014, p. 333). Digital literacies also enable rural residents to deal with some of the logistical difficulties of living far from regional services: a number of tasks that used to be completed in person could now be conducted online (Milbourne & Kitchen, 2014, p. 334). Additionally, digital technologies – always provided there is adequate technological infrastructure – can provide ready access to literacy and cultural materials for rural residents, as well as other educational services (Hibbert, 2013). Rural social life is thereby at once enabled, enriched and sustained.

More to the point, however, there are profound implications for the formation of social capital, in the provision of what has been described by Woolcock (2001) as 'bonding', 'bridging' and 'linking' activities, resources and initiatives: 'Essentially, each type is distinguished by the proximity and similarity of the people it works to connect' (Donehower, 2014, p. 101). This is an especially important point with regard to the role and significance of literacies, which clearly have much to offer, at least potentially, in (re)generating rural community as well as solidarity, and in connecting across differences of space-time as well as culture and history.

Literacies, ruralities, mobilities

In this chapter, we have argued that those who consider rural literacies must understand both rurality and literacy as productive (in)stabilities, neither of which is fixed in time, place or meaning. Although this might seem a tall order, there is an ethical, as well as an intellectual, imperative to resist a will to closure as we work to understand both rural places and literacies in this way.

Historically, fixity has been a quality all too often ascribed to rural communities, in the sense of being 'stuck in the past', conservative (if not reactionary) in politics and values. This interpretive frame has made it difficult to acknowledge rural diversity and has led to such policy proposals as the abandonment of rural places.[7] It has also fostered the notion that future-looking, creative, visionary activity is the province of cities, as Corbett (2006) describes. Corbett offers a pointed critique of US economist Richard Florida's futurist vision, one which presumes continued out-migration from rural areas to urban centres, to the economic and ecological benefit of all. Such 'images of rurality as persistent, place-attached ghosts haunting the educational project of modernity' (Corbett, 2006, p. 286) lead to educational policies, in particular, that treat rural communities as 'a bit of an embarrassment as well as an administrative inconvenience', or simply leave them out of planning entirely (Corbett, 2006, pp. 293–294).

Literacy, in similar fashion, has historically been a moving target represented as an absolute, fixed standard. As Graff (1987, 1991), Barton (1994) and others have argued, standards for what counts as 'literate' continually evolve as the uses and technologies of literacy evolve. However, the terms 'literate' and 'illiterate' – or the phrase that Graff considers, the 'literacy crisis' – are embodied in various assessment practices as stable, quantifiable, you-are-or-you-aren't concepts. The 'literate' individual, as both a fixed truth and a moving target, has been used for decades to devalue rural places and people,[8] and such practices conceal the rich and specific nature of rural literacies. This is especially so when rural literacy and education are framed more or less exclusively within human capital perspectives, as we have suggested. Taking appropriate and critical account of social capital,[9] within an expanded view of (rural) *capitals* (Cocklin & Dibden, 2005), may well offer possibilities in this regard.

In particular, in a new world order of global digital networks and constant mobility, it is important, and indeed increasingly urgent, to think carefully and creatively about the affordances of information and communication technologies in harnessing and mobilising rural knowledge, culture and capacity in ways that resist marginalisation and the power of the pre-constructed. Within this, a richly reconceptualised view of rural literacies has a significant role to play in (re)building institutional capacity and enhancing community development and social renewal in rural life more generally.

Notes

1   In this regard, see Cocklin and Dibden (2005, pp. 3–6) with reference to 'the concept of capitals … as a category within which to categorise and (where possible) measure community and social change' in rural Australia. See also, more generally, Bourdieu (1986).
2   This does not mean that there was no scholarly attention to mobility prior or at least parallel to Urry's work in rural studies (see, for example, studies of out-migration and the like in Lichter & Brown, 2011 and Corbett, 2007; also Cresswell, 2010, p. 17, on 'the importance of an historical perspective which mitigates against an overwhelming sense of newness in mobilities research'). Rather, it is to propose that the 'paradigm' identified with Urry and his associates represents a distinctive insight into what are arguably qualitatively different social, cultural and technological conditions, profoundly changing the nature of mobile phenomena in contemporary social existence.
3   Increasingly overlaid now, of course, with virtual forms of travel.
4   Brandt's description of the control of the flow of literacies resonates with Massey's (1994) call to consider 'the power geometry of space-time compression', in which 'different social groups have distinct relationships to differentiated mobility: some people are more in charge of it than others; some initiate flows and movement, others don't; some are more on the receiving-end of it than others; some are effectively imprisoned by it' (Massey, 1994, p. 149).
5   For discussion of 4-H as a rural literacy sponsor, see McCracken (2012).
6   A term taken originally from Collins (1995, p. 6) and used here to refer to the articulation of literacy and technology more generally, specifically in the context of the new media age.
7   For an example of the abandonment idea, see the 'Buffalo Commons' movement in the United States, as described by Popper and Popper (2006).
8   See, for example, Mortensen (1994).
9   For a critical review of the social capital literature, see Naughton (2014).

References

Barton, D (1994). *Literacy: An introduction to the ecology of written language*. Oxford: Blackwell.
Bell, M & Osti, G (2010). Mobilities and ruralities: An introduction. *Sociologica Ruralis* 50, 199–204.
Bourdieu, P (1986). The forms of capital. In J Richardson (Ed.), *Handbook of theory and research for the sociology of education* (pp. 241–258). New York: Greenwood.
Brandt, D (1990). *Literacy as involvement: The acts of readers, writers, and texts*. Carbondale, IL: Southern Illinois University Press.
Brandt, D (1998). Sponsors of literacy. *College Composition and Communication* 49(2), 165–185.
Brandt, D (2001). *Literacy in American lives*. Cambridge: Cambridge University Press.
Butler, T & Edmondson, J (2012). Sustaining a rural Pennsylvania community: Negotiating rural literacies and sustainability. In K Donehower, C Hogg & EE Schell (Eds), *Reclaiming the rural: Essays on literacy, rhetoric, and pedagogy* (pp. 223–238). Carbondale, IL: Southern Illinois University Press.
Caletrío, J (2012). Book review: The new mobilities paradigm, by Mimi Sheller and John Urry. Mobile Lives Forum. Connnexion, 11 December. Available at http://en.forumviesmobiles.org/publication/2012/12/11/book-review-502 (accessed 21 July 2014).
Castells, M (1996). *The rise of the network society*. Cambridge, MA: Blackwell.

Cocklin, C & Dibden, J (2005). Introduction. In C Cocklin & J Dibden (Eds), *Sustainability and change in rural Australia* (pp. 1–18). Sydney: University of New South Wales Press.

Collins, J (1995). *Architectures of excess: Cultural life in the information age.* New York: Routledge.

Corbett, M (2006). Educating the country out of the child and the child out of the country: An excursion in spectrology. *The Alberta Journal of Education Research* 52(4), 286–298.

Corbett, M (2007). *Learning to leave: The irony of schooling in a coastal community.* Halifax, NS: Fernwood Publishing.

Corbett, M (2015). Rural literacies: Text and context beyond the metropolis. In J Rowsell & K Pahl (Eds), *The Routledge handbook of literacy studies* (pp. 124–139). New York and London: Routledge.

Coulombe, S & Tremblay, J (2004). Literacy, human capital, and growth. Working Paper #0407E, Department of Economics, Faculty of Social Sciences, University of Ottawa, Canada.

Cresswell, T (2010). Towards a politics of mobility. *Environment and Planning D: Society and Space* 28, 17–31.

Donehower, K (2014). Connecting literacy to sustainability: Revisiting literacy as involvement. In J Duffy et al. (Eds), *Literacy, economy, and power: Writing and research after 'literacy in American lives'* (pp. 97–110). Carbondale, IL: Southern Illinois University Press.

Donehower, K, Hogg, C & Schell, EE (2007). *Rural literacies.* Carbondale, IL: Southern Illinois University Press,

Donehower, K, Hogg, C & Schell, EE (Eds). (2012). *Reclaiming the rural: Essays on literacy, rhetoric, and pedagogy.* Carbondale, IL: Southern Illinois University Press.

Gee, JP (1991). *Social linguistics: Ideology in discourses.* London: Falmer Press.

Gee, JP (1989). What is literacy? *Journal of Education* 171(1), 18–25.

Graff, H (1987). *The legacies of literacy: Continuities and contradictions in western culture and society.* Bloomington: Indiana University Press.

Graff, H (1991). *The literacy myth: Cultural integration and social structure in the nineteenth century.* New Brunswick, NJ: Transaction.

Green, B (2013). Literacy, rurality, education: A partial mapping. In B Green & M Corbett (Eds), *Rethinking rural literacies: Transnational perspectives* (pp. 17–34). New York: Palgrave Macmillan.

Green, B & Corbett, M (2013a). Rural education and literacies: An introduction. In B Green & M Corbett (Eds), *Rethinking rural literacies: Transnational perspectives* (pp. 1–16). New York: Palgrave Macmillan.

Green, B & Corbett, M (Eds). (2013b). *Rethinking rural literacies: Transnational perspectives.* New York: Palgrave Macmillan.

Hanifan, LJ (1916). The rural school community center. *Annals of American Academy of Political and Social Sciences* 67, 130–138.

Hedberg, C & do Carmo, M (2012a). Translocal ruralism: Mobility and connectivity in European rural spaces. In C Hedberg & M do Carmo (Eds), *Translocal ruralism* (pp. 1–9). London: Springer.

Hedberg, C & do Carmo, M (Eds). (2012b). *Translocal ruralism.* London: Springer.

Hibbert, K (2013). Reconfiguring the communicational landscape: Implications for rual literacy. In B Green & M Corbett (Eds), *Rethinking rural literacies: Transnational perspectives* (pp. 155–175). New York: Palgrave Macmillan.

Hicks, D (2013). *The road out: A teacher's odyssey in poor America.* Berkeley, CA: University of California Press.

Leander, K, Phillips, N & Taylor, K (2010). The changing social spaces of learning: Mapping new mobilities. *Review of Research in Education* 34, 329–394.

Lichter, DT & Brown, DL (2011). Rural America in an urban society: Changing spatial and social boundaries. *Annual Review of Sociology* 37, 565–592.

Massey, D (1994). *Space, place, and gender.* Minneapolis, MN: University of Minnesota Press.

McCracken, IM (2012). I pledge my head to clearer thinking: The hybrid literacy of 4-H record books. In K Donehower, C Hogg & EE Schell (Eds), *Reclaiming the rural: Essays on literacy, rhetoric, and pedagogy* (pp. 121–142). Carbondale, IL: Southern Illinois University Press.

Milbourne, P & Kitchen, L (2014). Rural mobilities: Connecting movement and fixity in rural places. *Journal of Rural Studies* 34, 326–336.

Mortensen, P (1994). Representations of literacy and region: Narrating 'Another America'. In P Sullivan & D Qualley (Eds), *Pedagogy in the age of politics: Writing and reading (in) the academy* (pp. 100–120). Urbana, IL: National Council of Teachers of English.

Naughton, L (2014). Geographical narratives of social capital: Telling different stories about the socio-economy with context, space, place, power and agency. *Progress in Human Geography* 38(1), 3–21.

Popper, D & Popper, F (2006). The buffalo commons: Its antecedents and their implications. *Online Journal of Rural Research and Policy* 1(6).

Prinsloo, M & Rowsell, J (2012). Digital literacies as places resources in the globalized periphery. *Language and Education* 26(4), 271–277.

Redhead, S (2011). *We have never been postmodern: Theory at the speed of light.* Edinburgh: Edinburgh University Press.

Sheller, M (2011). Mobility. *Sociopedia.isa* pp. 1–12.

Sheller, M & Urry, J (2006). The new mobilities paradigm. *Environment and Planning* 38(2), 207–226.

Smith, D (1999). *Writing the social: Critique, theory, and investigations.* Toronto: University of Toronto Press.

Street, B (1995). *Social literacies.* London: Longman.

Street, B. (2003). What's 'new' in new literacy studies? Critical approaches to literacy in theory and practice. *Current Issues in Comparative Education* 5(2), 77–89.

Urry, J (2000). *Sociology beyond societies.* London: Routledge.

Urry, J (2007). *Mobilities.* London: Polity.

Woolcock, M (2001). The place of social capital in understanding social and economic outcomes. *Canadian Journal of Policy Research* 2(1), 11–17.

48

Bodily Well-being and the Visceral Geographies of the Rural

Allison and Jessica Hayes-Conroy[1]

Introduction

Recent work in rural studies, like much of the social sciences at large, has been influenced by the so-called material or affective turn. Scholars have engaged with concepts of relationality, materiality and embodiment, using theoretical frameworks such as non-representational theory and the more-than-human to explore how the material body comes to matter in rural contexts. This chapter seeks to connect this recent work in rural studies to the concept of visceral geography, broadly, and more specifically to visceral difference. 'Visceral geography' is a broad term that encompasses a wide range of critical and materially oriented attempts to theorise the body as a geographic space of its own. Visceral difference examines diverse moments of bodily sensation, moods, feelings and physical states of being, and asks how these different moments drive the production of sociospatial experience in varied and uneven ways. In this chapter, we explore why visceral difference matters to rural studies, and, more specifically, why it matters to the promotion of bodily well-being within rural spaces, drawing from our own scholarship to explore various empirical examples related to food, contamination and non-violence. We use the case of the Slow Food movement to explain our focus on difference, and the case of the Fukushima disaster to explore risk management in radioactive landscapes. We end by drawing upon lessons from our research on social activism in Colombia in order to enable conversation between the global north and south.

What does it mean to experience the rural with one's body? This is a question recently made popular by Michael Carolan's (2008) article in *Sociologia Ruralis* titled 'More-than-Representational Knowledge/s of the Countryside: How We Think as Bodies'. Carolan opens the paper with a clear and catchy point: 'if we think with our bodies then we must think about the countryside with our bodies too' (Carolan, 2008, p. 408). The rest of Carolan's paper is dedicated to uncovering some aspects of life in rural Iowa that become evident through a focus on embodiment: the tractor–body connections, the smell of livestock, and many other aspects of being-in-[a rural]-world. He also offers a rich explanation of notions like *dwelling*, *doing* and *being* derived from Heidegger and Merleau-Ponty, among others. Carolan's depictions and analyses are vivid and interesting, yet partial.

Contrast Carolan's work with that of another scholar who has also offered great contributions to our understandings of the experience of the rural, Carolyn Finney. Finney's (2010) article, 'This Land is Your Land, This Land is My Land', does not ask directly about the countryside as an 'embodied' or 'lived' event, yet perhaps speaks more deeply to this query than even Carolan himself. Finney's article interweaves storytelling with a sharp discussion of, paradoxically, representation – representations of African Americans, the environment, and the relationship between the two. She also talks a lot about power: the power to make visible/invisible, the power to tell stories and the power of images and words. How could it be that a focus on representation ends up revealing more about the body than an article directly focused on more-than-representational, embodied, lived experience? We suggest that the reason might lie in Finney's focus on social difference.

In interweaving storytelling and critical analyses of representation, Finney *is* talking about bodies. We might say she is talking about what we, elsewhere, have called *visceral difference* (Hayes-Conroy & Hayes-Conroy, 2010). This term is at once simplistic and jargoned – a way to signal that social difference (including race, class, gender, sexuality and more) really does matter all the way down to our physical matter, our bodies. Finney is keenly aware of this mattering, as demonstrated in the historical accounts she offers of her own parents' relationship with a 12-acre woodland outside of New York City. To be clear, in saying that social difference matters to our bodies *physically* we do not imply an essentialist view of race, gender or other forms of difference. Indeed, to avoid this fallacy, social theorists interested in difference have been reticent to discuss the material body at all, for fear of stirring up the racist mistakes of biological determinism. However, recent work on the materiality of difference has given scholars a vibrant way forward (Brison, 2002; Ahmed, 2006; Saldanha, 2006, 2007; Slocum, 2008, 2011). This work – which assumes a fluid, 'biosocial' body (as opposed to a static, 'pre-social' body) – has allowed scholars to pay attention to the physical body *and* difference. The reason may seem obvious: social difference is not just an idea, it is also physically produced and lived, often in multifarious and dynamic ways. These points we will attend to below.

What we want to propose here is that the dissimilarities we note between Carolan's and Finney's articles are indicative of a broader rift, emergent in rural studies and elsewhere, between scholars who are interested in bodies and bodily experience and scholars who are interested in power and social difference. We see this rift as unhelpful, and hope that this chapter can begin to mend the divide by demonstrating how the physical body itself is a site where these realms can come together. Below we provide a framework for thinking about this reconnection through the work of visceral geography. Visceral geography is a scholarly approach that takes seriously the biosocial complexity of the body and, in doing so, invites deeper understanding of the material body's role in the unfolding of social, political and ecological processes. Using a visceral approach, we focus on the theme of bodily well-being in order to clarify how calls to attend to the physical body must also be calls for a critical awareness of the mechanisms of oppression and social stratification that produce rural life.

Whose rural bodies?

A comprehensive review of the two divergent perspectives posited in the introduction is beyond the scope of this chapter. Instead, in this section we carefully and deliberately point to some examples of divergence as well as to ways in which enquiry into the body and enquiry into social difference are coming together in rural studies. It is important to note that it is not our intention to set up straw-men categories to break down. Certainly research into both the body and social difference has been, if anything, variable. Even the language employed to talk about these two 'fuzzy' realms has been multiple. For example, enquiry into the body has been promoted by studies of materiality, embodiment, performance, phenomenology, more-than- or non-representational dimensions, affect, and so on. And, enquiry into social difference has emerged from feminist, critical race and decolonial theory, to name just a few perspectives. These trajectories have always, to a certain extent, intersected. At the same time, the epistemological and ontological underpinnings of these trajectories often appear distinct. That is, it is still relatively rare in rural scholarship to find studies that are interested in the material body – its physical being, states, affects and so on – and that also recognise difference as a dynamic part of this body.

Body-centred approaches like non- or more-than-representational theory are considered relatively new and potentially innovative within rural studies (Woods, 2010, 2012). As the name suggests, these studies seek to move beyond matters of representation, discourse or meaning, highlighting instead the importance of bodily experience and affect. For example, Phillips (2014) draws upon the work of affect scholars Anderson (2006) and Pile (2010), as well as Carolan (2008), in weaving the material body into an account of a gentrifying rural village. In addition, Barratt (2012), also following Carolan, as well as others working on athletic experience (Spinney, 2006; Dant & Wheaton, 2007), describes a complex interrelation between the climbing body, climbing gear and the physicality of place (ice, rock, etc.). Also, Waterton (2012) has valuably detailed a growing body of work on the non-representational aspects of landscape, mentioning the work of Ingold (1995, 2011), Waitt (2007) and Wylie (2005), among others. Certainly such approaches are bringing fresh perspectives and questions to scholarly engagement with the rural. Nevertheless, often in such accounts, discussion of social differences like race and gender is absent. If it is present, difference may be included as an analytical touch point, but is not often described as corporeal experience – part of living and feeling.

Elsewhere, rural studies scholarship that is critically engaging with race, ethnicity, indigeneity, gender, sexuality and other forms of difference is also considered to be vital and innovative (Panelli, Hubbard, Coombes & Suchet-Pearson, 2009). For example, Panelli, Hubbard, Coombes and Suchet-Pearson (2009) special issue on 'De-centring White Ruralities' in the *Journal of Rural Studies* provocatively engages with the 'White and Western hegemonies' that the contributors argue underlie social constructions of the rural. In doing so, they also call attention to the white privilege and assumptions that characterise rural studies as a scholarly field. To be sure, the rural literature that is centred on difference is rich, and much too vast to comprehensively address here. Instead, we suggest that Panelli, Hubbard, Coombes and Suchet-Pearson (2009) provide some key examples of current directions, albeit partial. The point we want to make is that on the whole, such studies may be less likely to engage *directly* with discussions of bodies, embodiment, materiality and a realm beyond-representation, yet they are, ironically, much more likely to narrate the often viscerally engaging and emotionally charged lived realities of social difference in rural places.

There are already signs of valuable overlap between the body-centred and difference-centred scholarship that we describe here. Askins (2009), writing as part of the above-mentioned special issue, provides one well-developed example calling on rural scholars to consider what she calls 'reflective embodiment' (which acknowledges power and identity) as well as 'unreflective embodiment' (which does not understand difference as material), citing scholars like Probyn (2005) and Tolia-Kelly (2006, 2007) as inspiration. Waterton (2012) also echoes concerns about body-centred scholarship 'los[ing] sight of the ways in which difference, power and control also figure within the mix' (p. 71). However, at issue here is not simply a mixing of representational and non-representational perspectives. Many scholars interested in body-centred approaches are intent on including representational accounts alongside non-representational discussions (Carolan, 2008; Halfacree & Rivera, 2012; Morse et al., 2014; Phillips, 2014). While such inclusions can themselves open up the possibility of discussing bodies and difference both, they may also reinstate an unhelpful boundary between the two, such that difference is always understood as representational and social, but not often considered affective and material. In the next section we discuss one way to transgress this boundary through attention to bodily well-being.

Visceral difference and bodily well-being

We start by clarifying why we choose to centre our discussion on bodily well-being. Our focus on well-being is a way to attend to the physical and psychic traumas of social inequality – to the ways that social difference plays out unevenly and often unjustly in rural (as well as urban) places. In other words, it is through an examination of bodily well-being that the uneven materialities of social difference can be revealed. For example, it is known that interpersonal experiences of racism among African American women constitute an independent risk variable for preterm delivery (Collins Jr et al., 2004). Eating disorders can also be triggered by the traumas of sexism, racism and heterosexism (Thompson, 1992). Also, much public health research is predicated on a 'social determinants of health' model, which seeks to intervene in the mechanisms of ill health that operate not individually but at the scale of social inequality (Hofrichter, 2003). Moreover, scholars of rural health have noted that these social determinants play out differently in rural and urban places (Dolan & Thien, 2008). Among Native and Indigenous peoples especially, the health of rural communities and ecologies is especially (and inextricably) linked to health of individual bodies (Wilson, 2005). For all of these reasons, we argue that in order to fully grasp the material relationship between the body and rural place, one must pay attention to the ways that bodily well-being unfolds within and through social difference.

In her recent book, *Belonging: A Culture of Place*, feminist scholar bell hooks recounts the impact of race and racism on the embodied experiences of trauma that have shaped black life in rural Kentucky. She writes:

> In our psycho history, meaning the culture of southern black folk living during the age of fierce legally condoned racial apartheid, the face of terror will always be white. And symbols of that whiteness will always engender fear. The confederate flag, for example, will never stand for heritage for black folks. It still awakens fear in the minds and imaginations of elder black folks for whom it signaled the support of a white racist assault on blackness
>
> *(hooks, 2009, p. 10)*

Hooks's quote makes clear that the physical and psychic well-being of black people in rural Kentucky is (and has long been) intimately connected to difference, hierarchy and oppression. The sensations of terror, anger, fear and sadness that hooks attributes to racism clearly matter to the way that she and other black Kentuckians experience rural place and to their well-being therein. Moreover, for hooks, well-being seems to integrate biological and social components in an irreducible fashion. In other words, it doesn't make much sense to try to untangle the representational and non-representational aspects of racism, nor to ask whether symbols, words or feelings matter more. Bodies and difference are collapsed in her account.

We previously chose to use the term 'visceral' to describe this kind of account – an account that sees the sensorial, biological body, and the person marked by social difference, hierarchy and power, as one and the same (Hayes-Conroy & Hayes-Conroy, 2010). In the way that we have conceptualised the term 'visceral', visceral experiences such as those described by hooks are biosocially produced; they are the physical bodily manifestations that arise through an interchange of our seemingly disparate (but ultimately hybrid) biological and social worlds.

They are the embodied experiences that emerge out of a complex exchange of energies, materials, ideas and conditions. Our contention here is not just that the visceral, as such, *matters* to the realm of the rural, but, more pointedly, that investigations into different and uneven visceral experiences of rural places can reveal why the material body is politically relevant and how it can lead us towards critical, progressive change.

Drawing from the above notion of the visceral, we wish to offer a conceptualisation of bodily well-being that is critical, process-oriented and biosocially hybrid. In this conceptualisation, we want to be especially attentive to how *difference* is conceived and produced as a matter of bodily health. More specifically, we want to eschew the ways that social difference – especially gender and race – are often produced as standardised and immobile facts of medicine (Epstein, 2007). Instead, we prefer an understanding of social difference that is fluid and context driven in relation to bodily well-being. That is, well-being is not predetermined by social difference, if only because social differences – like gender or race – are not themselves fixed categories. We suggest that bodily well-being is always emergent out of particular visceral geographies – geographies that are messy, complicated and ever-shifting, but nonetheless patterned in ways that can highlight wide-ranging sociostructural inequity.

In the section below we illustrate the above understanding through a discussion of specific empirical examples. We use three cases to demonstrate how bodily well-being emerges through different visceral connections to the matter and meaning of rural life.

Food, contamination and non-violence – three case studies

Bay Area, California, USA, and Nova Scotia, Canada

Our desire to merge research on bodies and social difference first came through our ethnographic exploration of the landscapes and spaces of the Slow Food movement organisation in Nova Scotia, Canada and Bay Area, California. Amidst the purportedly *natural* benefits, appeal and tastiness of Slow Food practices (e.g., gardening), places (e.g., local family farms) and provisions (e.g., heirloom stone fruit), our attention turned to the question of difference. Who was turned off by Slow Food? For whom was its tastiness not 'natural', not a given? For whom was its expected appeal not resonant? For whom was it less than beneficial? And, why? (Hayes-Conroy & Hayes-Conroy, 2010; Hayes-Conroy & Martin, 2010). While Slow Food leaders lamented the movement's lack of racial diversity, the overwhelming whiteness of Slow Food was assumed to be a matter of culture rather than physicality. That is, leaders assumed that learned cultural preferences between racial/ethnic groups could explain why it was mostly whites that chose to partake in the pleasures and (healthy) benefits of Slow Food. Rarely would slow foodies concede the possibility that the movement's natural, artisan foods and its pure, wholesome rural landscapes may not be physically beneficial to everyone.

Indeed this possibility – the idea that purported physical benefits of rural goods/activities/spaces may not be universal – only begins to make sense when we consider the biosocial nature of the human body. Yes, Slow Food may be taken into the body as clean, unprocessed and nutritious food; its activities may bring bodies into contact with fresh air and water, and scenic landscapes. Yet, Slow Food also may be felt as adverse; its goods, activities and spaces may create sensations of tedium, unease, shame, disconnection or disgust. Without recognising social and cultural difference as embodied, there is little room to respect that what some experience as natural, others may experience as white, Eurocentric, colonialist, heteronormative or otherwise not resonant with their own bodily sense of positivity (Guthman, 2008). There is also little room to recognise that healthy body–food relationships and body–land relationships are not a one-size-fits-all game.

In short, out of these uncomfortable realisations came the urge to explore difference *viscerally* – to examine how bodies feel, change and *do* difference, to pay attention to the ways in which health and difference co-develop and co-define each other in the body, and to pay attention to how bodies do not fit so simply into predetermined categories of difference, but actually dynamically create and become recreated within them. We have brought this impulse into our current projects in Japan and Colombia.

Fukushima, Japan

The Tohoku earthquake and tsunami of 11 March 2011 forever marked Fukushima, Japan as a site of radioactive disaster. In the aftermath of the disaster, residents navigated the uncertain prospects of life in a contaminated landscape. What is safe to eat and drink? Where should children play? What locations require evacuation? What level of radiation is safe? These are questions that seemingly cut across social difference, their answers illuminating health standards for all bodies, universally. Yet the pursuit of health within a radioactive landscape is never clear-cut. Indeed, there is much scientific and political dispute over how to measure and assess radiation dangers. Moreover, the complexities of contamination also extend beyond these disputes, and beyond the matter of radiation itself. In the summer of 2013, one of us (Jessica) travelled to Fukushima with a colleague (Sasha Davis) in order to study the relationship between bodily well-being and visceral experience in post-disaster Fukushima. As our interviews with residents revealed, striving to live a 'healthy' life within a contaminated landscape involves the navigation of various risks – an assessment of what is *felt* as more or less worrisome. Importantly, such assessments are taken up quite differently across lines of social difference, as we describe below.

In the immediate aftermath of the disaster, most everyone in Fukushima was concerned with the direct risks of radiation exposure. However, as interviews with several farmers illustrated, there were other risks to navigate as well. Older farmers, especially, risked losing their livelihoods – farms that had often been in the family for generations. Along with this, their identity and daily life routines as connected to these lands were also at risk. As many rural communities evacuated, it became clear to those who stayed that there was a lot more to fear than radiation exposure. Rural families and communities were torn apart as younger generations moved on, leaving the elders to care for family property. Family meals became sites of conflict as parents and grandparents disagreed on what was safe to eat. In these cases, navigating risk to well-being was not just about radiation, but also about the health of community, culture, tradition and the family as an institution.

One interview with a local dairy farmer was particularly telling. This farmer – we will call him Mr Nakahara – was in his 60s, and had worked on his farm for most of his life. Through a mandatory evacuation, Mr Nakahara had been forced to leave his farm, including his land, house and animals. He now lives in 'temporary' evacuee housing, in a small, box-like room with his wife and elderly mother. Mr Nakahara's life in this housing complex has not been easy. He has gained much weight as a consequence of his newly sedentary life. He doesn't find the food available to him satisfying or wholesome. He experiences serious bouts of depression. Further, the housing complex is in an area with not insignificant amounts of radiation itself. As we interviewed Mr Nakahara, decontamination workers dotted the hillside just outside the complex. We asked him why he chose to stay. Mr Nakahara revealed that his decision involved a complex navigation of various risks and enticements. The housing complex was a draw because it housed many elderly residents from their community. He worried that if they left, his mother would lose touch with friends. Moreover, the immediate radiation risks were not a huge concern, since cancers from low-dose radiation exposure frequently take years to develop – perhaps longer than their life expectancies. The housing complex was also near enough to his evacuated farm that he could return periodically to tend to the property, ensuring his connection to his family's land was not severed.

In short, Mr Nakahara's example illustrates how production of bodily well-being rests on a number of particular factors, including age, family responsibilities, sense of rural identity, and physical and emotional connection to rural lands. Mr Nakahara's current state of well-being is emergent from his specific embodied context, from the particular geographies that make up his complicated visceral relationship to the housing complex, his farmland and the Fukushima prefecture. While his physical and mental health is far from ideal, it is perhaps better (in his calculation) than what it might be if he severed ties to his community, family and farmland. Of course, other Fukushima residents may have visceral connections to this contaminated landscape that activate different risk factors, and different potential health outcomes. A younger mother with no particular ties to farming, and with deep-seated worries about radiation risks for her children, would likely calculate the pursuit of bodily well-being differently. Indeed, younger mothers and children were often the first to leave Fukushima – especially those that had enough money to comfortably evacuate, leaving behind jobs, property and sometimes other family members.

Clearly social difference, including gender, age, occupation, family history, geographic origin, community connections and class status, all play a role in how Fukushima residents differently navigate the health risks of landscape contamination – both what options are available to them, and what options seem most appealing. Yet, these examples also show that social difference in Fukushima is not something that operates parallel to the material body *but rather in and through it*, as a visceral compass that directs people in their risk-taking decisions. This compass is not innately natural; it arises out of the always-uneven structures of social difference that work to situate and materialise each person's unique relationship to radiation. Patterns are evident – such as those that align with residents' gender, age, occupation and class status. But the materiality of social difference as seen through the gauge of bodily well-being emerges as something much more complex, situated and fluid. Here, the *visceral* matters to the realm of the rural not just because it is the body that materialises rural experiences, but more particularly because the (social) unevenness of well-being reveals to us the political nature of rural life. It is through such a visceral account of social difference that we can begin to understand how to develop disaster management practices that are responsive to diverse needs of rural communities.

Antioquia, Colombia

Antioquia is a department (state) of Colombia boasting many mountainous areas, lowlands and a coastal region, as well as a number of towns and cities including Medellín, the departmental capital. In 2011 one of us (Allison) began a long-term ethnographic project in Antioquia with the Legion del Afecto, a youth initiative working for everyday peace and well-being in violence-affected communities. The Legion has inspired thousands of youth and is now present in multiple departments of Colombia, but it began in 2003 as an emotional urban-to-rural journey of 30 or so youth from the city of Medellín to the mountains and forests surrounding the rural township of Aquitania, Antioquia. Since this foundational trip, the initiative has placed central importance on the relationship between the journeying body and rural landscapes, spaces and people. The Legion seeks to potentiate collective well-being in part through attention to these embodied relationships.

The case of the Legion del Afecto offers another direct illustration of the importance of understanding well-being through simultaneous attention to bodies/bodily experience and power/social difference. While bodily well-being in the Fukushima example described above is tied to the direct and indirect impacts of nuclear disaster, in the case of the Legion, the pursuit of well-being emerges through the movement's attempt to help youth avoid what they call 'criminal death' (death as a result of targeted armed conflict, including gang-related homicides) as well as to help them deal with other physiological and psychic impacts of the country's multilayered conflict. Two brief reports from the Legion serve as telling examples.

The first has to do with the power of bodily needs themselves. A story is often narrated, from the early days of the Legion, in which dozens of Medellín youth found themselves in a far-away rural hamlet, trying to break the ice in conversation with a community that had been profoundly affected by armed conflict. Feeling frustrated, one of the young men from Medellín stood up to make an announcement: 'Here we are sitting here, talking as it gets dark, and not one of us knows where we will eat our next meal or sleep for the night.' In response, an elderly leader from the region stood up and announced to the youth not to worry, that the community would open their homes for them to eat and sleep. At that moment, the distance between the youth and the rural community was broken, because the youth were recognised not as urban strangers but as other bodies-in-need. Though a seemingly minor story, this anecdote profoundly shaped the development of the Legion, as the initiative built an identity around the bridging of communities through recognition of their physical connectedness (e.g., their shared needs for food, drink, sleep, affection and emotional support). Unlike many other state-funded social initiatives, the Legion refused to wear logo-marked vests that marked them as strangers – as members of an outside group. Instead, they insisted on arriving at targeted communities with song and dance as human beings – with bodily needs, feelings and sensations, proudly *sin chaleco* (without vest).

The second anecdote from the Legion has to do with the mobilising power of sensorial experience. The experience of an urban-accustomed body in rural settings could be exhilarating, frightening or somewhere in-between. For many of the youth in the Legion, journeying to rural areas has been an entirely new experience – one that has made them more aware of their own body's capacity for sensation and sensory awareness. On a 2013 trip to rural Antioquia, participating young men described experiencing new colours, smells, sounds and positive states of body and mind. Yet, importantly, while many youth in the Legion have direct experience with violence, rural sensorial experiences are not assumed to be therapeutic. Instead, the new sensorial experiences are discussed in the context of accompanying and getting to know others that also have been affected by violence – constructing well-being as intentionally collective, rather than implicitly individual. In this sense, the transformative power of sensorial experience in the Legion comes from the merging of rural experience with a powerful collective vision for social change.

The Legion demonstrates an interesting tension between bodily sameness and bodily difference, through which the movement pursues collective wellness. In the first example, the power to bridge differences came through recognising and securing similar biological necessities among urban and rural participants. In the second example, however, the transformative power came through *strategically producing* rather than assuming the benefits of rural journeying, a tactic that required recognition of bodily difference both within and between rural and urban participants. While the case of Fukushima reveals that the production of bodily well-being is socially varied and contextual, the case of the Legion demonstrates that the production of well-being *as an activist strategy* requires deliberate attention to both how bodies can (re)act differently and how (different) bodies can experience collectively. The Legion's example shows us that in any given social problem or initiative it may not be possible to fully understand the significance of bodily experiences of the rural without simultaneously considering how power for transformation is generated and how bodies may relate and react to that power differently.

Conclusions

Our three examples have explored the messy ways in which bodily well-being is created (or damaged) through day-to-day interactions that are neither solely sensorial/biological nor social, but instead are biosocial. In conclusion, we want to expand these examples to make three related points about rural studies scholarship.

First, and most generally, we appreciate that rural scholars, no matter the perspective or training, are most interested in capturing, explaining and accounting for rural life in as complete a way as possible. In particular, what has prompted renewed interest in the body and new excitement about perspectives-beyond-representation is the realisation that the *lived* aspects of life do not always make it into scholarly accounts. We see these realisations as valuable, and at the same time recognise that they should not overshadow the importance of building accounts that also reveal the workings of power and difference.

Second, if rural scholars are to write truthfully about power and difference, then it seems necessary to follow them into the body. Above we mention a few scholars who are already doing this. More generally, we want to note that feminist scholarship on the body has long been rich, vibrant and diversely engaged, and could provide multiple avenues for the rural scholar to develop body-centred means of analysis that take difference and power seriously.

Third, and finally, we have shown that a focus on bodily well-being provides a hybrid analytical frame with a common and familiar starting point (a well body). Importantly, if well-being is to be a framework for understanding social difference in and through the body, it must be addressed through much broader means than, for example, standard, predetermined health indicators allow. This demand for recognising bodily complexity and uniqueness, however, does not deny the possibility of commonality and connection. In fact, it is through the work of examining bodily difference – uncovering the ways that bodies feel, experience and live the rural differently – that we have also become attentive to the possibility and the importance of mutuality. Particularly through the work of the Legion del Afecto, we have been inspired by the body as a point of mutual connection. Unlike what we found in our earlier work on Slow Food, however, the potential for mutuality in the Legion comes directly out of a recognition of visceral difference. Thus, we propose that the body – in all of its dynamic difference – can and should be utilised as an important foundation for all types of progressive social projects that seek to promote and enhance rural well-being.

Note

1   The authors choose to write their names this way to indicate equal authorship.

References

Ahmed, S (2006). *Queer phenomenology: Orientations, objects, others.* Durham, NC: Duke University Press.

Anderson, B (2006). Becoming and being hopeful: Towards a theory of affect. *Environment and Planning D* 24, 733–752.

Askins, K (2009). Crossing divides: Ethnicity and rurality. *Journal of Rural Studies*, 25(4), 365–375.

Barratt, P (2012). 'My magic cam': A more-than-representational account of the climbing assemblage. *Area* 44(1), 46–53.

Brison, SJ (2002). *Aftermath: Violence and the Remaking of a Self.* Princeton, NJ: Princeton University Press.

Carolan, MS (2008). More-than-representational knowledge/s of the countryside: How we think as bodies. *Sociologia Ruralis* 48(4), 408–422.

Collins Jr, JW, David, RJ, Handler, A, Wall, S & Andes, S (2004). Very low birthweight in African American infants: The role of maternal exposure to interpersonal racial discrimination. *American Journal of Public Health* 94(12), 2132–2138.

Dant, T & Wheaton, B (2007). Windsurfing: An extreme form of material and embodied interaction? *Anthropology Today* 23, 8–12.

Dolan, H & Thien, D (2008). Relations of care: A framework for placing women and health in rural communities. *Canadian Journal of Public Health/Revue Canadienne de Sante'e Publique*, S38–S42.

Epstein, S (2007). *Inclusion: The politics of difference in medical research*. Chicago, IL: University of Chicago Press.

Finney, C (2010). This land is your land, this land is my land: People and public lands redux. *The George Wright Forum* 27(3), 247–254.

Guthman, J (2008). 'If they only knew': Color blindness and universalism in California alternative food institutions. *The Professional Geographer* 60(3), 387–397.

Halfacree, KH & Rivera, MJ (2012). Moving to the countryside … and staying: Lives beyond representations. *Sociologia Ruralis* 52(1), 92–114.

Hayes-Conroy, A & Hayes-Conroy, J (2010). Visceral difference: Variations in feeling (slow) food. *Environment and Planning* A 42(12), 2956–2971.

Hayes-Conroy, A & Martin, DG (2010). Mobilising bodies: Visceral identification in the Slow Food movement. *Transactions of the Institute of British Geographers* 35(2), 269–281.

Hofrichter, R (2003). *Health and social justice: Politics, ideology, and inequity in the distribution of disease* (Vol. 11). San Francisco, CA: Jossey-Bass.

hooks, b (2009). *Belonging: A culture of place*. New York: Routledge.

Ingold, T (1995). Building, dwelling, living: How animals and people make themselves at home. In M Strathern (Ed.), *Shifting contexts: Transformations in anthropological knowledge* (pp. 57–80). London: Routledge.

Ingold, T (2011). *Being alive: Essays on movement, knowledge and description*. London: Taylor & Francis.

Morse, CE, Strong, AM, Mendez, VE, Lovell, ST, Troy, AR & Morris, WB (2014). Performing a New England landscape: Viewing, engaging, and belonging. *Journal of Rural Studies* 36, 226–236.

Panelli, R, Hubbard, P, Coombes, B & Suchet-Pearson, S (2009). De-centring white ruralities: Ethnic diversity, racialisation and indigenous countrysides. *Journal of Rural Studies*, 25(4), 355–364.

Phillips, M (2014). Baroque rurality in an English village. *Journal of Rural Studies* 33, 56–70.

Pile, S (2010). Emotions and affect in recent human geography. *Transactions of the Institute of British Geographers* 35(1), 5–20.

Probyn, E (2005). *Blush: Faces of shame*. Minneapolis, MN: University of Minnesota Press.

Saldanha, A (2006). Reontologising race: The machinic geography of phenotype. *Environment and Planning D* 24(1), 9–24.

Saldanha, A (2007). *Psychedelic white: Goa trance and the viscosity of race*. Minneapolis, MN: University of Minnesota Press.

Slocum, R (2008). Thinking race through corporeal feminist theory: Divisions and intimacies at the Minneapolis Farmers' Market. *Social & Cultural Geography* 9(8), 849–869.

Slocum, R (2011). Race in the study of food. *Progress in Human Geography* 35(3), 303–327.

Spinney, J (2006). A place of sense: A kinaesthetic ethnography of cyclists on Mont Ventoux. *Environment and Planning D* 24, 709–732.

Thompson, BW (1992). 'A way outa no way': Eating problems among African-American, Latina, and White women. *Gender & Society* 6(4), 546–561.

Tolia-Kelly, D (2006). Affect – an ethnocentric encounter? Exploring the 'universalist' imperative of emotional/affectual geographies. *Area* 38, 213–221.

Tolia-Kelly, D (2007). Fear in paradise: The affective registers of the English Lake District landscape re-visited. *Senses and Society* 2, 329–352.

Waitt, G & Lane, R (2007). Four-wheel drivescapes: Embodied understandings of the Kimberley. *Journal of Rural Studies* 23, 156–169.

Waterton, E (2012). Landscape and non-representational theories. In *The Routledge companion to landscape studies* (pp. 66–75). London: Routledge.

Wilson, K (2005). Ecofeminism and First Nations Peoples in Canada: Linking culture, gender and nature. *Gender, Place and Culture* 12(3), 333–355.

Woods, M (2010). Performing rurality and practising rural geography. *Progress in Human Geography* 34(6), 835–846.

Woods, M (2012). Editorial: New directions in rural studies? *Journal of Rural Studies* 28, 1–4.

Wylie, J (2005). A single day's walking: Narrating self and landscape on the South West Coast Path. *Transactions of the Institute of British Geographers* 30, 234–247.

Part VIII

Power and Governance

Section editor: Lynda Cheshire

49

Power and Governance

Empirical Questions and Theoretical Approaches for Rural Studies

Lynda Cheshire

Introduction

In the first volume of *The History of Sexuality*, the French philosopher Michel Foucault observed that 'power is everywhere' (1981, p. 93), not because it has a hold on everything, but because it is produced at every moment and at every point. While Foucault's writing on power represented a distinct shift in the way power was understood and theorised within the social sciences, his observation about the pervasiveness of power in social relations and practices has long been shared, even among those who do not follow his theoretical stance. In the field of rural studies, this is evident in the way power has endured as a dominant theme on the research agenda. In tracking transformative, and sometimes more subtle, changes in rural society and the concomitant effects of those changes on rural power relations, and by engaging with theoretical advancements in the study of power more broadly, our understanding of how power is exercised in and upon rural areas has evolved over time. From stories of an egalitarian and distinctly rural way of life to processes of counter-urbanisation and contestations over the very meaning of rurality; from the role of local government as *the* locus of power in rural areas to the emergence of new forms of governance that reshape the state in both vertical and horizontal directions; from farmers as local political elites to their subsumption into a globalised and industrialised agro-food network; and from rural areas as spaces of decline and marginalisation to a reassertion of rural power through new social movements and politics, rural studies scholars have revealed the way power is bound up in each of these processes to serve the interests of some, but not others, and to generate marginalisation, inequality, conflict, resistance and change.

In this section, the composite chapters document some of the more recent trends in the way power is thought to operate in contemporary rural society, and their outcomes for rural people and communities. These begin with an examination by David Douglas of the changing structures and institutions of power in rural areas, notably the restructuring of rural local government witnessed across much of the global north, and the opportunities and risks afforded by this process. Among many of the challenges to the once-hegemonic authority of rural local government is the move towards new partnership arrangements that have brought a much wider range of interest groups and actors into the local decision-making arena. While the disruption of traditional power structures is thought to have created new opportunities for 'power sharing' among those once absent from the political elite, the chapter by Áine Macken-Walsh indicates to us that it also constrains opportunities for others who remain excluded.

The diffusion of rural power is also noted by Michael Woods in his chapter, but his focus is less on the formalised structures of power (however they might now be configured) and more on rural actors' sense of disillusionment with the ability of established rural groups (including the local and national state) to represent their views and interests. In the void created, a range of rural social movements and protest groups have emerged to oppose or reverse unpopular decisions, resist perceived threats to established ways of life, and fight for the right to maintain control of, and access to, rural resources. The capacity of rural dwellers to respond to externally imposed change is also addressed by Nathan Young. Whereas Woods frames such capacity for action through the lens of protest or resistance, Young engages with the concepts of resilience to explore how human agency can also be exerted through the adaptive capacities of rural people to plan for, and respond flexibly to, unknown contingencies. As Young notes, however, the renewed focus on agency rather than powerlessness in resilience thinking can be problematic if it remains blind to questions of power and inequality in the differential access to the resources that resilience depends upon, and in the way that discourses of resilience support, rather than challenge, a dominant neoliberal political agenda.

In the final chapter, Loka Ashwood and Michael Bell take a different perspective on rural power. They suggest that despite the symbolic power of rural areas – which the rural movements of Woods' chapter have sought to assert and protect – rural power in its material form has been eclipsed by the power of agriculture and agricultural constituencies, not only in policy terms, but also within academic research where the sociology of food and agriculture reigns supreme while sociology's rural subject is left to languish. For Ashwood and Bell, this has pulled academic and policy attention away from many rural issues, such as health, poverty and social justice, that are not oriented towards agriculture and disabled alternative politics in the countryside. However, they reject the inevitability of the rural's displacement, arguing that while rural studies scholars are influenced by the power-pull between rural and agriculture, they also help to create it, and thus have the power to unmake it and give the rural the renewed attention that it needs.

The remainder of this opening chapter provides the necessary context to these contemporary examinations of rural power by embedding them within a historical narrative of rural studies scholarship and its treatment of power as a topic of substantive interest and as an analytical concept. This account is necessarily brief and traverses a wide array of theoretical and substantive issues that have captured the attention of scholars over the last half-century. Despite their diversity, what they share in common is a concern to illustrate the way power has been exercised *within*, *over*, *by* and *about* the rural. Four core themes can be discerned.

In search of a rural ruling elite: community studies, class relations and the rural idyll

The first theme is the investigation of internal class and power structures in rural areas, which began with local 'community' studies and subsequently developed into a more critical exposition of the means by which the power of ruling elites was reproduced in rural areas, including through their dominance of local government decision making. During the 1970s, scholars debated whether local power structures were elitist or pluralist (Bachrach & Baratz, 1962), and whether it was class/production or status/consumption that provided the most coherent explanation for social inequality within rural areas (Oxley, 1974; Wild, 1974). In general terms, power was understood as having two dimensions or 'faces' (Bachrach & Baratz, 1962): the first when decision-making processes advantage one group over another; and the second in the exercise of control over the agenda-setting process, such that powerful actors determine which issues are brought to the decision-making arena in the first place.

The development of Lukes' (1974, 2005) more sophisticated conceptualisation of power, which identified a third dimension involving the manipulation of people's real interests so they come to share a particular view of the world, provided new insights into the way power could operate in ways that were both more subtle, but also more potent. This line of thinking came to influence rural studies as scholars identified how social structures and ideologies served to perpetuate the maintenance and reproduction of unequal class and power structures.

In the UK, this was heralded by the studies of Newby and colleagues (Newby, 1977; Newby, Bell, Saunders & Rose, 1978) on the class relationships between farmers and farm workers in East Anglia. While traditionally understood as potentially antagonistic, Newby and colleagues showed how class relations between propertied farmers and property-less farm workers were accepted by both parties as natural and unproblematic, which granted a high level of stability and legitimacy to a system that was otherwise profoundly unequal. More specifically, Newby, Bell, Saunders and Rose (1978) identified two components of rural life that contributed to the maintenance of these class structures. The first was the notion of rural areas as distinct and harmonious, along with ideologies of egalitarianism and community, which framed farmers and workers as being on the same side and disguised their opposing class interests. The second was the expression of these values in the course of local politics, which enabled rural elites to dominate local government and to justify their dominance through claims that what was good for the farmer, was also good for the (farming) community (see also Poiner, 1990; Gray, 1991). At that time, even the arrival of middle-class newcomers did little to disrupt these highly traditional power structures.

Globalisation, political economy and rural change

The second theme emerged from the ascent of a new phase of global capitalist accumulation in the 1980s which prompted a widespread programme of restructuring and deregulation in rural areas, embedding them in global and national relations of power. In response, and as Marsden and colleagues (1990) have since reflected, rural-based theory and research developed along two distinct lines, the first being the '"new" political economy of advanced agrarian systems' (Marsden, Lowe & Whatmore, 1990, p. 2). Influenced by Marxist writings on the inherently unequal and exploitative nature of capitalism development, contemporary scholars applied this lens to the way family farmers were being drawn into a transnationalised and increasingly techno-oriented agri-food system (Bonanno et al., 1994). While this exposure was often framed as offering farmers access to global markets, the reality was their growing dependence upon the technological inputs of large agribusinesses 'upstream', and on 'downstream' actors, such as supermarkets, who set the conditions for the production and distribution of farm products (Lawrence, 1990). In effect, farmers were seen to be engaging in a race to the bottom, competing for contracts with footloose capital on deteriorating terms of trade (Commins, 1990).

Despite its cogency as an analytical framework, the structuralist underpinnings of political economy were subsequently criticised for 'placing the whole process of social change ... largely beyond actors' practices and control' (Arce & Marsden, 1993, p. 296). The response was the adoption of more actor-oriented approaches to understanding global food systems that enabled researchers to position farmers as more active participants (Long, 1992). At the other end of the commodity chain, the process of 'deconstructing the powerful' (Murdoch, 2000, p. 410) was facilitated by the adoption of actor-network theory (Callon & Latour, 1981; Law, 1992), with corporate power understood as being contingent on the enrolment of a range of global and local actors into an actor–network and hence more susceptible to challenge and contestation than previously framed (Busch & Juska, 1997).

The second line of enquiry examined the uneven effect of these changes upon rural areas through the lens of 'rural restructuring'. In response to the demands of the globalised food system, family farms were becoming larger, more technologically oriented and more efficient, prompting a rapid decline in the rural workforce. At the same time, national governments were driving their own restructuring programmes according to economic rationalist imperatives that caused key services such as schools, hospitals and government agencies to close in areas where population levels no longer reached critical mass. Charting this 'dynamics of decline' (Lawrence & Williams, 1990), and noting how some rural areas were frequently performing worse than urban on a range of social and economic indicators, commentators declared a state of 'rural crisis' (Varley, Boylan & Cuddy, 1991; Lockie, 2000; Horton, 2005). Powerless against the forces of globalisation and the actors who drove it, these regions were seen to have become surplus to requirement and were rapidly becoming spaces of decline, marginalisation and exclusion (Herbert-Cheshire, 2003).

In contrast, rural areas that had high consumption value were experiencing the in-migration of a professional service class seeking its own rural idyll. As Newby (1980) saw it at the time, this 'quiet revolution' in the social composition of rural areas represented a significant challenge to the established structures of rural power, as disputes over land use and development turned rural areas into terrains of conflict, not only between locals and newcomers, but also among newcomers themselves (Woods, 1997). Coinciding with a 'postmodern turn' in the social sciences, these developments induced scholars to reflect that meanings of rurality were bound up in the exercise of power as actors were seeking to 'impose "their" rurality on others' (Murdoch & Pratt, 1993, p. 411). Academics were not immune from such criticism, but were viewed, alongside other elite groups, as attempting to make themselves powerful by marginalising alternative understandings of the rural (Murdoch & Pratt, 1994). Any attempt to define rurality was thus disparaged as an exercise of discursive power.

Rural governance and the reconfiguration of rural power

A third body of literature has taken the restructuring thesis in a different direction, citing the changing form and function of the nation state, and the shift from government to governance, as one of the most profound political processes to impact on rural areas. In broad terms, governance can be understood to represent a new mode of governing that is no longer enacted solely through the formal, coercive powers of the nation state, but is exercised through a range of governmental and non-governmental actors and entities operating at different spatial scales and across different sectors (Jessop, 1997; Stoker, 1998). Governance theorists have suggested that, through governance, political power has been reconfigured in both vertical (Jones & McLeod, 1999) and horizontal (Counsell & Haughton, 2003) directions. In terms of the former, the challenges of governing an increasingly globalised system have induced nation states to devolve many of their functions 'upwards' into the hands of supra-national bodies such as the European Union and the World Trade Organization. Simultaneously, they have also been devolved 'downwards' into the hands of sub-national and local actors on subsidiarity arguments that decision making should be enacted, where possible, at the level of authority closest to local people. Horizontal reconfigurations, on the other hand, are manifest in the positioning of local and regional actors who once operated beyond the formal authority of the local state as its 'partners' in new initiatives, indicating a blurring of the boundaries between state and civil society.

Rural scholars have charted the evolution of governance arrangements in rural policy and practice in the fields of rural development (Derkzen, Franklin & Bock, 2008; Shucksmith, 2010; Macken-Walsh & Curtin, 2013), natural resource management (Higgins & Lockie, 2002), agri-food systems (Le Heron, 2003) and planning (Morrison, Wilson & Bell, 2012). Core to this research have been questions about the operation of power within governance arrangements and the extent to which their structures, processes and outcomes are as democratic and empowering for rural people as they are frequently promoted. In this regard, scholars have been somewhat sceptical, scoping out a critical, theoretical and empirically informed research agenda into the practices and relations of power that play out in governance arrangements. What they have found is that the potential for power sharing is not always realised and that governance can foster new forms of inequality and exclusion (Woods, 1997). Despite the inclusion of a broader range of actors, governance initiatives can also remain elitist as the 'usual suspects' continue to dominate or are replaced by new rural elites who are skilled in project management and political lobbying (Osti, 2000; Kovách & Kučerova, 2009).

Despite the theoretical plurality of this work, Foucauldian governmentality analyses (Foucault, 1991) have been particularly influential in the past 15 years, viewing governance as an advanced liberal political practice that exerts power, first, by instrumentalising the self-governing capacities of individuals and communities according to certain prescribed ways of thinking and acting; and second, by classifying people and places on the basis of how well they conform to these demands. In strategies of rural development, for example, Cheshire (2006) has shown how local self-help groups are encouraged to seek their own solutions to the challenges of rural decline through enterprising community action. While those who conform to these policy prescriptions are celebrated for their 'can-do attitudes', those that cannot, or will not, are held responsible for their own failure and seen as undeserving of further support (Herbert-Cheshire & Higgins, 2004).

A reassertion of rural power: agency, resistance and protest

What each of the aforementioned themes share in common, aside from their critical interrogation of the exercise of power, is a propensity to view rural areas as spaces where power is exercised *on*, or at the least *in*, rather than necessarily *by*. In drawing attention to many of the challenges that rural areas have faced, rural scholarship has converged around a dominant narrative of rurality as passive to the influences of local elites, nation states and transnational actors who dictate their terms of engagement in the global economy, the nature and extent of their response (i.e., through community-based partnerships), and their very essence as particular kinds of rural spaces with particular trajectories (Halfacree, 2006). As Foucault pointed out, however, 'as soon as there is power relations, there is a possibility of resistance' (1980, p. 142), reminding us that even while power may seem immutable, the capacity to resist, negotiate and reshape the relations of rule are ever present. While the undue attention placed on the visibly powerful has, at various times, been countered by rural studies scholars, it is only recently that the assertion of rural power has become a topic of substantive interest, largely in response to the 'strange awakening' (Woods, 2005) of a mobilized rural populace once thought to be acquiescent.

This has been done in several ways. First, researchers have pointed to the myriad ways in which rural people exert agency through protest and political lobbying to reverse unpopular policy decisions, such as attempts to ban fox hunting in the UK (Woods, 1997), the proposed deregulation of the apple industry in New Zealand (McKenna, 2000), agricultural reform in France (Naylor, 1994) and dairy deregulation in Australia (Dibden & Cocklin, 2007). Second, these have been shown, at times, to lead to the emergence of national or global rural social movements as disparate groups with disparate agendas converge to defend a common interest against some externally imposed threat. In the global south, this has manifested itself in global peasant movements such as La Vía Campesina (Desmarai, 2002, 2008) and in the global north through a series of (sometimes militant) alliances that cohere around the preservation of a rural identity and lifestyle (however defined) that is seen as increasingly under threat (Woods, 2003). As Woods (2003) also observes, these movements have partially emerged in response to the perceived failings of traditional rural and farming organisations – including the local and national state – to adequately represent their interests, and the unwillingness of middle-class newcomers to accept the legitimacy of traditional rural elites.

Yet, Bell, Lloyd and Vatovec (2010, p. 205) also remind us that the reassertion of the rural voice is 'not necessarily cause for romantic celebration', since food scares, biosecurity threats and animal-borne viruses clearly exemplify the potentially destructive power that continues to reside within, and be exerted by, rural areas. In the language of actor-network theory, what these cases show us is that humans are not the only active agents in rural areas (Donaldson, Lowe & Ward, 2003). When nature is enrolled into 'hybrid' actor-networks to achieve actions such as food production or development, we are increasingly made aware of its limits through unintended outcomes such as loss of biodiversity, the impacts of climate change and disease. Recasting nature as no longer passive, Busch and Juska observe that we 'have barely begun to understand the impacts of radical disorganization of nature on our existence' (1997, p. 691).

Conclusion

The four themes briefly outlined in this introduction chart the intellectual development of power as a concept in rural studies research as scholars continue to grapple with emergent processes of change in rural areas. They also illustrate the evolution of conceptual understandings of power among rural researchers, illustrating the degree to which rural studies has engaged with, and contributed to, theoretical advancements in the social sciences more broadly. Rather than suggesting this work has unfolded in a linear manner, what this brief review has sought to show is the growing complexity of contemporary power relations in rural areas, the diverse ways in which power is exercised – and the corresponding diversity of the actors involved – and the plurality of theoretical approaches and frameworks through which scholarly analyses take place. The following five chapters illustrate the dynamic nature of this work while also demonstrating the ongoing centrality of rural power as a matter of substantive and theoretical concern.

References

Arce, A & Marsden, T (1993). The social construction of international food: A new research agenda. *Economic Geography* 69(3), 293–311.

Bachrach, P & Baratz, MS (1962). Two faces of power. *American Political Science Review* 56(4), 947–952.

Bell, M, Lloyd, S & Vatovec, C (2010). Activating the countryside: Rural power, the power of the rural and the making of rural politics. *Sociologia Ruralis* 50(3), 205–224.

Bonanno, A, Busch, L, Friedland, W, Gouveia, L & Mingione, E (Eds). (1994). *From Columbus to Conagra: The globalization of agriculture and food.* Lawrence, KS: University of Kansas Press.

Busch, L & Juska, A (1997). Beyond political economy: Actor networks and the globalization of agriculture. *Review of International Political Economy* 4(4), 688–708.

Callon, M & Latour, B (1981). Unscrewing the big leviathan: How actors macro-structure reality and how sociologists help them to do so. In K Knorr-Cetina & A Cicourel (Eds), *Advances in social theory and methodology: Towards an integration of micro and macro-sociologies* (pp. 277–303). Boston, MA: Routledge & Kegan Paul.

Cheshire, L (2006). *Governing rural development: Discourses and practices of self-help in Australian rural policy.* Aldershot: Ashgate.

Commins, P (1990). Restructuring agriculture in advanced societies: Transformation, crisis and responses. In T Marsden, P Lowe & S Whatmore (Eds), *Rural restructuring: Global processes and their responses* (pp. 45–76). London: David Fulton.

Counsell, D & Haughton, G (2003). Regional planning tensions: Planning for economic growth and sustainable development in two contrasting English regions. *Environment and Planning C: Government and Policy* 21(2), 225–239.

Derkzen, P, Franklin, A & Bock, B (2008). Examining power struggles as a signifier of successful partnership working: A case study of partnership dynamics. *Journal of Rural Studies* 24(4), 458–466.

Desmarais, A (2002). The Vía Campesina: Consolidating an international peasant and farm movement. *The Journal of Peasant Studies* 29(2), 91–124.

Desmarais, A (2008). The power of peasants: Reflections on the meanings of La Vía Campesina. *Journal of Rural Studies* 24, 138–149.

Dibden, J & Cocklin, C (2007). Contesting competition: Governance and farmer resistance in Australia. In L Cheshire, V Higgins & G Lawrence (Eds), *Rural governance: International perspectives* (pp. 175–190). London: Routledge.

Donaldson, A, Lowe, P & Ward, N (2003). Virus-crisis-institutional change: The foot and mouth actor network and the governance of rural affairs in the UK. *Sociologia Ruralis* 2(3), 201–214.

Foucault, M (1980). Powers and strategies. In C Gordon (Ed.), *Power/knowledge: Selected interviews and other writings 1972–1977* (pp. 134–145). New York: Pantheon.

Foucault, M (1981). *The history of sexuality.* Vol. 1: *An introduction.* London: Penguin.

Foucault, M (1991). Governmentality. In G Burchell, C Gordon & P Miller (Eds), *The Foucault effect: Studies in governmentality* (pp. 87–104). Hemel Hempstead: Harvester Wheatsheaf.

Gray, I (1991). *Politics in place: Social power relations in an Australian country town.* Cambridge: Cambridge University Press.

Halfacree, K (2006). Rural space: Constructing a three-fold architecture. In P Cloke, T Marsden & P Mooney (Eds), *Handbook of rural studies* (pp. 44–62). London: Sage.

Herbert-Cheshire, L (2003). Translating policy: Power and action in Australia's country towns. *Sociologia Ruralis* 43(4), 54–73.

Herbert-Cheshire, L & Higgins, V (2004). From risky to responsible: Expert knowledge and the governing of community-led rural development. *Journal of Rural Studies* 20(3), 289–302.

Higgins, V & Lockie, S (2002). Re-discovering the social: Neo-liberalism and hybrid practices of governing in rural natural resource management. *Journal of Rural Studies* 18(4), 419–428.

Horton, M (2005). Rural crisis, good practice and community development responses. *Community Development Journal* 40(4), 425–432.

Jessop, B (1997). The entrepreneurial city: Re-imaging localities, redesigning economic governance, or restructuring capital? In N Jewson & S MacGregor (Eds), *Transforming cities: Contested governance and new spatial divisions* (pp. 28–41). London: Routledge.

Jones, M & MacLeod, G (1999). Towards a regional renaissance? Reconfiguring and rescaling England's economic governance. *Transactions of the Institute of British Geographers* 24(3), 295–313.

Kovách, I & Kučerova, E (2009). The social context of project proliferation: The rise of a project class. *Journal of Environmental Policy and Planning* 11(3), 203–221.

Law, J (1992). Notes on the theory of the actor-network: Ordering, strategy, and heterogeneity. *Systems Practice* 5(4), 379–393.

Lawrence, G (1990). Agricultural restructuring and rural social change in Australia. In T Marsden, P Lowe & S Whatmore (Eds), *Rural restructuring: Global processes and their responses* (pp. 101–128). London: David Fulton.

Lawrence, G & Williams, C (1990). The dynamics of decline: Implications for social welfare delivery in rural Australia. In T Cullen, P Dunn & G Lawrence (Eds), *Rural health and welfare in Australia* (pp. 38–59). Wagga Wagga: Centre for Rural Welfare Research, Charles Sturt University.

Le Heron, R (2003). Creating food futures: Reflections on food governance issues in New Zealand's agri-food sector. *Journal of Rural Studies* 19(1), 111–125.

Lockie, S (2000). Crisis and conflict: Shifting discourses of rural and regional Australia. In B Pritchard & P McManus (Eds), *Land of discontent: The dynamics of change in rural and regional Australia* (pp. 14–32). Sydney: University of New South Wales Press.

Long, N (1992). From paradigm lost to paradigm regained? The case for an actor-oriented sociology of development. In N Long & A Long (Eds), *Battlefields of knowledge: The interlocking of theory and practice in social research and development* (pp. 16–43). London: Routledge.

Lukes, S (1974). *Power: A radical view.* London: Macmillan.

Lukes, S (2005). *Power: A radical view.* Hampshire and New York: Palgrave Macmillan.

Macken-Walsh, A & Curtin, C (2013). The case of the Rural Partnership Programme (RPP) in post-socialist Lithuania. *Sociologia Ruralis* 53(2), 246–264.

Marsden, T, Lowe, P & Whatmore, S (Eds). (1990). *Rural restructuring: Global processes and their responses.* London: David Fulton.

McKenna, M (2000). Can rural voices effect rural choices? Contesting deregulation in New Zealand's apple industry. *Sociologia Ruralis* 40(3), 366–383.

Morrison, TH, Wilson, C & Bell, M (2012). The role of private corporations in regional planning and development: Opportunities and challenges for the governance of housing and land use. *Journal of Rural Studies* 28(4), 478–489.

Murdoch, J (2000). Networks: A new paradigm of rural development? *Journal of Rural Studies* 1(4), 407–419.

Murdoch, J & Pratt, A (1993). Rural studies: Modernism, postmodernism and the 'post-rural'. *Journal of Rural Studies* 9(4), 411–427.

Murdoch, J & Pratt, A (1994). Rural studies of power and the power of rural studies: A reply to Philo. *Journal of Rural Studies* 10(1), 83–87.

Naylor, E (1994). Unionism, peasant protest and the reform of French agriculture. *Journal of Rural Studies* 10(3), 263–273.

Newby, H (1977). *The deferential worker: A study of farm workers in East Anglia.* London: Allen Lane.

Newby, H (1980). Trend report: Rural sociology. *Current Sociology* 28(1), 3–109.

Newby, H, Bell, C, Saunders, P & Rose, D (1978). *Property, paternalism and power: Class and conflict in rural England.* London: Hutchinson.

Osti, G (2000). LEADER and partnerships: The case of Italy. *Sociologia Ruralis* 40(2), 172–180.

Oxley, H (1974). *Mateship in local organization: A study of egalitarianism, stratification, leadership and amenities projects in a semi-industrial community of inland New South Wales.* Brisbane: University of Queensland Press.

Poiner, G (1990). *The good old rule: Gender and other power relationships in a rural community.* Sydney: Sydney University Press.

Shucksmith, M (2010). Disintegrated rural development? Neo-endogenous rural development, planning and place-shaping in diffused power contexts. *Sociologia Ruralis* 50(1), 1–14.

Stoker, G (1998). Governance as theory: Five propositions. *International Social Science Journal* 50(155), 17–28.

Varley, T, Boylan, TA & Cuddy, MP (Eds). (1991). *Rural crisis: Perspectives on Irish rural development.* Galway: Centre for Development Studies, University College of Galway.

Wild, R (1974). *Bradstow: A study of status, class and power in a small Australian town.* Sydney: Angus & Robertson.

Woods, M (1997). Researching rural conflicts: Hunting, local politics and actor-networks. *Journal of Rural Studies* 14(3), 321–340.

Woods, M (2003). Deconstructing rural protest: The emergence of a new social movement. *Journal of Rural Studies* 1(3), 309–325.

Woods, M (2005). *Contesting rurality: Politics in the British countryside.* Aldershot: Ashgate.

50

Power and Politics in the Changing Structures of Rural Local Government

David J. A. Douglas

Introduction

Local government in rural areas is at once the unit of government closest to rural communities, their agendas and priorities and at the same time a vehicle of policy, programme administration and resource allocation for so-called higher levels of government. In today's variegated and pervasive conditions of globalisation, a host of factors is conditioning the role and relevance of local government, while opening a diversity of as yet untested opportunities. Cutting across these realities, the emergence of a variety of 'wicked' problems challenges the connections between local government and the rural community itself, and its longer term development. Emanating from this dynamic, and from other sources, is the concept and practice of governance, which simultaneously appears to challenge the relevance of the institutionalised 'local state' while also potentially augmenting its role and relevance in the complexities of development.

Associated with some of these trends is the arrival of New Public Management or NPM (Osborne & Gaebler, 1993), and a range of ideological perspectives which have rendered the power and politics of rural local government and governance much more complex. These include the dominance of neoliberalism; the re-emergence of 'localism'; a concern with local democracy and social justice; growing attention to the role of the citizen and community organisations in environmental stewardship; and a concern with the central political issue of representation. And at the centre are the pivotal rural development questions of choice and control, both of which call forth the equally pivotal issues of subsidiarity and capacity. The central themes of power and capacity in rural local government also have to be understood in the context of some universal dimensions of rurality. These include the fundamentals of distance and density, and how these are changing with technology and other factors, and the associated question of scale (Reimer & Bollman, 2010). But they also include the significant diversity of rural contexts, from metro-adjacent zones to rural remote; from primary resource-based to modern knowledge-based economies; and from cultural homogeneity to diversity.

This chapter examines some of these and other issues through the lens of local government 'reform' or restructuring, a common preoccupation with national and provincial/state governments throughout most of the so-called developed world over the last several decades. It is acknowledged that most restructuring initiatives are for all local governments, and with some exceptions (e.g., Poland), rarely single out a defined 'rural'. Four interrelated concepts will be used to interpret this variegated record of local government restructuring. These are: power, decentralisation, governance and localism. To situate the restructuring process, the chapter begins with a review of four interrelated contexts through which rural local government restructuring has been conducted. It then notes some 'reform' options available to the state to recast local government, and recounts the fundamental roles and functions of local government, which underpin its very sustainability. This is followed by a brief examination of selected features of the diverse record of reform through restructuring, highlighting rationales and agendas relating to rural local government roles and functions, political and administrative structures, and access to resources. Illustrative outcomes are summarised, although space allows only a very selective coverage of the diversity of issues and jurisdictional contexts. In this overview of the restructuring record, the chapter alludes to key conceptual and critical issues, such as power, governance, subsidiarity, capacity and others relating to decentralisation, devolution, resources allocation and related matters germane to research, policy and practice. Finally, the developmental role of rural local government is critically addressed through a series of questions.

Restructuring: local government viability within the power and politics of four dynamic contexts

Restructuring local government involves changes in selected facets of the system from roles and functions, the number of local governments, levels, types and interrelationships, their spatial extent and configuration (e.g., boundaries), the amount and sources of resources, and more. Restructuring recasts the map of powers – responsibilities, authorities and resources. This is turn makes it a central consideration in rural development, and development planning (Forester, 1989).

Restructuring must address the central challenge in local government of 'balancing democracy, identity and efficiency' (CEMR, 2009). However, the operating contexts of rural local governments are not only extremely diverse, but they are often in a state of flux. 'Rurality' is contextually constructed through spatial arrangements, institutional inheritances and interests, national geopolitical contests and conditions, and the emergent forces of globalisation and advanced capitalism (Dicken, 2003; Timmons Roberts & Hite, 2003; Cloke, Marsden & Mooney, 2006; Reimer & Bollman, 2010). Four overlapping contexts can be identified.

First, rural local governments operate under different *spatial* contexts. The realities of transportation and telecommunications, accessibility and local economic base (narrow, resourced-based, specialised or seasonal) and other facts of life for smaller remote communities present a radically different set of challenges to those of metro-adjacent rural local governments (Woods, 2005; Reimer & Bollman, 2010). In some higher density rural regions, multi-community collaboration is feasible (e.g., southern Sweden); in other contexts the spatial configuration militates against this. Indeed, in many contexts, conditions do not even allow for the resourcing of local governments, and special service agencies are established.

Second, *institutional* contexts have a huge bearing on municipal roles, structures and sustainability, and hence restructuring options and dynamics. In some jurisdictions local governments have long functioned as extensions of the central government administration, with minimal own-source resources and limited mandates. In others, the array of functions beyond basic services such as physical infrastructure and waste management has extended to incorporate education, welfare and social services. Here, the political culture is one of considerable local autonomy and substantial resources, including the collection of income taxes.

In some contexts, the institutional environment is densely populated by a host of interests who guard their 'turf' in areas such as health care, conservation and economic development.

Related to the above are the contests and outcomes of *geopolitics* within which all rural local governments operate. Competitive interests of the central state and the local community come into play. The state seeks to economise on locally or regionally delivered services; achieve greater degrees of 'joining up' to reduce duplication and bureaucratic confusion; manage heterogeneous demands; offload selected responsibilities; impose service standards; generate more opportunities for the private sector; and reduce the overt size of 'government' itself. Sometimes countering this agenda, rural local governments strive for more local autonomy in order to effectively represent their constituencies, acquire and sustain a viable financial resources base, influence the nature and extent of services provided, and collaborate with other local governments, and other levels of government, as required. All attempts at restructuring have to be situated in this, at times volatile, intergovernmental dynamic.

Finally, there are the diverse and pervasive influences of *globalisation* selectively connecting regional and local systems of government to a host of supranational, corporate and global governance interests and agendas (Dicken, 2003; Woods & McDonagh, 2011). This has, in most instances, been investigated at the major urban and regional levels (Chisholm, 1990; GaWC, 2015) while rural and remote communities, and especially their local governments, have received scant attention. However, given the international governing systems that attend the relentless dynamic of global capital accumulation, there can be little doubt that local government in rural areas has also been directly and indirectly subject to its agenda. Deregulation, or, in some perspectives, re-regulation, favouring the unfettered movement of capital, pervades all dimensions of local government, such as the directives for local government procurement practices under trade agreements such as NAFTA (North American Free Trade Agreement) and the proposed Canada–EU Trade Agreement (CETA) (European Commission, 2015). It has also been evident in the interventions of the European Central Bank in some of the Eurozone states during the recent recession and of the EU more broadly in setting expectations for decentralisation, the enhancement of local government capacity and other undertakings in rural regions through schemes such as the LEADER programmes.

In addition to these four conditioning contexts, restructuring is only one of a number of means available to the state to enhance the efficacy of, and to control, its local government system. Depending on the political and institutional context, it can close, expand the role, size, numbers, multi-tier, and otherwise recast the political and administrative architecture of the system. Actually, much of the development of local government occurs through an evolutionary process of internal refinement, such as incremental legislative and regulatory amendments. This somewhat invisible state-led process is continuous and cumulative, and may have as dramatic an effect over time as other interventions.

But the first priority for rural local government is its viability. And this is in no way guaranteed. It is achieved by securing its capacity to attend to its dual role of service provision to individuals and property, and political representation of its community (Marshall & Douglas, 1997). The state will also have its own designs on local government (Regulski, 2003; Tindal & Nobes-Tindal, 2009; Brunet-Jailly & Martin, 2010) while the market sees in local government a variety of service provision opportunities, the presence of publicly supported competition, and a potential client for financial, public works and other services. Indeed the municipality itself can be 'in the market' for its resident electorate's custom, vying with neighbouring local governments (Boyne, 1996). So local governments' functions, and their requisite resource endowments, are socially and otherwise constructed, and the outcomes of sometimes lengthy power dynamics. In simple terms, these dynamics revolve around two key tensions between, on the one hand, increased *centralisation* versus increased *local autonomy*, and on the other, increased *fragmentation* versus increased *consolidation*. We will use local government restructuring as our principal perspective on power and politics in these contexts.

Restructuring: the interested parties, rationales and agendas

The interested parties in the political and administrative structures of local government include the state in all its forms, local governments themselves, and their collective groupings, the local electorate, local, regional and global business interests, issue-specific organisations (such as farming or conservation groups), parastatal organisations (such as energy companies), privatised energy and resources organisations, increasingly global governing agencies, and others.

Paraphrasing Borge and Rattsø (2012), the conventional agenda sees the centre as dominant, based on its priorities for distribution and stabilisation. For allocation purposes public goods must be centralised in areas with strong externalities and economies of scale, and homogenous preferences across regions. Any rationale for decentralisation is to achieve allocation gains for local public goods.

However, the multiplicity of relevant parties, and their respective agendas, has produced a complex set of factors leading to the diverse patterns of local government restructuring in rural areas that we see today across the developed world. These threads range from the potency of neoliberalism and its associated prescriptions of New Public Management (NPM), the influence of international capital in contemporary globalisation, and the various attempts to down-size and decentralise government, to the resurgence of community-based advocacy and the principles of subsidiarity. Despite this multiplicity of actors, the state remains the most interested and overtly active agent in the structure and restructuring of local government in rural areas, and the record here is extremely diverse (see, for example, Leemans, 1970; Dente & Kjellberg, 1988; Sancton, 1991; Wollman, 2004, 2012; Swianiewicz, 2010; de Vries & Sobis, 2013). However, with the impact of globalisation, alongside processes of rural restructuring and emergent patterns of multilevel governance, the state's agency has been significantly modified (Cloke, Marsden & Mooney, 2006; Tomaney, Pike & Rodriguez-Pose, 2010).

While the state's agenda is not always explicit, its influence over the direction of local government restructuring is evident. In Canada, for example, Ontario's introduction of regional municipalities in the 1970s was premised on the appropriateness of a new upper tier (in addition to the historical counties) to provide regional-level services such as waste disposal and policing, and to address metropolitan growth. The province's comprehensive redrafting of the entire local government landscape in the 1990s was unabashedly ideological and premised on largely unfounded claims of significant cost savings (Douglas, 2005; Tindal & Nobes-Tindal, 2009). Much of Denmark's latest restructuring agenda relates to the appropriate location of higher order services such as hospitals, while Ireland's extensive restructuring in 2014 reinforced the highly centralised characteristics of this country; addressed glaring inequalities in some electoral arrangements; introduced a lower-tier municipal district within the counties; and drove an overriding cost management (i.e., reduction) agenda (Oireachtas Library and Research Service, 2012; Breathnach, 2013).

Paraphrasing Swianiewicz (2010), the rationale for restructuring is that larger local governments have more capacity to provide a wider range of functions, so territorial consolidation allows an allocation of more services to the local level. Economies of scale also mean less expensive, more effective services provision, while it is asserted that local democracy is promoted as citizens have greater inclination to participate in local politics (Dahl & Tufte, 1973). In addition, there will be less income disparity among municipalities, thereby reducing pressure for horizontal equalisation, a costly and politically sensitive issue for the state. There can also be more effective planning and development policies, and the 'free rider' problems of fewer locally provided services being consumed by residents who live and pay local taxes in another jurisdiction are reduced in territorial consolidation. Finally, there is a better match between administrative boundaries and service catchment areas.

Decentralisation

Decentralisation, often far removed from any real devolution of power, authority and commensurate resources, has been a persistent theme throughout the local government restructuring project. It is associated with the substance and optics of 'the hollowing out of the State' (Jessop, 2004), addressing chronic public indebtedness, seeking to create more 'joined up' government agencies, and responding to the heterogeneous demands of spatially dispersed constituencies. Overlaying this, central government shrinking and downloading becomes common practice, placing even more pressure on local governments to amalgamate and gain economies of scale, enter into public–private partnerships, outsource services and privatise. Some governments – the 1980s Australian federal government being an instance – have encouraged extensive inter-municipal regional collaborations (through so-called Regional Organisations of Councils or ROCs) to foster regional economic development and deliver central government services (Marshall, 2010). Many of these developments have been addressed amid increased financial and fiscal integration between the centre and its rural local governments as de facto co-agents within the mature welfare state. Constraining and shaping the decentralisation agenda has been the long-term institutionalised structure of local government itself (e.g., embedded multi tiered relationships) with very uneven absorptive and operational capacities.

Associated with all agendas has been the reality of shifting thresholds relating to the economic feasibility of services and facilities provision such as hospitals and high schools. Technological developments in health provision, for example, have heralded changing minimal requisite serviced populations. So there is a moving spatial configuration to achieve the optimal allocation of scarce public resources. This has been a major consideration in a dictated, if contested, thinning out of key health and other services across rural areas (e.g., Saskatchewan, Ireland). Across this has been some recognition of the rationality of capturing the maximum of positive externalities from economic, social, amenity and other activities within a given local government's territory, an axiom of spatial matching.

Saarimaa and Tukiainen (2012, pp. 131–132) pose two questions on the contentious issue of decentralisation. The first relates to the way functions and revenue sources are assigned to different levels of government. Following Musgrave (1959) and Oates (1972), they argue that decision making should be decentralised 'so that public good provision can be matched to heterogeneous preferences of the voter population'. The second question revolves around the optimal size of municipalities, which they see as a trade-off of opposing forces. On the one hand, they argue, economies of scale and 'inter-jurisdictional spillovers' favour large municipalities. On the other hand, as local governments increase in size, they are faced with increased heterogeneity in the preferences and interests of their electorate, which makes it more difficult for them to tailor services to meet those needs (Alesina & Spolaore, 1997, 2003).

In effect, the *size* and *number* of municipalities is a key policy decision in achieving a welfare-maximising production of decentralised public services. Are there too many, and are they just too small? Northern Ireland's 'programme of reform' is just the latest of these where the 26 local governments will be reduced to 11 by April 2015 (www.nidirect.gov.uk/local-government-reform). And related to this agenda are questions of the most appropriate roles and functions for these rural governments, and central governments' contesting objectives of control and cost reduction, and associated offloading. From these foundational issues, the authority, responsibility and resources for rural local governments are in question. And from the latter, what proportion of resources should be own-sourced, how are they sourced (e.g., property taxes, user fees, income taxes), and what proportion should be centrally funded, whether designated or under block transfer arrangements?

Never to be dismissed in all of these issues is the popularly promulgated concern with 'too many municipalities', the emotive unease with 'too much government', burgeoning bureaucracy, putative duplication in services and facilities, and other contentious matters. Regardless of the evidence this agenda has not been without political traction as a force in local government 'reform'.

Localism

While some supra-national policies and programmes have created institutional conditions under which local government has been hollowed out, they have also contributed to the so-called bottom-up agenda of expanded endogenous development and increased autonomy associated with 'localism' (OECD, 2006). Examples of these initiatives include the EU's 1996 *Cork Declaration* (EU, 1997) and subsequent reinforcements of this manifesto; the commitment to subsidiarity in the Maastricht Treaty (1992); and the LEADER programme, now in its fourth generation. As the chapter by Macken-Walsh (this volume) illustrates in more detail, these have spurred on an interest in, and applications of, various forms of horizontal (across state, market and civil society) and vertical (between local, regional and international) partnership arrangements as a means of sharing powers, pooling resources, addressing the limitations of governments at all levels, and engaging the breadth of new partners in rural areas. This is most evident in bottom-up, place-based approaches to rural development which have been further fuelled by resurgent localism, along with societal concerns with various social justice issues, environmental challenges (such as climate change), sustainable development and the imperative of securing local democracy through broader and more effective participatory processes. These, and other local and regional threads, converge with varying degrees of tension and congruence with the agendas from the centre and from supra-national and other non-local sources.

The evolving case for the 'local' perspective has been articulated by Sansom and McKinlay (2013, p. 4) as follows:

> we are seeing a growing recognition of 'local' as the pivotal node for coordinating delivery of a wide range of services. This is occurring for a number of reasons, including the need for cost savings, the often ponderous nature and silo mentality of centralised bureaucracies, and the scope to draw on local knowledge and networks, to encourage co-design and co-production, and to strengthen the community's own institutions. The concept is very much one of a partnership between the state, the private sector and civil society.

However, all of this raises the question of who has a stake in localism. Is the 'local' being co-opted by central government and related interests, such as embedded regimes for coordination, cost management, joined-up delivery of services, streamlining and related managerial interests? Or is its central ethos of autonomy, self-determination, context-responsive policy and respectful practice the prevailing imperative?

The process of restructuring: a note

In changing the roles, functions and structures of local government, the approach taken by most states has been to promulgate the nature of the 'problem' (e.g., services duplication) or opportunity (e.g., increased competitiveness), legitimise the imperative, and move with some dispatch with a programme of 'reform'. The process varies enormously from little consultation to token panels and town hall meetings, on to in-depth surveys, collaborative research and analysis, and the ex-ante evaluation of alternatives. The process in the state of Victoria, Australia has been reported as autocratic, contrasting with more consultative processes in Tasmania, Queensland and South Australia (Marshall, 2010). In 2004, New South Wales adopted a top-down process to enforce amalgamations.

Referendums are rare (Tanguay & Wihry, 2008). Search for consensus among the array of interested parties, or a visible consensus being attained, are also rare (Moisio, 2012). Business representatives are rarely evident in the process of generating and negotiating alternatives (Batley & Stoker, 1991) while international and national local government organisations are rarely engaged. Processes associated with shared power and multi-stakeholder contexts that are typified as governance are the exception. Contrary to democratic principles, the use of fiat is not unknown (Douglas, 2005; Tindal & Nobes-Tindal, 2009). Plebiscites are occasionally used. The process often starts with legislation or a proposal for such, and a White Paper or equivalent setting out the central government's policy and reform intentions. Often characterised by occasional extended oppositional activities, and even litigation, restructuring has generally been completed within a five-year period.

In contrast to some federal systems the 16 Länder in Germany are highly constrained by the constitution in their attempts to rationalise their local governments. The counties (Landkreise) and their constituent Gemeinden have considerable powers of autonomy. They have also invested in extensive administrative reforms and improvements since the 1990s, and a range of intergovernmental collaborative arrangements to reduce costs and achieve requisite economies of scale for services such as hospitals and sports facilities. Similar inter-local government collaborative arrangements (such as syndicates or informal networks) are increasingly evident in the Czech Republic, France, the Netherlands, Finland, Hungary, Belgium and elsewhere (de Vries & Sobis, 2013).

Selected outcomes of restructuring

The most obvious and universal outcome of local government restructuring in rural areas has been the reduction in numbers and the increase in size of local government units. Examples include Norway going from 750 to 450 local governments in the 1960s, while Sweden's 2,281 local governments transformed into 816 after 1952; to 464 after 1971; and eventually to 290. Finland's voluntary process starting in 1945 reduced 560 municipalities to 460 by 1990, and 432 in 2005, followed by the PARAS reform incentives package to 336 by 2011. In Denmark, 1,000 parish municipalities and 80 towns in 1970 were transformed into 275 new local governments. In 2007, the 271 local governments were scaled up in size to 98, and the 14 counties redesigned as five regions. In 2012, Ireland reduced its county councils from 34 to 31, replaced the previous eight regional authorities with three regional assemblies, abolished town councils, and provided for new sub-county, town-centred municipal districts throughout the country (the capital city, Dublin, was an exception) (Oireachtas Library and Research Service, 2012). The Province of Ontario, Canada, culled 815 municipalities in 1996 to 445 in 2004, a 45% reduction. Québec's largely urban-focused amalgamations after 2000 reduced the number of municipalities from 1,306 to 1,115, followed by a series of highly contested 'de-mergers'. Australia saw a reduction from 826 local authorities to 626 (1991–1998), most of which took place in four states, while Japan experienced dramatic reductions throughout the 20th century, from 15,859 to 3,232 local authorities, and more recently from 2,395 in 2005 to 1,821 in 2006, under a vigorous decentralisation agenda (JLGC, 2006).

In terms of the substantive change in role and functions, as well as resource allocations, the pattern is more diverse, because the starting point for rural local governments was extremely diverse (in terms of authority, responsibility, resources and other characteristics), and the political climate across national contexts has varied considerably (CEMR, 2011). To illustrate this diversity, local government in Canada accounts for approximately 11% of total public expenditure (Douglas, 2006), whereas in Finland the proportion is around 40%, and while most Scandinavian local governments have gained functional powers, the Irish have lost them. In Poland, the outcomes have been much more dramatic. Since 1989 a structural transformation of what purported to be a local government system in the Soviet era has been achieved. Through three decades of intensive and at times highly contested proposals, counter-proposals and negotiations, a robust system of Gminas, Powiats and Vojvodships incrementally has been put in place. And refinement continues. A significant degree of decentralisation has occurred, greater than that evident in several longer standing local government systems (such as Ireland and England). Poland has succeeded in developing and streamlining its long-standing Vojvodships, investing in them as the primary vehicles for rural regional development in the country (Douglas, 2007).

In all cases, however, despite the diversity of outcomes, the continuing tension between centralisation, managerial pragmatism and political control, on the one hand, and on the other, localism, place-based autonomy and contested democratic choice in local self-reliance remains apparent.

Local government and rural development

It has been argued that 'the installation of a local government system, however rudimentary, would be generally regarded as a *sine qua non* of rural development' (Douglas, 2005, p. 231). Therefore, the ongoing development of this system would be integral to the development of rural society (Allen, 1987; Clark, Huxley & Mountford, 2010; Förschner, 2011). While it is not the purpose of this brief chapter to assess the contribution of local government restructuring to rural development, the imperative of rural development suggests a number of significant policy, practice and research questions to which this chapter might offer some preliminary insights, perhaps constituting a small part of the eventual answers.

Is it likely that local governments in rural areas are more efficient as a result of the various restructuring initiatives? The net effects of achieving some economies of scale with increased geographic size and a larger serviced population, minimising overlap and duplication in activities, accommodating some services that have been downloaded from the centre, and other facets of the restructuring, are not at all emphatically positive. The primary reason for this uncertainty is the evidence of substantial escalation in costs, or, at best, no cost savings (Sancton, 1996; Mavroyannis, 2002; Kushner & Siegel, 2005; Slack & Bird, 2012). Quoting from one of many critical reviews of the evidence, it is accepted that 'gains from consolidation are not a certainty. ... the extent of size economies will be lower than may be anticipated. ... there are likely to be significant transition costs ... The consolidated government will not be perfectly efficient and focused on attaining the expectations of the electorate or the national government' (Fox & Gurley, 2006, p. 35).

At the same time, it is also generally recognised that the record of amalgamations and upscaling has, however unevenly, brought some benefits in equalising the quality of services (such as housing) and providing new services (such as welfare) to residents of former smaller local governments, while enhancing the administrative capacities of the new local government itself (Marshall, 2010; Sancton, 2010). Some services, such as water and sewage treatment, fire protection and transit that have very substantial capital requirements, have manifested savings when spread over an enlarged population. But other services such as health and social welfare and support are much more labour intensive, and have greater heterogeneity in demand. Average calculations show ephemeral savings, if any. Optimal populations for services such as housing and youth services are set much lower than the populations often associated with local government consolidation. And it is into these service domains that more and more municipalities are entering.

Have these selective cost increases cancelled out whatever economies of scale (and scope) might have been achieved through local government restructuring? The balance of evidence and opinion suggests that, on average, they might have. But any definitive answer from across the spectrum of rural contexts awaits more systematic research.

Is it likely that local governments are more democratic as a result? Using the simple metric of population or electorate per locally elected politician, the evidence to date suggests a potential decline in local democracy. And much of the research literature has noted the almost universal pattern of upscaling and the associated diminution in representation (Mouritzen, 1989). Some jurisdictions (such as Ireland) have matched local government amalgamations with the creation of another tier of smaller units. Others have addressed the options of wards, community committees or councils, or other intermediary arrangements within the expanded municipality to address the contentious issue of increased distances between elected representatives and the electorate. In most instances, however, the pattern reveals substantial increases in the populations of local governments (e.g., England, Lithuania, Sweden, Netherlands). Some Australian experience appears to have publicly acknowledged the erosion of local democracy, but placed its faith in enhanced governance processes and citizen participation.

The pivotal concept of governance is very relevant here (Keating, 1998; Welch, 2002; Cheshire, Higgins & Lawrence, 2007). Many contexts have seen a considerable increase in the activity patterns of special interest groups, NGOs, business associations, landowners, and a great variety of others. Much of this is associated with the contested concept of rural restructuring (McDonagh, 2001; Cloke, Marsden & Mooney, 2006). But have these multifarious ventures in shared power arrangements, pooled resources and opportunistic organisations made up for the potential democratic deficit associated with the thinning out of formal political representation? Because of the transparency and accountability criteria associated with formal democratic systems, the answer is likely, no.

Is it likely that rural local governments' capacities to provide – in some cases more, and in all cases better – services have been enhanced? The record around this question is extremely mixed, and suggests the need for in-depth research. The series of restructuring episodes in, for example, the Danish case suggests an incremental process of negotiated functional allocations (e.g., education, health services) where financial resources and other facets of capacity were allocated and reallocated over time. The Ontario case was one of downloading by edict with minimal attention to fiscal and other capacities. The Norwegian case for regional development suggests a careful fitting of functions and capacity. The Polish case suggests a learning process of mismatches between functional allocations and the requisite resources, followed by some reactive compensating state subventions. But there is no clear universal pattern in the record of local government restructuring, and the sometime concomitant processes of decentralisation that would indicate a matching of functional shifts and capacity reinvestments. Again, Québec might be an instructive exception (Québec, Gouvernement du, 2006; Jean, 2010).

Is it likely that the restructuring processes have brought about greater political autonomy for rural local governments? This is not dissimilar to the question posed by Brunet-Jailly and Martin (2010) regarding the continuing subordination of local governments in Australia and Canada to their provincial/state overlords. The general evidence suggests an emerging increment in relative power for the larger metropolitan governments due to a variety of indirect effects associated with globalisation, increased national and provincial/state stakes in the metro region's competitive economic positioning, and their political critical mass as sophisticated bureaucratic entities with formidable strategic capacities. The same does not apply to most other local governments, notably the smaller rural municipalities. Even with some expansion of their functions, an increase in size, and their expanded roles in co-delivering services, there is little consistent evidence to suggest that these developments have been associated with any increase in their political autonomy. Are they gaining more sway through the complexities of intergovernmental processes, through multilevel governance dynamics, and through multi-municipal collaborative and related networking arrangements (Korsching, Borich & Stewart, 1992; Douglas, 1999)? This is far from certain, and awaits some in-depth comparative case study research.

Have the restructuring interventions brought about greater congruity between the spatial configuration of local governments and their functional domains? The answer for most local government services is likely, yes. And those services with lower population thresholds, such as kindergartens, have been nested within a schools system hierarchy with its own spatial configuration, which increasingly approximates the geographical reach of the extended restructured local government area. The challenges of capturing the public good benefits generated by a municipality within its statutory domain are more than likely addressed in the extended spatial reach of the fewer, and now larger, local governments' boundaries. It is very likely that the governmental, governance and other challenges posed by increased labour force, consumer, residential and other mobilities (Freshwater & Ward, 2014) have been addressed by the dominant process of spatial upscaling.

Have the various restructuring interventions facilitated the evolution of governance processes? Whether there is a cause and effect link here awaits the attention of further research. However, the literature (Phillips, 2010) and anecdotal evidence suggests that the extended processes of local government restructuring, and the accompanying debates and power struggles, have been associated with a vibrant array of governance initiatives. The great variety of interests that may be affected by the restructuring of local government arrangements (e.g., housing, agriculture, heritage) have taken a very visible role in the debates surrounding the proposed restructuring, and local governments, and often central government agencies, have joined an assortment of ad hoc organisations to address the spectrum of issues on hand.

Have the restructuring episodes been characterised by participation on the part of local governments and their representatives, and what has been the nature of this engagement? Of course local governments have been involved in the restructuring processes, some more as objects of the central government's designs, others as subjects of a collaborative process. In some instances, such as in Denmark, municipal organisations have been active on behalf of their constituency. In others, such as the state of Tasmania in Australia, the process from the start was very collaborative. The more recent Ontario case is one of circumscribed participation, with local government as the passive recipient of the provincial government's edicts, even in the capital city of Toronto. Other Canadian provinces (e.g., Saskatchewan) have more collaborative processes. In one instance, one province (Newfoundland and Labrador) devolved the entire process to local communities (e.g., Fogo).

The Polish record is instructive, displaying as it does the back-and-forth tensions between a reconstituted centre and an emerging local (Regulski, 2003). One very innovative episode had the basic units of local government, the Gminas, themselves designing the appropriate configuration of their second-tier local governments, the Powiats. Against the grain, Hungary and the Czech Republic have responded to local historical, cultural and political imperatives by facilitating the growth in numbers of new and smaller local governments (Fox & Gurley, 2006). Short-lived exceptions in diverse contexts (e.g., England, Finland, Sweden) have allowed for experimental and more bottom-up redesign alternatives. However, emerging from this considerable variety of process and engagement is the dominant agenda of the central government, with its admixture of cost savings and management, decentralisation and downloading, political control, management efficiencies, joined-up regional operations, and attempts to minimise the contradictions that go with the heterogeneity of spatially disparate service demands and centralised design and provision. The collaborative process, where it has existed, and the controlled degrees of participatory process, where they have been accommodated, have generally been subservient to the centre's hegemonic agenda.

Have the local government restructuring agendas and processes been explicitly linked to, or even integrated within, a broader rural development agenda? An attempt to answer this question is embedded in our speculations on the previous questions. And there is very little evidence in the literature of any explicit attempt to attach, let alone integrate, the local government restructuring project with a larger, comprehensive rural or even regional development initiative. Notwithstanding the institutional rhetoric of bodies such as the EU, this remains something of a puzzling deficit in rural development policy and practice (Douglas, 2005). The few exceptions might be found in Québec (Jean, 2010; Québec, 2006) and Norway (Aarsæther & Nyseth, 2007).

Summary

We are asserting that rural development extends far beyond resolution of the so-called Dahl–Tufte dilemma (Dahl & Tufte, 1973). The questions suggest a research agenda. We have unapologetically speculated on tentative partial responses to some of them, and surmised directions for possible answers. But that is all. The questions remain. They are important to policy making, professional practice, and rural development research priorities. In several instances (e.g., Douglas, 2005; Breathnach, 2013, 2014), it has been postulated that local government restructuring has been antithetical to rural development. These are serious claims. The questions posed here, and the rural development research agenda identified, are both warranted and urgent.

Not to be lost in this highly selective overview is Sassen's cautionary thesis that new (international) legal regimes will serve to 'un-bundle sovereignties' and 'denationalize territories', reconfiguring the links between rights and territories, with consequential 'disturbing repercussions for distributive justice and equity' (Sassen, 1996, pp. 28–30). So, is this changing landscape of restructured local governments simply ameliorating the internal contradictions of capitalist accumulation, straining the legitimacy of the now up-scaled government, falling between the two stools of a dangerously attenuated representative democracy and an over-extended participatory process, while stretching the capacities and tolerances of governance systems and associated networks? These, and equally fundamental, longer term potential outcomes for rural regions must be the subject of more independent and critical research.

David J. A. Douglas

References

Aarsæther, N & Nyseth, T (2007). Governance and innovations in the Nordic periphery. In L Cheshire, V Higgins & G Lawrence (Eds), *Rural governance: International perspectives* (pp. 51–65). London: Routledge.

Alesina, A & Spolaore, E (1997). On the number and size of nations. *Quarterly Journal of Economics* 112(4), 1027–1056.

Alesina, A & Spolaore, E (2003). *The size of nations*. Cambridge, MA: MIT Press.

Allen, H (1987). Decentralisation for development: A point of view. *Planning and Administration* 14(1), 23.

Batley, R & Stoker, G (1991). *Local government in Europe*. London: Macmillan.

Borge, L-E & Rattsø, J (2012). Fiscal federalism: International experiences and the Nordic response. In A Moisio (Ed.), *Rethinking local government: Essays on municipal reform* (pp. 15–41). Helsinki: Government Institute for Economic Research.

Boyne, GA (1996). Competition and local government: A public choice perspective. *Urban Studies* 33(4–5), 703–721.

Breathnach, P (2013). Regional governance and regional development: Implications of the Action Programme for Effective Local Government. *Administration* 61(3), 51–73.

Breathnach, P (2014). Creating city-region governance structures in a dysfunctional polity: The case of Ireland's National Spatial Strategy. *Urban Studies* 51(11), 2267–2284.

Brunet-Jailly, E & Martin, JF (2010). *Local government in a global world: Australia and Canada in comparative perspective*. Toronto: University of Toronto Press.

CEMR (Council of European Municipalities and Regions) (2009). *Balancing identity, democracy and efficiency: Changes in local and regional structures in Europe*. Paris: Council of European Municipalities and Regions.

CEMR (Council of European Municipalities and Regions) (2011). *Local and regional government in Europe: Structures and competences*. Paris: Council of European Municipalities and Regions.

Cheshire, L, Higgins, V & Lawrence, G (2007). Rural governance and power relations. In L Cheshire, V Higgins & G Lawrence (Eds), *Rural governance: International perspectives* (pp. 291–303). London: Routledge.

Chisholm, M (1990). *Regions in recession and resurgence*. London: Unwin Hyman.

Clark, G, Huxley, J & Mountford, D (2010). *Organising local economic development: The role of development agencies and companies*. Paris: OECD.

Cloke, P, Marsden, T & Mooney, P (Eds). (2006). *Handbook of rural studies*. London: Sage.

Dahl, R & Tufte, E (1973). *Size and democracy*. Berkeley, CA: Stanford University Press.

Dente, B & Kjellberg, F (1988). *The dynamics of institutional change: Local government reorganization in Western democracies*. London: Sage.

de Vries, M & Sobis, I (2013). Consolidation in local government: An international comparison of arguments and practices. *Administration* 61(3), 31–50.

Dicken, P (2003). *Global shift: Reshaping the global economic map in the 21st century*. New York: Guilford Press.

Douglas, DJA (1999). The new rural region: Consciousness, collaboration and new challenges and opportunities for innovative practice. In W Ramp, J Kulig, I Townsend & V McGowan (Eds), *Health in rural settings: Contexts for action* (pp. 39–60). Lethbridge: University of Lethbridge.

Douglas, DJA (2005). The restructuring of local government in rural regions: A rural development perspective. *Journal of Rural Studies* 21(2), 231–246.

Douglas, DJA (2006). The fiscal imbalance and rural municipalities. In Federation of Canadian Municipalities (Eds), *Building prosperity from the ground up: Restoring municipal fiscal balance* (pp. 88–94). Ottawa: FCM.

Douglas, D (2007). Local governance for economic development: A comparative analysis of Canadian and Irish conditions and its lessons for Poland. In S Giguère (Ed.), *Local innovations for growth in Central and Eastern Europe* (pp. 43–67). Paris: OECD.

European Commission (2015). http://ec.europa.eu/trade/policy/in-focus/ceta/index_en.htm#outcome (accessed 13 July 2015).

European Union (1997). The Cork Declaration 1996. *LEADER Magazine* Winter, No. 13. Available at http://ec.europa.eu/agriculture/rur/cork_en.htm (accessed 4 October 2015).

Forester, J (1989). *Planning in the face of power*. Berkeley, CA: University of California Press.

Förschner, M (2011). *Partnerships in the recovery: Rebuilding employment at the local level.* LEED, Handbook # 3. Paris: OECD.

Fox, WF & Gurley, T (2006). Will consolidation improve sub-national governments? World Bank Policy Research Working Paper 3913. Washington, DC: World Bank.

Freshwater, D & Ward, J (2014). *Local labour markets as a new way of organizing policies for stronger regional economic development in Atlantic Canada.* St. John's: The Harris Centre, Memorial University.

GaWC (Globalization and World Cities Network) (2015). http://www.lboro.ac.uk/gawc/ (accessed 13 July 2015).

Jean, B (2010). Negotiating 'rural' and constructing a development process: Rural development planning in Quebec. In DJA Douglas (Ed.), *Rural planning and development in Canada* (pp. 134–149). Toronto: Nelson.

Jessop, B (2004). Hollowing out the 'nation-state' and multilevel governance. In P Kennett (Ed.), *A handbook of comparative social policy* (pp. 11–25). Cheltenham: Edward Elgar.

JLGC. (2006). Newsletter article on municipal mergers in Japan: Japan consolidations. *JLGC Newsletter* 58, pp. 2–3. New York: Japan Local Government Centre.

Keating, M (1998). *The new regionalism in Western Europe.* Cheltenham: Edward Elgar.

Korsching, PF, Borich, T & Stewart, J (Eds). (1992). *Multicommunity collaboration: An evolving rural revitalization strategy.* Ames, IA: North Central Regional Centre for Rural Development.

Kushner, J & Siegel, D (2005). Are services delivered more efficient after municipal amalgamations? *Canadian Public Administration* 48(2), 251–267.

Leemans, AR (1970). *Changing patterns of local government.* The Hague: ULA.

Marshall, J & Douglas, DJA (1997). *The viability of Canadian municipalities: Concepts and measurements.* Toronto: ICURR Press.

Marshall, N (2010). Restructuring and reform: Australia. In E Brunet-Jailly & J Martin (Eds), *Local government in a global world: Australia and Canada in comparative perspective* (pp. 81–107). Toronto: University of Toronto Press.

Mavroyannis, M (2002). Is bigger better? Recent experiences in municipal restructuring. *Canadian Tax Journal* 50(3), 1011–1018.

McDonagh, J (2001). *Renegotiating rural development in Ireland.* Aldershot: Ashgate.

Ministère des Affaires municipales et des Régions (2006). *National policy on rurality – 2007–2014.* Québec: Gouvernement du Québec.

Moisio, A (Ed.). (2012). *Rethinking local government: Essays on municipal reform.* Helsinki: Government Institute for Economic Research. Vatt Publications, 61.

Mouritzen, PE (1989). City size and citizens' satisfaction: Two competing theories revisited. *European Journal of Political Research* 17(6), 661–688.

Musgrave, R (1959). *The theory of public finance: A study in public economy.* New York: McGraw-Hill.

Oates, WE (1972). *Fiscal federalism.* New York: Harcourt Brace Jovanovich.

OECD (Organization for Economic Co-operation and Development). (2006). The new rural paradigm: Policies and governance. Paris: OECD.

Oireachtas Library & Research Service (2012). *Local government reform.* Dublin: Spotlight, No. 12.

Osborne, D & Gaebler, T (1993). *Reinventing government.* New York: Penguin.

Phillips, S (2010). 'You say you want an evolution?': From citizen to community engagement in Canadian cities. In E Brunet-Jailly & J Martin (Eds), *Local government in a global world: Australia and Canada in comparative perspective* (pp. 55–80). Toronto: University of Toronto Press.

Québec, Gouvernement du. (2006). *Politique nationale de la ruralité.* Québec City: Ministère des Affaires Municipales et des Régions.

Regulski, J (2003). *Local government reform in Poland: An insider's story.* Budapest: Local Government and Public Service Reform Initiative, Open Society Institute.

Reimer, B & Bollman, R (2010). Understanding rural Canada: Implications for rural development policy and rural planning policy. In DJA Douglas (Ed.), *Rural planning and development in Canada* (pp. 10–52). Toronto: Nelson.

Saarimaa, T & Tukiainen, J (2012). Do voters value local representation? Strategic voting after municipal mergers. In A Moisio (Ed.), *Rethinking local government: Essays on municipal reform* (pp. 131–162). Helsinki: Government Institute for Economic Research. Vatt Publications, 61.

Sancton, A (1991). *Local government reorganization in Canada since 1975.* Toronto: ICURR Press.

Sancton, A (1996). Reducing costs by consolidating municipalities: New Brunswick, Nova Scotia, and Ontario. *Canadian Public Administration* 39(3), 267–289.

Sancton, A (2010). Restructuring and reform: Canada. In E Brunet-Jailly & J Martin (Eds), *Local government in a global world: Australia and Canada in comparative perspective* (pp. 108–129). Toronto: University of Toronto Press.

Sansom, G & McKinlay, P (Eds). (2013). *New century local government: Commonwealth perspectives*. London: Commonwealth Secretariat.

Sassen, S (1996). *Losing control.* New York: Columbia University Press.

Slack, E & Bird, R (2012). Merging municipalities: Is bigger better? In A Moisio (Ed.), *Rethinking local government: Essays on municipal reform* (pp. 83–130). Helsinki: Government Institute for Economic Research. Vatt Publications, 61.

Swianiewicz, P (Ed.). (2010). *Territorial consolidation: Reforms in Europe.* Budapest: Open Society Institute, Local Government and Public Service Reform Initiative.

Tanguay, G & Wihry, DF (2008). Voters' preferences regarding municipal consolidation: Evidence from the Quebec de-merger referenda. *Journal of Urban Affairs* 30(3), 325–345.

Timmons Roberts, J & Hite, A (Eds.) (2003). *From modernization to globalization: Perspectives on development and social change.* Oxford: Blackwell.

Tindal, C & Nobes-Tindal, S (2009). *Local government in Canada.* Toronto: Nelson.

Tomaney, J, Pike, A & Rodriguez-Pose, A (2010). Local and regional development in times of crisis. *Environment and Planning A* 42, 771–779.

Welch, R (2002). Legitimacy of rural local government in the new governance environment. *Journal of Rural Studies* 18, 443–459.

Wollmann, H (2004). Local government reforms in Great Britain, Sweden, Germany and France. Between multi-function and single-purpose organization. *Local Government Studies* 30(4), 639–665.

Wollmann, H (2012). Local government reforms in (seven) European countries: Between convergent and divergent, conflicting and complementary developments. *Local Government Studies* 38(1), 41–70.

Woods, M (2005). *Rural geography.* London: Sage.

Woods, M & McDonagh, J (2011). Editorial: Rural Europe and the world: globalization and rural development. *European Countryside* 3, 153–163.

51

Governance, Partnerships and Power

Áine Macken-Walsh

Introduction

The concept of power is potent in the field of rural development and agriculture, resonating with debates on the powerlessness of rural people in highly regulated top-down agriculture policy making on one hand, and possibilities for greater bottom-up influences in multi-sectoral approaches to development on the other. Partnerships, typically theorised as institutions of governance, provide a mechanism for devolving power to local actors in designing and implementing development interventions (Ray, 2000). The mainstreaming of partnership approaches to rural development and agriculture across much of the world may appear to constitute a greater accession of power to rural regions and people. In exploring whether or not this is the case, the governance literature has been preoccupied with questions such as how partnerships disrupt traditional statutory powers and succeed in 'opening up' development design and implementation processes to a diversity of non-statutory actors. Such questions have led important areas of enquiry, identifying implications arising for how we understand changing power structures and outcomes for rural people.

As explained by Stoker (1996, p. 4), governance reconceptualises power as a matter of social reproduction rather than social control, suggesting, as Stone (1989, cited in Goodwin, 1998, p. 10) does, that 'what is at issue is not so much domination and subordination, as a capacity to act and accomplish goals'. The shift from government to governance is often described as a shift from 'power over' to 'power to' (Goodwin, 1998, p. 10), following the central idea that power is devolved to local communities to identify and pursue their own development goals. Rural development partnerships, thus, are typically organised territorially and adopt an inter-sectoral approach as a strategy to ignite between private, public and third-sector actors the type of cross-cutting 'transverse debate' required for development to be addressed in a sufficiently creative and integrated way (Caspar, Farrell & Thirion, 1997, p. 7). Considering the potential for variation in how partnerships operate, not least because of the myriad actors and interests involved, questions arise as to what implications governance institutions have for the power of rural people.

Haugaard's power theory (2002, 2012) offers a useful lens for examining the way power operates in and through governance arrangements. In particular, it orients analysts to both the structures of partnerships and their goals. Structural or dispositional power, defined as 'structured rules of the game' (Haugaard, 2012, p. 37), has a particular association with governance. With governance, it is postulated that there has been a shift from crude or coercive domination of government to more subtle forms of 'constitutive, positive and disciplinary' power (Haugaard, 2012, p. 36, citing Foucault, 1979 and Elias, 1994). To exert such power, partnerships as governance institutions require legitimacy, which is thought to be achieved by non-statutory and statutory actors working together to build common purpose through deliberative arenas (Connelly, Richardson & Miles, 2006).

However, power theory also reminds us that 'structures and institutions are always goal-specific and frequently actor specific' (Haugaard, 2002, p. 309). If this is the case, and partnerships are both goal-specific as well as structure-specific, it follows that they encourage the inclusion of some actors and the exclusion of others. The empirical literature examining how partnerships operate in practice has found that they provide new opportunities that are empowering of some actors to pursue their goals. However, constraining powers that limit the engagement of multiple sectors within decision-making processes are also identified. These forms of 'power over', exerted, for example, by extra-local funders or dominant local actors, illustrate the 'organising in' of some development interests and the 'organising out' of others (Haugaard, 2012).

This chapter seeks to examine some of the crucial intersections between Haugaard's power theory and partnerships as governance institutions, elucidating the structural and goal-oriented aspects of how partnerships function. The first section focuses specifically on how partnerships operate at the local level, exploring the local structural factors that explain the emergence of some actors as prominent and powerful. Second, the analysis widens to focus on the power of extra-local factors in exerting 'push' and 'pull' influences on both the structures and goals of rural partnerships, and in favouring the participation of some actors while excluding others. Third, the focus shifts to those whose goals are excluded from rural governance, highlighting how actors' conscious resistance to participation in rural partnerships may represent power rather than powerlessness. Fourth, an overview of the expansion of meta-governance structures to include sectors such as agriculture is presented. This broadened participatory nexus proposes a wider population with new opportunities for (non-)participation and power accumulation, raising interesting implications for our current understandings of power and powerlessness in the context of the rural governance project universally.

Local powers

We may understand from the literature that without the meaningful participation and representation of diverse local actors, the partnership approach is no different to top-down forms of authority (Gore, 2008). However, because many partnerships are organised at the local level and involve local actors, they are inevitably shaped by the established structures of power that pre-exist them. Diverse local contexts do not represent a 'blank canvas' where, upon the initiation of new partnerships, established powers cease to have influence (Edwards, Goodwin, Pemberton & Woods, 2001, p. 291; Macken-Walsh & Curtin, 2013). Instead, the normal workings of power in any given locality are likely to impact on how partnerships operate in practice (Richardson & Cashmore, 2011; Clegg, 2014).

For example, empirical studies have frequently concluded that statutory representatives of top-down governing are powerful and dominant in rural partnerships (Curtin & Varley, 1997; Edwards, Goodwin, Pemberton & Woods, 2001; Furmankiewicz, 2012; Furmankiewicz & Macken-Walsh, forthcoming). Such statutory actors, having gained the upper hand in traditional local government processes, may attempt to monopolise partnerships to maintain their status or to prevent new elites emerging through rural partnerships (Edwards, Goodwin, Pemberton &

Woods, 2001; Convery, Soane, Dutson & Shaw, 2010; Furmankiewicz, Macken-Walsh & Stefańska, 2014; Furmankiewicz & Macken-Walsh, forthcoming).[1] In other studies, private sector actors such as artisans and tourism operators are noted to be powerful actors, motivated by funding opportunities offered by partnerships that are compatible with their business goals (Osti, 2000, p. 176). In other contexts, larger scale multinational industries, such as those exploiting the natural resources of rural areas, are found to instigate and lead rural partnerships in an effort to mediate challenges to their own legitimacy (Cheshire, 2010). The third sector, particularly in contexts where private sector interests are relatively absent (Cheshire, 2010), has also emerged as powerful in promoting social and cultural goals through rural partnerships (Macken-Walsh & Curtin, 2013).

A growing body of literature indicates that characteristics other than sectoral affiliation explain how certain actors become prominent in rural partnerships. Those occupying the category of the powerful and dominant in rural partnerships are often identified as the 'usual suspects' (Curtin & Varley, 1997), whomever, at the local level, the usual suspects may be. Such actors may be trusted members of their communities, including those who do not have formal representative roles, and actors such as mayors whose legitimacy and power are distinctively associated with personal attributes rather than their status as elected representatives (Convery, Soane, Dutson & Shaw, 2010). Other powerful actors may be employees of local government, such as cultural house workers in post-socialist states, whose occupational roles are normatively associated with work for the public good (Macken-Walsh & Curtin, 2013).

Various types of structures at the local level thus impact on how partnerships take shape. From a governance theory perspective, there is a hybridity of legitimacy discourses at the local level that underpin how different sectoral representatives come to be powerful in rural partnerships (Connelly, Richardson & Miles, 2006). In such a vein, Derkzen, Franklin and Bock (2008) draw attention to the way partnerships allow for power struggles to arise between existing and new powers, thereby potentially offering opportunities for new elites to emerge. However, other empirical studies have highlighted that little or no rule breaking takes place within partnerships (Connelly, Richardson & Miles, 2006), finding that actors tend to conform to local legitimacy structures.

In this light, the territorial frame in which partnerships operate arguably makes them susceptible to established local power structures and, potentially, to dynamics of cronyism, clientelism and professional dependency (Heanue & Macken-Walsh, 2012; Furmankiewicz, Macken-Walsh & Stefańska, 2014; Furmankiewicz & Macken-Walsh, forthcoming). Furthermore, empirical studies show that rural actors can be compelled to comply not only with local power structures, but also with the structures that are determined externally by actors such as sponsors or funders of rural partnerships. The implications of extra-local structure and goal setting for the power of local communities become apparent in such contexts, and it is to this question that we now turn.

Extra-local powers

It is typical for rural partnerships to have external funders, whether they are large multinational corporations (Cheshire, Everingham & Lawrence, 2014), the state (Curtin & Varley, 1997) or the supra-state, such as the EU. Furthermore, partnerships are increasingly becoming units of large multilevel or 'meta' governance systems that are rationalised remotely from individual rural territories. These extra-local influences are frequently found to exert significant power over the operation of local partnerships in practice (Convery, Soane, Dutson & Shaw, 2010; Macken-Walsh & Curtin, 2013). However, what are the means by which local actors accede to such distant forms of power and how is power legitimised at the multi- or meta-governance level?

According to Haugaard (2012, p. 36) and drawing on Foucault (1979), governance represents a move from the 'crude domination' of government to more subtle 'constitutive, positive and disciplinary' power. However, because of the close association between governance and the potential for empowerment, governance structures are often 'presented as intrinsically good and their legitimacy as self-evident' (Connelly, Richardson & Miles, 2006, p. 268). Large multi- and meta-governance structures tend to attach to core legitimacy claims that are underpinned by particular policy belief systems, such as grounds of 'increased effectiveness' or 'norms of openness and inclusiveness', which are drawn from theories of deliberative democracy (Connelly, Richardson & Miles, 2006, p. 269).

Multi- and meta-structures of governance are challenged with garnering coherent legitimacy as a whole, which inevitably must emerge from what Connelly, Richardson and Miles (2006, p. 70) describe as 'a mass of overlapping, individually imperfect deliberative processes'. Such processes, seeking to be representative of diverse local actors, are operationalised through partnerships that typically follow an inter-sectoral structure. However, inter-sectoral structures may not necessarily correspond with the structures of rural territories. Drawing attention to why this is problematic, Edwards, Goodwin, Pemberton and Woods (2001, p. 297) observe: 'Partnership is demonstrated by the involvement of a tick-list of established institutions who are perceived to "represent" different interests within the town … implying no necessity either for the enrolment of non-establishment organisations, or for the actual engagement of the people who live in the town.'

Having partnerships adhere to structures prescribed by extra-local powers, such as inter-sectoral membership, means that extra-local powers can foster structural formulae for the achievement of certain norms and goals. This has crucial implications for how local actors may exert power in pursuing their interests through rural partnerships. An example cited frequently in studies of policy-sponsored rural partnerships is imposed bureaucratic procedures and rules that have the effect of inculcating a professionalised culture in how rural partnerships operate internally (Delin, 2012; Marquardt, Möllers & Buchenrieder, 2012). The 'organising in' by extra-local powers of certain actors, together with the 'organising out' of others, has the effect of placing added parameters around who and what activities are included, and in creating what Kovach and Kucerova (2006) termed the favoured 'project class'. Funders of rural partnerships are found to have a role in deciding not only 'who is to be admitted as legitimate partners … and how the partnerships are actually to operate' but also 'what is required to be done' (Curtin & Varley, 1997, p. 142). Similarly, O'Toole and Burdess (2004, p. 433) observe how 'higher levels of governance "steer" the self-governing processes of small rural communities, expecting them to "row" for themselves'. In power theory, an analogous image is presented as 'the transition from the sword (government) to the plough (governance)' (Haugaard, 2012, p. 36).

If we are to believe that 'organisation is the mobilisation of bias' (Haugaard, 2012, p. 38 citing Schattschneider, 1975), governance structures may be understood as instrumental to delivering particular development goals. There is a close relationship between partnership structures and goals: the nature of the goals promoted by partnerships can themselves be postulated as adhering to principles of equal representation and embodying opportunities for empowerment. 'Public good' projects, such as housing and service provision promoted by privately initiated partnerships in rural Australia (Cheshire, 2010), provide an example of how partnership goals and structures may be intertwined and legitimated as intrinsically good. In the EU, a convergence is identified in the literature between 'design value' rural enterprise projects and their capacity to 'raise local consciousness of territorial identity … and raise confidence in the ability of the area to regenerate itself' (Lowe et al., 1998, p. 54). Through the valorisation of local custom, tradition and skill, it is claimed that higher status jobs may be created for local people with local inhabitants, as producers or guardians, placed in control of the management of local resources (Lowe et al., 1998, p. 57). Underpinned by such claims, the distinctive development goals of rural partnerships appear to be confluent with the structures of partnerships, with both claimed to empower rural actors.

Through a lens of power theory, however, such claims have weak foundations. Rural partnerships' provision of a supportive structural locus for the pursuit of particular development goals is potentially empowering for those who are interested in pursuing those goals. However, extra-local powers that 'organise in' some development interests and 'organise out' others have an inevitably stifling effect on the potential for partnerships to ignite the type of inclusive debate on which partnerships such as the LEADER approach are principled (Caspar, Farrell & Thirion, 1997). For those who participate in partnerships but whose goals are 'organised out' of partnerships, they may rationally not engage in 'power struggles' when there is little or no chance for them to prevail. In such a scenario, we see partnerships delivering a structural reconfiguration rather than a redistribution of power among the actors involved (Edwards, Goodwin, Pemberton and Woods, 2001). For excluded actors, whose structures and interests preclude any involvement in rural partnerships, it may be perceived that they are powerless in the context of rural governance. However, if we are to understand governance as fundamentally premised on actors' exertion of power in determining their outcomes, we must recognise multiple sites for the exertion of power that are not confined to the deliberative arenas of particular rural partnerships.

The power of non-participation

Shortall (2008) reminds us that engagement in partnership structures or the pursuit of goals fostered by partnerships may not be assumed to be the natural choice of rural inhabitants and nor can it be assumed that 'to participate is the default position of the social norm, or that non-participation is exclusion' (Shortall, 2008, p. 455). It follows that those who 'self-exclude' or consciously resist participation in rural partnerships may not be powerless, but may in fact be potentially powerful.

But, how does such conscious non-participation or resistance manifest itself and how may it be recognised as potentially powerful? Within scenarios of domination and the 'organising out' of particular interests, Haugaard (2012) identifies scope for those who are perceived to be excluded to exercise empowering 'power to'. Some of these forms of power relate to how actors consciously subscribe to, and comply or otherwise with, the powerful structures and/or goals that prescribe what is 'reasonable thought and action' in any given context. For those who comply with partnership structures, not to achieve goals but because they perceive that it is reasonable to participate and that not to do so would provoke scrutiny or some form of sanction, they are being dominated by 'power over'. However, for those who consciously decide that they do not wish to participate because they evaluate partnership structures and goals to be uninteresting, undesirable or illegitimate, they are exerting empowering 'power to'.

A social group that has been noted to be inactive in many rural partnerships across the EU is primary producers: those whose economic and social problems are said to have led to the introduction of the LEADER[2] programme, a programme that has operationalised the partnership approach across EU rural regions since 1991 (Varley & Curtin, 2006). Farmers and fishers are noted to be marginalised – not in all, but in many rural partnerships (Osti, 2000; van der Ploeg, 2003; Esposito-Fava & Lajarge, 2009; Macken-Walsh, 2009). Their marginalisation has not typically given rise to power struggles *within* partnerships, as Derkzen, Franklin and Bock (2008) have identified, but, rather, to a marked absence of debate and conflict, particularly considering the large population of primary producers in rural areas. A focus both on structures-oriented and goals-oriented issues is necessary to explore this.

Understanding structures as essentially the 'rules of the game', it is immediately apparent that rural partnerships are not the only 'game' in EU rural areas. Farming organisations, ranging from representative lobby groups to large cooperatives, have an established presence in many rural areas. While it is beyond the scope of this chapter to comment on the power dynamics of these organisations, their continuing strong presence offers a clue as to why many primary producers are not engaging with or challenging partnerships[3] – they have their own structures. As we understand from Haugaard (2012), it may be conducive to the power of primary producers for structures that do not concern them to operate independently of them. For as long as the structures survive and prosper, it is less likely that they will acquire interests infringe on primary producers, potentially resulting in power challenges and redistribution. Thus, power struggles failing to transpire between primary producers[4] and the eligibly powerful in rural partnerships is protective of each group's structures and goals rather than a diminution of their power, which is consistent with the analysis of Derkzen and colleagues (2008).

Aside from this partial explanation as to why farmers and fishers tend to not engage with rural partnerships, a focus is warranted on the particular goals of rural partnerships. Despite rural partnerships having been prompted by problems of 'crisis proportions' experienced by primary producers, such as steeply declining numbers at work in agriculture, low agricultural incomes and the high proportion of officially categorised non-viable farms (Kearney et al., 1995, cited in Curtin & Varley, 1997), in many cases primary producers are less likely than other social groups to take up the rural economic diversification opportunities offered by LEADER. While some primary producers may be considered as lacking power to engage with LEADER due to factors such as having skills and experience that do not match up with 'design value' enterprises, research has highlighted that both farmers and fishers may not wish to engage in such enterprises. Farmers and fishers are found to have strong social and cultural identities based on occupational practices of farming and fishing, which are fundamentally different to the service, design and commodification activities of enterprises supported by LEADER. Farmers and fishers are core groups of indigenous rural communities on whom a core development strategy of rural partnerships is based – 'the revival of local traditions, the renovation of local monuments, and the re-creation of rural/local images' (Kovach, 2000, p. 181). However, empirical research has highlighted the capacity for primary producers to reject such development strategies on the basis that they constitute the '"trinketisation", commercialisation, and trivialisation of culture' (Kneafsey, 1998, p. 113) and because they are incompatible with their subjectively esteemed forms of occupational knowledge and skill (Macken-Walsh, 2009, 2012). For a range of reasons, therefore, primary producers may reject both the structures and the goals of rural partnerships.

Resistance is associated with rural people in particular, potentially contributing to strategies of resilience and offering a protective function towards lay and localised forms of knowledge, skill and custom (Macken-Walsh & Byrne, 2015). The types of ontological insecurity that cause people to comply with structures of partnerships, even when they are not furthering their own goals, may be weakly present among rural actors such as primary producers who can have structures and goals of their own. Furthermore, primary producers are noted to have resilient identities that may be less permeable to legitimacy sources, such as expert or reified knowledge, that challenge 'what is locally considered reasonable behaviour … (and) whereby the conventionality of structures disappears from view from the perspective of the social actor' (Haugaard, 2011, p. 23). It is in such a context that Byrne, Edmondson and Fahy (1993, p. 253) note that 'when indigenous inhabitants ... gradually abandon local criteria regulating forms of reasonable thought and feeling, they will have become much more similar to people everywhere else'. Such integration, paradoxically, would run contrary to the rhetoric of empowerment, indigenisation and cultural valorisation that accompanies the goals of rural partnerships.

Van der Ploeg (2005) focuses on the significance of the rural peasantry as offering 'pockets of resistance' against the hegemony of mega-projects such as governance. He advocates the exploration of 'uncapturedness, the struggle for autonomy and the creation of noncontrollability wherever they emerge' and recognition of such as a powerful, 'actively constructed response' to the domination of the mega-project (van der Ploeg, 2005, p. 15). He notes an 'intriguing "traveling" of the peasant principle', the significance and power of which represents an important part of the real picture of how multilevel governance is evolving and the power of non-participation as well as participation.

Rural partnerships' exclusion of goals and actors' non-participation through self-exclusion stifle the structural capacity of partnerships to integrate development interests within and across rural territories. The absence of power struggles within partnerships is generative of other forms of structural power that operate independently from partnerships. Contrary to the aims of rural partnerships, what has emerged in many contexts is a deepening divide between the rural development sector on one hand and the primary production sector on the other (Macken-Walsh, 2009). Relevant to this particular conundrum of rural partnerships is the broadening of rural governance to include a wider variety of structures and goals. Such diversification of the participatory nexus of rural governance is exemplified by the recent expansion of the EU governance project, which will now take our focus.

The governance 'mega-project'

The European Innovation Partnership (EIP), instigated in 2014, is the umbrella policy under which new forms of partnerships and their interrelationships are organised in a highly integrated multilevel system. The most subsidiary partnership of the EIP is called an Operational Group (OG), which is officially described as a partnership established by two or more different actors collaborating to address any agriculture-related idea or problem (Europa, 2014). OGs are described as 'demand-driven partnerships – using bottom-up approaches and linking farmers, advisors, researchers, businesses, and other actors' (van Oost, 2012, p. 6). While the operationalisation of OGs is in progress, their design compares and contrasts in interesting ways with the myriad rural partnerships examined previously in the literature.

The structures and goals of OGs have characteristics that contrast with rural development partnerships. While the occupational roles of the members of OGs must be different (farmers, researchers and agribusiness, for example), they are pursuing common development goals within a single sector. In contrast to inter-sectoral partnerships, OGs must not represent any particular constellation of actors, avoiding the potential arbitrariness of the 'tick-list' approach to membership that presumes different interests are represented simply when all establishment institutions are involved (Edwards, Goodwin, Pemberton & Woods, 2001). This may potentially lead to goals and structures of OGs being more relevant to, and representative of, the occupational actors involved.

OGs may be organised nationally and there is no limit on the number of OGs that can be established within single territories. Therefore, unlike rural development partnerships, OGs do not require actors within territories to collaborate within a single partnership, and multiple (small or large) OGs may coexist in the same territorial or sectoral space. This arguably liberates the operation of OGs from the constraints of local power structures that have impacted on many existing rural partnerships. Conceivably, in contexts where there are incompatibilities or power struggles, there is no rule preventing actors from establishing multiple OGs. Possibilities are thus presented to generate power beyond the struggles identified as instrumental for empowerment processes in rural development partnerships (Derkzen, Franklin & Bock, 2008) through an alternative route of collaboratively building mutual interests and synergies. Goals that are 'organised out' by some OGs may be 'organised in' by others.

Such characteristics of the EIP governance project may appear to enable a greater diversity of rural actors to exert power in more diverse ways, prompting interesting research questions. However, broadened governance structures that extend the rules of the game by 'organising in' a wider diversity of interests create new opportunities for the mobilisation of bias. While it is clearly stated that any agriculture-related problem is eligible to underpin the establishment of an OG, clearly not all OGs will be funded, and criteria will be used for the purposes of allocating funding. Clues as to what might frame such criteria are presented in how the structures and goals of EIP partnerships are articulated in the policy and academic literatures. Throughout, one core theme emerges: knowledge.

The literature on governance and power pays attention to the concept of knowledge. Literature focusing on EU multilevel governance structures in other policy areas that pre-exist the EIP have highlighted processes of 'expertification' (Smismans, 2006) and the emergence of a 'professional European lobbying class' (Knodt, Greenwood & Quittkat, 2011, p. 353). Those with expert knowledge generate legitimacy and power through their status as what Haugaard (2011, p. 24) calls 'specialists in truth production'. In this context, the significance of the role of the 'innovation broker' in the EIP warrants attention. The role of the innovation broker is singled out in the policy literature as crucial for catalysing and supporting the establishment of OGs in cases where single actors encounter difficulty in finding partners to 'get an innovation project going' (van Oost, 2012). While the innovation broker may not necessarily be involved in the action pursued by the OG, s/he can assist in helping to formulate and articulate new ideas, linking partners and searching for funding (van Oost, 2012).

Such functions make apparent the potential for innovation brokers to have powerfully deterministic roles on the focus, outcomes and participants in OGs. As highlighted by authors such as Smismans (2006) and Knodt, Greenwood and Quittkat (2011), the dominant 'expertified' class emerges across actor types, transcending occupational or sectoral boundaries. For example, rather than having skills specific to the area of policy concern, dominant actors are more likely to be communications and law professionals (Smismans, 2006). Smismans (2006, p. 271, citing Habranski, 2004), with reference to an existing agriculture interest group that exerts influence through various participatory structures in the EU, observes how all staff who are tasked with lobbying the EU have university education but '[t]hey have never worked for any of the national Farmers' Unions before or had a career in the farming sector'. As evidenced in the existing literature on governance and power, expert knowledge can become hegemonic, with powerful actors becoming 'remarkably Eurocentric in their thinking' (Lowe et al. 1998, p. 68) and, resonating with Smismans (2006), expanding 'their authority to spheres not justified by their knowledge' (Haugaard, 2011, p. 23).

The significance of expert or reified knowledge has a special association with how governance structures acquire legitimacy to 'organise in' particular actors and goals. In addition to applying existing analytical frameworks to explore how the structures and goals of OGs take shape in practice, a research agenda focusing on the crucial question of knowledge and power will provide an interesting focus in research on the meta-governance project henceforth.

Conclusion

Haugaard's power theory assists us in understanding the nuances of what it means for actors to participate or not participate in rural partnerships and to draw conclusions that elucidate the intricacies of how actors may be empowered or dominated in different operational cases. If governance is to be truly understood as a 'nobody in charge world' (Stoker, 1996, p. 4), it follows that those actors who do not participate in partnerships are recognised as having the potential to be equally as powerful as those who do participate.

It may not be concluded that those who participate in the development activities of rural partnerships are empowered or powerful, since the picture is far more complex. The power of participants is underpinned by both local and extra-local structures that regulate the scope of their actions. Nonetheless, they are exercising empowering 'power to' if the development structures and goals of partnerships are conducive to their interests. On the other hand, those who are not powerful in rural partnerships because the structures and goals have 'organised out' their interests, may be powerless if they continue to participate in partnerships. Non-participants, by contrast, may be powerful if they consciously decide to have no involvement in partnerships because they cannot see their goals being furthered. The latter category is particularly resonant with van der Ploeg's (2005) 'pockets of resistance', recognised as powerful in their own right, despite operating outside the participatory mechanisms of rural governance.

Liberalisation of the most recent incarnation of partnerships operating under the EIP to organise at the national and international levels potentially opens up opportunities for actors within the agriculture sector to exercise greater power. However, as they have before, phenomena such as 'expertification' threaten to curtail opportunities for diverse occupational actors to become powerful. Notwithstanding this, Clegg (2014, p. 388) reminds us that '[c]ircuits built on ideology that seek to dominate, to attain hegemony, are the most fragile and vulnerable'. Such circuits are omnipresent in governance but, as in government, are open to disruption, most powerfully by 'pockets of resistance' in which new oppositional powers can emerge. Although the bureaucratic literature does not confront the theory of power in any robust way, there are decipherable convergences between policy discourses of multi-actor innovation delivered through multilevel governance and an understanding of power which recognises that it 'is much more efficient to govern through freedoms, however illusory, than repressions' and that circuits of power which 'stress system integration and allow for diversities and pluralities in social integration are more resilient and robust' (Clegg, 2014, p. 388). Now entering into an unprecedented 'mega-project' of multilevel governance, the 'pockets of resistance' that will emerge henceforth appear all the more powerful in this context.

Notes

1 As the analysis of Furmankiewicz and Macken-Walsh (forthcoming) highlights, statutory representatives on boards of partnerships may be professionally dependent on more senior statutory employees and may be relatively inactive silent members in the activities of partnership boards.
2 Liaisons Entre Actions de Developpement de l'Économie Rurale (LEADER).
3 However, farming lobby groups have sought to challenge the increasing diversion of funding from agriculture to rural development (Shucksmith, 2010).
4 Osti (2000, p. 176) presents a counterpoint to farmers' powerful non-participation in rural partnerships, noting that farmers are 'bewildered from losing their privileged channels of influence'.

References

Byrne, A, Edmondson, R & Fahy, K (1993). Rural tourism and cultural identity in the West of Ireland. In B O'Connor & M Cronin (Eds), *Tourism in Ireland: A critical analysis*. Cork: Cork University Press.

Caspar, R, Farrell, G & Thirion, S (1997). *Organising local partnerships. Innovations in Rural Areas*. Notebook No 2. LEADER European Observatory / AEIDL. Brussels.

Cheshire, L (2010). A corporate responsibility? The constitution of fly-in, fly-out mining companies as governance partners in remote, mine-affected localities. *Journal of Rural Studies* 26(1), 12–20.

Cheshire, L, Everingham, JA & Lawrence, G (2014). Governing the impacts of mining and the impacts of mining governance: Challenges for rural and regional local governments in Australia. *Journal of Rural Studies* 36, 330–339.

Clegg, S (2014). Circuits of power/knowledge. *Journal of Political Power* 7(3), 383–392.

Connelly, S, Richardson, T & Miles, T (2006). Situated legitimacy: Deliberative arenas and the new rural governance. *Journal of Rural Studies* 22(3), 267–277.

Convery, I, Soane, I, Dutson, T & Shaw, H 2010. Mainstreaming LEADER delivery of the RDR in Cumbria: An interpretative phenomenological analysis. *Sociologia Ruralis* 50(4), 370–391.

Curtin, C & Varley, T (1997). Take your partners and face the music: The state, community groups and area-based partnerships in rural Ireland. In P Brennan (Ed.), *L'Irlande, identités et modernité* (pp. 141–155). Centre de Gestion des Revues, Université Charles de Gaulle, France.

Delin, M (2012). The role of farmers in local action groups: The case of the national network of the local action groups in the Czech Republic. *Agricultural Economics - Zemědělská ekonomika* 58(9), 433–442.

Derzken, P, Franklin, A & Bock, B (2008). Examining power struggles as a signifier of successful partnership working: A case study of partnership dynamics. *Journal of Rural Studies* 24(4), 458–466.

Edwards, B, Goodwin, M, Pemberton, S & Woods, M (2001). Partnerships, power, and scale in rural governance. *Environment and Planning C: Government and Policy* 19(2), 289–310.

Elias, N (1994). *The civilizing process*. Oxford: Basil Blackwell.

Esposito-Fava, A & Lajarge, R (2009). Territorialisation, return or death of agriculture in rural policies? Paper presented to the XXII Congress of the European Society for Rural Sociology (ESRS), Vaasa, August 2009.

Europa (2014). *Operational Groups under Rural Development Programmes*. http://ec.europa.eu/eip/agriculture/sites/agri-eip/files/operational-groups_en.jpg (accessed 15 January 2015).

Foucault, M (1979). *Discipline and punish*. Harmondsworth: Penguin.

Furmankiewicz, M (2012). LEADER+ territorial governance in Poland: Successes and failures as a rational choice effect. *Tijdschrift voor Economische en Sociale Geografie* 103(3), 261–275.

Furmankiewicz, M & Macken-Walsh, A (forthcoming). Government within governance? Polish rural development partnerships through the lens of functional representation. *Journal of Rural Studies*.

Furmankiewicz, M, Macken-Walsh, A & Stefańska, J (2014). Territorial governance, institutional networks and power: The case of cross-sectoral partnerships in rural Poland. *Geografiska Annaler, Series B: Human Geography* 96(4), 299–401.

Goodwin, M (1998). The governance of rural areas: Some research issues and agendas. *Journal of Rural Studies* 14(1), 5–12.

Gore, T (2008). Collaborative governance and territorial rescaling in the UK: A comparative study of two EU Structural Funds programmes. *GeoJournal* 72(1–2), 59–73.

Haugaard, M (2002). *Power: A reader*. Manchester: Manchester University Press.

Haugaard, M (2011). Rethinking power. Social Science Research network (SSRN). Available at http://ssrn.com/abstract=1913739 (accessed 15 June 2014).

Haugaard, M (2012). Rethinking the four dimensions of power: Domination and empowerment. *Journal of Political Power* 5(1), 33–54.

Heanue, K & Macken-Walsh, A (2012). Static structures and dynamic processes of participation and access: A case study of Connemara community radio. *Irish Communications Review* 13(7), 28–41.

Kearney, B, Boye, GE & Walsh JA (1995). EU LEADER 1 Initiative in Ireland, Evaluations and Recommendations, Department of Agriculture, Food and Foresty, Agriculture House, Dublin, Ireland.

Kneafsey, M (1998). Tourism and place identity: A case-study in rural Ireland. *Irish Geography* 31(2), 111–123.

Knodt, M, Greenwood, J & Quittkat, C (2011). Territorial and functional interest representation in EU governance. *Journal of European Integration* 33(4), 349–367.

Kovach, I (2000). LEADER, a new social order, and the Central and East European countries. *Sociologia Ruralis* 40(2), 181–189.

Kovach, I & Kucerova, E (2006). The project class in Central Europe: The Czech and Hungarian cases. *Sociologia Ruralis* 46(1), 3–21.

Lowe, P, Ray, C, Ward, N, Wood, D & Woodward, R (1998). *Participation in rural development: A review of European experience*. Centre for Rural Economy (CRE), Research Report, University of Newcastle-upon-Tyne, February 1998.

Macken-Walsh, A (2009). *Barriers to change: A sociological study of rural development in Ireland*. Carlow, Ireland: Teagasc.

Macken-Walsh, A (2012). Operationalising contemporary rural development: Socio-cultural determinants arising from a strong local fishing culture. *Human Ecology* 40(2), 199–211.

Macken-Walsh, A & Byrne, A (2015). Cooperation in Irish family farming. In D Meredith (Ed.), *Family farming in Ireland: Continuity and change*. Dublin: Royal Irish Academy.

Macken-Walsh, A & Curtin, C (2013). Governance and rural development: The case of the Rural Partnership Programme (RPP) in post-socialist Lithuania. *Sociologia Ruralis* 53(2), 246–264.

Marquardt, D, Möllers, J & Buchenrieder, G (2012). Social networks and rural development: LEADER in Romania. *Sociologia Ruralis* 52(4), 398–431.

Osti, G (2000). Leader and partnerships: The case of Italy. *Sociologia Ruralis* 40(2), 172–180.

O'Toole, K & Burdess, N (2004). New community governance in small rural towns: The Australian experience. *Journal of Rural Studies* 20(4), 433–443.

Ray, C (2000). The EU LEADER programme: Rural development laboratory. *Sociologia Ruralis* 40(2), 163–171.

Richardson, T & Cashmore, M (2011). Power, knowledge and environmental assessment: The World Bank's pursuit of 'good governance'. *Journal of Political Power* 4(1), 105–125.

Schattsschneider, EE (1975). The Semisovereign People: A Realist's View of Democracy in America. Wadsworth.

Shortall, S (2008). Are rural development programmes socially inclusive? Social inclusion, civic engagement, participation, and social capital: Exploring the differences. *Journal of Rural Studies* 24(4), 450 457.

Shucksmith, M (2010). Disintegrated rural development? Neo-endogenous rural development, planning and place-shaping in diffused power contexts. *Sociologia Ruralis* 50(1), 1–14.

Smismans, S (2006). *Civil society and legitimate European governance*. Cheltenham: Edward Elgar.

Stoker, G (1996). *Governance as theory: Five propositions*. Mimeo, Department of Government, University of Strathclyde, UK.

van der Ploeg, JD (2003). Rural development and the mobilisation of local actors. Conference paper presented to 'Planting Seeds for Rural Futures: Rural Policy Perspectives for a Wider Europe', the European Conference on Rural Development, Salzburg, November, 2003.

van der Ploeg, JD (2005). Empire and the peasant principle. Paper presented to the XXI Congress of the European Society for Rural Sociology, Keszthely, Hungary, 22–26 August.

Van Oost, I (2012). The European Innovation Partnership (EIP) agricultural productivity and sustainability: Moving agriculture ahead! Paper presented to 'Best Practice in Extension Services: Supporting Farmer Innovation', Aviva Stadium, Dublin, 1 November 2012.

Varley, T & Curtin, C (2006). The politics of empowerment: Power, populism and partnership in rural Ireland. *The Economic and Social Review* 37(3), 423–446.

625

52

Confronting Globalisation?

Rural Protest, Resistance and Social Movements

Michael Woods

Introduction

The increasing integration of rural communities into transnational social and economic networks has unsettled the politics of rural regions across the globe. Through much of the 20th century, rural economies and societies in the advanced industrial nations of Europe, North America, Japan and Australasia (the 'global north') were defined and governed in relation to national political interests. Agriculture was regulated to support national food security (or, within Europe's Common Agricultural Policy, European food security), and forestry, mining and other resource industries were similarly managed in the national interest (often as nationalised industries). At the same time, rural development programmes were implemented to address regional inequalities and mitigate the disruptive effects of mass internal migration while conservation measures were introduced to protect sites of national environmental or cultural significance. These policies reflected a broadly consensual view of what the countryside was for, shared and reproduced by stable policy communities that excluded dissenting discourses whilst providing a non-confrontational route for rural representation through mainstream farm unions, interest groups and political parties.

The first challenges to the rural political settlement also came from domestic trends: the success of productivist agricultural policies that paradoxically weakened the power of farmers in rural communities and created a vacuum in rural leadership; the rise of counter-urbanisation and the arrival of in-migrants to rural communities, eager to step into the leadership void but often with very different ideas about rural life and priorities than traditional elites; and the popularisation of economic, environmental and animal welfare discourses that questioned agricultural exceptionalism. Accordingly, the earliest skirmishes were localised conflicts around specific developments, land management issues or public services, which escalated over time into regional or national campaigns and debates, targeted at regional or national governments (Mormont, 1987; Woods, 2005).

However, the focus on the local, regional and national political realms has served to disguise the hidden hand of neoliberal globalisation as a driving force behind many of the most critical pressures on rural communities. For instance, the struggle for survival by family farmers in the global north has been compounded by intensified competition resulting from stretched commodity chains and the dismantling of trade barriers, including ideological pressures on national governments to phase out production subsidies as obstacles to competition; the loss of traditional rural employers has followed relocation to cheaper production sites abroad by transnational corporations; demands on housing and land, and cultural tensions, come not only from domestic migration but also from international migration and tourism; and so-called 'urban' viewpoints on environmental protection and animal welfare reflect a broader 'globalisation of values' stoked by transnational NGOs and the global media.

Yet, in contrast to the global south – where rural movements that emerged from issues around peasant farming, land reform and indigenous rights have recognised neoliberal globalisation as a common enemy and coalesced into transnational solidarity networks, such as La Via Campesina (Borras, Edelman & Kay, 2008; Woods, 2008) – rural protests in the global north have rarely explicitly referenced globalisation, and instances of transnational organising are uncommon. As such, it might be suggested that rural movements have been mis-targeted. Certainly, the limited capacity of national governments to react to rural concerns has contributed to disillusionment in the established rural interest groups that formed part of historic policy communities, and to the emergence of new rural protest groups, some of which have targeted non-state actors such as transnational corporations. At the same time, though, relational perspectives have demonstrated that globalisation is characterised not by the concentration of power but by the diffusion of power (Massey, 2005; Woods, 2007). Impacts of globalisation in rural localities require the enrolment and acquiescence of local actants, giving them some (limited) capacity to resist, subvert or modify global processes. Accordingly, even localised rural conflicts can be seen as part of the contesting of globalisation.

There are, therefore, at least five arenas in which rural activists can be observed to be confronting globalisation, directly or indirectly. These include:

- *Agricultural protests* by farmers in several countries including Britain, Ireland, France, Germany, Belgium, Poland, Australia, New Zealand and the United States, reacting to industry restructuring that has dismantled the protectionism of the postwar period, increased competition and squeezed the incomes of small producers. Farmers' protests have tended to be targeted at national governments and national policy reforms, including early mass demonstrations in the United States in the 1970s and in Australia and New Zealand in the 1980s (Stock, 1996; Halpin, 2004). Yet, the Australian and New Zealand protests were against deregulation that was part of the rollout of neoliberal globalisation. Similarly, in Europe, farmers' protests have contested reforms to the Common Agricultural Policy that have been implemented as outcomes of global trade negotiations, such as the withdrawal of milk quotas. European farmers have also protested against the effects of trade liberalisation within the European Union, with imports blockaded or seized by direct action in Britain and France (Naylor, 1994; Woods, 2005), whilst opposition to new trade agreements has mobilised mass demonstrations in South Korea and much more limited demonstrations by farmers in Australia (Lee, Kim & Wainwright, 2010; Woods, 2015). At the same time, some farmer activism has started to be directed against transnational corporations, including protests across Europe against fuel companies in 2000, and against supermarkets in 2014 opposing cuts in payments for milk driven by world market prices, as well as direct action and rallies against genetically modified crops in France and Poland.
- *Opposition to industrial restructuring* in sectors other than agriculture, including forestry, mining, food processing and manufacturing, commonly associated with corporate reorganisation, trade liberalisation and the relocation of production within a globalising economy. Campaigns have mobilised, for example, around the closure of sawmills in

Canada, food processing plants in Australia, and textile factories in Britain, often initially involving industrial action and public rallies to resist restructuring, but in some cases transmuting into more proactive initiatives to support economic diversification and community regeneration (see, for example, Larsen, 2008; Prudham, 2008). Although such actions are shaped by the backdrop of economic globalisation, they are mostly highly localised movements, rarely developing into translocal alliances.

- *Struggles over land rights* of various complexions and configurations. Although the struggle for land reform and resistance to 'land-grabbing' is primarily associated with rural movements in the global south, issues around land have also become increasingly significant for rural politics in the global north. International land investments in Australia and parts of Eastern Europe have been contested by local opponents, prompting, for example, protests by farmers in Poland in early 2015. Beyond agriculture, foreign purchases of Scottish landed estates in the 1990s reignited debates over the concentration of land ownership in Scotland, which gained traction with political reforms introduced by the devolved Scottish government after 1999 that have empowered communities to organise to buy their own land (Mackenzie, 2006; Wightman, 2010). Conversely, the rights of landowners have been asserted in conflicts over the appropriation of property for industrial and infrastructural developments including reservoirs, airports, roads and energy projects, often pitting local landowners against transnational corporations. The 'Lock the Gate' campaign in Australia, for example, has mobilised farmers to block access to land for coal seam gas exploitation; whilst conflict over mining development in Rosia Montana, Romania, has revolved around pressure on property owners to sell land to a Canadian-owned mining corporation (Velicu, 2012). From a different direction, the reassertion of the land rights of Indigenous peoples in North America, Australia and New Zealand has become a contentious political issue in rural regions that engages with globalisation on multiple scales, from recognising the injustices of colonial dispossession to the participation of Indigenous groups in resource struggles with transnational corporations (Gedicks, 2001; Larsen, 2008).

- *A defensive politics of rural identity* that is mobilised in opposition to perceived threats from cultural globalisation and the promotion of universal standards in environmental management and animal welfare. This includes tensions around the impact of immigration and tourism on traditional rural cultures, and associated conflicts over new housing and tourism developments, the presence of migrant workers, and the settlement of refugees and asylum seekers (Hubbard, 2005). It also includes rural resistance to new laws and regulations that restrict, for example, hunting and shooting wild animals, or traditional farm husbandry practices, and confrontations with transnational NGOs that are active in campaigning on these issues. In several parts of Europe, including Italy, France and Belgium, demonstrations against the introduction of European Union regulations on shooting wild birds were framed as a defence of rural tradition; whilst in Britain, the mobilisation of mass demonstrations by the Countryside Alliance between 1997 and 2004 was driven primarily by opposition to legislation to ban the hunting of wild mammals with dogs (Woods, 2005, 2015; Mischi, 2013).

- *Environmental protests* that concern the use or conservation of rural ecosystems and landscapes. These include actions to protect rural sites from development or exploitation by global resource industries, which can involve the forging of alliances between local protesters and transnational environmental organisations, as in the case of industrial forestry in western Canada (Magnusson & Shaw, 2003), or the Rossport oil pipeline in Ireland (Gilmartin, 2009). In other instances, however, transnational environmental NGOs can come into conflict with rural activists, for example in campaigning to promote global environmental values with respect to animal welfare or farming practice, as discussed above, or around the scale at which environmental concerns are framed. Most notably, the development of renewable energy schemes in rural settings – supported by transnational NGOs as a response to climate change – have been frequently opposed by groups concerned at the impact on local rural landscapes and environments, with wind farm developments in particular sparking a plethora of rural conflicts in Britain, Spain, Australia, the United States and elsewhere (Woods, 2003b; Zografos & Martinez-Alier, 2009; Phadke, 2011).

All of the above arenas of conflict, however, involve the contestation of power in rural society and engage with its redistribution in the context of globalisation. In some cases the focus is on power over rural resources such as land and water; in other cases it concerns the power to make decisions that affect employment in rural localities or the prices paid for agricultural products; and in yet others the question revolves around the power to define rurality itself. Indeed, the proliferation of rural protests and conflicts reflects the ambiguities arising from the erosion of traditional rural power structures – for instance, as power has been removed from rural communities and concentrated by corporate restructuring in globalisation, or as the influence of interest groups such as farm unions has been weakened. Rural protests thus frequently respond to a sense of disempowerment by rural communities and are discursively targeted at a perceived new power centre, articulated through binaries such as local/global, rural/urban, and native/incomer. In practice, however, the dynamics of rural restructuring are embedded in far more complex relations of power that extend within rural communities, with inequalities structured around class, ethnicity, indigeneity, gender and so on. Negotiating these internal power relations to blend resources and build alliances can be critical to enabling rural protest movements to assemble a capacity to act – or in other words, to obtain *power to* achieve their desired outcomes.

The remainder of this chapter examines the resurgence of rural protests and their role in confronting globalisation through three conceptual lenses. First, it positions rural protests as part of a new 'politics of the rural' shaped by contests between competing discourses of rurality that are focused on the perceived meaning and experience of rurality. Second, the chapter considers whether contemporary rural protests represent a return of class politics, and their contribution to struggles over global capitalism. Third, the chapter turns to social movement theory as a framework for analysing the dynamics and organisation of rural protests and their variable geography. Finally, the chapter concludes by assessing the efficacy of rural protests in confronting globalisation and their legacy for rural society.

From rural politics to the politics of the rural

The emergence of rural protest movements over the last three decades has challenged rural social scientists to rethink our conceptual frameworks for the analysis of rural policy and politics. Conventionally, rural politics had been conceived in terms of the management and distribution of resources, notably land. Although tensions might occasionally arise over land use, or access to water or minerals, these were understood as resource conflicts between competing interest groups, which could involve local campaigns and demonstrations but which were normally resolved within the mechanisms of state policy making. The concept of 'policy communities' provided a framework for understanding the negotiated management of rural resources by a small group of interest group representatives, whilst the introduction of broader perspectives could be positioned as a transition to a more open form of policy network (Smith, 1993; Winter, 1996).

However, studies in the 1980s and 1990s had started to record the proliferation of rural conflicts that did not fit this model: dissenting from the consensus, involving new, often ad hoc campaign groups and more confrontational tactics, and often revolving around more emotive or symbolic concerns that could not be explained by economic rationalism. As Mormont (1987, p. 562) observed, 'If what could be termed a rural question exists it no longer concerns issues of agriculture or of a particular aspect of living conditions in a rural environment, but questions concerning the specific function of rural space and the type of development to encourage within it.'

The shift was conceptualised in Woods (2003a) as a move from 'rural politics' – concerned with the management of rural resources – to a new 'politics of the rural', in which the central issue is the meaning and regulation of rurality. This conceptualisation was informed by the recognition as part of the cultural turn in rural studies that the 'rural' is not only a socially constructed category, but that different actors will construct their idea of rurality differently, and that these constructs can have a powerful influence on individuals' perceptions and behaviours. As such, the politics of the rural can be understood as the clash of competing 'discourses of rurality' (Woods, 2005).

The politics of the rural can be observed playing out in internal struggles within rural areas between factions with competing notions of rural life and the use of rural land around issues such as new housing developments (Murdoch & Marsden, 1994; Woods, 1998), wind farms (Woods, 2003b; Zografos & Martinez-Alier, 2009; Phadke, 2011), access to land (Parker, 2002), hunting (Woods, 2005; Mischi, 2013) and industrial agriculture (Smithers, Joseph & Armstrong, 2005). Such conflicts are sometimes represented as tensions between 'locals' and 'incomers', and indeed disputes can develop from the determination of in-migrants to protect their financial and emotional investment in an imagined rural lifestyle; however, the local/ incomer dichotomy oversimplifies both the heterogeneity of in-migrants and the divergence of perspectives within rural communities as the hegemony of traditional industries has waned and as people have become more exposed to mainstream media.

Similarly simplistic dualisms are also present in a second expression of the politics of the rural: the mobilisation of protesters in defence of an imagined rural against perceived external threats, which are often framed as a rural–urban conflict. The mass mobilisation of rural campaigners by the Countryside Alliance in Britain in the late 1990s and early 2000s exemplified this, with a specific proposal to legislate to ban the hunting of wild mammals with hounds portrayed as a broader assault on 'the rural way of life' by 'urban prejudice' (Woods, 2005). This representation, which was reproduced through the imagery and rhetoric of the campaign, as well as by its strategy of holding mass demonstrations in London, both imposed a particular discourse of rurality as the 'true' countryside behind which all rural people must rally, and alienated any dissenting perspectives as being non-rural – thus ignoring both anti-hunting sentiment in rural communities and the strong *urban* ties of many of the movement's activists. Moreover, whilst the Countryside Alliance campaign was focused on domestic politics, its discourse evoked a wider 'other'. The appropriation of patriotic symbols such as flags and national anthems as part of its protest dramaturgy reinforced the historic association of British national identity with the countryside and hinted at the pollution of urban thought by foreign influences (Wallwork & Dixon, 2004).

The conflation of rural and national identities has also been present in farmers' protests against trade deals, imports and deregulation in Britain, France, Australia and elsewhere (Strijker, Voerman & Terluin, 2015). In making the association, such protests implicitly resist globalisation, yet by adopting nationalistic rhetoric and positioning foreign farmers as rivals, they stop short of building a transnational solidarity movement against neoliberal globalisation. Only in a few exceptional cases have rural protesters explicitly represented neoliberal globalisation as posing a threat to an imagined rural identity, most notably in the Confédération Paysanne's targeting of McDonald's as a symbol of globalisation's impact on an idealised French peasant existence (Woods, 2015).

The return of the class struggle?

As a conceptual framework, the 'politics of the rural' can be critiqued, like other expressions of the cultural turn in rural studies, for overemphasising the importance of symbols and discourses and understating the material basis of rural protests. Farmers' protests, or the resistance of workers to a mill closure, may incorporate rhetoric about the loss of rural tradition or the impact on a rural way of life, but they are grounded in material concerns about the loss of jobs and incomes. In seeking to capture these material drivers of rural protest, we perhaps need to revisit the political economy approach in rural studies and refocus attention on the significance of class.

Class conflict was rife in the countryside of the late 19th and early 20th centuries, finding expression, for example, in the pioneer trade unionism of the English Tolpuddle Martyrs, the Australian Shearers' Strike, and the brief popularity of socialism in the farmlands of the American Midwest. By the mid-20th century, however, the potential for working-class mobilisation had been repressed by the assertion of paternalistic power structures that aligned the interests of rural workers with those of the farming elite, reinforced by discourses of the 'apolitical countryside' in Britain and 'countrymindedness' in Australia. Moreover, deindustrialisation and the mechanisation of agriculture depleted the rural working class and marginalised its position in rural politics, such that researchers in the 1980s and 1990s pointed not to inter-class conflict in rural communities, but to intra-class conflict between competing middle-class factions (Cloke & Thrift, 1987).

Heley (2015) suggests that class analyses had all but disappeared from rural studies by the mid-1990s, but notes a recent revival of interest associated with renewed investigation of inequalities in rural society. This includes research into gentrification processes through which working-class residents have been displaced from rural property markets. By and large this has occurred with significantly less resistance than has been observed in cases of urban gentrification, but there are exceptions, especially in localities where the impact of gentrification has been particularly intense, such as Hebden Bridge in northern England, or localities where gentrification has particularly taken the form of property purchases as holiday homes, as in parts of Wales. Similarly, protests have been mobilised against luxury developments aimed at international tourists or amenity migrants in settings as diverse as Scotland and Japan. Moreover, in Scotland, where large tracts of land are still held in large quasi-feudal estates, tenant opposition to the sale of the North Lochinver estate and the Isle of Eigg to foreign buyers, in 1989 and 1995 respectively, acted as a catalyst for a resurgent land reform movement and for legislation for a community 'right to buy' (Wightman, 2010).

At the same time, however, it can be difficult to disentangle anti-gentrification campaigns from more reactionary middle-class actions to protect their property interests by opposing further developments (Murdoch & Marsden, 1994; Woods, 2005). The case of Queenstown, New Zealand, described by Woods (2011), is a case in point, with campaigning to halt the rapid tourism- and amenity migration-driven pace of development led by affluent in-migrants, including some international property owners, but resisted by a pro-development local elite which insisted that ongoing development was necessary to permit local residents to benefit from the boom and to prevent the district becoming an exclusive preserve of the global super-rich, an 'Aspen of the South Pacific'. Moreover, the mobilisation of pro-hunting protests in Britain by the Countryside Alliance was characterised by critics as an elite-led defence of privilege. The Countryside Alliance responded with billboards and adverts depicting working people such as nurses who were supporters (Burridge, 2008), yet its leadership was disproportionately comprised of the aristocracy and landed gentry, and its objective was to defend an institution that had underpinned the rural class structure in 20th-century England (Woods, 2005). This profile contrasts with pro-hunting groups in Europe, which have a stronger working-class and anti-authority base (Mischi, 2013). As such, the class politics of rural protests are more complex than might initially be imagined.

Alongside struggles over property and housing, rural labour struggles have also been stoked by economic globalisation. The internationalisation of labour supply in quintessentially rural occupations such as agricultural production, meat-processing and salad-packing, forestry and mining, has on the one hand provoked anti-migrant worker sentiment and support for right-wing populist parties in regions such as the east of England, and on the other hand prompted renewed rural trade unionism as migrant workers organise to fight exploitation, with varying degrees of success. The United Farm Workers union in the United States, for example, mobilised up to 50,000 Latino migrant workers in the 1970s, before losing most of its members and many of its hard-won concessions (Bardacke, 2011). In other contexts, labour has organised to contest the neoliberal logic of corporate restructuring decisions that have closed down mills and factories deemed to be uncompetitive in globalised markets, as Prudham (2008) documents for a Canadian sawmill.

In his analysis, Prudham draws on Karl Polanyi's notion of the 'double movement' (Polanyi, 1944) to emphasise the interconnected dynamics of struggles around global capitalism and over local economic and environmental conditions and social relations. Polanyi proposed that the ebb and flow of laissez-faire or self-regulating market capitalism can be understood as the product of struggles between social forces over 'fictitious' commodities such as money, land and labour, and argued that attempts to 'free up' the circulation of such elements are met by countervailing pressures from civil society to regulate their allocation and restrict unfettered capitalism. Moreover, Polanyi diverges from orthodox Marxism in positioning the commodification of nature (in the form of land) alongside the commodification of labour as a source of political struggle. Thus, in the context of resource deindustrialisation, Prudham (2008) identifies the 'double movement' in play in neoliberal reforms that facilitate the withdrawal of global capital from the forestry town of Youbou in Canada on the one hand, and in the mobilisation of a worker-based local movement – the Youbou Timberless Society (YTS) – on the other, and particularly in the transition of the YTS's focus from protecting jobs to articulating a critique of globalist forestry and championing regulatory practices aimed at enhancing local social, economic and environmental sustainability.

Interestingly, Polanyi is also deployed by Birchfield (2005) to analyse the counter-globalisation activism of José Bové and the French Confédération Paysanne, contending that 'in both theory and practice the Bové phenomenon (and its resonance beyond France) embodies the core values of Polanyi's [work]' (Birchfield, 2005, p. 592). Birchfield argues that there are parallels between the analysis of 19th-century capitalism presented by Polanyi in *The Great Transformation* (Polanyi, 1944), and Bové's critique of contemporary agri-food globalisation in *Le Monde n'est pas une Marchandise* [*The World Is Not for Sale*] (Bové & Dufour, 2001), and especially his criticism of the excessive commodification of all forms of human activity. Furthermore, Birchfield sees Bové and the Confédération Paysanne's mixing of protest politics and sustainable agricultural practice, and their alliance building with peasant movements and counter-globalisation activists globally, as embodying the civil society response to unfettered capitalism envisaged by Polanyi.

The Polanyian analyses of Birchfield and Prudham locate rural protests in the broader context of struggles over global capitalism, but both also note limitations to the framework, particularly for understanding the translocal and multi-scalar dynamics of the protests. To understand these we need to turn to social movement theory.

Rural protests as social movements

The diverse array of contemporary rural protests, and their sometimes elite and reactionary character, has fed a reluctance by some commentators to classify them as social movements. Reed (2008), for example, has argued that the pro-hunting and farmers' demonstrations in Britain at the turn of the century were not popular movements, but rather were 'led by elite actors attempting to defend old privileges in new ways' (Reed, 2008, p. 209) (see also Mamonova & Visser, 2014 on 'phantom movements' in rural Russia). Others, such as Woods (2003a, 2008), have contended that this view reflects too narrow a definition of social movements, and asserted that rural protests are consistent with Diani's definition of a new social movement as 'a network of informal interactions between a plurality of individuals, groups and/or organisations, engaged in political or cultural conflict on the basis of a shared collective identity' (Diani, 1992, p. 13). Although the plethora of rural protests in the global north do not have the organisation interconnectivity or the ideological coherence of the transnational agrarian movement in the global south (Borras, Edelman & Kay, 2008), they do arguably share a mobilising collective identity as rural, and therefore constitute *rural social movements*, if not a singular *rural movement*.

Certainly, concepts from social movement theory have been widely drawn on by researchers to analyse the dynamics and organisation of rural protests. These include the notion of *frame alignment*, which plays a fundamental role in the mobilisation of social movements by converting individual discontent into collective action (Snow, Rochford, Worden & Benford, 1986). The translation of the financial difficulties faced by individual farmers, or the concerns of a specific community such as hunters, into 'rural issues' that can serve as the basis for mass mobilisation is a classic example of frame alignment (Woods, 2003a). Not only does it give disparate individuals a collective identity, it also defines the object of activism, mostly commonly through the frame of an imagined rural–urban conflict (as discussed above). At the same time, this framing closes down other possibilities for collective action, such as around class solidarity, and other targets, such as neoliberal globalisation.

Whilst rural identity cements internal coherence, rural movements have also sought to build broader alliances through acts of *frame transformation* that associate their causes with wider popular tropes. For example, the pro-hunting Countryside Alliance in Britain drew on frames of liberty and civil rights to try to position their demonstrations in a historical lineage of political struggles and to draw comparisons with oppressed Indigenous groups worldwide (Woods, 2005), assisted by a sympathetic press that played a key role in frame reproduction (Woods, 2009). Similarly, many rural protest groups, including the Countryside Alliance, have appropriated patriotic and nationalistic rhetoric and iconography (Wallwork & Dixon, 2004), implicitly recognising globalisation as a driver of change, but simultaneously rejecting alignment with transnational counter-globalisation movements (arguably, only the Confédération Paysanne in France has successfully combined these two elements).

Frame alignment is important to rural movement recruitment, but other concepts from social movement theory can also help to understand the mobilisation of individuals. Resource mobilisation theory (McCarthy & Zald, 1977) has traction in explaining the activism of farmers and property owners to defend capital interests, but less so mobilisations around less tangible notions of rural identity. Recent scholarship on emotions and social movements can be helpful

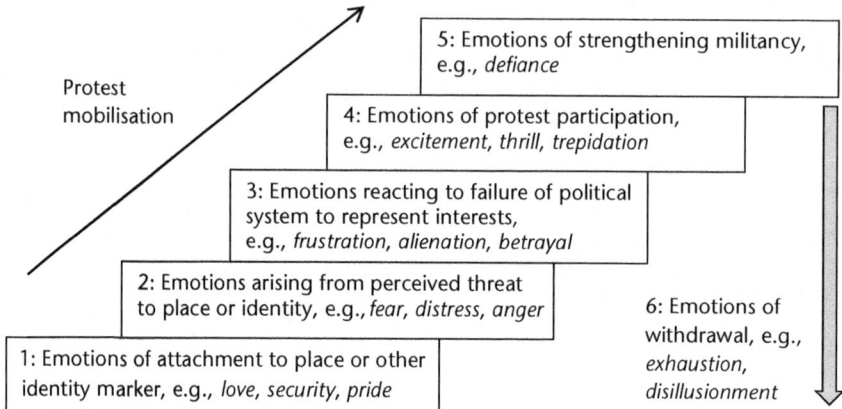

Figure 52.1 The ladder of emotions in protest mobilisation

here, with Woods, Anderson, Guilbert and Watkin (2012), for example, tracing rural activism in Britain along a 'ladder of emotions' from emotional attachment to rural places and tradition to feelings of fear, betrayal and desperation, 'forced' mobilisation, pride and enjoyment, and finally emotional exhaustion and withdrawal from protest participation (Figure 52.1).

This reading reinforces impressions of rural protests as impulsive and insurgent, conforming to the representation of social movements as 'rhizomic' in nature – that is, lacking leaders, central organisation or clear boundaries. Indeed, Woods and colleagues (2013) identify the rise of rural protests with discontent with established, more formal or 'arborescent' rural interest groups, but also critique the rhizomic/arborescent dichotomy by arguing that established rural organisations tacitly encourage radical outriders, whilst rhizomic social movements tend towards arborescent forms as they more seriously engage with the state.

All these dimensions are factors in the uneven geography of rural movements – with protests erupting in different countries at different times, around different issues, with different repertoires of action, and with different magnitudes of mobilisation – and thus their failure to cohere into a truly global movement. As Figure 52.2, taken from Woods (2015), indicates, globalisation forms a common background, but the trajectory of rural movements is shaped by national political contexts and cultures, political societalisation, and the influence of institutional structures and geography on capacities to act. Accordingly, rural movements continue to be largely circumscribed by national contexts, and only rarely break through to more global prominence, as in the case of Bové or struggles around forestry in British Columbia. As Magnusson and Shaw (2003) argue with respect to the latter, such cases do not so much jump scales, but collapse scale, so that the local and global become blurred. In other words, they act as what Routledge (2003) calls convergence spaces, or temporary alignments of diverse actors around specific issues which have been framed as common causes.

Conclusion: confronting globalisation and the efficacy of rural movements

Rural protests have become a feature of the 21st-century countryside, yet they remain an evasive and ephemeral phenomenon. For all the disruption and media attention that they have occasionally (though not universally) generated, their efficacy in achieving objectives is highly questionable. The pro-hunting demonstrations in Britain failed to stop anti-hunting legislation,

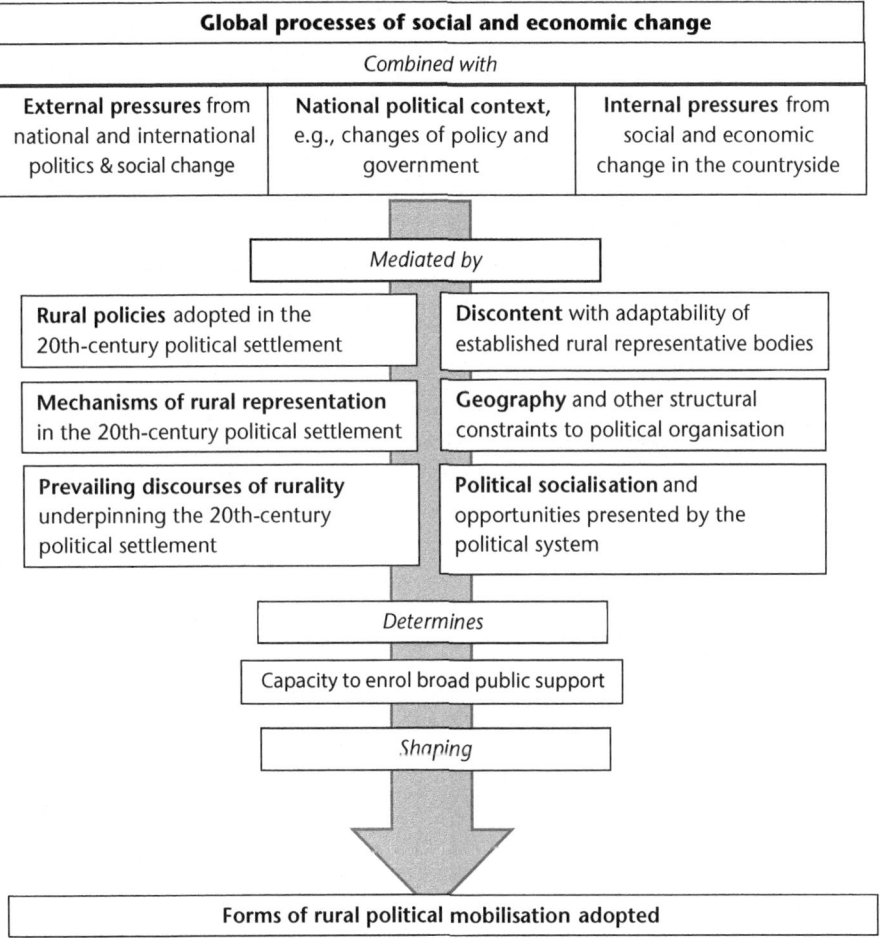

Global processes of social and economic change		
Combined with		
External pressures from national and international politics & social change	**National political context,** e.g., changes of policy and government	**Internal pressures** from social and economic change in the countryside

Mediated by

Rural policies adopted in the 20th-century political settlement	**Discontent** with adaptability of established rural representative bodies
Mechanisms of rural representation in the 20th-century political settlement	**Geography** and other structural constraints to political organisation
Prevailing discourses of rurality underpinning the 20th-century political settlement	**Political socialisation** and opportunities presented by the political system

Determines

Capacity to enrol broad public support

Shaping

Forms of rural political mobilisation adopted

Figure 52.2 Model of factors in contemporary rural mobilisation

just as hunting protests in Europe have failed to block EU directives. Farmers' protests have had little impact on prices, trade, subsidy reforms or the practices of transnational corporations. Anti-development campaigns have had more sporadic success in defeating proposals for roads or wind farms or reservoirs, but often only to displace development (and conflict) elsewhere. These outcomes may be explained by the limited resources and capacities of grassroots rural activists, including the difficulty of organising across dispersed rural areas, but also by the mis-targeting of mobilisations, the misleading message of key frames and the failure to organise transnationally against neoliberal globalisation.

However, this is not to say that rural protests have left no legacy. They have emboldened and politicised participants, and spawned more constructive initiatives for rural activism. Indeed, the most successful rural movements have been those that have eschewed protest and confrontation for the more practical construction of alternatives to neoliberal globalisation: the land rights movement in Scotland; the rural community movement in Scandinavia; community forestry in North America; back-to-the-land pioneers and organic farmers, among others (Halhead, 2006; Mackenzie, 2006; Halfacree, 2007; Prudham, 2008; Reed, 2008). Through such initiatives, rural actors are shaping the future of rural identities, not by confronting globalisation, but by co-constructing the emergent global countryside.

References

Bardacke, F (2011). *Trampling out the vintage: Cesar Chavez and the two souls of the United Farm Workers.* London and New York: Verso.

Birchfield, V (2005). José Bové and the globalisation countermovement in France and beyond: A Polanyian interpretation. *Review of International Studies* 31, 581–598.

Borras, SM, Edelman, M & Kay, C (Eds). (2008). *Transnational agrarian movements: Confronting globalisation.* Chichester: Wiley-Blackwell.

Bové, J & Dufour, F (2001). *The world is not for sale.* London and New York: Verso.

Burridge, J (2008). 'Hunting is not just for blood-thirsty toffs': The Countryside Alliance and the visual rhetoric of a poster campaign. *Text and Talk* 28, 31–53.

Cloke, P & Thrift, N (1987). Intra-class conflict in rural areas. *Journal of Rural Studies* 3, 321–333.

Diani, M (1992). The concept of social movement. *The Sociological Review* 40, 1–25.

Gedicks, A (2001). *Resource rebels: Native challenges to mining and oil corporations.* Cambridge, MA: South End Press.

Gilmartin, M (2009). Border thinking: Rossport, Shell and the political geographies of a gas pipeline. *Political Geography* 28, 274–282.

Halfacree, K (2007). Trial by space for a 'radical rural': Introducing alternative localities, representation and lives. *Journal of Rural Studies* 23, 125–141.

Halhead, V (2006). Rural movements in Europe: Scandinavia and the accession states. *Social Policy and Administration* 40, 596–611.

Halpin, D (2004). Transitions between formations and organisations: An historical perspective on the political representation of Australian farmers. *Australian Journal of Politics and History* 50, 469–490.

Heley, J (2015). Reviewing and renewing class: The prospects for a twenty-first century rural class analysis. In E Kasabov (Ed.), *Rural co-operation and development in Europe* (pp. 102–119). Basingstoke: Palgrave Macmillan.

Hubbard, P (2005). 'Inappropriate and incongruous': Opposition to asylum centres in the English countryside. *Journal of Rural Studies* 21, 3–17.

Larsen, S (2008). Place-making, grassroots organizing, and rural protest: A case study of Anahim Lake, British Columbia. *Journal of Rural Studies* 24, 172–181.

Lee, S-O, Kim, S-J & Wainwright, J (2010). Mad cow militancy: Neoliberal hegemony and social resistance in South Korea. *Political Geography* 29, 359–369.

Mackenzie, AFD (2006). A working land: Crofting communities, place and the politics of the possible in post-Land Reform Scotland. *Transactions of the Institute of British Geographers* 31, 383–398.

Magnusson, W & Shaw, K (Eds). (2003). *A political space: Reading the global through Clayoquot Sound.* Minneapolis: University of Minnesota Press.

Mamonova, N & Visser, O (2014). State marionettes, phantom organisations or genuine movements? The paradoxical emergence of rural social movements in post-socialist Russia. *Journal of Peasant Studies* 41, 491–516.

Massey, D (2005). *For space.* London: Sage.

McCarthy, JD & Zald, MN (1977). Resource mobilization and social movements: A partial theory. *American Journal of Sociology* 82, 1212–1241.

Mischi, J (2013). Contested rural activities: Class, politics and shooting in the French countryside. *Ethnography* 14, 64–84.

Mormont, M (1987). The emergence of rural struggles and their ideological effects. *International Journal of Urban and Regional Research* 7, 559–578.

Murdoch, J & Marsden, T (1994). *Reconstituting rurality.* London: UCL Press.

Naylor, E (1994). Unionism, peasant protest and the reform of French agriculture. *Journal of Rural Studies* 10, 263–273.

Parker, G (2002). *Citizenships, contingency and the countryside.* London: Routledge.

Phadke, R (2011). Resisting and reconciling big wind: Middle landscape politics in the new American West. *Antipode* 43, 754–776.

Polanyi, K (1944). *The great transformation: The political and economic origins of our time*. Boston, MA: Beacon Press.

Prudham, S (2008). Tall among the trees: Organizing against globalist forestry in rural British Columbia. *Journal of Rural Studies* 24, 182–196.

Reed, M (2008). The rural arena: The diversity of protest in rural England. *Journal of Rural Studies* 24, 209–218.

Routledge, P (2003). Convergence space: Process geographies of grassroots globalisation networks. *Transactions of the Institute of British Geographers* 28, 333–349.

Smith, MJ (1993). *Pressure, power and policy: State autonomy and policy networks in Britain and the United States*. New York: Harvester Wheatsheaf.

Smithers, J, Joseph, AE & Armstrong, A (2005). Across the divide (?): Reconciling farm and town views of agriculture – Community linkages. *Journal of Rural Studies* 21, 281–295.

Snow, DA, Rochford, BE, Worden, S & Benford, R (1986). Frame alignment processes, micromobilization and movement participation. *American Sociological Review* 51, 464–481.

Stock, CM (1996). *Rural radicals: Righteous rage in the American grain*. Ithaca, NY: Cornell University Press.

Strijker, D, Voerman, G & Terluin, I (Eds). (2015). *Rural protest groups and populist political parties*. Wageningen: Wageningen Academic Publishers.

Velicu, I (2012). To sell or not to sell: Landscapes of resistance to neoliberal globalisation in Transylvania. *Globalisations* 9, 307–321.

Wallwork, J & Dixon, J (2004). Foxes, green fields and Britishness: On the rhetorical construction of place and national identity. *British Journal of Social Psychology* 42, 21–39.

Wightman, A (2010). *The poor had no lawyers: Who owns Scotland (and how they got it)*. Edinburgh: Birlinn.

Winter, M (1996). *Rural politics*. London: Routledge.

Woods, M (1998). Advocating rurality? The repositioning of rural local government. *Journal of Rural Studies* 14, 13–26.

Woods, M (2003a). Deconstructing rural protest: The emergence of a new social movement. *Journal of Rural Studies* 19, 309–325.

Woods, M (2003b). Conflicting environmental visions of the rural: Windfarm development in Mid Wales. *Sociologia Ruralis* 43, 271–288.

Woods, M (2005). *Contesting rurality: Politics in the British countryside*. Aldershot: Ashgate.

Woods, M (2007). Engaging the global countryside: Globalisation, hybridity and the reconstitution of rural place. *Progress in Human Geography* 31, 485–507.

Woods, M (2008). Social movements and rural politics. *Journal of Rural Studies* 24, 129–137.

Woods, M (2011). The local politics of the global countryside: Boosterism, aspirational ruralism and the contested reconstitution of Queenstown, New Zealand. *Geojournal* 76, 365–381.

Woods, M (2015). Explaining rural protest: A comparative analysis. In D Strijker, G Voerman & IJ Terluin (Eds), *Rural protest groups and populist political parties* (pp. 35–62). Wageningen: Wageningen Academic Publishers.

Woods, M, Anderson, J, Guilbert, S & Watkin, S (2012). 'The country(side) is angry': Emotion and explanation in protest mobilization. *Social and Cultural Geography* 13, 567–587.

Woods, M, Anderson, J, Guilbert, S & Watkin, S (2013). Rhizomic radicalism and arborescent advocacy: A Deluzo-Guattarian reading of rural protest. *Environment and Planning D: Society and Space* 31, 434–450.

Zografos, C & Martinez-Alier, J (2009). The politics of landscape value: A case study of wind farm conflict in Catalonia. *Environment and Planning A* 41, 1726–1744.

53

Responding to Rural Change

Adaptation, Resilience and Community Action

Nathan Young

Introduction

Rural scholars have long paid close attention to the dynamics between stability and change, tradition and novelty, continuity and disruption. In recent years, however, discussions of rural change have taken on particular urgency. Rural regions and communities in highly developed nations are being seriously challenged by a range of forces, including economic globalisation, environmental change, new technological developments and a renewed post-financial crisis commitment to austere forms of neoliberalism. These are dynamic forces whose combined effects are multiple, variable and often unpredictable. Available evidence suggests that some communities and regions are having great difficulty responding to these changes, while others have been able to maintain and even improve local economies, community services and general quality of life (Shucksmith et al., 2012; Parkins & Reed, 2013). To address these discrepancies, rural scholars are increasingly using concepts first developed in ecology and ecosystem science – namely resilience, adaptation and adaptive capacity – to understand rural people's and communities' abilities to respond to both known and unforeseen changes and challenges. These concepts challenge the notion that rural residents and communities are powerless in the face of external forces, suggesting that local social, political and ecological processes and assets play a significant role in determining rural futures.

As we will see, there have been growing pains in this emerging field of enquiry. The applicability of ecological concepts to human affairs is one source of controversy. Another surrounds the role of government and ideology in promoting community-level adaptation. Policy makers, think-tanks and non-governmental organisations (NGOs) from across the political spectrum have taken a keen interest in resilience and adaptation scholarship and initiatives. While much of the academic work to date is progressive in intent (aiming to help communities assess or develop adaptive capacity), some critics argue that encouraging communities to adapt and change absolves senior governments of their broader responsibilities to protect rural livelihoods, services and environments (e.g., Bristow, 2010).

The chapter proceeds as follows. The first section discusses the unique challenges facing rural communities in an increasingly globalised, fast-paced and environmentally precarious world. These challenges are demanding unprecedented nimbleness and flexibility at the local level, requiring many communities to reimagine their futures and plan for unknown contingencies. The second section discusses the ecology-derived concept of resilience and its recent influence on rural studies. I will argue that while this concept is intriguing for the social sciences (including rural studies), its utility is mostly metaphorical. The third section addresses the more precise concept of adaptive capacity, which also has roots in ecology but is more directly useful for studying human affairs. For social scientists, adaptive capacity generally refers to the ability of a group or community to 'learn, experiment, and foster novel solutions in complex social–ecological circumstances' (Armitage & Plummer, 2010, p. iii). As such, I argue that adaptive capacity is both an important concept for understanding rural resilience, and a gateway for examining critical issues of local governance, power relations, norms, skills, knowledge and equity. In other words, it provides researchers with a means of investigating the potential and limitations of community-level power and action under challenging circumstances. The fourth and final section addresses criticisms of this emerging field, and points to new potential research directions.

Rural change in the developed world: a perfect storm

This is a moment of profound change for rural regions and communities across the developed world (Shucksmith & Brown, this volume). The causes of these changes are complex, but four converging forces are particularly relevant to this discussion. The first is economic globalisation, which is reshaping the global geography of primary production, secondary manufacturing and (increasingly) tertiary services. Simply put, economic globalisation grants tremendous power to the orchestrators of global supply chains or networks to acquire raw materials and process them in regions of greatest cost advantage (Carolan, 2012). This is having a significant impact on both agricultural regions (particularly in countries that have minimised agricultural subsidies and protections) and areas traditionally reliant on resource extraction. Small producers in particular are being squeezed by globally structured economics of scale, and by the increasing dominance of large conglomerates and retailers in agriculture and commodities markets (Dauvergne & Lister, 2011).

The second force is rapidly evolving technology, particularly Internet-enabled commerce, production and work. In some rural regions, these technologies are encouraging in-migration of professionals and creative types capable of conducting at least some of their work at a distance. The Internet also allows rural firms to connect with far-away clients, partners and networks (although the empirical data are mixed about how often this happens – see Young, 2010; Tunberg, 2014). Unfortunately, these technologies also facilitate labour shedding, as agricultural production and resource work are increasingly rationalised and computerised (Kaloxylos et al., 2012), as well as capital flight from local businesses, as online retailers and service providers expand their reach into rural territories.

The third force is global environmental change, particularly, but not limited to, the emerging effects of climate change. Rural regions are particularly vulnerable to environmental changes given their heavy cultural and economic reliance on landscapes and physical systems. Climate change heightens rural vulnerability to both slow-onset problems (such as drought) and rapid-onset ones (floods, fires, damaging weather). Single-industry and less diversified communities are thought to be especially vulnerable to both types of event (Adger, 2000). Intensive production methods such as monocropping and clear-cut logging also enhance local vulnerability to environmental pressures.

The fourth converging force spurring change in rural regions is a shift in governance methods and strategies. Over the last 20 years or so, rural development policy across the developed world has taken a distinctly neoliberal turn, characterised by an emphasis on regional competitiveness, local entrepreneurialism, and devolution of key responsibilities for economic planning and development (Herbert-Cheshire & Higgins, 2004; Skerratt, 2013). The financial crisis of 2007–2008 did not end neoliberal hegemony, as some hoped it might, but rather married it even more closely with the austerity agenda of market discipline and diminished social welfare services (Shucksmith & Brown, this volume). As a consequence, rural communities are expected to face down economic and environmental problems with less institutional support than even a few years ago.

These converging and rapidly evolving forces are combining to create significant uncertainty about rural futures, as well as a renewed academic focus on whether and how rural communities might react, respond to and even thrive in this new environment. The concepts of resilience, adaptation and adaptive capacity have emerged as a way to investigate and explain the highly variable responses of rural communities to such changes.

'Resilience thinking' comes to rural studies

As mentioned previously, rural scholars have long studied how rural residents and communities respond to exogenous and endogenous change. In recent years, however, this work has increasingly centred on the notion of resilience. Resilience theory began in the 1970s in ecology, as a movement to reconceptualise how natural systems work (Davoudi, 2012). Early advocates of 'resilience thinking', such as C. S. Holling, Lance Gunderson, Brian Walker and Carl Folke, argued against the accepted wisdom that ecosystems are generally static entities that tend towards equilibrium unless disturbed (Folke et al., 2010). Instead, they posited that ecosystems are constantly changing – going through cycles of increasing and decreasing complexity and interconnectivity – in which disturbances play a crucial and continuous role. According to this view, an event like a forest fire – which appears to be devastating – can in fact be a positive development in the life of a resilient forest ecosystem, prompting it to renew, adapt and change. Ecological resilience is therefore defined as 'the capacity of a system to absorb disturbance and reorganise while undergoing change so as to still retain essentially the same function, structure, identity, and feedbacks' (Walker, Holling, Carpenter & Kinzig, 2004, p. 4).

This definition has two important ramifications. First, resilience does not always involve a return to the status quo. Change or 'reorganisation' is a desirable outcome if it preserves the 'essence' of the system. Second, it suggests that if a disturbance is so great that it overwhelms a system's capacity for resilience, a *qualitative* transformation occurs in which the system flips into a different state (identity) altogether. A classic example is the Canadian Atlantic cod fishery – once one of the most abundant fisheries on the planet that was driven to the brink by overexploitation. The fishery was closed in 1992 in the hope that a temporary moratorium would allow stocks to rebound. Unfortunately, they never have – the disturbance to the cod was too great, and new species and ecosystem dynamics have taken their place (Finlayson & McCay, 1998).

From the beginning, proponents of resilience thinking have argued that similar dynamics of cyclical change, disturbance (or crisis), recovery, adaptation and transformation are observable in human systems and societies (e.g., Holling, 2004). Many social scientists have found this argument compelling, and have worked to incorporate resilience thinking into traditional social science domains (e.g., Homer-Dixon, 2006; Gotts, 2007). Ecological resilience does not translate perfectly to human affairs, however. Human beings have unique capabilities, and human communities do not always behave like biophysical ecosystems. As such, debates continue about the role of complex human processes like agency, learning and planning in determining resilience outcomes (e.g., Davidson, 2010; Berkes & Ross, 2013). To date, resilience thinking has made the greatest inroads in subfields such as environmental sociology, the sociology of natural disasters, and studies of war and conflict zones. With respect to rural studies, resilience thinking has thus far had its strongest impact on the study of Indigenous, remote and/or resource-dependent communities. Prominent social scientists such as Fikret Berkes (working mostly in the Canadian North) (see Berkes, Colding & Folke, 2003; Berkes & Ross, 2013) and W. Neil Adger (in the coastal tropics) (2000, 2003; see also Adger & Barnett, 2009) have used the term 'social-ecological resilience' to investigate the close intertwining of human and natural systems in these places. The core argument in these works is that the health and viability of communities is directly linked to the surrounding ecology, and that vulnerability and resilience dynamics in one sphere have direct effects on the other.

The integration of resiliency thinking has been slower on the more mainstream side of rural studies – that largely concerned with issues such as agriculture, labour, migration, and local culture and social structures. Nevertheless, resiliency thinking is being increasingly applied in these areas. Christopherson, Michie and Tyler (2010, p. 3) argue that the concept resonates in economic-themed rural and regional research because, 'at base, [resilience] addresses a very old and enduring question: why do some regions manage to overcome short-term or long-term economic adversity to maintain a high quality of life for residents, while others fail?' Resiliency thinking's focus on local attributes and processes fits neatly with the influential literature on clusters, learning regions and local innovation systems that emerged in the 1990s (Hassink, 2010). It also dovetails with economic geography's analyses of regional economies as the product of long 'path dependencies' that lock economies into more and less flexible configurations (Martin, 2012). On social issues, resilience has worked its way into discussions of 'rural social sustainability', or the community attributes that enhance cooperation and quality of life (McManus et al., 2012; Wilson, 2012a).

Despite its increasing popularity, one of the major difficulties in applying the concept of resilience to human affairs is that it works much better as a metaphor than as a measurable property or process. In a recent overview essay, Davoudi (2012, p. 299) concludes that while 'resilience is replacing sustainability [as a term of choice among academics and policy makers] … it is not quite clear what resilience means, beyond the simple assumption that it is good to be resilient'. Resilience has given us an interesting way to think about change – as being non-linear, constant, and variable according to both internal and external factors. It has also provided cause to reflect on the range of community-level responses to these changes. For instance, several scholars explicitly or implicitly suggest that a resilience continuum exists. In some circumstances, 'coping' at the household and community level is enough to ride out short-term disturbances, for instance by providing help to individuals or families affected by the loss of a major employer. In other cases, 'adaptation' is needed, which implies a longer-term adjustment in community processes, such as the formation of new community organisations (for micro-finance or community branding, for example). At the extreme, 'transformation' may be required in order to ensure a community's long-term viability, such as when a resource-dependent community reinvents itself as a tourist destination. These examples are common-sense illustrations of resilience in action, but when it comes to measuring resilience levels, or comparing resiliency across communities, the breadth and imprecision of the resilience metaphor becomes a significant liability. For resilience to be a useful concept for rural studies, it must be more than an 'I know it when I see it' phenomenon. Thankfully, a better concept exists that, although lacking in metaphorical resonance, provides more analytical direction for social scientists looking to understand community responses to change.

Adaptive capacity

Like resilience, 'adaptive capacity' is originally an ecological term, defined by Gunderson (2000, p. 427) as 'the ability of an ecological system to remain in a stability domain … despite the alteration of key [environmental] variables'. For ecologists, adaptive capacity refers to the elasticity of system components to continue functioning despite changes in underlying conditions, such as the introduction of an invasive species or a shift in local climate. In the social sciences, however, 'capacity' has a different meaning – one that is closely tied to human characteristics such as agency, learning, creativity and collaboration. In the social sciences, capacity refers to the ability to act or exert influence – powers that can be enabled and constrained by a range of local and extra-local forces. Capacity is therefore a concept that social scientists can more readily work with, and that connects more closely with the traditional topics and concerns of rural studies.

Most studies of adaptive capacity in rural regions attempt to identify factors associated with greater and lesser abilities of individuals, households and communities to enact intentional changes that mitigate risks in the face of actual or potential disturbances (Armitage & Plummer, 2010; Gupta et al., 2010). It is unsurprising that these studies have gone in multiple directions, given the range of factors that could possibly impact the adaptive capacity of communities. In the following sections, I summarise in broad strokes where the literature has gone thus far.

Learning and knowledge

The literature is near unanimous that learning and knowledge are essential components of rural adaptive capacity. Knowledge comes in many forms, and includes formal and technical skills, general awareness of political, economic and environmental forces (such as globalisation and climate change), and local, traditional or experiential knowledge of landscapes, ecosystems and community dynamics (Brown & Westaway, 2011, p. 324). While each type of knowledge is valuable, Gupta et al. (2010, p. 463) stress the importance of 'learning capacity', which is the ability to synthesise information from multiple sources, to experiment and draw lessons from experimentation, to trust the knowledge that others bring to the table, and 'to question socially-embedded ideologies … and assumptions that dominate [status quo approaches to] problem-solving'. In a similar vein, some researchers stress that depth of learning is critical to successful adaptation. The distinction among single-loop, double-loop and triple-loop learning is made in several analyses (e.g., Diduck, 2010; Gupta et al., 2010). According to Armitage et al. (2011, p. 996), 'single-loop learning involves fixing errors from routines [such as] modifying harvest strategies; double-loop learning involves correcting errors by rethinking management goals or adjusting … policies; and triple-loop learning involves more fundamental changes in [local] governance norms and protocols'. Each level involves more ambitious, abstract and difficult applications of acquired knowledge.

A less developed branch of this literature looks at the role of imagination and creativity in community-level adaptive capacity. A range of studies have shown that rural residents frequently take a conservative approach to environmental and economic disturbances, preferring to 'ride it out' using individual and collective coping strategies rather than engaging in more radical adaptive or transformative action (e.g., Bullock, 2013; Raymond & Robinson, 2013). The ability to imagine different possible futures is therefore a key stepping stone on the way to deeper changes (Davis & Reed, 2013), although these imaginings can also be a site of conflict within a community, particularly when there is disagreement about the cause of economic and environmental difficulties, and what may be done at the community level to counter them (Young, 2013).

Community capitals

A second key theme of rural adaptive capacity research focuses on what Magis (2010, p. 406) calls 'community capitals', or 'community resources that are strategically invested in collective endeavours to address shared community objectives'. Depending on the study, these capitals include financial capital, human capital, political capital, civic capital, natural or environmental capital, built capital, social capital and social networks, and trust (see Table 53.1). The core finding of this research is that communities with high levels of place-based capital resources are better able to resist temporary changes (coping) and engage in the more difficult and long-term processes involved in adaptation and transformation (Wilson, 2012a). The flip side is that communities lacking these resources are disproportionately harmed by social-ecological disturbances or crises (Goulden, Adger, Allison & Conway, 2013).

Wilson (2010, 2012a) argues that a community's adaptive capacity is enhanced not only by the presence of capitals, but by their diversity and complementarity. For instance, a community that is reliant on a single industry or employer may have highly developed economic capital, but likely low social and environmental capital, and is thus highly vulnerable to economic and environmental shocks that affect the key industry or employer. Adaptive capacity is strongly enhanced by a balance of what Wilson terms 'multifunctional' capitals – capitals that have multiple origins and expression points, and are not exclusively derived from, or over-dedicated to, a small number of sources or projects.

Adaptive capacity is also enhanced when capitals are both well grounded in the community and extend outside of it to distant places and others. For instance, rural businesses that are exclusively tied to local markets fare worse in a crisis than those that have external clients (Brewton, Danes, Stafford & Haynes, 2010). Community leaders (elected and volunteer) with diverse connections beyond the community and region are also thought to be a major advantage (Skerratt, 2013). Social networks that are diverse and geographically mixed enhance adaptive capacity by broadening the pool of information, advice, reciprocity and influence available to a community.

Table 53.1 Dimensions of 'community capitals'

Property	Description
Financial capital	Assets, wealth, income and financial resources, including ability to fundraise and/or borrow on favourable terms
Human capital	Skills, knowledge, expertise, experience, credentials and accreditations
Political capital	Connections to key political decision makers or administrators; legitimacy in the eyes of the governed
Civic capital	Levels of citizen commitment to and engagement with local institutions and organizations
Natural or environmental capital	Soil, water, forest, animal, landscape and nature-aesthetic resources; biodiversity and ecosystem resilience
Built capital	Infrastructure, including services, technologies, amenities; housing stocks; commercial and industrial properties
Social capital	Networks of reciprocity, help, obligation, information-gathering or influence, within and beyond the community or region
Trust	Interpersonal trust as a basis of collective action; institutional trust as the basis of multi-scalar coordination

Sources: Adger (2003), Magis (2010), Wolfe (2010) and Wilson (2010, 2012a, 2012b).

The literature also suggests that a mix of bonding, bridging and linking ties is a substantial advantage (Pelling & High, 2005). Bonding ties are based on close affinity, and are a strong basis of collective action at the local level. Bridging ties are typically across social groups, allowing people to access information and skills that may not exist within a tightly bonded network. Linking ties are those that reach up and down a hierarchy, for instance to senior politicians, bureaucrats or employers. All are advantageous at different times and in different ways, depending on the nature and duration of the challenge.

Institutions

A third theme in rural research on adaptive capacity involves the study of institutions. 'Institution' has a double meaning, and studies of adaptive capacity touch on both. On the one hand, institutions refer to the formal entities that are purposely created and structured to accomplish tasks (in strict sociological terms, these would be called organisations, but the distinction is seldom made in the literature). On the other hand, institution refers to 'the habituated and customary dimensions of social life' (Matthews & Sydneysmith, 2010, p. 224) that include formal and informal rules, norms, habits, customs and expectations.

Institutions are of great interest because they have a strong influence on local behaviour, and because they serve as a bridge between different scales of social organisation (Agrawal, 2010). Opinion on the role of institutions in fostering or inhibiting adaptive capacity is mixed, however. Some scholars argue that local institutions are inherently conservative, and therefore constrain the efforts of individuals to change their behaviours, as well as those of senior governments or outside organisations to instil a more flexible ethos at the community level (e.g., Gupta et al., 2010). According to this view, local institutions tend to reflect the 'stability domain' that exists prior to disturbances. The lock-in of these arrangements lessens a community's adaptive capacity because they tend to favour existing industries and power structures, 'and therefore unnecessarily slow down [economic] restructuring as well as indirectly hampering the development of indigenous potential and creativity' (Hassink, 2010, p. 48).

Others, however, see local institutions as an asset. For instance, authors working in the common pool resources (CPR) and social ecology traditions see local institutions as central to environmental governance (e.g., Berkes, Colding & Folke, 2003; Dietz, Ostrom & Stern, 2003). Far from being rigid, these schools of thought see local institutions as flexible and dynamic, able to adjust harvest levels and internal distribution rights and obligations on a season-by-season basis. This prompts Armitage et al. (2011) to argue that responsibility lies primarily with the state to create new programmes that build on local institutional strengths rather than overruling them (Adger, 2003 makes a similar point). According to this view, governments and outside organisations seeking to enhance adaptive capacity must first clear an important legitimacy hurdle. Programmes that seek to engage local institutions rather than 'reshaping' them (or going around them) are more likely to kick-start or enhance the learning and experimentation that is critical to adaptation (Raymond & Robinson, 2013). When structured appropriately, inclusive efforts such as the co-management of resources or collaborative research initiatives can facilitate the multi-scalar connections and coordination that build local capacity for intentional change.

Community characteristics and dynamics

While the literature is by no means unanimous, it is clear that community characteristics and dynamics play a central role in adaptive capacity (Smit & Wandel, 2006, p. 287). For example, local economic diversity can help mitigate certain types of disturbance, such as a commodity market downturn or the loss of a major employer. There is also evidence that demographically diverse communities are similarly advantaged (Pendakur & Young, 2013), as are communities in which women play prominent economic and leadership roles (Agarwal, 2009). Communities that are physically closer to major centres also have more adaptation options than those that are geographically marginalised (Ryser & Halseth, 2010).

Community dynamics are strongly influenced by local politics and alliances. Communities dominated by 'growth coalitions' comprised of traditional economic and political elites appear to be less likely to innovate and experiment with new economic and environmental priorities and arrangements (Swindal & McAreavey, 2012). These coalitions are powerful and deeply entrenched in many communities, making it difficult for new voices and entrants to access levers of power or participate in key community-level exercises such as economic planning. This points to an important distinction between 'adaptive capacity' and 'adaptive action' (Adger & Barnett, 2009). In short, a community can have high levels of community capital and institutional resources, but this potential may go unfulfilled if access to key processes is blocked by elites with a stake in traditional political and economic arrangements.

Finally, research shows that intangibles such as sense of place, belonging and trust matter for adaptive capacity (Kulig, Edge & Joyce, 2008). In a study of farming communities in the Australian outback, McManus et al. (2012, p. 20) found that a sense of belonging and commitment to place is pivotal for engendering 'robust levels of ongoing engagement between farmers and town communities [that] are important in maintaining rural populations and services'. Engagement and commitment are critical variables because successful collective adaptation takes a tremendous amount of time and energy on behalf of rural residents. Similarly, research shows that high levels of trust facilitate collective adaptation by encouraging risk taking, while low levels of intra-community trust prompt individuals and households to act more conservatively and avoid experimentation (Groenewald & Bulte, 2013).

Critiques and limitations of the literature

The literature on rural resilience, adaptation and adaptive capacity has grown exponentially in recent years, yielding important insights into community responses to change. However, this field has also been strongly (yet sympathetically) criticised on multiple fronts. This section reviews those criticisms, and uses them as bases for discussion of where rural resiliency research goes from here.

The first major critique of the resiliency and adaptation literature is that it has a strong systems bias that reflects the ecological origins of these concepts. As mentioned earlier, ecosystems do not exhibit agency, creativity, customs and relationships in the same manner as human communities. Bristow and Healy (2014) argue that many studies of rural and regional resilience neglect this fact, and place too much emphasis on demographic and economic performance indicators as measures of resilience, such as trends in population growth or decline, output, employment and income. Hudson (2010) similarly argues that community resilience is not always reducible to economic indicators, and that in many cases greater economic self-sufficiency – rather than further integration into global markets – is a more common-sense direction for community adaptation, particularly if it lightens the local environmental footprint and thus enhances long-term sustainability (see also Young, 2013). Instead, these critics suggest that resiliency and adaptation ought to be conceptualised as context dependent, and rooted more in community-level processes and decision making than in the machinations of abstract (economic) systems (see also Berkes & Ross, 2013).

The second critique is that many studies of resiliency give little consideration to questions of power, governance and inequality. Few studies explicitly address inequalities and divisions at the local level, for instance. As mentioned earlier, blanket assumptions that communities are egalitarian or that local governments, networks and organisations are broadly inclusive or representative are highly problematic. The distinct voices of minorities, women, Indigenous people and youth are too often subsumed under the moniker of 'community resilience'. Similarly, discussions of capitals – particularly physical, built and environmental capital – are often surprisingly silent (or ignorant) on issues of property rights and exclusion. A good deal of rural property around the world is privately held, which at the very least complicates their utility for community-level action and responses to change.

At the macro level, several authors have argued that resilience thinking is highly compatible with dominant pro-capitalist narratives of competitiveness and neoliberal market disciplining. For instance, Bristow (2010, p. 159) argues that senior governments and think-tanks have been quick to embrace resilience-themed language and policy as a means of pushing communities to adopt a more business-friendly stance, reinforced by external consultants armed with metrics to 'impel regions to benchmark and adopt best-practice lessons from elsewhere, while periodically measuring their competitive success relative to other regions or rivals'. According to this view, resilience is another way of imposing market discipline on communities, while responsibilising them for the (inevitable) failures that afflict many places (MacKinnon & Derickson, 2012). Hudson (2010) also points out that market-driven adaptation often leads to increased specialisation, as local businesses try to find and develop niches in an increasingly globalised economy. Perversely, this can lead to increased vulnerability, as a single community has little influence over global prices and demand for highly specialised commodities, goods or services. Finally, Pike, Dawley and Tomaney (2010) argue that resilience language (like sustainability before it) is inherently imprecise, and is often implicitly used to support business interests. To illustrate, these authors point to the restructuring of the British coal mining sector in the 1980s, which nominally made individual companies more resilient (i.e., competitive) but had devastating impacts on labourers and communities. They argue that the key question in any discussion of resilience ought to be 'what kind of resilience and for whom?', suggesting that in many cases the term has been surreptitiously hijacked to support powerful interests.

The third major criticism of the existing literature is that it is silent on key normative and moral issues. The resilience and adaptation literature generally assumes that local-level change is a desirable response to outside disturbances. The distinction between positive and negative change is rarely considered, nor is the possibility of maladaptation (adaptation that creates further harm). As Bohensky, Stone-Jovicich, Larson and Marshall (2010, p. 27) argue, it is entirely possible that 'enhancing adaptive capacity at one scale may undermine adaptive capacity at other scales: a sector may benefit at the expense of a region, or individual at the expense of a community … similarly, short-term adaptive capacity may differ from long-term adaptive capacity'. Change of all types creates winners and losers, and the resilience and adaptive capacity literatures need to integrate this fact into all analyses of community responses to change.

Finally, and related to the above, most resilience research is silent on the issue of resistance. The a priori assumption that adaptation is desirable, and that adaptive capacity is an asset to be cultivated and maximised, closes off consideration of any meaningful role for local resistance to outside forces. This is a significant blind spot. For instance, in many settler societies, rural Indigenous people contest and oftentimes resist the appropriation of land and natural resources for private gain. This resistance is often pursued in the name of equity and justice, collective rights, local control over development, and environmental sustainability – all of which are at least nominally consistent with resilience thinking. Some researchers have moved in this direction, arguing that the resilience metaphor does not capture the range of possible progressive community-level responses to change. MacKinnon and Derickson (2012), for instance, suggest that the community resilience metaphor be replaced by 'community resourcefulness', as this does not prejudge the character, intent or outcome of community-level action. Resourcefulness can include resistance and protest alongside the deployment of capitals, assets and learning. The fact is that resistance and acceptance of change can exist simultaneously within a community, and the tension between them is dynamic and oftentimes creative (Young, 2013). At the very least, the possibility of resistance needs to be brought into the academic conversation about resilience and adaptation. The study of community responses to change is incomplete without it.

Conclusion

Rural communities across the developed world are facing significant challenges from evolving economic, environmental, technological and political conditions. Recently, rural scholars have drawn on the ecological concepts of resilience, adaptation and adaptive capacity to understand local-level responses to these challenges. In this chapter, I have argued that while resilience is a useful metaphor that encourages us to rethink how change happens and how communities respond to it, as a social science concept it is lacking. Far more useful is the notion of adaptive capacity, which places emphasis on the facilitators and barriers to individual and community agency, creativity and innovation. This in turn prompts us to look at adaptation as a dynamic multidimensional process that is strongly influenced by local and extra-local factors. Both senior governments and local residents play a role in enhancing community abilities to respond to change – even if those responses involve resistance or a turn away from further integration into global markets and towards self-sufficiency and valorisation of place.

In short, the growing literature on rural resilience, adaptation and adaptive capacity shows that these are deeply contextual phenomena – meaning that a 'resilient community' looks different in different places under different circumstances. This should not be seen as a weakness of current research in the field, but rather as an invitation to further develop resiliency-related concepts and perform more in-depth case research that will help refine our understanding of community-level responses to accelerating rural change.

References

Adger, WN (2000). Social and ecological resilience: Are they related? *Progress in Human Geography* 24, 347–364.

Adger, WN (2003). Social capital, collective action, and adaptation to climate change. *Economic Geography* 79(4), 387–404.

Adger, WN & Barnett, J (2009). Four reasons for concern about adaptation to climate change. *Environment and Planning A* 41, 2800–2805.

Agrawal, A (2010). Local institutions and adaptation to climate change. In R Mearns & A Norton (Eds), *Social dimensions of climate change: Equity and vulnerability in a warming world* (pp. 173–198). Washington, DC: World Bank.

Agarwal, B (2009). Gender and forest conservation: The impact of women's participation in community forest governance. *Ecological Economics* 68(11), 2785–2799.

Armitage, D, Berkes, F, Dale, A, Kocho-Schellenberg, E & Patton, E (2011). Co-management and the co-production of knowledge: Learning to adapt in Canada's Arctic. *Global Environmental Change* 21, 995–1004.

Armitage, D & Plummer, R (2010). *Adaptive capacity and environmental governance*. Berlin: Springer-Verlag.

Berkes, F, Colding, J & Folke, C (2003). *Navigating social-ecological systems*. New York: Cambridge University Press.

Berkes, F & Ross, H (2013). Community resilience: Toward an integrated approach. *Society and Natural Resources* 26(1), 5–20.

Bohensky, E, Stone-Jovicich, S, Larson, S & Marshall, N (2010). Adaptive capacity in theory and reality: Implications for governance in the Great Barrier Reef region. In D Armitage & R Plummer (Eds), *Adaptive capacity and environmental governance* (pp. 23–42). Berlin: Springer.

Brewton, KE, Danes, SM, Stafford, K & Haynes, GW (2010). Determinants of rural and urban family firm resilience. *Journal of Family Business Strategy* 1, 155–166.

Bristow, G (2010). Resilient regions: Re-'place'ing regional competitiveness. *Cambridge Journal of Regions, Economy and Society* 3, 153–167.

Bristow, G & Healy, A (2014). Regional resilience: An agency perspective. *Regional Studies* 48(5), 923–935.

Brown, K & Westaway, E (2011). Agency, capacity, and resilience to environmental change: Lessons from human development, well-being, and disasters. *Annual Review of Environment and Resources* 36, 321–342.

Bullock, R (2013). Mill town identity crisis: Reframing the culture of forest dependence in single-industry towns. In J Parkins & M Reed (Eds), *Social transformation in rural Canada* (pp. 269–290). Vancouver: UBC Press.

Carolan, MS (2012). *The sociology of food and agriculture*. New York: Routledge.

Christopherson, S, Michie, J & Tyler, P (2010). Regional resilience: Theoretical and empirical perspectives. *Cambridge Journal of Regions, Economy and Society* 3, 3–10.

Dauvergne, P & Lister, J (2011). *Timber*. Malden, MA: Polity.

Davidson, D (2010). The applicability of the concept of resilience to social systems: Some sources of optimism and nagging doubts. *Society and Natural Resources* 23(12), 1135–1149.

Davis, EJ & Reed, MG (2013). Governing transformation and resilience: The role of identity in negotiating roles for forest-based communities of British Columbia's interior. In JR Parkins & MG Reed (Eds), *Social transformation in rural Canada* (pp. 249–268). Vancouver: UBC Press.

Davoudi, S (2012). Resilience: A bridging concept or a dead end? *Planning Theory & Practice* 12(2), 299–307.

Diduck, A (2010). The learning dimension of adaptive capacity: Untangling the multi-level connections. In D Armitage & R Plummer (Eds), *Adaptive capacity and environmental governance* (pp. 199–218). Berlin: Springer-Verlag.

Dietz, T, Ostrom, E & Stern, PC (2003). The struggle to govern the commons. *Science* 302(12), 1907–1912.

Finlayson, AC & McCay, BJ (1998). Crossing the threshold of ecosystem resilience: The commercial extinction of northern cod. In F Berkes & C Folke (Eds), *Linking social and ecological systems* (pp. 311–337). New York: Cambridge University Press.

Folke, C, Carpenter, SR, Walker, B, Scheffer, M, Chapin, T & Rockstrom, J (2010). Resilience thinking: Integrating resilience, adaptability and transformability. *Ecology and Society* 15(4), 20–29.

Gotts, NM (2007). Resilience, panarchy, and world-systems analysis. *Ecology and Society* 12(1), 24–37.

Goulden, MC, Adger, WN, Allison, EH & Conway, D (2013). Limits to resilience from livelihood diversification and social capital in lake social-ecological systems. *Annals of the Association of American Geographers* 103(4), 906–924.

Groenewald, SF & Bulte, E (2013). Trust and livelihood adaptation: Evidence from rural Mexico. *Agriculture and Human Values* 30, 41–55.

Gunderson, LH (2000). Ecological resilience – In theory and application. *Annual Review of Ecological Systems* 31, 425–439.

Gupta, J et al. (2010). The adaptive capacity wheel: A method to assess the inherent characteristics of institutions to enable the adaptive capacity of society. *Environmental Science & Policy* 13, 459–471.

Hassink, R (2010). Regional resilience: A promising concept to explain differences in regional economic adaptability? *Cambridge Journal of Regions, Economy and Society* 3, 45–58.

Herbert-Cheshire, L & Higgins, V (2004). From risky to responsible: Expert knowledge and the governing of community-led development. *Journal of Rural Studies* 20, 289–302.

Holling, CS (2004). From complex regions to complex worlds. *Ecology and Society* 9(1), 11–21.

Homer-Dixon, T (2006). *The upside of down*. Toronto: Alfred A. Knopf.

Hudson, R (2010). Resilient regions in an uncertain world: Wishful thinking or practical reality? *Cambridge Journal of Regions, Economy and Society* 3, 11–25.

Kaloxylos, A et al. (2012). Farm management systems and the future internet era. *Computers and Electronics in Agriculture* 89, 130–144.

Kulig, JC, Edge, DS & Joyce, B (2008). Understanding community resiliency in rural communities through multimethod research. *Journal of Rural and Community Development* 3(3), 76–94.

MacKinnon, D & Derickson, KD (2012). From resilience to resourcefulness: A critique of resilience policy and activism. *Progress in Human Geography* 37(2), 253–270.

Magis, K (2010). Community resilience: An indicator of social sustainability. *Society and Natural Resources* 23(5), 401–416.

Martin, R (2012). Regional economic resilience, hysteresis, and recessionary shocks. *Journal of Economic Geography* 12, 1–32.

Matthews, R & Sydneysmith, R (2010). Adaptive capacity as a dynamic institutional process: Conceptual perspectives and their application. In D Armitage & R Plummer (Eds), *Adaptive capacity and environmental governance* (pp. 223–242). Berlin: Springer-Verlag.

McManus, P, Walmsley, J, Argent, N, Baum, S, Bourke, L, Martin, J & Sorenson, T (2012). Rural community and rural resilience: What is important to farmers in keeping their country towns alive? *Journal of Rural Studies* 28(1), 20–29.

Parkins, JR & Reed, MG (Eds). (2013). *Social transformation in rural Canada: Community, cultures, and collective action.* Vancouver: UBC Press.

Pelling, M & High, C (2005). Understanding adaptation: What can social capital offer assessments of adaptive capacity? *Global Environmental Change* 15, 308–319.

Pendakur, R & Young, N (2013). Putting on the moves: Individual, household, and community-level determinants of residential mobility in Canada. *Demographic Research* 29, 767–796.

Pike, A, Dawley, S & Tomaney, J (2010). Resilience, adaptation and adaptability. *Cambridge Journal of Regions, Economy and Society* 3, 59–70.

Raymond, CM & Robinson, GM (2013). Factors affecting rural landholders' adaptation to climate change: Insights from formal institutions and communities of practice. *Global Environmental Change* 23, 103–114.

Ryser, L & Halseth, G (2010). Rural economic development: A review of the literature from industrialized economies. *Geography Compass* 4(6), 510–531.

Shucksmith, M, Brown, DL, Shortall, S, Vergunst, J & Warner, ME (2012). *Rural transformations and rural policies in the US and UK.* New York: Routledge.

Skerratt, S (2013). Enhancing the analysis of rural community resilience: Evidence from community land ownership. *Journal of Rural Studies* 31(1), 36–46.

Smit, B & Wandel, J (2006). Adaptation, adaptive capacity and vulnerability. *Global Environmental Change* 16, 282–292.

Swindal, MG & McAreavey, R (2012). Rural governance: Participation, power and possibilities for action. In M Shucksmith, DL Brown, S Shortall, J Vergunst & ME Warner (Eds), *Rural transformations and rural policies in the US and UK* (pp. 269–286). New York: Routledge.

Tunberg, M (2014). Approaching rural firm growth: A literature review. *Journal of Enterprising Communities* 8(4), 261–286.

Walker, BH, Holling, CS, Carpenter, SR & Kinzig, A (2004). Resilience, adaptability and transformability in social–ecological systems. *Ecology and Society* 9(2), 5.

Wilson, G (2010). Multifunctional 'quality' and rural community resilience. *Transactions of the Institute of British Geographers* 35, 364–381.

Wilson, GA (2012a). *Community resilience and environmental transitions.* New York: Routledge.

Wilson, GA (2012b). Community resilience, globalization, and transitional pathways of decision-making. *Geoforum* 43, 1218–1231.

Wolfe, D (2010). The strategic management of core cities: Path dependency and economic adjustment in resilient regions. *Cambridge Journal of Regions, Economy and Society* 3, 139–159.

Young, N (2010). Business networks, collaboration, and embeddedness in local and extra-local spaces: The case of Port Hardy, Canada. *Sociologia Ruralis* 50(4), 392–408.

Young, N (2013). Visions of rootedness and flow: Remaking economic identity in post-resource communities. In JR Parkins & MG Reed (Eds), *Social transformation in rural Canada* (pp. 232–248). Vancouver: UBC Press.

54

The Rural–Agriculture Power Play

Loka Ashwood and Michael M. Bell

Introduction

Over 30 years ago, rural studies took a marked turn away from the symbolism of its rural footing. In the midst of a farm crisis, failed social interventions and misplaced support of productivism, rural sociologists recognised it was time for theoretical innovation and change in the discipline. And how better to turn the passive sociological support of technocratic agribusiness into a razor-edged refute than through the sociology of agriculture? Newby's (1983) now classic critique offered the sociology of agriculture as a counter to the failed sociology of the rural. Agriculture and its labour enabled a materialist approach rooted in political economy that classic writers like Marx and Kautsky could speak to. And although the rural may not matter to everyone, eating and the means for doing so do, ensuring disciplinary relevance. Instead of the population decline and regressive politics of the rural, which Marx famously characterised as the 'idiocy of rural life' (Marx & Engels [1848] 1972, p. 477), the sociology of agriculture offered a rebirth of the discipline through theoretical tools not specific to the rural, like commodification, mechanisation, extraction and exploitation.

Therein arose a tradition that remains strong within the discipline today, perhaps even eclipsing the language of 'rural sociology'. Considered as one hand of what scholars came to see as the 'agri-food system', the sociology of agriculture provided a means to address rural problems in concert with the potential solutions provided by urban linkages (Goodman & DuPuis, 2002; Carolan, 2012). This rural–urban unity of purpose and consequence is mostly positive. We note, however, an incidental contrast in positioning. Agriculture in this literature speaks of action and possibilities, while – at least implicitly – the rural falters with inaction and impossibility. While successful in its aim of thwarting uncritical rural sociology, the sociology of agriculture has helped to disarm activities of the rural that are not necessarily agricultural.

Why does agriculture hold such power over the rural? Many scholars have questioned the very meaning of the rural, and even called for the elimination of the term or predicted its demise (Hoggart, 1990; Urry, 1995). Yet despite dramatic changes in agriculture that relate closely to changes in the rural, there has been limited analytical critique of the term (Friedland, 2002).

Here, we revisit the critiques afforded to rural meaning and politics and adapt their application to agriculture. As the birthplace of the sociology of agriculture and the site of its most prevalent application, we focus attention on the United States to analyse the power play at the rural–agricultural nexus. We use Bell, Lloyd and Vatovec's (2010) analytical categories of the material – *rural power* – and the symbolic – *power of the rural* – to study agriculture. We transform these categories into *agricultural power* and *power of agriculture* to discuss the material and ideological pre-eminence of agriculture. Ideas have material consequences as much as the other way around, in both the rural and in agriculture. We argue that the materialist focus on farming and food through the agricultural frame has prompted the treatment of the rural as a passive place of less importance. Agriculture has become material while the rural has become immaterial, or so recent scholarship seems to suggest.

Thus, where Bell, Lloyd and Vatovec (2010) argued that the rural has both material and symbolic powers, and constituencies that build around these powers, we suggest a curious orthogonal axis of conflict. Increasingly, the rural is only symbolic and agriculture is powerful material truth. Following the language suggested by ell, Lloyd and Vatovec (2010), it is as if we have only agricultural power and the power of the rural, with the former in ascendance and the latter in decline. Rural power and the power of agriculture have already slipped from view. Soon, perhaps, only agricultural power will remain.

We contend that all four powers – the material and symbolic powers of the rural and agriculture both, and their constituencies, remain analytically crucial for rural sociology. But we also call for recognising a *power play* between the two, fuelling the disempowerment of the rural and the empowerment of agriculture. We worry that the sociology of agriculture implicitly promotes the very tendency that has been its principal object of critique: productivism, reducing the rural to a narrowly economic phenomenon, a space of production and not much else.

Moving forward, we suggest that attention to the dialogue between the rural and agriculture symbolically and materially can help better reveal unfolding injustices and powerful political constituencies shaping the rural vulnerabilities of the day. The rural is as much agricultural as agriculture is rural. As the classic study by Goldschmidt (1978) pointed out decades ago, when the mechanical cultivation of the land displaces human labour, the decline of farmers takes its toll on rural viability. Rural misery, it seems, knows well the company of agriculture, and vice versa. Moreover, power plays can reverse. By identifying the existence of this power play, we hope to find the capacity to overcome it, restoring both scholarly and practical balance. Like agriculture and its people, the rural and its people matter and our ideas help ensure that both remain of concern.

The life (and death?) of agriculture and the rural in US rural scholarship

As noted in the introduction, in comparison to the rural, agriculture seems alive, well and thriving in scholarly and research circles in the USA. Academically, colleges of agriculture persist across the country, still standing on the land grant history of many public universities. Rural sociology departments no longer remain by name, shuffled into other agricultural social science disciplines like agricultural economics and agricultural education, or rebranded as environmental, developmental and community. Only four departments continue to include rural sociology in their title: Auburn University's Agricultural Economics and Rural Sociology; University of Idaho's Agricultural Economics and Rural Sociology; University of Missouri's Rural Sociology; and – with a stretch – South Dakota State's Department of Sociology and Rural Studies. A number of programmes also include a graduate specialisation termed 'rural sociology', such as Oregon State within its School of Environment and Natural Resources and Penn State within its Department of Agricultural Economics, Sociology, and Education. But not much remains of rural sociology institutionally, at least by that name.

The United States also falters in terms of rural funding. The centrepiece of agricultural and rural funding is the Farm Bill, which is typically reauthorised every five years to support the US Department of Agriculture (USDA). It lists its 2014–2018 economic implications for its US$489 billion in funding as follows: 80% nutrition, 8% crop insurance, 6% conservation, 5% commodities and 1% other (USDA, 2015).[1] The rural does not register as an economic implication. Rather, funding aims to 'enable USDA to further expand markets for agricultural products at home and abroad, strengthen conservation efforts, create new opportunities for local and regional food systems and grow the biobased economy [and] maintain important agricultural research' (USDA, 2015).

In other countries, terms like 'rural' and 'rural sociology' have more vitality, with a reasonable clutch of rural sociology or rural development departments showing up in developing nations, as well as a few in developed nations. More impressive is the status of the rural in government, especially in the UK, where the sense of rural space as more than a zone of agricultural production has deep cultural roots and continues to support major tourist and real estate industries, and where tight urban planning (at least compared with the USA) puts most rural space within commuting distance of cities. In 2002, the UK even changed the title of its formerly productivist-sounding Ministry of Agriculture, Fisheries and Food to the Department for Environment, Food and Rural Affairs, dropping the word 'agriculture' altogether. The UK government also maintains a Department of Agriculture and Rural Development for Northern Ireland, which retains the word 'agriculture' and a more narrowly economic framing of the rural as 'rural development', but does use the 'R-word'. The phrase 'rural development' is also common for government departments in developing countries, such as India's Department of Rural Development.

In terms of funding, the European Commission's Common Agricultural Policy (CAP) for many years has organised its funding around two 'pillars': agricultural production support and 'rural development'. In the 2014–2020 reauthorisation of the CAP, €277 billion have been set aside for direct payments and market support, as well as €85 billion for the second pillar (European Commission, 2013). While rural development funding is only a third of agricultural payments, the new CAP also aims to link the two pillars more closely, which is another win for the 'rural', even if the language remains economistic. 'Farming is not just about food,' an overview of CAP explains, 'It is about rural communities and the people who live in them' (European Commission 2014, p. 4).

So, is the decline of the rural in the face of agriculture's ascent a US-specific phenomenon? Perhaps. Or, better put, it seems likely that this shift is most strongly pronounced in the United States, including US scholarship, government and culture. However, given the USA's hegemonic tendencies, as well as the hegemonic tendencies of productivism more generally, we think it is of broad interest to trace the power play of the rural and the agricultural in the USA.

The shift from rural to agriculture in the USA

Ironically, in the same year that Goldschmidt (1978) published his study of the interplay of the rural and the agricultural, the US-based Rural Sociological Society (RSS) convened its first meeting of the Sociology of Agriculture sub-group – today known as the Sociology of Agriculture and Food Research Interest Group (RIG). Shortly afterwards, Newby (1983) issued a highly influential call for a new rural sociology refocused on the sociology of agriculture. Agriculture rapidly became *the* mechanism to explain rural loss through theory rooted in political economy, a popular stance that persists today. As of 2015, membership in the Sociology of Agriculture and Food RIG attracts the most members of any RIG, with 171 – 40% of RSS members who renew yearly.[2] Second is the Natural Resources RIG with 121, while subgroups with 'rural' as part of their title file in much further behind: Rural Poverty (64 members), Rural Policy (50 members), Rural Studies (56 members), Rural Gender Issues (46 members) and Rural Racial and Ethnic Minorities (37 members). But this shift has not staunched the bleeding of interest in the RSS. Over the last 15 years, membership numbers have dropped nearly 50%, from 1,013 in 2000 to 559 in 2014.[3]

While the interdependency of agriculture and the rural has been verified repeatedly since Goldschmidt's classic work, there remains an implicit danger in such thinking. The majority of US rural residents make their living through work that does not pertain to agriculture, and the percentage still in agriculture continues to decline markedly. As of 2004, only 6.2% of non-metropolitan jobs pertained to agriculture (Parker & Kusmin, 2006). As of 2013, only 3.6% of non-metropolitan jobs were related to fishing, farming, ranching, hunting, managing agricultural land, or working as a labourer related to those fields.[4] Agriculture may feed the world, but it is not feeding the wallets of most rural Americans.

The issue of work is an important one for rural Americans, since rural people on average are poorer than urban dwellers. Rural black and American Indian/Alaskan Native residents are the poorest demographics in the USA: 37.4% and 34.4% live in poverty respectively (USDA ESR, 2015). Certainly, employment in agriculture and food production could potentially play a part in lowering these figures, improving the livelihoods and health of rural residents through better pay and better working conditions in a fair food economy. And scholars could help turn the tide. As Kloppenburg (1991, p. 520) pointed out, it is the 'task' of those who recognise that contemporary agricultural production 'is neither socially just nor ecologically benign' to reform the types of knowledge informing it. Rural sociologists produced ample evidence challenging industrial agriculture – a task little addressed by other academics in colleges of agriculture (Welsh, 1997; Constance & Bonanno, 1999; Magdoff, Foster & Buttel, 2000; Hendrickson & Heffernan, 2002; Bonnano & Constance, 2006; Lobao & Stofferahn, 2007). This challenge remains of vital importance in sociology related to food, agriculture or the rural. But it also suggests a conundrum: the predominance of agriculture as *the* problem and *the* solution for the rural. Meanwhile, the focus on agriculture and food diverts attention from the many other activities that contribute to, and even potentially resolve, rural issues today.

The urban connection to agriculture via food, and the rise of urban agriculture, further elevates the position of the urban relative to the rural as the space of analysis. Although each is important in its own right, studies of food and urban farming have become ways for rural sociologists to expand the otherwise limited pools of funding and audience that they face (Hinrichs, 2000; Goodman & Redclift, 2002). The increasingly poor, hungry and disadvantaged rural population has less political representation, and less relevance in the private sector, even among non-profit organisations. Pender (2015), in a study of US foundations, concluded that only 6.3% of grants were designed with rural benefits in mind in the period of 2005–2010. 'Considering that the rural share of the U.S. population was 19% in 2010, all of these estimates suggest an urban focus of foundation grants' (Pender, 2015, p. 2). Latest estimates show the rural share of the US national population decreasing further to only 15% (USDA ERS, 2015). Even globally, a minority of the population – 46% – lives in rural places (United Nations, 2014). But 100% has to eat, so food and agriculture speak directly to urban populations. Moreover, the visual consumption of the rural (Urry, 1995) by the urban through tourism is an increasing share of the limited flows of capital back to the rural.

For rural sociology to remain viable, agriculture provides a subtle, linguistic switch in focus that many scholars – ourselves included – have found attractive (e.g., Bell, 2004; Ashwood, Diamond & Thu, 2014). But agriculture's vivacity may not be quite as strong as the comparative rural case makes it seem. In a 2015 Google search, the words 'death of the rural', registered 322,000 hits. But 'death of agriculture' garnered 11,700,000 hits: a ratio of over 36 to 1. In part, this descriptive evidence supports the general trend that more people think and care about agriculture than the rural. But it also suggests something equally important: there is widespread concern that agriculture is dying too, just like the rural.

This is unsurprising, since the very meaning of 'agriculture' merges the materiality of the land with the people who cultivate it, mixing up the tangibility of earth with the malleability of societal norms. Agriculture begins with the field. *Agri*, from the Latin *ager*, captures the land, the soil, the terrain – those parts of a field ready to support growth; *cultura* tails *agri*, tying the meaning of a field to husbandry or the care it is afforded, a Latin noun that also means culture. Agriculture, that is, *agri* and *cultura*, is defined by three interlinked parts: (1) the land rendered a field; (2) a field made ready for growth (hoeing, sowing, tilling and so forth); and (3) growth made possible by cultivators – historically, human ones, as *cultura* suggests. When tractors replace people, and confinement buildings replace fields, *cultura* and *agri* make less sense ideologically. Friedland (2002) points to the increasing difficulty of agriculture sustaining its initial meaning as spiralling mechanisation strips people and animals from the land. Combine that with climate change, declining soil fertility and urban encroachment, and agriculture may be next up for material and symbolic grabs.

All this points to a central question for those with rural and agricultural interests, grappling with debates over content and concepts: what *power plays* pull our analytical attention towards agriculture, and away from broader rural concerns? Our question makes clear that the two are not mutually exclusive. Agriculture is not always rural and rural is not always agriculture. And the disempowerment that now plagues the rural may well face agriculture in coming years. By highlighting the play of power between the material and the ideal, agriculture and the rural, we seek to identify the pulls that try to yank all to one conceptual side or the other. In this case, we use power plays to understand the relationship between the empowerment of agriculture and the disempowerment of the rural.

The rural–agriculture power play

Agricultural power is vast. Our economy and ecology vest land and fields with abundant materiality. Even when some layers are extracted, others still follow below. This permanence of what we might, drawing on Bell (2007), call *first agriculture* – the materiality of agriculture, to which we typically grant priority over its symbolic manifestations – stands against the seeming impermanence of the rural. People move away, cultures change, but the land stays. Rural impermanence as part of mobilities research prompted Hoggart (1990) to boldly suggest, 'Let's do away with the rural', in a bout of frustration with the dramatic changes in rural places. Urry (1995, p. 229) predicted rural places becoming 'consumed, used up, wasted, dissipated'. Through its focus on land and fields, but not always people, agriculture appears immobile, rather than transient like people are. In contrast, the explicit connection of people to place as part of rural meaning, an ontological connection of environs with the constitution of people themselves, seemed to some scholars to render the rural no longer a pertinent category. Rather than simply changing, the category 'rural' appeared fundamentally and irreparably reconfigured and unrecognisable.

The land, though, stays put, even when people move away. The stability of land and fields quickly turns material agricultural power into a power of agriculture ideology, what we might also call *second agriculture* – the ideal or symbolic moment in the dialogics of agriculture, which we typically regard as secondary to the material – where immobile materiality denotes what is symbolically lasting. It's an irony in part: land can change hands quickly, and access to a field can end abruptly, dependent upon the social constructs that provide rights. Moreover, how we use land, and therefore what it materially does, can vary widely across time and culture, as in the conflict between Indigenous understandings of how land should be used and that of European settler cultures. And how we use land shapes our symbolic values and understandings of it through a dialogue (Bell & Ashwood, 2016). Despite this interrelationship between the ideal and the material, land continues to hold lore as permanent in agricultural understandings, unlike the people upon it, with all their symbolising.

This is from where agricultural empowerment and rural disempowerment largely derive their sense. In *Gone With the Wind*, Gerald O'Hara tells Scarlett that 'the land is the only thing in the world worth working for, worth fighting for, worth dying for, because it's the only thing that lasts'. This lasting sense of land's materiality evokes ideological passions, especially for those like Bull McCabe, lead character in John B. Keane's play *The Field*. When an outsider threatens the continuance of his husbandry over a beloved field, McCabe kills in an enraged attempt to prevent it. A stark lesson unfolds as McCabe himself later dies after having sacrificed his own sanity and that of his family's in the pursuit of owning a field. As McCabe so vividly experienced, what lasts is not necessarily what one can stand or sit upon. Nonetheless, the material focus of agriculture separates the dependency of what is material from the ideologies that accompany it. First agriculture trumps second agriculture. Land itself becomes coupled with ownership, a supposedly permanent pairing ideologically pre-eminent in American agriculture and its institutions. Those who live in rural spaces and do not own land, or very little of it, fade from the prevailing view. It is a power play where those outside of land ownership fare poorly in the predominant ideologies of agriculture.

Land's material power in agriculture works down to the molecular level. Many branches of agricultural science root knowledge within the land's materiality without reference to the human. For example, when a soil scientist establishes threshold values for phosphorus and nitrogen applications, materially there seems little reason for anyone to follow a different route. After all, soil needs only so many nutrients to produce a crop, and not any more than a particular threshold. Soil scientists may be driven to madness when carefully executed plans for nutrient management go awry in the fields of everyday life, where farmers have other concerns, other understandings, which shape their application rates: the tallest corn and the neatest rows (McGuire, Morton & Cast, 2012; Harden, Ashwood, Bland & Bell, 2013).

Another materialism tells us why they like tall corn and neat rows, say rural sociologists: the symbolism of productivism, an ideological superstructure that arises *from* capitalist accumulation. Here we see an argument where one materialism trumps another. The soil scientist's advice that money is wasted on over-application nonetheless falls to the needs of capital. Materiality reigns prominently here, whether the particulars of nutrient application or the exploitation necessary in capitalism. Ideology comes into the analysis, but as a *result* of materialism, not mutually constitutive of it. Agricultural power thus subsumes the power of agriculture.

These explanations – the soil scientist's recommendations, the social scientist's political economic theories, the sense of the land's permanence – are all symbolic understandings. Ontologically, a materialism divorced from the symbolic is itself an ideology. But these explanations are not only symbolic, or only ideological. They all arise from the interplay of agricultural power and the power of agriculture, the material and the symbolic both. But the pull of rope leans now more to the side of agricultural power, often heavily so.

The disjointing of the human from materiality, and the unloading of people issues onto rural sociologists, builds a materialist agricultural power narrative that prompts another problem. Rural sociologists' responses can be too farmer-based, as the nutrient example suggests, where the resolution lies in the hands of a farmer applicator. Research unfortunately reverts to a small segment of the rural population. The material–ideal dichotomy this creates is part of a broader critique that Goodman (1999) makes of agri-food studies' nature–human, modernist dualism.

In addition to this ontological separation, issues of justice abound. Returning to our example of phosphorus and nitrogen overloading, other players vested with an interest in clean water can be rendered voiceless, such as the water itself, hypoxia in the Gulf and lakes and streams across the country, dead fish and others that fall victim to toxic algae blooms, or other non-agricultural (but perhaps rural) actors contributing to overloading. The analytical focus on farmers encouraged by human-free physical science separates these broader ecological concerns from the decision making of an elite few. It empowers particular agricultural players invested in such an approach by giving time and money to a small segment of applicators and less so to the broader costs. It is a power of agriculture frame that works against lasting ecology and justice.

Meanwhile, the rural, now separated from these various materialities of agriculture, becomes a catch-all for the *cultura* of agriculture, the community, husbandry and humanity attached to the agricultural endeavour. The rural – both a component of agriculture and a place separate from it – makes little sense against an absolutist view of materiality's eminence. Considering agriculture as a part-human construction threatens the material framings that help maintain the status quo.

Agriculture and its constituencies

Here is where the constituencies that form around rural and agricultural powers become most crucial, the crux of politics. Bell, Lloyd and Vatovec (2010) distinguish between two forms of power: *power-from* and *power-over*. Speaking of the rural, power-from describes how power comes to exist from its rural roots, either materially or symbolically. Like the land, the animals, or the ideas of freedom either conjure, these are powerful materialities and symbolisms that come *from* the rural. But at the power-from stage, power has yet to be enacted into politics. It is simply potential. Bell, Lloyd and Vatovec (2010) capture the enactment of power through the term *rural constituencies* (of material power) and *constituencies of the rural* (of symbolic power) – that grant power *over* the rural. Constituencies capture the potential to turn power-from into an active embodiment of power-over. Any successful constituency is likely in part to be formed of both forms of constituency, drawing on material and symbolic rural powers to turn power-from into power-over.

A parallel set of terms applies to agriculture. For our purposes, *agricultural constituencies* form social relations of power based on the material powers of agriculture, and *constituencies of agriculture* form social relations of power based on the symbolic powers of agriculture (see Figure 54.1). To become a constituency, a power must be utilised, until which time it remains a realisation. Realisations are stable, though – they exist without being capitalised upon. When power is practised over agriculture, it becomes an actual social and political relation.

Farmers are the most obvious example of an *agricultural constituency*, manifested in farmers' organisations, based on the material argument that we are on the land and what we produce from it everyone materially needs. This is the critical moment of mobilisation that attracts much attention in sociology. Certainly, a realisation of the importance of land can exist without forming a social movement around it. But the point of collective action is a relation that achieves power-over. A less obvious agricultural constituency might be phosphorus mining companies and their various lobbying organisations, seeking market share and regulations friendlier to their interests, based on the argument that phosphorus is a material need of agriculture that others ignore at their peril.

An example of a *constituency of agriculture* is those who adhere to private property as a right based in Lockian and Jeffersonian land-centric ideas, and support policies that uphold them. Such a constituency might include farmers, but also many who do not work land themselves.

Stabilisation	Material	Symbolic	Stabilisation
Power-From	Agricultural power	Power of agriculture	Realisations
Power-Over	Agricultural constituencies	Constituencies of agriculture	Relations
Mobilisation	First agriculture	Second agriculture	Mobilisation

Figure 54.1   Politics of agriculture

Soviet-style collectivism would never feed us, urban Americans may contend, thus gaining a measure of their own control over agriculture, albeit far less direct than the power over agriculture such an ideology grants farmers. Other symbolic arguments, however, can form the basis of an even more powerful constituency of agriculture. Think of the neoliberal use of private property *rights* to achieve ends that ironically may lead to dispossession, as in corporate land grabs gaining power over the agricultural landscape. Key here, like in the formation of any constituency, is the development of alliances of those whose interests may differ. Given the fading of the rural, agricultural constituencies seem now to be gaining far more power over agriculture than rural constituencies are gaining over the rural.

A paradox of agricultural powers

But the strange thing is, as we noted earlier, farmers and peasants are fewer and fewer every year. As agricultural powers increase, the people who control them decrease. For power has a habit of concentrating.

Farmers and peasants remain an undeniably important piece in the agriculture puzzle. They are the cultivators, in the original Latin sense, who persist even in the face of industrialisation. A litany of research has examined this shrinking sub-group of the rural population: their movement from conventional to sustainable farming (Bell, 2004); their marginalistion in industrial agriculture (Kloppenburg, 1991; Watts, 1994; Constance, 2008); their crises (Heffernan & Heffernan, 1986); their cultural roots (Salamon, 1992); their decision-making patterns and values (Saltiel, Bauder & Palakovich, 1994; Burton, 2004); and their politics (Gilbert, 2015). This is only the tip of an enormous body of research. In a quick search of the content of *Rural Sociology,* the leading US journal on rural sociology, farmers garnered 544 related articles. Agriculture? 716. But race? 374. Poverty? 435. A small minority of rural people attracts by far the majority of rural sociology's attention. As mentioned earlier, only 3.6% of the rural population makes its money from farming, ranching, hunting, managing agricultural land or working as a labourer related to those fields.

Our sense is that the well-intentioned analyses of farmers and agriculture, in an effort to curb the damaging consequences of industrialisation, in part advantages the frames that many sociologists are working against: big agriculture, big money and big power. Agriculture and farming carry extensive rights earned by constituencies of agriculture and agricultural constituencies that sometimes disable alternative politics in the countryside. Through narrative privileging and legal statutes, the few making money in industrial agriculture can do so at the expense of their neighbours, as in the case of concentrated animal feeding operations (Ashwood, Diamond & Thu, 2014). Think of the activities of the infamous Farm Bureau – a dual constituency of agriculture and agriculture constituency – that has immense influence over state and federal politics. Its power-over agriculture lends to some big agribusiness ends. This is not to say all alternative rural politics outside of agricultural ones are the just ones. Rural extremism is a particularly disturbing example (McNicol Stock, 1996). But it is a disturbing example that warrants more attention.

Affording agriculture exclusive symbolic authority in the countryside can disadvantage rural frames distinct from farming and food, and push other troubling trends out of the picture. A slippery slope pervades the rural. If there are fewer farmers, then the rural warrants less attention. Agricultural transformations become inevitable, fuelling the passivity of the rural, rather than fostering recognition that it is quite active and alive. Just perhaps not with agriculture as the heartbeat of its reality.

Conclusion

The power-play between agriculture and the rural in the USA reveals some troubling trends. The materialist first, ideas second approach predominant in agricultural sciences disjoins humans from nature. It creates a power of agriculture ideology suited to agricultural constituencies and constituencies of agriculture that benefit from consolidation and productivist agriculture. In this frame, rural is an inconvenience better sidelined in research concerns. Second, materialist ideologies displace humanity from its central position in any agricultural research, and instead render people the exclusive domain of rural sociologists. Rural sociologists can face pigeon-holed research that demands human solutions to materialist problems, rather than recognising their interaction from the start. Even under the political economy view, the same trap can apply. With capitalism as the ultimate materiality responsible for agricultural consolidation, ideas equal outcomes. Third, the agriculture-first focus eclipses broader rural concerns, pulling attention away from many rural issues such as health, environment, justice, poverty, work, recreation and tourism that are not necessarily agricultural. The rural becomes only a space of production, and agriculture becomes only a means of production.

There is no inevitability or permanence to the current power pull between agriculture and the rural. This moment of agricultural power and power of agriculture may quickly change. Where the rural is displaced today, it could be the firebrand of tomorrow. Where agriculture reigns today, its constituencies could find it less useful tomorrow. As rural studies scholars, we are no exception to these power pulls. We find ourselves in them and help create them. Playing into the cards of materialist ideologies disables rural scholarship seeking reform in the countryside. What possibilities and players are we missing by focusing so much attention on agriculture? With renewed attention to the rural in all its complexity, we can better achieve goals for social and ecological justice everywhere.

Notes

1   It's a similar situation for US research funding.
2   Figures are drawn from the 2014 RSS Annual Council meeting Executive Director Report – a total of 559 members. Since RIG numbers rely on payment of yearly membership fees, to compute the percentage we subtracted Lifetime, Emeritus and Emeritus Sustaining, and Distinguished from the membership numbers, leaving a final number of 431 members. These were the most recent numbers available, and our thanks go to Scott Sanders and Cindy Struthers for guidance finding them. The RIG numbers are provided from the 2015 Mid-Year Council Meeting RIG Committee Report.

3 Drawn from the 2006 RSS Calendar Year Membership Report: 1988–2006.
4 Data were computed using the ACS 1-year estimate data set and analysing Table B24010. We totalled the following fields for men and women: (1) farming, fishing and forestry occupations, including first-line supervisors of farming, fishing and forestry workers; agricultural workers; fishing and hunting, and forest, conservation and logging workers; and (2) farmers, ranchers and other agricultural managers. A total of 700,181 men and women worked in these areas out of a total of 19,408,187 non-metropolitan workers in 2013. We thank Tim Kusmin of the USDA's Economic Research Service for guiding our acquisition of these data.

References

Ashwood, L, Diamond, D & Thu, K (2014). Where's the farmer? Limiting liability in Midwest industrial hog production. *Rural Sociology* 79(1), 2–27.
Bell, MM (2004). *Farming for us all*. University Park, PA: Pennsylvania State University Press.
Bell, MM (2007). The two-ness of rural life and the ends of rural scholarship. *Journal of Rural Studies* 23(4), 402–415.
Bell, MM & Ashwood, L (2016). *An invitation to environmental sociology* (5th edn). Thousand Oaks, CA: Pine Forge Press.
Bell, MM, Lloyd, SE & Vatovec, C (2010). Activating the countryside: Rural power, the power of the rural and the making of rural politics. *Rural Sociology* (50)3, 205–224.
Bonanno, A & Constance, D (2006). Corporations and the state in the global era: The case of seaboard farms and Texas. *Rural Sociology* 71(1), 59–84.
Burton, RJF (2004). Seeing through the 'good farmer's' eyes: Towards developing an understanding of the social symbolic value of 'productivist' behaviour. *Sociologia Ruralis* 44, 195–215.
Carolan, M (2012). *The sociology of food and agriculture*. London and New York: Routledge.
Constance, D (2008). The southern model of broiler production and its global implications. *Culture & Agriculture* 30(1, 2), 17–31.
Constance, D & Bonanno, A (1999). CAFO controversy in the Texas panhandle region: The environmental crisis of hog production. *Culture & Agriculture* 21(1), 14–26.
Economic Research Service. United States Department of Agriculture (2015). Overview. Available at http://www.ers.usda.gov/topics/rural-economy-population/population-migration.aspx#.U1FW3scwjC4 (accessed 23 June 2015).
European Commission (2013). Overview of CAP Reform 2014–2020. Agricultural Policy Perspectives Brief. No. 5. European Union.
European Commission (2014). *The EU's Common Agricultural Policy (CAP): For our food, for our countryside, for our environment*. Luxembourg: Publications Office of the European Union.
Friedland, WL (2002). Agriculture and rurality: Beginning the 'final separation'? *Rural Sociology* 67(3), 350–371.
Gilbert, J (2015). *Planning democracy: Agrarian intellectuals and the intended new deal*. New Haven, CT: Yale University Press.
Goldschmidt, W (1978). *As you sow: Three studies in the social consequences of agribusiness*. Montclair, NJ: Allanheld, Osmun and Company.
Goodman, D (1999). Agro-food studies in the 'age of ecology': Nature, corporeality, bio-politics. *Sociologia Ruralis* 39(1), 17–38.
Goodman, D & DuPuis, ME (2002). Knowing food and growing food: Beyond the production–consumption debate in the sociology of agriculture. *Sociologia Ruralis* 42(1), 5–22.
Goodman, D & Redclift, M (2002). *Refashioning nature: Food, ecology and culture*. London and New York: Routledge.
Harden, NM, Ashwood, LL, Bland, WL & Bell, MM (2013). For the public good: Weaving a multifunctional landscape in the Corn Belt. *Agriculture and Human Values* 30(4), 525–537.
Heffernan, WD & Heffernan, JB (1986). Impact of the farm crisis on rural families and communities. *The Rural Sociologist* (6), 166–170.
Hendrickson, MK & Heffernan, WD (2002). Opening spaces through relocalization: Locating potential resistance in the weaknesses of the global food system. *Sociologia Ruralis* 42(4), 347–369.
Hinrichs, C (2000). Embeddedness and local food systems: Notes on two types of direct agricultural markets. *Journal of Rural Studies* 16(3), 295–303.

Hoggart, K (1990). Let's do away with rural. *Journal of Rural Studies* 6(3), 245–257.

Kloppenburg, J (1991). Social theory and the de/reconstruction of agricultural science: Local knowledge for an alternative agriculture. *Rural Sociology* 56(1), 519–548.

Lobao, L & Stofferahn, CW (2007). The community effects of industrialized farming: Social science research and challenges to corporate farming laws. *Agriculture and Human Values* 25, 219–240.

Magdoff, F, Foster, JB & Buttel, FH (2000). *Hungry for profit: The agribusiness threat to farmers, food, and the environment.* New York: Monthly Review Press.

Marx, K & Engels, F ([1848] 1972). Manifesto of the Communist Party. In RC Tucker (Ed.), *The Marx Engels reader* (pp. 331–362). New York: WW Norton.

McGuire, J, Morton, LW & Cast, AD (2012). Reconstructing the good farmer identity: Shifts in farmer identities and farm management practices to improve water quality. *Agriculture and Human Values* 30(1), 57–69.

McNicol Stock, C (1996). *Rural radicals: Righteous rage in the American grain.* Ithaca, NY: Cornell University Press.

Newby, H (1983). The sociology of agriculture: Toward a new rural sociology. *Annual Review of Sociology* 9, 67–81.

Parker, T & Kusmin, L (2006). *Rural employment at a glance.* Economic Information Bulletin No. (EIB-21). United States Department of Agriculture.

Pender, JL (2015). *Foundation grants to rural areas: From 2005 to 2010: Trends and patterns.* Economic Information Bulletin No. (EIB-141). United States Department of Agriculture.

Salamon, S (1992). *Prairie patrimony: Family, farming, and community in the Midwest.* Chapel Hill, NC: North Carolina University Press.

Saltiel, J, Bauder, JW & Palakovich, S (1994). Adoption of sustainable agricultural practices: Diffusion, farm structure, and profitability. *Rural Sociology* 59(2), 333–349.

United Nations (2014). *World urbanization prospects: The 2014 revision.* New York: United Nations.

Urry, J (1995). *Consuming places.* London: Routledge.

USDA (US Department of Agriculture) (2015). *Agriculture Act of 2014: Highlights and implications.* Available at http://www.ers.usda.gov/agricultural-act-of-2014-highlights-and-implications.aspx (accessed 16 July 2015).

USDA ERS (US Department of Agriculture Economic Research Service) (2015). *Poverty demographics.* Available at http://www.ers.usda.gov/topics/rural-economy-population/rural-poverty-well-being/poverty-demographics.aspx (accessed 17 April 2015).

Watts, M (1994). Life under contract: Contract farming, agrarian restructuring, and flexible accumulation. In P Little & M Watts (Eds), *Life under contract* (pp. 21–77). Madison: University of Wisconsin Press.

Welsh, R (1997). Vertical coordination, producer response, and the locus of control over agricultural production decisions. *Rural Sociology* 62(4), 491–507.

Conclusion

55

Conclusion

Rural Studies: The Challenges Ahead

Mark Shucksmith and David L. Brown

Introduction

Rural studies examines the interrelationships between substantive domains including economy, polity, social organisation, population change, and the natural environment. It is a comprehensive approach to examining structure, agency and rural transformation in the broadest sense. Hence, rural studies, and this Handbook in particular, is an inherently interdisciplinary project. Moreover, rural studies is an applied approach to social science inquiry. Studies are motivated by the joint goal of contributing to social science knowledge, theory and method while at the same time responding to real-life social problems including underdevelopment, social exclusion, population decline, environmental displacement, poverty, ineffective governance, under-employment and environmental pollution. Equally, it examines social, political and economic structures and processes that enhance opportunity and inclusion, making rural areas desirable places to live for many. Accordingly, rural scholars strongly believe that knowledge and practice are equal parts of an integrated process of discovery, engagement and education.

A thematic approach

In our introduction we set out four cross-cutting themes for contributors to this volume to address, namely: (a) more deeply interrelated places; (b) rising inequality; (c) fiscal crisis of the state and impacts of the great recession; and (d) rural as a site of resistance/reproduction of neoliberalism.

The growing interrelation between places is reflected in most of the contributions, not only in terms of closer urban–rural relations but even more ubiquitously in referring to globalisation and the 'annihilation of space', a phrase used not only by Castells in 1996 but interestingly also in 1852 by Frederick Douglass to describe the effects of the railway, steamship and telegraph. We have written elsewhere of the 'mobilities turn' and its implications for rural studies (Shucksmith, Brown & Vergunst, 2012). Urry (2007) argues that economies and societies have been reconfigured around mobilities, founded upon an emergent 'mobilities complex', a new globalised system which remakes consumption, pleasure, work, friendship and family life, and which is becoming an increasingly potent stratifying factor of our late modern or postmodern times. At one level this raises questions for rural studies in terms of migration, commuting, retirement, poverty and social exclusion, tourism, global divisions of labour and climate change.

More fundamentally, the mobilities turn calls into question the notion of 'place' itself, endogenous development, the rural–urban binary implicit in rural or urban studies and the lineal space that comprises the rural–urban interface. Nevertheless, 'while the extent and nature of mobility have increased in contemporary society, and new forms of mobility are restructuring people's social and economic lives, people still solve the challenges of everyday life in geographically bounded communities' (Shucksmith, Brown & Vergunst, 2012, p. 291), albeit constructed by the various kinds of mobility happening within and through them. Contemporary mobilities are therefore restructuring the nature of rural–urban and global–local relationships, rather than diminishing the importance of place.

With heightened mobilities and more deeply interrelated places comes the potential for increased or diminished rural agency, reflecting the implicit tension between freedom and interdependence in a networked world (Mulgan, 1997). In her contribution to this volume (p. 593), Lynda Cheshire reviews succinctly how our understanding of the exercise of power in and upon rural areas has evolved:

> From stories of an egalitarian and distinctly rural way of life to processes of counter-urbanisation and contestations over the very meaning of rurality; from the role of local government as *the* locus of power in rural areas to the emergence of new forms of governance that reshape the state in both vertical and horizontal directions; from farmers as local political elites to their subsumption into a globalised and industrialised agro-food network; and from rural areas as spaces of decline and marginalisation to a reassertion of rural power through new social movements and politics, rural studies scholars have revealed the way power is bound up in each of these processes to serve the interests of some, but not others, and to generate marginalisation, inequality, conflict, resistance and change.

Indeed many contributions to this volume have highlighted inequalities, most notably around gender and ethnicity, access to land, employment, housing and public services, and it is clear that social and economic inequalities are again increasing within rural areas themselves in many countries. An important irony discussed by Kai Schafft in his introduction to the Handbook's section on social institutions is that increased education of rural youth, an unambiguous goal of virtually all rural policies, typically leads to youth out-migration and a continuing cycle of underdevelopment, extreme population ageing, economic decline and institutional decay.

The global financial crisis has played a significant role here, producing 'new poor' among the middle classes and self-employed, with those who were already vulnerable driven deeper into poverty with less social protection from the state as a result of austerity measures and neoliberal imperatives, as described in Bock's contribution and others in this volume. Thus the percentage of citizens with incomes below the poverty line reached 35.7% in Greece and 27.3% in Spain, while youth unemployment in these two countries reached 52.4% and 53.2% respectively (Eurostat, 2015). The working poor are a special problem in rural areas whose economies are often characterised by a lack of occupational diversity and a preponderance of low-wage, low-skill jobs. Regardless of their work effort, these persons cannot obtain enough hours of work, or well-paid work, to earn a secure income. Underemployment is a major determinant of rural poverty and income inequality, and demonstrates that economic structure, not work effort, is largely to blame. There are simply too many workers chasing too few well-paying jobs in many rural economies today. David Freshwater and Bruce Weber engage with this issue and suggest that effective networks linking rural workers with well-paying urban jobs is a way to overcome chronic low income among a disproportionate share of rural workers. They observe that the traditional economic base of the rural economy is increasingly integrated within the modern economy through national and international trade and other types of 'distance killing' processes. Of course, rural areas lacking effective links with national and international markets are vulnerable to chronic social and economic decline.

Bettina Bock notes that it is not yet clear how the financial crisis has affected rural areas. An EU study suggests that 'rural areas have been hit by the closure of plants, loss of employment in industry and construction, and the cuts in public budgets and resulting loss of services, although agriculture has been relatively protected through the Common Agricultural Policy' (European Commission, 2011). In the United States, rural areas appear to have been somewhat shielded from the worst impacts partly because house lending was more responsible and fewer households were faced with unpayable mortgages. In addition, the situation may differ considerably between rural areas, depending on factors such as geographical location, institutional capacity and civic engagement. Rural youth out-migration from southern Europe has increased substantially, as one might expect, yet some rural areas receive young people returning from the cities to seek refuge from the crisis on their families' farms, bringing their skills, energies and networks. One important question is whether rural destination communities can fully utilise these skills and talents, and retain in-migrants in rural areas after economic recovery. If not, then their migration to rural areas during the financial crisis may be somewhat equivalent to a 'boom and bust' cycle experienced by many rural mining and extractive economies.

'In addition, throughout Europe, citizens in rural areas take up the initiative to maintain services despite budget cuts through collaboration with business, non-profit and governmental organisations and the development of novel business and service delivery models. Here, the rural areas are not victims to the crisis but sites of resistance and social innovation', says Bock. This theme of rural social reproduction is embedded in many of the Handbook's chapters and especially in the section on social institutions. In some instances this leads to resilience and enhanced agency (Faircloth & Hynds) while Schafft shows how many sociocultural modes, practices and discourses reflect and reproduce rural marginality.

In her contribution, Katrina Rønningen sees the financial crisis as only one of a set of dramatic shifts in the place of the rural in the global north, triggered both by short-term shocks but also by wider shifts and challenges in the relationship between nature and society on a planetary scale. 'There are three dynamics: a return to resource extraction (including fracking and renewables); the reconfiguring of urban–rural relationships and power asymmetries; and the neo-productivist turn within agriculture linked to the 2007/8 crisis, food security and land-grabbing.' For this reason she argues (p. 270) that

> we are not experiencing the end of a long trajectory of rural development that culminated in the multifunctional project in agriculture and rural land management. Rather, we seem to be at the start of a series of transitions, partly triggered by specific crises since 2008 and partly driven by wider crises of intensifying inequality and climate change (and their interactions). In this context, we are not consolidating past approaches, epistemologies and theories. Rather we are searching for new critical social scientific approaches to new, planetary-scale, problems.

The question then arises of how far rural areas may be sites of resistance to neoliberalism, where alternative models may emerge from local action and social innovation. In his contribution, Geoffrey Lawrence expresses concern that 'a neoliberal calculus has been increasingly applied to state-funded research in the US, with an assessment by governments that such public investment is "useless" if it is not commercialised (Glenna, Lacy, Welsh & Biscotti, 2007; Glenna & Henke, 2014)'. Even more worryingly, Leland Glenna and Elizabeth Ransom posit that, under neoliberalism, there is a concerted effort to convert R&D in public universities into privately owned goods from which profits can be extracted, skewing research away from non-commercial but publicly beneficial areas of investigation. Moreover, in 2016 the UK government proposed that academics in receipt of government funds should not be allowed to comment on policies or to make policy recommendations arising from their research.

In her contribution, Cheshire also sees dangers in a focus on resilience thinking 'if it remains blind to questions of power and inequality in the differential access to the resources that resilience depends upon, and in the way that discourses of resilience support, rather than challenge, a dominant neoliberal political agenda'. More hopefully, Kiah Smith's contribution sees recognisable discursive and political changes being driven by grassroots peasant farmer movements as well as by enlightened leaders in peak food policy organisations. She argues that through emerging civic–intergovernmental pacts and multi-stakeholder deals, key players are identifying new ways of creating a more just global food system.

An 'international' perspective?

An 'international handbook of rural studies' should incorporate an international perspective and the authors of our chapters have responded to this challenge in various ways. One aspect of this has been a recognition throughout the chapters of the significance for rural areas of global processes – for example, of marketisation, financialisation and deregulation – which in turn are bound up with neoliberalism and the mobilities complex (Urry, 2010). Global–local relations has been a recurring theme. A few authors have written primarily from the experience of a single country and have endeavoured to relate this to international literatures to a greater or lesser degree. A few of the contributions to this volume have included some discussion of relations between the global south and north, but the primary focus of the authors has been the global north. However, rather than being a homogeneous space, the research shared in this Handbook shows that the global north is filled with complexity and diversity.

Several authors have attempted a truly international perspective, drawing on literatures from many parts of the world to identify what is universal and what is particular, as best one can in a short contribution. Some authors have focused primarily on one part of the world, such as Europe, Australia or North America, while acknowledging less familiar literatures to a degree. It has been fascinating, as editors, to see authors confronting, perhaps for the first time, evidence from other countries which contradicts taken-for-granted ideas and reveals them as historically and culturally contingent. For example, consider counter-urbanisation. Once proposed as a universal aspect of post-industrial development, we now know that this process of population deconcentration is not experienced similarly across the global north. In fact, it only occurs at certain times, and under particular circumstances. It is often said that travel gives one a new perspective on one's own familiar surroundings. Lowe (2012) quotes T.S. Eliot's poem *Little Gidding* in this context: 'And the end of all our exploring / Will be to arrive where we started / And to know the place for the first time.'

An international perspective helps us then to distinguish what is universal from what is particular to different situations or locations. Of course, as Shortall and Alston (2016) warn, comparative analysis needs to be wary of making universal claims but also of becoming mired in national uniqueness and particularism (Hantrais, 1999). If social sciences can discern what is general and what is specific, this will help practitioners judge whether and how knowledge gained in a particular context can be applicable elsewhere (Lowe, 2012). This argument resonates with Burawoy's (1998) discussion of the 'extended case method': he contends that the extended case method extracts the general from the unique thereby moving the researcher from micro to macro, and connecting present with past. It is often suggested that concepts developed in the West, and particularly in English, tend to dominate comparative analysis (Holmwood, 2007). In Europe it has been noted that researchers from the UK have a disproportionate influence because of the dominance of English as the working language, perhaps generating a new form of discursive imperialism (Hantrais, 2009), and this charge may also be levelled at rural studies (Lowe, 2012). A truly international perspective may help to mitigate this.

Emerging issues in rural studies

Change, not stability, is the typical situation experienced by rural communities throughout the global north. Many of these processes of change – for example, population ageing, counter-urbanisation, social exclusion, transformations of the structure of agriculture – engage with issues that have commanded the attention of rural scholars and policy makers for a long time. In contrast, other issues are only now emerging. While not according emerging issues a higher priority for research or policy development, we seek to identify and discuss some of these new issues and encourage researchers to consider engaging with them in the future. These emerging issues interrogate new aspects of the four themes that motivate this Handbook.

The urban/rural dichotomy is increasingly inappropriate

Many of the Handbook's chapters have emphasised the growing interdependence of places in contemporary society. These heightened interrelationships are produced by a wide range of mobilities that are made possible by advances in information technology, modern transportation, and societal and global transformations facilitated by deregulation, devolution of authority, ever more mobile capital and labour, and heightened corporate penetration throughout national and global space. Accordingly, contemporary rural scholars must resist the inclination to dichotomise rural from urban, difficult though this may be in practice. This rural/urban dichotomy is increasingly illusory and inappropriate in the global north, which has been characterised by Castells (1989) as a 'space of flows'. Of course, when data are available that allow us to compare places which are classified as rural and urban, this is hard to resist and may indeed be revealing. Nevertheless, rural scholarship should resist lapsing uncritically into the rural/urban dichotomy, and seek to focus instead on the interrelationships that give meaning to both urban and rural space, and especially to the rural–urban interface which is a space of intense social and economic interaction, not a boundary delineating separate social, economic and environmental spheres (Lichter & Brown, 2011).

Rural people and communities are increasingly precarious in today's world

During the recent economic crisis, the social protection offered in the global north has been challenged and redefined in many ways. The recent recession has shown that the social contract is increasingly fragile in today's neoliberal world. In the face of rising financial instability and sovereign debt, many nations significantly diminished the social protections offered to residents and citizens. While Greece is an exemplar for externally imposed withdrawal of social protection, many other nations have also pulled back on social protections heretofore taken for granted, and often made eligibility for receipt conditional on certain behaviours or attributes. In the EU, for example, Spain, Italy, Ireland and Greece all experienced a significant decline in real public spending during 2010–2012 compared with 2007–2009 (Giovannini, 2014). In the USA, the rate of absolute poverty grew by 43% between 2000 and 2010 (Clark, 2015). Increased

667

economic insecurity affects urban and rural people alike. Accordingly, future rural research would be well advised to examine the impacts of macroeconomic policies on rural well-being.

Some research points to the emergence of a 'precariat' class in Europe and North America (Standing, 2011), whose lives are dominated by insecurity both because of the flexibilisation of labour markets (insecure contracts, agency working, zero-hours contracts, part-time work, youth unemployment) and because of the withdrawal and conditionality of social protection. Underlying both of these is the declining power of organised labour, which Mason (2015) argues is the most pernicious purpose of neoliberalism. According to Choonara (2011), the concept can be traced back to Bourdieu, 'who described precarity as a "new mode of dominance" resulting from restructuring of the economy that "forced workers into submission". Bourdieu argued that globalisation and fragmentation of the labour market had created a new generalised and permanent state of insecurity for workers.' Standing goes further, arguing that precarious workers now form a distinct social class with separate conditions and interests from other workers, although others such as Choonara disagree. There appear to have been few studies yet of a rural precariat as such, and yet many rural households tend to experience persistent low pay, lower unionisation and less access to social protection. This is another pressing avenue for future research by rural scholars.

Neoliberal policies not only affect the well-being of persons and households, but also place rural communities at the risk of being left even farther behind. Experts disagree on the most effective ways of dealing with the economic transformations occurring today, for example, with uneven spatial development that is produced by economic deskilling, offshoring of rural manufacturers, and human capital deficits resulting from long-term out-migration of well-prepared youth. As Brown and Schafft (2011, p. 226) observed, 'The rural policy choice can be understood as a debate between *equity advocates* who argue that ... governments should play a key role in promoting rural development, and *efficiency advocates* who argue that rural economies are experiencing a "natural" transformation , and that public policy should not interfere with this process of change.' Clearly, efficiency advocates are in the driver's seat in today's neoliberal world. They see communities as interchangeable sites of production and not as valued social contexts. Capital flight from inefficient rural locations is considered 'natural' and necessary for overall national development even if it results in further rural underdevelopment. Hence, we encourage tomorrow's rural scholars to examine the impacts of neoliberal policies on rural communities and economies as well as on individuals and households.

Nature and rural society are inextricably intertwined

Social scientists have struggled with the relationship between nature and society. Sociological human ecology, for example, included environment in the ecological complex along with population, organisation and technology, but environment was typically seen as *social* context, not nature (Hawley, 1968). Environmental sociology developed as a specialisation within sociology during the 1980s, but even this balanced approach included a starting assumption that the physical and social should be separated analytically (Buttell, 1987). By the 1990s, however, this perspective began to change with the publication of influential articles contending that natural and social forces are *conjointly constituted*. As Freudenberg and his colleagues (1995, p. 387) observed, 'To emphasize either the social or the physical aspects of resource use in isolation, or even to acknowledge that both have importance, is to run the risk of failing to grasp the inherent interplay of the two.' Similarly, Raymond Murphy (1995, p. 703) observed that 'Unidirectional determinisms and reductions – of the social by natural or the reverse – need to be replaced by a perception of the dialectical relationship between the two.' Hence, in contemporary practice, environmental social science, including that examining rural areas, tends to examine what are called 'coupled natural–human systems'. One illustration of this is the growing currency of the concept of the *anthropocene*, a proposed epoch that begins when human activities started to have a significant global impact on Earth's ecosystems (Crutzen & Stoermer, 2000).

This new perspective of coupled natural–human systems opens up a whole range of environmentally related issues to rural scholarship, and re-energises other areas of research that had become dormant over time. Nowhere is this dialectical relationship between nature and society more relevant than in considering climate change and rural society. Scholars have a full agenda in examining rural practices like carbon-based energy production, animal agriculture or long-distance commuting that increase carbon emissions thereby adversely affecting the environment; and similarly examining how more erratic weather, increased or decreased rainfall, more severe storms and other environmentally based perturbations affect rural economy and society. These concerns also offer opportunities for the clandestine exercise of discursive power, for example to prevent new housing development, as we noted in the introduction to this volume.

In addition, the advent of new energy extraction technologies such as horizontal hydraulic fracturing ('fracking'), deep water drilling, and recovering oil from high-sulphur tar sands has re-energised decades-old areas of rural research that study the impacts of boom and bust cycles on community organisation, how temporary workers and their families affect community organisation, and institutional capacity such as law enforcement, education and general governance (Freudenberg & Grambling, 1992). This bundle of environmentally based rural issues will undoubtedly occupy a much higher place on the rural research agenda in the future.

Migration and displacement

Rural scholars have studied migration for decades (Brown, 2002; Argent, this volume), yet the nature of population mobility affecting rural areas has dramatically changed in contemporary society. In previous decades, the main focus of rural migration research was on internal migration and population redistribution. For most of modern history in the global north, people left rural areas for cities and contributed to greater and greater levels of urbanisation. Then, around the 1970s, counter-urbanisation became a prominent phenomenon in the USA, UK, much of continental Europe, Australia and elsewhere (Brown & Wardwell, 1980; Champion, 1989). However, by the 1980s the complexity of this process became apparent as nations like the USA reverted to net rural migration loss while counter-urbanisation continued in others like the UK.

While internal migration is still an important issue for rural research, it has been superseded in importance by migration from abroad. In recent decades, rural areas have become destinations for both direct or onward migration from lower income countries or zones of political instability, whether they be from the EU's eastern periphery and beyond, from Mexico and Latin America, or from North Africa and the Middle East. Cities are still the primary destinations for such migration, but rural areas are getting their share. This is particularly true in the United States where Hispanic migration has brought large non-English-speaking populations to places that hitherto were mostly Anglo-Saxon and English speaking. In the UK and continental Europe, and especially countries in the Schengen zone, migrants have flowed from east to west, filling important economic niches but also raising social challenges (De Lima, Parra & Pfeffer, 2012). Recently, social and political turmoil in Syria, Iraq and elsewhere in the Middle East has resulted in huge flows of refugees fleeing violence and/or looking for a more stable place to live and work. Data are not available to determine what share of these refugee streams will end up in rural communities, but it will probably be substantial, especially relative to the size and socioeconomic composition of existing populations. This migration will pose both challenges and opportunities for the communities involved, and a fertile area for rural social science research.

It is likely that such displacement will be an important and continuing feature of the 21st century, according to Betts (2015). Globally, one in every 122 humans is now either a refugee, internally displaced, or seeking asylum (UNHCR, 2015). In general terms, the number of refugees in the world is broadly a function of the number of wars and human-rights-abusing dictatorships at any given time. However, Betts argues, 'there are also grounds to believe that refugees and displacement are likely to become a defining issue of the 21st century. Two global trends in particular suggest this: fragility and mobility. In both cases the international community is struggling to come up with viable collective responses.' Chronic fragility characterises a growing number of states, whose weak governance renders them unable to ensure basic human rights and forces many people then to cross borders in search of fundamental rights and security. This fragility may be exacerbated by climate change and disputes over land and resources. On top of this, Betts (2015) argues that 'with globalisation, the opportunity and inclination to move is greater than ever' and states have found themselves unable to control immigration. The 1951 convention on the status of refugees is crucial but outdated, requiring modification to cope with the increasingly complex sources of cross-border displacement today. Social science research, including that on rural migration, can contribute to revising this essential treaty to reflect contemporary realities and protect human rights.

A problem-focused rural studies

In the introduction to this volume we advocated a problem-oriented approach to rural studies in which scholars contribute more effectively to policy and practice through their research. We also recognised that this is not straightforward for many reasons. It requires working across boundaries between academic disciplines; between universities and society; between research, teaching and engagement; and between nations. Each of these requires recognition of, and sensitivity to, other cultures, practices and knowledges. Moreover, the processes through which research feeds into policy and practice are rarely simple, linear, transparent, or unidirectional. Nevertheless, we maintain that researchers have a responsibility to contribute to public understanding and debates if we are to realise the public value of our universities and justify our public funding and academic freedom.

But how should rural scholars proceed to engage? What strategies might we use to bring our evidence into policy and practice? This, of course, depends on how we conceive of the policy process. Moreover, the notion of 'evidence-based policy' has been critiqued by a number of scholars (Nutley, 2003; Pawson, 2006; Nutley, Walter & Davies, 2007; Stevens, 2007; Denzin, 2009; Monaghan, 2010; Shortall, 2012). One model that recognises the inherently political nature of the process is the 'advocacy coalition framework' (Sabatier, 1987). In this pluralistic model, civil society organisations with shared or complementary interests form shifting coalitions to pursue these interests. Such advocacy coalitions are eclectic mixes of organisations and social actors, including academics, which form on an issue-by-issue basis. Evidence from academics is deployed (often as 'killer facts' or powerful narratives) essentially as a weapon in the power struggle between competing interests. Once their research is in the public domain, scholars have little or no control over its use. As a US government policy maker once commented to one of this chapter's authors (Brown), 'I just want a few numbers to abuse.' Engaging in this political process, it can be hard to distinguish 'public social science' from the uncritical, unreflexive sale of knowledge to 'clients' which Burawoy (2005) disdains.

A modification of the advocacy coalition model is offered by Stevens (2007). His Darwinian analysis of the survival of ideas that fit argues that ideas may be findings, facts or recommendations produced by an array of groups, including academics, lobby groups and journalists, some of which will appeal to powerful supporters. Those that have powerful supporters have an 'evolutionary' advantage, and will survive. Stevens is very clear that it is not the power of the idea that matters, but the power of its supporters (2007, p. 28) which might be policy makers, business or pressure groups (Shortall, 2012). Similar arguments are made by McLaughlin and Neal (2007) and by Denzin (2009).

The actors in the policy process include not only interest groups and academics, of course, but also politicians, civil servants and institutions. Their interests are recognised by political scientists and in the advocacy toolkits developed and employed by organisations such as Oxfam and Greenpeace. Shortall (2012) shows how accepted ideas of priorities become embedded in organisations such as government departments over time, and close relationships are developed with certain interest groups: the example of ministries of agriculture and farmers' unions is often quoted. Policy priorities that become embedded in this way tend to be those that are favourable with the public, stakeholder groups and politicians, and there may be no appetite for evidence that threatens the status quo. Moreover, politicians use evidence selectively to create powerful narratives which will secure them a good press and re-election; civil servants also use evidence selectively to advance their careers, justifying particular policies within government and developing proposals which will find favour with their superiors (Stevens, 2011; Shortall, 2012).

Seeking to inform policy and practice with research-based evidence, hence, can be a tricky business. It requires far more 'craft' than simply publishing in academic journals. At the very least, it requires either the researcher, an advocate or a knowledge-broker to have some awareness of the 'field' (in Bourdieu's terms) and how this is infused with power.

Another way in which evidence informs policy and practice is via the public intellectual. The precise meaning of this term is rightly contested (Issitt & Jackson, 2013), but a public intellectual is popularly understood to refer to an intellectual who participates in the public realm in addition to their academic and professional affairs. They have necessarily gained distinction in their own field of expertise and in addition contribute to public debate, perhaps also giving policy advice, whether in relation to their own field of expertise or more generally. Some scholars have found it difficult to balance scholarly and political roles. Amitai Etzioni (1996) is an example. A past president of the American Sociological Association (ASA), Etzioni is now better known as the leader of the Communitarian Movement, a social movement focused on enhancing collective engagement while tempering individualism. In contrast, another past president of the ASA, Michael Burawoy, seems better able to pursue his scholarly role while promoting 'public sociology' (Burawoy, 2005). Public scholarship is widely remarked upon and valued by many of those engaged in the policy process. A key finding of Talbot and Talbot (2014) is that senior civil servants value academics' general expertise and reputation as much as, or more than, they do specific research. Moreover, such interactions as participation in advisory boards, or as trustees, are a frequent way in which academic research is accessed over a long period by third-sector organisations as well as by many in government (Bastow, Dunleavy & Tinkler, 2013). Bourdieu argues that academics should make their voices heard directly in all the areas of public life in which they are competent, promoting intellectual argument rather than the ubiquitous 'slander, sloganisation and falsification' of political life, so fulfilling academics' 'function of public service and sometimes public salvation' (Bourdieu, 1998, p. 9; see also Sassower, 2014). On this basis, academics may engage in networked rural development or place-shaping, for example, as well as in high-level policy advice and public debates, as a public service obligation, provided this is accompanied by critical reflexivity (Shucksmith, forthcoming).

In each of these models, the production of evidence tends to be seen as primarily the preserve of academics. However, there is a growing acknowledgement that academia has no monopoly on knowledge or evidence, reflected in a tendency to speak less of 'knowledge transfer' but instead of knowledge exchange, knowledge mobilisation or co-creation of knowledge. This has the advantage of incorporating not only 'scientific' knowledge but also practical knowledge and experiential insight. While this may risk being seen as less 'objective' and independent by critics, conversely the findings may be more trusted by those involved. Brewer (2013) argues that in addressing the 'wicked problems' which now face us, public social science must collaborate with other social actors and publics, including government, NGOs and civil society, through co-production of knowledge to lessen the gap between researchers and the 'real world' of wicked problems. Necessarily this requires social scientists 'to write to make themselves understood rather than for professional acclaim' (Brewer, 2013, p. 11) and for their research activity to be engaged and accessible. But connecting with other social actors and publics goes beyond effective dissemination, communication and open access, requiring genuine involvement of different publics in the formulation of the research problem and subsequent conversations with relevant publics at all stages of the research process (Brewer, 2013).

Rural studies has embraced the validity and worth of co-creation and knowledge exchange, more in practice in some disciplines and countries than others, with numerous examples referred to amongst the contributions to this Handbook (e.g., Corbett & Bæck; Donehower & Green; Faircloth & Hynds; Symes & Phillipson) as well as those mentioned in our introductory chapter (Marika, Yunupingu, Marika-Mununggiritj & Muller, 2009; Ramzan, Pini & Bryant, 2009). The 2015 Congress of the European Society for Rural Sociology included a working group considering 'Co-production of Land Use Knowledge', and *Sociologia Ruralis* in 2013 published a special issue on 'Sociology, Knowledge and Evidence in Rural Policy-Making', which included papers on co-production of knowledge and knowledge exchange in/with rural communities. Notwithstanding this, there is scope for more use of, and reflection on, co-creation and knowledge exchange in rural studies.

The scope for bringing research to policy and practice depends, of course, on the institutional structures and arrangements of different countries as well as academic cultures and capacities. Thus, Shucksmith and colleagues (2012) discussed the diminished scope for US rural sociology to inform policy at the present time, despite its having historically responded to an external policy demand. This is explained in terms of the legitimacy of government intervention at all levels being disputed by the ascendancy of the political right and the reliance on ideology over evidence. In the UK and EU, on the other hand, there have been numerous channels through which rural policy makers have sought research-based evidence, even if often the policies which ultimately emerge only partially reflect that evidence (Shucksmith, Brown & Vergunst, 2012; Shortall, 2012). Again there is scope for further discussion in rural studies of 'science into society', as some would frame this, or more broadly of the politics of rural studies: what strategies might we adopt to bring our work to inform policy and practice, and what issues might this raise for the critically reflexive scholar?

Finally, we would be remiss if we did not observe that academic institutions are ambivalent at best in their support of public scholarship. Applied research is generally considered less prestigious than purely disciplinary research, and academic reward structures seldom incentivise public engagement. This may be beginning to change as the public role of universities in society is being interrogated, and renegotiated. For example, both of our universities, Newcastle and Cornell, have recently established well-funded public engagement initiatives. Still, junior scholars tend to avoid highly applied pursuits until they have obtained a measure of job security through their disciplinary contributions. To do otherwise would be risky business, until the synergies between engagement and research are better recognised, and engagement is defined, as it should be, as a legitimate from of scholarship. Regardless of these institutional barriers, and the constraints to public engagement discussed above, we recommend that rural research should be planned with public engagement in mind from its very inception. In other words, we believe that such engagement is an integral part of the research process itself, and should not be an afterthought once the analysis is complete. We contend that research and engagement can be integrated within any research tradition from the most highly quantitative analyses of secondary data to ethnographic studies. Rural research can and should influence policy discourse, but the system is not simply demand driven. Scholars and policy makers must be engaged in ongoing relationships, and researchers must build effective bridges between their world and policy and practice.

Final words

The 21st century will bring rapid, transformational change, much of it in ways we have not foreseen and to which people in rural areas (as elsewhere) will have to adapt as best they can. Some will flourish, riding the waves of change to their advantage, while many others will struggle. In this volume we have reported on some aspects of the changes that are currently under way, including growing inequality and fiscal restraint in the wake of the great recession; closer interdependencies between places in an increasingly networked, globalised world; the rise of neoliberal hegemony; and the prospect of climate change and political instability both of which displace peoples around the world. This volume's contributions also show evidence of people in rural areas adapting successfully to change, indeed often thriving, and exerting agency in negotiating and resisting some of these processes. The capacity to act, collectively and individually, is crucial but this cannot be a matter purely for self-help, for 'sink or swim', as some resilience discourses might imply (Cheshire, Esparcia & Shucksmith, 2015). The responsibility for thriving in the face of these changes is a shared responsibility between people in place and governments and other institutions at many levels.

What contribution might rural studies offer in these challenging times? Certainly we must continue to provide research-based evidence to inform policy and practice, and become smarter about how to bring that evidence to bear in fields which are heavily policy infused. Beyond that, rural studies can deconstruct political positions and unveil hidden power relations, 'unveiling the unknown mechanisms of the established order, of symbolic violence, and sharing this knowledge in a reflexive and political alliance with the dominated – the "downtrodden" – as a counter power' (Deer, 2008, p. 208), as well as speaking truth to power. Above all, rural studies can hold up a mirror to society to foster public deliberation and debate about what we understand to be a 'good society' and a 'good life' (Shucksmith, forthcoming). As Brewer (2013, p. 14) argues, 'the social sciences are the way in which society can find out about itself and in so doing generate the idea of society itself', helping in the development and dissemination of key social values that render society possible, such as trust, altruism and tolerance. The challenge for rural studies, then, as for the social sciences in general, is to 'help us understand the conditions which both promote and undermine these values and identify the sorts of public policies, behaviours and relationships that are needed in culture, the market and the state to ameliorate their absence and restore and repair them' (2013, p. 15).

Acknowledgement

The authors wish to acknowledge our colleagues in the Trans-Atlantic Rural Research Network (TARRN) for helping us scope out some of the emerging issues in this chapter.

References

Bastow, S, Dunleavy, P & Tinkler, J (2013). *The impact of the social sciences: How academics and their research make a difference*. London: Sage.

Betts, A (2015). Human migration will be a defining issue of this century. *The Observer*, 20 September 2015.

Bourdieu, P (1998). *Acts of resistance: Against the new myths of our time*. Cambridge: Polity.

Brewer, J (2013). *The public value of the social sciences*. London: Bloomsbury.

Brown, DL (2002). Migration and community: Social networks in a multi-level world. *Rural Sociology* 67(1), 1–23.

Brown, DL & Schafft, K (2011). *Rural people and communities in the 21st century*. Cambridge: Polity.

Brown, DL & Wardwell, J (Eds). (1980). *New directions in urban–rural migration: The population turnaround in rural America*. New York: Academic Press.

Burawoy, M (1998). The extended case method. *Sociological Theory* 16(1), 4–33.

Burawoy, M (2005). 2004 Presidential address: For public sociology. *American Sociological Review* 70, 4–28.

Buttell, F (1987). New directions in environmental sociology. *Annual Review of Sociology* 13, 465–488.

Castells, M (1989). *The informational city: Information technology, economic restructuring, and the urban regional process*. Oxford: Blackwell.

Champion, T (Ed.). (1989). *Counterurbanization: The changing pace and nature of population deconcentration*. London: Edward Arnold.

Cheshire, L, Esparcia, J & Shucksmith, M (2015). Community resilience, social capital and territorial governance. *ager: Journal of Depopulation and Rural Development Studies* 18, 7–38.

Choonara, E (2011). Is there a precariat? *Socialist Review* (October).

Clark, T (2015). *Hard times: Inequality, recession, aftermath*. New Haven, CT: Yale University Press.

Crutzen, P & Stoermer, E (2000). The Anthropocene. *Global Change Newsletter* 41, 17–18.

De Lima, P, Parra, P & Pfeffer, M (2012). Conceptualizing contemporary immigrant integration in the rural United States and United Kingdom. In M Shucksmith, DL Brown, S Shortall, J Vergunst & M Warner (Eds), *Rural transformations and rural policies in the US and UK* (pp. 79–99). London: Routledge.

Deer, C (2008). Doxa. In M Grenfell (Ed.), *Pierre Bourdieu: Key concepts* (pp. 119–130). Stocksfield: Acumen.

Denzin, N (2009). The elephant in the living room: Or extending the conversation about the politics of evidence. *Qualittive Research* 9(2), 139–160.

Etzioni, A (1996). *The golden rule*. New York: Basic Books.

European Commission (2011). *Poverty in rural areas of the EU*. EU Agricultural and Economic Brief 1. Brussels: EC DG Agriculture and Rural Development.

Eurostat. (2015). *Unemployment statistics: Statistics explained* and *People at risk of poverty or social exclusion: statistics explained*. Luxembourg: Eurostat.

Freudenberg, W, Frickel, S & Grambling, R (1995). Beyond the nature/society divide: Learning to think about a mountain. *Sociological Forum* 10(3), 361–392.

Freudenberg, W & Grambling, R (1992). Community impacts of technological change: Toward a longitudinal perspective. *Social Forces* 70, 937–955.

Giovannini, A (2014). 5 Facts about social welfare in Europe. *Eutopia* (June). Retrieved 25 October 2015 from http://eutopiamagazine.eu/en/alessandro-giovannini/columns/5-facts-about-social-welfare-europe.

Glenna, L & Henke, C (2014). Agricultural technologies and the structure of the North American agrifood system. In C Bailey, L Jensen & E Ransom (Eds), *Rural America in a globalising world: Problems and prospects for the 2010s* (pp. 85–102). Morgantown: West Virginia University Press.

Glenna, L, Lacy, W, Welsh, R & Biscotti, D (2007). University administrators, agricultural biotechnology and academic capitalism: Defining the public good to promote university–industry relationships. *Sociological Quarterly* 48(1), 141–164.

Hantrais, L (1999). Contextualization in cross-national comparative research. *International Journal of Social Research Methodology* 2(2), 93–108.

Hantrais, L (2009). *International comparative research: Theory, methods and practice*. Basingstoke: Palgrave Macmillan.

Hawley, A (1968). Human Ecology. In D Sills (Ed.), *International encyclopedia of the social sciences* (pp. 328–337). New York: Crowell, Collier and Macmillan.

Holmwood, J (2007). Sociology as public discourse and professional practice. *Sociological Theory* 25(1), 46–66.

Issit, J & Jackson, D (2013). What does it mean to be a public intellectual? Higher Education Academy Research Seminar, 12 March 2013. https://www.heacademy.ac.uk/resource/what-does-it-mean-be-public-intellectual.

Lichter, D & Brown, DL (2011). Rural America in an urban society: Changing social and spatial boundaries. *Annual Review of Sociology* 37, 565–592.

Lowe, P (2012). The agency of rural research in comparative context. In M Shucksmith, DL Brown, S Shortall, J Vergunst & M Warner (Eds), *Rural transformations and rural policies in the US and UK* (pp. 18–38). London: Routledge.

McLaughlin, E & Neal, S (2007). Who can speak to race and nation? *Cultural Studies* 21(6), 910–930.

Marika R, Yunupingu, Y, Marika-Mununggiritj, R & Muller, S (2009). Leaching the poison – The importance of process and partnership in working with Yolngu. *Journal of Rural Studies* 24, 404–413.

Mason, P (2015). *Postcapitalism: A guide to our future*. London: Allen Lane.

Monaghan, M (2010). Adversarial politics and evidence utilization: Modelling the changing evidence and policy connection. *German Policy Studies* 6(2), 17–52.

Mulgan, G (1997). *Connexity: How to live in a connected world*. Boston, MA: Harvard Business Review Press.

Murphy, R (1995). Sociology as if nature did not matter: An ecological critique. *British Journal of Sociology* 46(4), 688–707.

Nutley, S (2003). Bridging the research/policy divide: Reflections and lessons from the UK. Keynote paper presented at 'Facing the Future: Engaging Stakeholders and Citizens in Developing Public Policy', National Institute of Governance Conference, Canberra, 23 April.

Nutley, S, Walter, I & Davies, H (2007). *Using evidence: How research can inform public services*. Bristol: Policy Press.

Pawson, R (2006). *Evidence-based policy: A realist perspective*. London: Sage.

Ramzan, B, Pini, B & Bryant, L (2009). Experiencing and writing indigeneity, rurality and gender. *Journal of Rural Studies* 24, 435–443.

Sabatier, P (1987). Knowledge, policy-oriented learning, and policy change. *Knowledge* 8, 649–692.

Sassower, R (2014). *The price of public intellectuals*. Basingstoke: Palgrave Macmillan.

Shortall, S (2012). The role of subjectivity and knowledge power struggles in the formation of public policy. *Sociology* 47(6), 1088–1103.

Shortall, S & Alston, M (2016). To rural proof or not to rural proof: A comparative analysis. *Politics & Policy* 44(2).

Shucksmith, M (forthcoming). Re-imagining the rural: From 'rural idyll' to 'good countryside'. A provocation. *Journal of Rural Studies*.

Shucksmith, M, Brown, M & Vergunst, J (2012). Constructing the rural–urban interface: Place still matters in a highly mobile society. In M Shucksmith, DL Brown, S Shortall, J Vergunst & M Warner (Eds), *Rural transformations and rural policies in the US and UK* (pp. 287–303). London: Routledge.

Standing, G (2011). *The precariat: The new dangerous class*. London: Bloomsbury.

Stevens, A (2007). Survival of the ideas that fit: An evolutionary analogy for the use of evidence in policy. *Social Policy and Society* 6, 25–35.

Stevens, A (2011). Telling policy stories: An ethnographic study of the use of evidence in policy-making in the UK. *Journal of Social Policy* 40(2), 237–255.

Talbot, C & Talbot, C (2014). *Sir Humphrey and the professors: What does Whitehall want from academics?* Policy@Manchester, University of Manchester.

UNHCR (2015). *Global trends report: World at war*. Geneva: United Nations High Commissioner for Refugees.

Urry, J. (2007). *Mobilities*. Cambridge: Polity.

Urry, J. (2010). Consuming the planet to excess. *Theory, Culture & Society* 27(2–3), 1–22.

Index